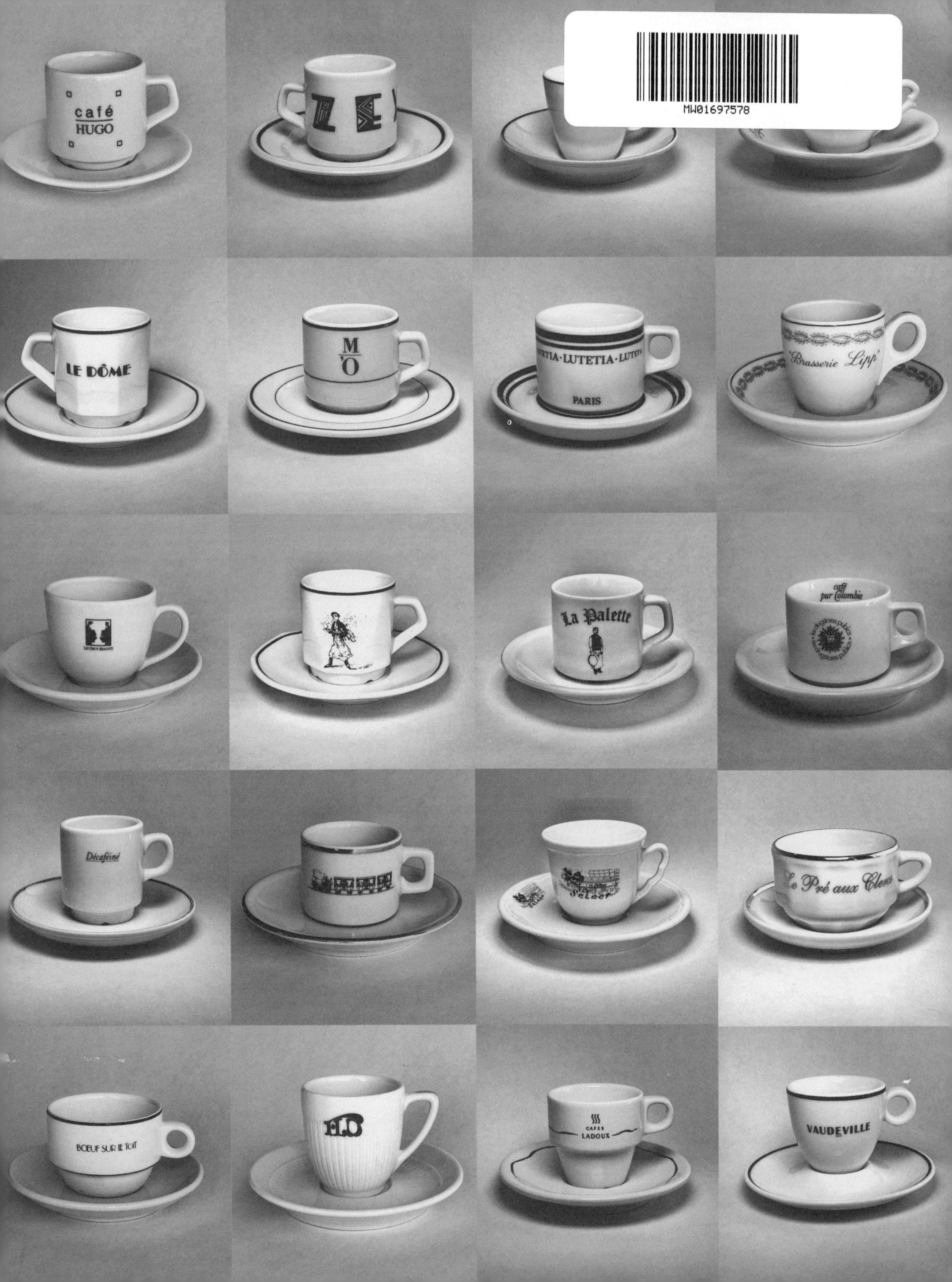
café
HUGO
LE DÔME
M
'O
LUTETIA
PARIS
"Brasserie Lipp"
La Palette
café
pur Colombie
Décaféiné
Le Pré aux Clers
BOEUF SUR LE TOIT
CAFES
LADOUX
VAUDEVILLE

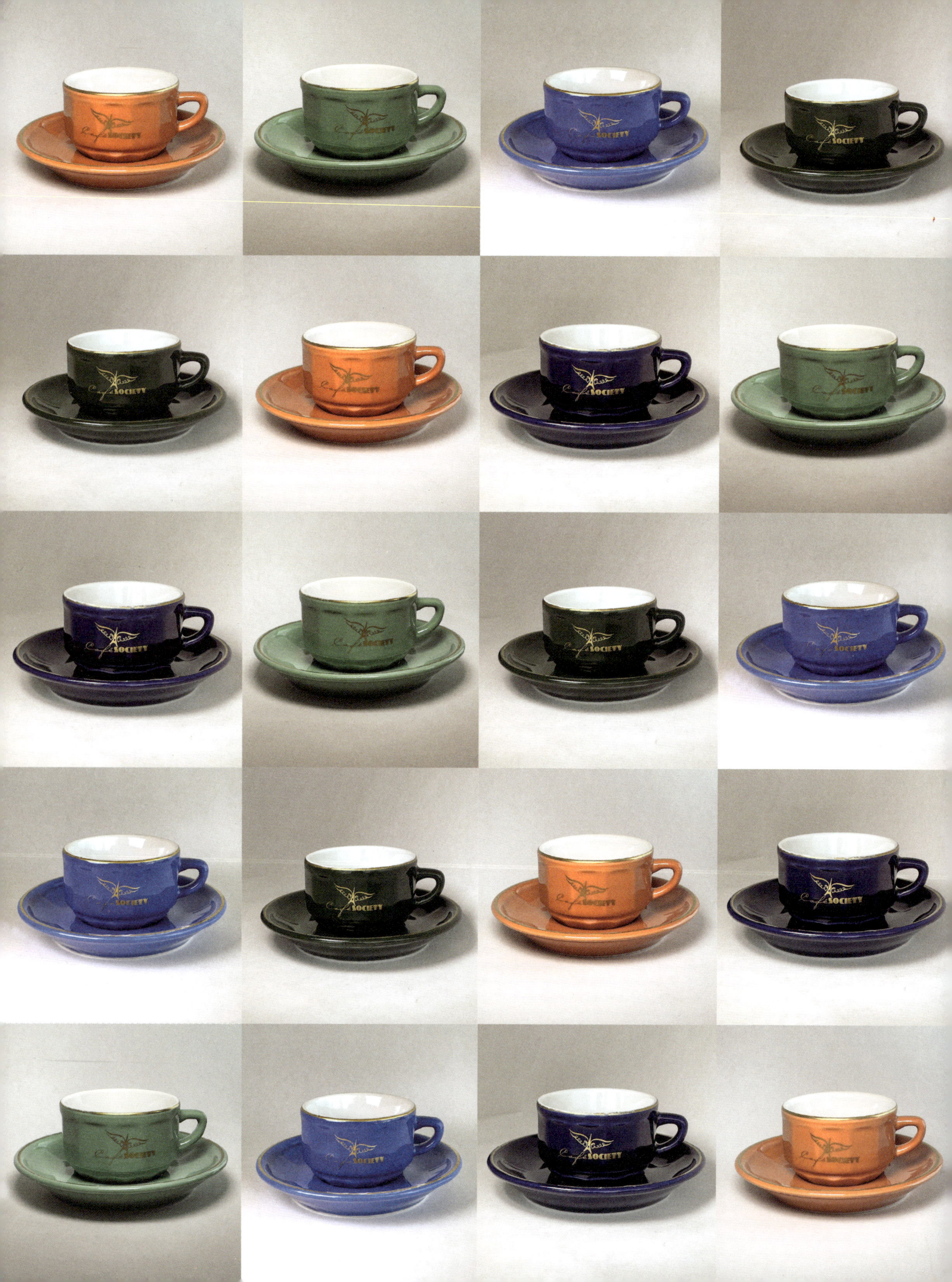
Cafe SOCIETY

CAFÉ SOCIETY

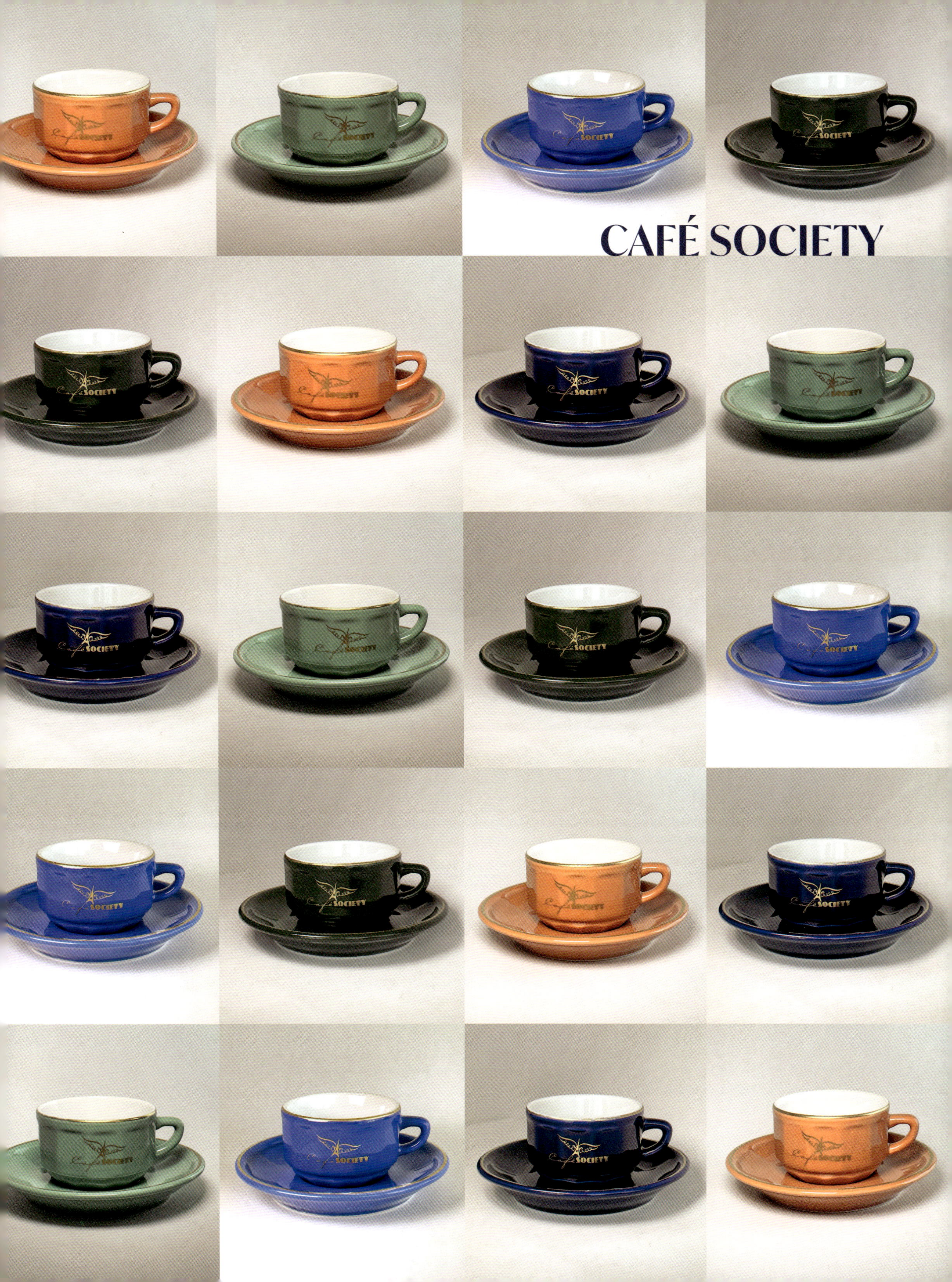

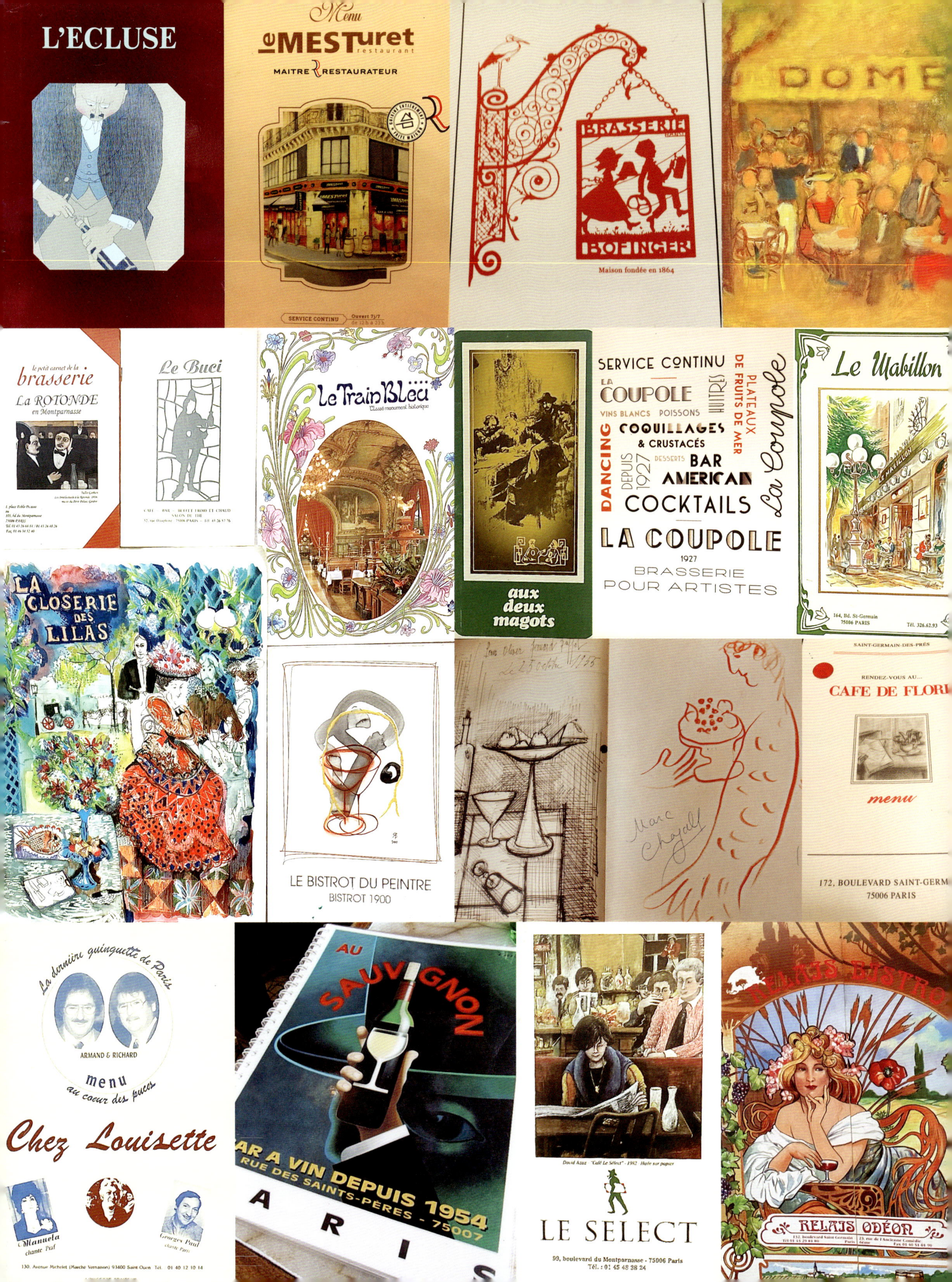

L'ECLUSE
Menu
le MESTuret restaurant
MAITRE RESTAURATEUR
SERVICE CONTINU
Ouvert 7j/7
BRASSERIE
BOFINGER
Maison fondée en 1864
DOME
le petit carnet de la
brasserie
La ROTONDE
en Montparnasse
Le Buci
Le Train Bleu
Classé monument historique
aux deux magots
SERVICE CONTINU
LA COUPOLE
VINS BLANCS POISSONS
COQUILLAGES
& CRUSTACÉS
HUITRES
PLATEAUX DE FRUITS DE MER
DANCING
DEPUIS 1927
DESSERTS
BAR AMERICAN
COCKTAILS
La Coupole
LA COUPOLE
1927
BRASSERIE
POUR ARTISTES
Le Mabillon
164, Bd. St-Germain
75006 PARIS
Tél. 326.62.93
LA CLOSERIE DES LILAS
LE BISTROT DU PEINTRE
BISTROT 1900
Marc Chagall
SAINT-GERMAIN-DES-PRÉS
RENDEZ-VOUS AU...
CAFE DE FLORE
menu
172, BOULEVARD SAINT-GERM
75006 PARIS
La dernière guinguette de Paris
ARMAND & RICHARD
menu
au coeur des puces
Chez Louisette
Manuela
chante Piaf
Georges Paul
130, Avenue Michelet (Marché Vernaison) 93400 Saint Ouen Tél. : 01 40 12 10 14
AU SAUVIGNON
BAR A VIN DEPUIS 1954
RUE DES SAINTS-PÈRES - 75007
PARIS
David Azuz "Café Le Sélect" - 1982 Huile sur papier
LE SÉLECT
99, boulevard du Montparnasse - 75006 Paris
Tél. : 01 45 48 38 24
RELAIS BISTRO
RELAIS ODÉON

CAFÉ SOCIETY

Time Suspended: The Cafés & Bistros of Paris

Joanie Osburn

To Larry,

Vive les cafés et bistros de Paris!

Joanie Osburn

June 13, 2023

goff BOOKS

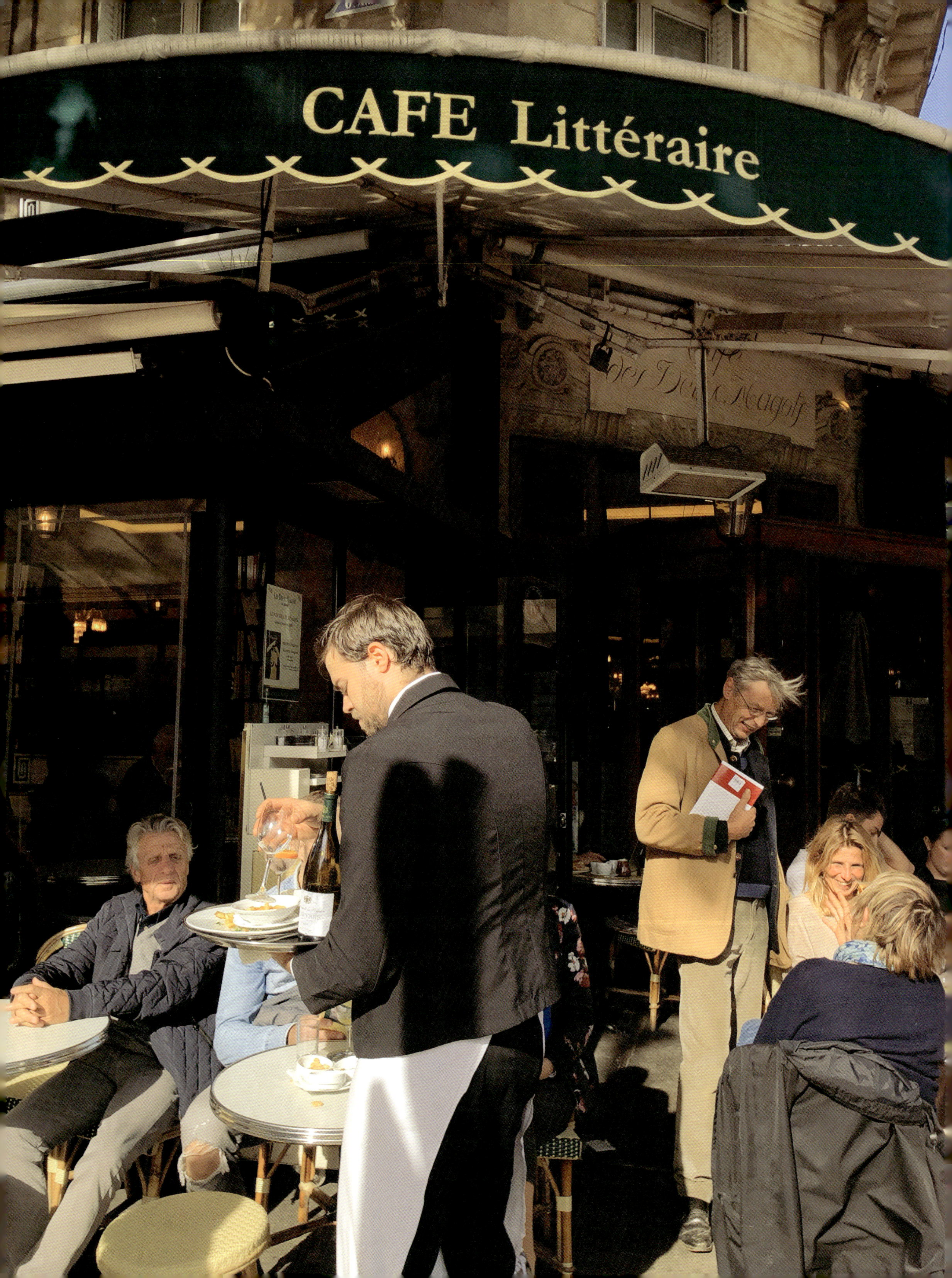
CAFE Littéraire

Contents

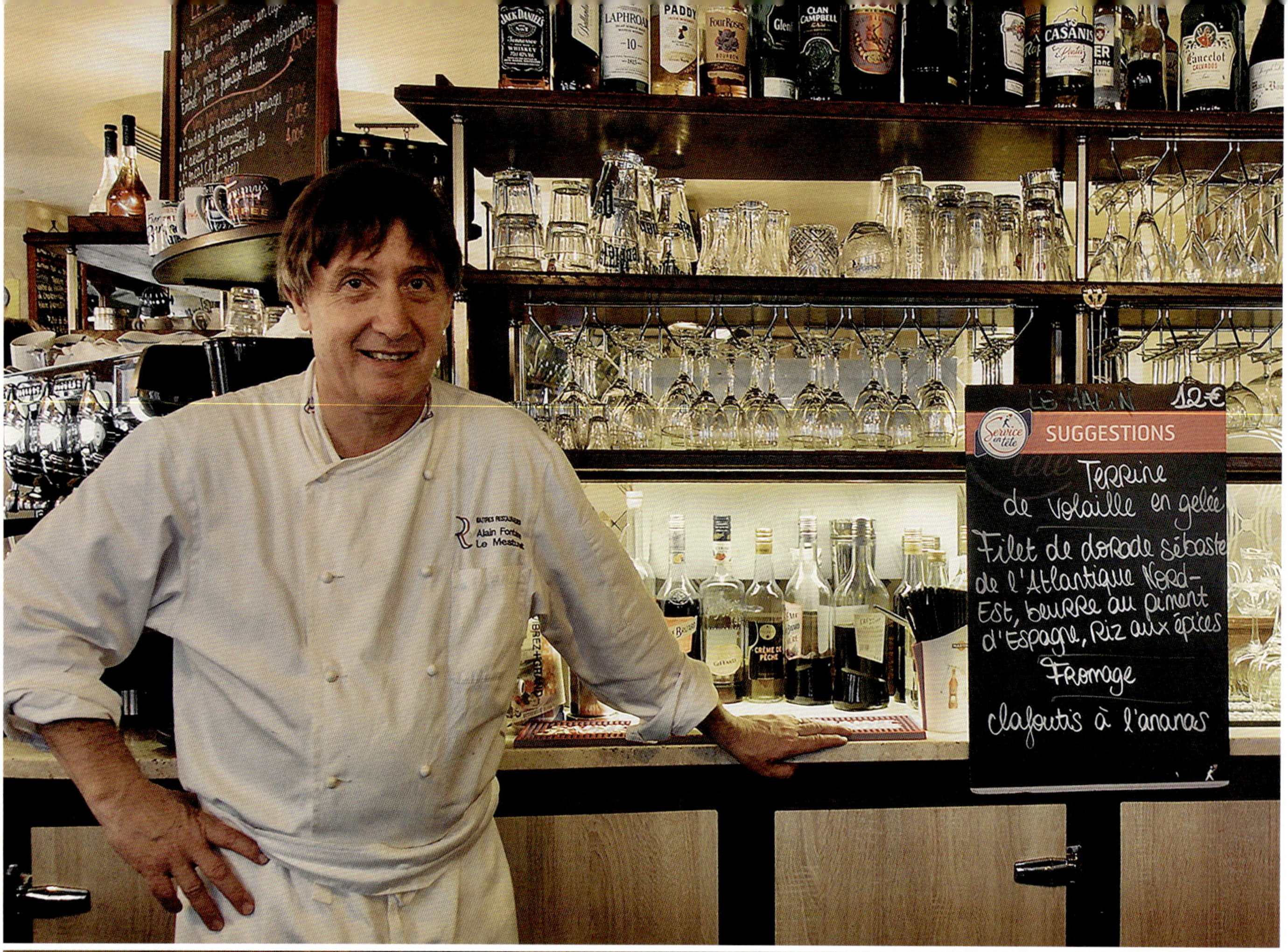
SUGGESTIONS
12€
Terrine de volaille en gelée
Filet de dorade sébaste de l'Atlantique Nord-Est, beurre au piment d'Espagne, Riz aux épices
Fromage
clafoutis à l'ananas

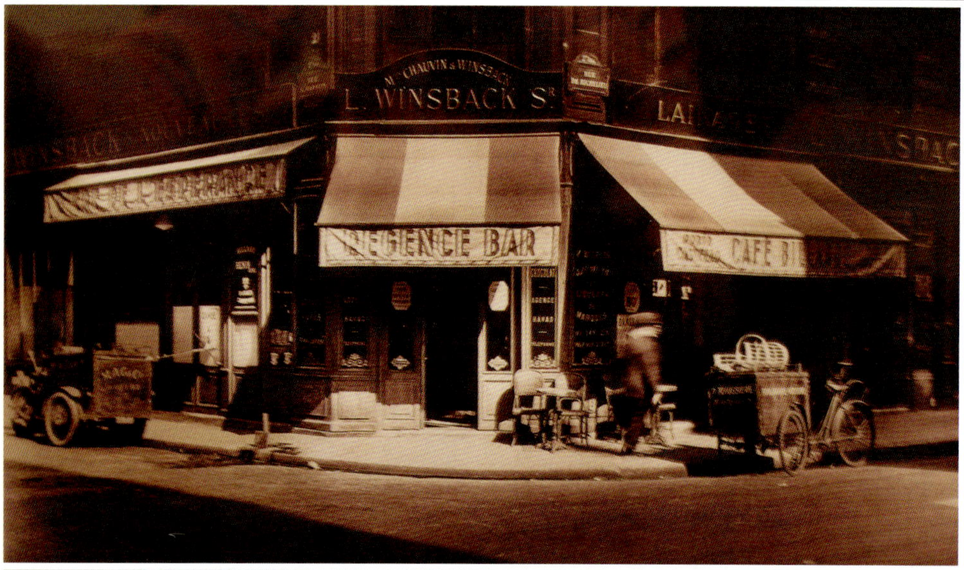
L. WINSBACK Sr
REGENCE BAR

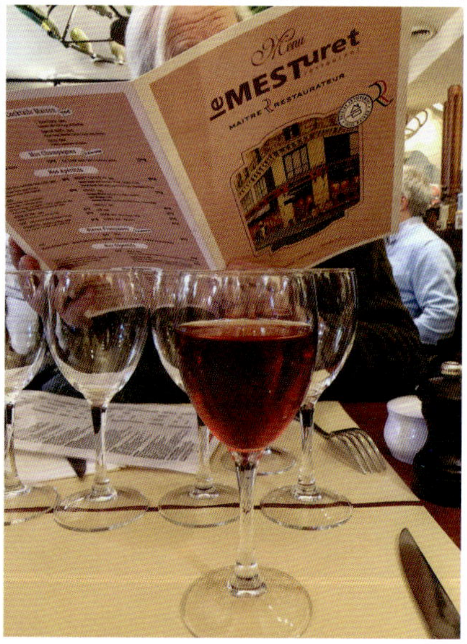
Menu
MESTuret
MAÎTRE RESTAURATEUR

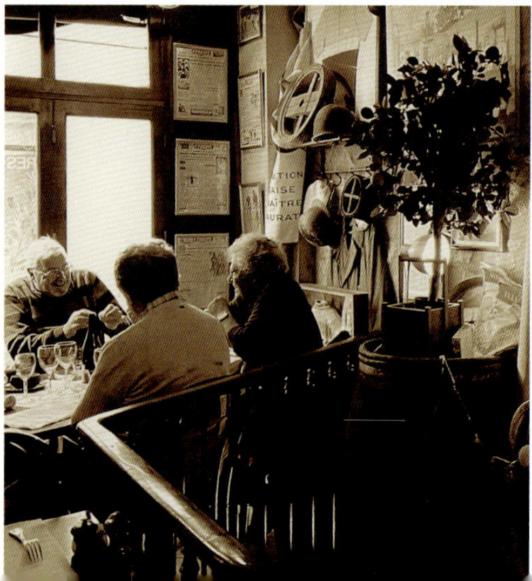

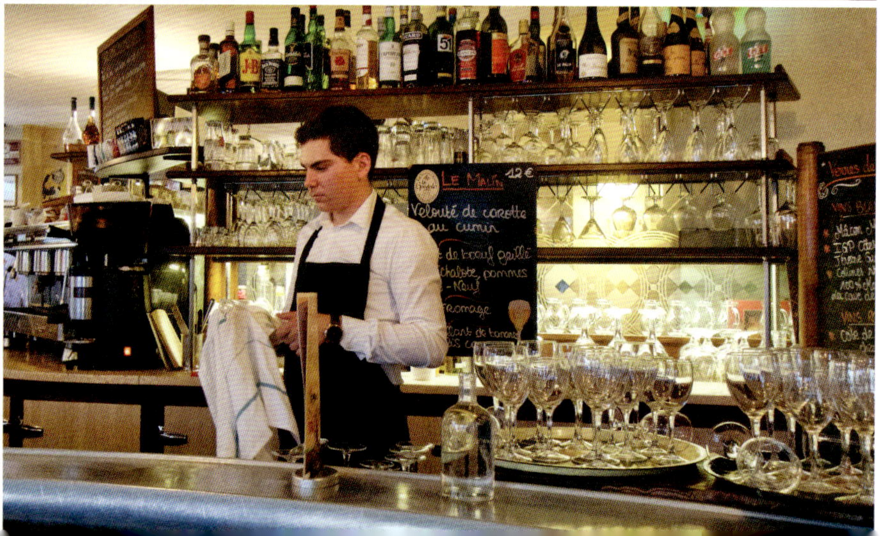

Foreword

Je voulais féliciter Joanie Osburn qui a su capter l'art de vivre des cafés et bistrots parisiens avec justesse et bienveillance.

A la lecture de son remarquable livre, on comprend d'emblée que cet art de vivre si parisien est en réalité offert aux touristes du monde entier, à tous les amoureux de Paris et des parisiens.

Il fallait le regard particulier d'une "Américaine à Paris" pour raconter ce qui nous semble tellement naturel : le plaisir des terrasses, le goût des produits de qualité travaillé avec soin, le fumet d'un café au comptoir, coude-à-coude avec un étranger qui l'est tout d'un coup bien moins, le goût des autres...

Au détour des pages, on se prend à flâner dans les rues de la capitale, à se rappeler des rencontres entre amis, des moments de convivialité autour des comptoirs de nos bistrots.

C'est toute l'âme du peuple de Paris que Joanie évoque avec talent, sans oublier bien sûr les femmes et les hommes qui travaillent au quotidien à rendre leur ville accueillante, agréable et plus humaine.

Ce beau livre est un manuel poétique pour mieux profiter de l'expérience parisienne, pour comprendre que chaque café, chaque bistrot possède une âme particulière. A chacun de trouver l'établissement qui lui correspond le mieux ! Entre enseignes mythiques et cafés de quartier, nous partageons la même convivialité.

Le Paris que décrit Joanie n'est pas nostalgique, il est bien vivant et nous travaillons tous les jours à le préserver pour nos clients à venir.

Je suis très touché que l'auteure soit si attachée à ces personnages hauts en couleur qui se retrouvent dans nos cafés et bistrots parisiens, échappés d'un film, d'une chanson ou d'un roman.

Merci à elle et longue vie à *Café Society, The Cafés and Bistros of Paris* !

I wish to congratulate Joanie Osburn, who has captured the art of living in Parisian cafés and bistros with accuracy and benevolence.

Reading her remarkable book, we immediately understand that this Parisian art of living is in fact offered to tourists from all over the world, to all Paris lovers and Parisians.

It took the special eye of an "American in Paris" to recount what seems so natural to us: the pleasure of the terraces, the taste of quality products prepared with care, the aroma of a coffee at the counter, side by side, elbow-to-elbow with a stranger who is suddenly much less so, the taste of others...

As we turn the pages, we find ourselves strolling through the streets of the capital, remembering meetings between friends, moments of conviviality around the counters of our bistros.

It is the whole soul of the people of Paris that Joanie evokes with talent, without forgetting of course the women and men who work every day to make their city welcoming, pleasant, and more human.

This beautiful book is a poetic manual to a better enjoyment of the Parisian experience, to understand that each café, each bistro has a particular soul. It's up to everyone to find the establishment that suits them best! Between legendary brasseries and neighborhood cafés, we share the same conviviality.

The Paris that Joanie describes is not nostalgic, it is very much alive and we work every day to preserve it for our future clients.

I am very touched that the author is so attached to these colorful characters who find themselves in our Parisian cafés and bistros, escaped from a movie, a song, or a novel.

Thank you to her and long life to *Café Society, The Cafés and Bistros of Paris*!

Alain Fontaine

Founder of the restaurant Le Mesturet, president of the Association Française des Maîtres Restaurateurs

Flâneuring on the Streets of Paris

"A walk about Paris will provide lessons in history, beauty, and in the point of Life."

Thomas Jefferson

Daily life plays out on Paris's streets alongside traces of centuries rich with history. As in all big cities, the Parisians rush through the streets to reach their work and rendezvous on time, but despite the hurry, they appreciate and find joy in their city, punctuated with bursts of creativity: impromptu group dancing, fancy skating on a bridge, children posing on Buren's interactive columns, a clown walking through Arc de Triomphe du Carrousel on a snowy day, perhaps a wedding party at the Tour Eiffel, or a bride running through the rain-soaked street. Then we reach the illustrious Shakespeare & Co., which pays homage to San Francisco's renowned City Lights and charms us with its own café. However, frequent strikes by students, transit workers, even lawyers, called *grèves,* and *manifestations*, do not delight, and hamper the usual modes of transportation. Paris makes a great backdrop for all this and more. A city on the move, not resting on its laurels, is one of the world's most popular destinations. Who can forget Humphrey Bogart's "We'll always have Paris" in *Casablanca*? No matter when you experience the city, the memory of Paris is destined to endure.

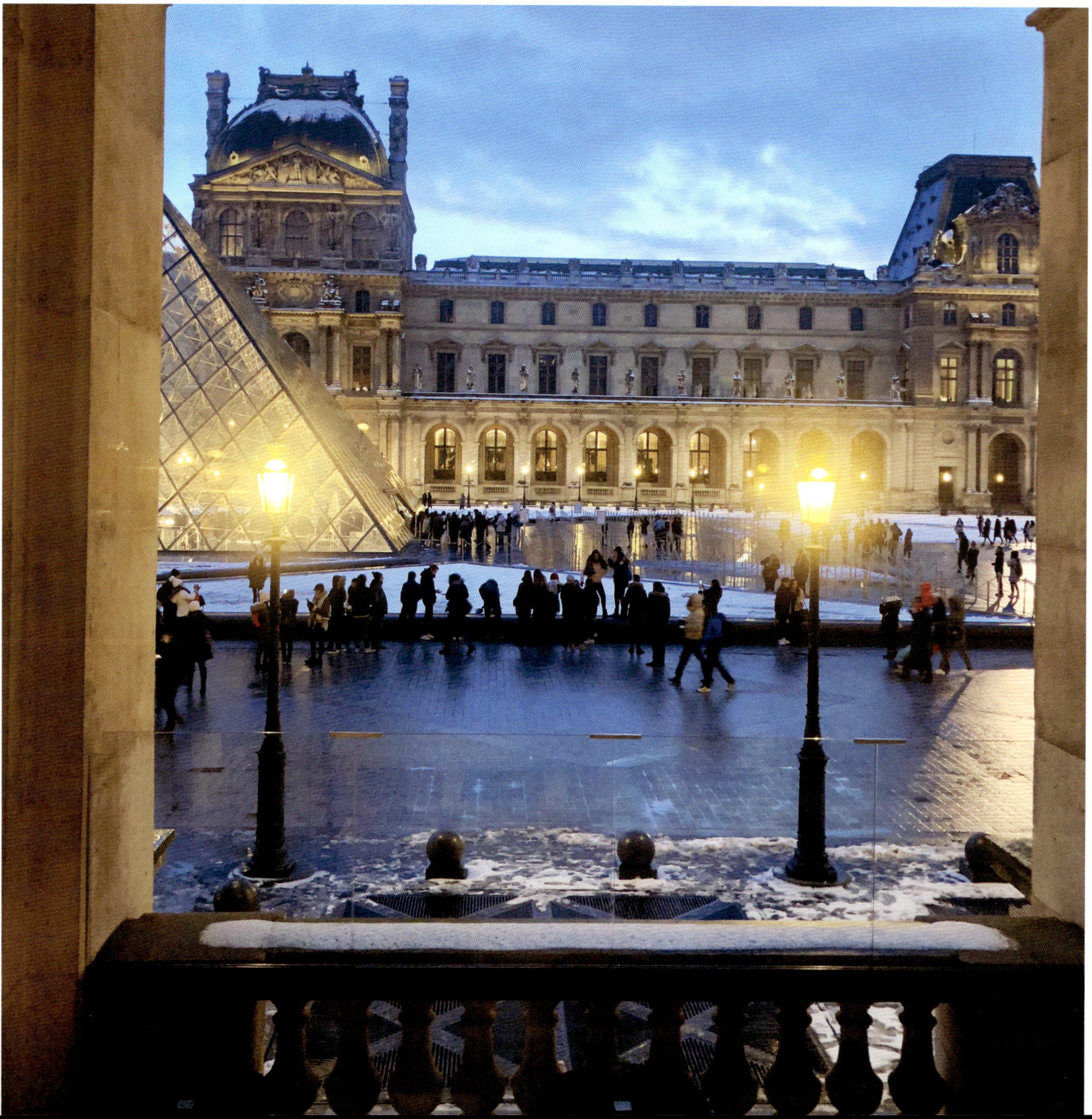

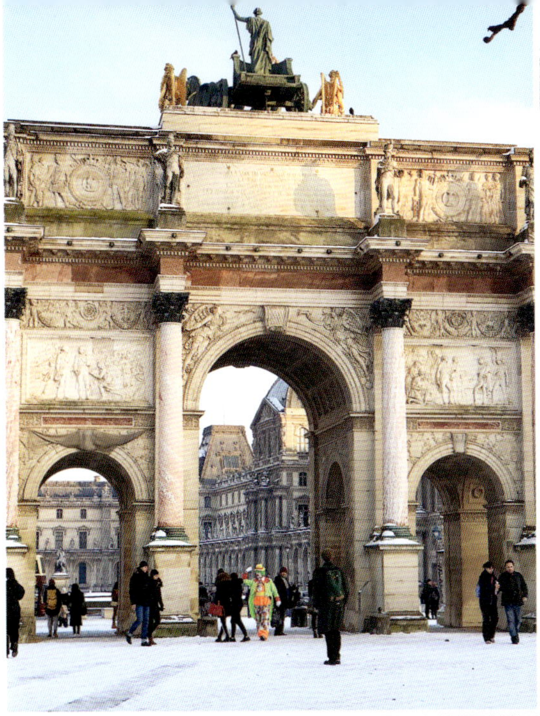

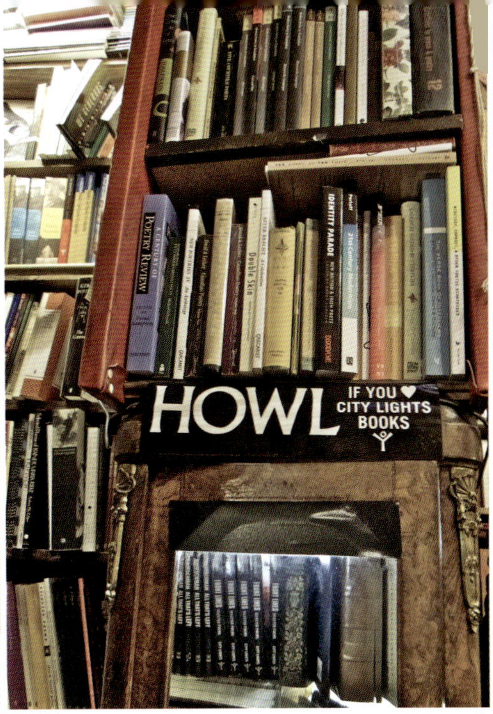
HOWL
IF YOU ♥ CITY LIGHTS BOOKS

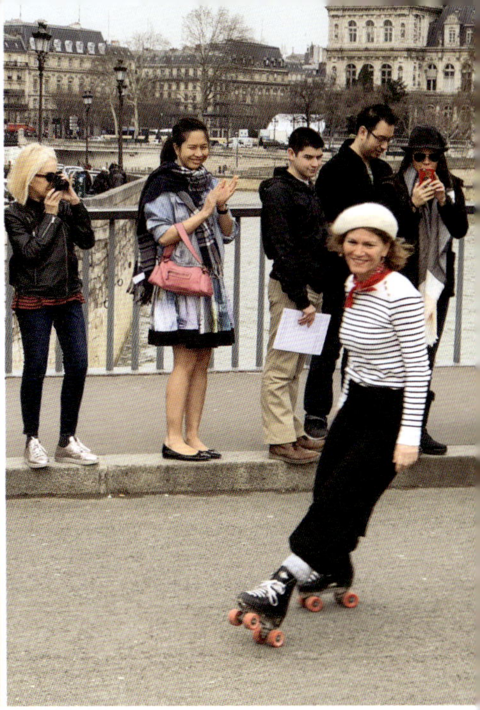

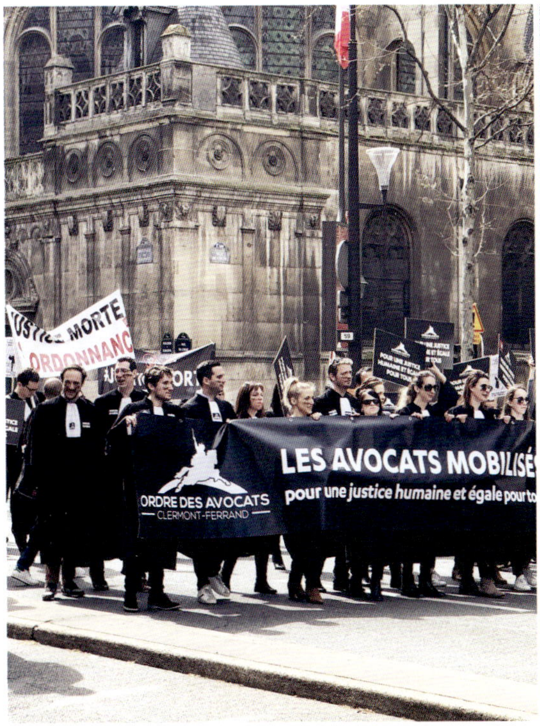
LES AVOCATS MOBILISÉ
pour une justice humaine et égale pour to
ORDRE DES AVOCATS
CLERMONT-FERRAND

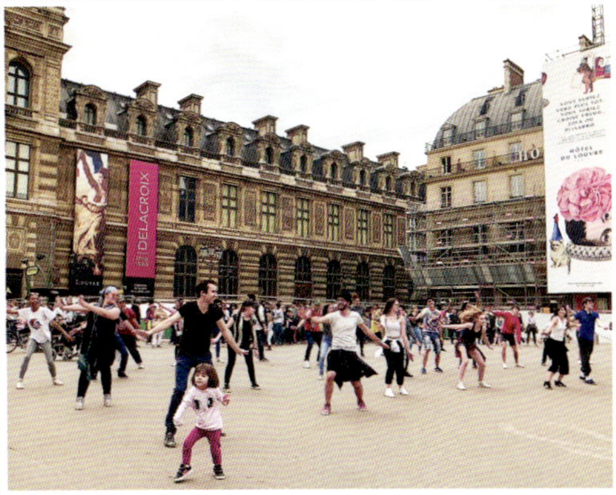
DELACROIX

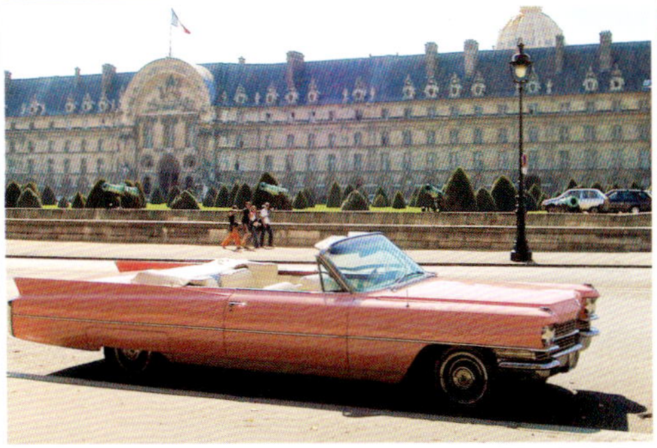

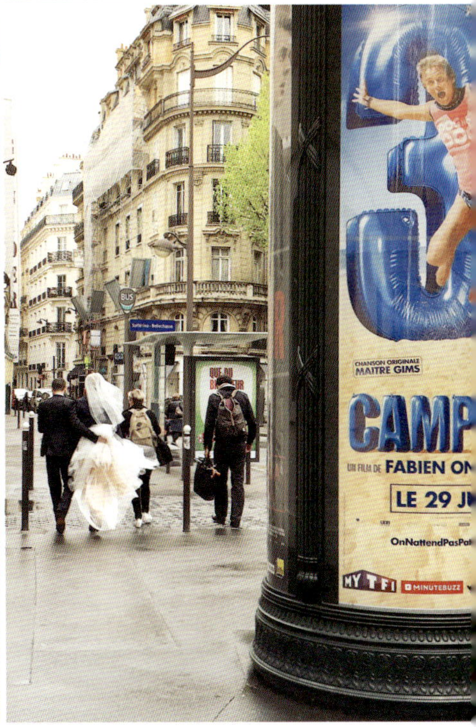
CHANSON ORIGINALE
MAITRE GIMS
CAMP
FABIEN ON
LE 29 J

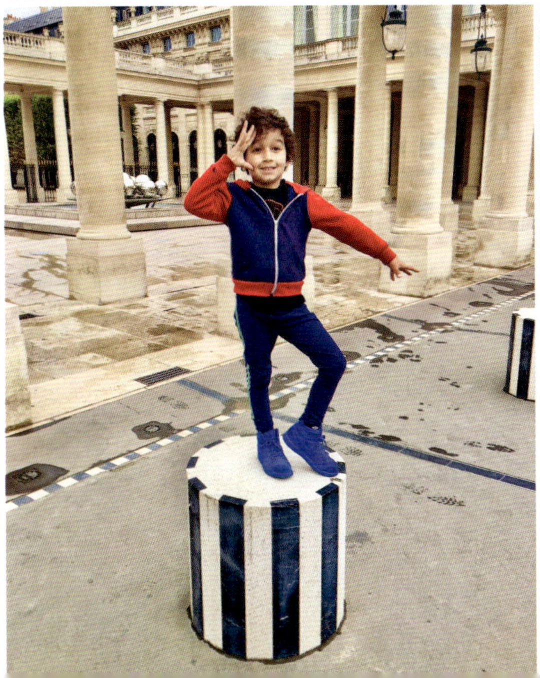

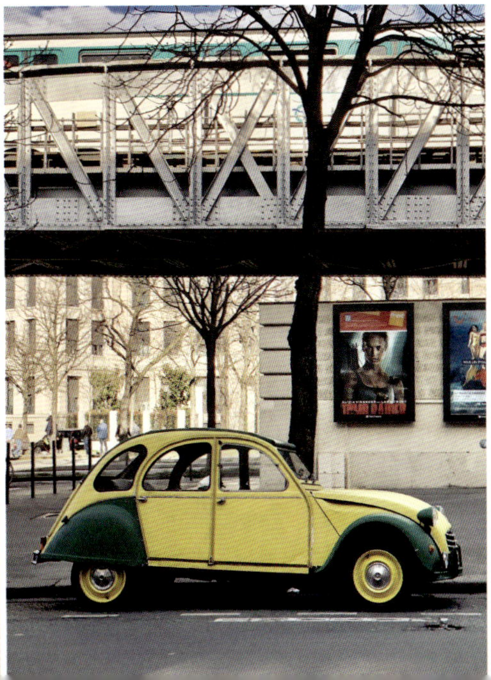

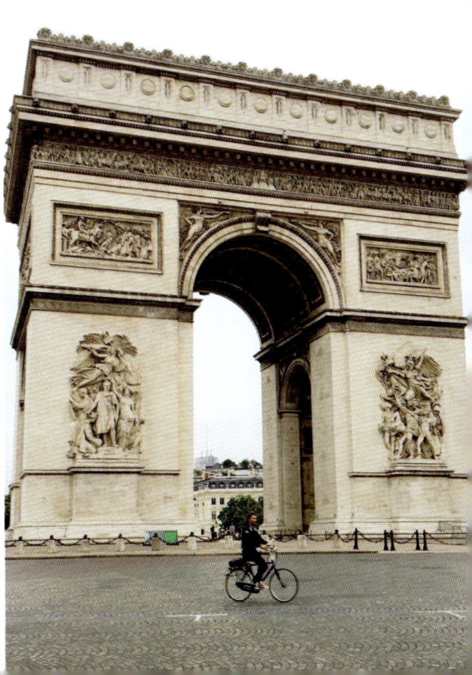

Expect the Unexpected

"To err is human, to stroll is Parisian."
Victor Hugo, *Les Misérables*

A walk through the streets of Paris elicits all the senses: the sound of the rain, the street music, the traffic, the children playing. Sure, the eye is pleased by the magnificent monuments, yet also by the architecture, window displays, outdoor sculptures, manicured parks, fashionable people on the move, and the unexpected, unpredictable bursts of Parisian creativity that seems so natural. Who cannot be captivated by the fragrance of exquisite florists' displays spilling onto the street, the scent of chickens roasting on outdoor rotisseries, or the inviting aroma emanating from cafés, bistros, and patisseries? Unlike the US, where people routinely walk the streets with paper cups of sugary coffee drink, in Paris, it is not about drinks to go but rather about the aroma of espresso radiating from the café where one wants *to stay* and enjoy. How delicious is the taste of a freshly made crêpe from a street cart, roasted chestnuts from a corner stand, croissants from a patisserie, gelato from Berthillon, or something unexpected from an open-air food market that one passes through *en flâneur*? We want to touch the locks on the bridges (before the authorities remove them), the bouquiniste's books, the enticing items in the pretty boutiques. We must take care to watch our step as we walk with our heads turned sideways toward the tempting window displays. After an exhilarating promenade, we are quite ready to take a café break and calm our senses.

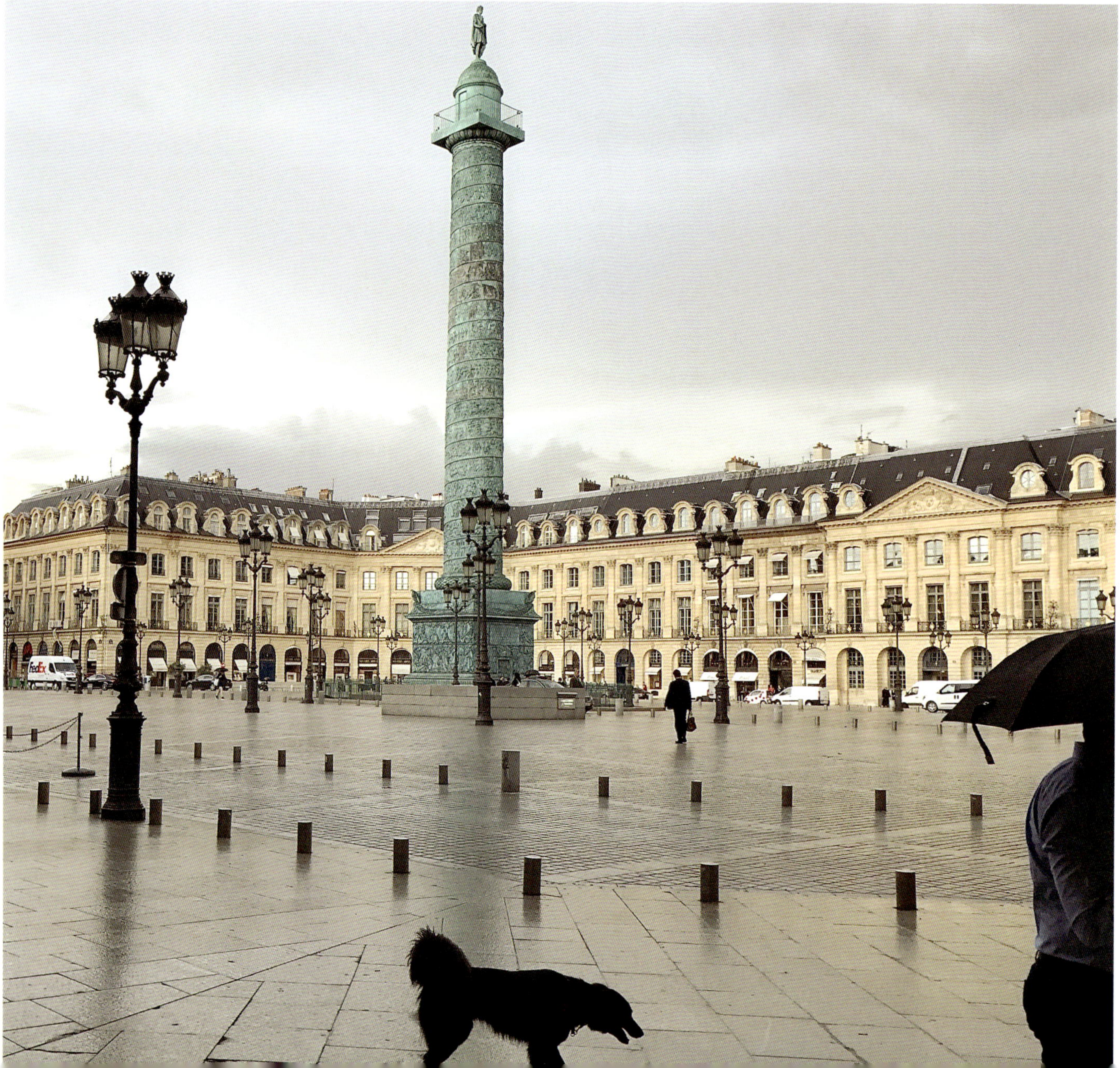

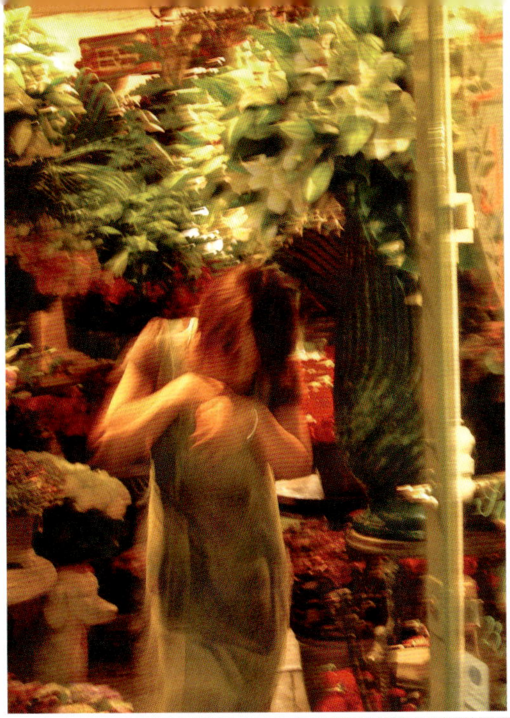
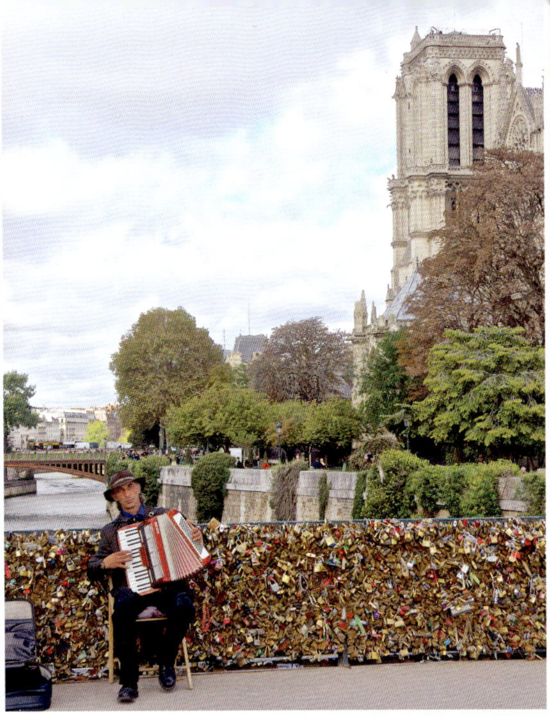
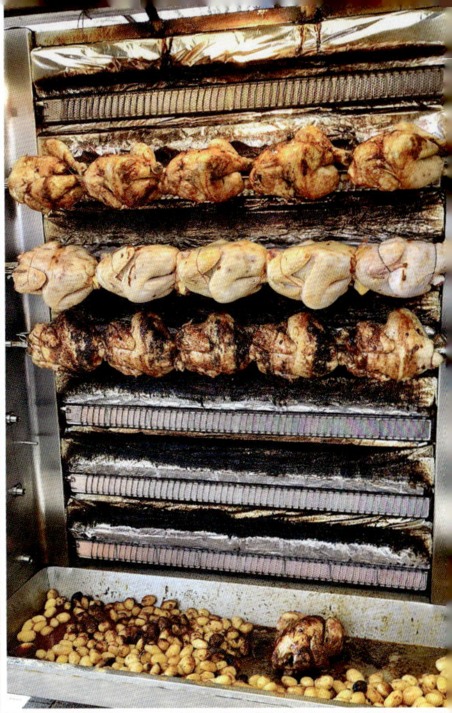
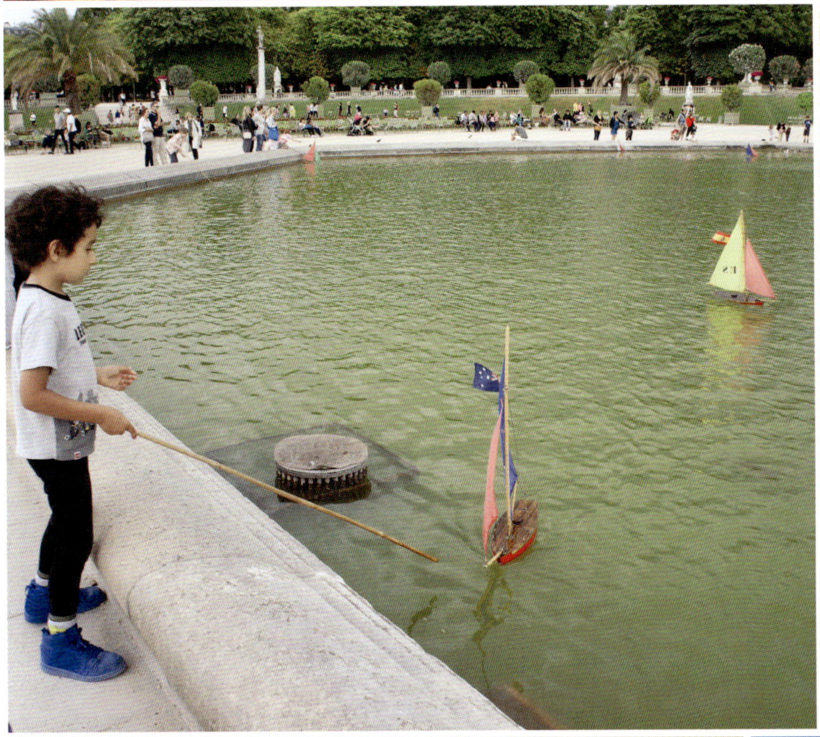
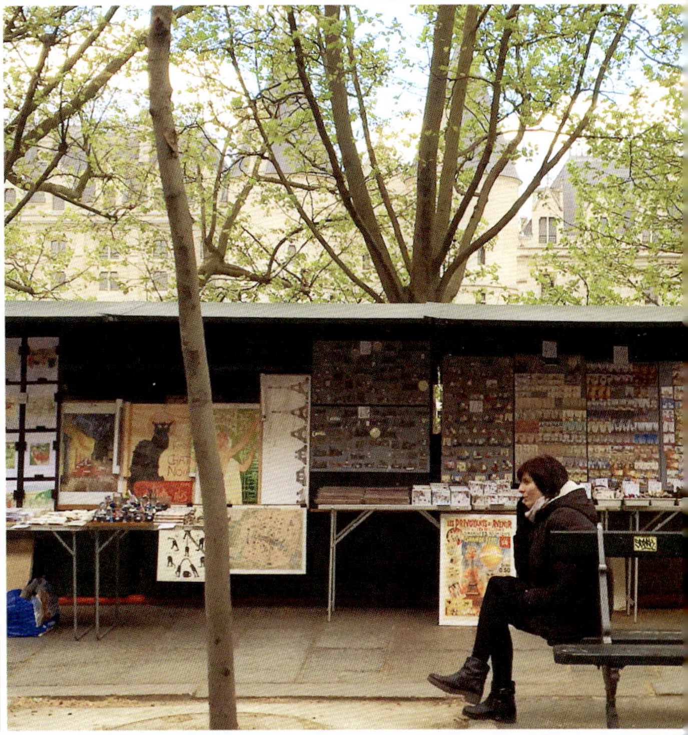
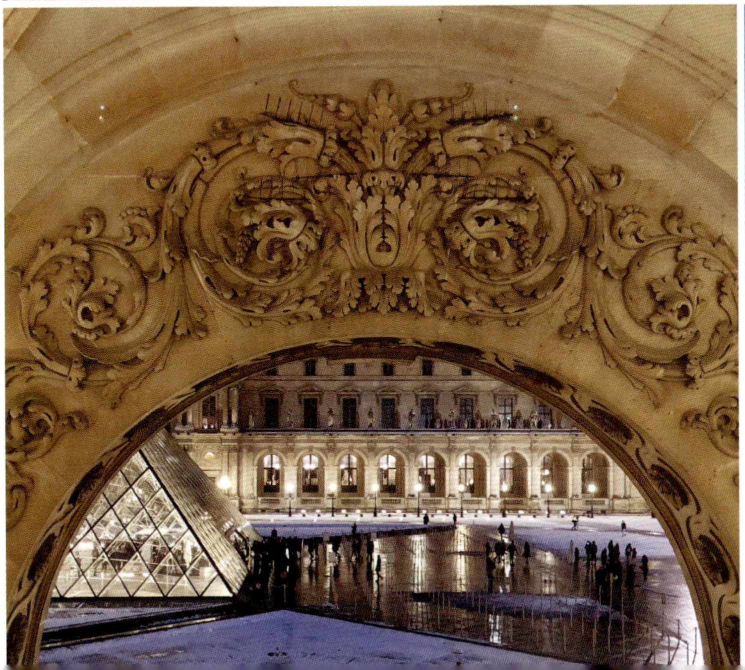
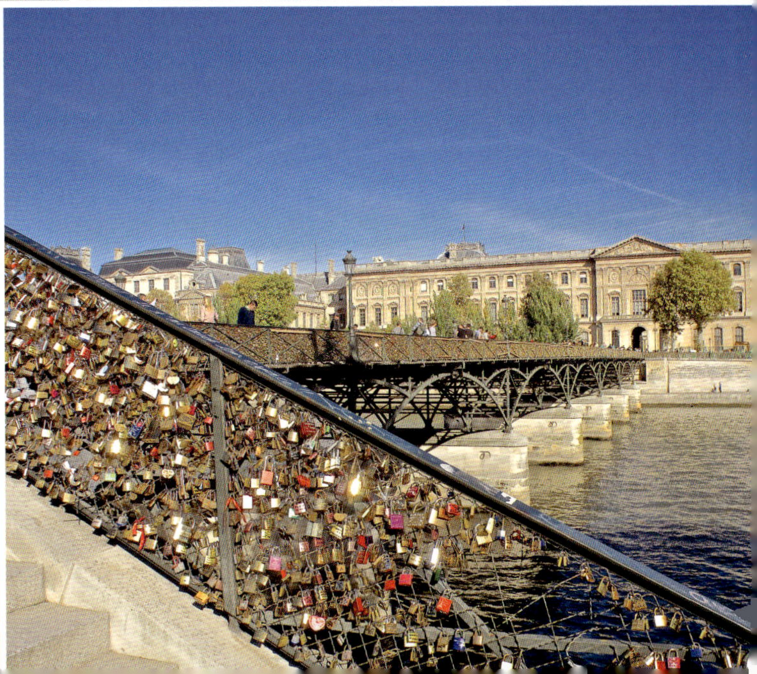

Poetry, Art, Flowers & Ice Cream

"To know Paris is to know a great deal."

Henry Miller

A Rimbaud poem written on a wall, paintings on a street corner, a bird perched on the head of a golden Joan of Arc. Everywhere you look, the beauty dotting the streets perchance delivers as much visual excitement as the magnificent interiors in the galleries and museums of Paris. And nature peeks out between the concrete and limestone, with around 484,000 trees—more than any other European capital—including beautifully sculpted plane trees and chestnut trees planted with chestnuts from Thomas Jefferson's Monticello. Along with the glorious Luxembourg Gardens, Paris has 480 other parks and manicured gardens meticulously curated each season, which deliver fresh compositions year-round. These impeccable gardens, along with the exquisite Parisian artisan florists, burst forth with color, fragrance, and stunning design that softens the streetscape.

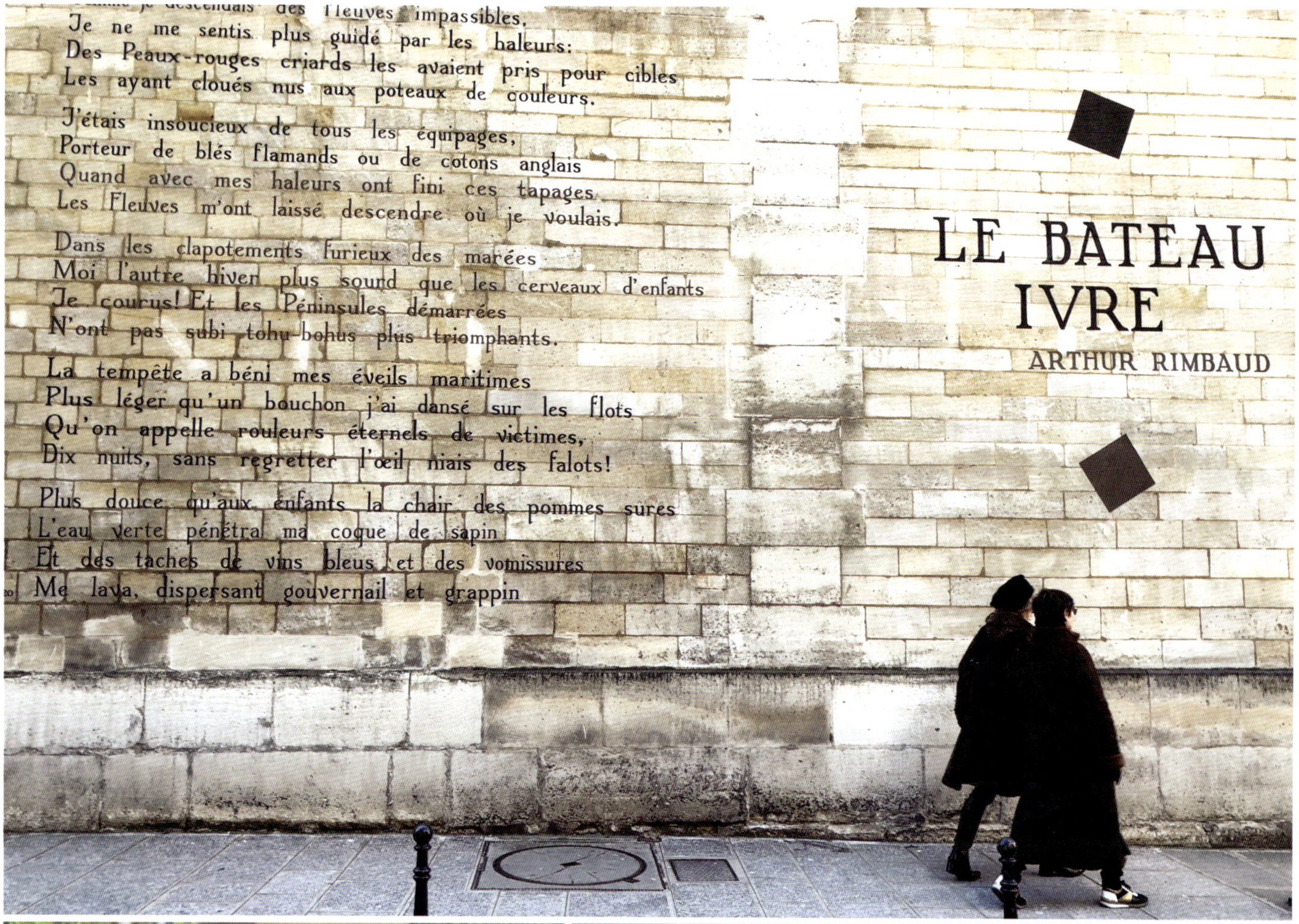

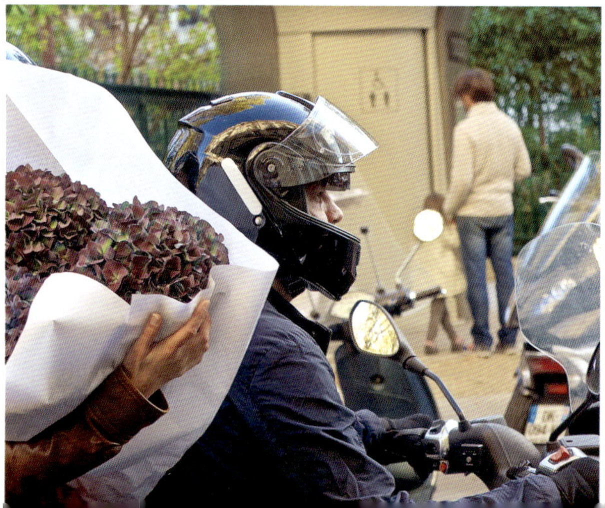

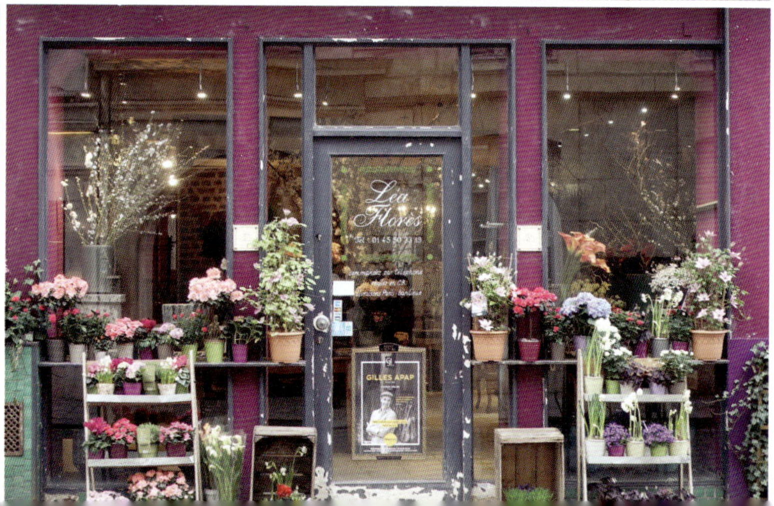

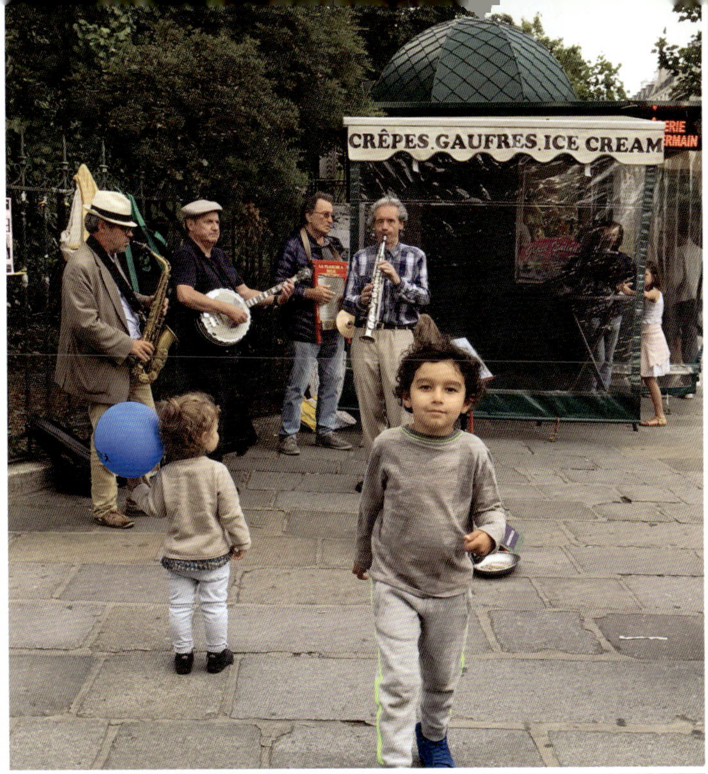
CRÊPES GAUFRES ICE CREAM

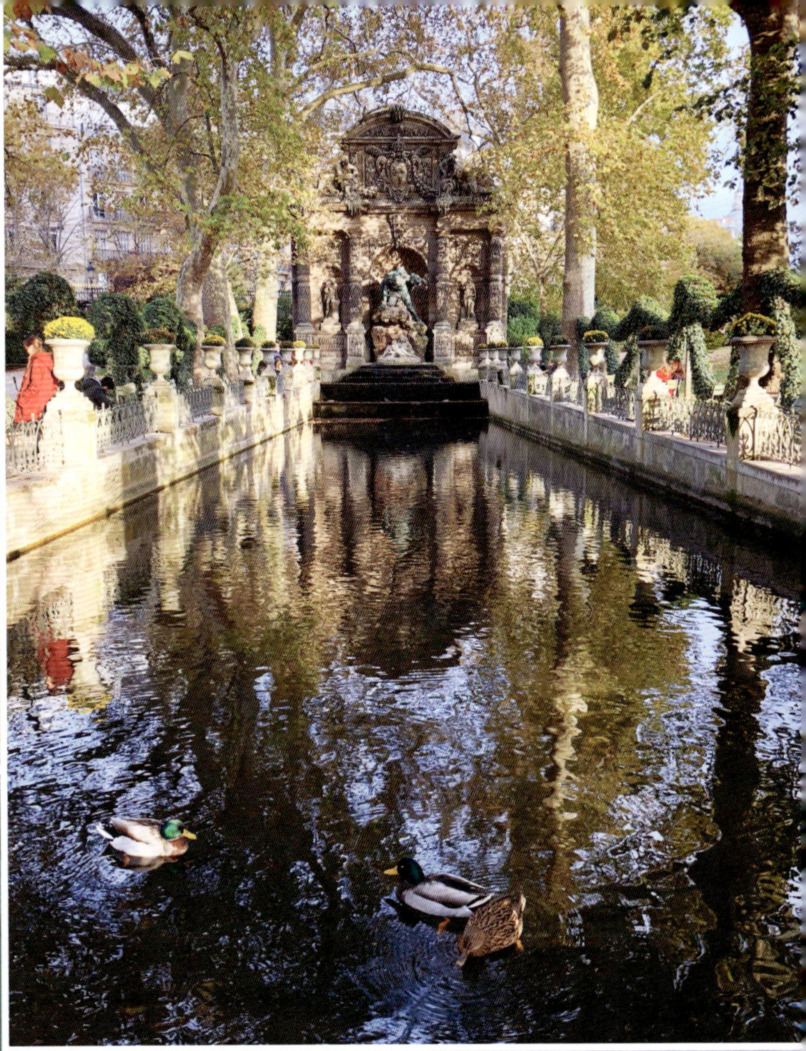

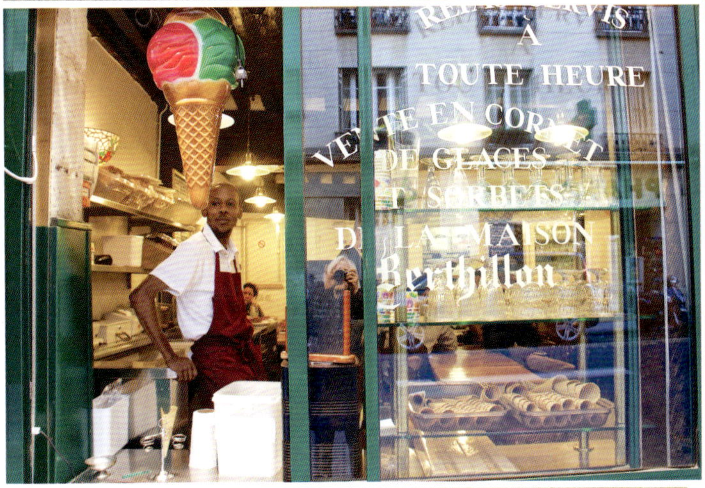
TOUTE HEURE
Berthillon

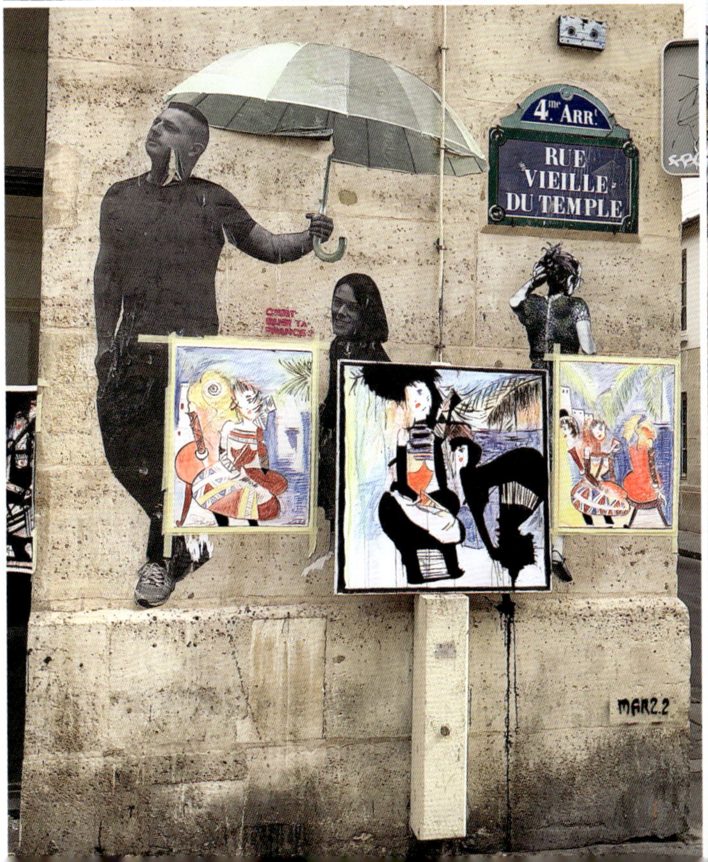
4me ARR.
RUE VIEILLE DU TEMPLE
MAR22

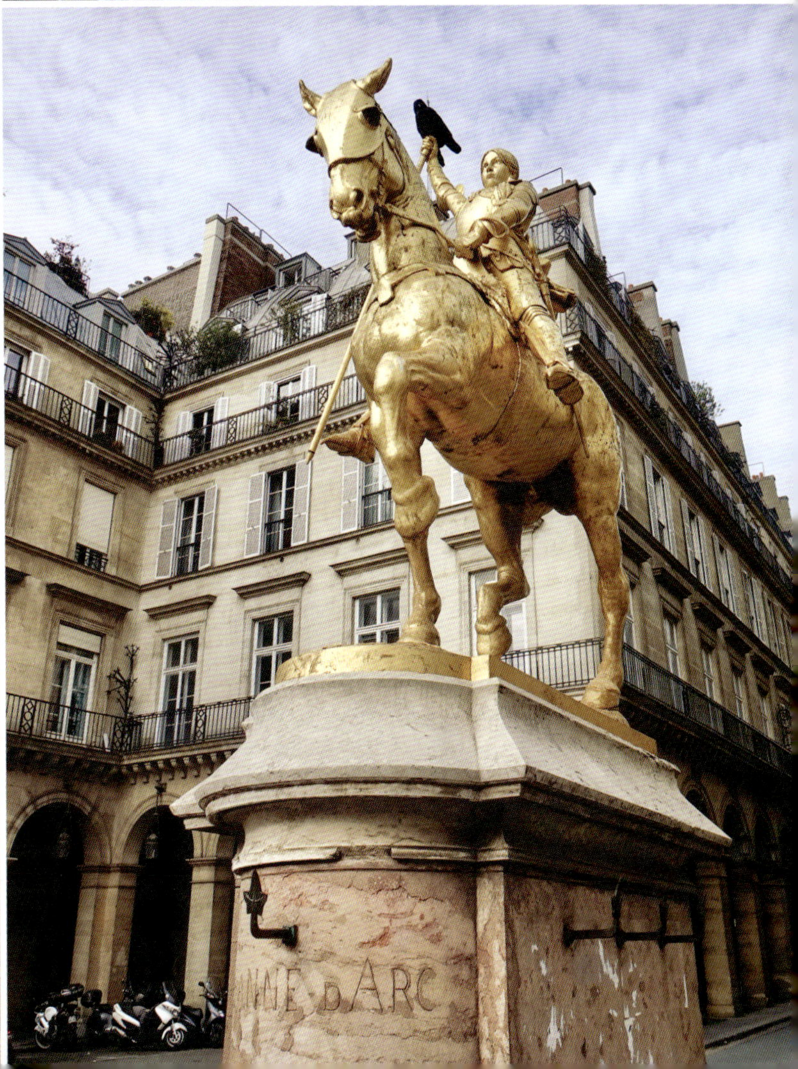

Spotted all Over Paris: The Eiffel Tower

> "There is an attraction and a charm inherent in the colossal that is not subject to ordinary theories of Art."
>
> **Gustave Eiffel**

From the Left to the Right Bank, the iconic Tour Eiffel can be seen all over Paris, through trees, across and under bridges, from balconies, atop buildings, behind Napoleon's cannons, and, most magnificently, at the Trocadéro. Before he created the Eiffel Tower for the 1889 Exposition Universelle—completed in two years, two months, and five days—master engineer Gustave Eiffel built hundreds of creative metal structures worldwide, including the Statue of Liberty. Though criticized by artists and writers of the day, the tower was an immediate success with two million visitors during the Exposition alone, followed by seven million visitors a year. Electrified at the turn of the 20th century, technology has since progressed to display spectacular light shows emanating from the tower. The Tour Eiffel, freshly painted a brighter yellow-brown for the 2024 Summer Olympics, stands tall as a symbol of Paris, a marvel of engineering and aesthetic design, as majestic and elegant today as it was in 1889.

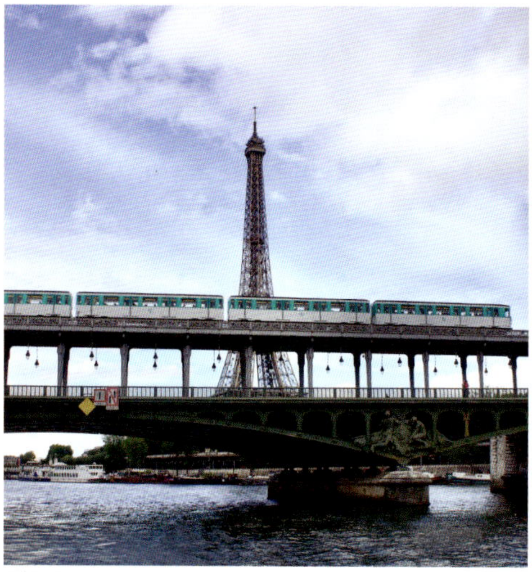

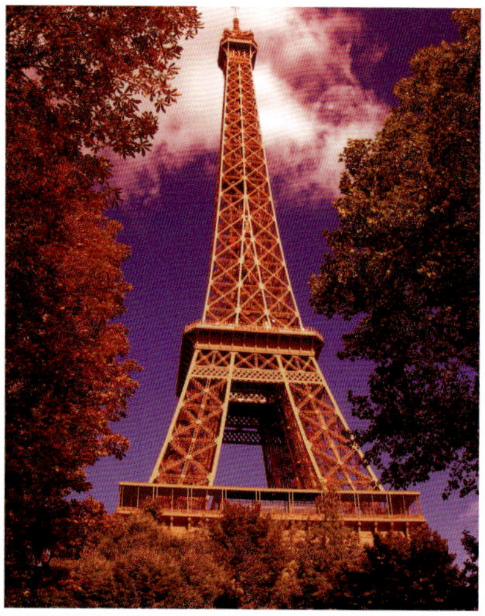

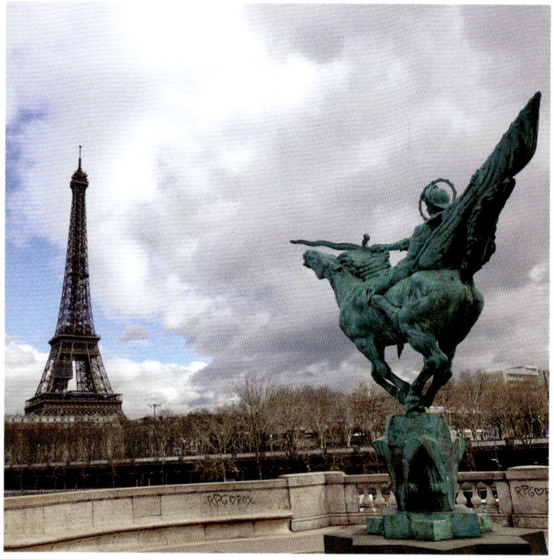

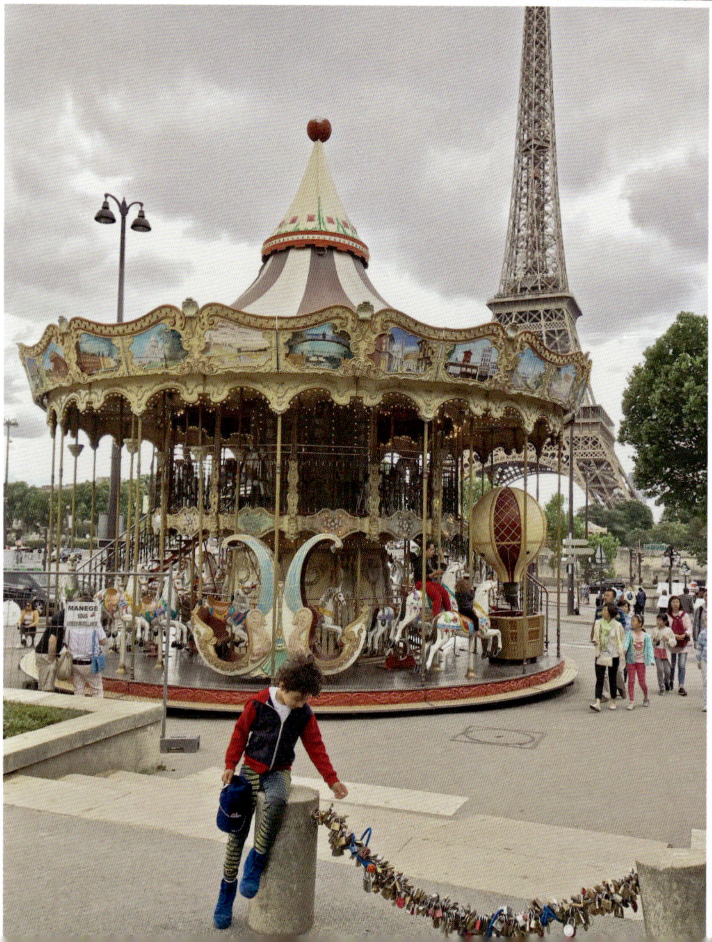

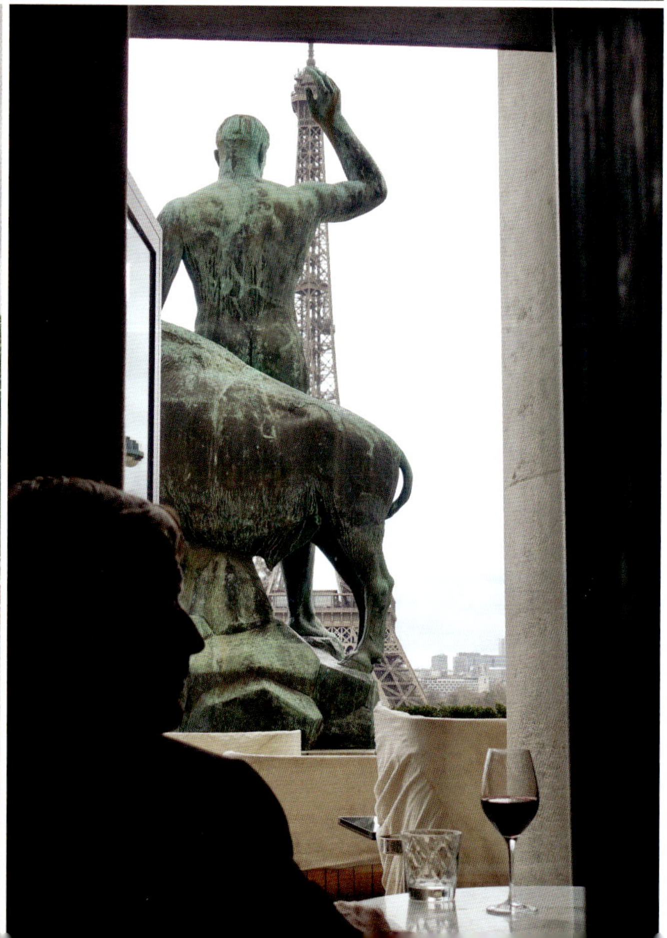

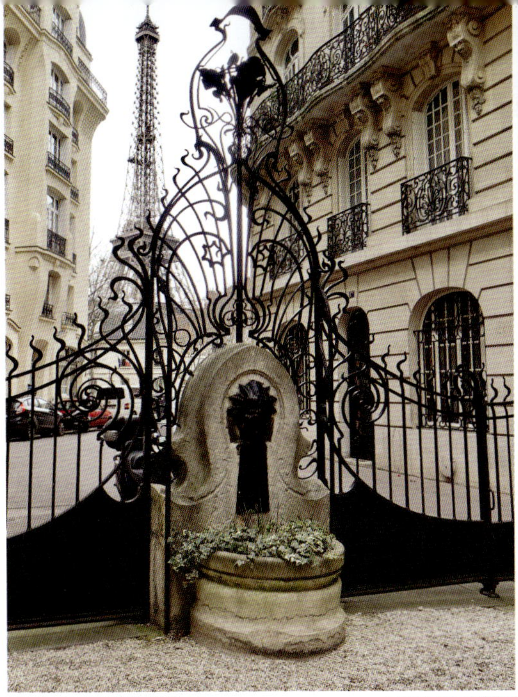
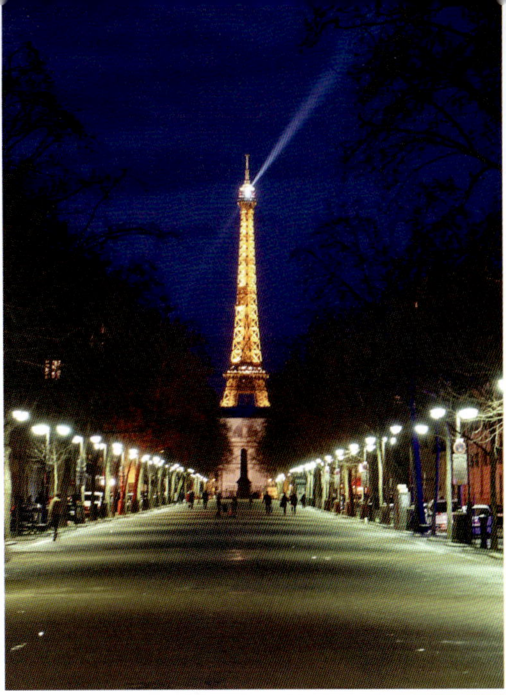
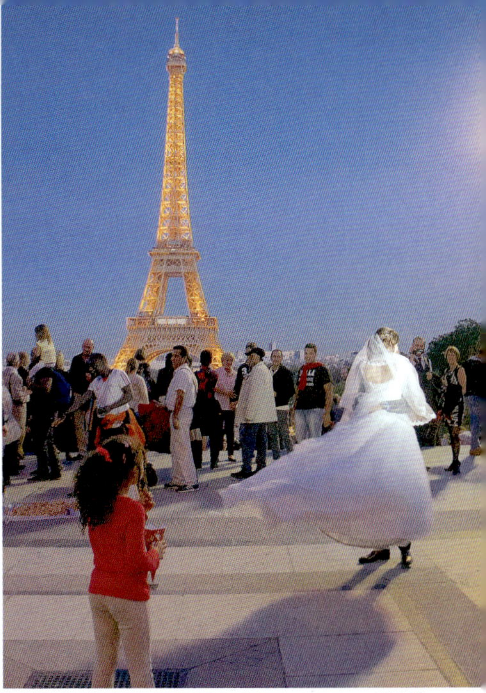
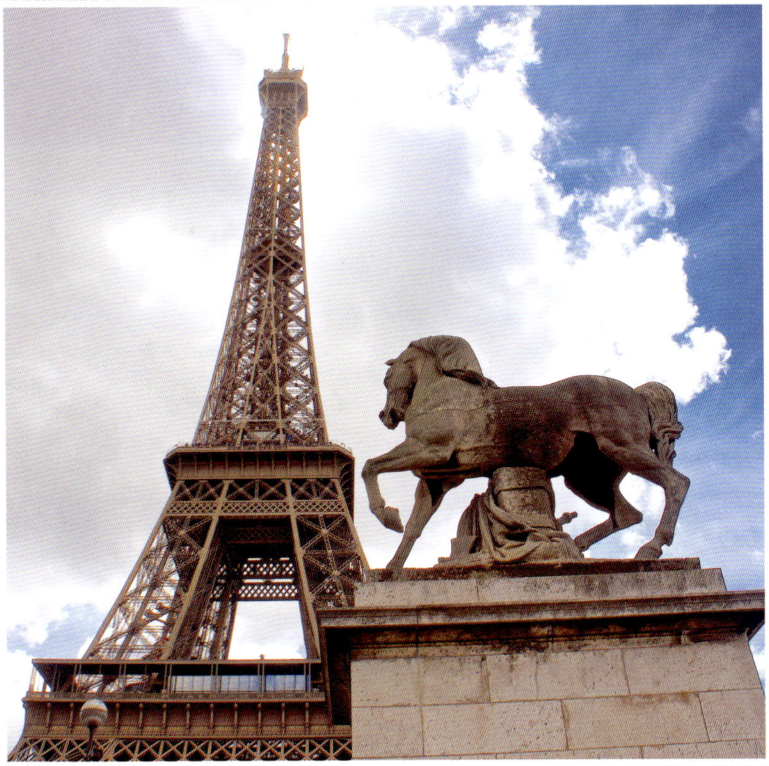
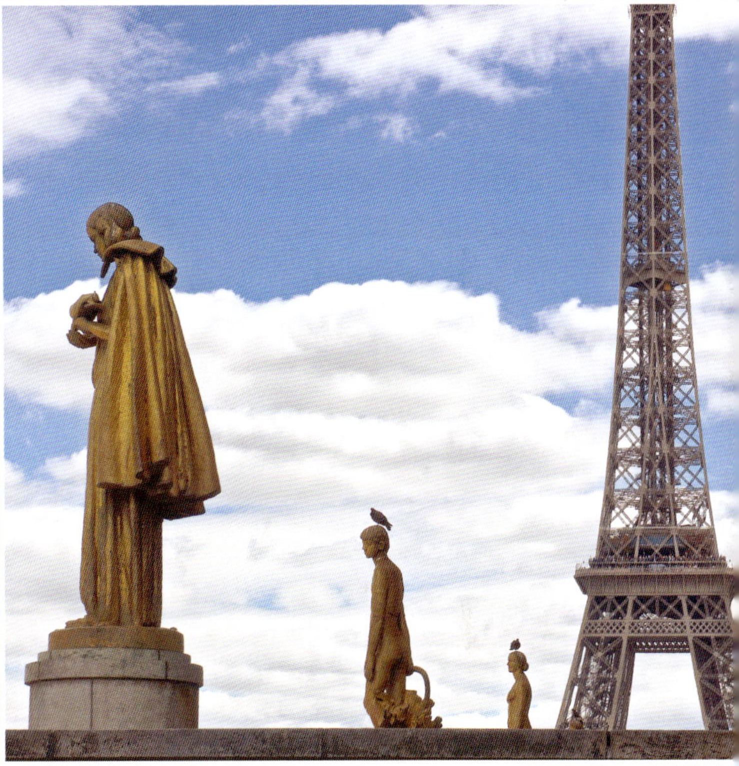
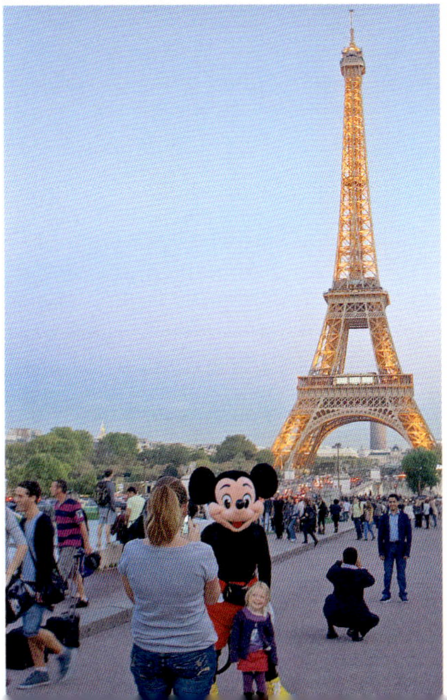
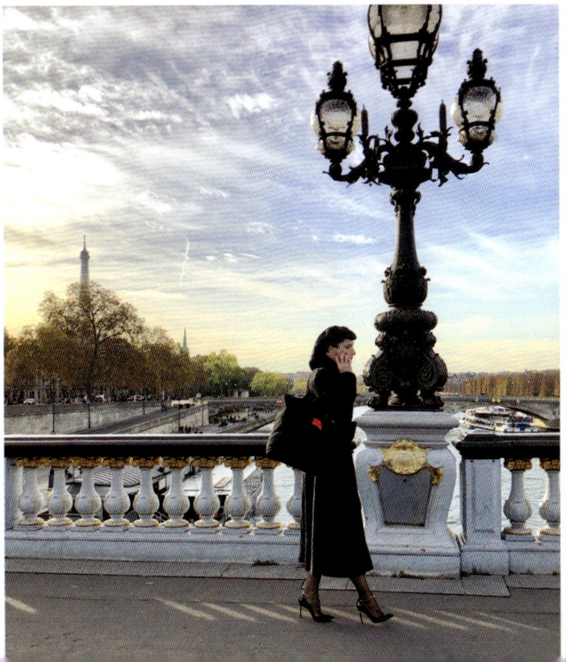
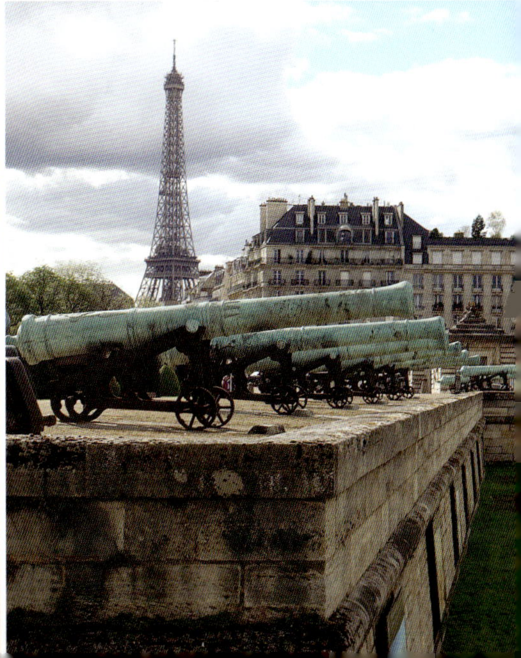

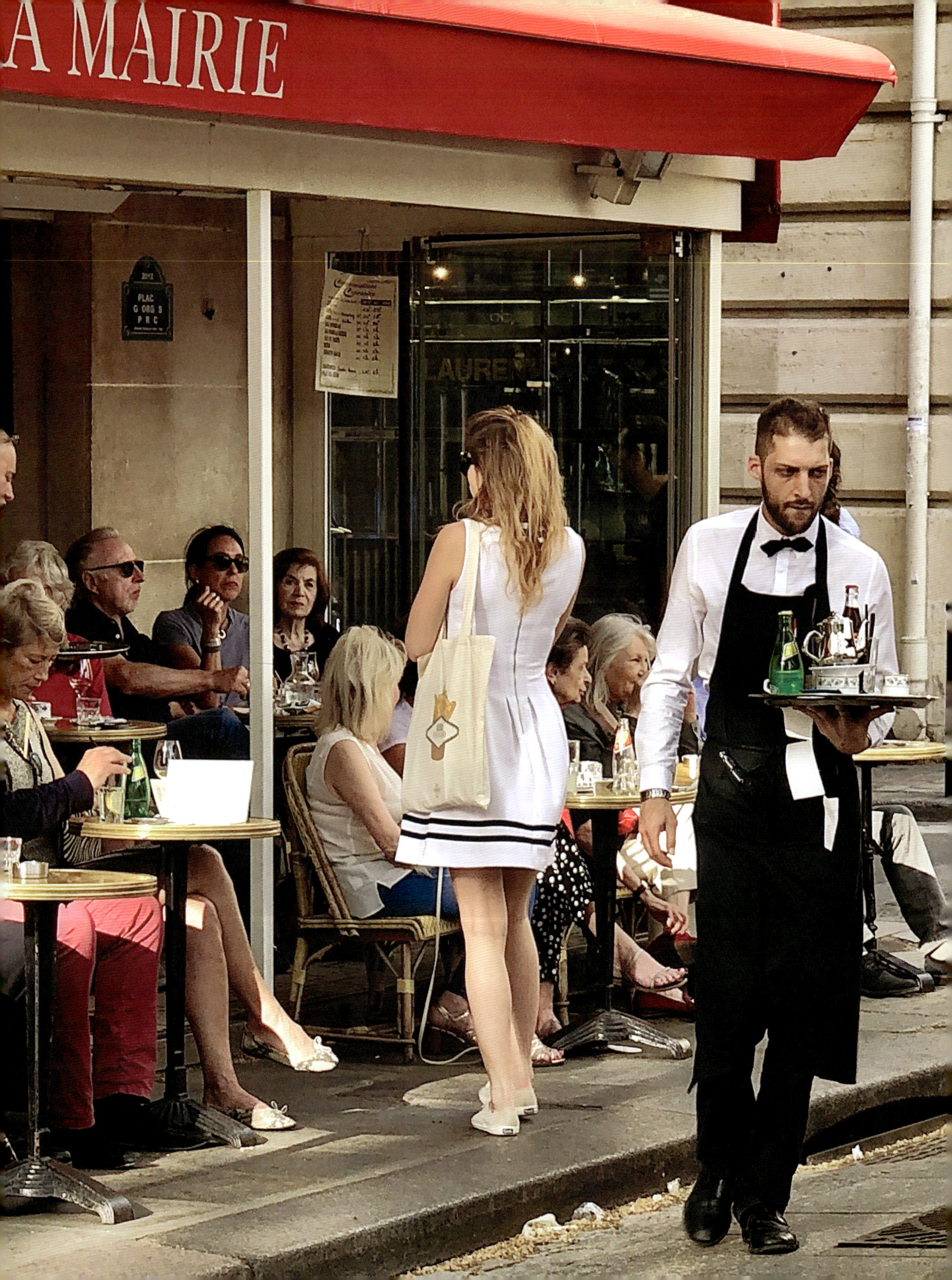
A MAIRIE

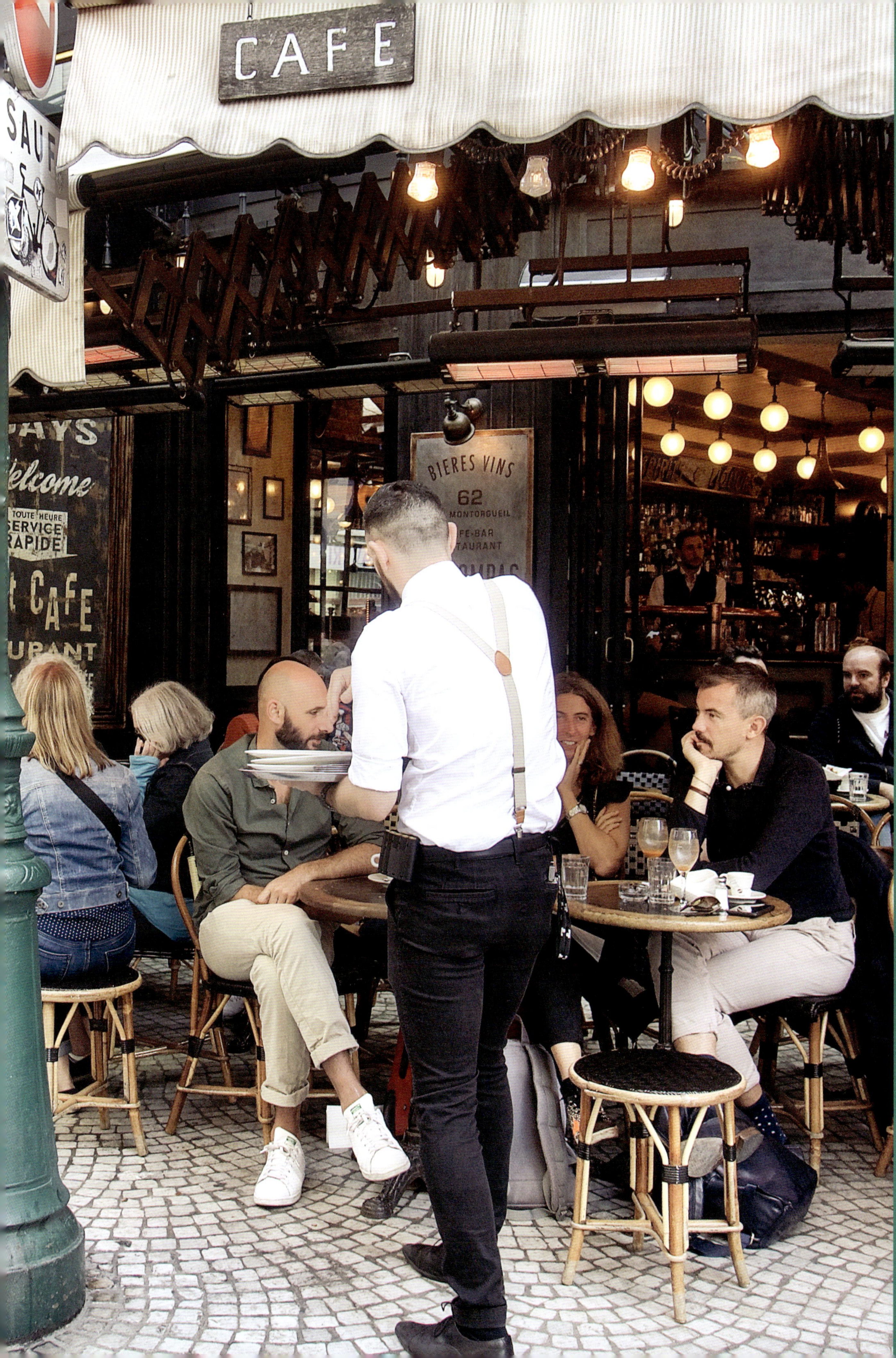

PART 1 Paris & its Cafés

PARIS... & its Cafés

"I believe it was the Irish writer George Moore or was it Stendhal? who, in reply to the question how might art be best promoted, gave the remarkable answer: 'Establish cafés!'"

René Prévot

Over the centuries, countless artists have tried to capture its essence in photos, songs, films, plays, books, paintings, and poems, making Paris-dreamers of people everywhere, many of whom have never been fortunate enough to visit the "City of Light" (*La Ville Lumière*). For those who visit or live in Paris, the experience is far more than its storied food and wine, museums and galleries, monuments and statues, architecture and interiors. It is more than the Seine, the bouquinistes, the haut fashion, the long summer nights, the sparkling streets after another rain, more than the dark winters and bright summers, and the plane trees with their colorful flaky bark. Yes, Paris is all that and still more; yet, above all, Paris is simply "always a good idea," as Audrey Hepburn once said.

There must be a reason why hundreds of songs are written about Paris and why poets, artists, architects, writers, filmmakers, lovers, and travelers have flocked to this magical city for hundreds of years. With always so much to see, do, savor, study, and absorb, the Parisians' creative energy, still flowing through the streets and incorporated into the city's fiber, makes it glow in our times. Not only do the celebrated sights and museums capture the essential spirit of Paris, but so does the everyday life of the cafés with their terraces and zinc bars, which are as much a part of Paris as the Eiffel Tower or the Louvre. Indeed, both Parisians and tourists spend more time in cafés than visiting monuments and museums.

To know Paris, one needs to understand the *café esprit*, for the café naturally exists as the center of the Parisian lifestyle where Parisians savor the time apart from work, school, and home. The café is tied to the identity of Paris; it is part of its signature. Historically, the people gathered at their local café for warmth, conviviality, gossip, and newspapers, meeting friends, family, and colleagues; habitués even received their mail and later phone calls. Today, with the inviting aromas, the sounds of plates rattling, espresso machines hissing, lively conversations in every language, the café remains an antidote to isolation and satisfies the innate need for human connection. Cafés are so integral to French culture that you would be hard-pressed to find a French movie without a café featured somewhere in the film (have you ever seen one?), and lingering in a café can feel like being in a French film.

In recognition of the timeless historic cafés, bistros, and brasseries known for their exemplary design and often legendary artistic, political, and literary habitués, France has bestowed upon many of them the designation of "Historic Monument." Numerous designated historic cafés, bistros, and brasseries are featured in this book. Among them: Brasserie Bofinger, Brasserie Lipp, La Palette, Café Procope, Bouillon Chartier Montparnasse, Le Bistrot du Peintre, Clown-Bar, La Coupole, Au Chien Qui Fume, L'Escargot Montorgueil, Le Grand Véfour, Le Rocher de Cancale.

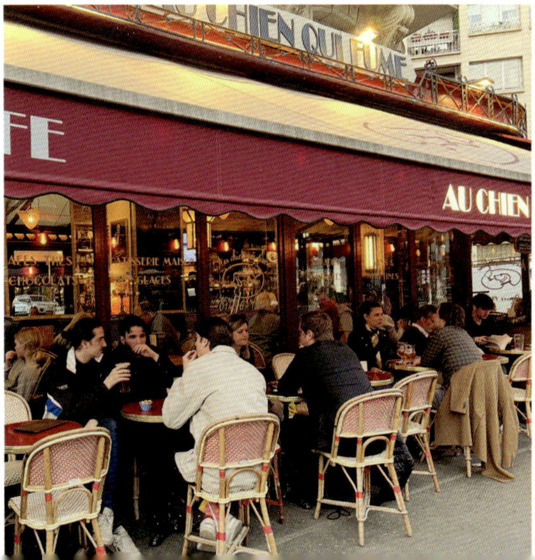

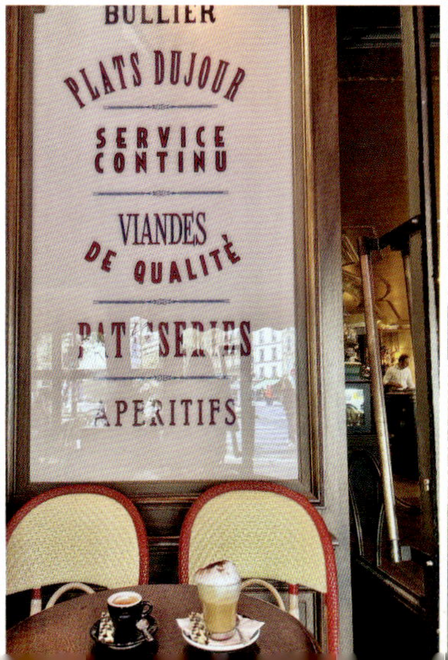

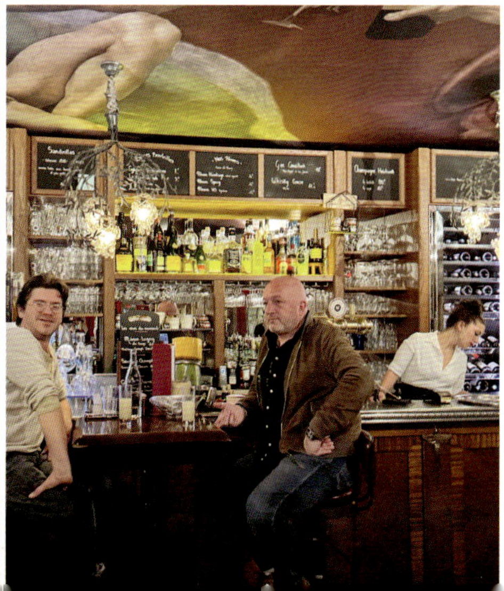

All the Streets in Paris Lead to its Cafés

"I do not believe there is another city on earth so beautiful as Paris
nor another people with such an appreciation of the beautiful as the French..."

Edward Hopper

Only in Paris do all the streets, metros, buses, autos, bicycles, and even the river, guide us to the cafés; café dwelling is simply the way of life for the French, no matter the weather, the time of day, or the time of year.

Paris is the capital of cafés. Everyone is welcome in this most democratic establishment: well-known and unknown artists, models, writers, poets, filmmakers, composers, stage and film stars, politicians, royalty, moguls, workers, tourists, and expats continue to grace its tables for hours at a time.

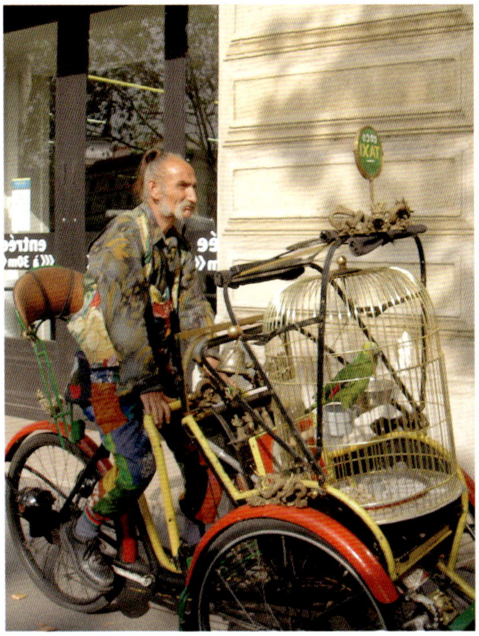

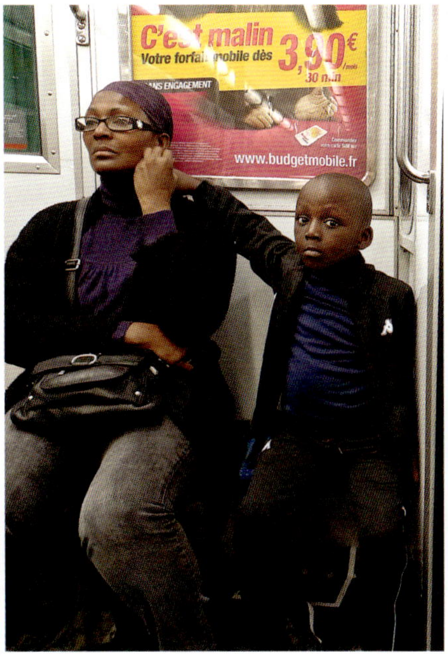

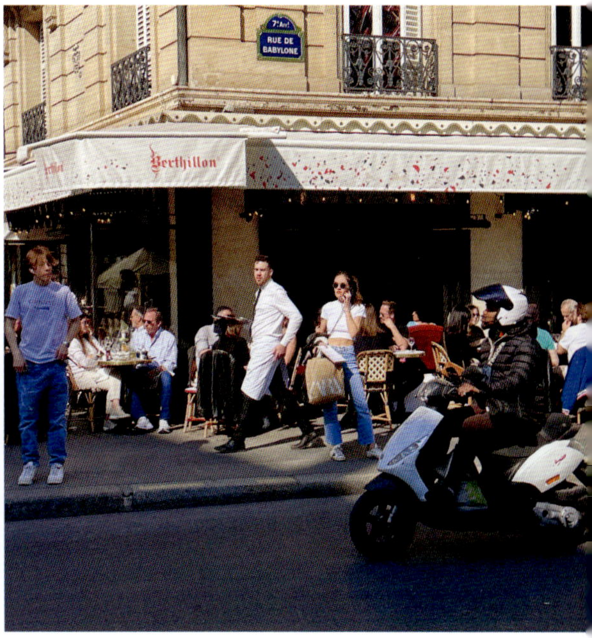

"When I sit in Paris in a café, I don't sit casually—
I go over a certain sonata in my head and discover new things all the time."

Arthur Rubinstein

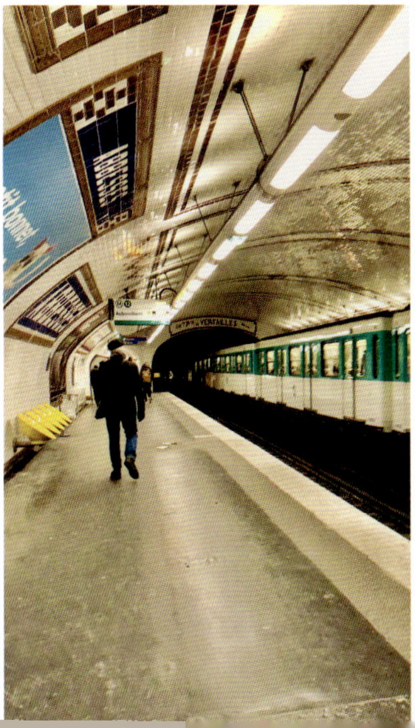

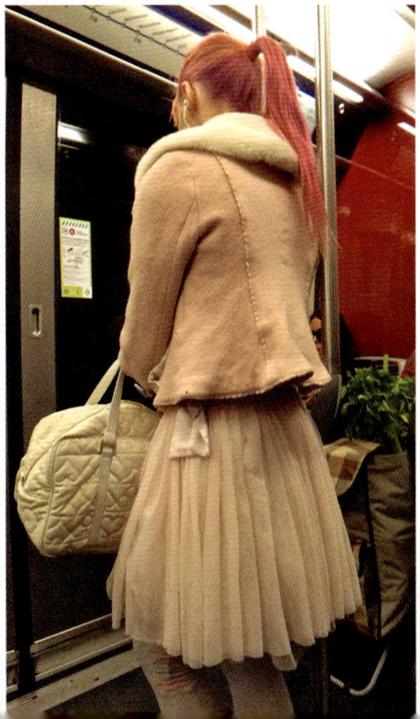

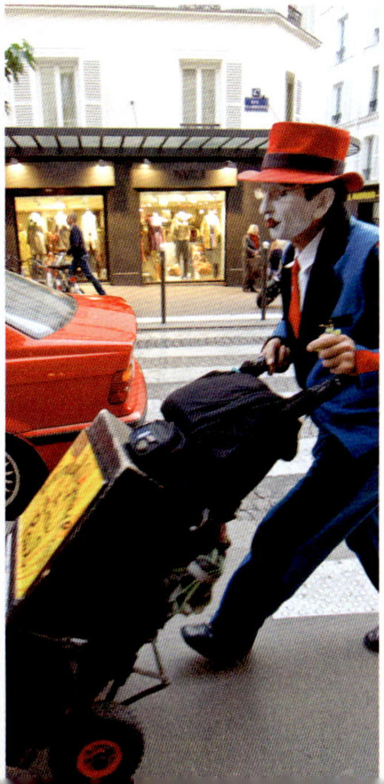

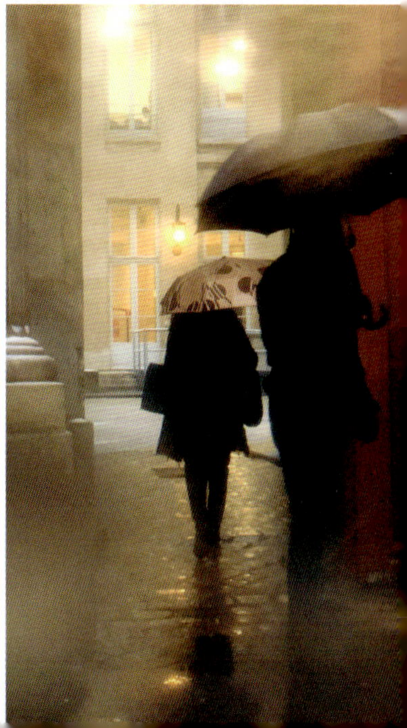

A Certain Alchemy

"I no longer know which humorist rightly claimed in the past that we could write a history of civilization by limiting its study to that of cafés."

Léon-Paul Fargue

What is it about the Parisian café and bistro that draws us in? Why does the French café lifestyle capture the heart as well as the appetite? What makes a Parisian café or bistro in Paris distinct from a Parisian "style" café or bistro elsewhere in the world? When so many other countries emulate French cafés and bistros, it seems clear that, while the Parisian café has universal appeal, its authenticity is solely achieved in Paris. The reasons are mysterious: Could the magic be embedded in the Parisian DNA, honed by history, expertise, and love? Or, does the City of Light have the perfect *lumière* and *terroir* found nowhere else? The French café is a gathering place to see and be seen and a refuge where one can be alone without the interruptions and pressures of everyday life. Here we can put time on hold to enjoy meaningful and illuminating conversation, linger, reflect, know oneself and others better, relax and appreciate the art and beauty of life. While a place for contemplation, the café is also a place to observe city life's flow and vitality. Inclusivity is integral to café society, which is open to all who appreciate the café lifestyle. There may be cafés worldwide, but as Enlightenment economist Ferdinando Galiani once said, "Paris is the café of the world." Indeed, the Parisian café is undoubtedly the oft-mentioned *third* place, where one can suspend time and just be who you are, where you are.

The role of the café in French society fires the imagination. Historically, artists, writers, performers, politicians, traders, and travelers met and cross-fertilized their ideas and schemes to create movements in art, politics, literature, and more. Here culture, change, civilization, coffee, wine, and food commingle. Aperitifs, assignations, and artistry; coffee, conversation, and camaraderie; people-watching, passing the time, pondering the news; revelry, resistance, revolution, and romance—anything and everything happens in the cafés of Paris. Part of the fabric of the city, they are institutions of sociability, culture, and heritage.

Through the centuries, from their inception, Parisian cafés have been incubators for many revolutions in France. Revolutionaries have comfortably gathered in cafés and plotted the overthrow of royalty, emperors, dictators, and capitalists. Oh, it isn't just the French who conspired in cafés; many political exiles came to Paris to plan their own revolutions, including Ho Chi Minh, Lenin, Trotsky, and Karl Marx. Deposed from their own country's leadership, others come to Paris to plot their return to power and enjoy the food and wine, no doubt.

There is always too much to see and do in Paris for a tourist, and for a Parisian, there is often so little time after the responsibilities of work and daily life to slow down, be still, and enjoy the moment in a café. However, despite the hurry of life, the very Parisian *l'art de vivre*, as much a part of the Parisian experience for tourists as it is for the Parisians, is very much alive and well, and dwells in the cafés and bistros of Paris.

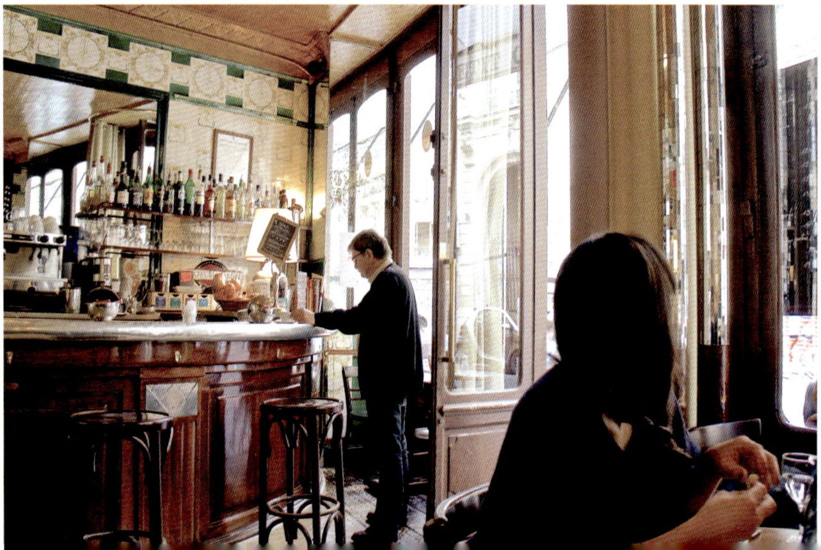

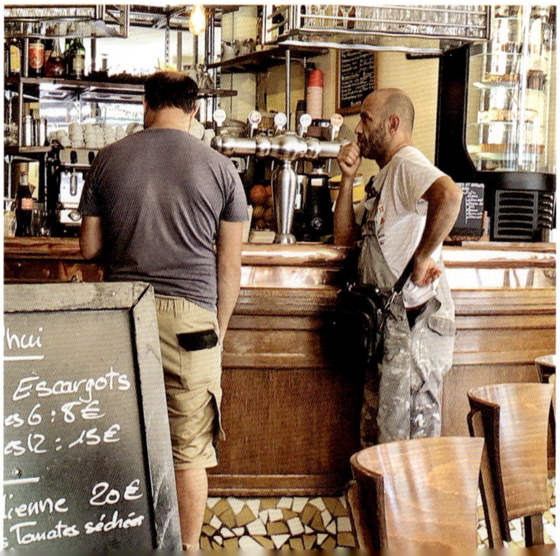

"There is never any ending to Paris and the memory of each person who has lived in it differs from that of any other. We always return to it no matter who we were or how it was changed nor what difficulties nor what ease it could be reached. It was always worth it and we received a return for whatever we brought to it."

Ernest Hemingway

One might argue that the best way to discover Paris is as a flâneur, an urban stroller, a dreamer, wandering Paris with no other purpose than to let it unfold before you; to be an observer on its streets and in the cafés. Honoré de Balzac described flânerie as "the gastronomy of the eye" and what better place to take a flâneuring break than in a Parisian café or even flâneuring from café to café? This book does just that.

Everyone who has lived in or visited has a uniquely personal view of Paris and its cafés. *Café Society* is about my vision of Paris's cafés and bistros, savored from years of flâneuring; seen through the gaze of an American in Paris, one of a continuous line from Benjamin Franklin and Thomas Jefferson over the centuries up to the present. Paris continues to be an evocative voyage for people the world over, including countless American visitors, Francophiles, and expats; its cafés are an alluring draw. We cannot claim to be experts, though we are most certainly appreciators, each with our own lens on The City of Light.

With thousands of cafés, bistros, and brasseries in Paris, here is but a taste, a dollop, a nibble, rather than a comprehensive compendium; meant to tempt, not overwhelm. Some are where you come to enjoy the food; others pull you in for reasons as simple as just being there, in the moment, pressing an image in your memory book. Not every café photographed is named; there are those taken in passing that afford a hint of the discoveries to be made while flâneuring. Photos scattered throughout the book and featured in Part 10, "In Search of Lost Time," have been captured over several decades, and cafés, for better or worse, may not look the same now as they were in this book. Many of the featured cafés have been refreshed, renovated, or modernized—some well, some not; a few have endured for over a century intact, merely polished; others, sadly, have disappeared. In the 21st century, cafés and bistros are 20% fewer in number than in 1999 and continue to grow fewer each year. The survival of the café lifestyle where café-goers may spend hours over an espresso or glass of wine, browsing a newspaper (still), or smartphone (everywhere), meeting friends, or just being, is now in peril, and heed must be taken. Can you imagine Paris without its cafés and bistros? It would be like the proverbial day without sunshine (though there are many of those in an often-gray Paris). While the food and design have been copied worldwide, restaurateur Alain Fontaine sagely says, "the Parisian bistro and café have a certain alchemy that can only be found in Paris."

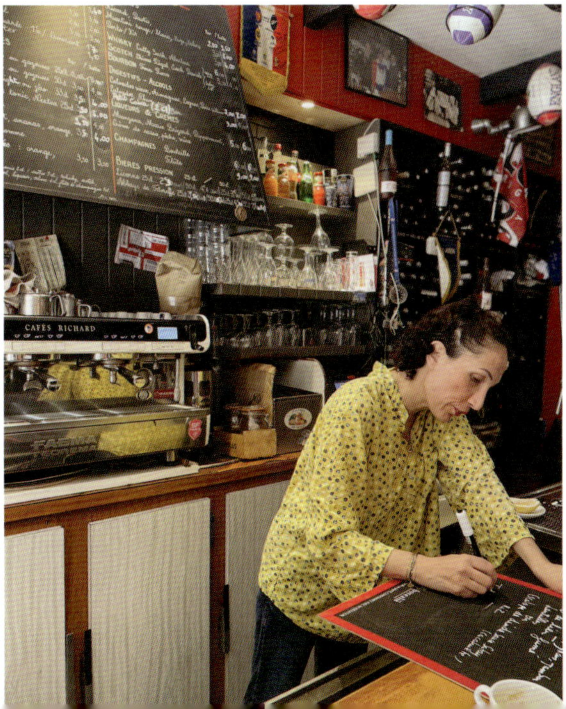

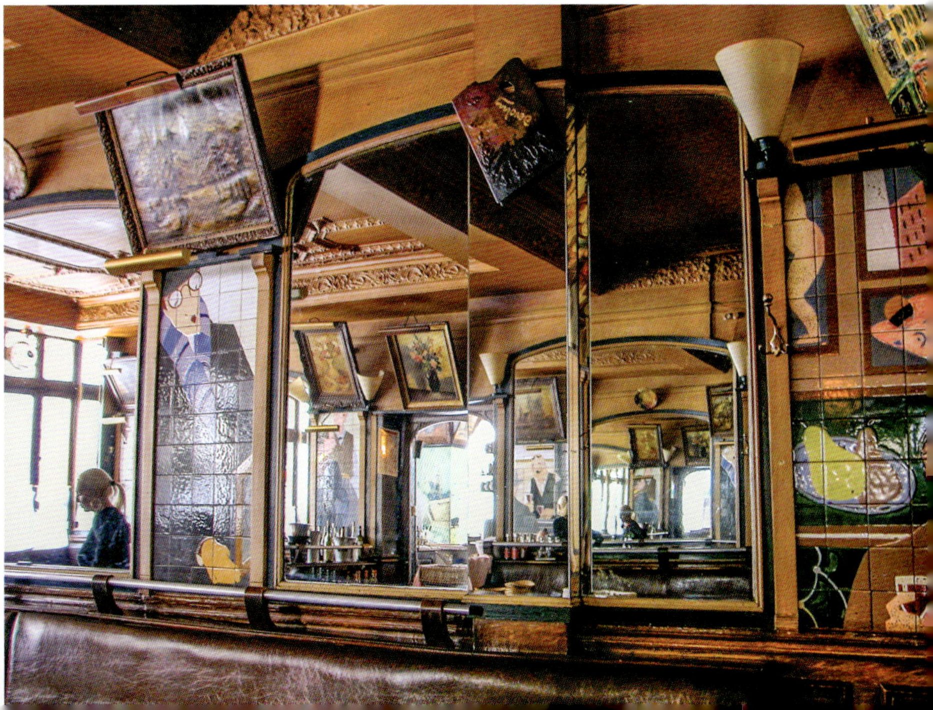

Definitions of Paris Cafés & Bistros

> "I ate and drank what I wanted in Paris. Butter, duck fat, liver fat, triple-cream brie, deep cherry-red wines, pear, clementine and lavender jelly, crème cakes, caviar, escargot in sautéed pine nuts, and garlic butter."
>
> **Sarah Schmidt**

How does one classify eating establishments in 21st-century Paris? Some exterior awnings tick several boxes: café, bistro, brasserie, restaurant, and bar. The catch-all "restaurant" or *au courant* "resto" is often used by food writers, customers, and the establishments themselves as an addition to the other labels. Our focus is on the cafés, bistros, and brasseries—the significant pillars of Parisian eateries. While historic definitions are now blurred, some classifications remain relevant.

CAFÉ: Never mistake a café for a coffee shop that only serves coffee drinks and pastries, sometimes prepared refrigerated food. Classic cafés have full kitchens and a bar, traditionally made from zinc, with food cooked to order throughout the day. In the morning, the café serves the quintessential French breakfast of coffee, tea, or hot chocolate, croissant, tartine, confiture, sweet butter, and fresh-squeezed orange juice. The classic French lunch is often a spin on salads, sandwiches, buttery omelet, *croque monsieur*, warm *plat du jour*. Dinner dishes (often also served at lunch) are simple—duck *confit*, *poulet*, *poisson*, *steak frites*. Dessert is enjoyed after a meal rather than a snack in between. Espresso or *noisette* (with a dollop of milk) are to be had all day and night; a cappuccino or other major milk or cream drink only at breakfast. Drinks at the zinc bar cost less than sitting at a table though occupying a table for hours over an espresso or aperitif is quite typical. Café design can vary from informal neighborhood eatery to elegant Art Nouveau or Art Deco showplace. Iconic outdoor terraces have chairs facing the street where smoking is permitted and people watching plentiful. Cafés are usually open all day from 7 am to 11+ pm.

BISTRO: Sometimes spelled *bistrot*. Their design is usually small, cozy, sometimes rustic, sometimes elegant, ofttimes family run, always lively and genial. Bistros serve hearty portions of simple classic French dishes, often grandma's recipes, for a reasonable price, along with new creations. Parisian bistros have been a veritable French institution since the mid-19th century when the Auvergnats came from the Massif Central to Paris and provided inexpensive meals to the population. Menus are frequently augmented with specials written on the blackboard; regional wines are available by the glass, carafe, or bottle. Bistros are usually open during lunch and dinner hours. Some are open daily, others weekdays only.

BRASSERIE: Originating in Alsace, brasserie is the French word for brewery, and before 1850 brasseries were breweries; after 1850, they became beer-drinking establishments as well. In 1870, with France's defeat in the Franco-Prussian War, many Alsatians left the newly German-occupied region for Paris. They brought with them their local food—often one-dish meals like *choucroute garnie* and enormous *plateaux de fruits de mer*—and began serving them along with the beer. Brasseries are often large spaces with high ceilings and elegant Art Nouveau or Art Deco design. Many classic brasseries, no longer family owned, are run by large corporations that restore the historic interiors and maintain the quality of the food. New (neo) brasseries with celebrated young chef-owners are becoming in vogue. They are often open early to very late.

RESTAURANTS: Parisian restaurants usually have white tablecloths and serve intricate dishes on a *prix-fixe* (appetizer, entrée, and dessert) or a la carte menu with flawless service. Many serve classic food, while others offer original, creative dishes. Like bistros, restaurants are usually open only during meal hours and are often closed on Sundays or Mondays.

PLUS: Currently, there are all sorts of eating establishments to be found, from classic bouillons, crêperies, cabarets, and guinguettes, to take-out and food trucks. You can find pizzerias, tapas, tacos, bagels, boba, sushi, falafel, poke and more. World food trends (fast and slow) are ubiquitous.

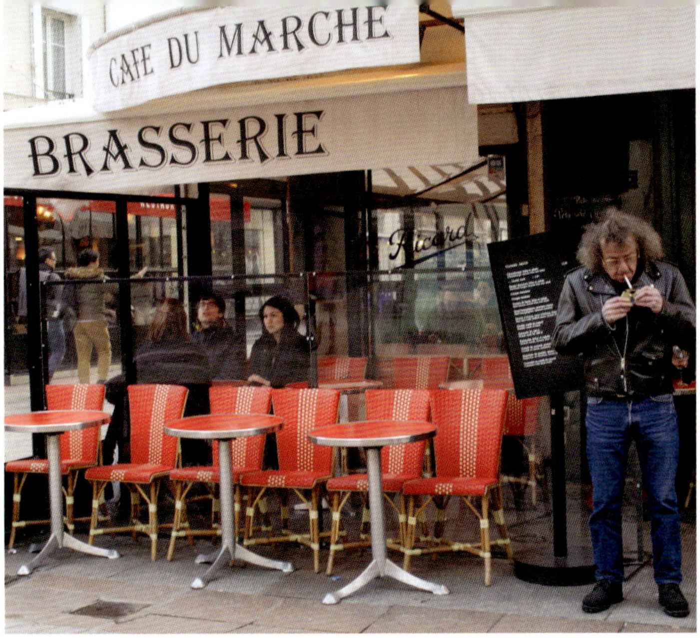
CAFE DU MARCHE
BRASSERIE

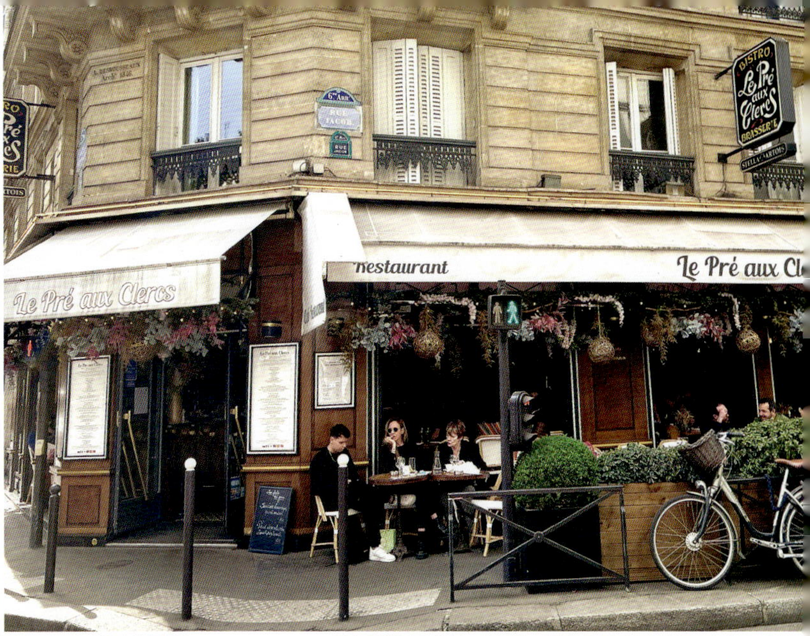
Le Pré aux Clercs
restaurant

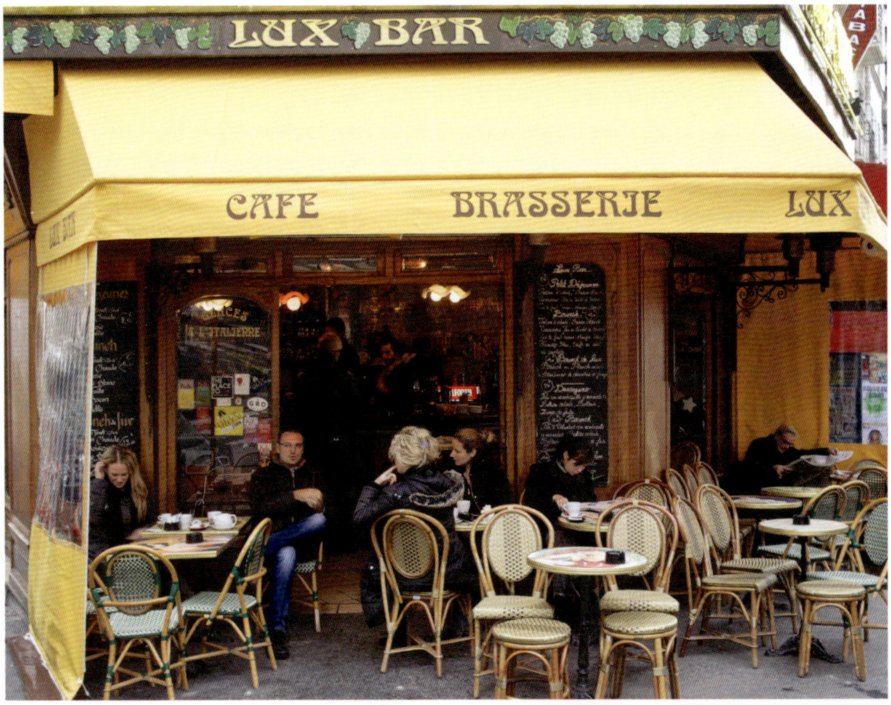
LUX BAR
CAFE
BRASSERIE
LUX

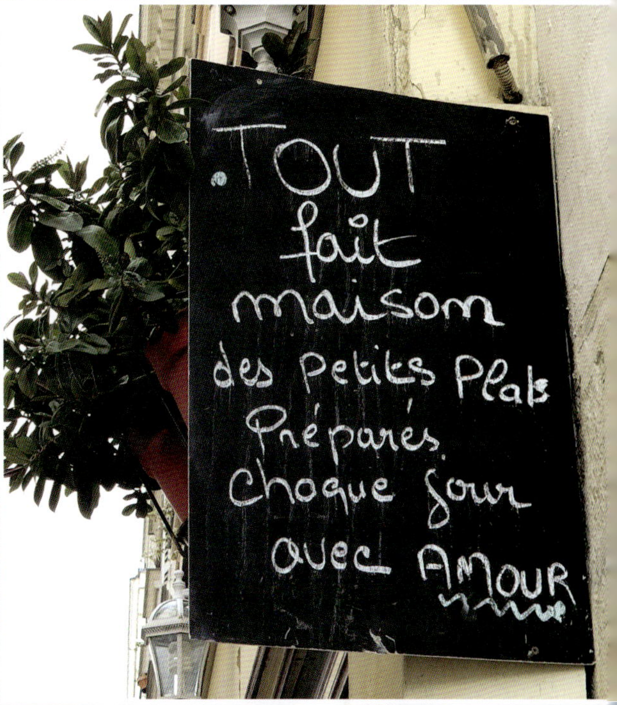
TOUT
fait
maison
des petits plats
Préparés
Chaque jour
avec AMOUR

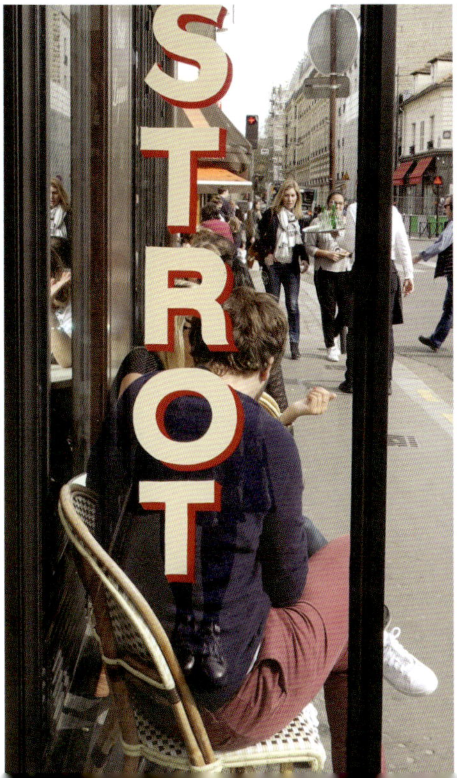
STROT

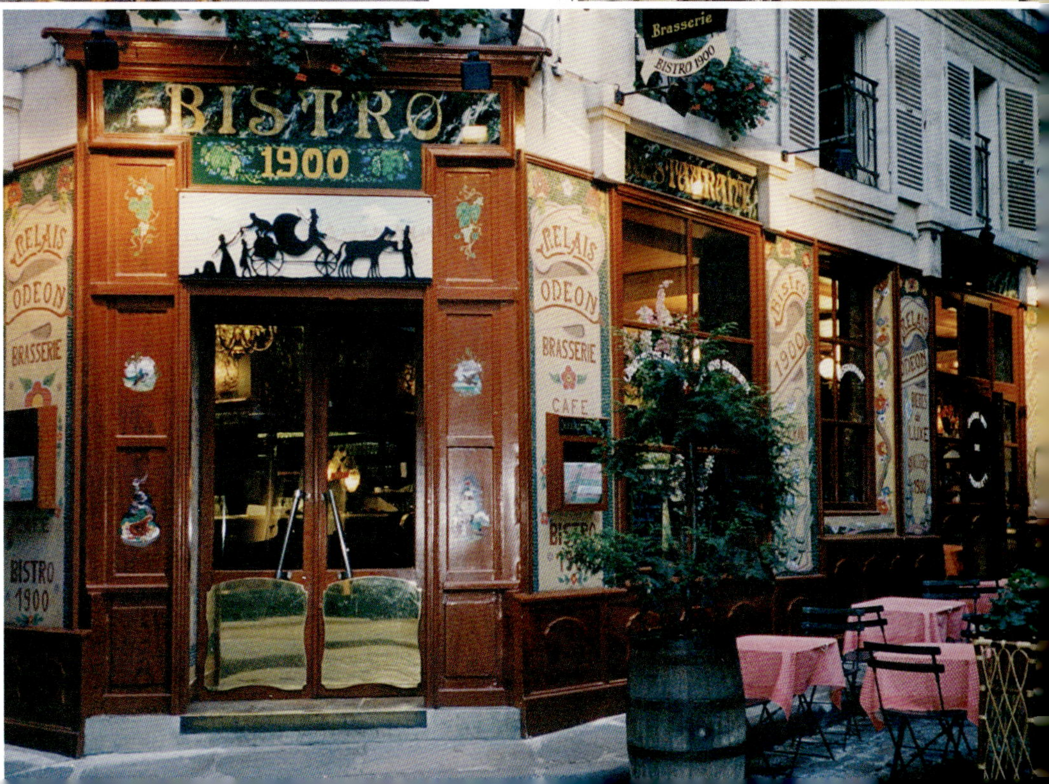
BISTRO
1900
RELAIS
ODEON
BRASSERIE
CAFE
Brasserie

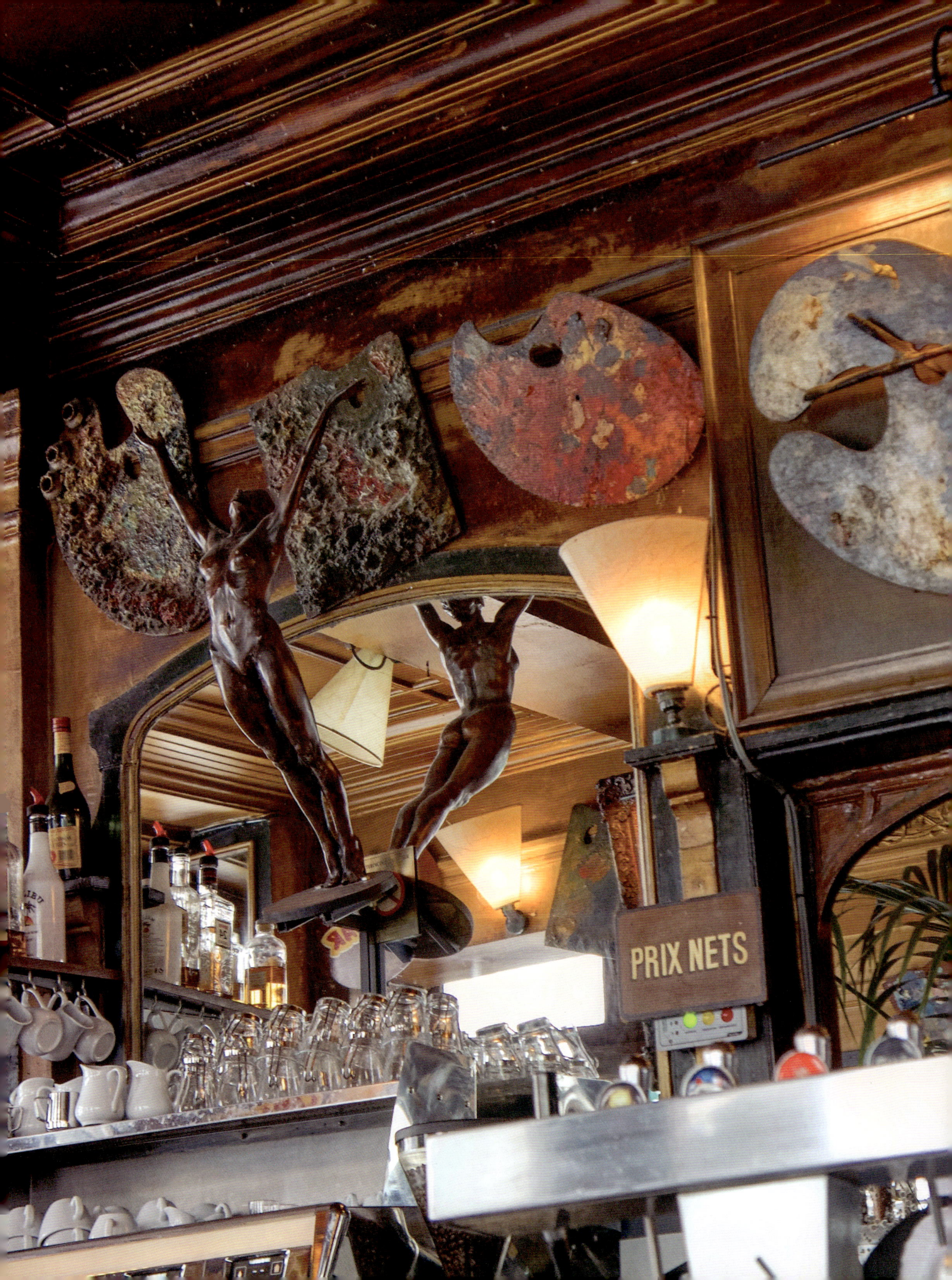
PRIX NETS

PART 2 The Look & Feel

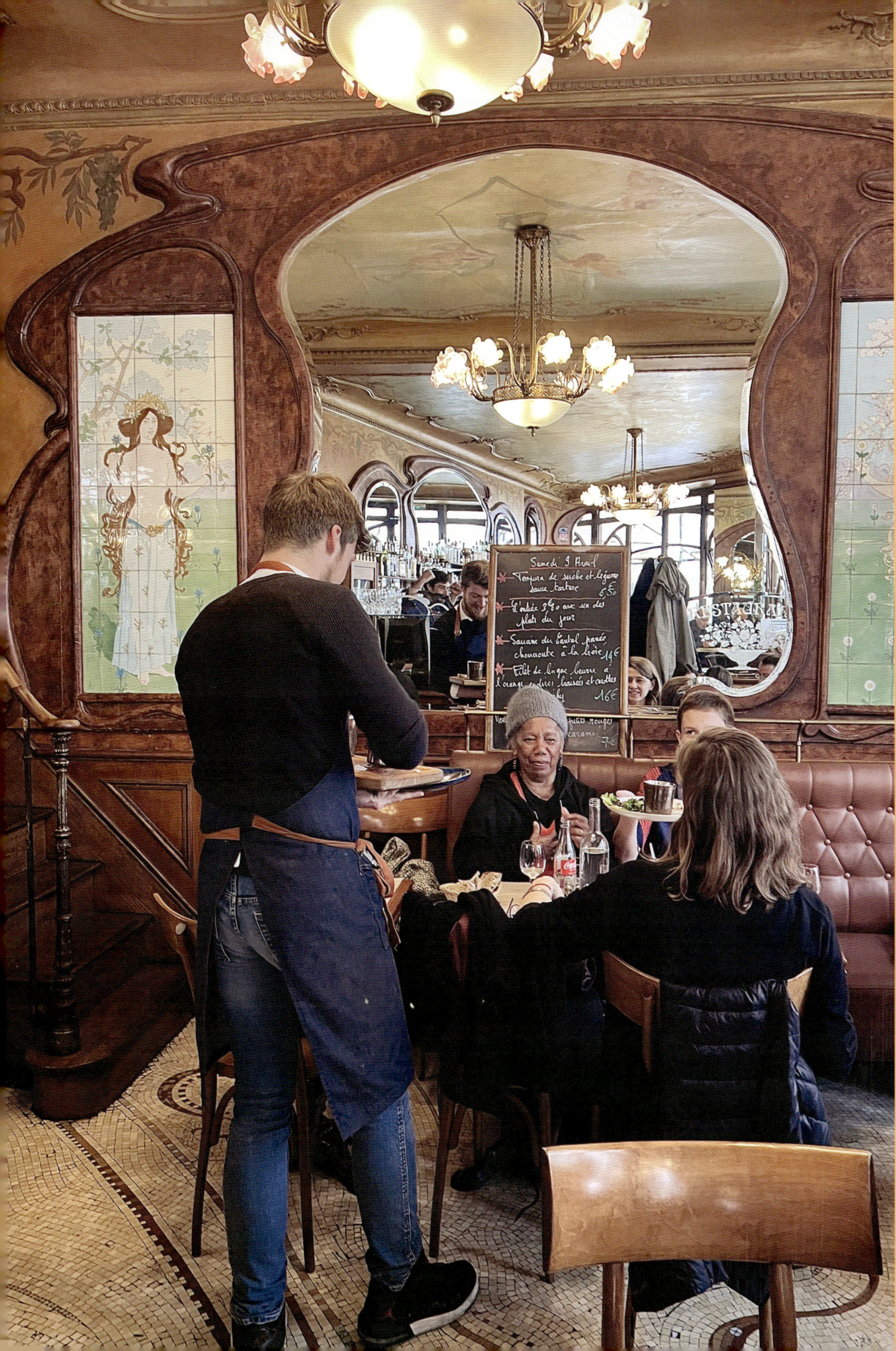

The Look & Feel

"Mystery is not about traveling to new places but about looking with new eyes."

Marcel Proust

The character of Paris is defined as much by its cafés as by its monuments. While cafés across the world have been serving coffee for hundreds of years, Paris still dazzles as the café of the world. Every street and street corner bustles with cafés, and the café lifestyle persists as a vital component of daily life. The Golden Age of cafés likely began during La Belle Époque (from 1890 until WWI) and continued through the period between the wars, ending with the start of WWII. Though most of the elegant cafés of this era have vanished, some remain gloriously intact. Sadly, classic cafés and bistros are evaporating, falling prey to expensive rents, at-home Nespresso machines, fast food, and delivery services, along with changing tastes. Fortunately, there are still some wonderfully preserved venues, as well as worthy upstarts, where, for a reduced price, you can stand and order an espresso or glass of wine at a zinc bar, where there is a terrace as well as a beautiful interior space, where one can see and feel the Paris of today, and where the Paris of yesterday still resonates and stirs the soul. These cafés, bistros, and brasseries are the superstars where the look and feel of the Paris café and Paris itself endures. Perhaps, if attention is paid to design as well as cuisine, this could be the time to usher in a new golden age?

Do you want to sit inside or outside? Or inside looking out? Or outside looking out? (Parisian cafés have chairs facing out toward the life of the street). Choose a seat on the terrace or in the cozy interior, or stand inside at *le zinc* with *le vrai français*—knocking back an espresso or a *verre de vin*. The weighty choice is between people watching and smoking (or dodging smokers) vs. a cozy and convivial interior. Many cafés have window walls that open to the terrace so that one can be inside yet feel outside. Or you can sit outside next to an opening to the interior and view both the street scene and the heart of the café. The interior is often beautiful, with quiet voices engaged in lively conversations and no smoking. A patron will often get up and go outside, sometimes quite often—even during a meal—for a smoke. Whether inside or on the terrace of an authentic Parisian café or bistro, there is no mistaking that you can only be in Paris and nowhere else in the world.

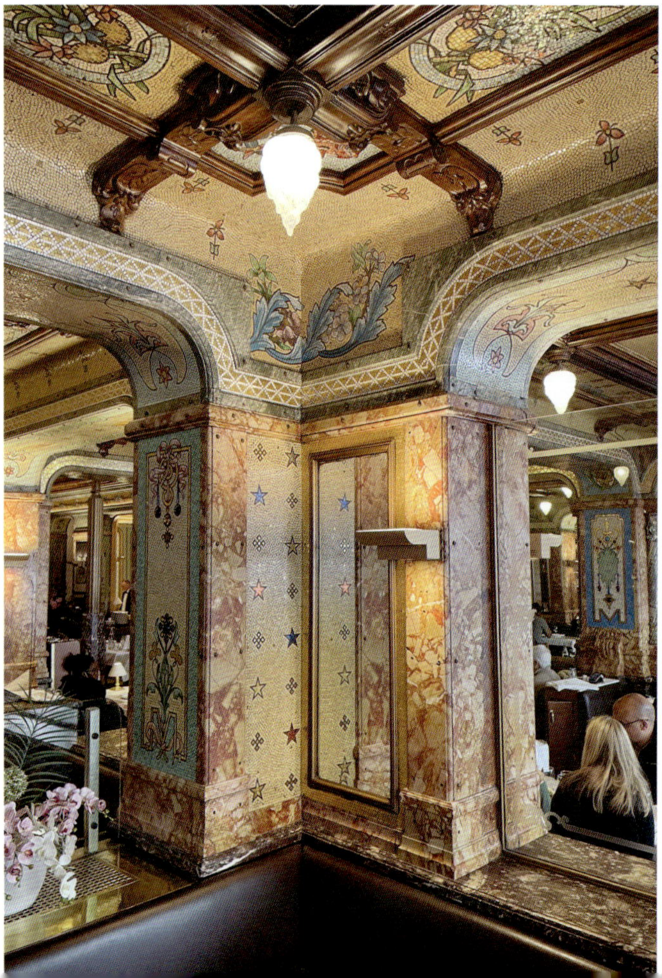

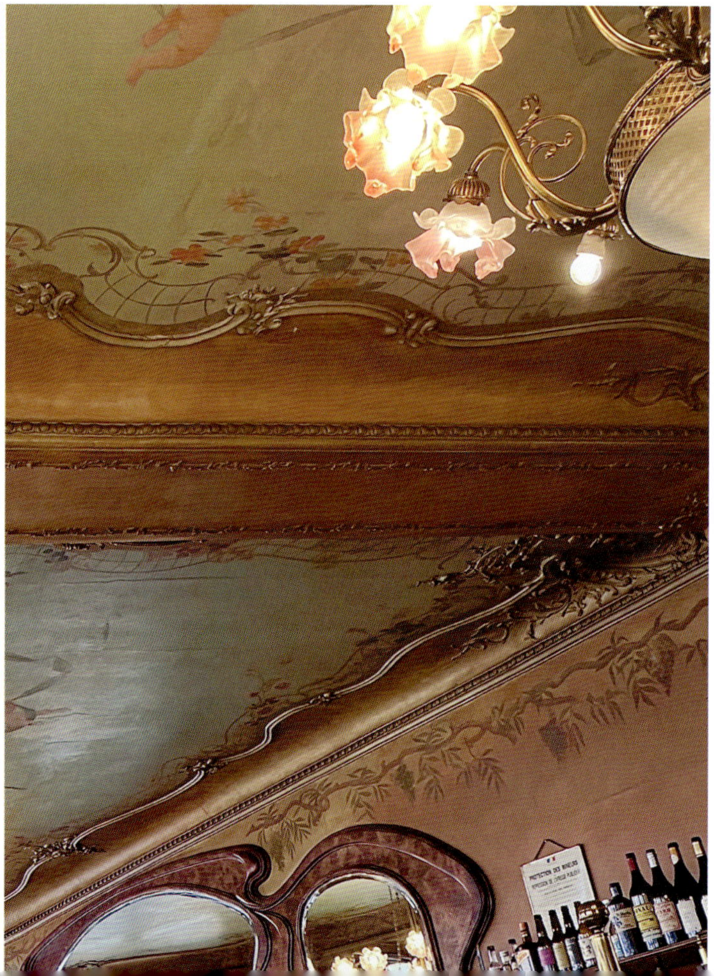

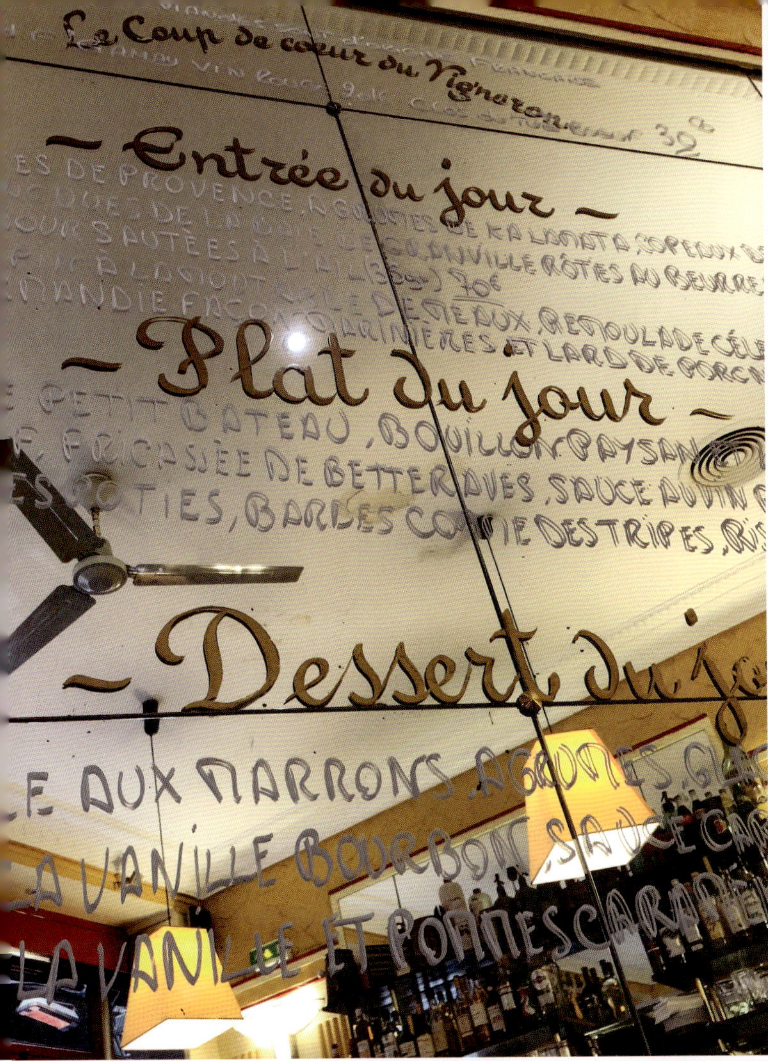
Entrée du jour
Plat du jour
Dessert
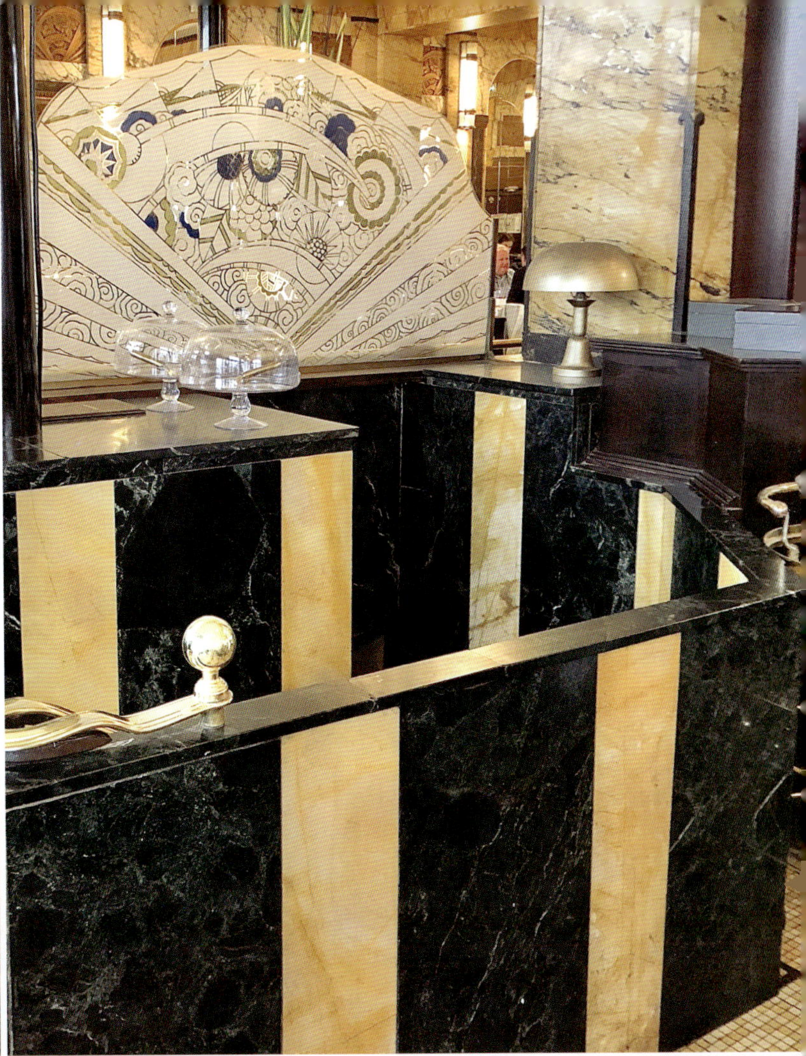
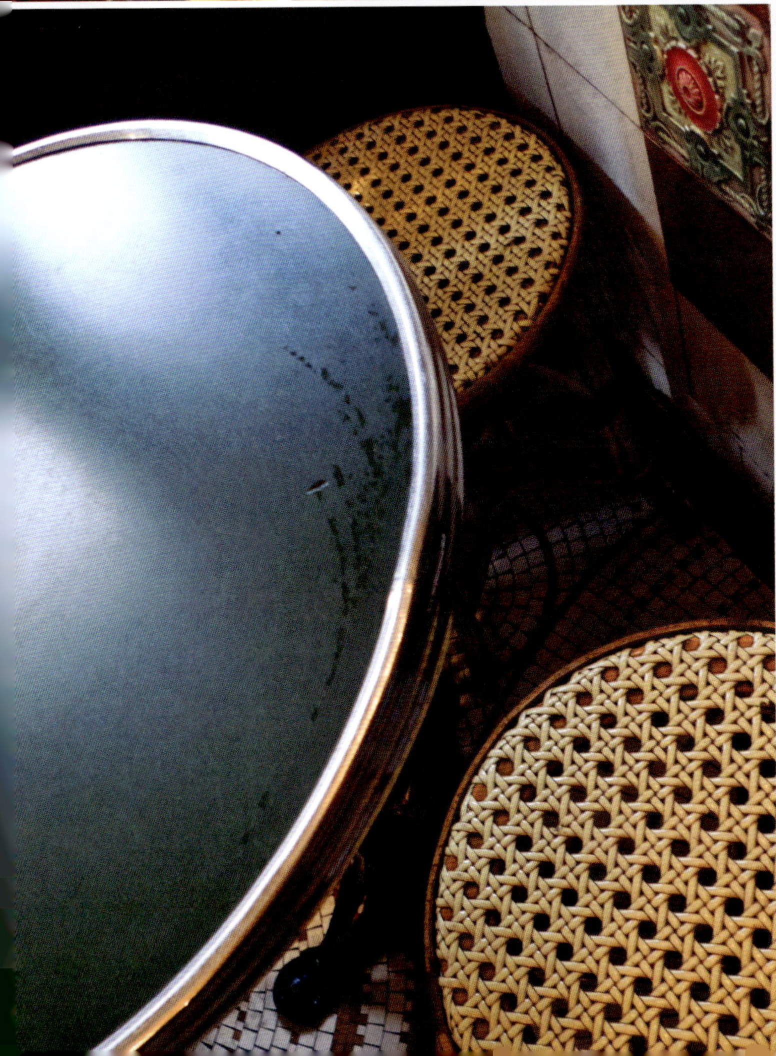
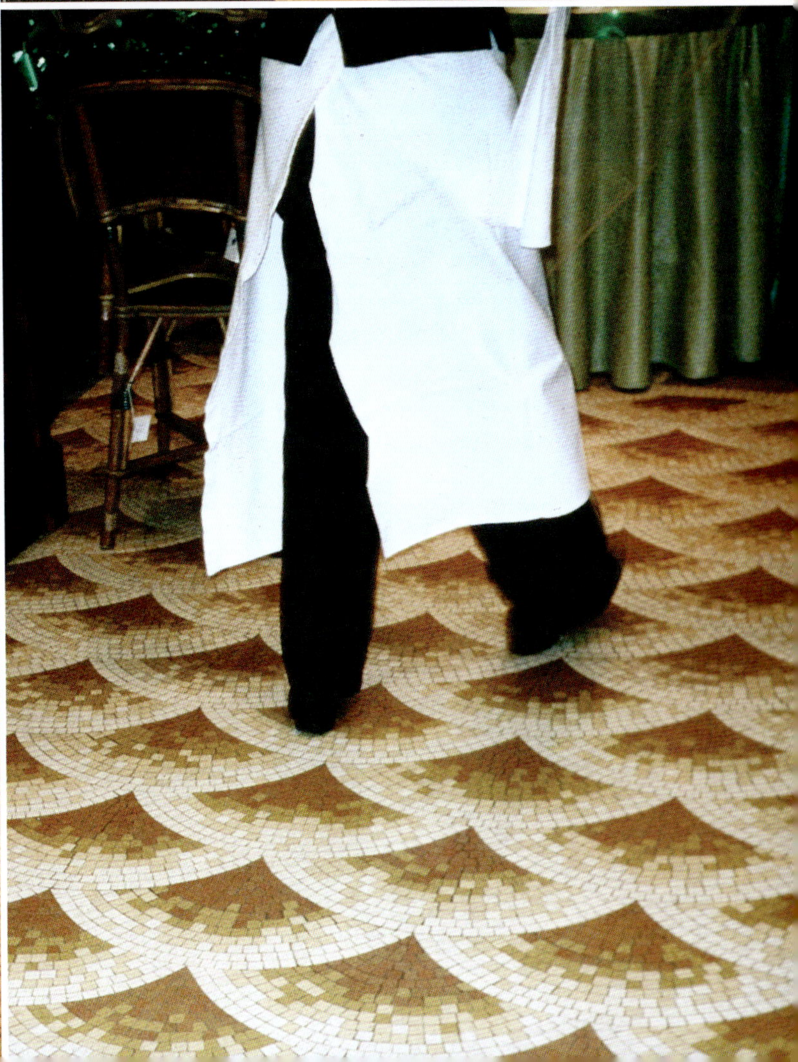

La Terrasse

"They line sprawling avenues and stand on corners of tiny streets like sidewalk academies where one learns Bohemian life, scorn for the middle classes, humor, and how to hold a glass."

Léon-Paul Fargue

Colorful awnings with trademark logos and lettering announce each café with an elegant flourish, beckoning strollers to rest and renew. With their metal-rimmed marble gueridon tables, patterned Rilsan and rattan chairs facing the street, and signature awnings, Paris's café terraces are as legendary as the Tour Eiffel and much more accessible. People-watching on a terrace has its own expression: *flâner en terrasse*.

The awnings provide protection from rain, snow, and sun (though the French often shun awnings and relish the sun for their *de rigueur* tan). With the prohibition of cigarettes inside, smokers have taken to the terrace, so non-smokers need to be wary of where they sit and how the wind blows. Brimming with life day and night, even on a snowy winter's day, blankets, and glass enclosures ensure the terraces are cozy and animated year-round.

By expanding the café's territory onto the sidewalk, terraces are essentially the outdoor living rooms of Paris. Enlivening the sidewalks with customers' comings and goings—Left Bank, Right Bank, all around town—lively café terraces invite the public to enjoy a quintessential Parisian street scene.

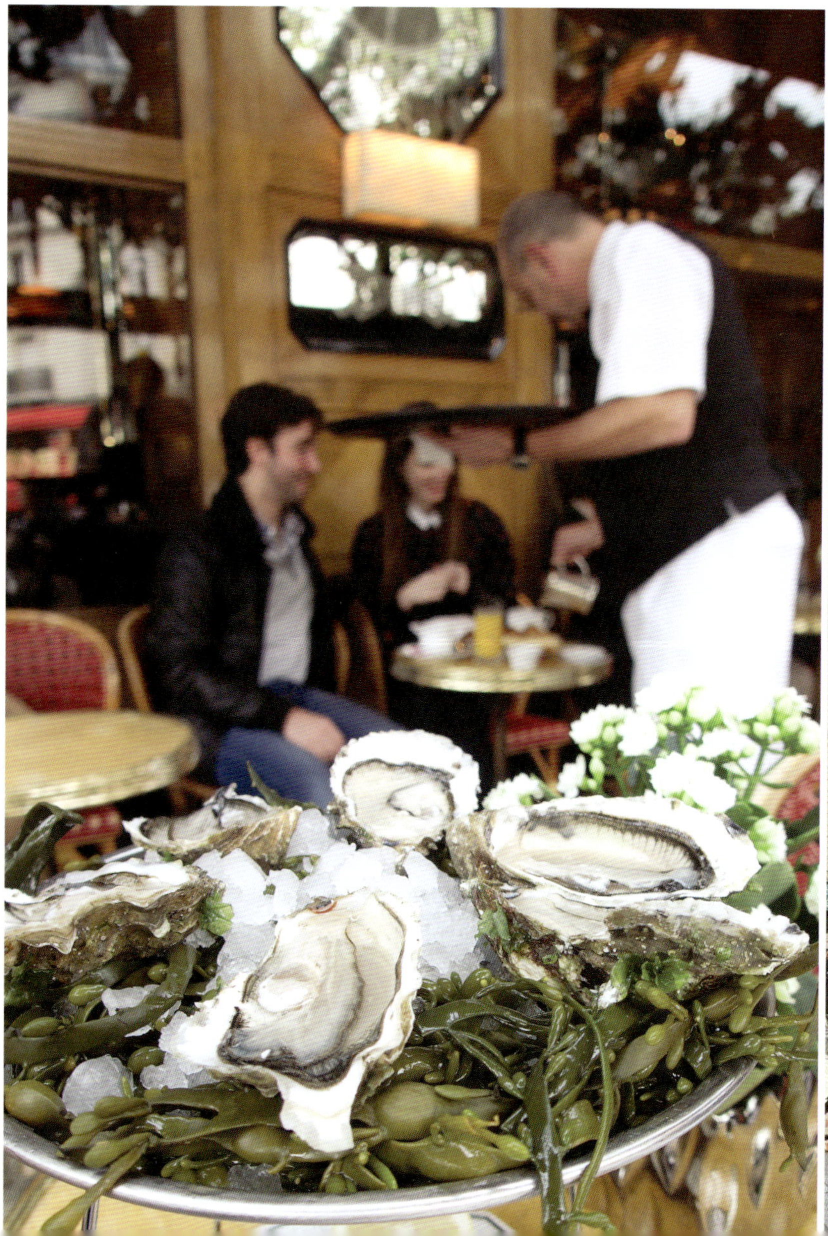

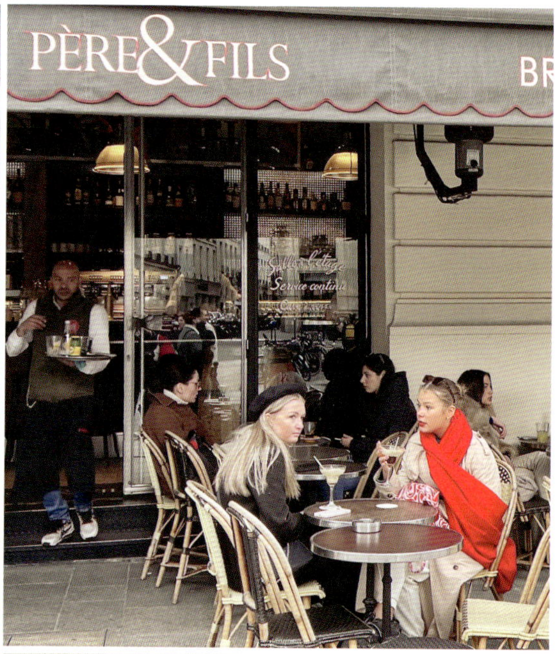

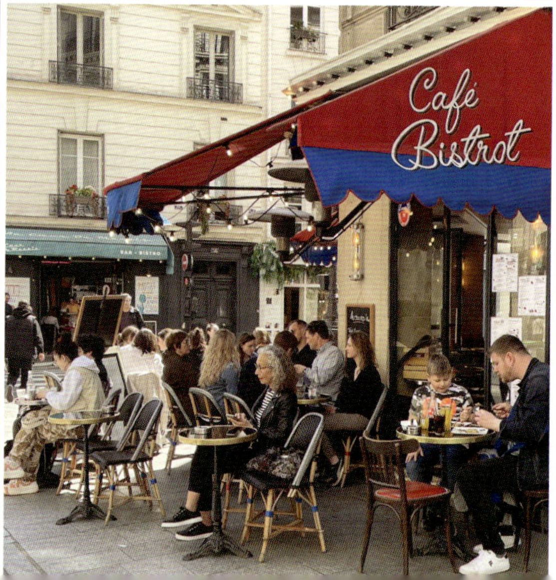

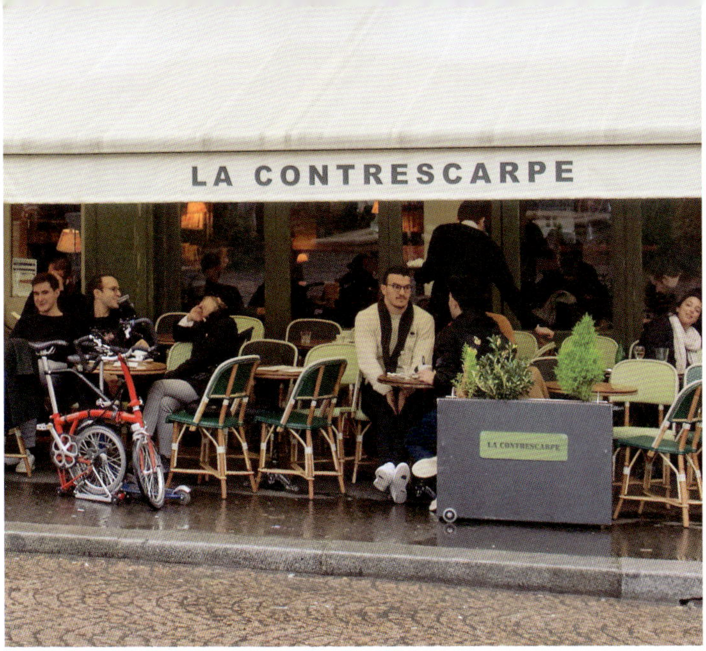
LA CONTRESCARPE

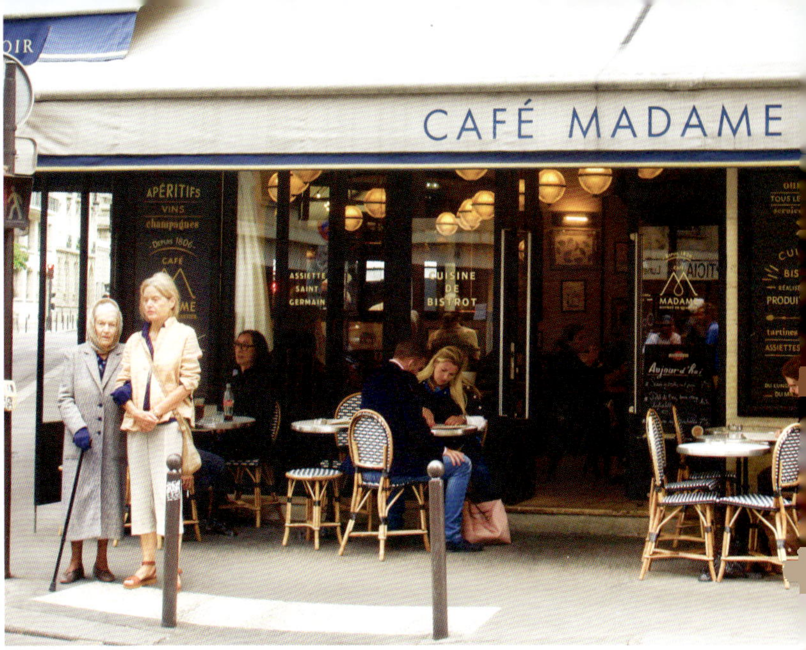
CAFÉ MADAME
APÉRITIFS
VINS
champagnes

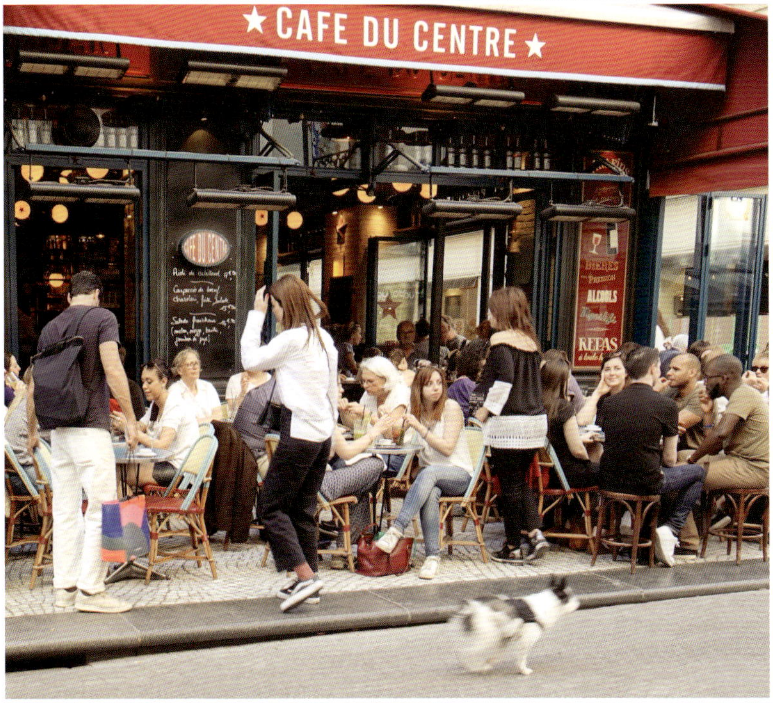
★ CAFE DU CENTRE ★
ALCOOLS
REPAS

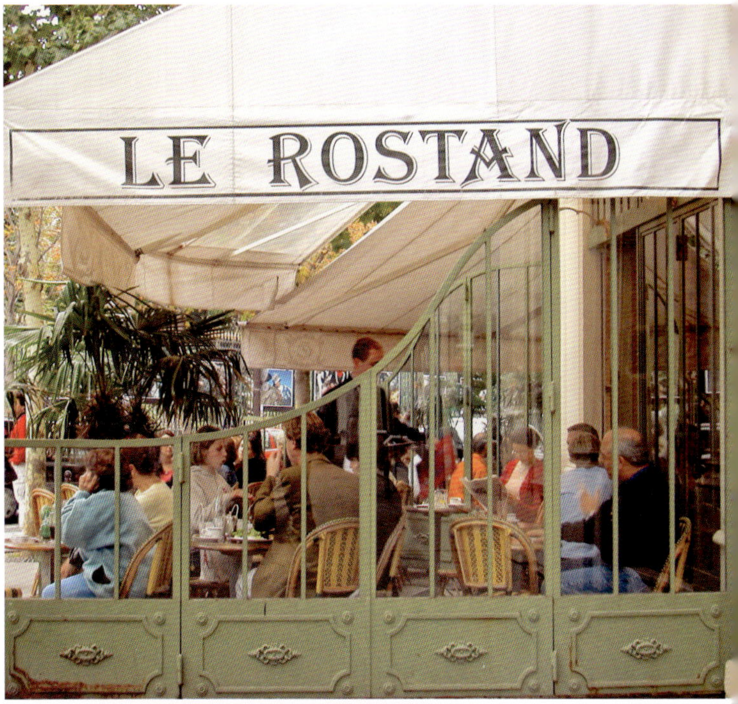
LE ROSTAND

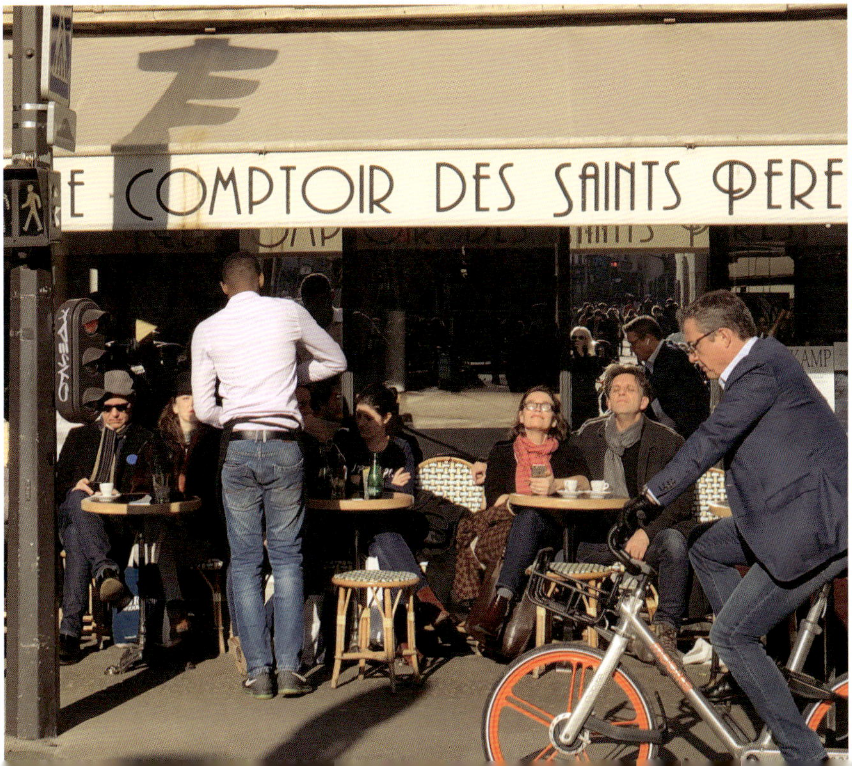
E COMPTOIR DES SAINTS PERE

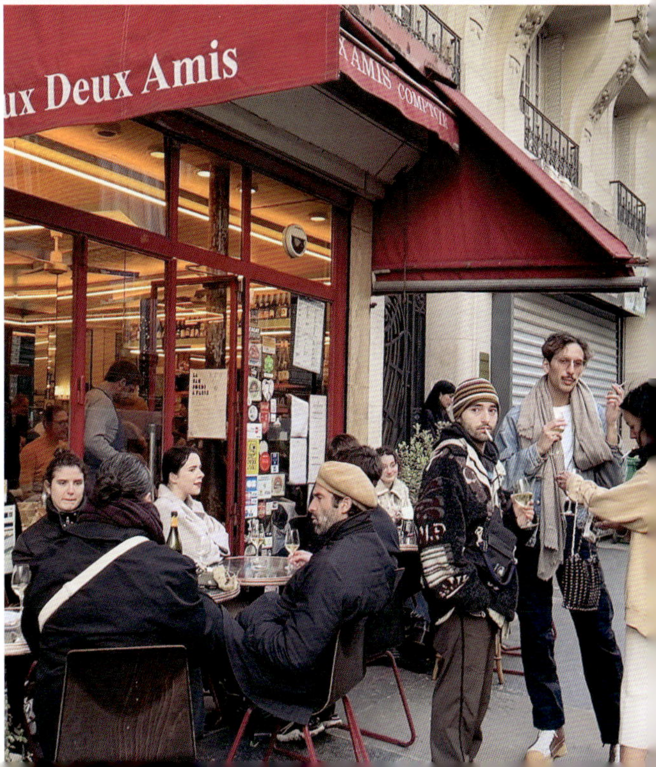
ux Deux Amis

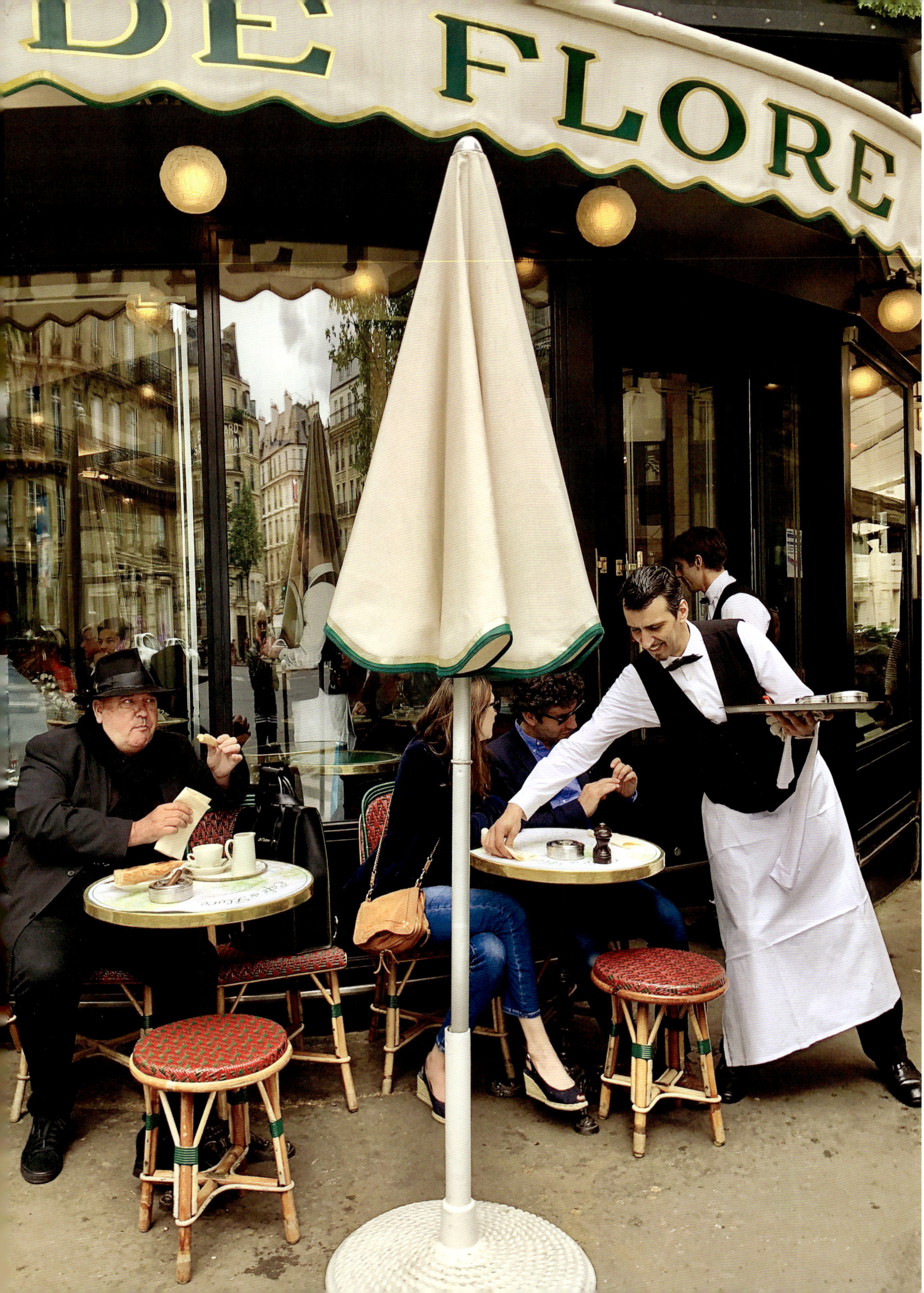
DE FLORE

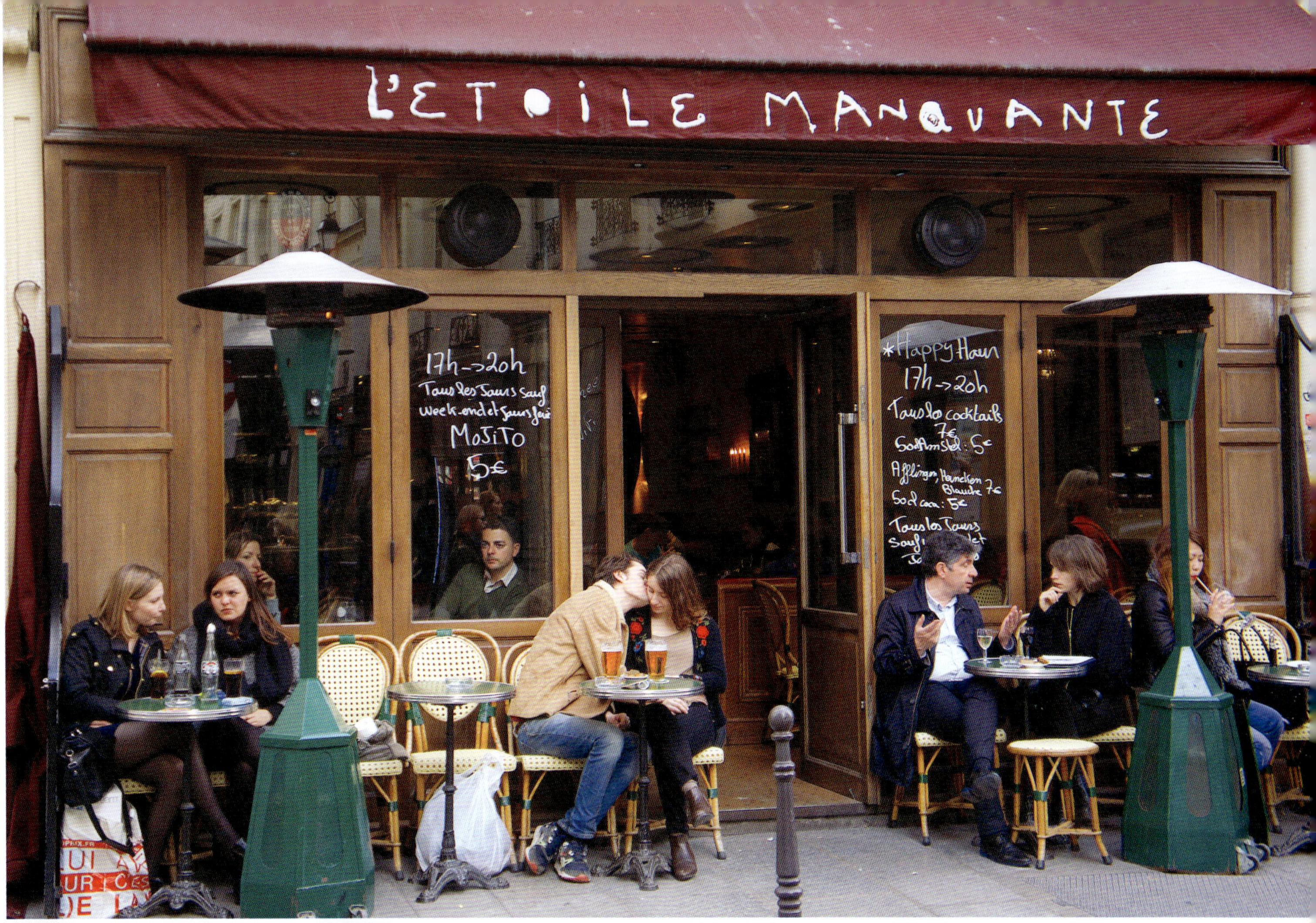
L'ETOILE MANQUANTE
17h->20h
MOJITO
5€
*Happy Hour
17h->20h

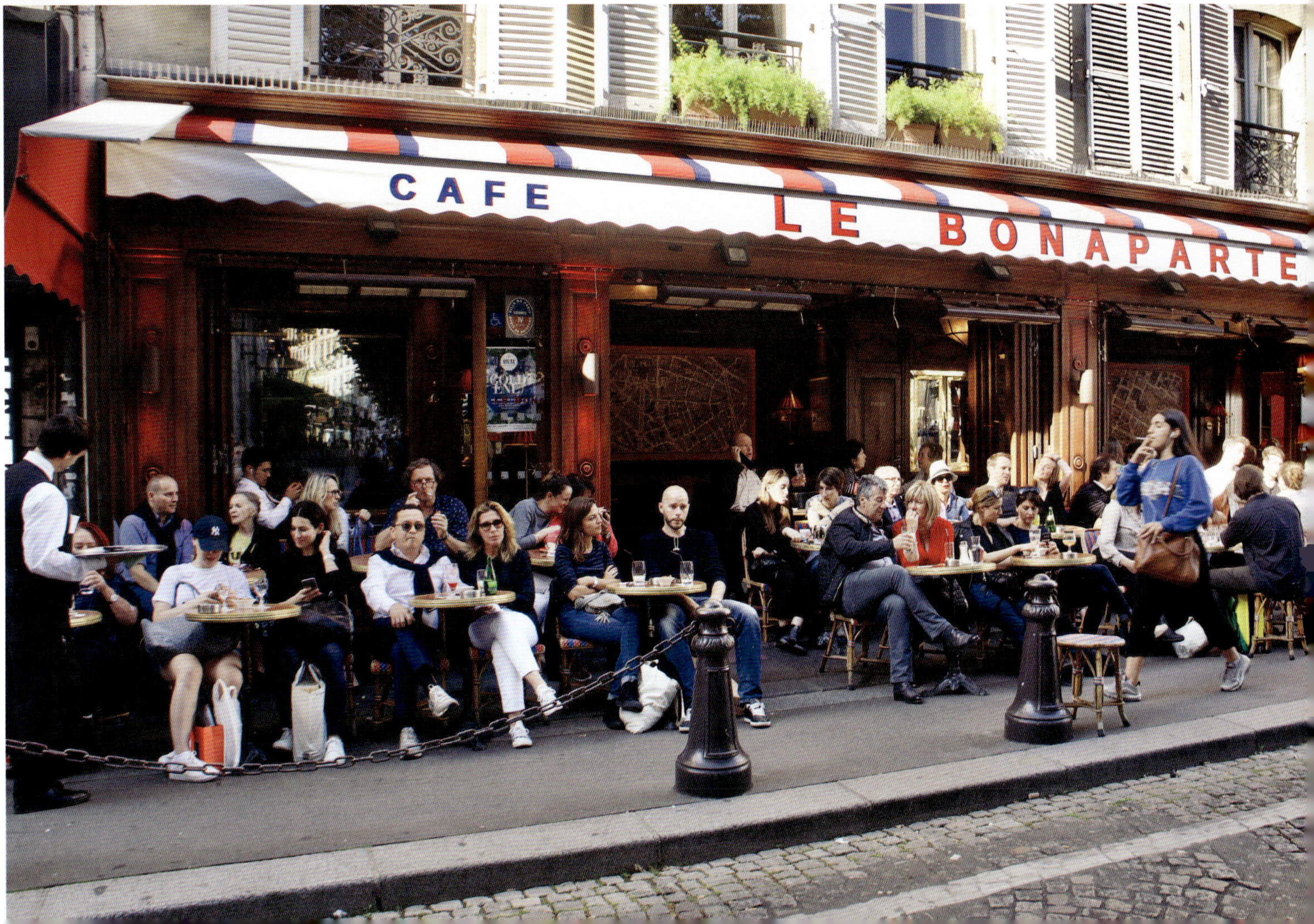
CAFE
LE BONAPARTE

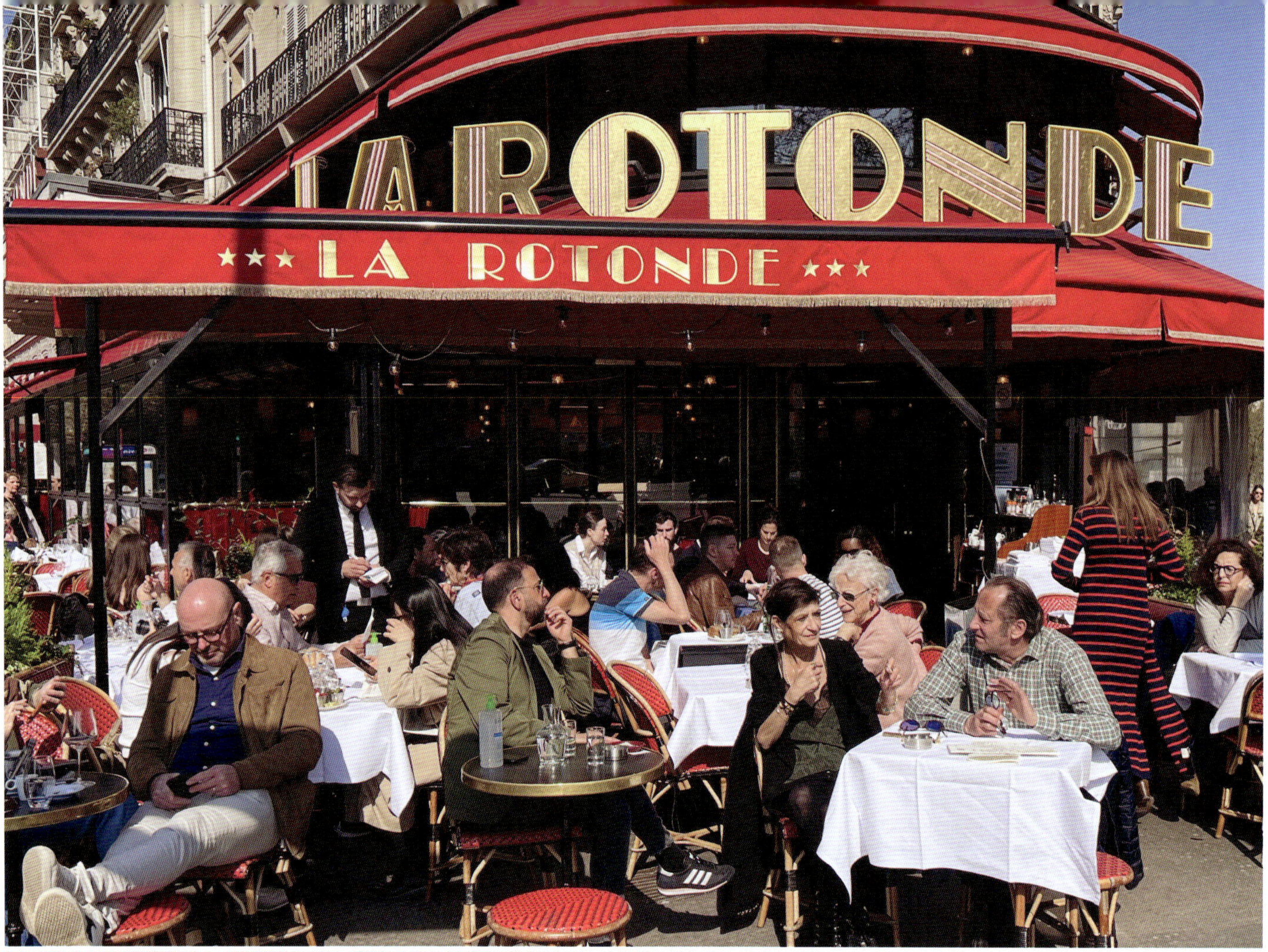
LA ROTONDE
LA ROTONDE

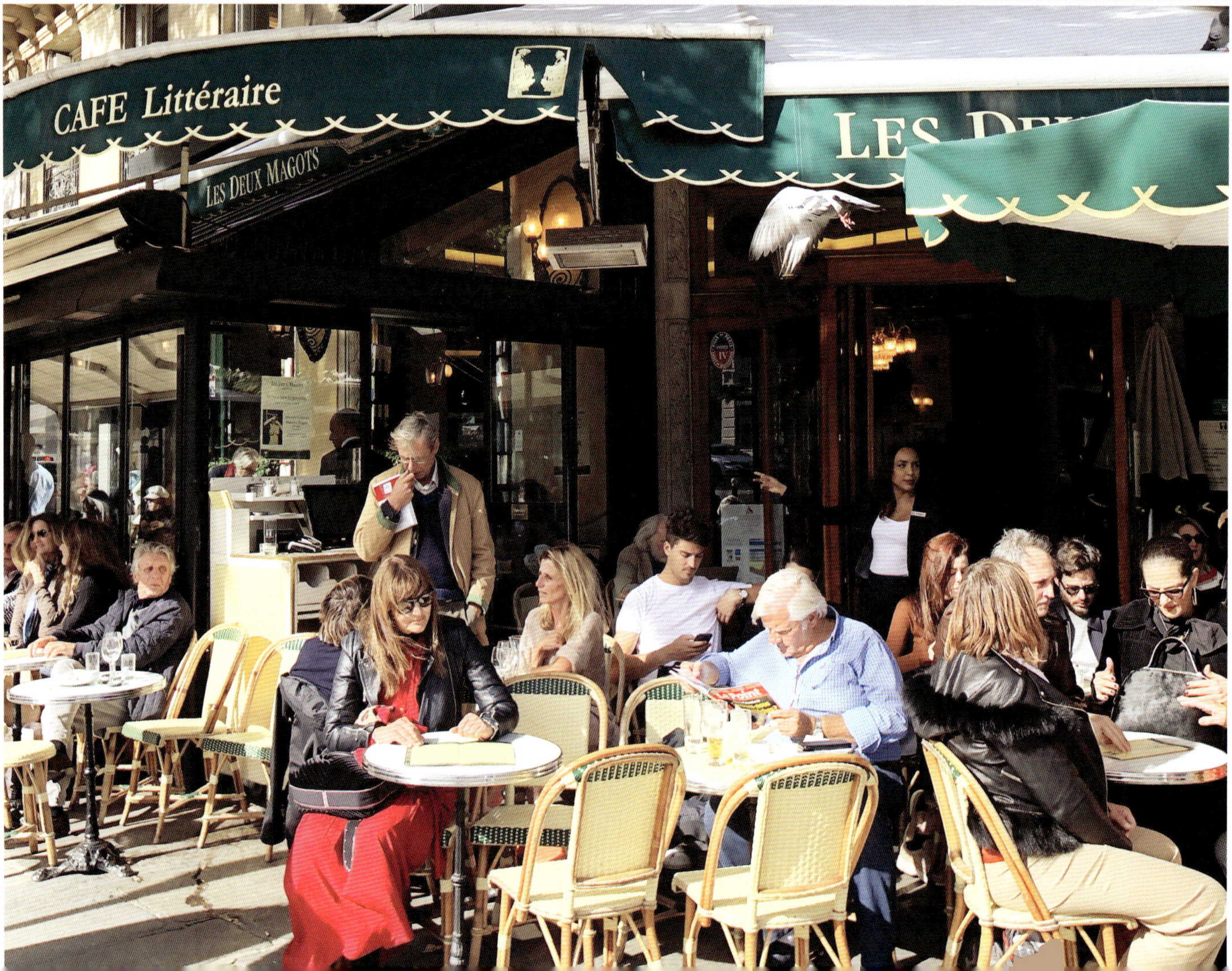
CAFE Littéraire
LES DEUX MAGOTS

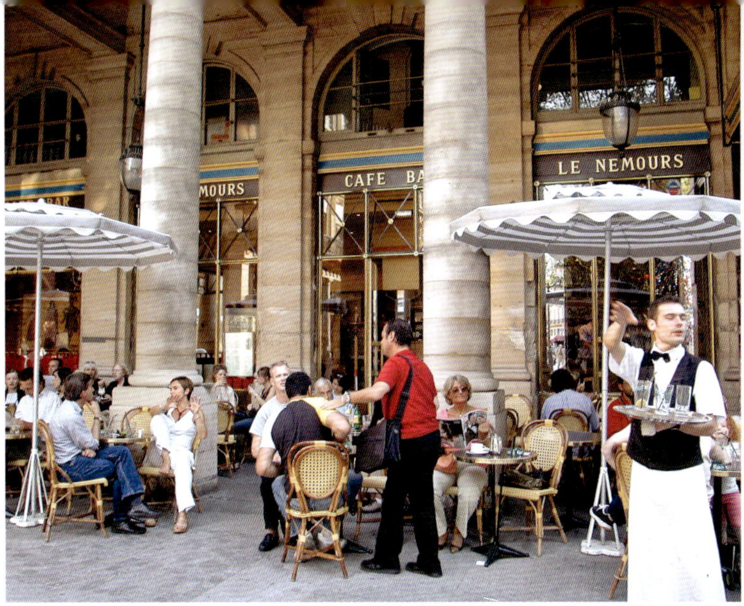
LE NEMOURS
CAFE BA
MOURS

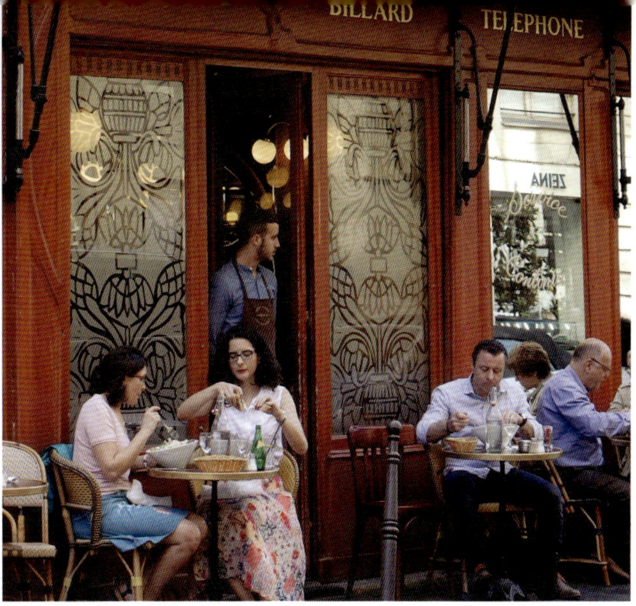
BILLARD

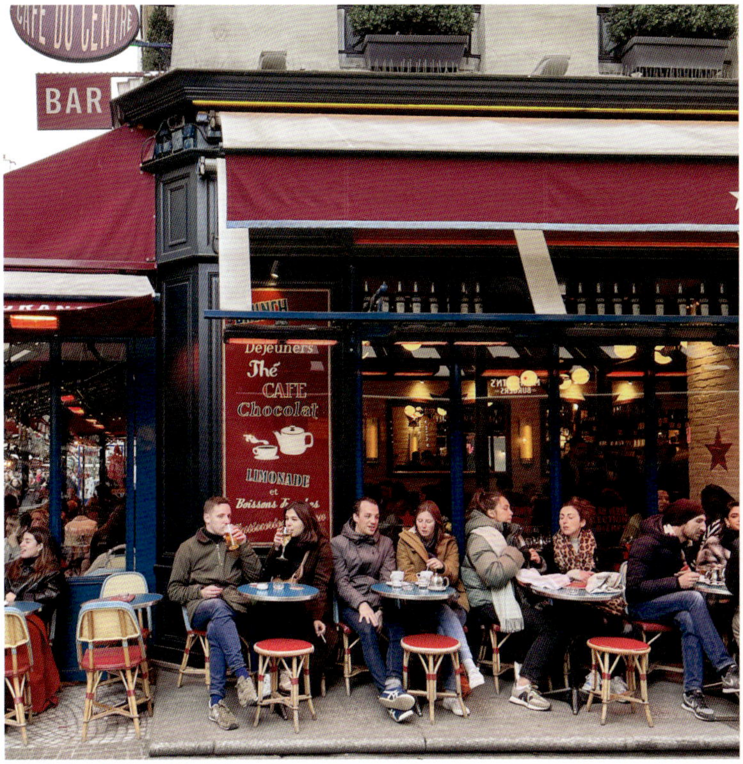
BAR
Dejeuners
Thé
CAFE
Chocolat
LIMONADE

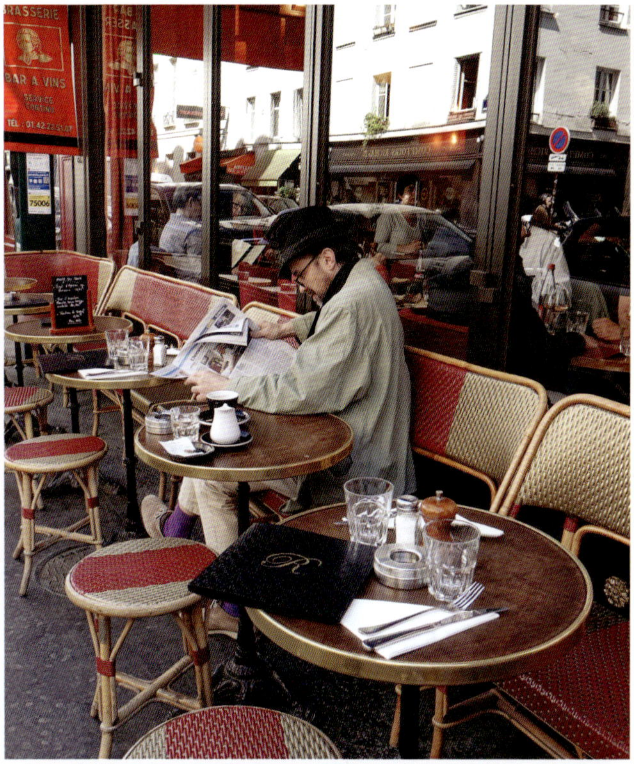

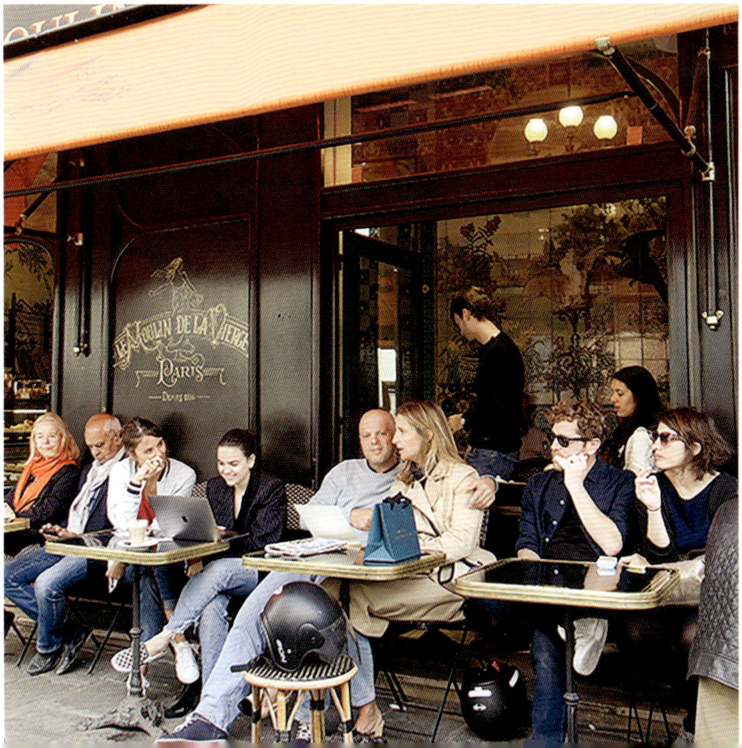

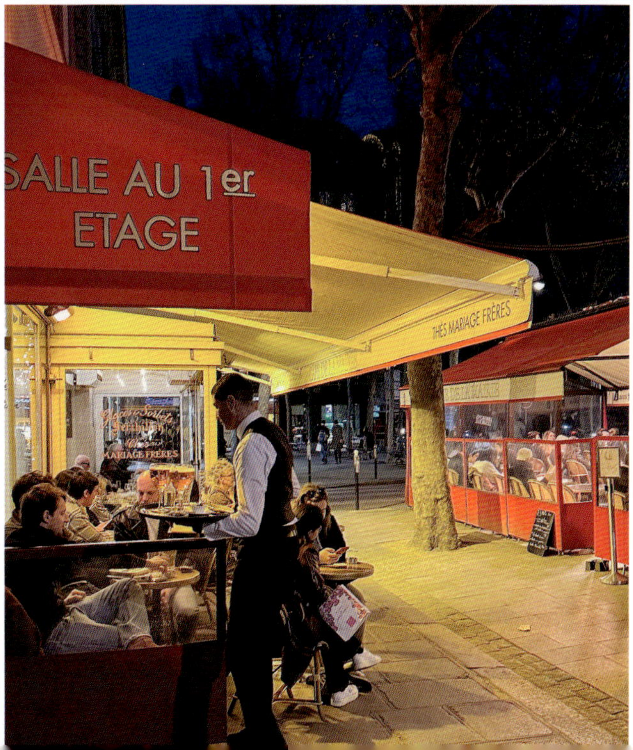
SALLE AU 1er
ETAGE

L'Intérieur

"It is certain that the café by itself with its tables, its booths, its mirrors, its light, its smoky atmosphere, and the sounds of voices, rattling saucers, and footsteps which fill it—the café is a fulfillment of being."

Jean-Paul Sartre

Café interiors come in various sizes, shapes, and styles, from classic Art Nouveau and Art Deco to mid-century modern, sophisticated 20th & 21st-century, funky fun, industrial, or something less than good design. While we appreciate and delight in every creative and beautiful café no matter the era, preserving the remaining historic cafés is critical to the look and feel of the city of Paris itself. In a classic Parisian café, every element of the design matters: the architecture, furniture and furnishings, waiters' attire, tableware, plating, even the cloth napkins that can be as sizable as a tablecloth. Rare is the classic café or bistro today that has kept its original design intact; too many have been destroyed, with structural and decorative elements sold or even stolen like Roman ruins. There is an unfortunate trend to renovate inexpensively with inferior design and materials rather than restore the original interior. Cafés, bistros, and brasseries that retain time-honored elements like moleskin banquettes, wooden chairs (often Thonet) and tables, zinc counters, mirrored walls, decorative mosaic floors, elegant lighting, and brass coat racks, are to be treasured and celebrated. Here, even the restrooms—often down a narrow winding staircase—can be worth a journey because of their vintage, beautiful, or surprising design.

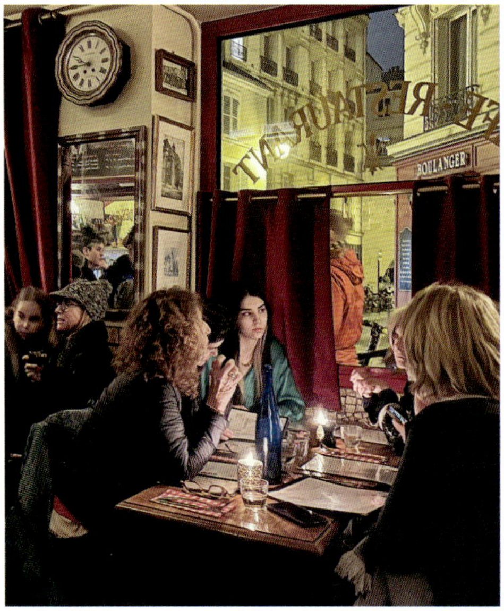

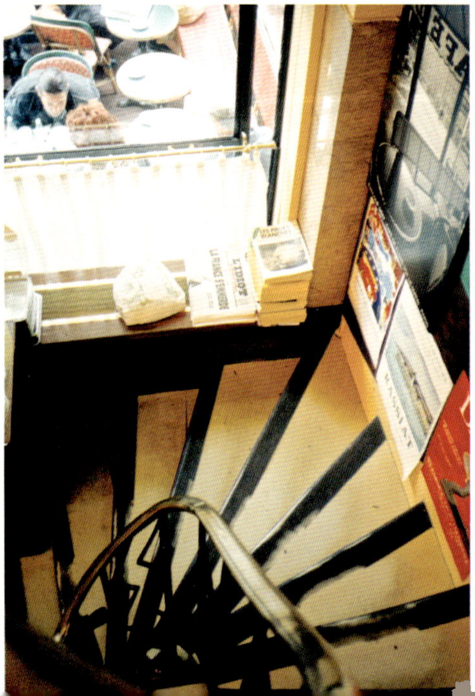

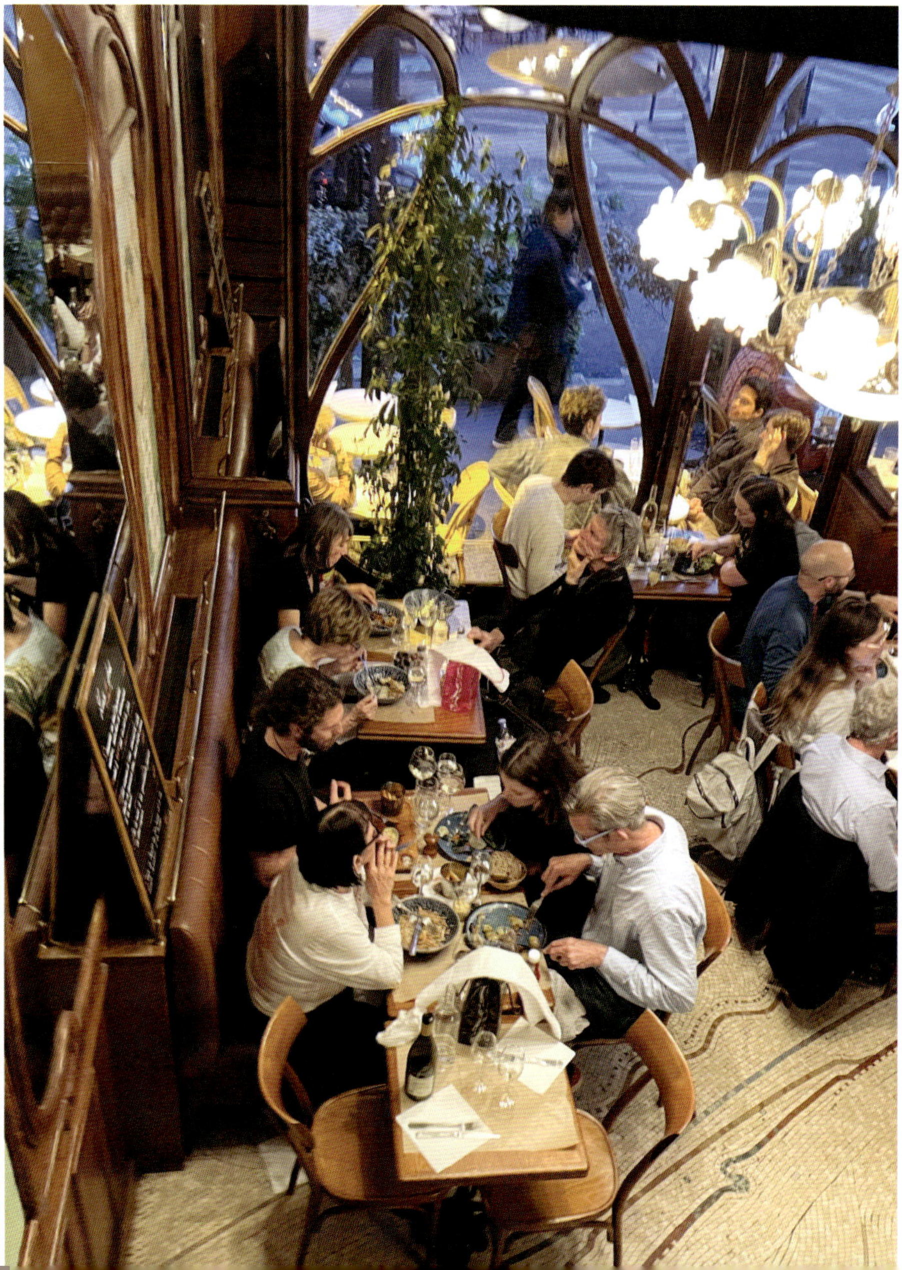

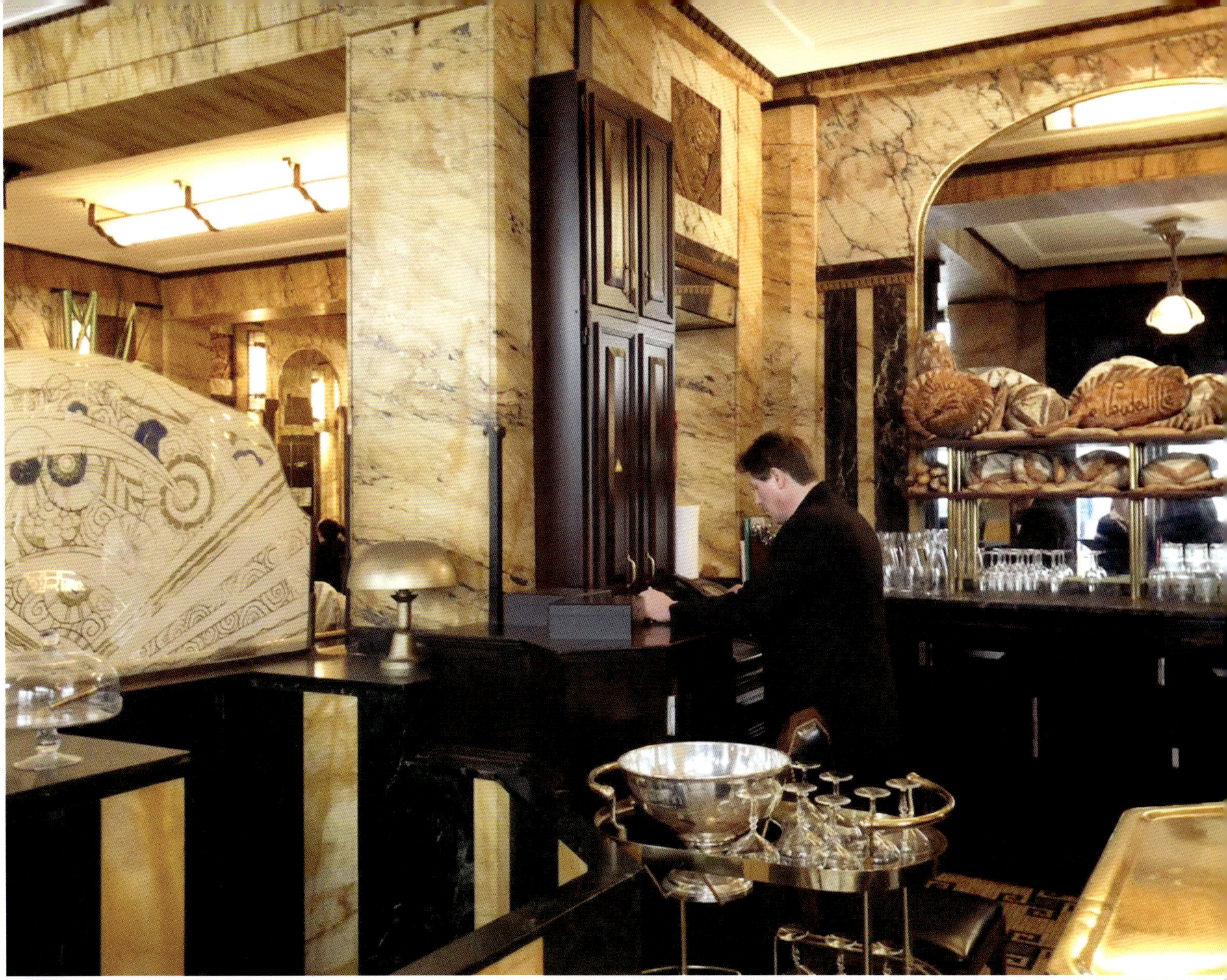
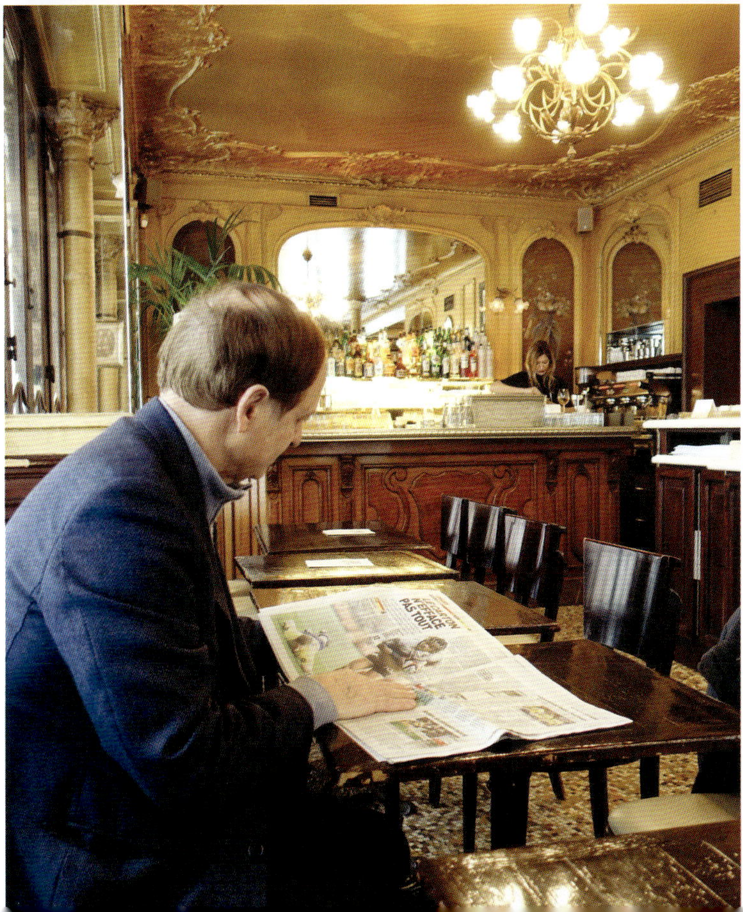
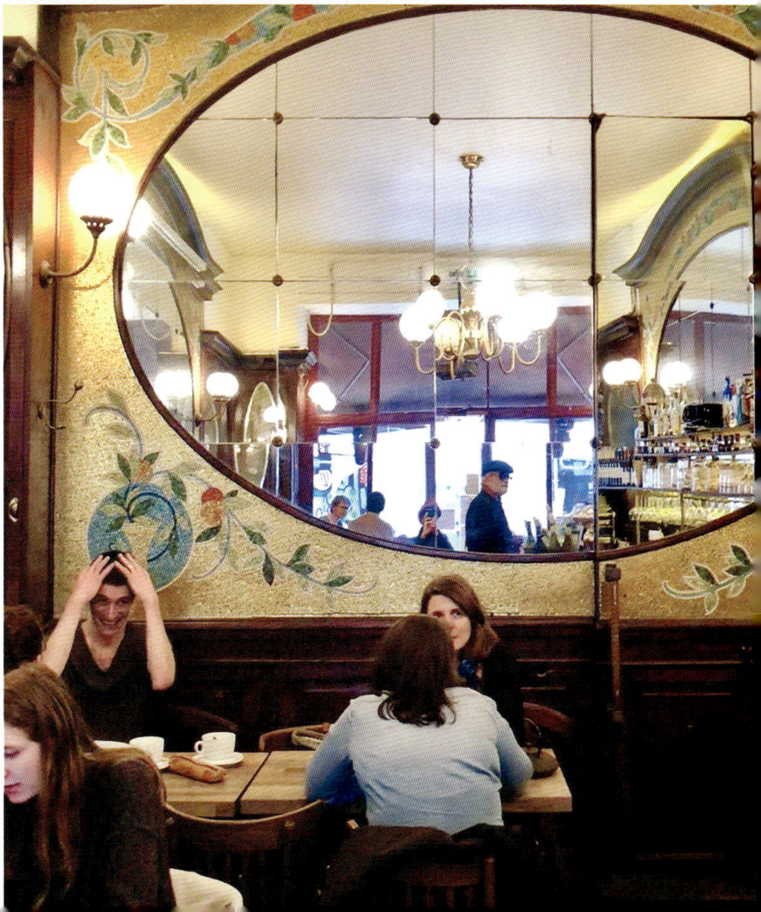

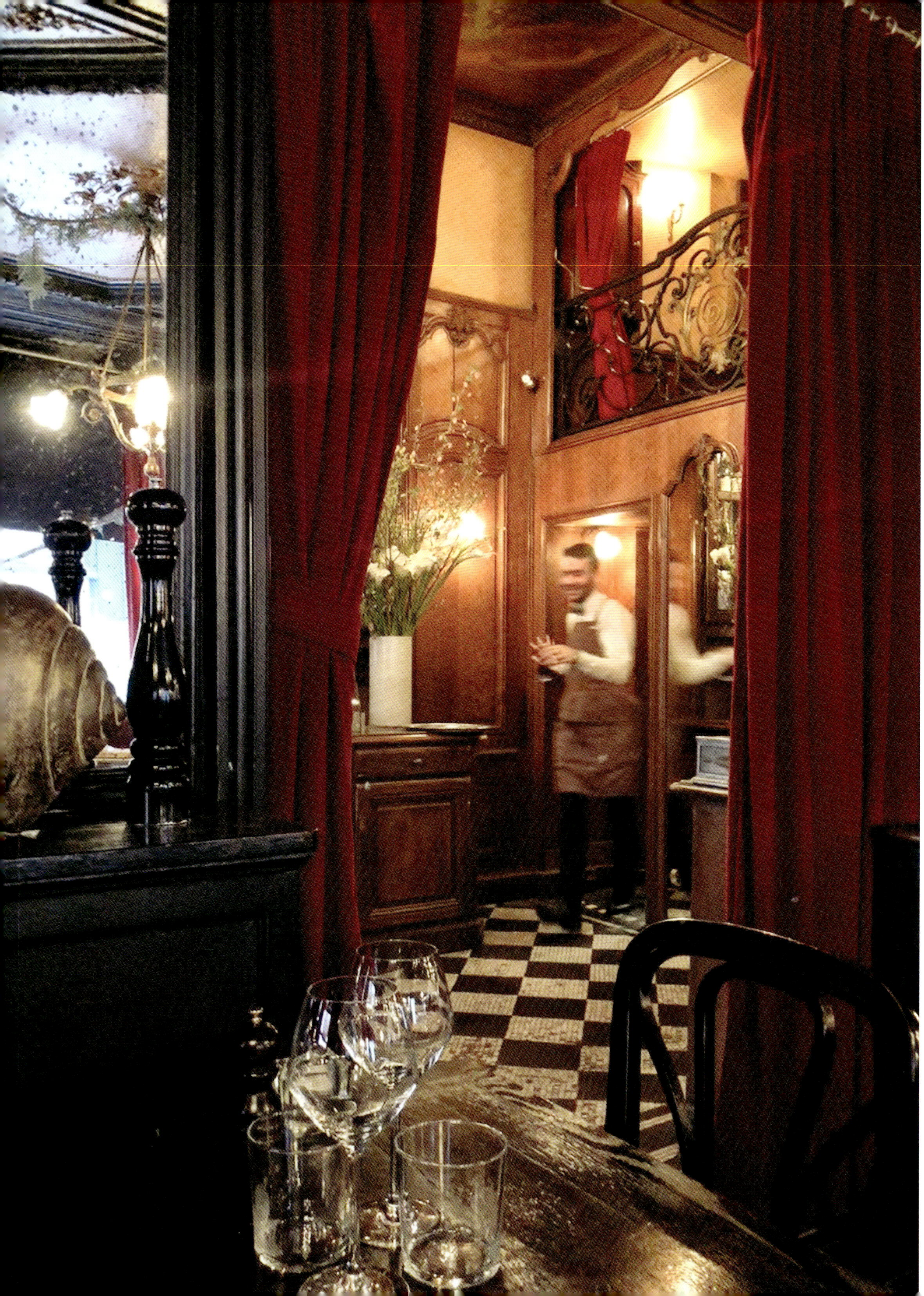

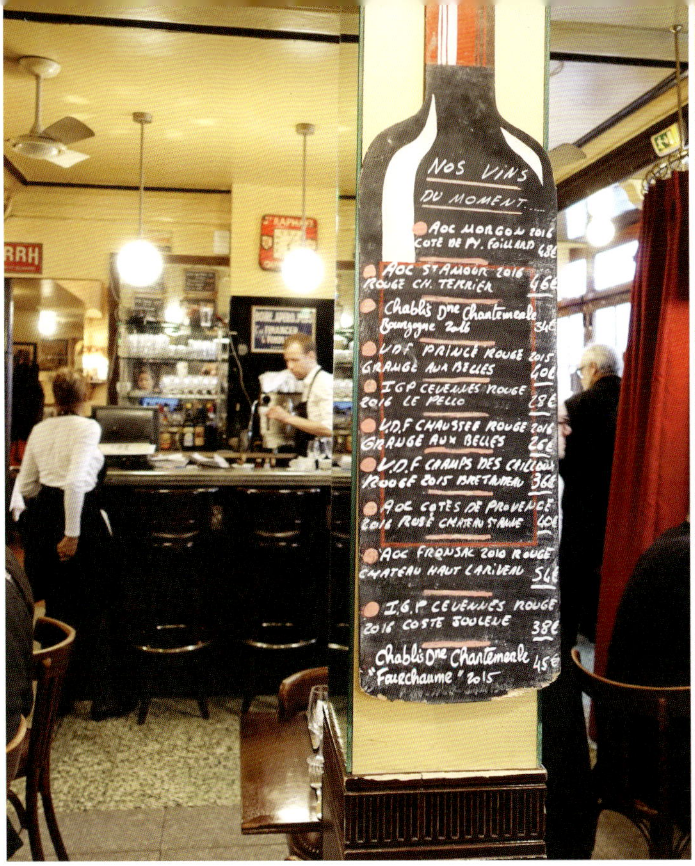

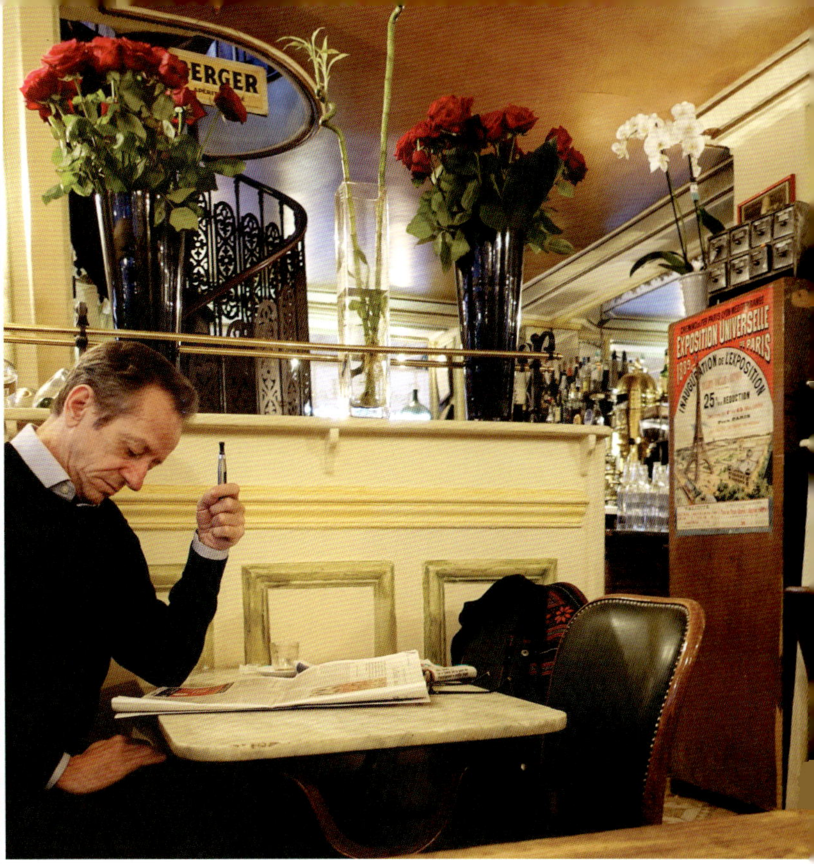

L'Escargot Montorgueil (OPPOSITE PAGE), established in 1828, has been serving its escargot (now in a myriad of preparations) for almost 200 years. The exquisite downstairs dining rooms, designated as a historic monument, were refreshed, not remodeled in 2014. Marcel Proust, Sarah Bernhardt, Salvador Dalí, among other notables, have dined here (and no, it doesn't only serve escargot).

Bistrot Paul Bert (ABOVE LEFT), Café Louis Philippe, Au Petit Fer à Cheval (BELOW LEFT), and Brasserie Floderer (BELOW RIGHT) boast authentic, evocative interiors and serve faultless dishes befitting their ambiance.

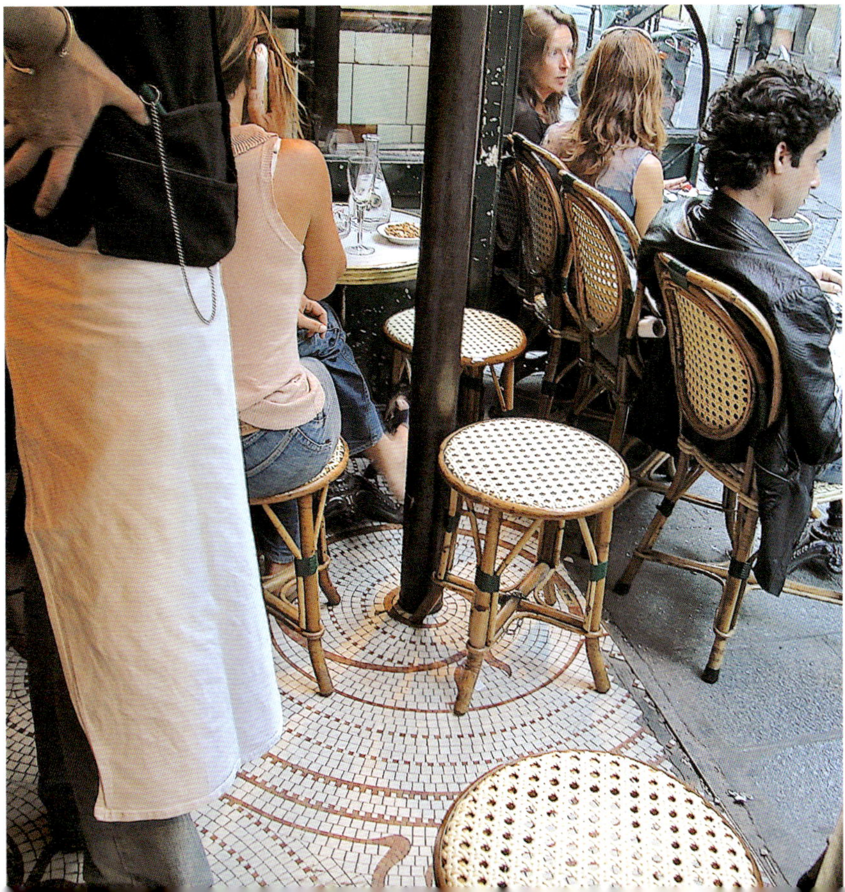

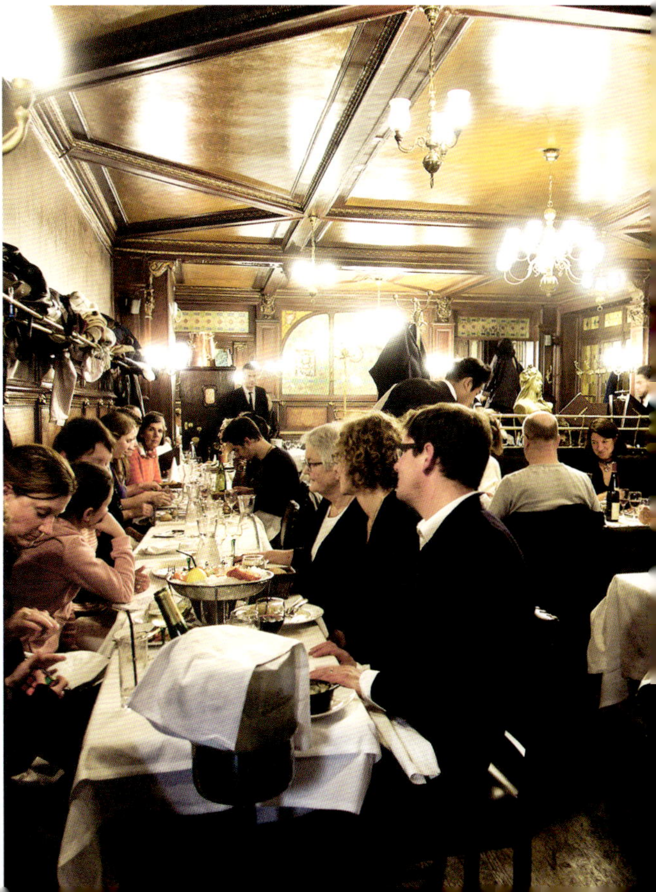

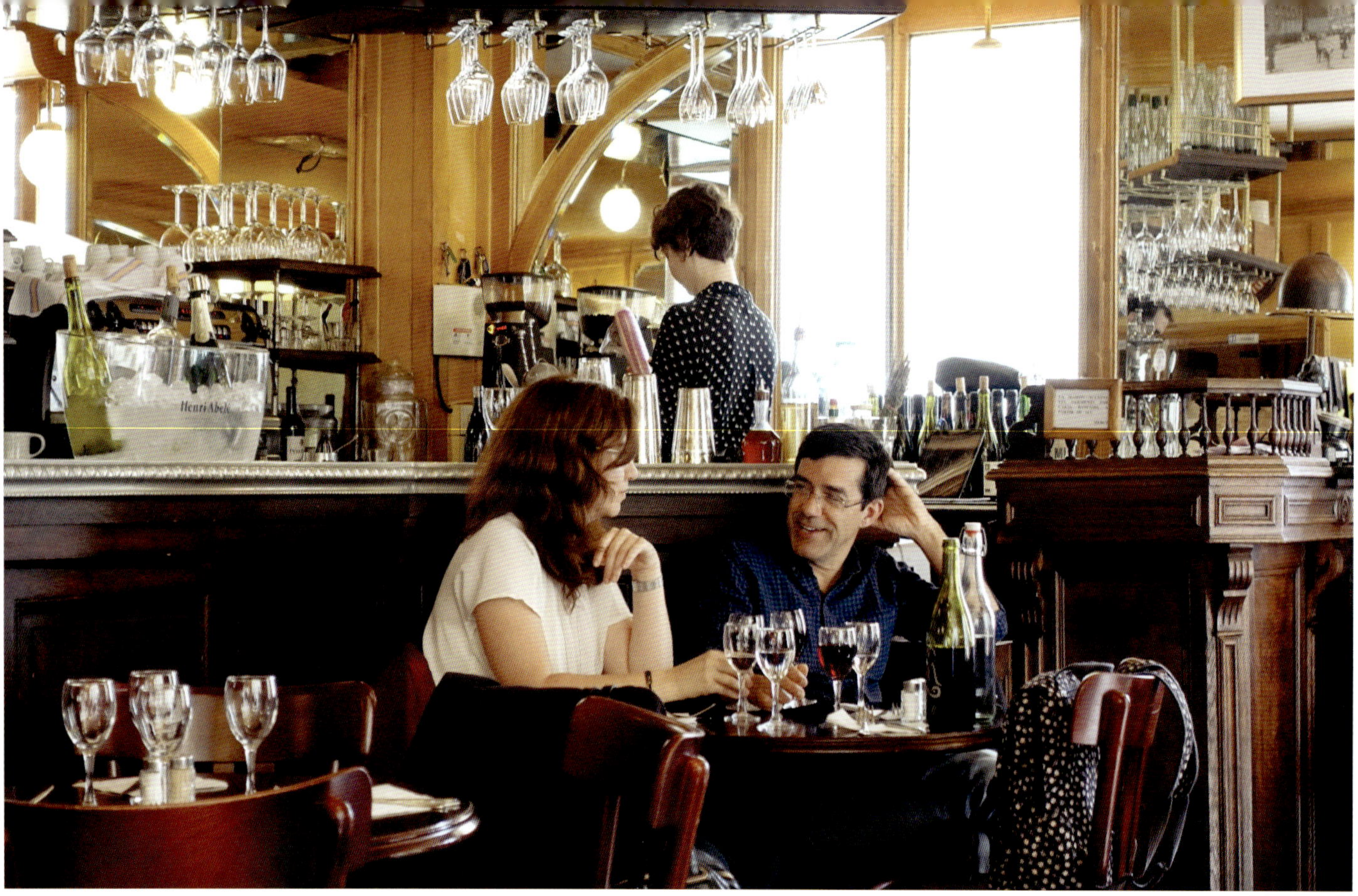

Two charming bistros on the Right Bank are worthy of a meal as well as a photo shoot: Bistrot Victoires (ABOVE), which has been around since 1802, and early 20th-century favorite La Tartine (BELOW LEFT), whose cigarette-toned ceiling is now freshly painted.

Bouillon Chartier Montparnasse (OPPOSITE TOP), founded in 1896, has retained its elegant 1906 Art Nouveau interior and traditional food at modest prices. Featuring elegantly carved wood, ceramics, mirrors, glass paintings, and roof, it remains perfectly preserved. Le Charbon (BELOW RIGHT), created in 1863, retains an authentic flavor with their classic with an asian twist dishes from the chef, and a festive interior that remains of the "époque."

Since 1925, the bistro turned brasserie, Terminus Nord (OPPOSITE BOTTOM), near the Gare du Nord, has welcomed travelers to its Art Deco space, featuring a sublime rounded bar. Daily menus are hand-written on the blackboard.

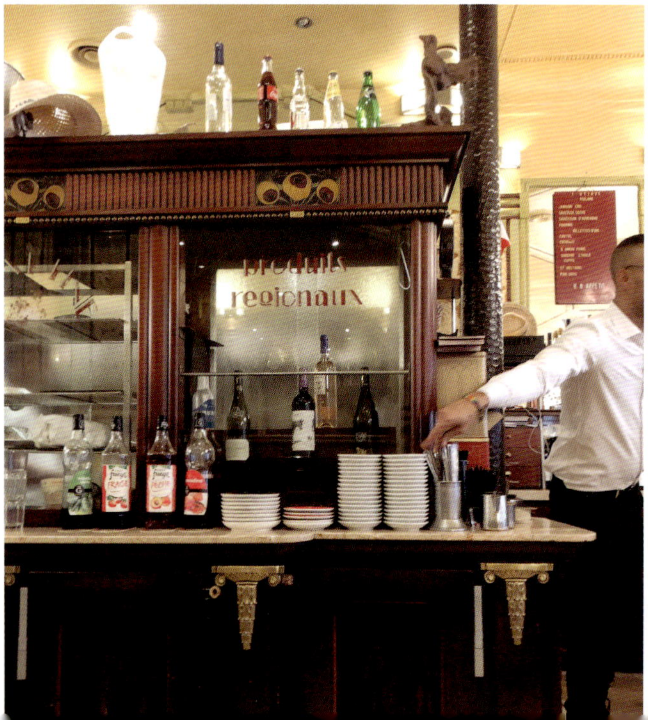

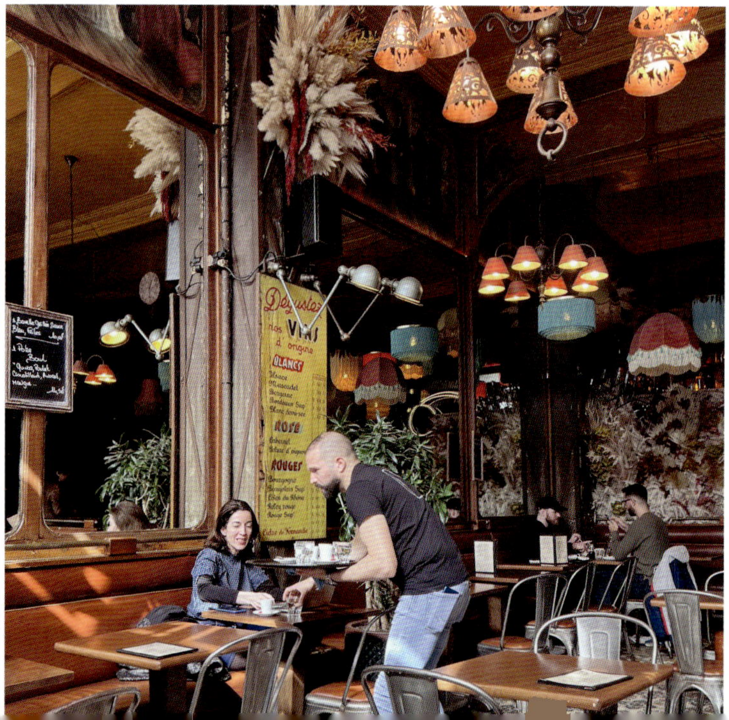

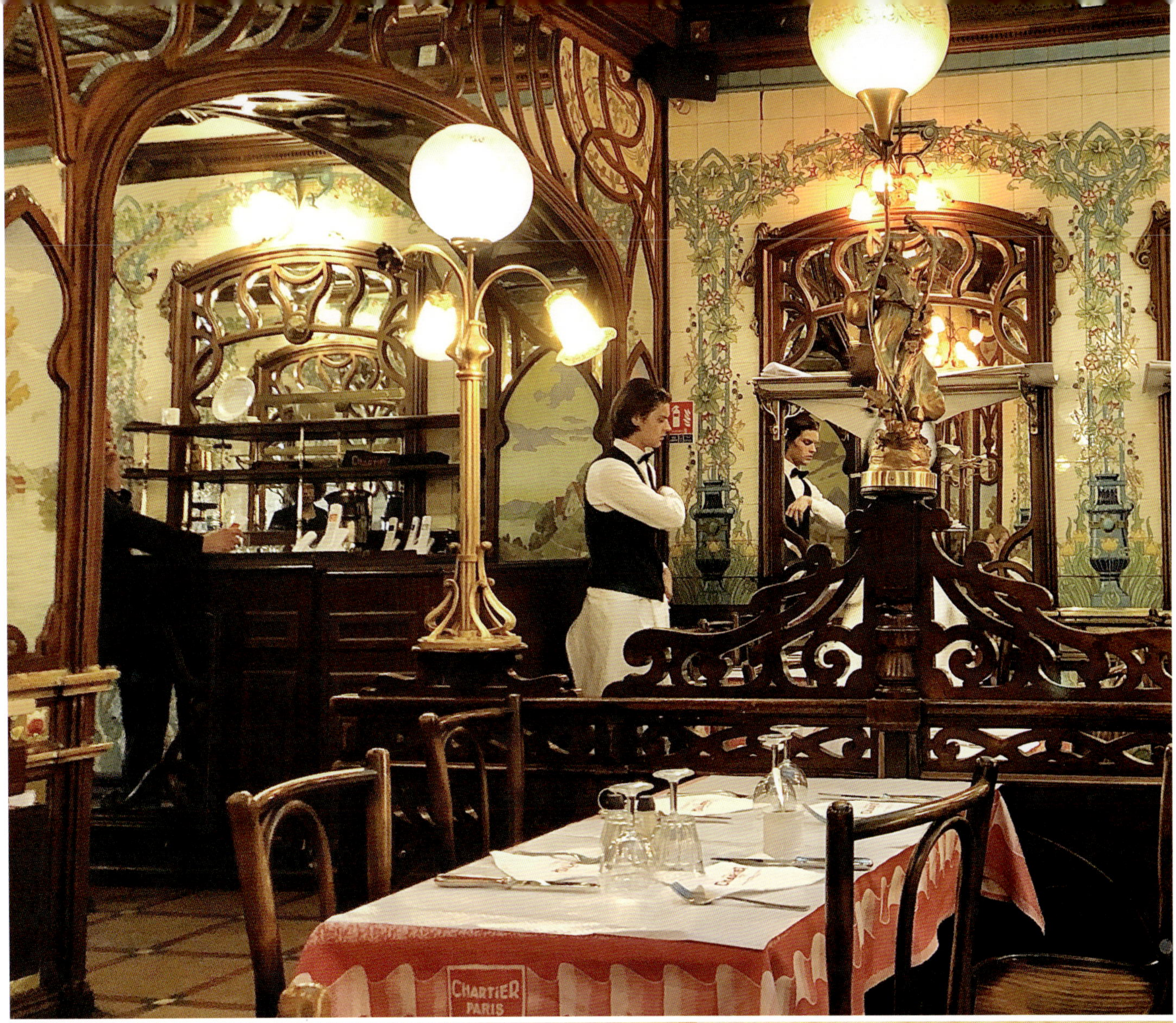
CHARTIER
PARIS

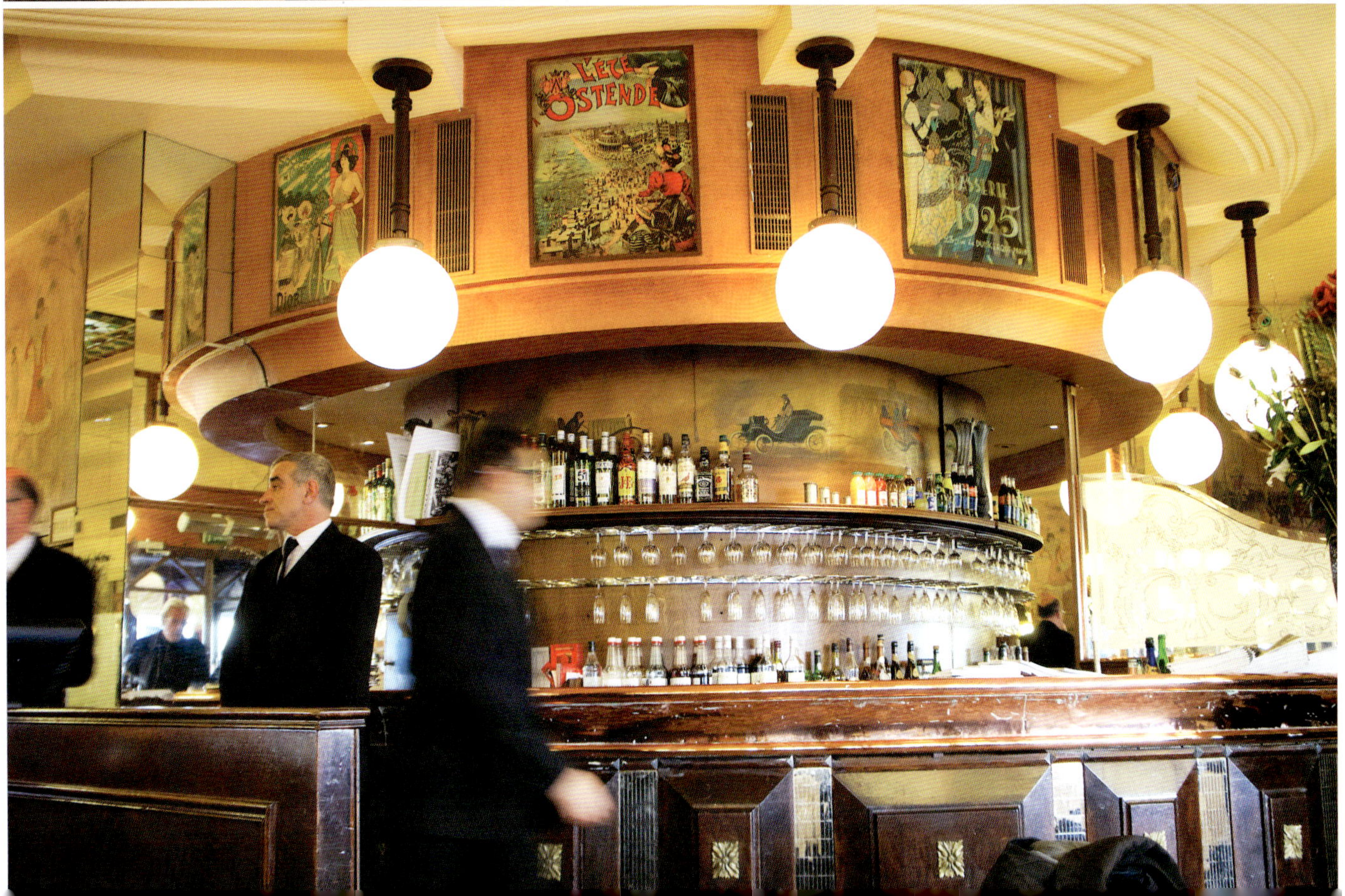
OSTENDE
1925

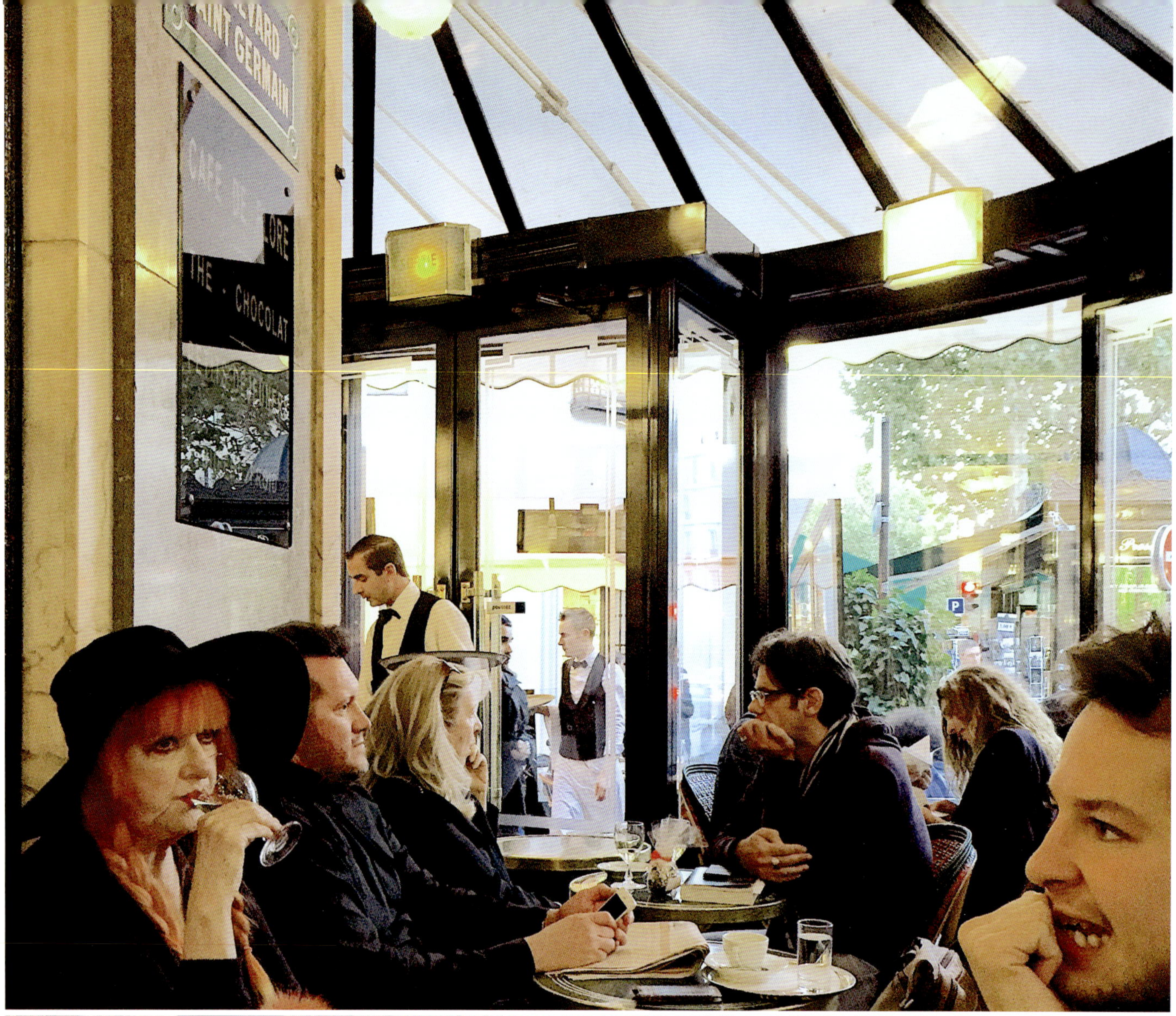
THE . CHOCOLAT

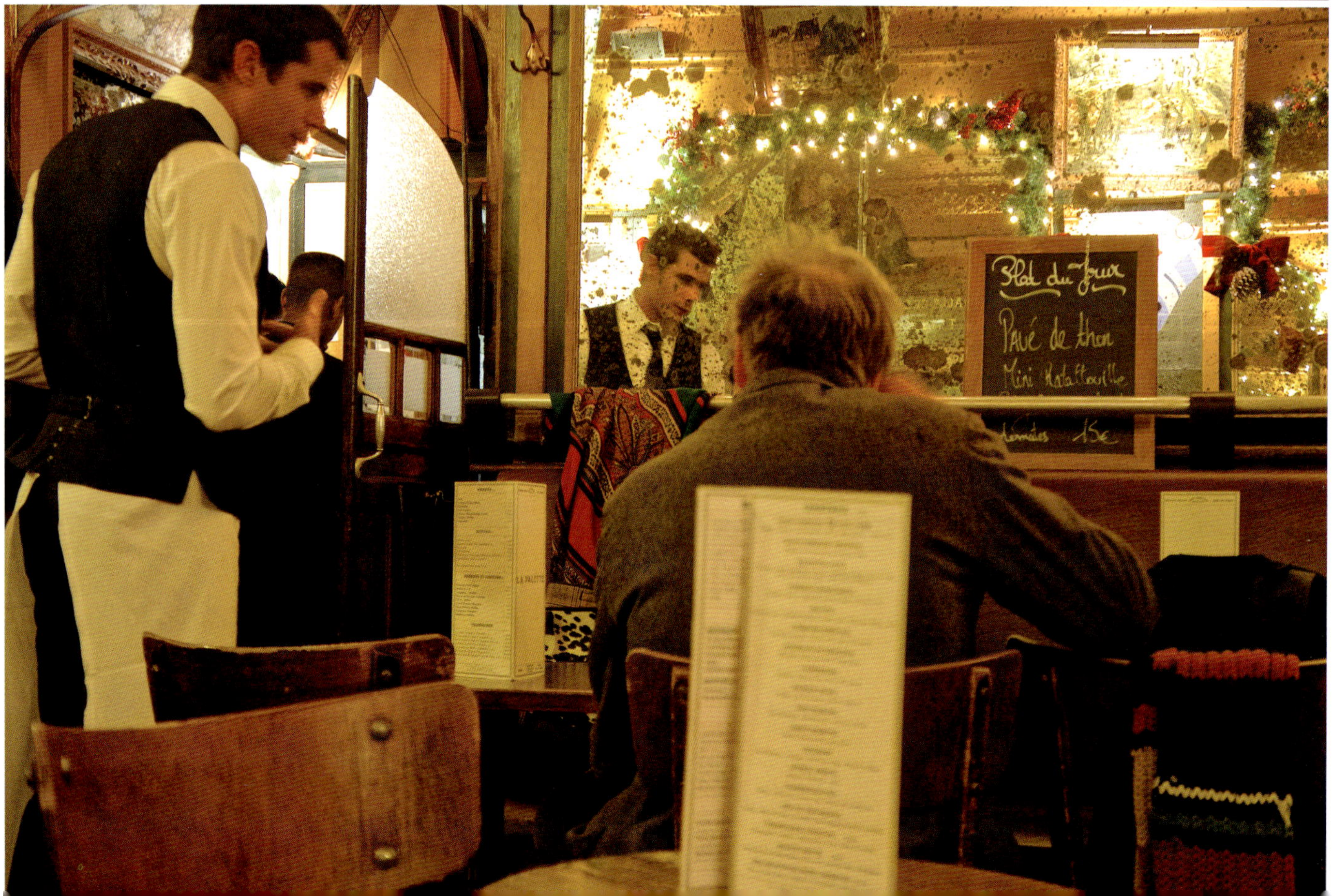
Plat du Jour
Pavé de thon
Mini Ratatouille

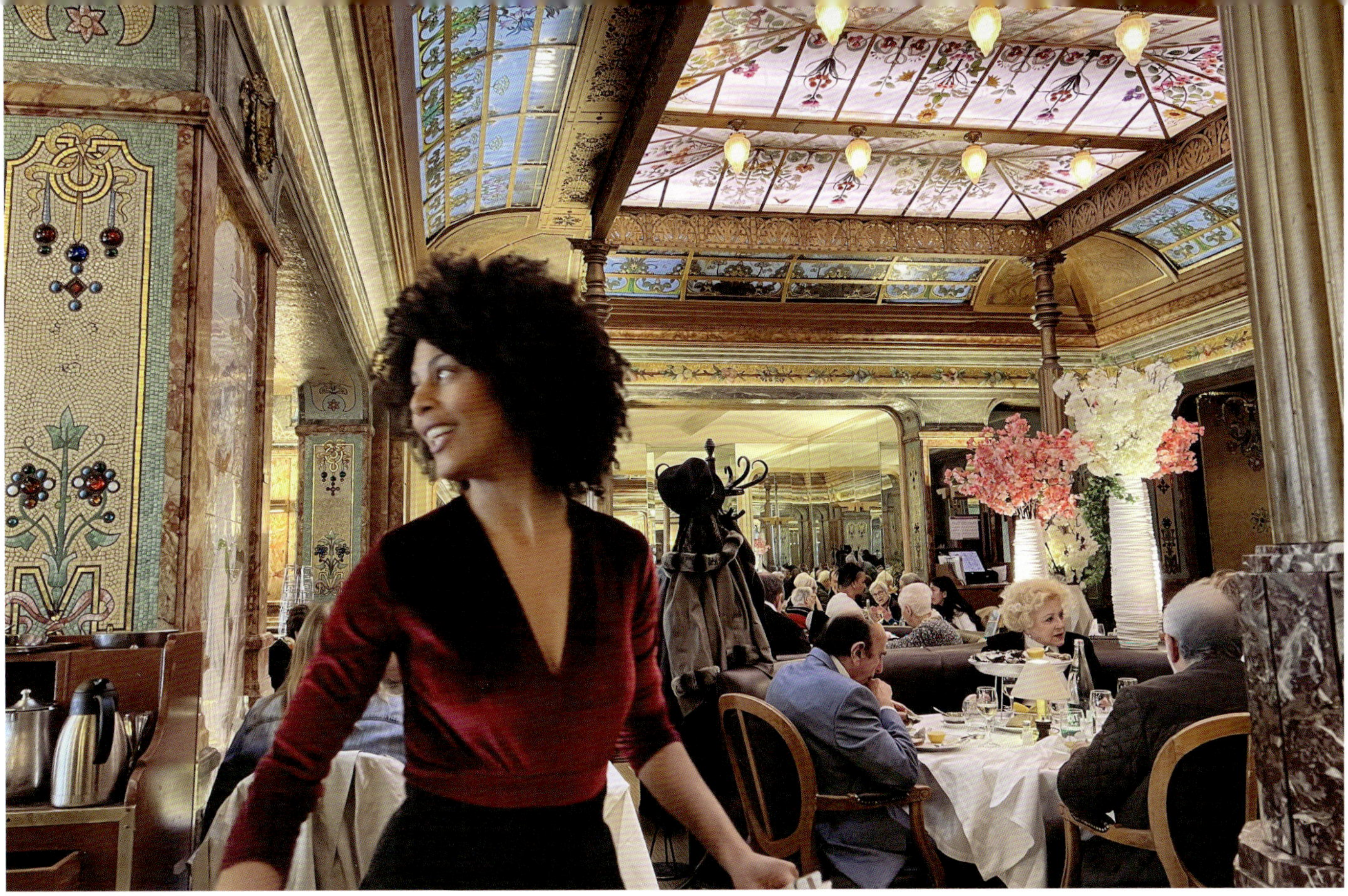

Floor to ceiling glass windows and doors, oversized mirrors, and soft, flattering lighting, all hallmarks of the mise-en-scene where everyday life flows seamlessly from early morning to late evening. With the sounds of plates clattering, espresso machines hissing, people conversing in a babble of languages, feeding the innate need for human contact, the café celebrates being alive and in the world, whether together with friends, colleagues, family, or solo. Austrian critic Alfred Polgar put it beautifully: "for all who wish to be alone but need sociability for this; in this setting, one finds an antidote to isolation."

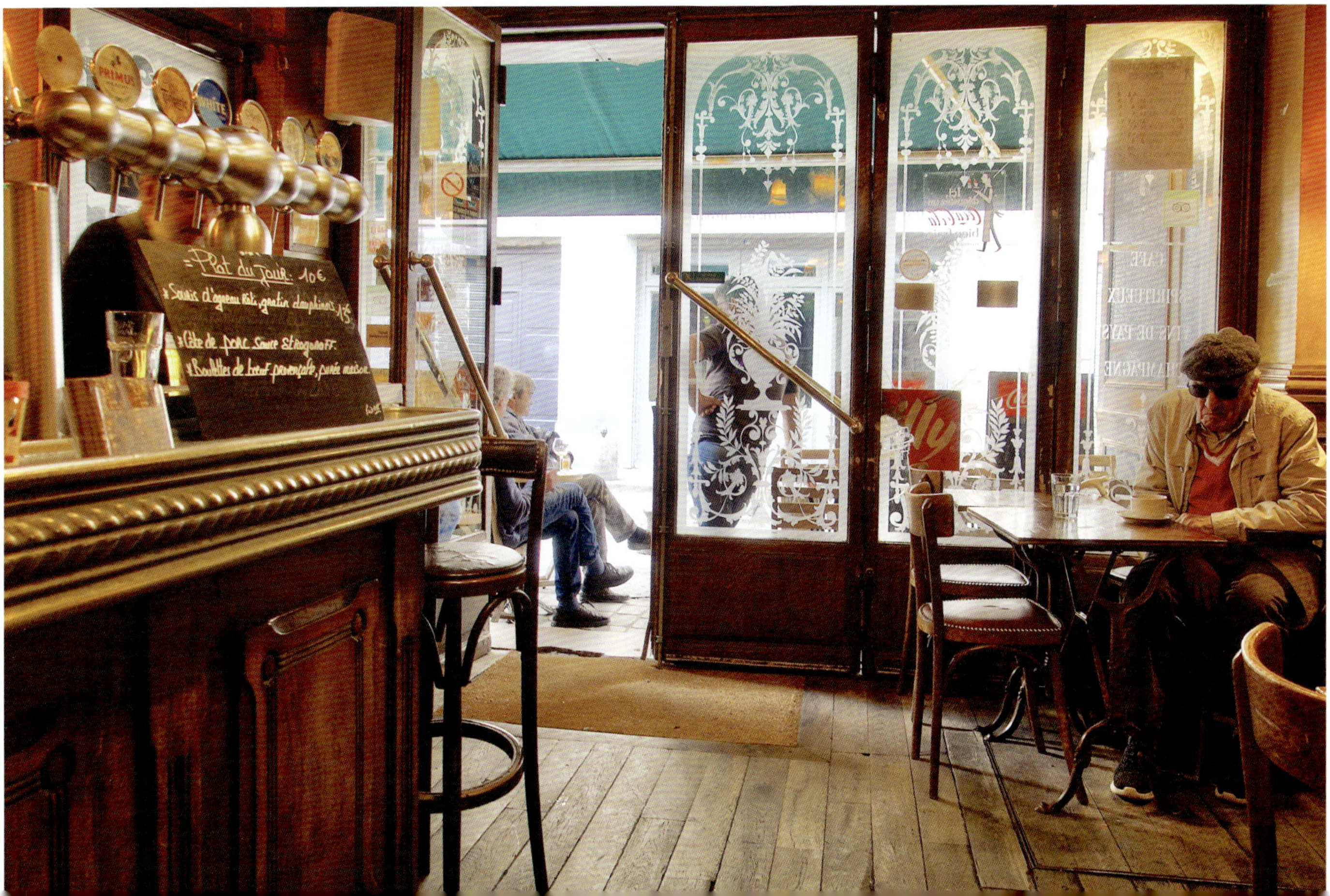

Le Zinc

"The bar of a cafe is the parliament of the people."

Honoré de Balzac

Ah, *le zinc*—the quintessential Parisian counter or bar and the common term for a café or bistro—was developed by the joiner Emile Verrière in 1821 and first fabricated by zinc roofers. By the mid-19th century, before Paris had a water supply network and indoor plumbing or heating, the hard-working Auvergnats from the Auvergne or Aveyron of France's Massif Central sold and delivered water, coal, and firewood to the population from their simple kiosks. To sweeten the deal, they added wine, coffee, lemonade, and then simple one-dish meals. A zinc counter provided the ideal surface behind which a husband-and-wife team would preside and serve their customers. The owners were king and queen behind *le zinc*, often witnesses to marriages, spies for local police, and arbiters of neighborhood gossip and disputes. Habitués, feeling at home, often lived at *le zinc* from opening to closing, with only work to interrupt. Workers from nearby factories began their day early with their newspaper and companions, by *tuer le verre* (killing the glass) of white wine for breakfast, followed by drinking and eating breaks throughout the long workday and into the evening. Rarely were stools provided—you stood at the bar to drink, socialize, read the newspapers, argue politics. In the right café at the right time, these prototypical men can still be found at *le zinc* from early morning on through the day until the last aperitif.

The Belly of Paris by Émile Zola, published in 1873, has the first recorded mention of *le zinc*. The novel takes place in and around Les Halles, where the Auvergnats founded the bistros of Paris, complete with iconic zinc bars. These Auvergnat entrepreneurs and their descendants have continued to run almost three-quarters of the humble and prominent bistros and cafés throughout Paris in the 20th and 21st centuries, including the illustrious Le Flore, Le Dôme, La Coupole, and Les Deux Magots in the 6th arrondissement. A few of the originals endure, some transformed utterly, others, thankfully, preserved.

Technically, a bar can be manufactured with marble, wood, copper, or even Formica and still be called *le zinc*. In the late 1880s, zinc counters in Paris numbered 70,000. During the German occupation in WWII, most zinc bars in Paris were melted down by the Germans and used for weapons. Fortunately, after the war, production of these sturdy bars with finely decorated edges resumed. In the 21st century zinc bars can be found in a multitude of cafés, bistros, brasseries, and bouillons, often crafted in the traditional way—by hand—by the same families in the same factories.

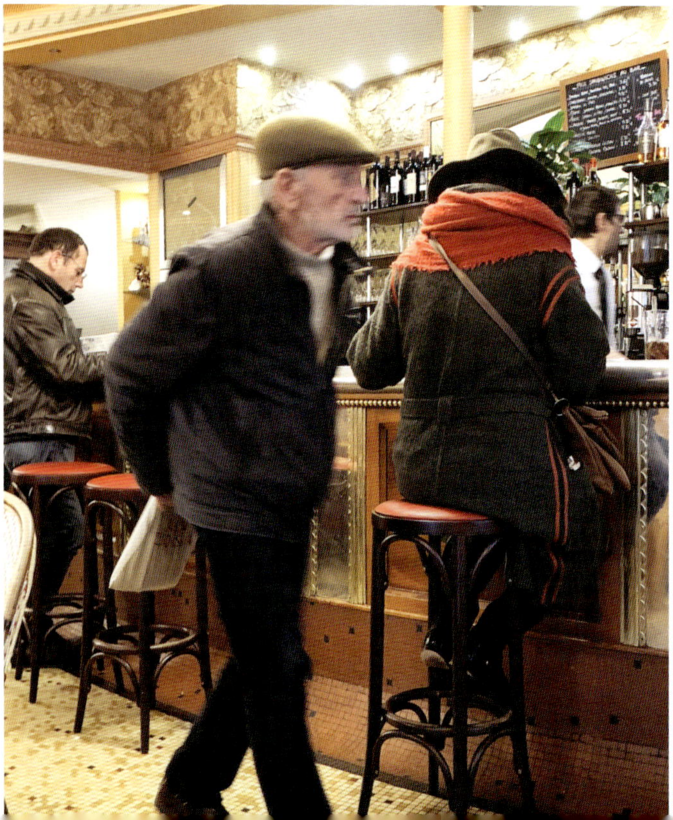

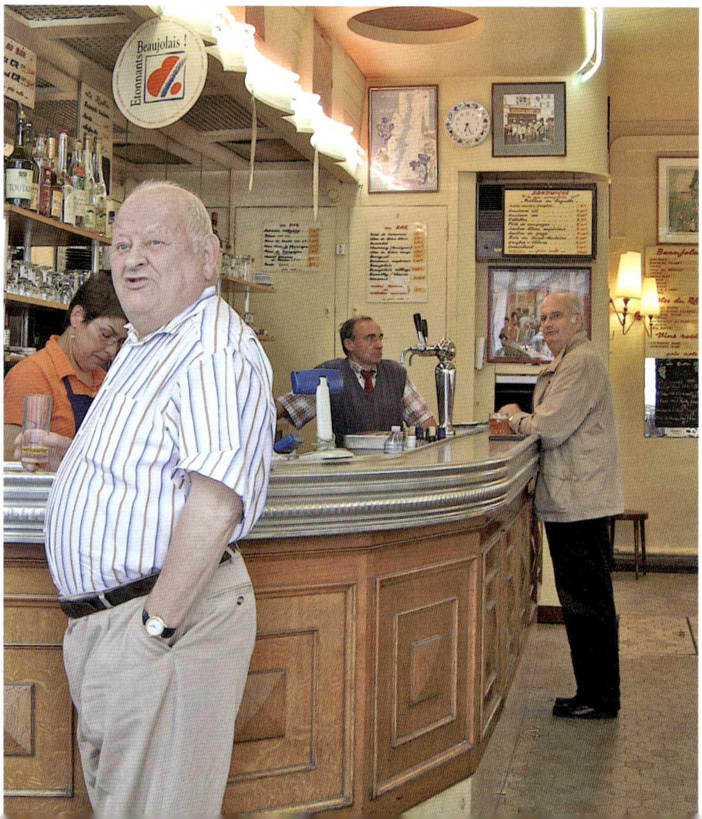

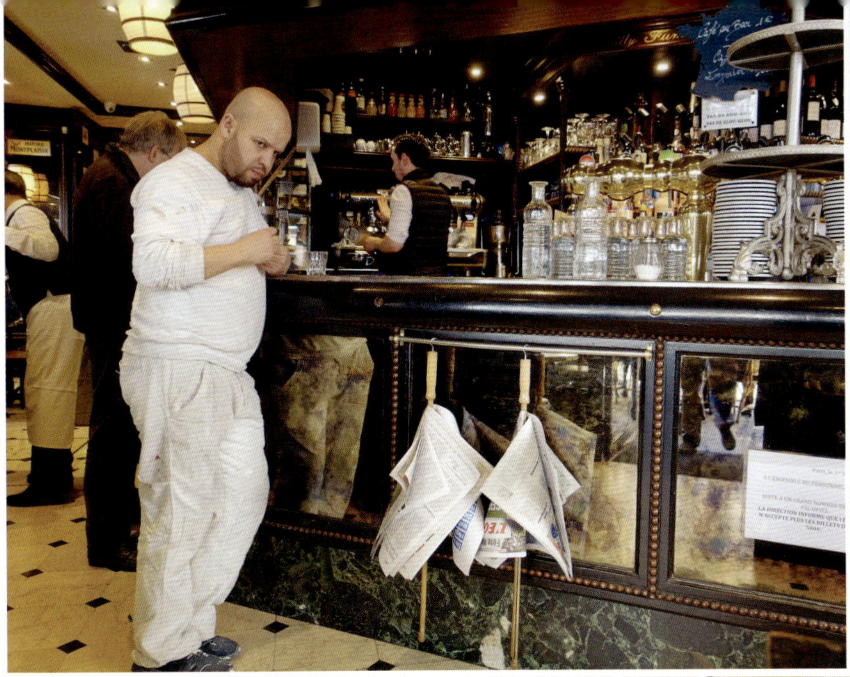
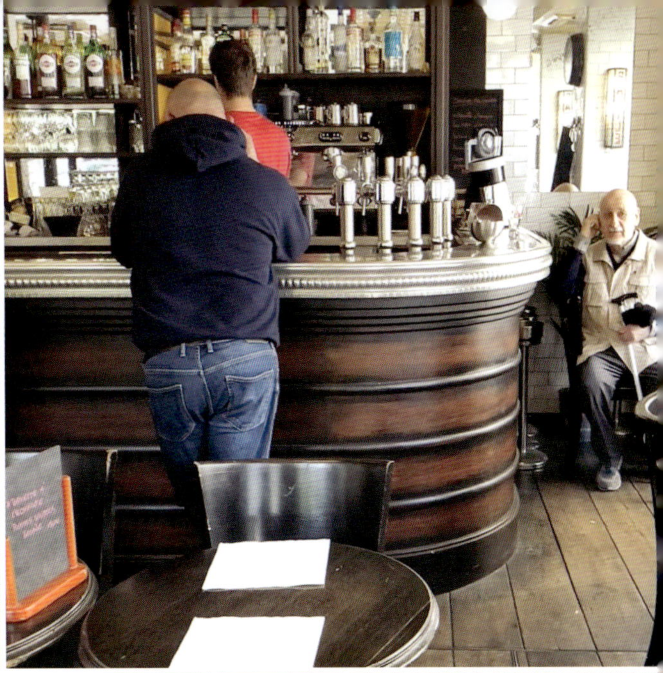
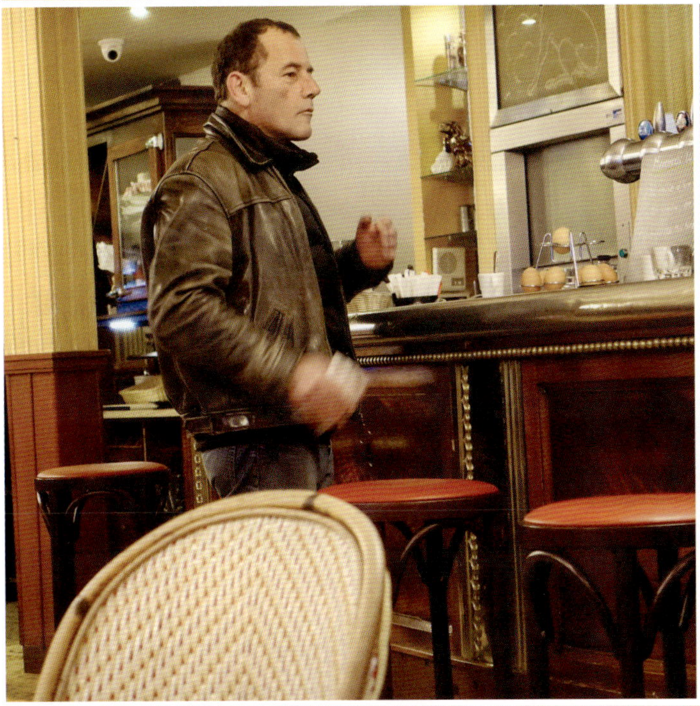
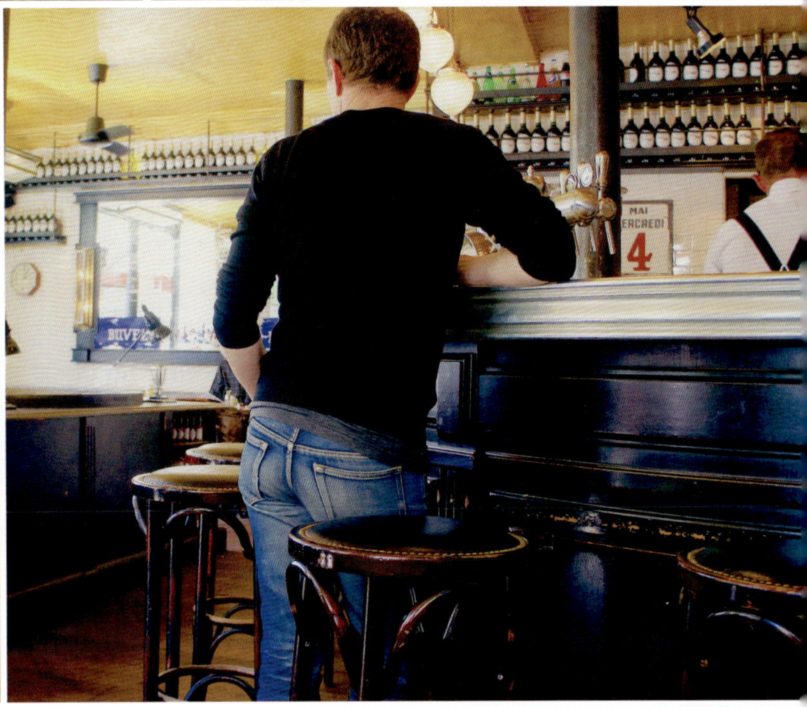
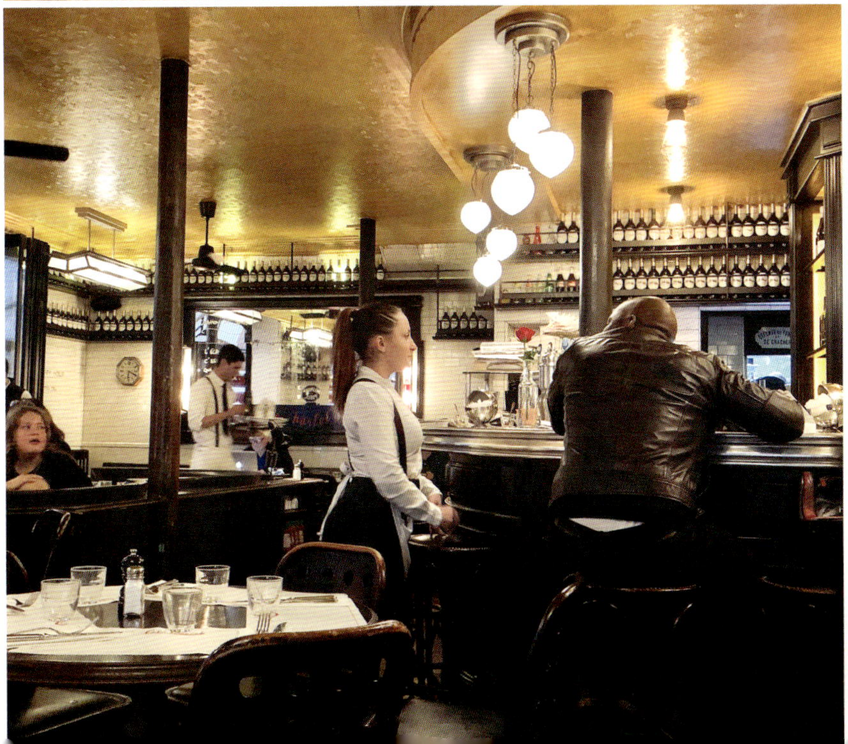
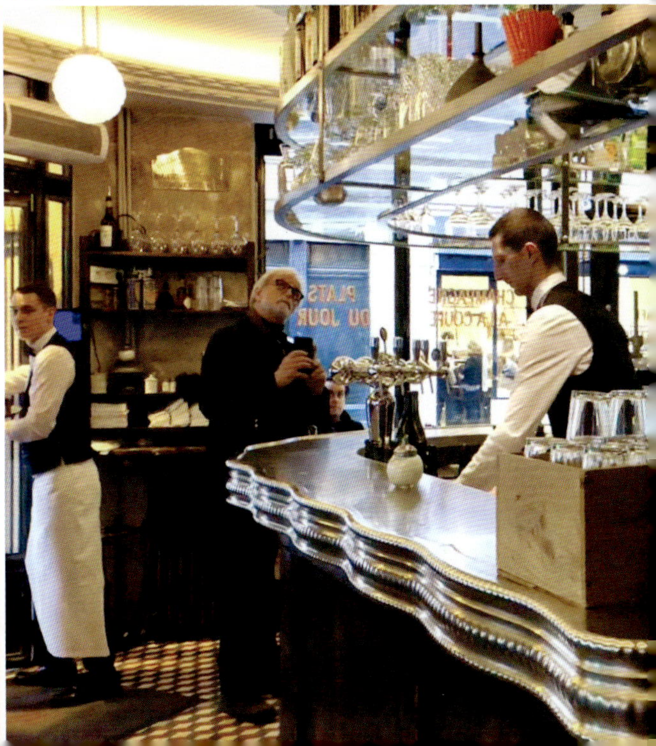

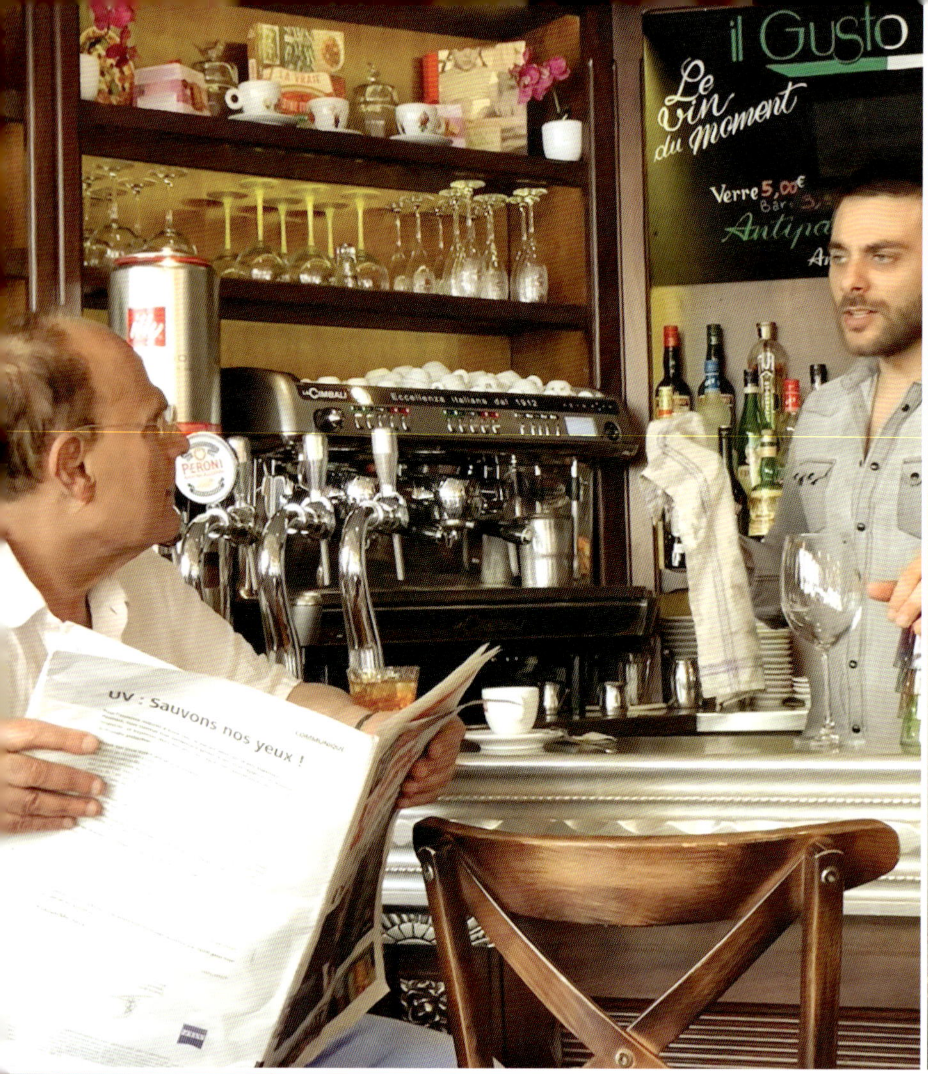
il Gusto
Le vin du moment
Verre 5,00€
PERONI
UV : Sauvons nos yeux !

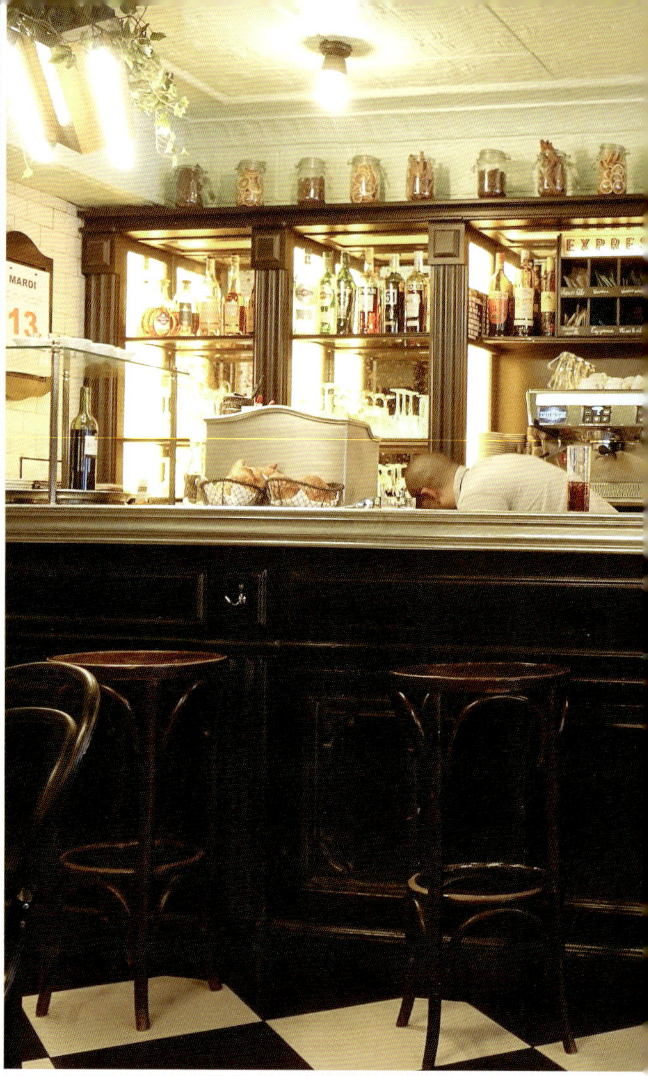
MARDI
13

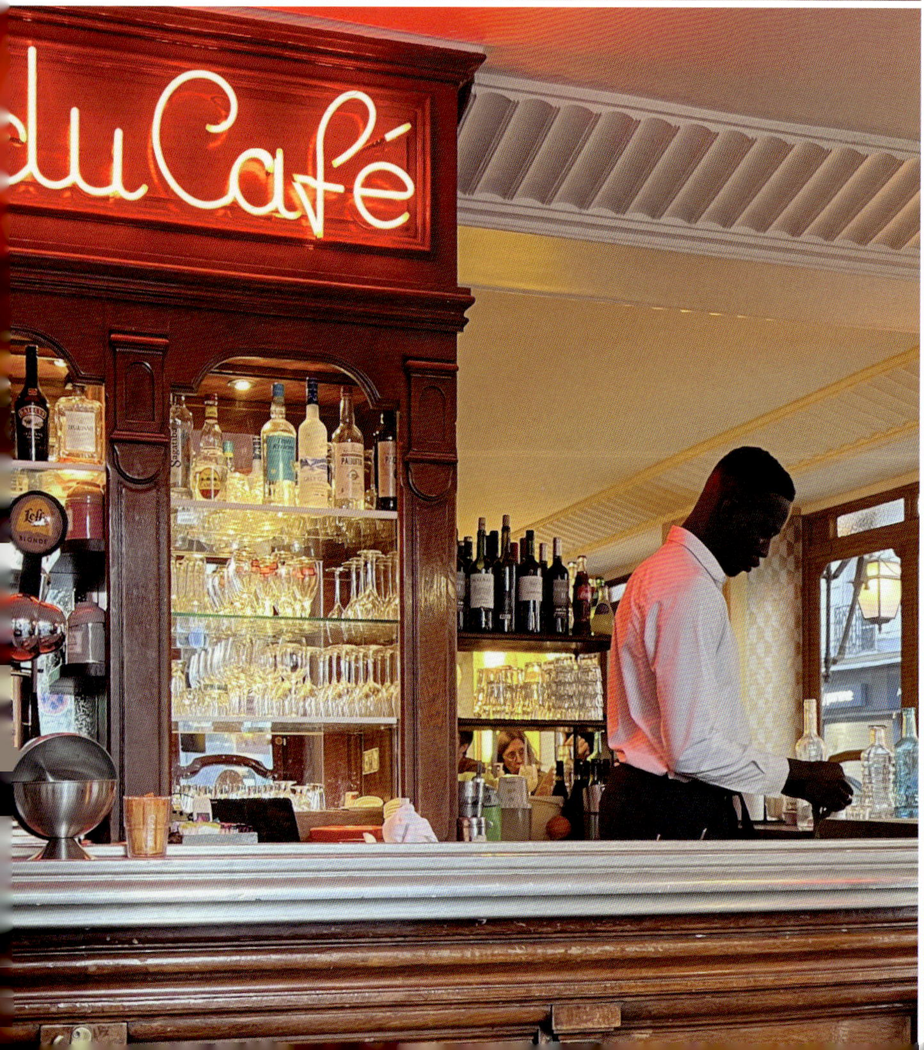
du Café

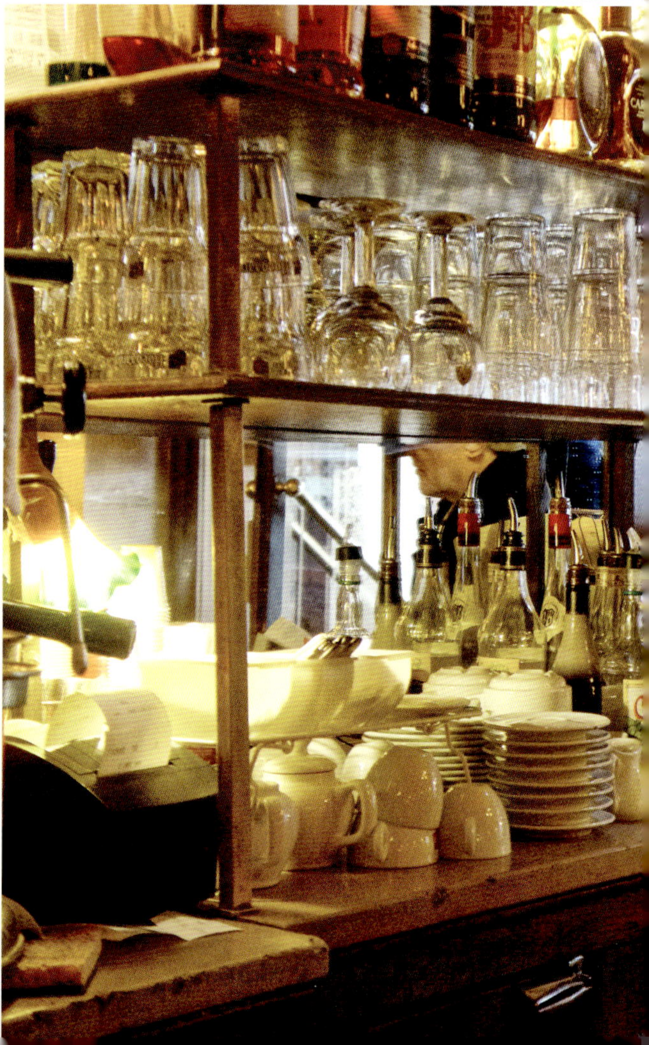

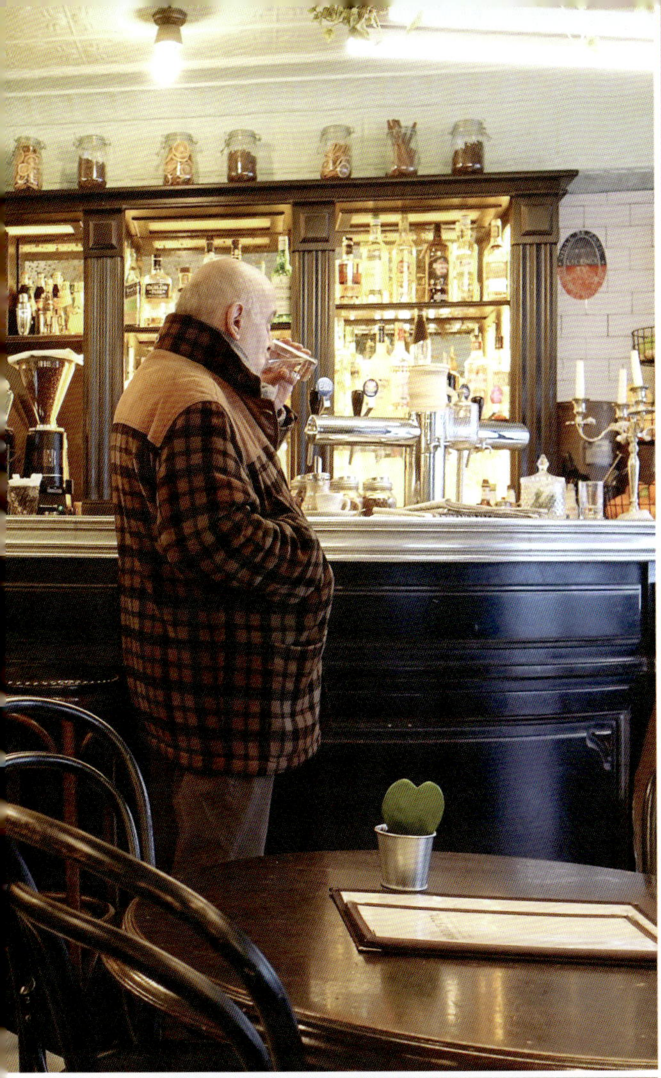

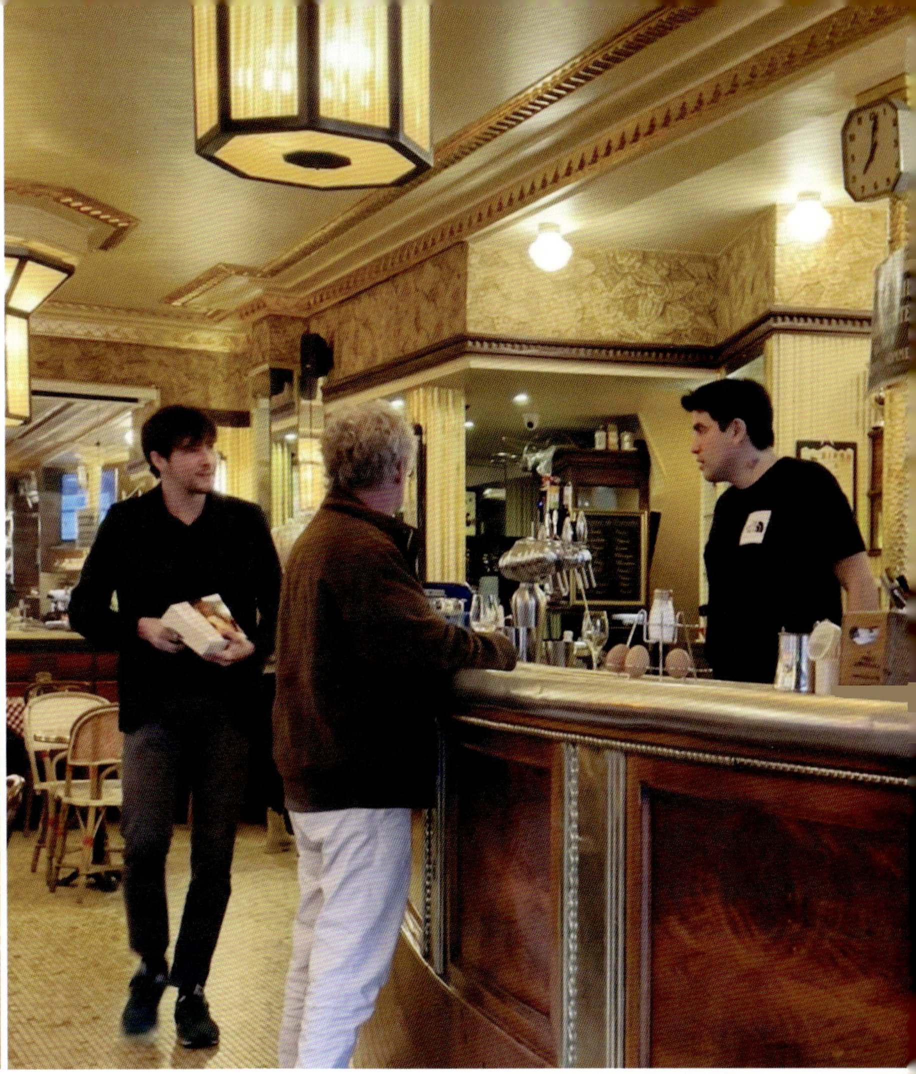

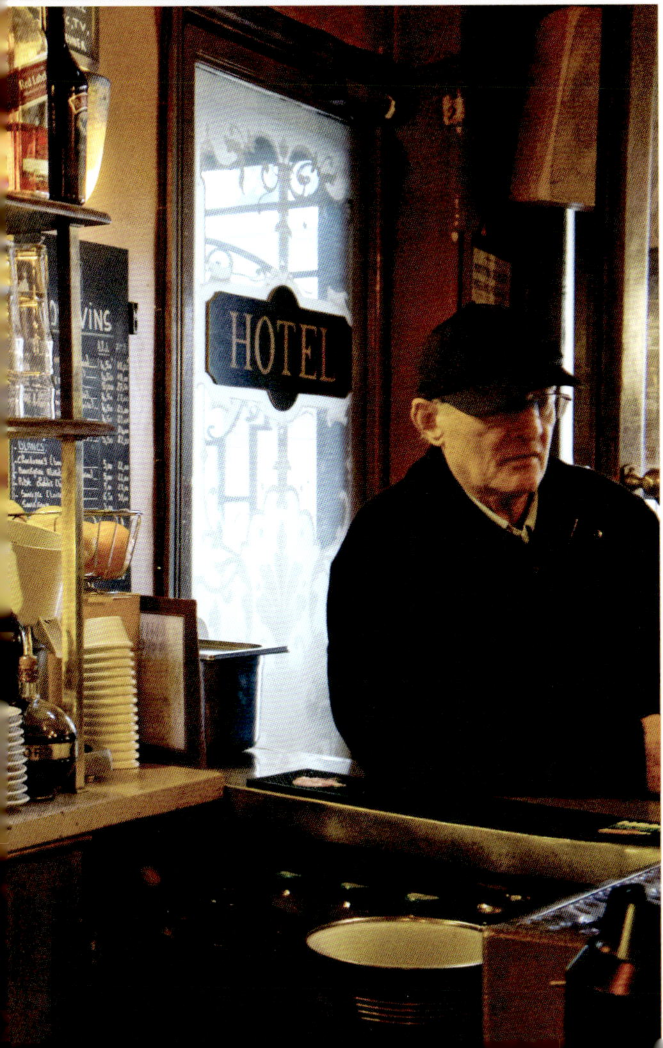
VINS
HOTEL

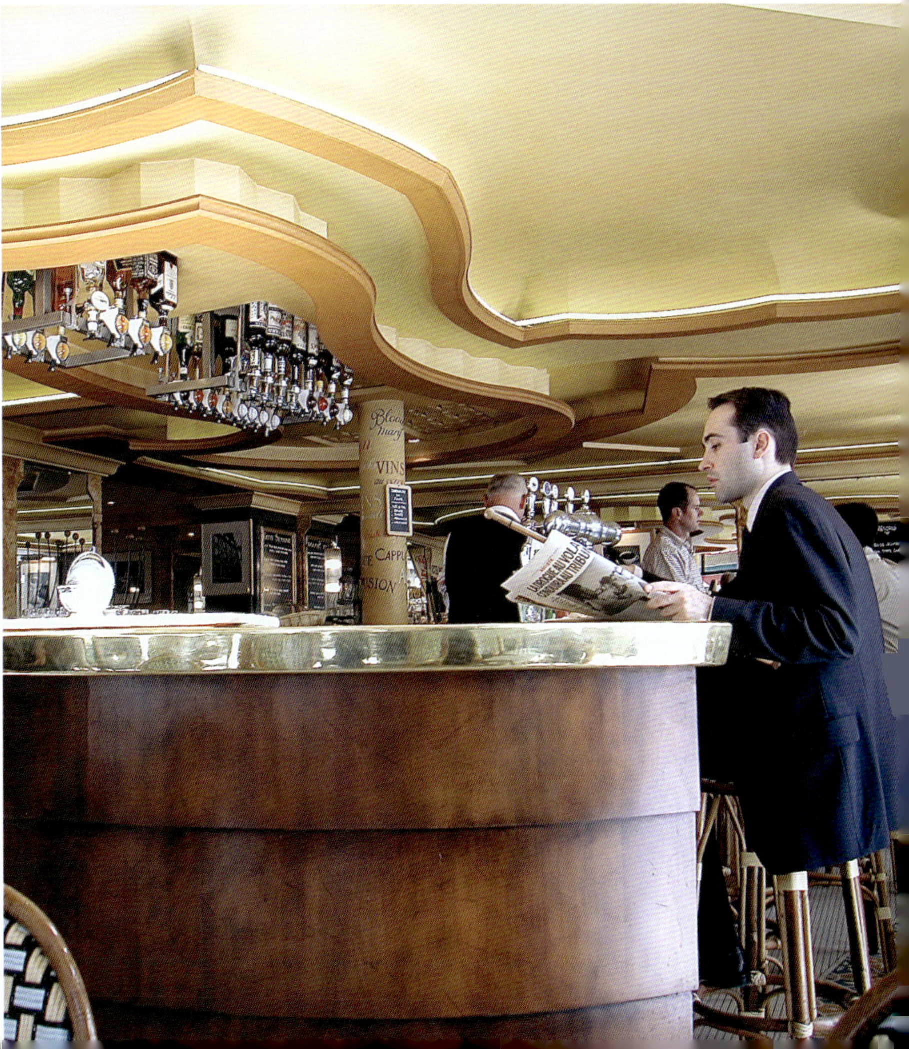
VINS

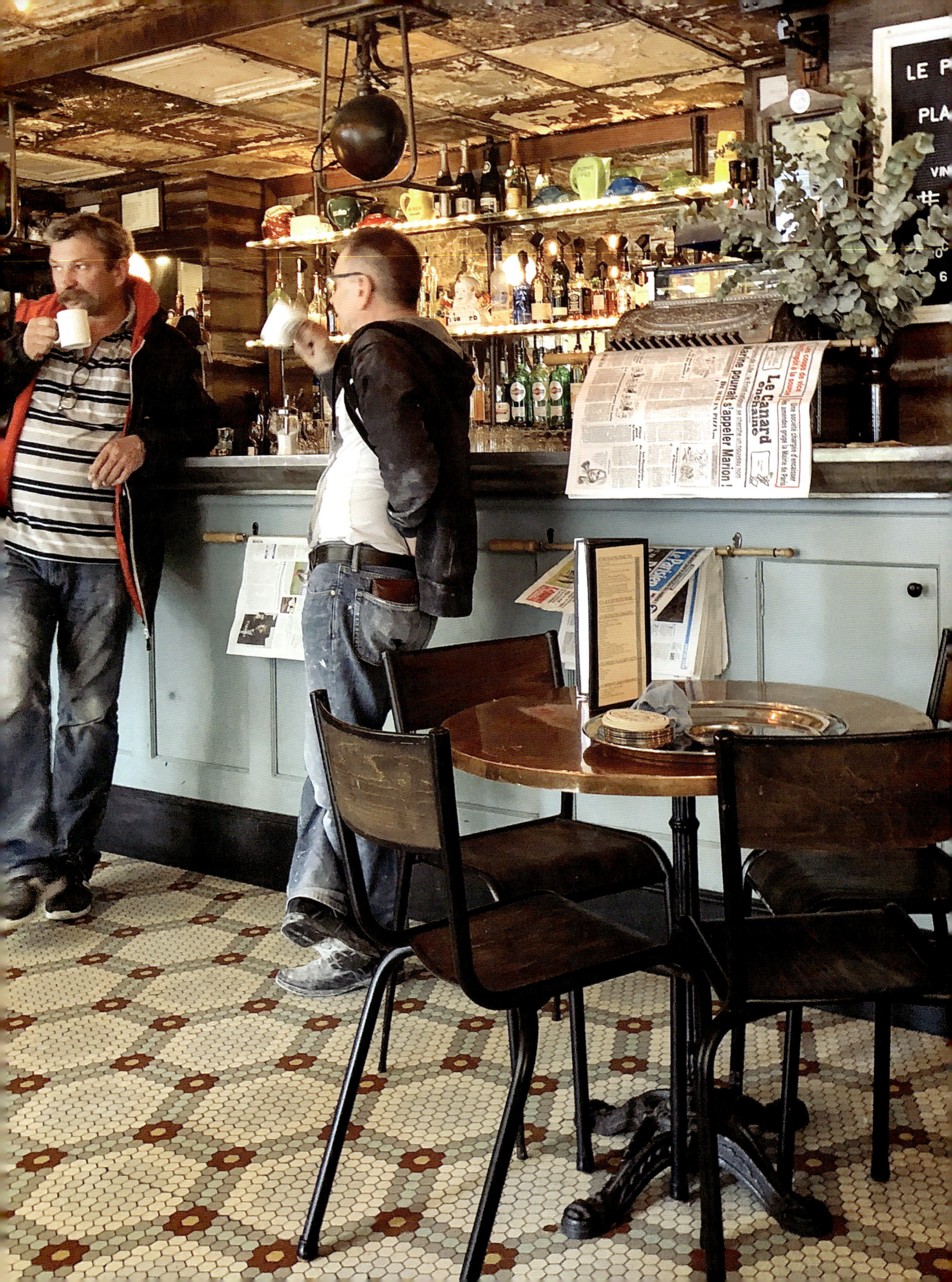
Le Canard enchaîné
pourrait s'appeler Marion !

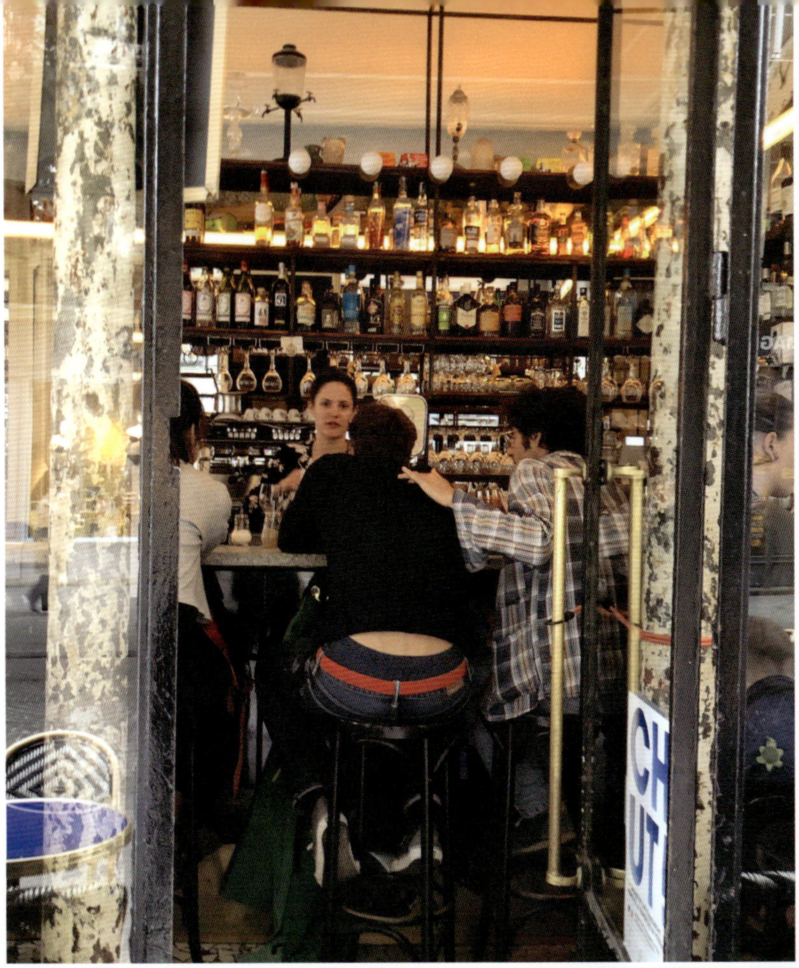

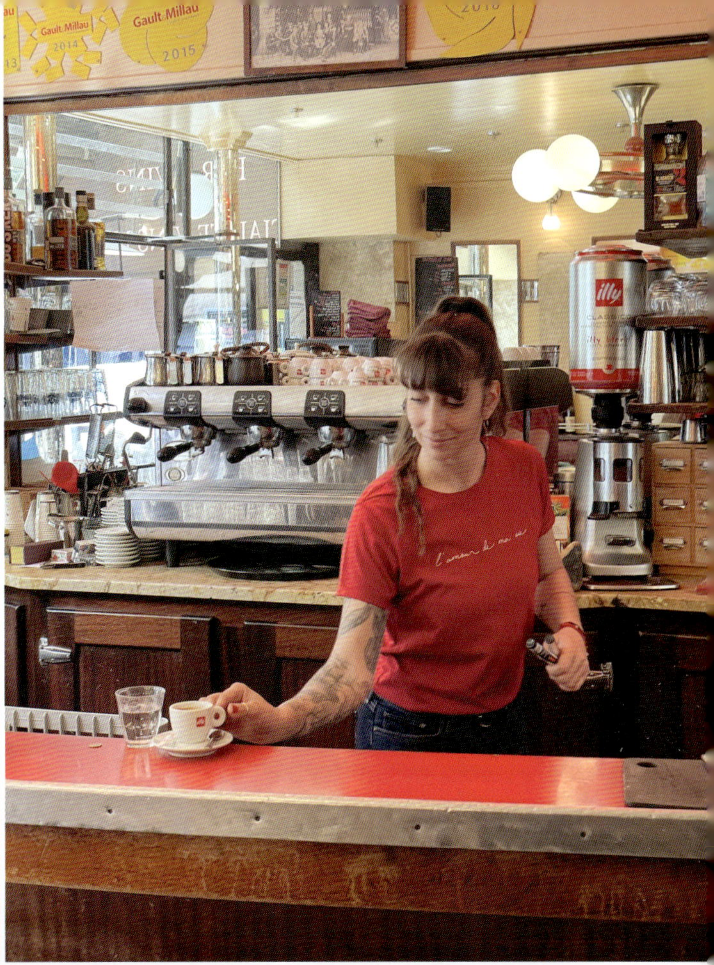
Gault Millau
2014
Gault Millau
2015
illy

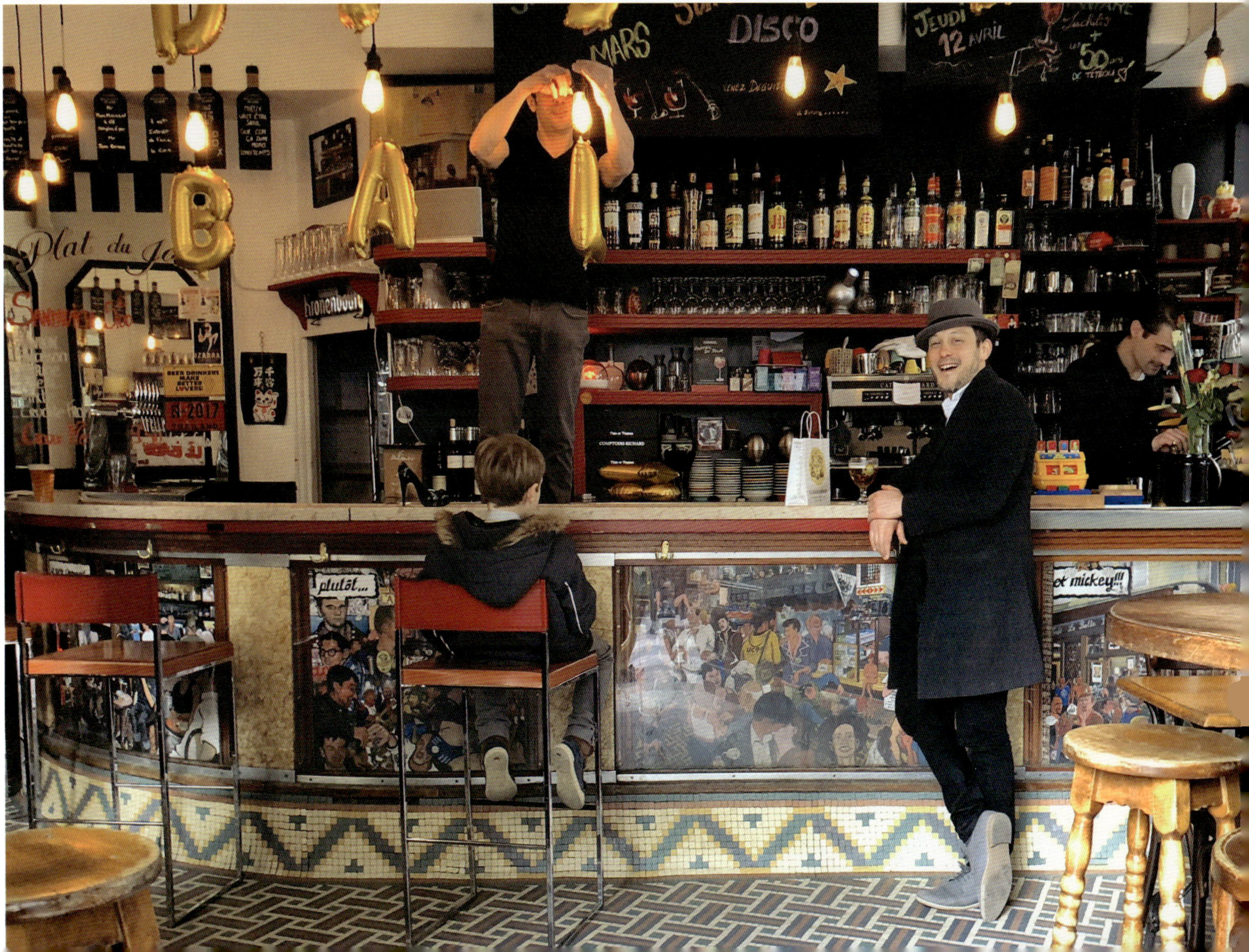
MARS
DISCO
JEUDI
12 AVRIL
Plat du Jo
plutôt...
et mickey!!!

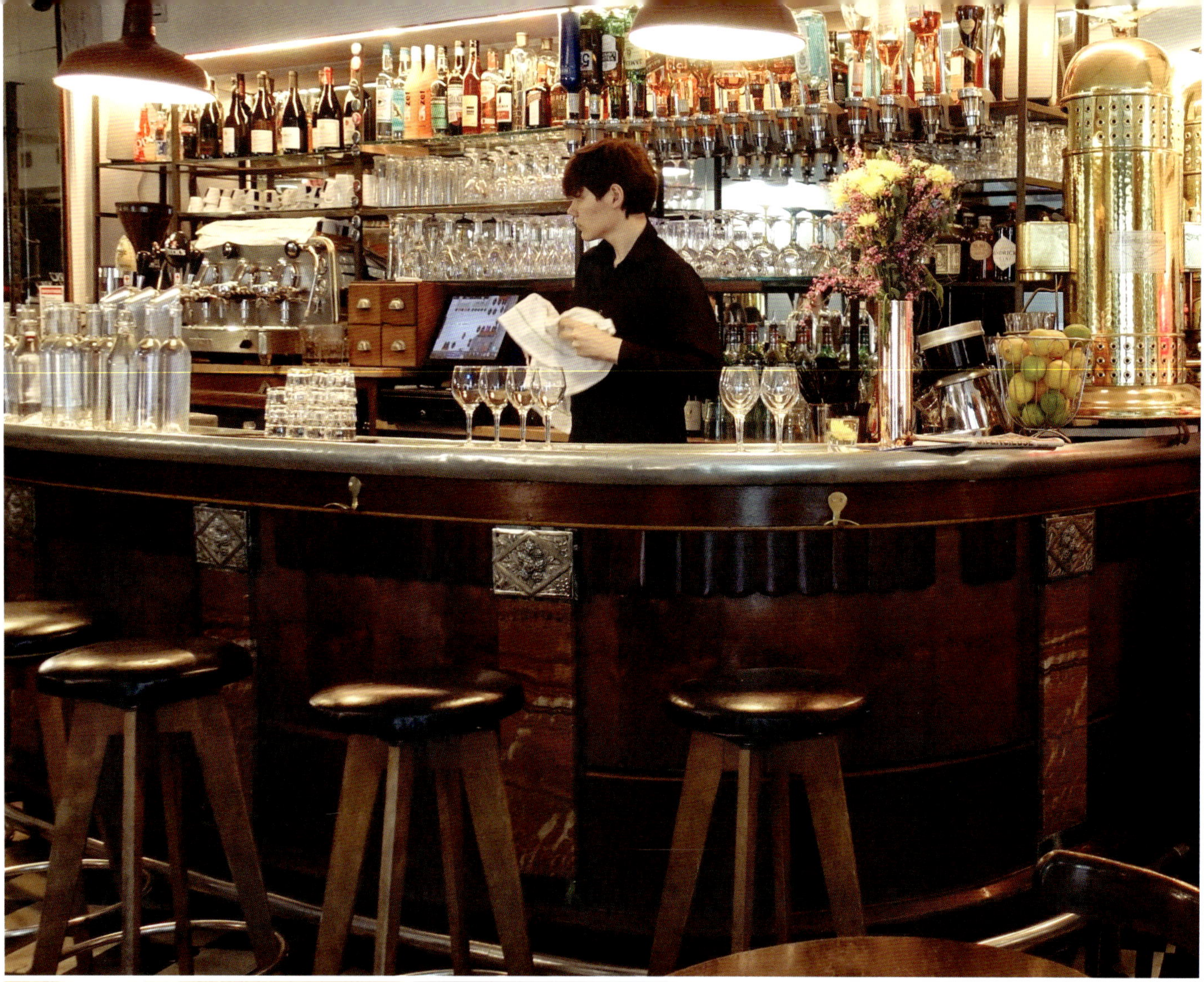

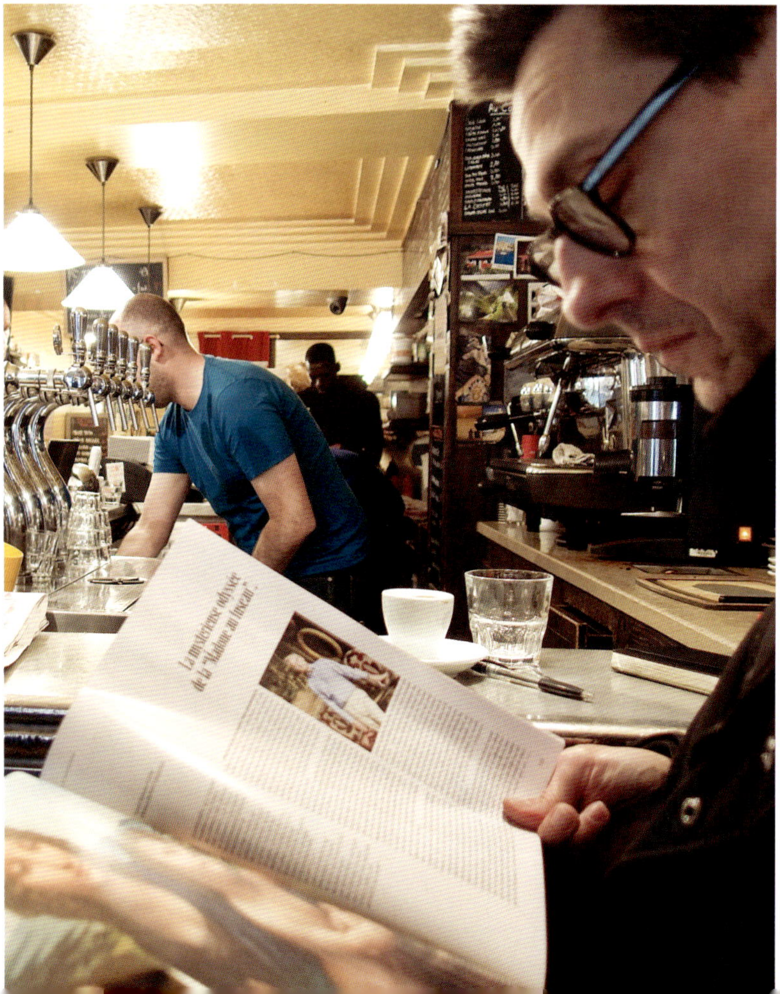

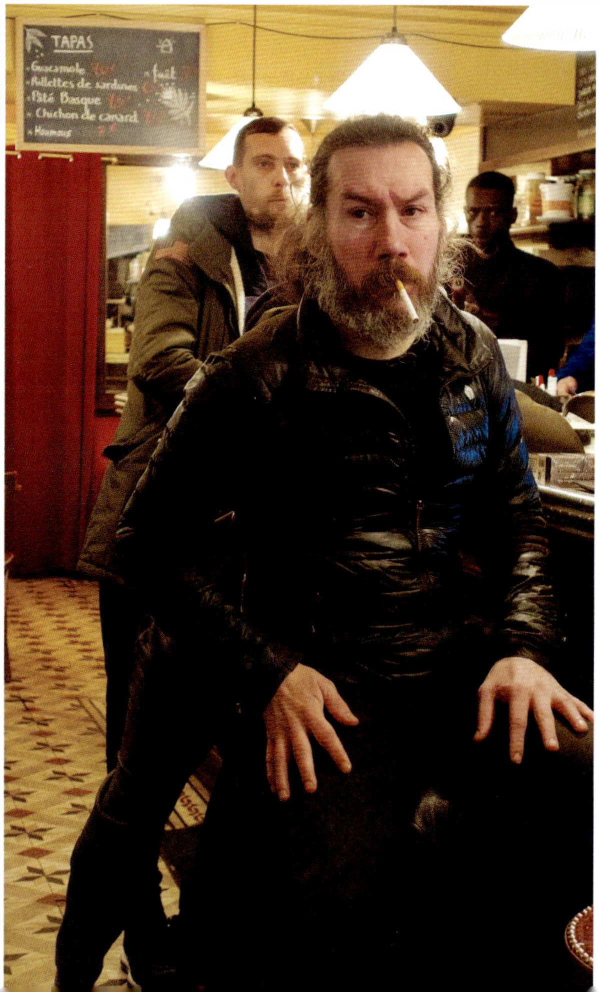
TAPAS
Guacamole
Pâté Basque
Houmous

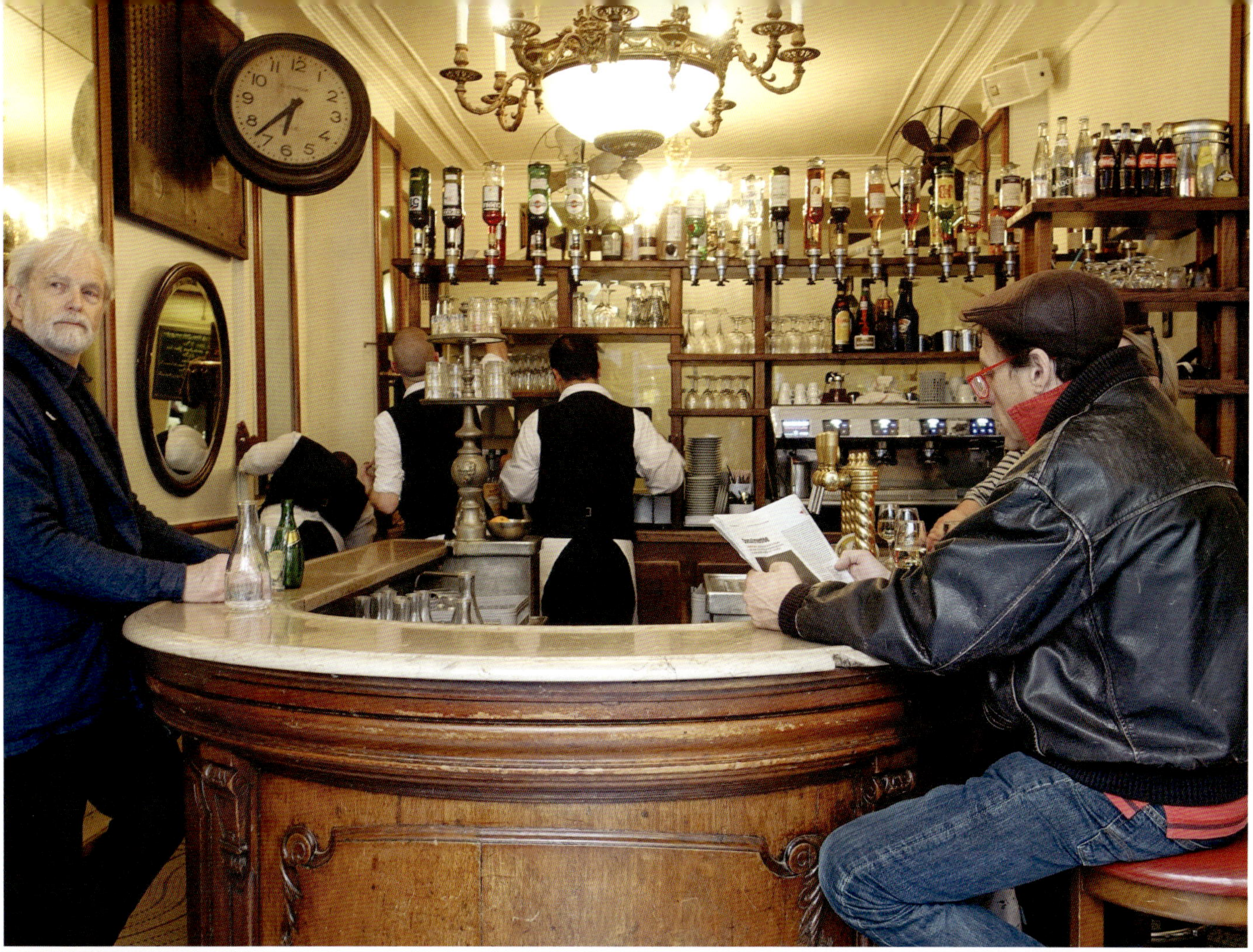

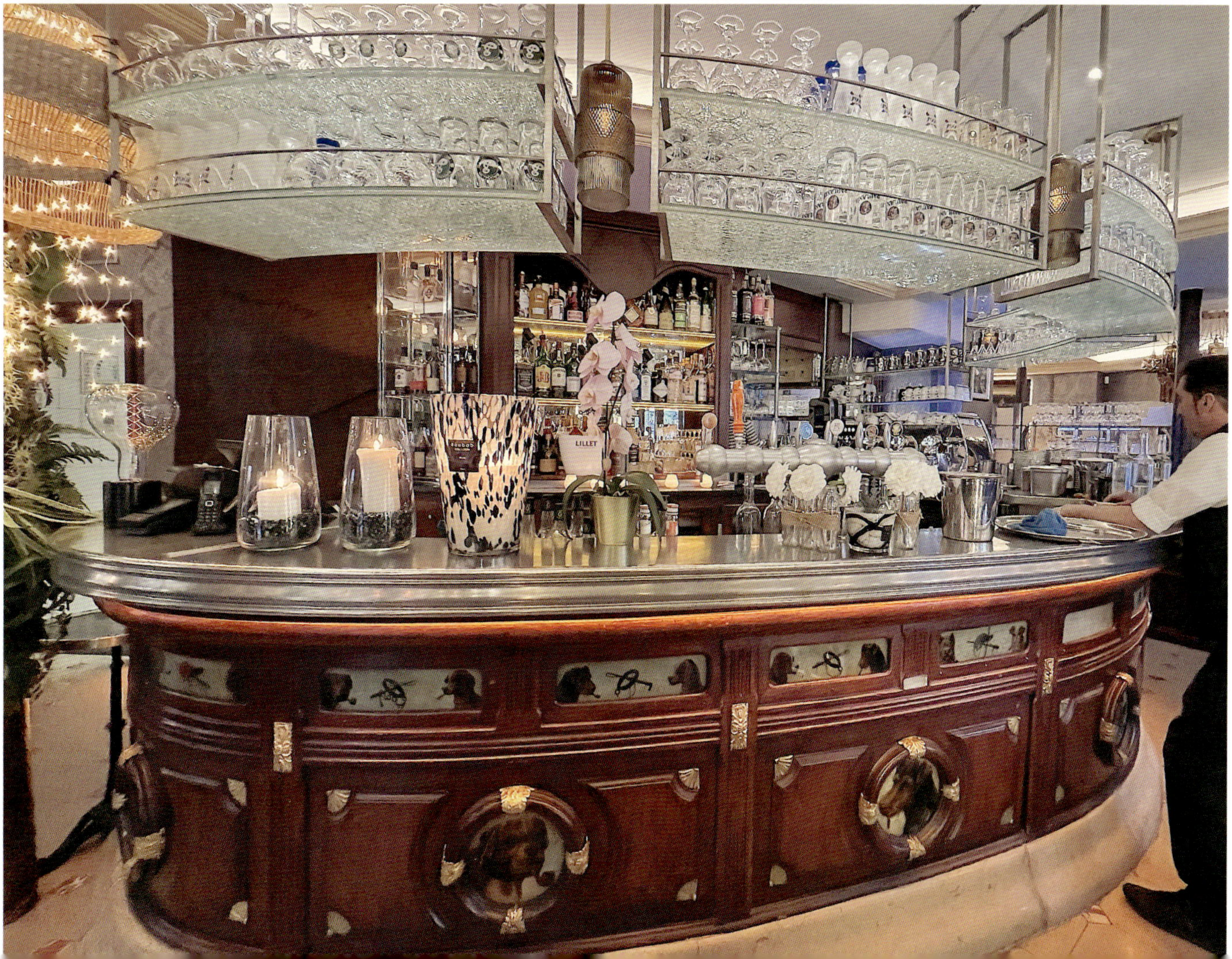
LILLET

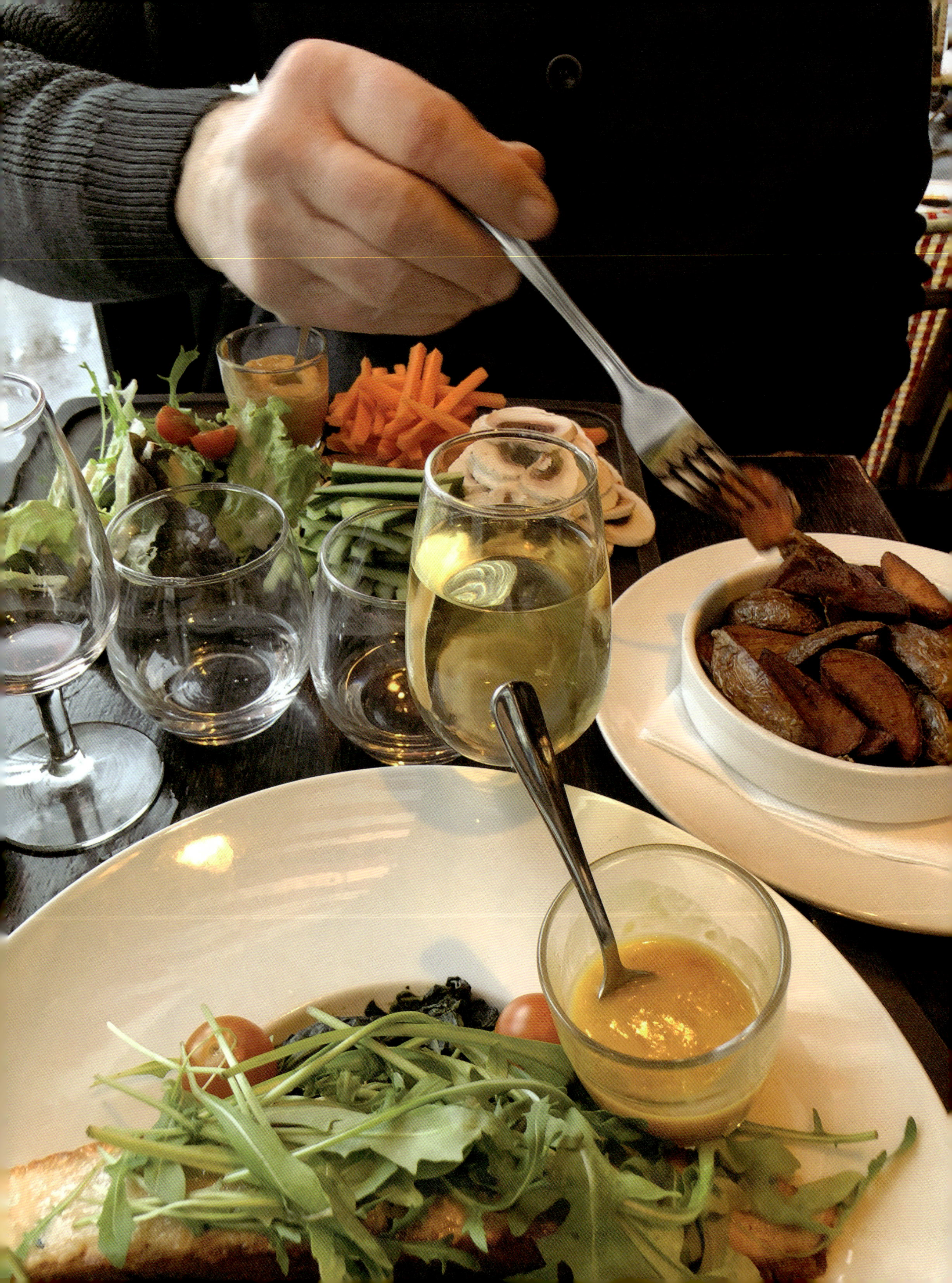

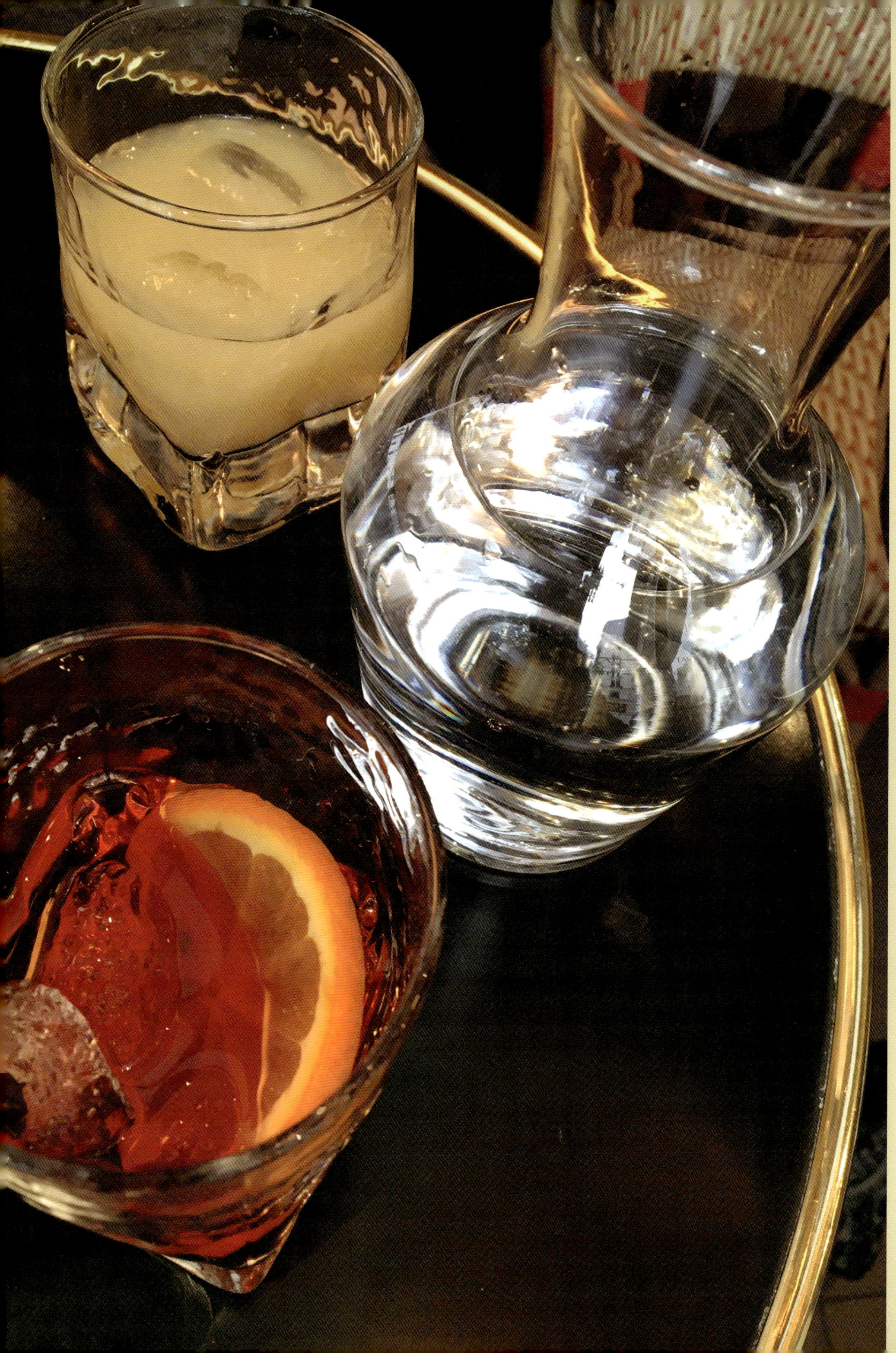

PART 3 The Food & Drink

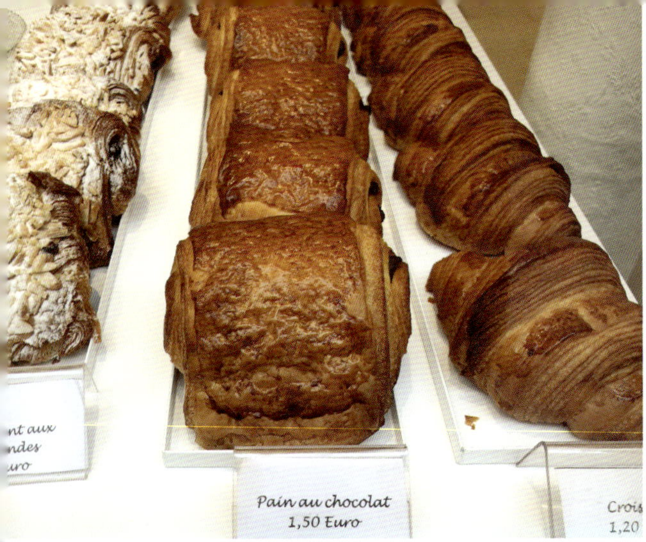

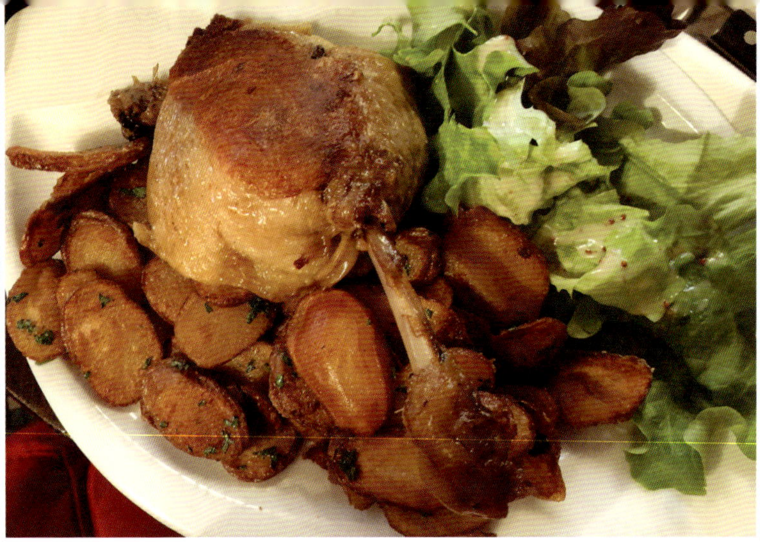

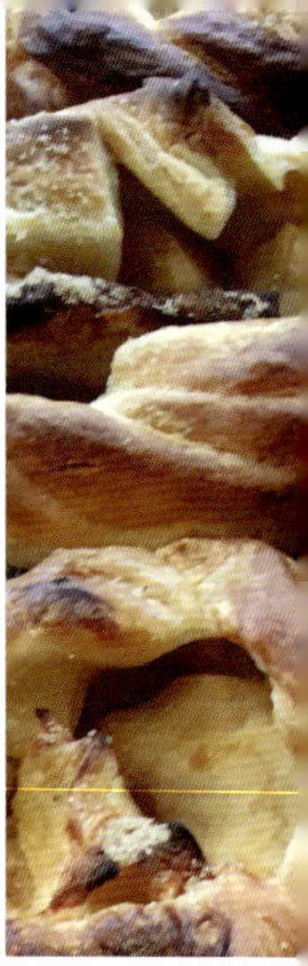

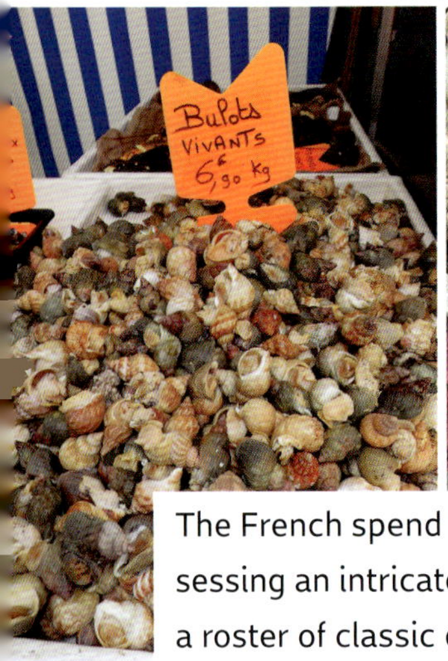

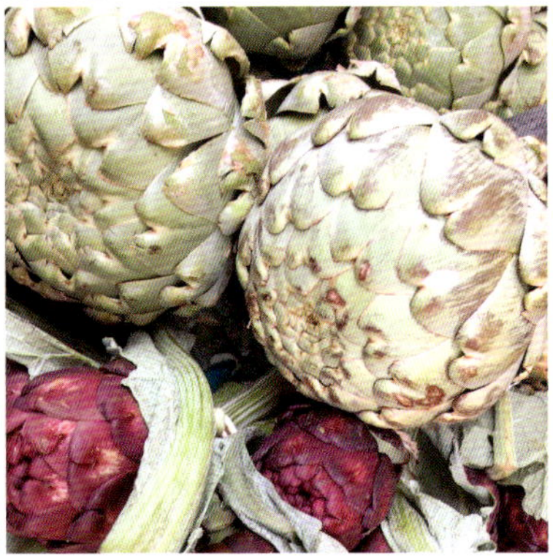

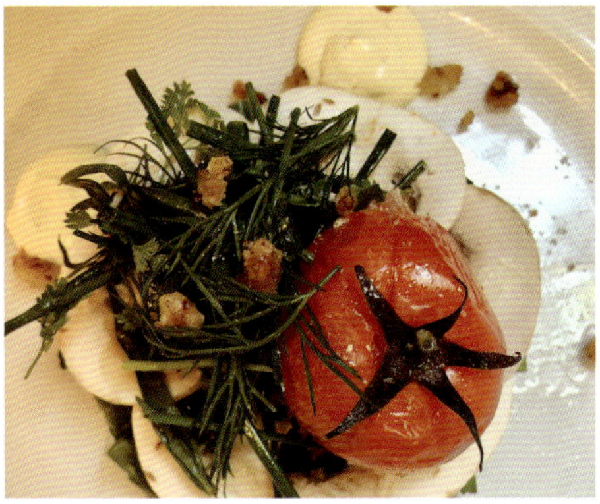

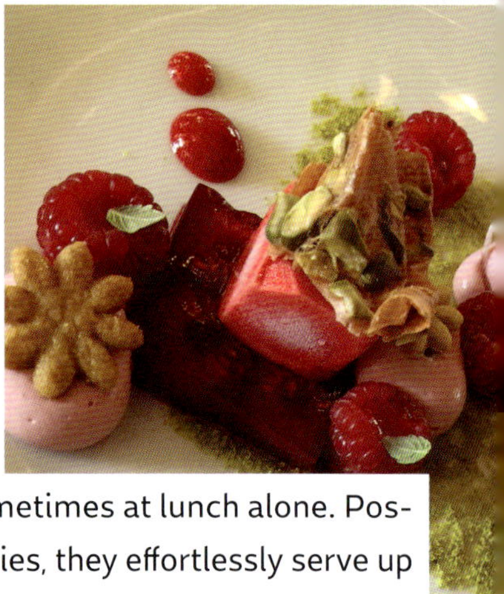

The French spend more time eating than any other nation—more than two hours a day, sometimes at lunch alone. Possessing an intricate understanding of ingredients and food pairing perfected over the centuries, they effortlessly serve up a roster of classic dishes on their tables: foie gras with sweet jam and fruit bread, duck *confit* with sautéed potatoes and warm arugula, *moules-frites*, *choucroute garnie*. Adding to the classic mix is a perpetual French penchant for inventing new dishes and minting or adapting culinary trends. Thus, whoever travels to Paris can be assured that eating well is, indeed, the best revenge. The difficulty will be pacing oneself when confronted by too many choices in too few days.

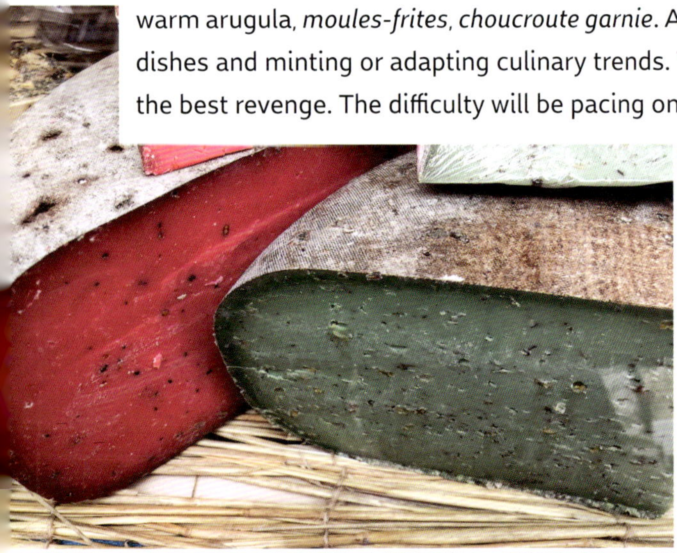

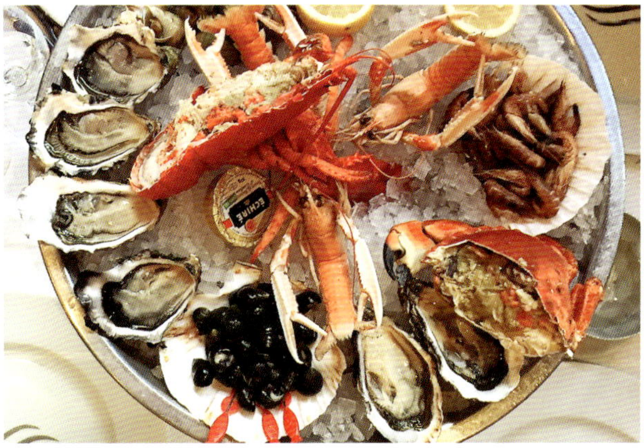

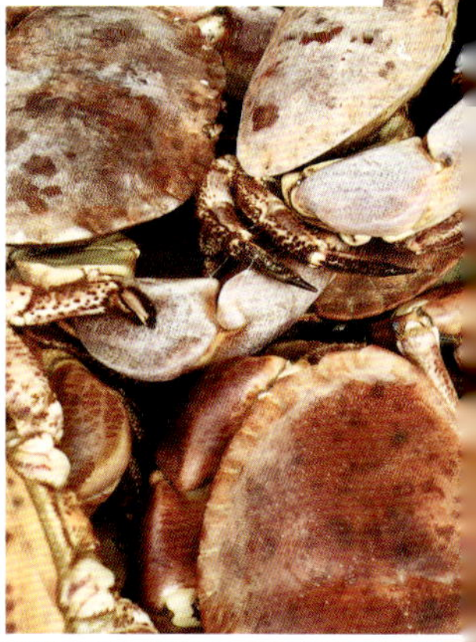

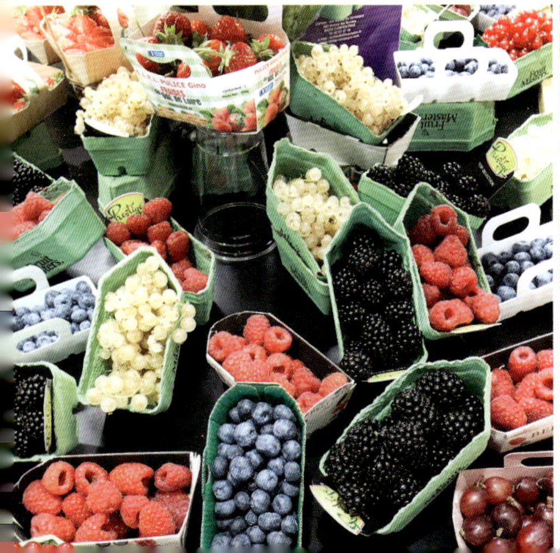

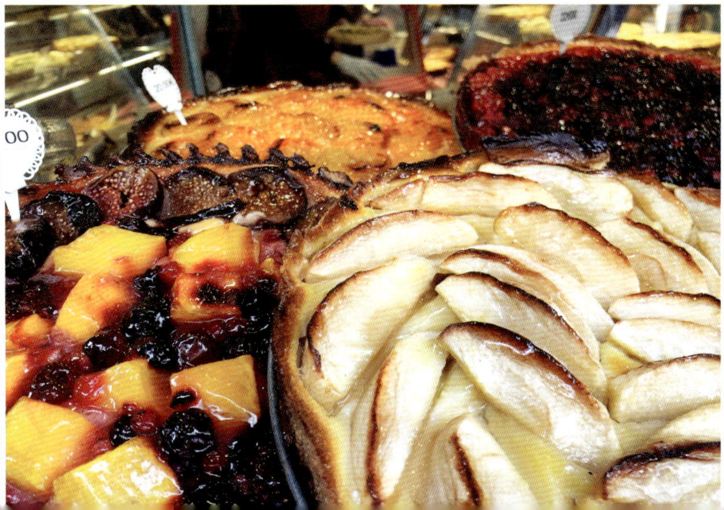

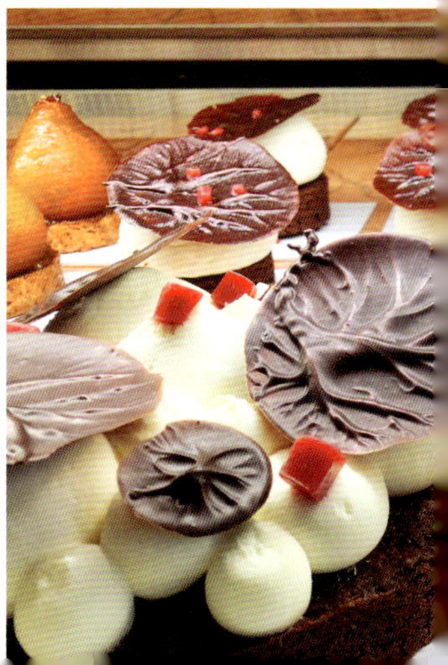

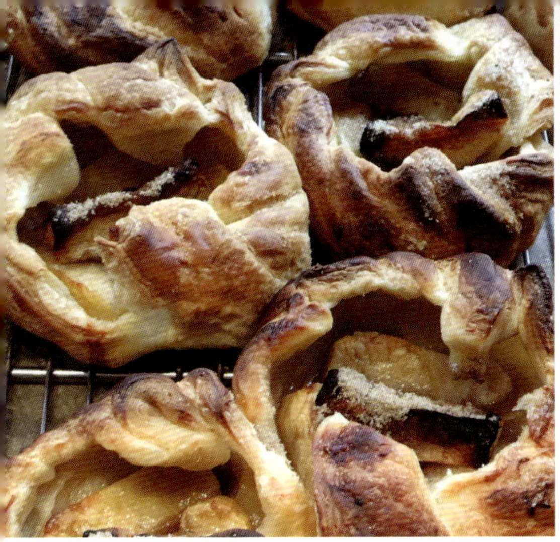
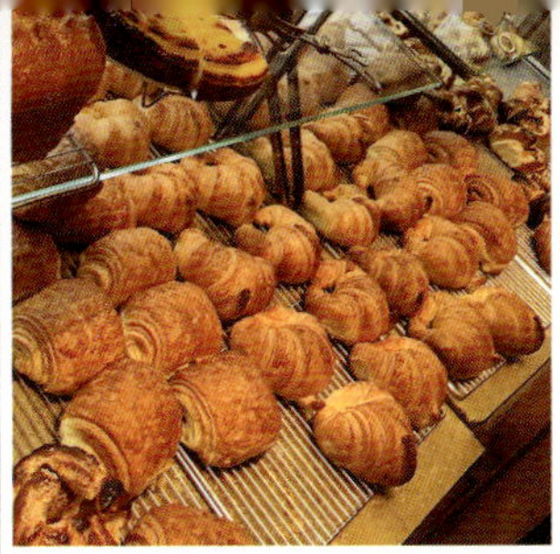
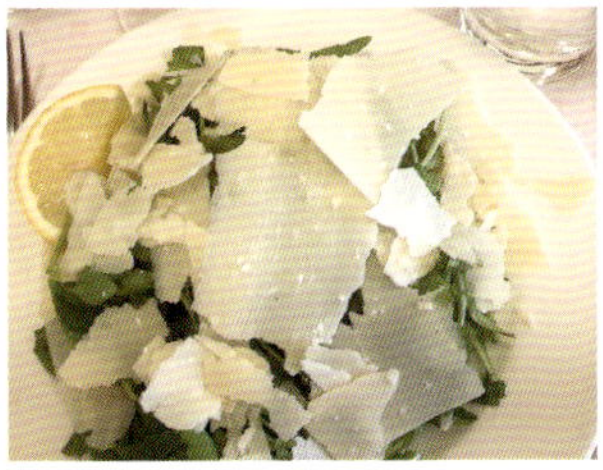
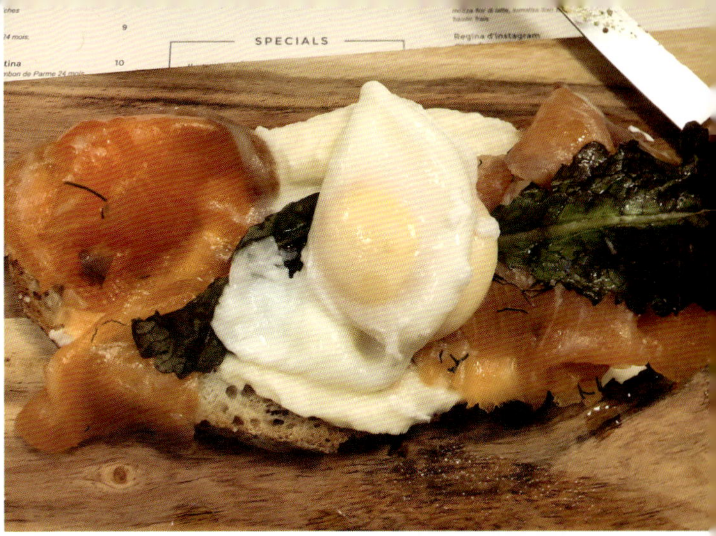
SPECIALS
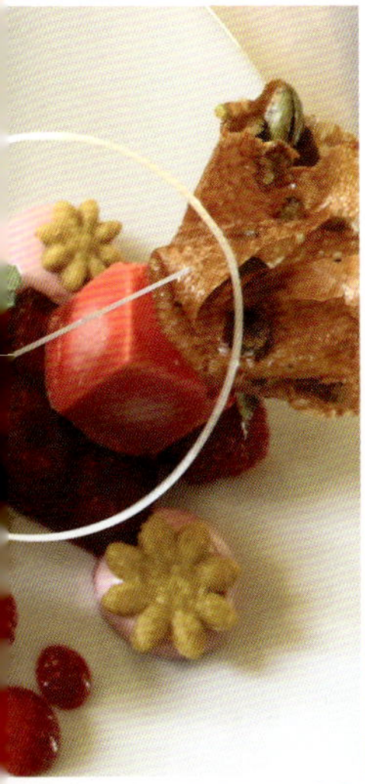
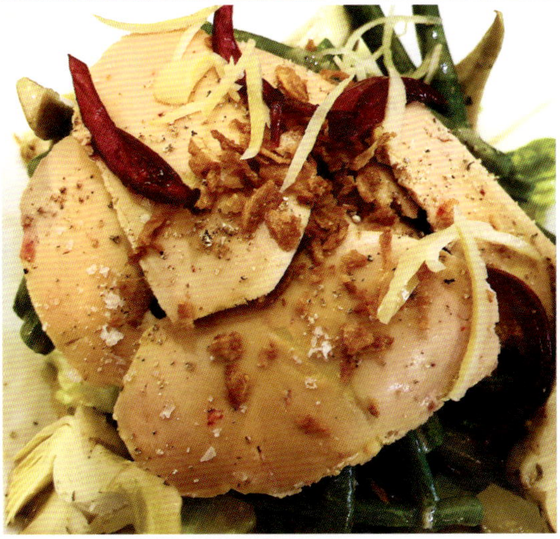
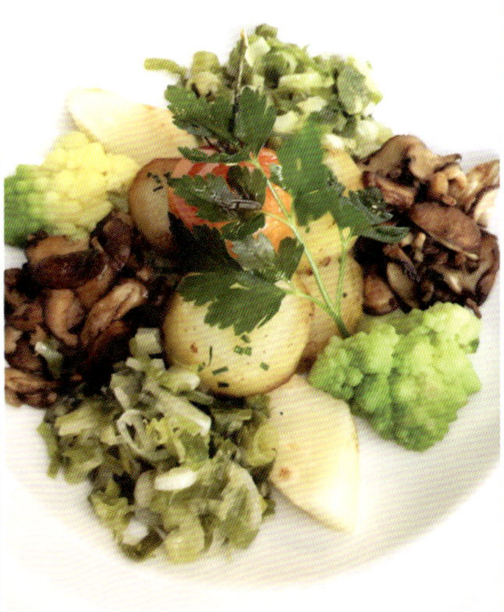
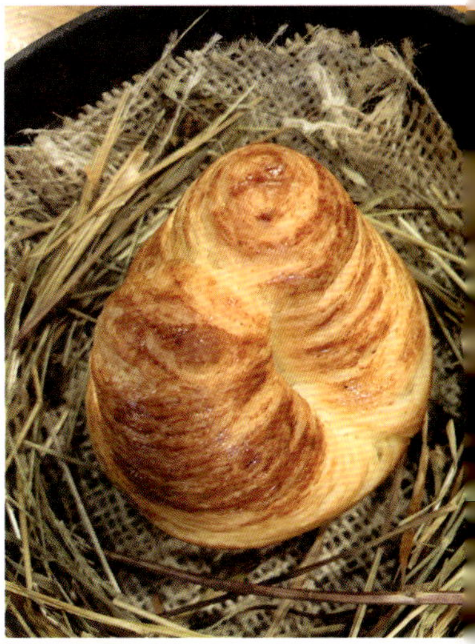
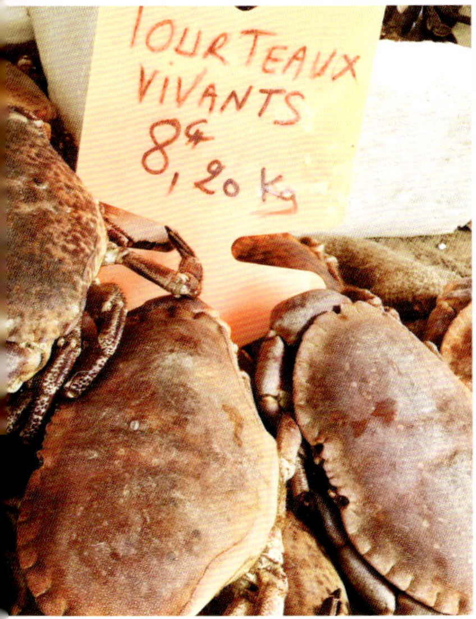
VIVANTS
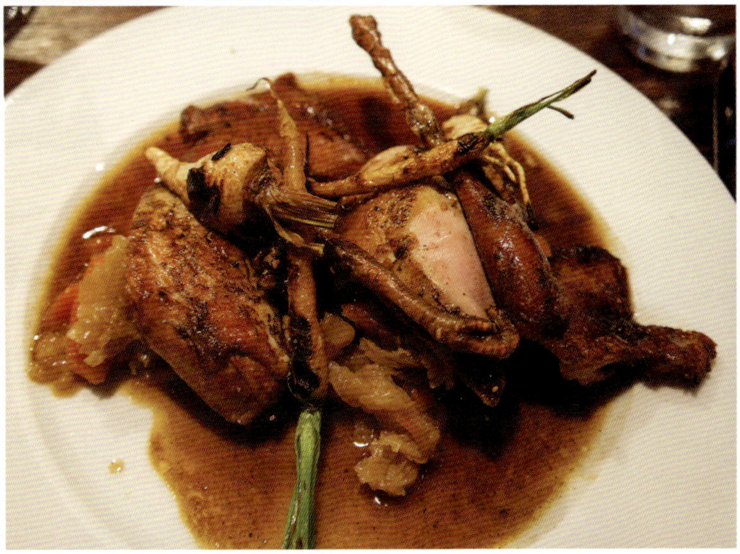
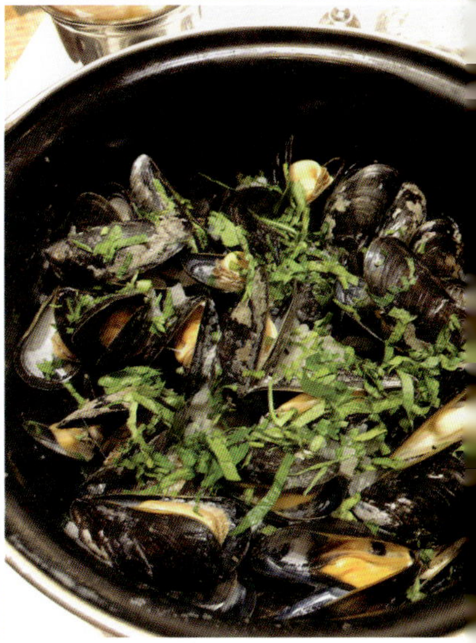
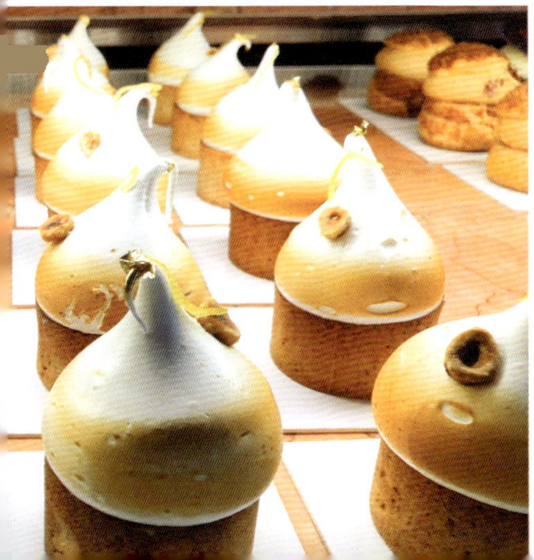
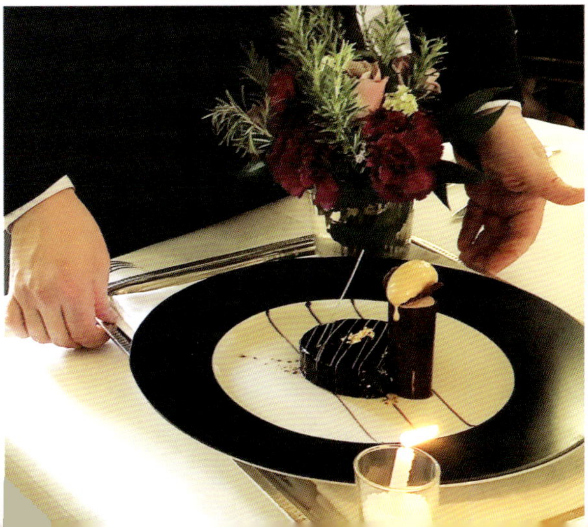
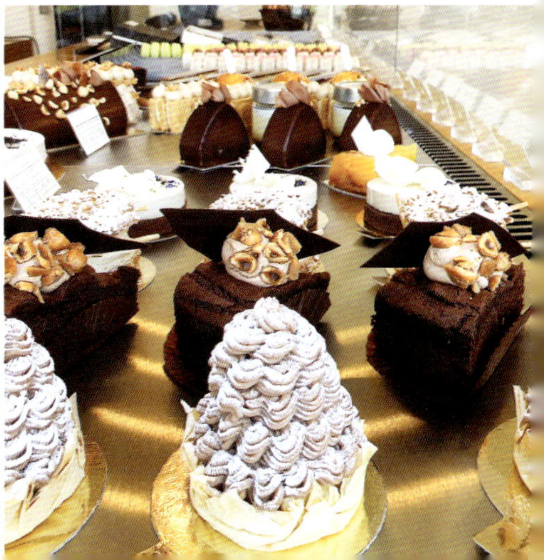

L'Apéritif

"Let me be mad, then, by all means! Mad with the madness of Absinthe, the wildest, most luxurious madness in the world! *Vive la folie! Vive l'amour! Vive l'animisme! Vive le Diable!*"

Marie Corelli, *Wormwood: A Drama of Paris*

Champagne, Kir, Pastis, Byrrh, Dubonnet, or Absinthe? Once seated for dinner or maybe even at lunch, your waiter will ask if you would like to "*prendre un apéro*." A long-held ritual in France, not only is the aperitif a luscious drink, it is meant to prepare the appetite for dining and allow a relaxed transition from the day's bustle to the ensuing meal. So as not to overwhelm in light of the substantial food to follow, *l'apéro* is served only with a small, light, salty snack. The French do not nibble between meals, so *l'heure de l'apéro* is the only time they snack, albeit lightly. "*Chin-chin*," the ubiquitous toast, and a gentle clinking of glasses always precede *l'apéritif*. Cheers!

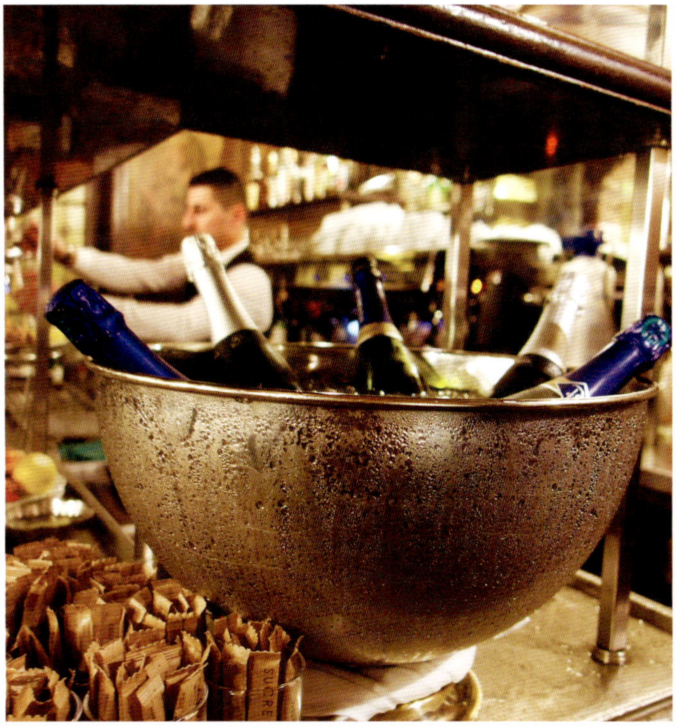

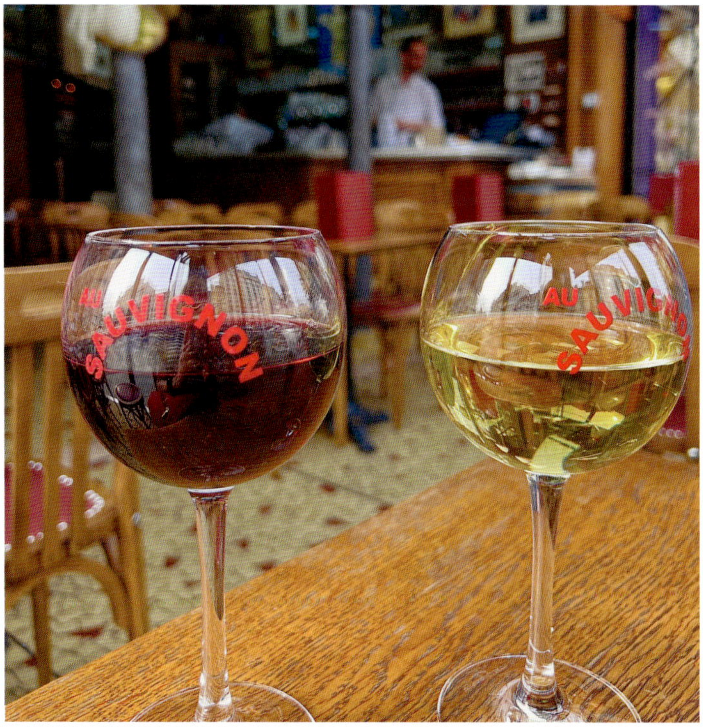

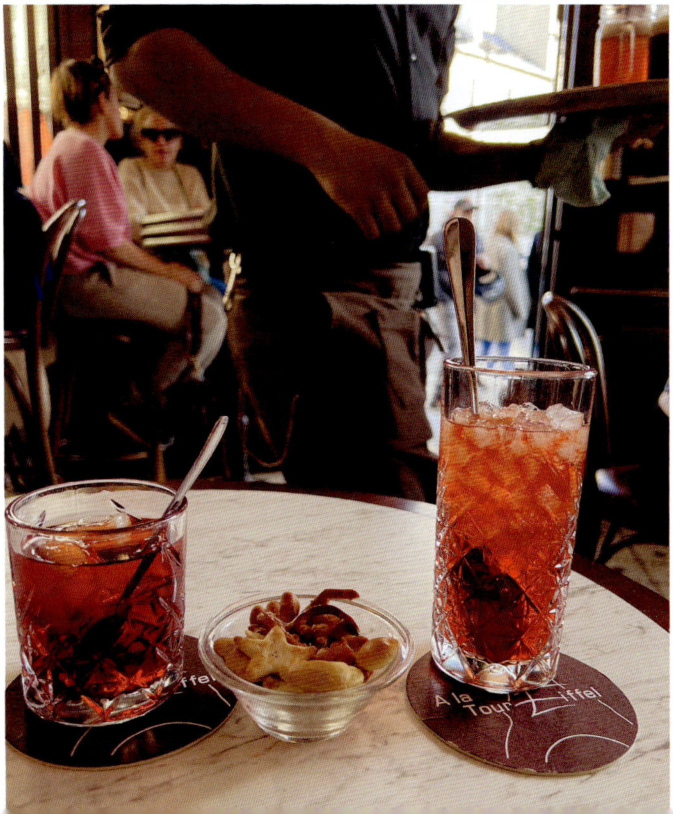

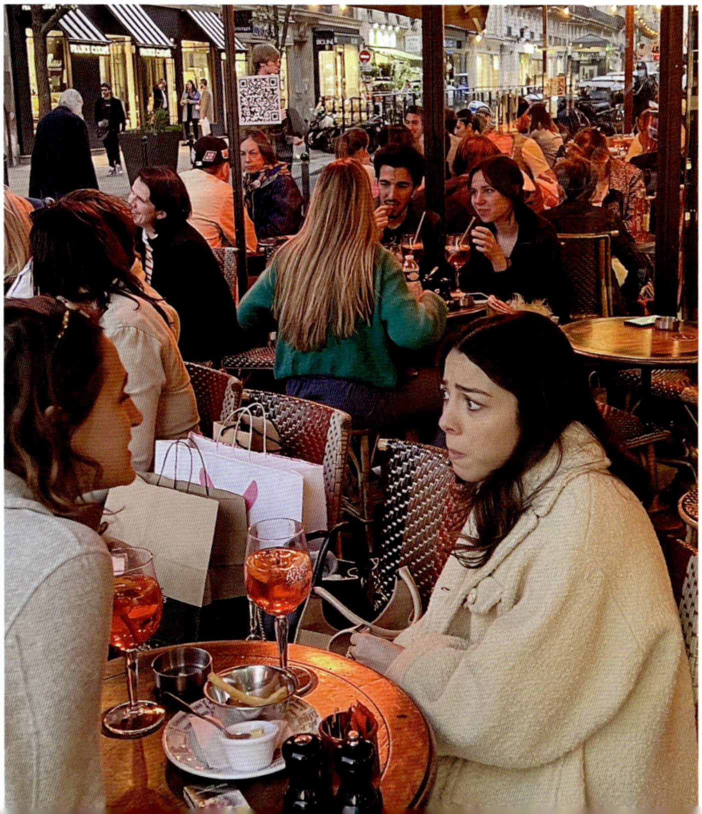

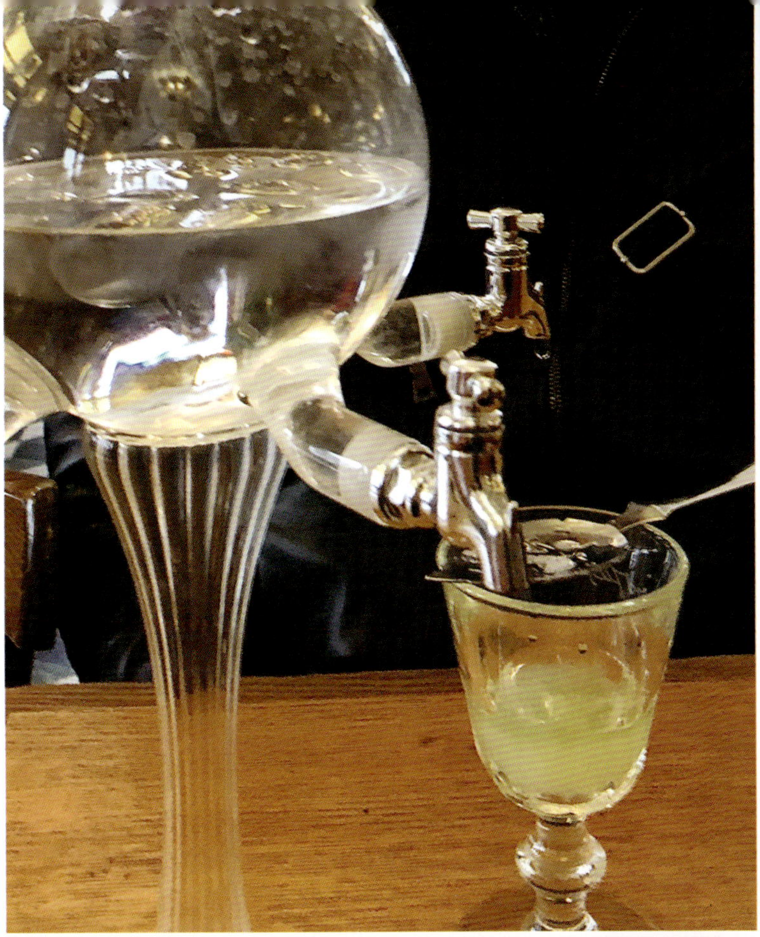

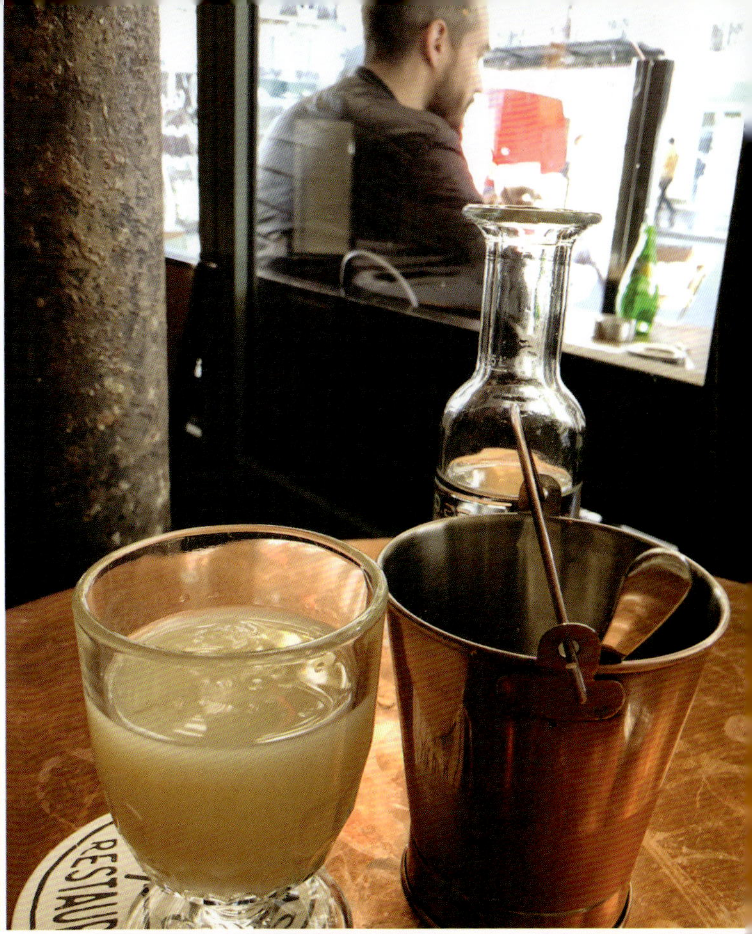

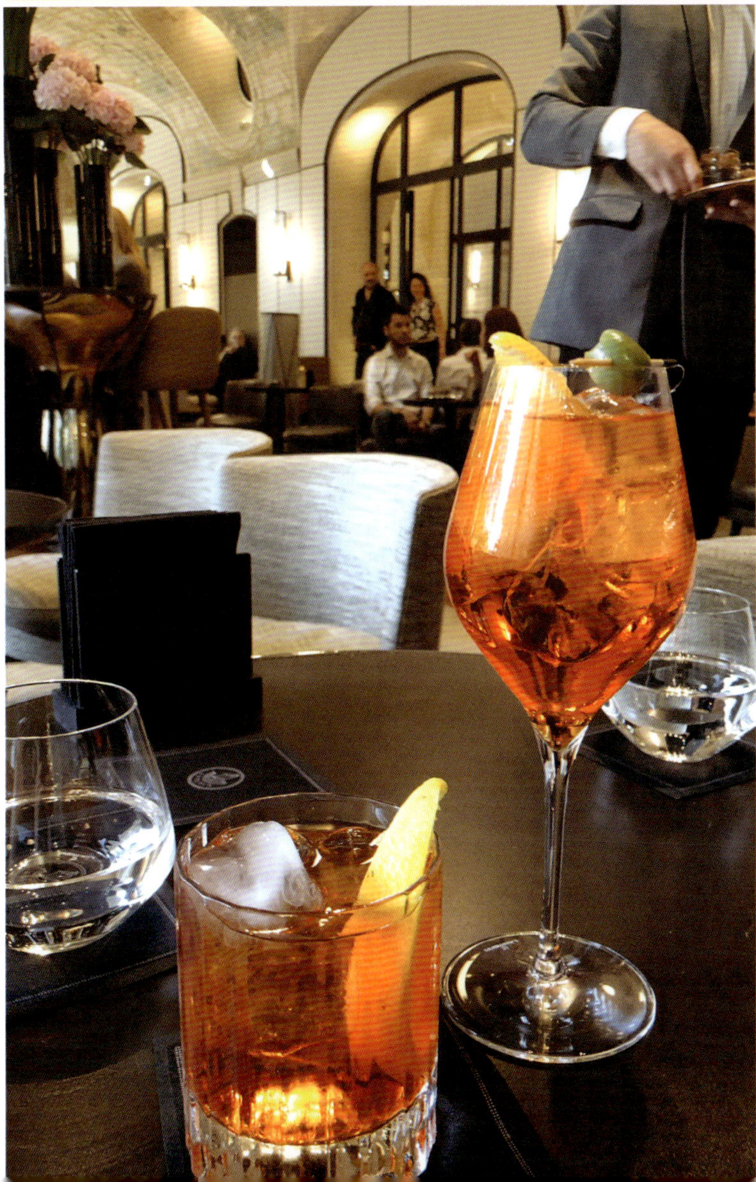

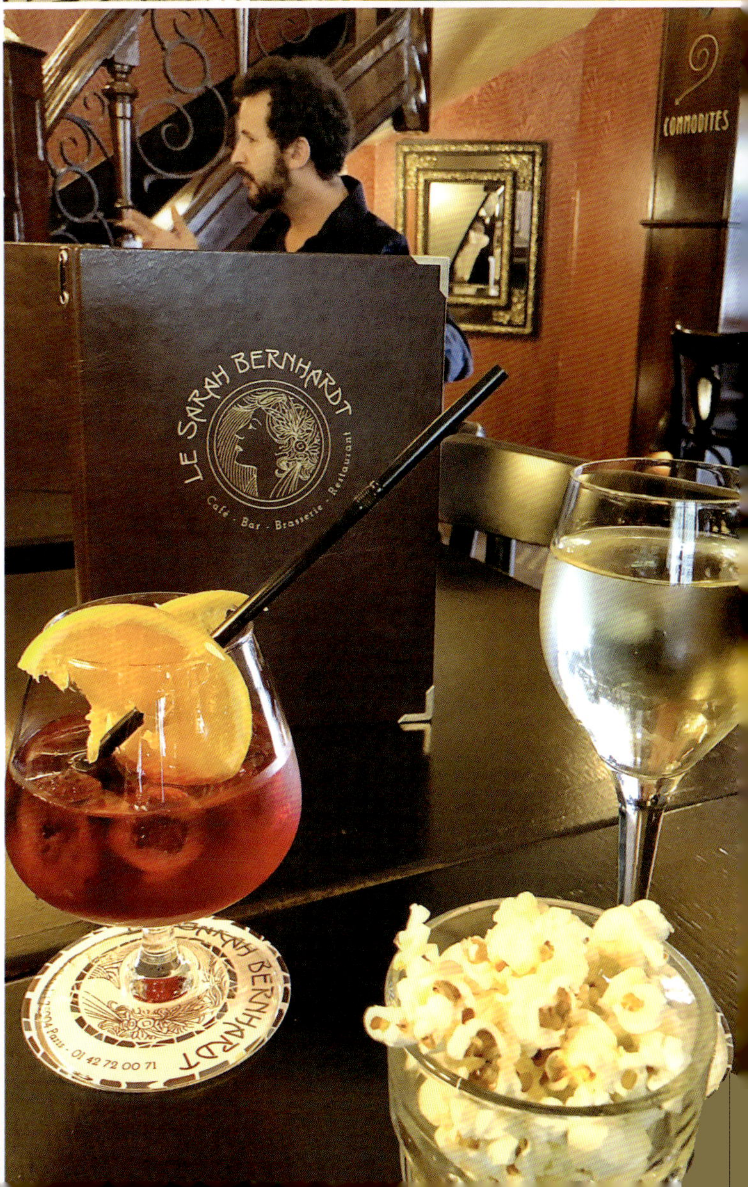
COMMODITES
LE SARAH BERNHARDT
Café · Bar · Brasserie · Restaurant
SARAH BERNHARDT
01 42 72 00 71

L'Entrée

> "It's pronounced wee but spelled O-U-I. It's all you'll want to say when you're sitting at one of the thousands of little cafés that line the streets, and you're looking at a menu full of foods you just want to eat for days."
>
> **Giada De Laurentiis, *Paris!***

In France, the entrée (*entrer* means enter) is the first course of a meal rather than the main course. Oysters, escargot, moules, foie gras, or something lighter, perhaps vegetarian? Or a salad—possibly even *with* foie gras? Classic or newly invented? In Paris, choices are abundant, all good. While it is easy to snobbishly pan the traditional Parisian eateries, many of these hallowed institutions, including Bofinger, Le Dôme, and Le Select, have maintained consistent quality over multiple decades and have invigorated their classic cuisine with fresh dishes. Added to these are the extraordinary Parisian innovators who delight us by forever creating new and exciting cafés, bistros, and brasseries. Both kinds of addresses are worth a journey.

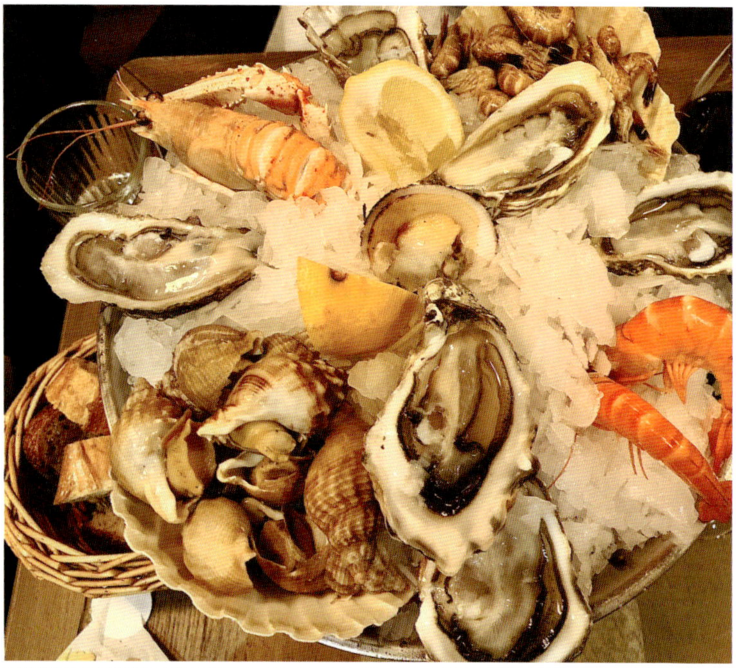

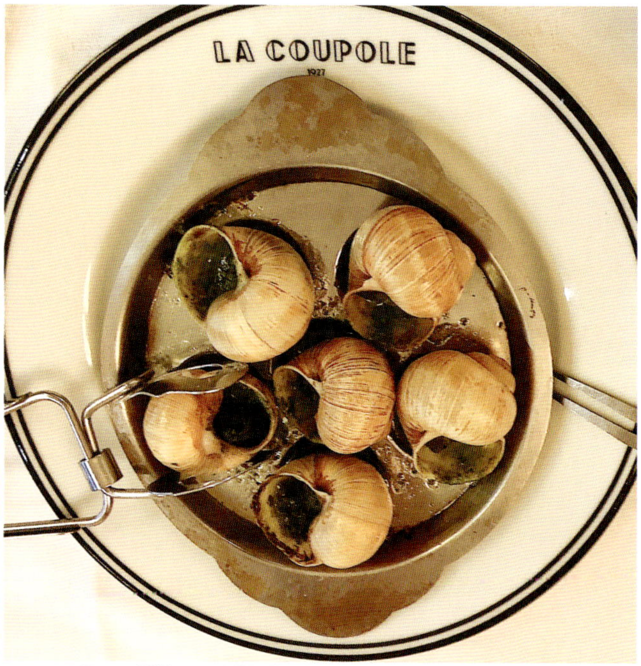

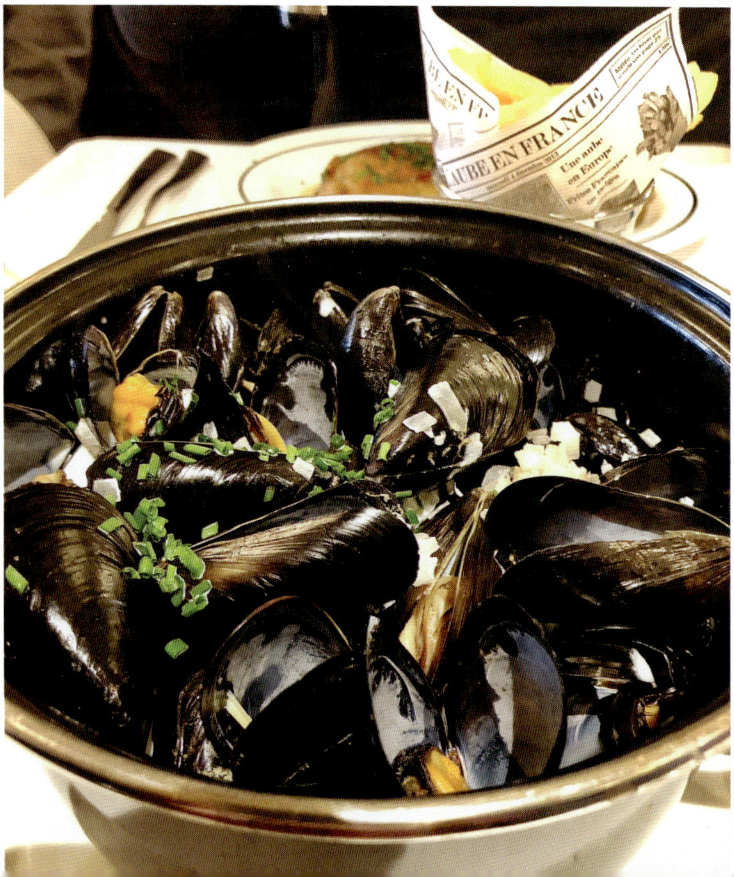

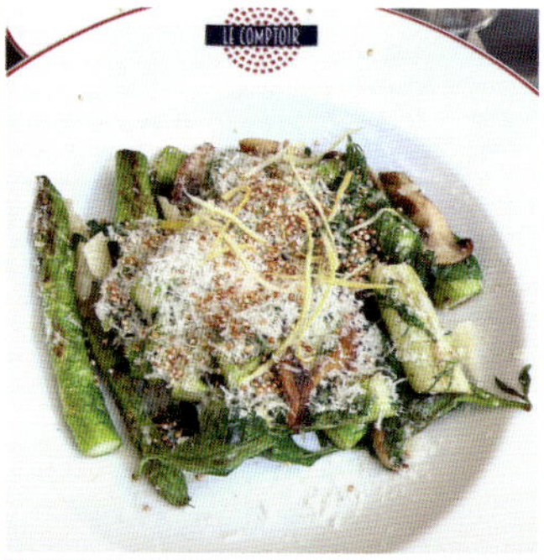

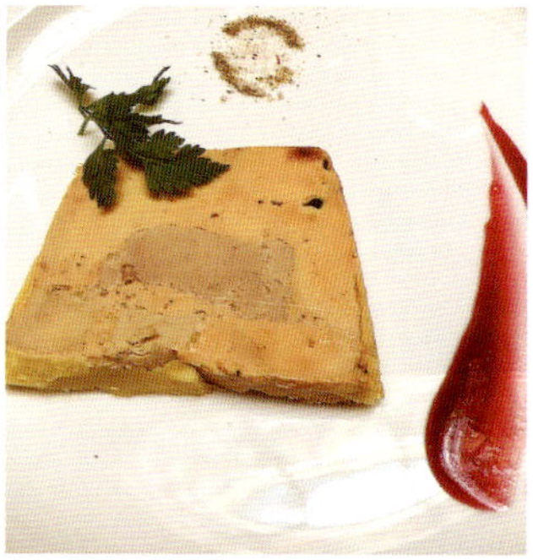

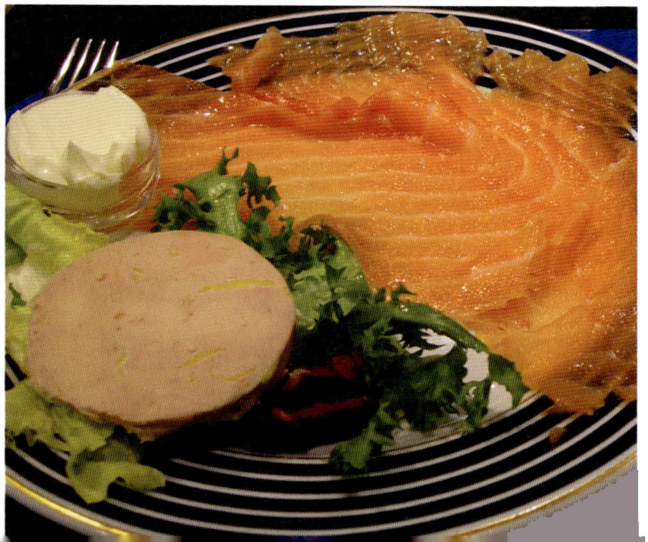

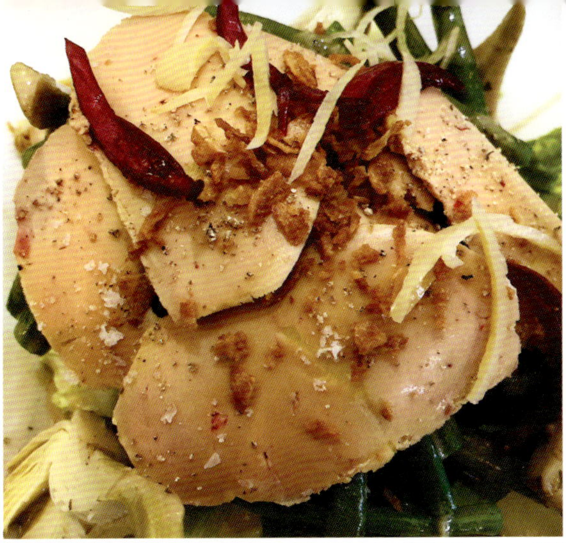
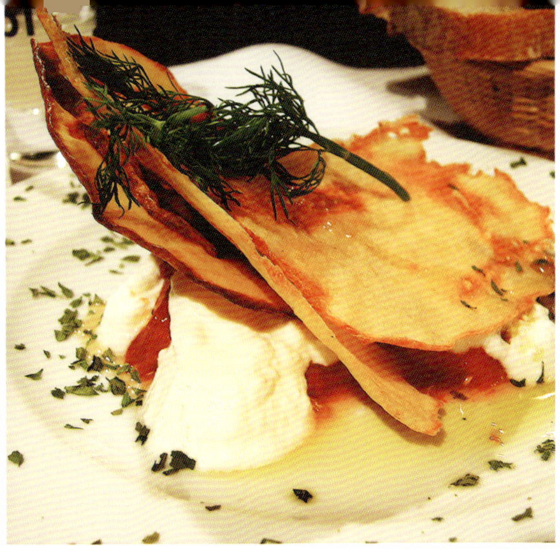
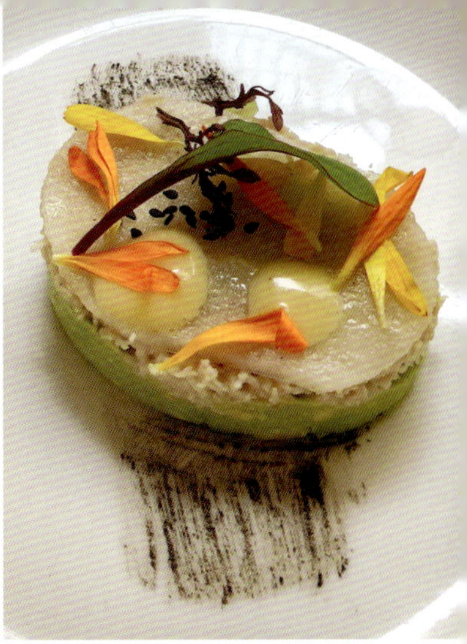
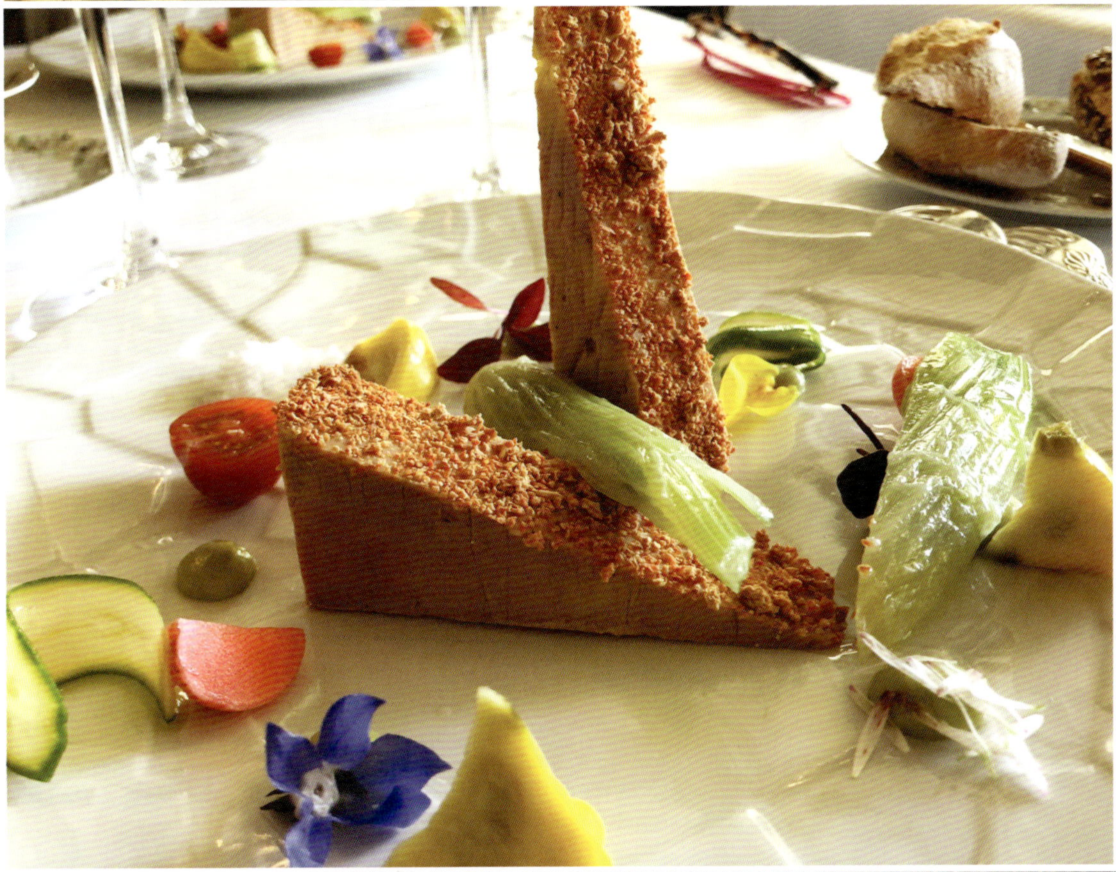
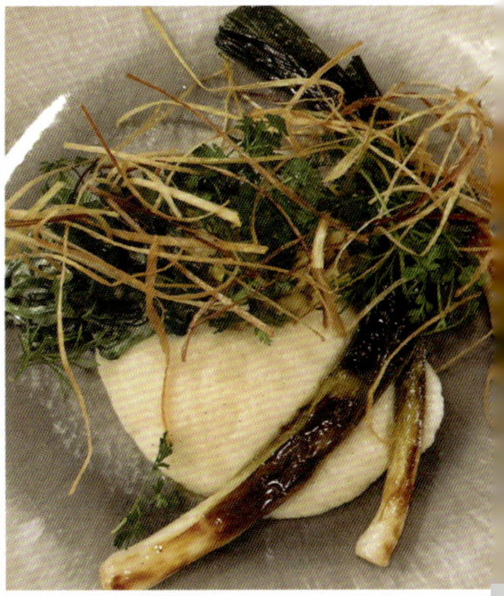
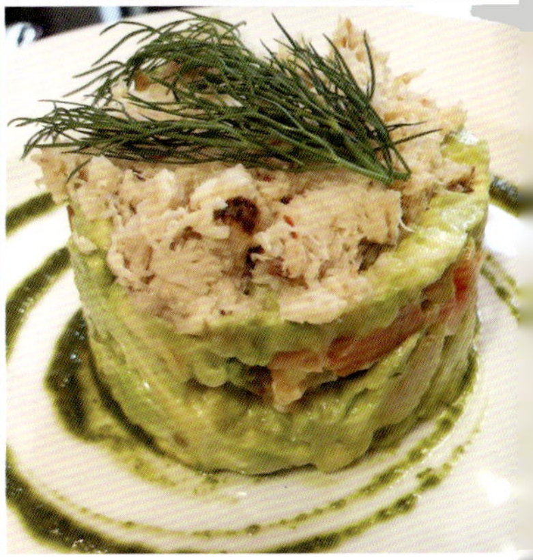
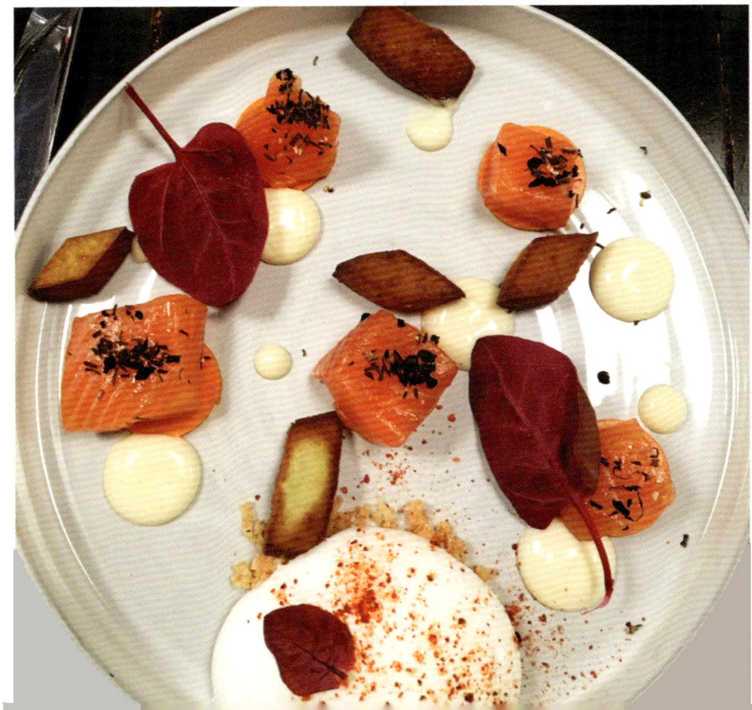
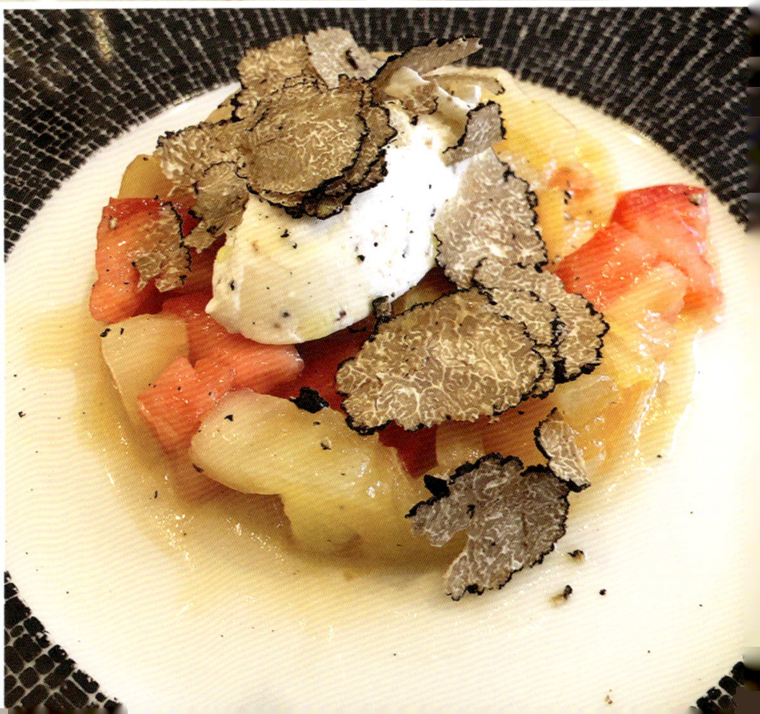

Le Plat

"I'd love to be a tabletop in Paris, where food is art and life combined in one, where people gather and talk for hours."
Maureen Johnson, *The Last Little Blue Envelope*

Meat (in various incarnations) and potatoes remain the mainstays of many French diets, with a wealth of exquisite freshly caught seafood and a variety of poultry is gaining ground (including rabbit, which is considered poultry in France).

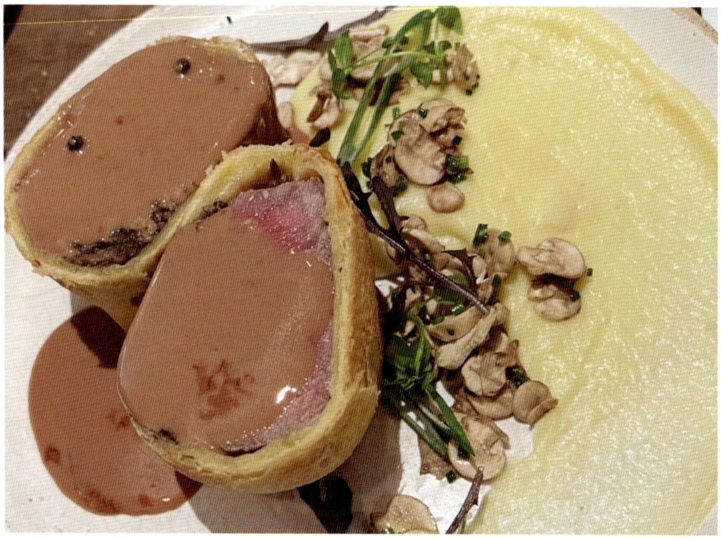

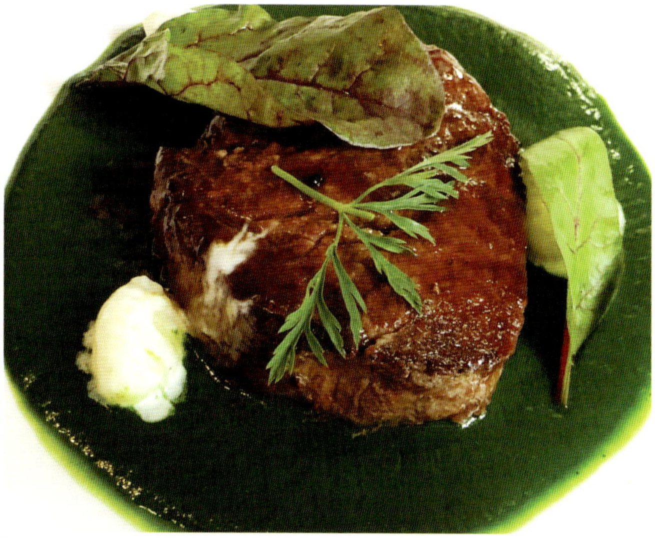

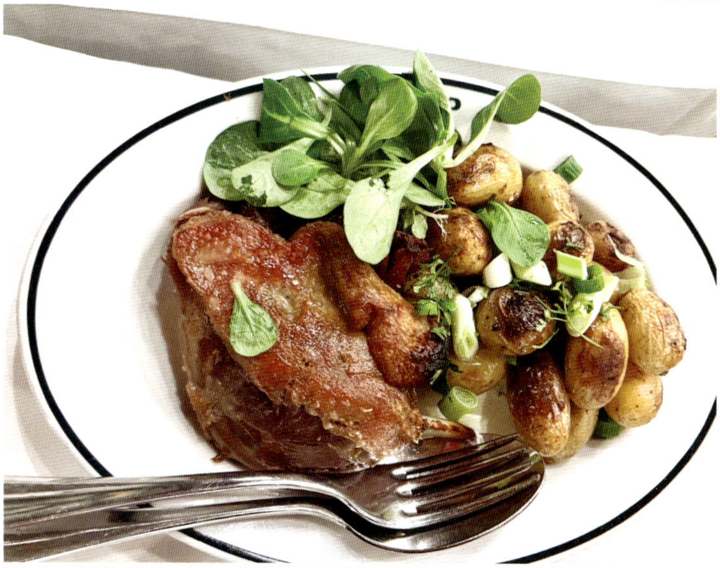

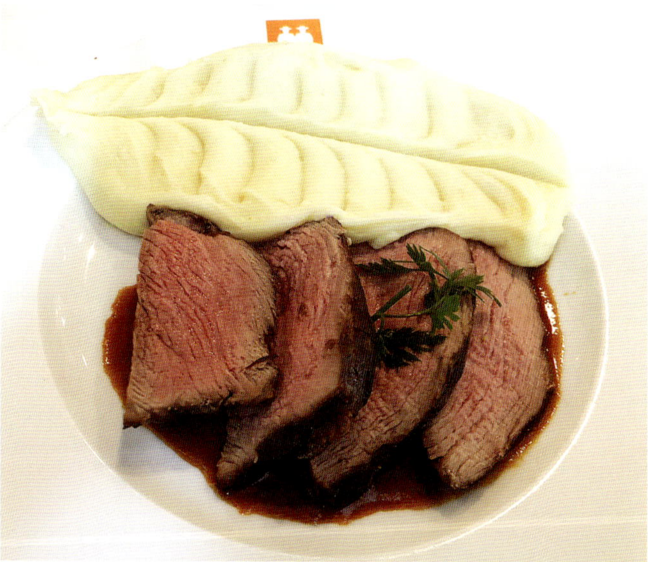

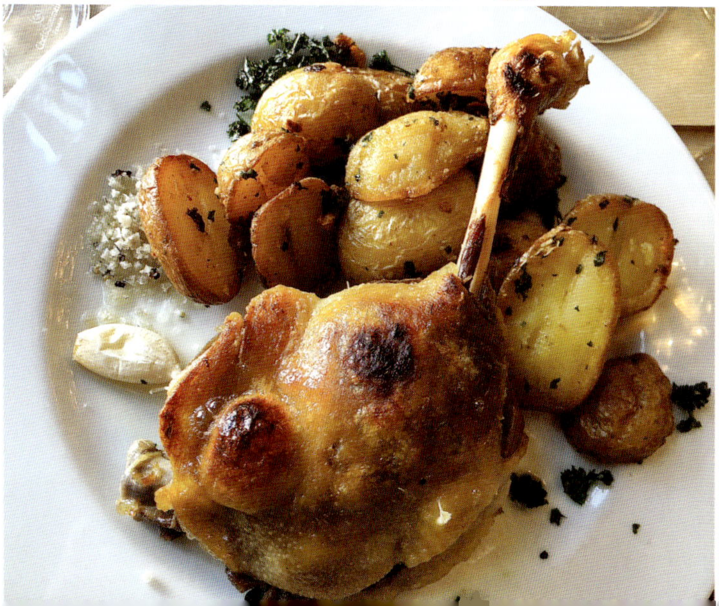

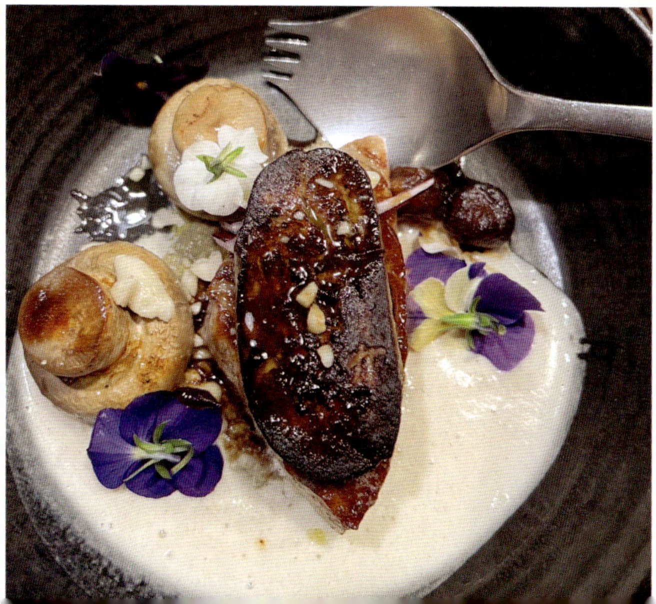

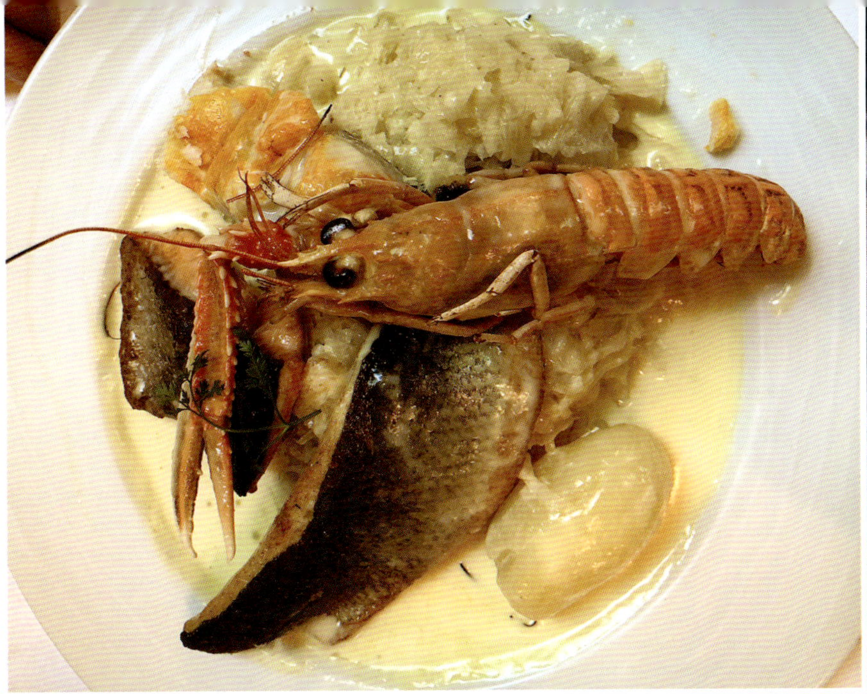
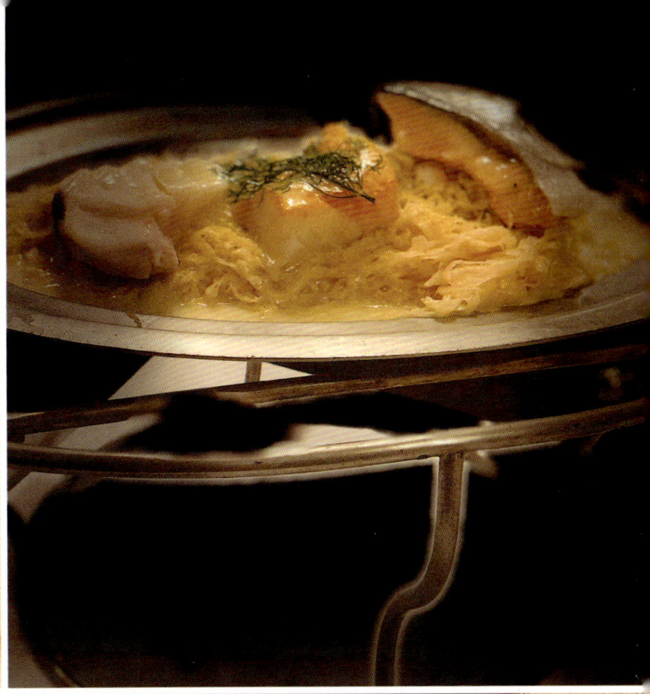
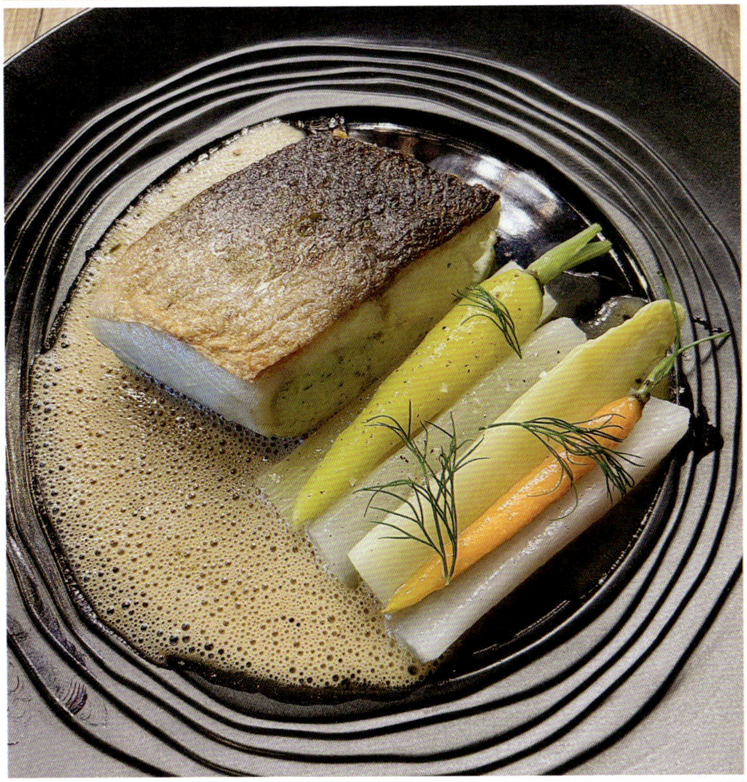
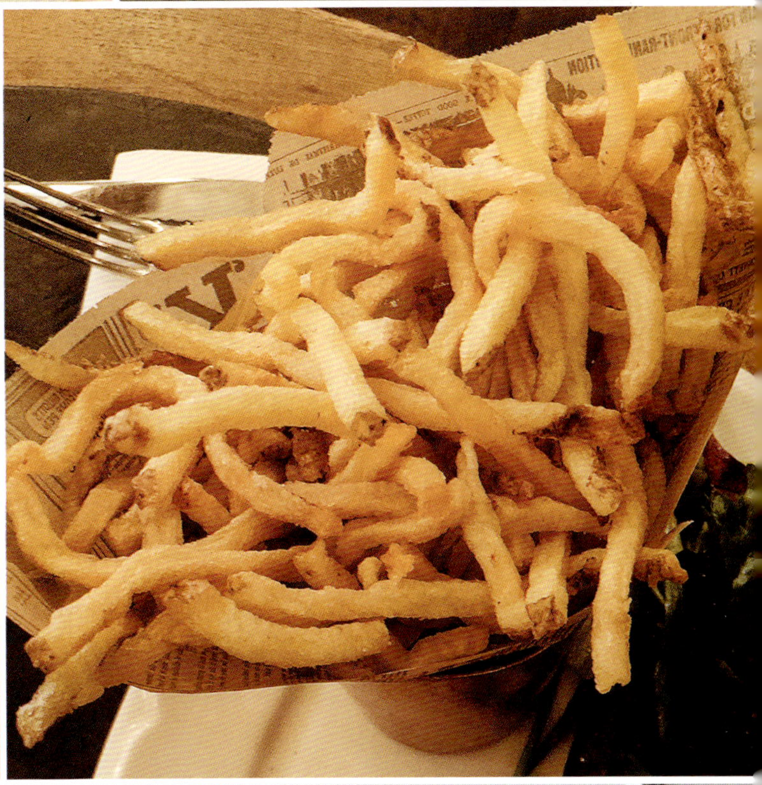
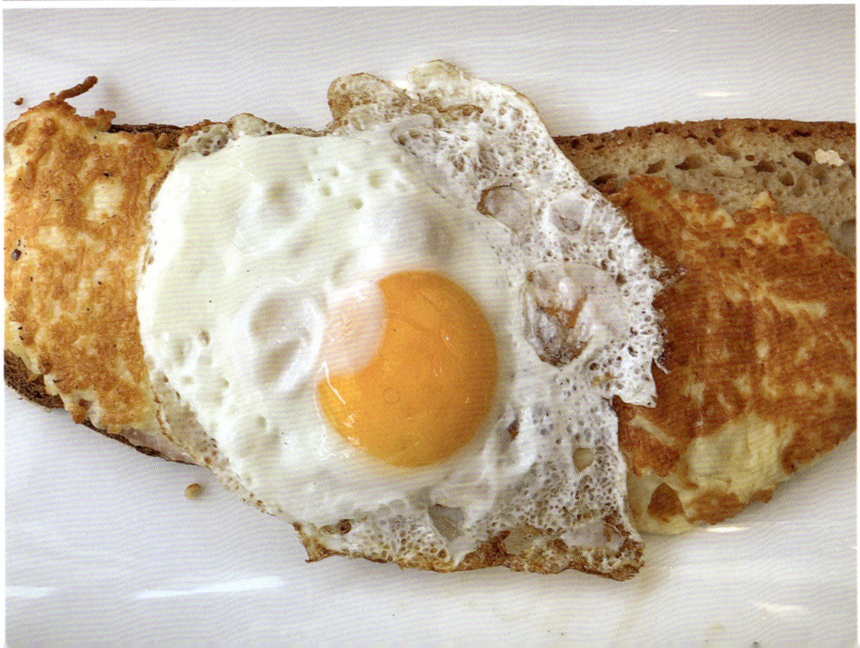
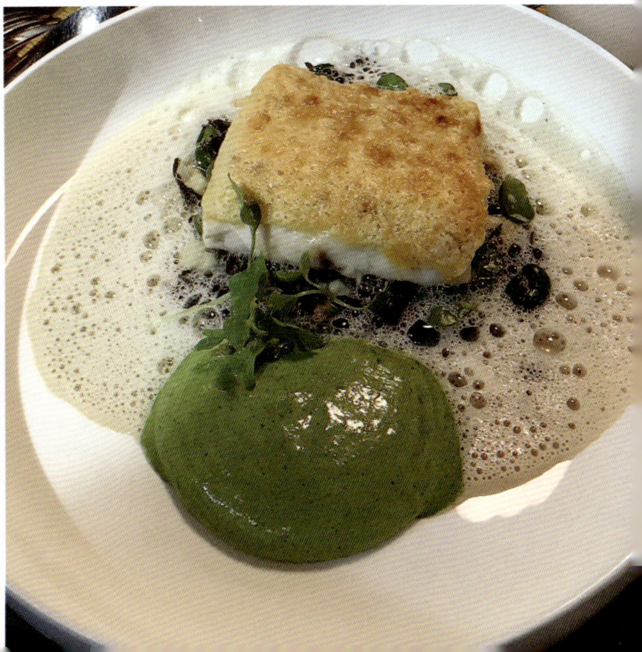

Le Plat

"The discovery of a new dish does more for the happiness of mankind than the discovery of a star."

Jean Anthelme Brillat-Savarin

It hasn't always been easy going green, but a remarkable trend toward more beautiful vegetables on the plate is now widespread. Unlike in past decades, one might work the system and ask for special preparation—*pas de beurre, pas de crème*—without a shrug and a sour look surfacing on the waiter's face.

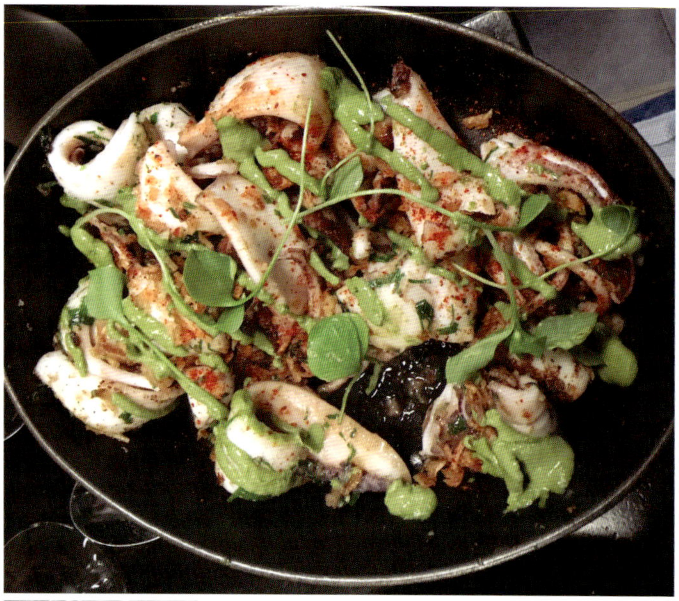

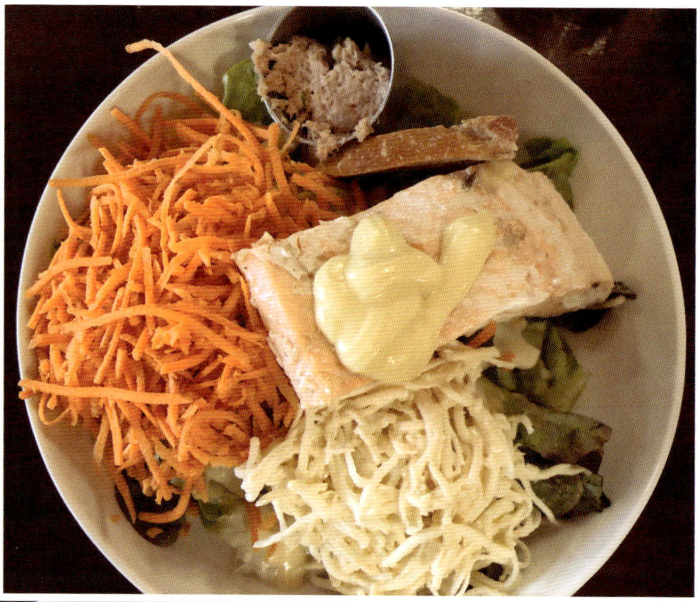

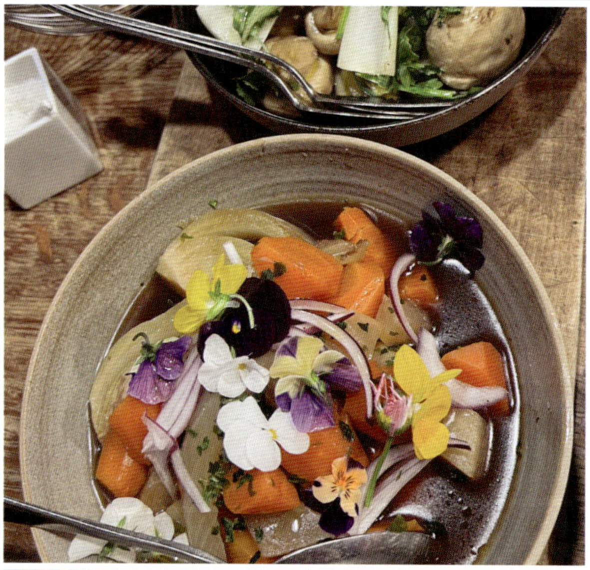

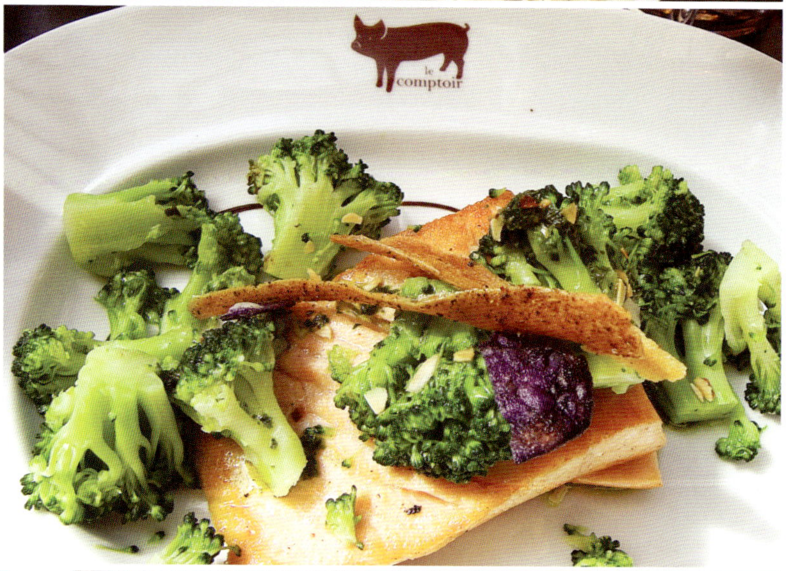

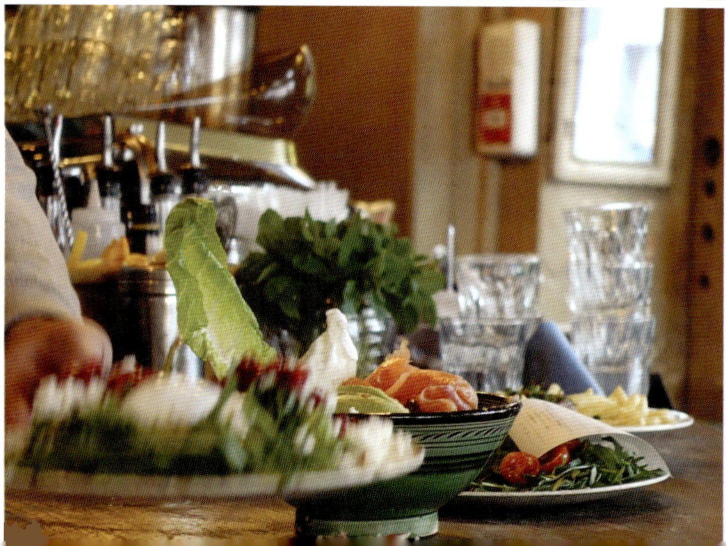

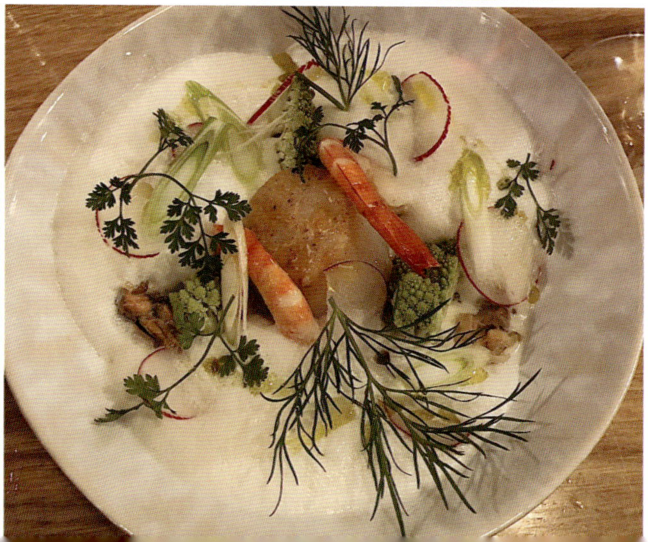

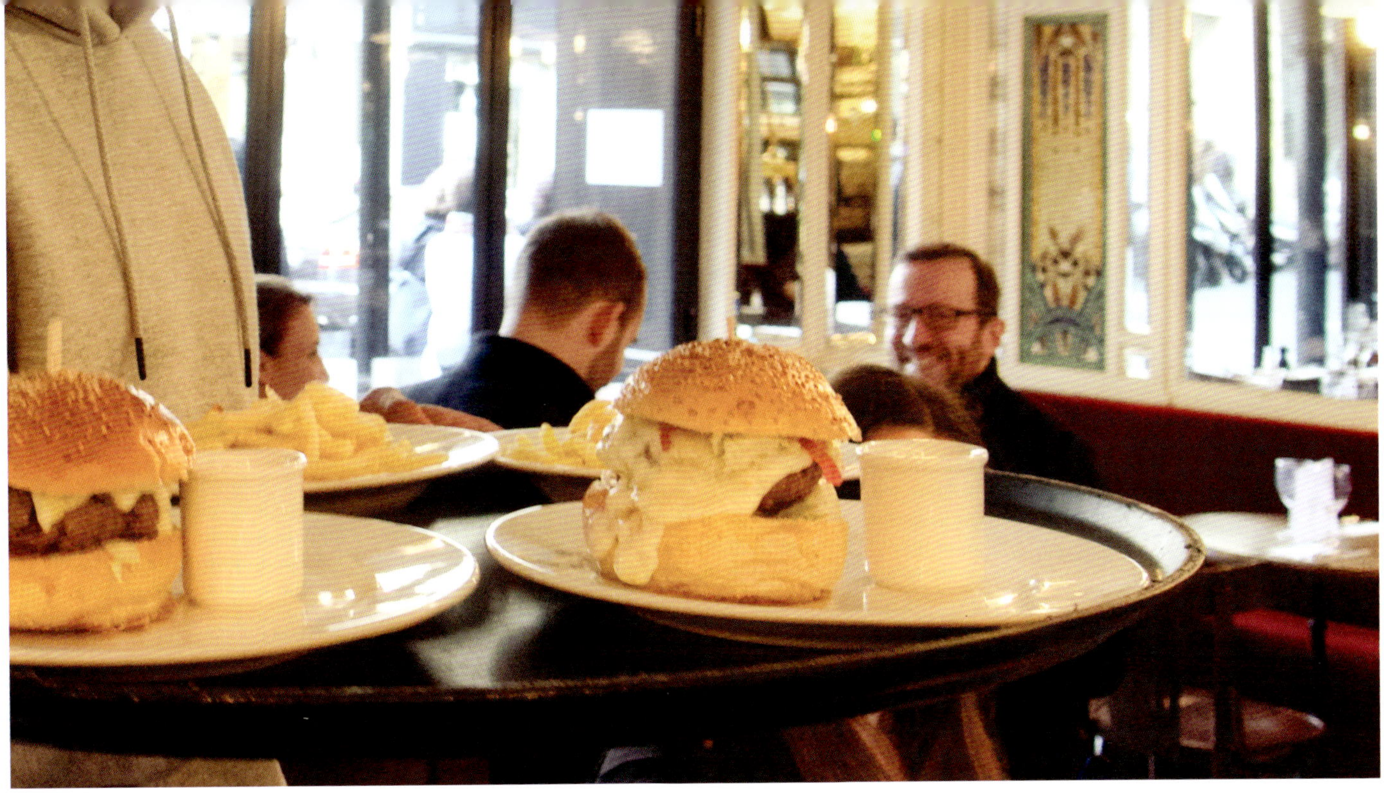

Oh, and the hamburger—prettier than the US standard—seems to have infiltrated nearly 85% of French eateries, including cafés, bistros, brasseries, and starred restaurants. Ketchup can be requested; however, flavorful French mustard, a staple often found on the table next to the salt and pepper, is the preferred condiment. It seems to pair well with French cuisine, including their version of burgers. But, of course, the best version may just be Le Mesturet's duck confit burger, sans beef.

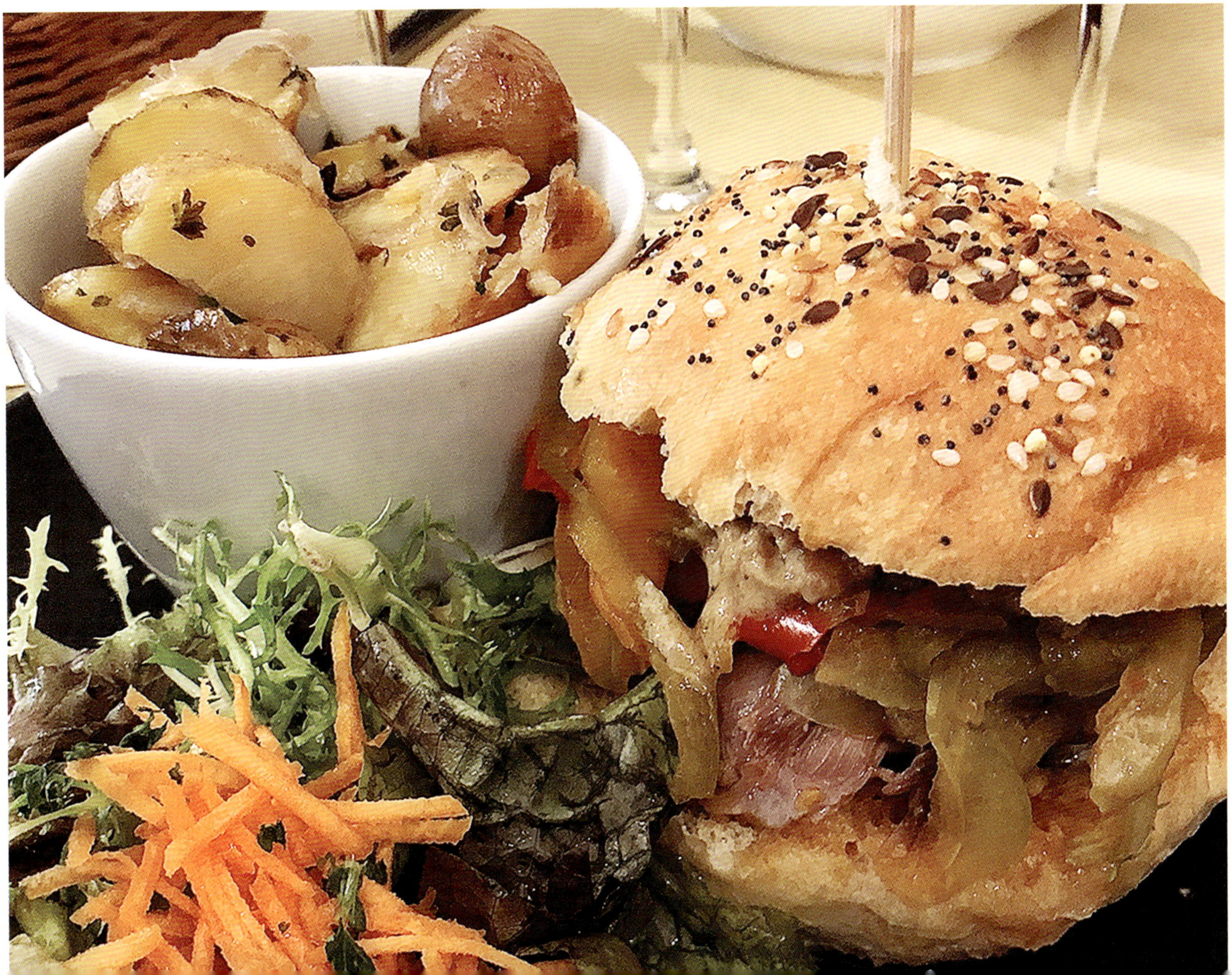

Le Dessert

"The French bring to the table the same appreciation, respect, intelligence, and lively interest that they have for the other arts, for painting, for literature, and for the theatre."

Alice B. Toklas

French pastries are world-renowned, and who doesn't fall for the exquisite lusciousness of these intricately crafted delicacies? Yes, sugar, cream, and butter work magic on the taste buds, and the elegant forms and colors of each creation bring joy to the eye. However, we cannot ignore *beaucoup de* other incomparable French desserts, including mouthwatering ice cream and cheese. Not to be missed is an ice cream pilgrimage to Berthillon on Île Saint-Louis, where the flavors are natural, and the lines form no matter the weather. Those with a cheese tooth rather than a sweet tooth can order the ubiquitous cheese course. As De Gaulle once said, "how can you govern a country which has 246 varieties of cheese?" Shall we also savor a moment of reverence to taste Proust's madeleine? You must walk a lot in Paris to keep fit because the temptations are worth the indulgence.

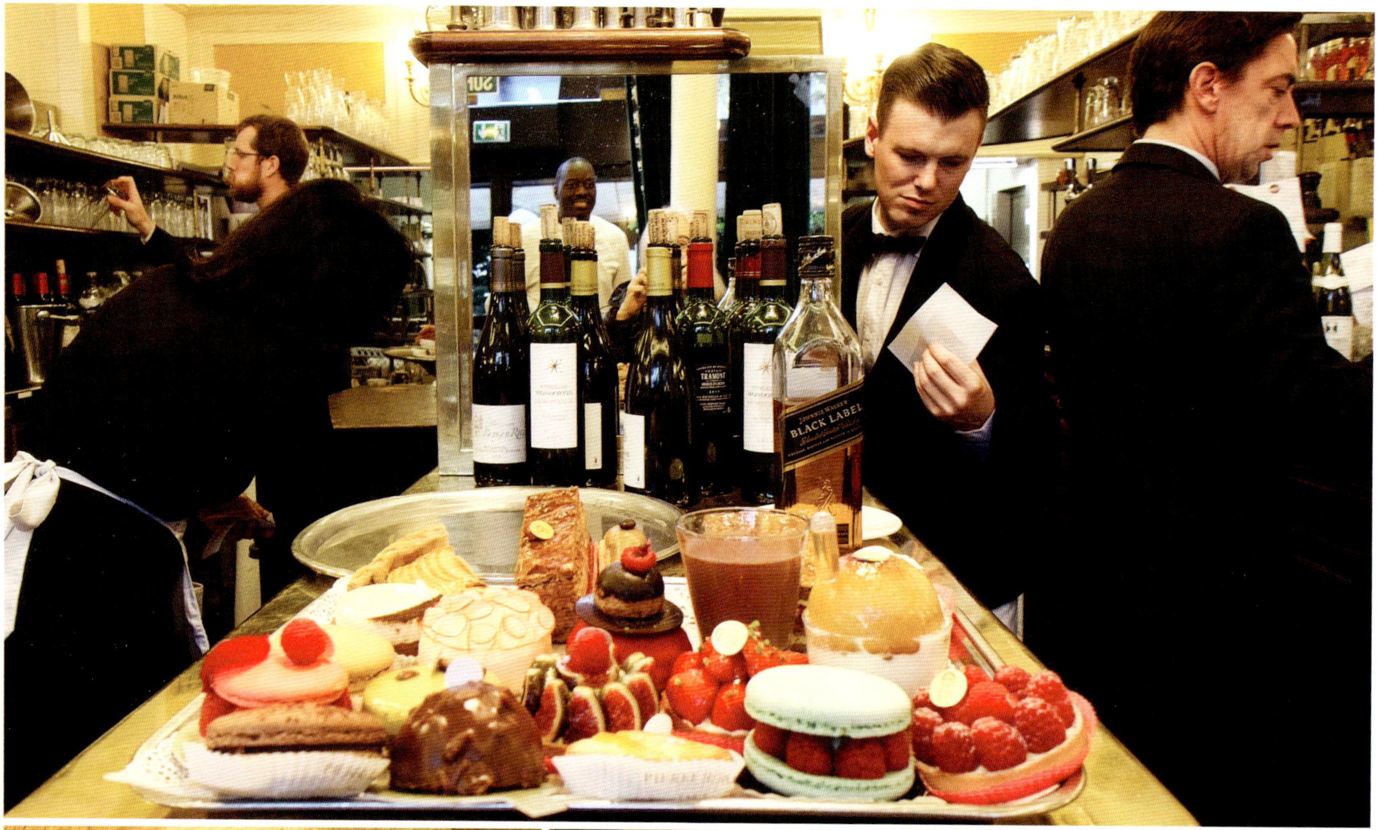

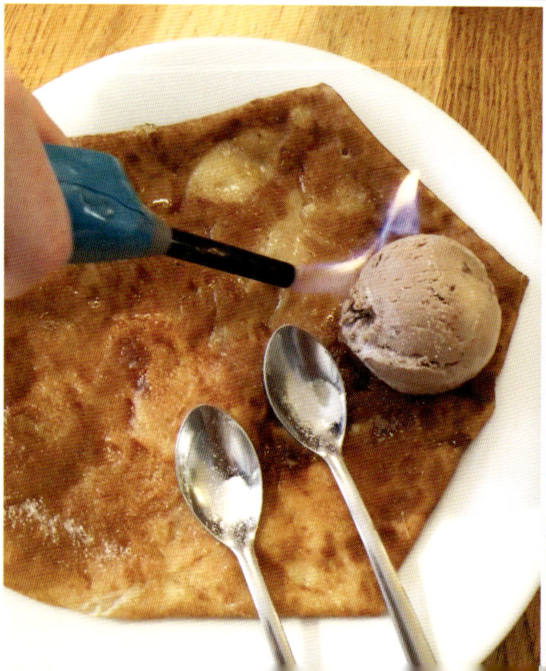

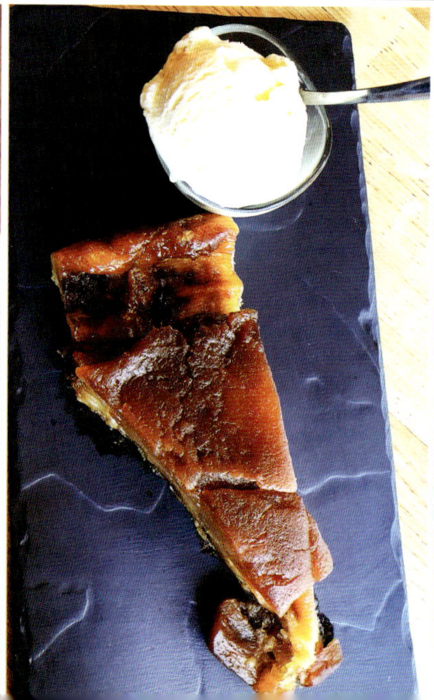

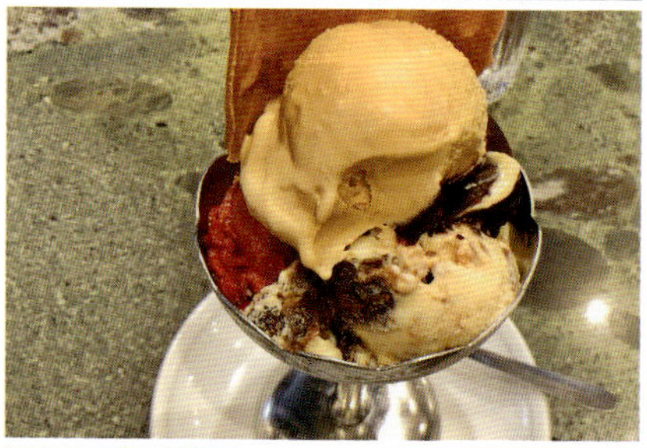

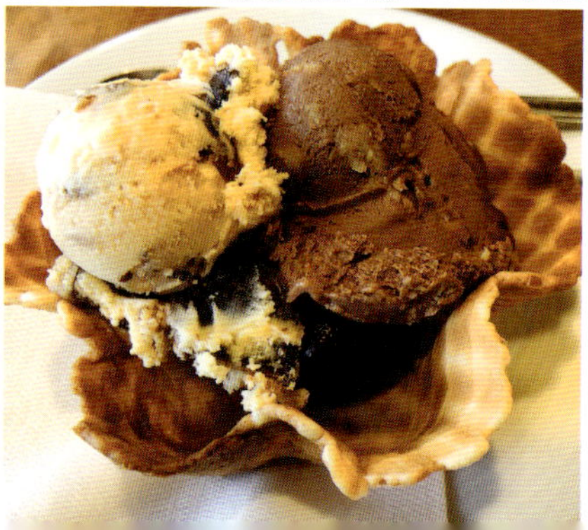

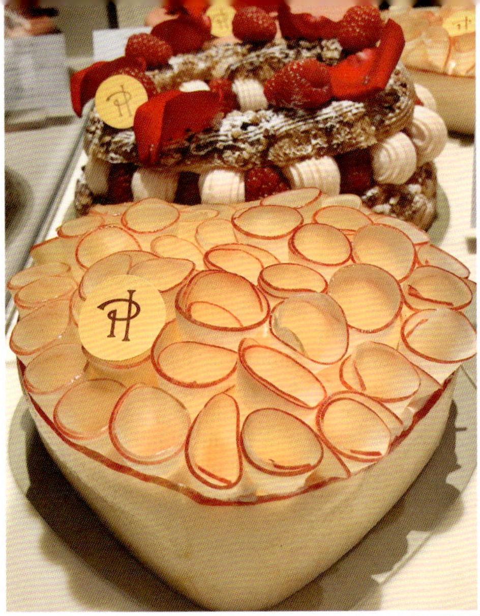
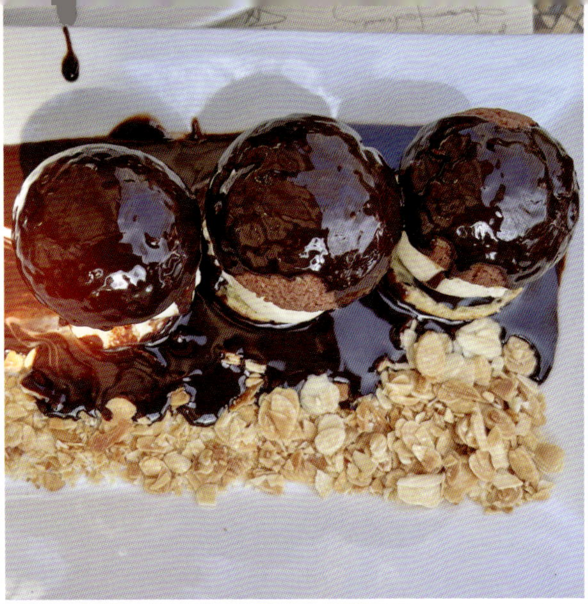
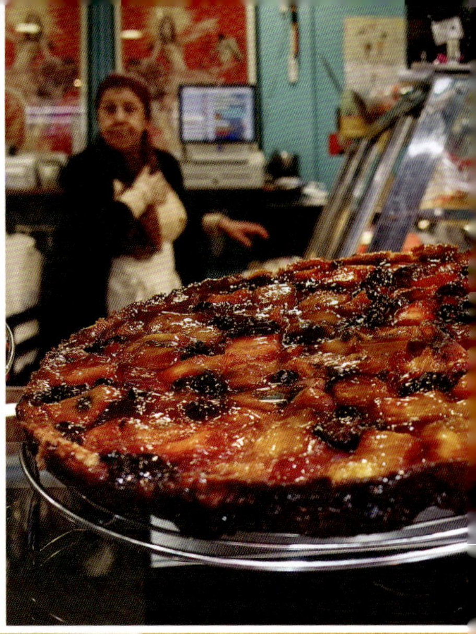
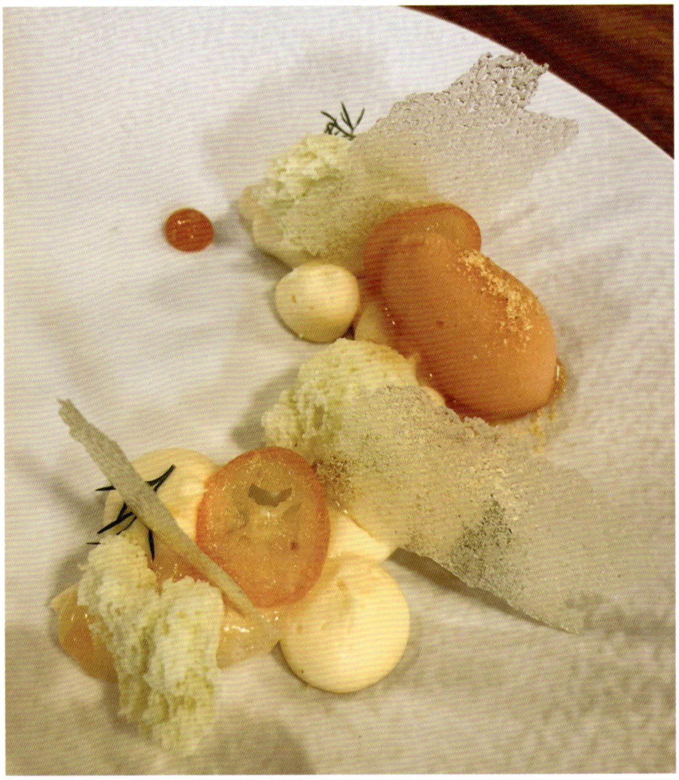
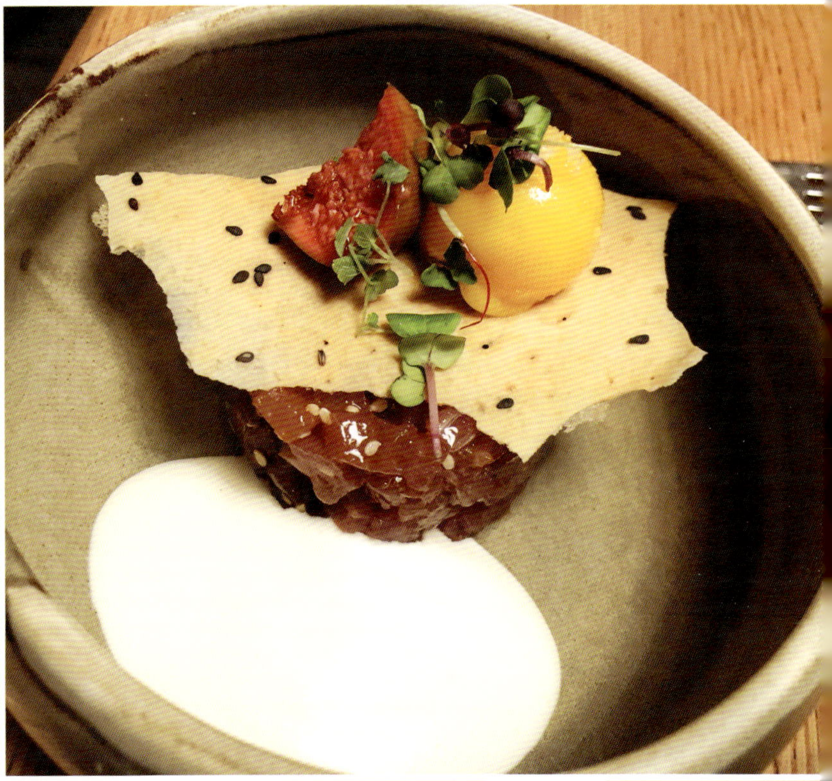
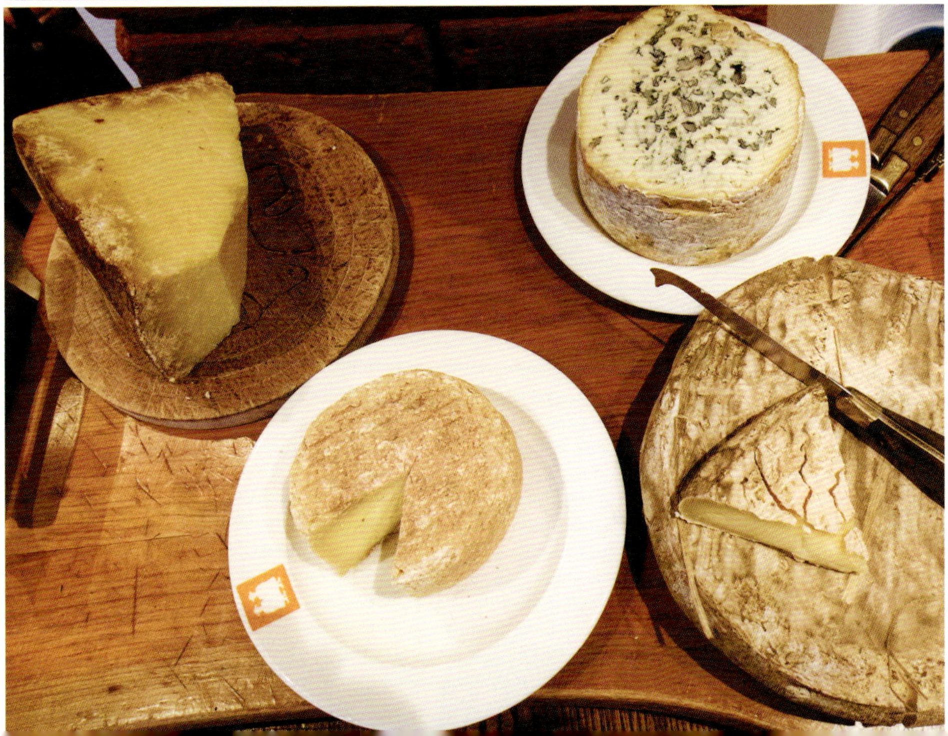
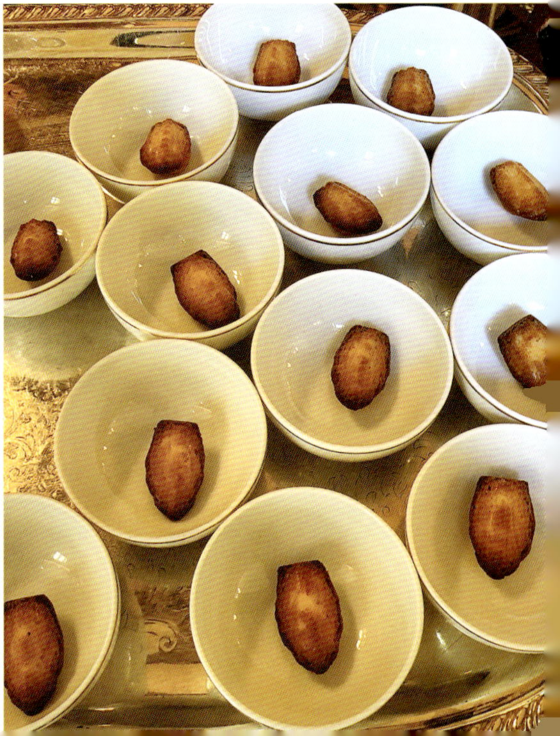

Les Boissons

> "The glass of wine has become the universal ritual of communication. The bistro is our oasis."
>
> **Edgar Morin**

For breakfast, it's a simple choice of café, *thé*, or chocolat. The natural beverage chronology for lunch is wine during, espresso after. Dinner invites an aperitif before, wine during–red and/or white depending on the course—espresso, after, sometimes followed by a digestif. Beer is acceptable any time after breakfast, especially in a brasserie where it is a natural choice.

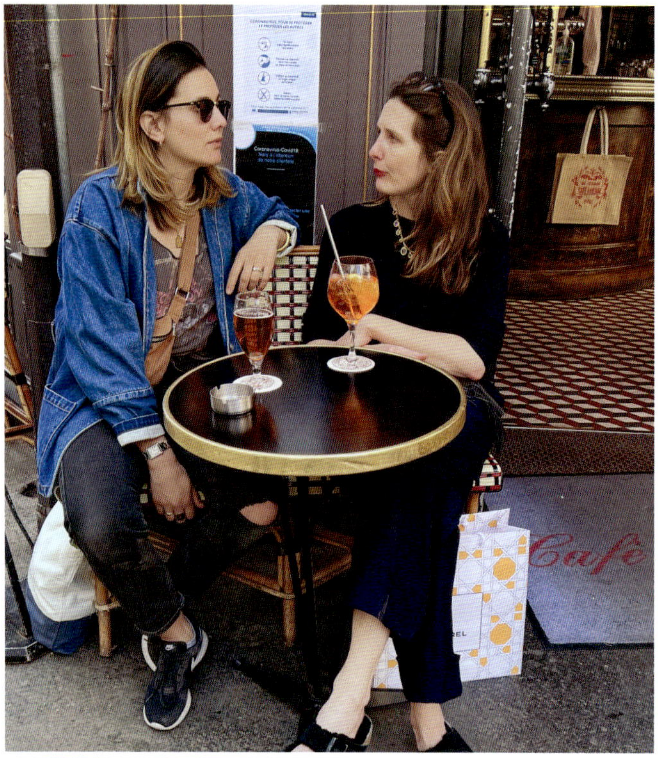

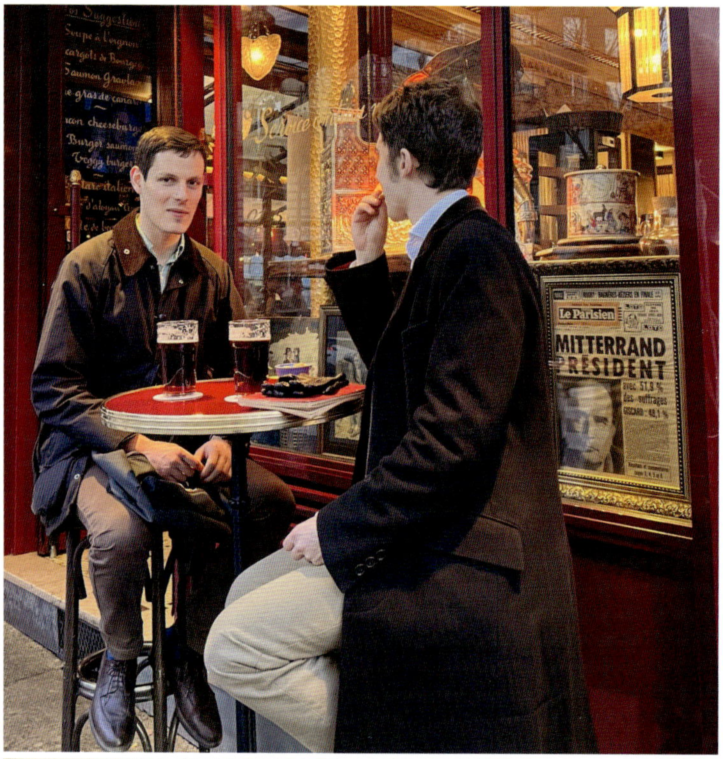

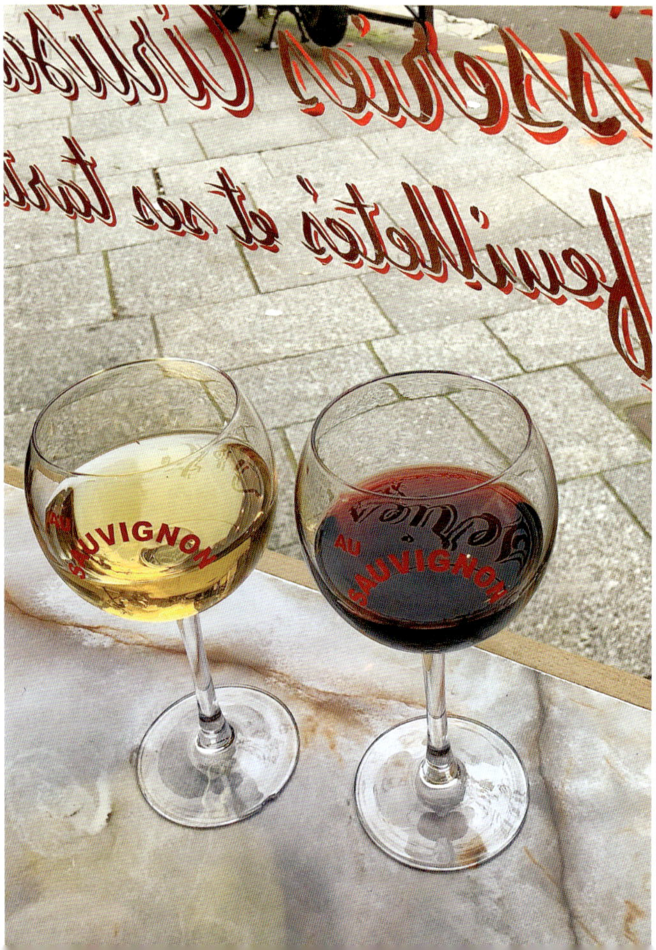

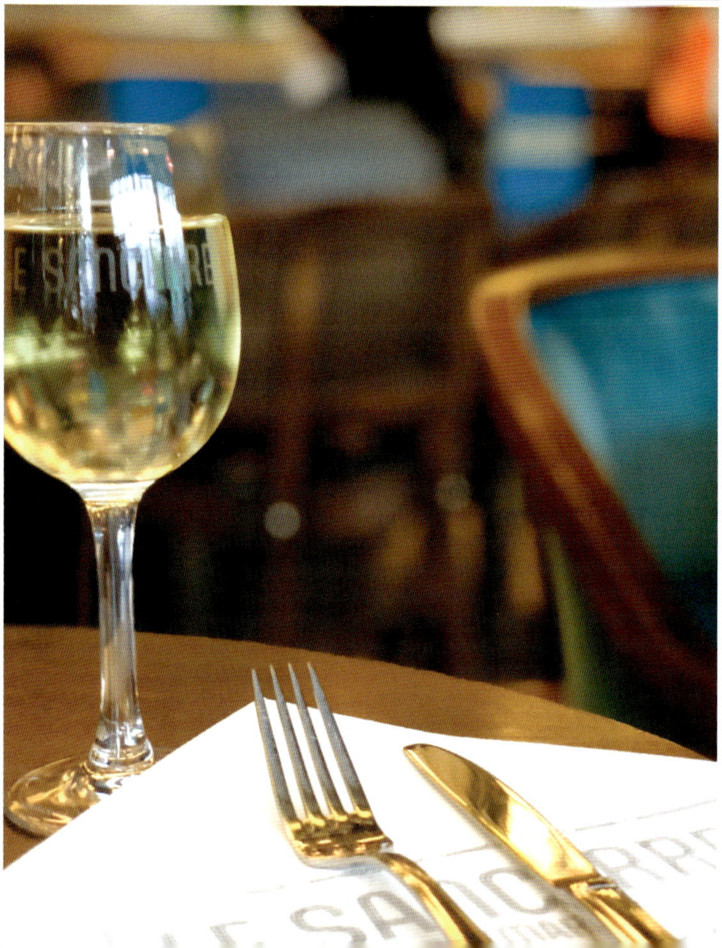

"... but you drank your black coffee by choice, believing that Paris was sufficient alcohol."

Malcolm Cowley, *Exile's Return: A Literary Odyssey of the 1920s*

Even though Paris is "sufficient alcohol," a meal without wine is possible but not commonplace in Paris, whether you choose a *vin de table* or a Bordeaux. Tracing their origins back to the 6th century BCE, the wines of France are indeed a wonder of the world.

Like Sartre and de Beauvoir and the generations before and after them, café-goers sit for hours, nursing one drink of espresso, tea, Perrier, hot chocolate, wine, or an aperitif. No one is rushed or intimidated—every beverage and person is treated equally, with respect, and often with good humor by the waiter or the barman.

The democracy of the café allows a choice of drinks at any time of day; however, tourists might want to understand the heavy-duty French traditions: a cappuccino only in the morning, espresso or noisette the rest of the day. A glass of white wine at the zinc counter in a classic worker café is just fine for breakfast; it will telegraph your sophistication to the barman and the neighboring *habitués*, though promenading may be a bit wobbly after.

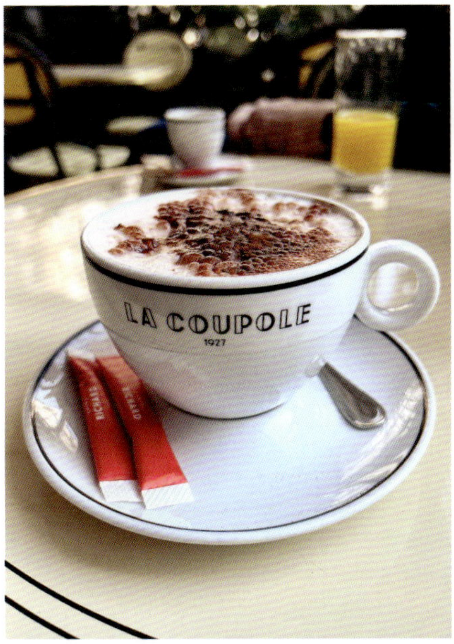

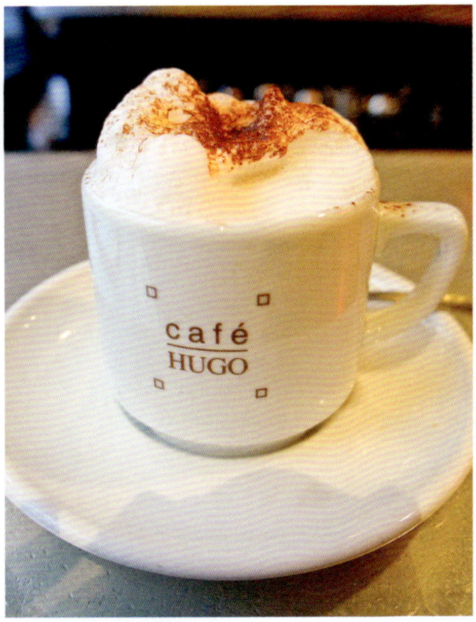

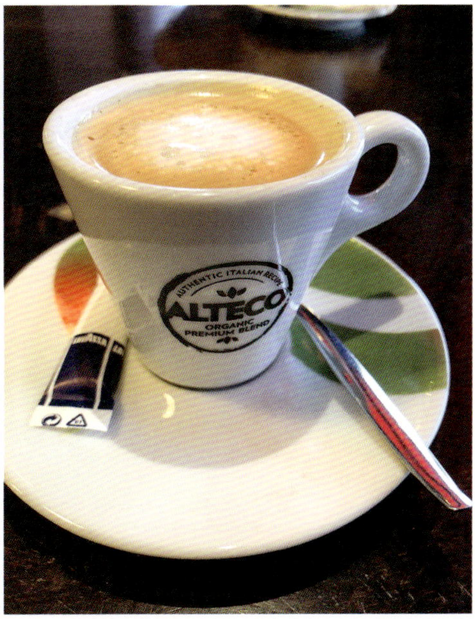

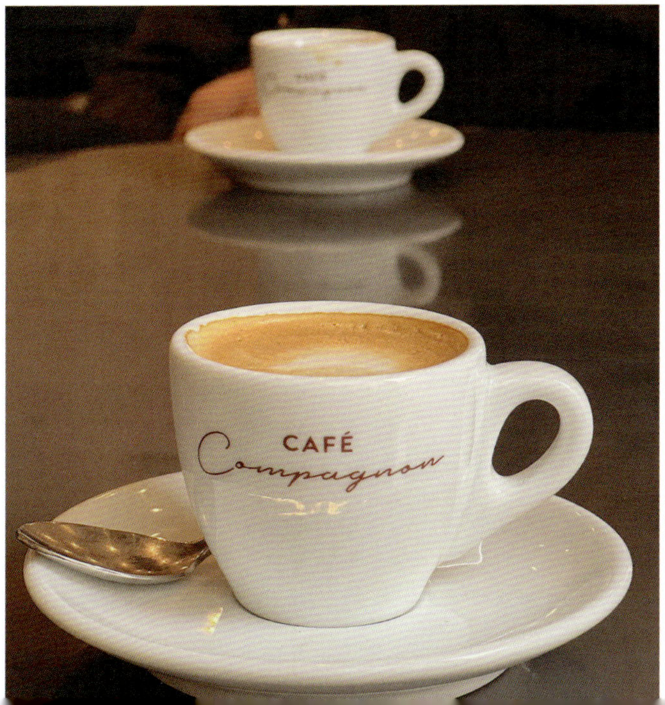

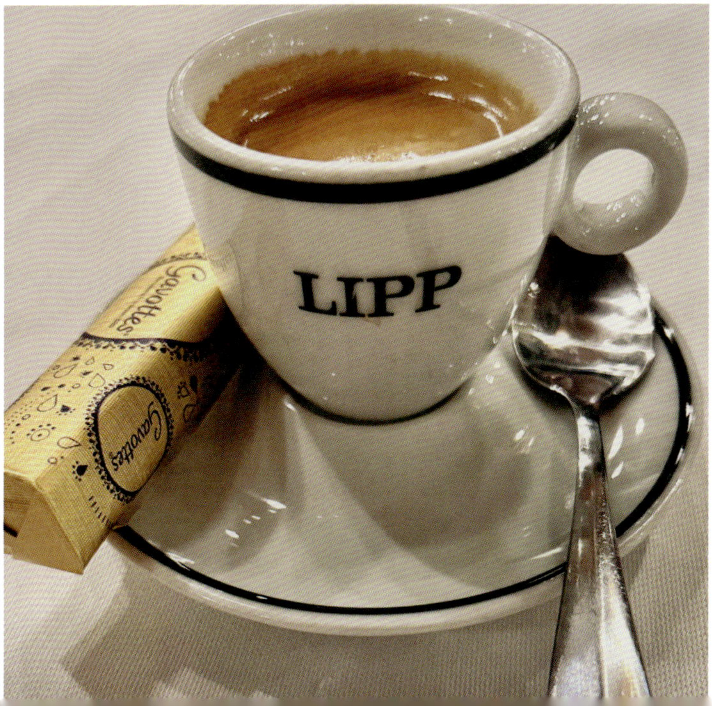

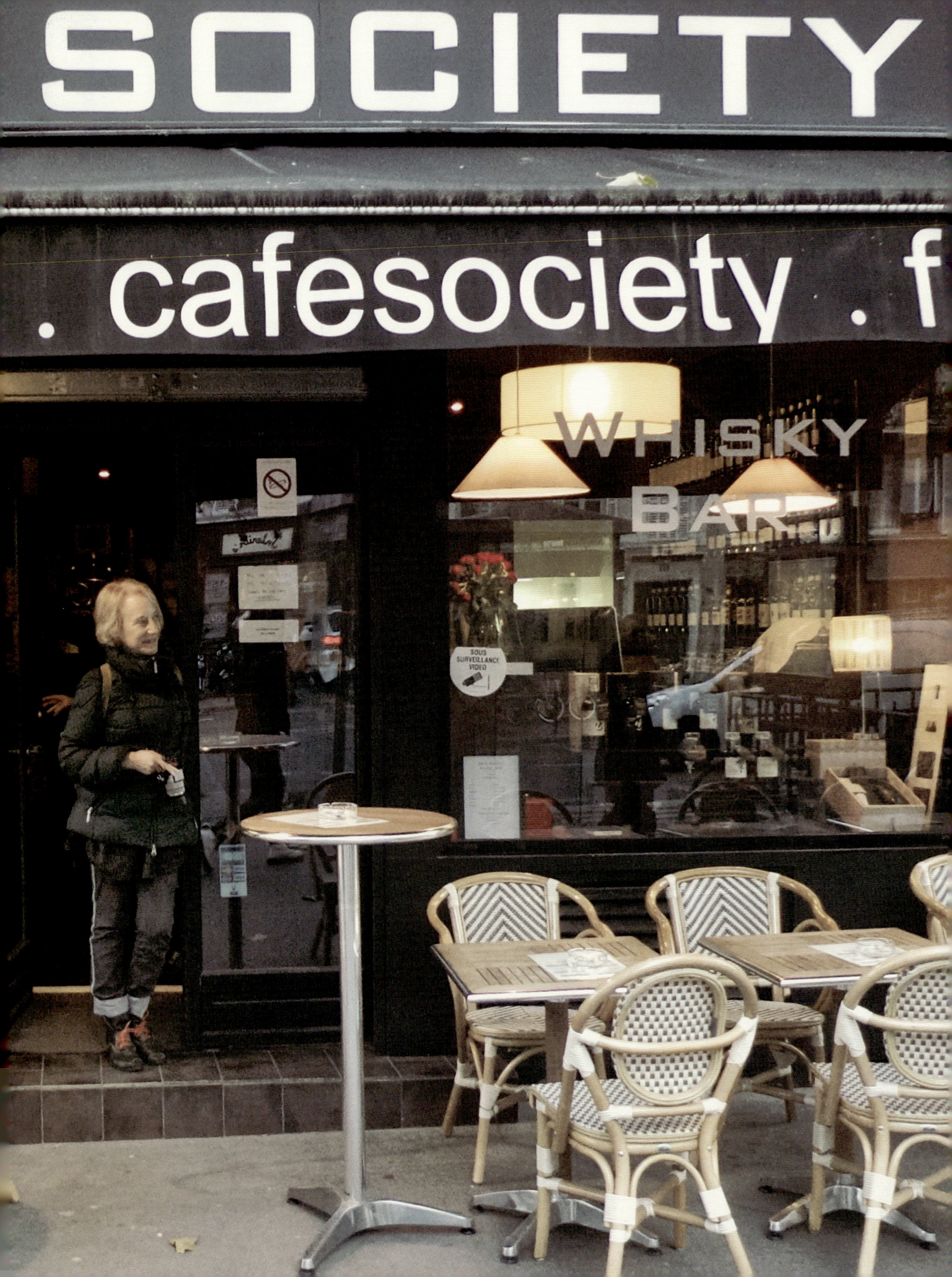
SOCIETY
. cafesociety . f
WHISKY
BAR
SOUS SURVEILLANCE VIDEO

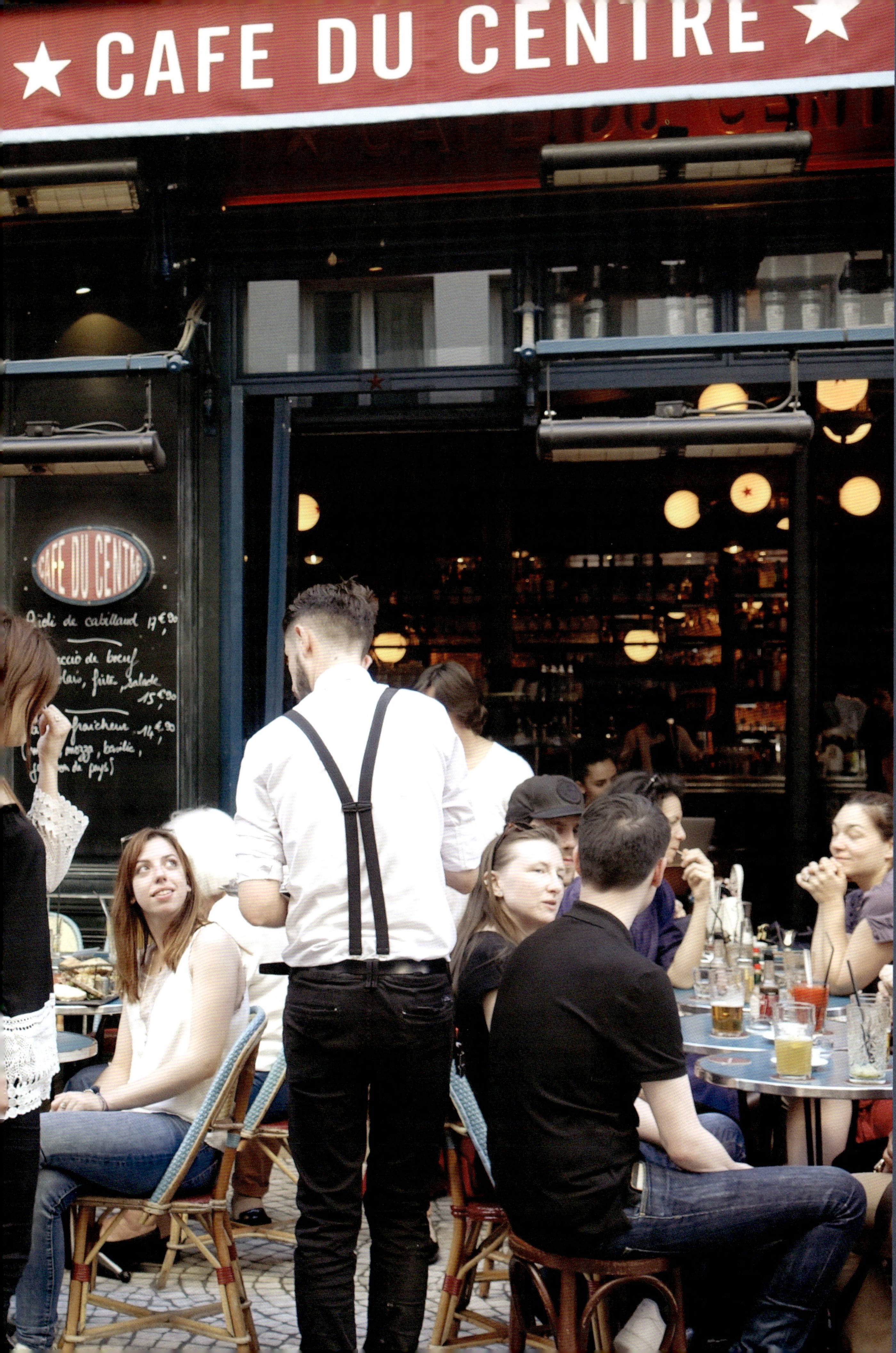

PART 4 Café Society

A Lively Social Network

"Frequenters of cafés are supposed to be in perpetual exuberance of spirits, always witty, always happy, and each one the best fellow in the world."

Charles Dickens

The social networks of Paris for centuries, cafés serve as a hub, where people meet to share an espresso, a glass of wine, or a meal. Face-to-face encounters have helped shape many of the personal, artistic, and political issues of the day. The café persists as a lively social network even in the current era—despite screen technology where the virtual replaces the actual. Humans crave the in-person connection cafés provide, accompanied by good food and drink to boot.

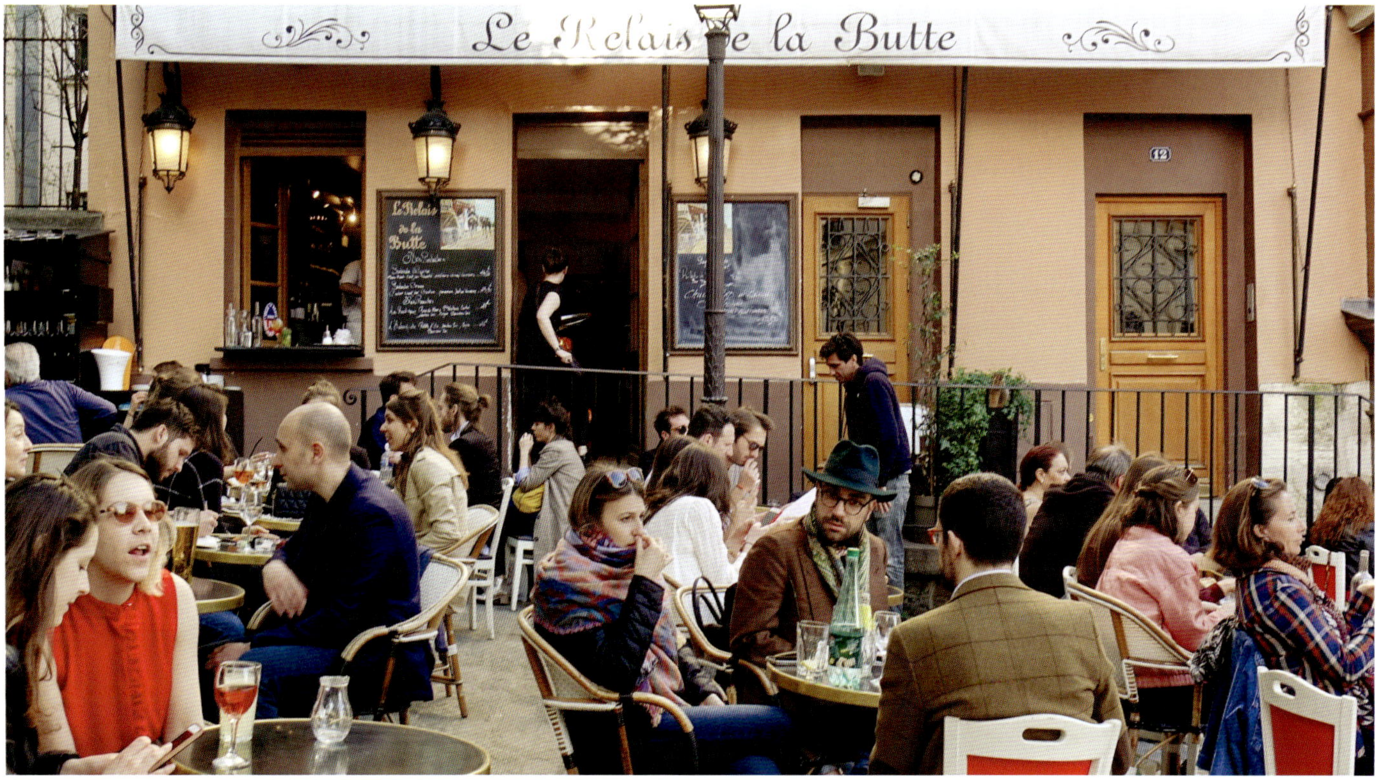

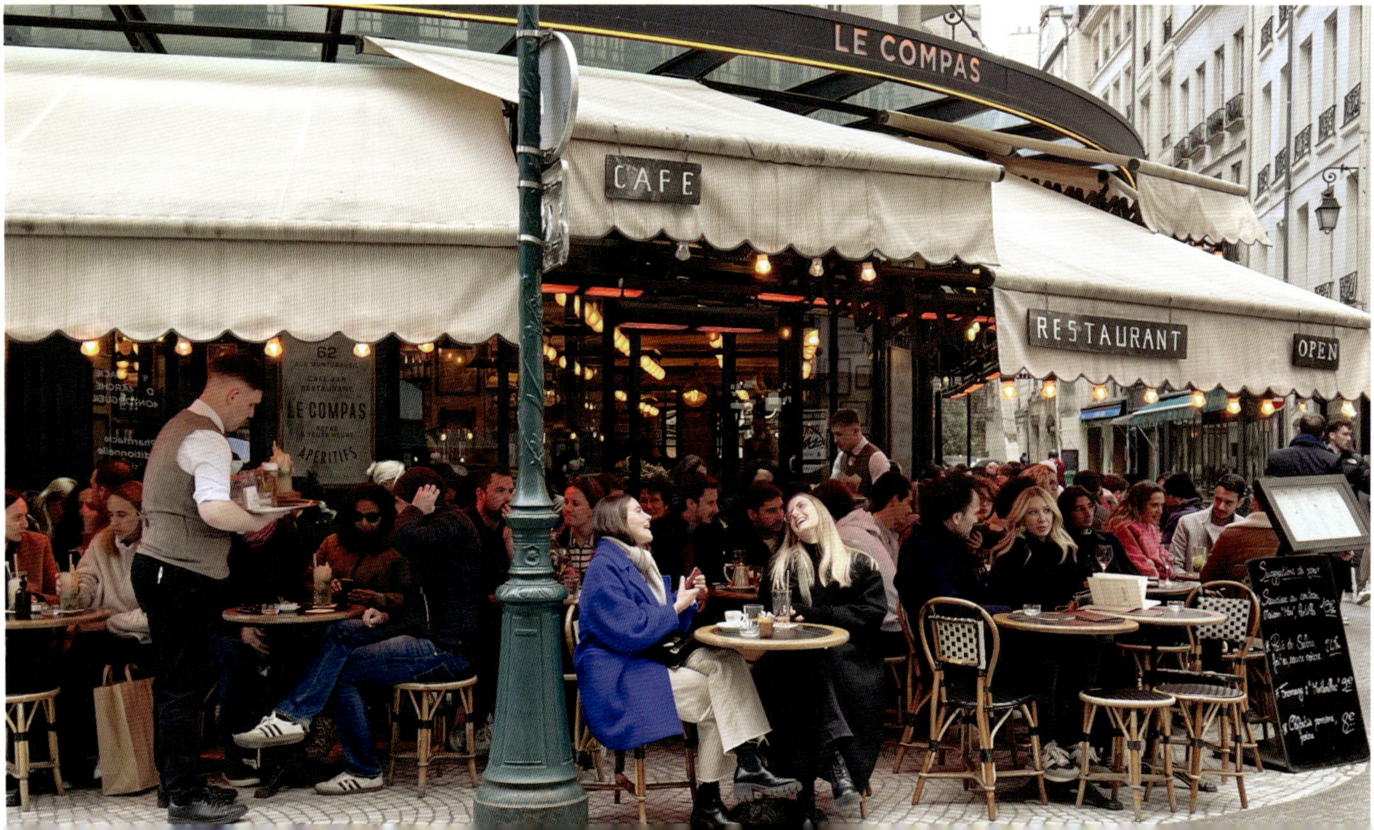

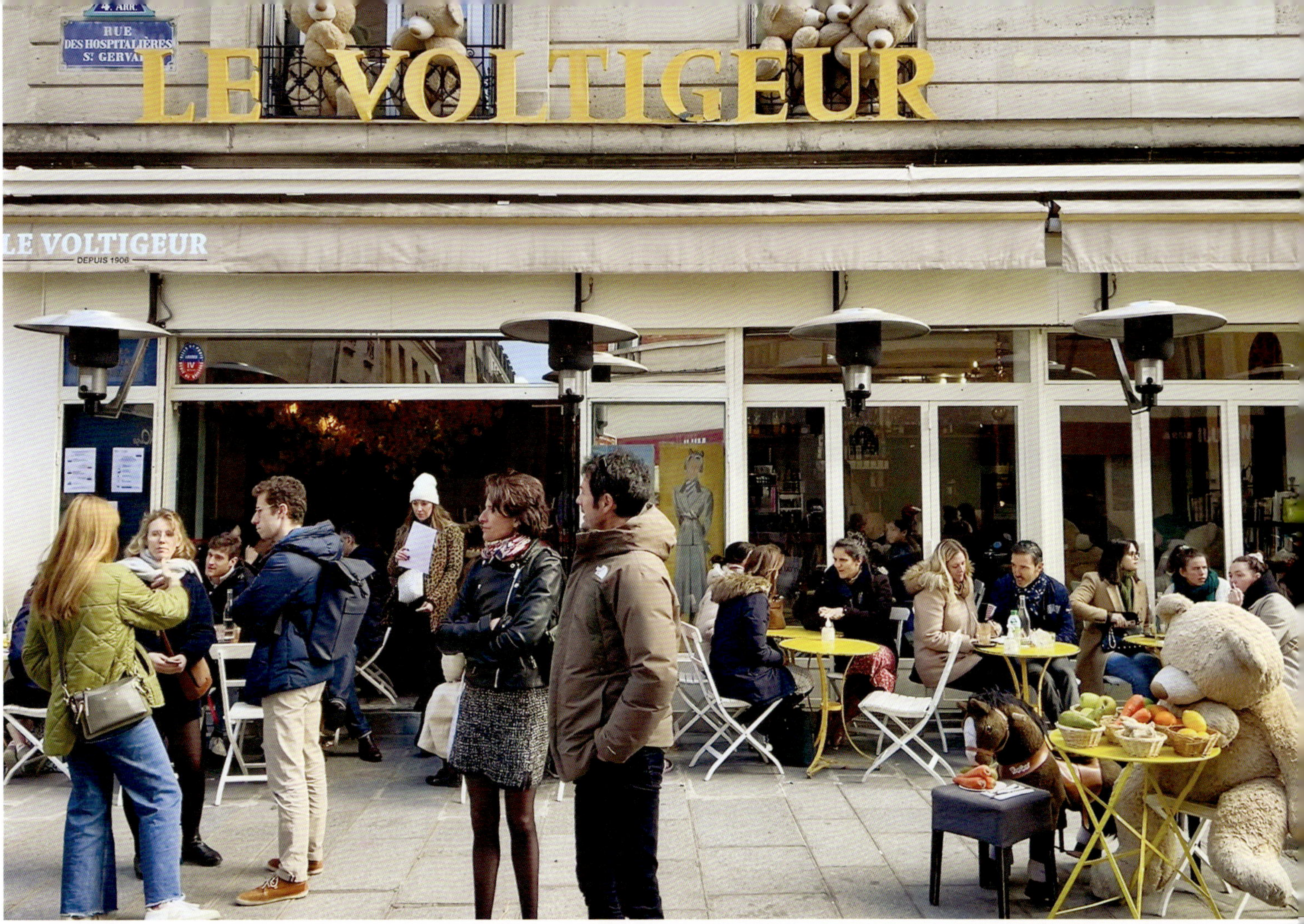
4. ARR.
RUE DES HOSPITALIÈRES ST GERVAI
LE VOLTIGEUR
LE VOLTIGEUR
DEPUIS 1906

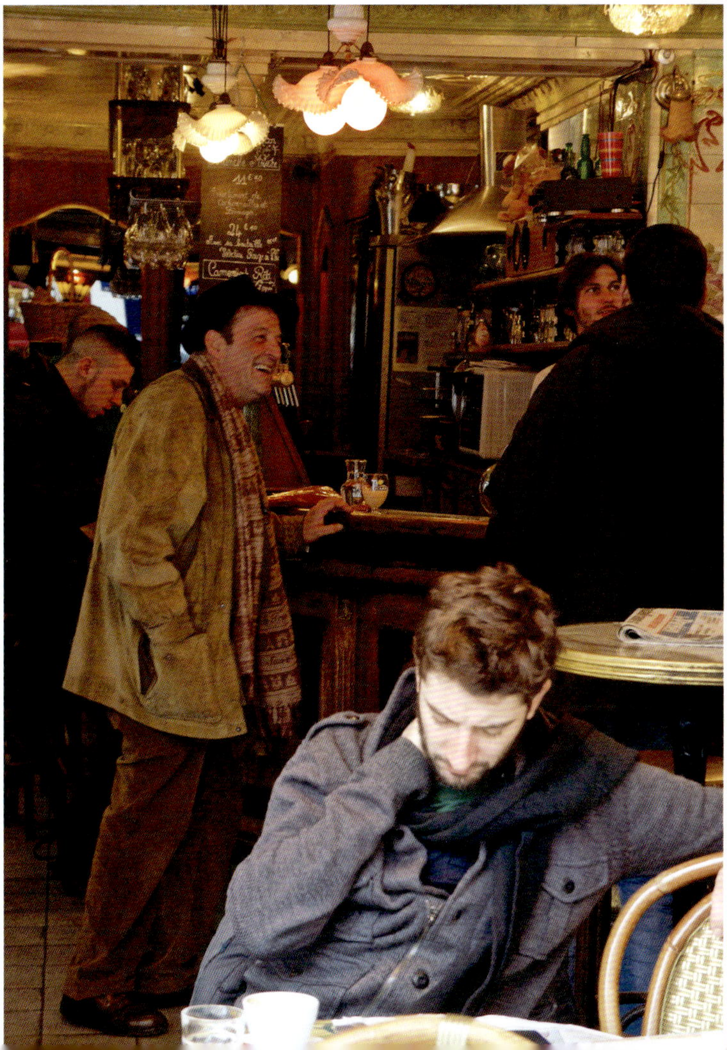

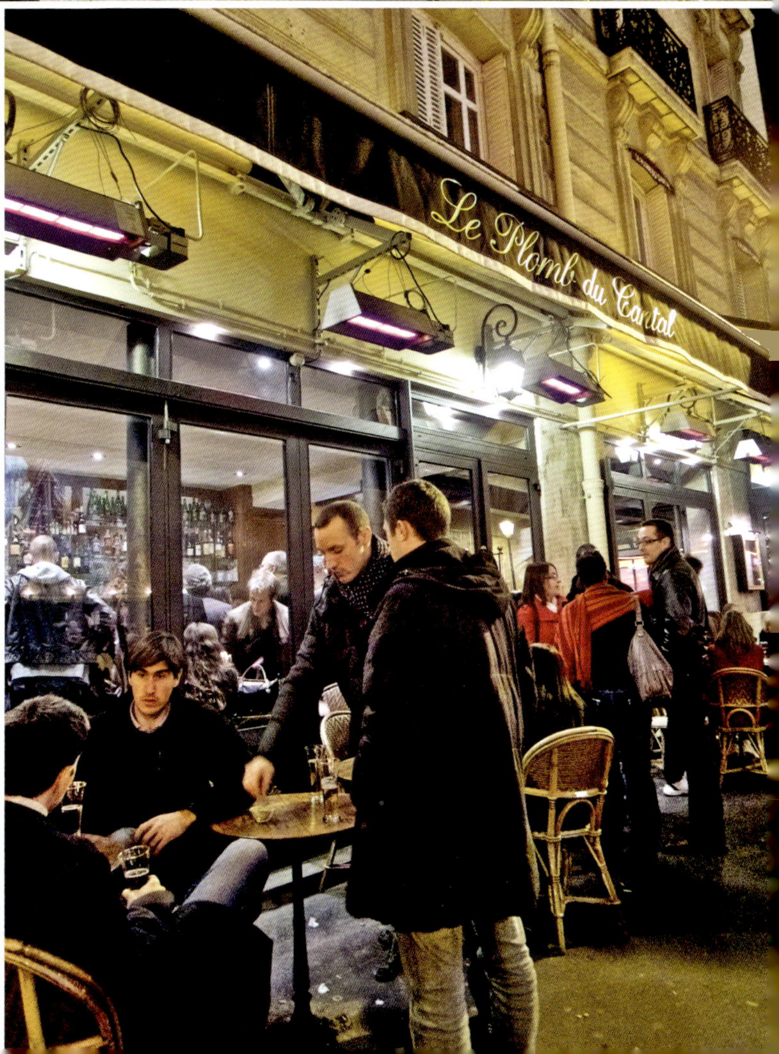
Le Plomb du Cantal

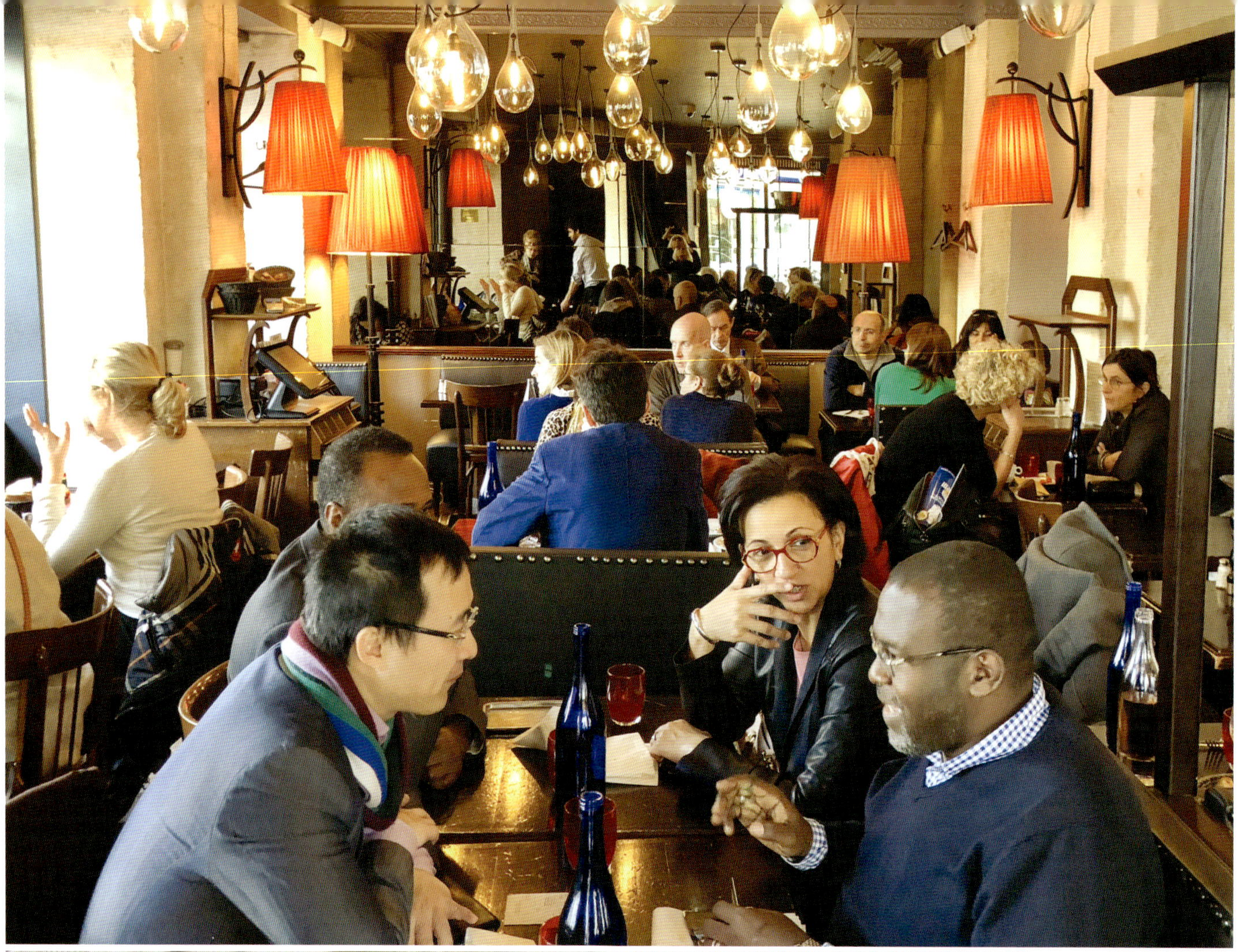

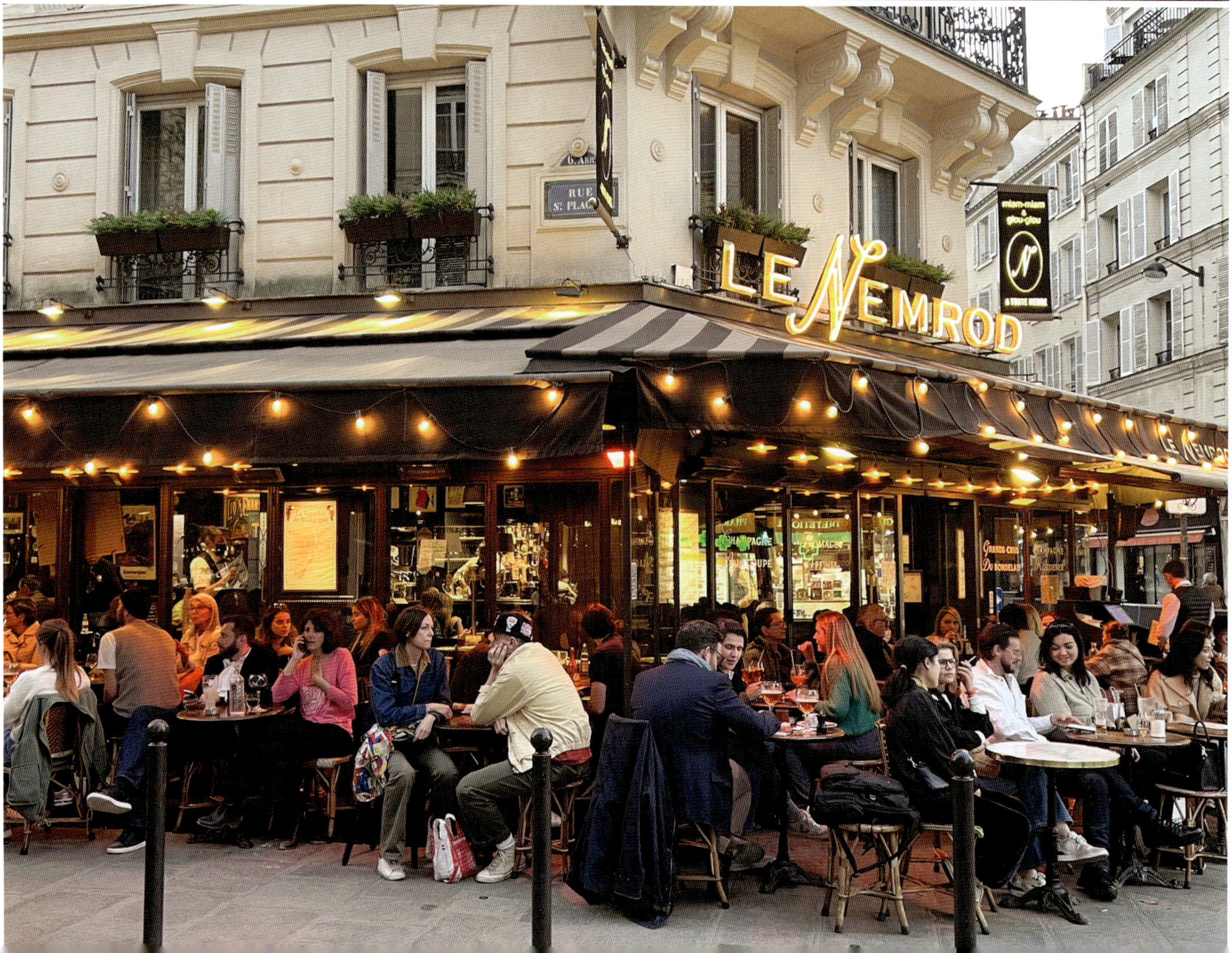
LE NEMROD

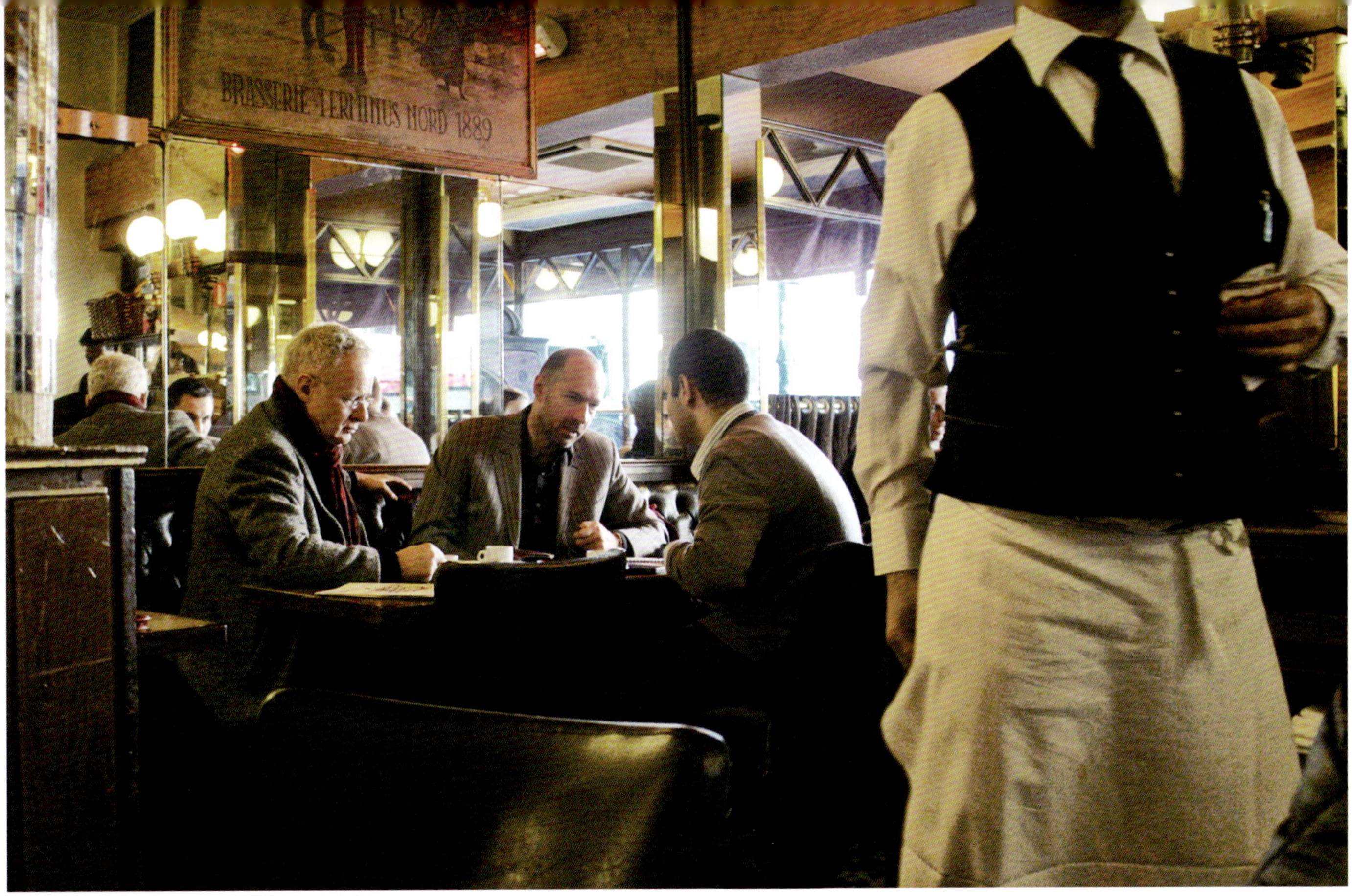

Democracy rules in cafés and bistros. Everyone is welcome; every nationality, ethnicity, gender, age, profession or trade, political opinion, and pocketbook. Anyone can be and is automatically a member of café society because it is open to all. The importance of social interaction, often taken for granted in normal times, became urgently clear in the early 2020s with the impact of the isolation caused by the worldwide pandemic. In Paris, it is the normalcy of café life that one hungers for: to be out and about and in the world. To be in Paris.

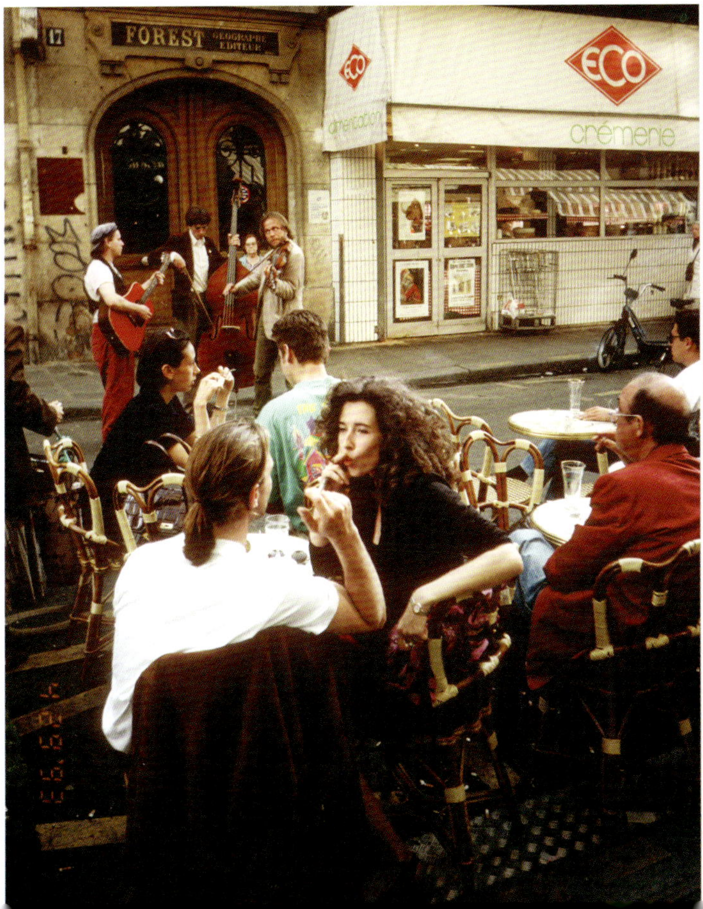

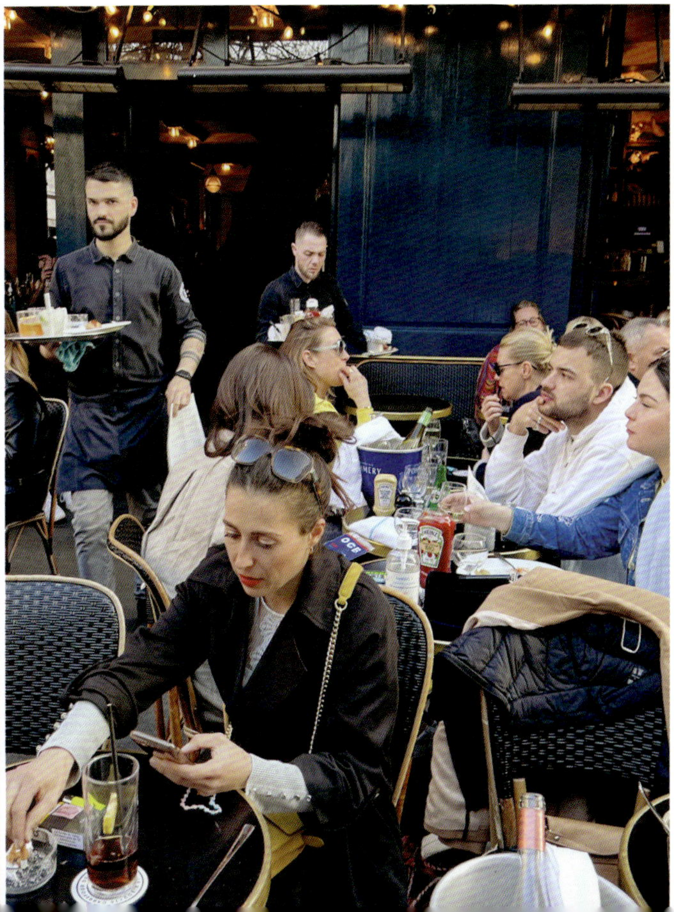

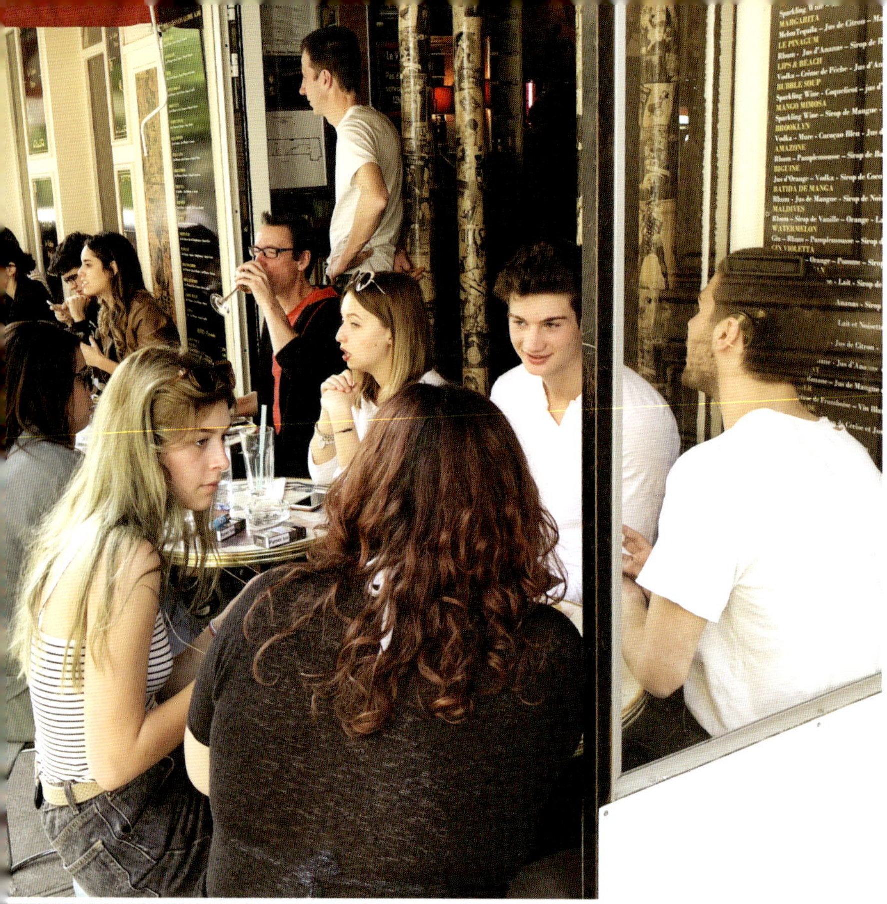

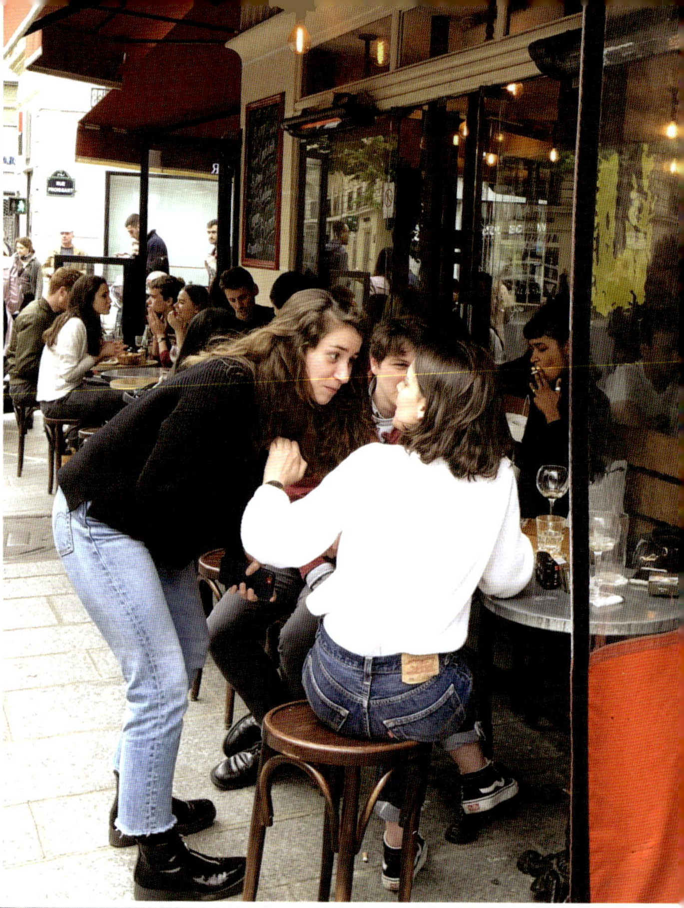

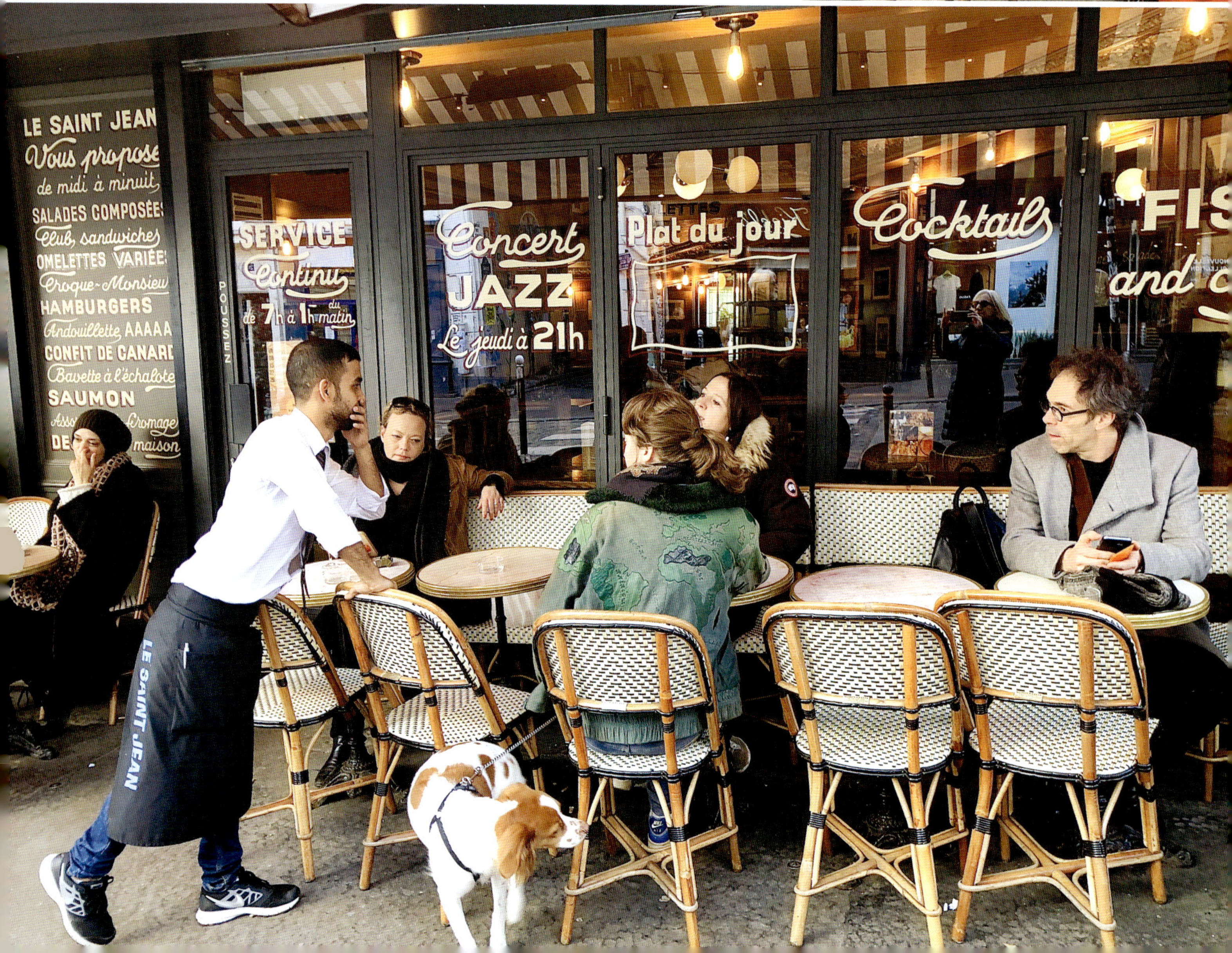
LE SAINT JEAN
Vous propose
de midi à minuit
SALADES COMPOSÉES
Club, sandwiches
OMELETTES VARIÉES
Croque-Monsieur
HAMBURGERS
Andouillette AAAAA
CONFIT DE CANARD
Bavette à l'échalote
SAUMON
SERVICE
Continu
POUSSEZ
Concert
JAZZ
Le jeudi à 21h
Plat du jour
Cocktails
LE SAINT JEAN

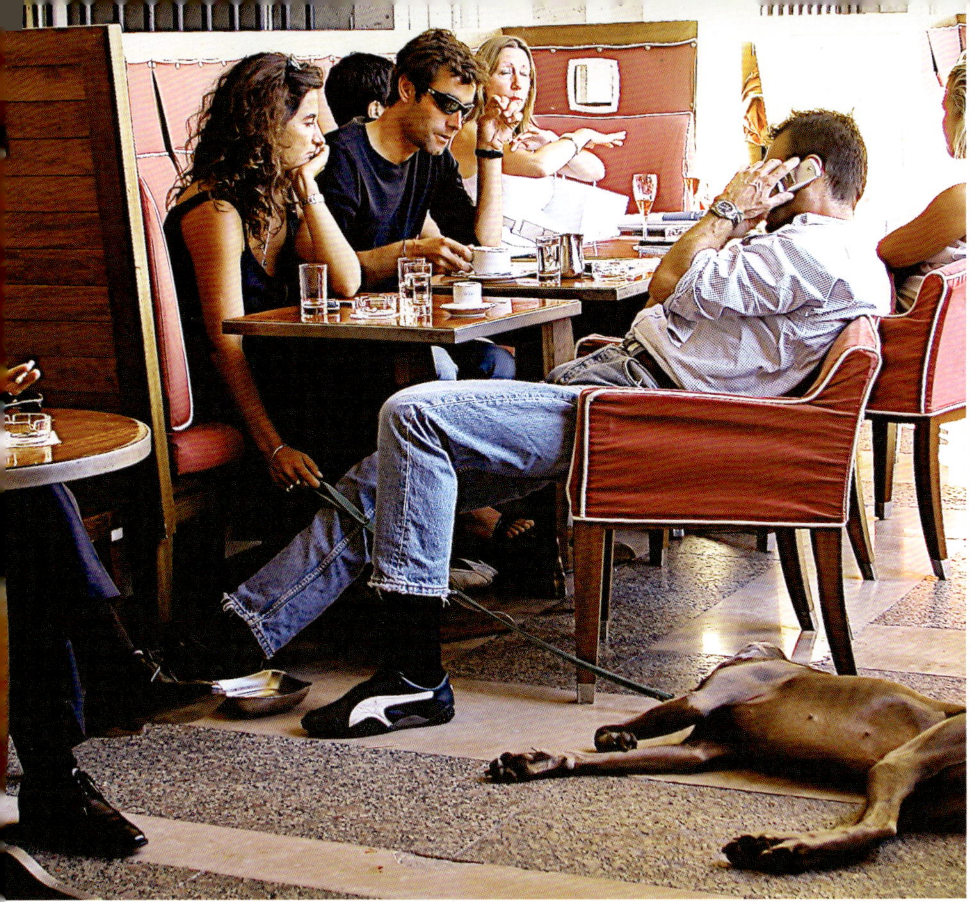

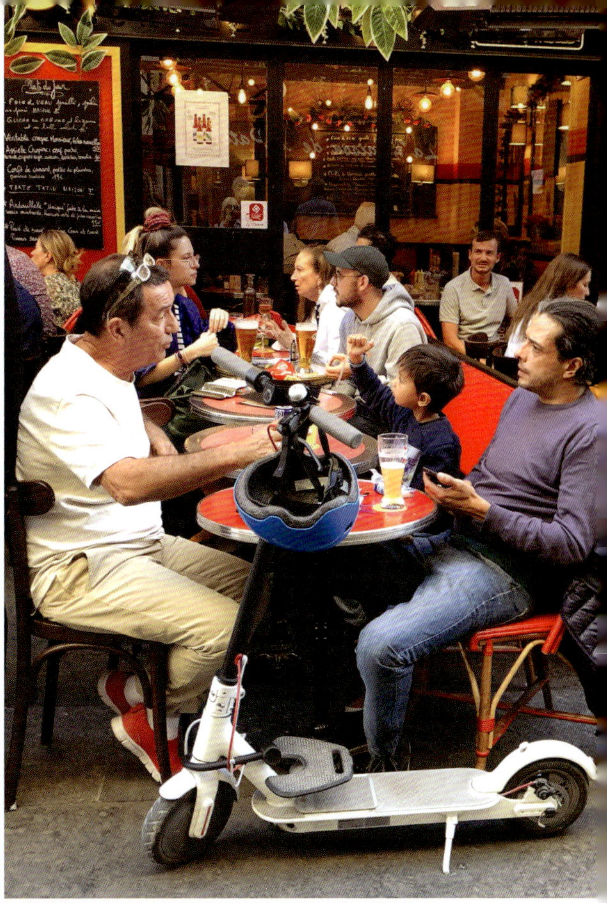

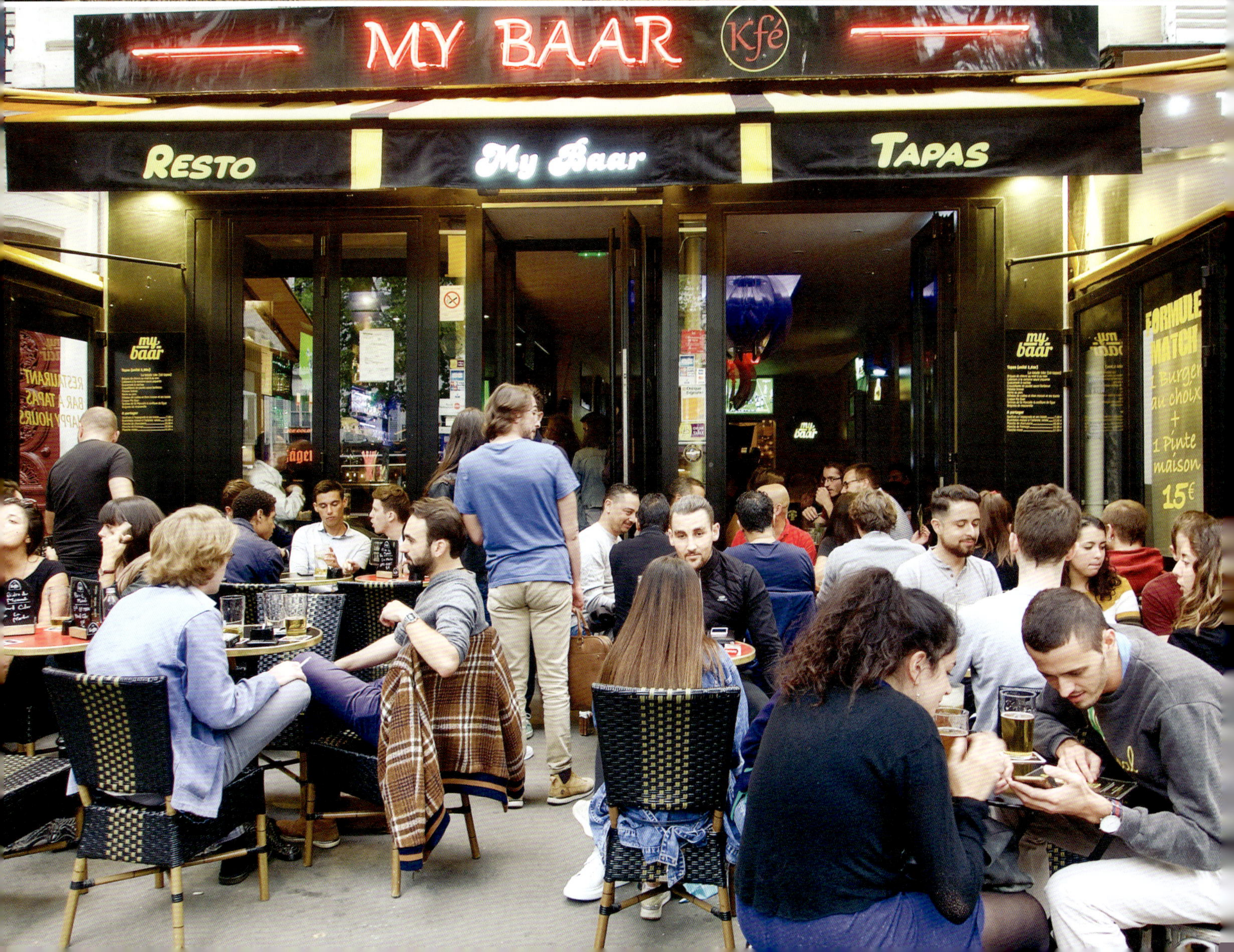
MY BAAR
Kfé
RESTO
My Baar
TAPAS
FORMULE MATCH
1 Burger au choix
+
1 Pinte maison
15€

The Things to Do: From Work to Play

"Paris...is loath to surrender itself to people who are in a hurry; it belongs to the dreamers."

Julian Green, *Paris*

Originating as coffeehouses serving simply coffee and sweets, along with conversation, in the 17th century, these establishments expanded to employ full kitchens with food and beverage service from early morning into the wee hours and so became cafés. Although there has been a proliferation of third-wave coffeehouses in the last couple of decades, the relevance of the traditional café to the Parisian lifestyle has not changed. The classic cliché that the café is the Parisian's living room continues to ring true. The idea of the café as a home away from home originated in the French worker café where the common people gathered before, during, and after work. These differed significantly from the elegant bourgeois cafés where people dressed to the nines and arrived to see and be seen. No matter the style then or now, a lot happens in the daily life of a café. There is a natural flow from early morning to late at night, of people reading newspapers and books, meeting and conversing with family, friends, co-workers, and even strangers; people-watching, smoking on terraces, playing games, working on laptops, flirting during a romantic rendezvous, talking and texting on smartphones, and daydreaming, always daydreaming.

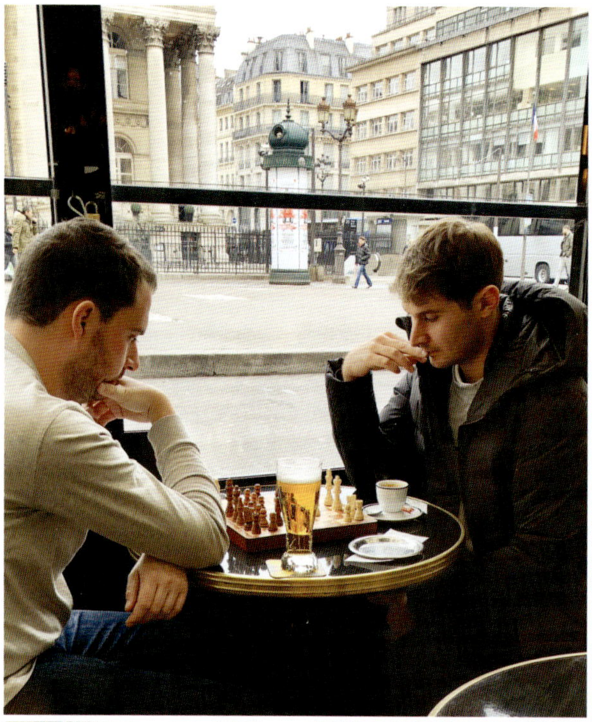

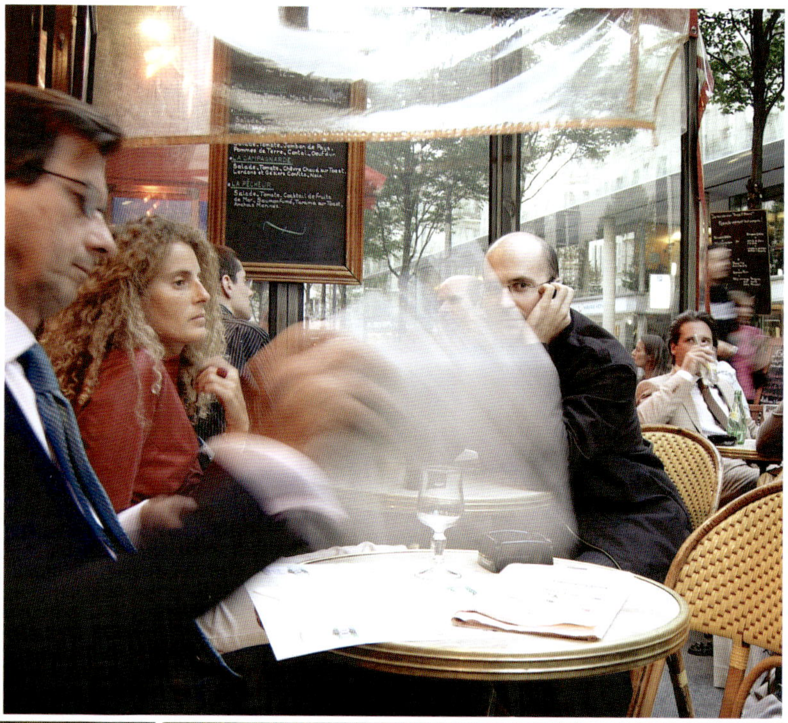

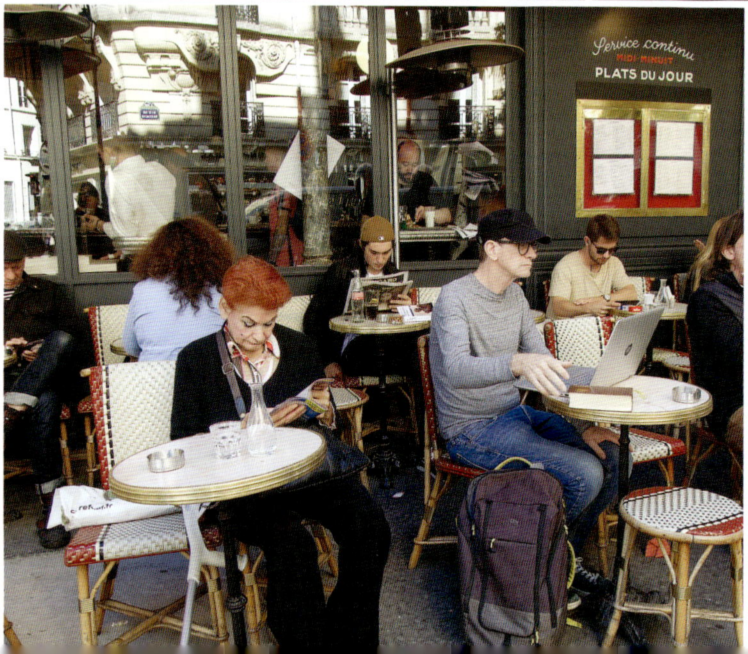

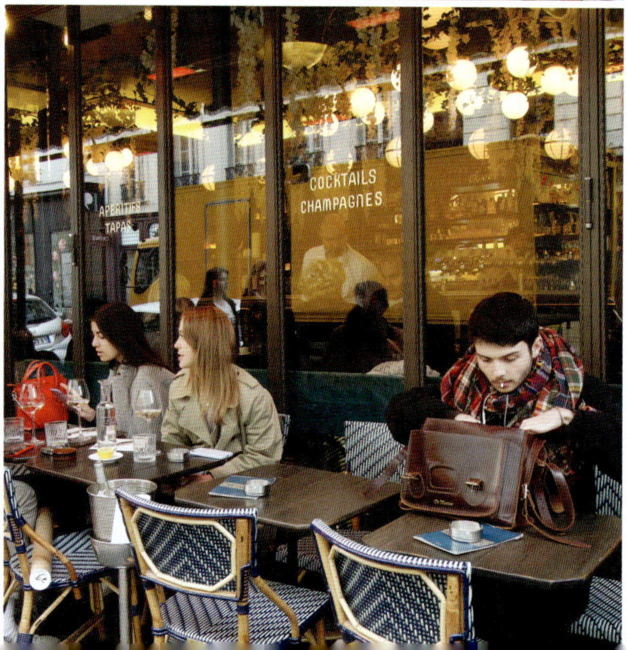

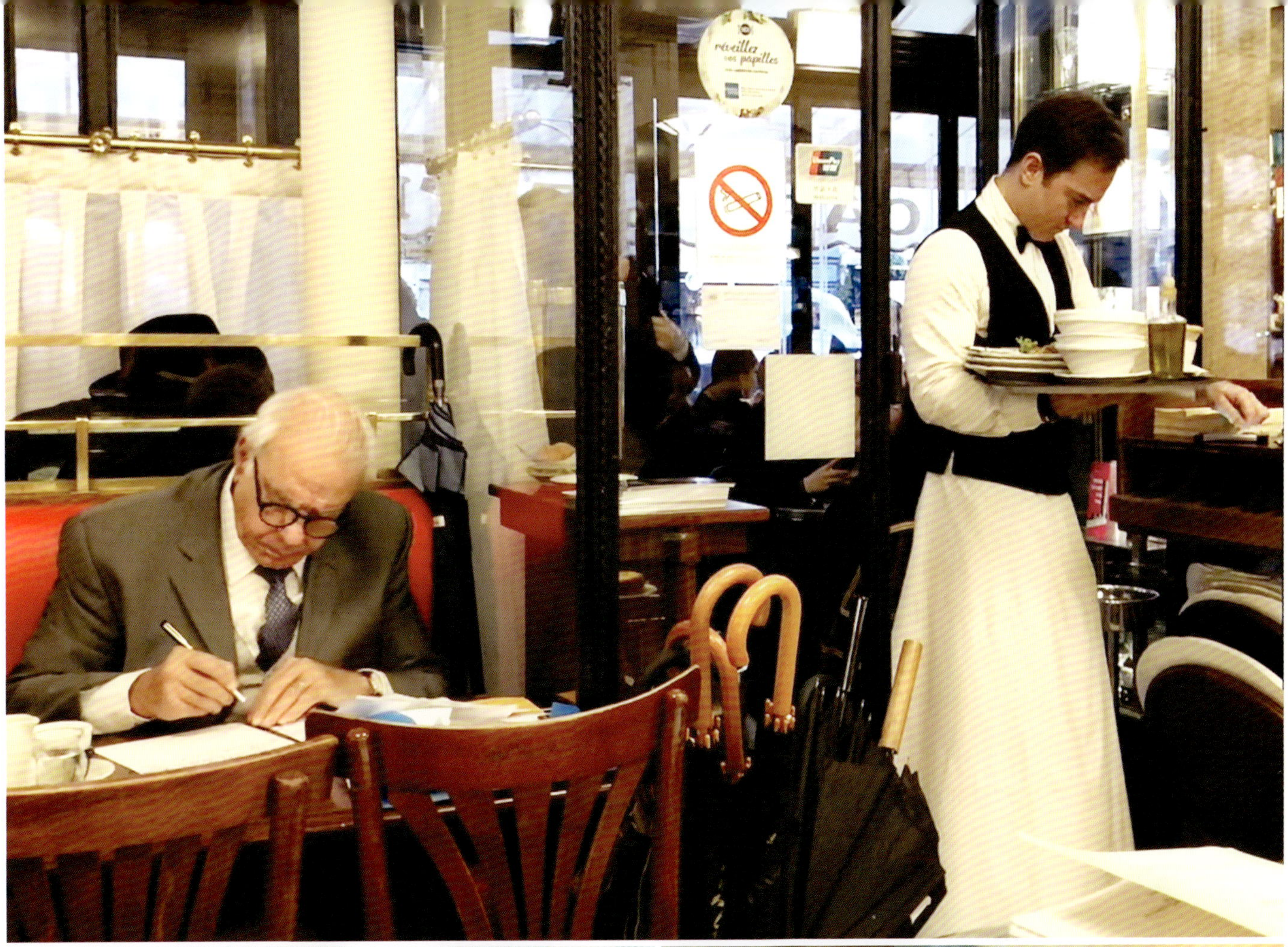

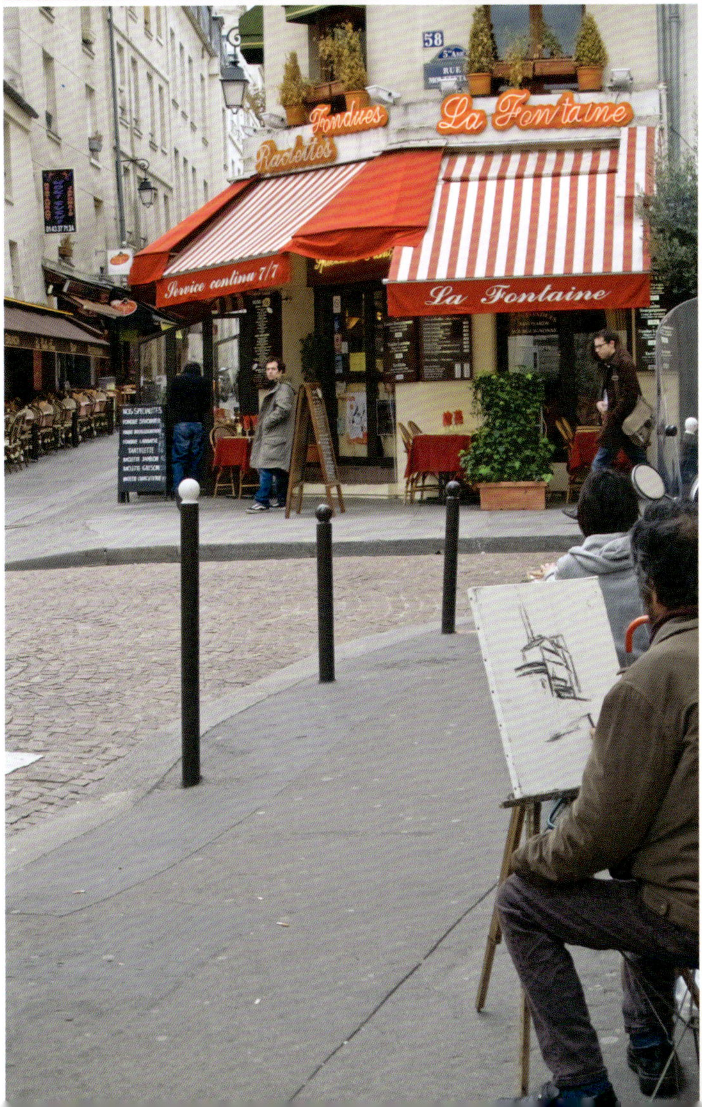
Fondues
La Fontaine
Raclettes
Service continu 7/7
La Fontaine

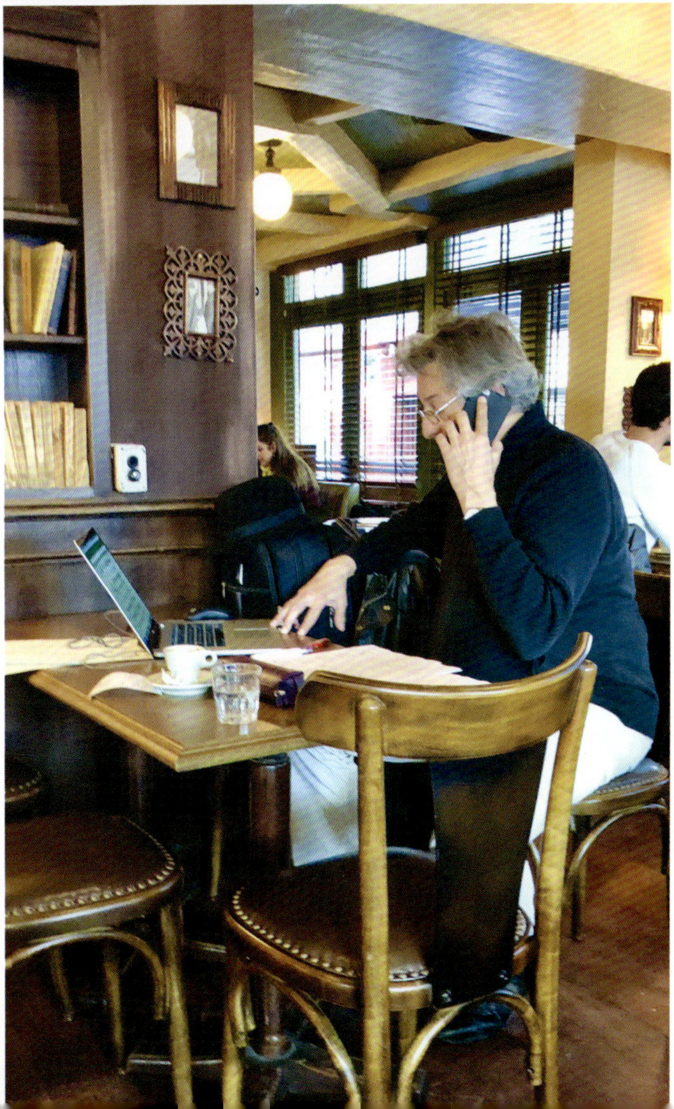

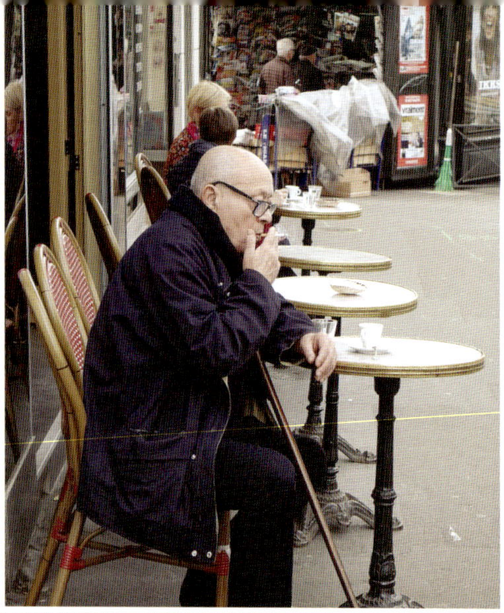

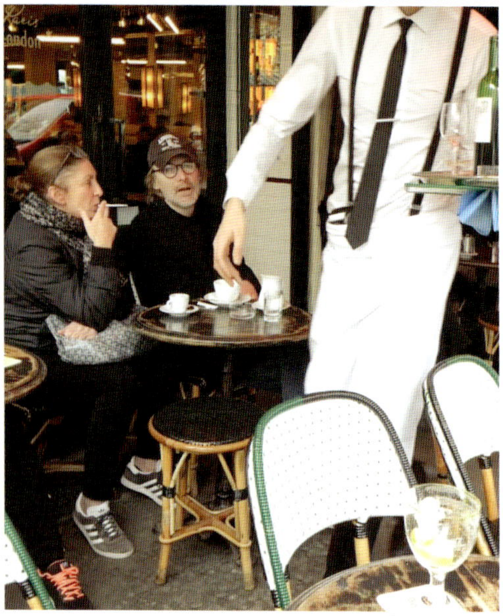

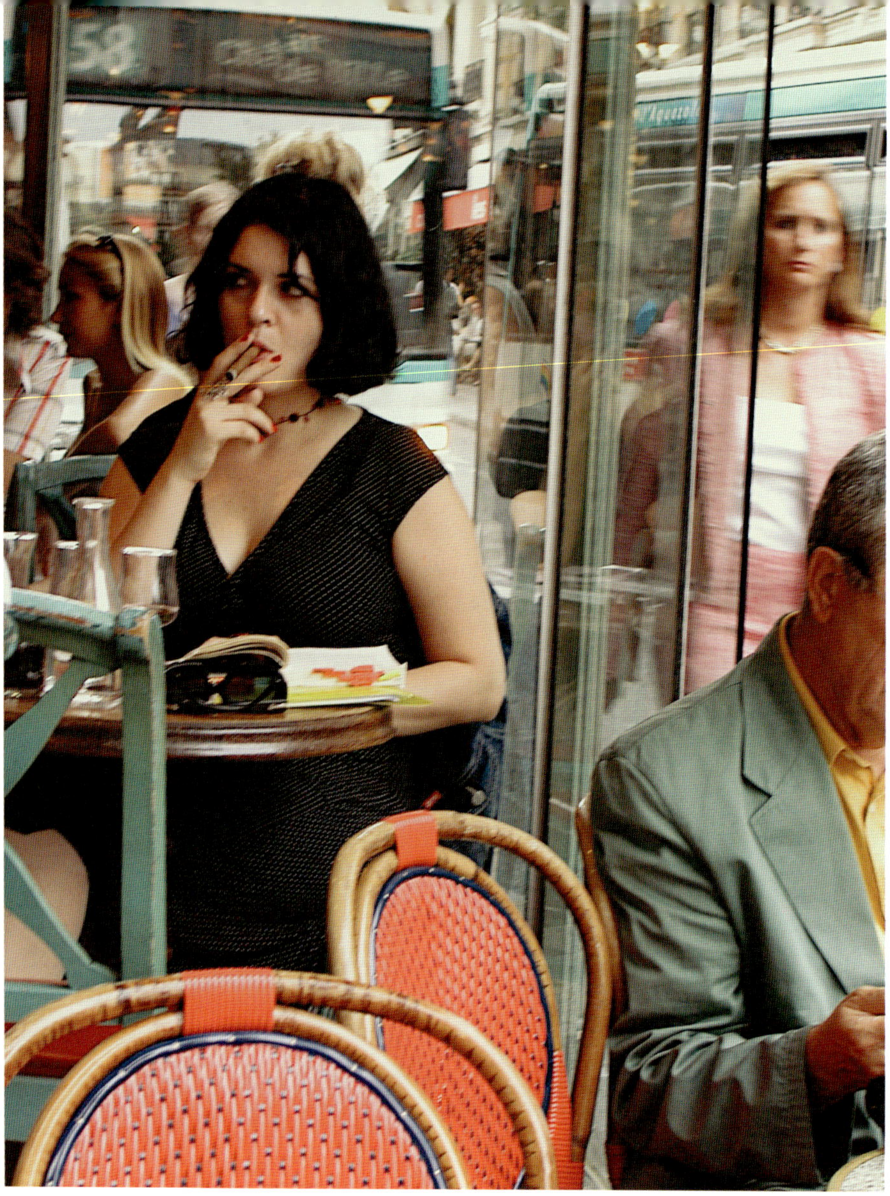

While smoking was banned in enclosed public places in 2006, it is still allowed on café terraces. Yes, on the terraces, in the streets, and apartments, smoking endures; vaping as well.

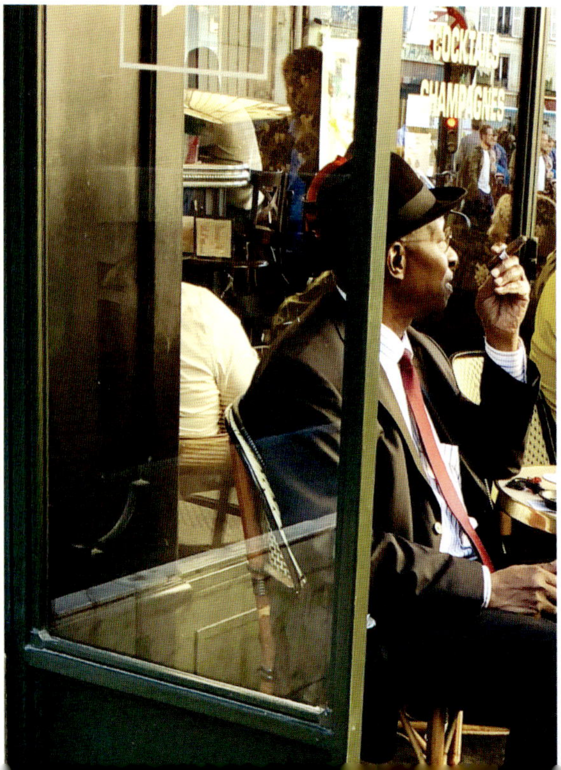

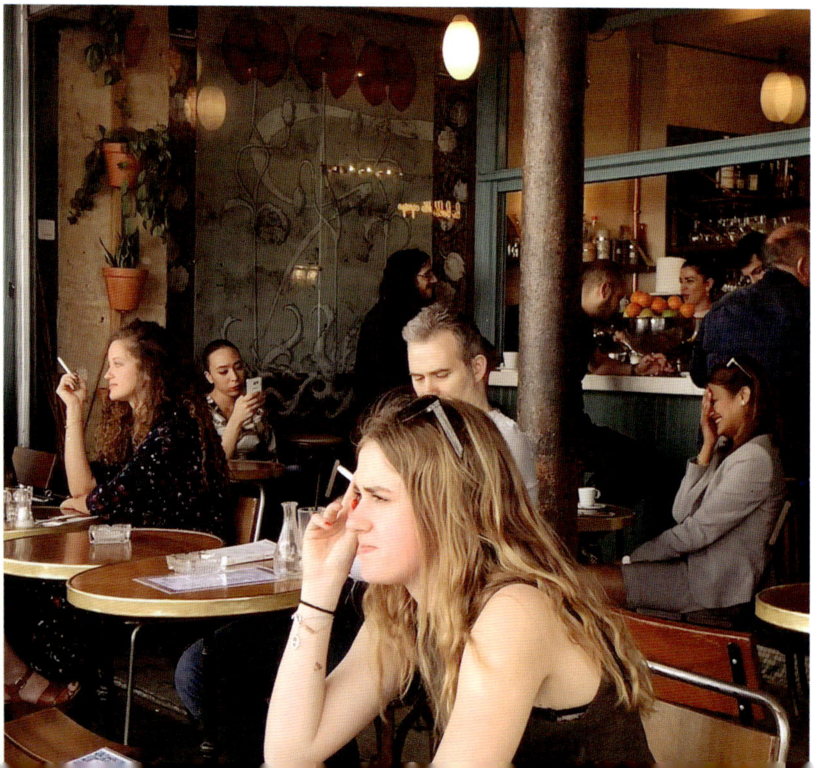

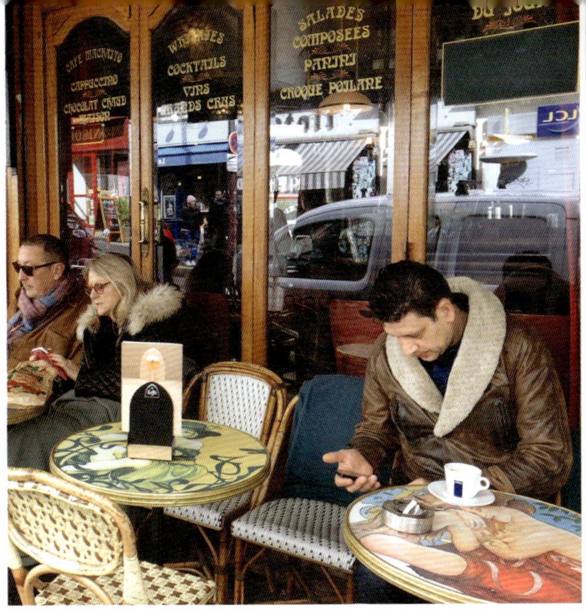
CAFE MACHIATO
CAPPUCCINO
CHOCOLAT CHAUD
COCKTAILS
VINS
SALADES
COMPOSEES
PANINI
CROQUE POILANE
LCL
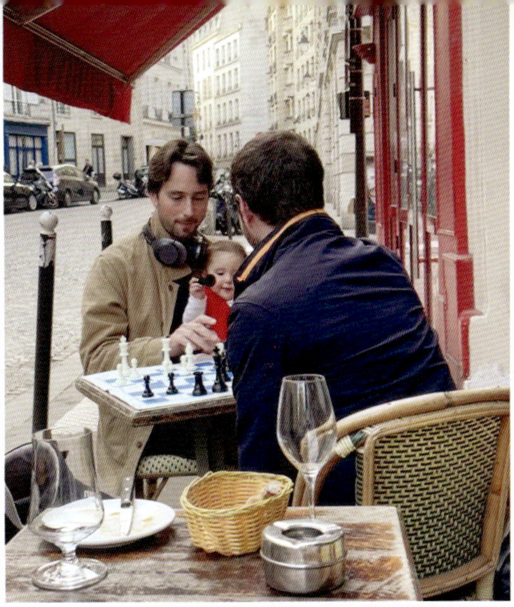
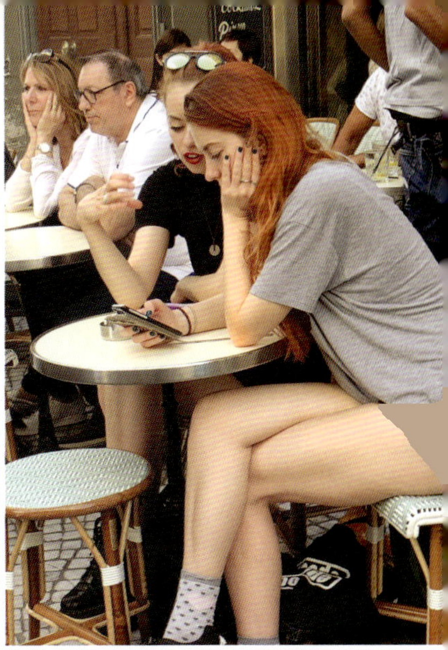
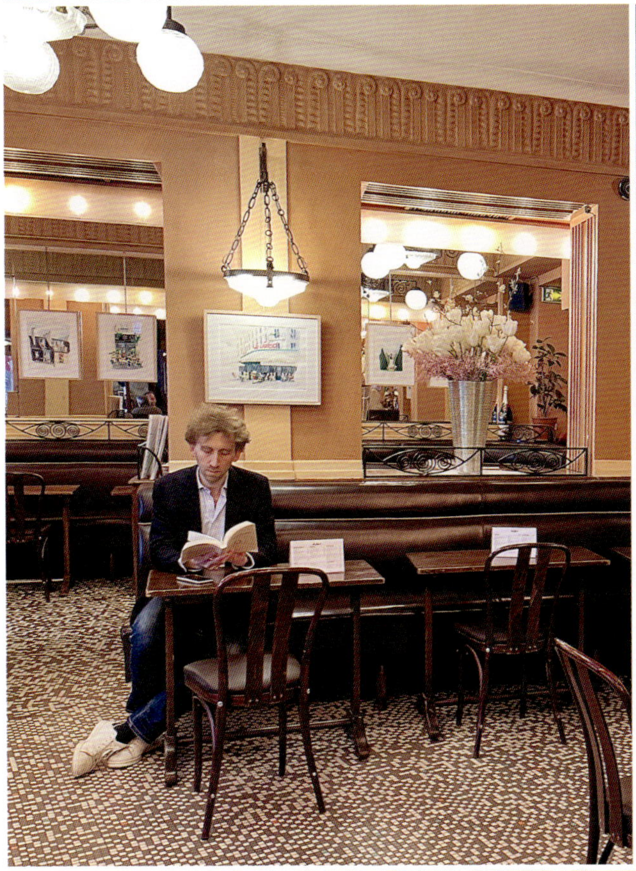
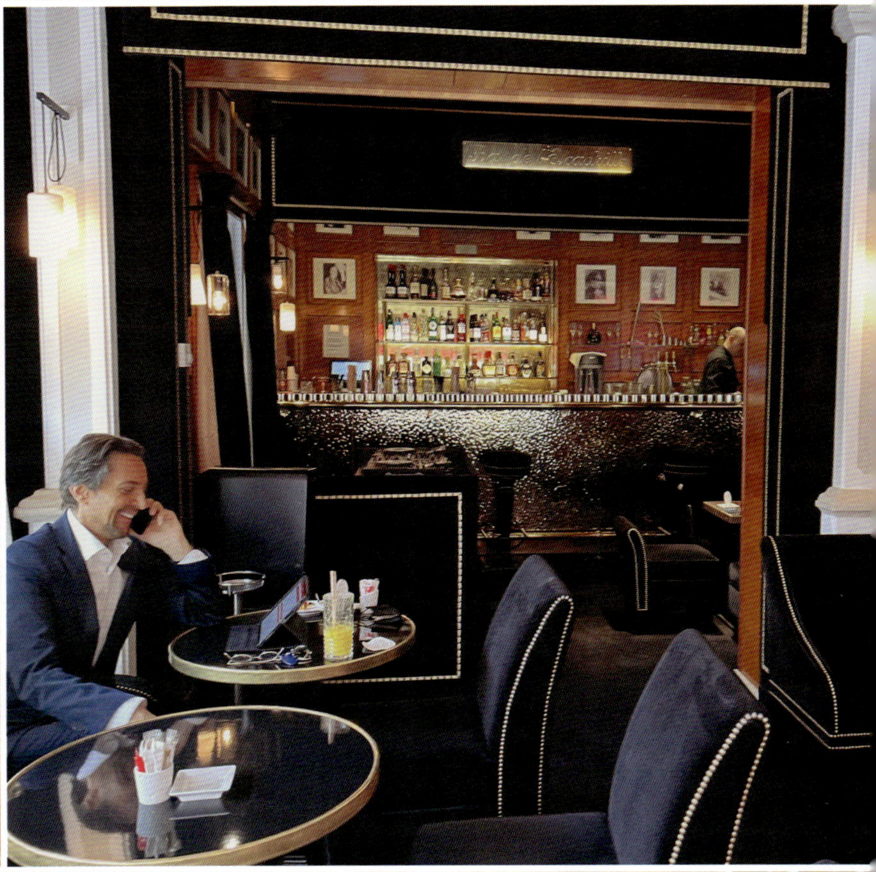
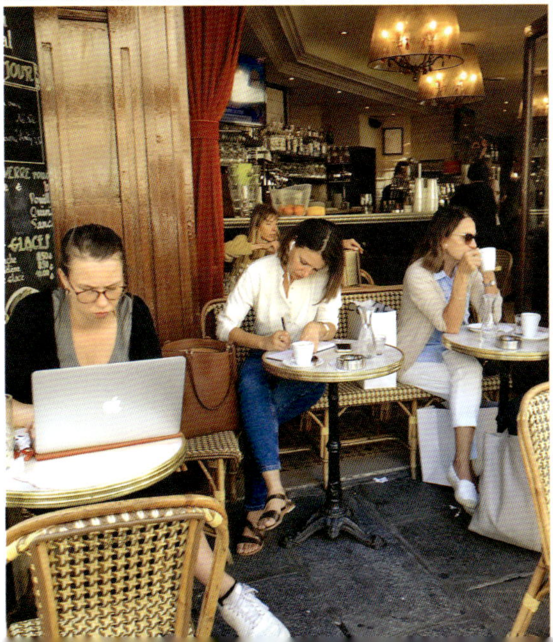
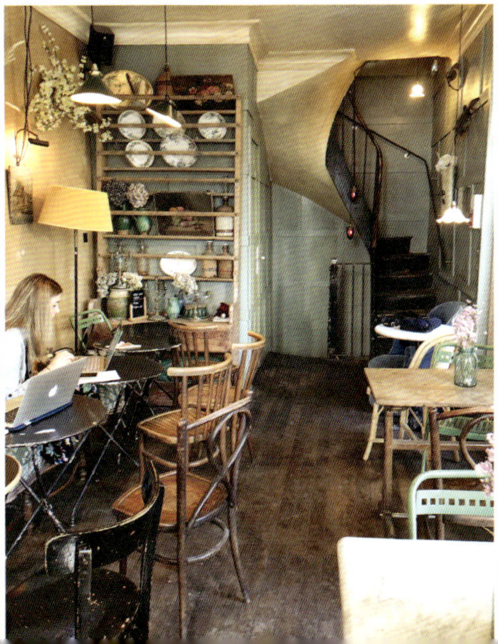
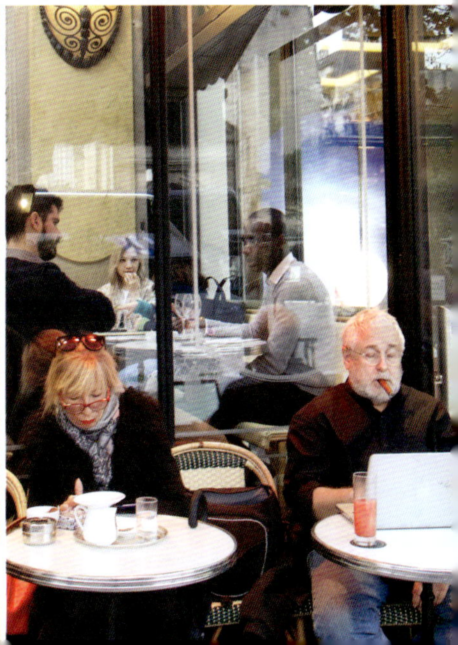

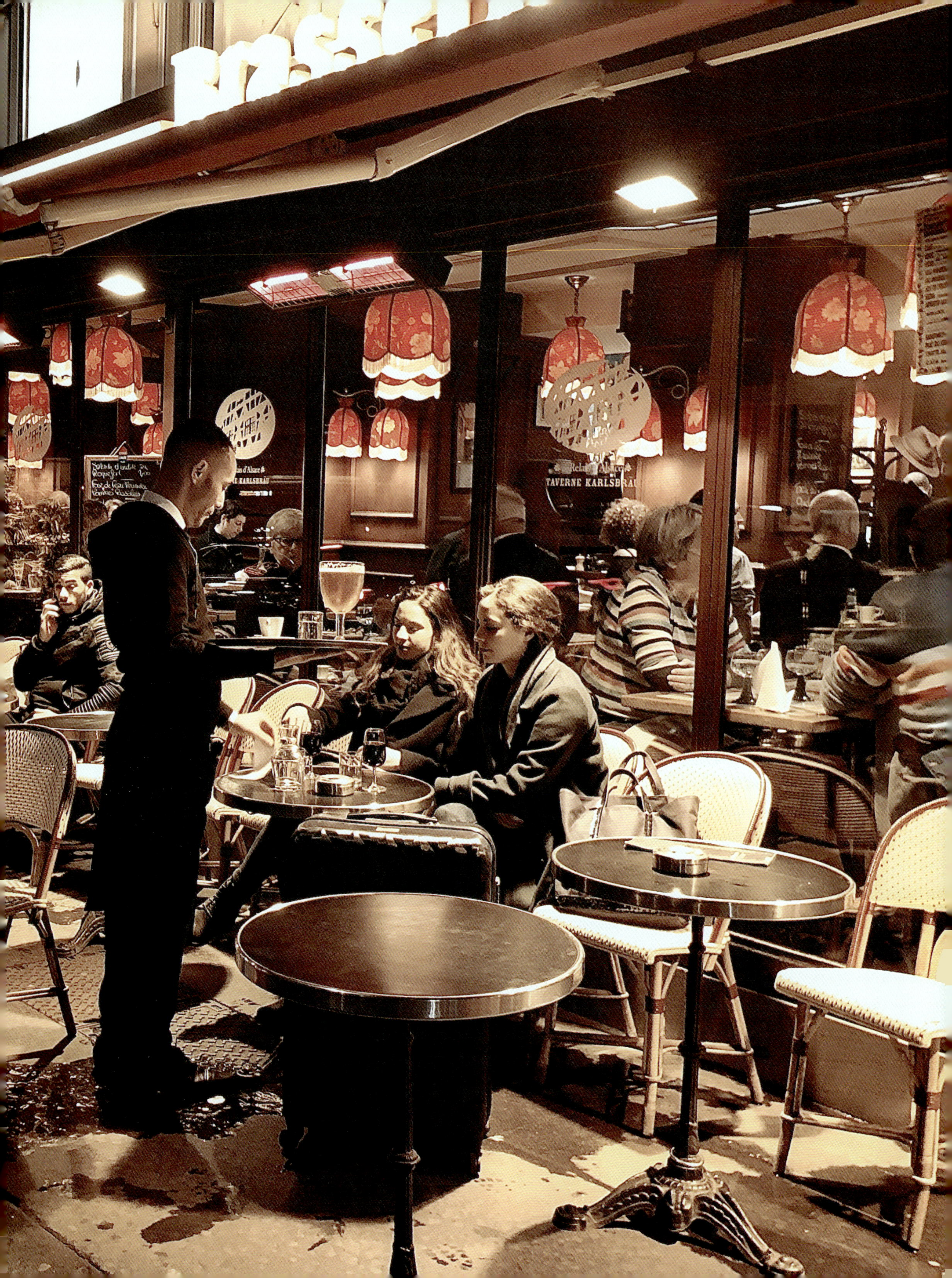
TAVERNE KARLSBRAU

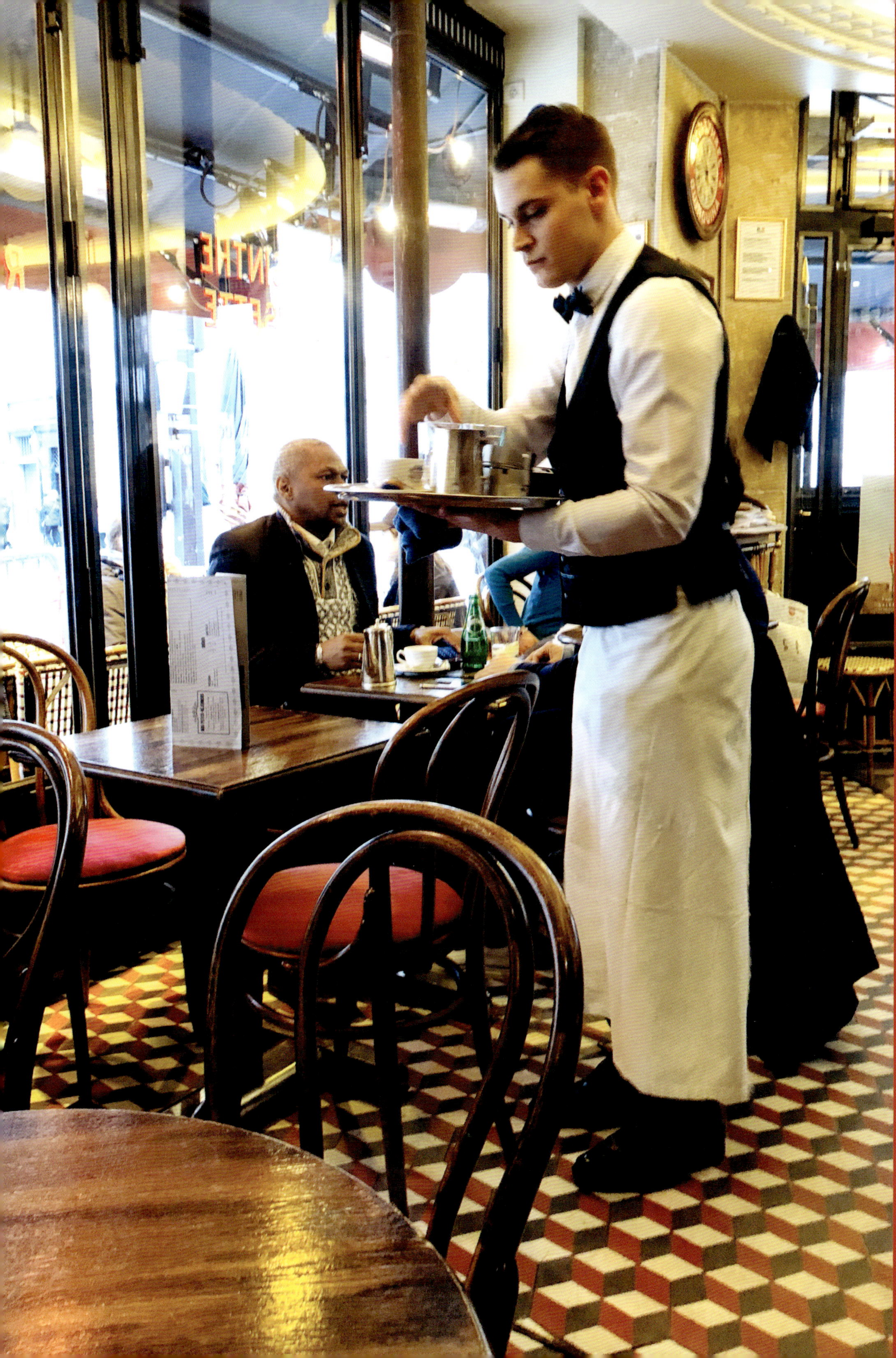

PART 5 The People Who Make Café Society

The Patrons

"What are they going to look for on the moon? I bet there isn't even a Bistro up there."
(from a Maurice Chevalier song)

Long a gathering place of a diverse clientele that includes artists, writers, intellectuals, students, lovers, and revolutionaries, the French café is an animated hangout. The vibe can be bohemian, bobo, chic, working-class, business-suited, snob, artistic, historic, or trendy. Locals, regulars, expats, tourists, couples, singles, colorful misfits, groups of friends, children, and animals all are welcome in the democratic cafés and bistros of Paris. Come on in. Or linger on the terrace. Not only is everyone welcome, but anything can happen and everything does in a Parisian café, including genuine, long conversations where you can sort out or share life or work issues and events. The lost art of conversation is to be found in the café.

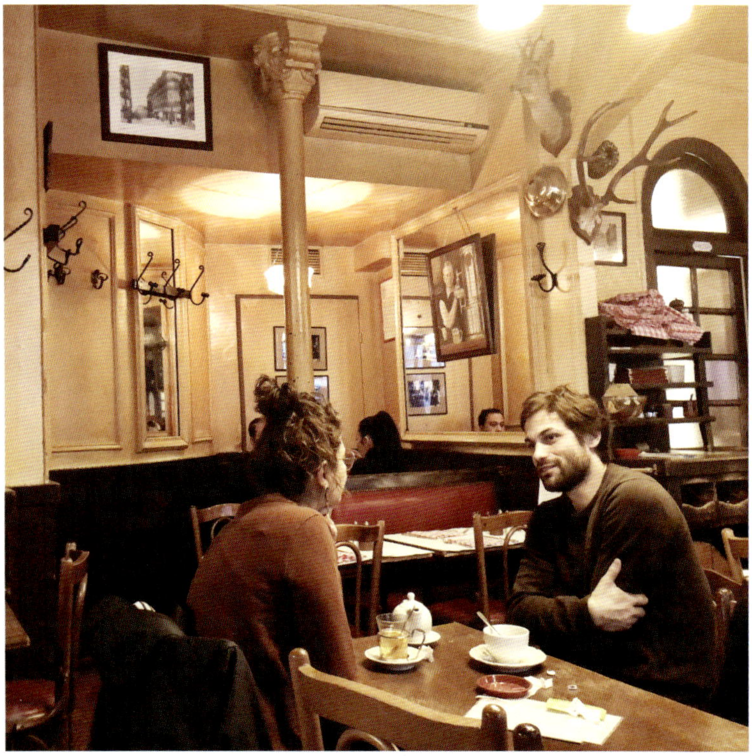

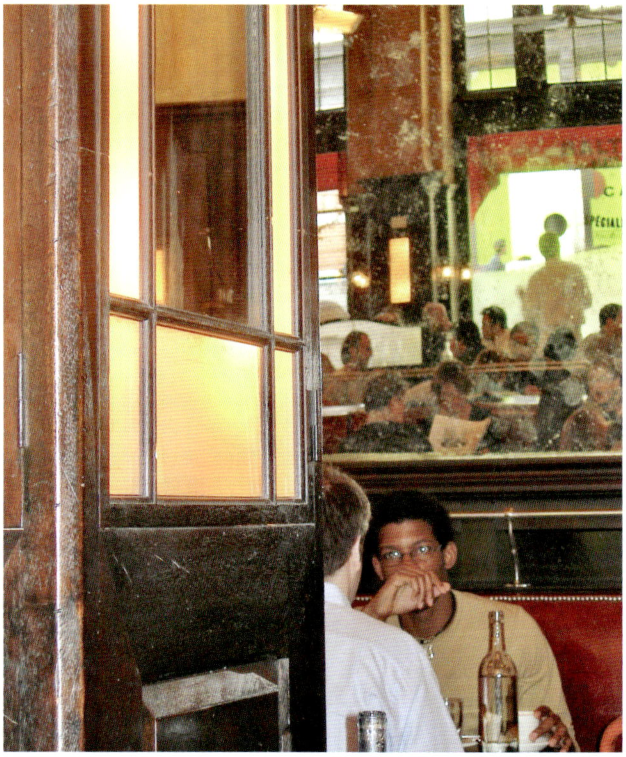

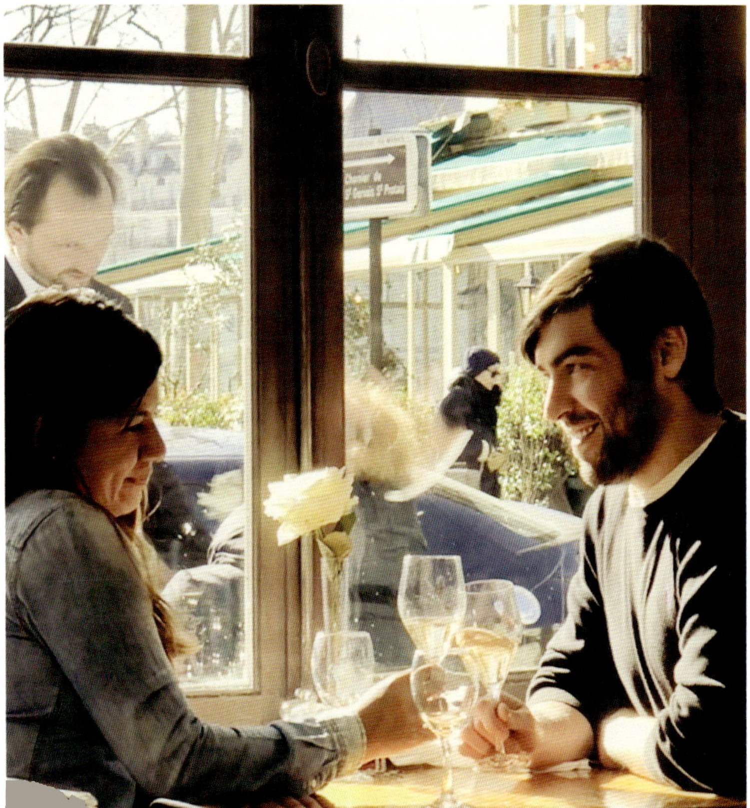

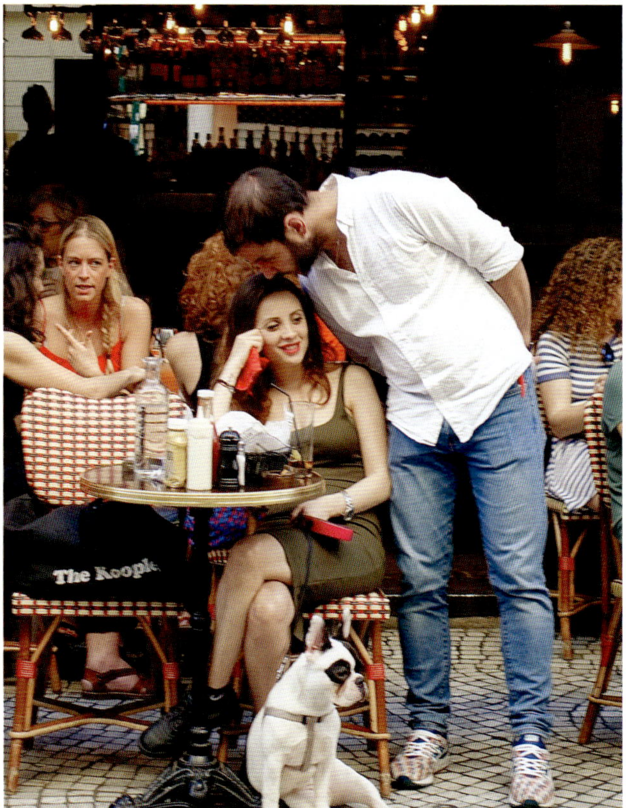

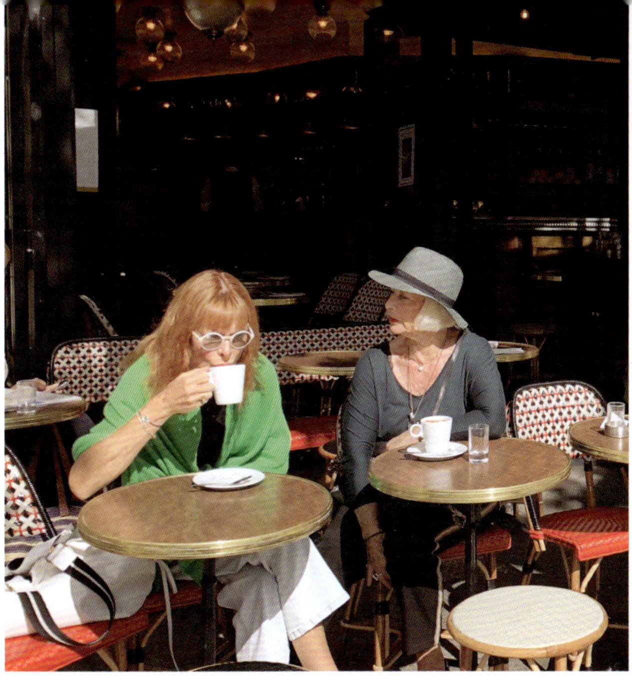

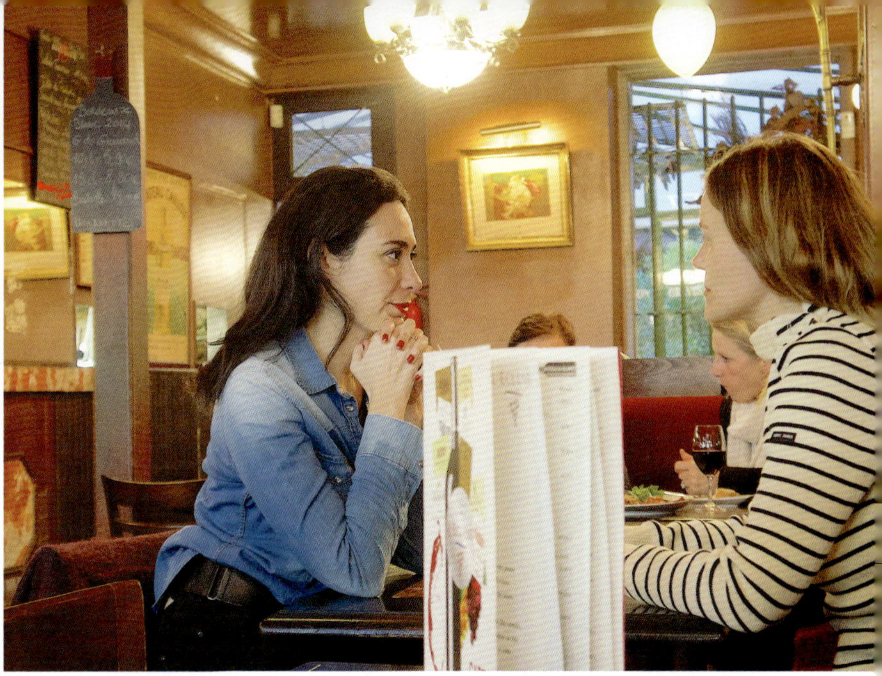

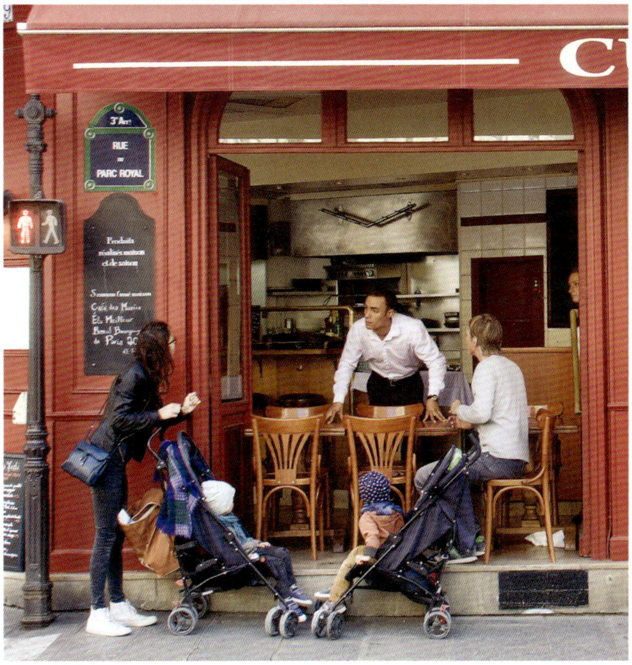
RUE
PARC ROYAL

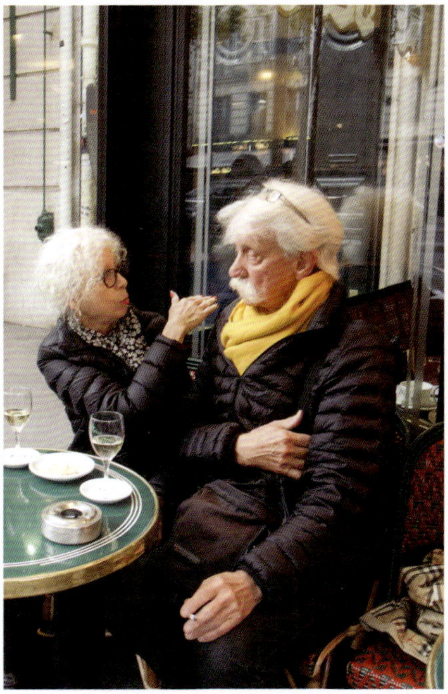

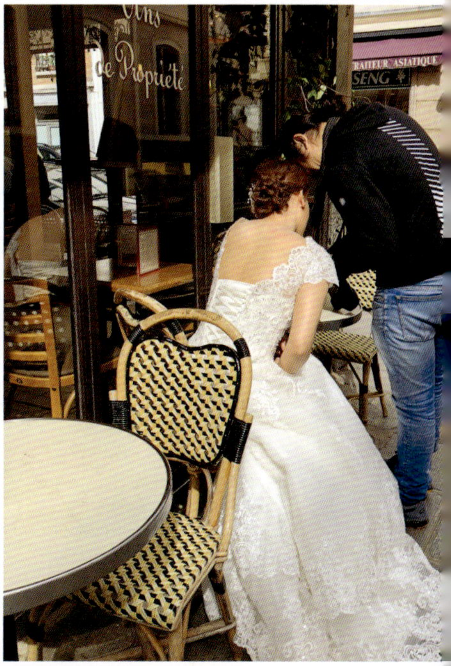
TRAITEUR ASIATIQUE
SENG

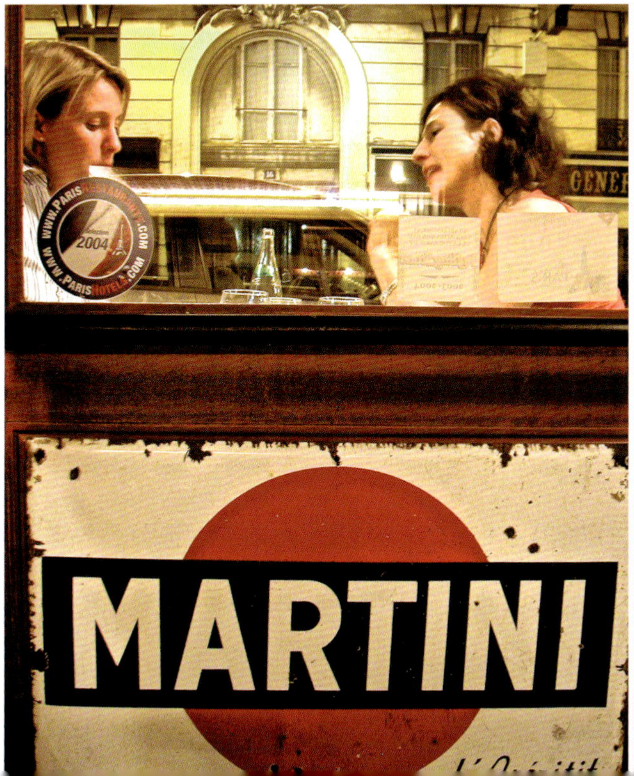
2004
MARTINI

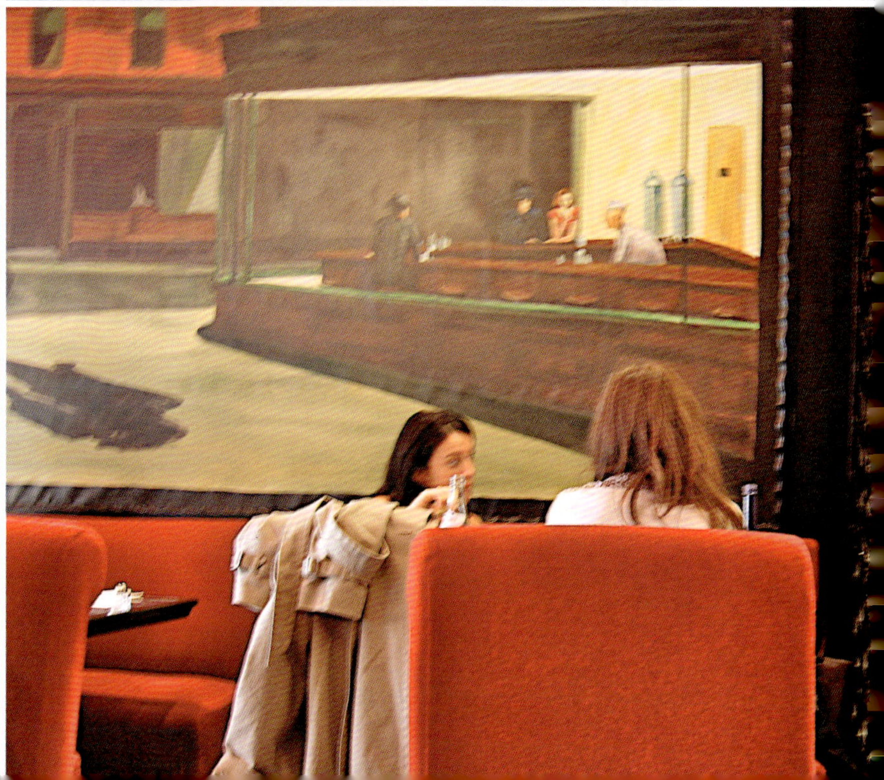

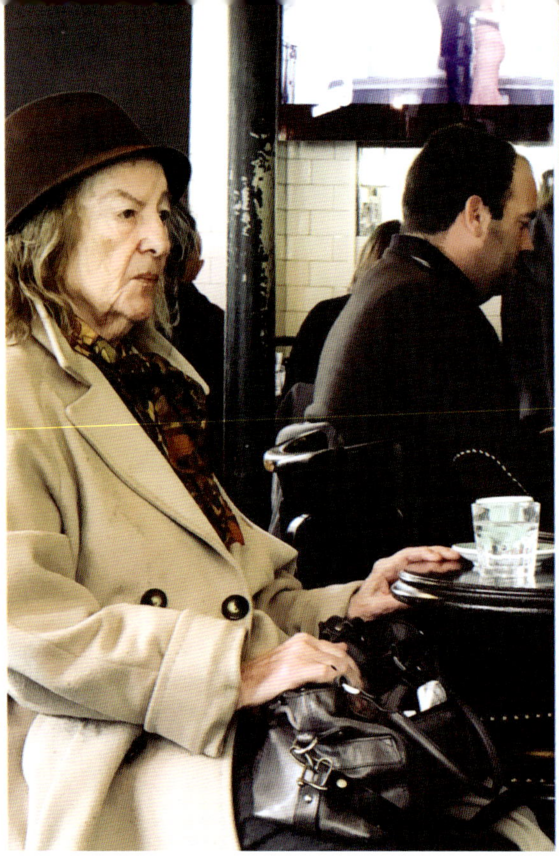

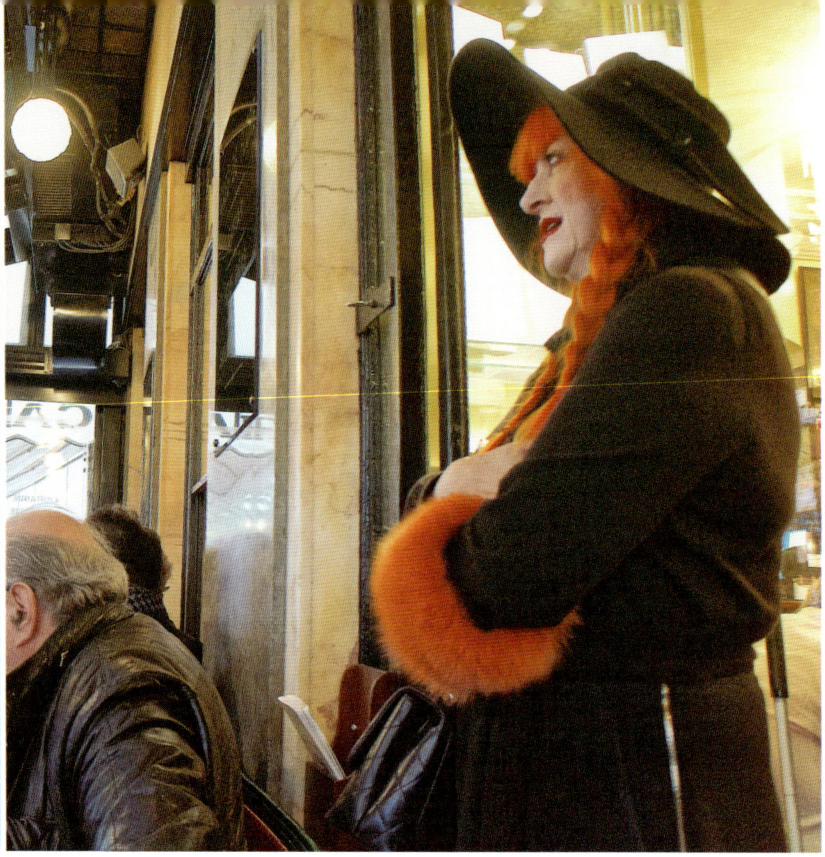

A table for one is never awkward in a Parisian café because everyone feels welcome but private, an observer, a flâneur out in the world, taking time to ponder, to dream, or maybe even to work. Alone, one is never lonely because the tables are close and the waiter, the barman, and the other diners observe and engage. In Paris, it is the café that one hungers for where one can feel at home away from home.

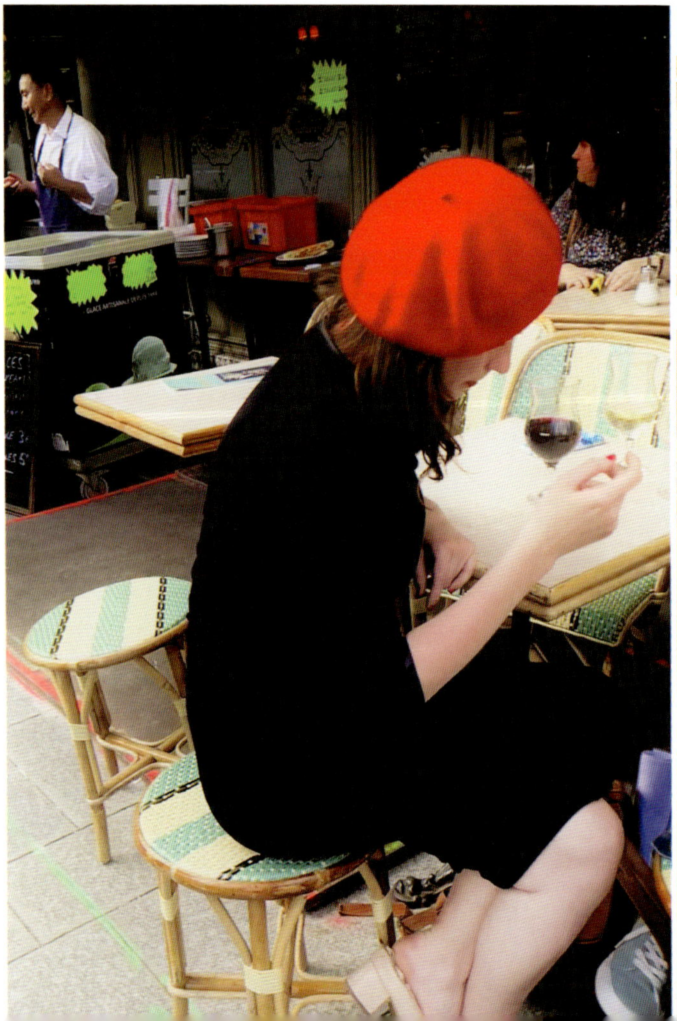

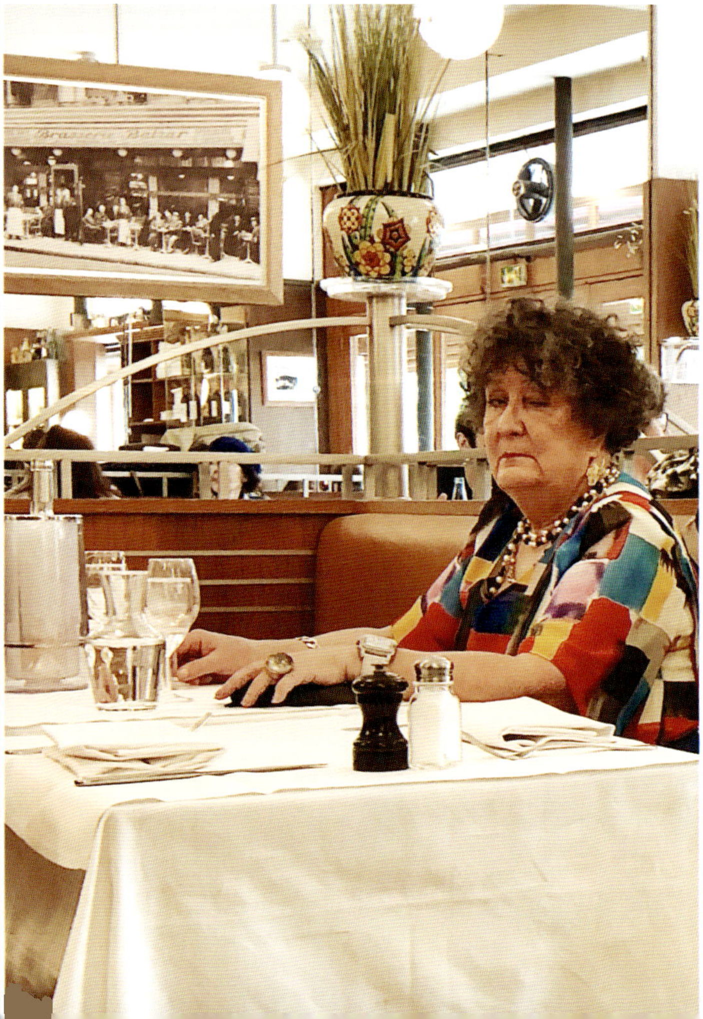

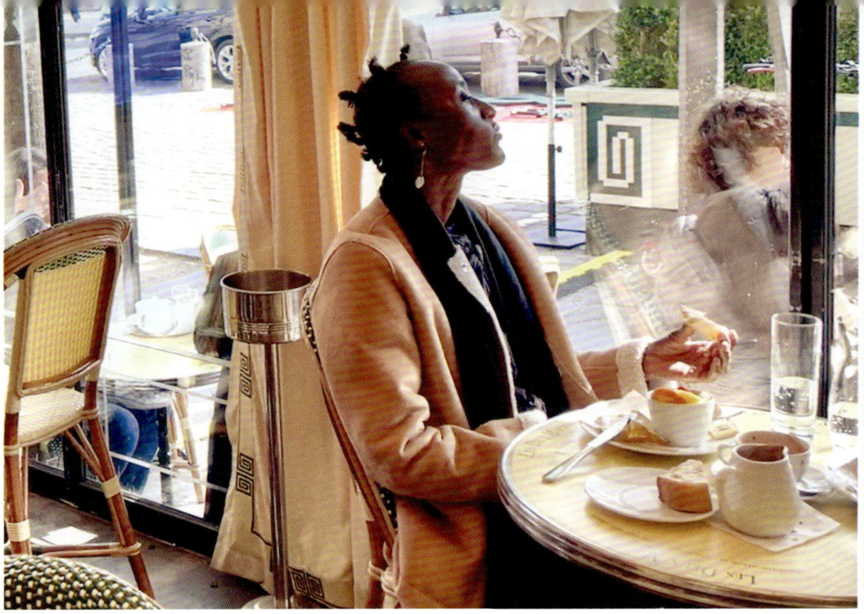
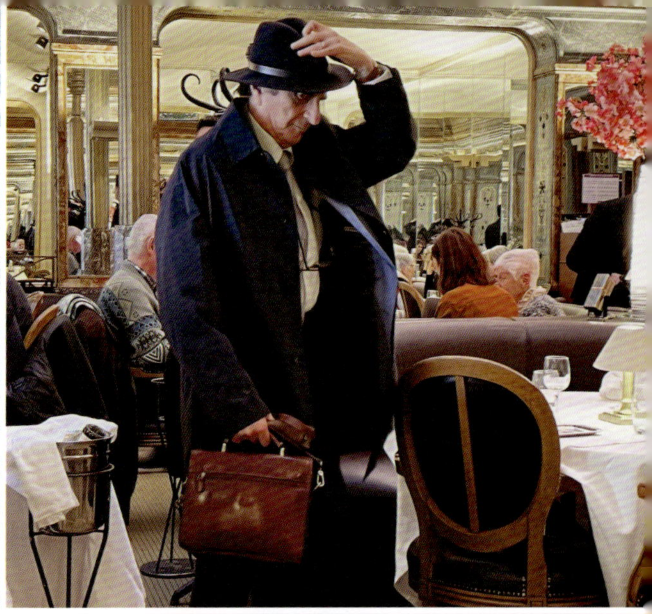
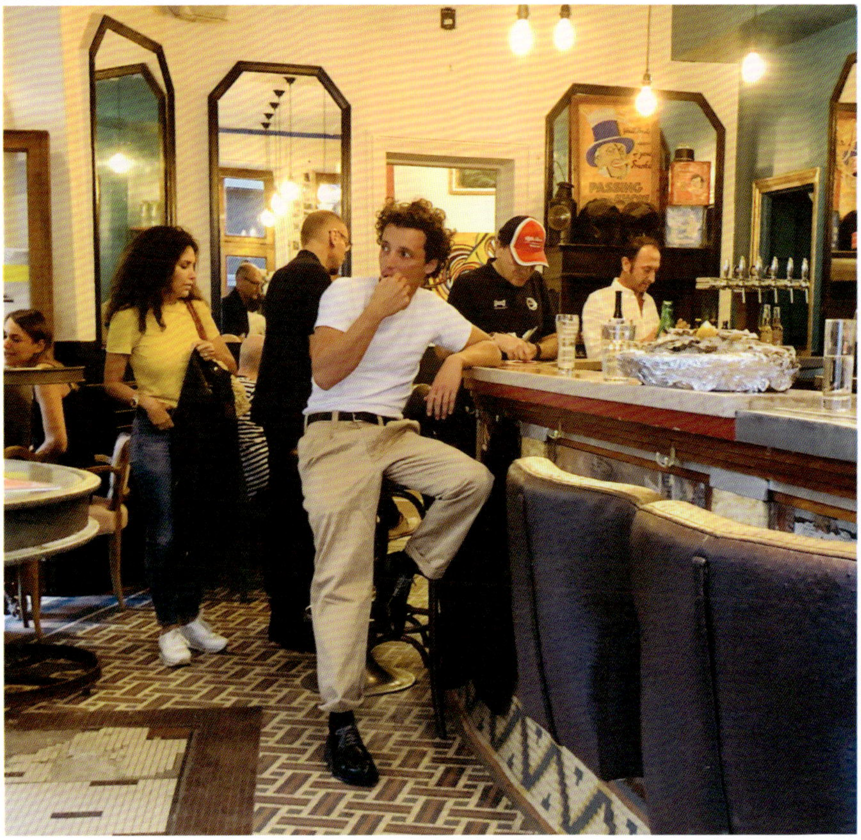
PARKING
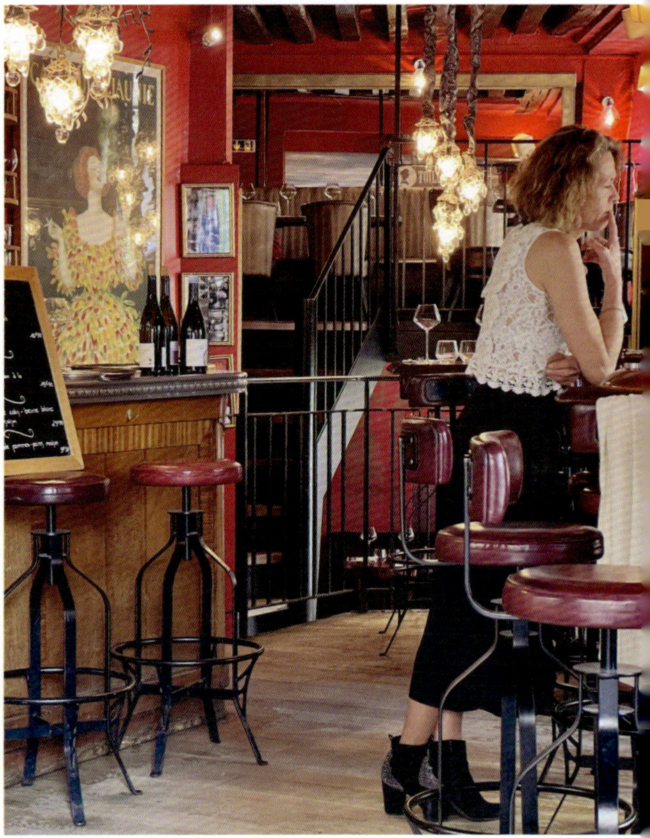
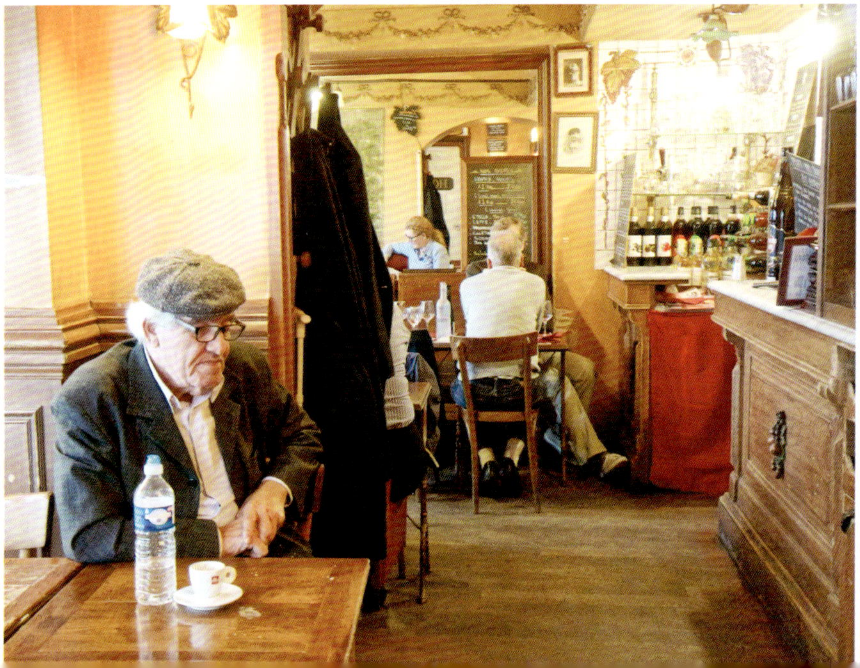
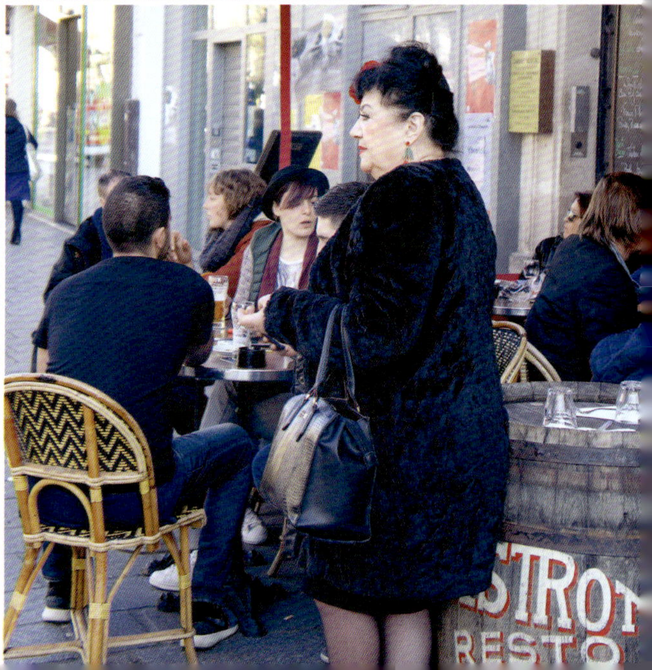

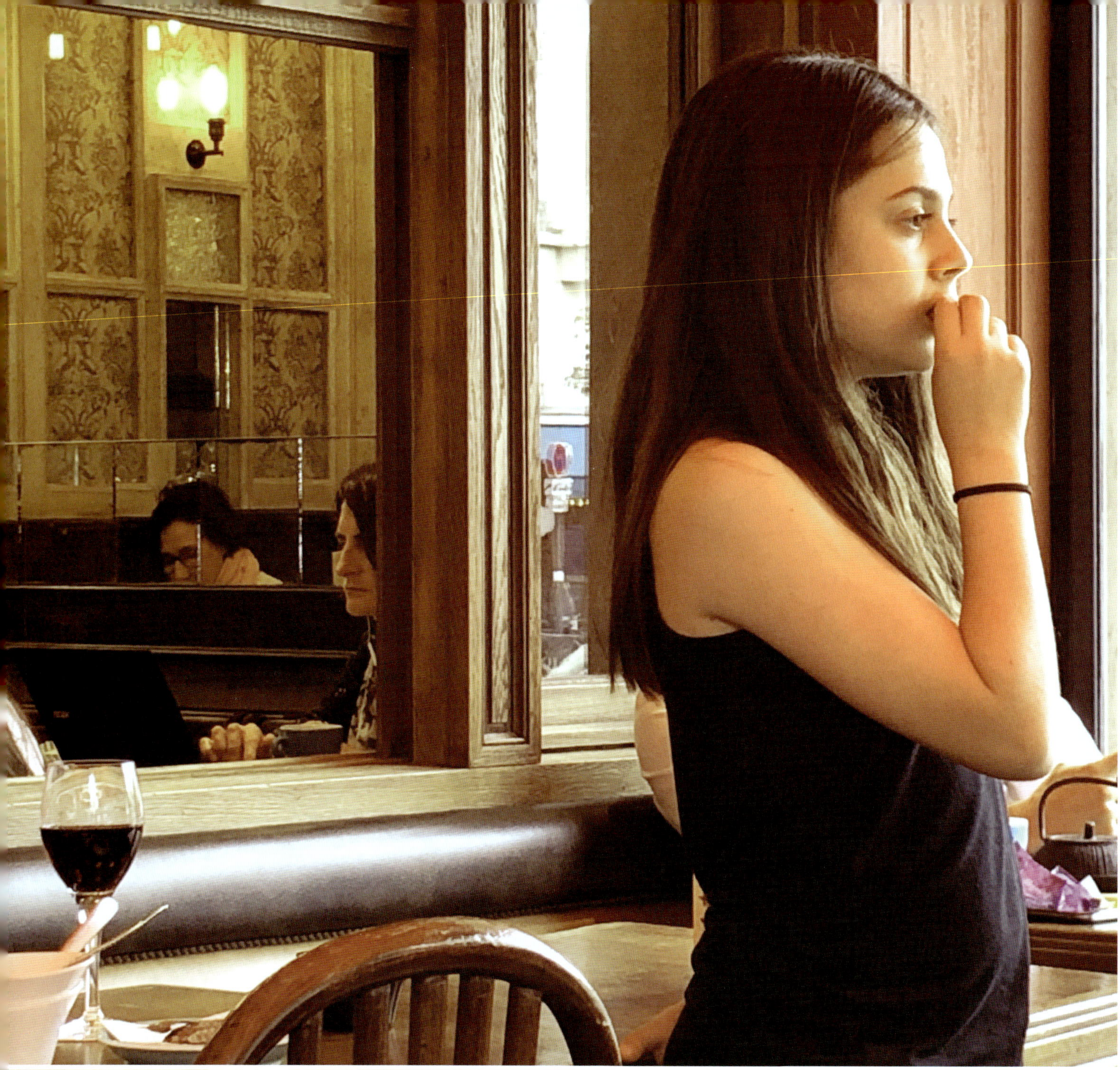

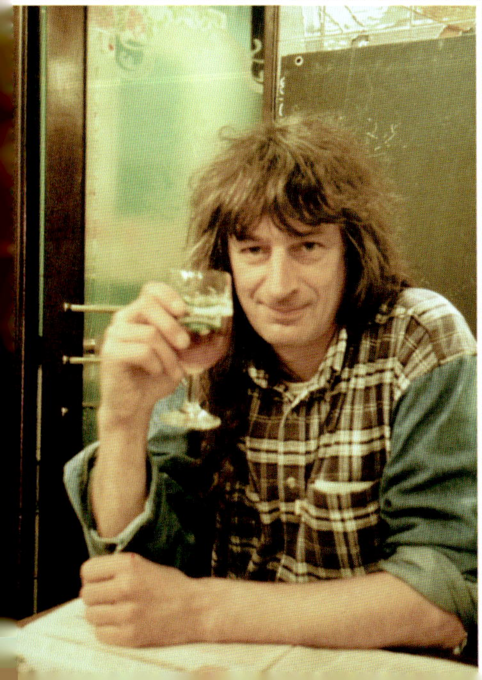

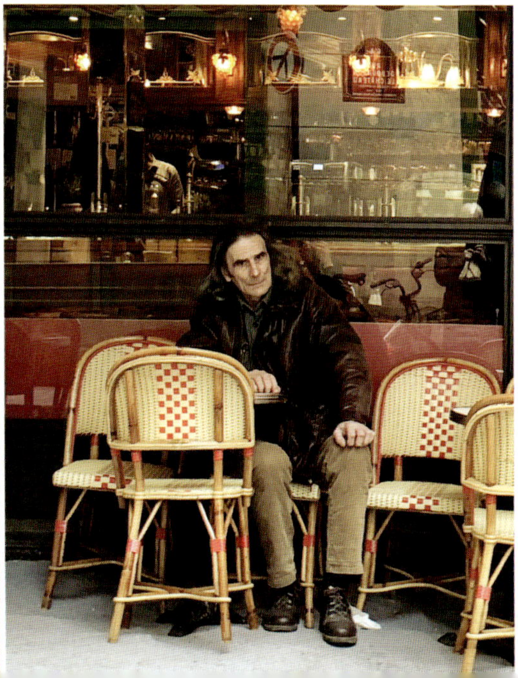

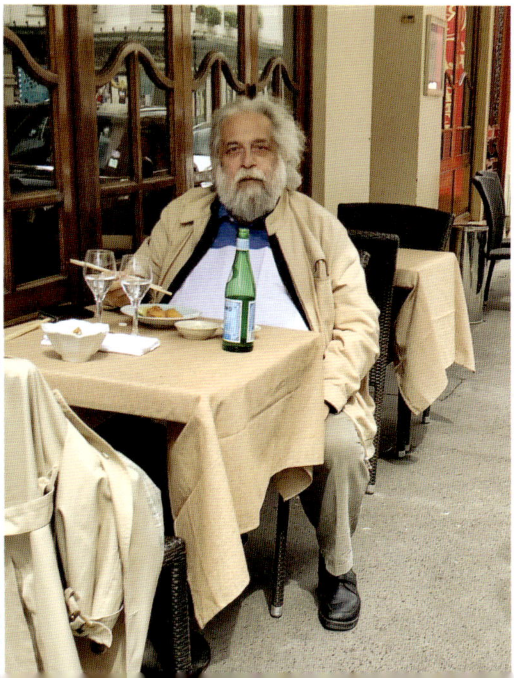

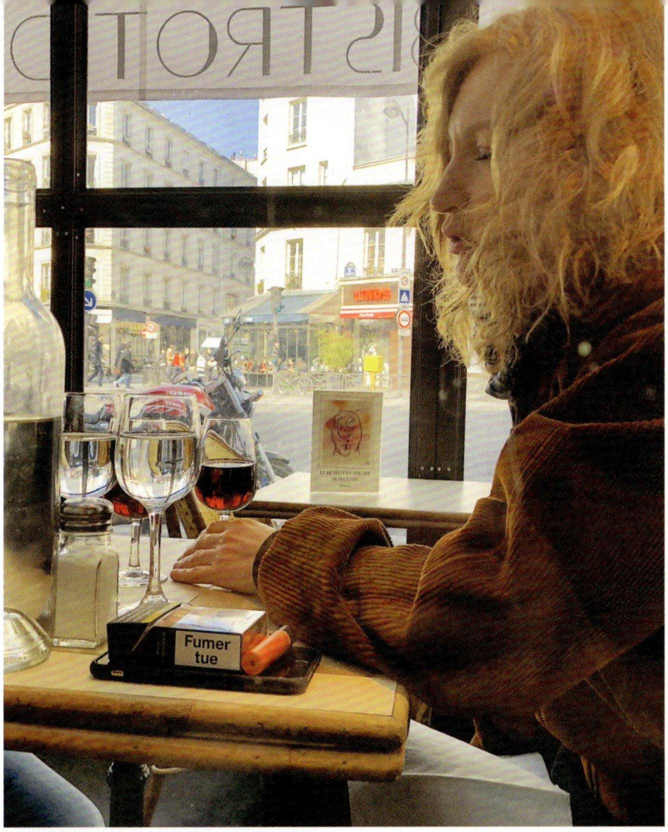
Fumer
tue

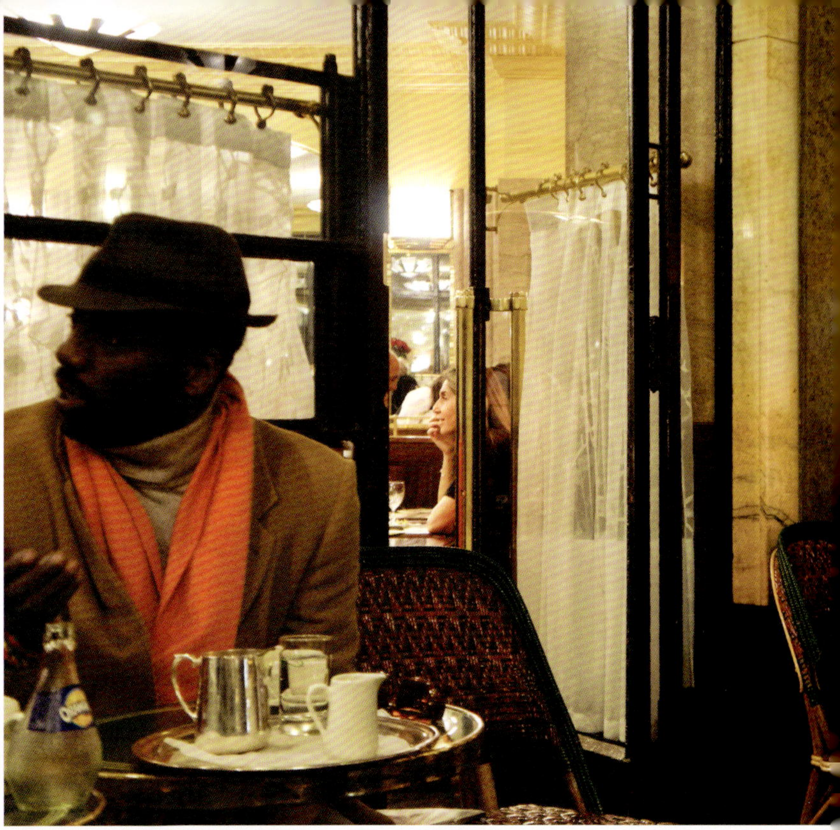

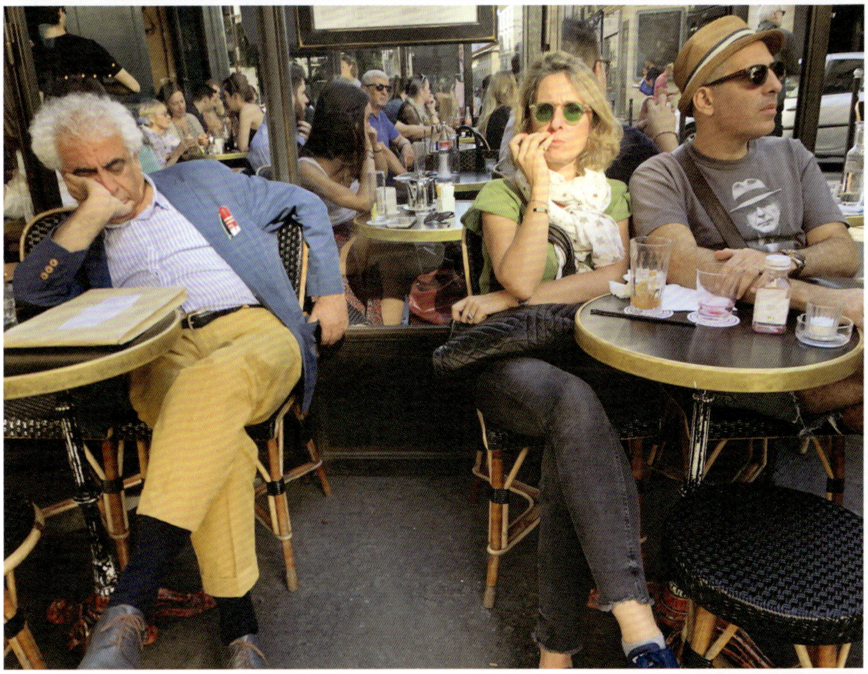

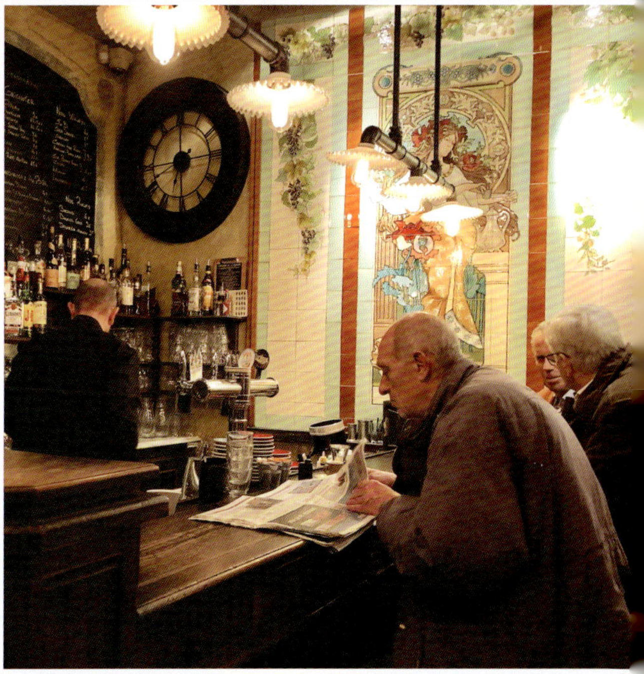

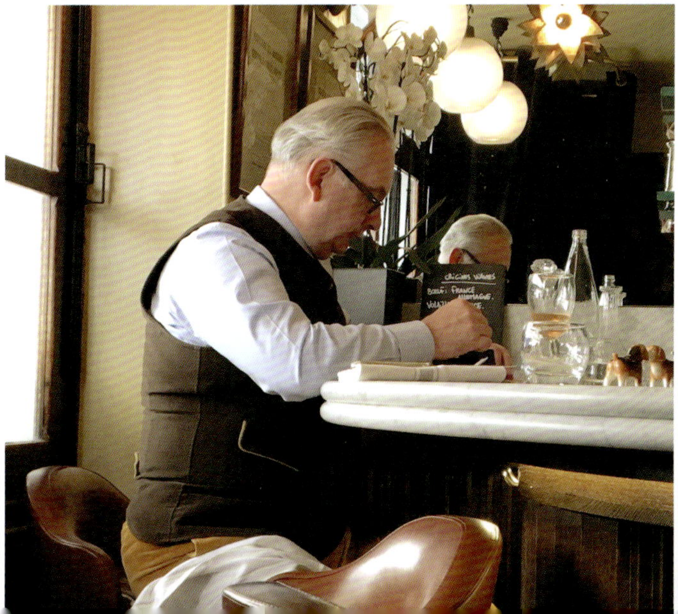

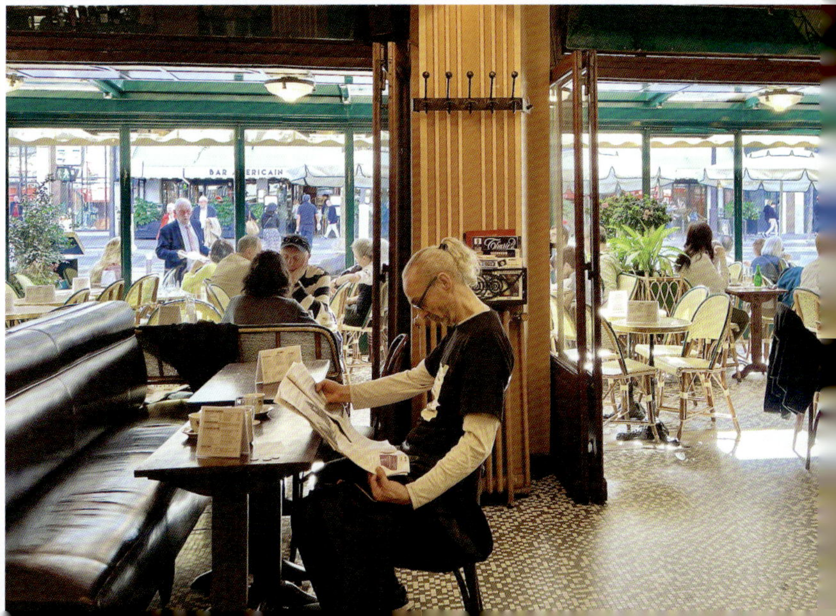

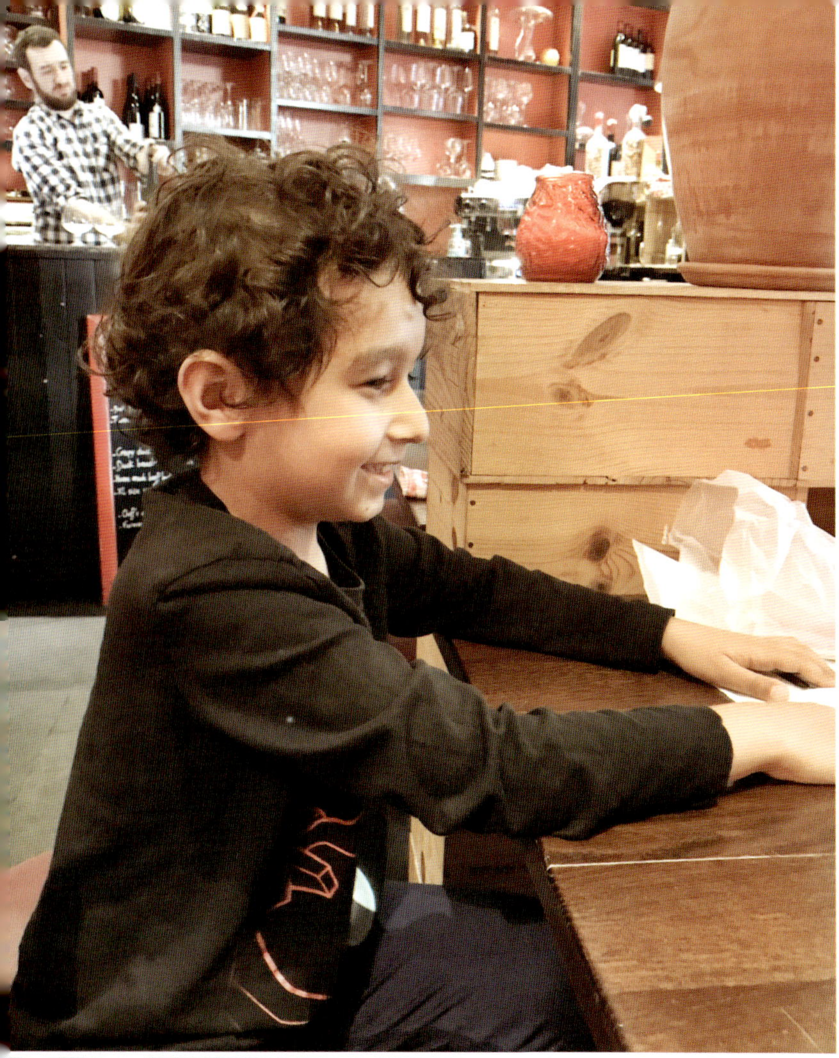
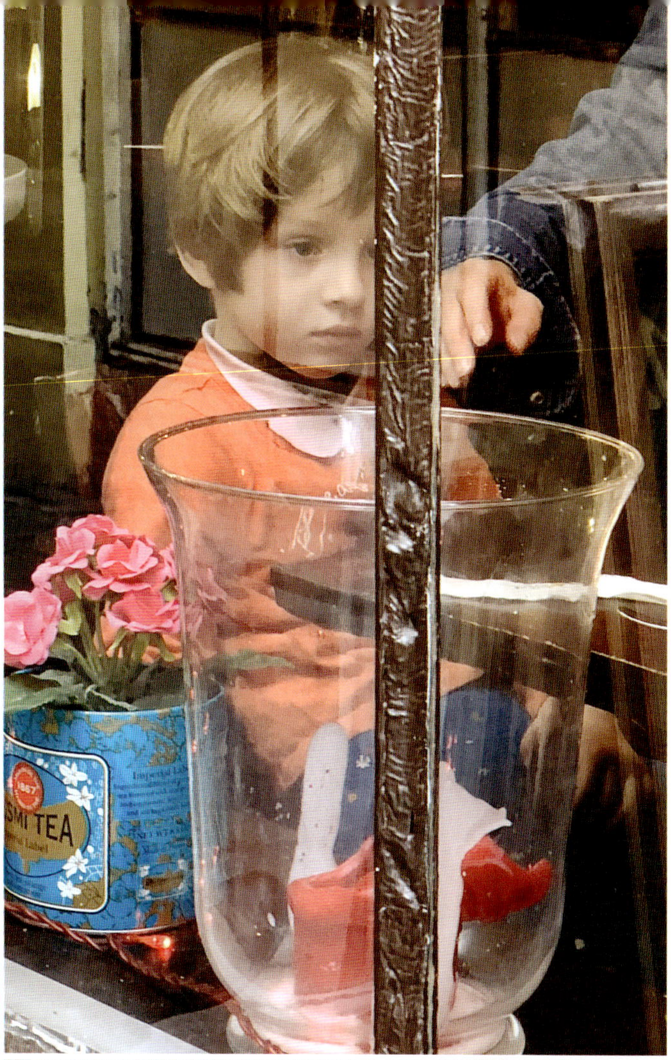
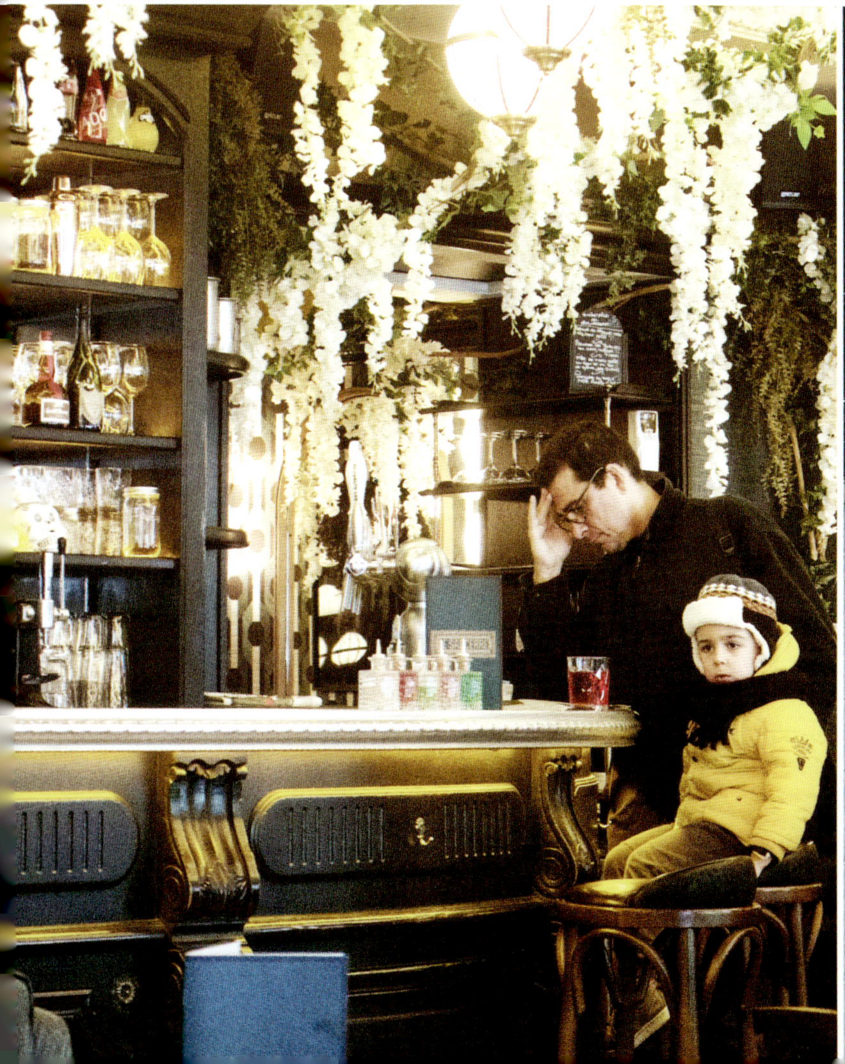
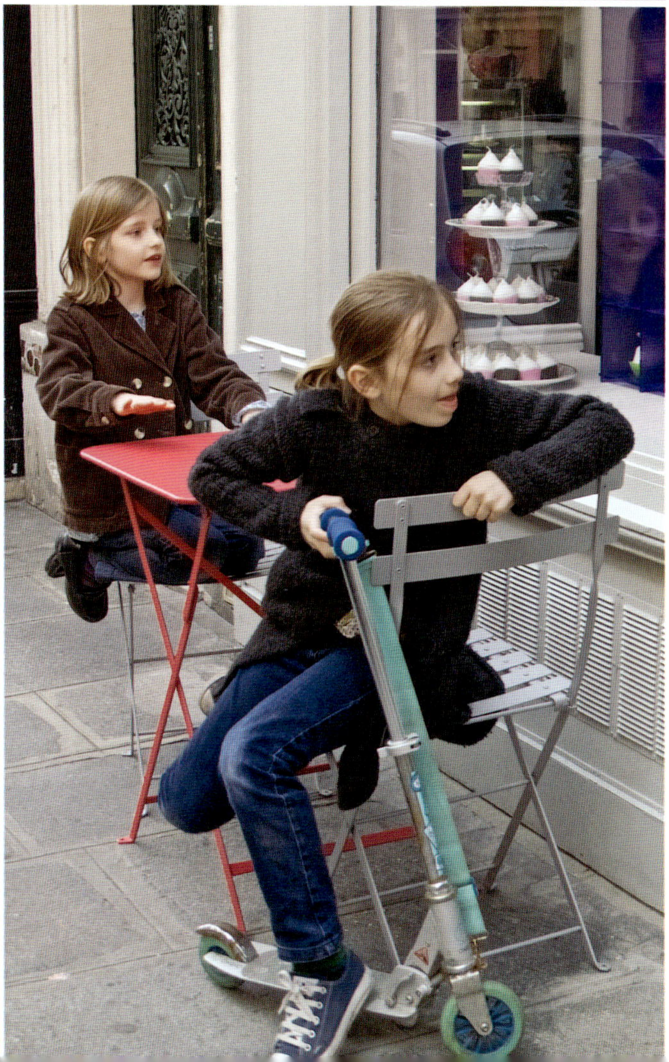

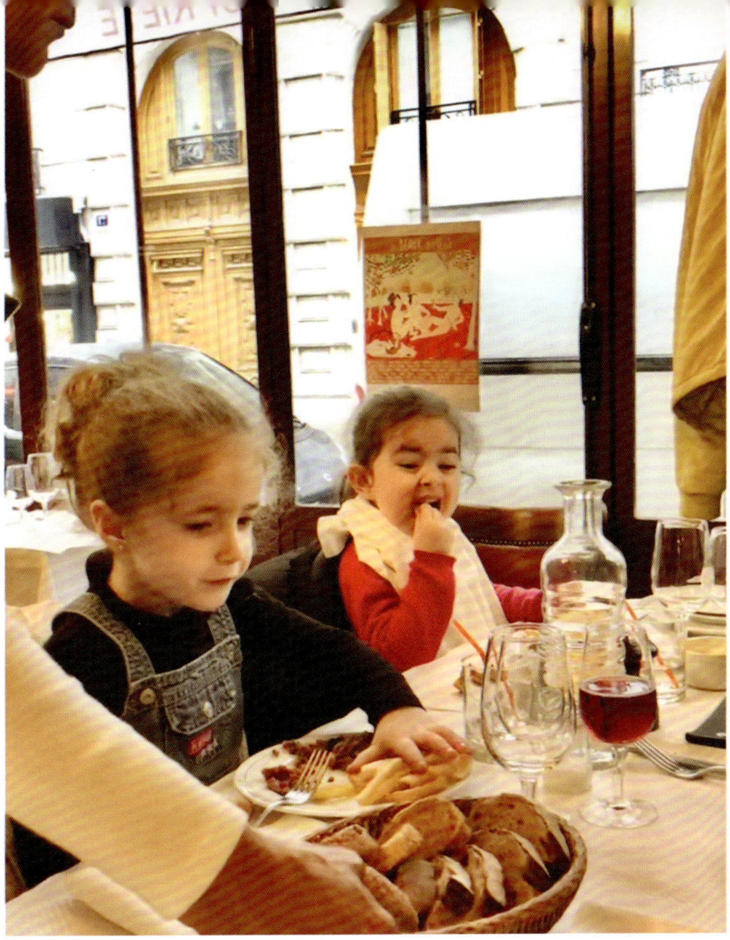

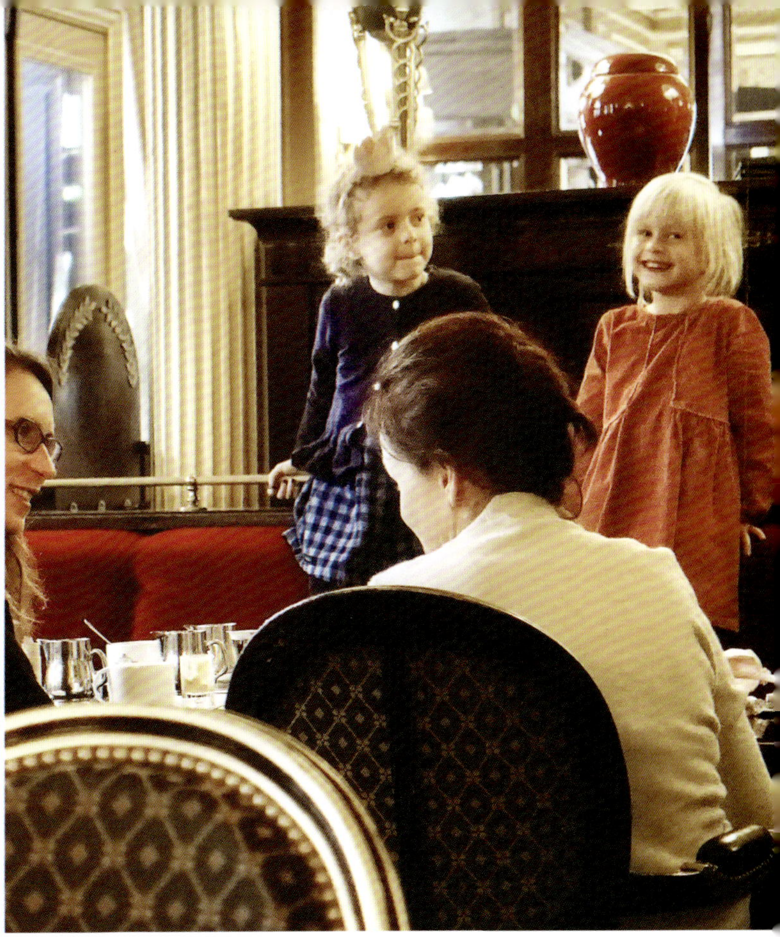

Whether bellying up to the bar or doing homework, small fry are esteemed members of café society. Children are treated with respect, like miniature adults. They learn café behavior and lifestyle from an early age; it is part of their heritage. From babyhood on, as they grow into schoolchildren, teenagers, and young adults, with family and friends, they regularly dwell in cafés.

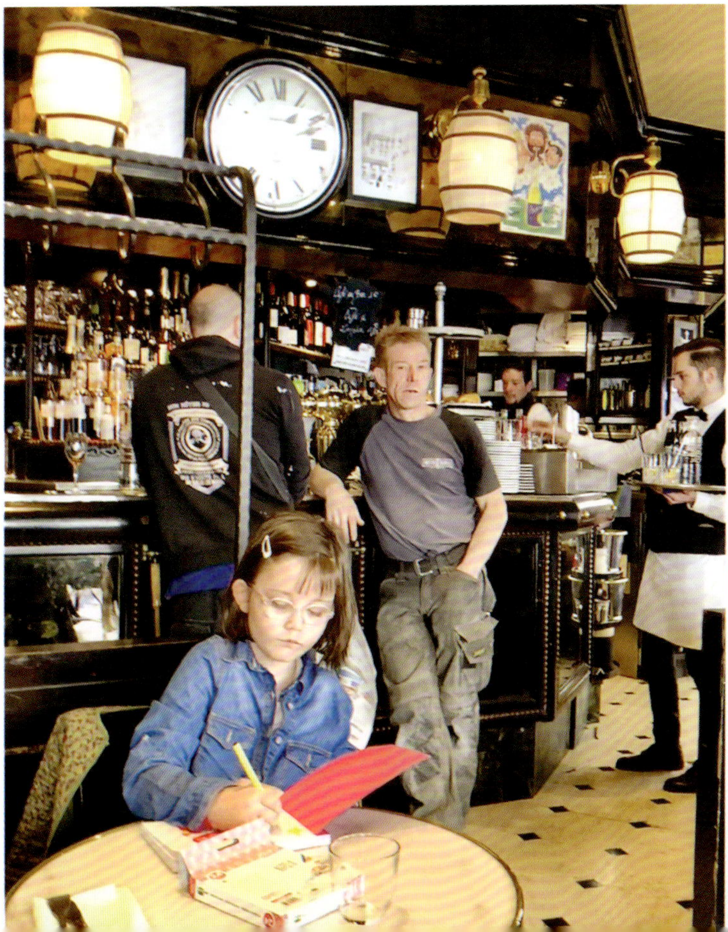

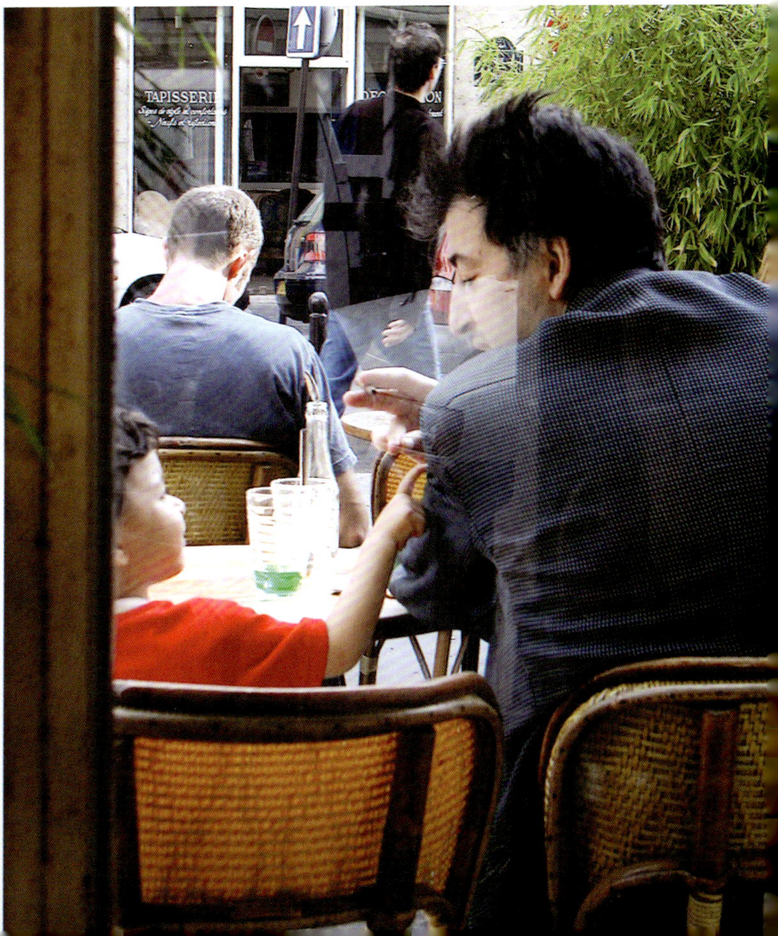

The Waiter

"The older waiter said, 'Each night I am reluctant to close up because there may be someone who needs the café.'"

Ernest Hemingway

The Parisian waiter moves like lightning, tending tables and kitchen with grace and efficiency. They are adept acrobats, ever performing a dance, as they navigate tight, busy spaces, balancing heavy trays laden with food and drink. Kitchens can often be upstairs or downstairs, so the waiter's agile ballet becomes ever more precarious. For the Parisian waiter, this is a profession—*un métier*—taken seriously, with dignity, often with a sense of humor despite their reputation for surliness. The always-busy Parisian waiter, a consummate professional, knows when to provide perfect service and when to disappear, allowing the customer to just be for as long as they want. Their hallmark style includes a classic white shirt, black bow tie, black vest with multiple pockets for various coins, black trousers, short black jackets (when the weather requires), and a waist-to-floor white apron—called a rondeau. The classic attire and finesse carried forth into the 21st century—albeit with some mix of style and gender—comfortably affirms that you are in a Parisian café.

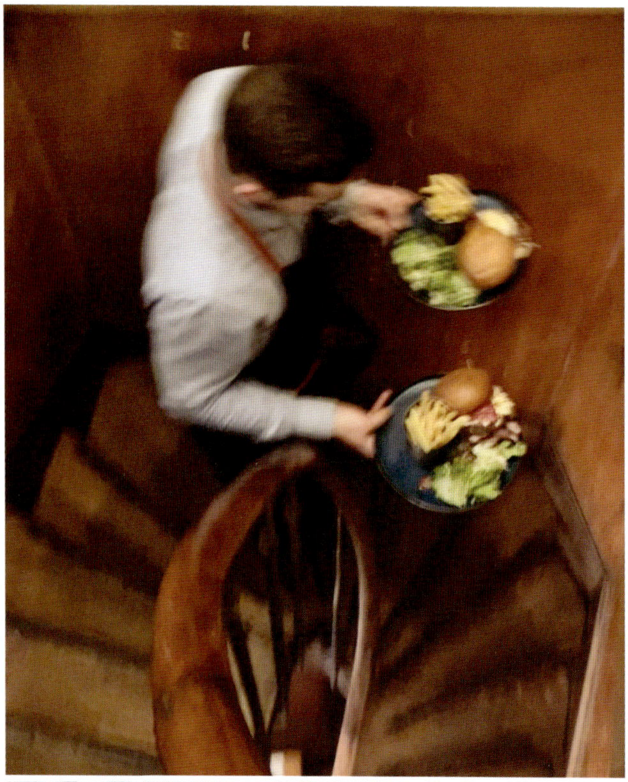

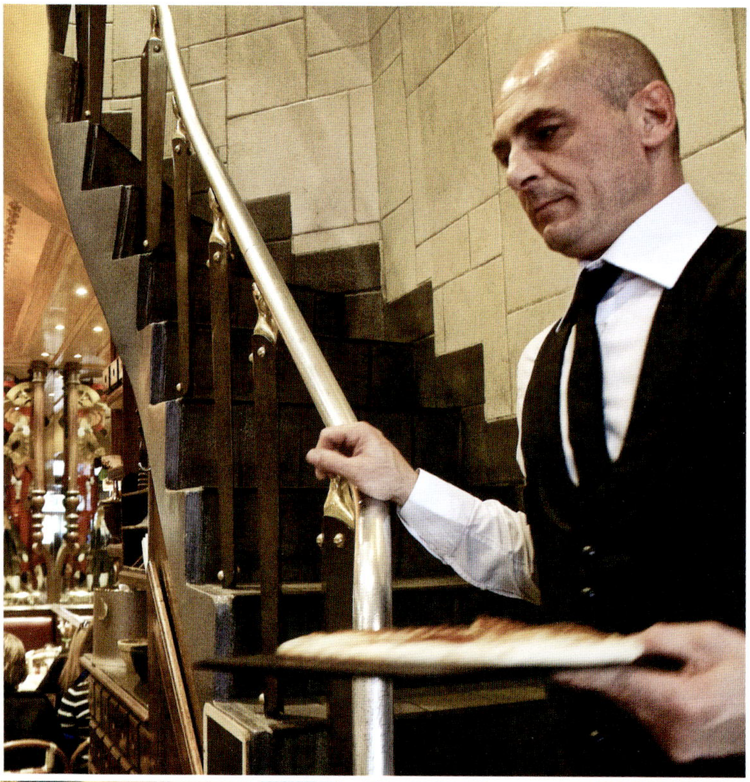

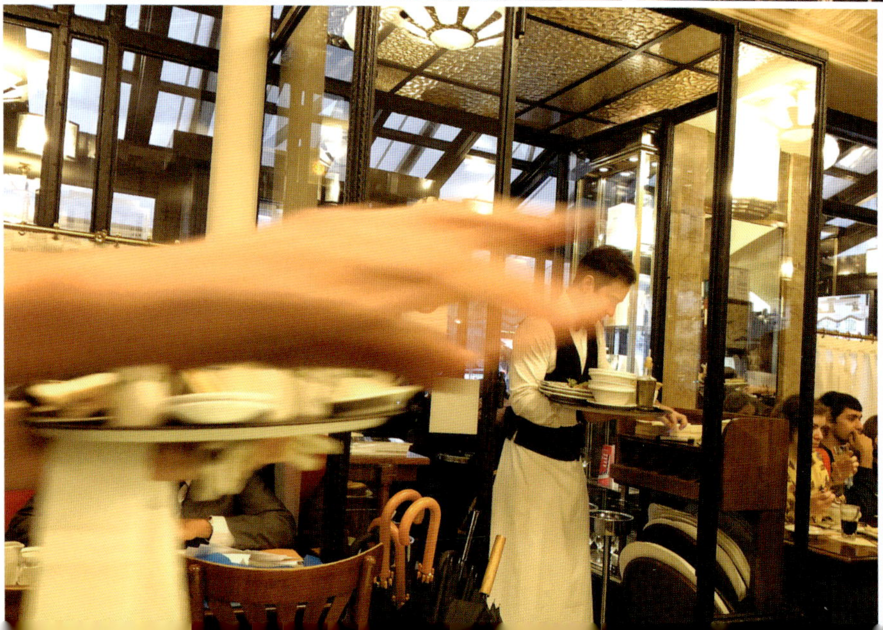

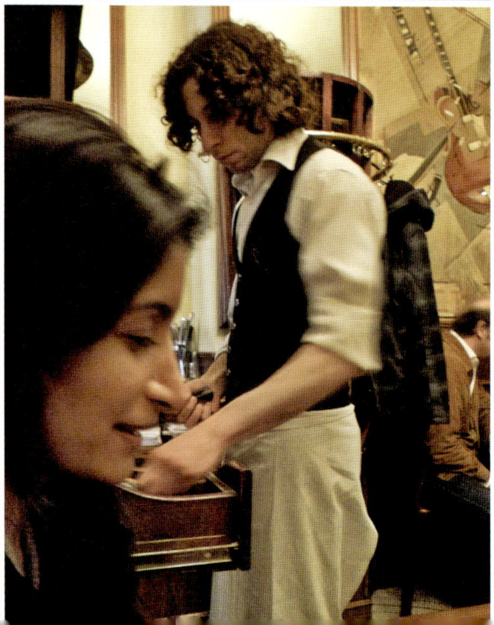

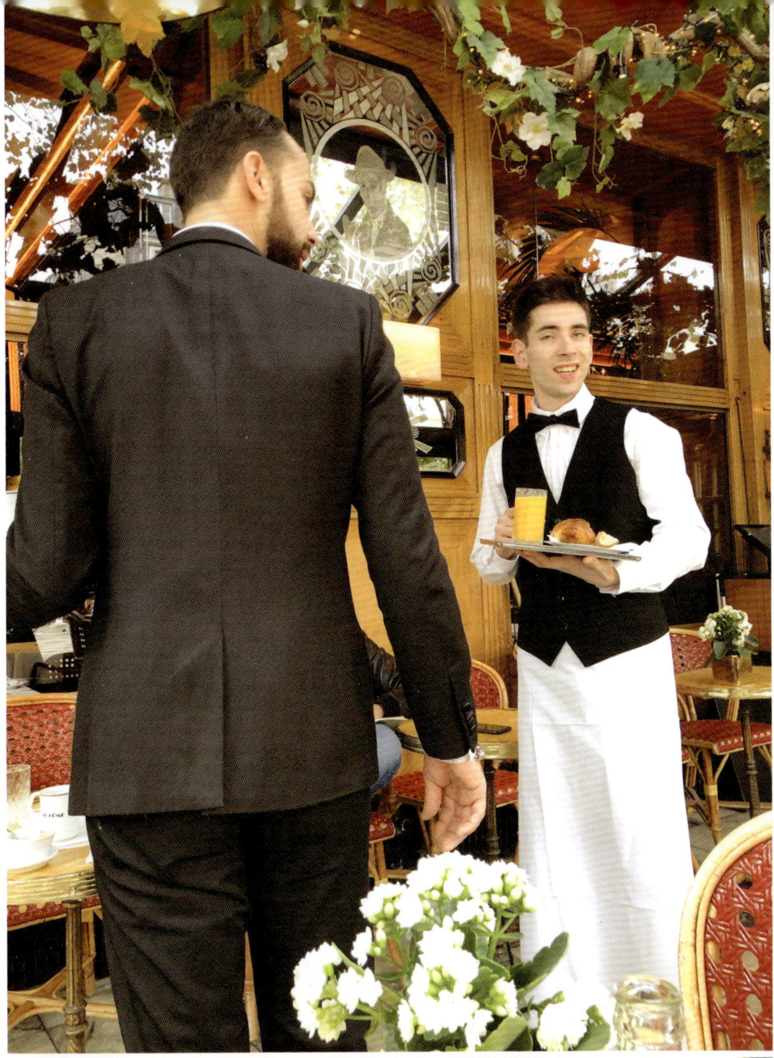

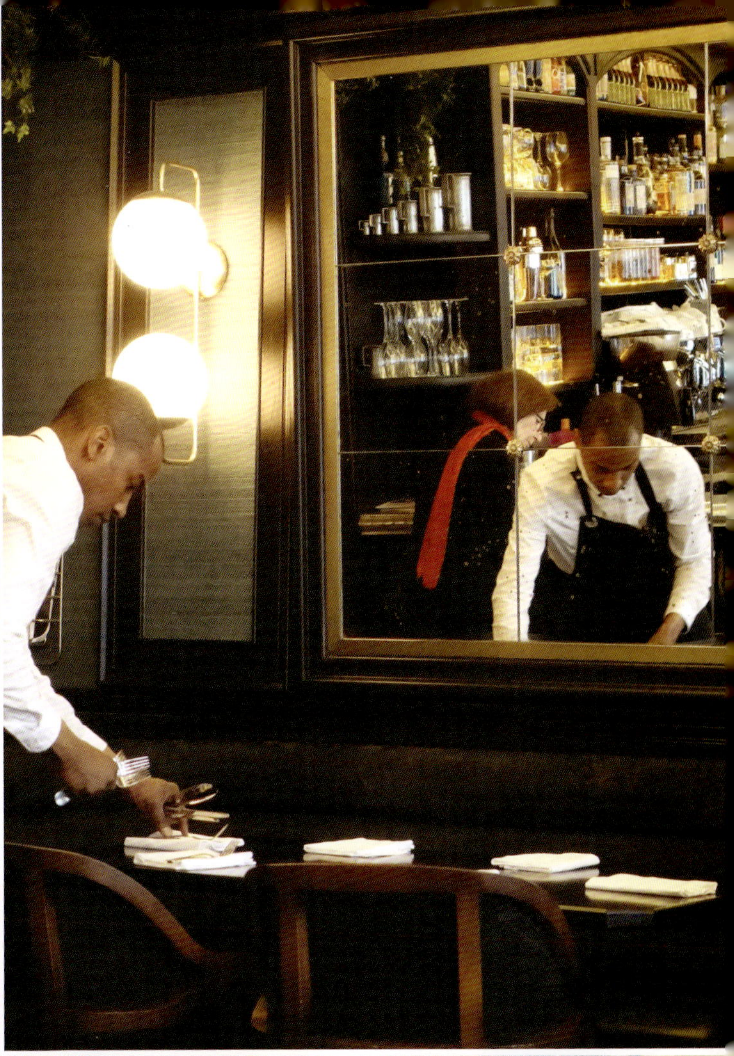

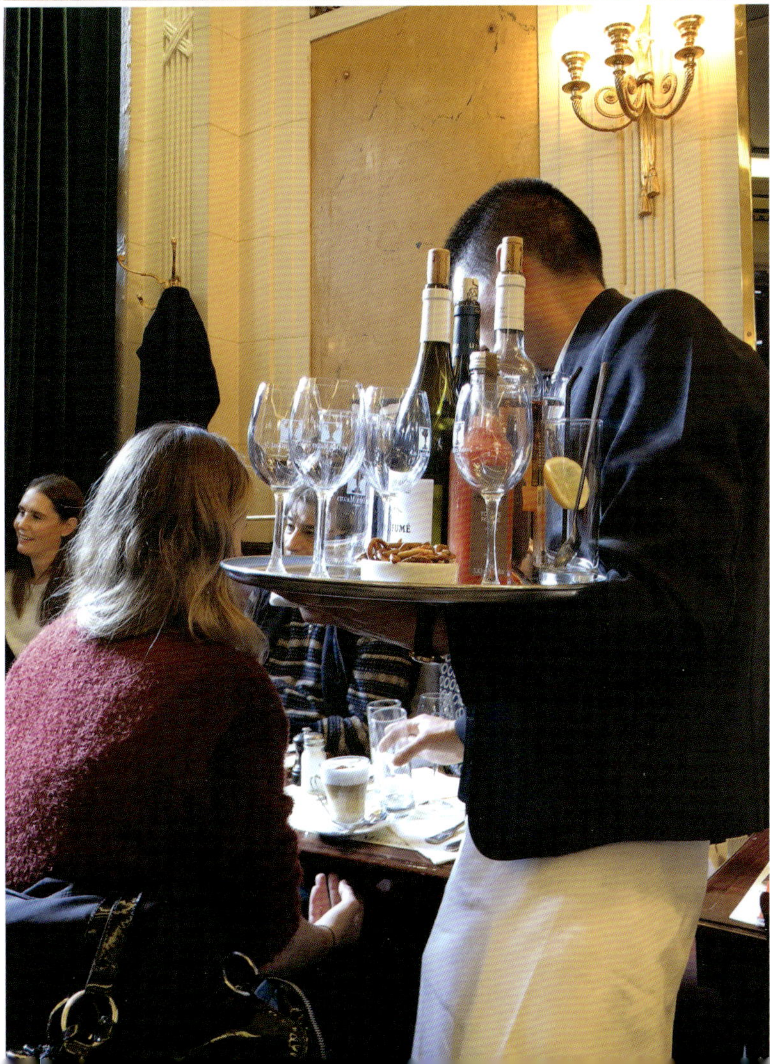

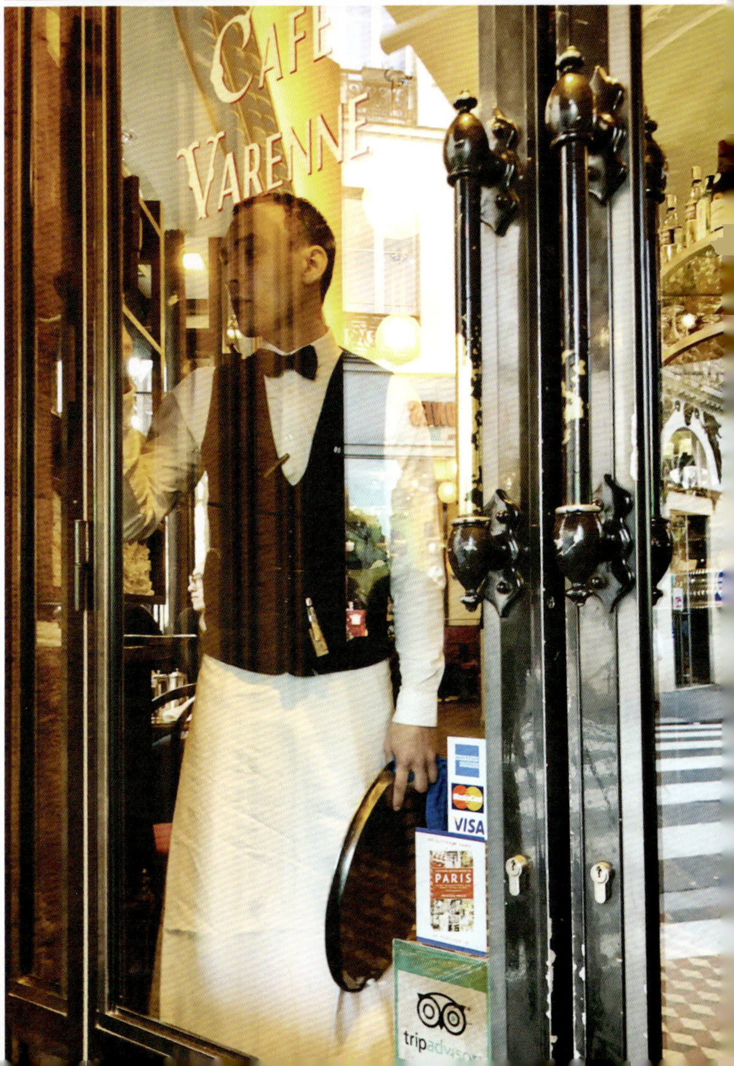
CAFE
VARENNE
VISA
PARIS

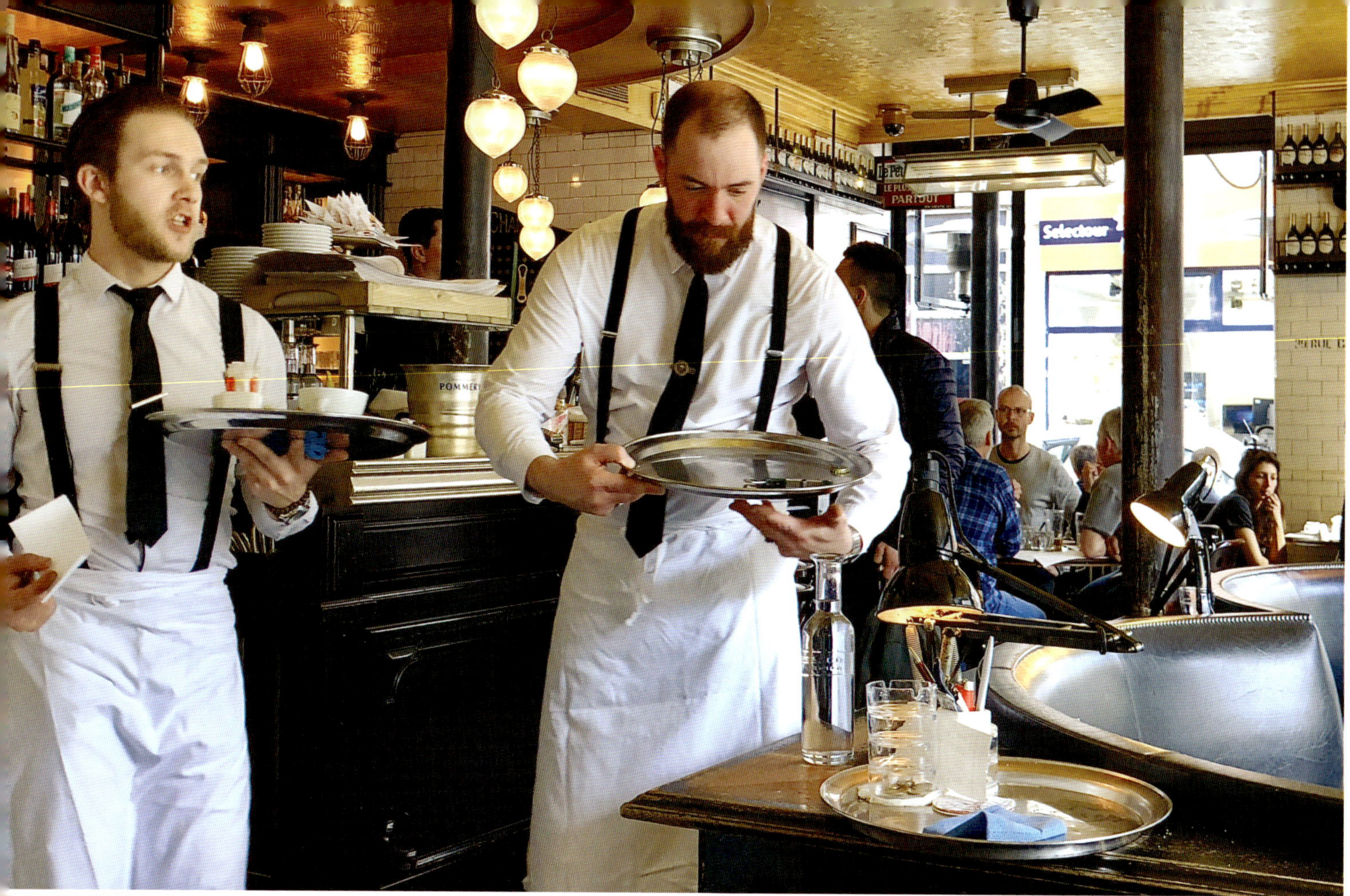
POMMERY
Selectour

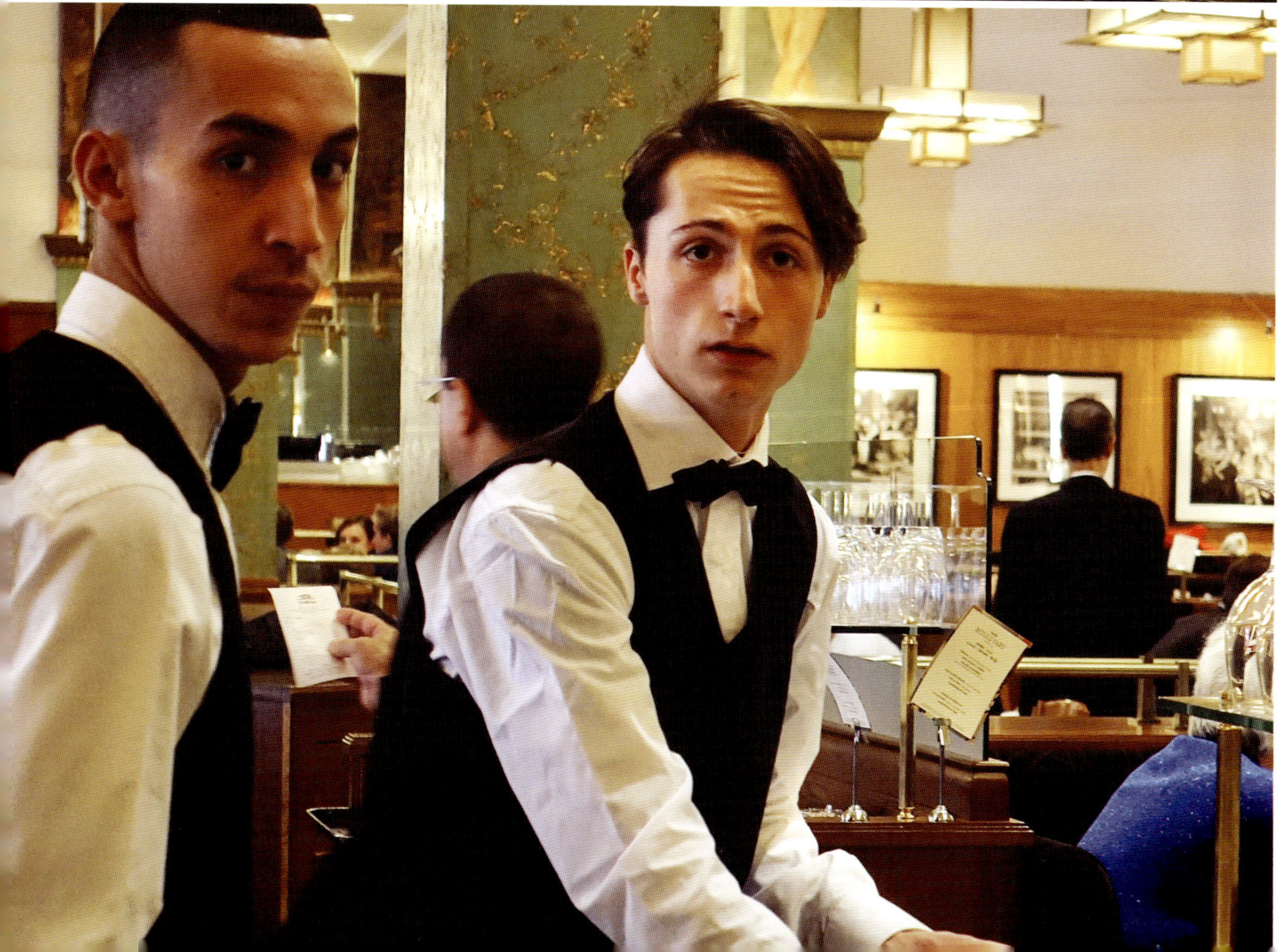

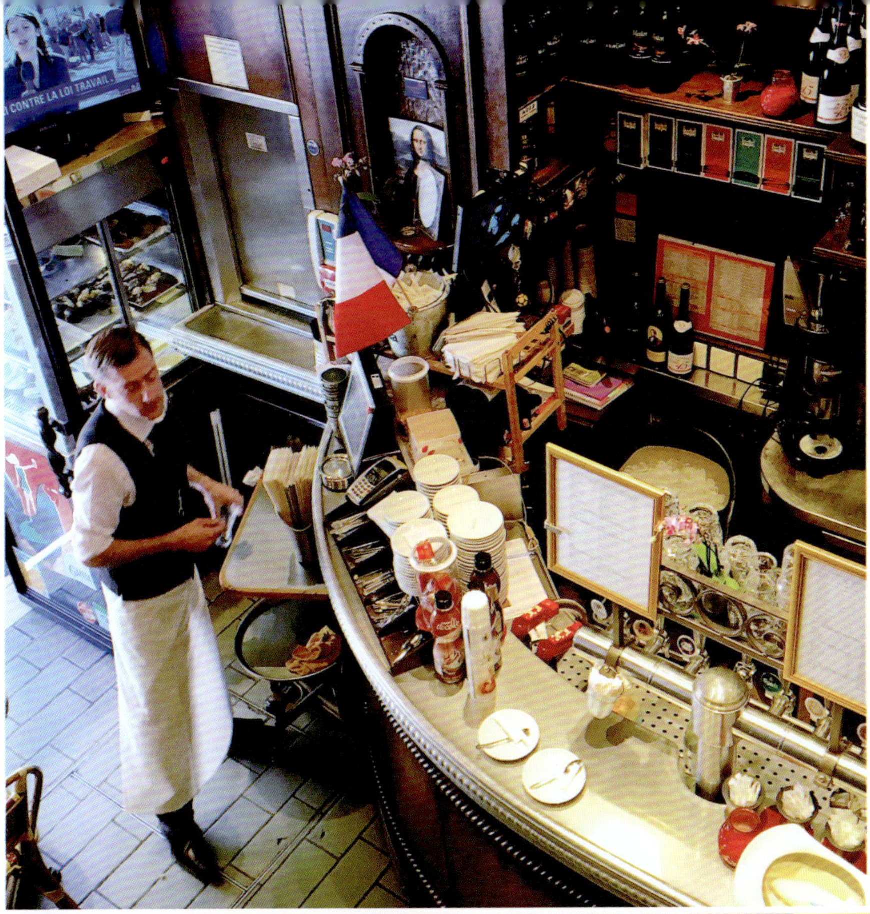
CONTRE LA LOI TRAVAIL !

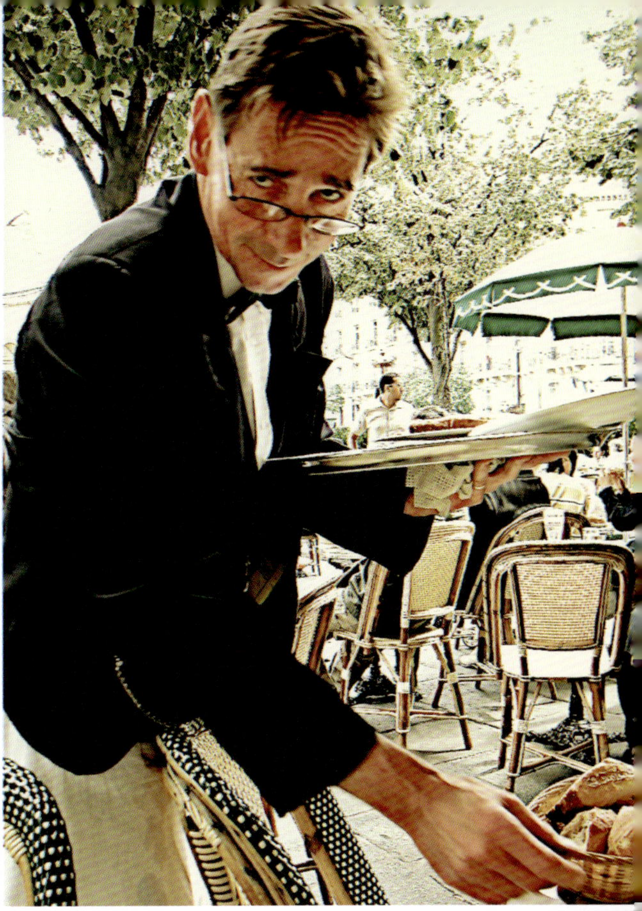

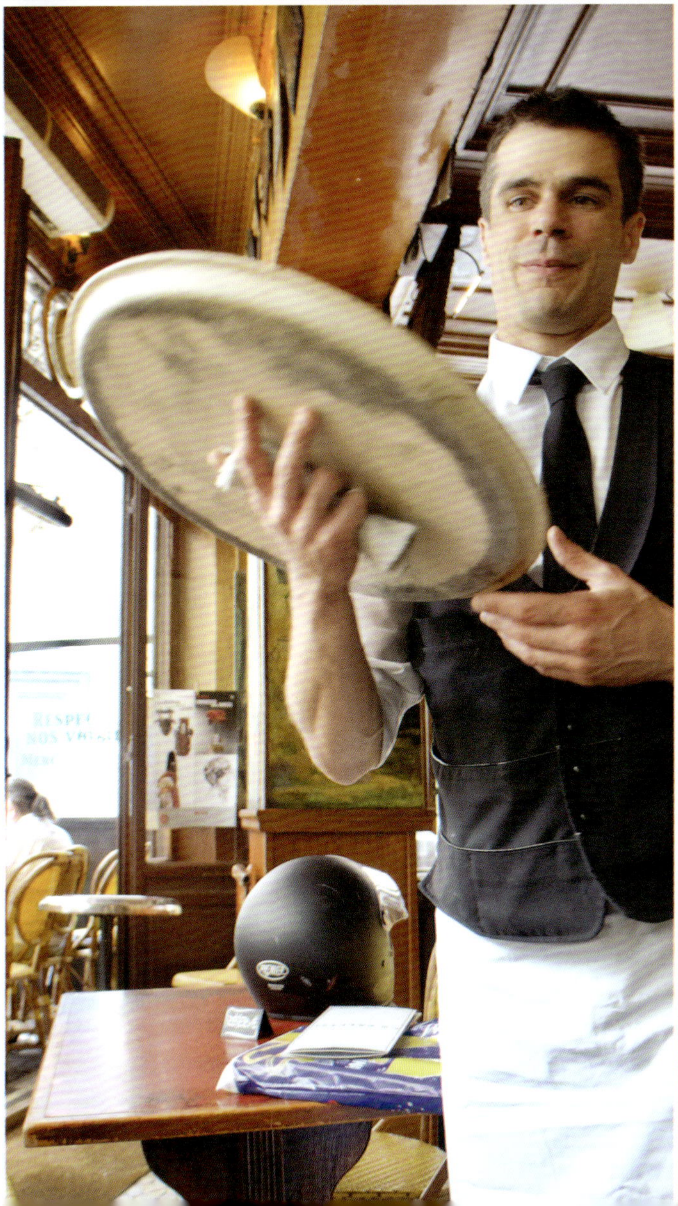

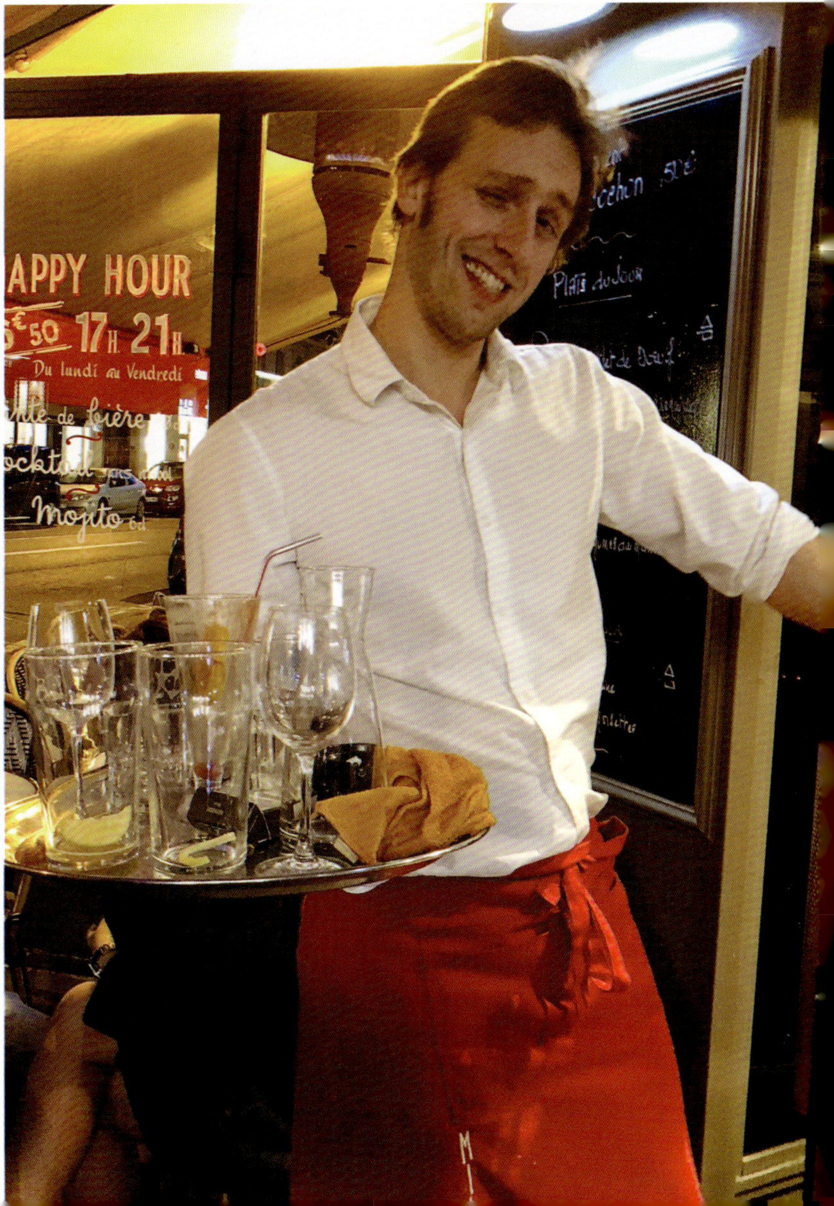
APPY HOUR
17H 21H
Du lundi au Vendredi
Mojito
Plat du Jour

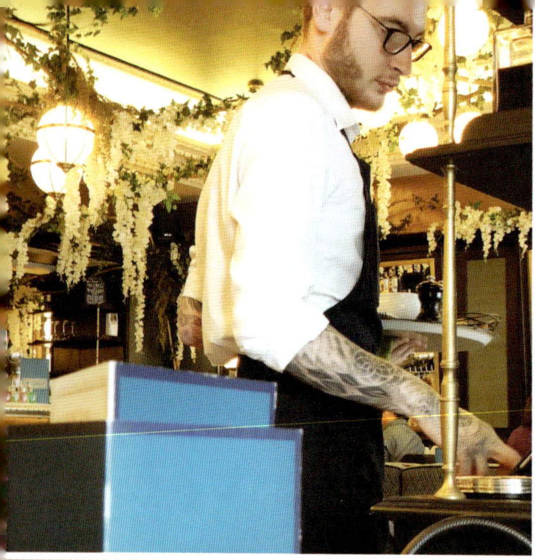
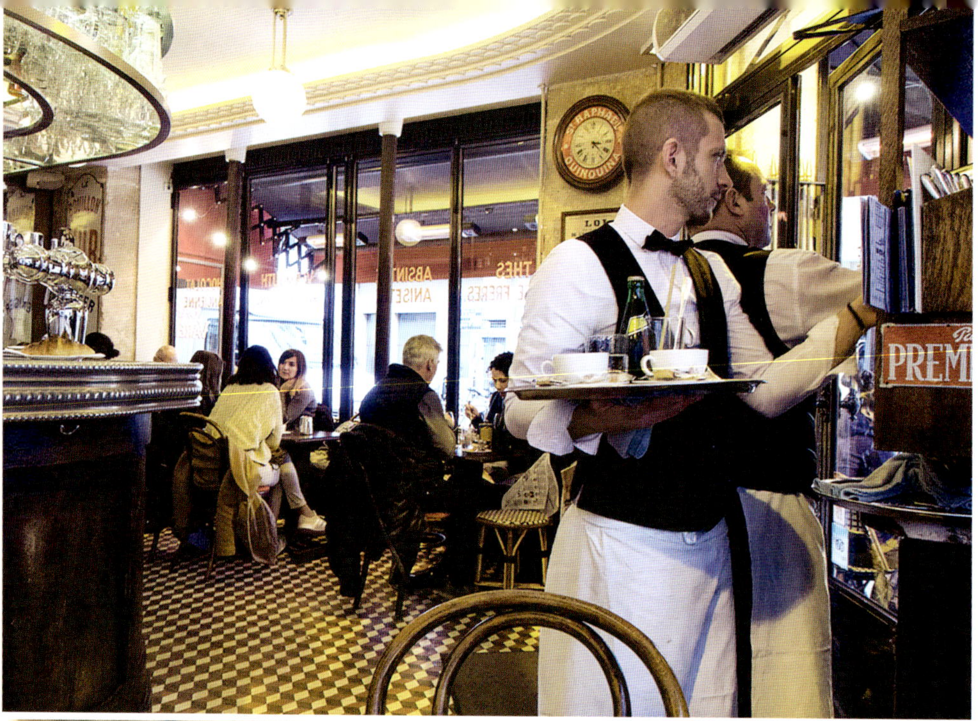
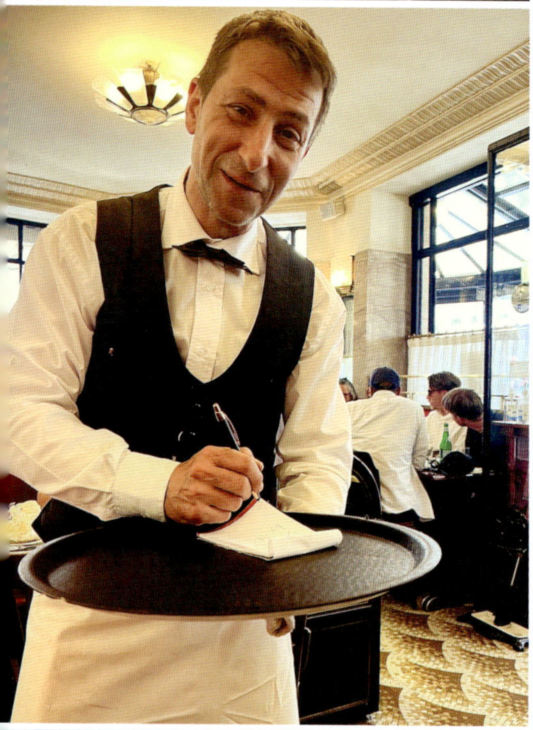
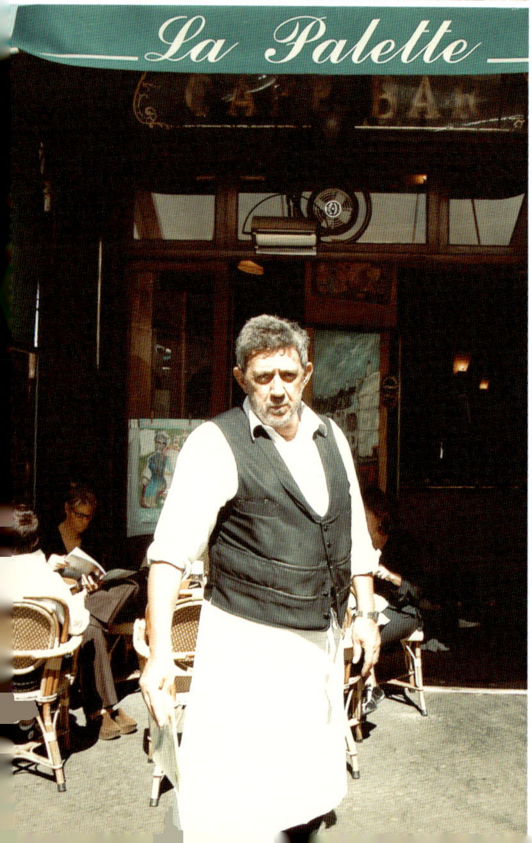
La Palette
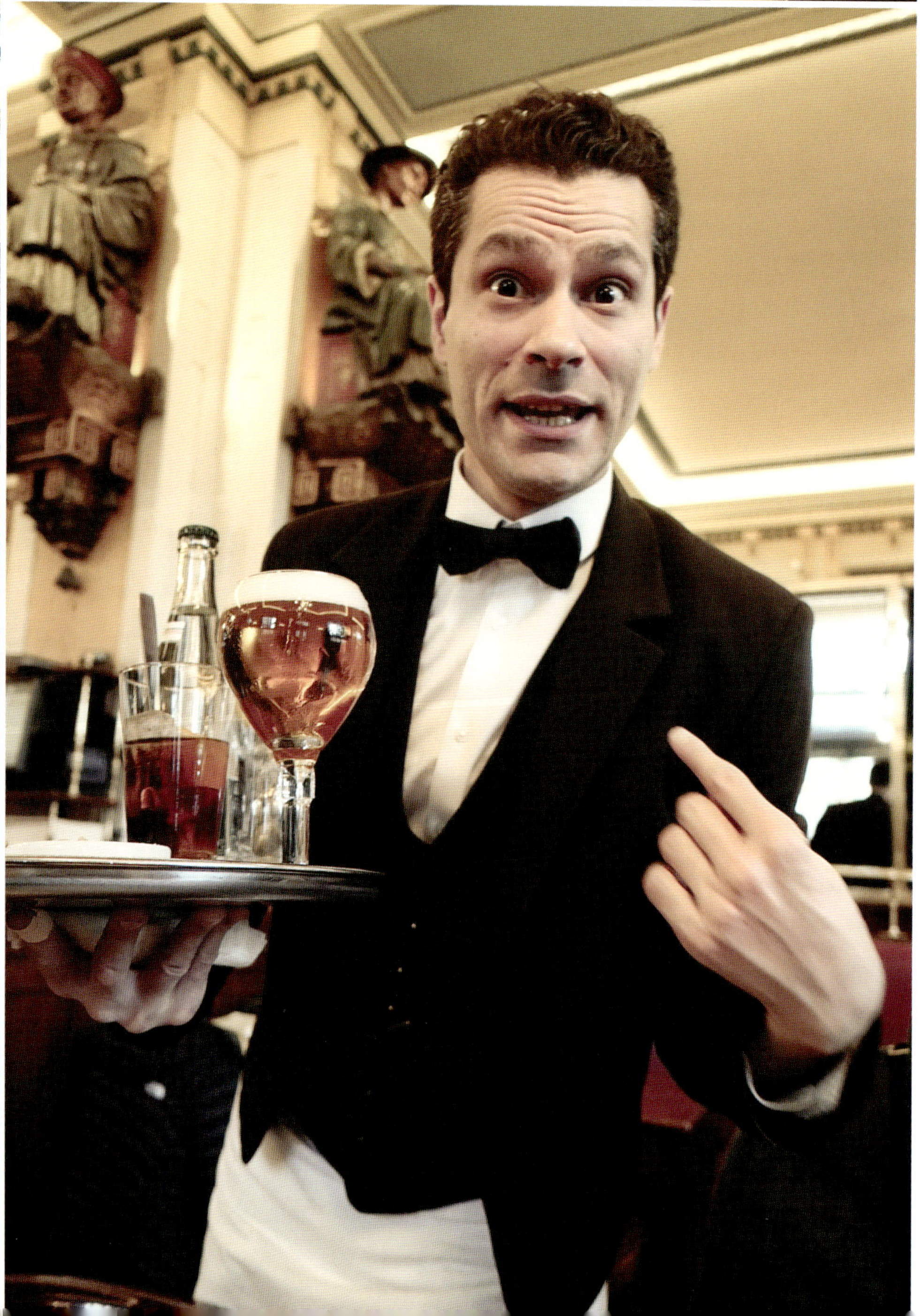

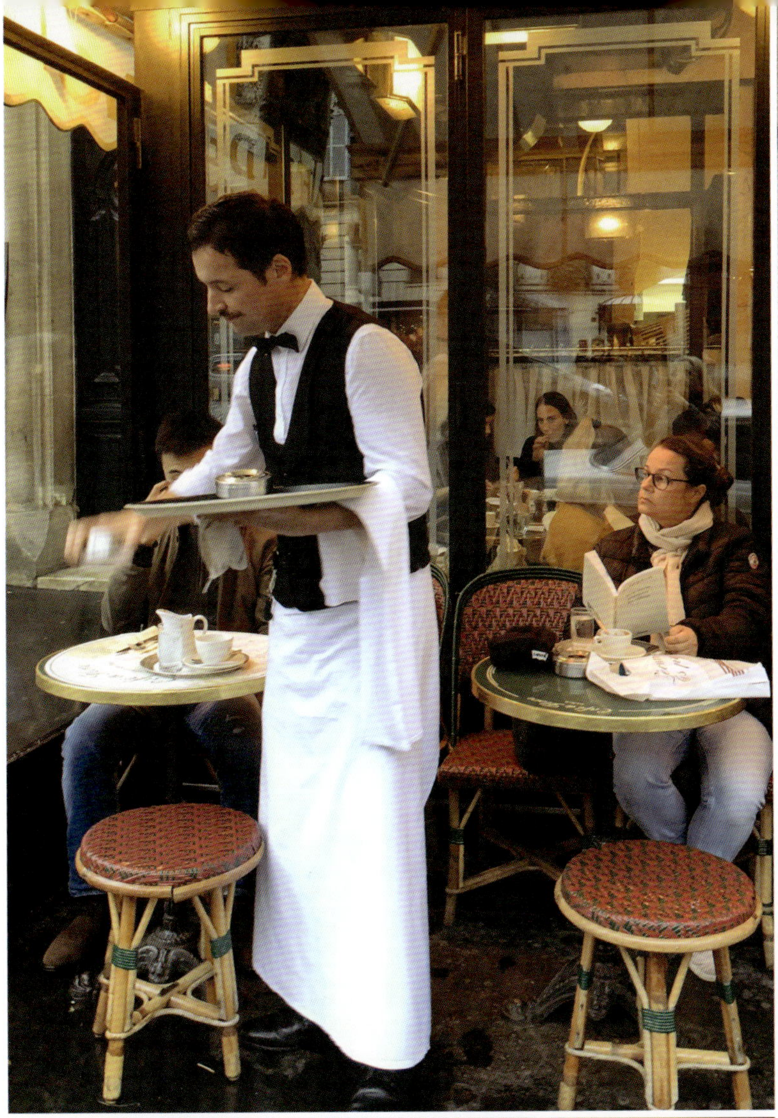

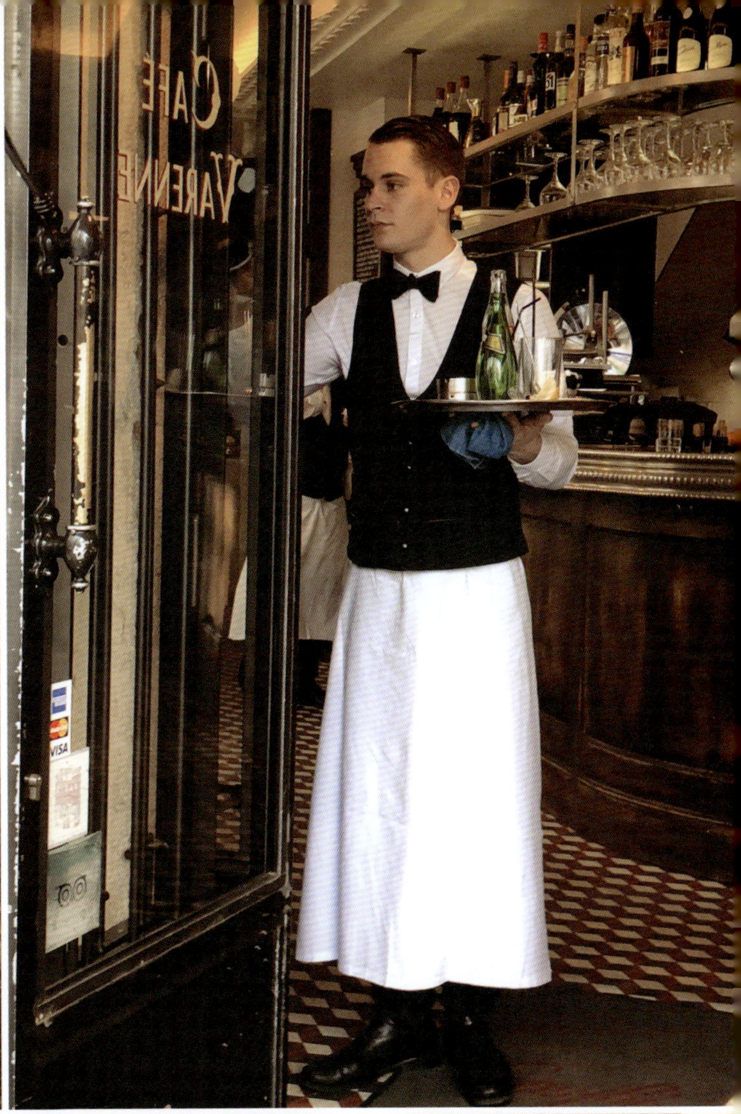

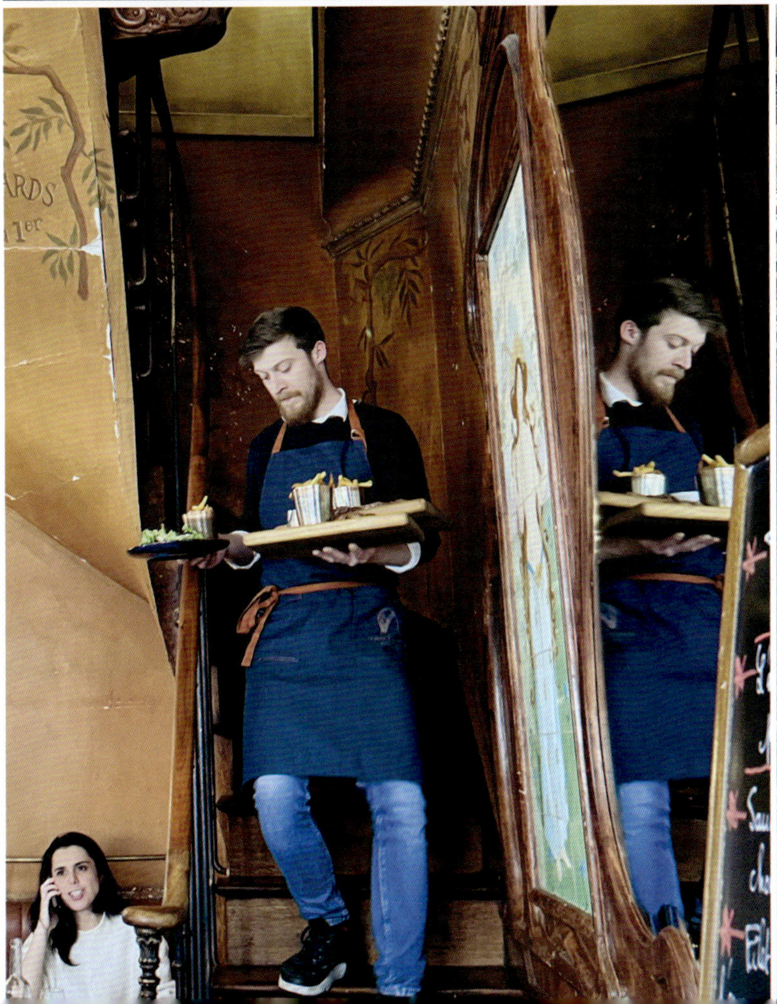

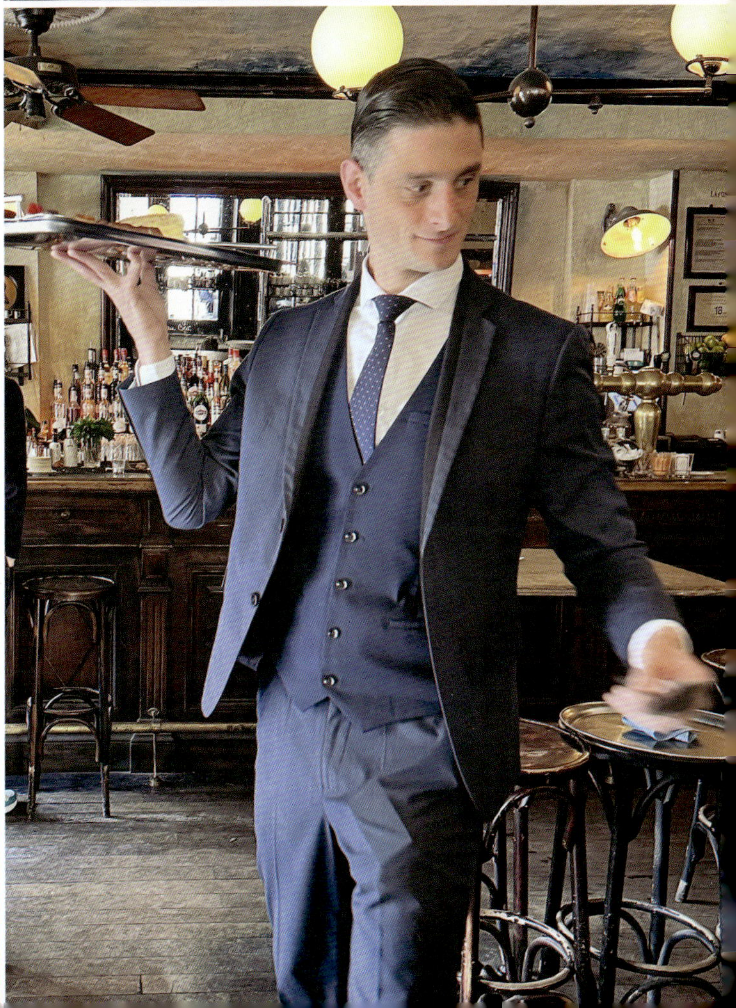

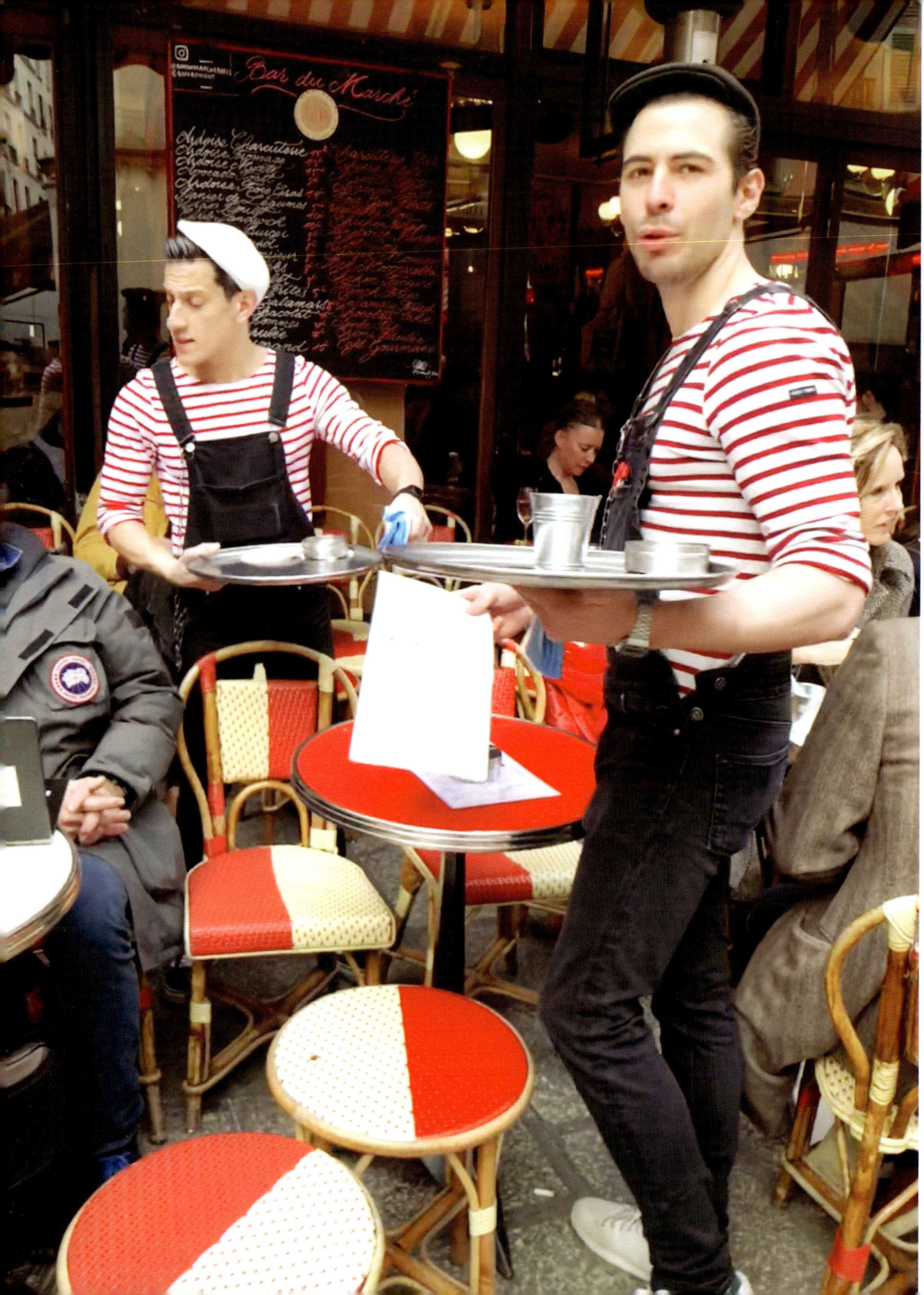
Bar du Marché

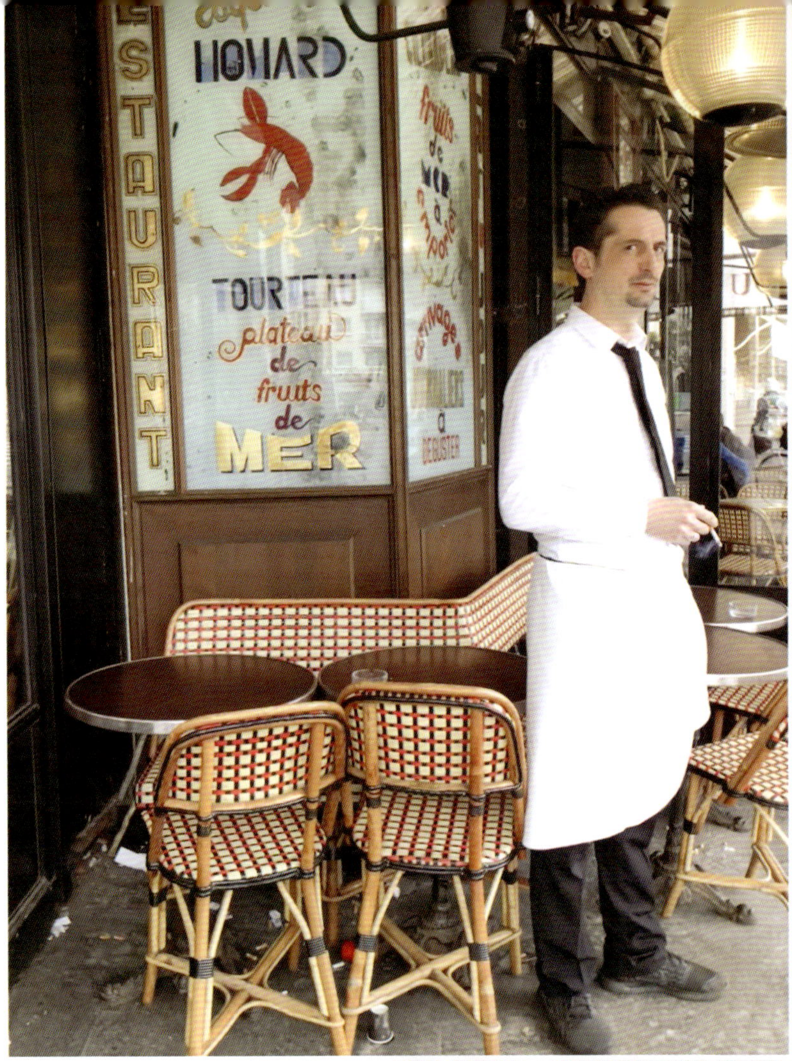
HOMARD
plateau
de
fruits
de
MER

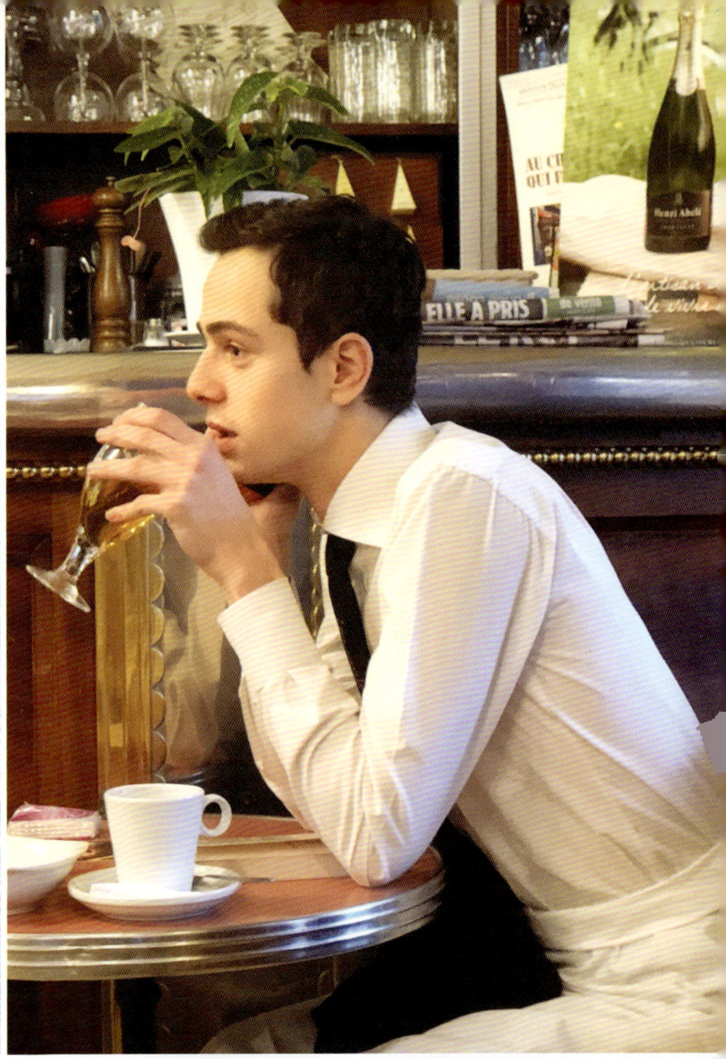
ELLE A PRIS

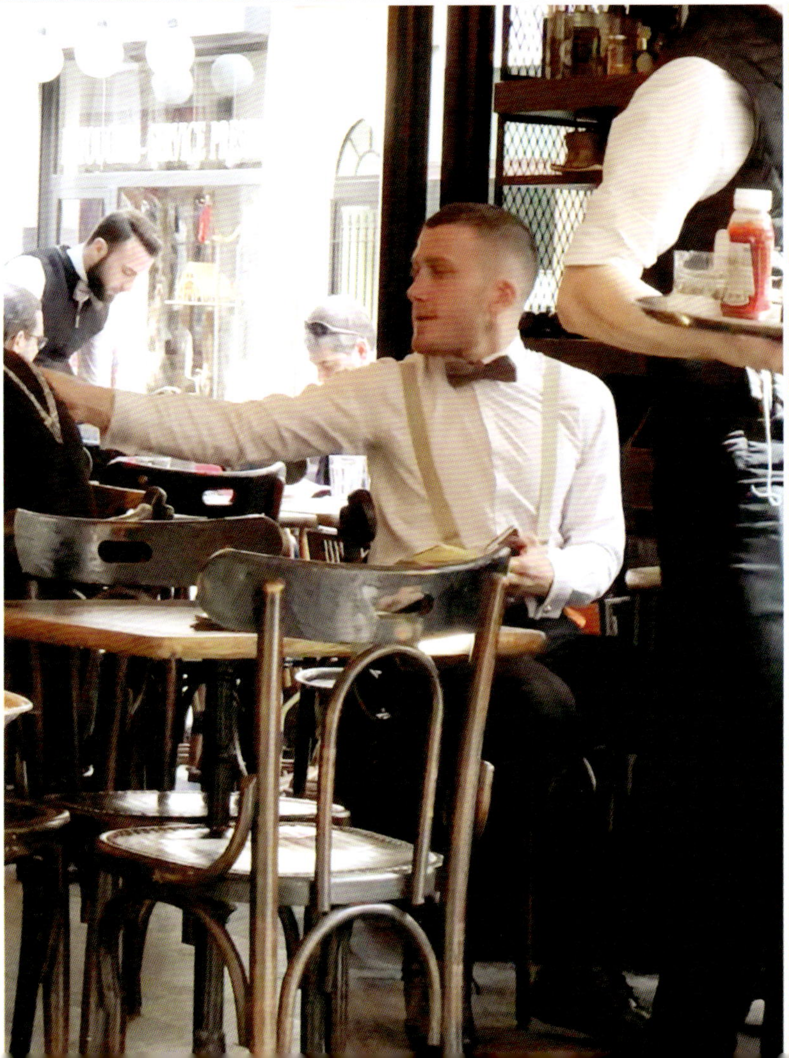

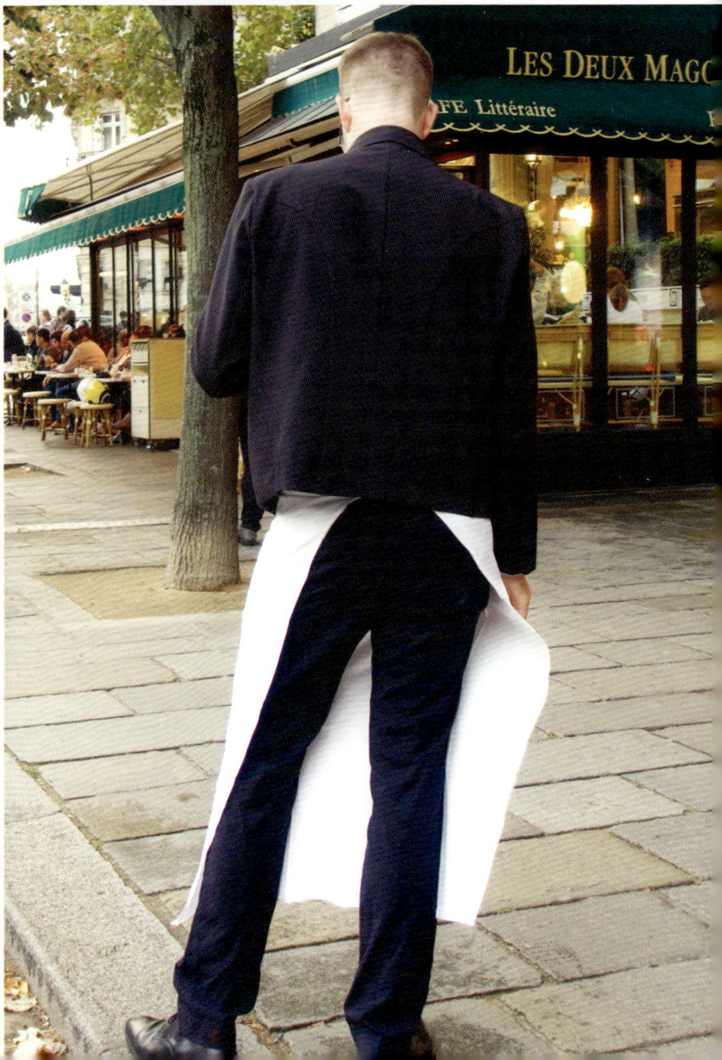
Littéraire

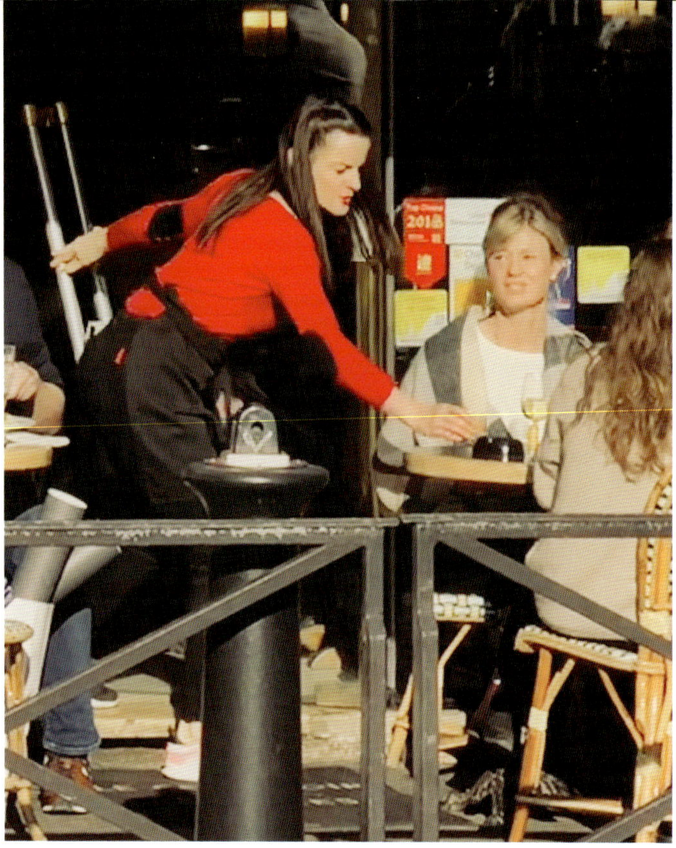

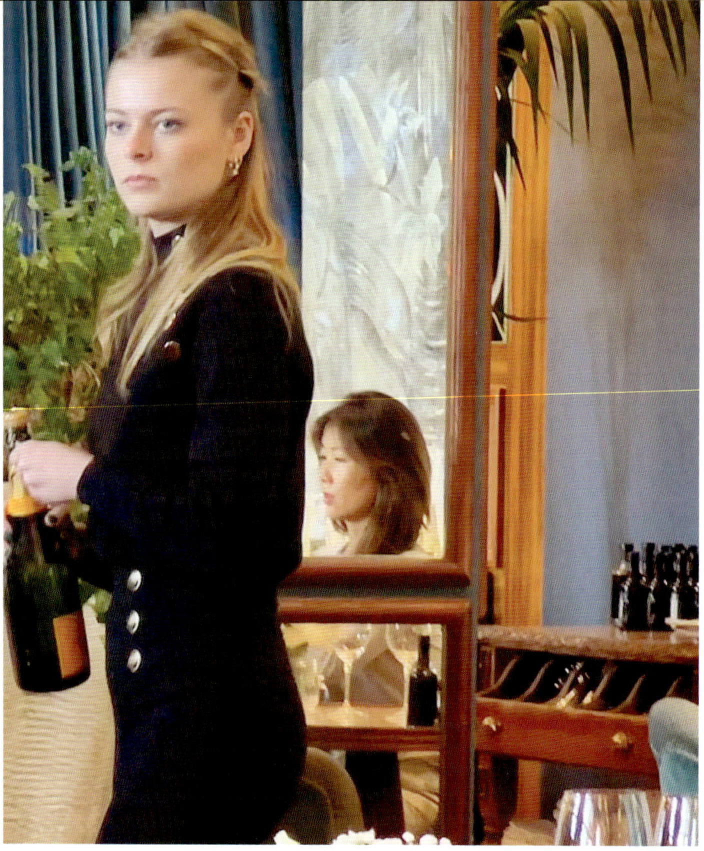

The *serveuse*, or waitress, climbs up and down the same kitchen stairs, carries the same overloaded trays, dodges the same customers and workmates, and dances the same dance as her male counterparts. She executes each movement with agility and grace.

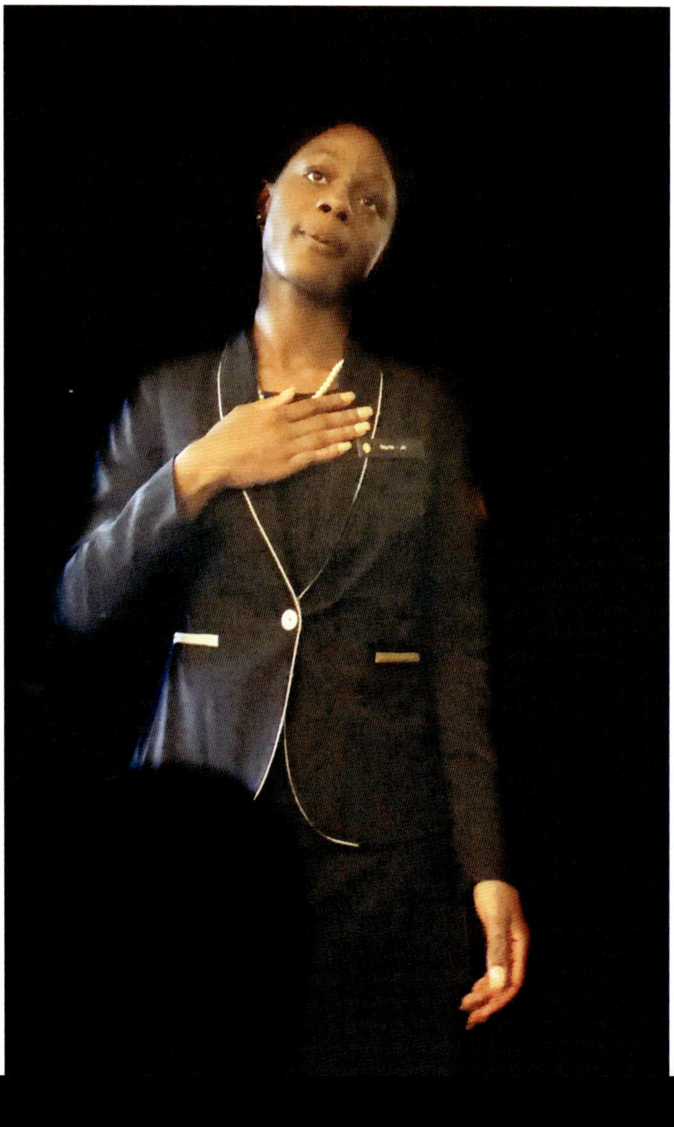

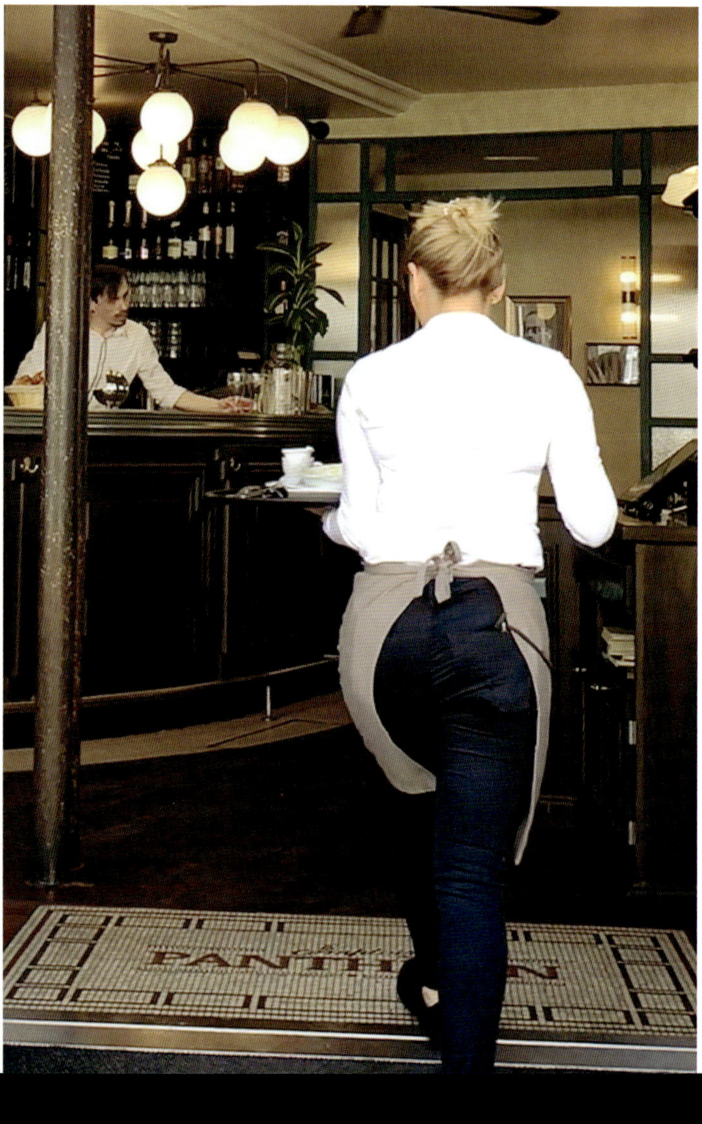

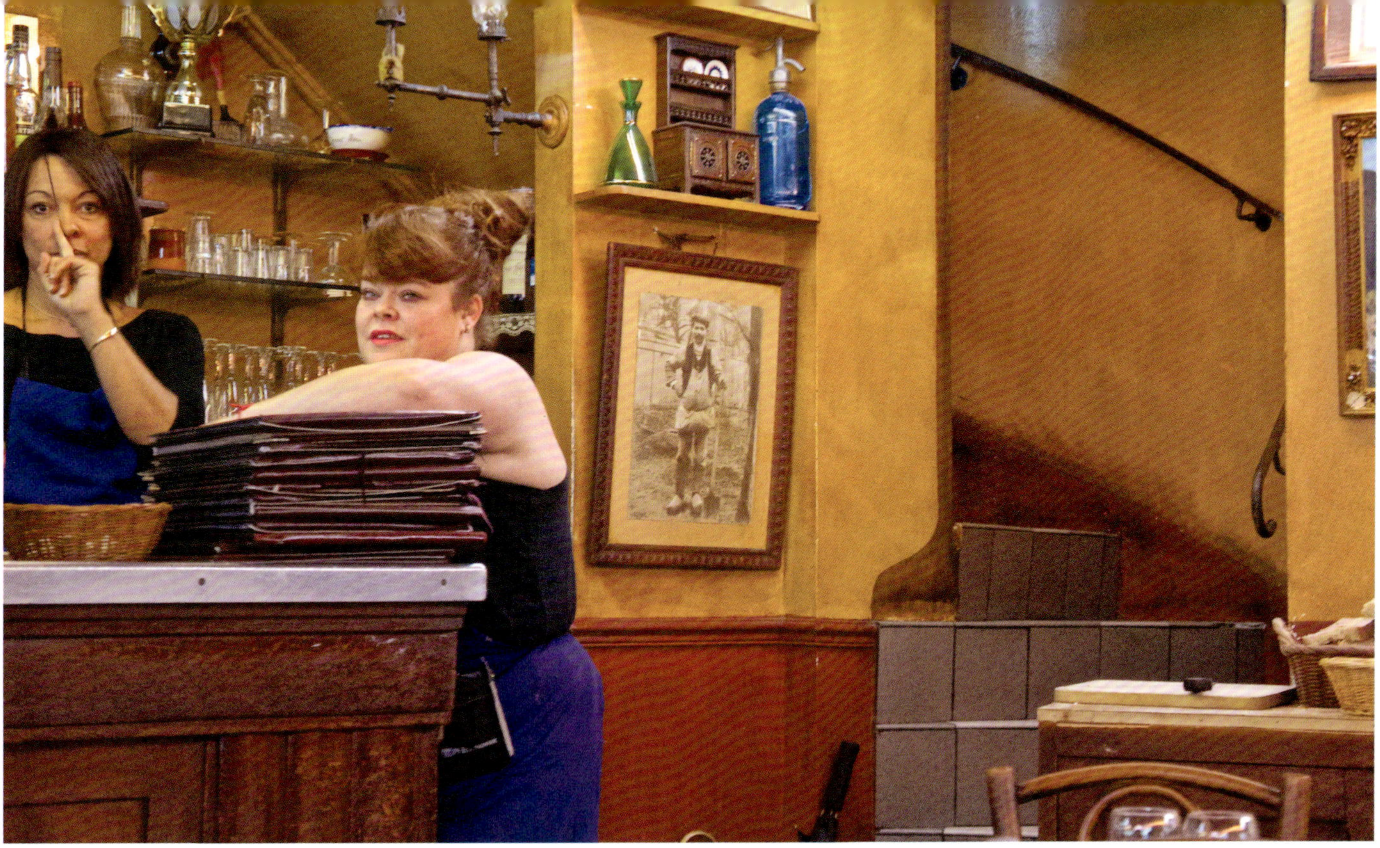

A waitress seemingly from another era graces Chez Paul with her skills and style. Her presence in this bistro, opened in 1900, back in the day of *charbon* and *limonadiers*, (coal and lemonade makers/café owners), along with the classic food and ambiance, lends an air of time suspended.

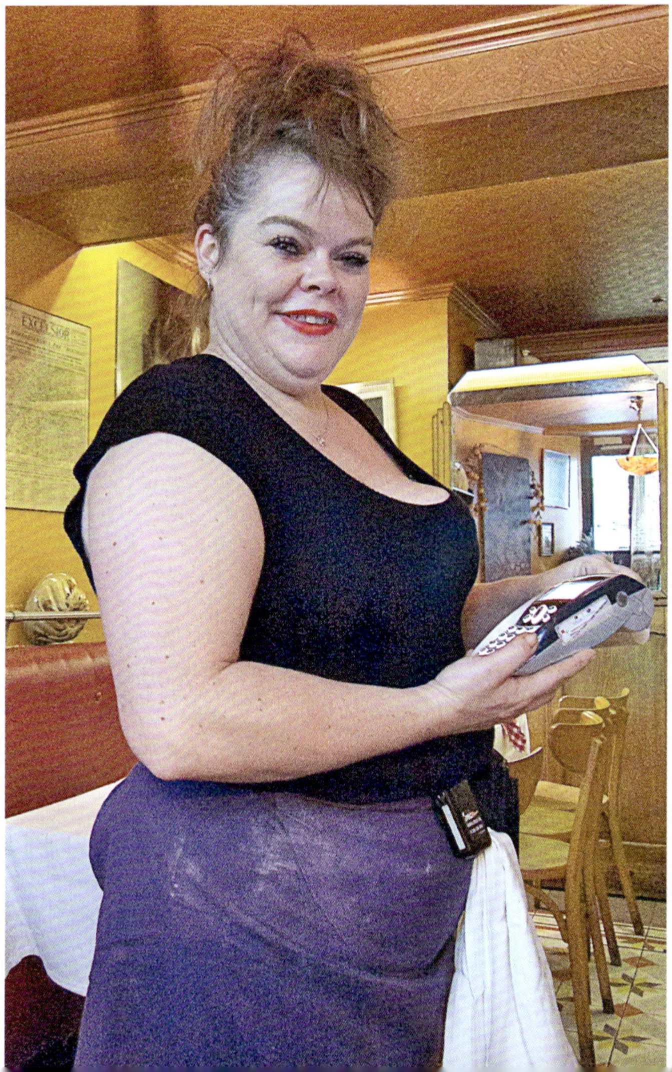

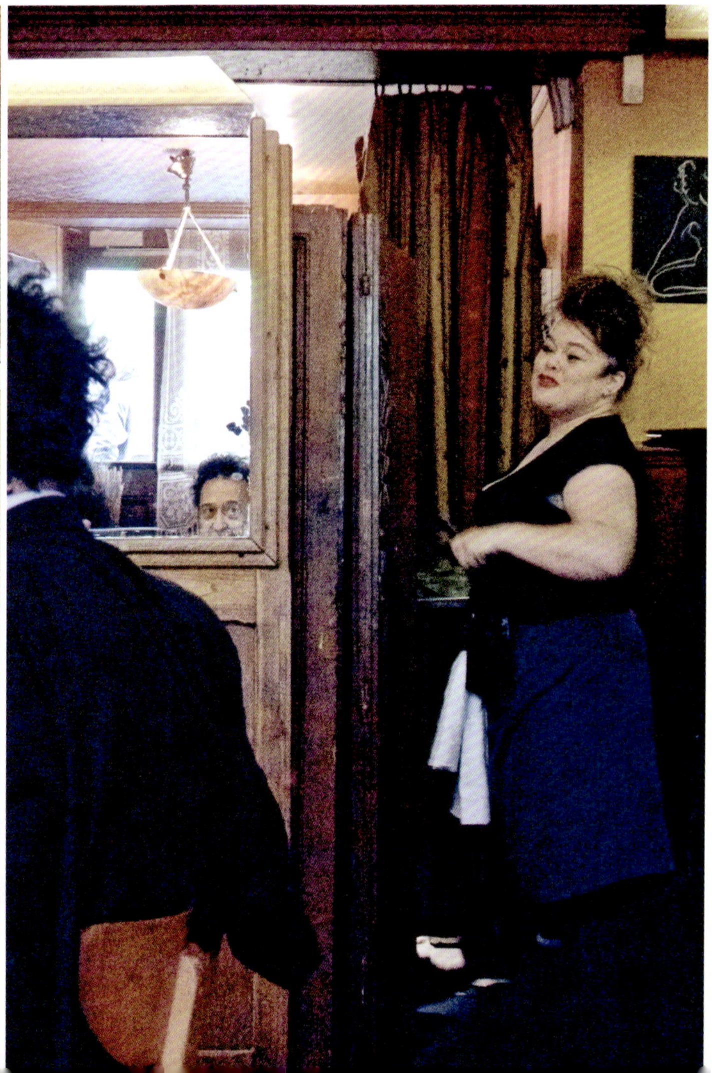

The Barman

"Of course, one should not drink much, but often."
Henri de Toulouse-Lautrec

The star at *le zinc* is the barman or barwoman, as skilled at conversation as they are at knowing your "usual." They move with precision, never missing a beat, while preparing and serving with elegant finesse. The bar and barman or barwoman have supported many lively discussions and lifetime friendships. This role of facilitator and connector originates from the counter's very beginnings as a social network when the proprietor held court at *le zinc* and orchestrated much of French daily life: food, cash, gossip, matchmaking, and conduct, sometimes even acting as an informant for the police.

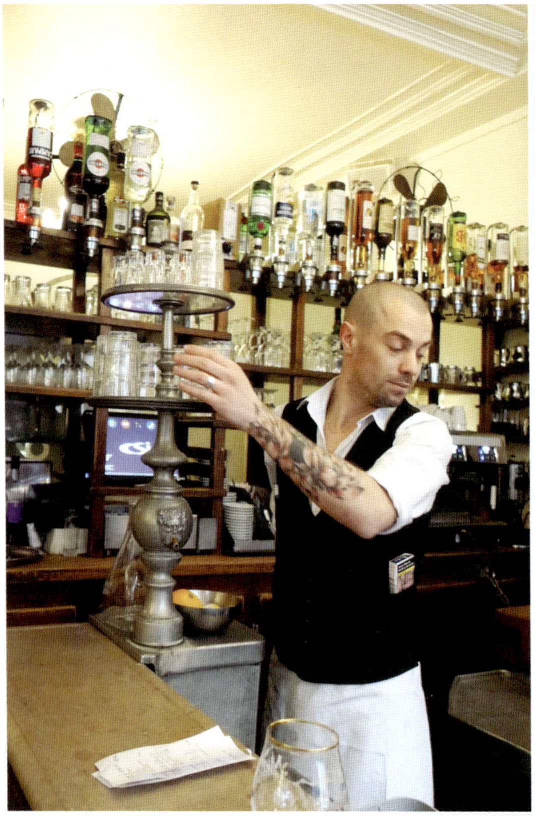

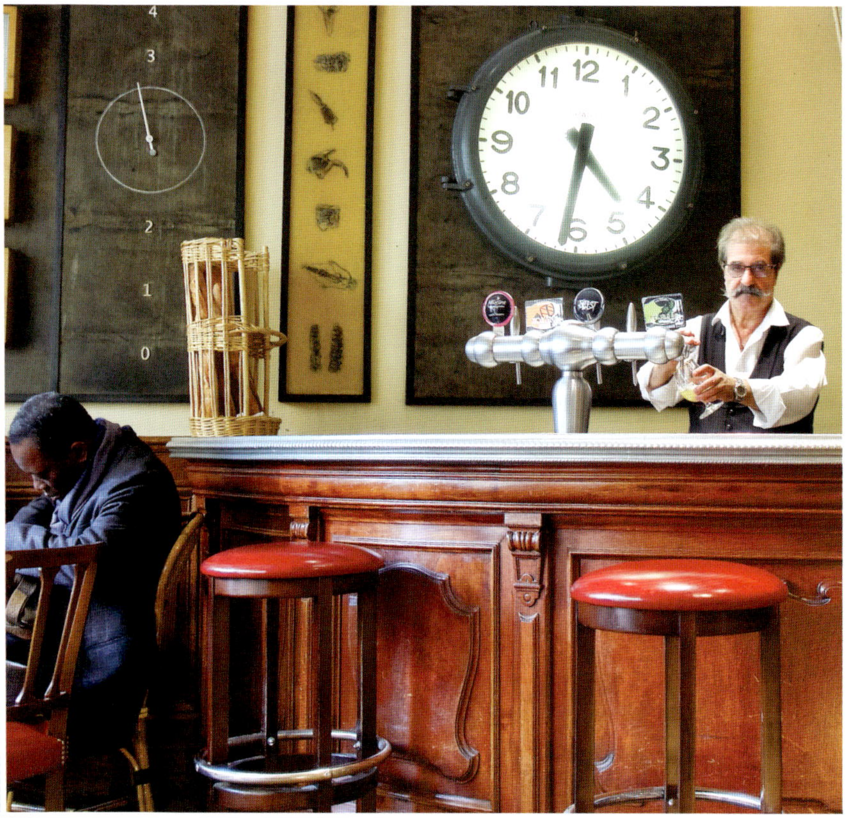

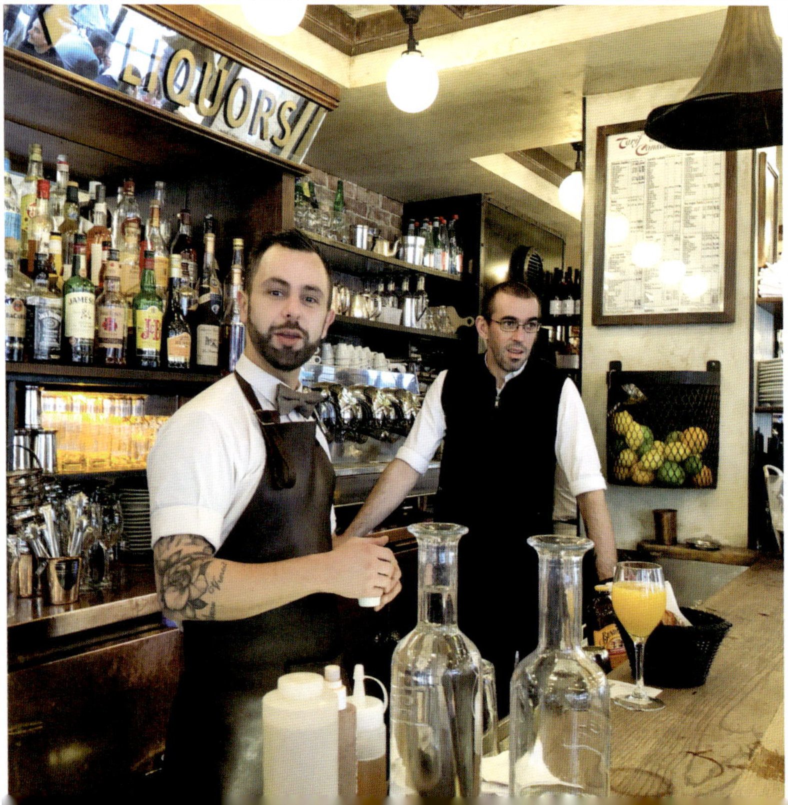

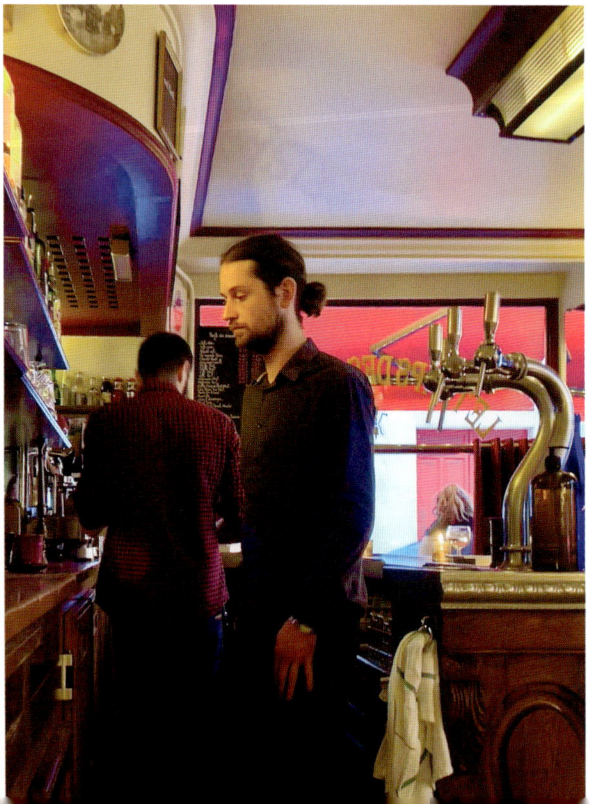

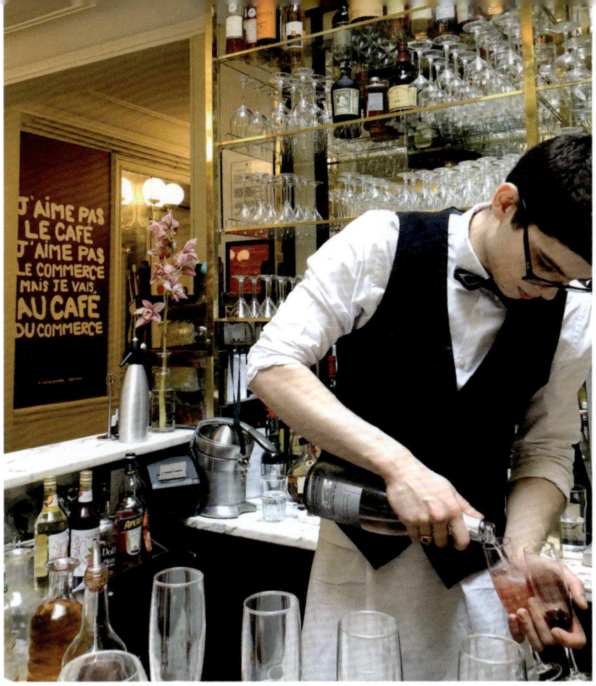
J'AIME PAS
LE CAFE
J'AIME PAS
LE COMMERCE
MAIS JE VAIS
AU CAFE
DU COMMERCE

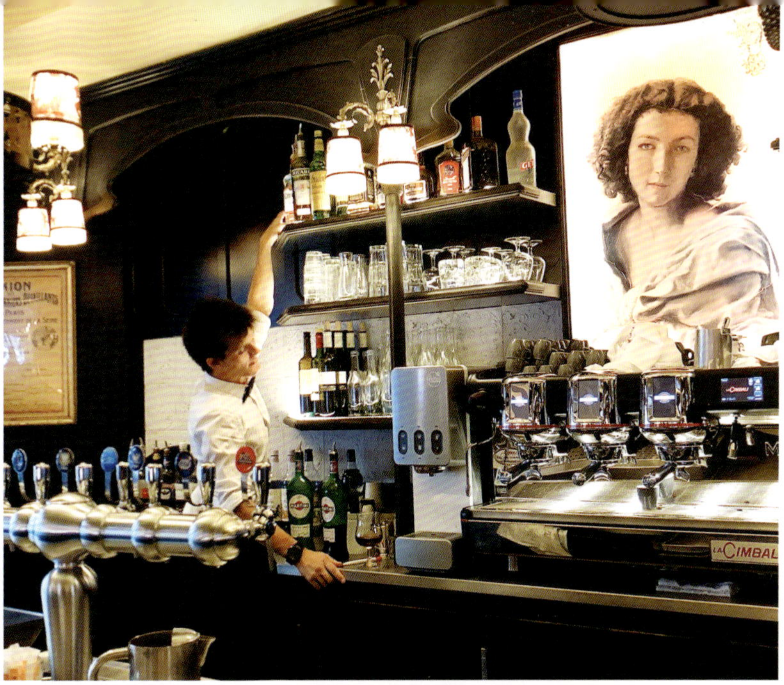

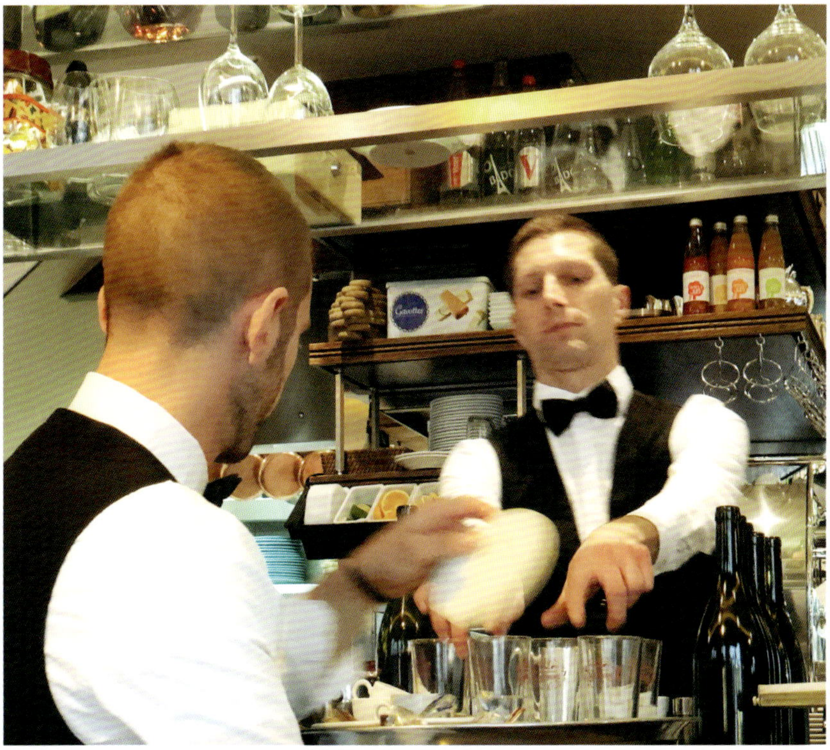

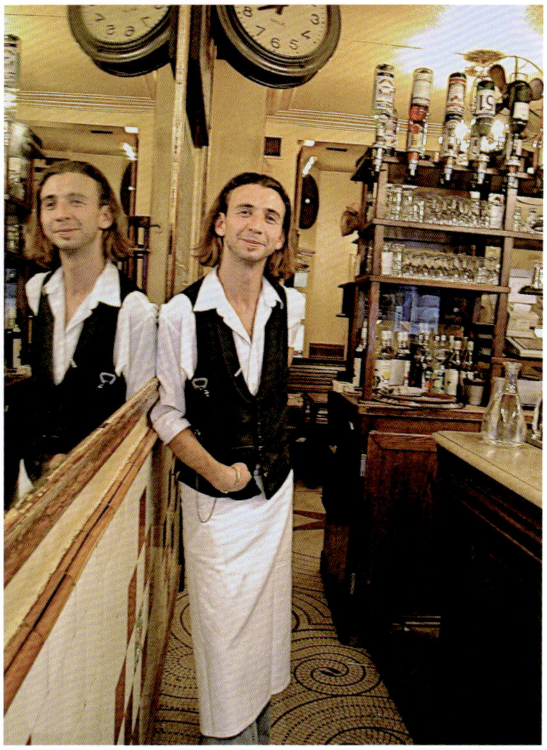

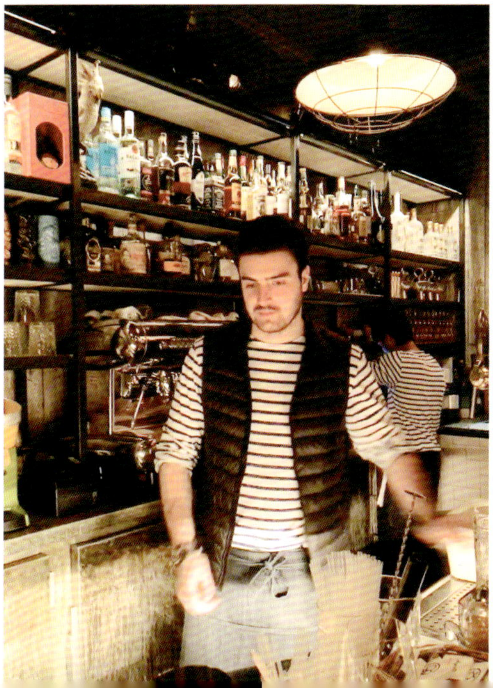

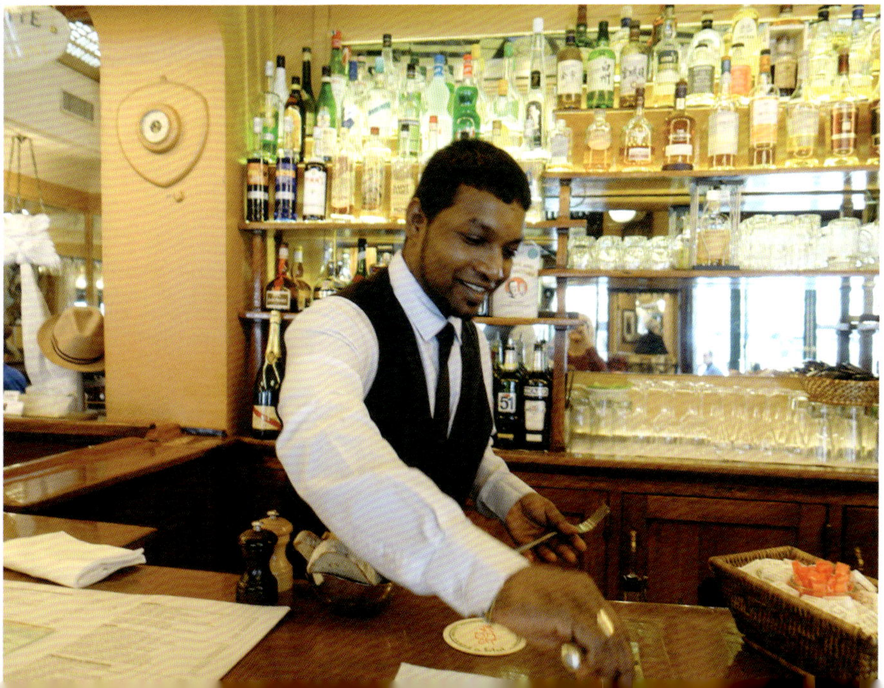

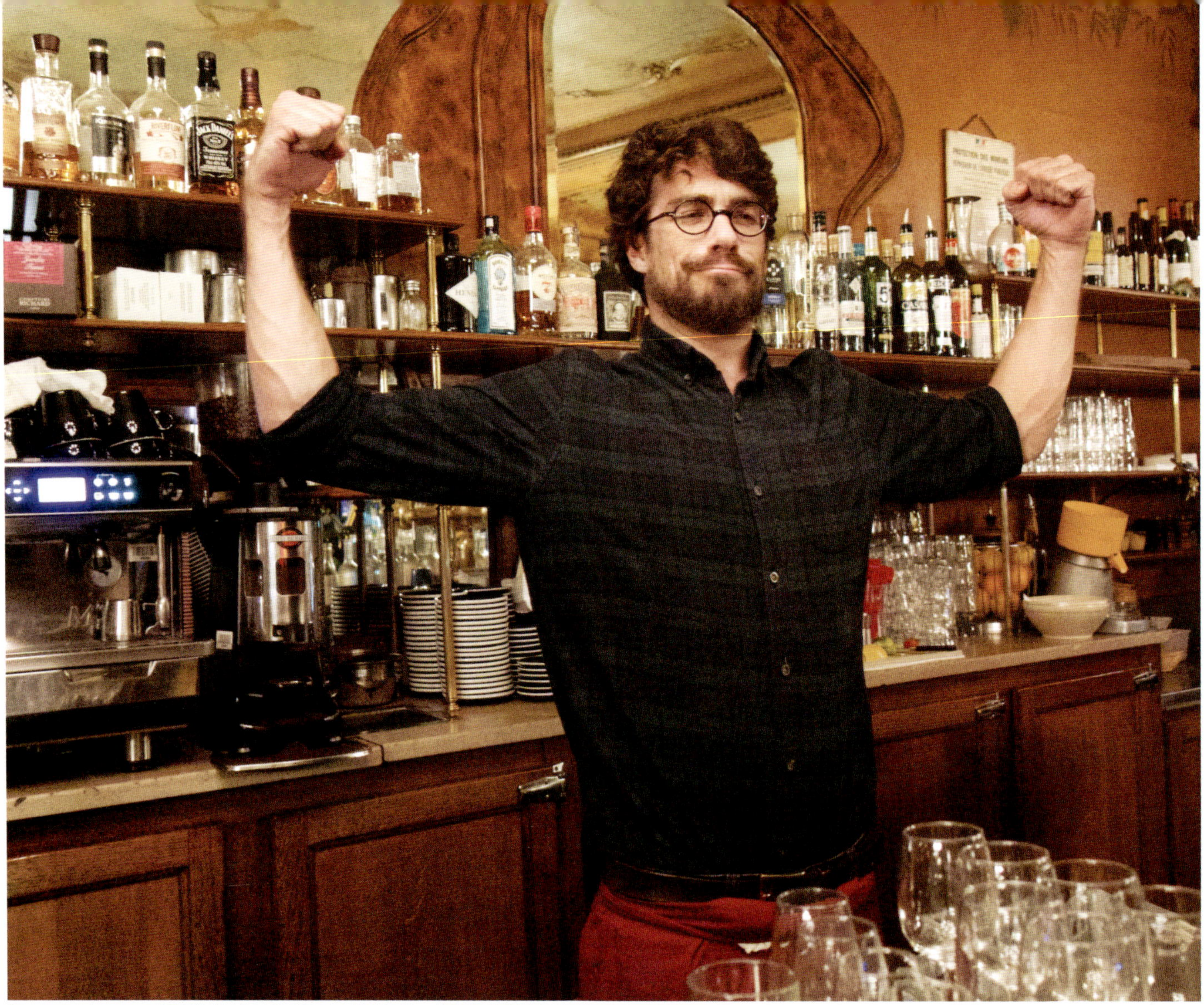

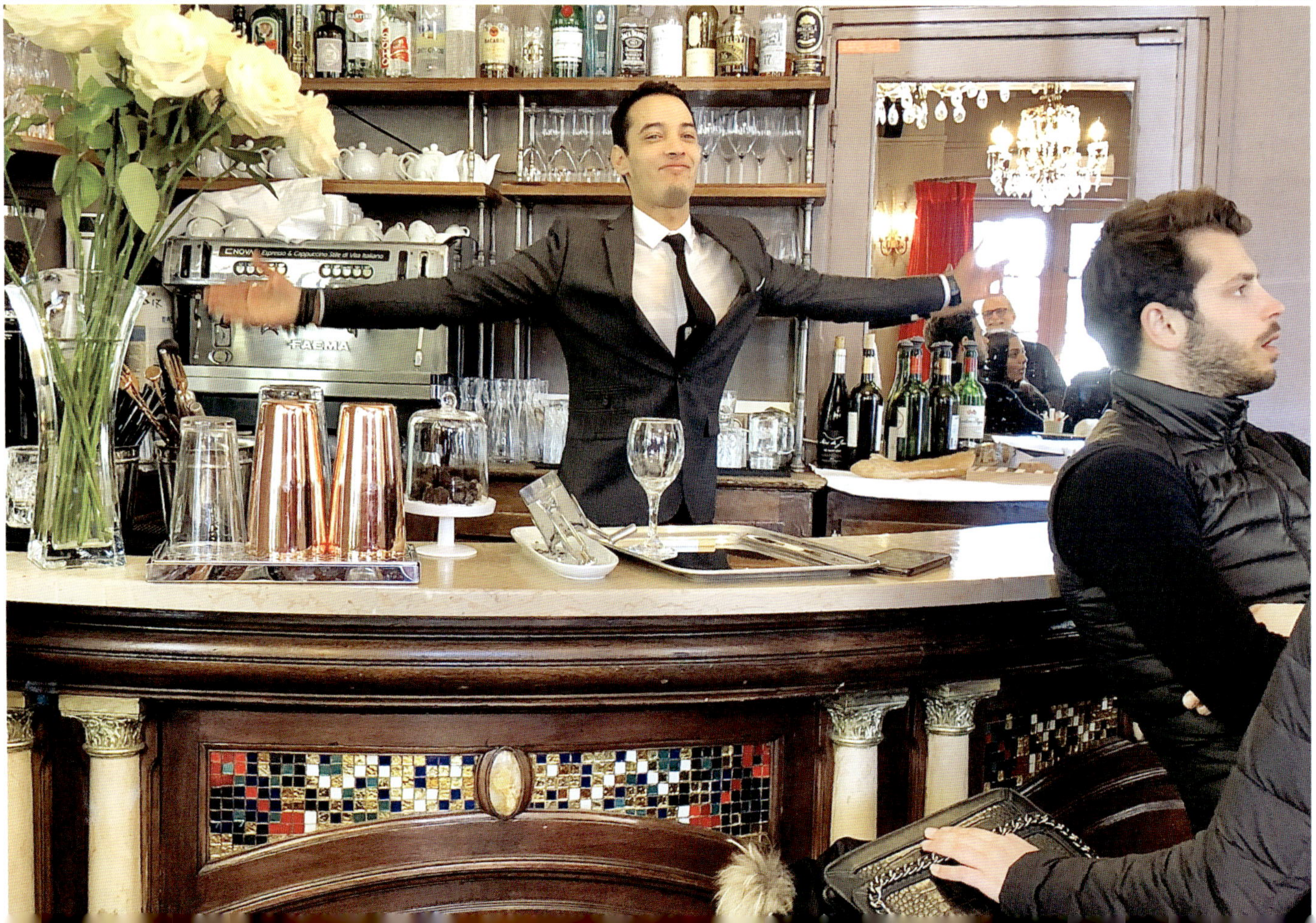
FAEMA

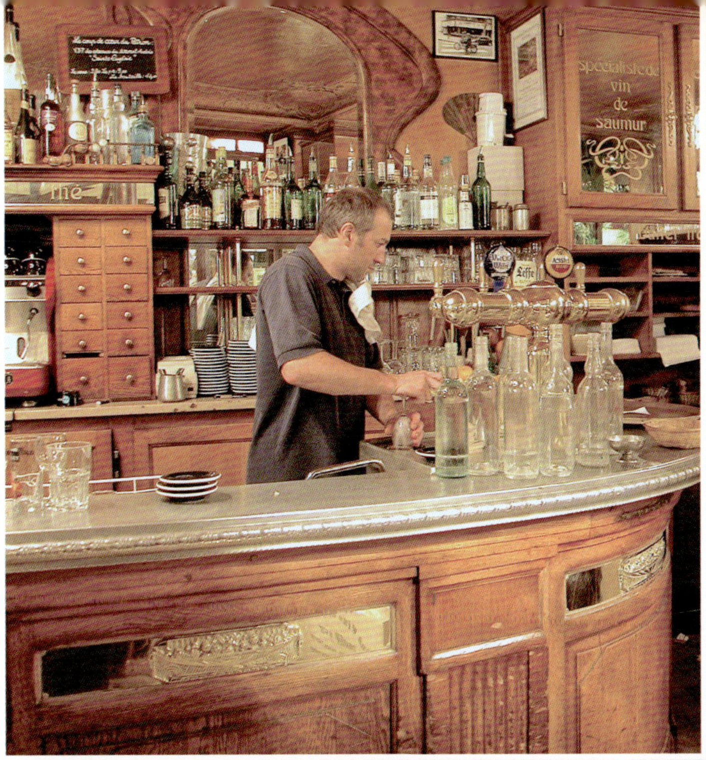

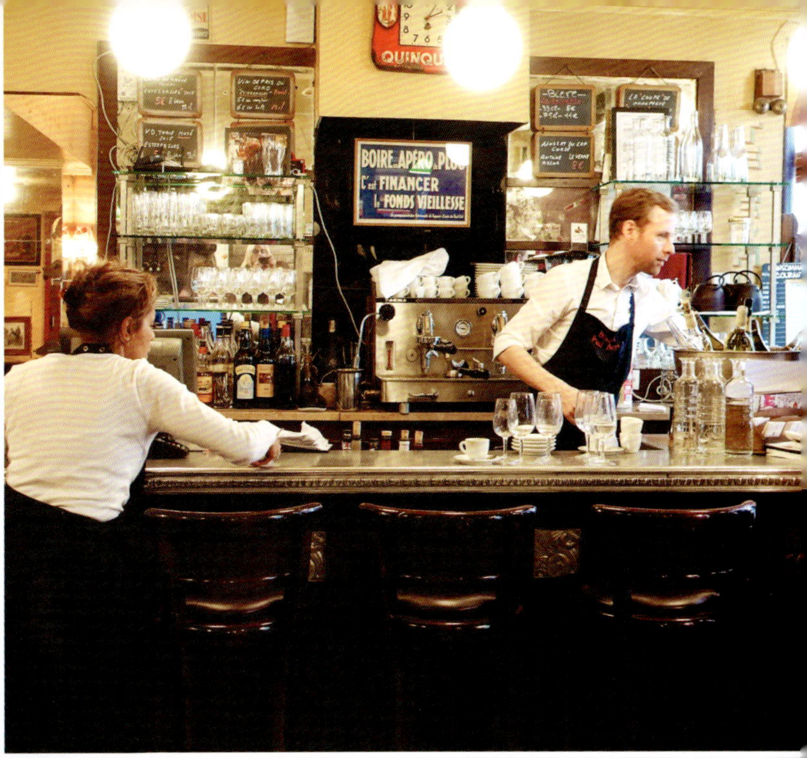
FINANCER

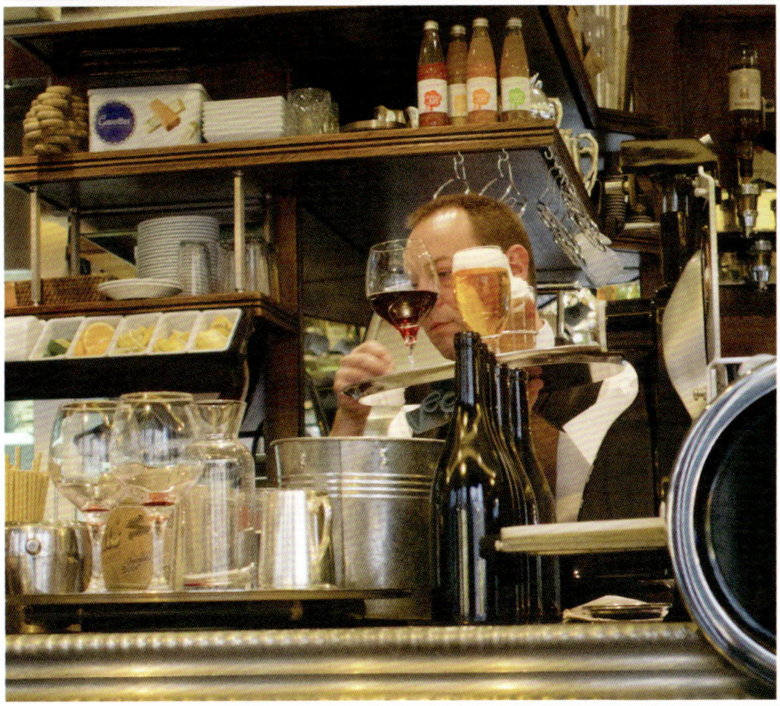

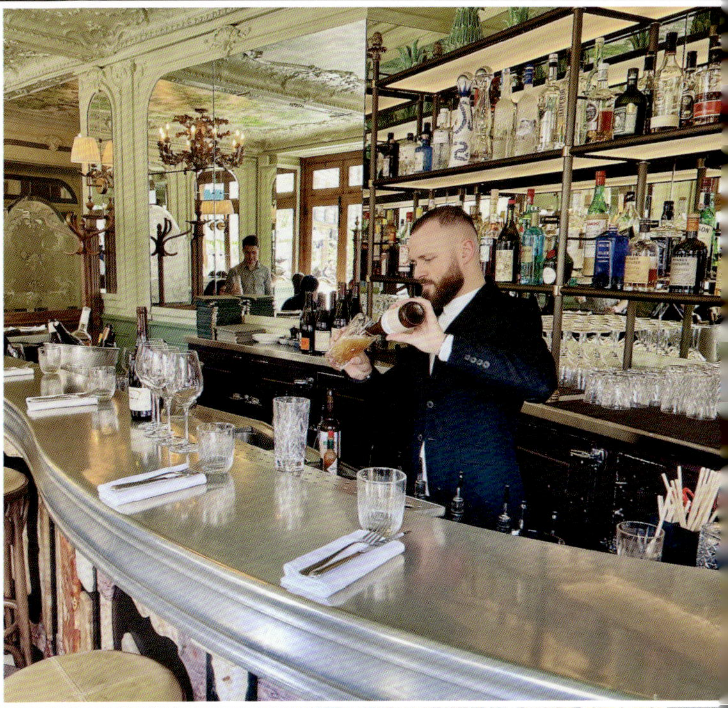

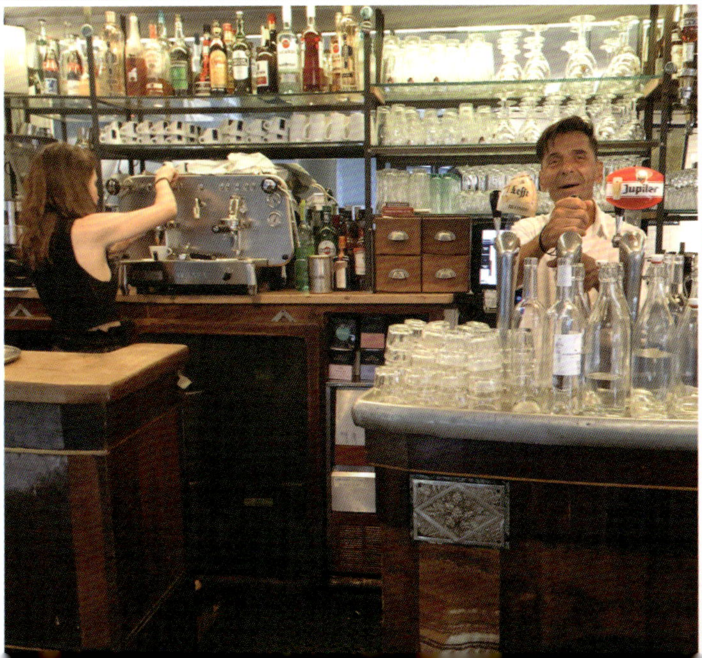
Jupiler

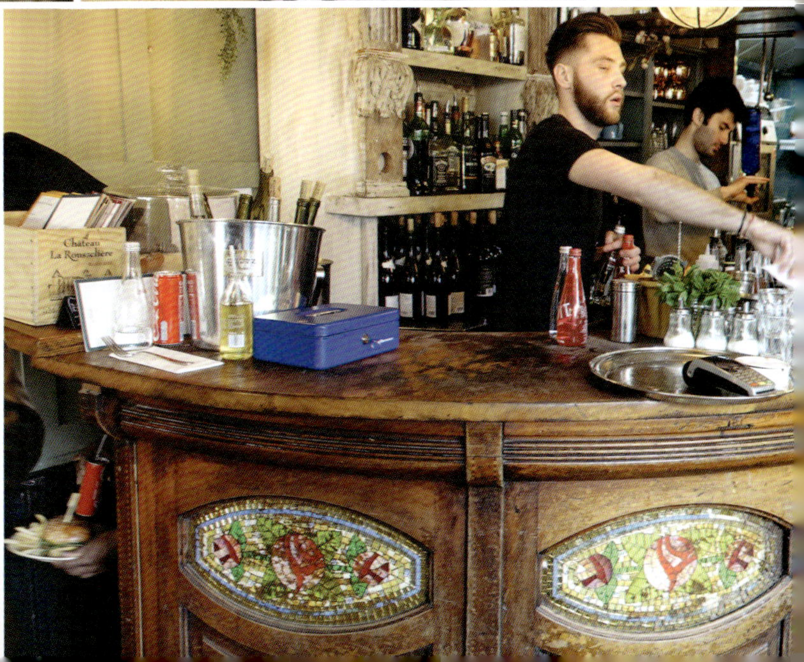

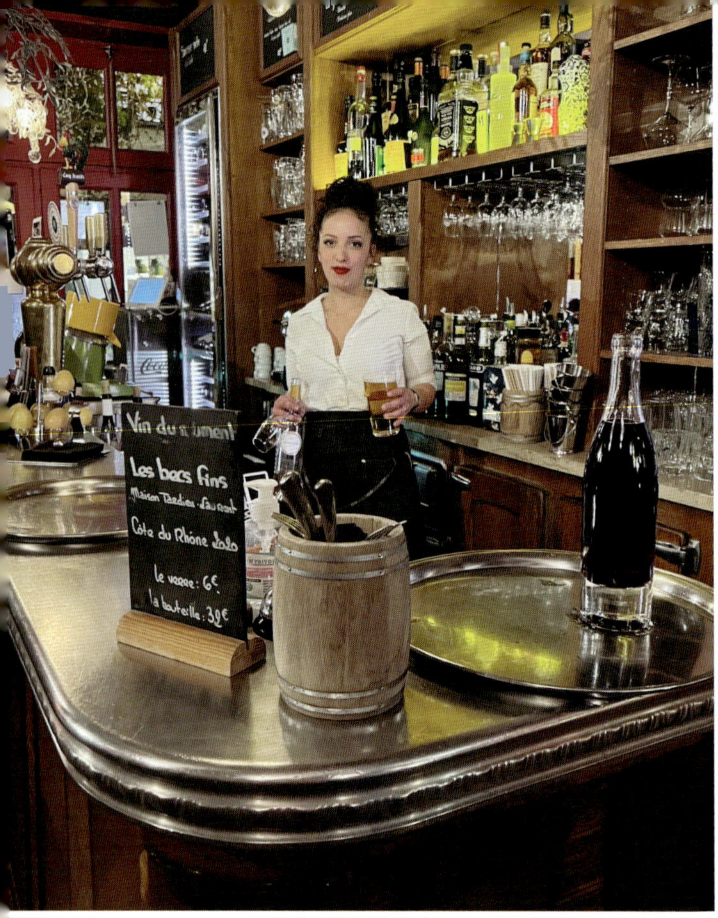
Maison Tardieu-Laurent
Côte du Rhône 2020
le verre : 6€
la bouteille : 32€

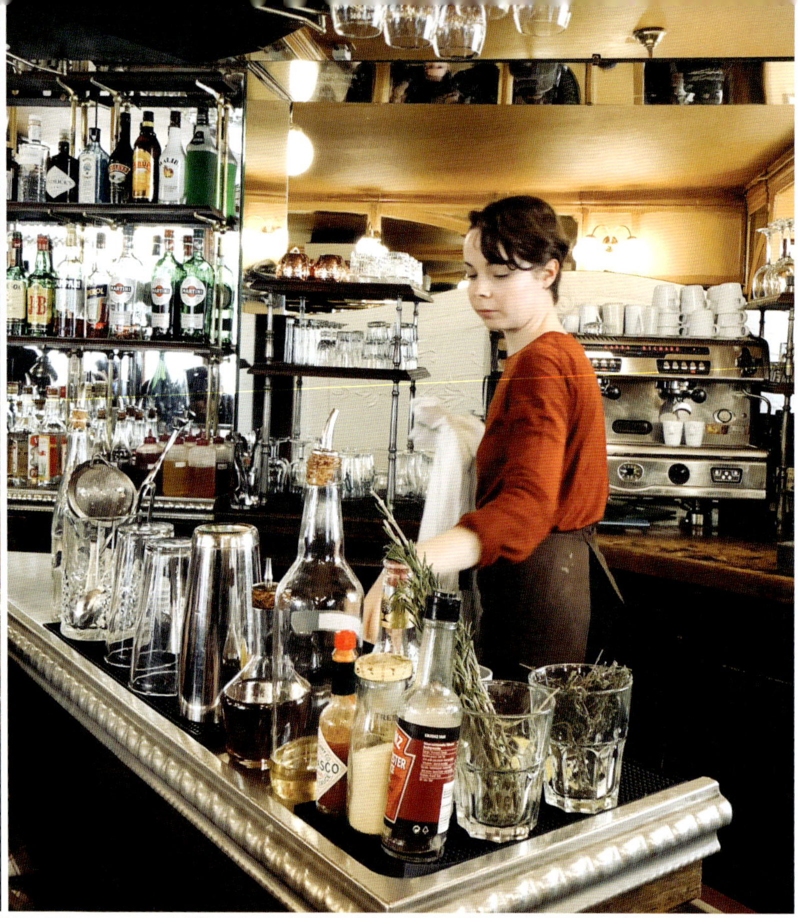

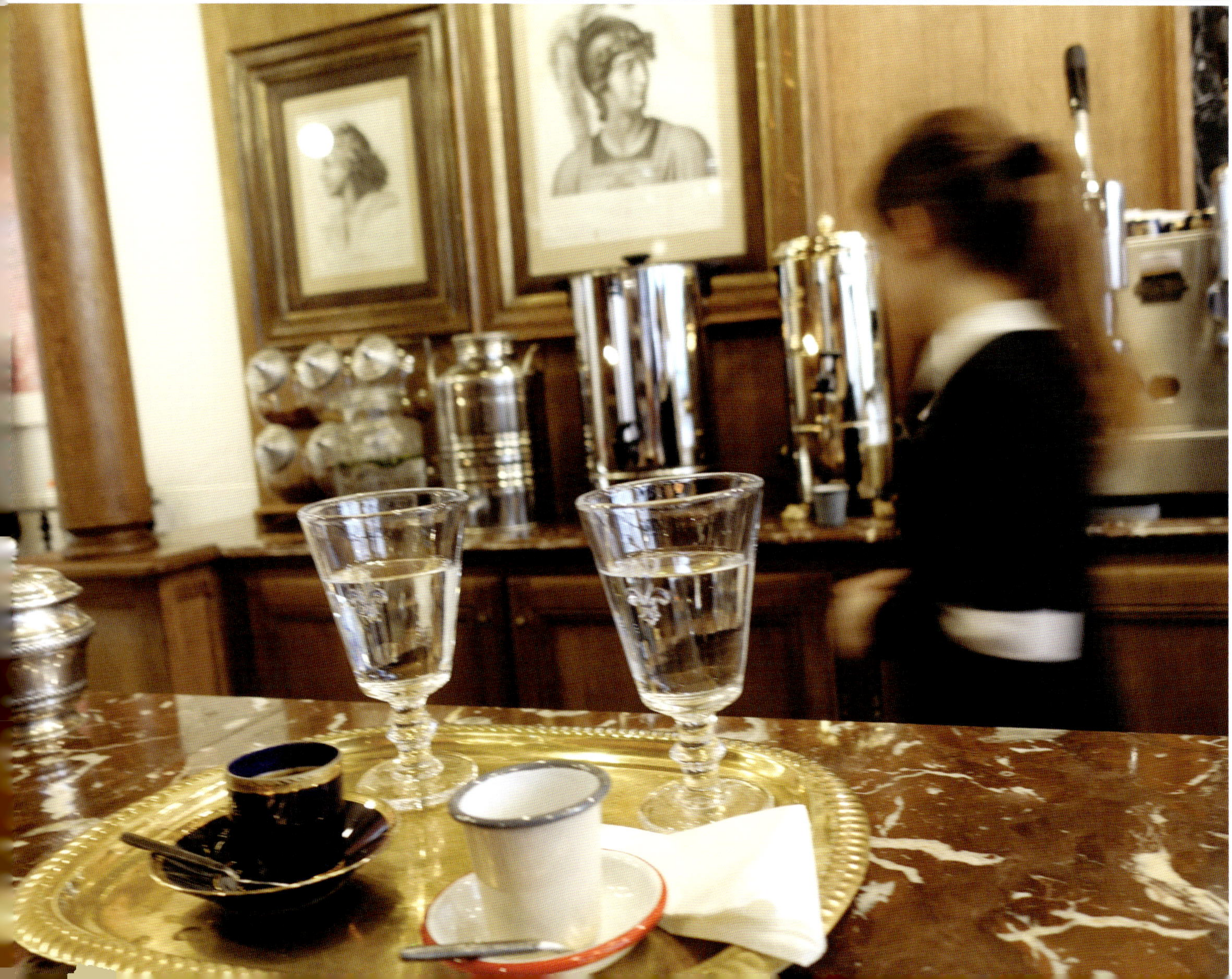

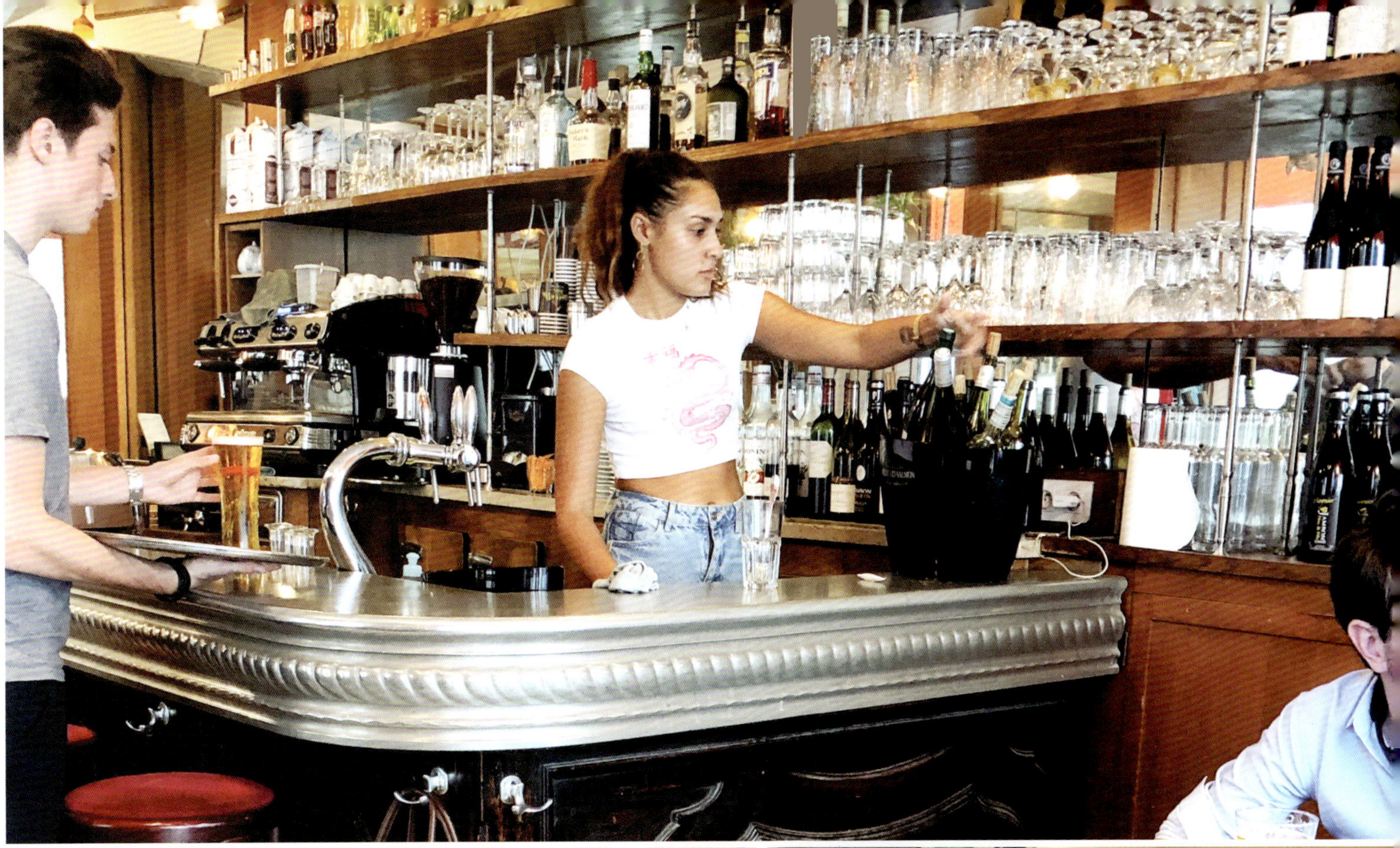

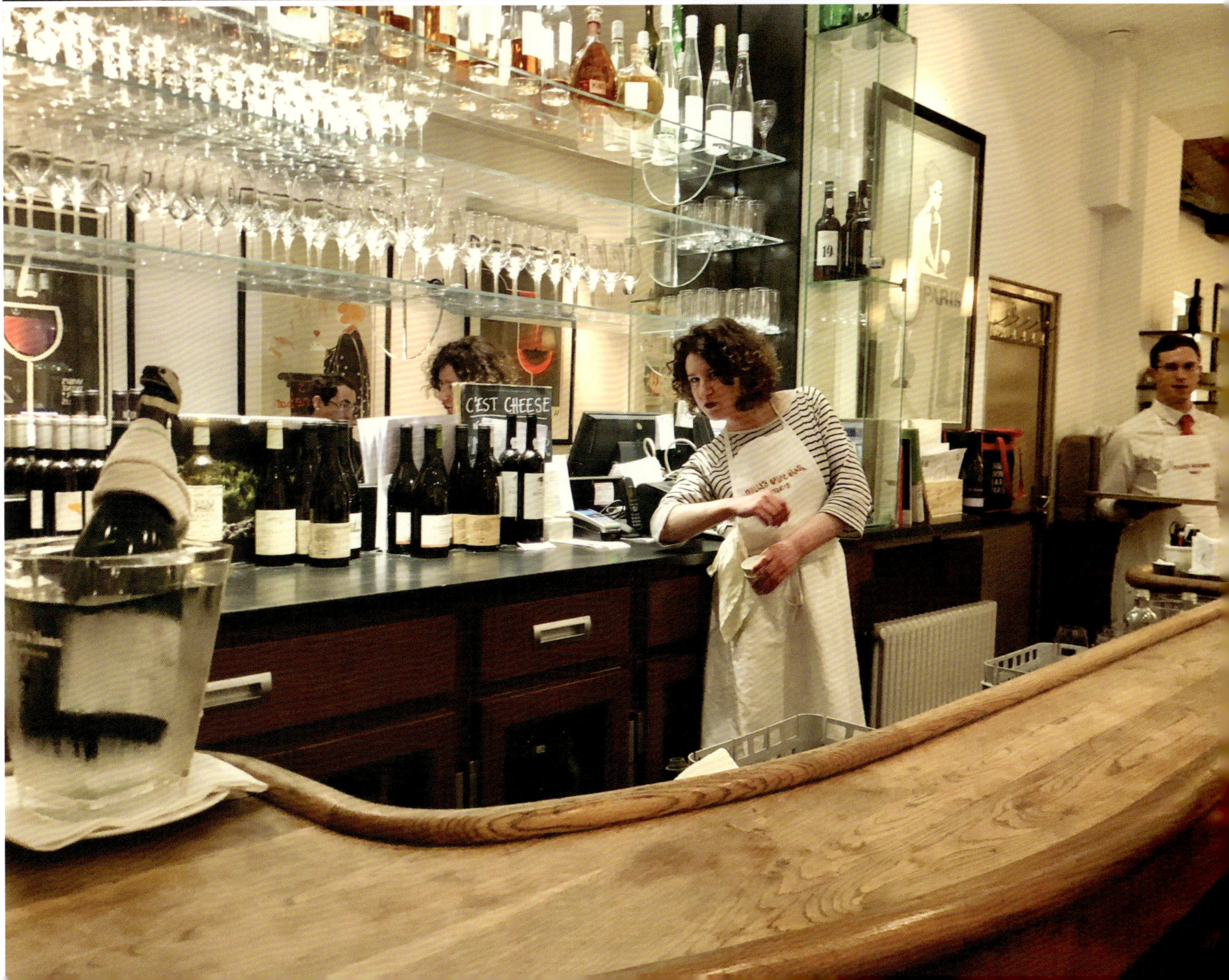
C'EST CHEESE
PARIS

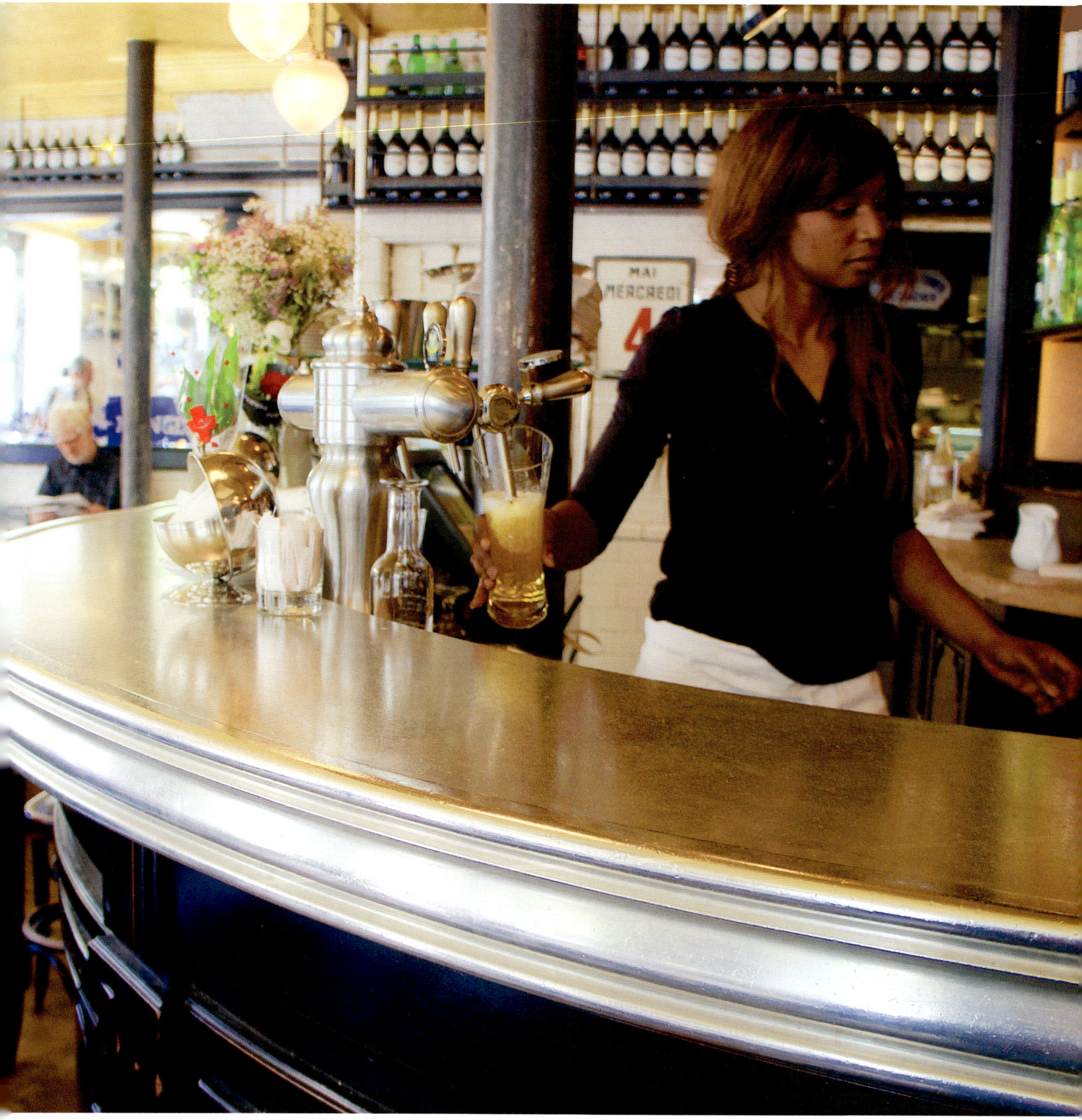
MAI
MERCREDI

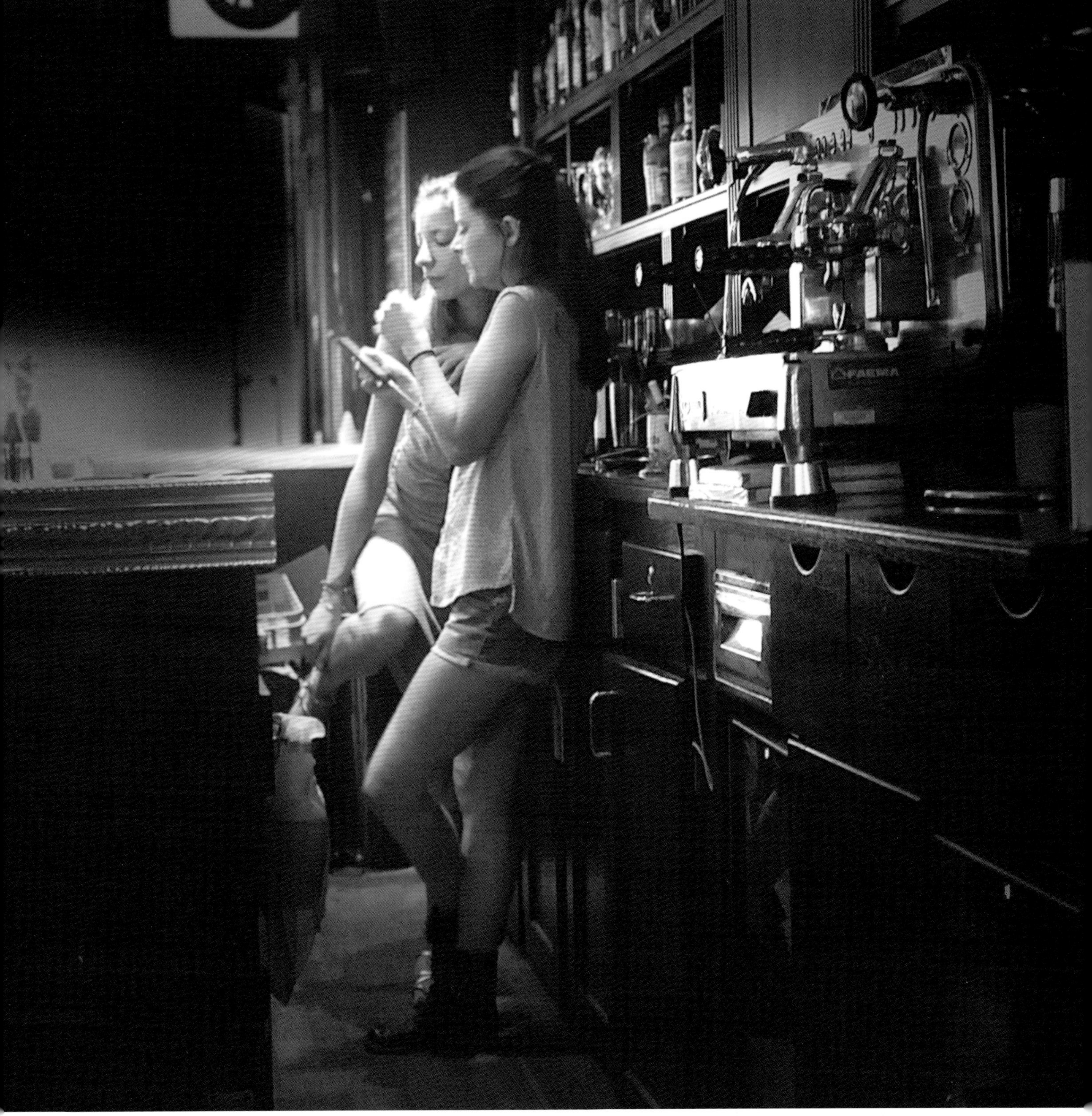
FAEMA

The Chef

"Good cooking is the basis of true happiness."

Auguste Escoffier

In the provinces and Paris (in earlier days), the husband traditionally worked as the chef, and the wife oversaw the dining room. Sometimes still in Paris, the husband-and-wife team can be found in neighborhood bistros and cafés. Nevertheless, many Parisian cafés and bistros now have cooks rather than chefs, and the enterprise is no longer a family affair. Fortunately, there is a growing trend for chefs, and chef-owners, often in their 20s and 30s, to preside over the kitchen and create fantastic cuisine. Discovering these treasured spots is worth the effort because, with these young chefs' hard work, talent, and dedication, the results are memorable. Immersed in their kitchens, chefs work from early morning to late at night behind the scenes. From time to time, they will emerge to greet their delighted guests. As long as the food is fresh and *fait maison*, the cooking can be delicious in Paris, regardless of title or ownership.

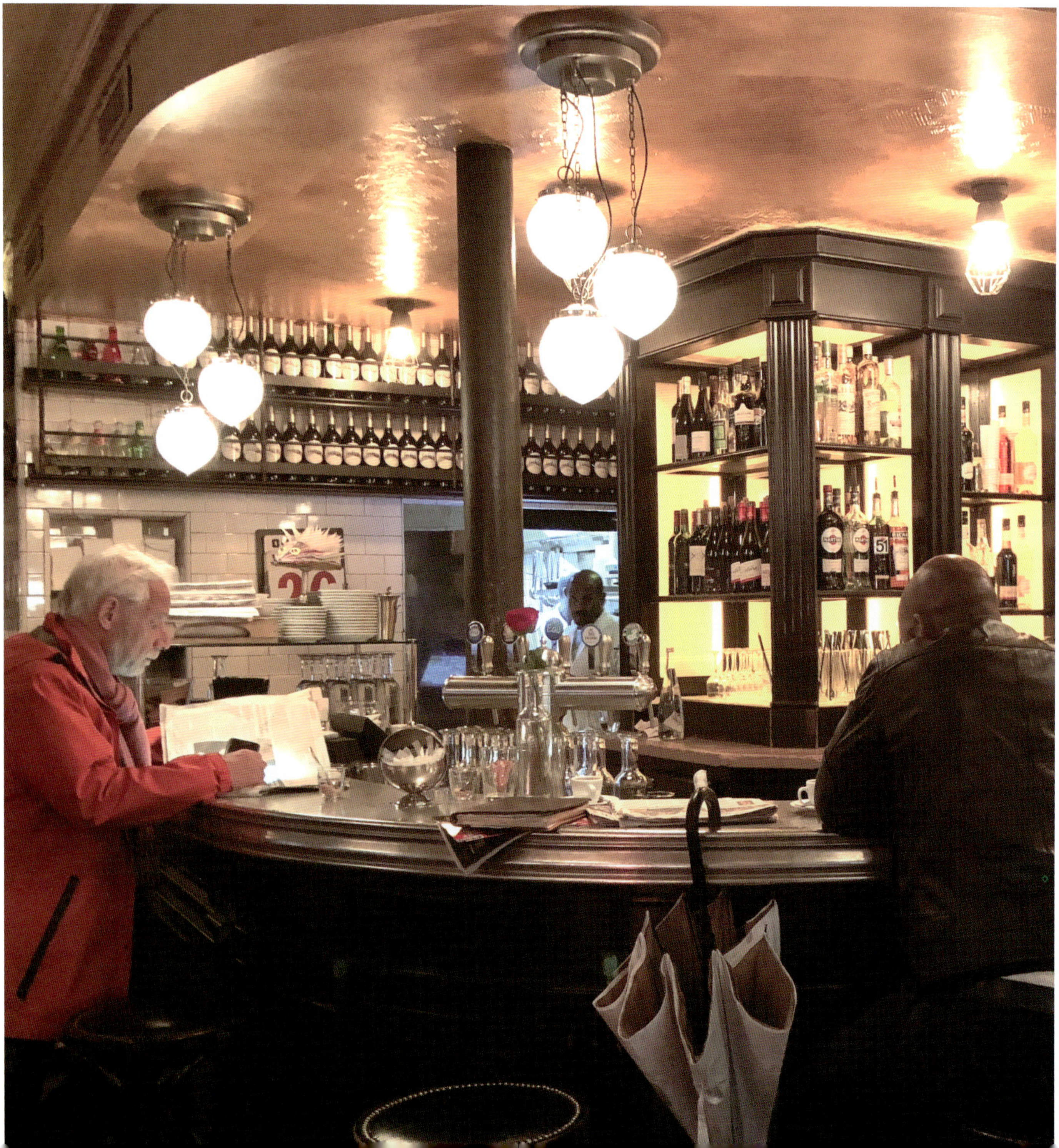

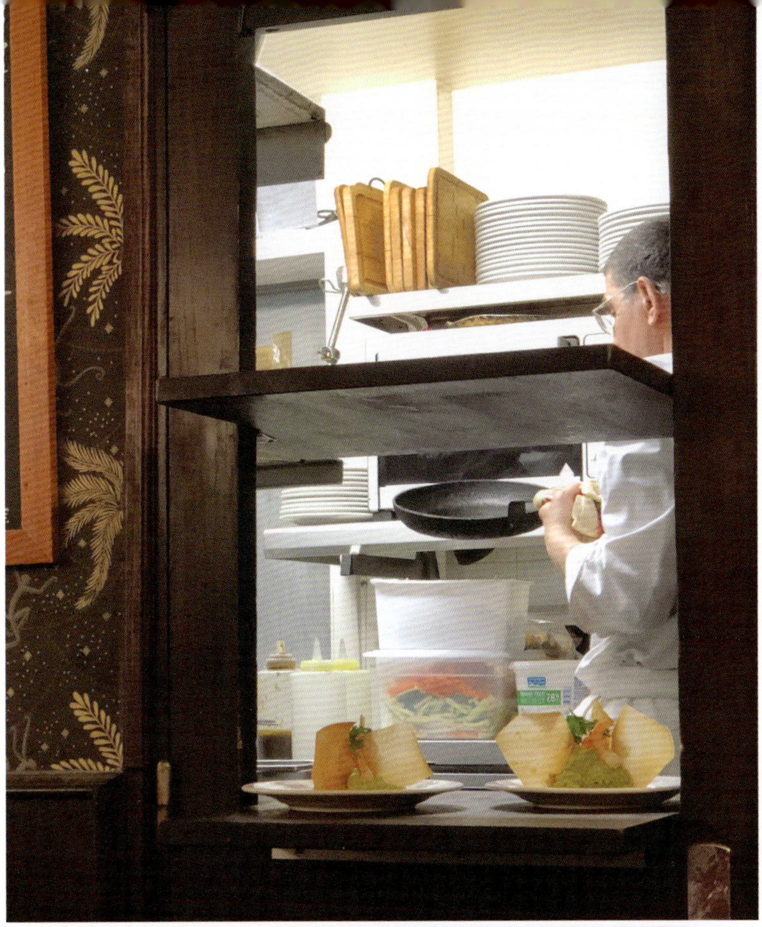

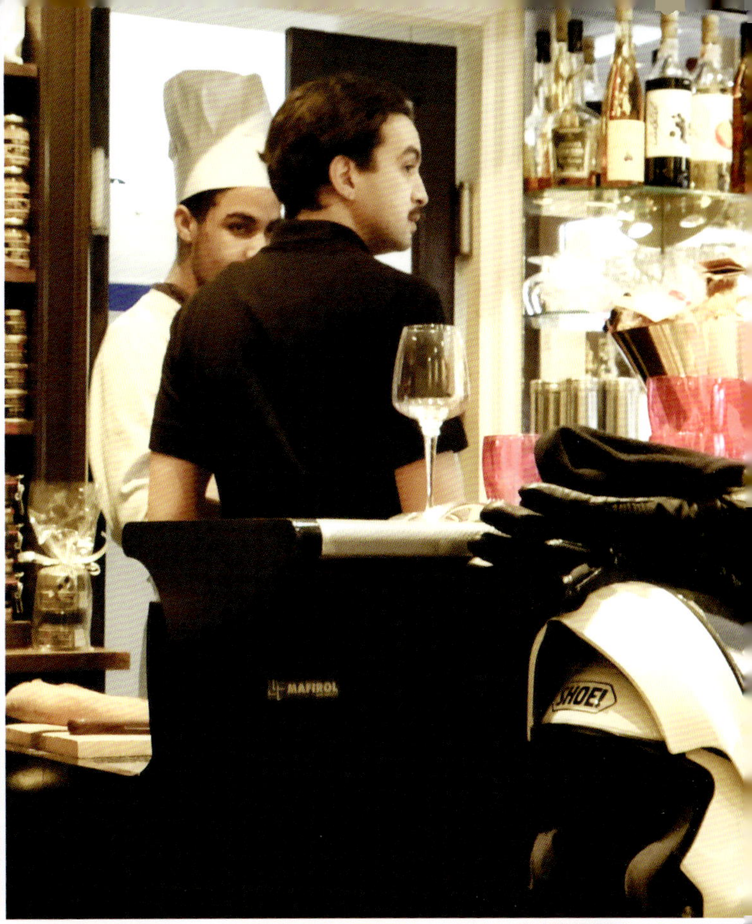
MAFIROL
SHOEI

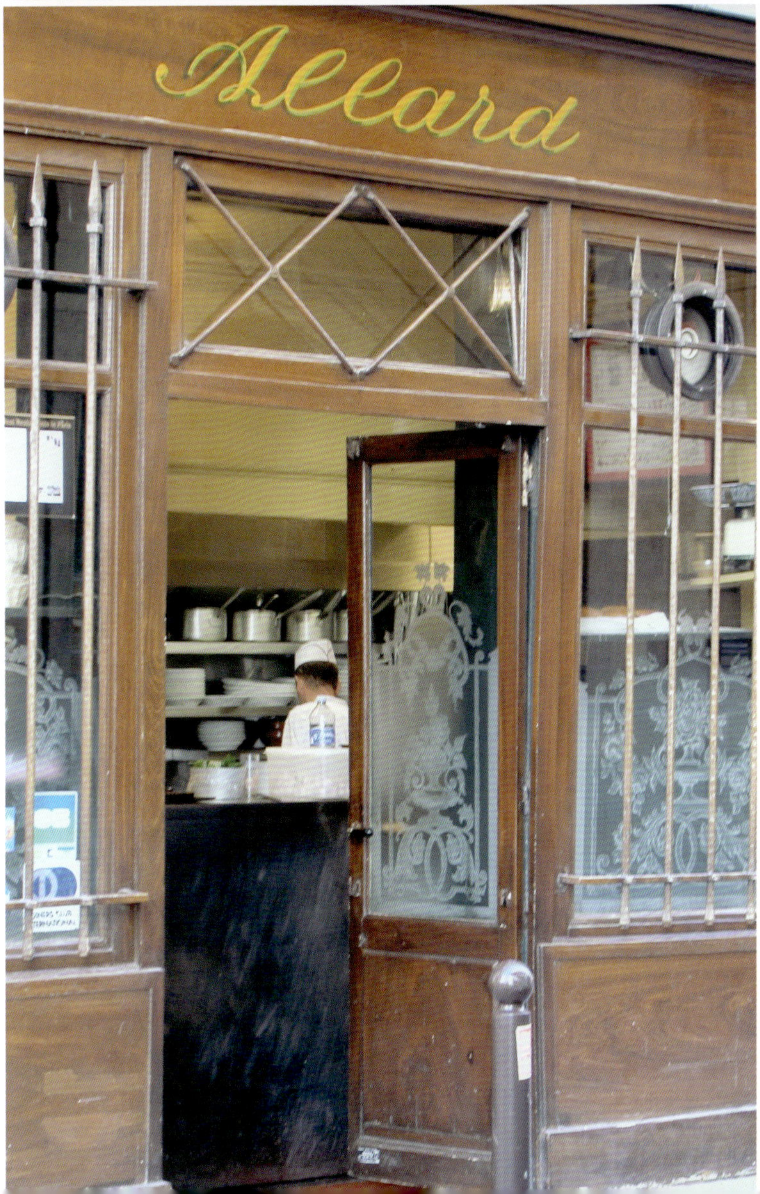
Allard

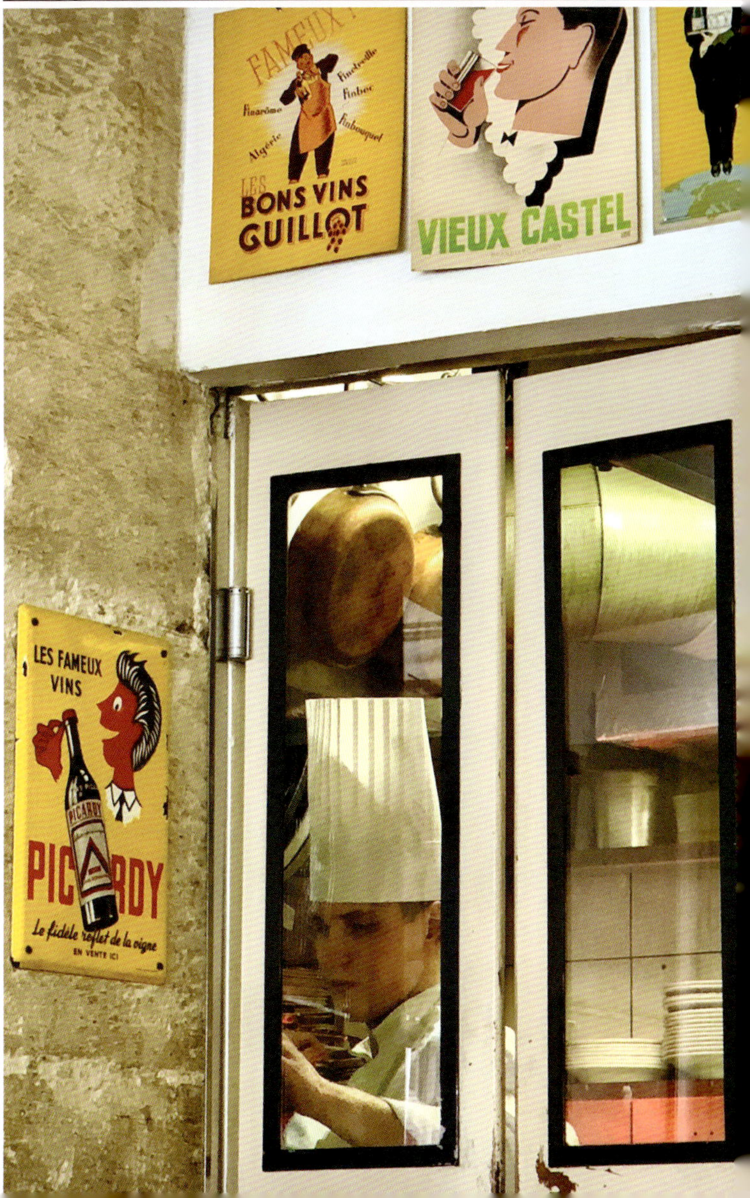
LES
BONS VINS
GUILLOT
VIEUX CASTEL
LES FAMEUX
VINS
PICARDY
Le fidèle reflet de la vigne
EN VENTE ICI

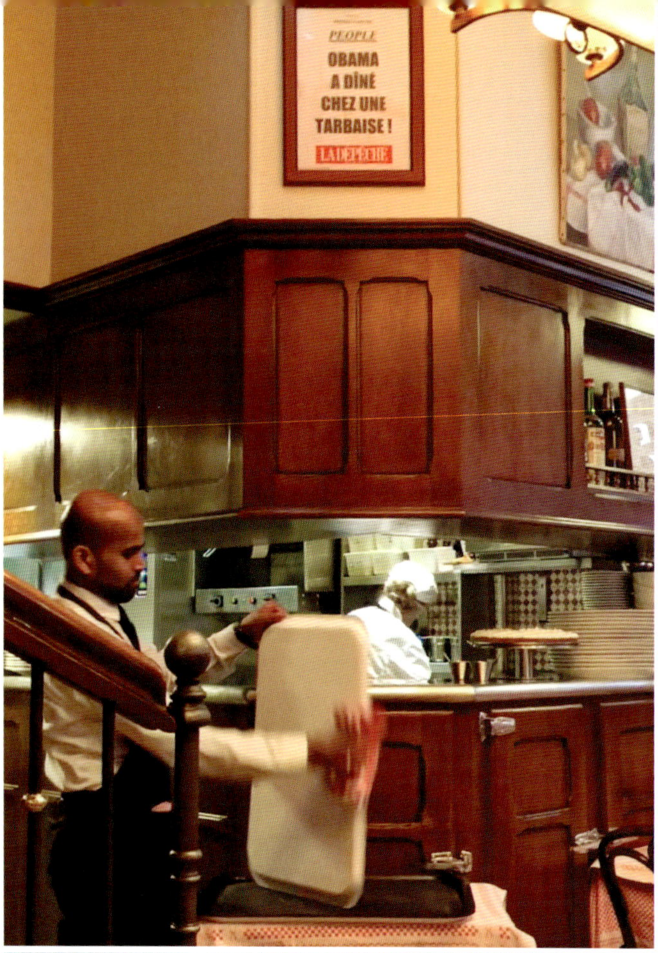
PEOPLE
OBAMA
A DÎNÉ
CHEZ UNE
TARBAISE !
LA DÉPÊCHE

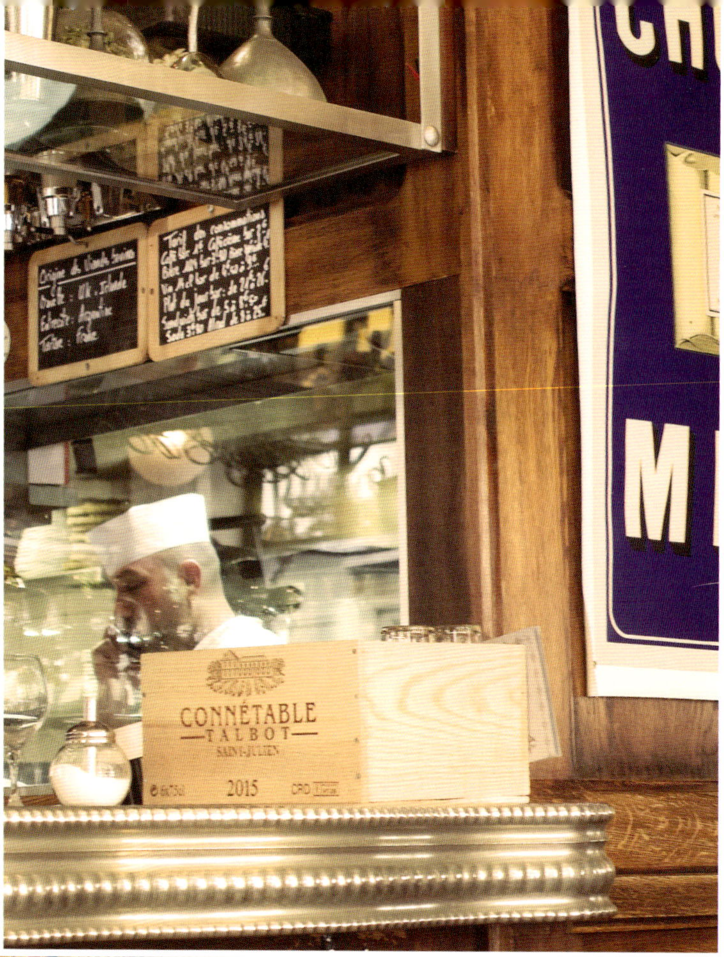
CONNÉTABLE
TALBOT
SAINT-JULIEN
2015

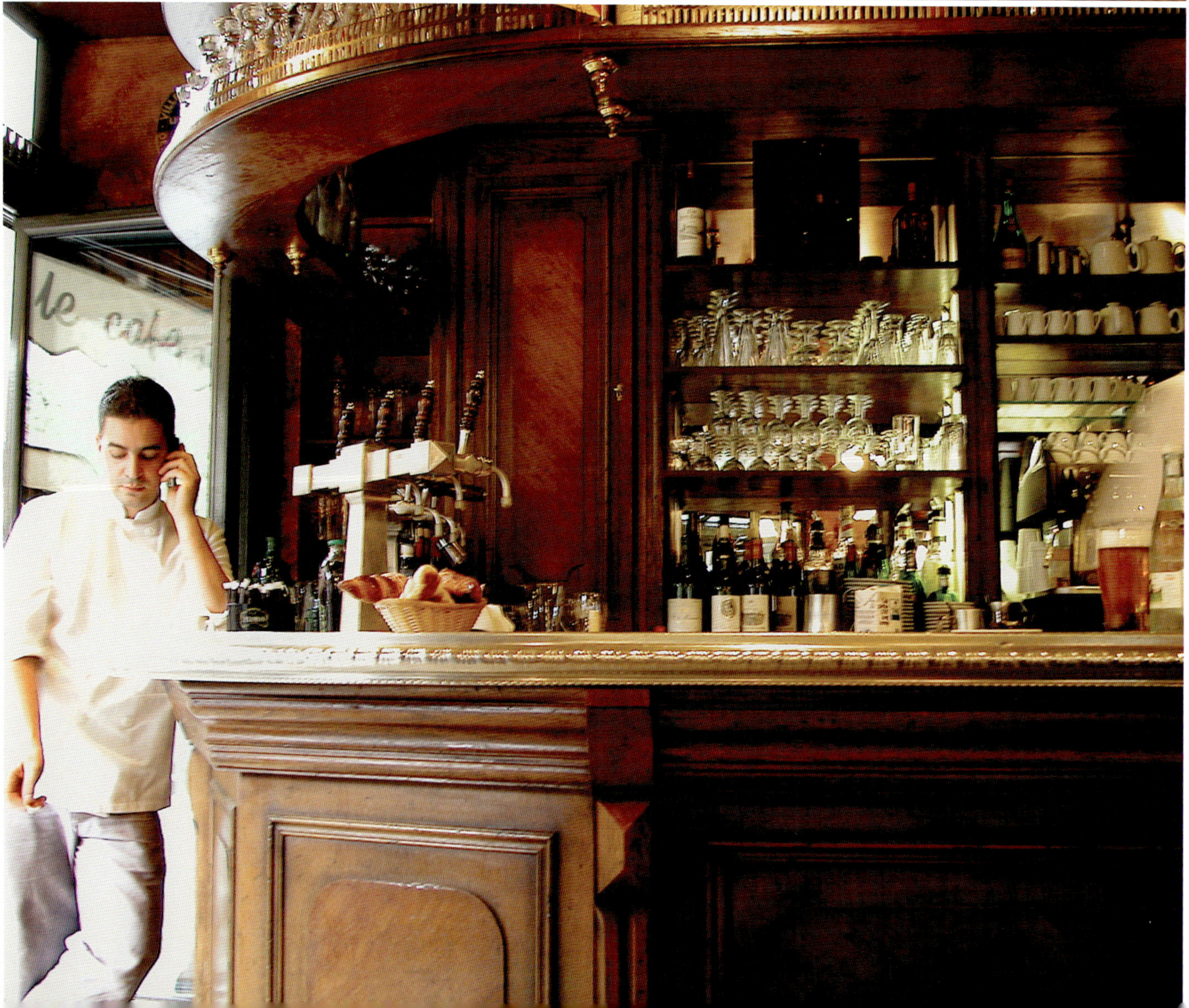

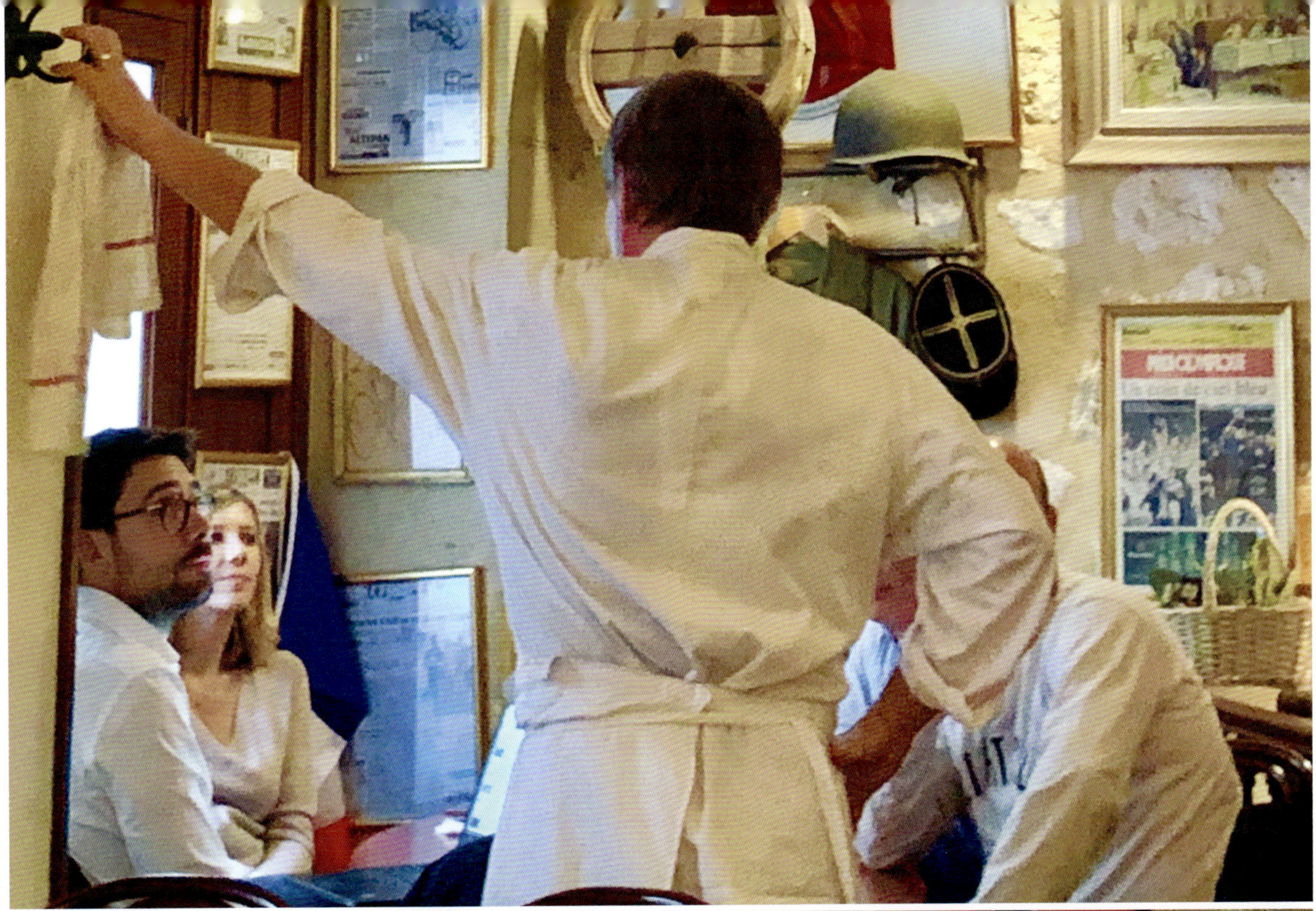

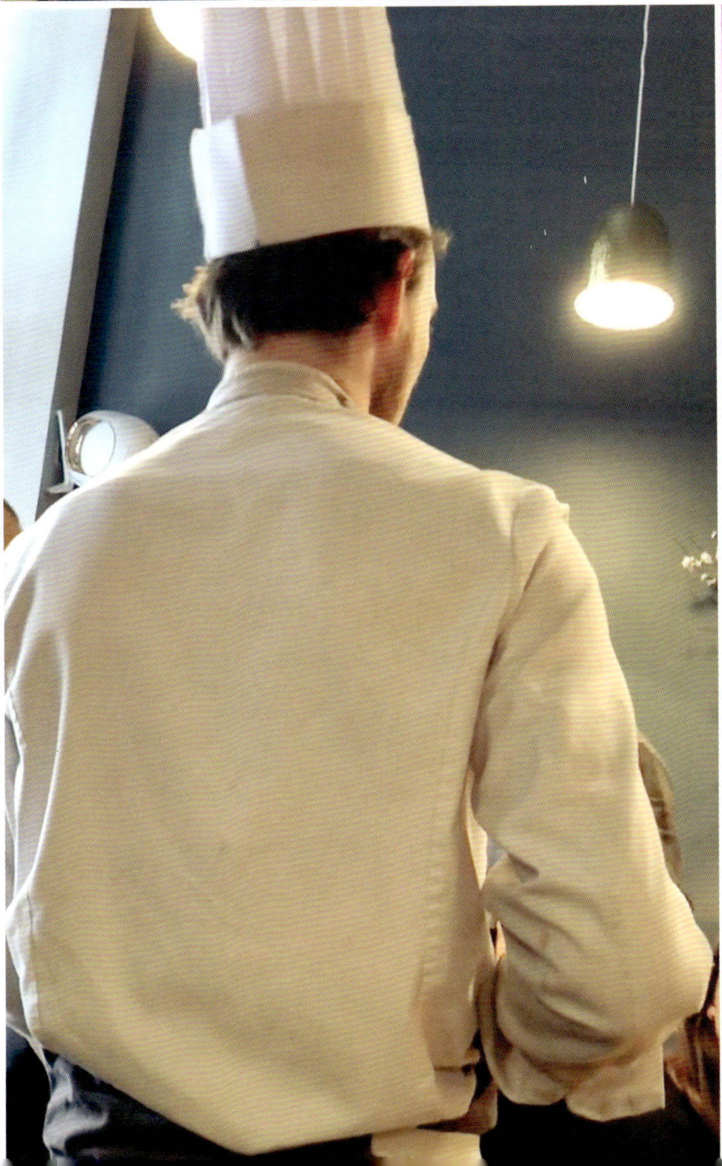

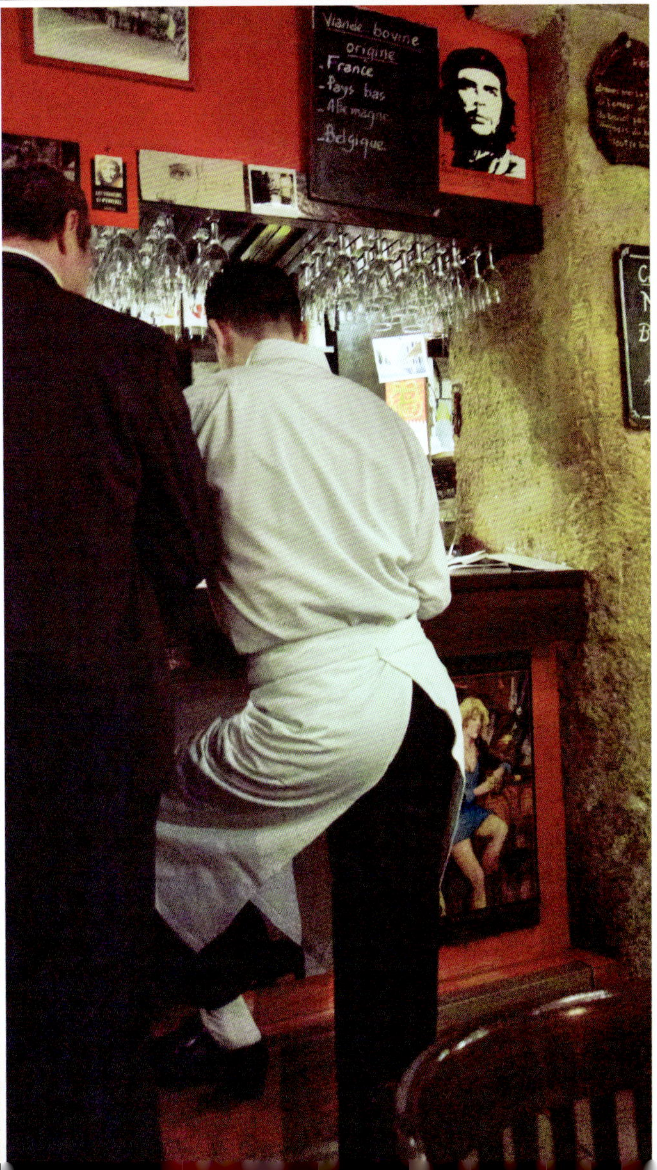
Viande bovine
origine
-France
-Pays bas
-Allemagne
-Belgique

The Animals

"Whoever does not visit Paris regularly will never really be elegant."

Honoré de Balzac

Animaux bienvenus. Indeed, democracy rules in Parisian cafés and bistros, even for animals; it seems there are more regulations for them in parks than in food establishments. The French adore cute animals, and with a canine population that counts one dog for every seven Parisians, they are naturally welcome customers. Parisian dogs, sometimes even cats (or giant teddy bears), are well-behaved customers and invariably adorable. They add smiles and animation without exception to the place.

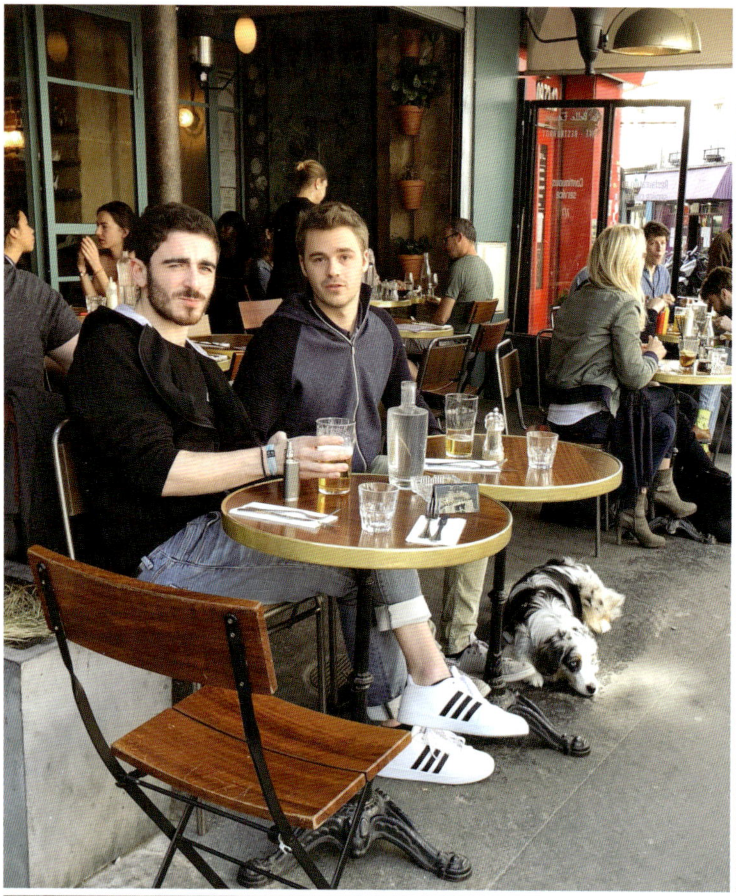

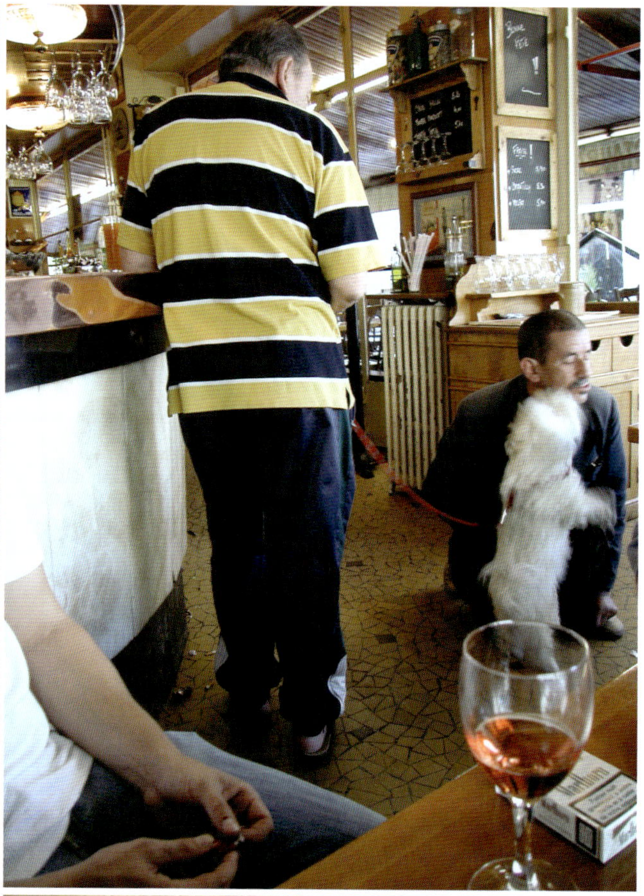

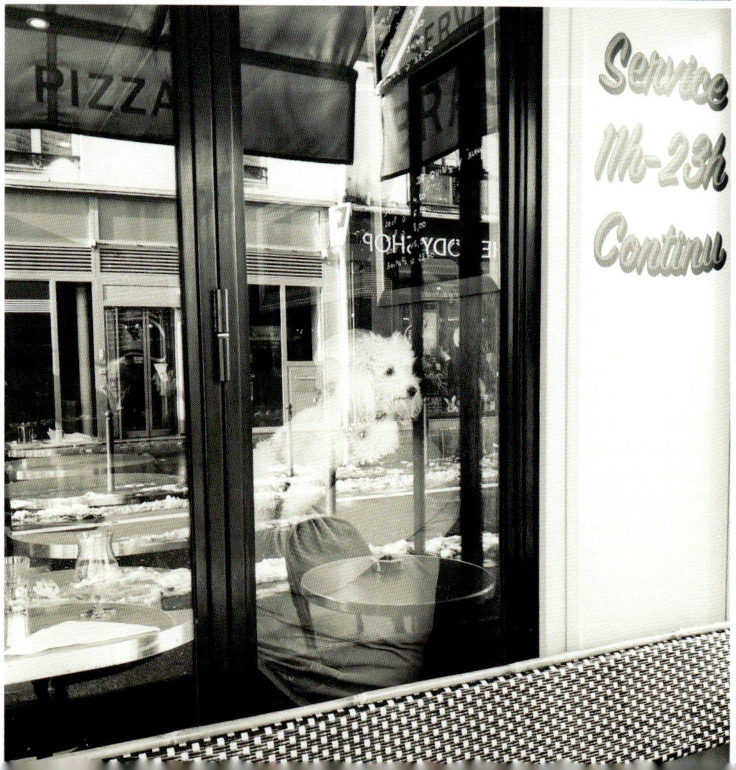

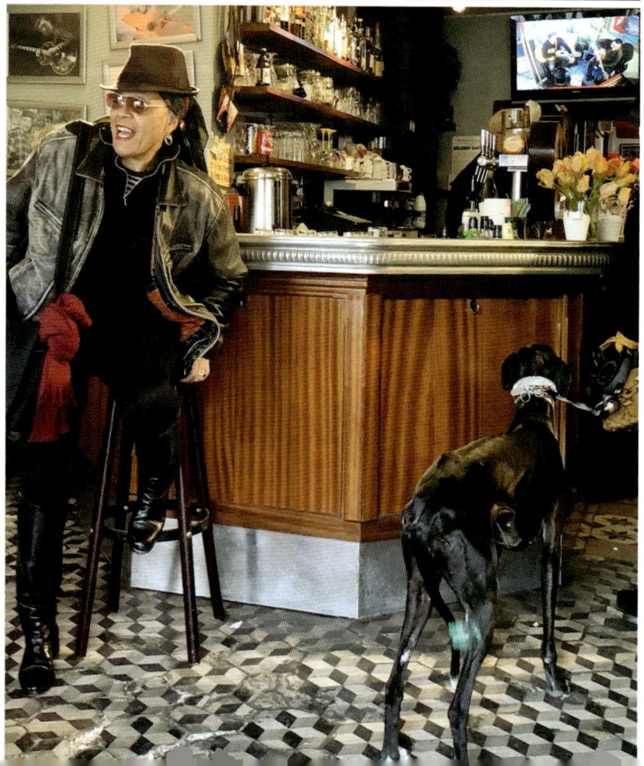

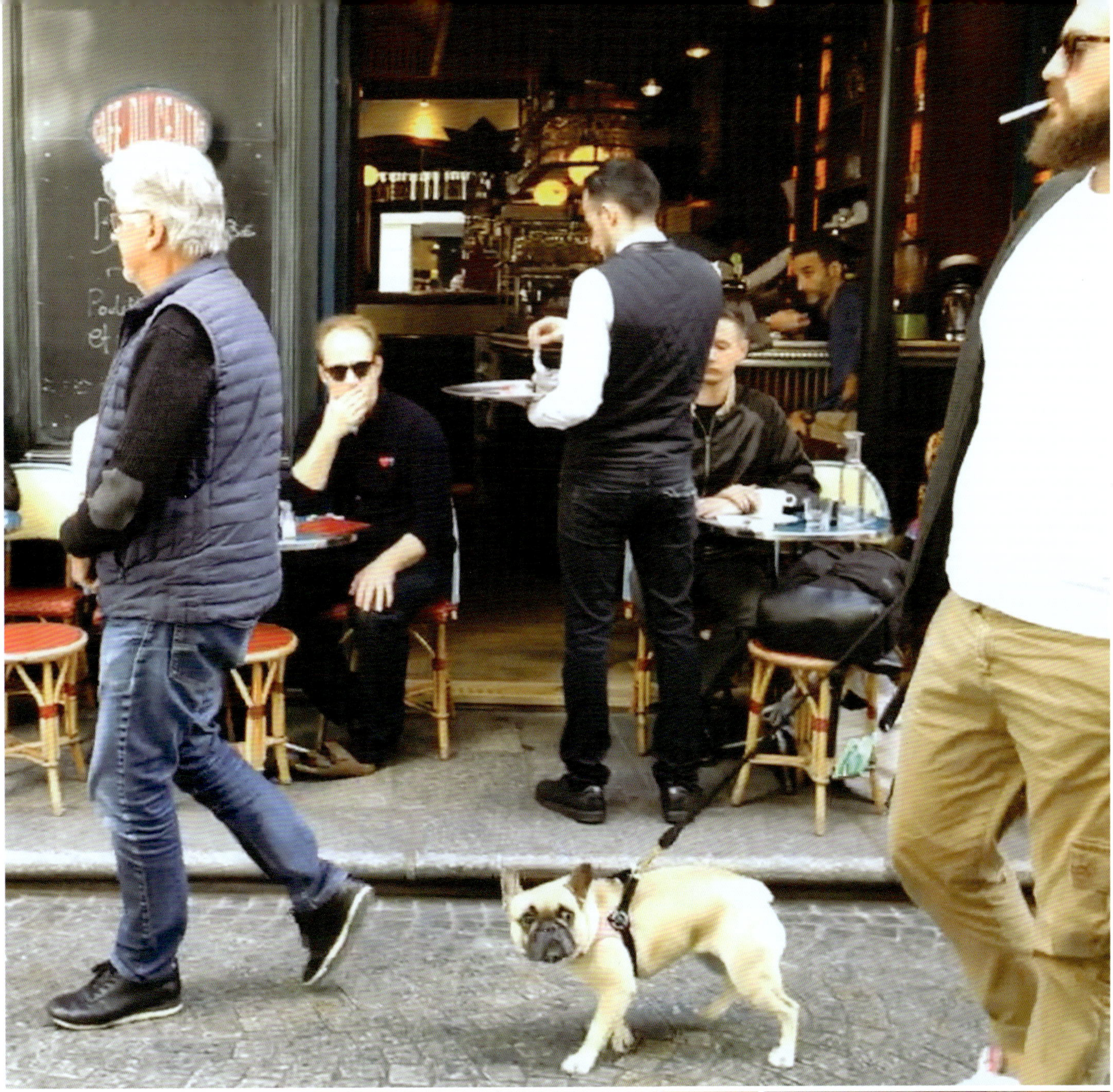

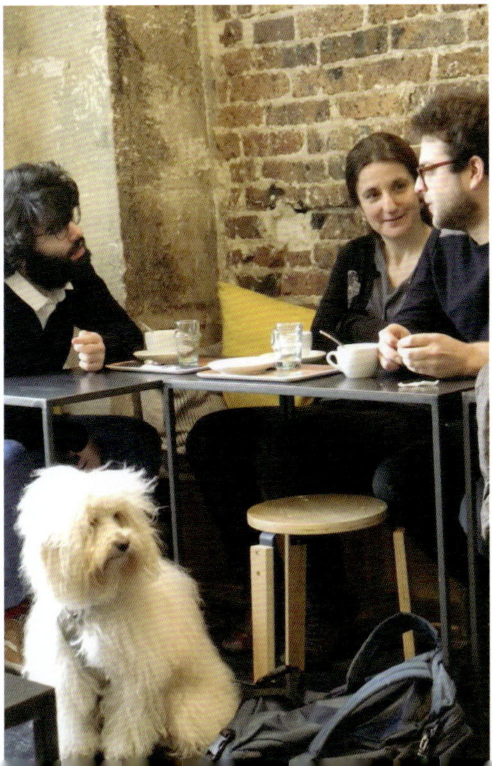

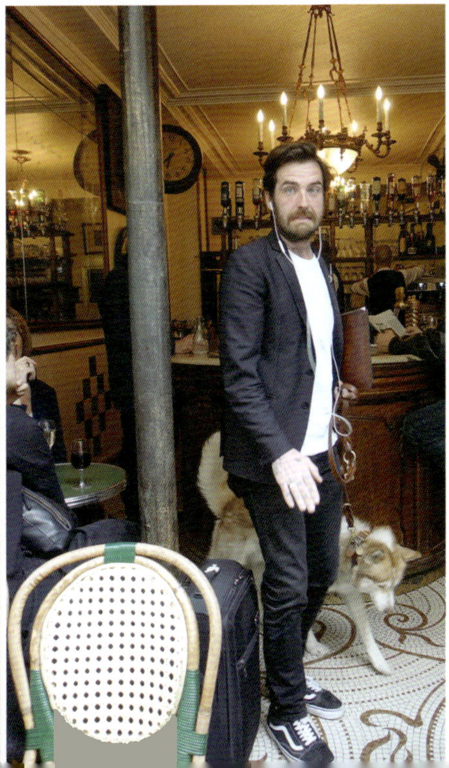

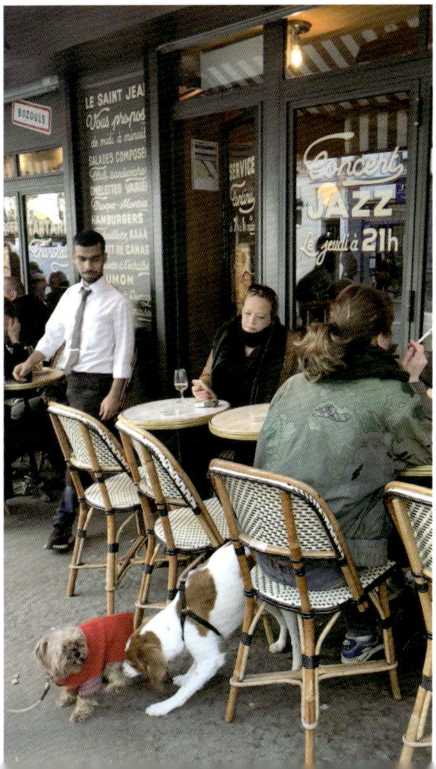
HAMBURGERS
Concert
JAZZ
Le jeudi à 21h

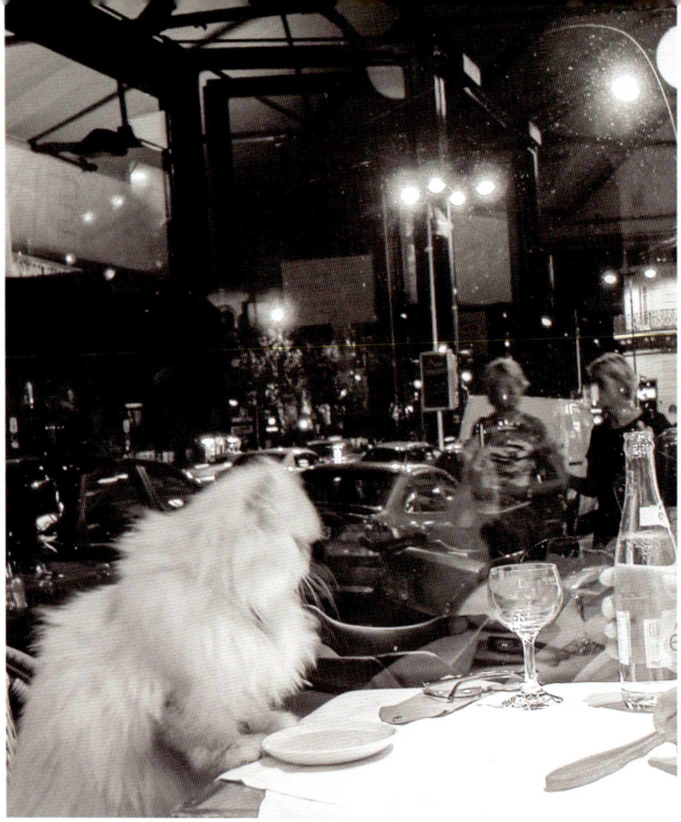

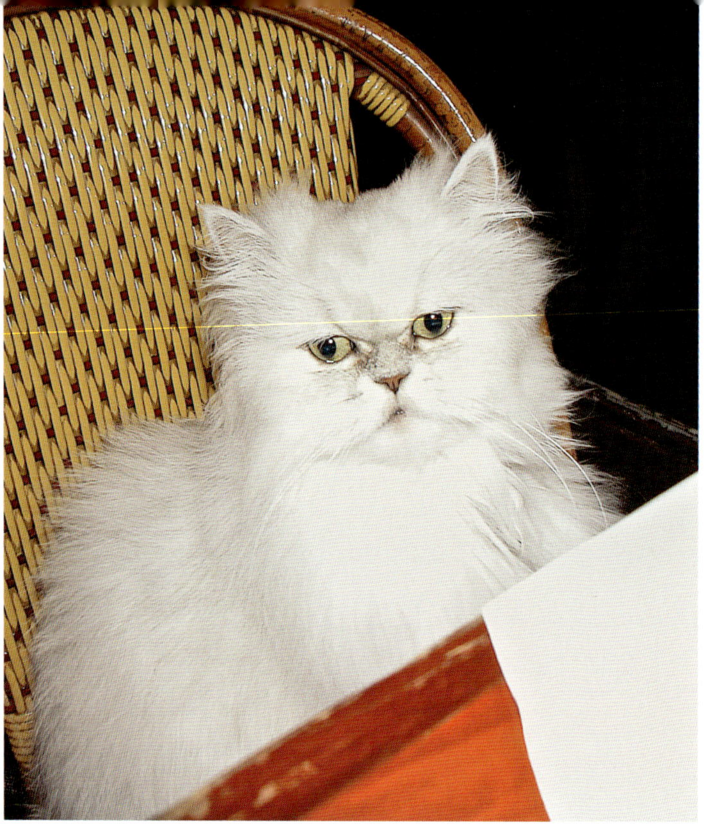

The white cat is comfortably seated at legendary Brasserie Lipp, where the likes of notables such as Colette, Picasso, Gide, Hemingway, Ernst, de Chirico, and Giacometti once dined, and politicians still gather. She is a regular whose owner pours Evian into her white plate while he sips his wine at this otherwise proper ultra-formal historic brasserie at Saint-Germain-des-Prés.

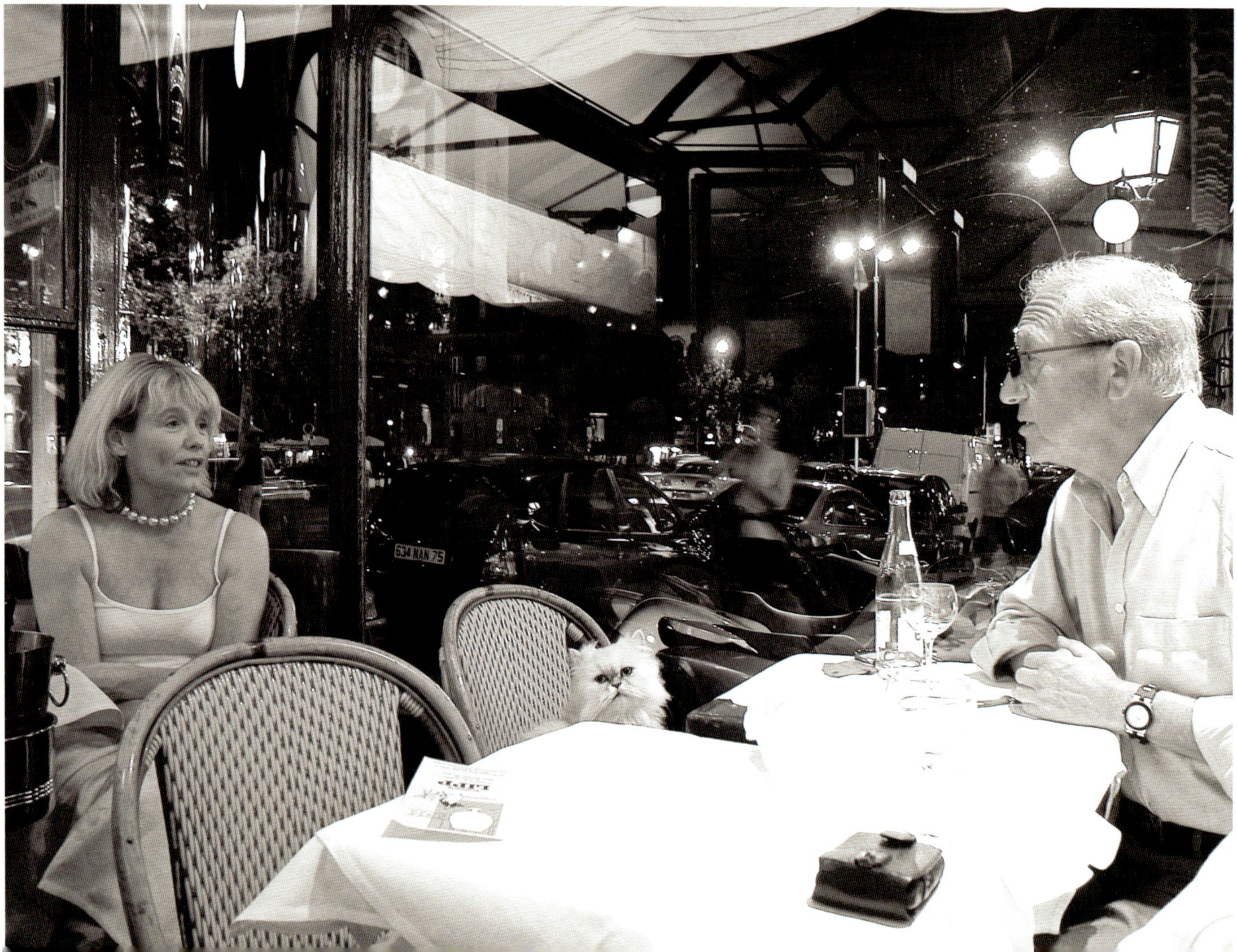

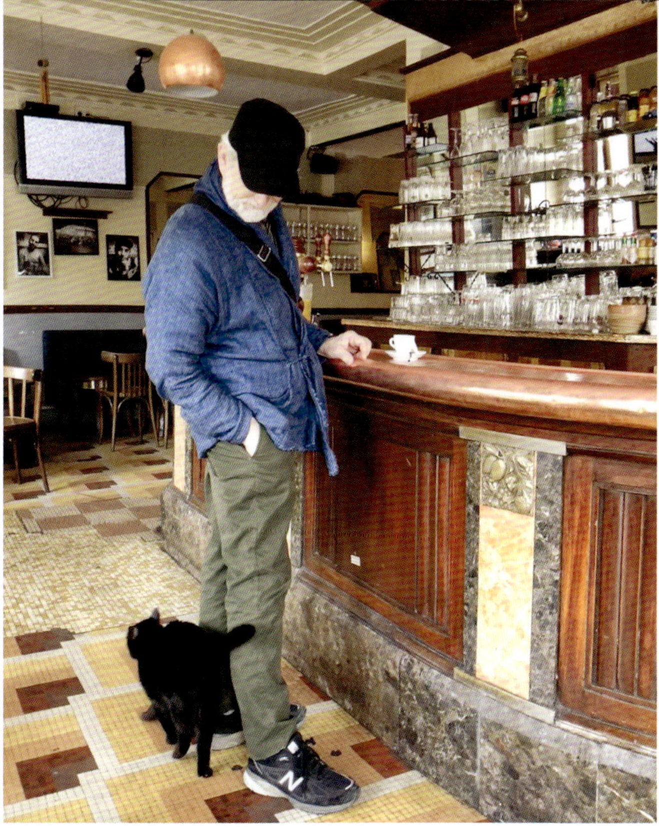

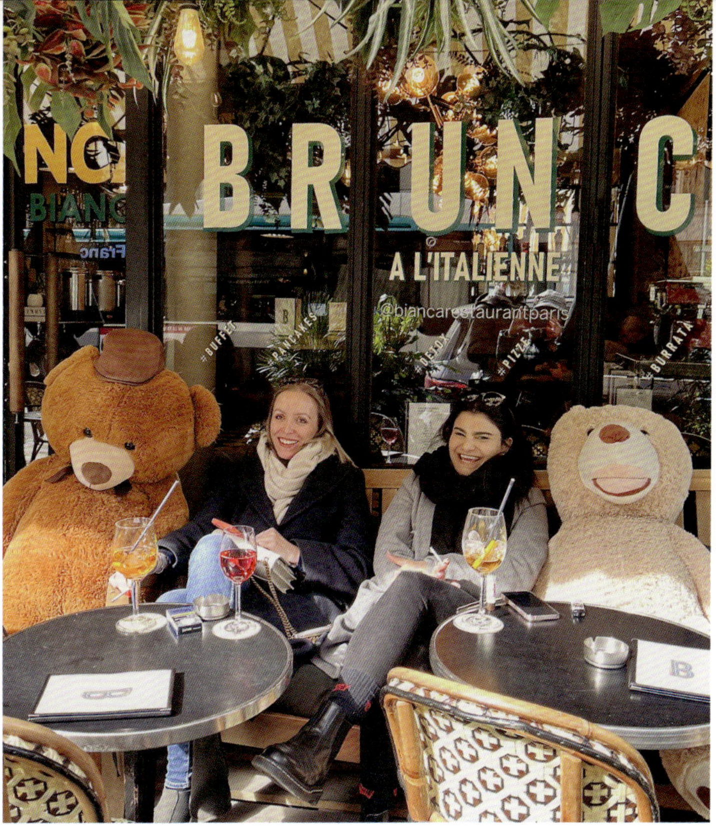

Les Nounours des Gobelins (*nounours* in French means "teddy bear"), started by a bookshop owner in 2018, spread all over Paris and became a playful way to create social distancing in cafés during COVID by placing large teddies on seats. Mickey, the mascot cat at the renowned Le Select, has passed on to cat heaven, but her portrait and memory linger at the bar where she stood guard and slept comfortably.

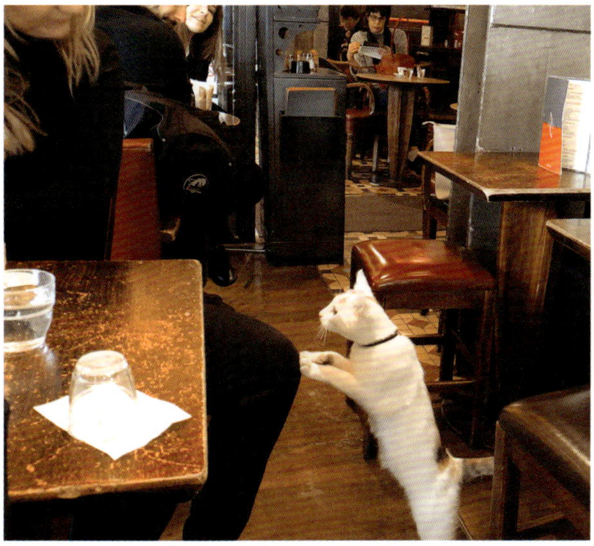

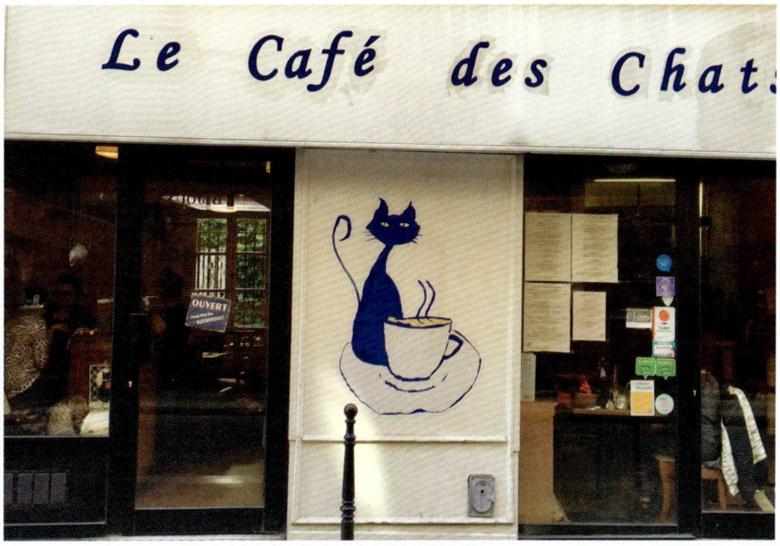

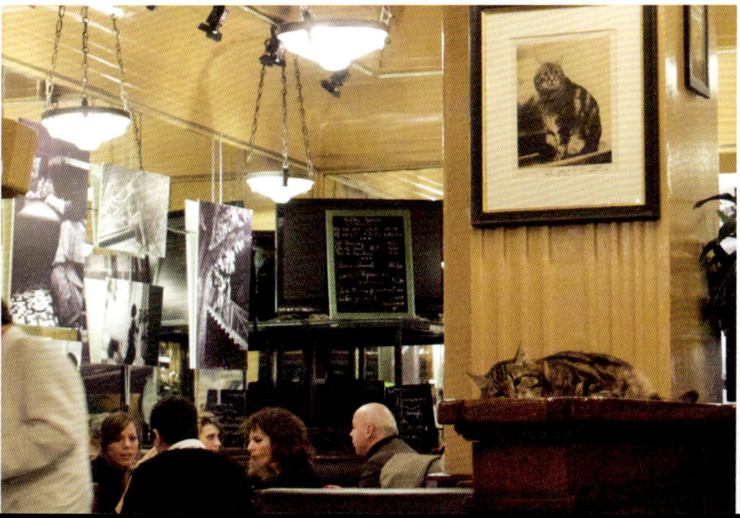

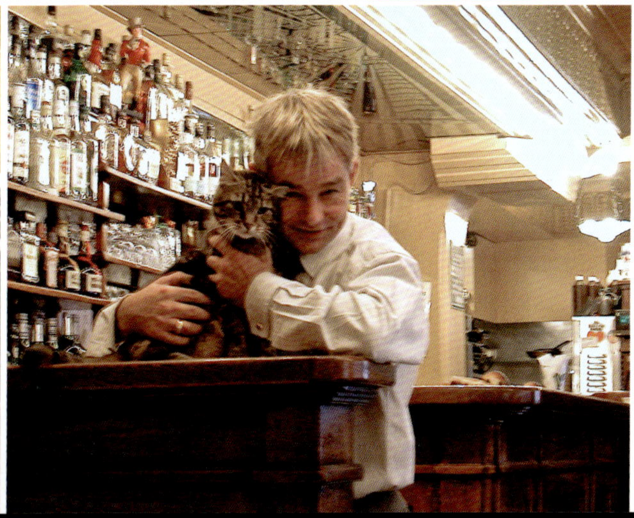

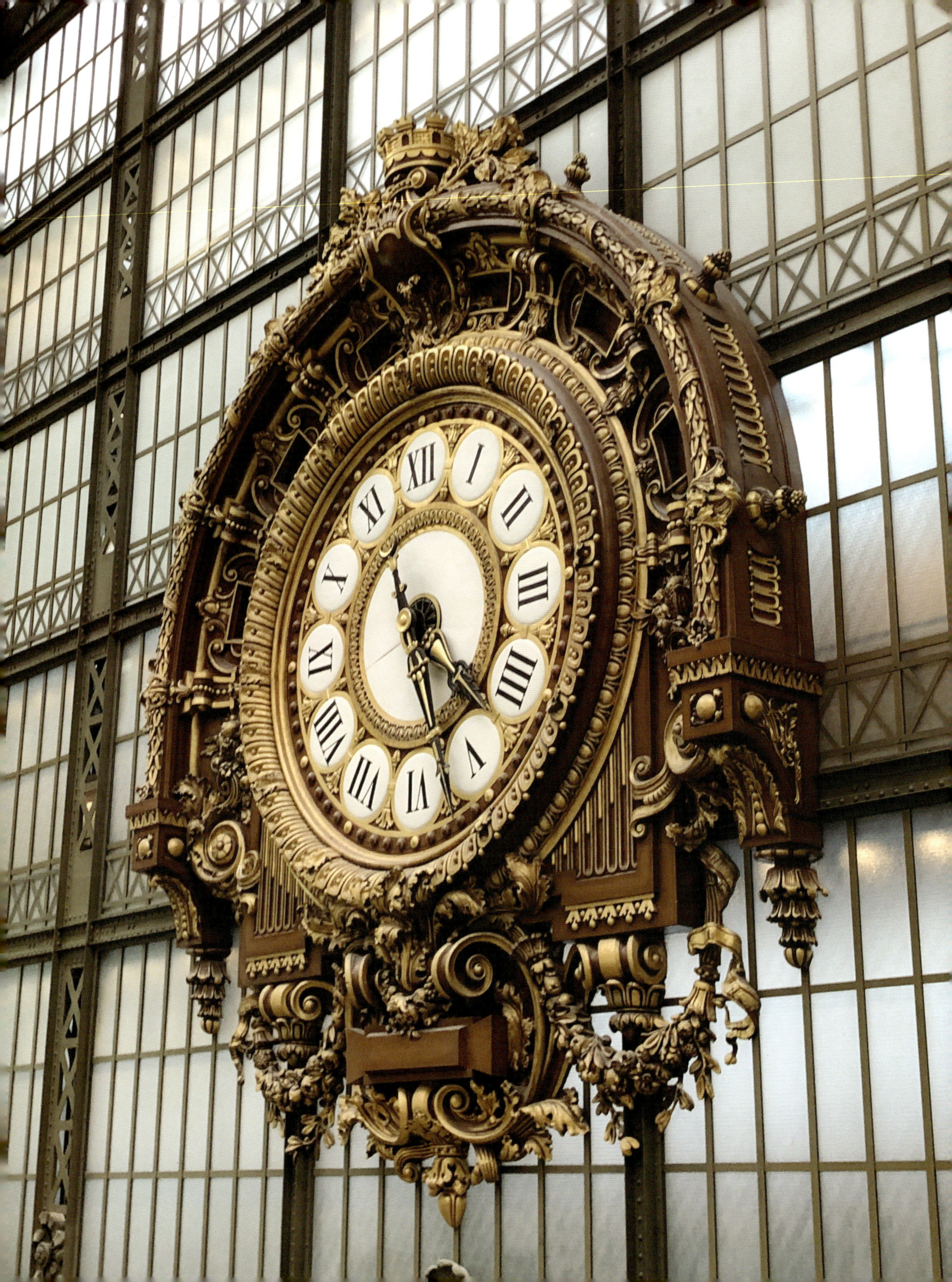

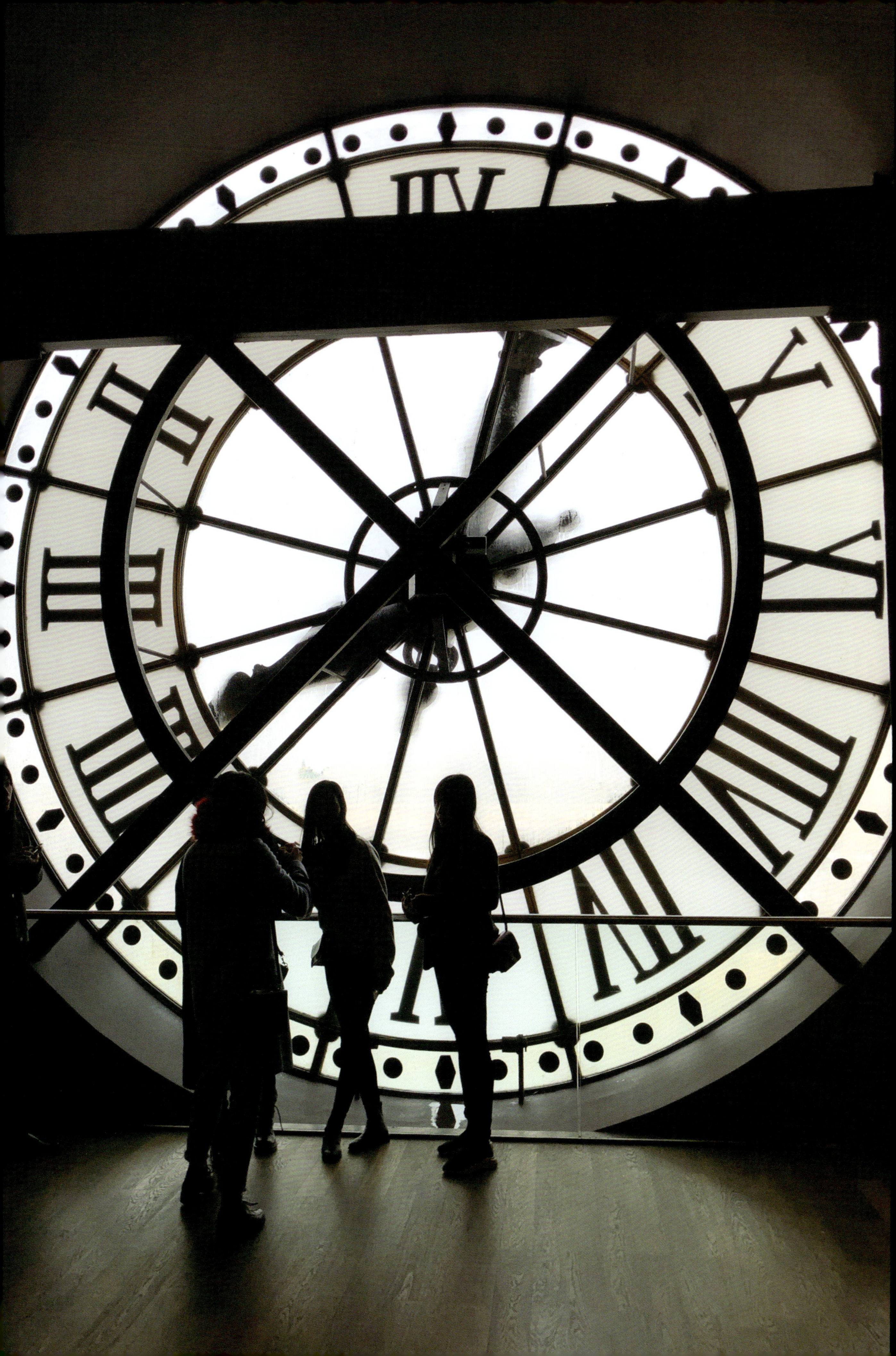

PART 6 The Time of Day

Petit Déjeuner

> "You start at a café table because everything in Paris starts at a café table.
> You end at a café table because everything in Paris ends at a café table."
>
> **Irwin Shaw**

For the French, breakfast is the least important meal of the day. The morning café meal is simple: a croissant, brioche, or tartine with fresh preserves and sweet butter, orange juice squeezed fresh at the bar immediately before being served, coffee (possibly café au lait in a bowl), tea, tisane, or *chocolat chaud*. That's it. There is the possibility of hard-boiled eggs in some cafés, but omelets are more common at lunchtime. If you want milk in your coffee, this is the time to indulge because post-breakfast, it's just espresso or a noisette (with a dollop of milk), usually after a meal or on its own any time of the day. And it's coffee-to-stay, not coffee-to-go. The proper *Parisiens* do not walk in the street with paper cups filled with sugary coffee concoctions. Linger as long as you want or quickly be on your way, it is no matter to the wait staff. In recent decades many hotels have begun to serve food-laden buffets, and long-held traditions are rapidly changing in cafés as well: omelets are now on some breakfast menus, various coffee drinks can be had throughout the day, and Starbucks-inspired paper cups to-go appear on more streets daily.

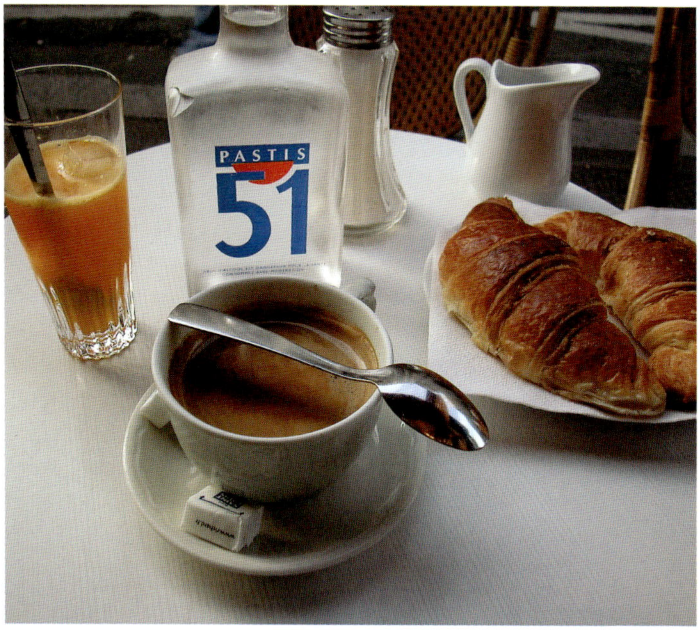

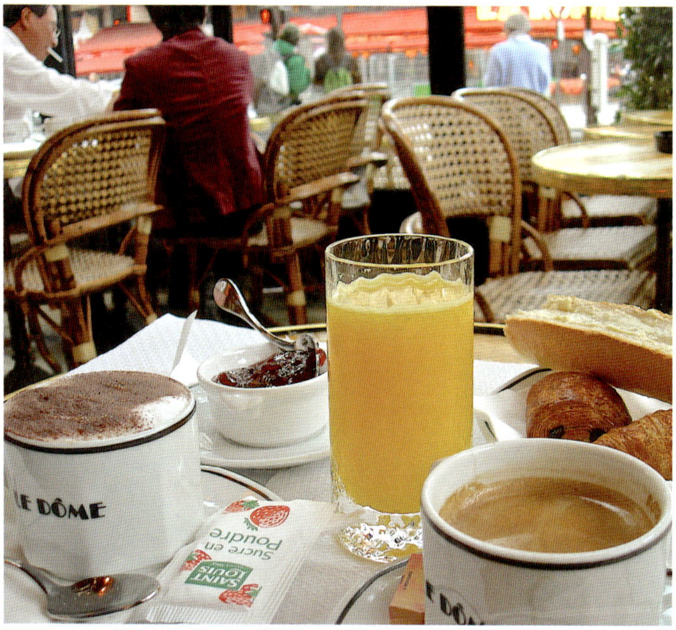

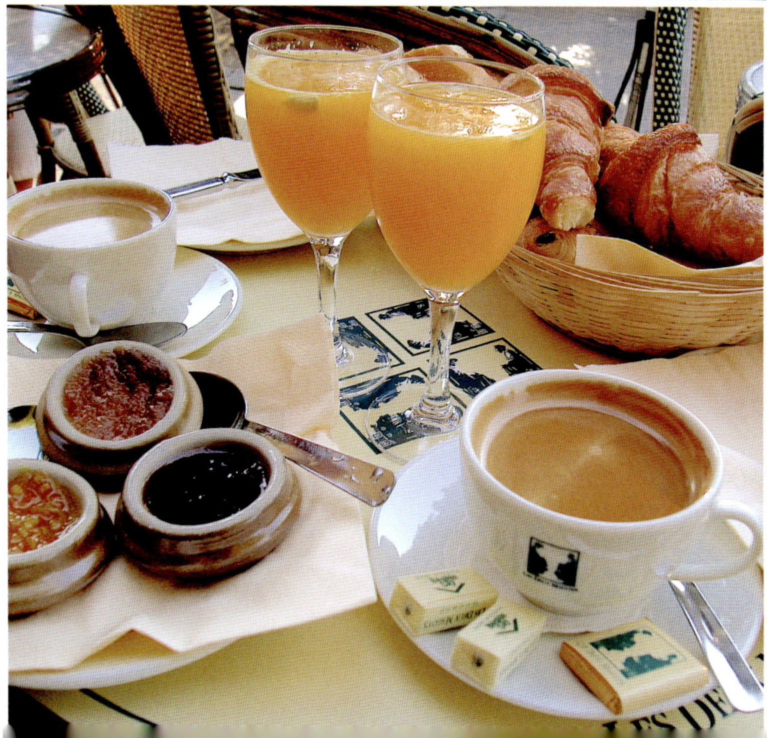

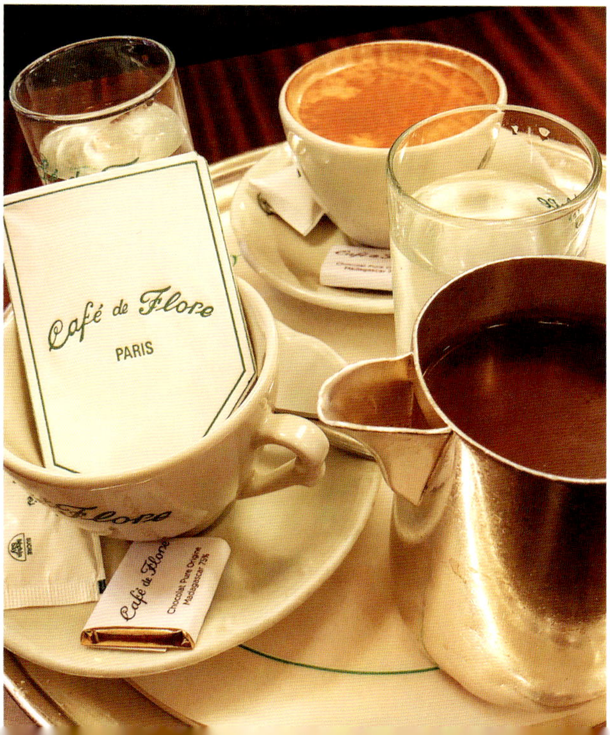

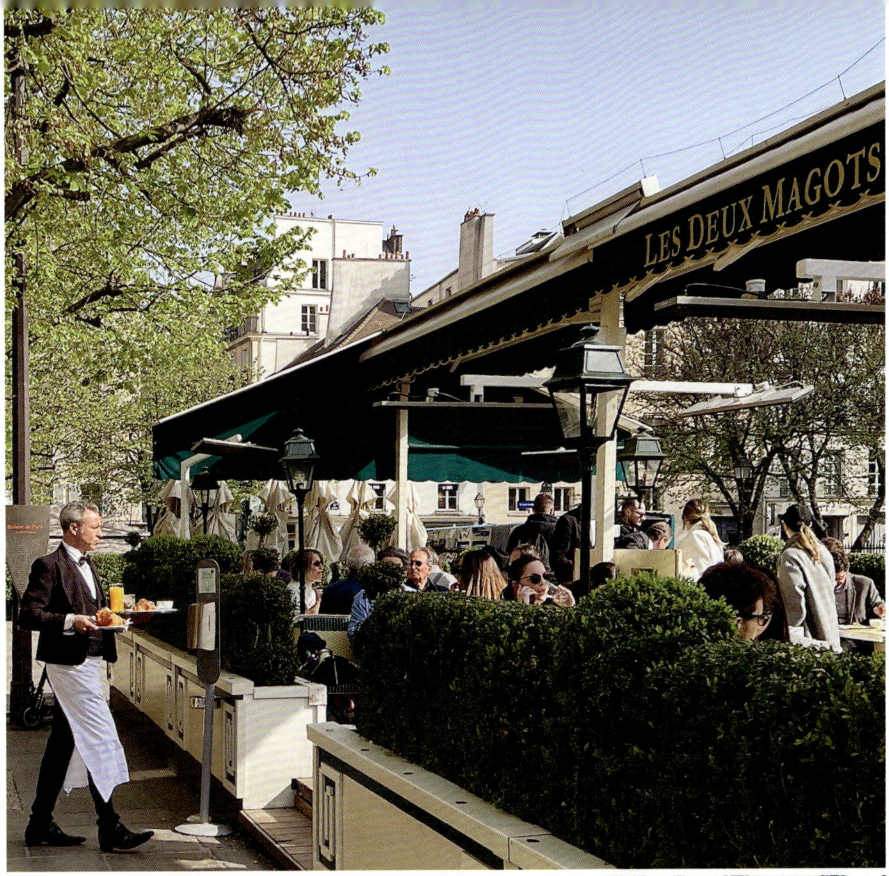
LES DEUX MAGOTS

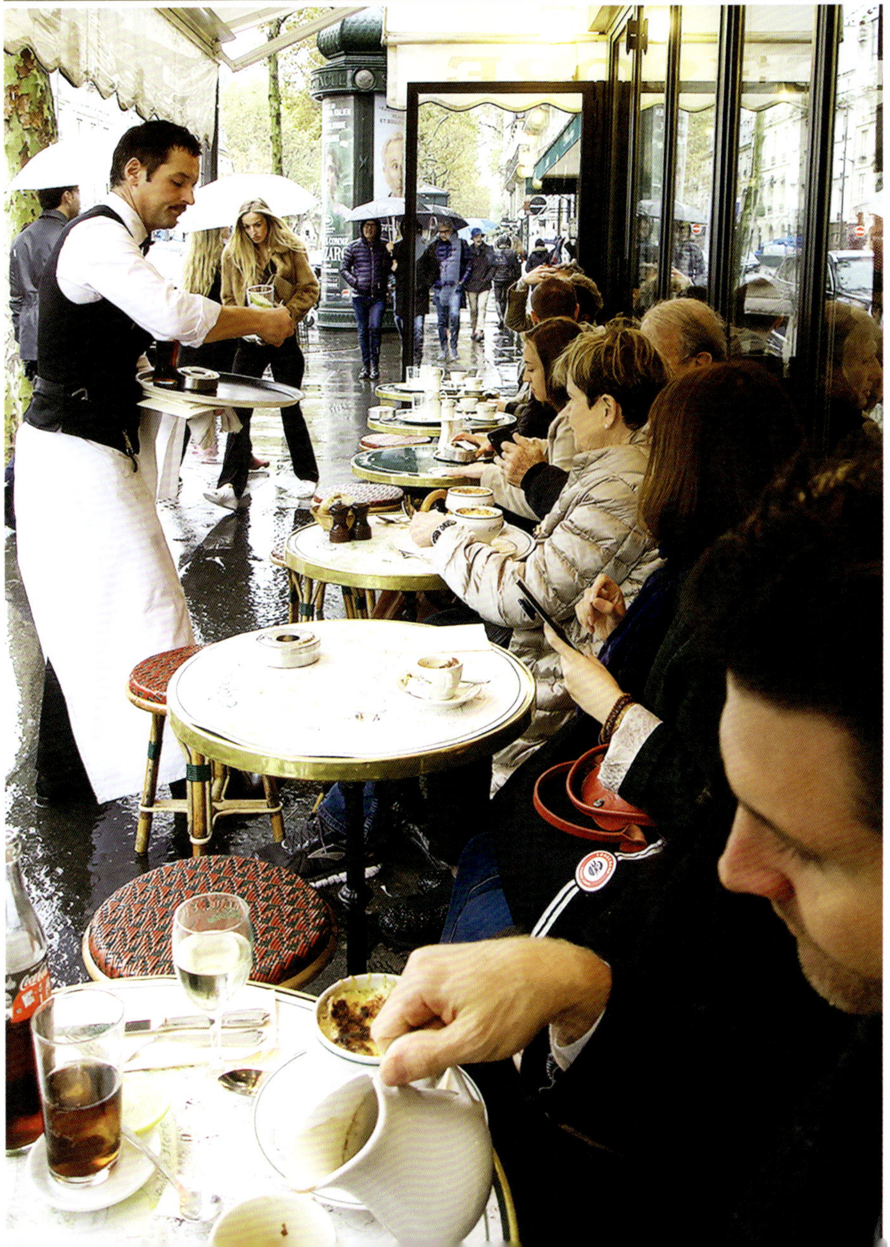

Le Déjeuner

"To have left even the tiniest morsel in the dish would have shown as much discourtesy as to rise and leave a concert hall before the end of a piece under the composer's very eyes."

Marcel Proust

After a light protein-free breakfast and hours of strolling the streets of Paris, a bounteous lunch in a café, bistro, or brasserie is the perfect way to power up for whatever comes next. Often considered the most important meal of the day, the French honor this experience, taking the time to appreciate the food and camaraderie. Lunch can last two hours, even during the workweek, and the French have longer lunch breaks than in any other country. French schoolchildren eat three-course lunches that are cooked, not prepackaged. That may be open for change now since many workers and students grab a sandwich and eat at their desks. *Parisiens* usually take their lunch starting from 1-1:30, so tourists can generally find tables free from noon to 1 pm, even without a reservation. However, it is helpful to reserve in advance for the best seating and service. Be aware that, around lunch and dinner hours, some tables are designated for diners and others for those who want "just a drink." Those set with tablecloths, napkins, and silverware are for diners and bare tabletops for those who simply want an espresso or aperitif. Some cafés have heated sections where smoking is allowed—technically deemed "*terrace*"—between the outside and the interior. Put your red boxing gloves beside your bicycle, your shopping bags under the table, and sit yourself down in close proximity to neighboring tables, as the French personal space in cafés is cozy and convivial.

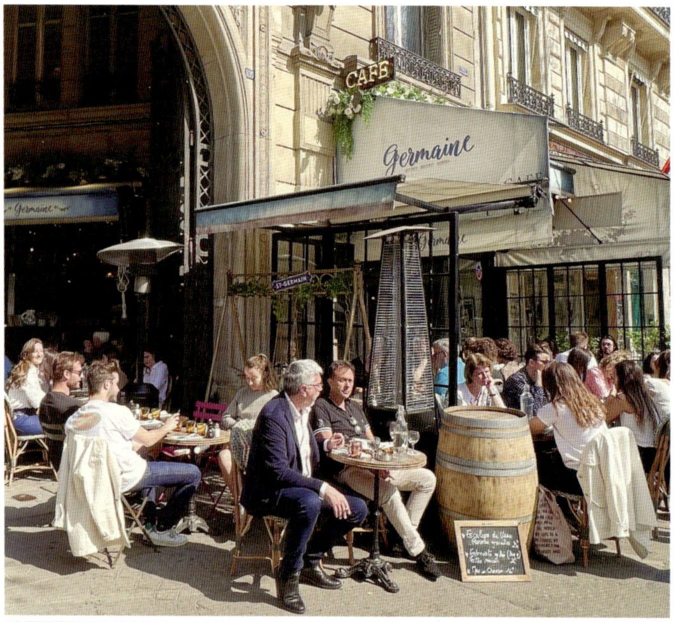

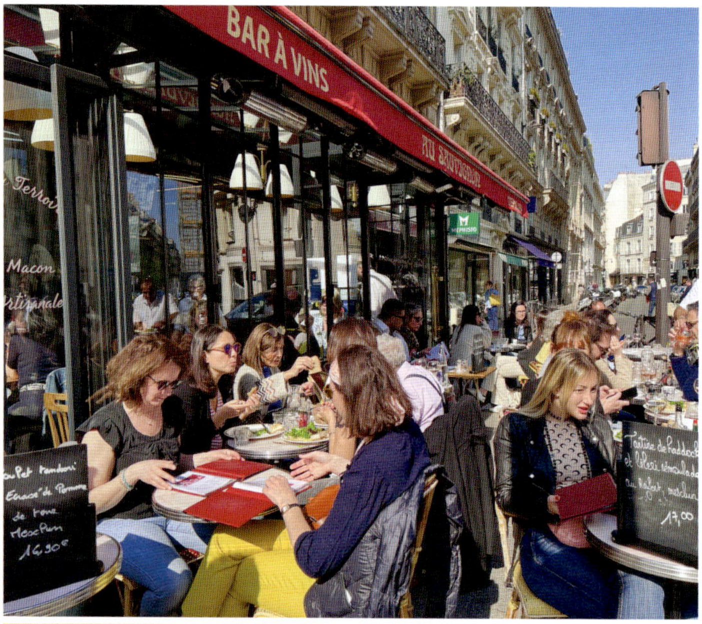

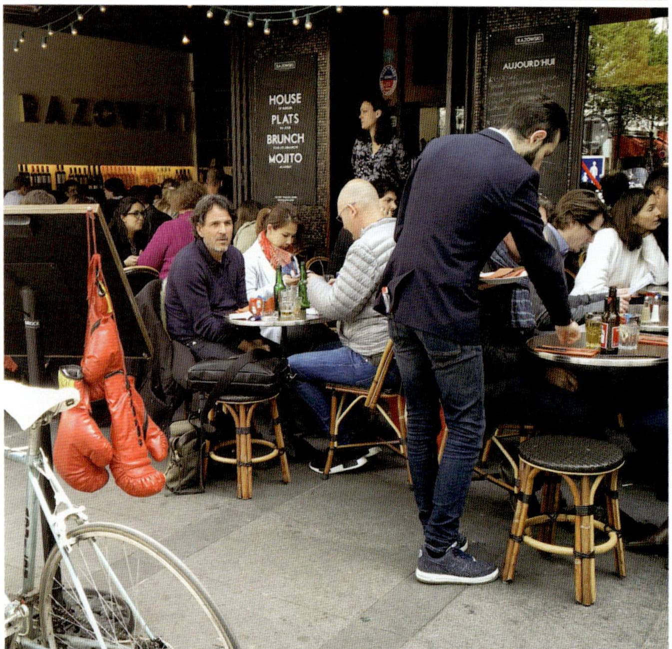

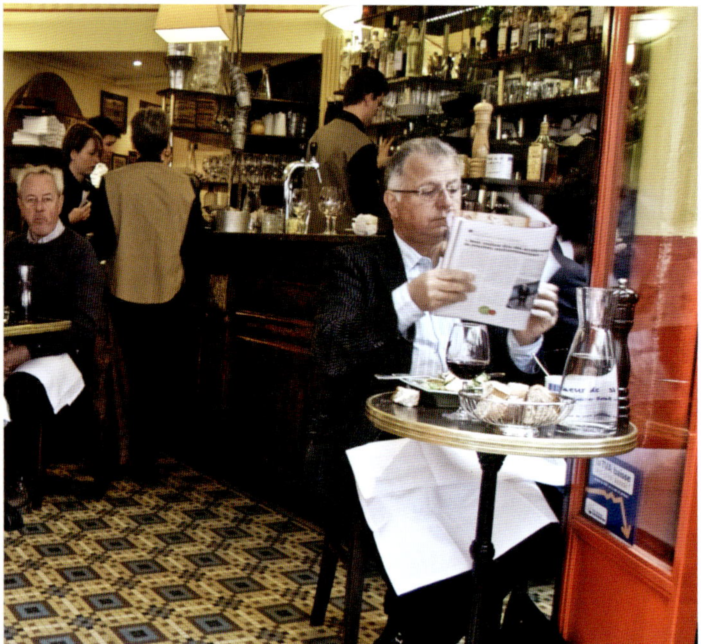

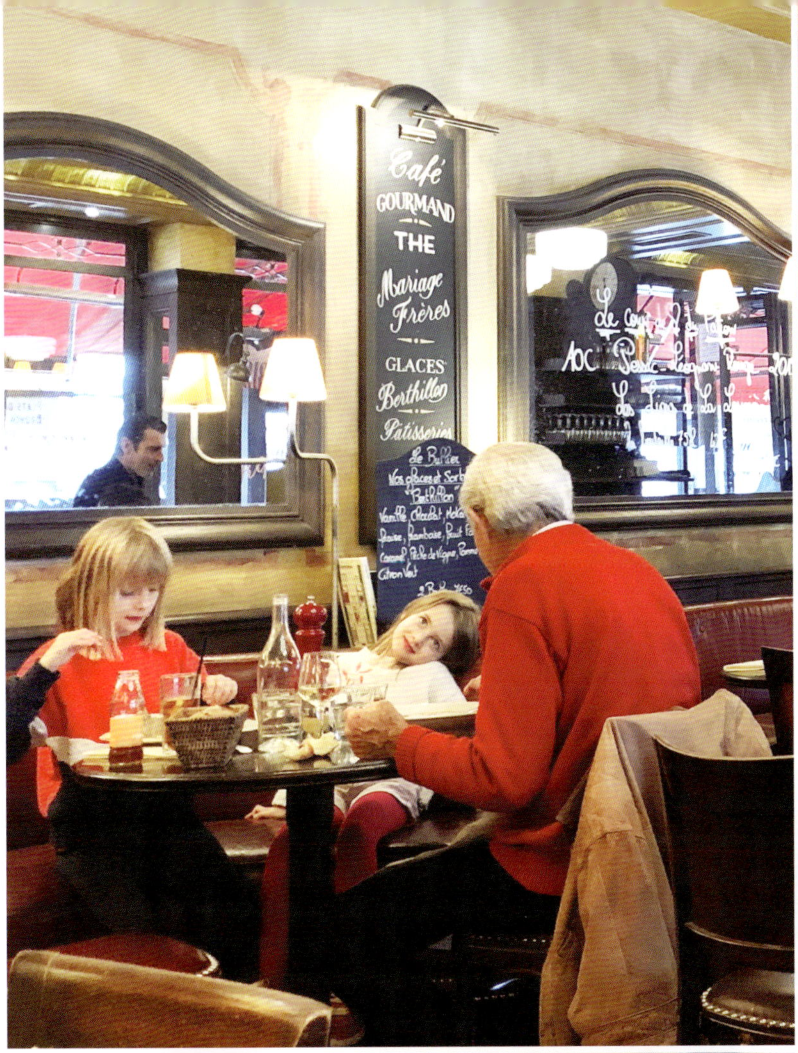
Café
GOURMAND
THE
Mariage
Frères
GLACES
Berthillon

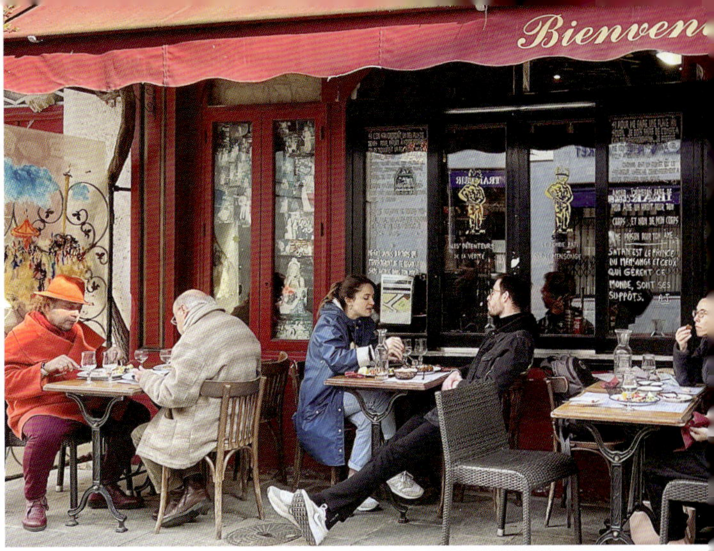

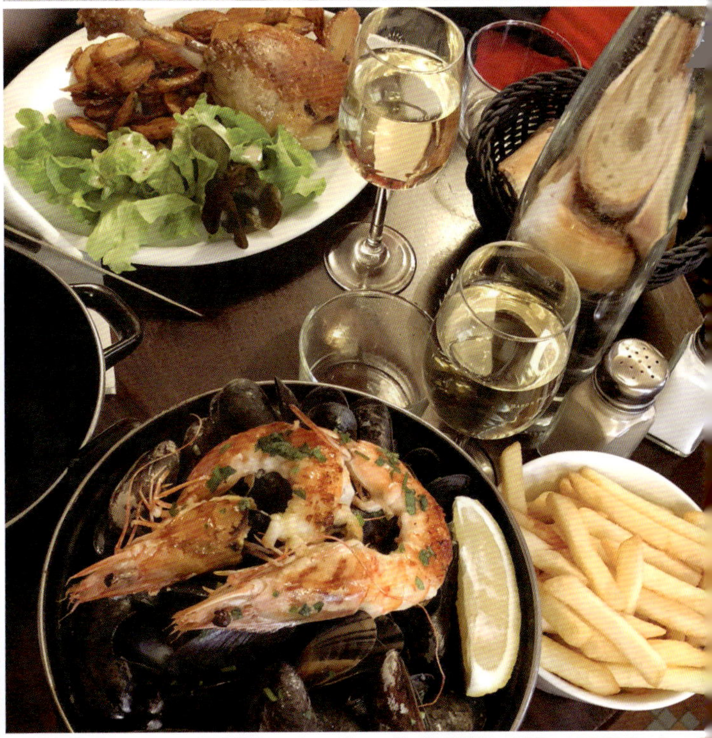

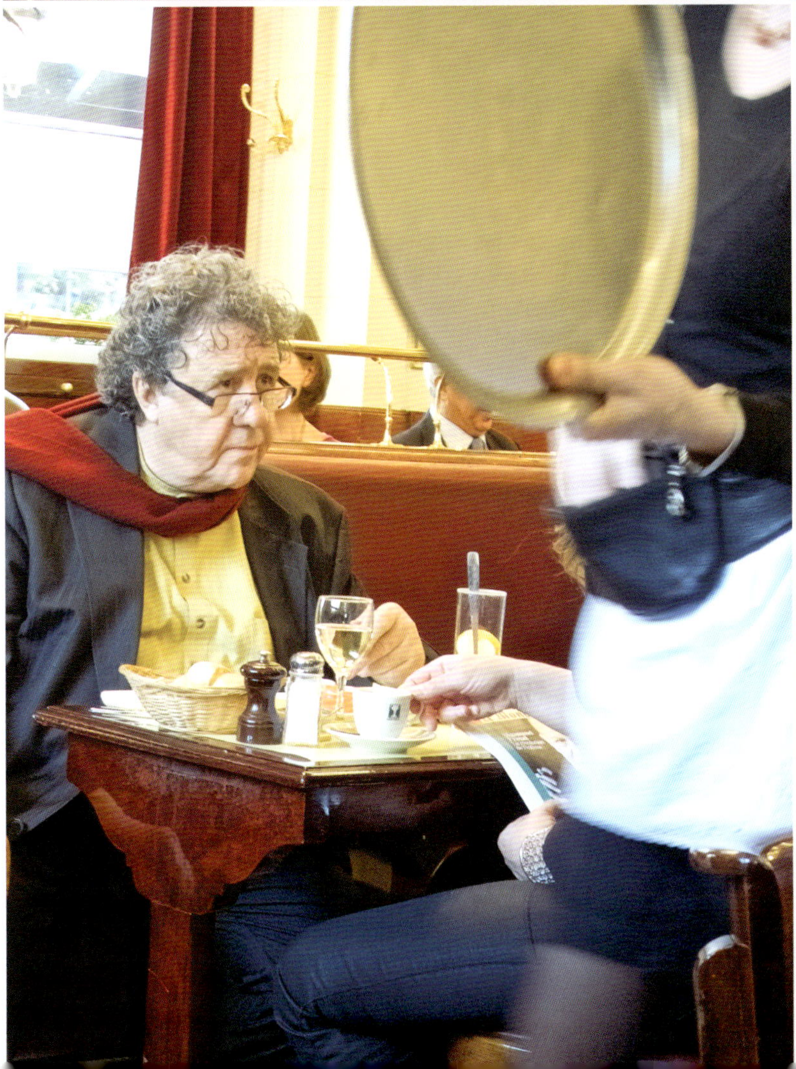

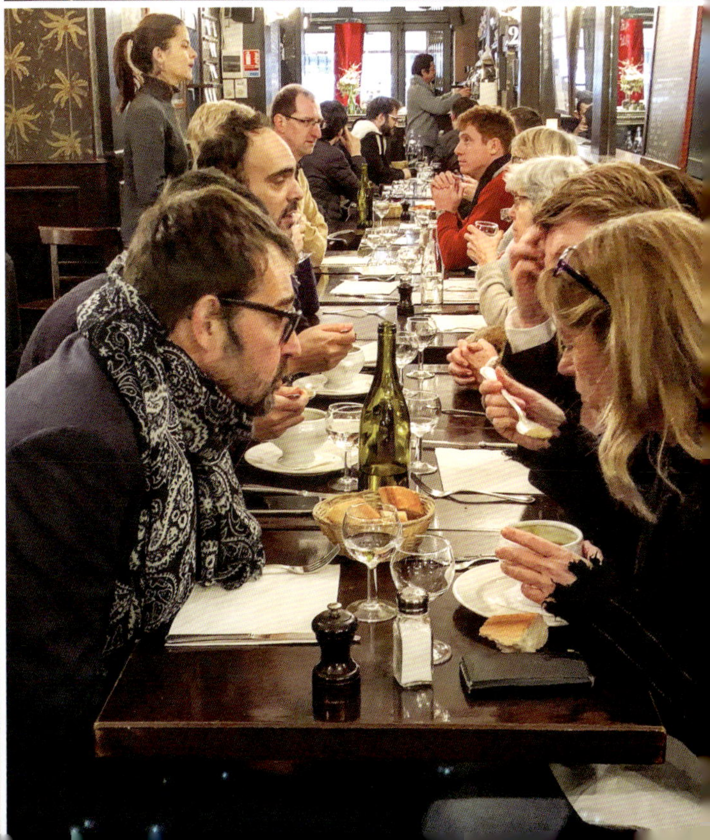

L'Après Midi

"Great silent crowds watching the street live."
Emile Zola

Stopping in a café for *l'après-midi* ("afternoon") beverage break keeps one hydrated and allows a moment in the day to be mindful and slow the scramble of daily life. Maybe even a sweet nibble during *L'heure du goûter* between 4 and 6 pm? It can be a time to meet friends and deny the fading French pride in not snacking between meals. It's never grab-and-go snacking, but rather about pausing to sip a tea, espresso, or Perrier, or indulging in a *chocolate chaud*, pastry, or *glace*. Why not take this time to refresh, renew, savor, and watch the world go by from the terrace of your favored café? There will be plenty of locals doing the same.

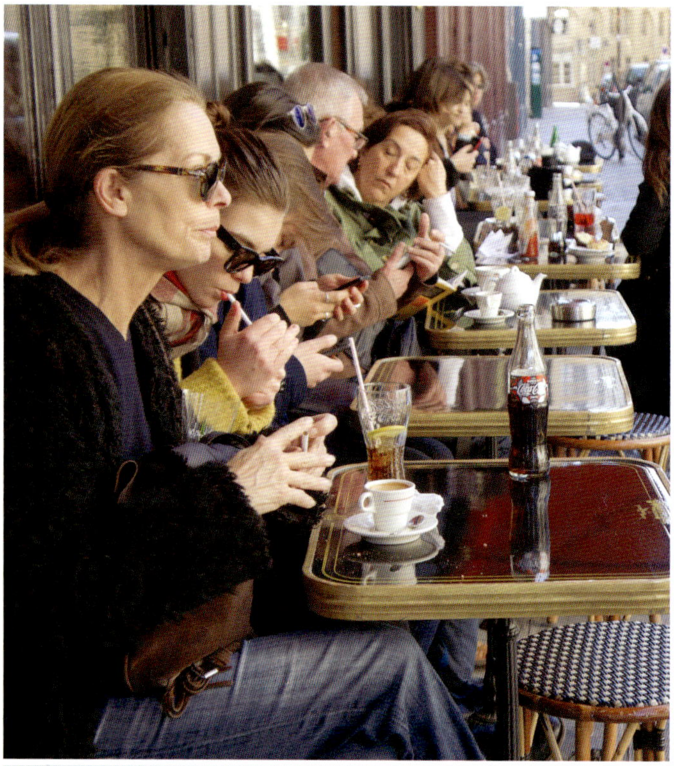

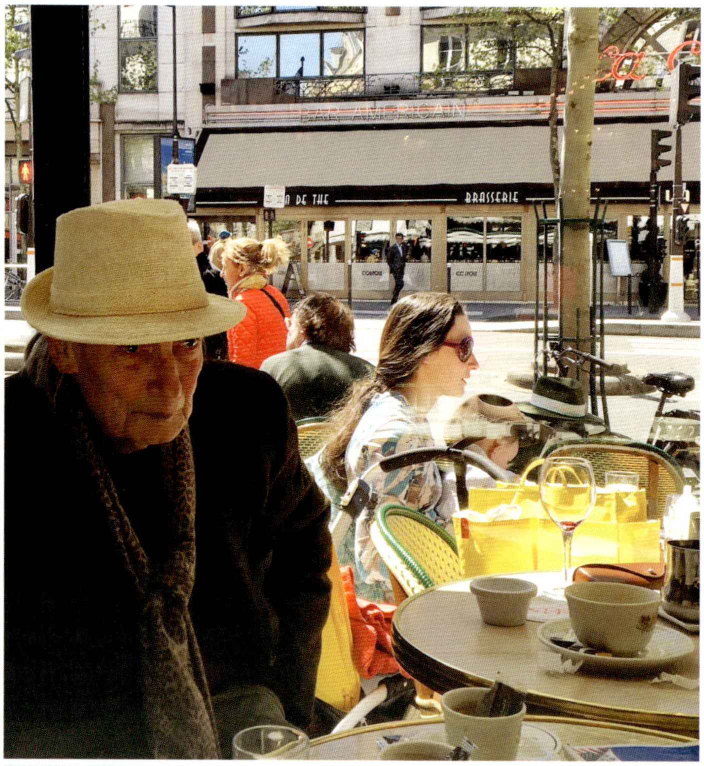

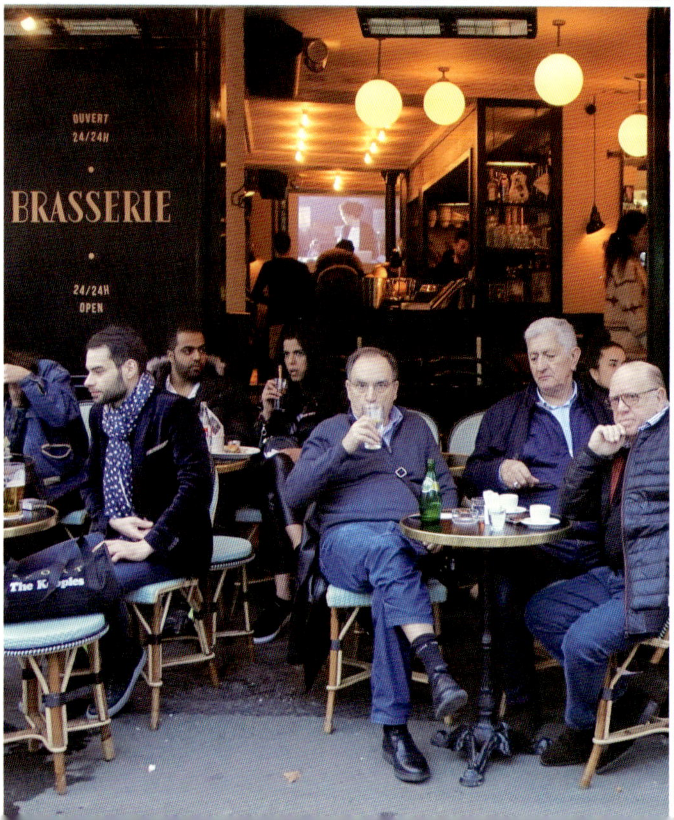

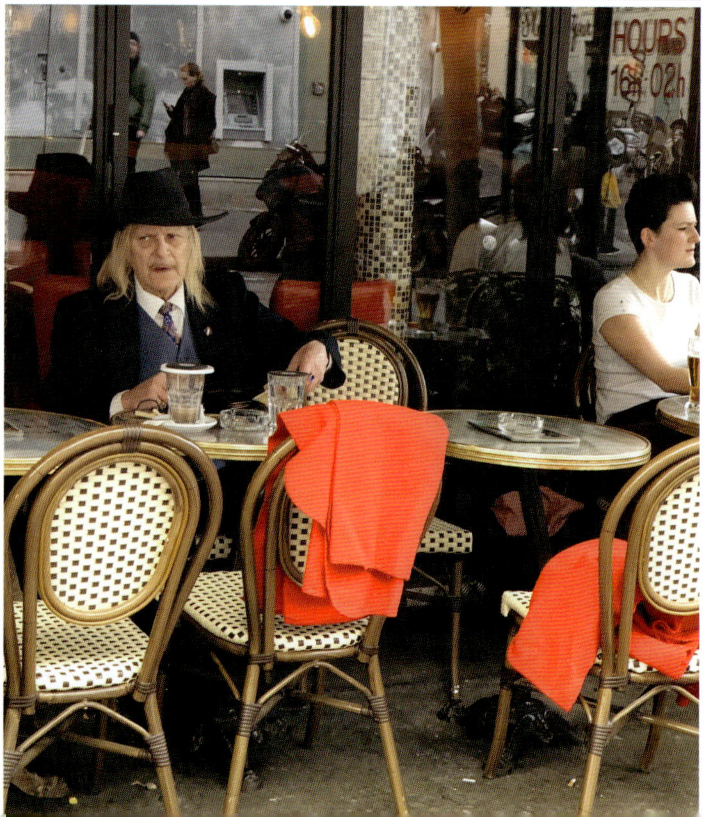

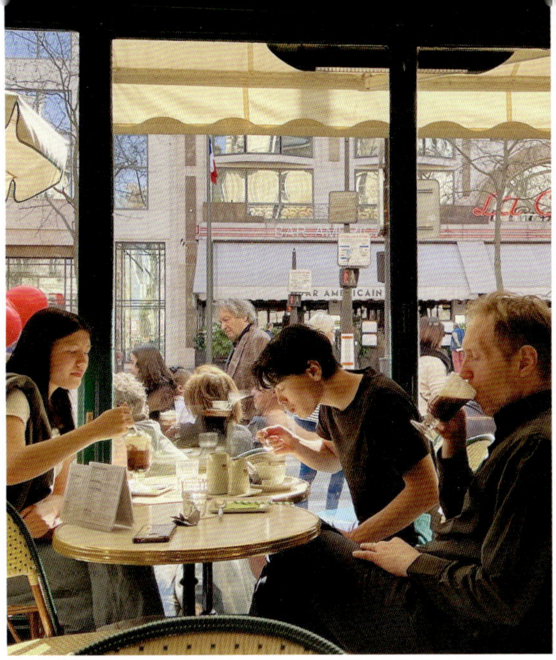

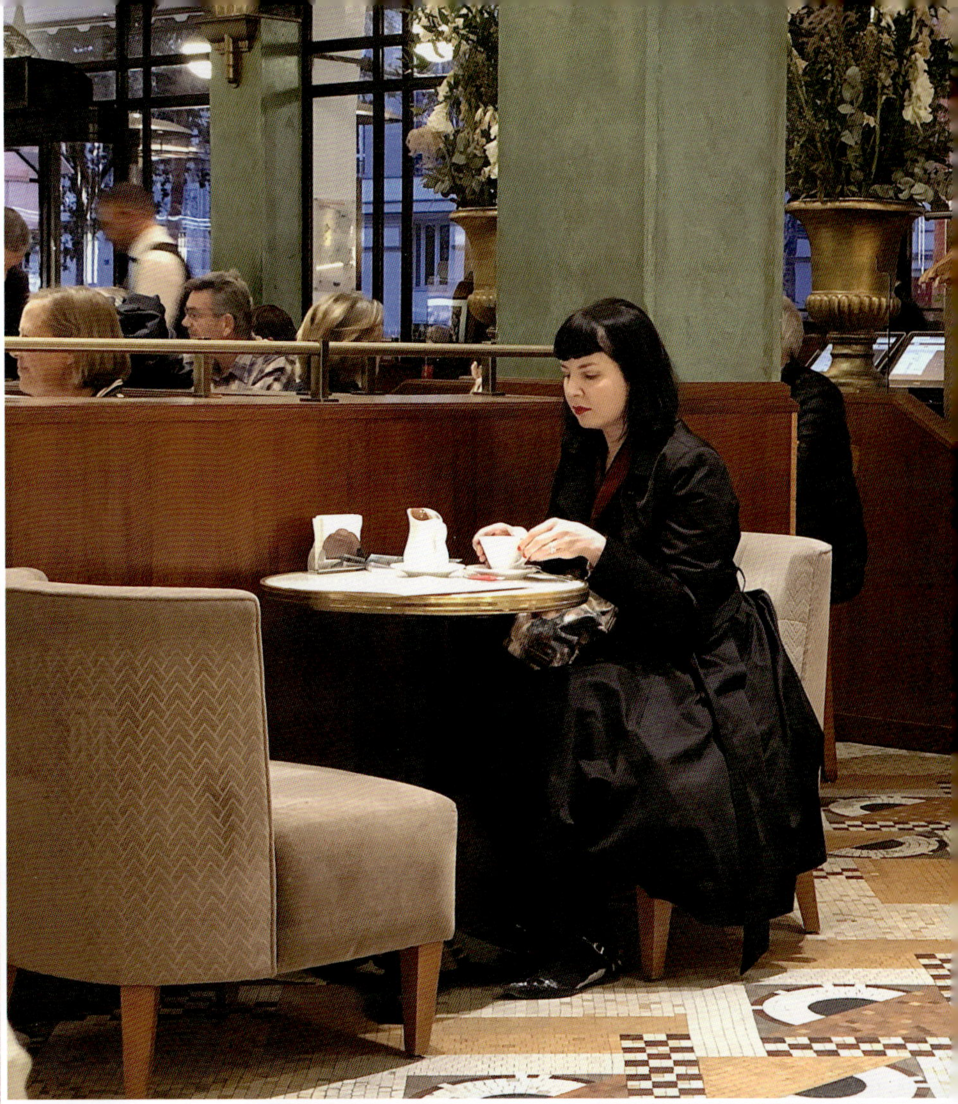

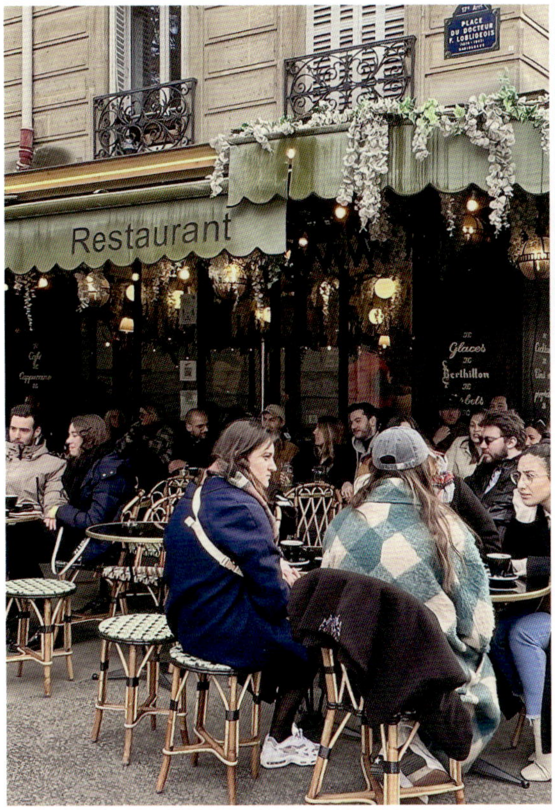
Restaurant

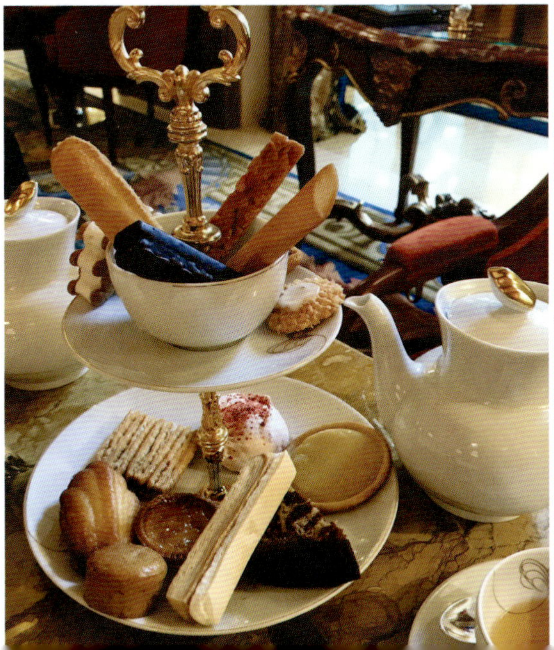

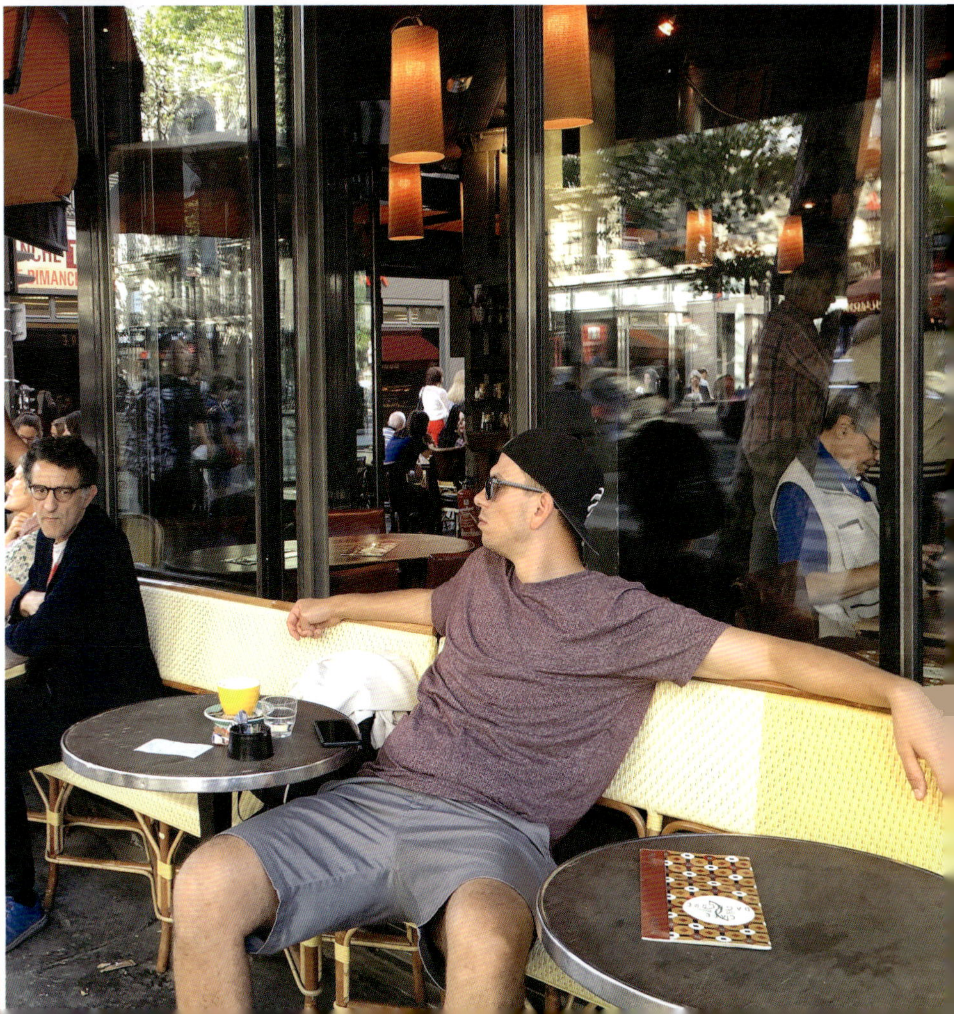

L'Heure de l'Apéro/Happy Hour

"Actually, Paris wakes up when it comes time for an apéritif."

Irving Stone

L'heure de l'apéro, from around 6-8 pm, is the mellow time after work and before dinner when the French traditionally relax with friends over an *apéritif*. They do not hurry to dine but rather enjoy each phase of their meal, all in good time. Don't confuse *apéritifs* with cocktails made with hard liquor. Instead, they are made with wine, aromatic herbs, and spices; some have quinine and were initially considered health tonics. Sweet vermouth, invented in Turin in 1786, was introduced to France by chemist Joseph Dubonnet in 1846. By mixing wine with bitter quinine softened with herbs and spices, Dubonnet created a delicious concoction while battling malaria with a beverage. An anise-flavored *apéro*, Absinthe, developed in Switzerland in the late 19th century, was enjoyed by the artists of Montmartre and Montparnasse; thought to be hallucinogenic, it was banned in 1915. A few years later, a young Paul Ricard commercialized anise-flavored wormwood-free Pastis to substitute for the favored but illegal Absinthe. The popularity of Pastis was immediate and continues to this day. Absinthe, *la fée verte* (the green fairy) is now legal, and certain cafés serve it with a traditional slotted sugar spoon and glass fountain. Absinthe and Pastis are the cloudy greed drinks seen in Paris every day at *l'heure de l'apéritif*.

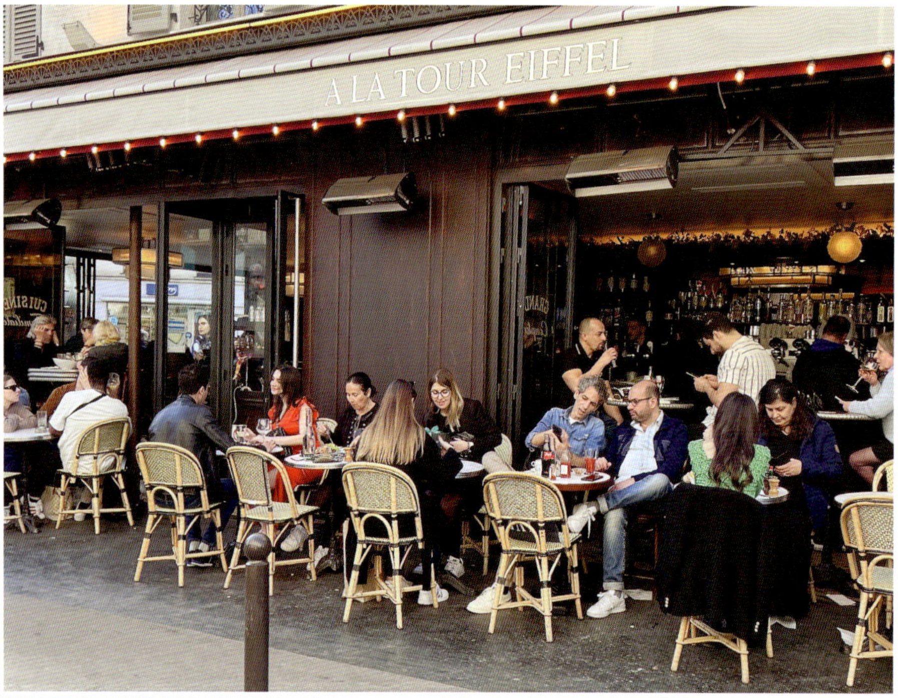

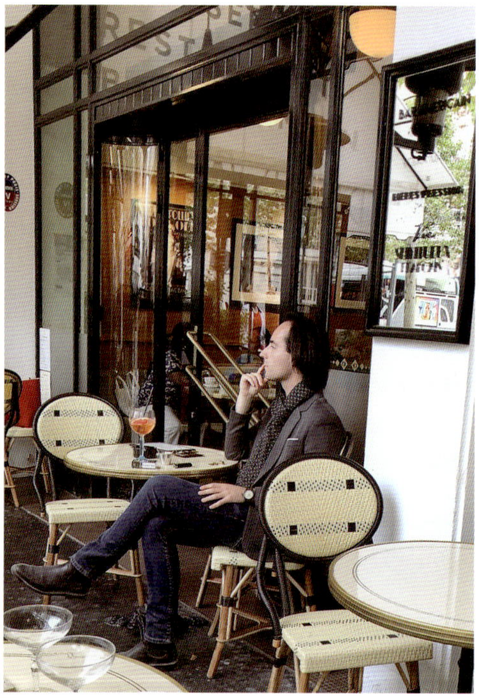

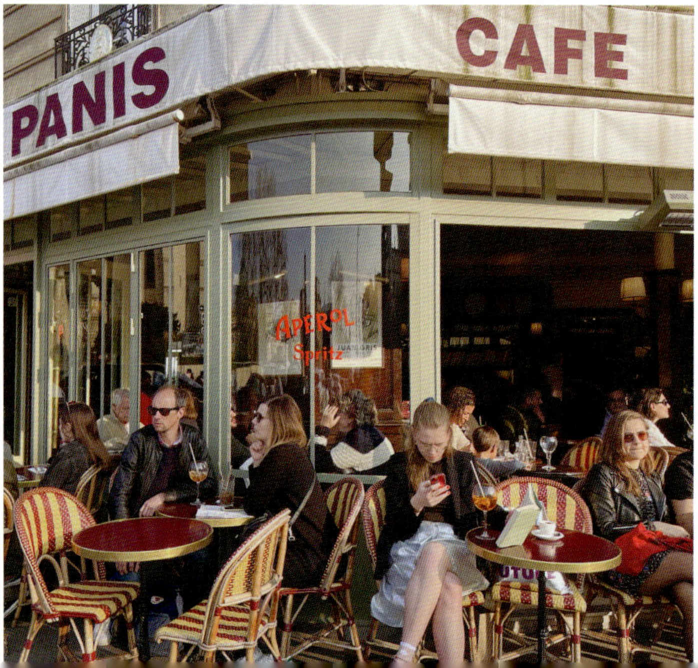

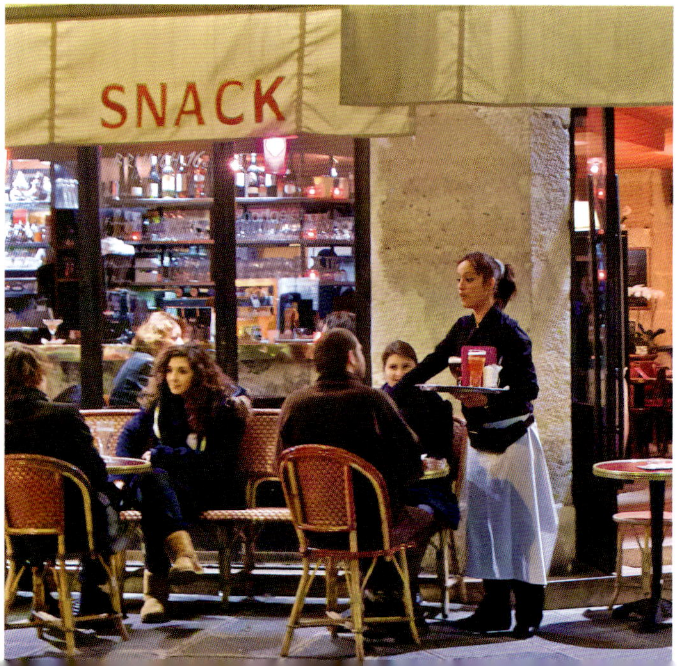

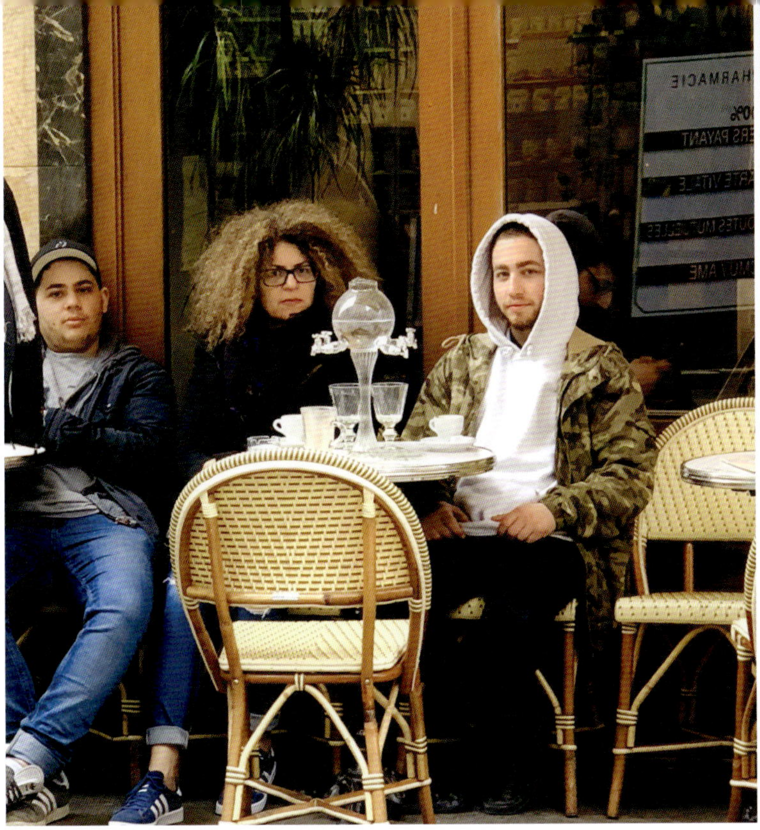

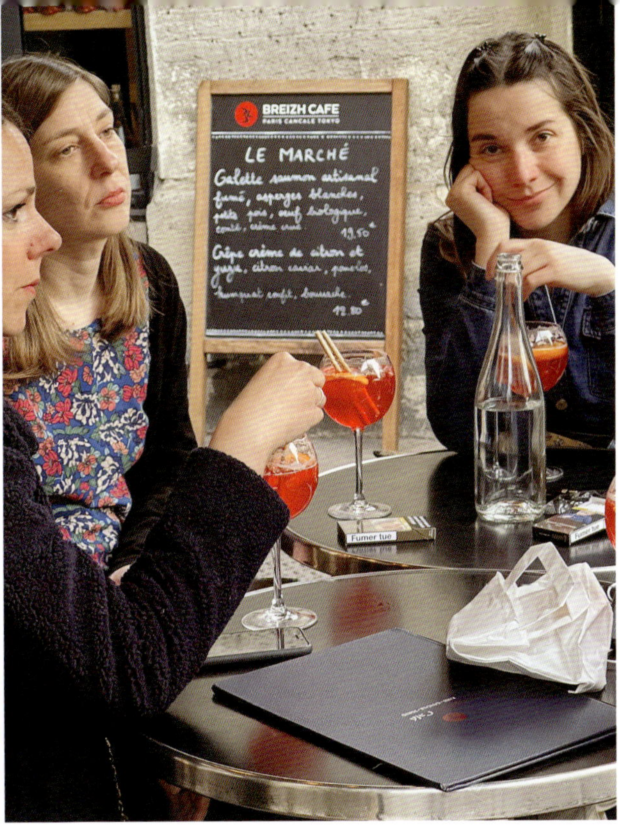

Aperitifs often have a slightly bitter taste and are designed to whet the appetite for dinner rather than cause an alcohol-induced buzz. Served with a little salty nibble, perhaps potato chips, nuts, olives, nothing more, they are meant to prime, not dampen the appetite. In addition to vermouth and Pastis, options for *l'apéritif* are quite varied and can include wine, Kir & Kir Royal (with champagne), champagne, port served over ice, beer, and Perrier. However, the original libations with their still-secret recipes are delicious and the most interesting.

Happy hour and trendy cocktail bars in Paris serving craft cocktails long past *l'heure de l'apéritif* have nothing to do with the sacred French *l'apéro* tradition. Still, they continue a trend beginning as far back as the 1840s, hitting its stride in 1871 when the first elegant Bar Americain opened in the new Grand Hotel at two rue Scribe. By the 1920s, American cocktails took center stage, and cafés with a Bar Americain were all the rage. In those days, the French served cocktails primarily to Americans and Brits, and the French stuck to their aperitifs, beer, and wine. Now craft cocktails, organic wine, and craft beer, as well as aperitifs, are imbibed by choice during *l'heure de l'apéro*, happy hour, and whenever the mood strikes.

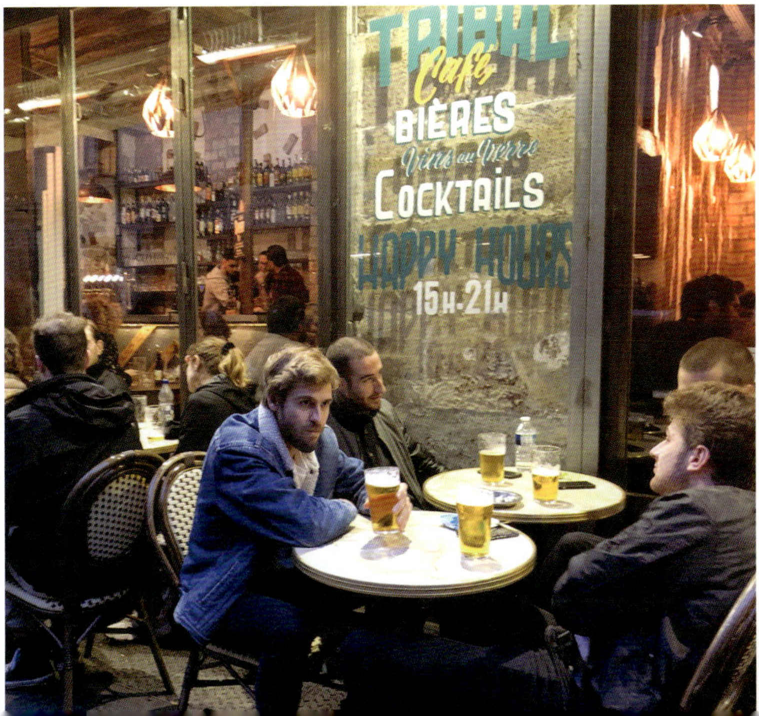

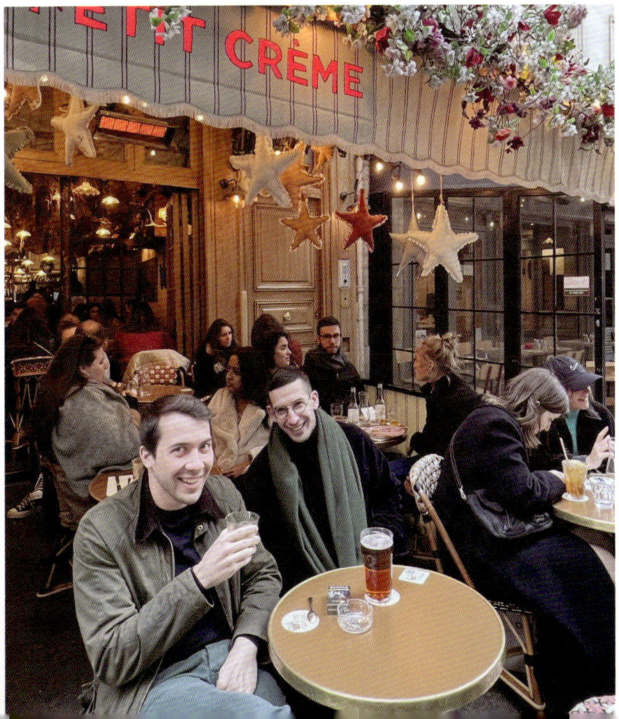

Le Dîner

"Everything ends this way in France – Everything. Weddings, christenings, duels, burials, swindlings, diplomatic affairs – Everything is a pretext for a good dinner."

Jean Anouilh

The streets of Paris are alive each night, with people spilling in and out of bistros cheerfully celebrating an evening meal among friends. After a late lunch and an *apéro*, Parisians dine long and late, usually from 8-11+ pm. Those who prefer to eat earlier will be sharing the experience mostly with tourists. In the off-season, it is easy to get a table early on, but it's always a good idea to reserve for the best tables and service. Parisians have specific rituals for dining, and it's instructive to watch their expertise at using their utensils to gather every morsel elegantly. At lunch and dinner in France, un café is taken after dessert as it is considered a separate course often served with a wrapped square of dark chocolate; in fine establishments, your espresso is served with *mignardise*—bite-sized sweets. A dessert after a dessert is a delectable reward after long Paris promenades.

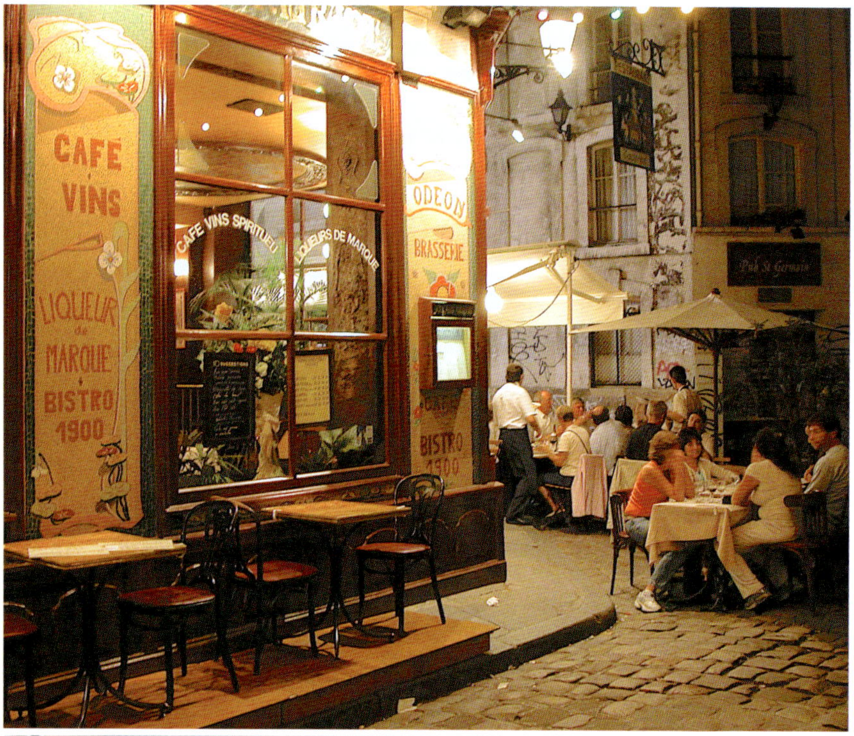

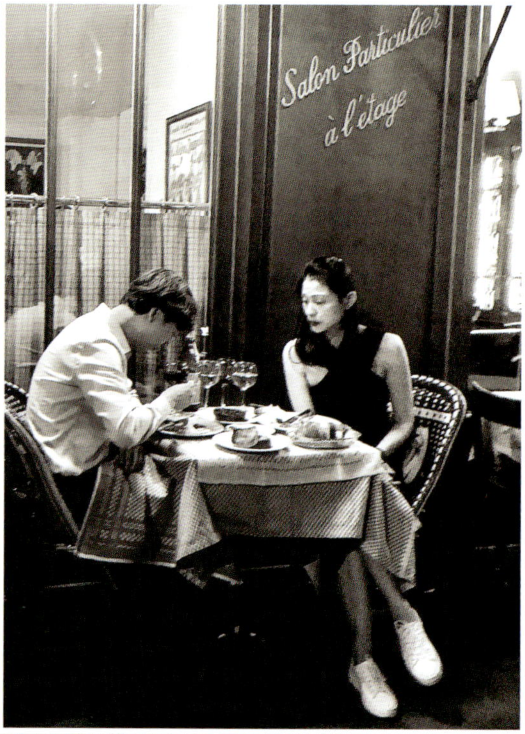

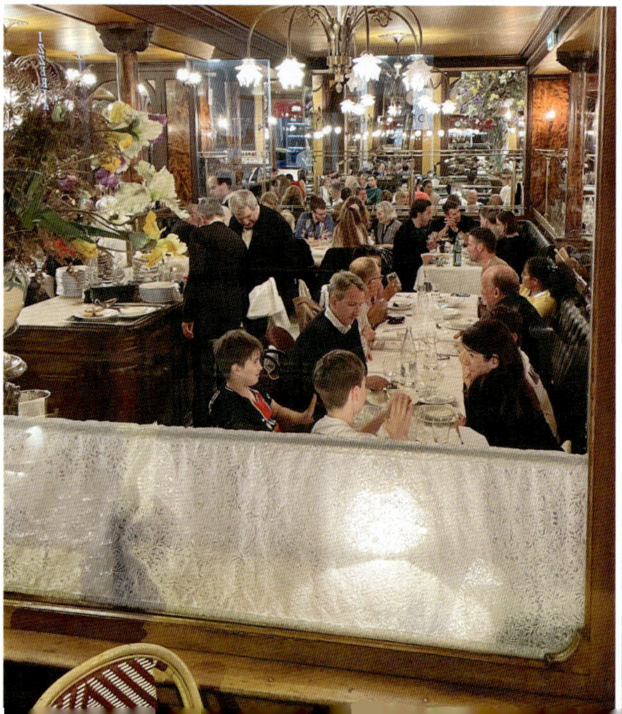

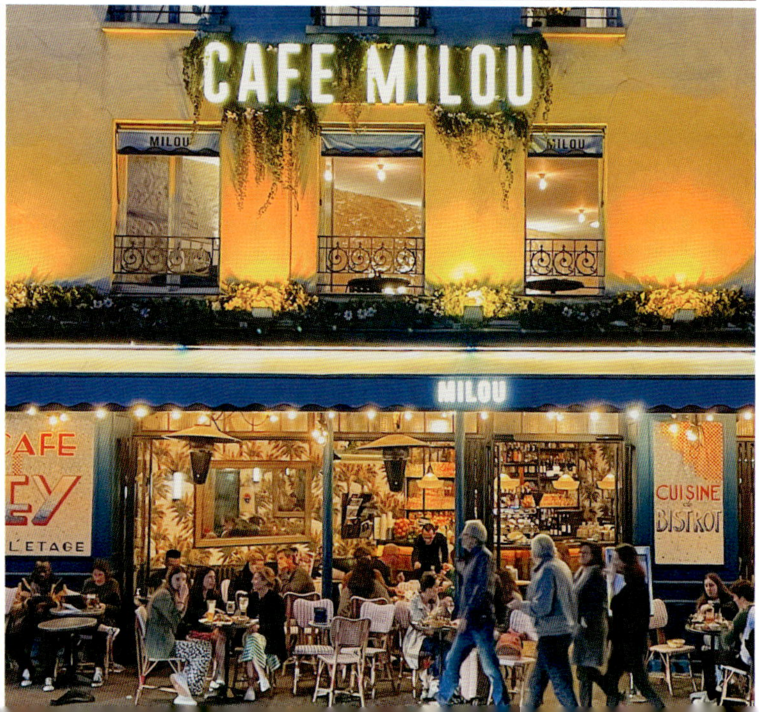

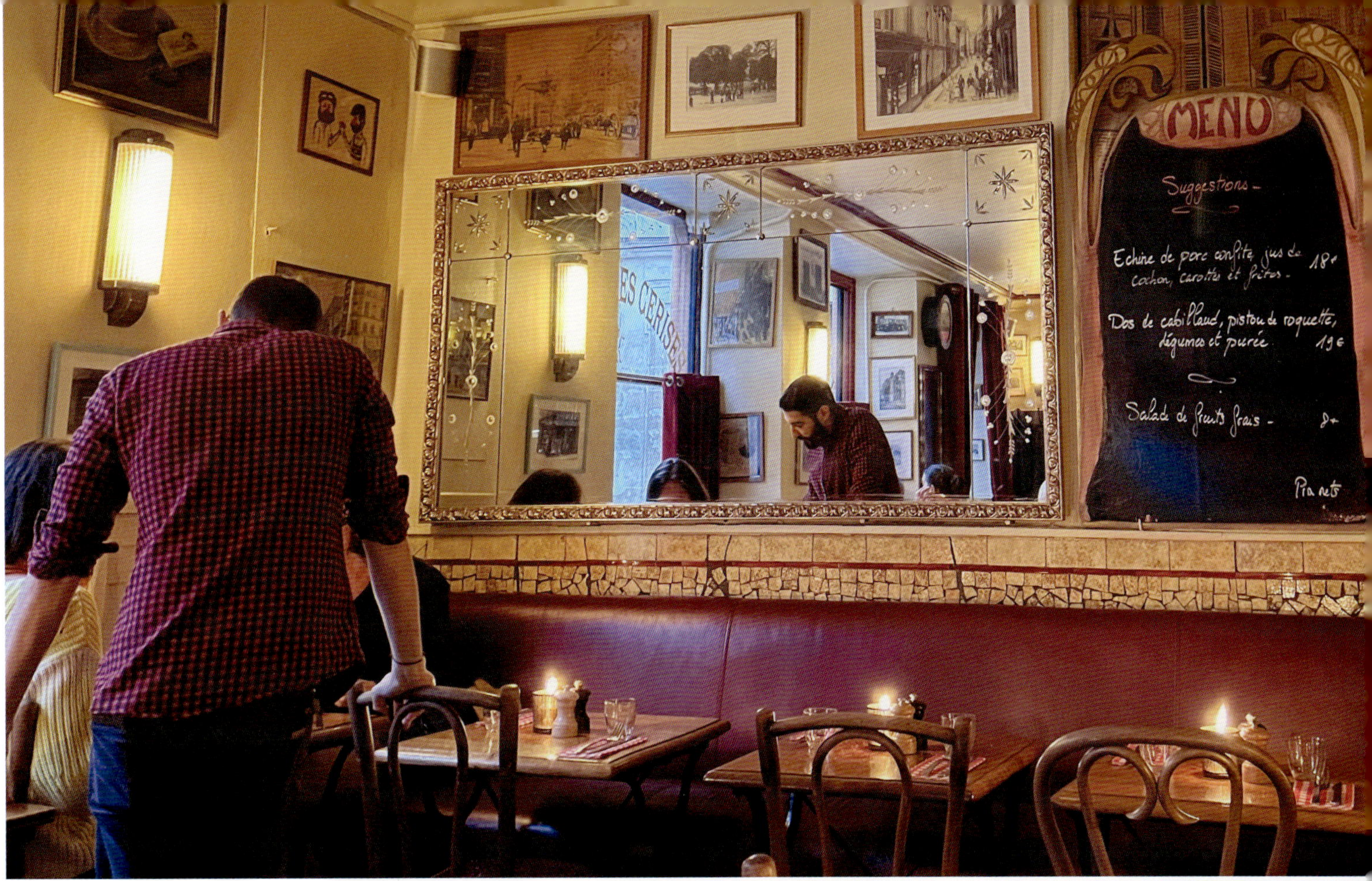

MENU
Suggestions -
Echine de porc confite, jus de cochon, carottes et frites - 18€
Dos de cabillaud, pistou de roquette, légumes et purée 19€
Salade de fruits frais - 8€

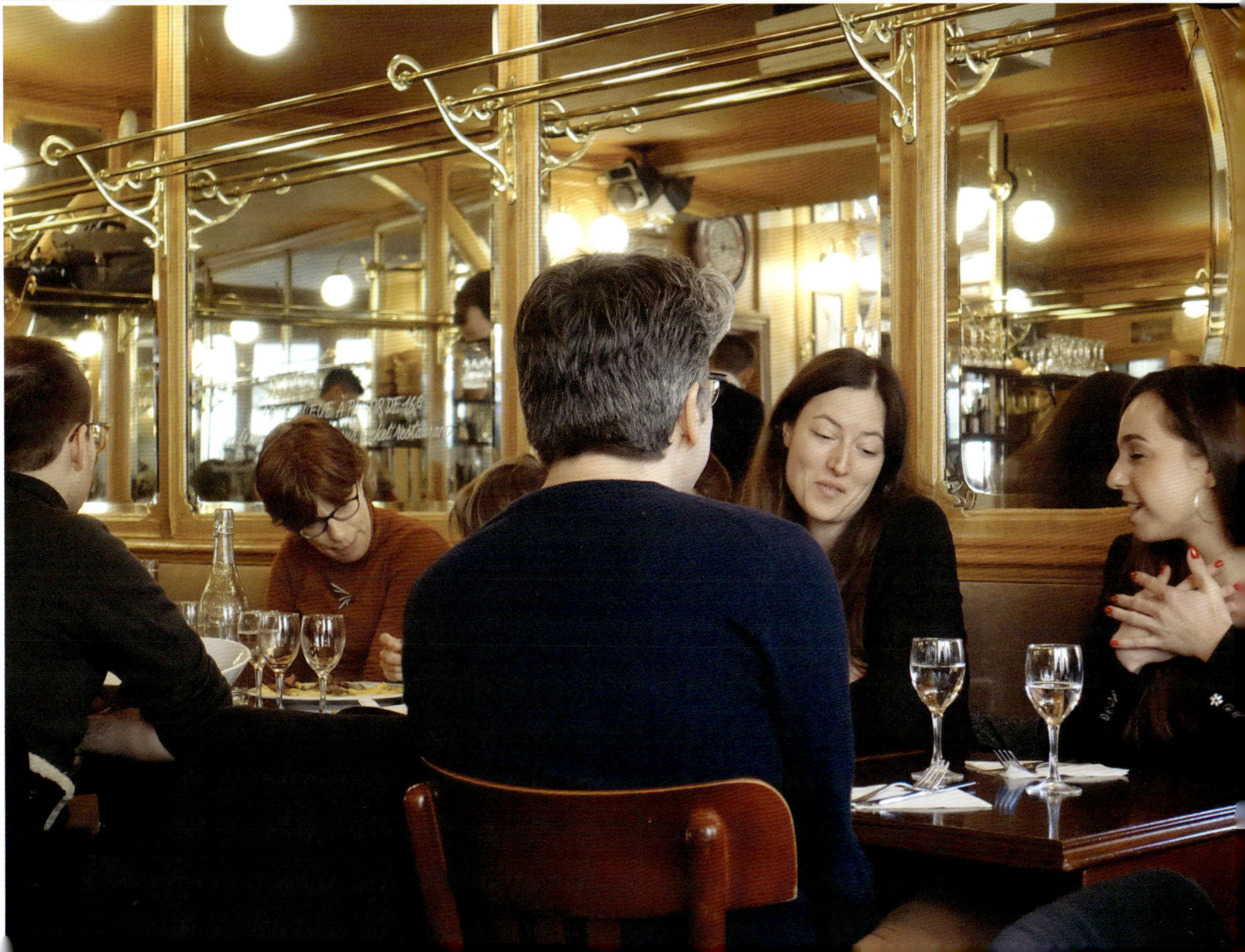

La Nuit

"It is in the Bistrots that I have often drawn most of my dialogues and surely the most beautiful scenes of my films."

Claude Lelouche

A nightcap? Given a 35-hour workweek, with starting hours for many at 9 or 10 am, weeks of vacation time, expanded holiday weekends, and summer daylight until 10 pm, Paris has a thriving nightlife. Watering holes abound, from cafés to bars, jazz venues, cabarets, clubs, and theaters, plus hidden sites that you have to be in the know to discover. Some of the liveliest *quartiers* for nightlife can be found in La Bastille, Le Marais, St. Germain, Le Quartier Latin, Montmartre, Pigalle, République, and Oberkampf. Can the days in the city of light be stretched any further?

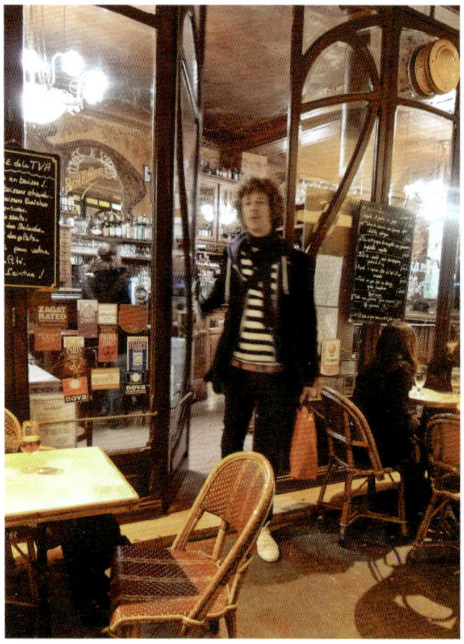

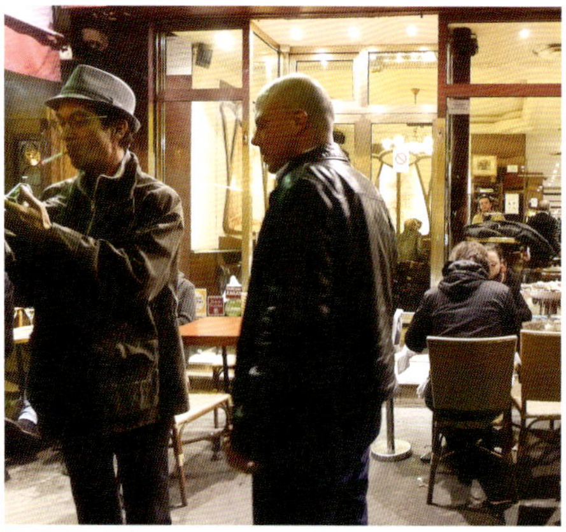

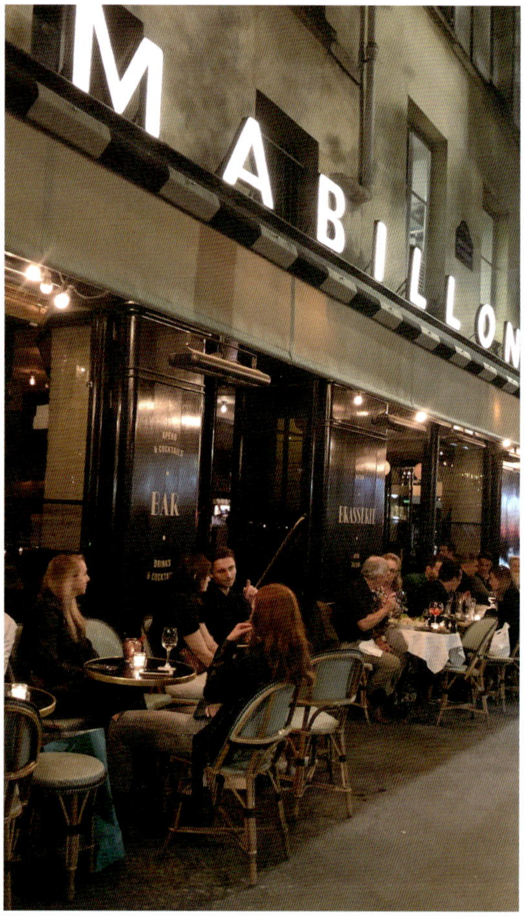

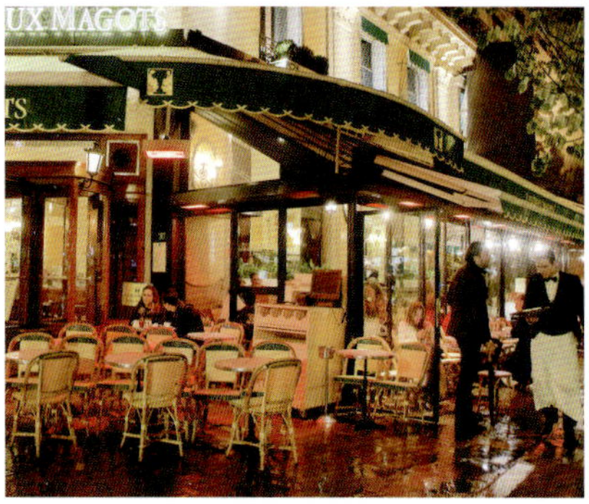

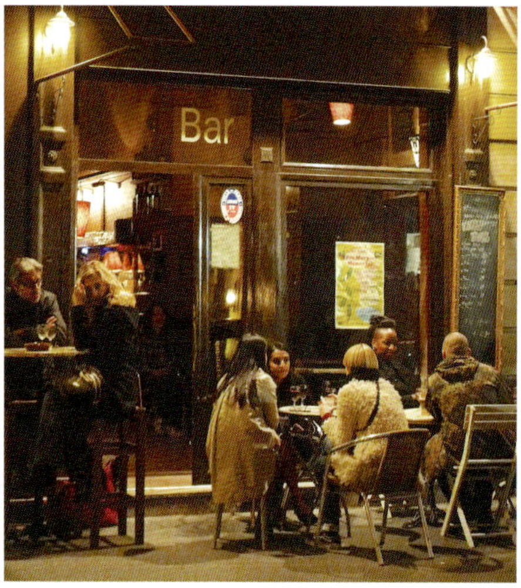

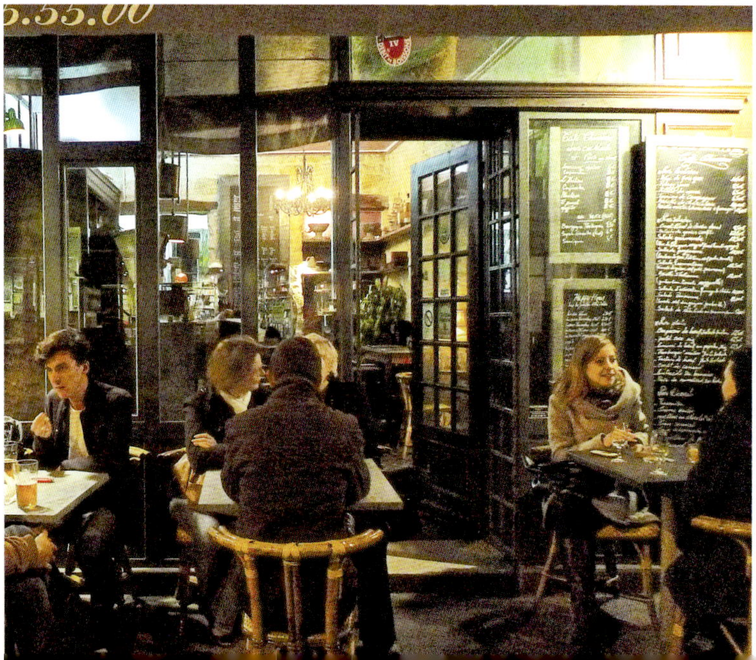

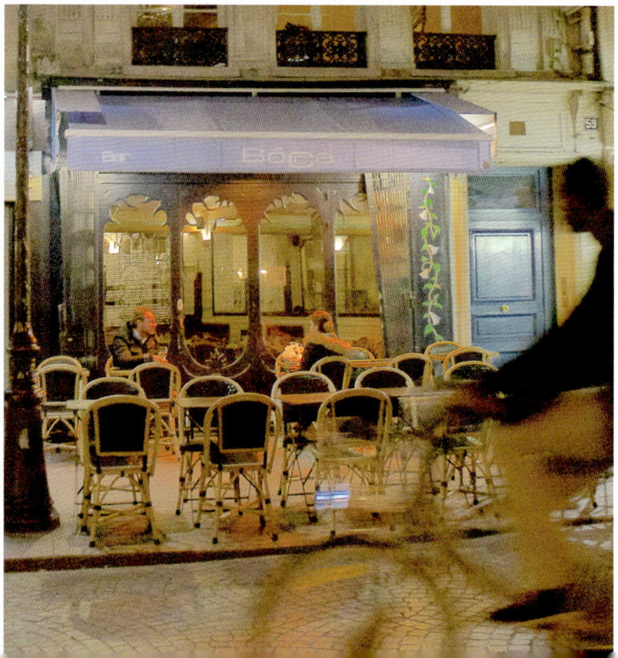

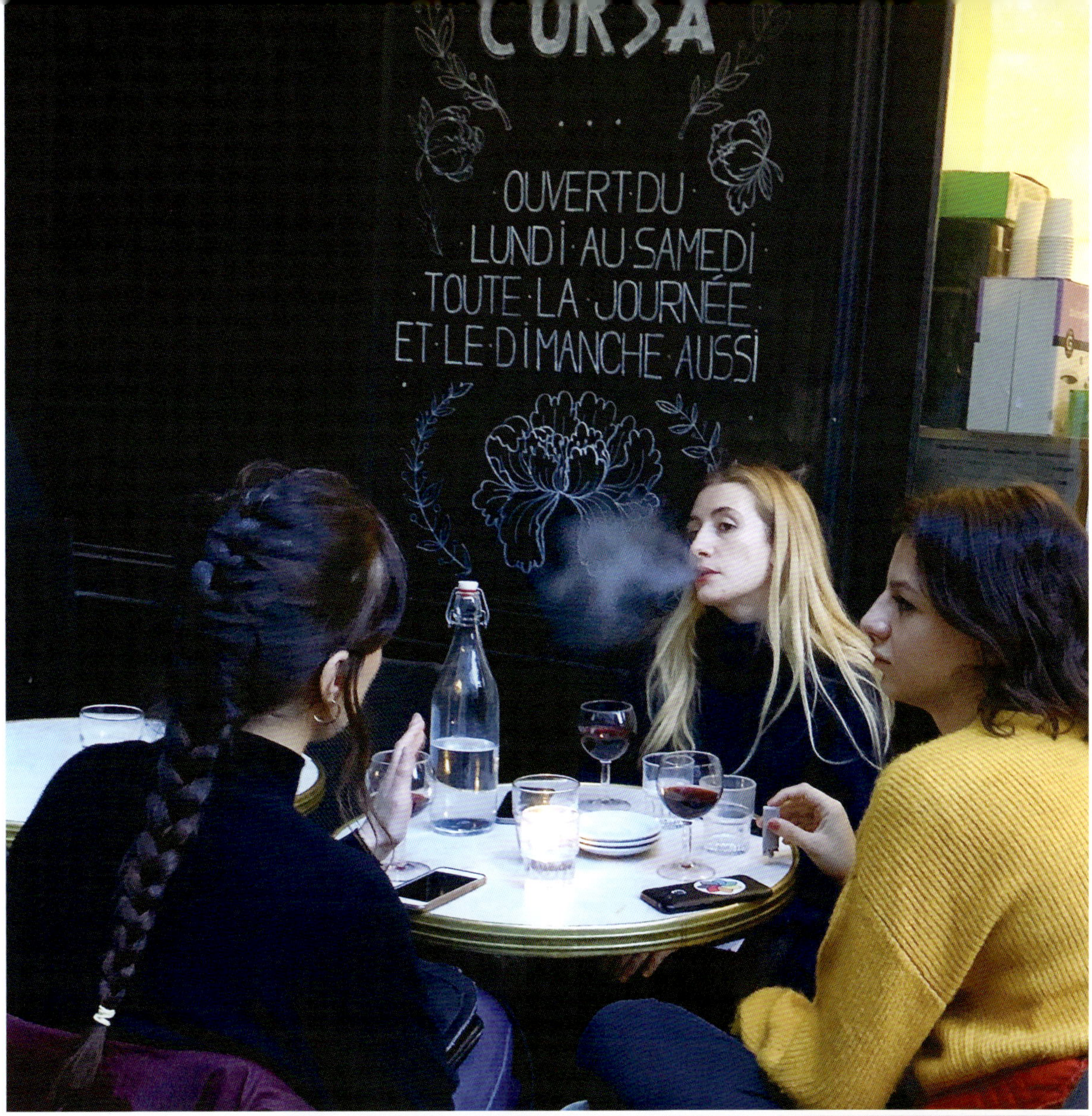
CORSA
OUVERT DU
LUNDI AU SAMEDI
TOUTE LA JOURNÉE
ET LE DIMANCHE AUSSI

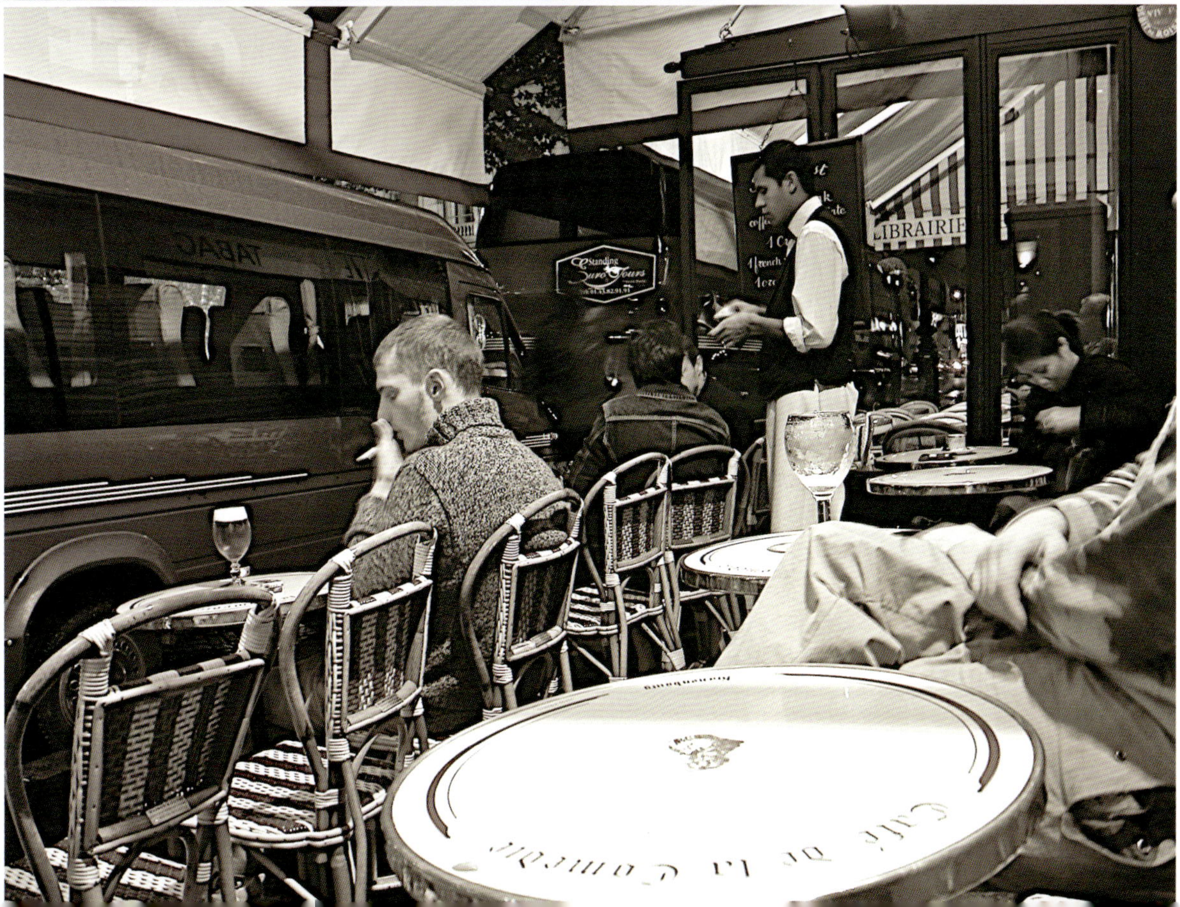
LIBRAIRIE

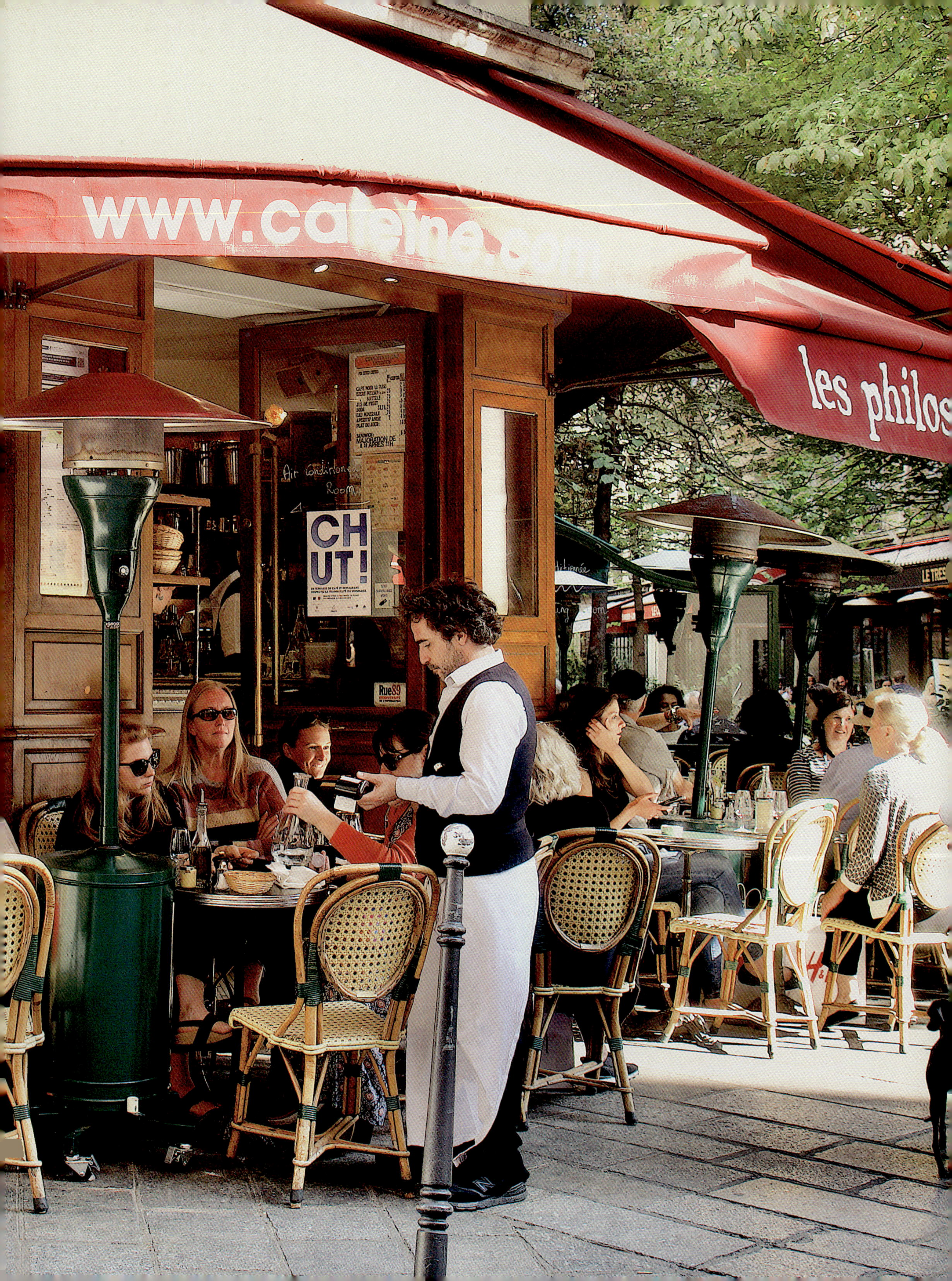
www.cafeine.com
les philos
CHUT!
Rue89

PART 7 The Time of Year

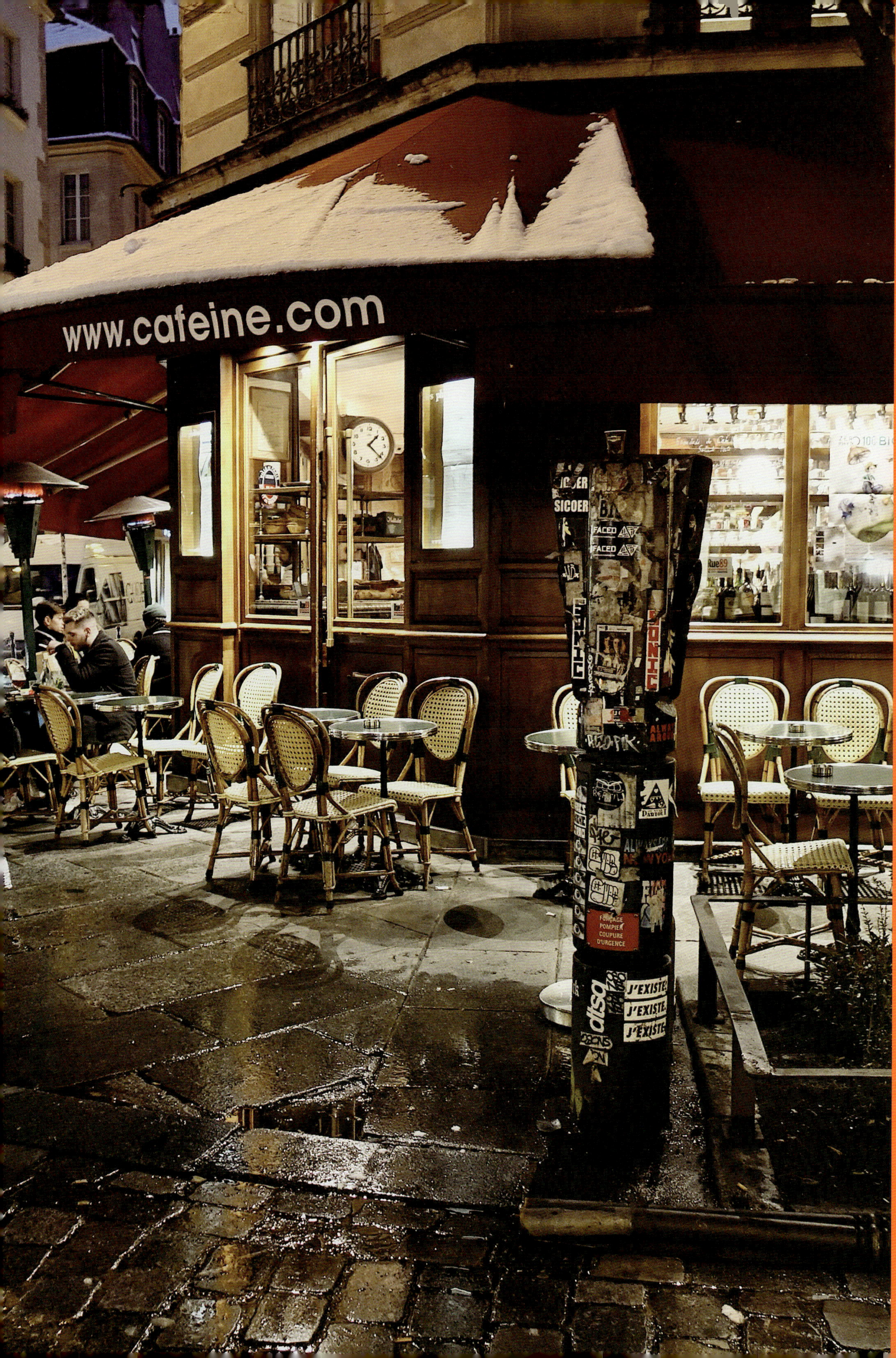

L'Été

"I love Paris in the summer, when it sizzles."
Cole Porter

It's summer in the city and the Parisians retreat to parts known and unknown, leaving a quieter playground for global tourists. Not everyone leaves, though, and many French now vary their respective exoduses, some in July, others in August. Thus, there are still Parisians to be found in summer, and they look gorgeous in their summer fashions. Many businesses are closed, but festive café terraces remain open throughout the day, hosting French sun worshippers and tourists from the world over. Top this off with sixteen hours of sunshine before late summer sunsets, and the humidity becomes more tolerable.

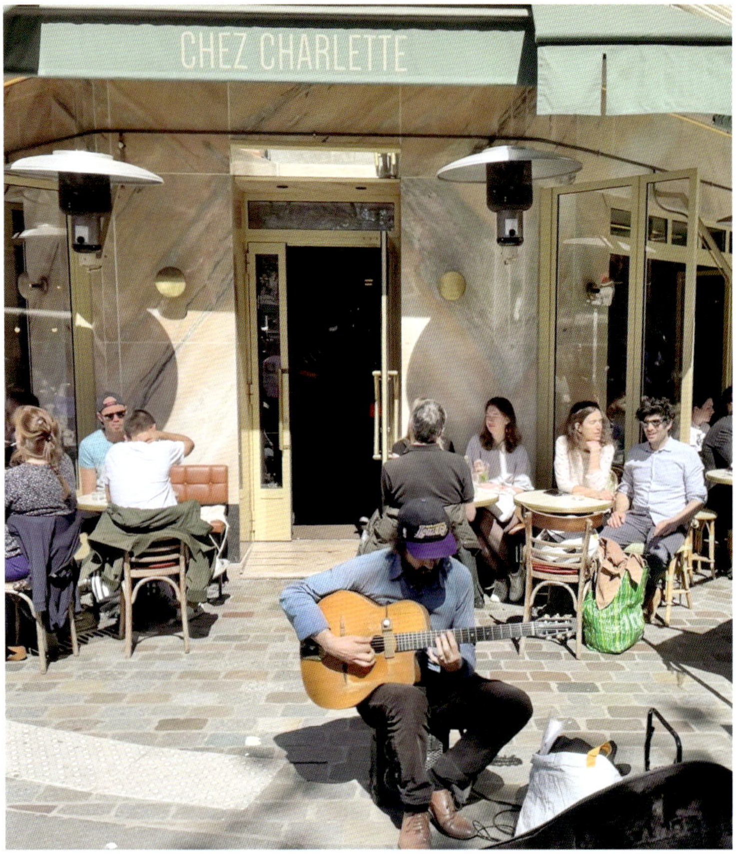

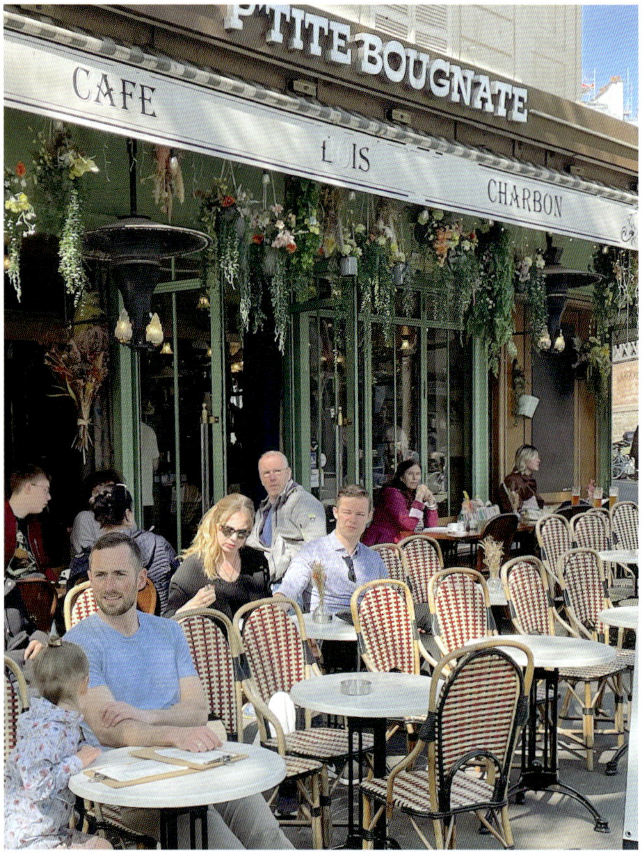

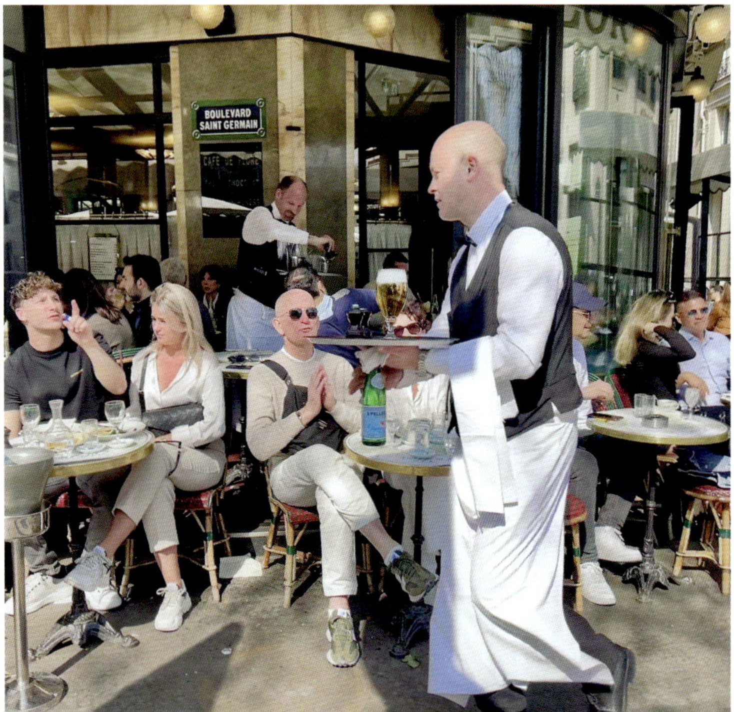

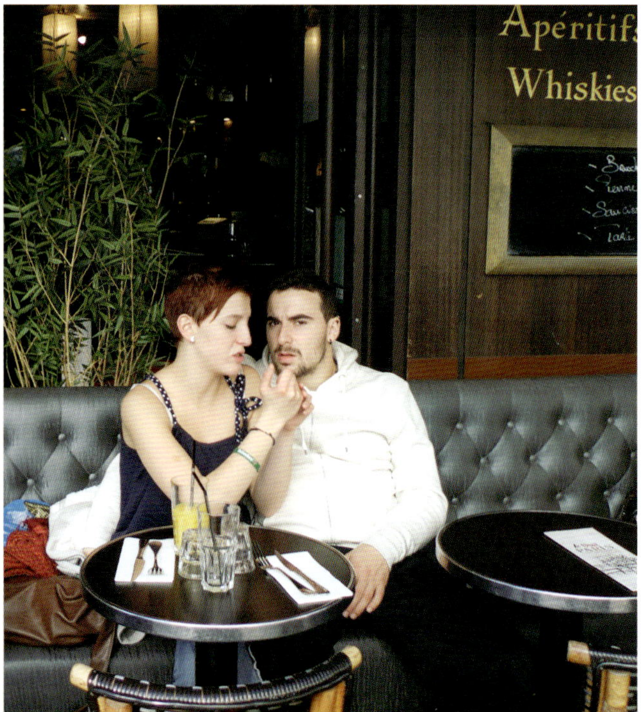

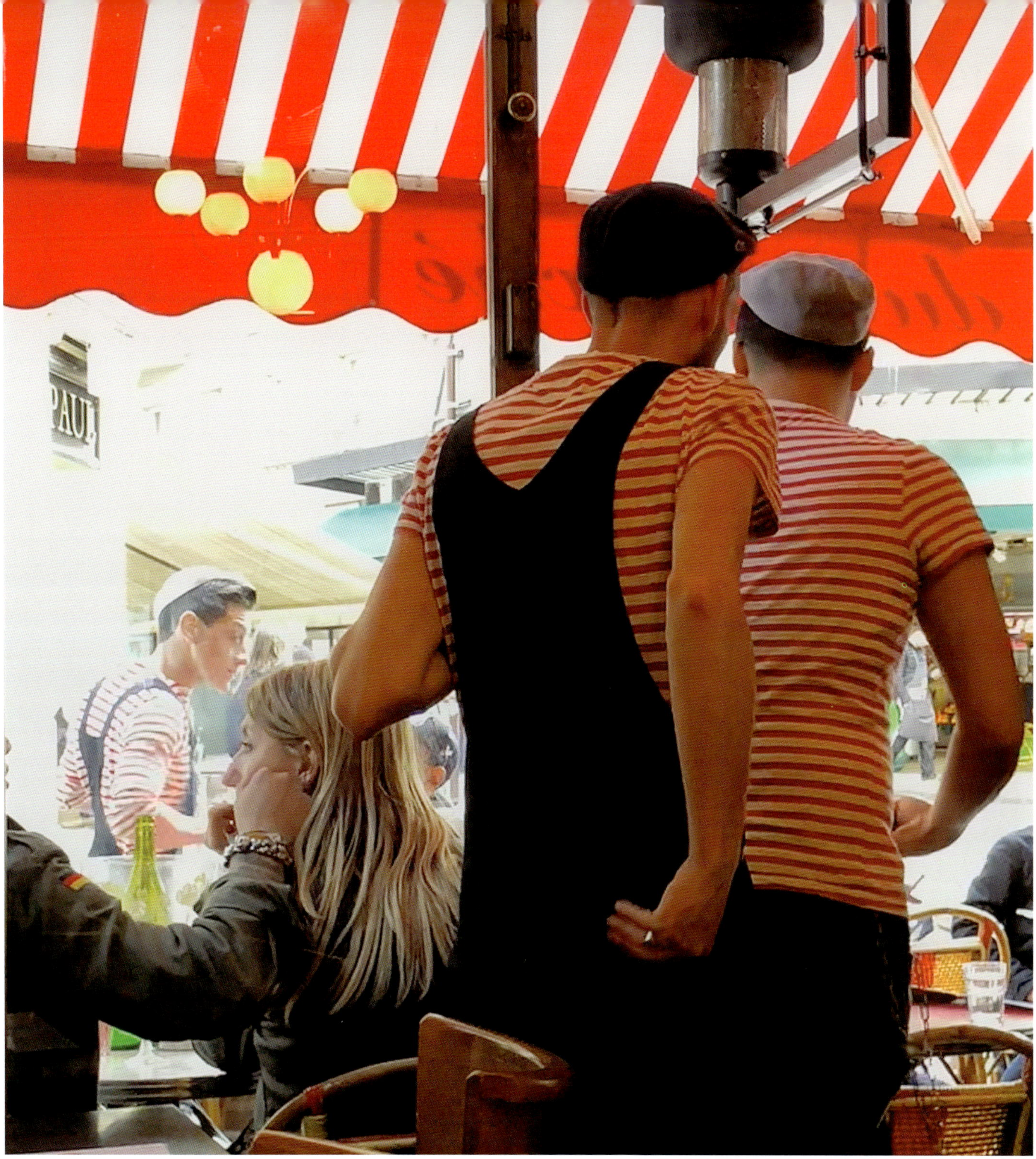
PAUL

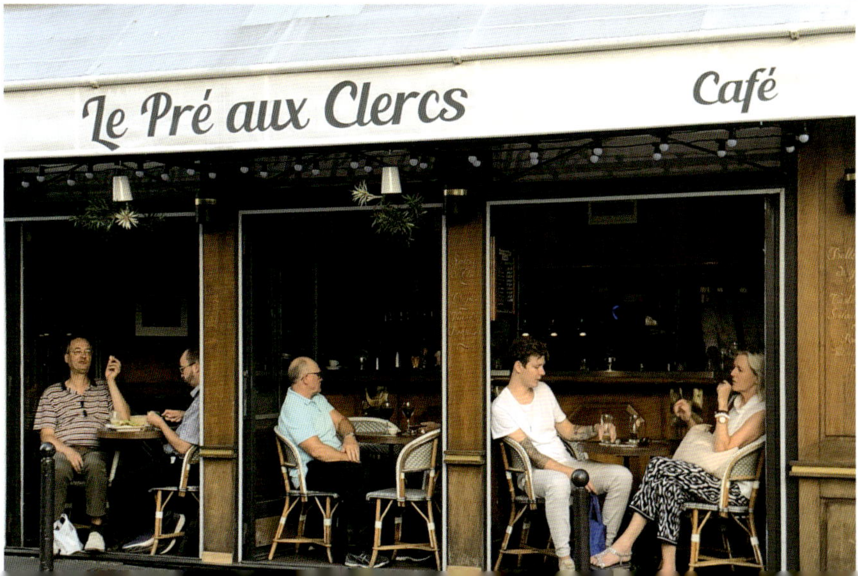
Le Pré aux Clercs
Café

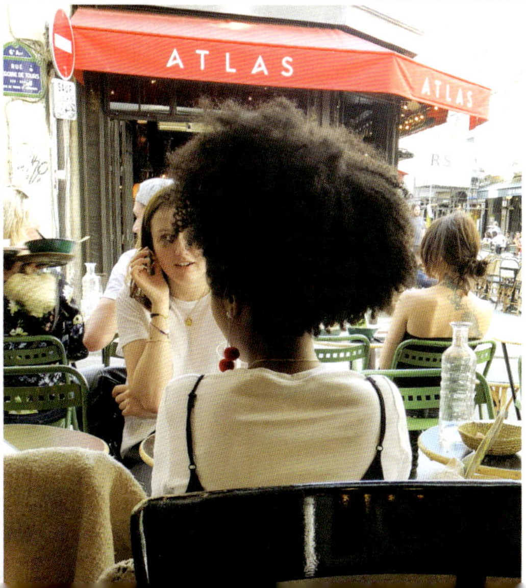
ATLAS
ATLAS

L'Automne

"The hours I have spent in cafés are the only ones I consider living apart from writing."

Anäis Nin

Ah, *La Rentrée*! The beginning of September is when the French return from vacation and go back to school and work; cultural events resume, restaurants reopen, new novels are released, and a new energy, a new beginning is in the offing. Nature's vibrant fall colors make Paris even more beautiful. As the days cool, chic scarves, hats, and gloves pop out all over the city. (This is a good time for fashionistas to study the French art of intricate scarf-wrapping.) The autumn air exhilarates during long Paris walks; the cafés a cozy stop with familiar red blankets, called "*le plaid*," draped over chairs on the terraces to warm the body. Paired with a hearty meal accompanied by *vin chaud* to warm the soul, and all's well in Paris.

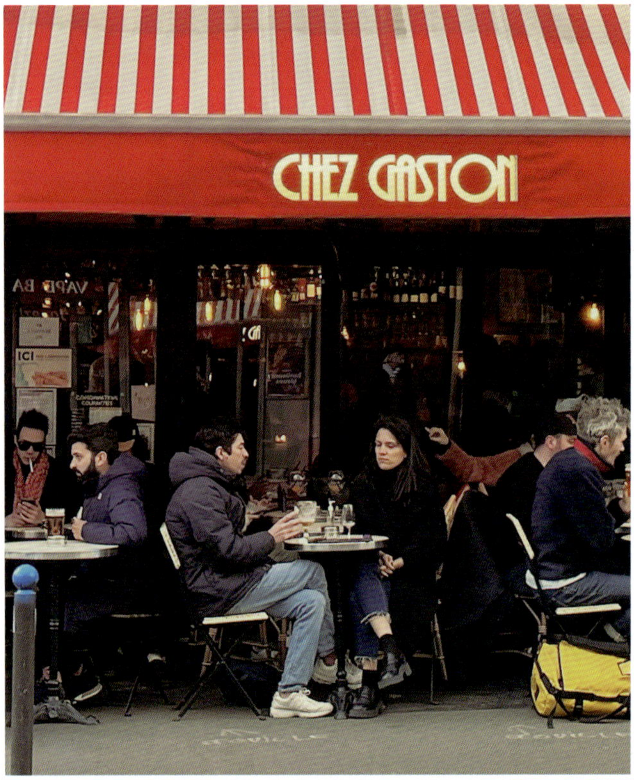

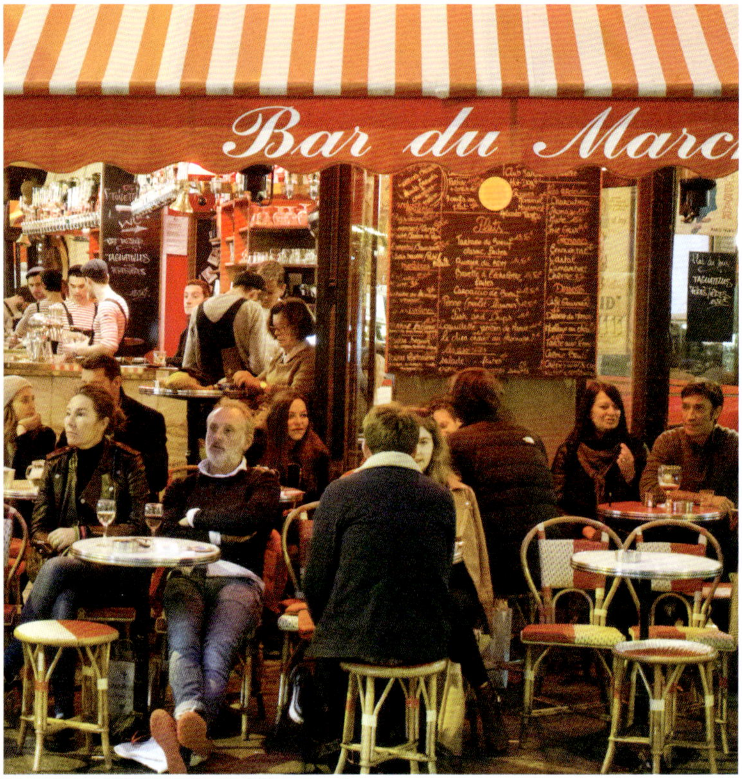

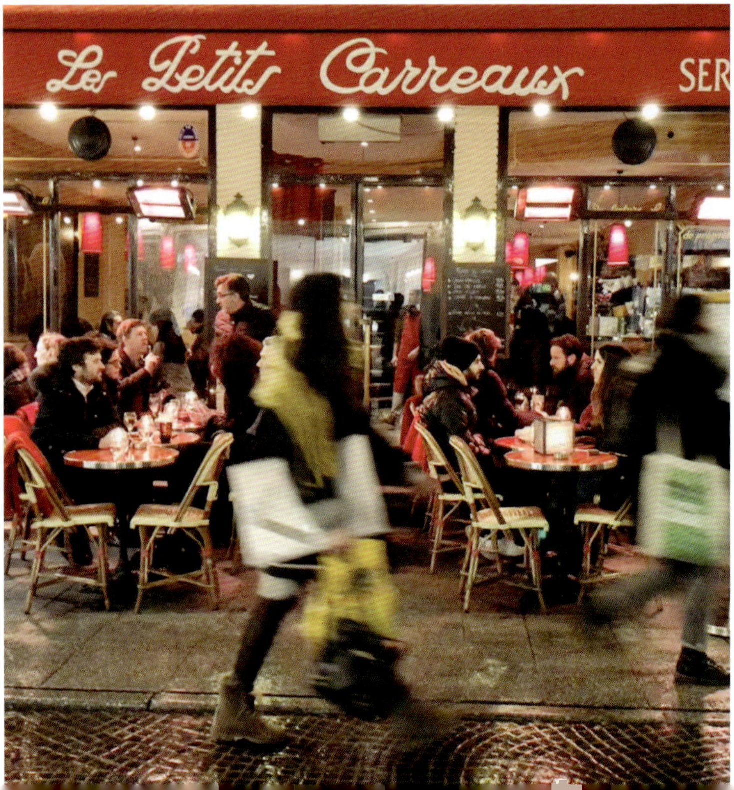

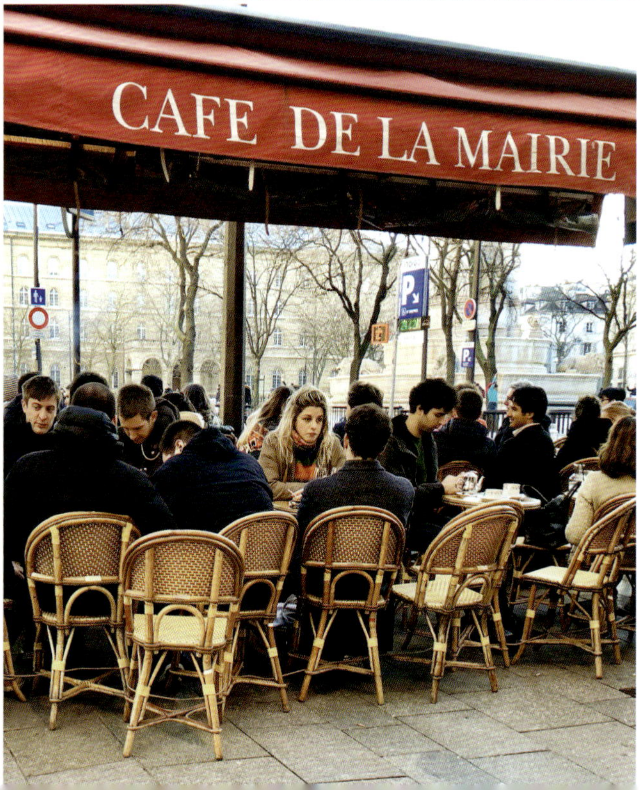

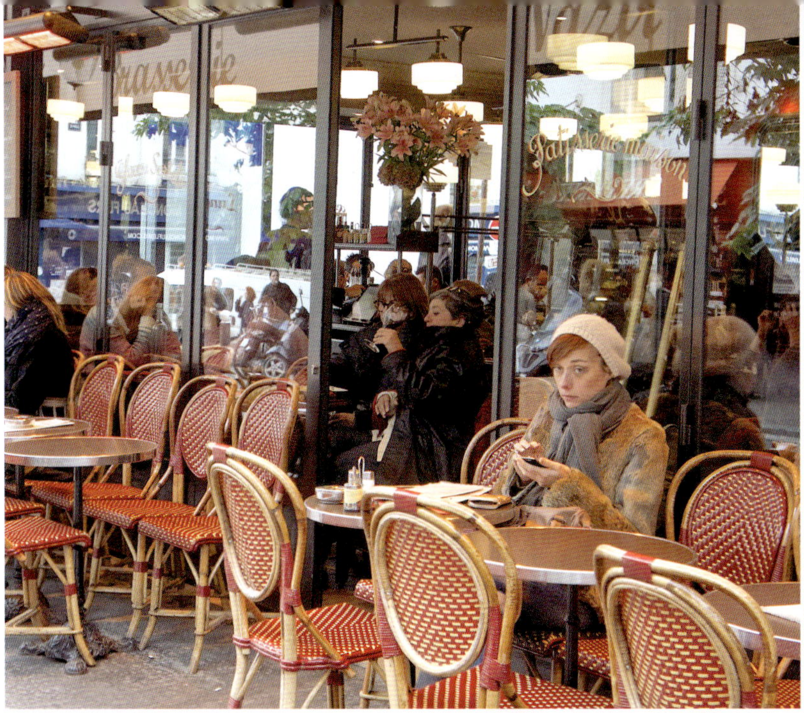

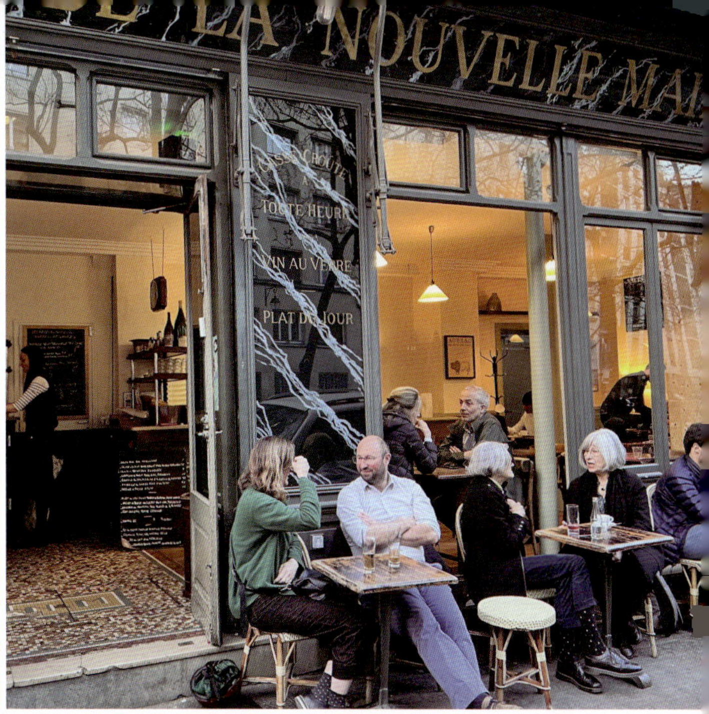
VIN AU VERRE
PLAT DU JOUR

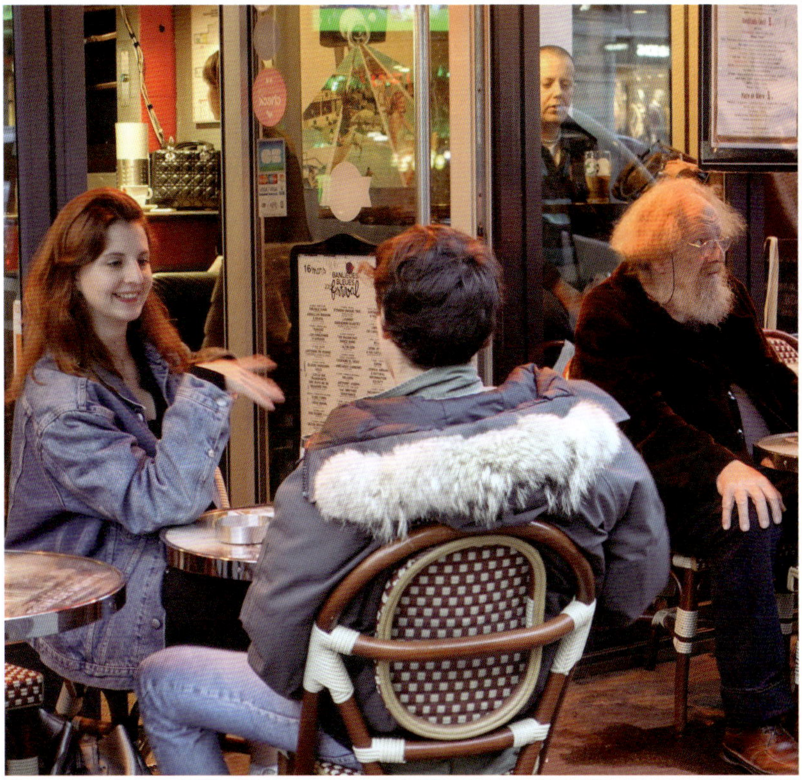

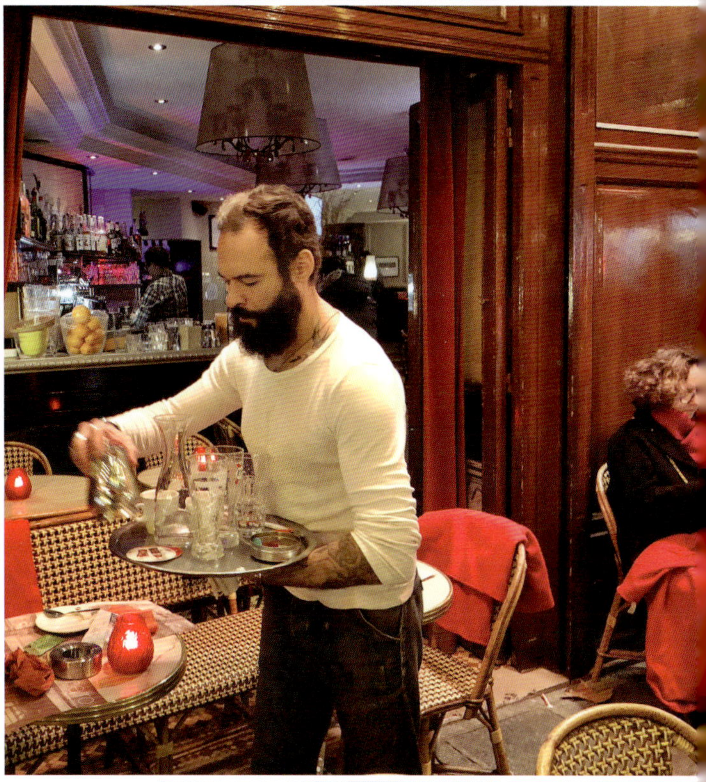

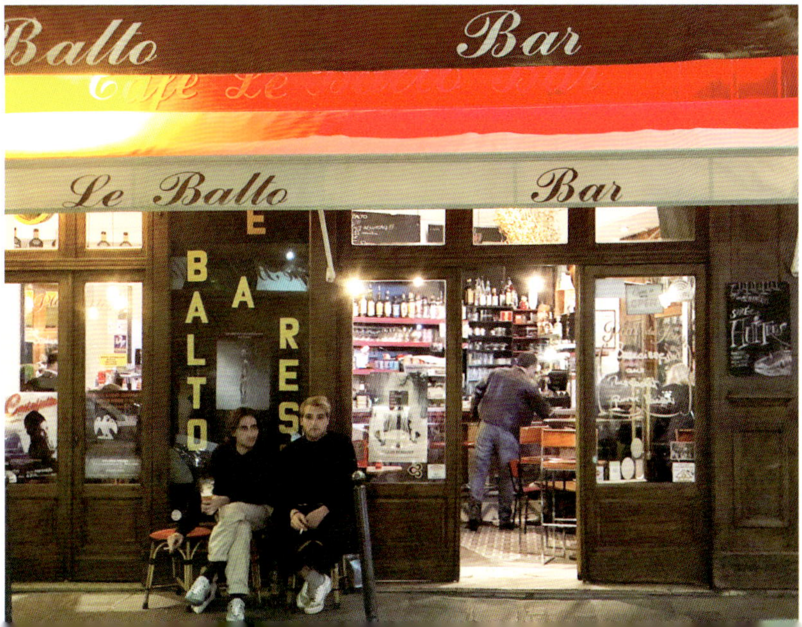
Balto Bar
Le Balto Bar

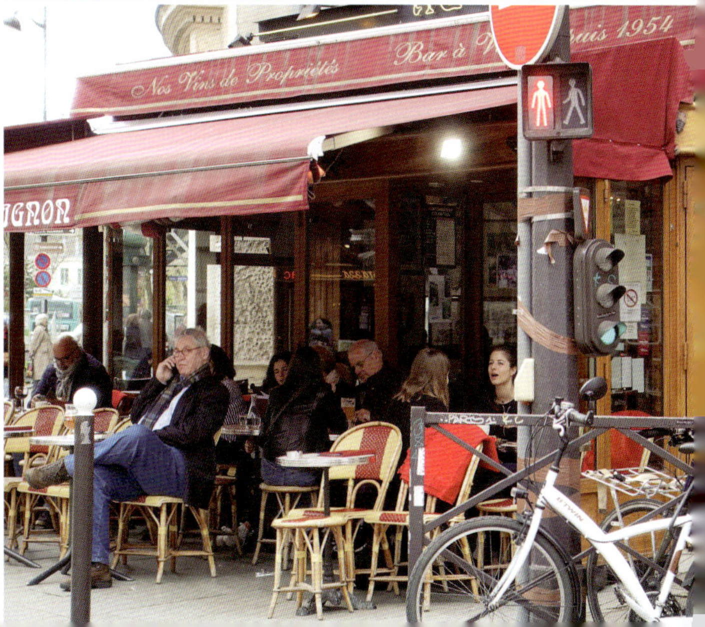
Nos Vins de Propriétés

L'Hiver

"In the depth of winter I finally learned that there was in me an invincible summer."

Albert Camus

Ok, it rains a lot in Paris almost any time of year. They say it rarely snows, but that happens too. Rain and snow, however, do not stop life on the street or the cafés. Just carry an umbrella and pop into a cozy café and wait for the rain to stop—which it does. Dining outside in all weather was commonplace, with outdoor heaters warming 70% of café terraces from 2008 (when smoking was banned in enclosed places) until April 1, 2022, when the heaters were banned to save 500,000 tons of CO2 each year. Many café terraces have glass enclosures that create a conservatory-style shelter in the winter months that is almost like an outdoor terrace.

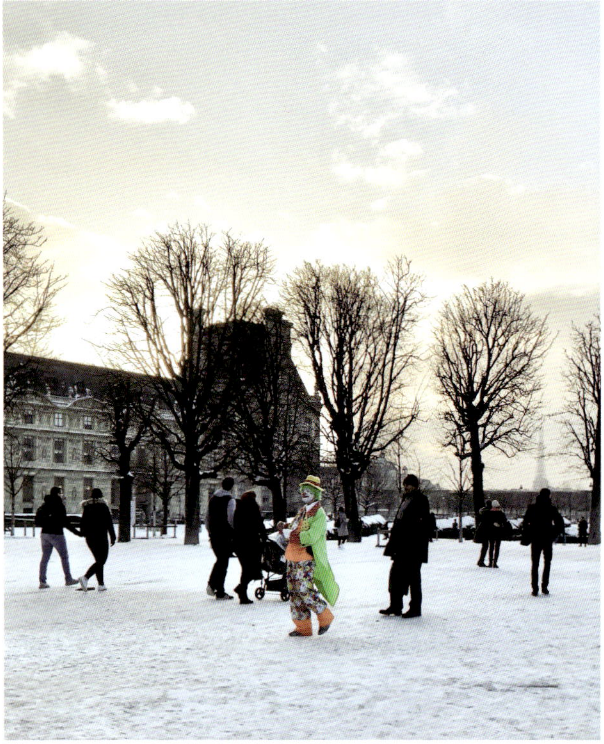

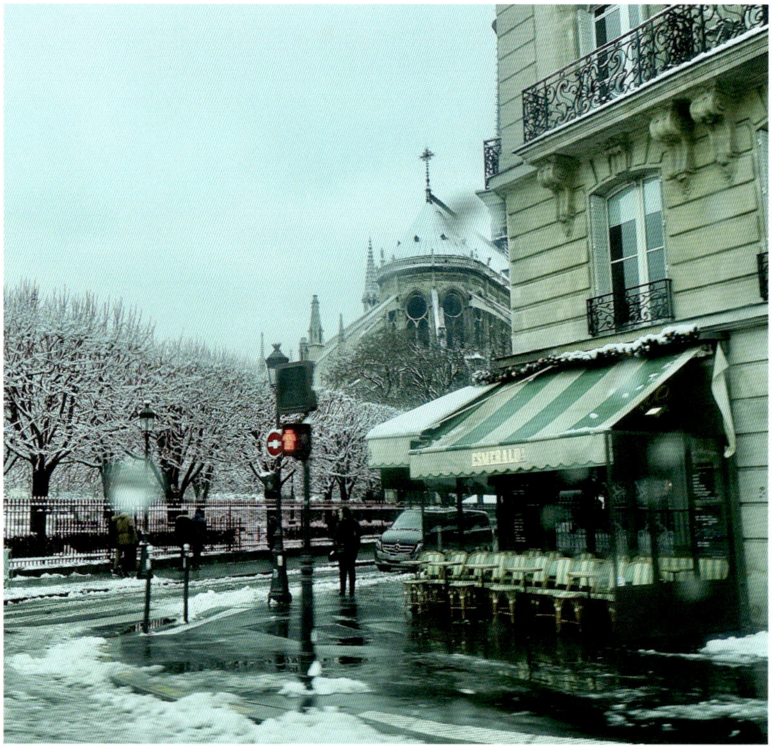

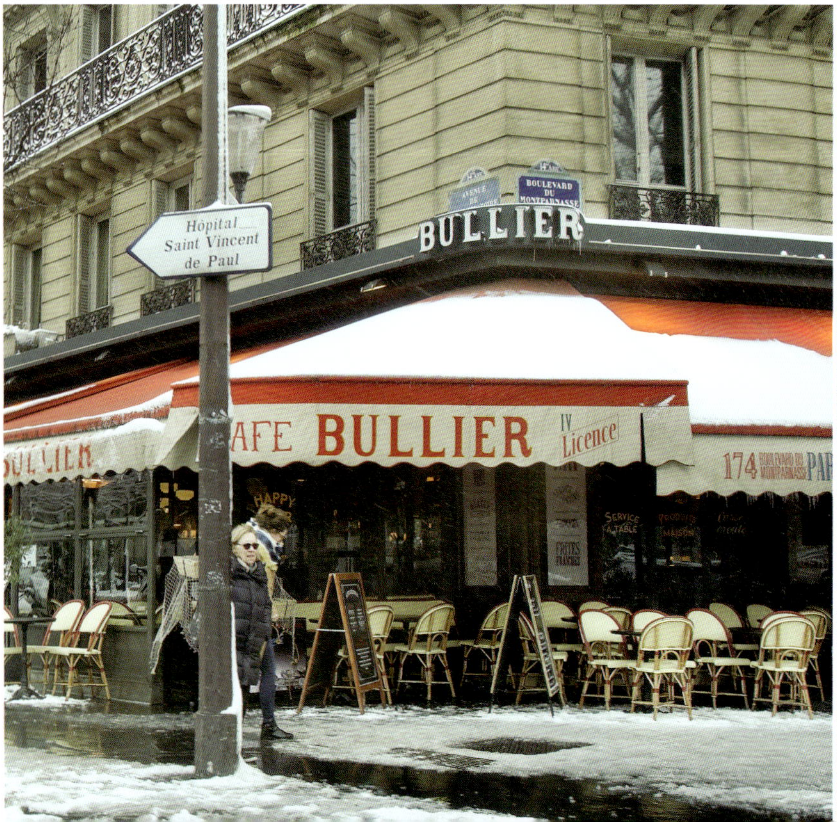

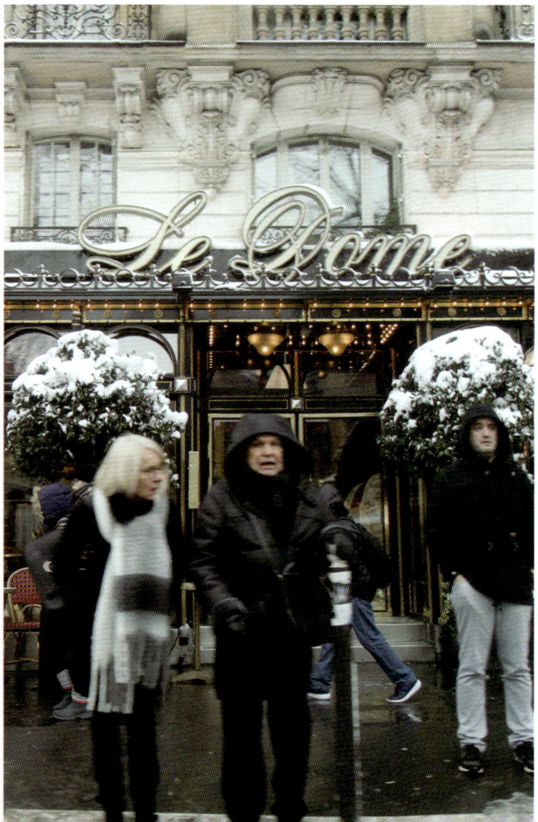

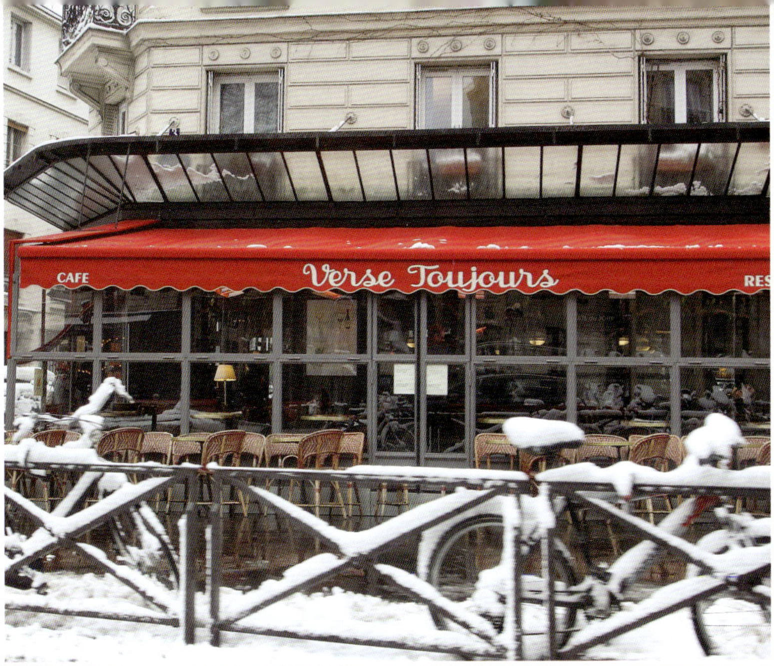
CAFE
Verse Toujours
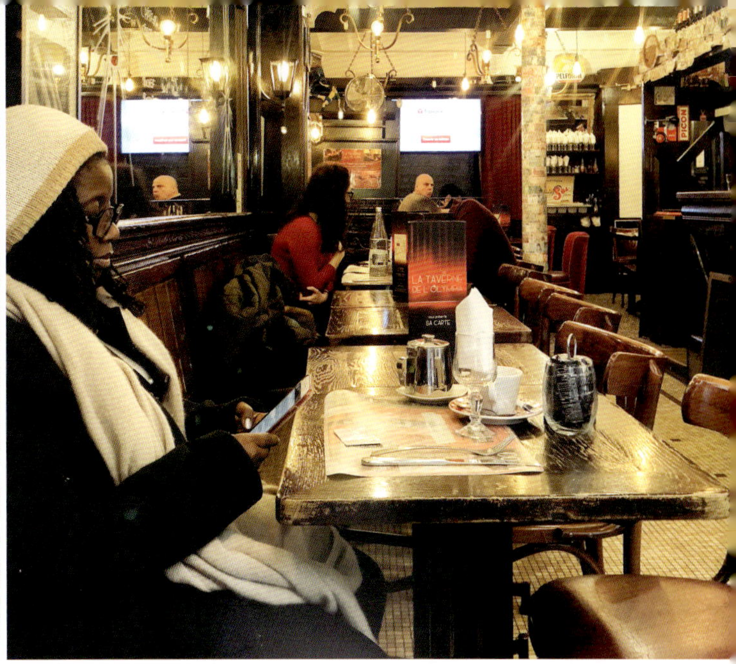
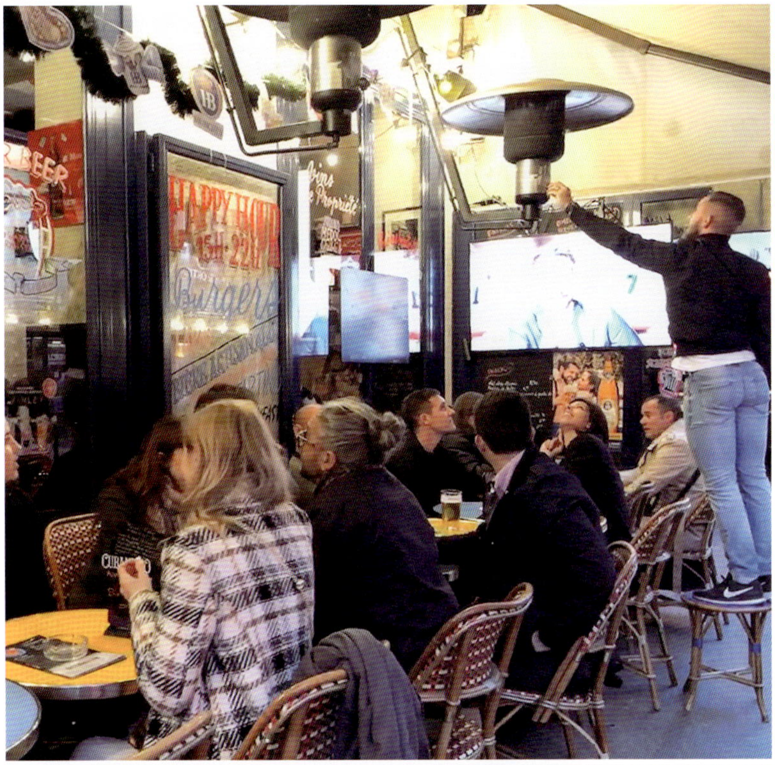
Burgers
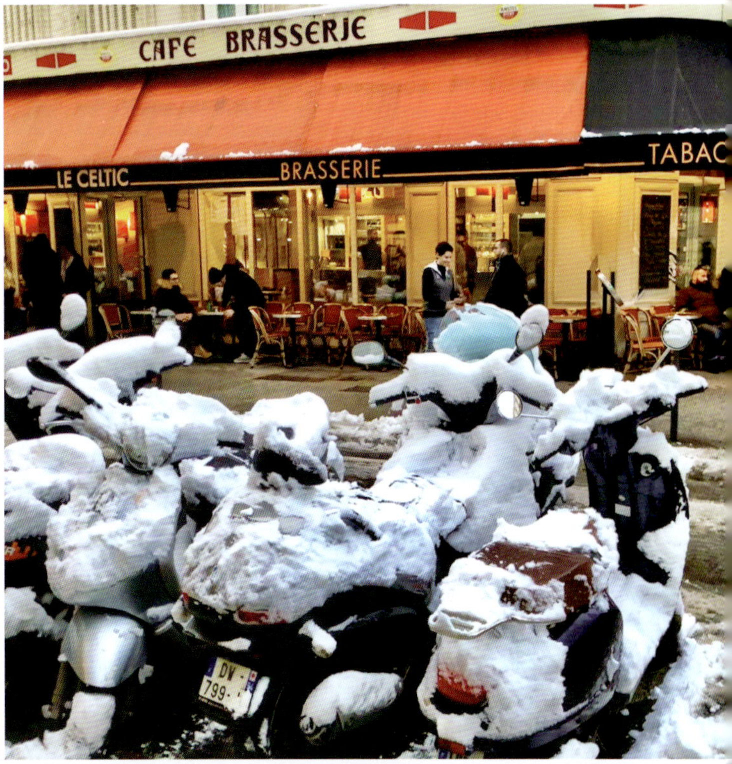
CAFE BRASSERIE
LE CELTIC
BRASSERIE
TABAC
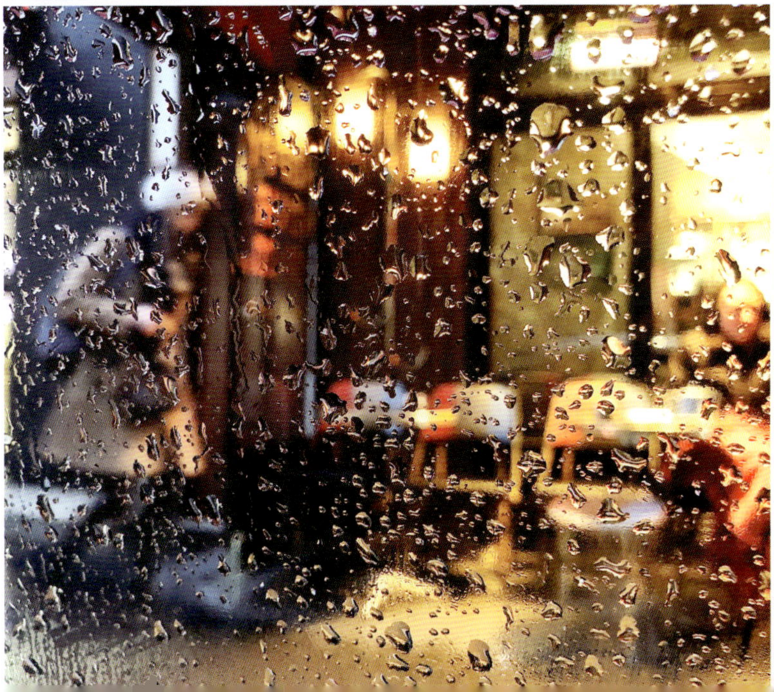
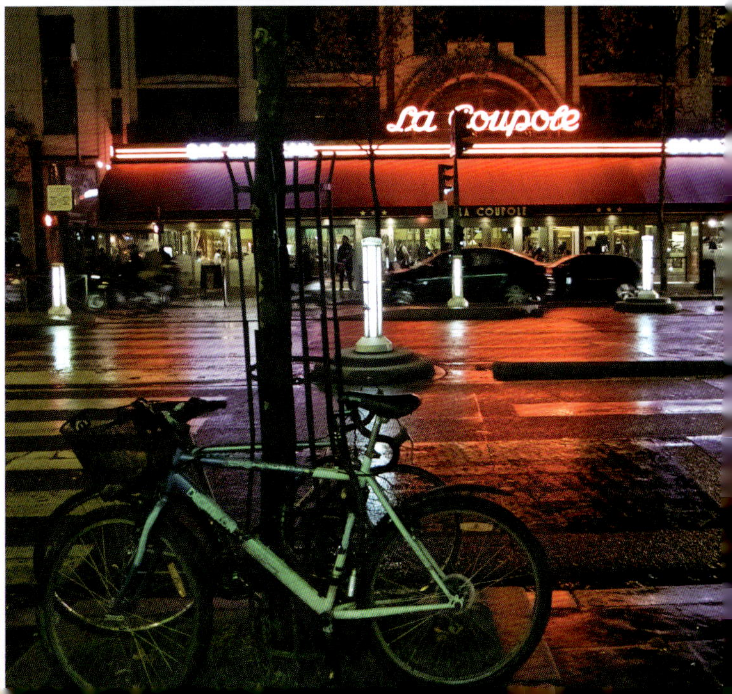
La Coupole

Le Printemps

"When spring comes to Paris, the humblest mortal alive must feel that he dwells in paradise."

Henry Miller

Time for the red blankets to cushion the seat rather than wrap the shoulders and for jackets to hang on the back of the Rilsen and rattan chair. Spring calls for a walk or run through Luxembourg's immaculately manicured gardens bursting with exquisitely arranged spring hues. Now is the time for the fresh leaves on the trees and flowers in the ground to bathe the city in luxurious, living colors. Inspired by what nature has unearthed, the Parisian florists go wild with imagination. The genius of their selection and arrangements is a breath of fragrant air and *un coup de foudre*. After celebrating the wonder of nature's rebirth at the end of the long, dark winter, there is always time for a café break.

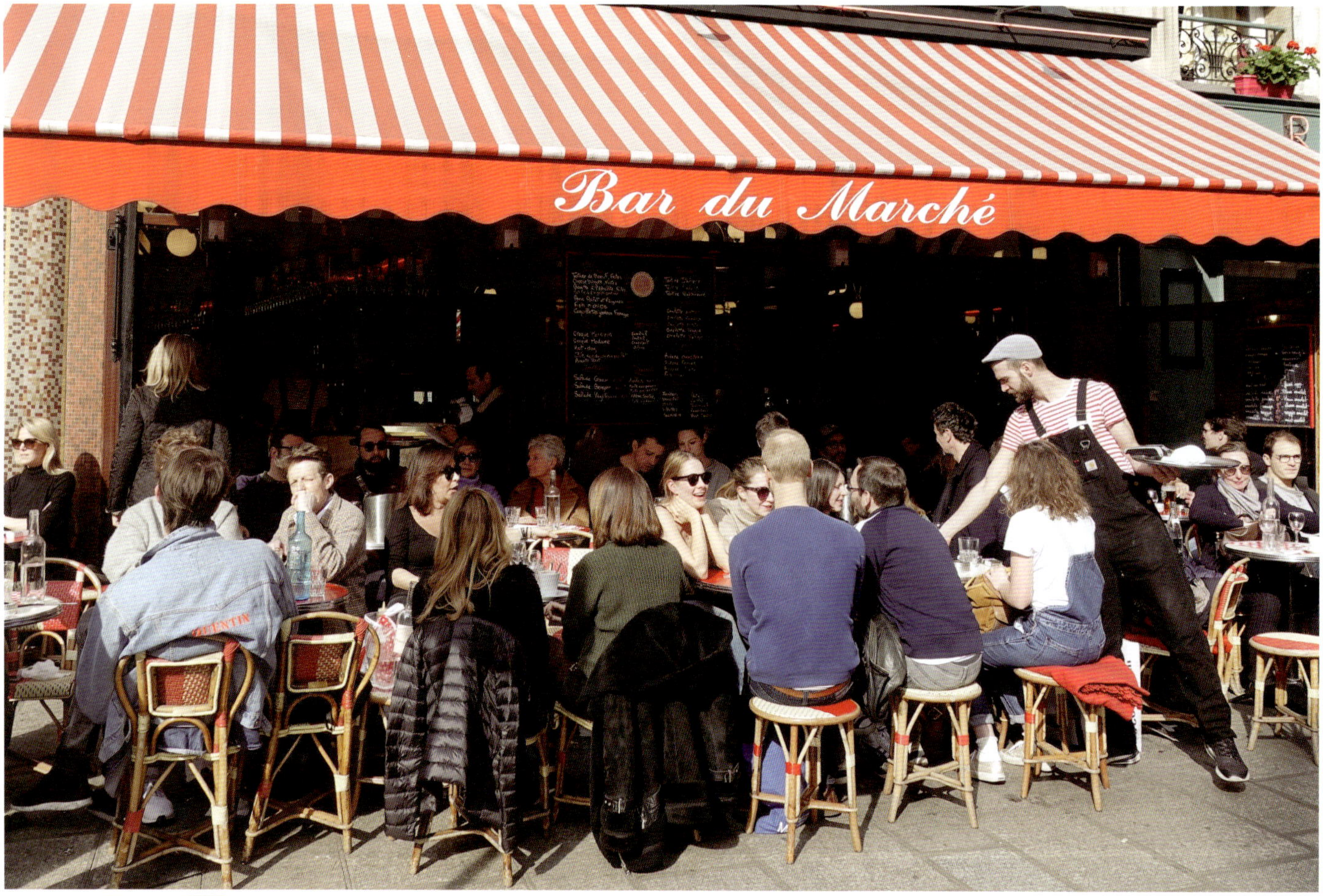

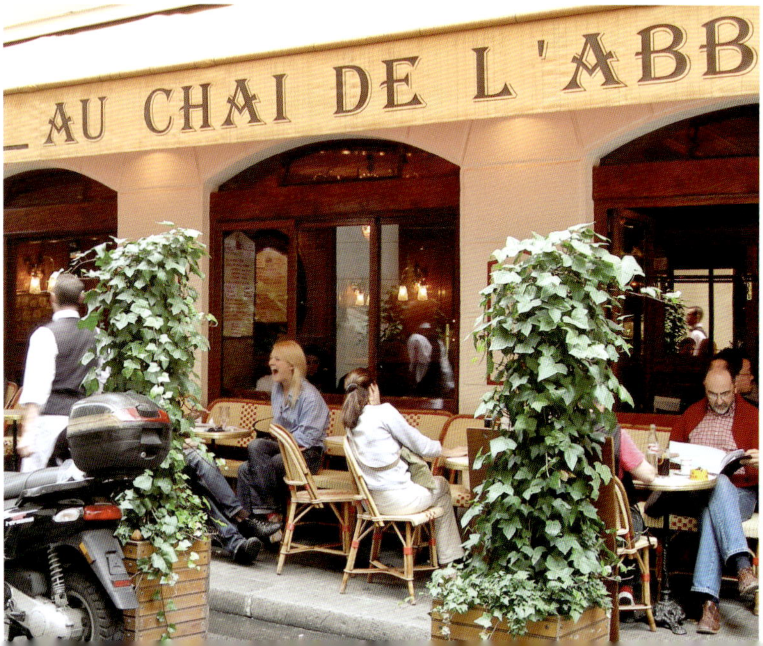

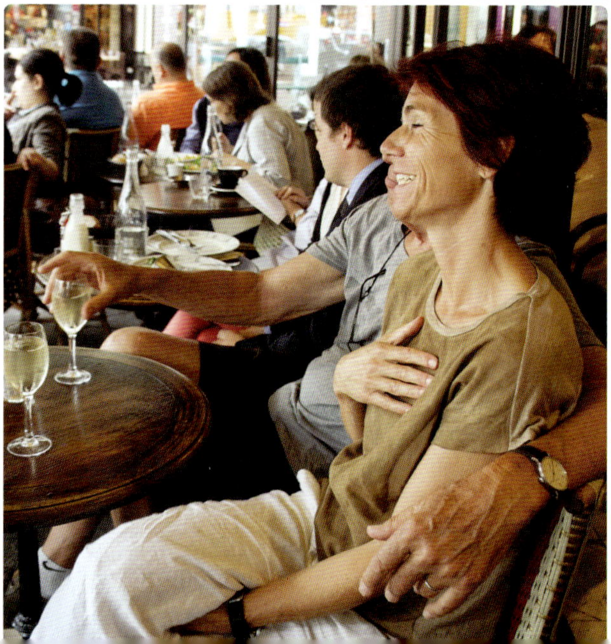

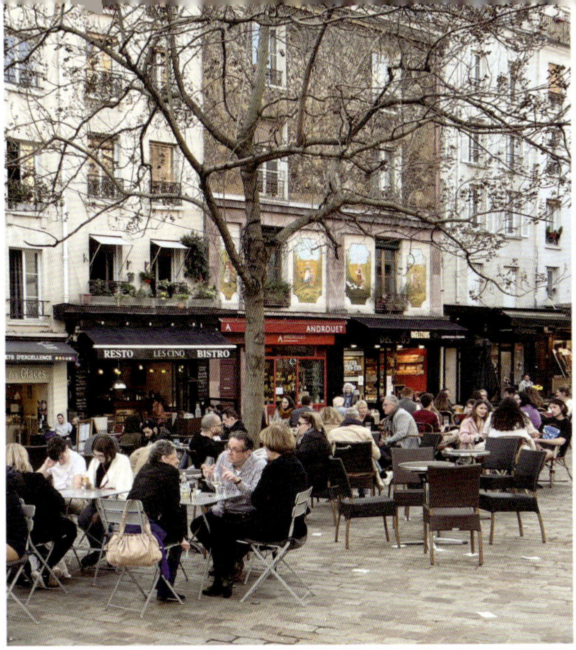
RESTO
BISTRO
ANDROUET

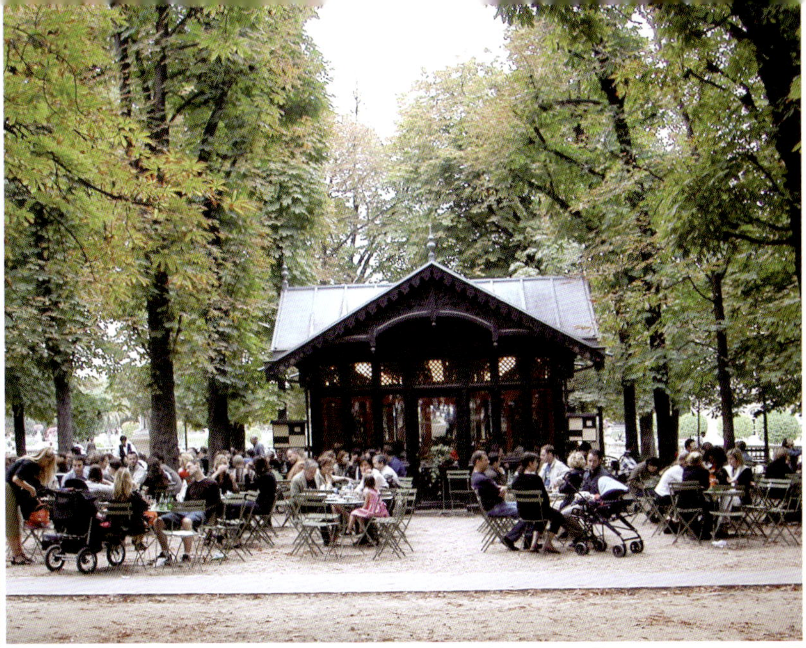

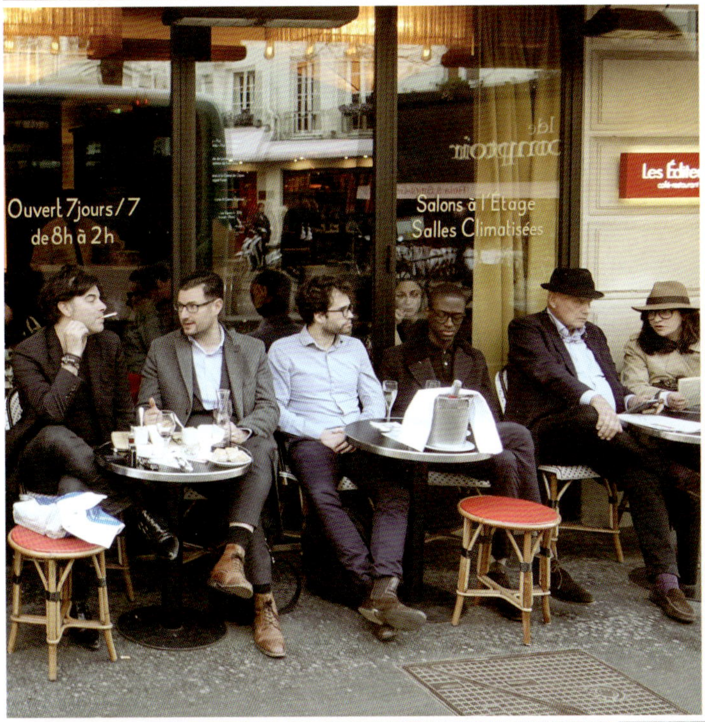
Ouvert 7jours/7
de 8h à 2h
Salons à l'Etage
Salles Climatisées

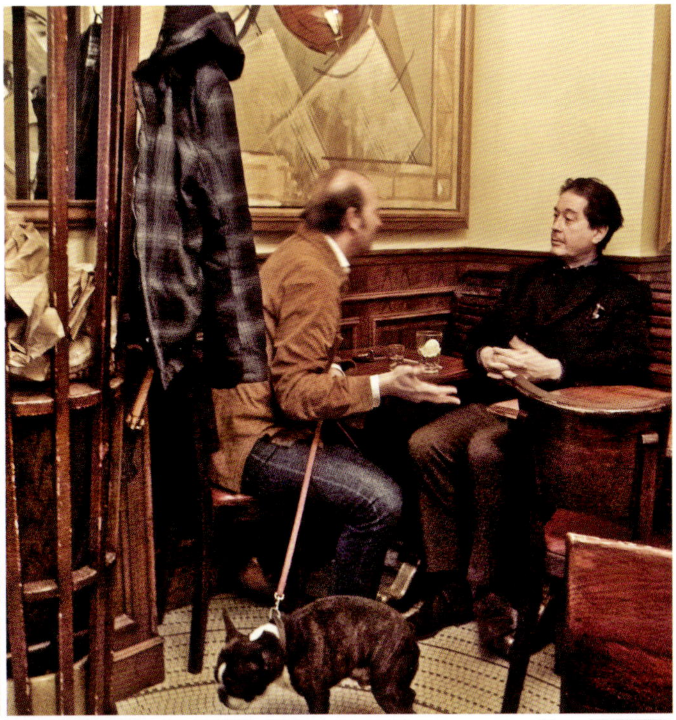

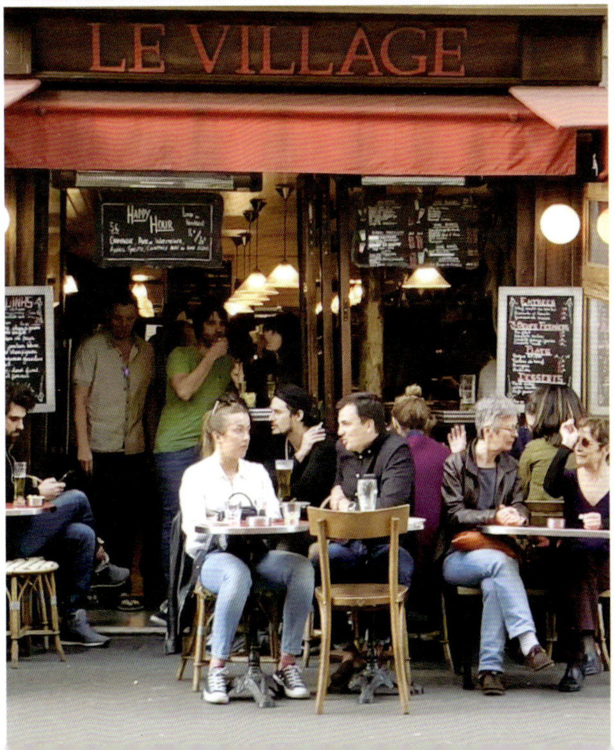
LE VILLAGE

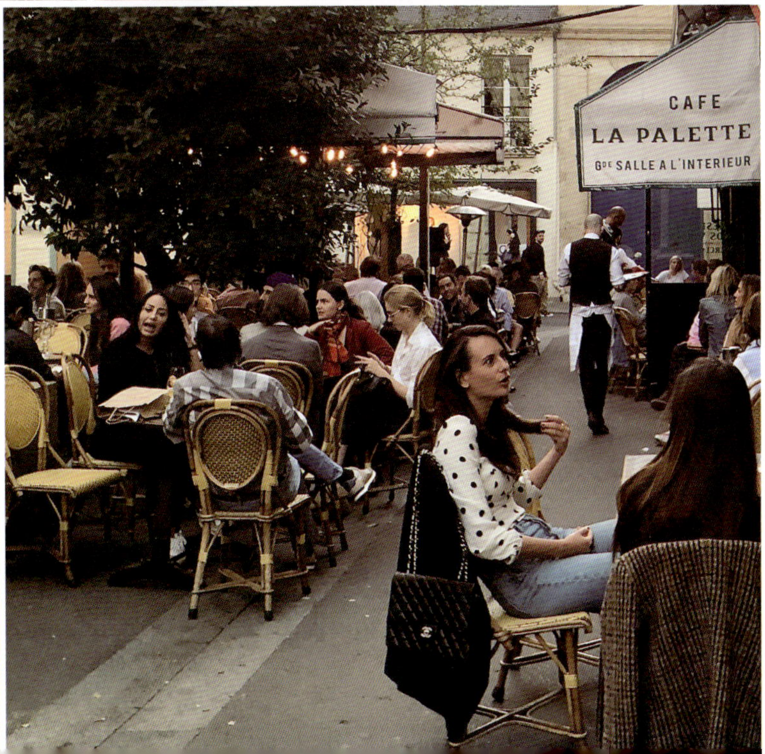
CAFE
LA PALETTE
Gde SALLE A L'INTERIEUR

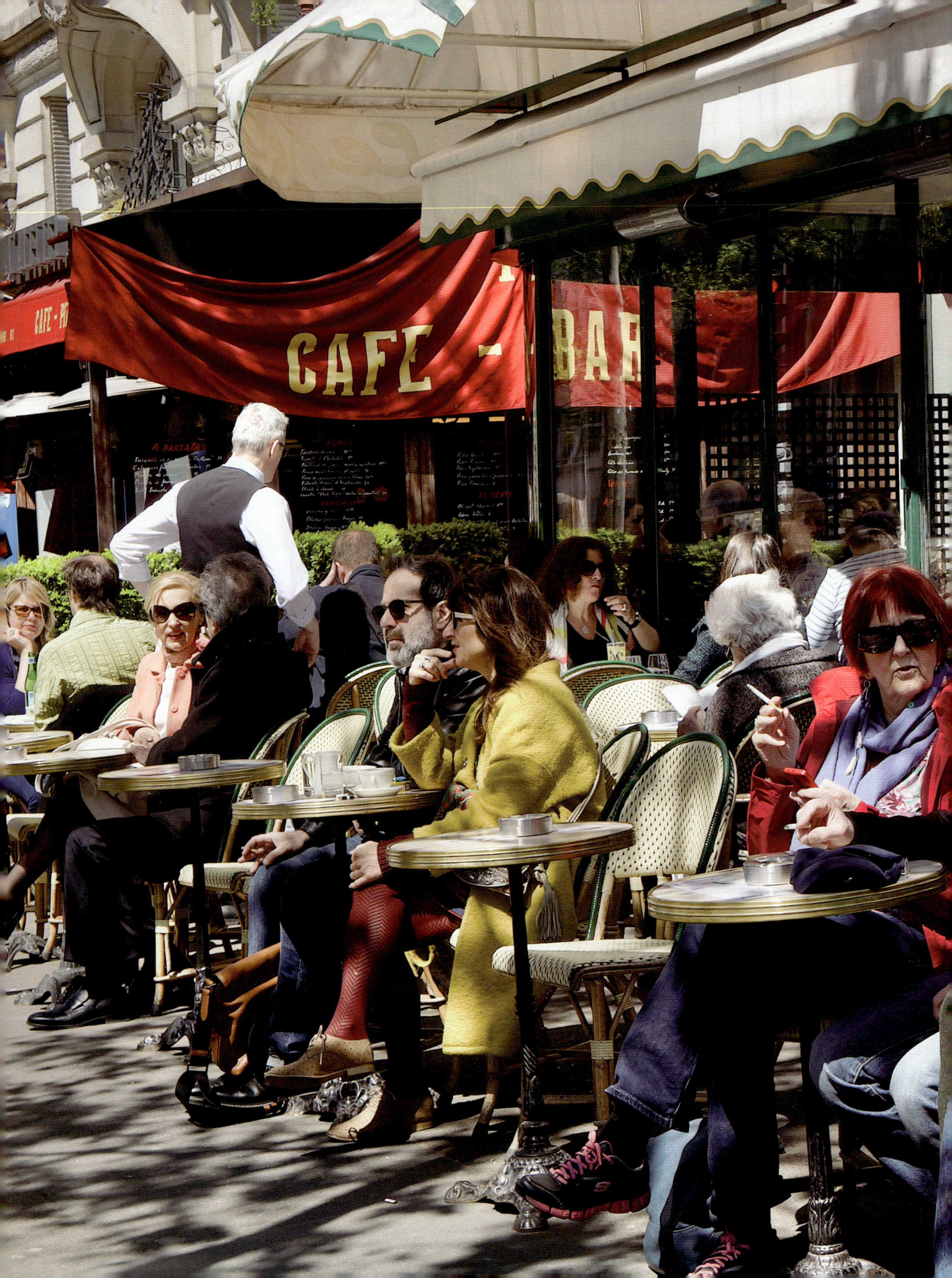
CAFE - BAR

PART 8 Les Quartiers: Historic, Trendy, & Local Haunts

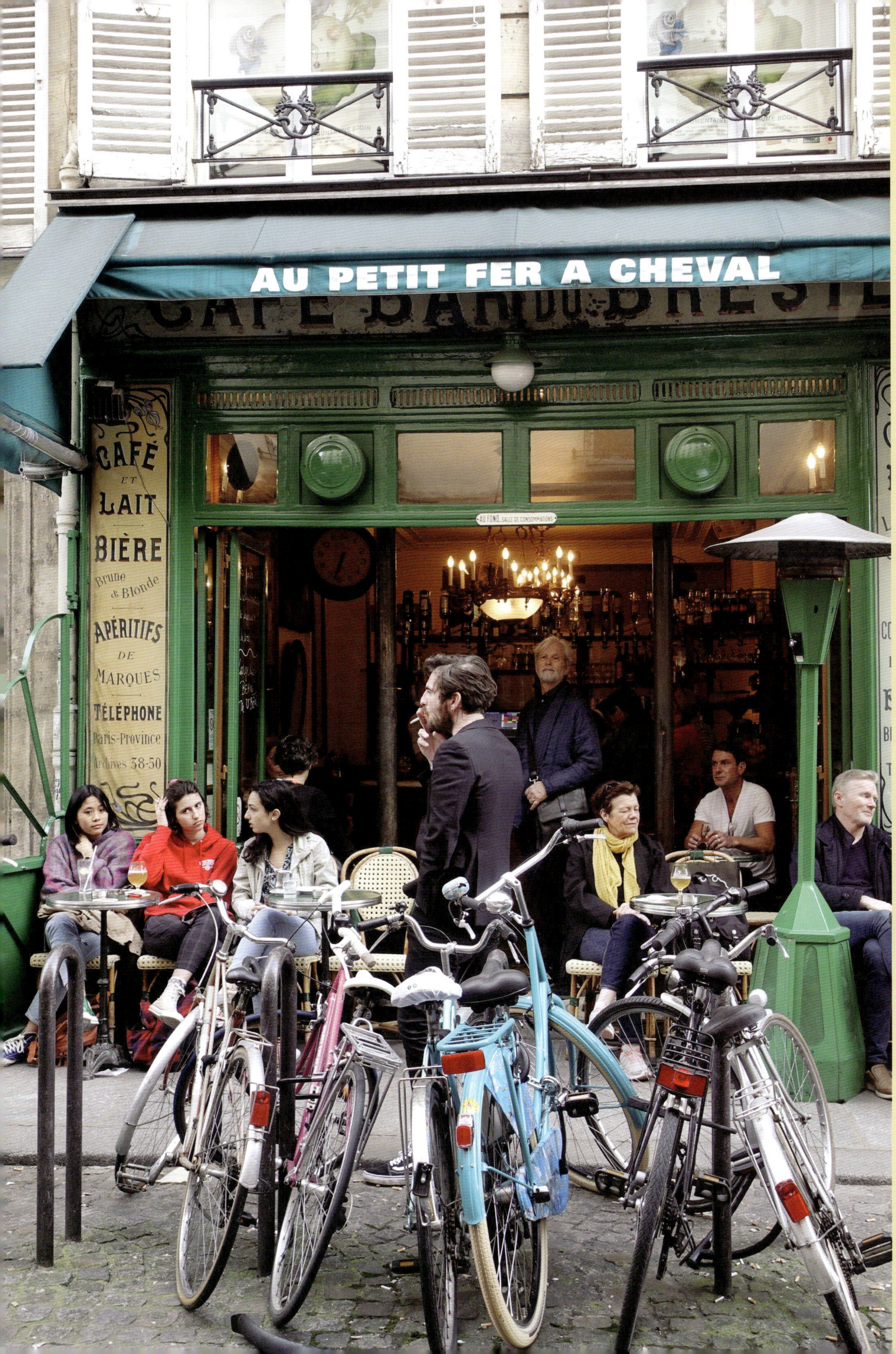

Odéon

"The strong coffee of St. Domangue drunk by Buffon, Diderot, and by Rousseau, added its heat to warm souls, sharpening the vision of the prophets in the assemblies at the Procope, who saw the radiant future of 1789 at the bottom of the black beverage in their cups."

Jules Michelet

Three years after the Grand Turk presented Louis XIV with the gift of coffee in 1669—introducing coffee to France—Armenian immigrant, Pasqua Rosée, along with an Italian chef from Sicily, Francesco Procopio dei Coltelli, sold coffee beans and brewed coffee for 2.5 sous at their kiosk in the Marché Saint-Germain on the Left Bank. Seventeen years later, in 1686, Procopio opened Café Procope. It was the first documented café in Paris and the first to serve Italian gelato and sorbet, having been awarded a royal license from Louis XIV to sell the dessert exclusively. Ideally located across from the Comédie Française, it became a meeting place for actors, politicians, philosophers, and the literary set. Still in operation today, Procope is remembered as a historic gathering place for the anti-royalists of the Revolution and graced by the likes of Moliere, Voltaire, Zola, Rousseau, Diderot, Beaumarchais, Alfred de Maupassant, Rabelais, Benjamin Franklin, Thomas Jefferson, Marat, Robespierre, Desmoulins, Danton, Napoleon, George Sand, Balzac, and Victor Hugo among other luminaries. It is where Benjamin Franklin worked on the Constitution, and Lafayette collaborated with Jefferson to write the first draft of the revolutionary document, "The Rights of Man."

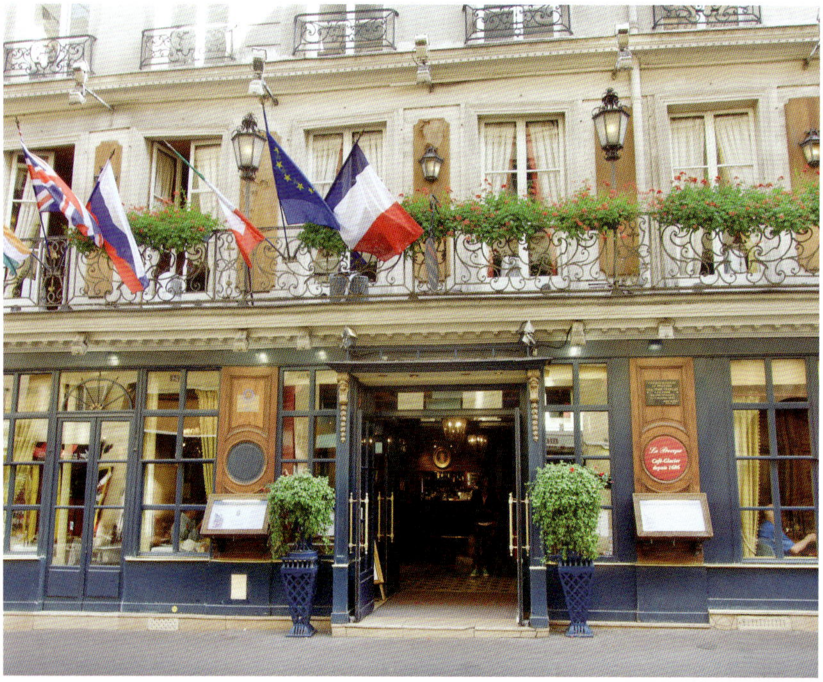

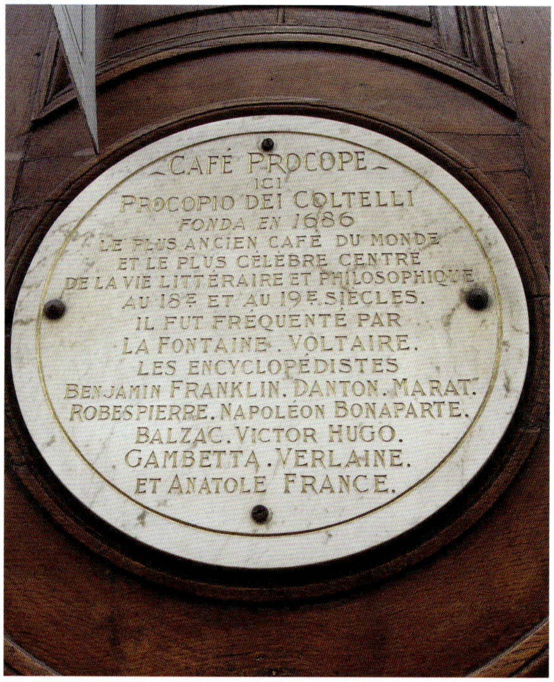

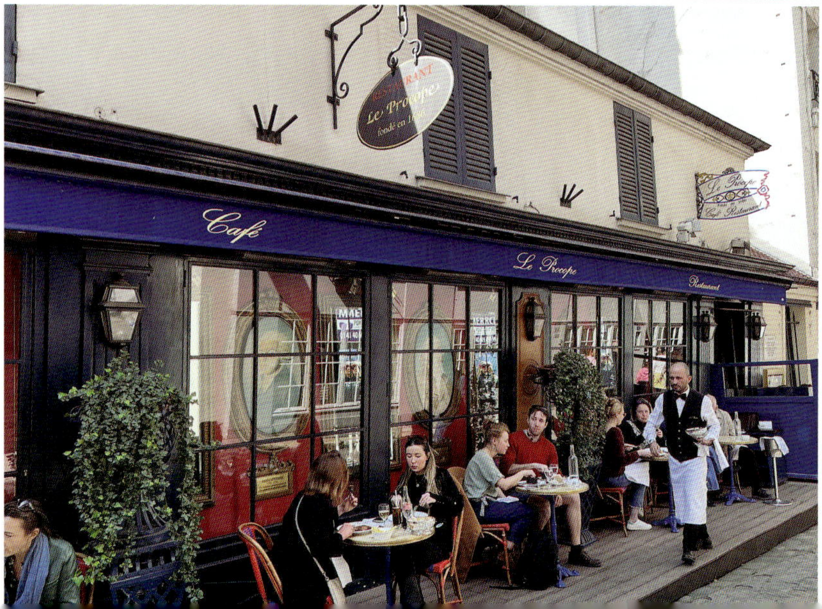

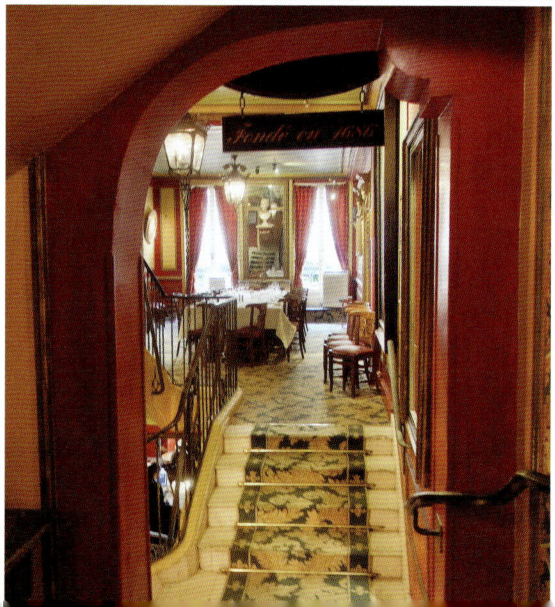

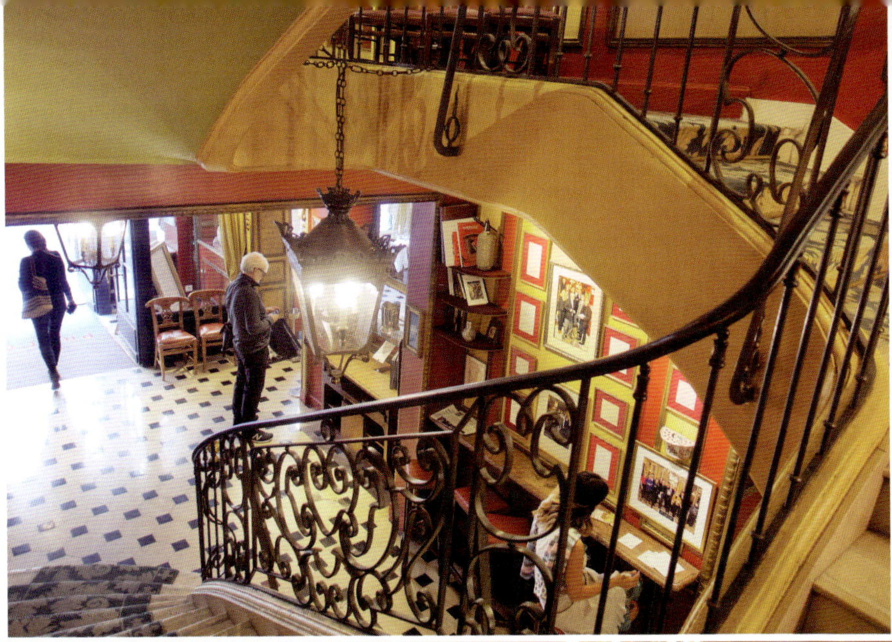

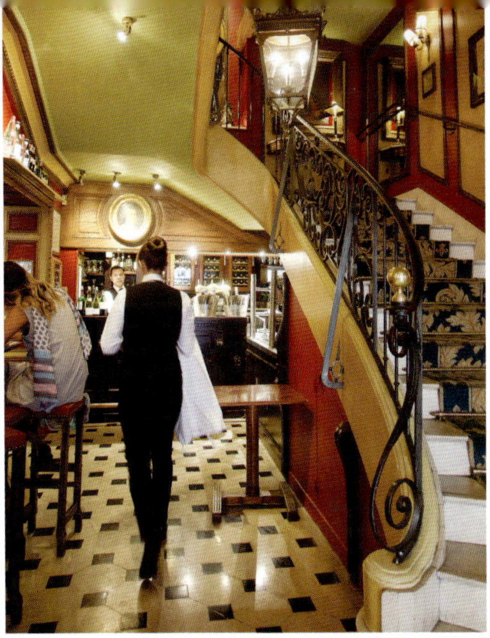

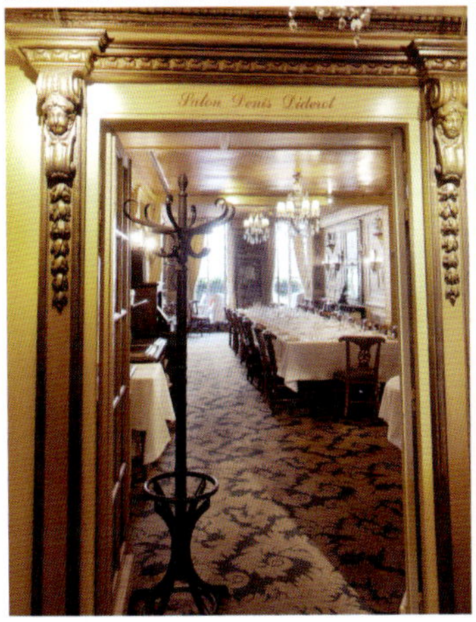

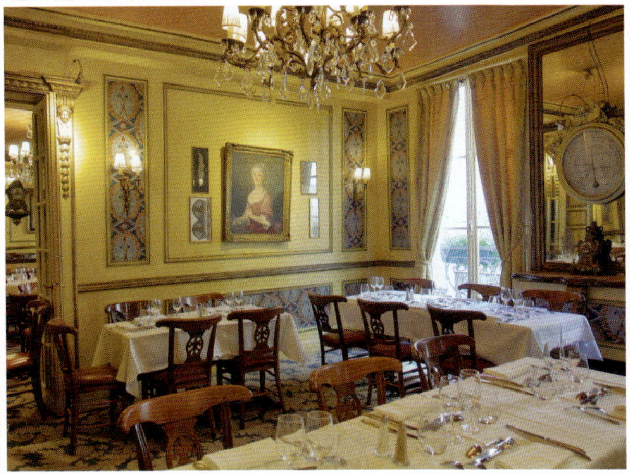

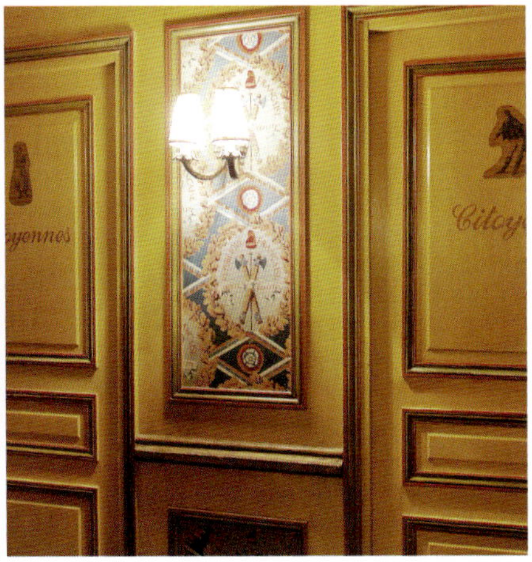

A more prosaic footnote is that Voltaire had his office upstairs at Procope and drank 40 cups of coffee-chocolate blend a day. Voltaire called Procope "the first salon where one's spirit was the only invitation necessary." Diderot made Procope an intellectual center during the French Enlightenment. Marat wrote every day on the third floor in a room now called the Salon Marat. A young Bonaparte left his hat at the Procope as security to pay for a drink, having forgotten to bring his money. The hat is still there, now on display. Along with a full classic menu, espresso, sorbet, and gelato remain staples in this exquisite café museum that fortunately endures.

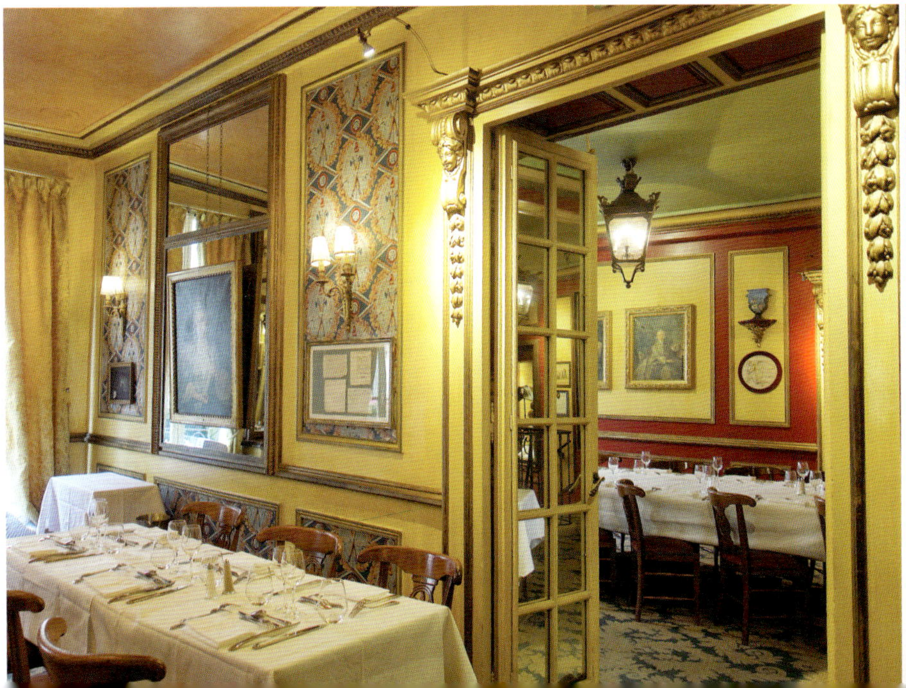

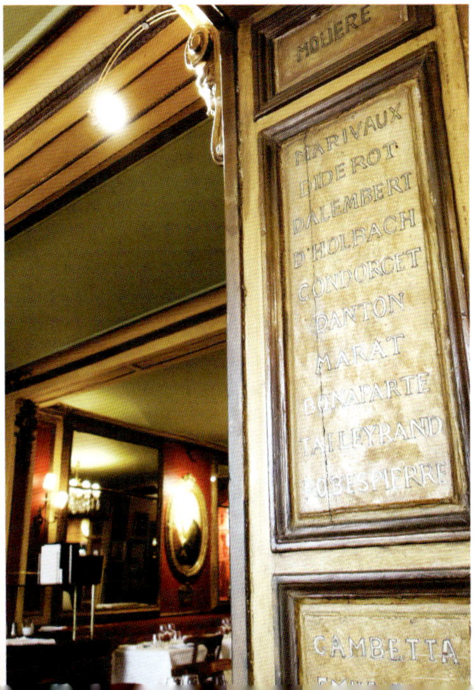

Palais Royal

"In all weathers, wet or fine, it is my practice to go toward five o'clock in the evening to take a turn in the Palais Royal...If the weather is too cold or too wet, I take shelter in the Café Régence. Nowhere in the world do they play chess as skillfully as in Paris and nowhere in Paris as they do at this coffeehouse."

Diderot (***Rameau's Nephew***)

Before Louis XIV moved the royal court to the Louvre and then to Versailles in 1682, the Palais Royal, created by Cardinal Richelieu in 1633, was home to the royal court. During the reign of Louis XIV, twenty-five elegant cafés flourished in and around the Palais Royal. Perhaps inspired by Versailles, these grand cafés were fitted with colossal mirrors, enhancing the interior's space, light, and sociability. Chess was played at almost every café—French chess players were the best in the world from the mid-18th to the mid-19th century, with notable players in important competitions at the literary Café Régence. Cafés supplied newspapers, magazines, and writing papers to patrons, providing information to the public and fostering political discourse, sometimes even revolution. It was not only the place to see and be seen for the privileged and intellectuals of café society but host to the political element. Two days before the Bastille fell in 1789, journalist Camille Desmoulins, standing on a marble-topped table in Café de Foy, urged the crowd to take arms and hasten to the Bastille. Away they marched: "*Vive la révolution!*" To get rid of this bothersome revolutionary clientele, Café de Foy's owner increased the price of the drinks.

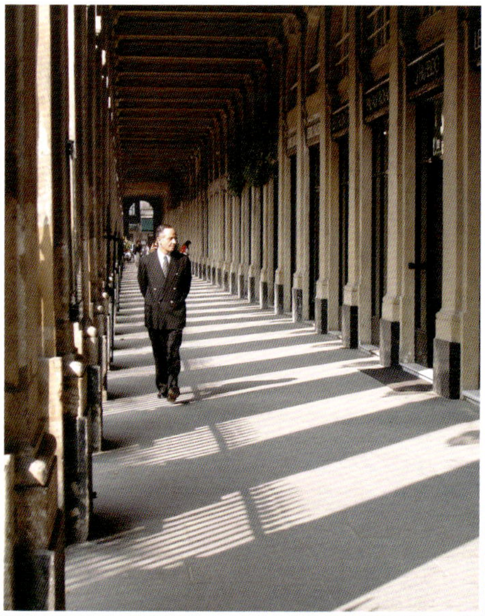

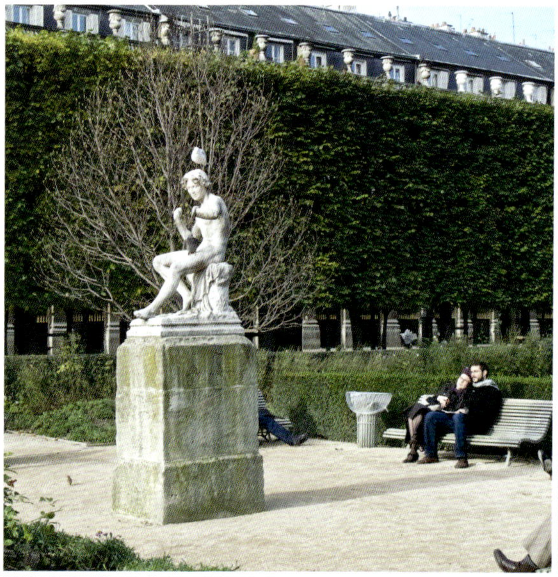

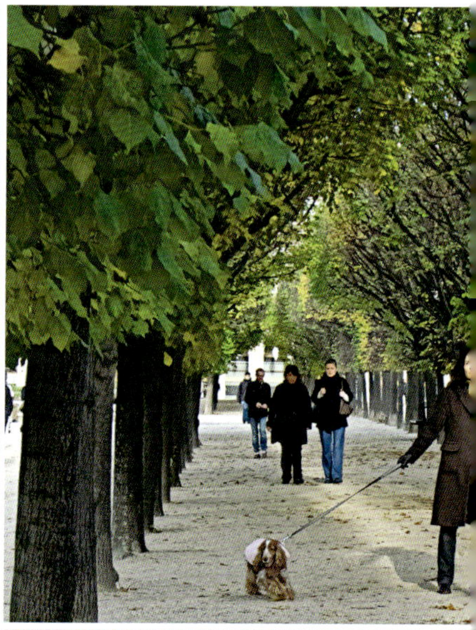

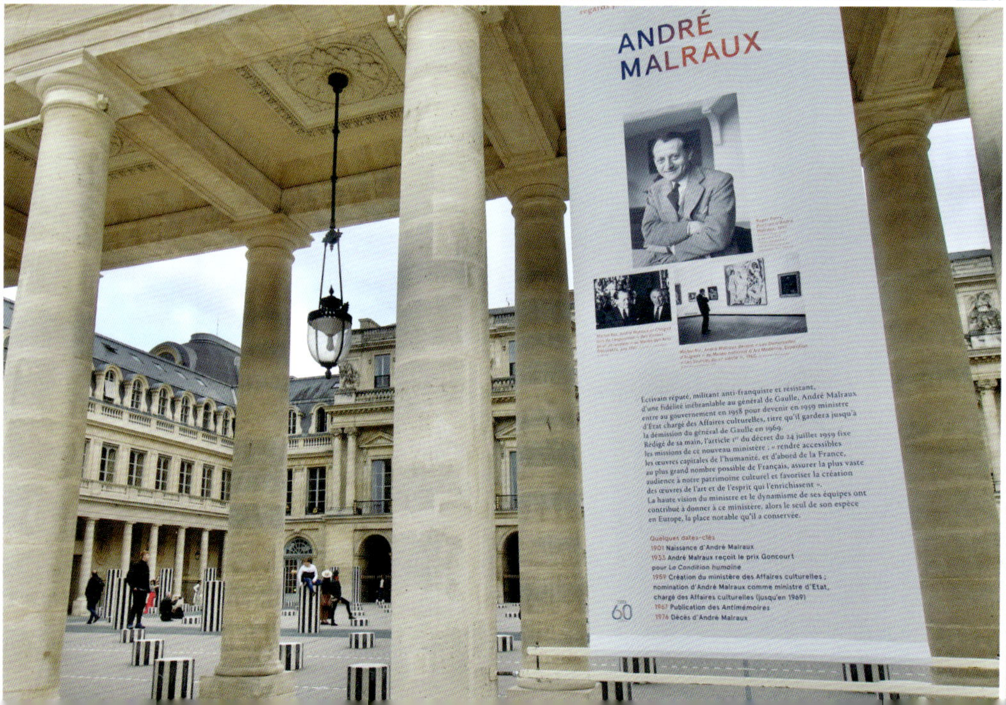

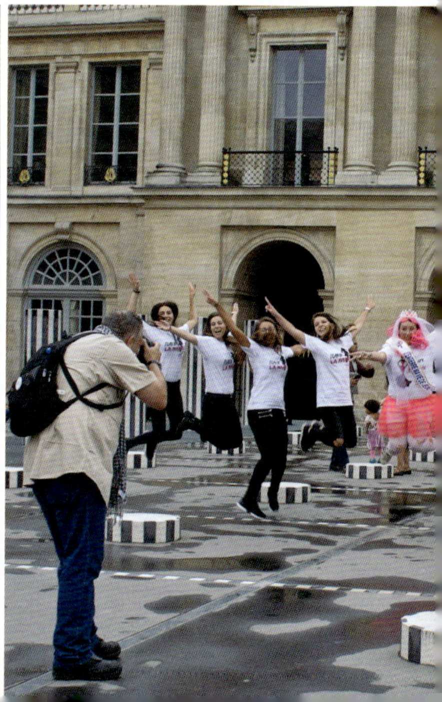

"Business people come to consume and play chess and draughts, distinguished strangers are eager to settle down...you pay six deniers for a so-called cup of mocha when you can get an excellent cup for five deniers at the café du Pont-Saint-Michel. But we are at the Palais Royal."

Mayeur de Saint-Paul

During the Palais Royal's heyday in the 18th century, cafés served as a hub for Parisians who participated in every sort of activity, savory and unsavory, political and otherwise. Café Corazza became the Jacobins' headquarters and later a haunt of Napoléon's. "At the Café Corazza, the Jacobins gathered...the politicians established clearly and by example that it was the right of the French citizen to read the gazettes, to talk loudly, and to enjoy all the other advantages of a café, on the condition of ordering one cup of coffee or a single thimbleful of brandy during the space of at least six hours...the Frenchman does not go to a café for the sake of drinking, nor does he drink at the café for the sake of drinking much less because he is thirsty: he drinks simply because he wants to go to the café." (Theodore Child, *Harper's New Monthly Magazine*, April 1889) RIP Café Corazza, born 1787, died in 2019, only to become a Manolo Blahnik boutique. Today Palais Royal retains its beautiful architecture and gardens, further animated in 1986 by Daniel Buren's 260 black-and-white-striped columns of varying heights where people of all ages pose, dance, and play. Pol Bury's two fountains filled with giant reflective stainless-steel balls are pure joy. The magnificent architecture currently houses government buildings as well as boutiques and art galleries, but only a few eating establishments.

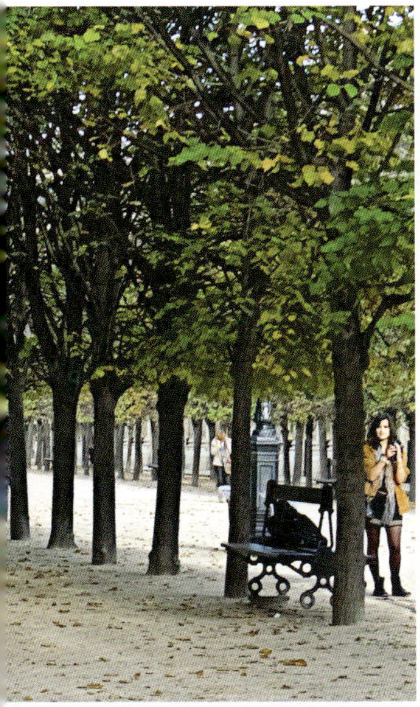
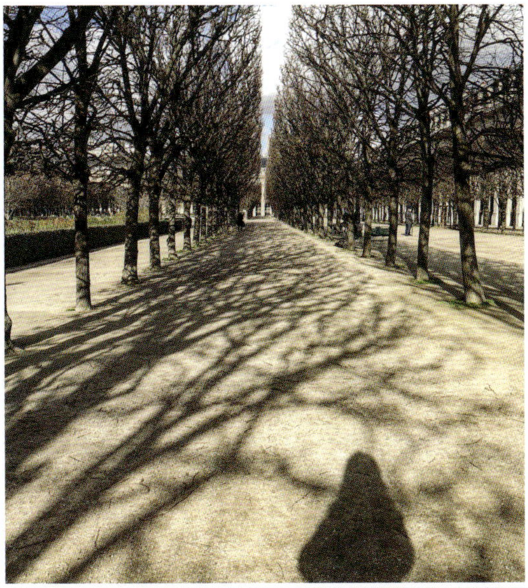
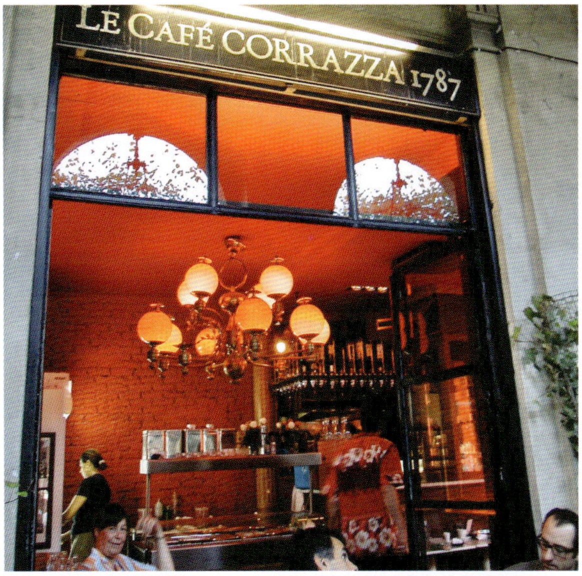

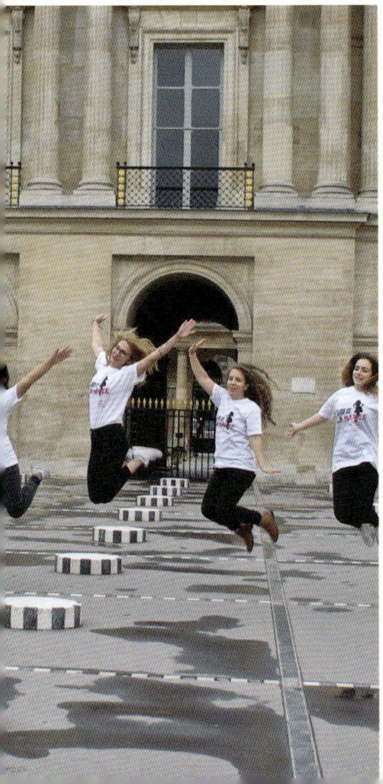
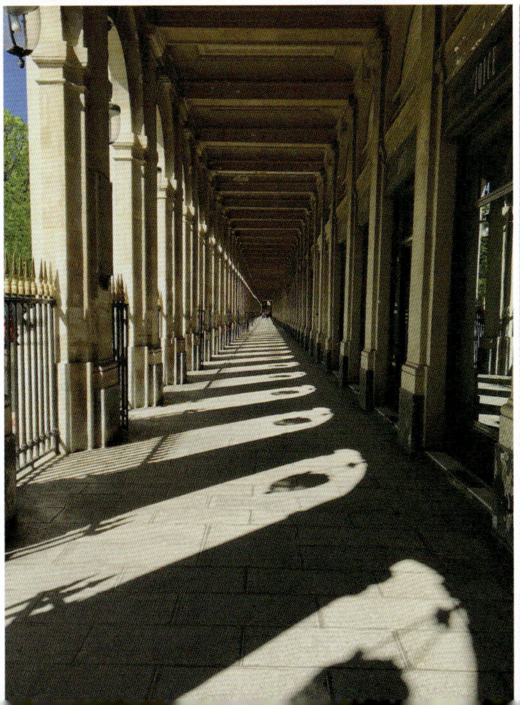
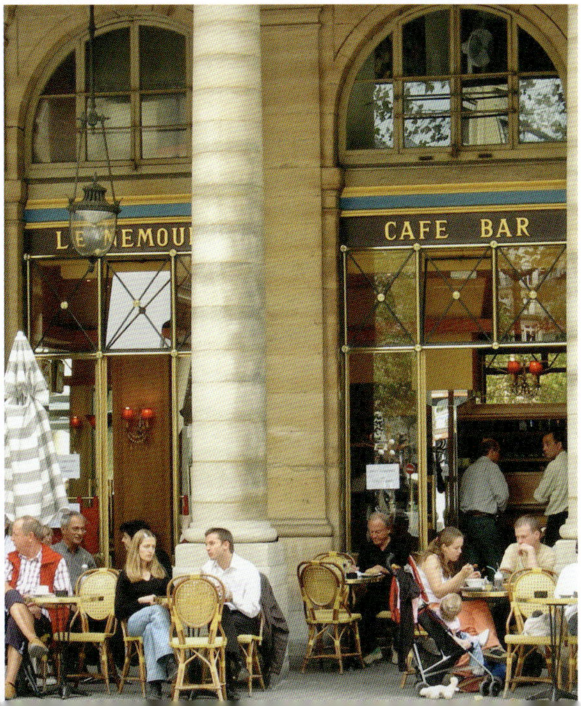

LE GRAND VÉFOUR

The Palais Royal cafés, centers of political activity preceding, during, and following the Revolution, were divided between royalists and revolutionaries. Opened in 1784, Café de Chartres, now the Michelin-starred Le Grand Véfour, was a meeting place for the Royalists, while other nearby cafés were home to the anti-royalist revolutionaries. After the Revolution, it became the gathering place of young aristocrats who escaped the guillotine and made plans to restore the monarchy. Changing hands and shifting from glory to neglect to glory through the centuries, Café Véfour has hosted notables including Murat, the Duke of Berry, Brillat-Savarin, Colette, Jean Cocteau, Marcel Pagnol, Jean Genet, André Malraux, and Juliette Gréco. Fragonard was a regular and died here in 1806 while eating ice cream. The artful mirrored elegance of its 18th-century design lingers along with the regal food, allowing 21st-century diners the opportunity to enjoy its present brilliance while envisioning a taste of the past.

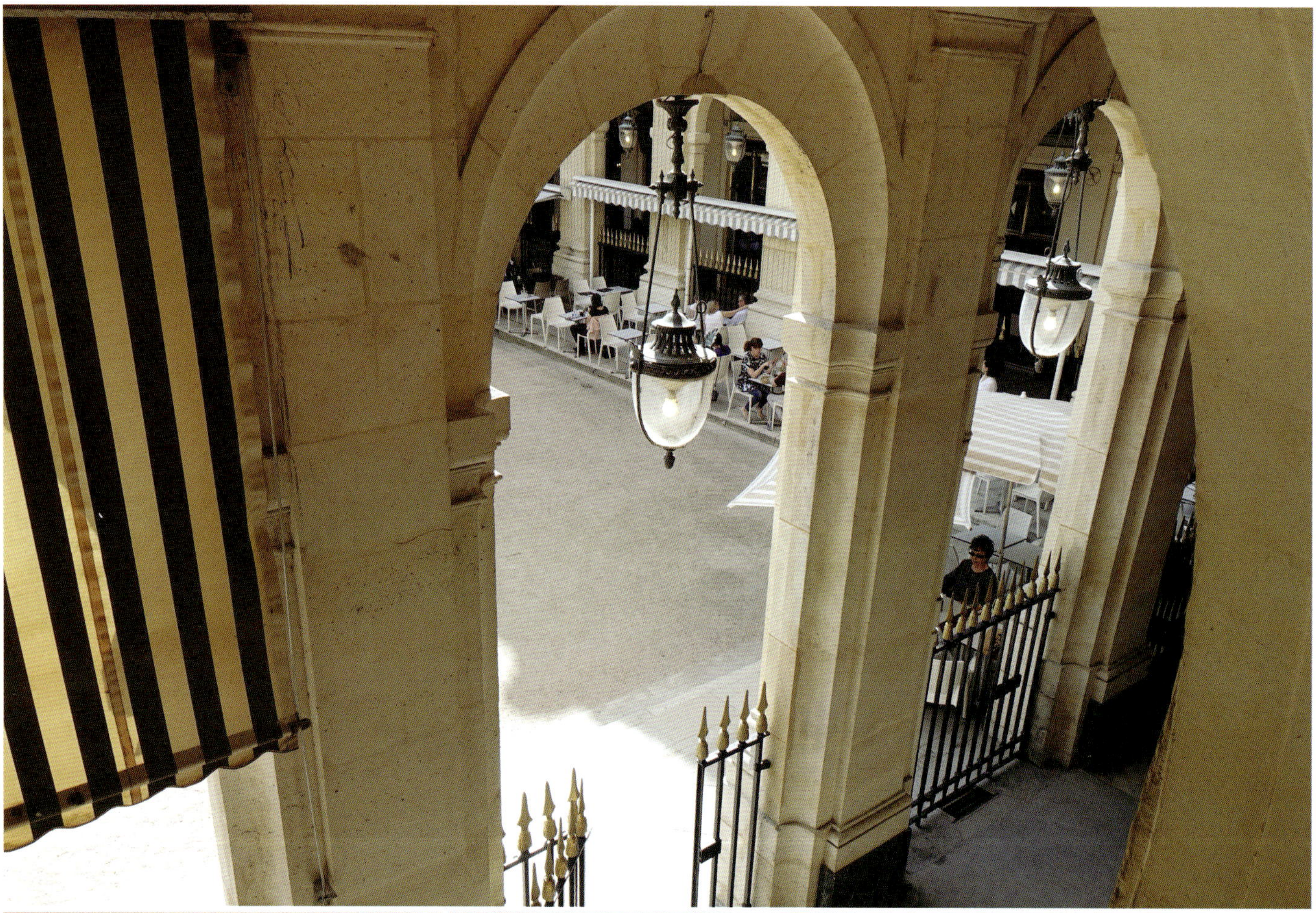

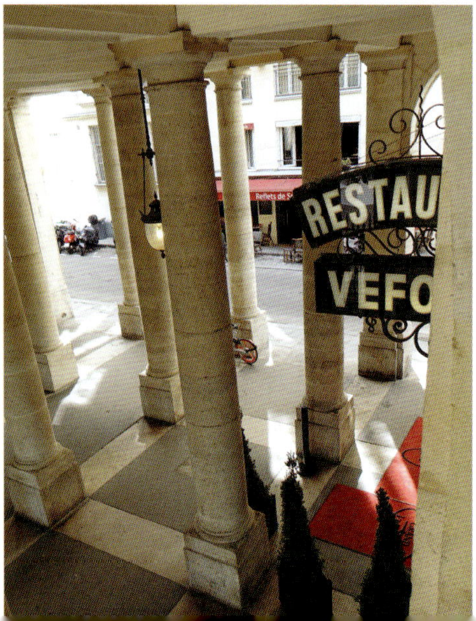

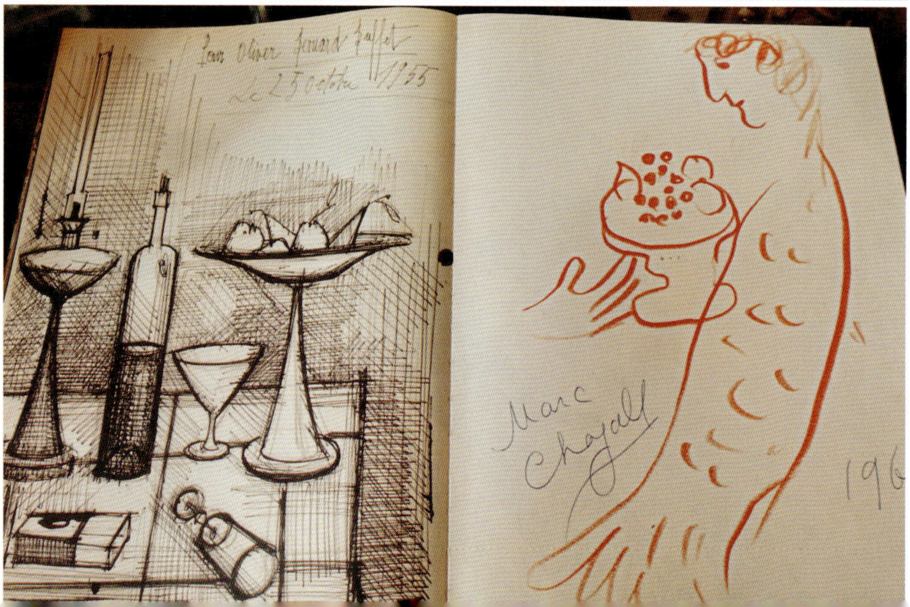

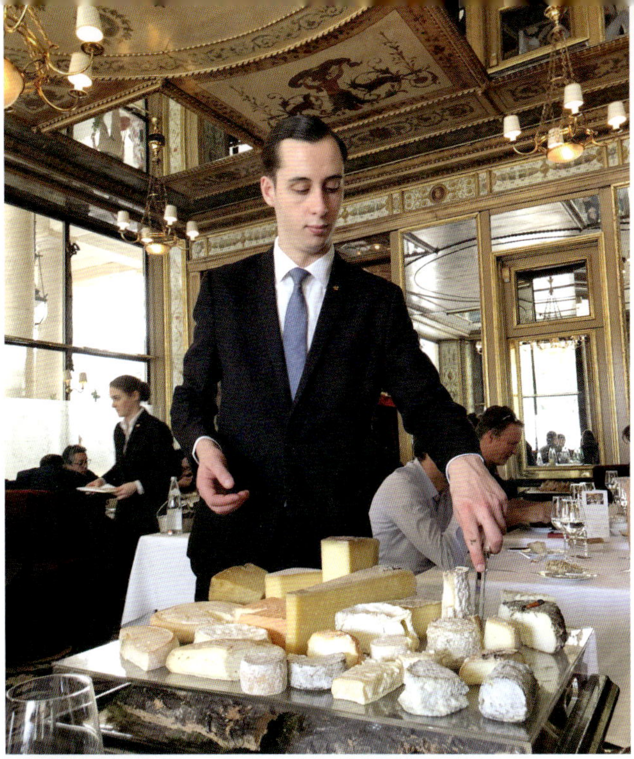
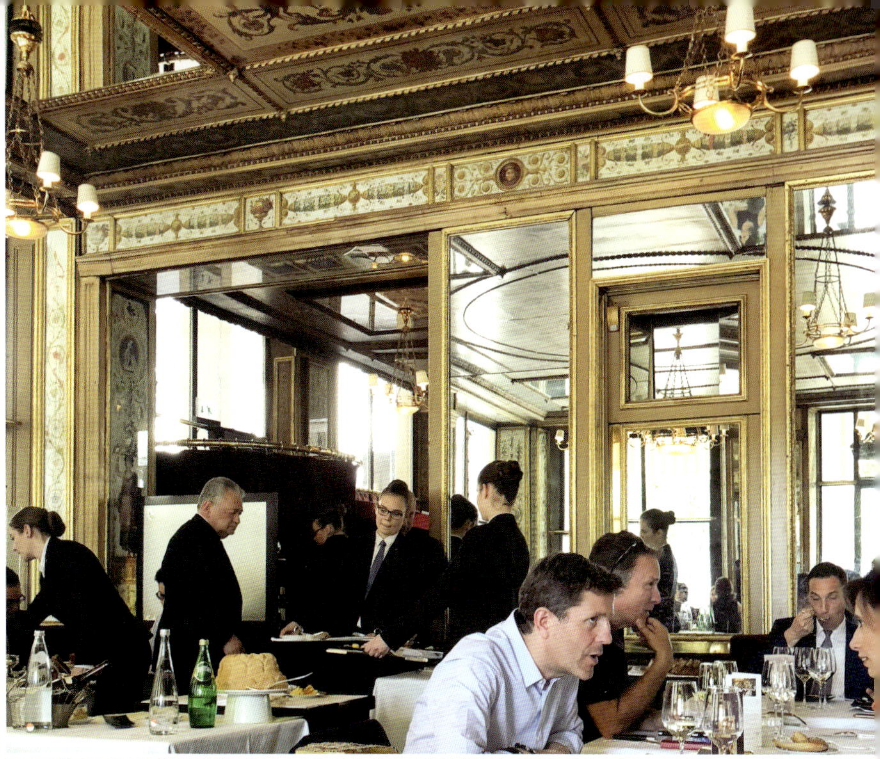
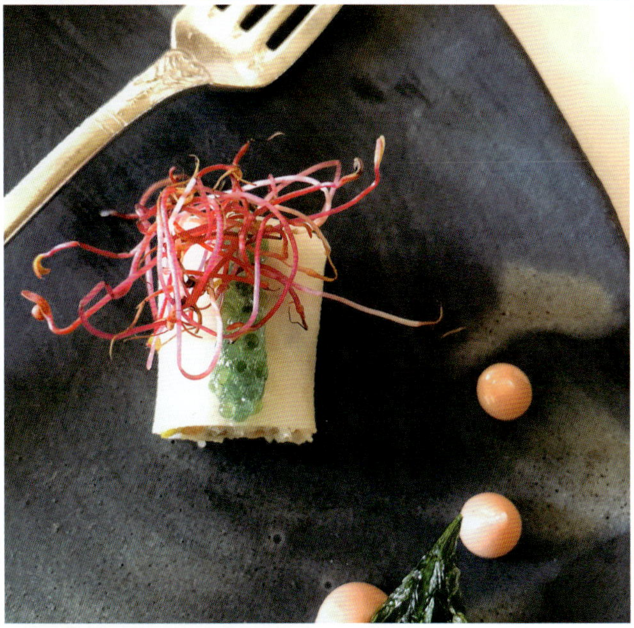
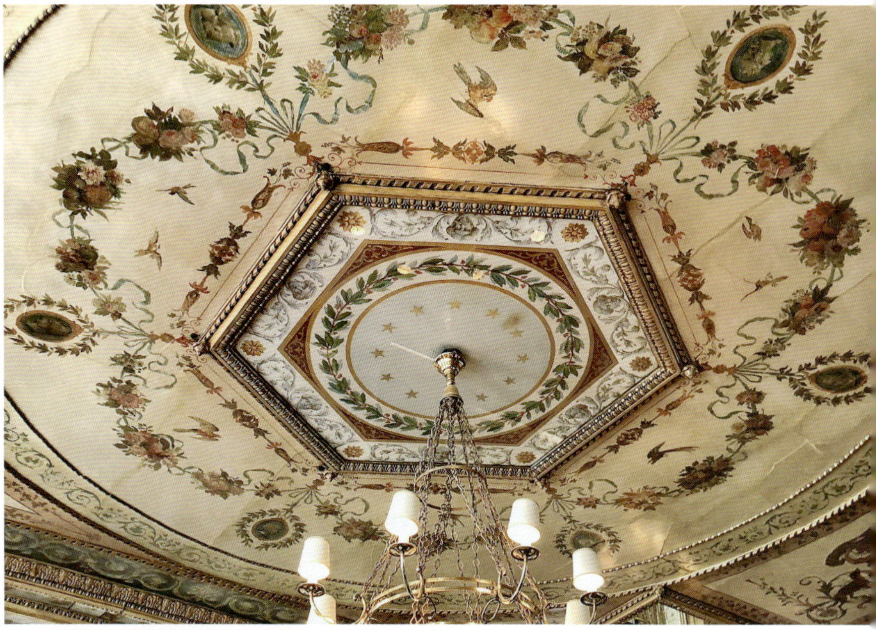
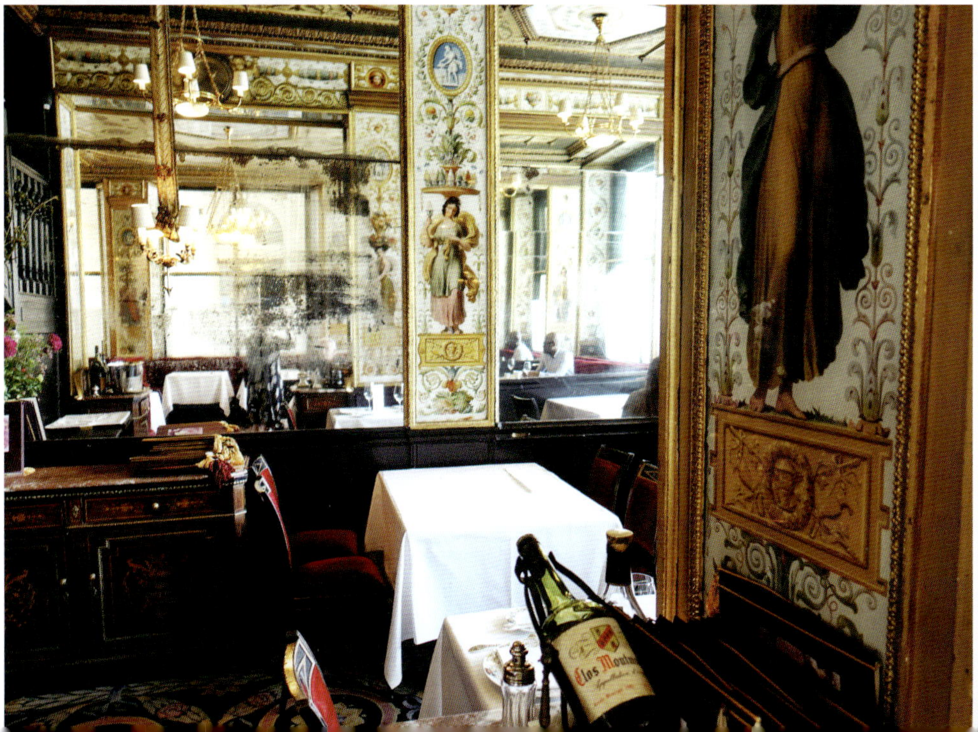
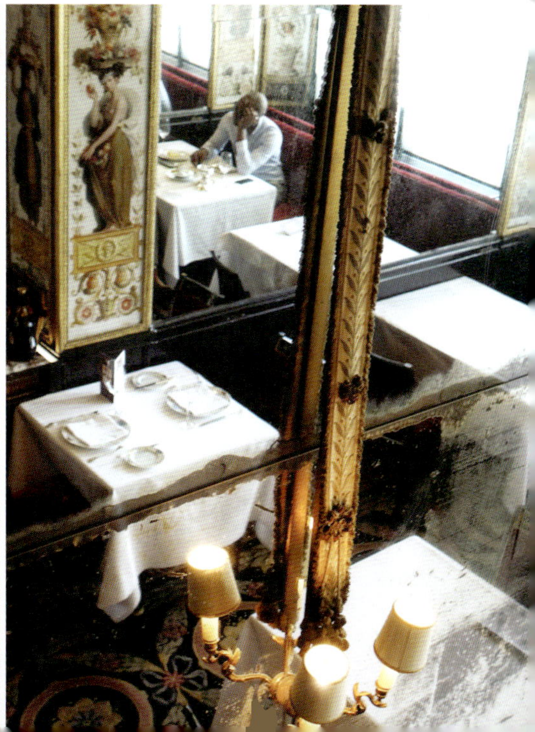

Les Grands Boulevards

"The cafés are a hub for people who live alone, young people but also the elderly. Their closure creates a real deficit in terms of sociability. But this lack does not only concern customers, occasional or regular. When walking in a city, cafés and their terraces punctuate the gaze, open the exterior to the interior, and vice versa."

Anne Steiner

Grand Boulevards and grand cafés. Follow the fashionistas and, in the 19th century, the opulent cafés of the Right Bank, near the Opera Garnier, the Bourse, theaters, elegant shops, arcades, and palatial department stores, were the place to see and be seen—after a showy promenade on the Grands Boulevards. The wide streets and sidewalks carved by Emperor Napoleon III's "Prefect of the Seine," Baron Haussmann, including Beaumarchais, Opéra, Madeleine, Montmartre, Capucines, Italiens, Temple, and Haussmann (of course), was part of Paris's grand mid-19th-century remodeling. Filled with fashionable Parisian society, the stylish cafés and terraces of these Grands Boulevards were where the bourgeois could display their wealth and status. Reflecting the elegance of the surrounding architecture, nearly all the notable cafés, Café Riche, Café Hardy, Café Anglais, and the venerable Café Tortoni are lost to history. Only the revered Café de la Paix, opened in 1862 across from the Opera Garnier, endures. A haunt of Second Empire imperialists, Café de la Paix is where Arthur Conan Doyle worked on the Sherlock Holmes books, and Victor Hugo, Émile Zola, Diaghilev, King Edward VII, Noël Coward, Gide, Oscar Wilde, the Duke of Windsor, Charles De Gaulle, and other luminaries dined along with visitors from around the world. Contributing to its prestigious history, Escoffier was once the chef here, and for those in the know, it was a haven for spies. It was restored and refreshed numerous times in its 160 years, most recently in 2021 by architect Pierre-Yves Rochon, who pledged to "preserve the heritage with a touch of modernity." It remains a historic monument. Choose to sit inside the elegant, evocative interior rather than outside with the tourists.

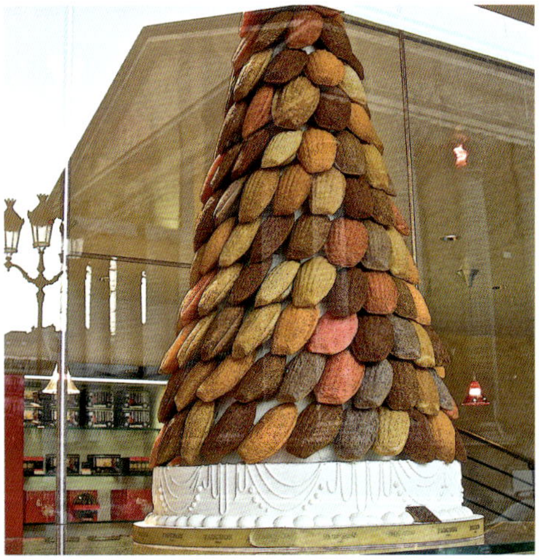

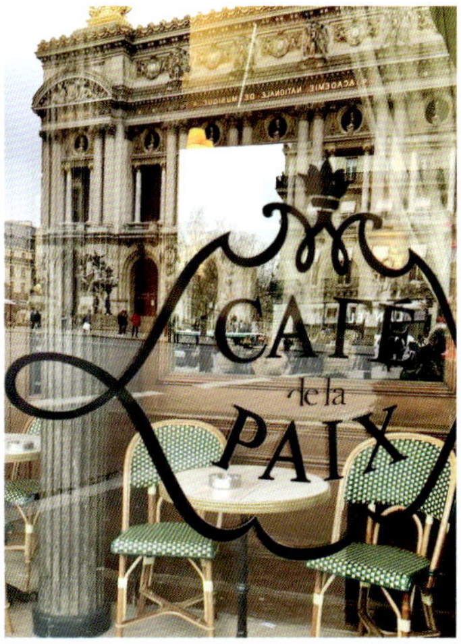

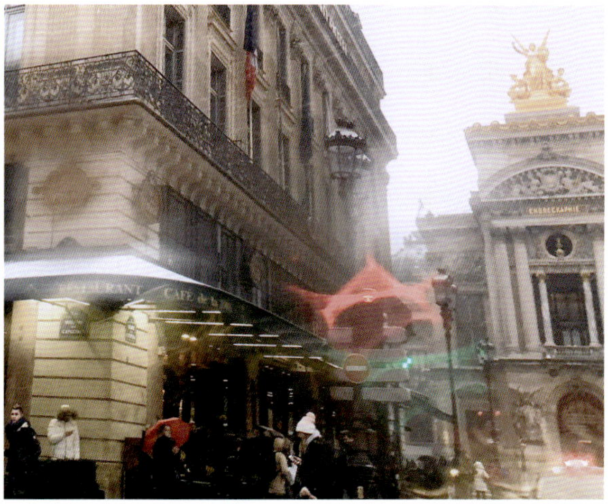

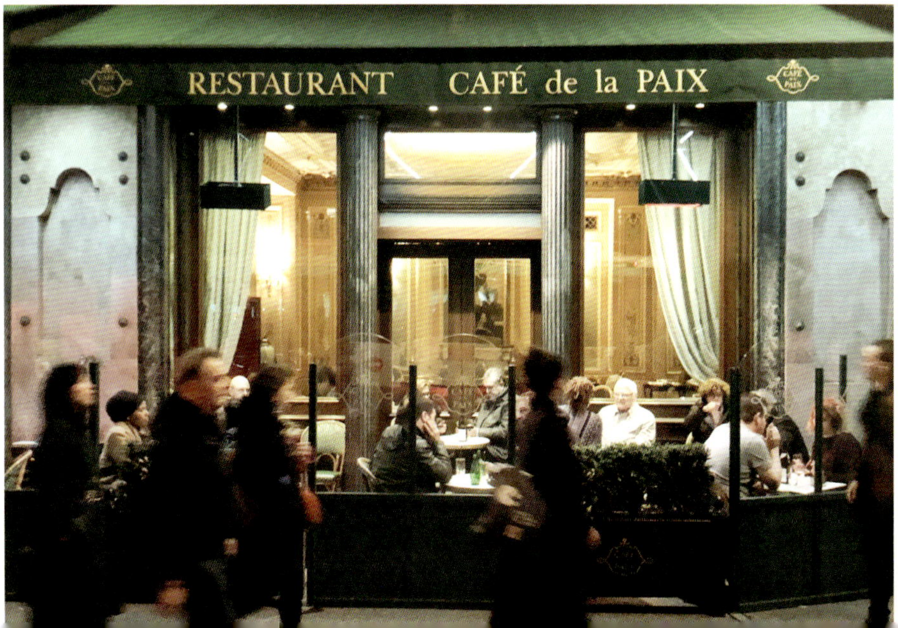

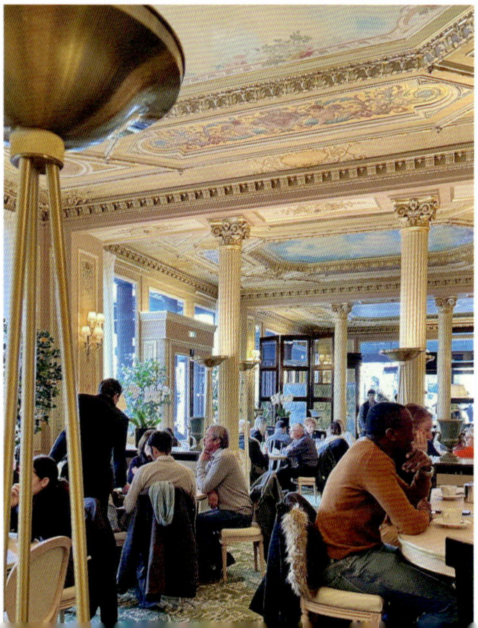

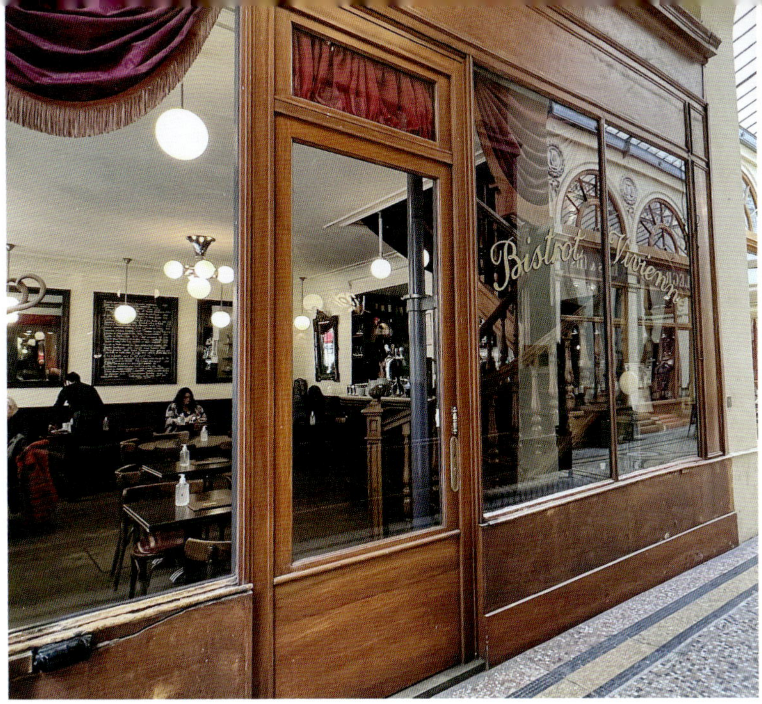

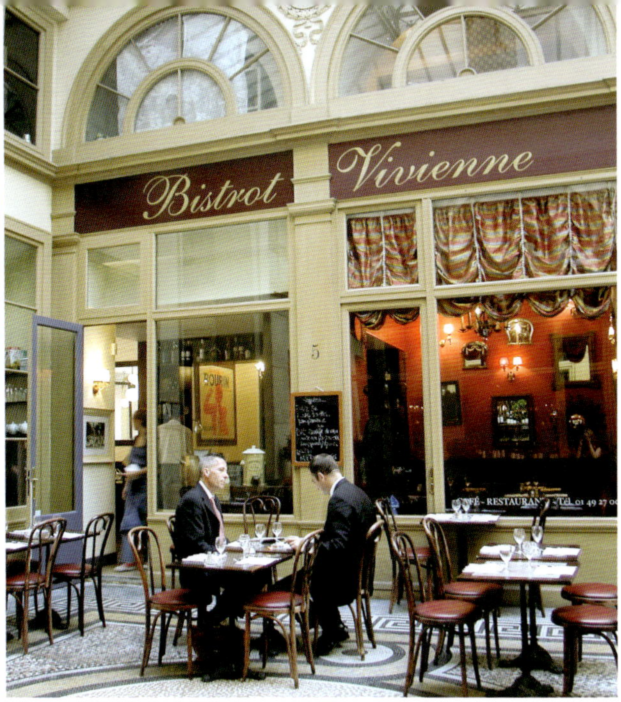

Of the 150 19th-century passages near the Grands Boulevards and Palais Royal, twenty-four survive today. They feature intricate tile (often mosaic) floors, detailed wood storefronts, enormous glass, and iron sconces, along with glass and iron roofs pouring natural light into the space. Their beautifully preserved architecture is a window into 19th-century Paris and ever so much lovelier than the ubiquitous shopping malls elsewhere in France and around the globe.

Bistrot Vivienne (ABOVE), frequently photographed and gloriously classic, with mirrors, banquettes, and wooden tables, is located at one of the magnificent Galerie Vivienne entrances. Serving a modest but sophisticated menu with locally sourced ingredients and Berthillon ice cream, it is one of Paris's treasured bistros.

Opened in 1865, Le Brébant (BELOW LEFT) was one of the grand cafés on the Grands Boulevards. Intellectuals of the day dined quite sumptuously there in great numbers for long hours, including Zola, Flaubert, Goncourt, Dumas *père*, and Delacroix. Now but a remnant of its former self, albeit with some architectural vestiges of its 19th-century grandeur, it boasts a long undulating zinc bar that serves up fancy cocktails into the wee hours. Studded with funky touches, this festive venue appeals to a young crowd. Open from 7:30 am to 4:30 am.

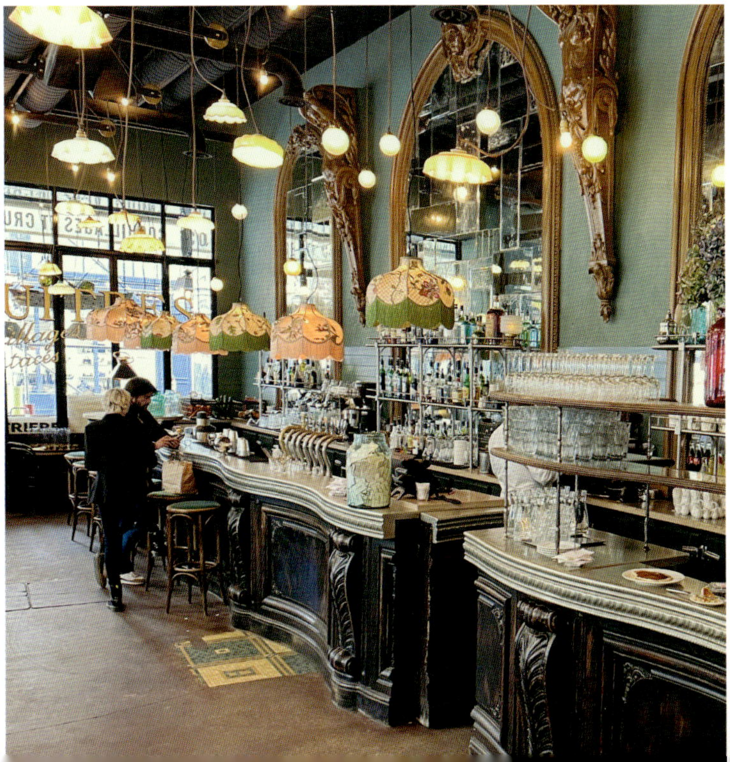

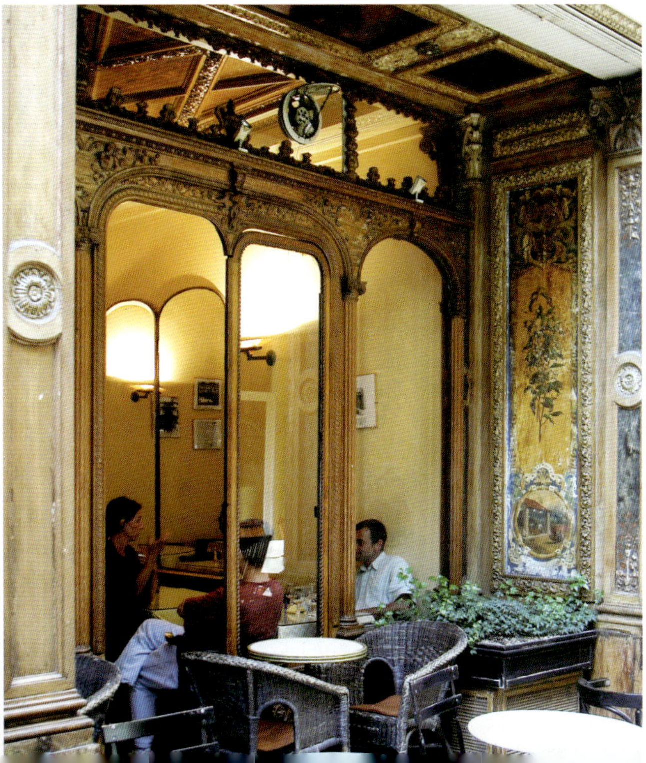

Le Quartier Latin

"I dreamt of being a writer once I started to read. I started to write *Bonjour Tristesse* in bistros around the Sorbonne. I finished it, I sent it to editors. It was accepted."

Françoise Sagan

The 2,000-year-old rue Saint-Jacques, in the Latin Quarter, is the oldest street in modern Paris, dating from the era when Paris was the Roman village of Lutetia. From the Middle Ages until 1789, students at the Sorbonne studied in Latin; thus, the neighborhood was dubbed the Quartier Latin. Allowing a glimpse into centuries past, many of the narrow, winding cobblestone streets here were untouched by Haussmann during his recreation of Paris in the mid-19th century. The Latin Quarter is animated and festive, filled with bookstores and cafés catering to students of the Sorbonne and other nearby institutions of learning. Linger on the Place de la Contrescarpe and rue Mouffetard (constructed in the 3rd century) for a taste of the intellectual bohemian days of yore.

Pedestrian-friendly and oh-so-mellow, Place de la Contrescarpe, at the center of the 5th arrondissement, is filled with music in the summer and lively all year round. Perch in one of its café terraces any time of the day in all seasons, and imagine Hemingway or James Joyce taking a break from their typewriters and wandering the streets and cafés hoping for inspiration.

Le Delmas, whose terrace directly faces the fountain on Place de la Contrescarpe, has a simple, on-trend menu and is open daily from 8 am to 11:00 pm. Planted on the ancient rue Mouffetard since 1870, tiny Le Verre à Pied ("stemmed glass") is a memento of the past and well worth a visit to hang out with the locals at *le zinc* (BELOW).

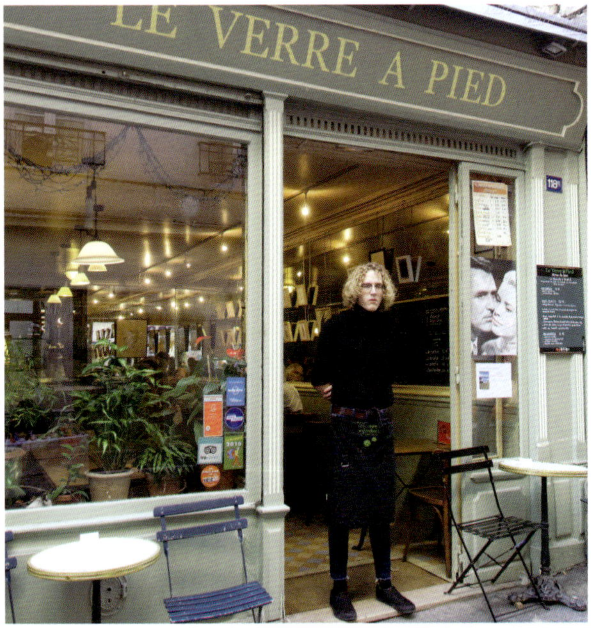

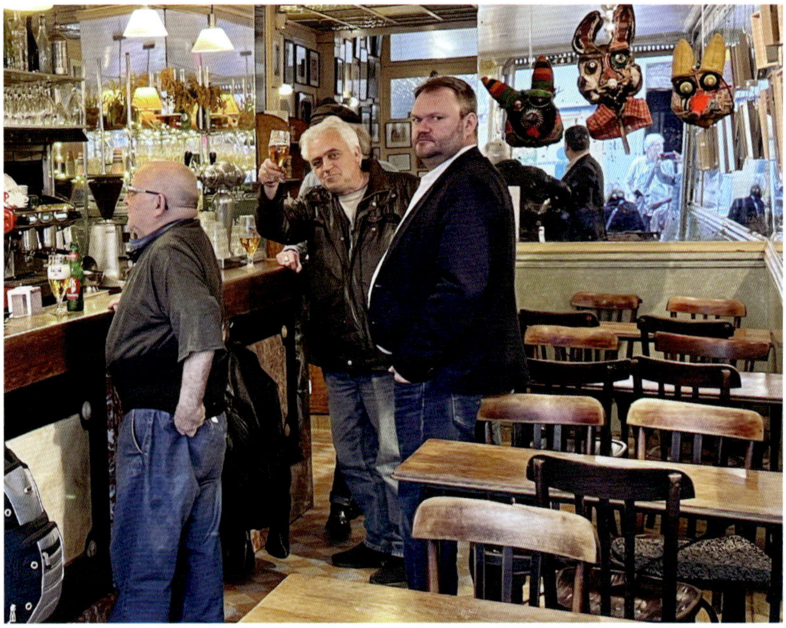

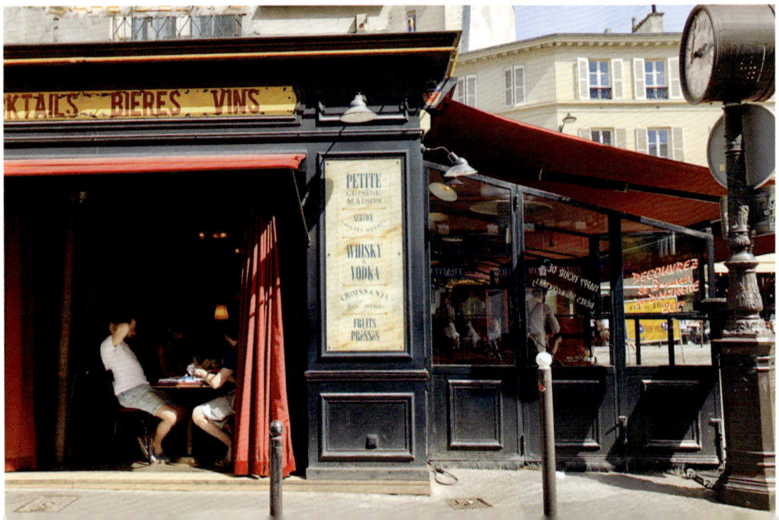

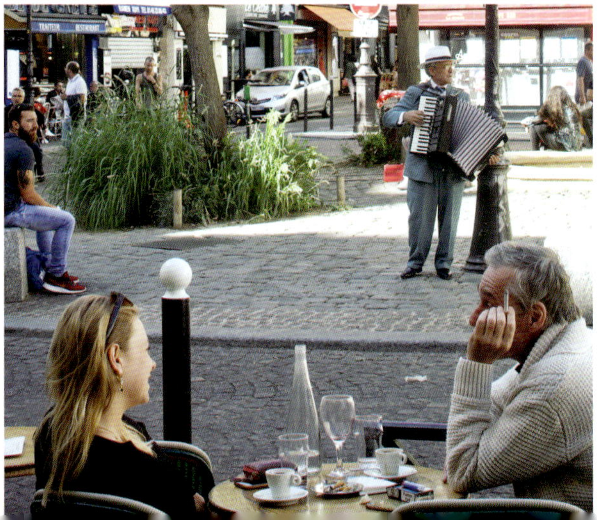

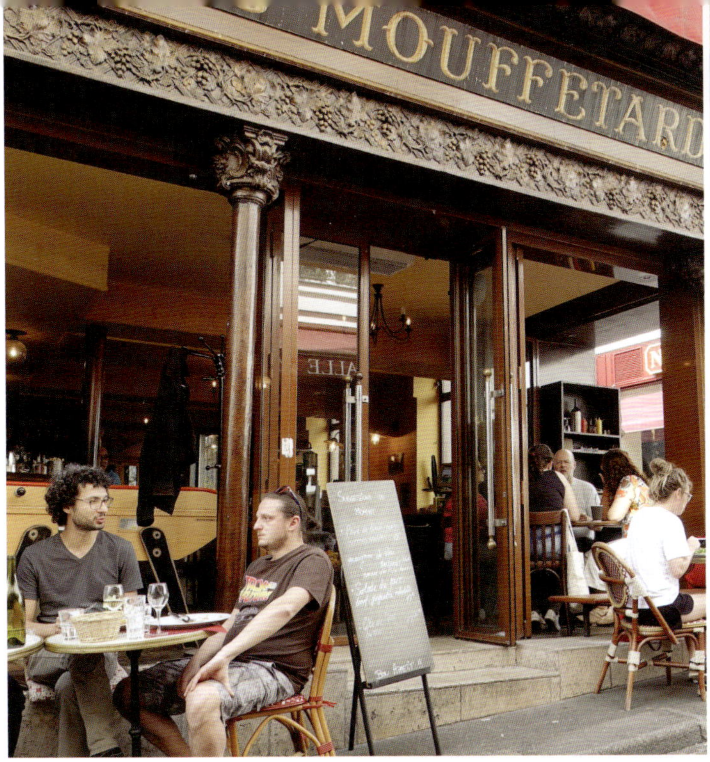

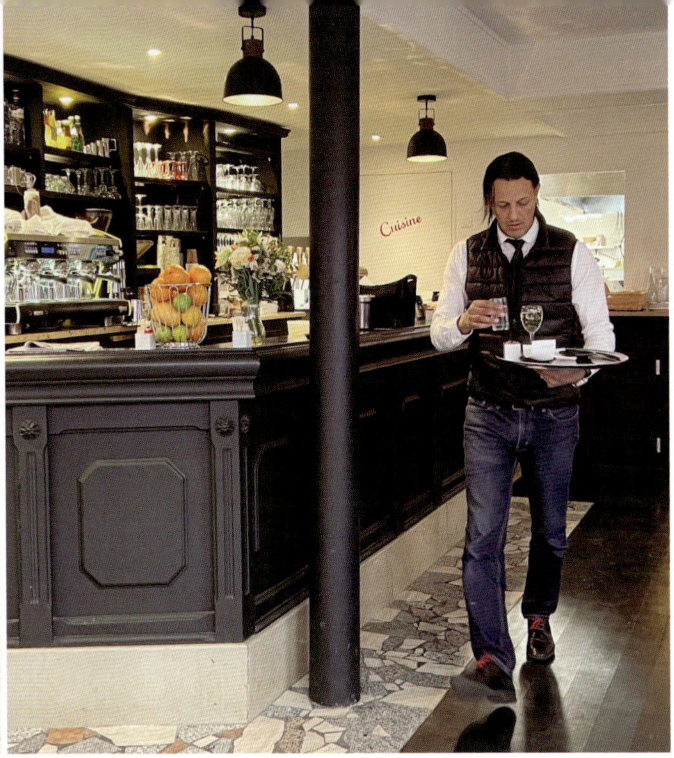

Le Mouffetard (ABOVE), the oldest food enterprise on rue Mouffetard, has evolved with the times and has an attractive, inexpensive, creative menu. Since the warm interior with the foosball machine (shown here) has been remodeled, it's best to grab a table on the terrace rather than in the now-sterile white interior.

Escargot is paired with biodynamic wine in the authentic Paris-in-the-'50s *bar à vin*, Au Doux Raisin (BELOW). The friendly, celebratory spirit and small, ultra-classic menu tilted toward Burgundy wine and dishes full of butter and garlic can tempt on a cold, rainy day. It is known for some of the best escargots in Paris, along with magnificent platters of cheese and charcuterie, *apéritifs* of yesteryear such as Cardinal and Communard, as well as *au courant* organic natural wines. The place is like a trip back through time with a nod to the present. Photos, stills, and posters of Gabin, Brassens, and filmmaker Audiard complete the homage to the '50s.

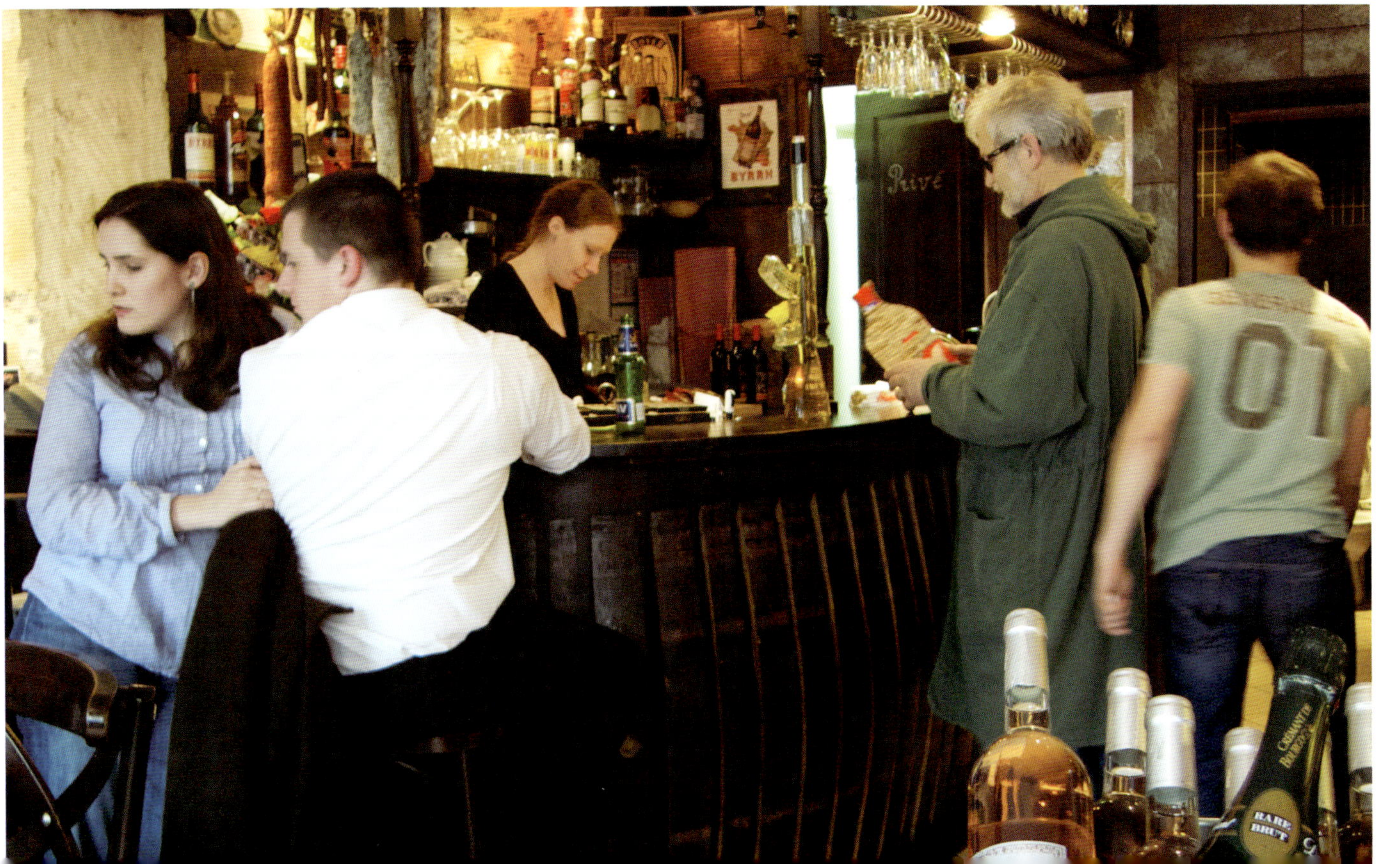

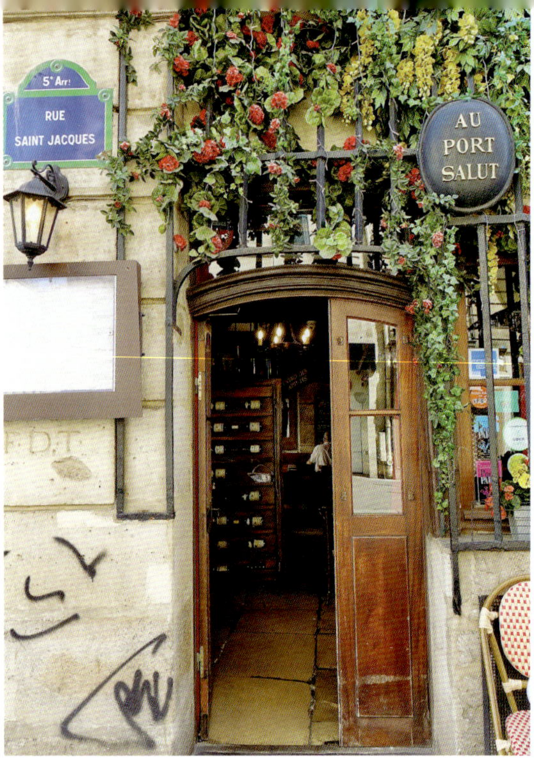

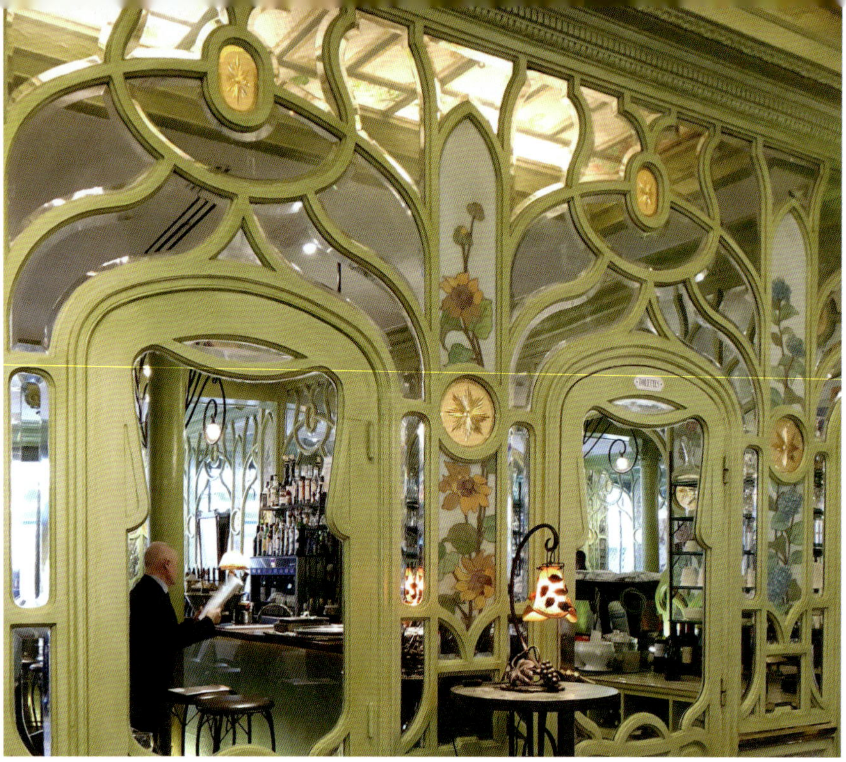

Au Port Salut fills the spot of a former 18th-century inn. In the mid-20th century, it was a cabaret where artists such as Serge Gainsbourg began their careers. Along with classic cuisine, this designated historical monument features live jazz every evening.

Since 1906, Bouillon Racine (ABOVE RIGHT), an Art Nouveau work of artistry, was one of the 250 Bouillons serving inexpensive, often one-dish meals such as soups during the Belle Époque. Far fewer now, Bouillons have regained popularity in Paris as a place for an economical meal in grand surroundings.

Opened in 1845 as a *crèmerie*/restaurant near the Sorbonne, Polidor (BELOW) has been refreshed—yet thankfully, unspoiled—by artisans in 2020. Steeped in history, Polidor persists as an inexpensive haunt for students, artists, writers, intellectuals, and professors. We can easily imagine the days when students hung out with André Gide, James Joyce, Jack Kerouac, Eugene Ionesco, René Clair, Paul Valéry, Henry Miller, Paul Verlaine, and Arthur Rimbaud. Ernest Hemingway wrote about it in *A Moveable Feast*, and Woody Allen featured it as the rendezvous spot in his nostalgic film, *Midnight in Paris*. With communal tables and nothing fancy in terms of food or design, it remains authentic, unspoiled, and unforgettable. Reservations unnecessary.

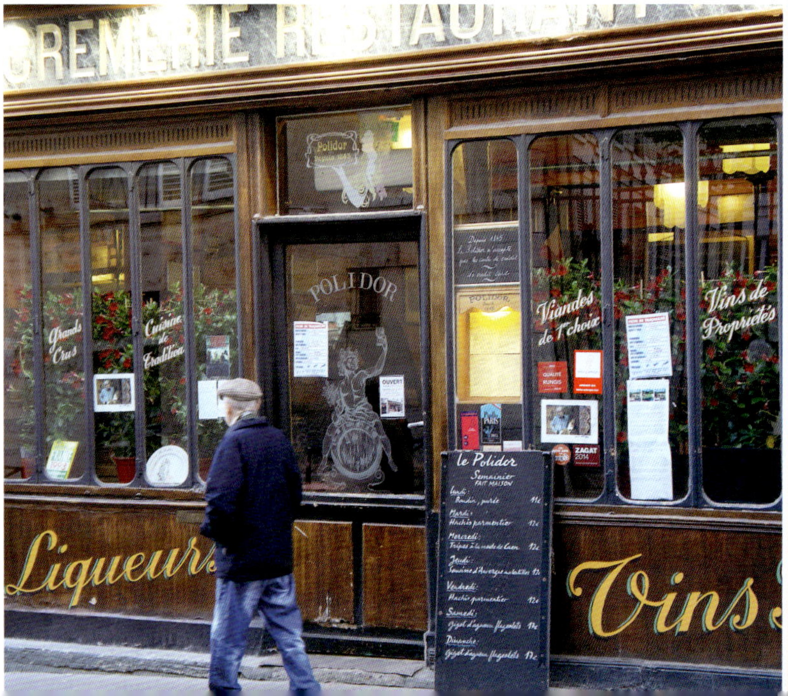

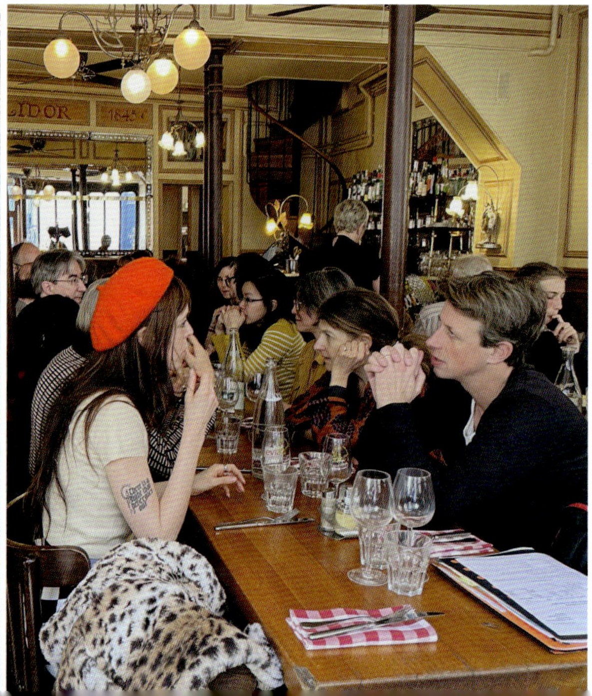

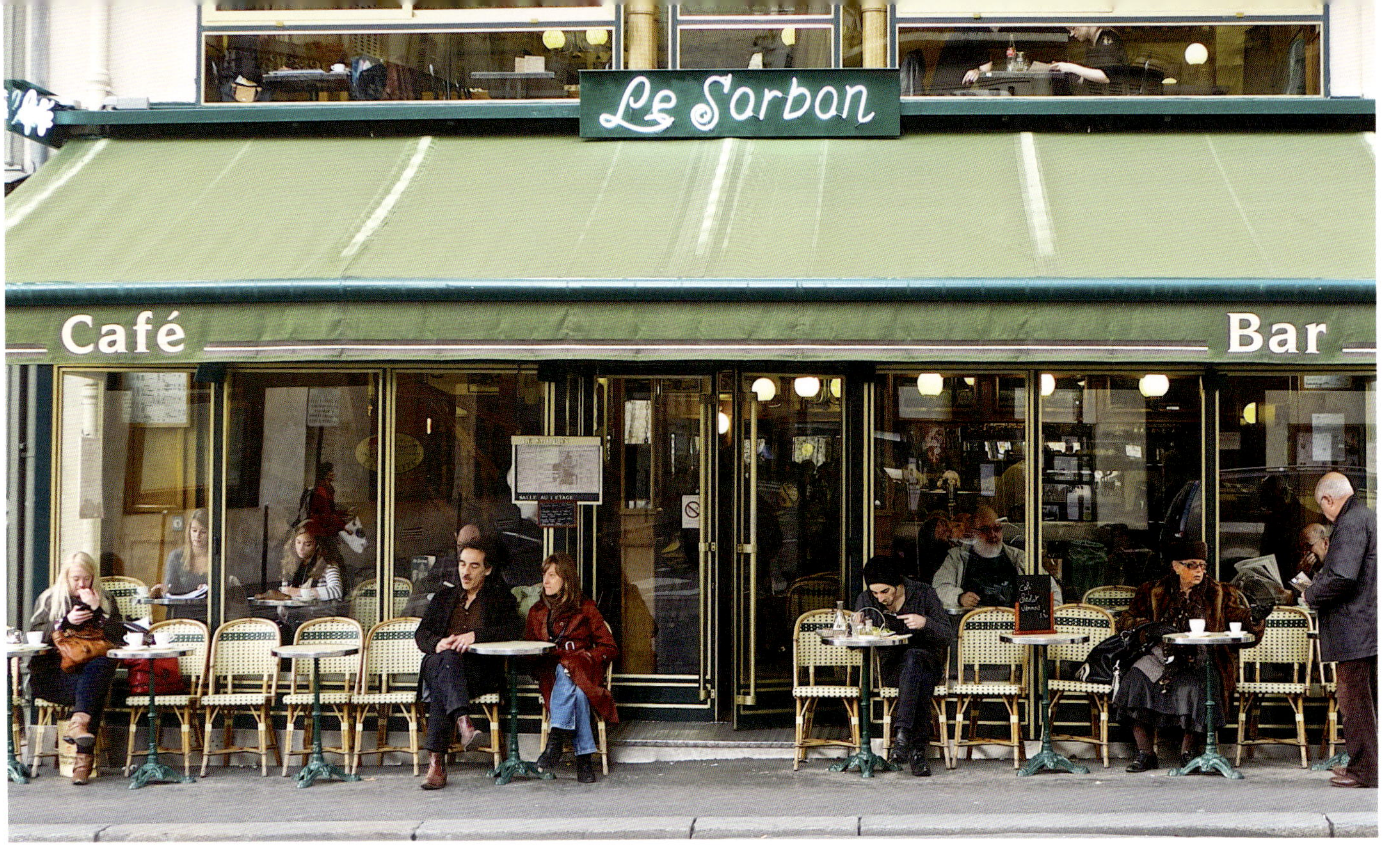

A neighborhood heavily populated by students, the Latin Quarter is home to plenty of inexpensive eateries with generous portions, often of good quality. Between regular mealtimes, it's fun to wander, sans reservations, check out the menus, peek at the plates, and take a chance. It's just one meal, and that's how discoveries are made.

Brasserie Balzar has been serving up classic brasserie cuisine since 1886 (as printed on some of their older awnings) or 1894 (as written on their website). As time goes by and memory is lost, many historic café, bistros, and brasseries have disputed dates. Balzar does not have the grand, elegant interiors of the best Parisian brasseries, nor is the food what it once may have been. However, it played host to numerous intellects of the 19th and 20th Century and if these walls could talk...

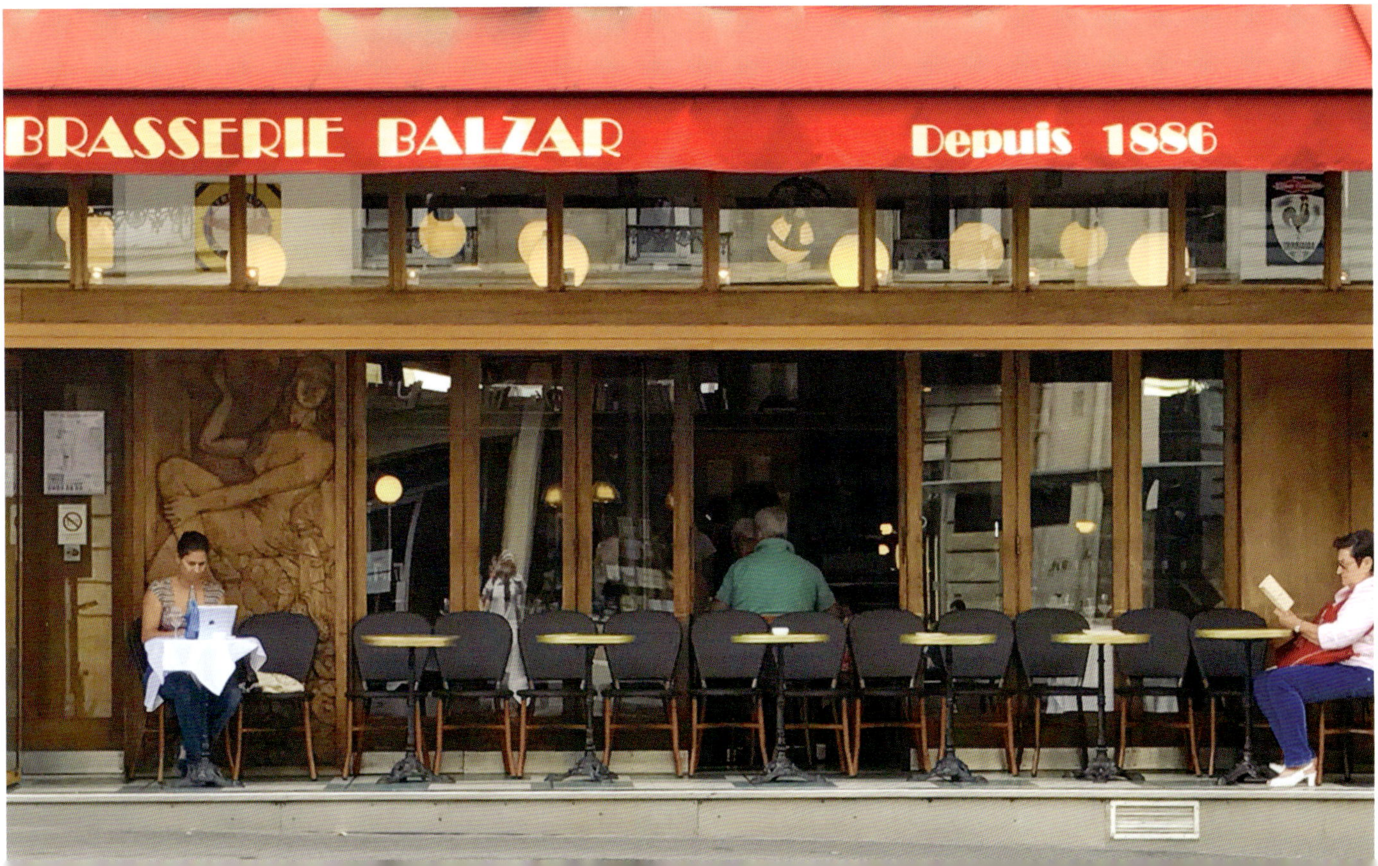

Montmartre

"Major art movements are planned and announced with cold determination in cafés."

René Prévot

Flush with vineyards, the 18th arrondissement in Paris, once considered the countryside, was established only in 1860. By the 1880s, Montmartre had become a party scene with its cafés and cabarets. Artists flocked to Montmartre, where the rent was low and the cafés and cabarets lively. Utrillo, Picasso, Renoir, Duffy, Henri Matisse, André Derain, Suzanne Valadon, Edgar Degas, Henri de Toulouse-Lautrec all lived in the neighborhood in those days. Today, there is the tourist Montmartre, and then there is the village Montmartre. One can cleverly skip the Place du Tertre, filled with tourists and "artists," and discover the village, set apart in every way from the rest of the City of Light. Head over to one of the best walking streets in Paris, rue des Abbesses, where the cafés are abundant and soulful and the shops as chic as any in Paris. Go café-hopping to Le Chinon, Le Sancerre, Le Petit Paris, Le Saint-Jean, and Café Bruant—named after renowned Montmartre cabaret singer, Aristide Bruant. Walk these village streets to Le Consulat, then find Amelie's café on rue Lepic. Gertrude Stein would often walk from the 6th arrondissement up to Montmartre to visit the studios of Picasso and other artists. While it looks daunting, it is just a vigorous three-and-a-half-mile walk across Paris and up the hill. From there, wander the back streets where the incomparable view unveils another Paris.

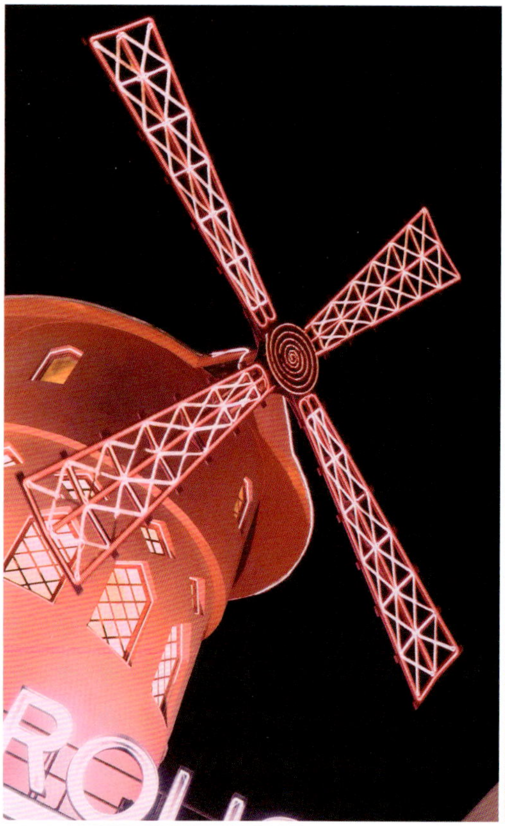

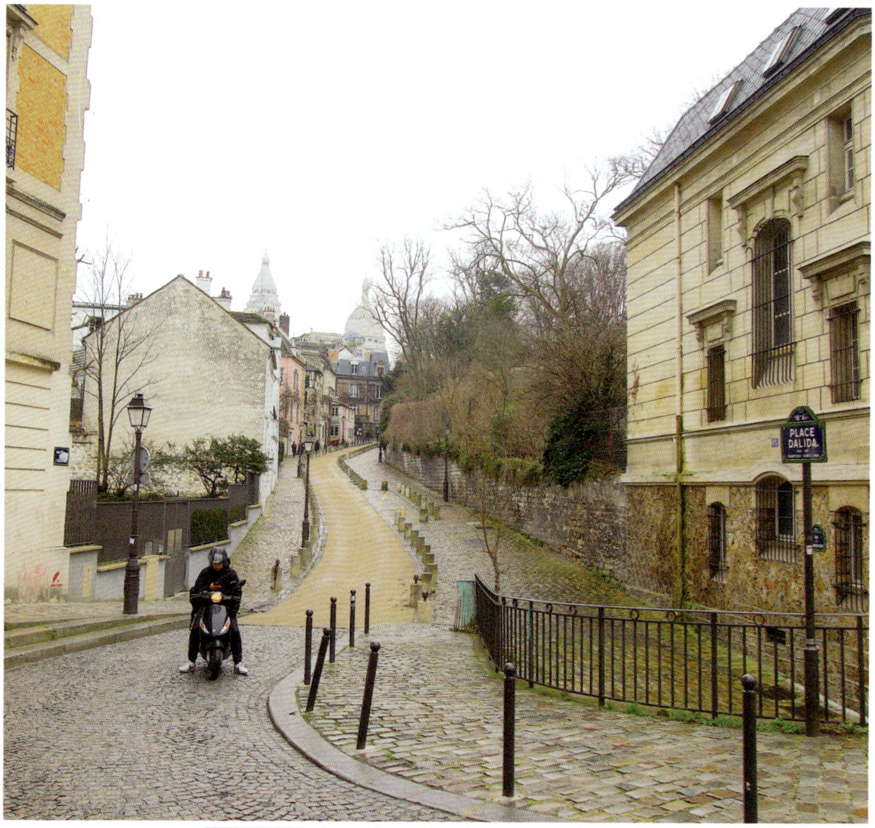

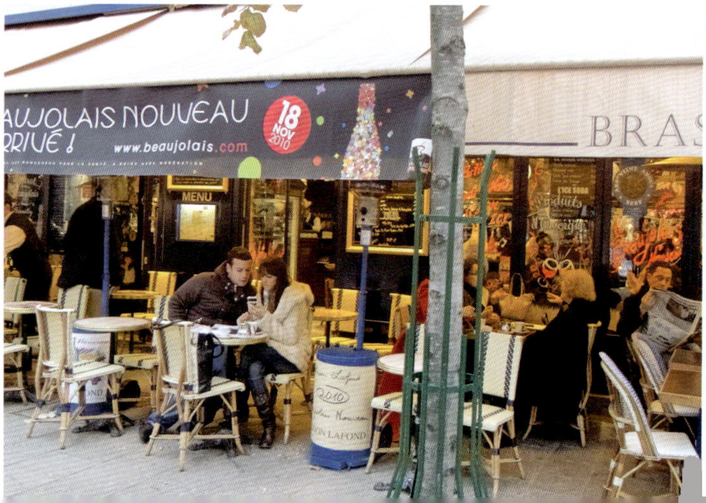

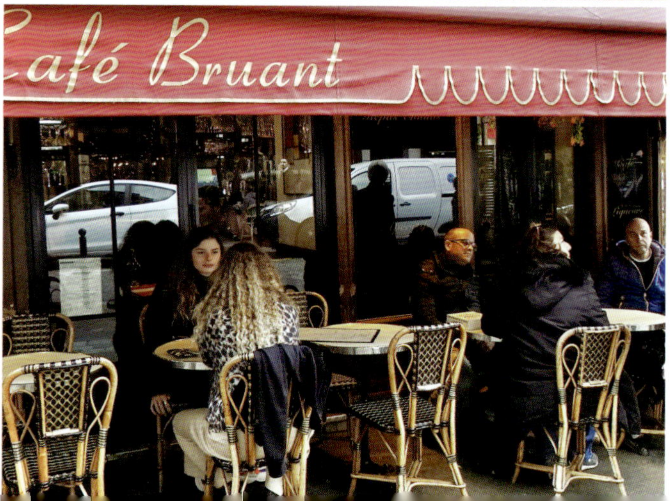

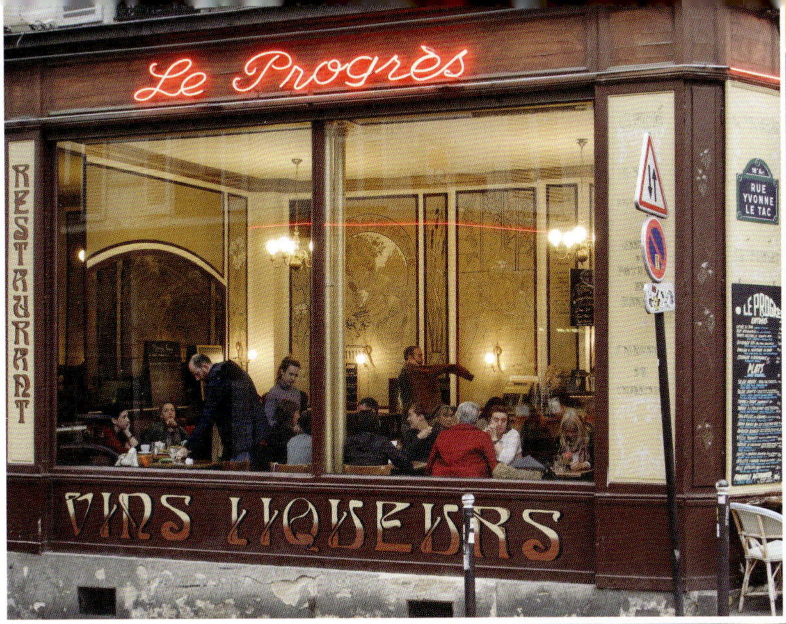
Le Progrès
RESTAURANT
VINS LIQUEURS
RUE YVONNE LE TAC
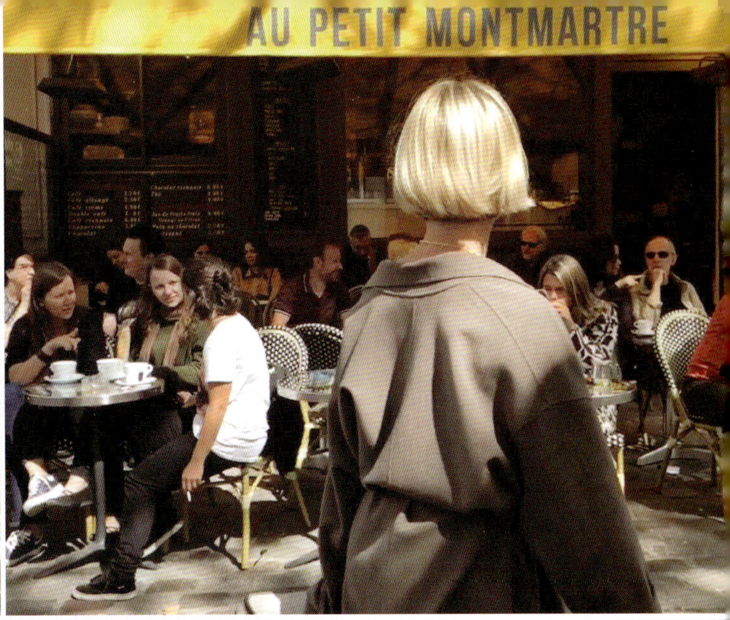
AU PETIT MONTMARTRE
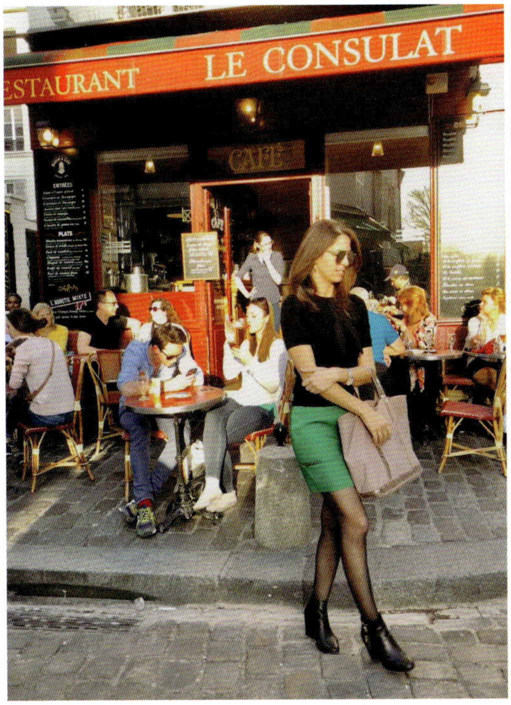
ESTAURANT LE CONSULAT
CAFE
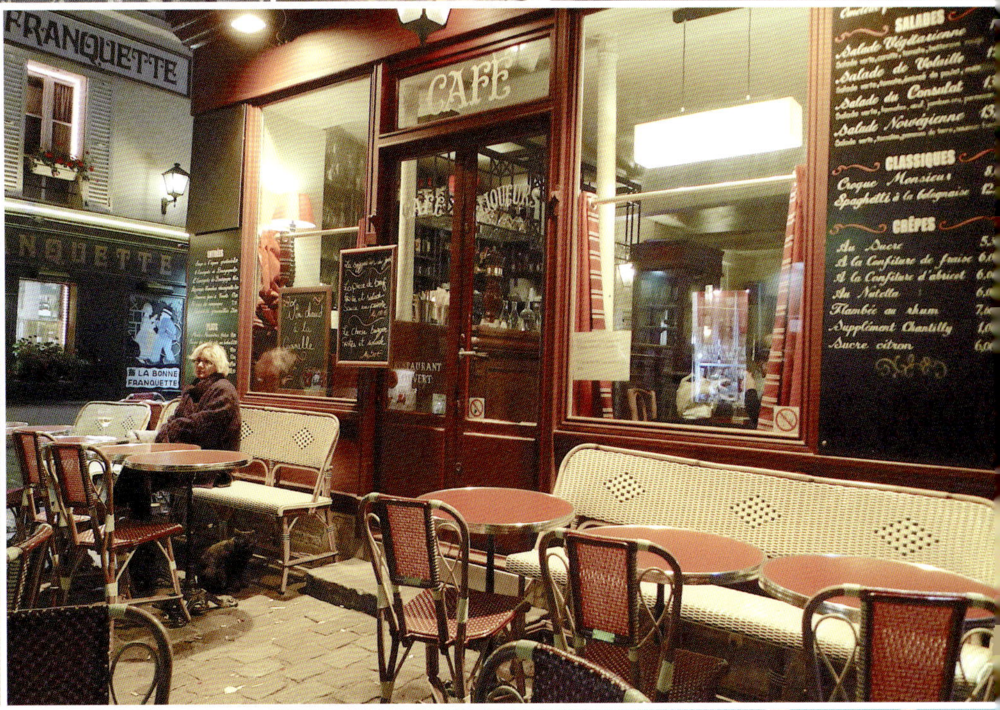
FRANQUETTE
CAFÉ
SALADES
Salade Végétarienne
Salade de Volaille
Salade du Consulat
Salade Norvégienne
CLASSIQUES
Croque Monsieur
Spaghetti à la bolognaise
CRÊPES
Au Sucre
À la Confiture de fraise
À la Confiture d'abricot
Au Nutella
Flambée au rhum
Supplément Chantilly
Sucre citron
LA BONNE FRANQUETTE
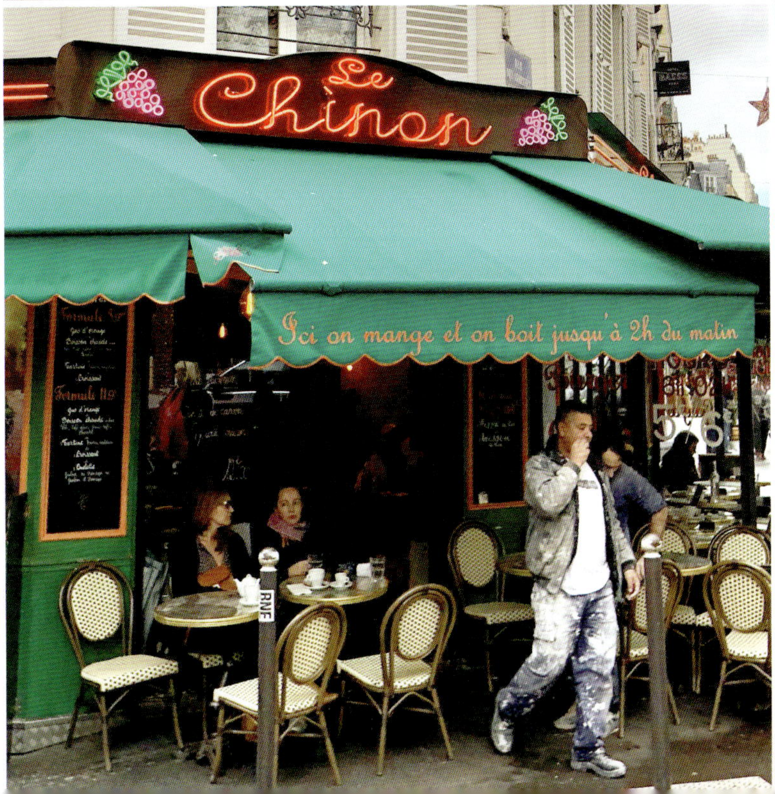
Le Chinon
Ici on mange et on boit jusqu'à 2h du matin
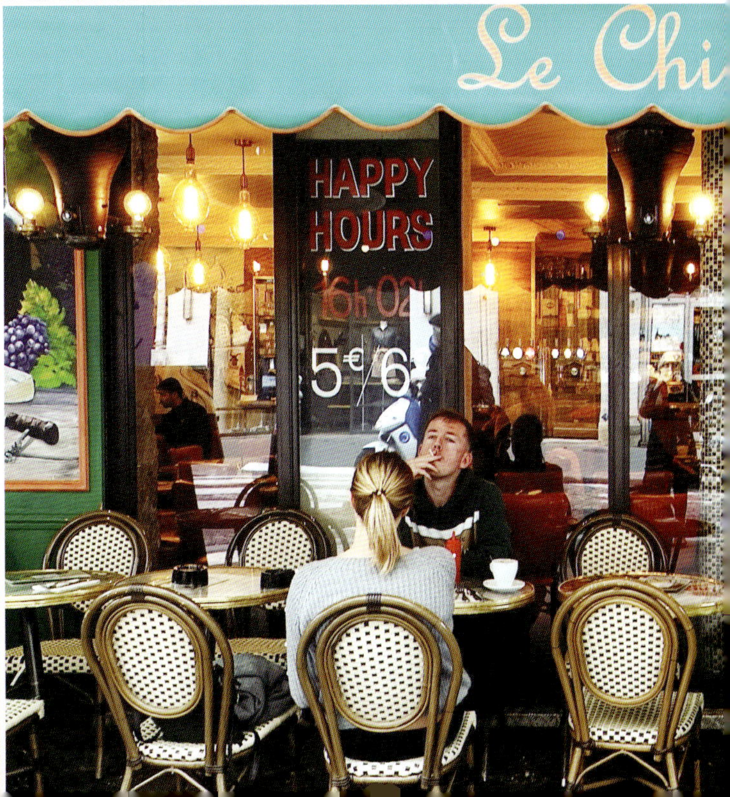
Le Chi
HAPPY HOURS

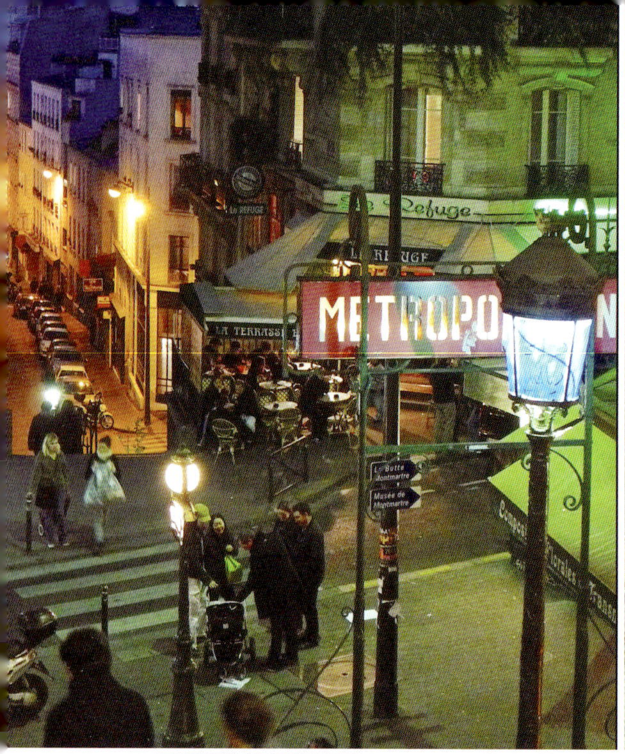
Le Refuge
LA TERRASSE

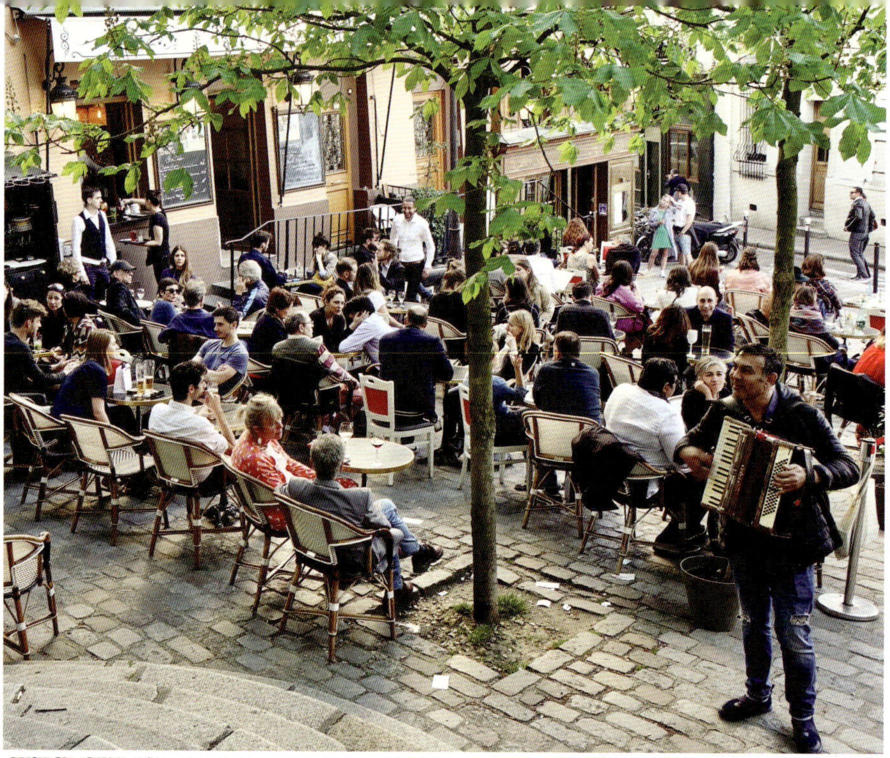

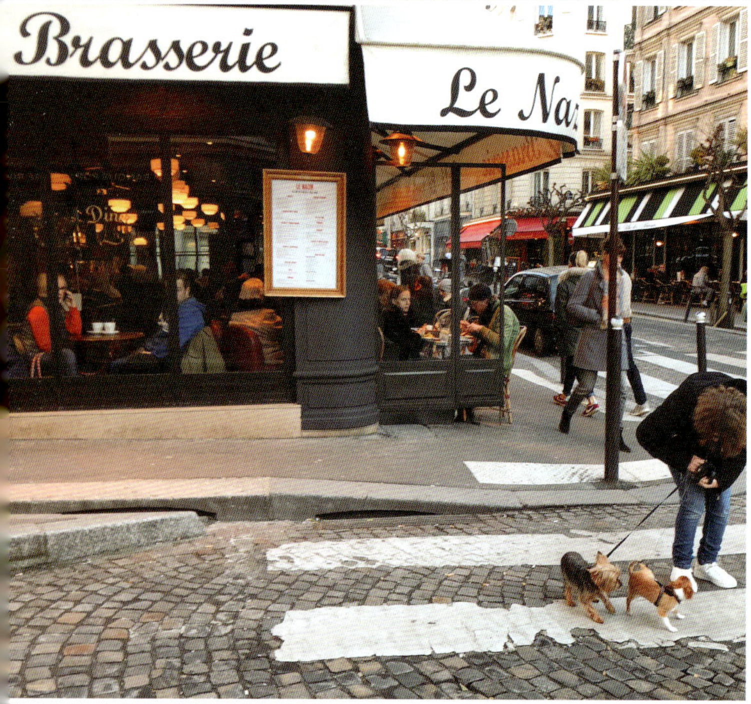
Brasserie

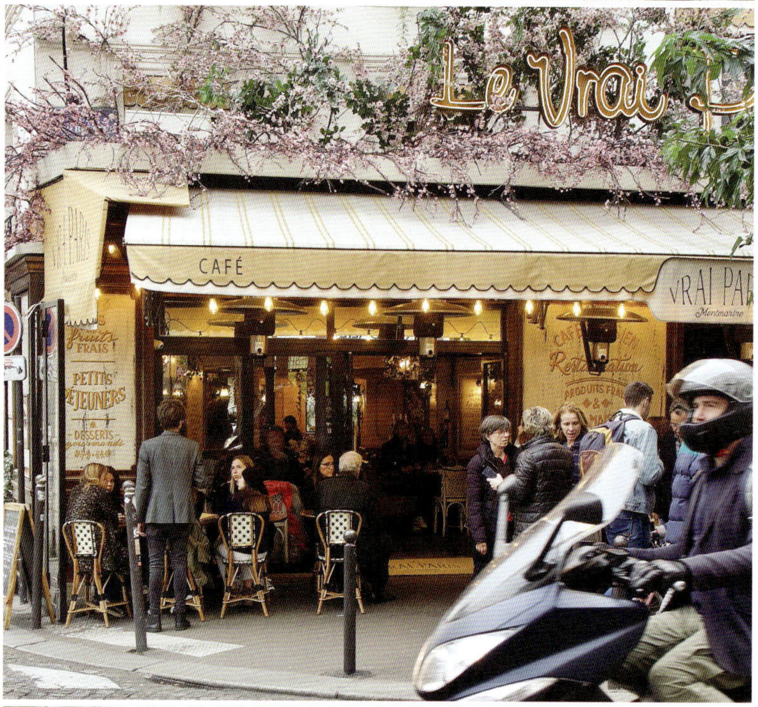
Le Vrai
CAFÉ
PETITS DÉJEUNERS

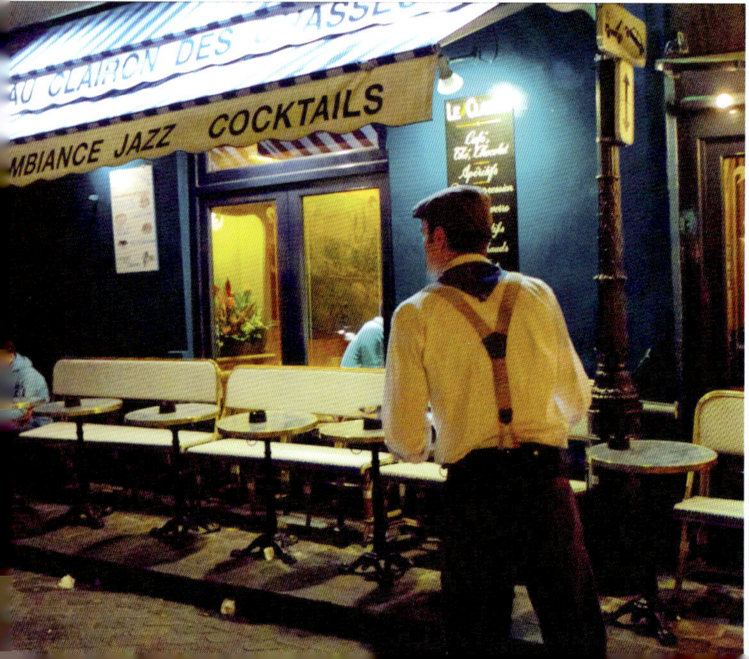
AU CLAIRON DES
JAZZ COCKTAILS

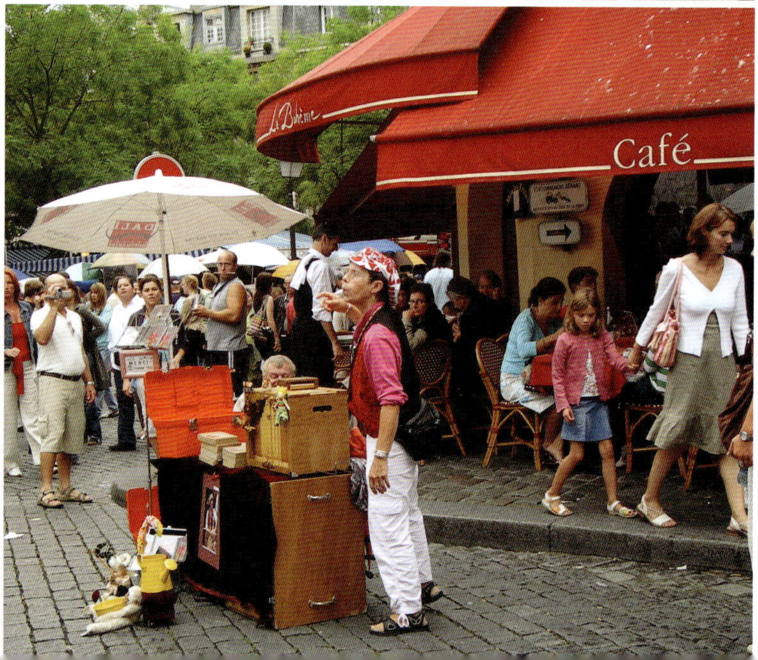
La Bohème
Café

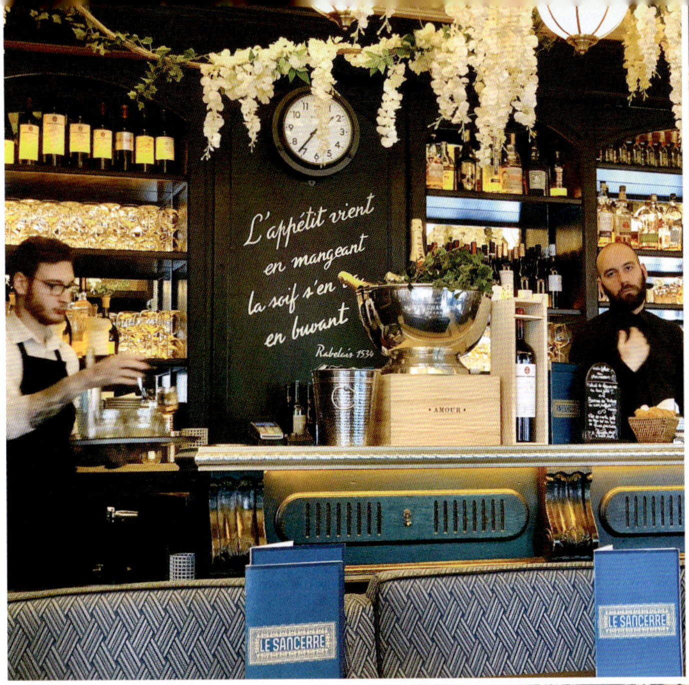
L'appétit vient
en mangeant
la soif s'en
en buvant
Rabelais 1534
LE SANCERRE
LE SANCERRE

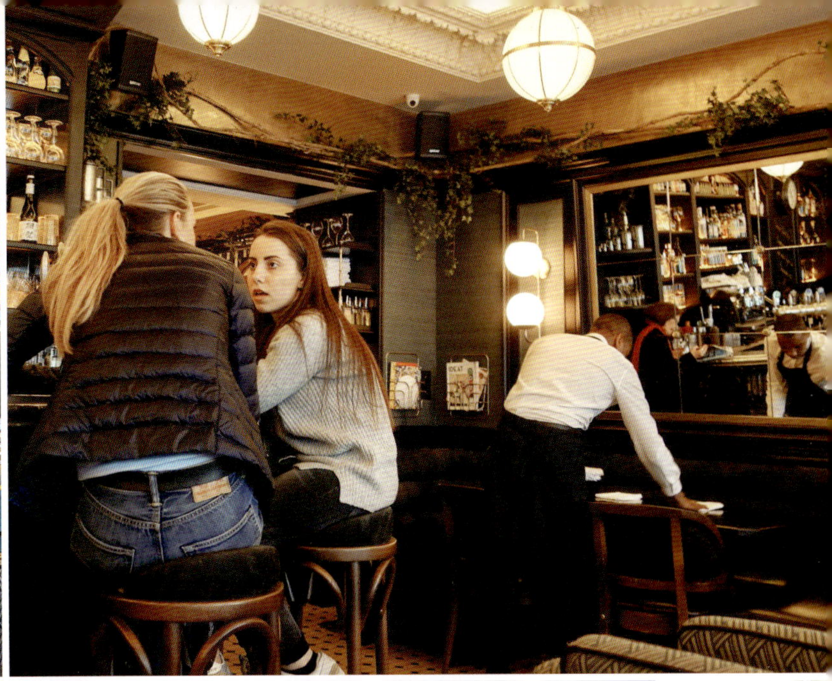

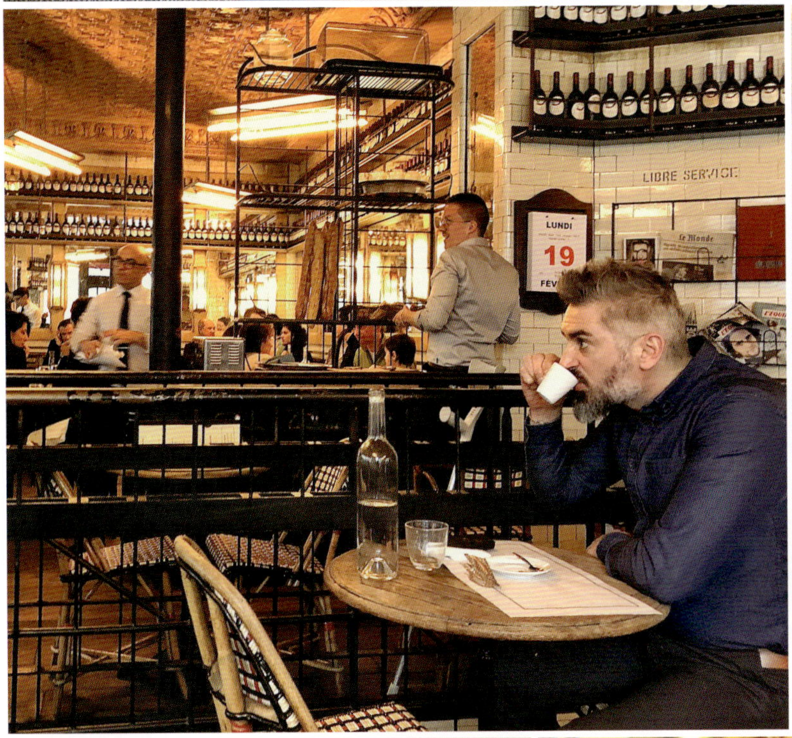
LIBRE SERVICE
LUNDI
19
Le Monde

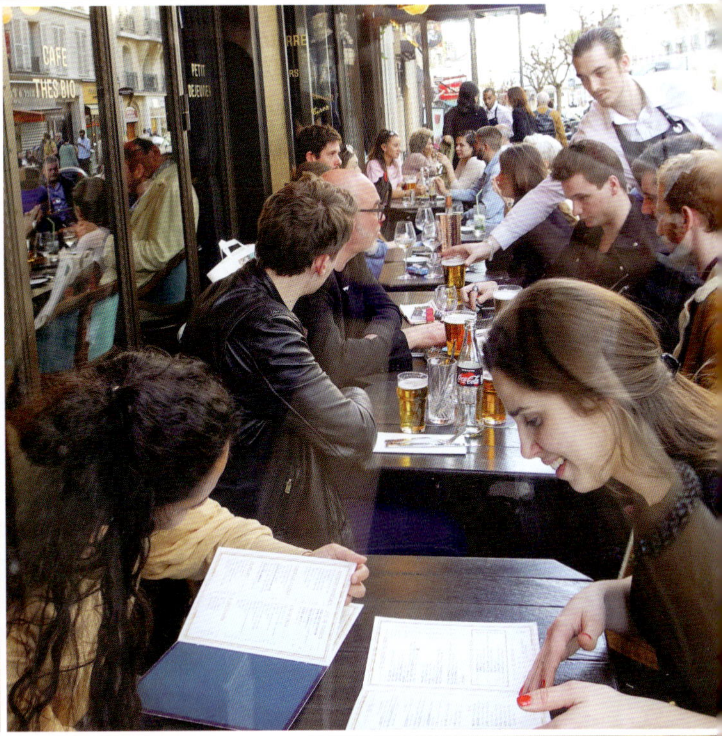
CAFE
THES BIO

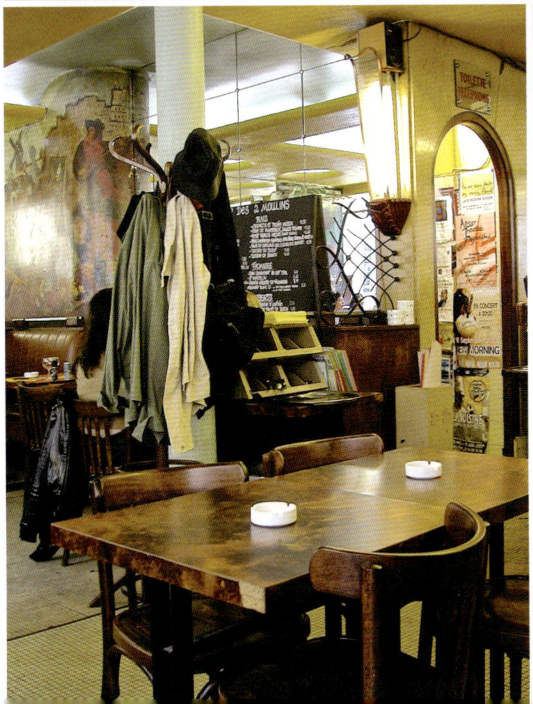

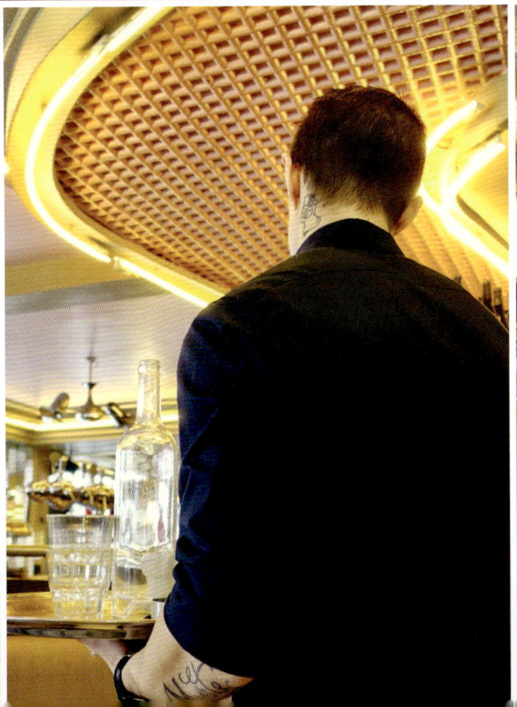

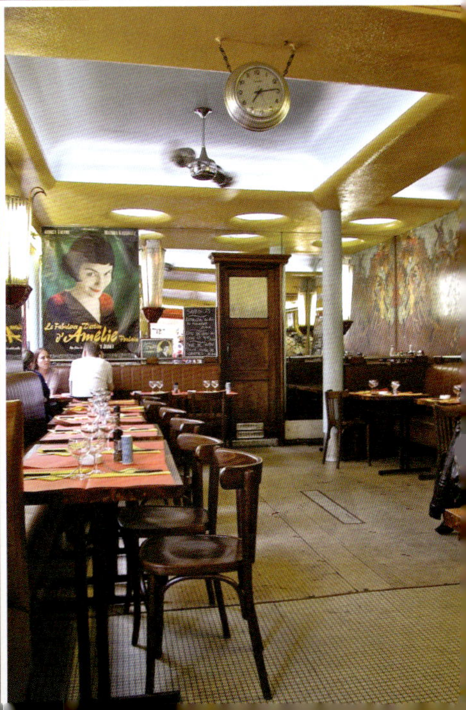

Montparnasse

"The Montparnassians sleep in the morning and in the afternoon and spend the evening and the neo-evening upon the terraces of the Dôme, the Rotonde, the Select, and other neighboring cafés. They have dark circles under their eyes, have read parts of *Ulysses*, and are likely to be self-made Freudians."

Elliot Paul

Montparnasse and *Les Années Folles* (the crazy years aka "The Roaring Twenties") are linked forever in Paris café lore. After WWI, artists moved en-masse from Montmartre to Montparnasse, colorfully dubbed "the navel of the world" by Henry James. Gertrude Stein coined the term the "Lost Generation" to describe the writers, artists, musicians, and intellectuals living and working in Paris after the Great War's devastation. These bohemians gathered in the cafés here to share their ideas and arguments accompanied by good food and drink. As was her style, Stein declared simply, "Paris was where the twentieth century was." In those days, the US dollar was strong and the French franc weak. Floating from La Closerie des Lilas to Le Dôme, to La Rotonde, to Le Sélect, then, La Coupole, American literary expatriates Henry Miller, Ernest Hemingway, F. Scott Fitzgerald, James Baldwin, Gertrude Stein, and others, mingled with the neighborhood artists, some French, others expats, and their muses and models. Soutine, Modigliani, Matisse, Picasso, Chagall, Giacometti, Derain, Léger, Man Ray, Brassaï, Kiki de Montparnasse, and Josephine Baker all encamped in these cafés. In that era between the two great wars, Paris was mad for American Jazz. F. Scott Fitzgerald minted the phrase "the Jazz Age," which ushered in a time when Black American musicians and performers were wildly popular. Expats came in large numbers, and artists of various nationalities frequented their chosen cafés along with the French. To some extent, Americans tended to gather at the Select, Germans and English at the Dôme, the Polish and Spaniards at the Rotonde, and a mix of international expats and locals at La Coupole. Fast-forward to our time, and we can but dream of the jazzy background music of that era. The fashion now around town is for hip-hop or electronic playlists, even in classic cafés—a thoroughly discordant note more appropriate for trendy cafés. Perhaps this is but a passing trend, and the sounds of Charles Trenet, Django Reinhardt, and Ella Fitzgerald will once again float through these hallowed dining halls. One hundred years later, in the Montparnasse of the 2020s, Bohemia lurks only in the shadows, and the legendary Montparnos are ghosts of another era. Still, these cafés are splendid.

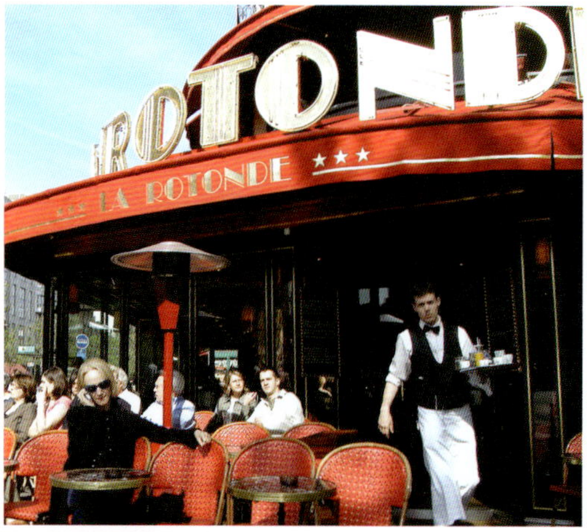

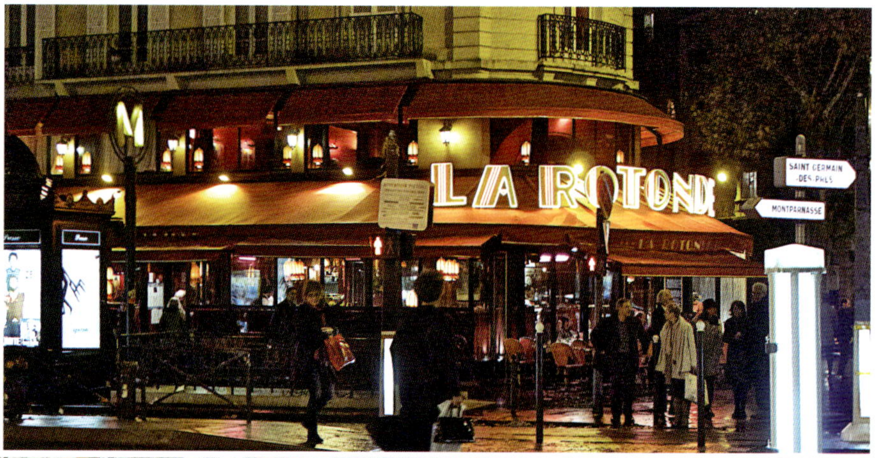

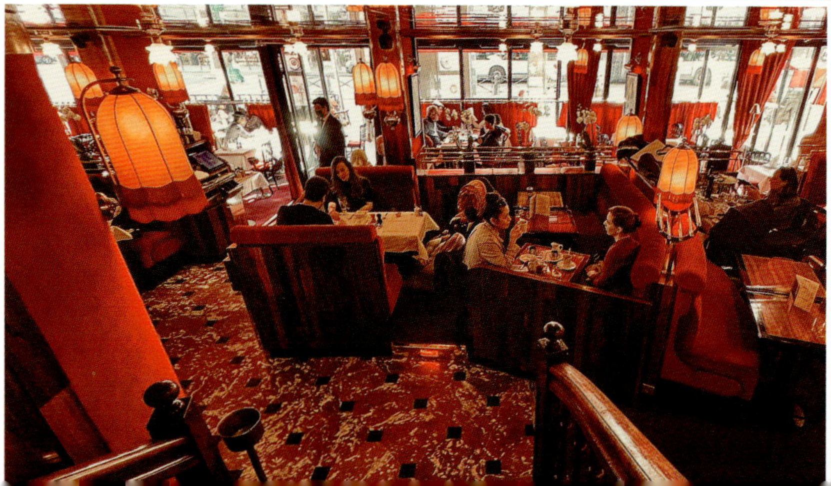

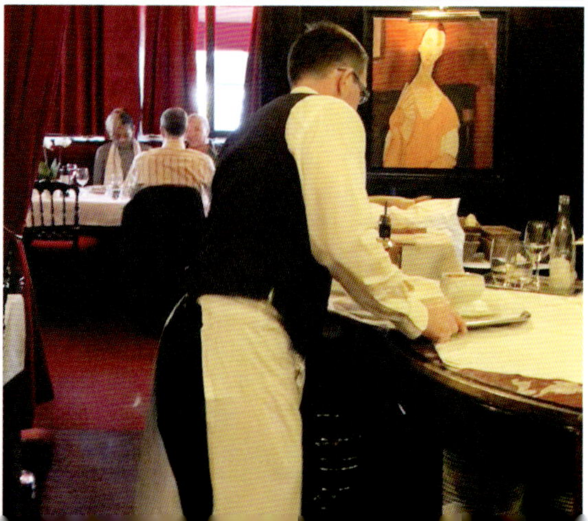

"The Café du Dôme served as the front porch, reception hall, parlor, and sitting room in one. It is home.""

Stephen Longstreet

Founded by Victor Libion in 1911, La Rotonde was one of the centers of Montparnasse café culture during *Les Années Folles*. The "*Rotondists*" included French and immigrant artists Picasso, Braque, Modigliani, Vlaminck, Derain, Lipchitz, Kisling, Foujita, Soutine, Van Dongen, Diego Rivera, Zadkine, Cocteau, Juan Gris, Gustave Moreau, and Man Ray. Impoverished Modigliani practically lived at La Rotonde, paying the supportive owner with his drawings and paintings, sometimes created right at the café table. Having been a fixture at La Rotonde, it is fitting that reproductions of his paintings now adorn the upstairs walls. "No matter what cafe in Montparnasse you ask a taxi driver to bring you to from the right bank of the river, they always take you to the Rotonde," wrote Ernest Hemingway in *The Sun Also Rises*.

Opened in 1897, Le Dôme is the oldest café/bistro/brasserie/restaurant (its designations and cuisine have become interchangeable over the decades) in Montparnasse. During and following the Belle Époque, it was one of the meeting places for known and soon-to-be-known painters, sculptors, writers, poets, models, and dealers, including habitués Simone de Beauvoir, Anaïs Nin, Khalil Gibran, Wassily Kandinsky and Giacometti. Lenin, Trotsky, and other revolutionaries found tables here as well. Apollinaire set the scene in 1912 when he coined the term "Dômier"—referring to the international artists who were regulars—and said, "Le Dôme is a café on the corner of Boulevard Raspail & Montparnasse...the Dômiers are the German painters who frequent it. It is here that they show their professional admiration for such and such a French painter."

After World War I, British and American expats including Gertrude and Leo Stein, Ezra Pound, Man Ray, Duke Ellington, and James Baldwin assembled here, and it's here that Dizzy Gillespie's jazz band made its Paris debut. "Before the outbreak of war in 1939, I remember sitting on the terrace of Le Dôme at certain times of day and hearing every language in the world being spoken," wrote Jean-Marie Drot, the documentarian of Montparnasse. In our epoch, Le Dôme is heralded for its magnificent seafood platters and fresh fish.

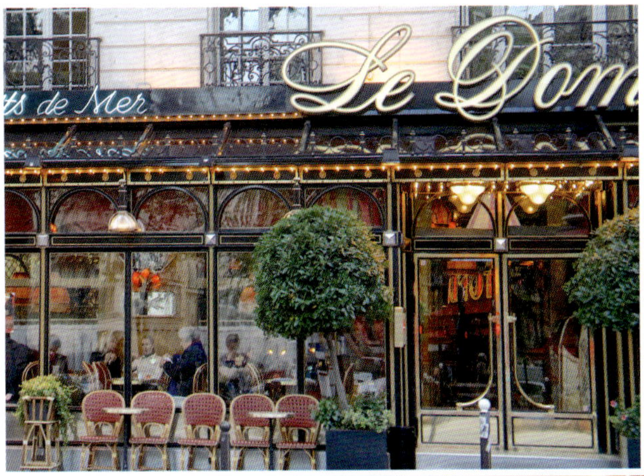

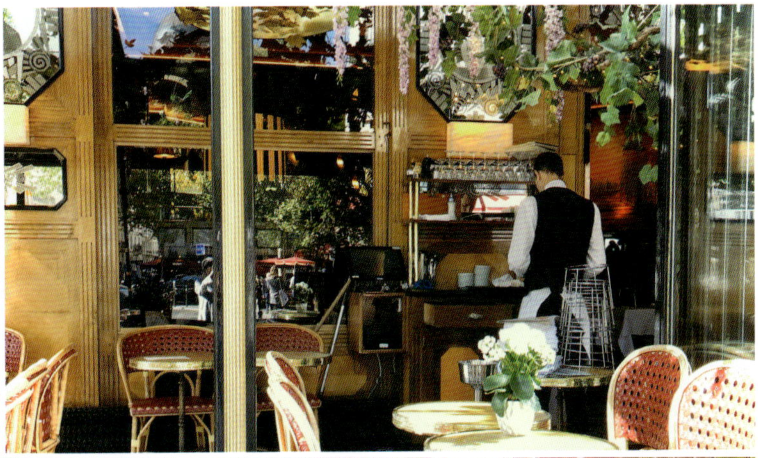

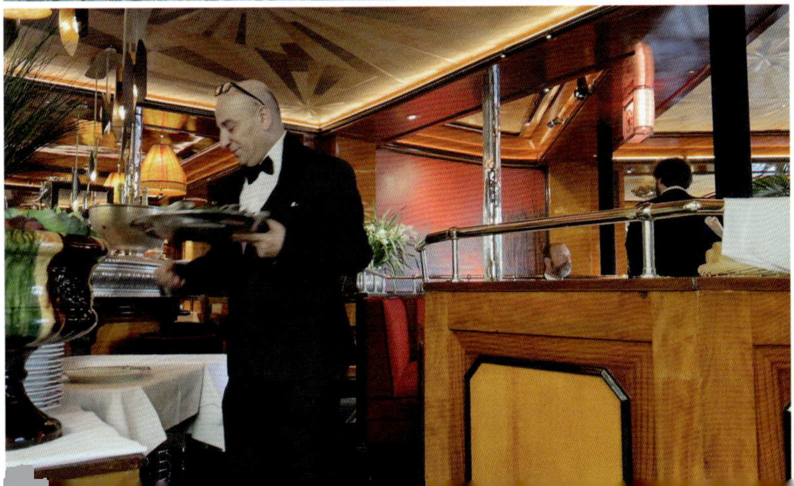

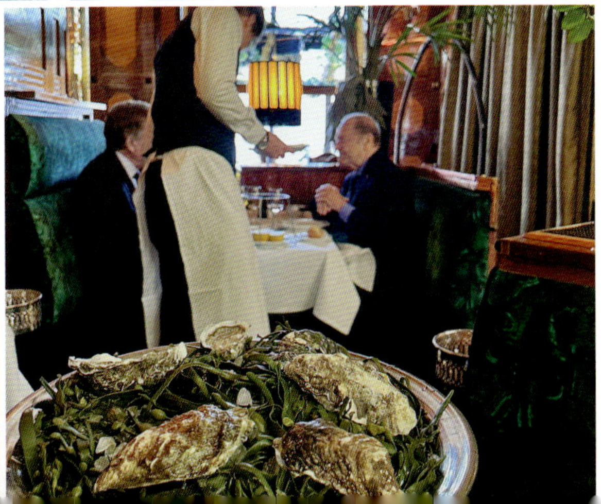

LE SELECT

"Talk for a moment with one of these exiles who have been sitting around in Paris for ten or fifteen years...One of these Hungarian counts who was once Prime Minister and who had parted with all his property. He sat next to us in the Café Select and played chess with himself."

Klaus Mann

Established in 1924, Le Select was the first café in Montparnasse to stay open all night. It was a watering hole for the Lost Generation writers, artists, composers, and filmmakers who congregated and exchanged ideas. Over the years, Ernest Hemingway, Henry Miller, John Dos Passos, James Baldwin, Samuel Beckett, Henri Matisse, Chaïm Soutine, Foujita, Alberto Giacometti, Salvador Dalí, Louis Buñuel, Erik Satie, Léon-Paul Fargue, Jean-Luc Goddard, Stuart Davis, Isamu Noguchi, and Alexander Calder, among others, shared tables and passions. During those days, here as in the other cafés, sometimes too much zeal fueled with too much alcohol led to actual fistfights. Arriving from Hungary in 1924, habitué Brassaï lived in an apartment above the café and took iconic photos of his Montparnasse neighborhood. Hemingway placed Le Select in *The Sun Also Rises*. You can still find regulars at the Select, some in the same seat daily, some, perhaps even writers, artists, composers, and filmmakers you may recognize. At the time of this writing, ever-smiling James, one of the top barmen in Paris, is at *le zinc* to welcome you. Is it a café, a bistro, a brasserie, or a restaurant? Maybe all four, and perhaps it doesn't matter. What matters most is that Le Select is unchanged, unspoiled, and unpretentious. Its history, food—some say the best croque-monsieur in Paris—and authenticity make it a memorable spot where one wishes to return time after time.

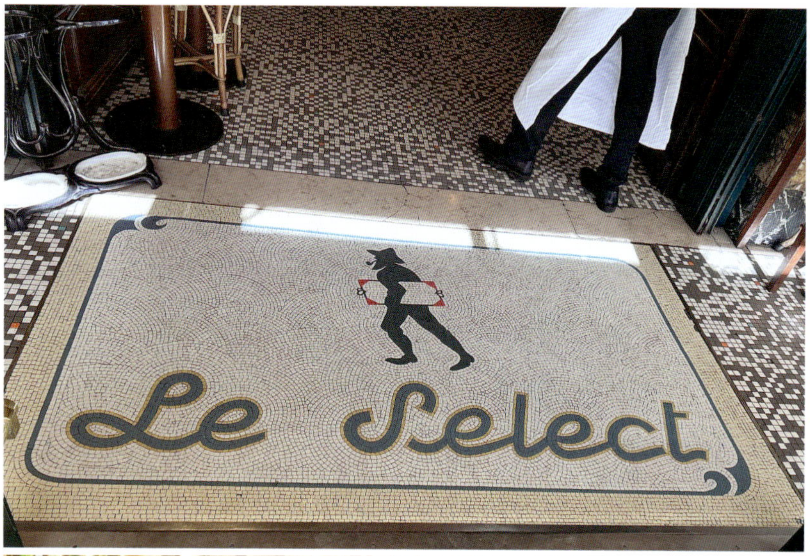

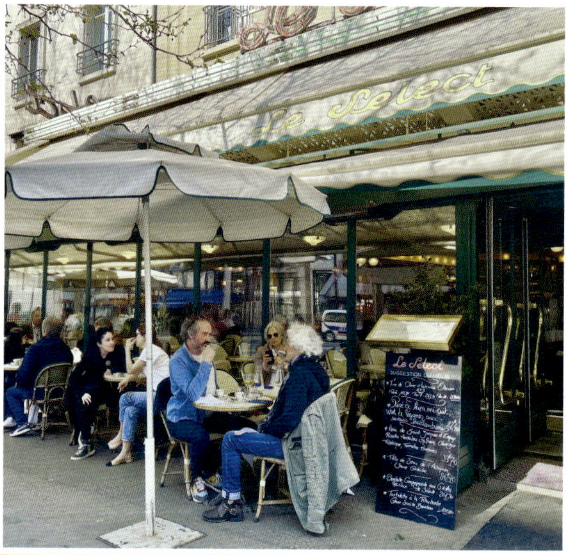

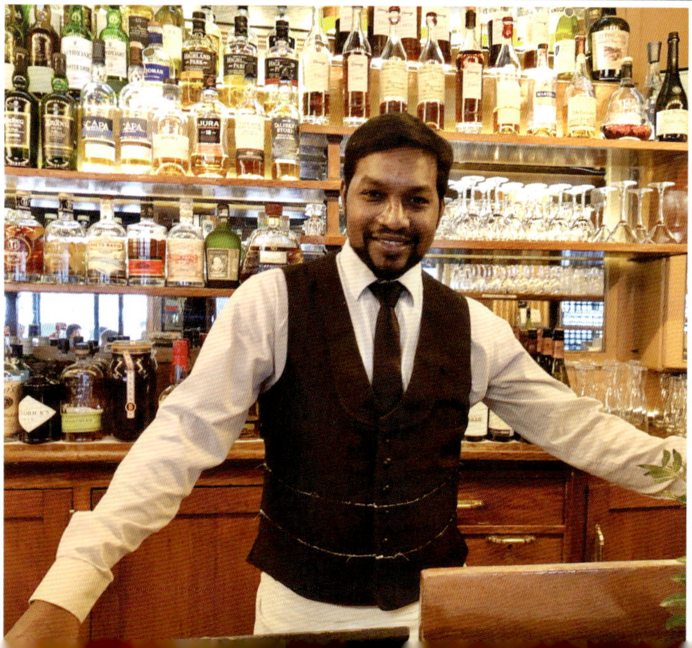

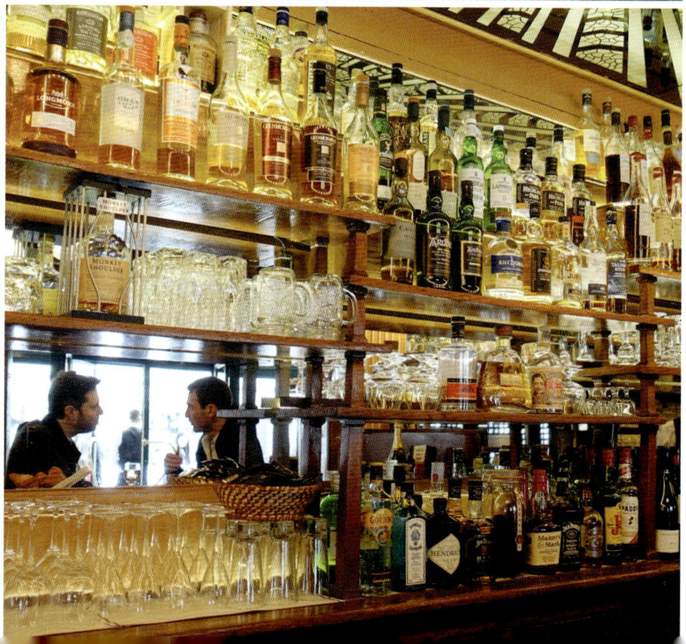

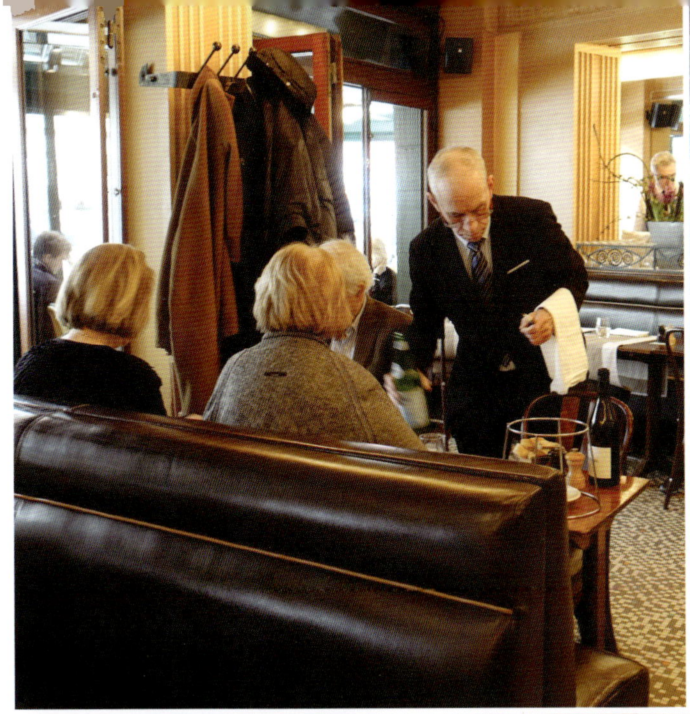

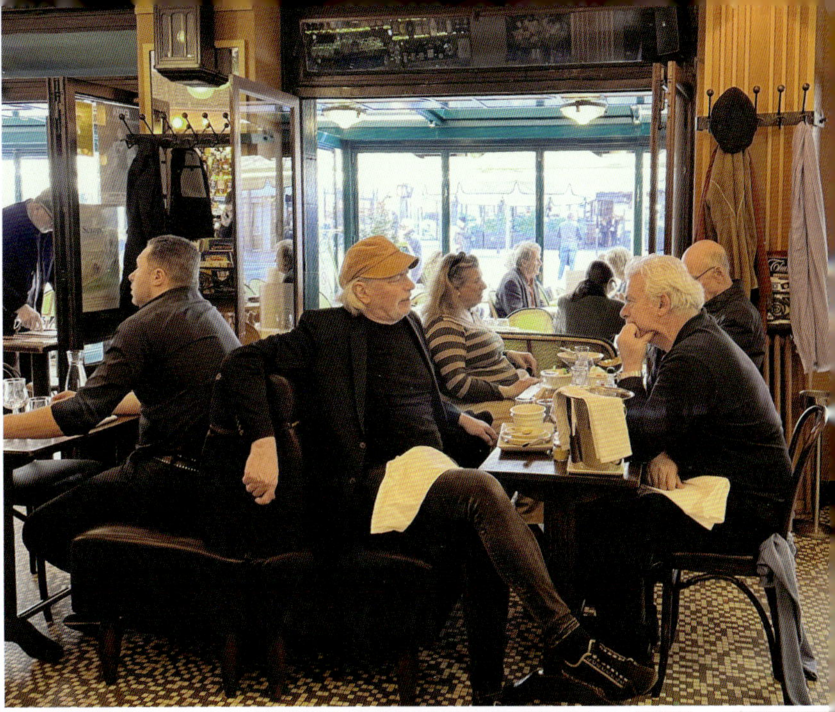

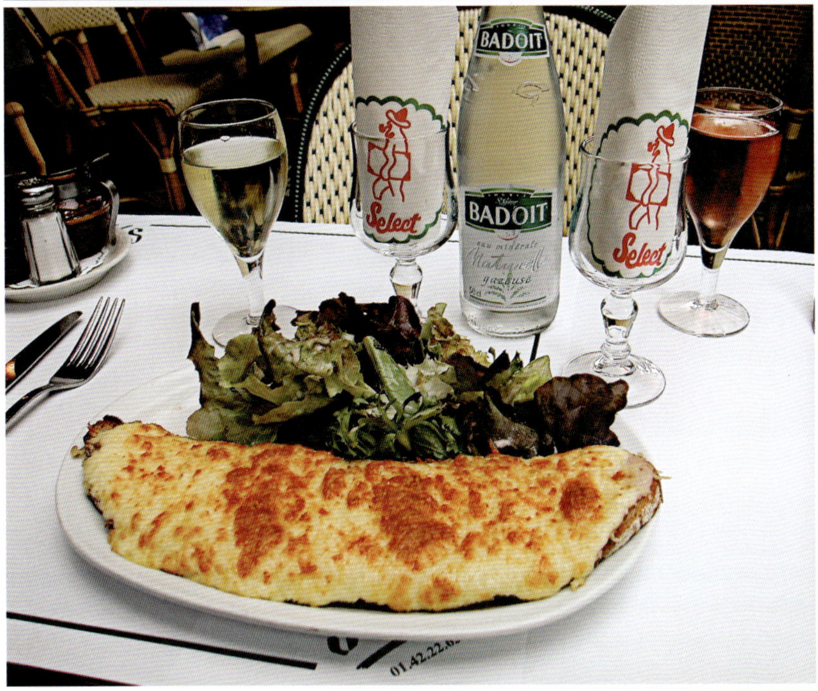
BADOIT
BADOIT
Select
Select

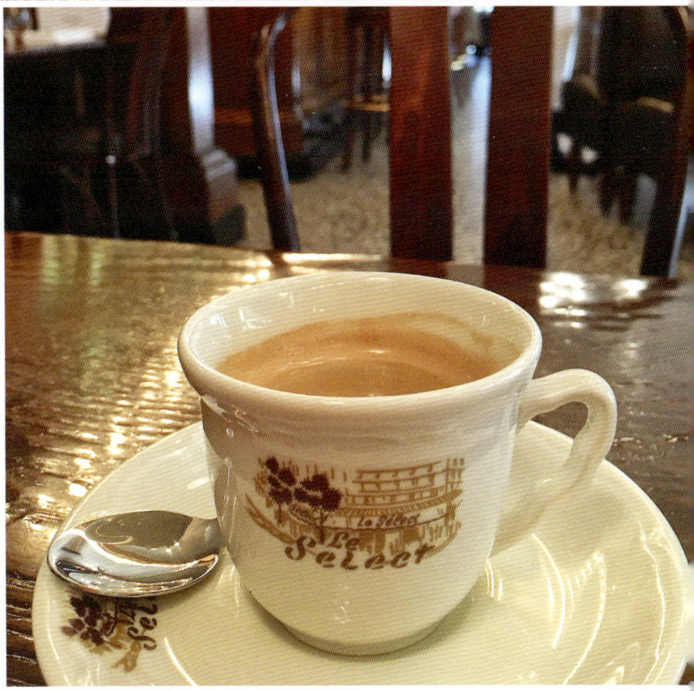
Le Select

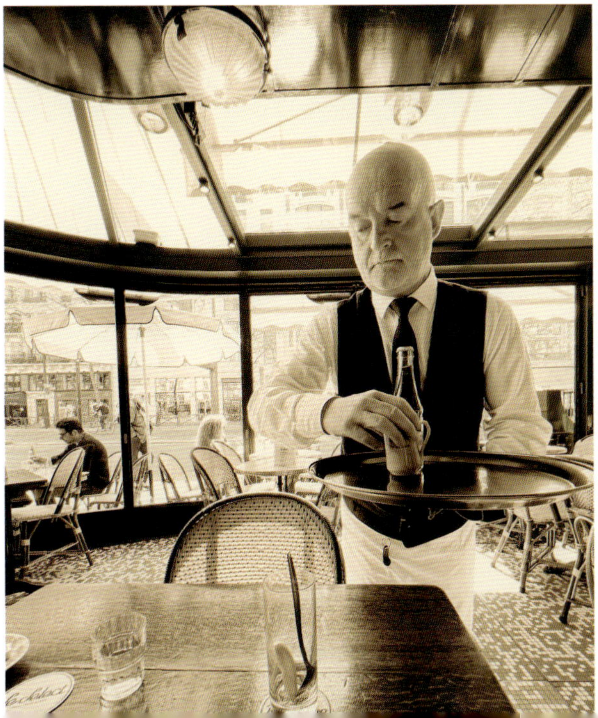

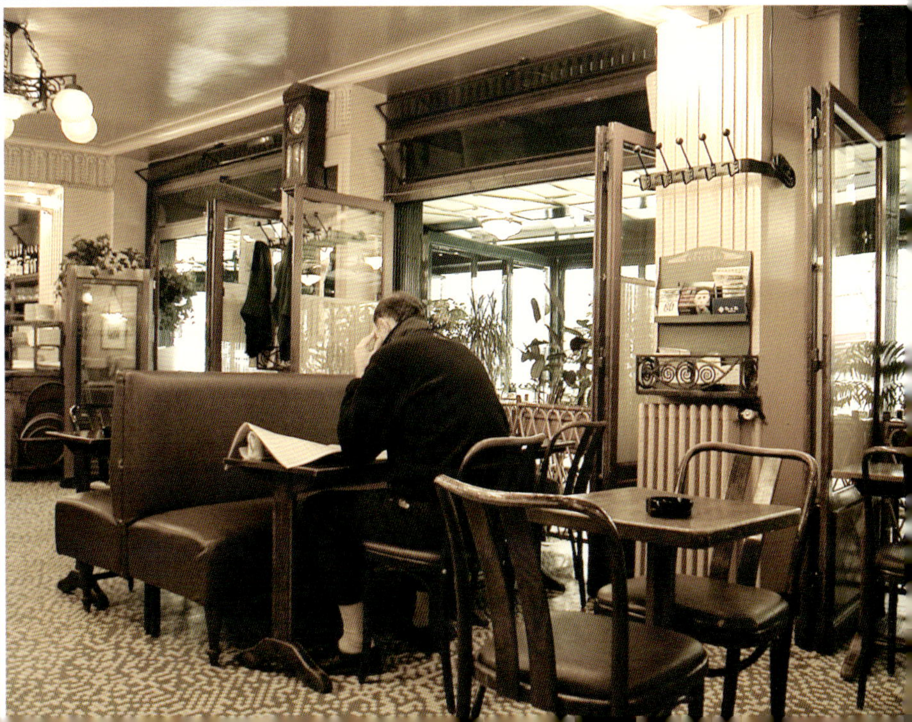

LA COUPOLE

> "La Coupole was the place of international painters and sculptors. Giacometti held court there; the affluent young came from all over to meet the master."
>
> **Iris Clert**

When La Coupole opened in 1927 with a lavish soirée celebrated by 2,500 of *Le tout Paris*, it was the event of the year in Montparnasse. Writers and artists enjoyed more than 1,500 bottles of Mumm champagne (reportedly not enough for the crowd) and thousands of oysters. The gorgeous Art Deco brasserie, with 32 columns painted by students of Fernand Léger (later enhanced by a central figurative sculpture rotating below an ever-changing colored dome), and a Bar Americain, became a favorite of French and Russian artists along with other expats between the two world wars. Prokofiev, Eisenstein, Chagall were at the Soviets' table; the American table seated a familiar cast of glamorous expats: Hemingway, F. Scott Fitzgerald, Gershwin, Calder, Henry Miller, Man Ray, and Josephine Baker. Then there was the table-hopping of a great mix of notables from the world over, including Ford Maddox Ford, Louis Buñel, Max Jacob, Colette, James Joyce, Laurence Durrell, Kandinsky, Robert & Sonia Delaunay, Lipchitz, Brancusi, Cocteau, Vlaminck, Picasso, and the magnificent muse Kiki de Montparnasse. At La Coupole in the early 20th century, George Simenon worked on the Maigret mysteries, Camus celebrated his Nobel prize, and Josephine Baker brought her cheetah on a leash. Years later, Patti Smith played her guitar on the terrace, and François Mitterrand enjoyed his last meal here. Despite the entire building being toppled by new construction in the '80s and a slew of ownership changes, the interior remains mostly intact. In 2018, the new owners elevated the quality of the food, revived dancing, and hosted *Soirées Paris Follies* in the lower-level dance hall where scenes of the *Last Tango in Paris* were shot. The exterior now sports the original designed chairs. On Saturday night, La Coupole is still the place to be, with diners displaying their stylish *Parisien* flair and filmmakers, publishers, artists, and intellectuals lending gravitas and continuity to its past glory.

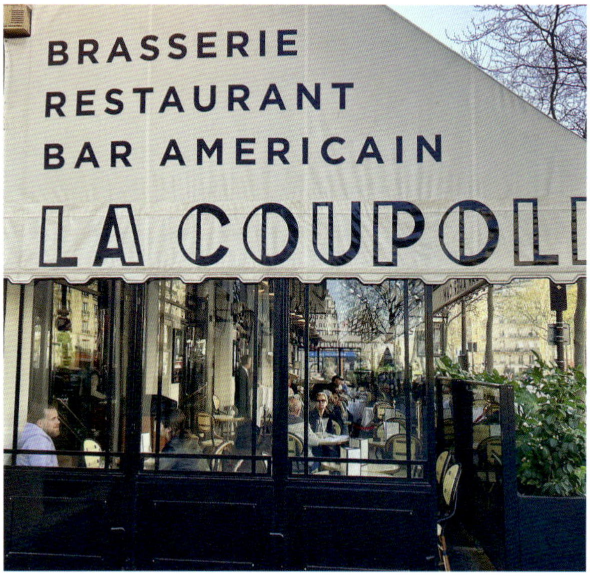

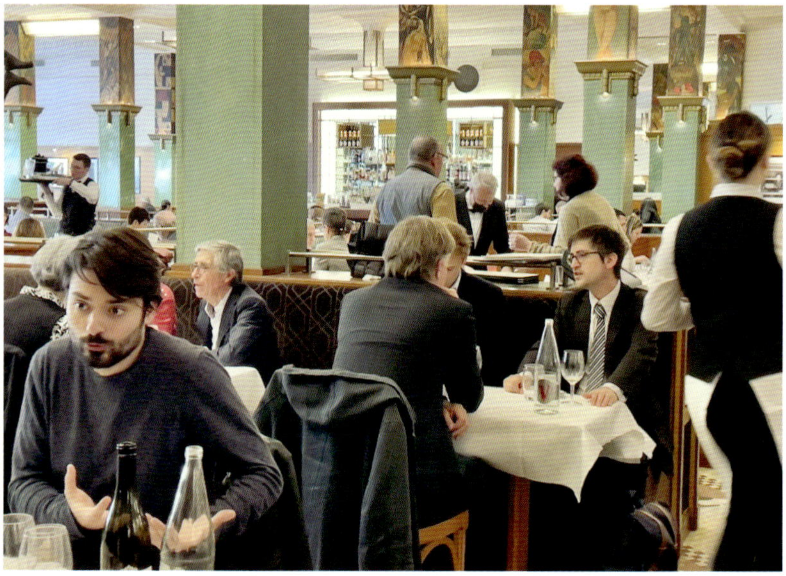

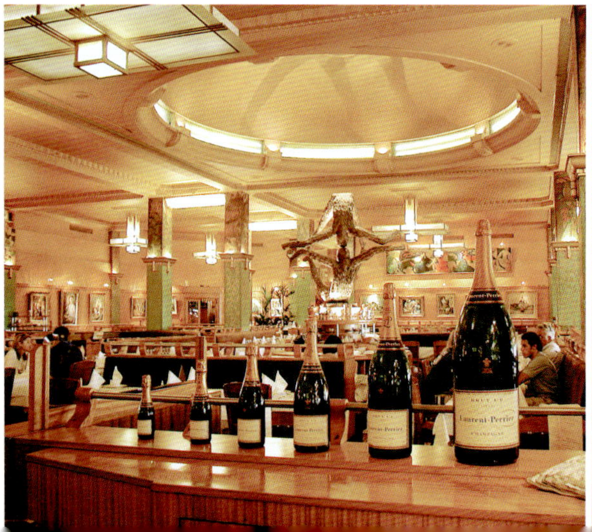

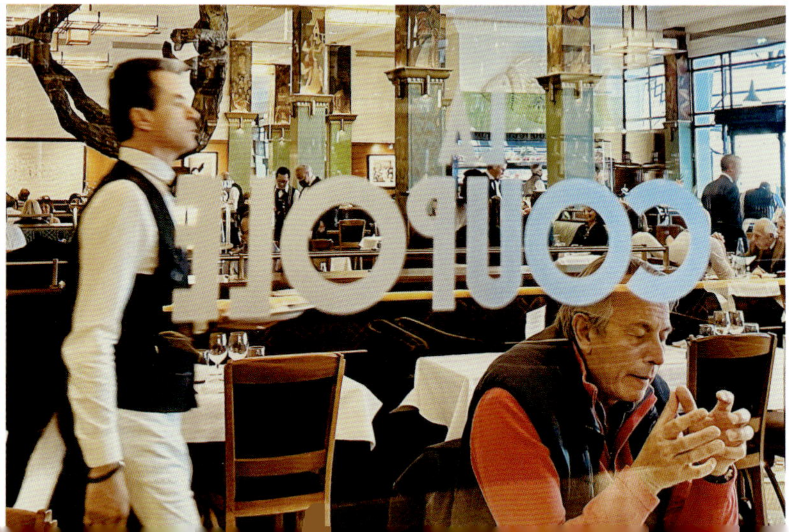

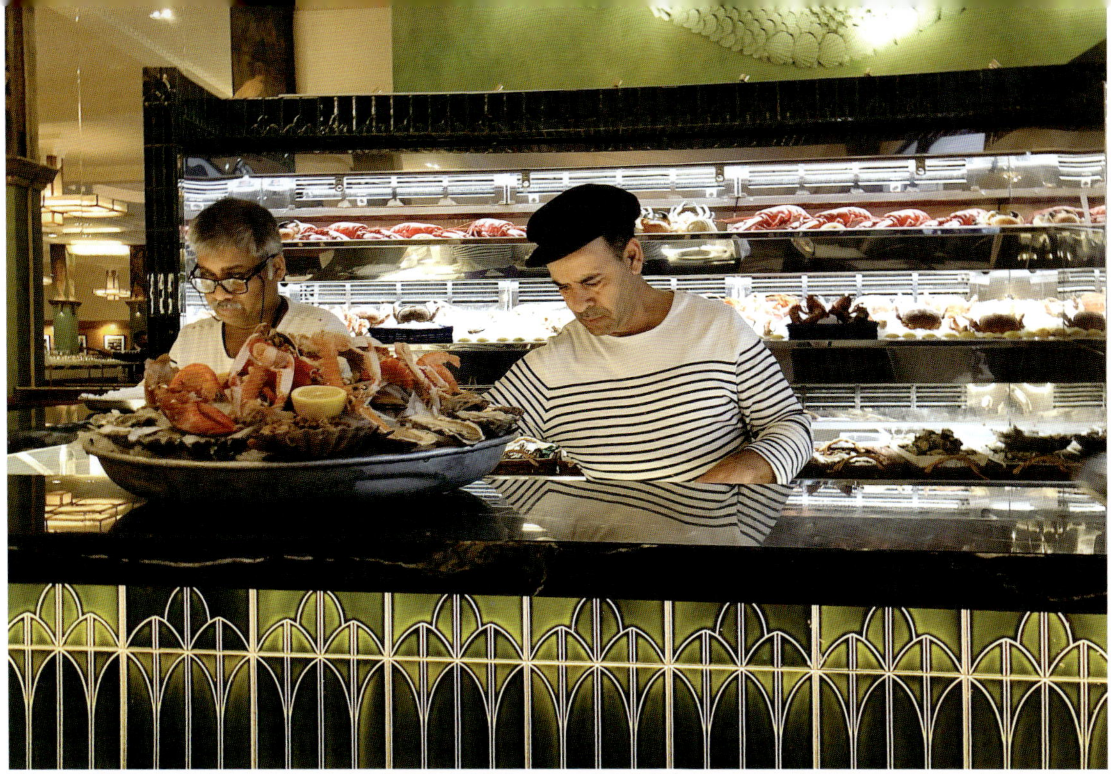

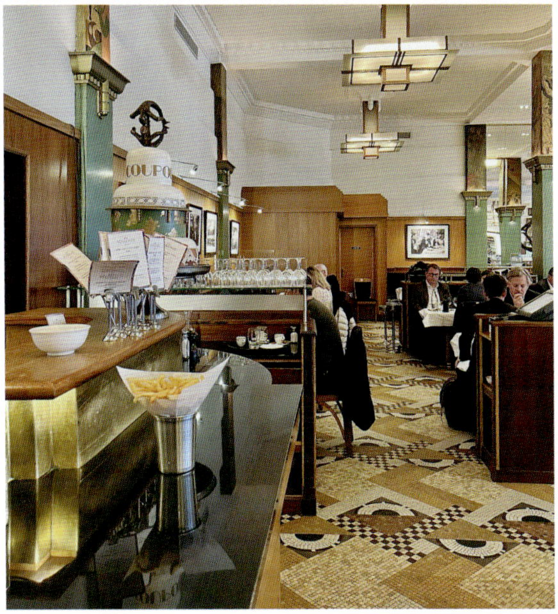

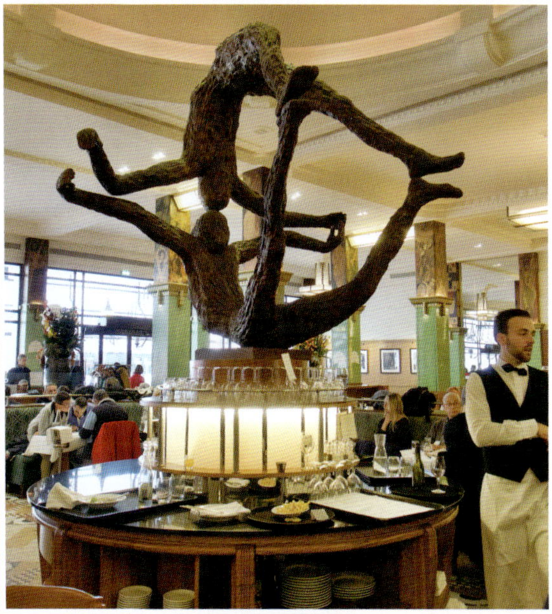

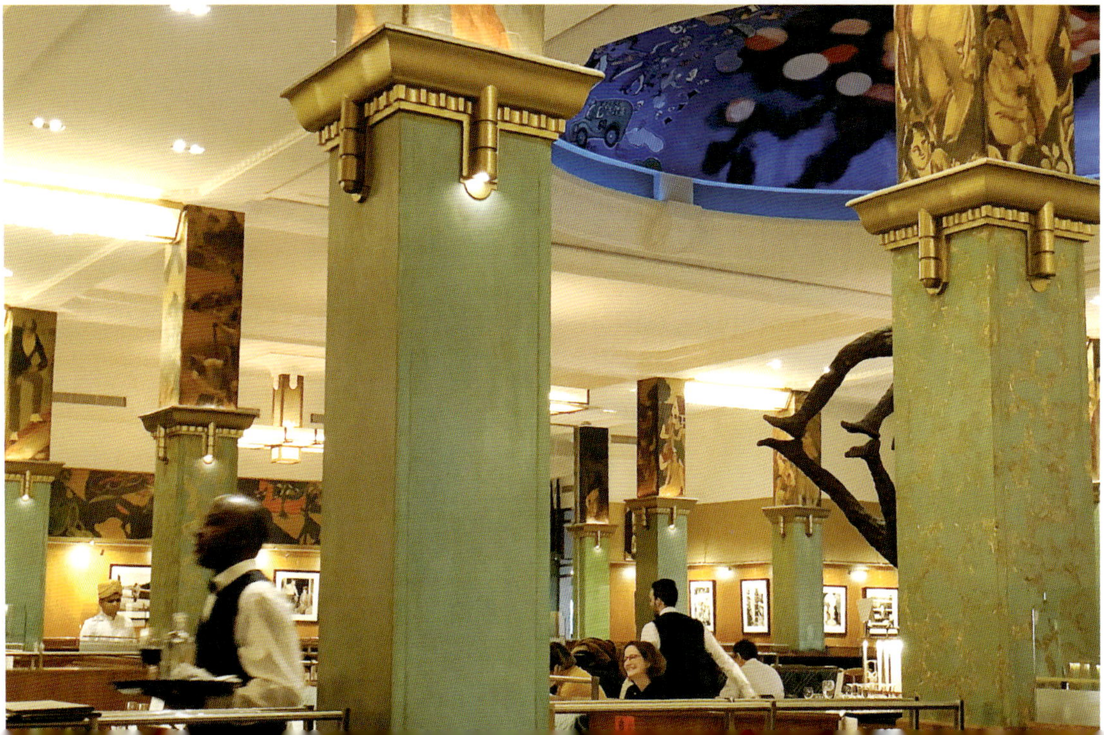

LA CLOSERIE DES LILAS

"...I thought of the waiter at the Closerie de Lilas who had been forced to cut his mustache when they made the American bar at the Closerie...."

Ernest Hemingway, *A Moveable Feast*

On the edge of Montparnasse, La Closerie des Lilas, with its lilac terrace, planted there since 1847, was originally a country inn, then a café, followed by a bistro; and now it's a brasserie, restaurant, and piano bar. Historically a home base for artists, politicians, composers, and writers, Charles Baudelaire, Honoré de Balzac, and Émile Zola were habitués in the 19th century, and Paul Cezanne, Samuel Beckett, Paul Verlaine, August Strindberg, Georges Braque, Pierre Bonnard, André Derain, Amadeo Modigliani, Pablo Picasso, Gertrude Stein, Vladimir Lenin, André Gide, Oscar Wilde, Ezra Pound, F. Scott Fitzgerald, and Samuel Beckett frequented the establishment in the 20th century. Hemingway wrote about it in *A Moveable Feast* and penned some of *The Sun also Rises* in-situ. Its literary prize is given to women who write in French, and there are brass plates with the names of the famous patrons who all delighted in the terrace, an enchanting lilac (*lilas)* garden.

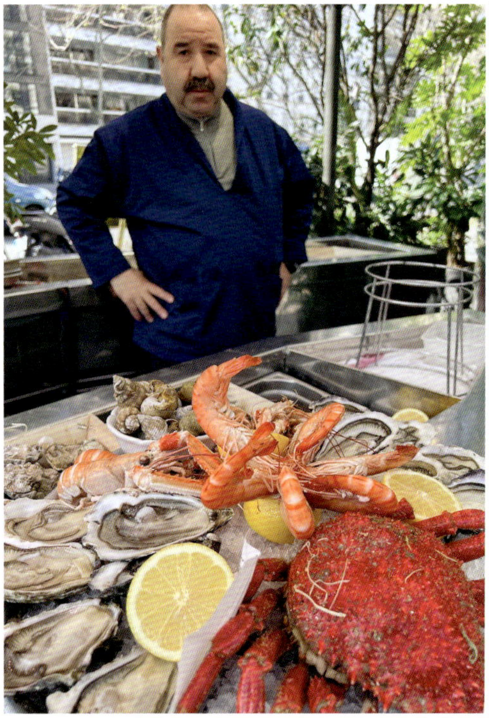

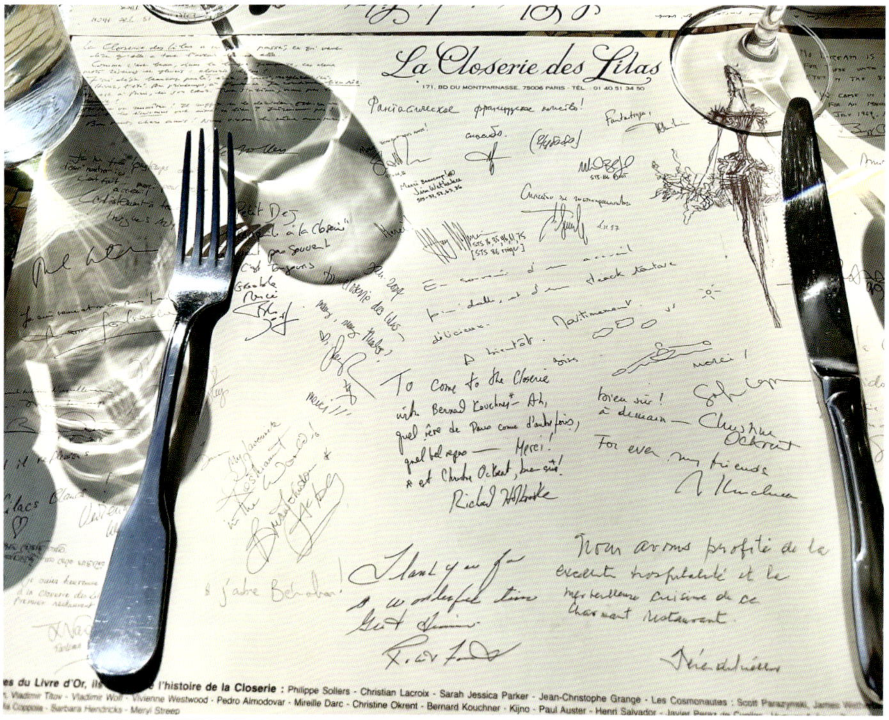

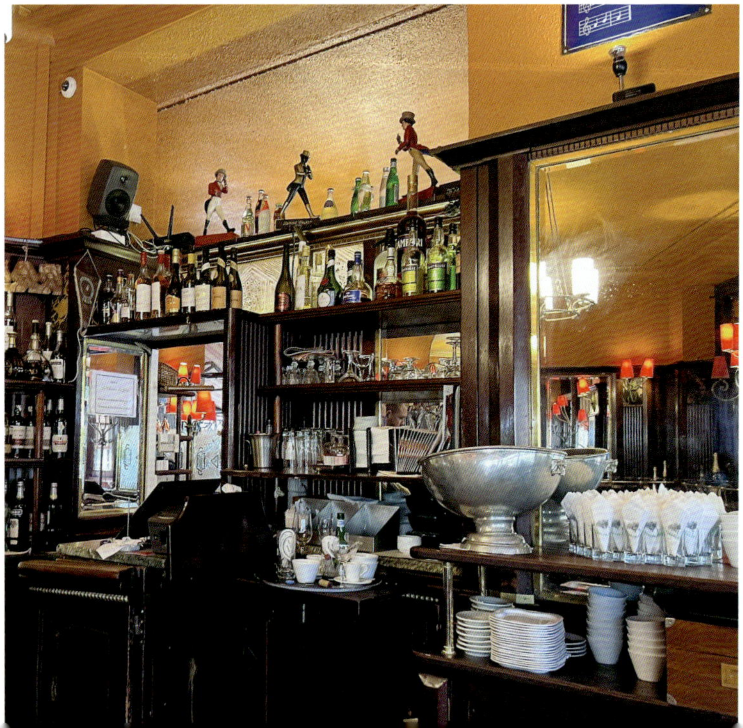

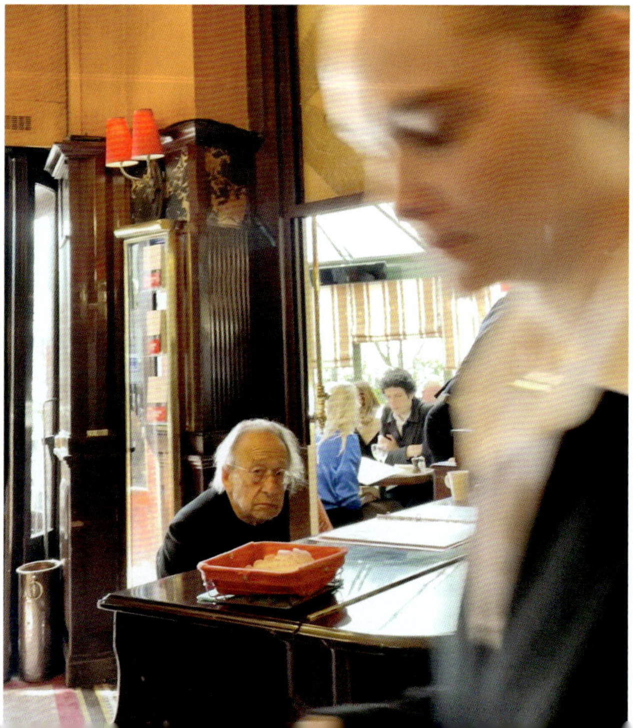

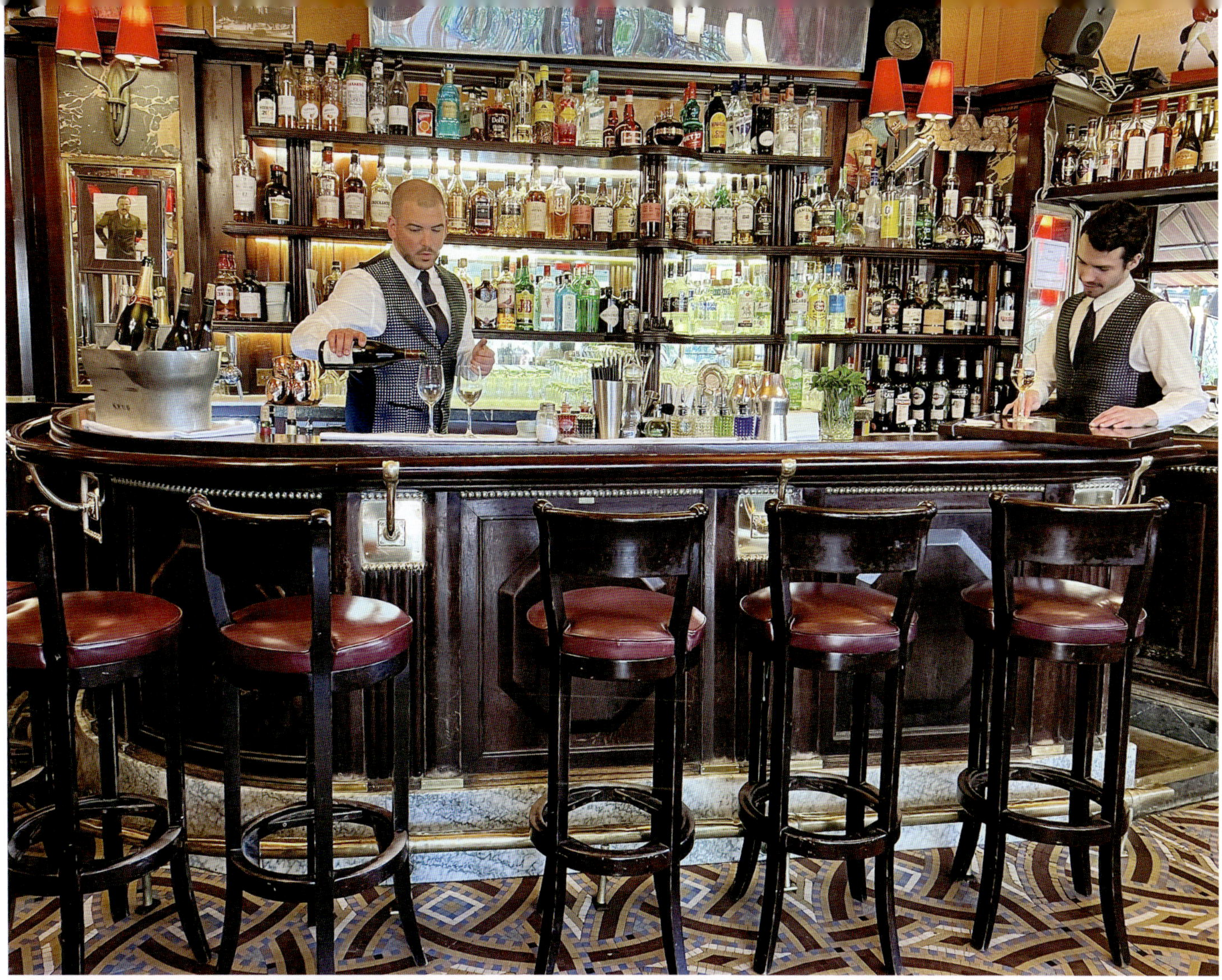

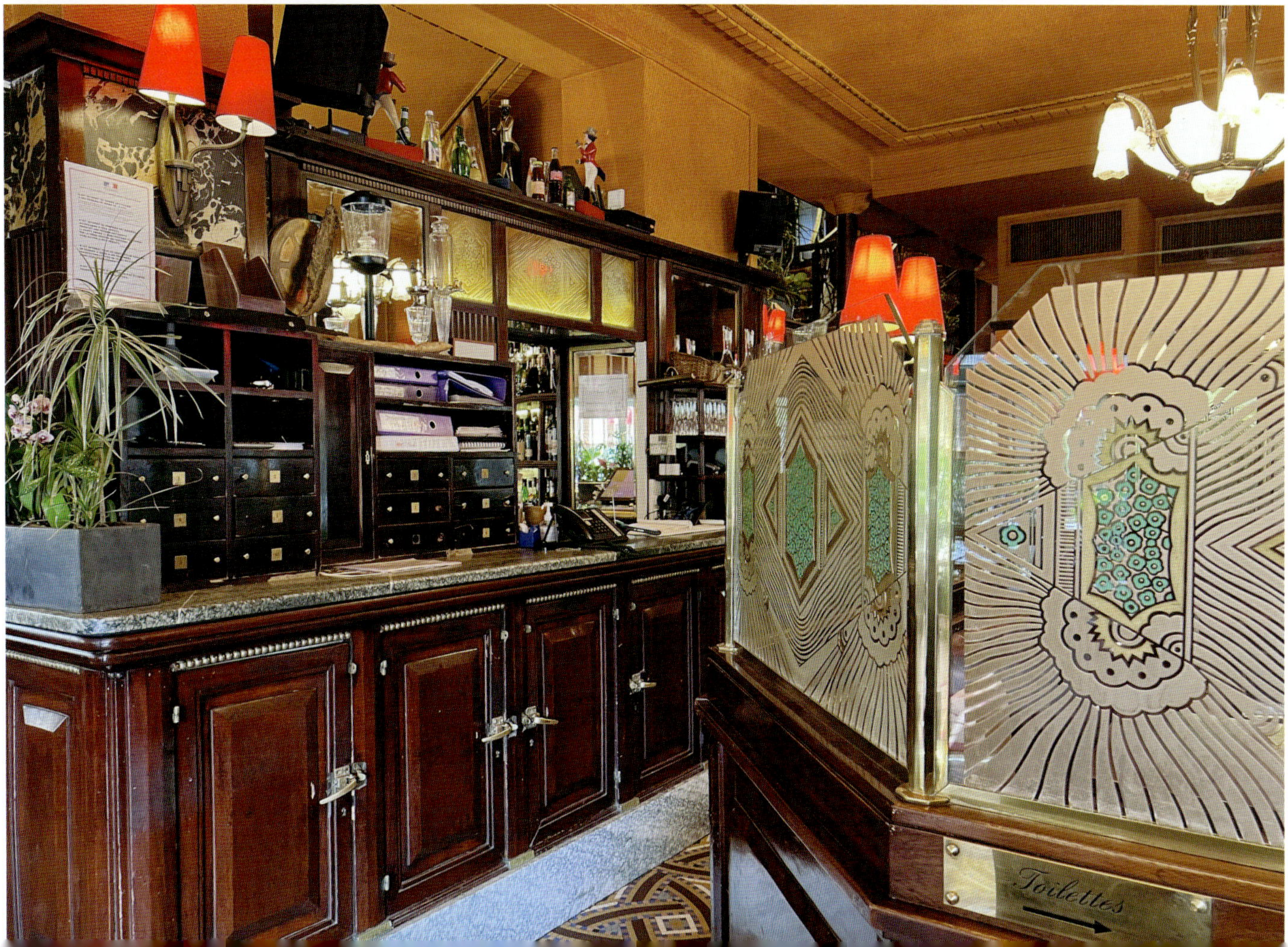
Toilettes

Saint-Germain-des-Prés

"One's home and studio are private, but in the evening, one did not have to be lonely because one could always walk into certain cafés and find friends gathered there...it was unplanned, free, casual."

Anaïs Nin

The legendary Saint-Germain-des-Prés quarter in the 6th arrondissement, is filled with a multitude of cafés, bistros, and brasseries. However, the fabled four still stir our imagination and, despite the tourists and the tariffs, are always worth a journey. While neighbors and rivals, Deux Magots and Café Flore, were established in the late 19th century, their great renown came in the early-to-mid-20th century when these cafés became the central axis for Surrealism, Existentialism, Feminism, and New Wave filmmakers. Famous habitués Jean-Paul Sartre, Simone de Beauvoir, and Albert Camus could be seen at their regular tables writing and arguing about politics, literature, and philosophy while sipping a single espresso for hours on end. Just across Saint-Germain, the historic Brasserie Lipp was founded in 1880 by Alsatian Léonard Lipp, one of the many who fled Alsace when it was annexed to Germany after the Prussian War. The fourth storied haunt, Le Bonaparte, is just around the corner on rue Bonaparte; where else?

The lavish 1920s interior at the legendary Brasserie Lipp is encrusted with decorative hand-painted tile by Léon Fargues, surrounded by expansive mirrors, and topped with Italianate painted ceilings. These are a backdrop for the correct, authentic brasserie food enjoyed by such luminaries as Colette, Proust, Gide, Hemingway, Max Ernst, de Chirico, Picasso, Giacometti, Calder, Riopelle, Sam Francis, Joan Mitchell, and every French president from Charles de Gaulle to Emmanuel Macron. During the 1930s it was a hotbed of political intrigue. Maintaining a menu that hasn't changed for decades and an upright and polished staff, the literati and politicians continue to meet in this frozen-in-time institution.

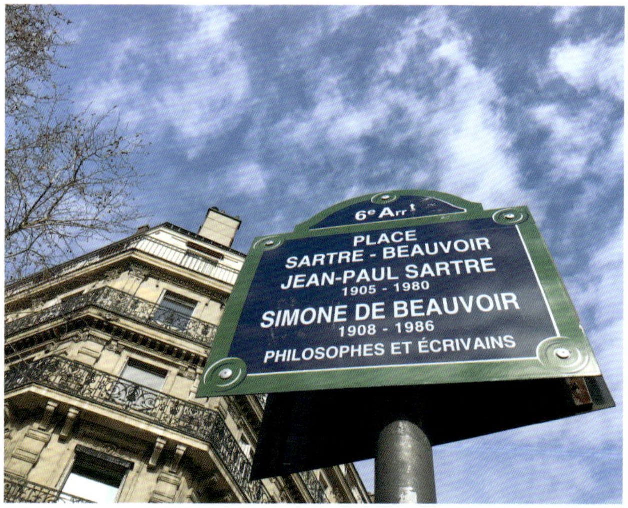

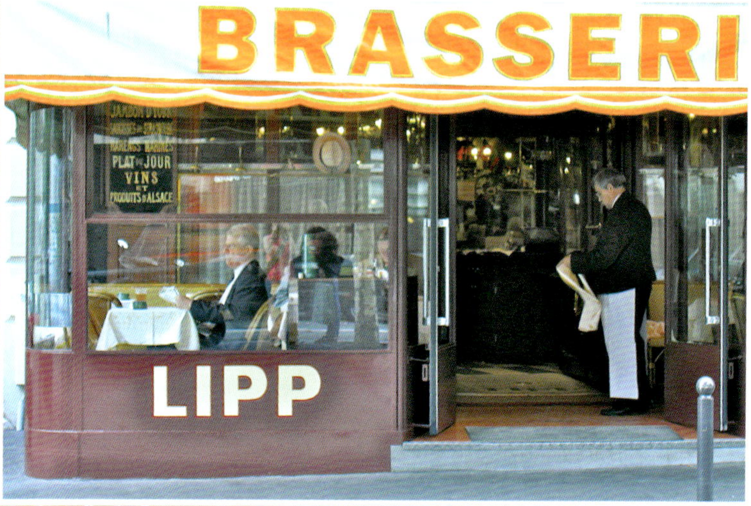

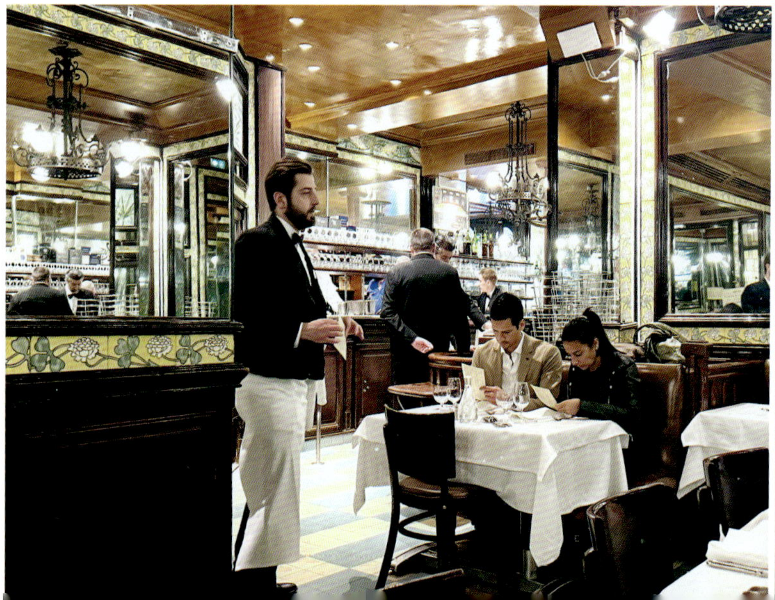

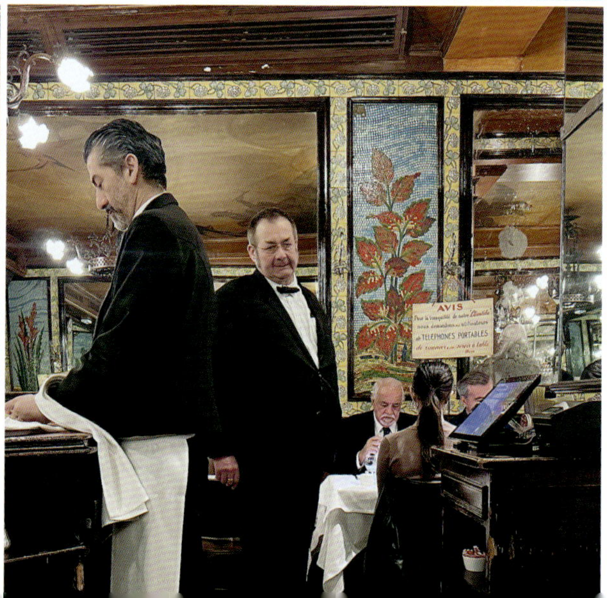

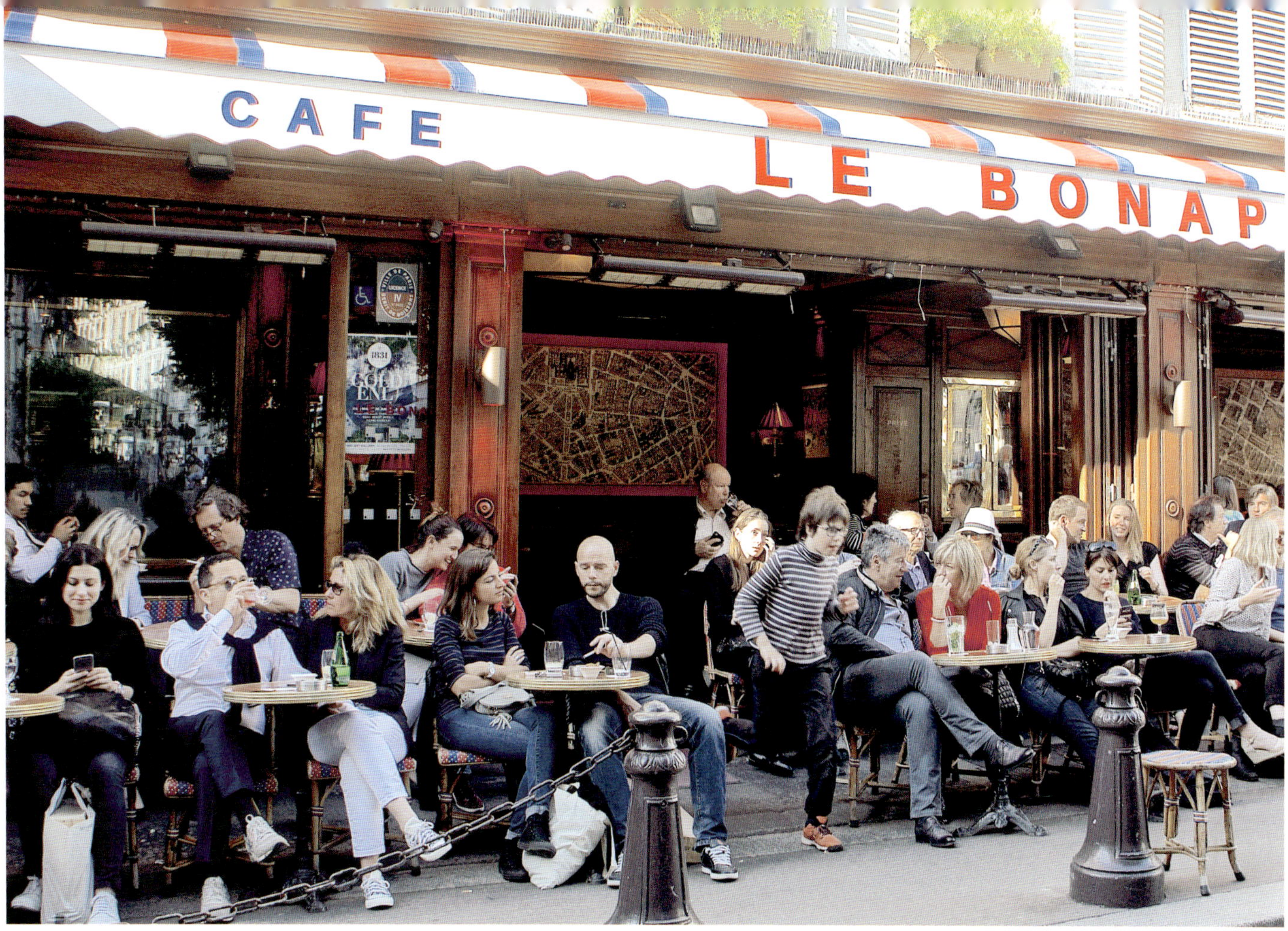

Classic with a twist: Café Bonaparte has been on the corner of the rue Bonaparte since 1873 and, though less illustrious than its three legendary neighbors, its view of Saint-Germain-des-Prés, along with its softer vibe and light, organic offerings are well worth a stop before or after traversing rue Bonaparte, awash with antique and art galleries leading to *La Seine*.

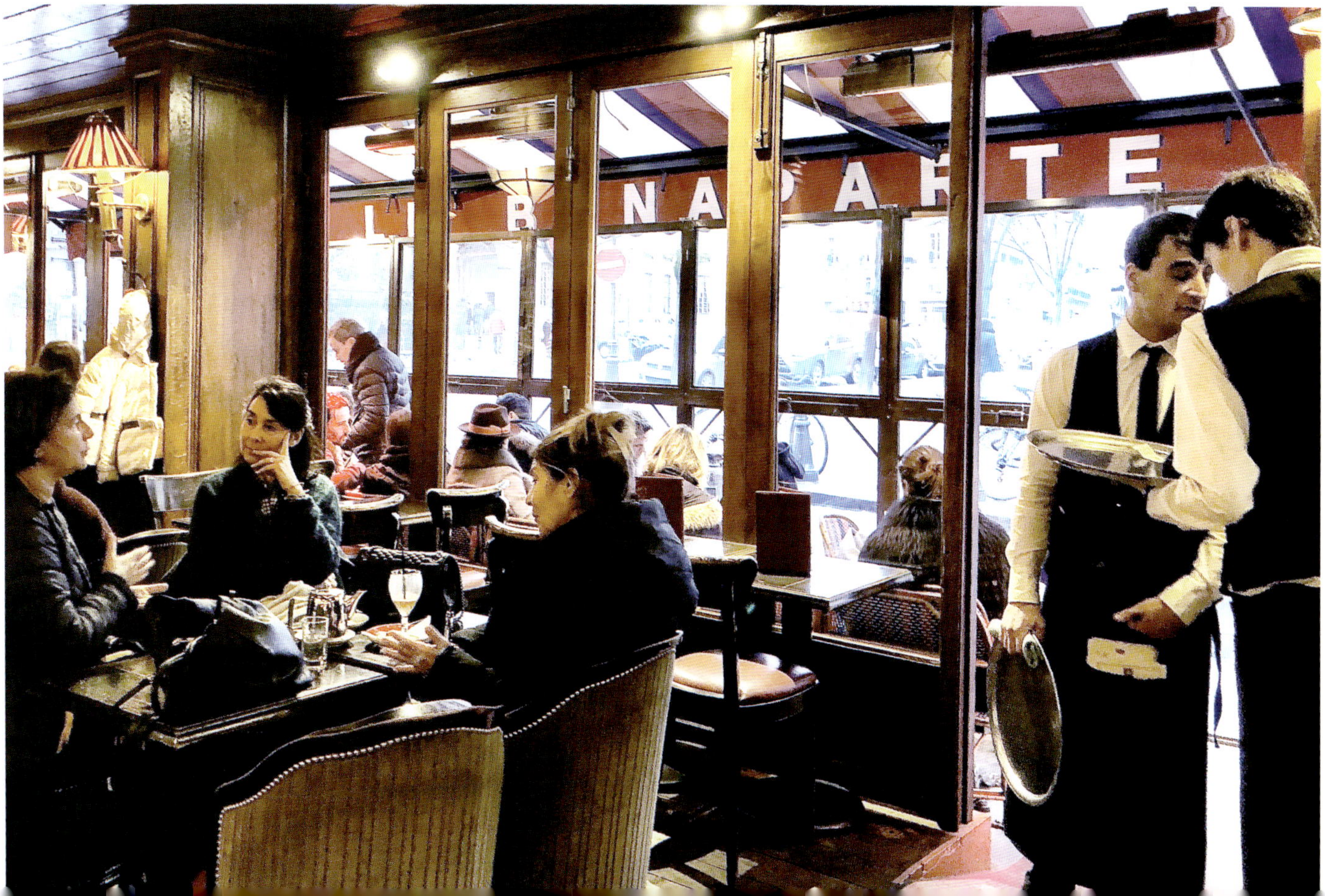

CAFÉ DE FLORE

"The roads of the Flore have been the roads of liberty."
Jean-Paul Sartre

No need to be deterred when you find its terrace brimming with tourists; simply wait a bit, and a table will be liberated shortly. Inside, you will be led to a table, outside it's catch as catch can. Café de Flore arrived on the Paris scene sometime between 1875-1887 (the actual date now in dispute) on the magnificent new Haussmann boulevard, Saint-Germain. Over the decades, a diverse procession of notables including Laurence Durrell, Truman Capote, Chagall, Picasso, Hemingway, the Giacometti brothers, Derain, Zadkine, Trotsky, Zhou Enlai, Brigitte Bardot, Alain Delon, Juliette Gréco, and Jean-Paul Belmondo have installed themselves at its tables. Here, Apollinaire and Breton invented Surrealism, and James Baldwin wrote *Go Tell It on the Mountain*. Between the wars, it became a workspace for the likes of Simone de Beauvoir (who never entirely abandoned Le Dôme), Jean-Paul Sartre, and Sartre's nemesis, Albert Camus. The warmth of the large heater placed in the center of the space in 1939 by new owner Paul Boubal reached all the way to the upper floor, providing a warmer living space than most Paris apartments. Le Flore continues to attract celebrities who, like de Beauvoir and Sartre, are more likely to select a discreet indoor table than the crowded terrace. Yes, an espresso is expensive, but you do not come to Le Flore or any legendary Paris café for an espresso. You are there to take a seat, to savor the moment, to experience the café lifestyle, and to step back into another time to another Paris. You are there to create a memory—your memory. In the morning, you accompany the experience with the perfect *petit déjeuner*; in the afternoon, the delicious profiteroles or *chocolat chaud*, perhaps a pastis at *l'heure de l'apéritif*—all served with the polish of the expert waitstaff. Café de Flore is indeed worth the price of admission.

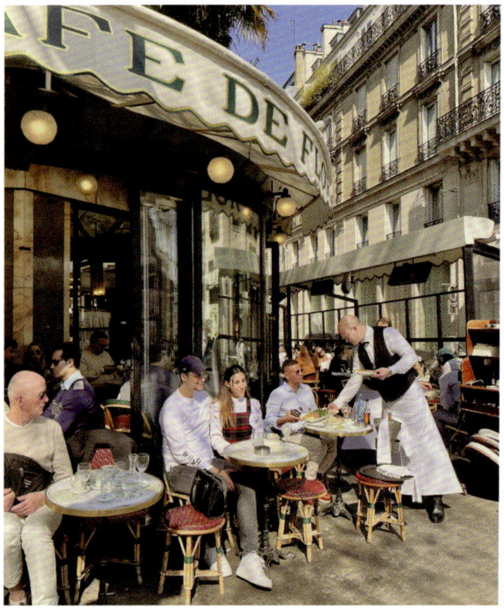

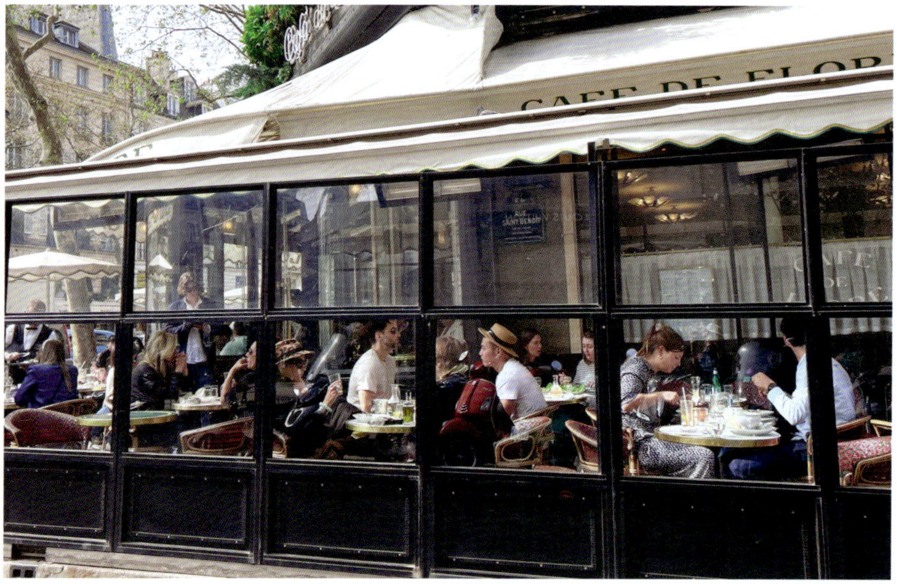

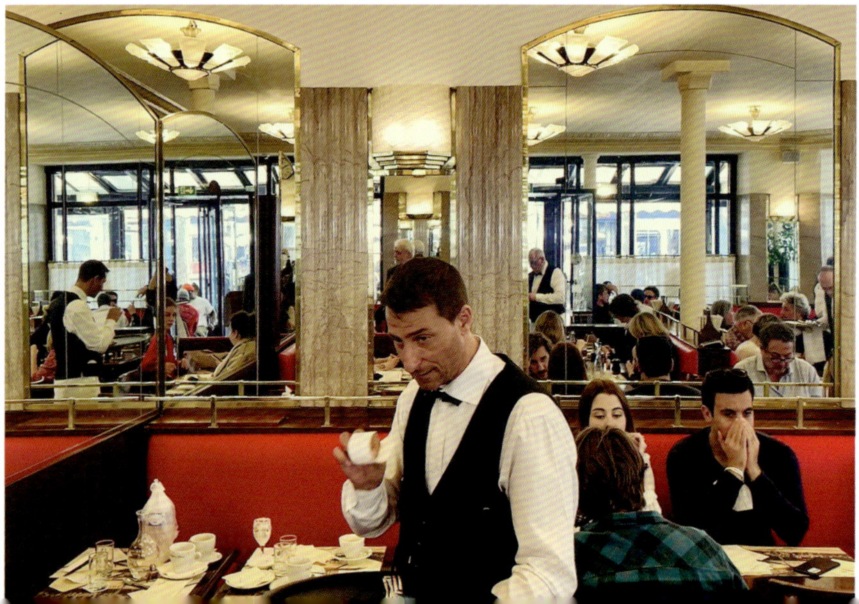

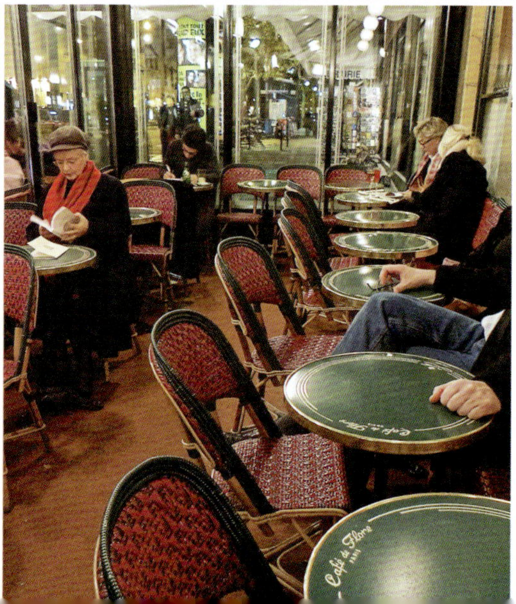

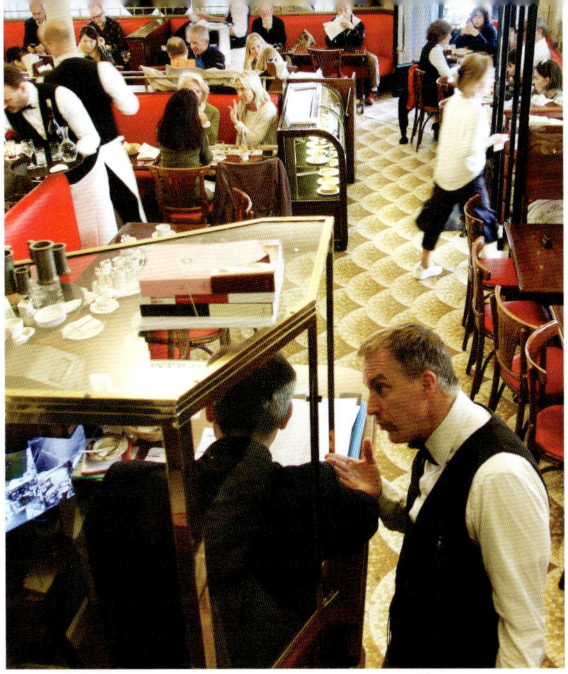

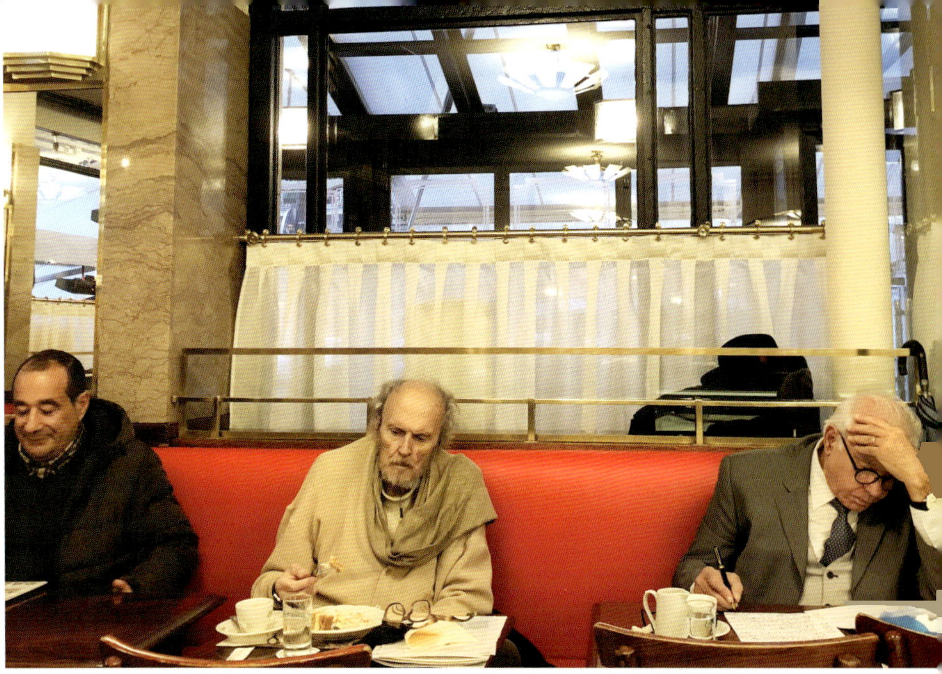

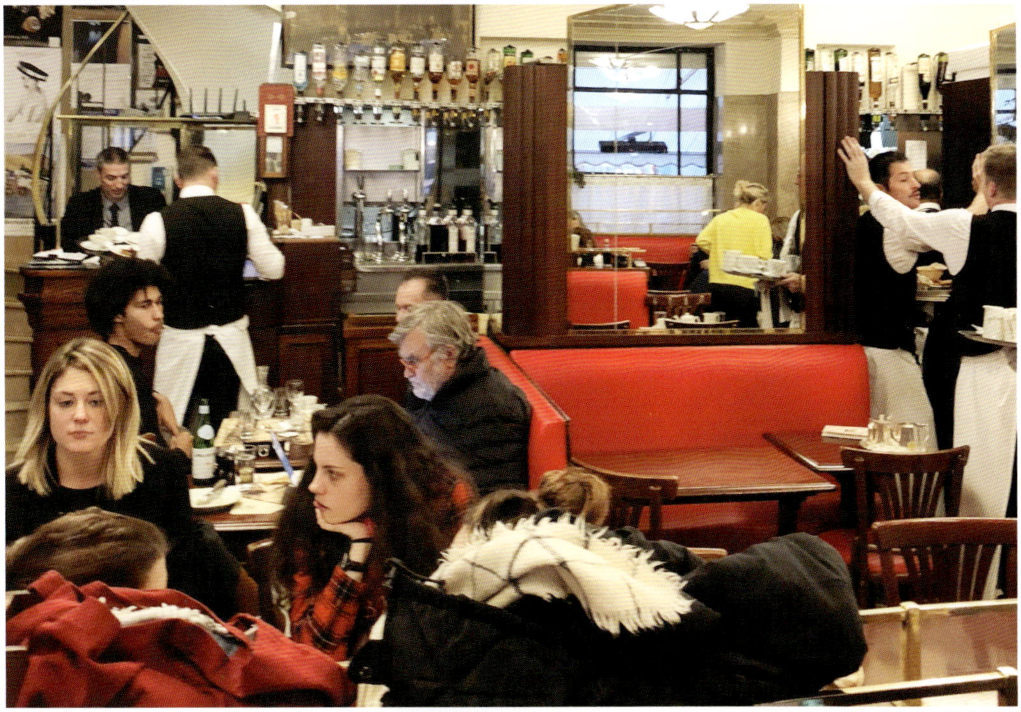

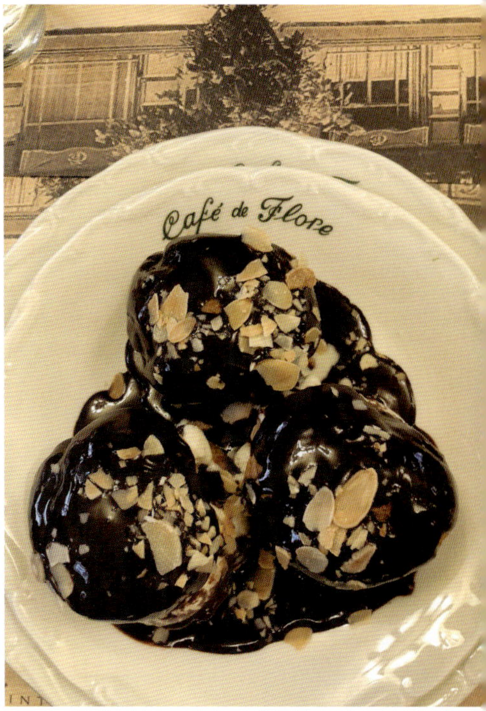
Café de Flore

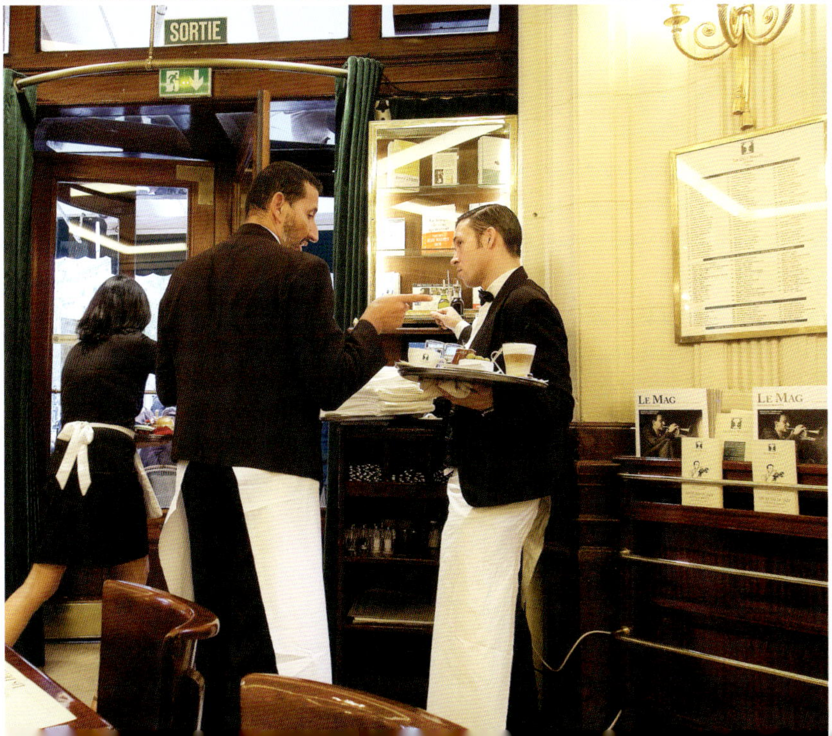
SORTIE
LE MAG
LE MAG

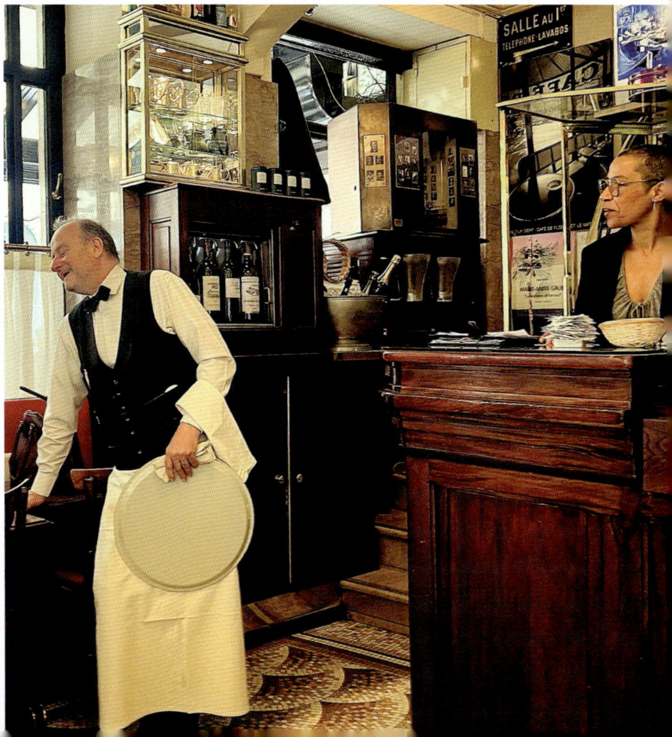
SALLE AU 1er
TELEPHONE LAVABOS

LES DEUX MAGOTS

"On Sundays, we sat at the Deux Magots and watched the people, devout as an Opera Chorus, enter the old doors or else watched the French read newspapers."

Zelda Fitzgerald, 1924

Hosting perhaps even more tourists on its terrace than its neighbor, Café de Flore, Les Deux Magots—originally a shop selling fabric and novelties—was transformed into a café in 1885. The original Deux Magots sculptures of Chinese mandarins ("*magot*" means Chinese figurine) still watch over the interior from on high. Every few decades, the name morphs from the original "Aux Deux Magots" to "Café des Deux Magots" to "Les Deux Magots," today's moniker. Many of the literary and artistic set regularly rotated between the Deux Magots and its rival, Café de Flore, and in 1945, Sartre and de Beauvoir quit the latter for Deux Magots. Proudly boasting "*Café Litteraire*" on its awning, Deux Magots, like several other historic literary cafés, has given out a literary prize since 1933. Paul Verlaine, Guillaume Apollinaire, André Breton, Arthur Rimbaud, Stéphane Mallarmé, Oscar Wilde, Pablo Picasso, Alberto Giacometti, Francis Picabia, André Derain, Fernand Léger, Louis Aragon, Paul Éluard, James Joyce, Ernest Hemingway, Bertolt Brecht, Stefan Zweig, Aldous Huxley, André Gide, Le Corbusier, and Juliette Gréco were among the celebrated habitués. At these tables, Oscar Wilde, in his last year of life, came every morning for breakfast and every evening for a glass of Absinthe. It is here that Picasso met Dora Maar and here that Apollinaire and Breton invented Surrealism (though Le Flore has claimed this as well)! Today, as in the past, rivalries between the two cafés remain among tourists and regulars, who sometimes embrace either Flore or Deux Magots or sometimes drift between the two. Contemporary notables—artists, writers, editors, publishers, filmmakers, and journalists—still choose the more private interior, often at quiet times of the day.

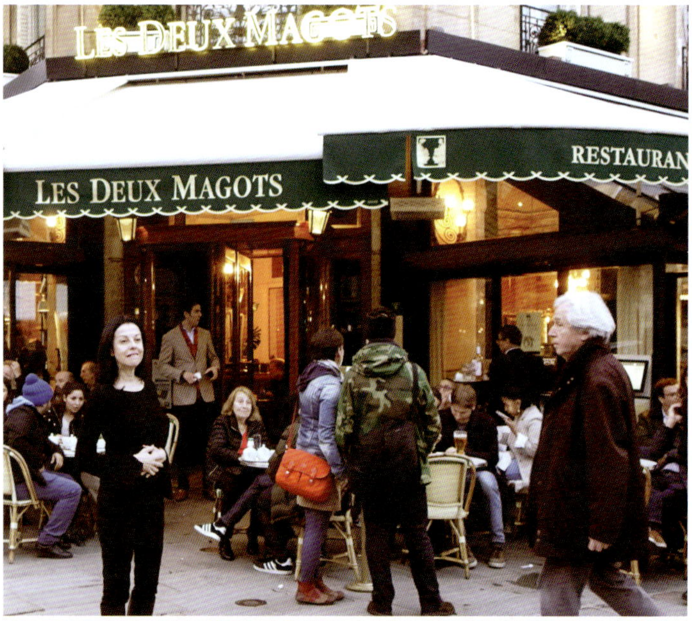

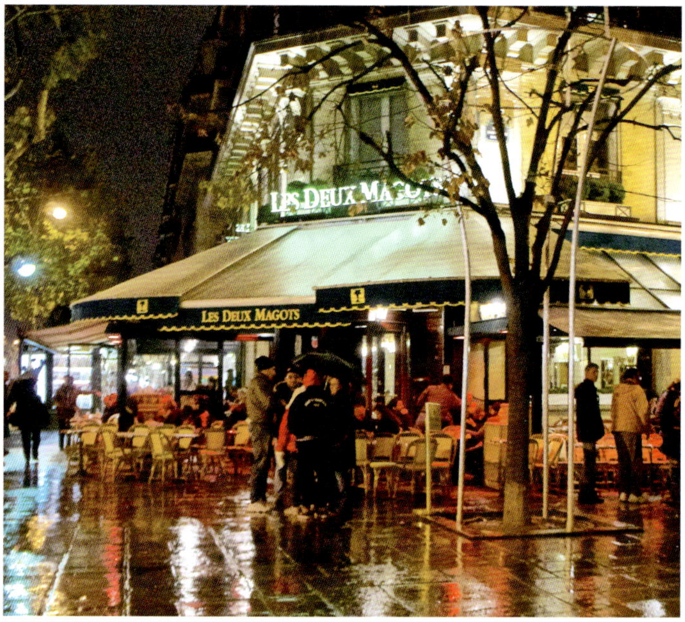

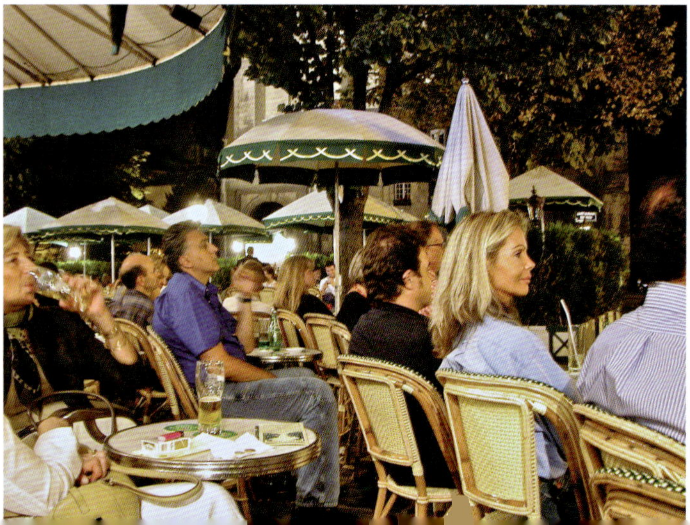

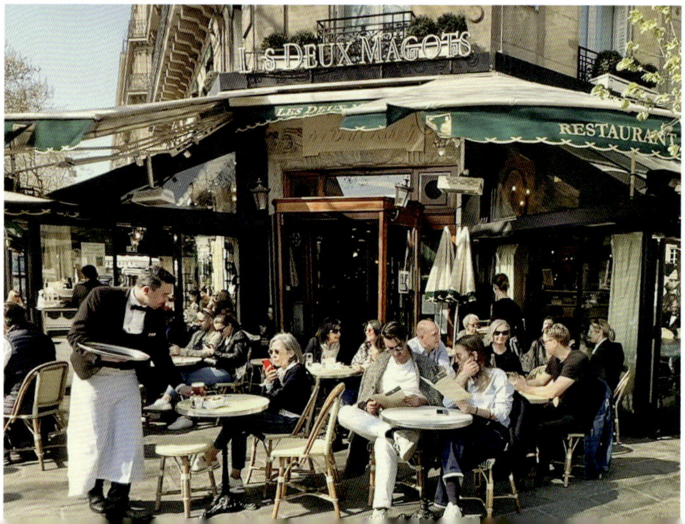

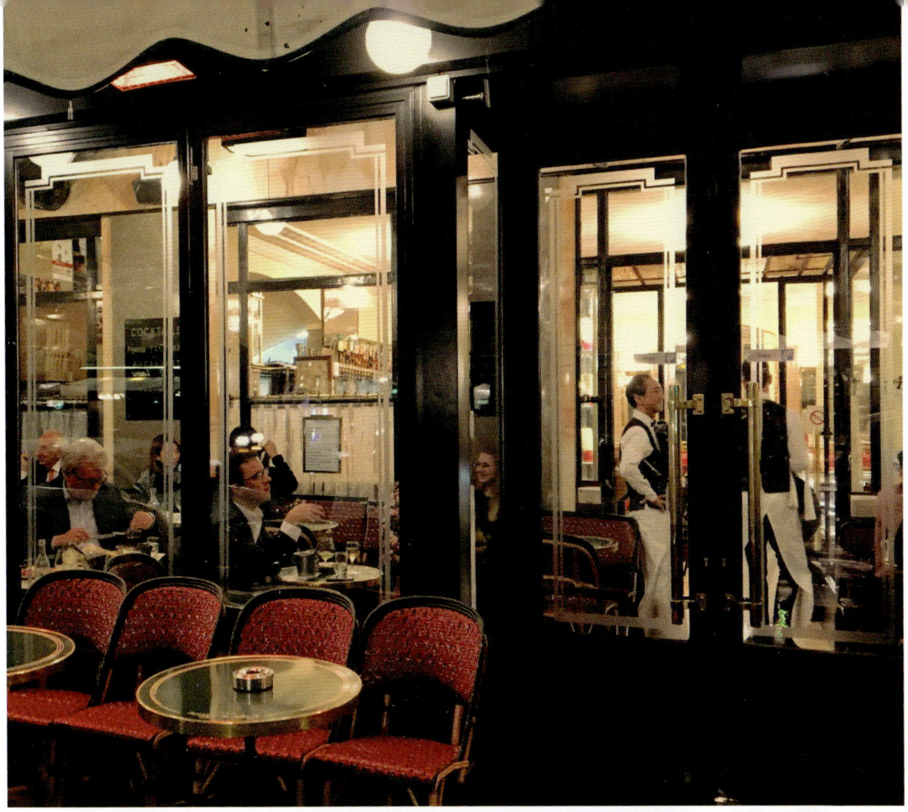

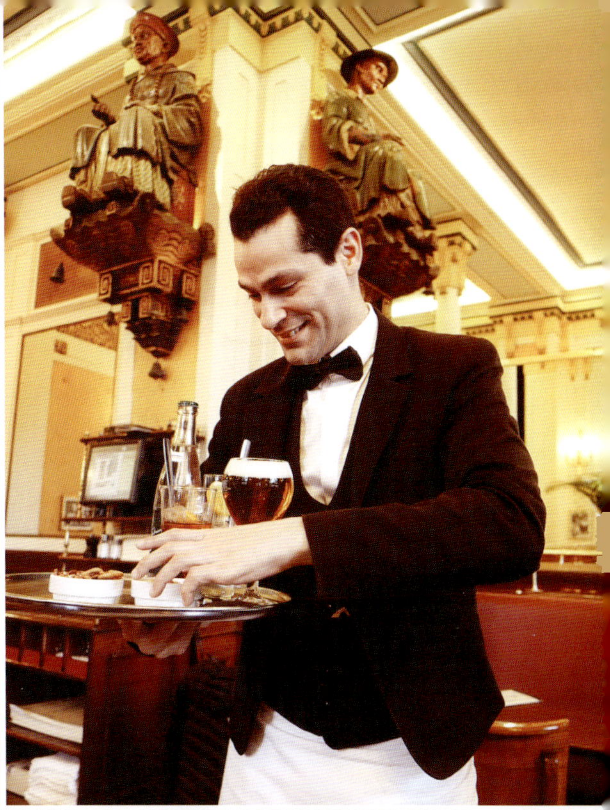

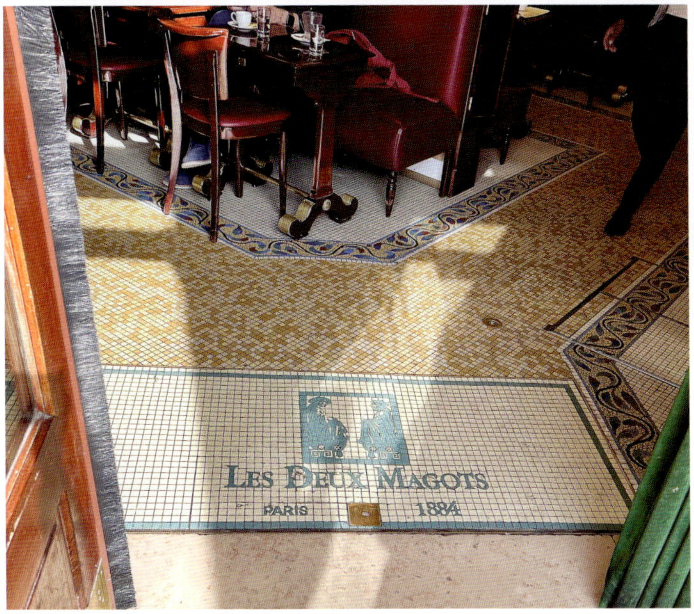
LES DEUX MAGOTS
PARIS 1884

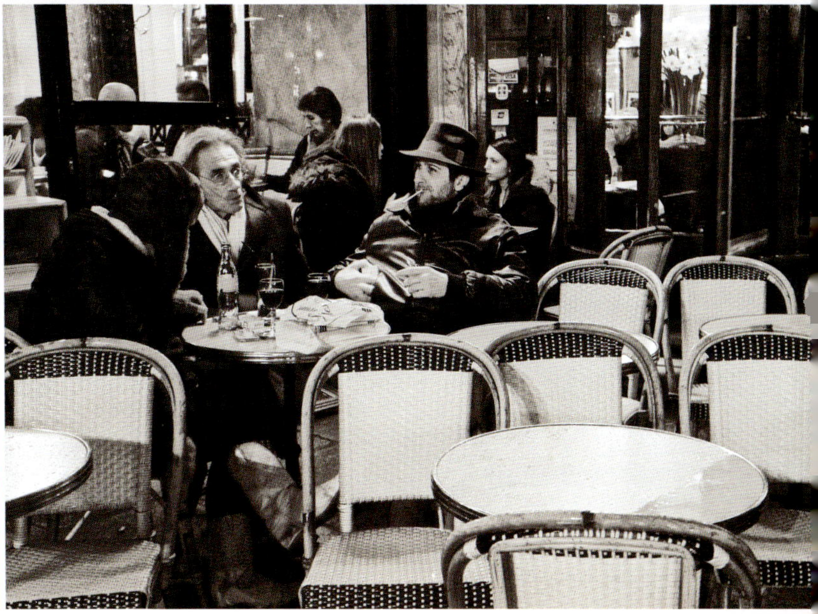

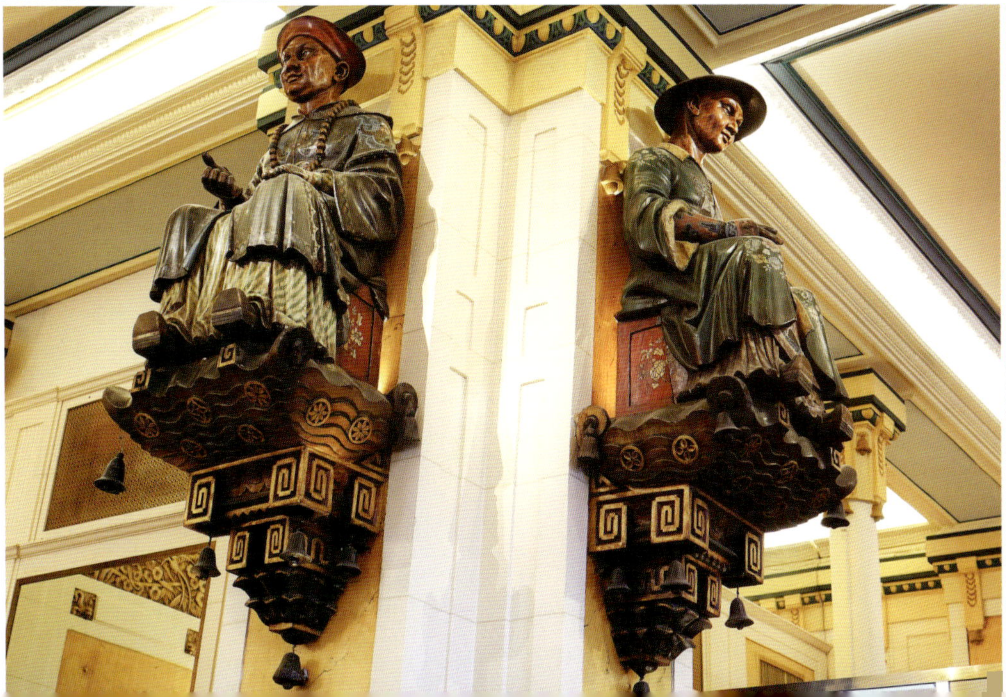

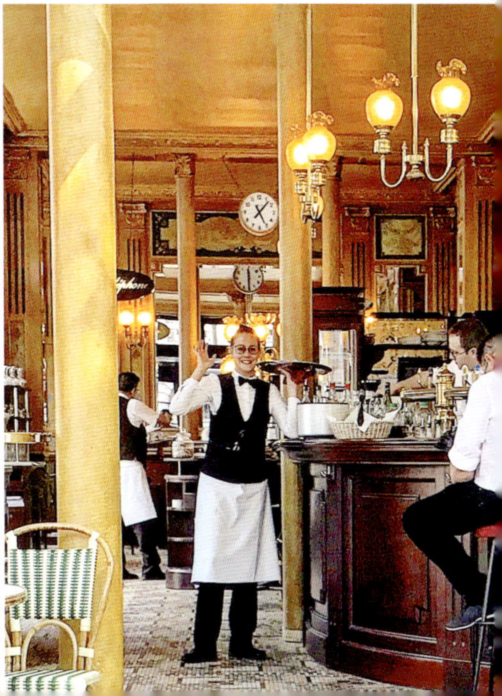

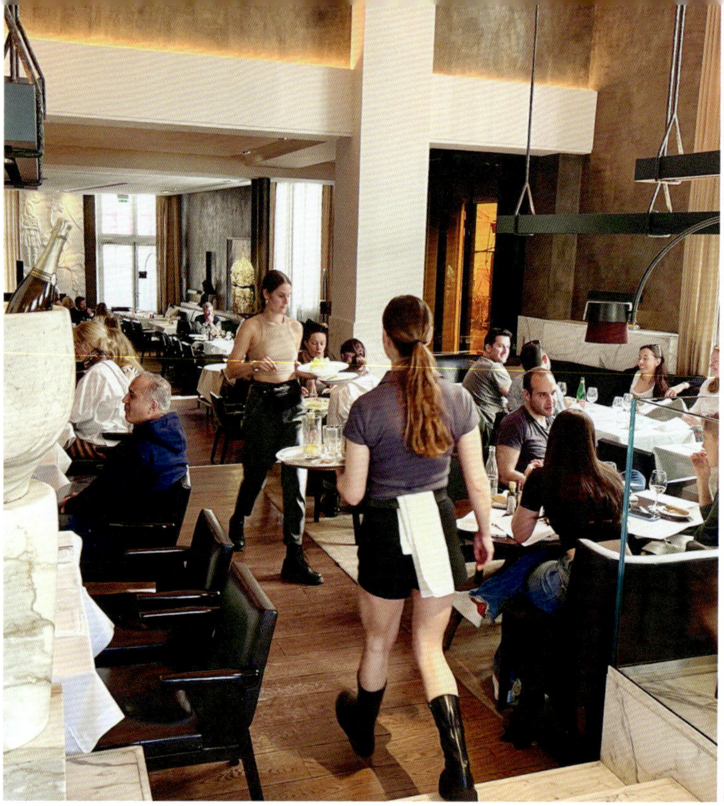

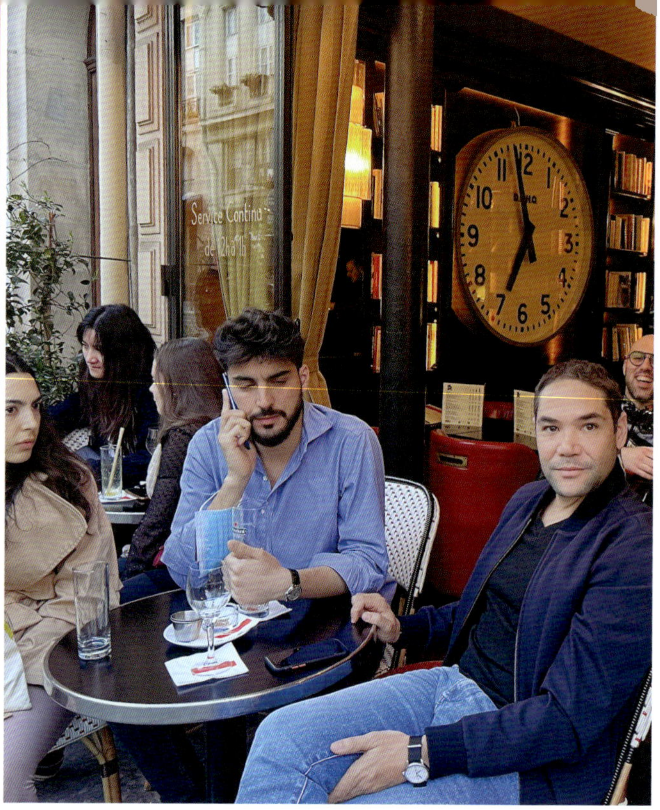

The Costes Brothers have brought the oh-so-chic and elegant La Société to the legendary bastion of Café Society in Saint-Germain-des-Prés. Designed by Christian Liaigre and frequented by well-known personalities, this clearly 21st-century café serves a fresh, organic menu.

Step away from Saint-Germain-des-Prés in any direction and an abundance of cafés fill the vistas. Along with boutiques, art galleries, antique shops, bookstores, cozy museums, the Luxembourg Gardens, and Le Bon Marché, the legendary bohemian, intellectual 6th arrondissement is chock full of more marvelous cafés than one can visit in a year. While the historic, artistic, literary cafés beckon, this most elegant neighborhood invites a stop at a myriad of charming cafés and bistros.

With terraces rounding the corner of the much-traversed intersection of rue Bonaparte and rue Jacob, Le Pré aux Clercs serves classic French dishes, including crêpes, with a taste of vegetarian fare. Family-owned since its opening in 1954, the Au Sauvignon wine bar serves a light fare that highlights delicious regional wines by the glass.

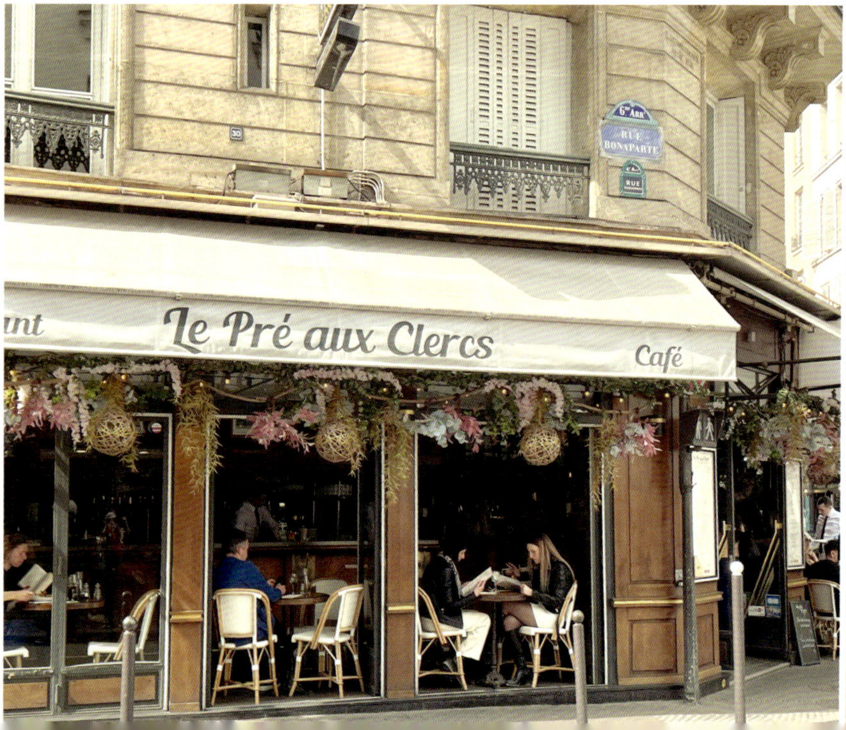

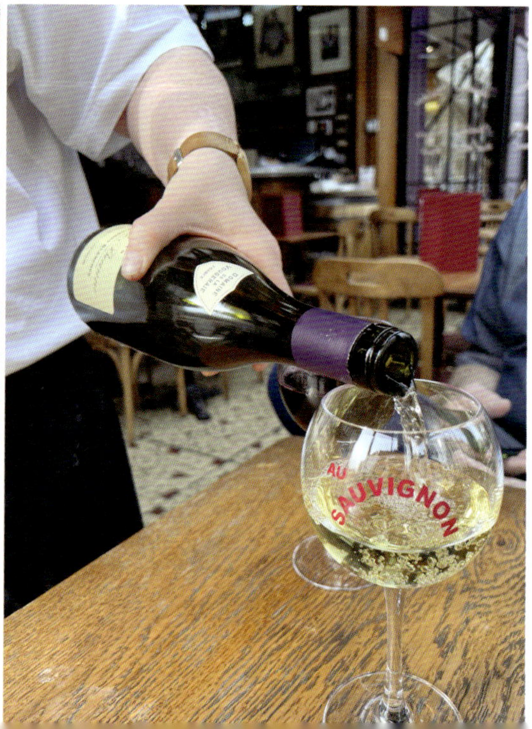

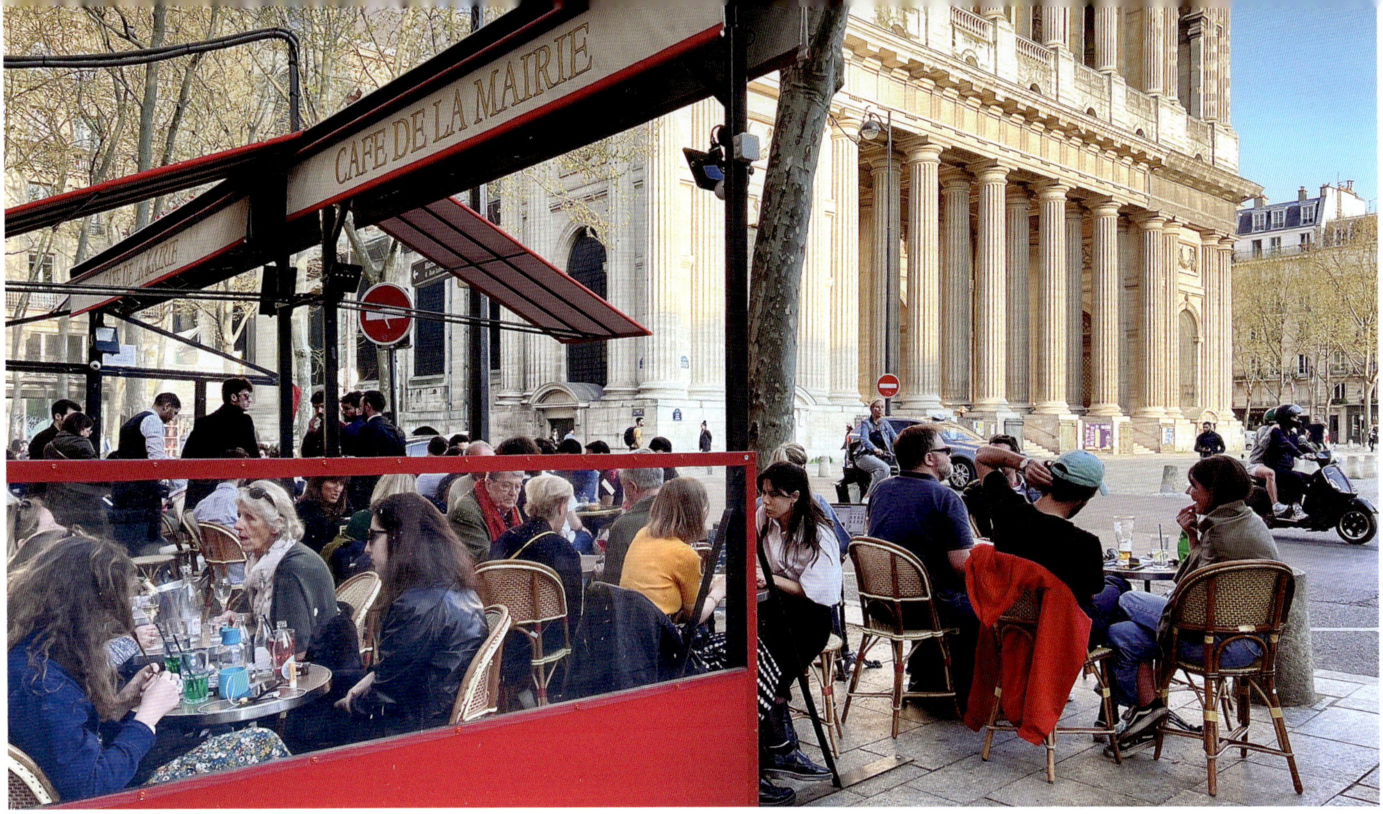

Facing St. Sulpice and sporting an overflowing two-part terrace and a Formica and brass detailed interior, Café de la Mairie harkens back to Paris in the '70s. Come for the view and its salads full of meat, seafood, and cheese, with but a few lettuce leaves.

At the historic Le Tournon, African-American writers, artists, and musicians gathered, Duke Ellington played Jazz, and the circle around George Plimpton's *Paris Review* met in the '40s and '50s. The establishment delivers a well-executed bistro menu near the Sénat and Luxembourg Gardens.

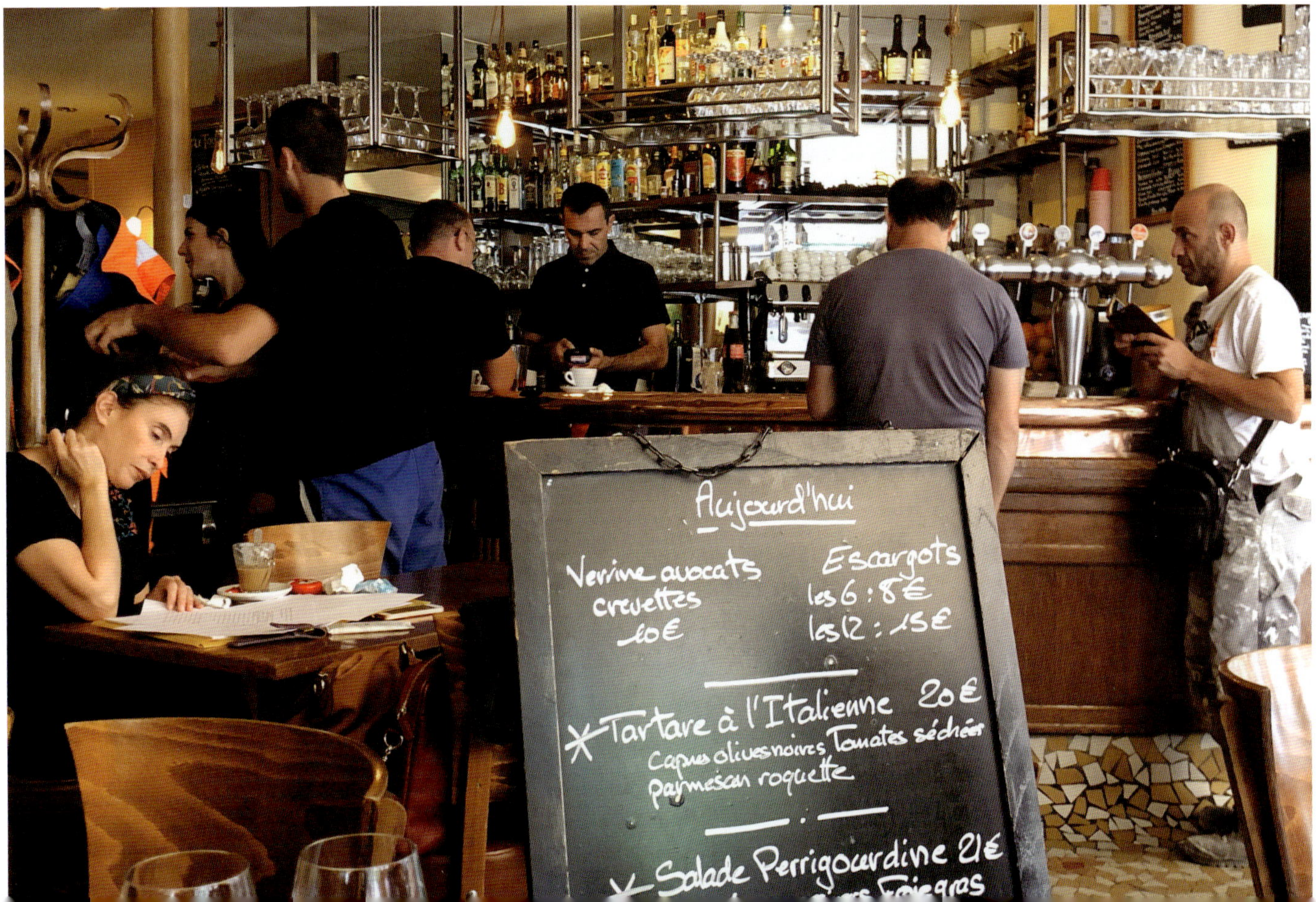

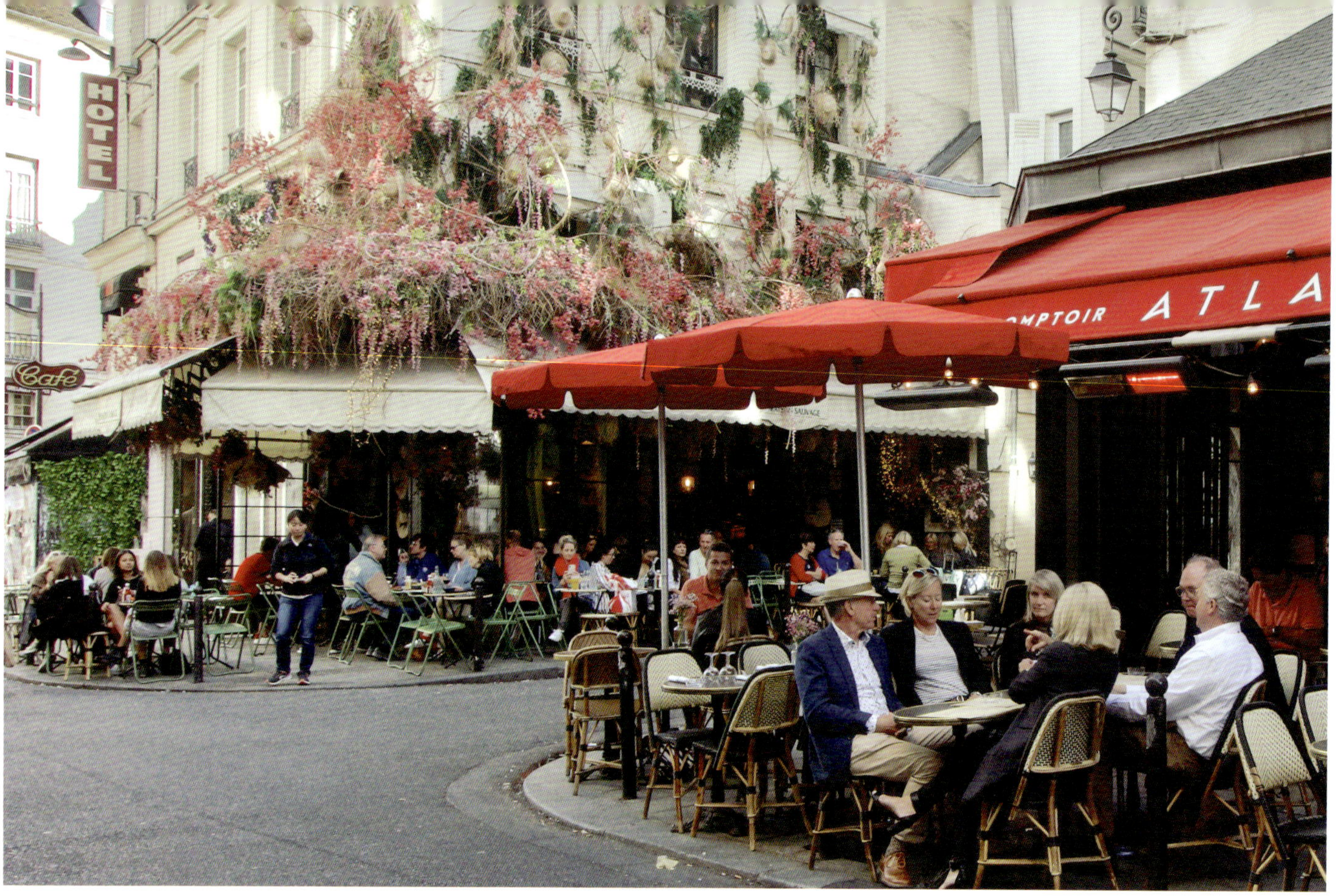

One of the oldest streets in Paris, rue de Buci, remains a beloved pedestrian street with an outdoor market—one of over 75 neighborhood markets in Paris—Tuesday through Sunday. Here, café terraces adorning both sides of the road attract a youthful crowd.

With absolutely charming design from the exterior to the cozy interior up to the second floor, Maison Sauvage serves simple, mostly healthy dishes. Those tempted by fresh seafood would do well to try L'Atlas across the street rather than take in Sauvage's fanciful design and simple fare.

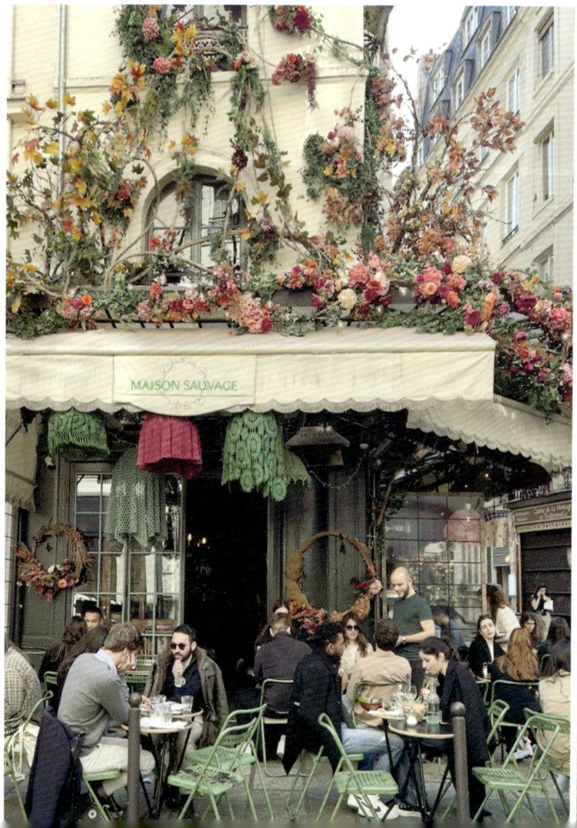

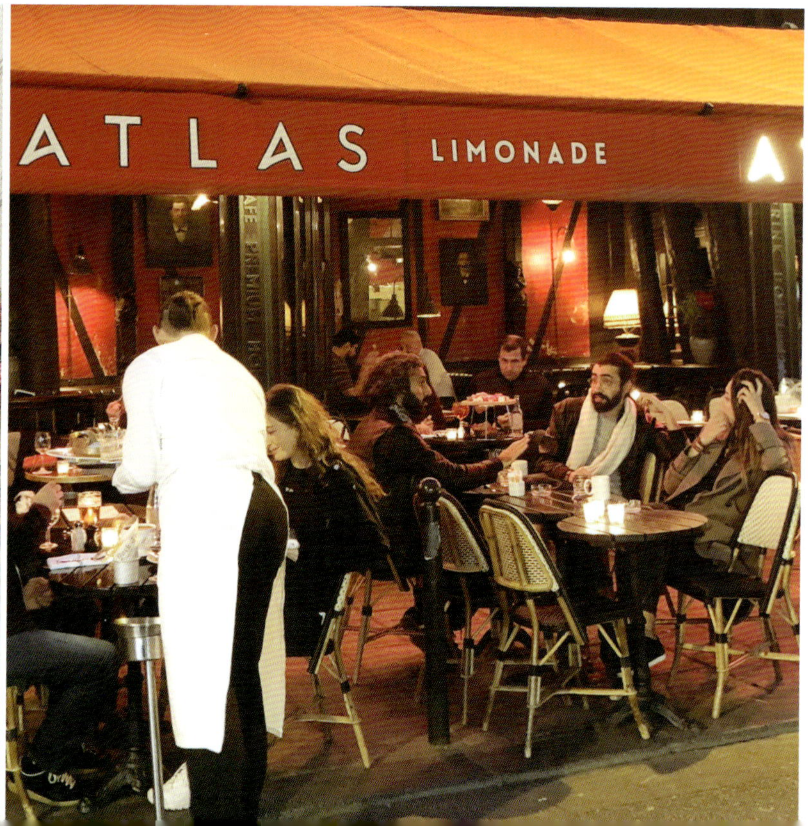

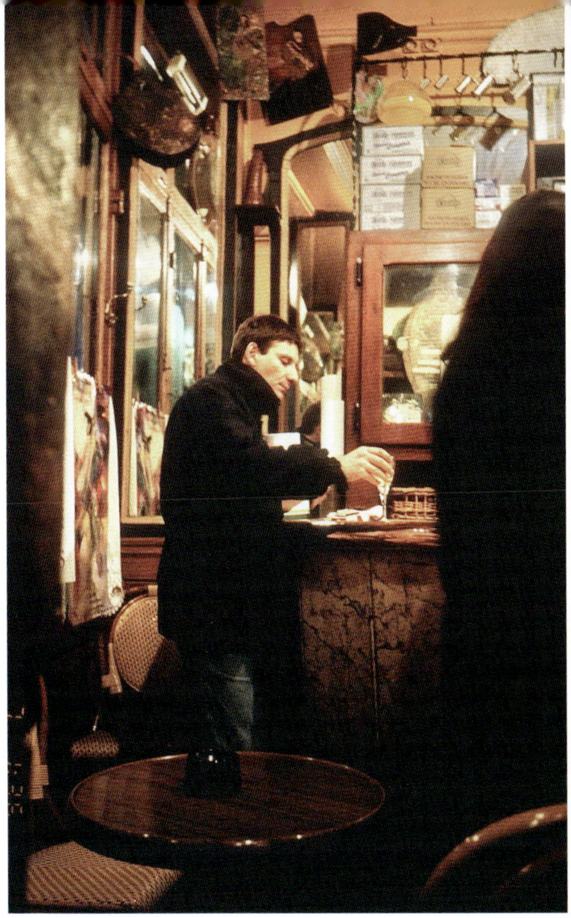

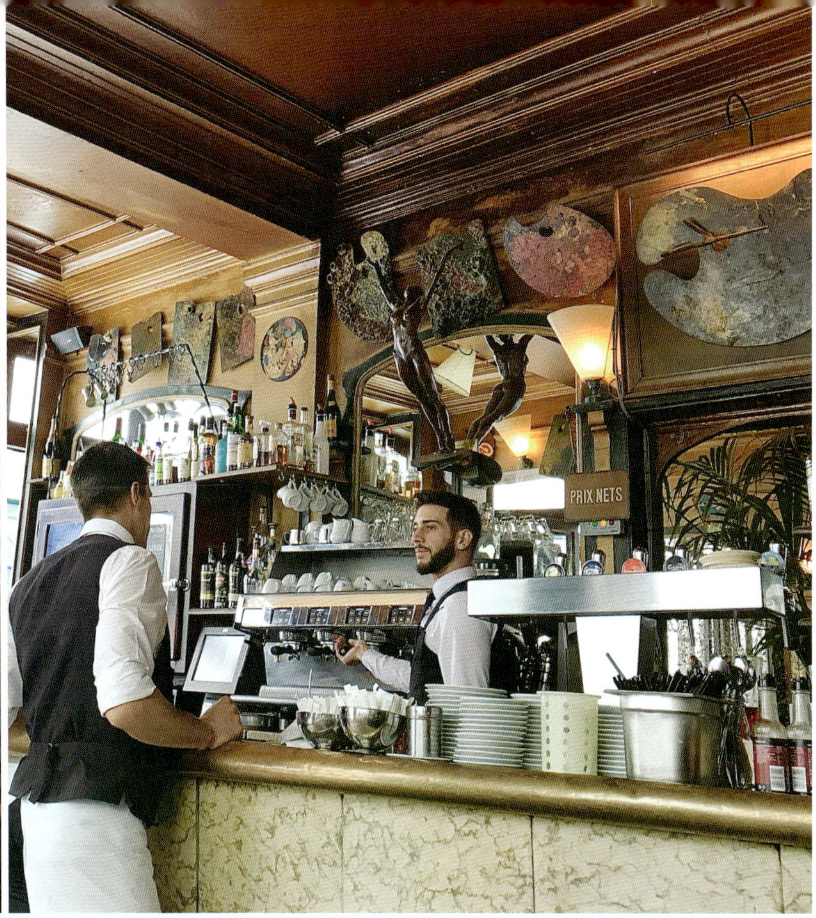

Located on art gallery lush, rue de Seine, near the École des Beaux-Arts, a visit to La Palette provokes a dilemma as to whether to sit on the lively terrace or in the overwhelmingly appealing vintage interior. The terrace is always hopping, overflowing with artists, art lovers, students, locals, and tourists, spilling out into the street in summer. Yet it's tempting to sit inside because the interior is glorious and gets even better the further back you go, past the bar with genuine artists' palettes. From its inception in the 1930s, it has received an art-world clientele of gallery owners, artists, writers, musicians, connoisseurs, and superstars like Cézanne, Picasso, Hemingway, Georges Braque, Jim Morrison, and former French president Jacques Chirac, who was a regular. La Palette's front window and backroom were listed as a Historical Monument on May 23, 1984.

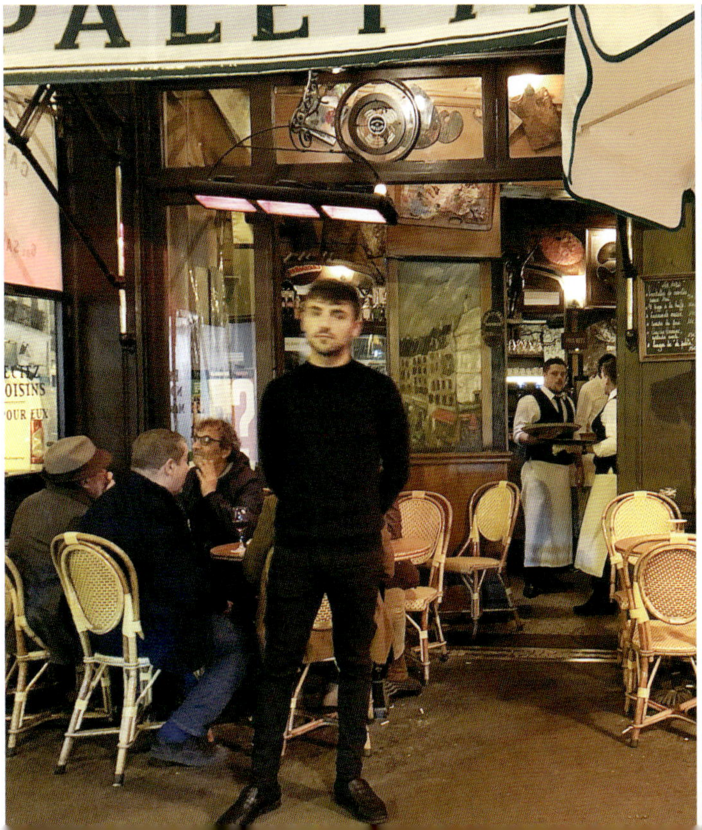

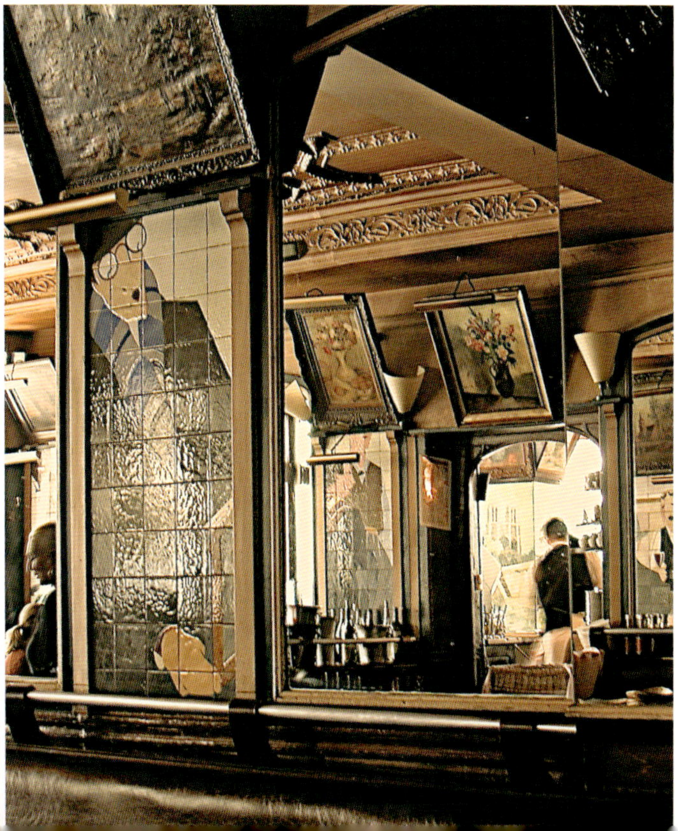

Le Marais

"Discovering a new street in Paris, or a new café, is much more interesting to me than visiting an old château or cathedral in some godforsaken hamlet."

Anaïs Nin

The gorgeous Place des Vosges in the Marais, originally the Place Royale, was built by Henri IV in the early 17th century as residences for the nobility around a lovely garden. It is the oldest planned square in Paris and became a prototype for the European square. This aristocratic neighborhood, spread across the 3rd & 4th arrondissements, fell into disrepair after the Revolution. Restored and preserved in the mid-to-late 20th century, the Place des Vosges and the Marais has again become one of Paris's most stylish quarters with trendy cafés, fashion houses, museums, hip galleries, and creative shops. From classic Ma Bourgogne, and elegant Carette, to trendy Café Hugo, stopping for an espresso, an *apéritif*, or a meal, under the arched arcades of the Place des Vosges, is a meditation. Wandering from here and crisscrossing the back streets, you'll find the treasures of the Marais and the "Haut Marais," cafés and bistros that span the gamut from historic to trendy and are waiting to be discovered.

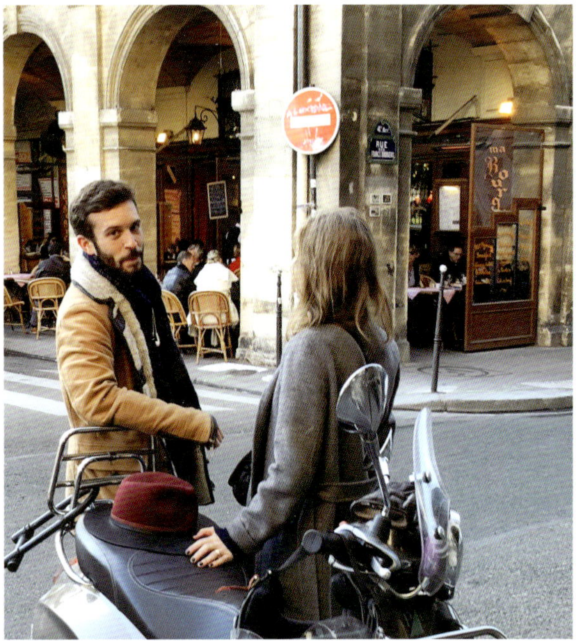

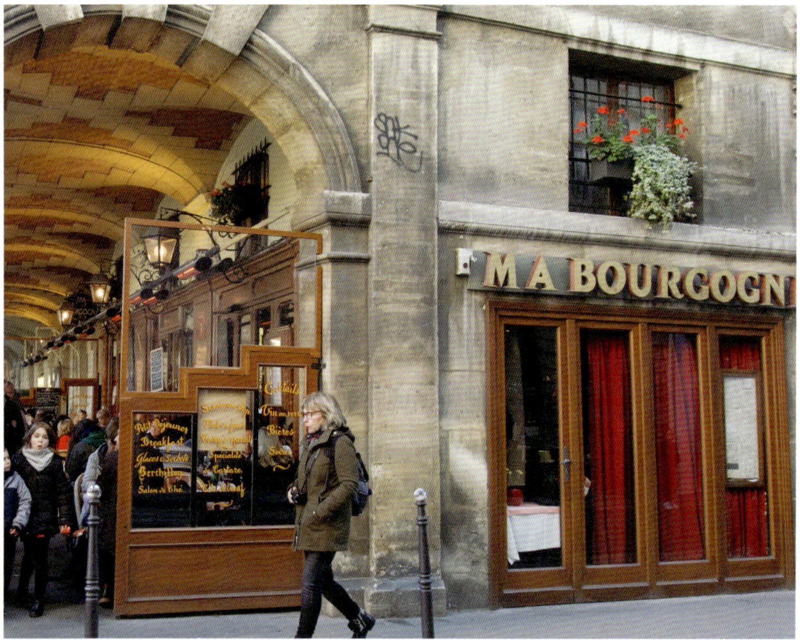

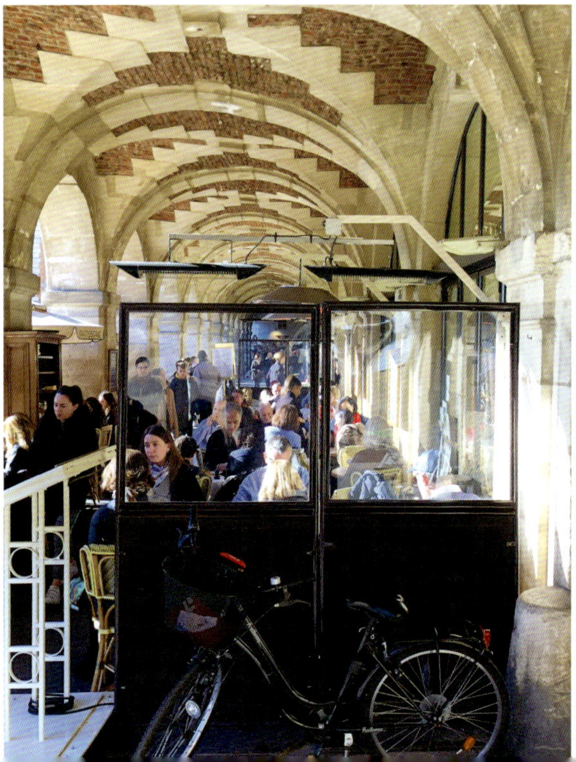

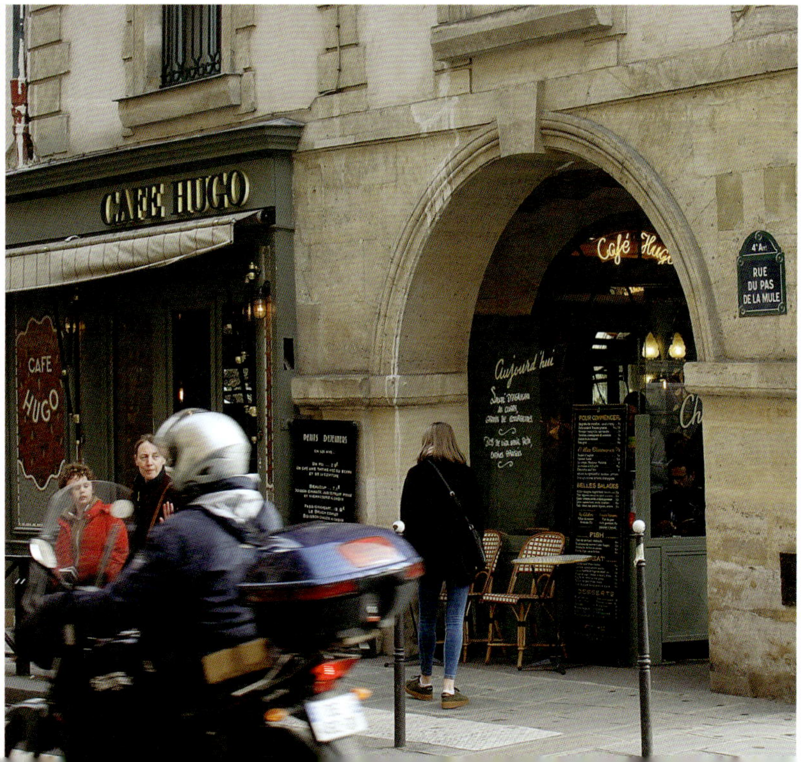

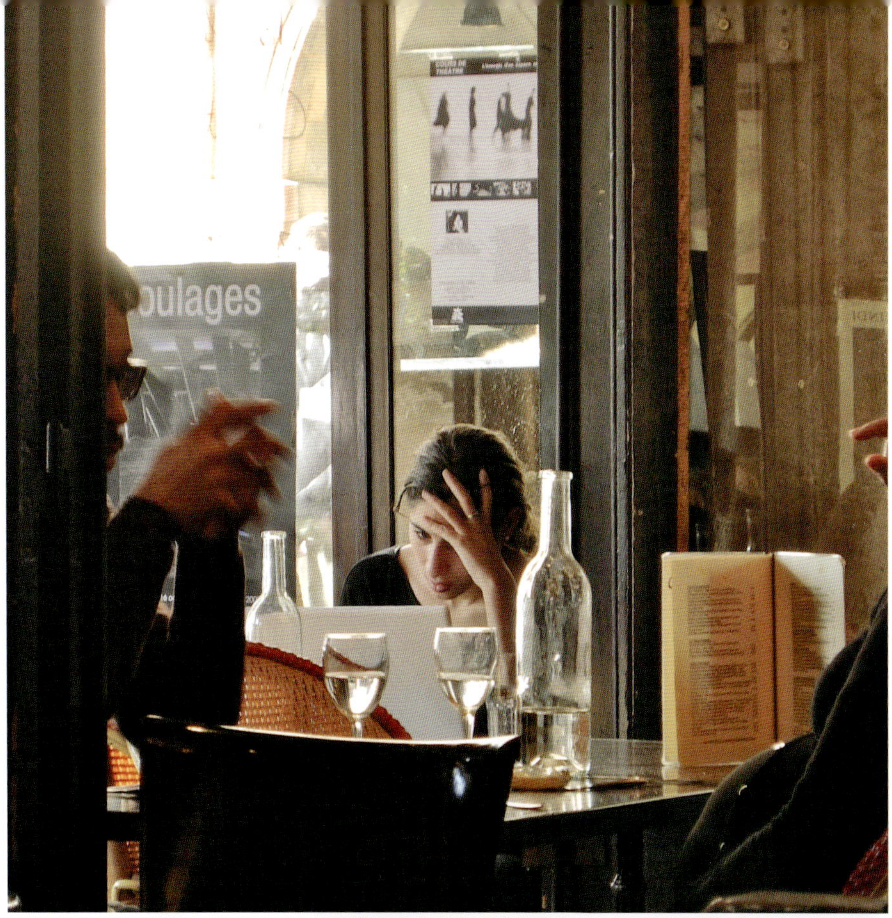

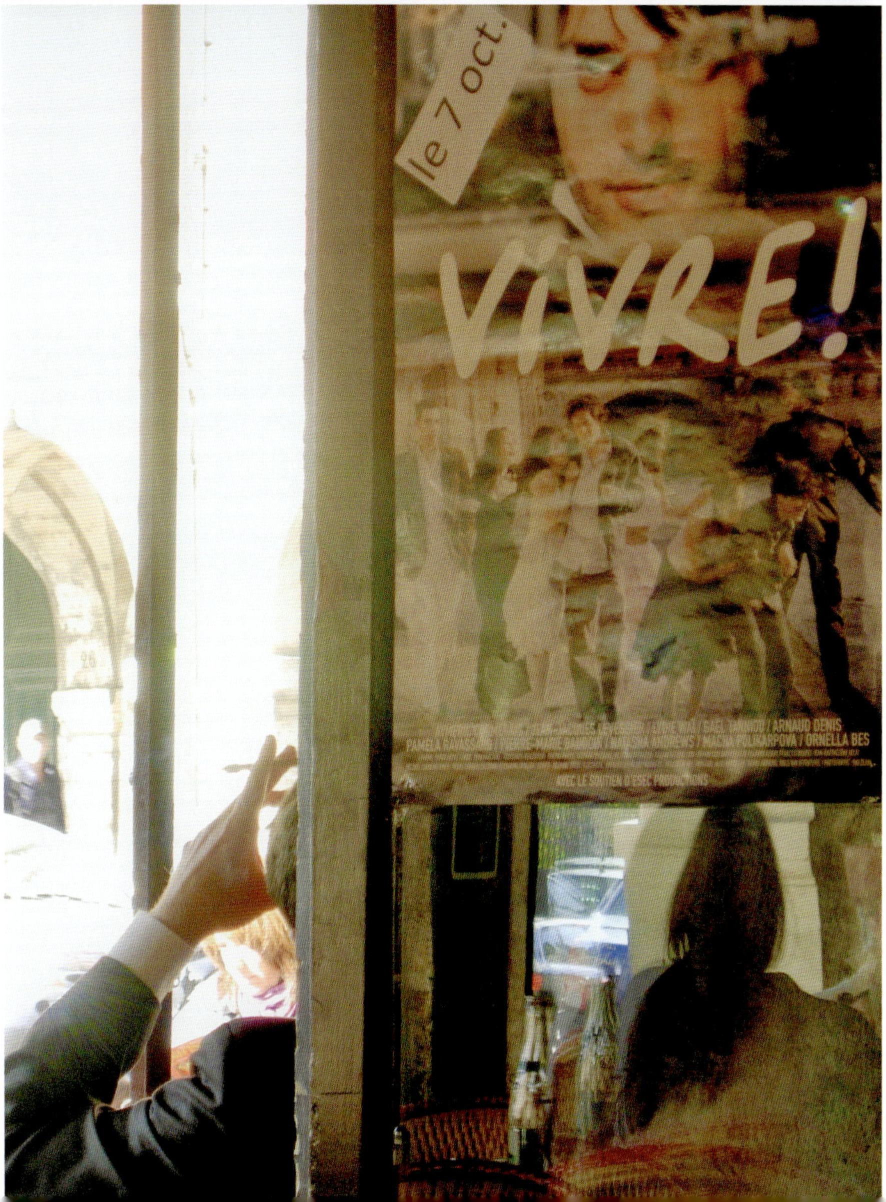
le 7 oct.
VIVRE!

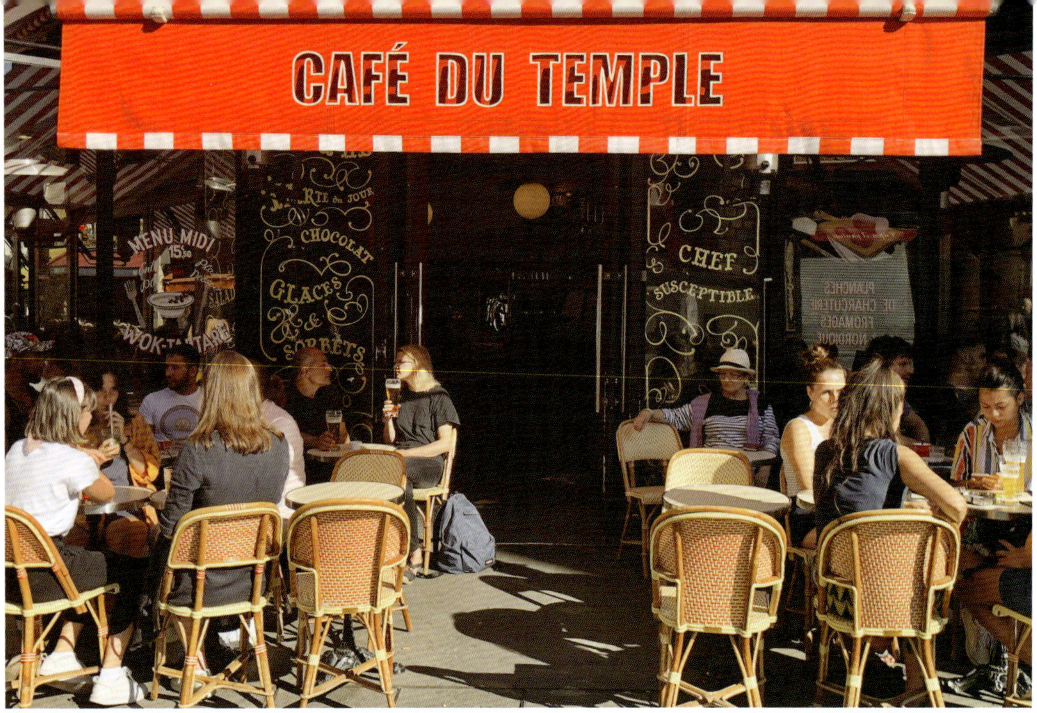
CAFÉ DU TEMPLE
MENU MIDI
CHOCOLAT
GLACES & SORBETS
CHEF SUSCEPTIBLE

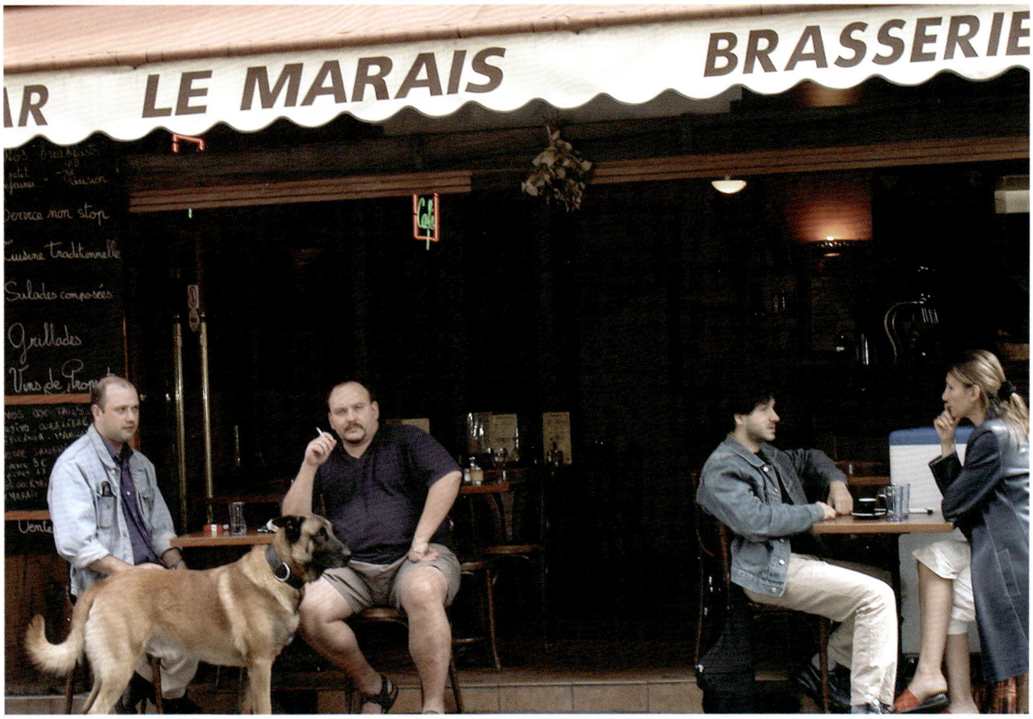
LE MARAIS
BRASSERIE
Service non stop
Cuisine traditionnelle
Salades composées
Grillades

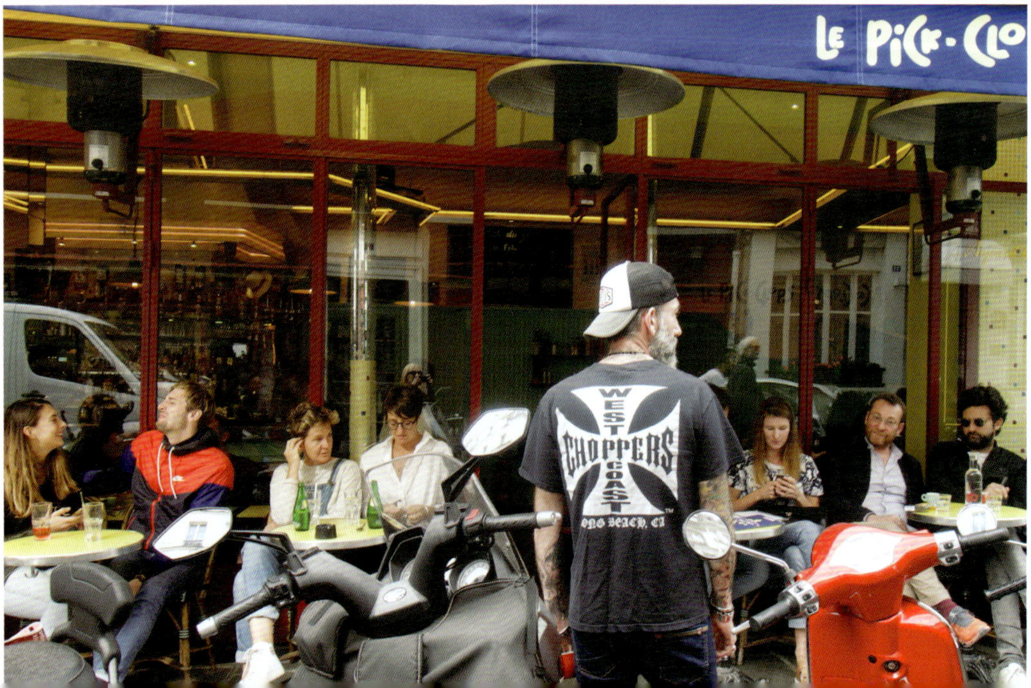
WEST COAST CHOPPERS

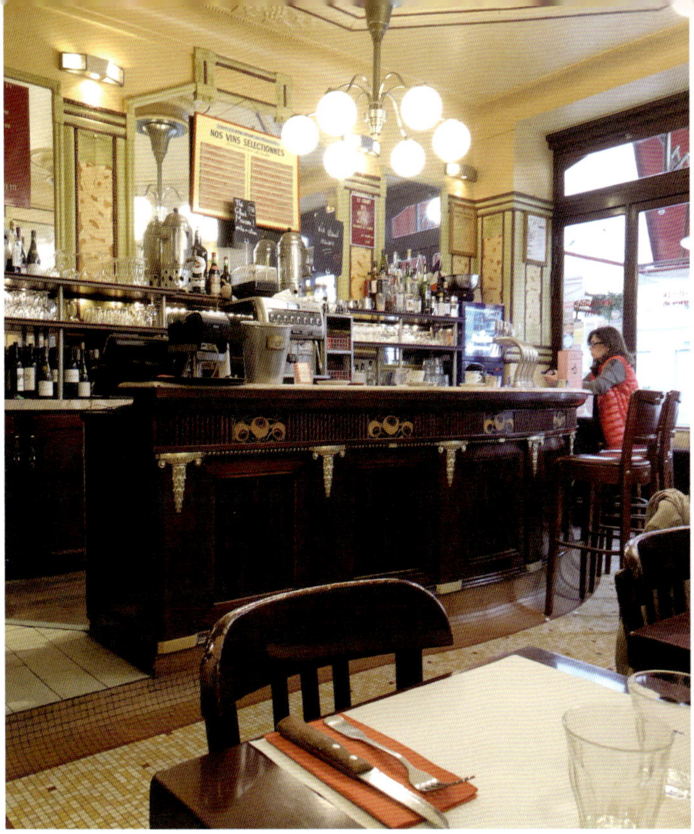

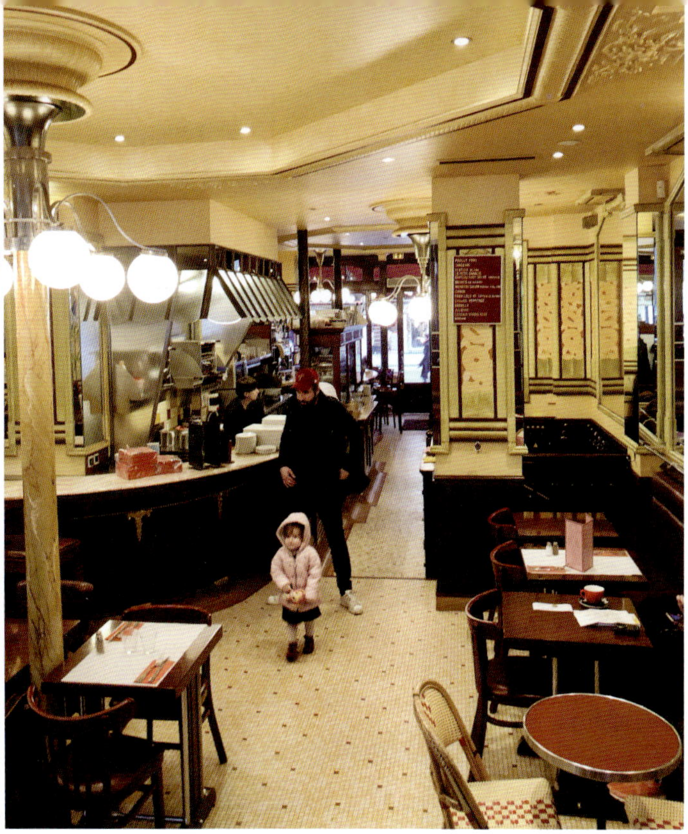

Boasting a bar that has been called the most photographed in Paris, pretty La Tartine, on rue de Rivoli, has hosted a clientele as diverse as Vladimir Lenin and James Joyce. These days, the café morphs into a *bar à vin* with an energetic vibe in the evening.

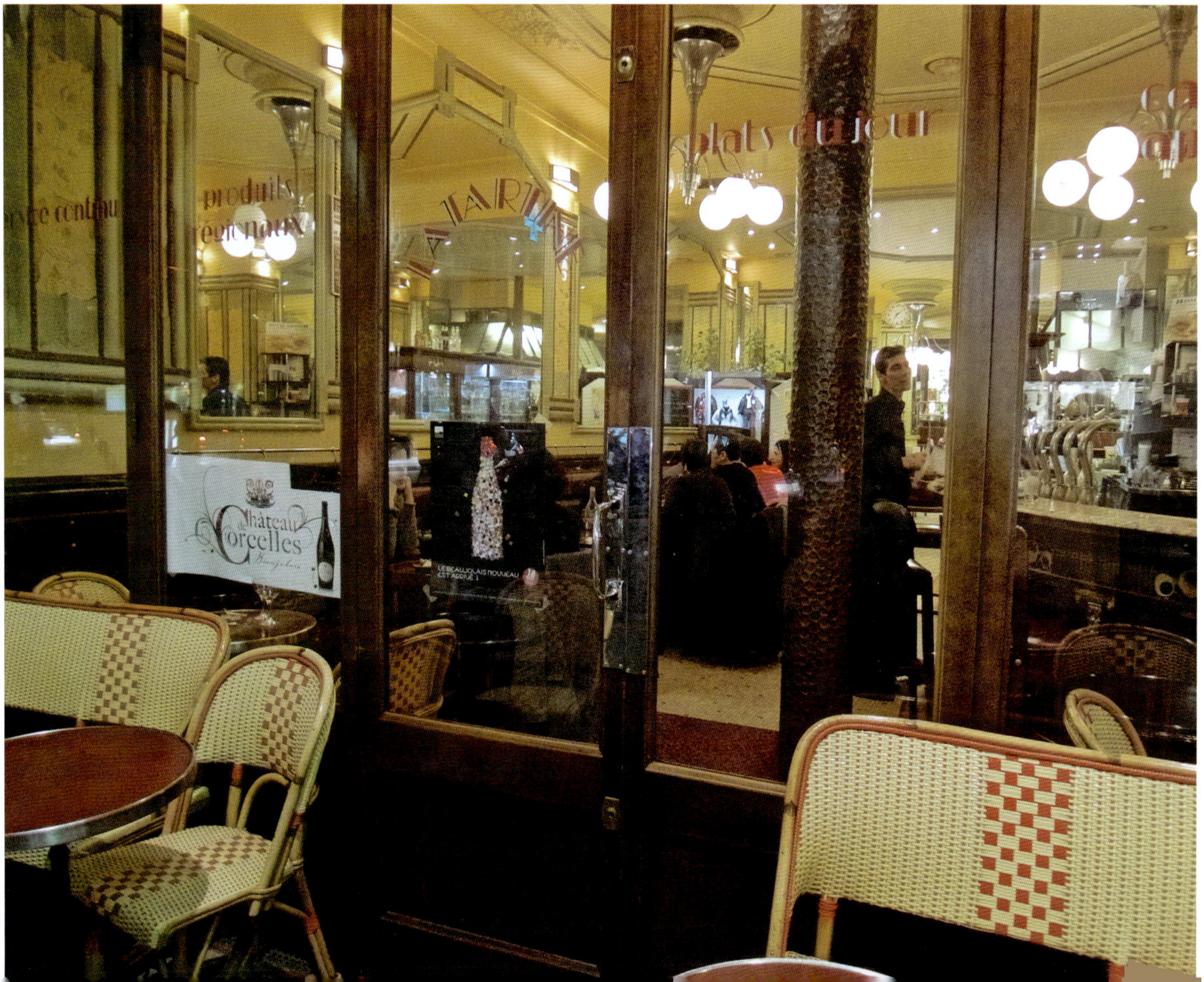

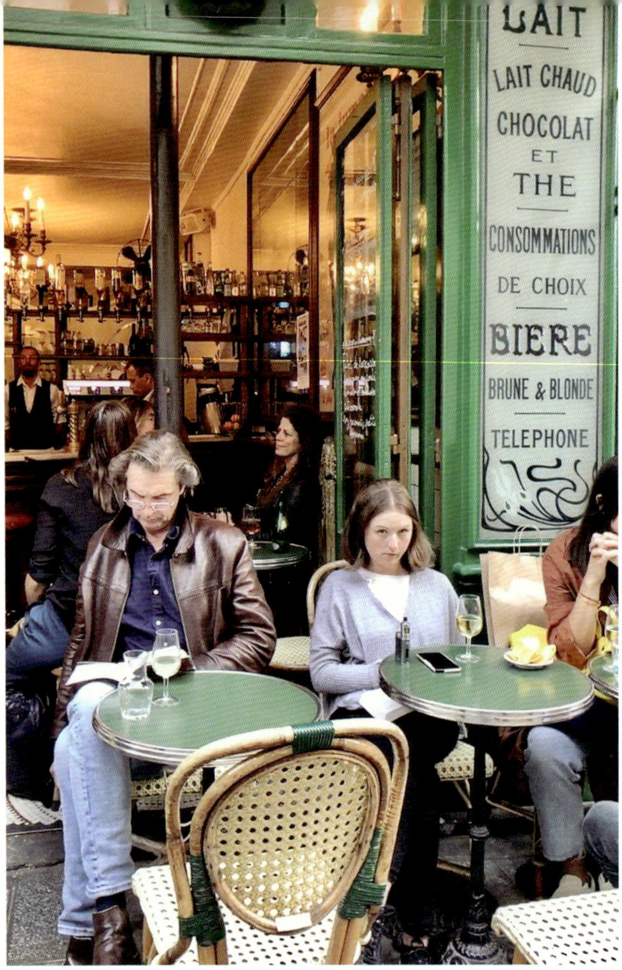

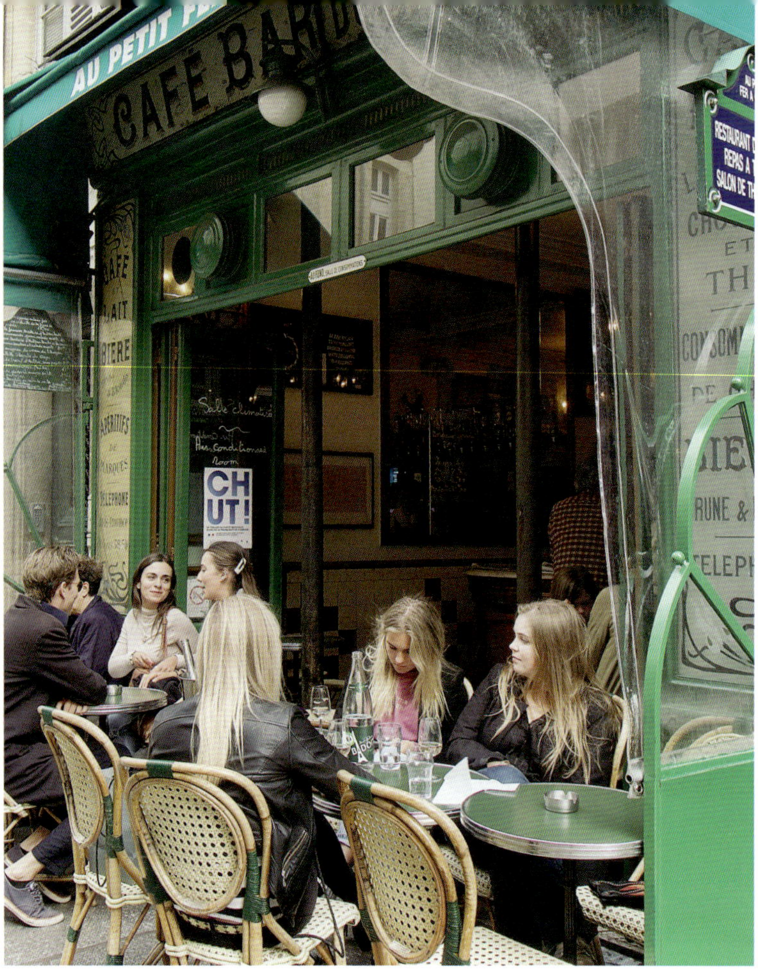

Au Petit Fer à Cheval, "The Little Horseshoe" with its horseshoe-shaped bar, opened as Café du Brésil in 1903. Xavier Denamur purchased it in 1989—the first of his bistros in the Marais. All Denamur's bistros retain authenticity in design and serve fresh, seasonal *bio* food from small farms. You have to love the fanciful names of his bistros and the name of his website: cafeine.com. In Les Philosophes ("The Philosophers"), and next door, La Chaise au Plafond ("The Chair on the Ceiling"), the authentic food and style are central to the spirit of the modern Marais and well worth a visit.

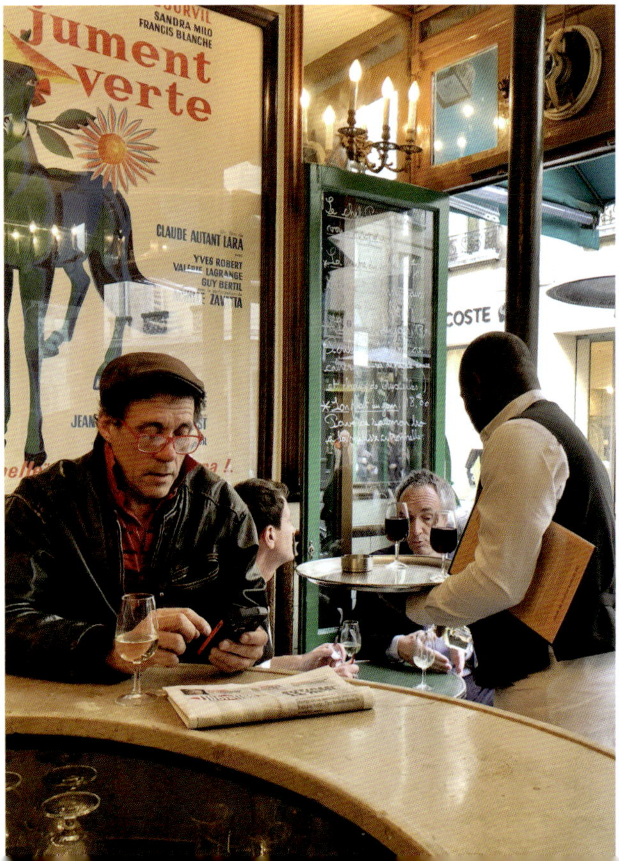

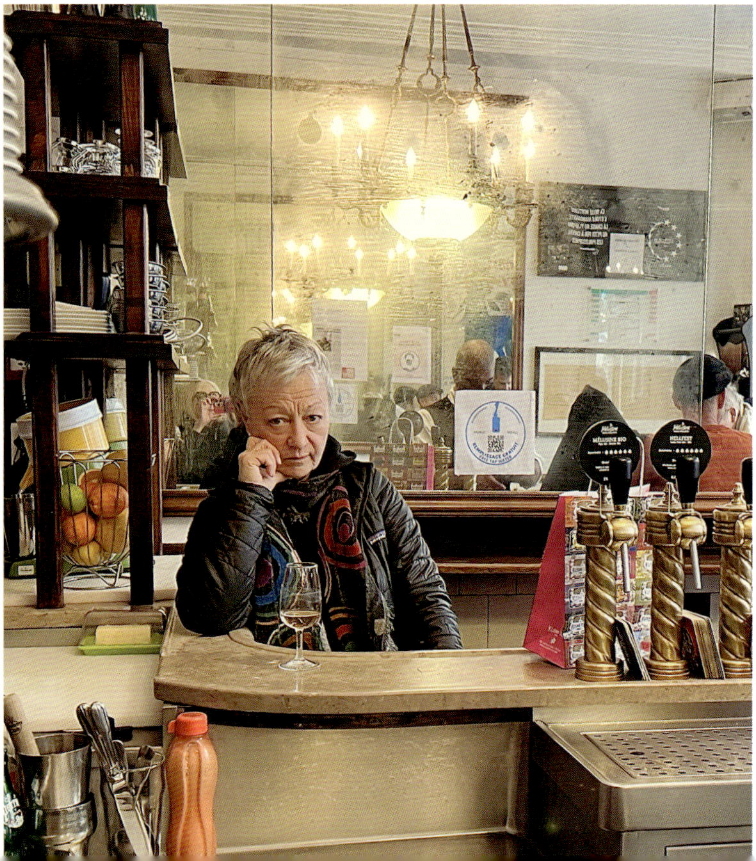

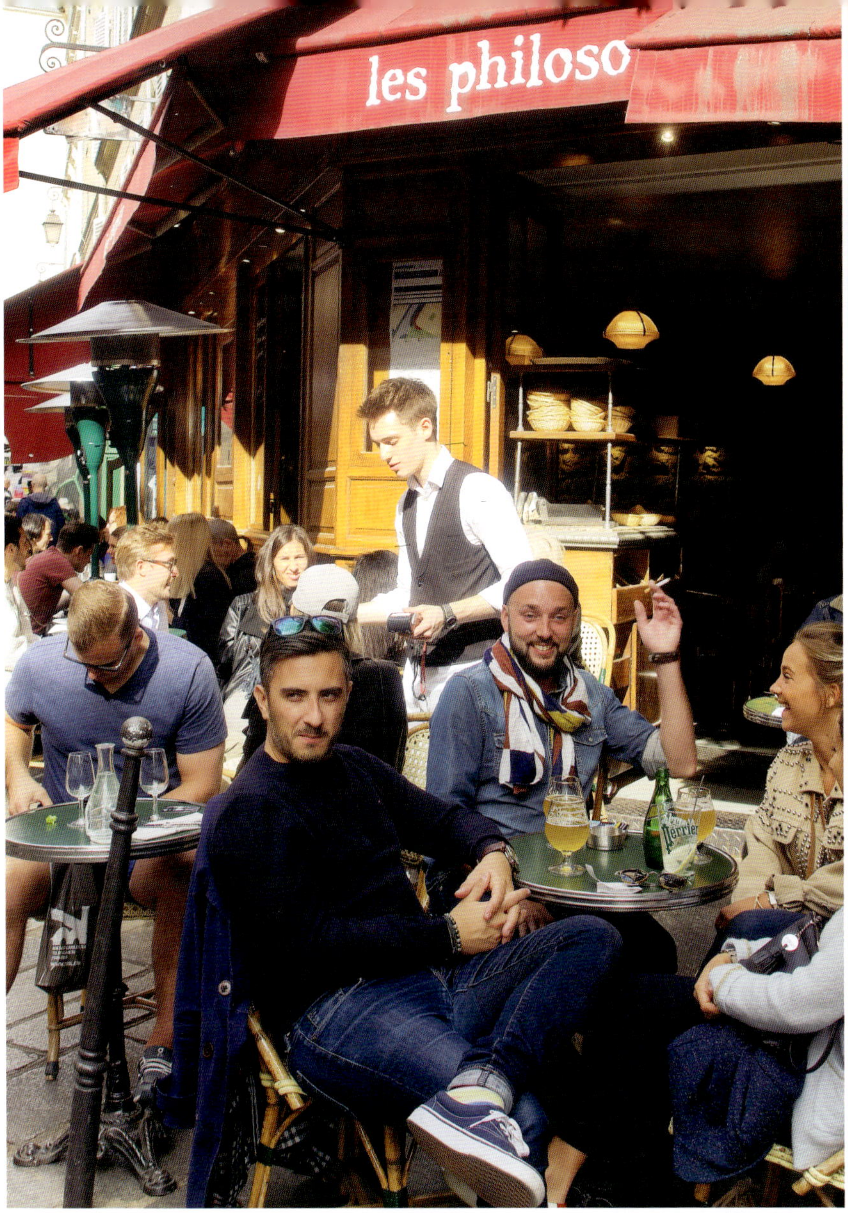
les philoso
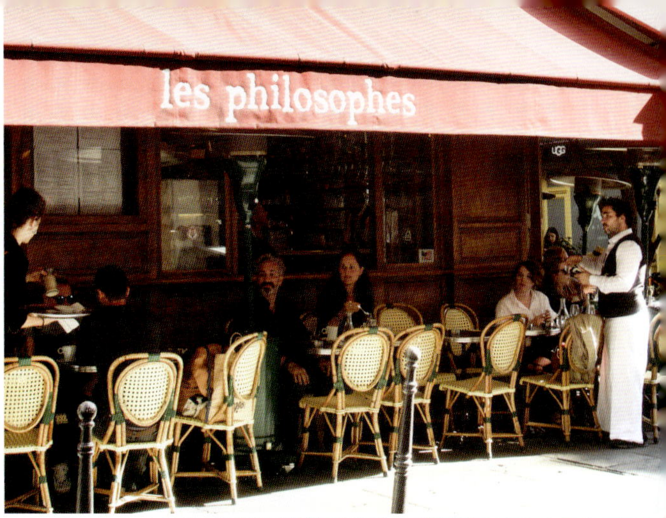
les philosophes
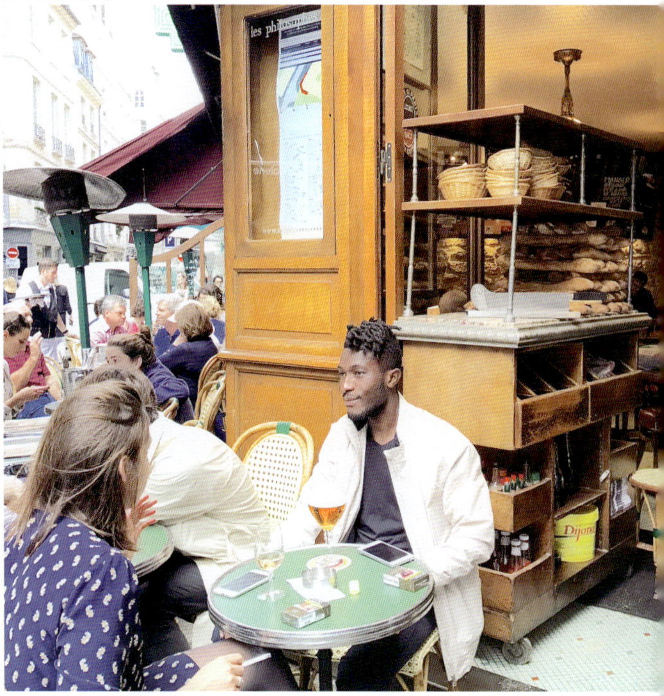
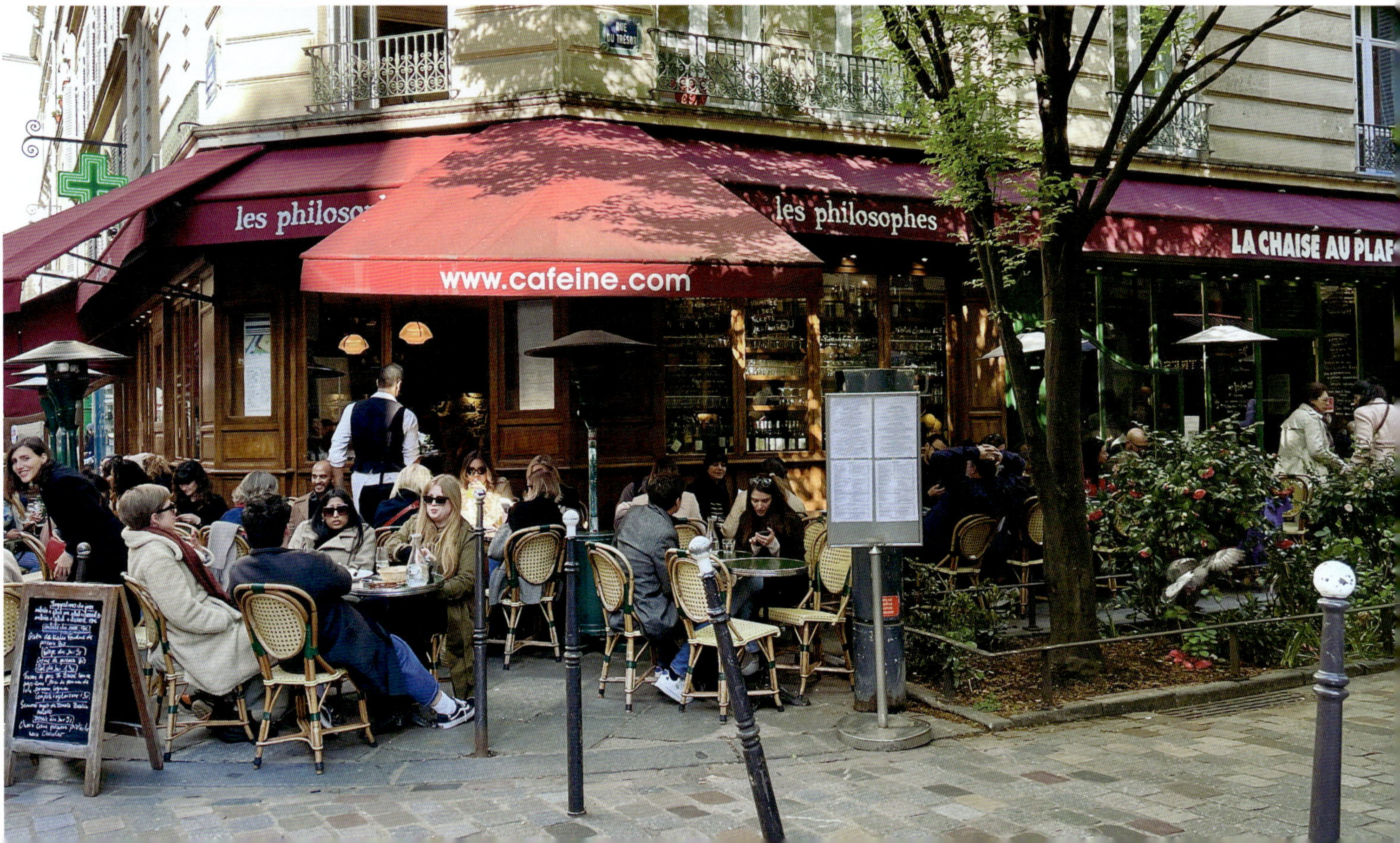
les philoso
www.cafeine.com
les philosophes
LA CHAISE AU PLAF

La Bastille

"'*Aujourd'hui, rien.*' That's what Louis XVI wrote in his diary on the day of the storming of the Bastille."

Jo Walton

All that is left of La Bastille is the name, the lore, some relics in the Bastille Metro and some scattered about Paris. After the revolution, the structure was dismantled, the stones taken as souvenirs or used for roads, bridges, and walls. The central column of Place de la Bastille is called the Colonne de Juillet and commemorates the revolution of 1830 rather than the July 14, 1789 revolution. While tales of the Bastille are plentiful in history and continue apace in the 21st century, today, the Place de la Bastille is the site of an architecturally controversial opera house as well as ongoing protest movements. The surrounding 4th, 11th, and (formerly gritty) 12th arrondissements have some of the top small museums and are brimming with superb, reasonably priced, funky-chic cafés, bistros, and brasseries, both hip Neo-Bistros, and iconic classics.

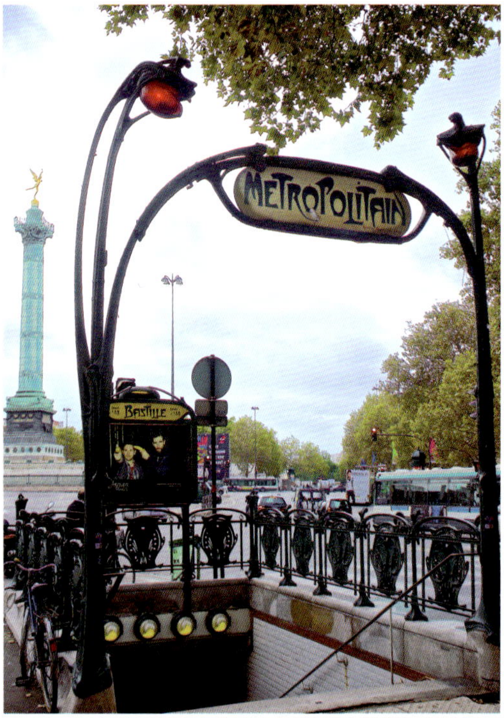

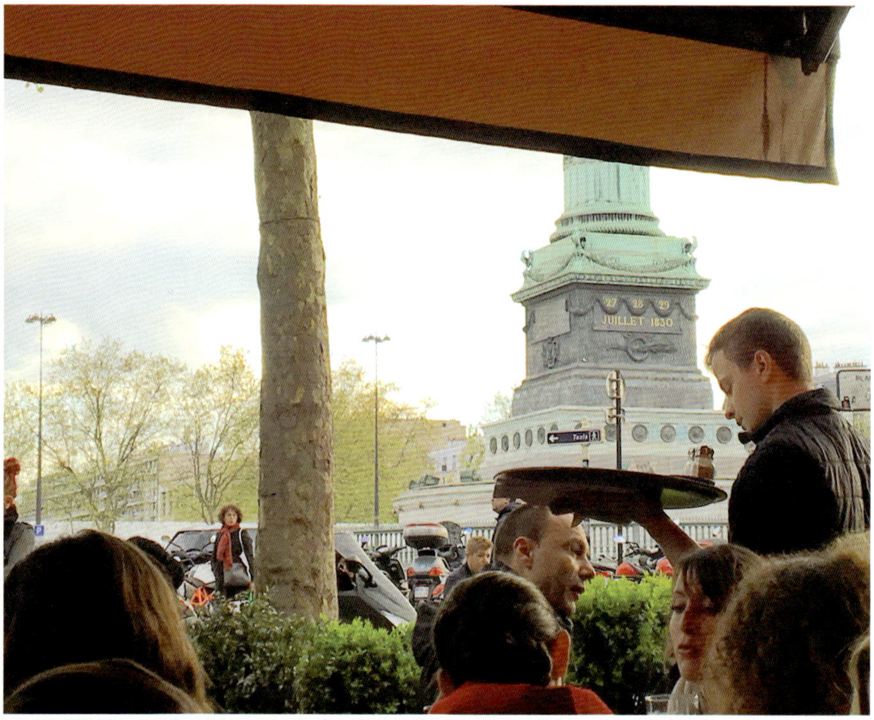

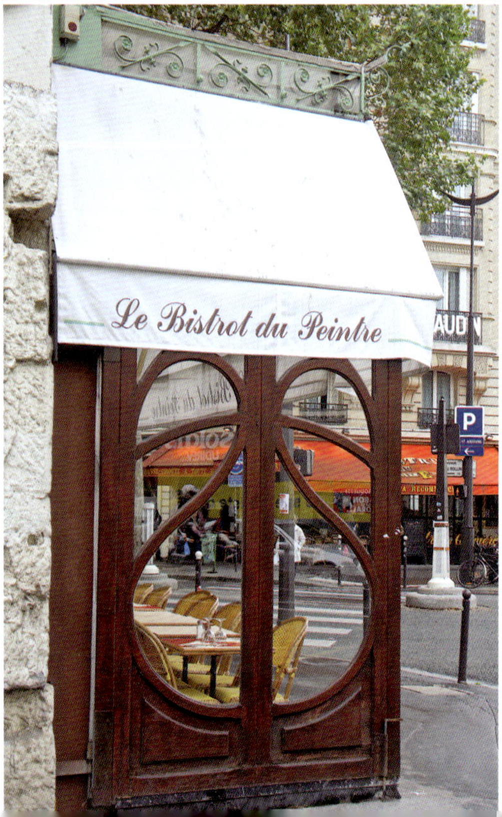

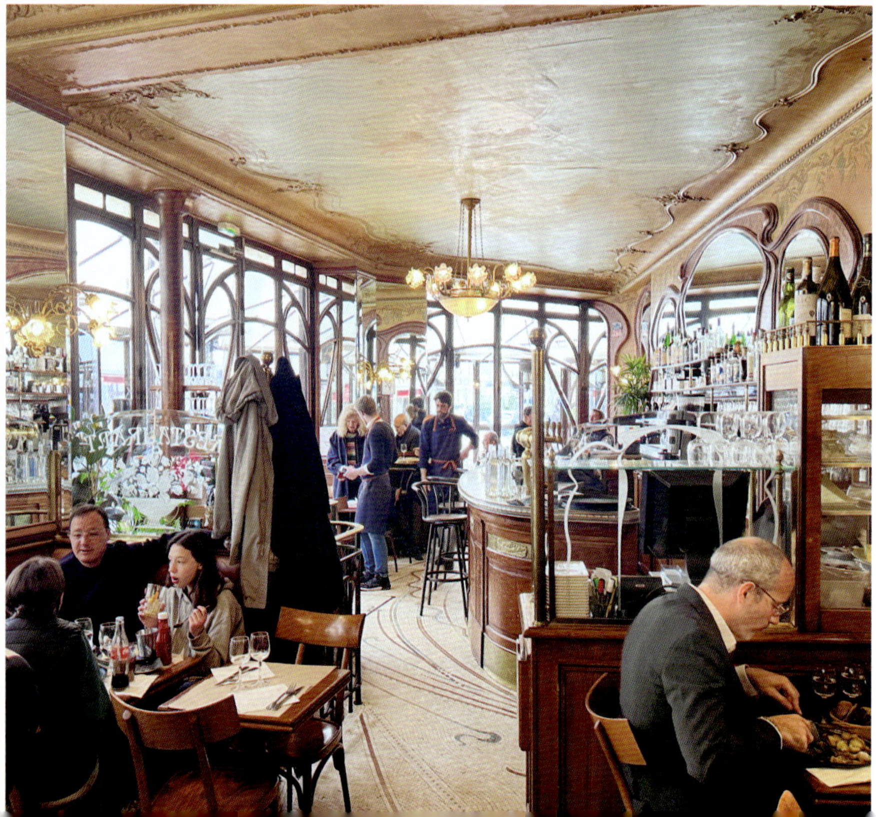

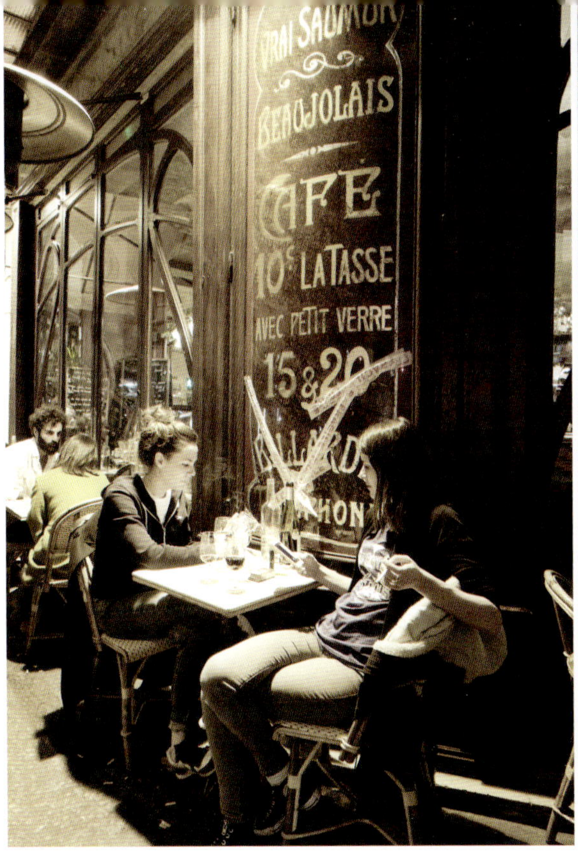

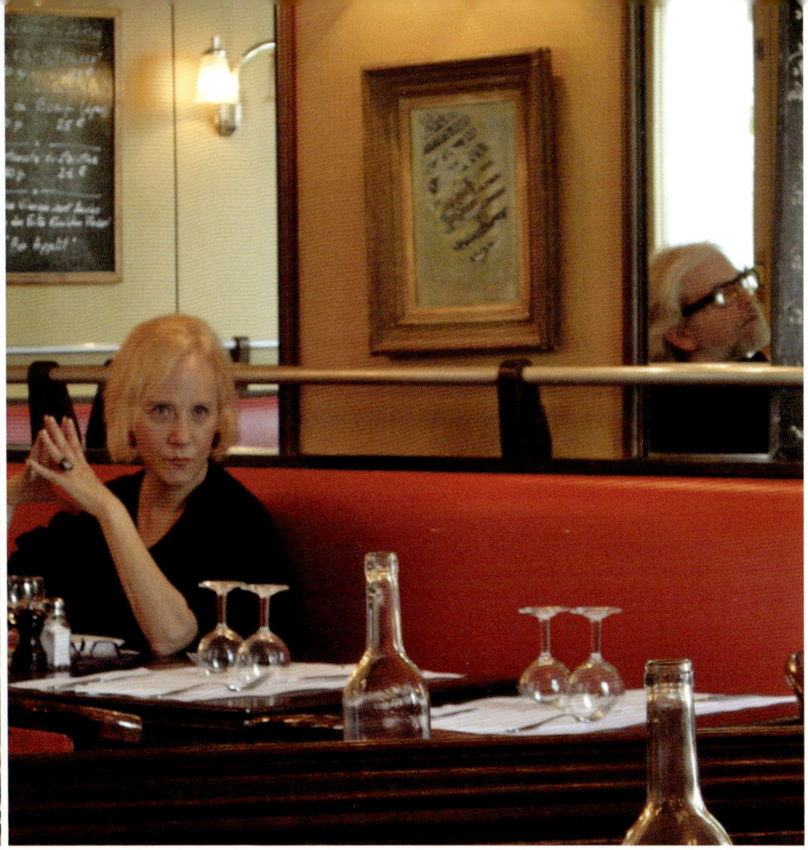

Le Bistrot du Peintre, opened in 1902 in the currently *branché* 11th arrondissement, is one of Paris's most delicious and evocative bistros. While the terrace and interior are always lively, the upstairs space is as inviting as the ground floor and quieter—pleasant for a large group. Its gorgeous Art Nouveau style is designated a Historic Monument. Auvergnat owner Hervé Bonal can be found behind *le zinc*, expertly curating and serving up a wide-ranging list of wines. Following in the footsteps of the 19th-century Auvergnats, Hervé started his career at Le Bistrot du Peintre as a waiter in 1991, then managed the restaurant from 1993 before taking it over in 2003. The classic-with-a-twist menu is seasonal, inexpensive, and always yummy.

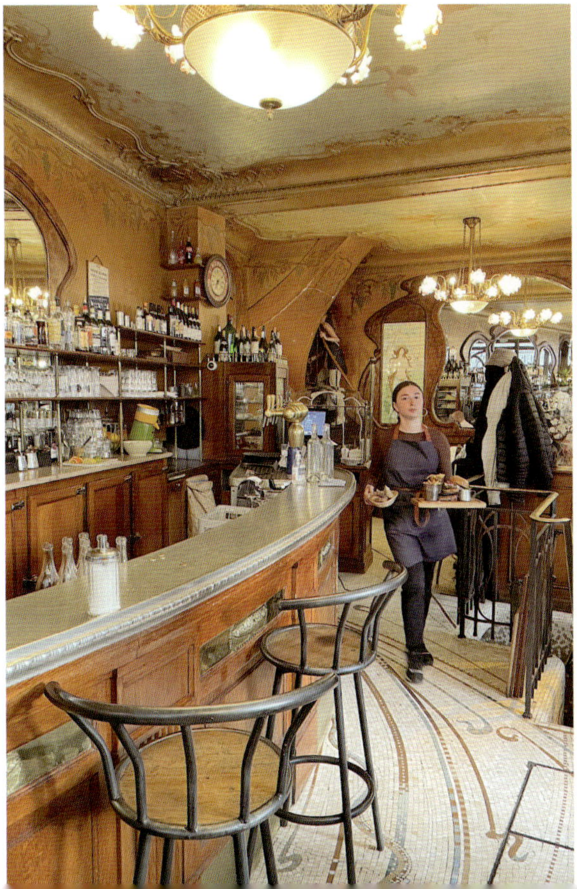

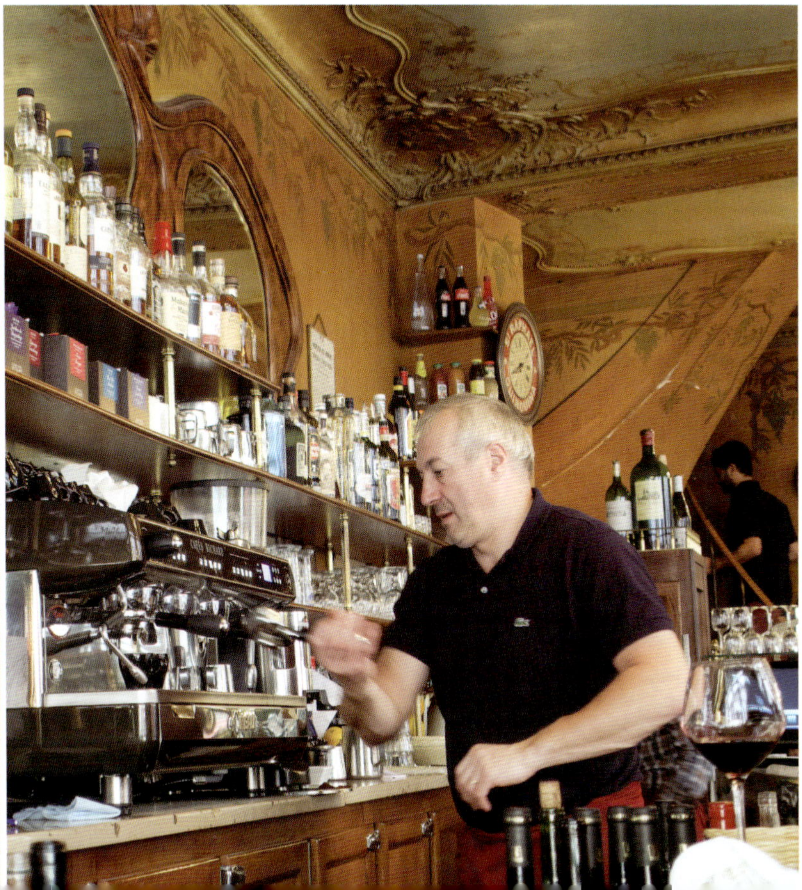

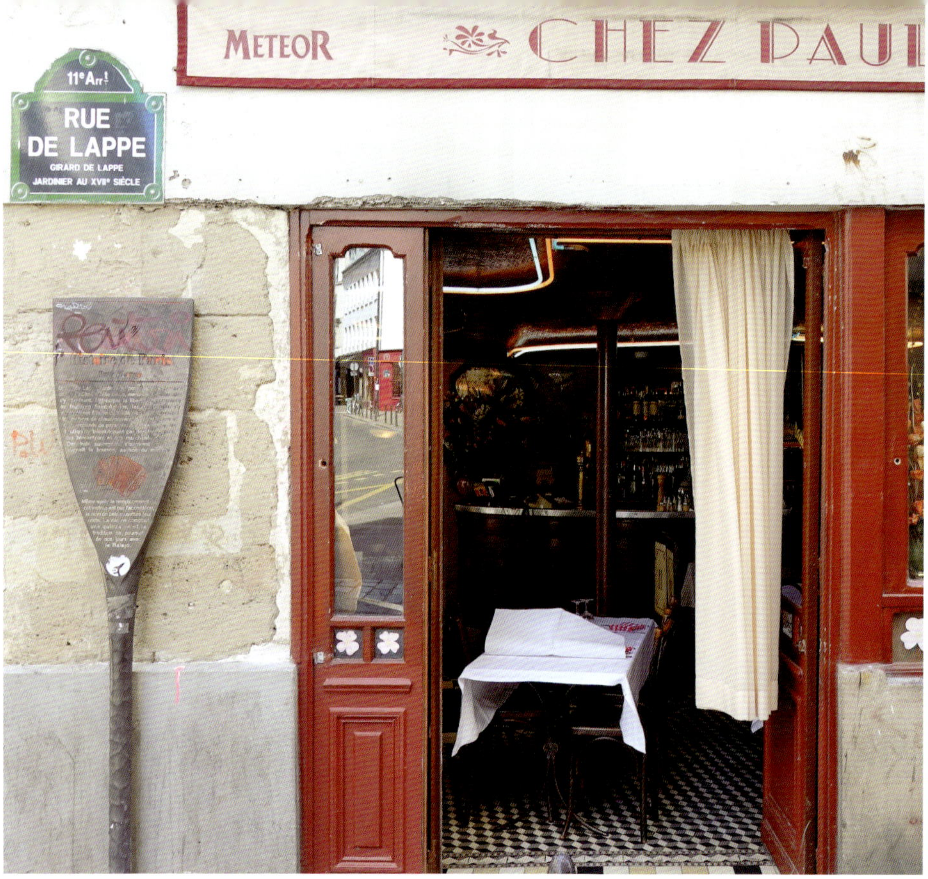

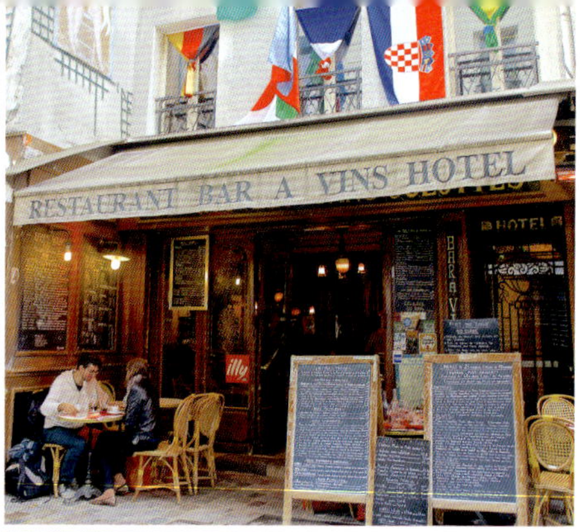

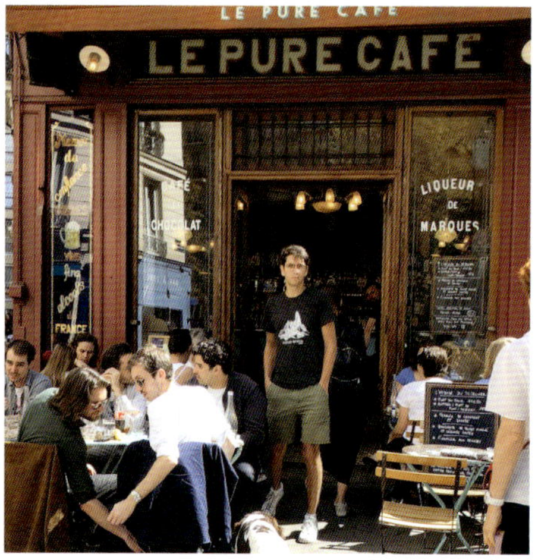

In the mid-19th century, the rue de Lappe was the hub for the Auvergnats who opened their *charbon* cafés and held court at their zinc bars. Now the heart of a lively neighborhood packed with cafés, bistros, bars, clubs, and brasseries, it's jumping when the sun goes down. Chez Paul stands ready to welcome you for a truly authentic, convivial, fun trip to your French grandma's kitchen (and her generous portions), with fresh, local, seasonal ingredients prepared perfectly and served by the most adorable waitress in Paris.

Featured in the film *Before Sunset*, Le Pure Café is too cool for words. Its funky vintage interior and simple, inexpensive menu dotted with modern touches make it a magnet for a young clientele. Newer to the classic bistro scene (established in 2000), though seemingly from a much earlier era due to its proper look and feel, menu, and vibe, Bistrot Paul Bert (BELOW LEFT), is no secret to either locals or tourists. Owner Bertrand Auboyneau often welcomes guests himself and makes sure everything is fresh and cooked to order, including the marvelous *frites*.

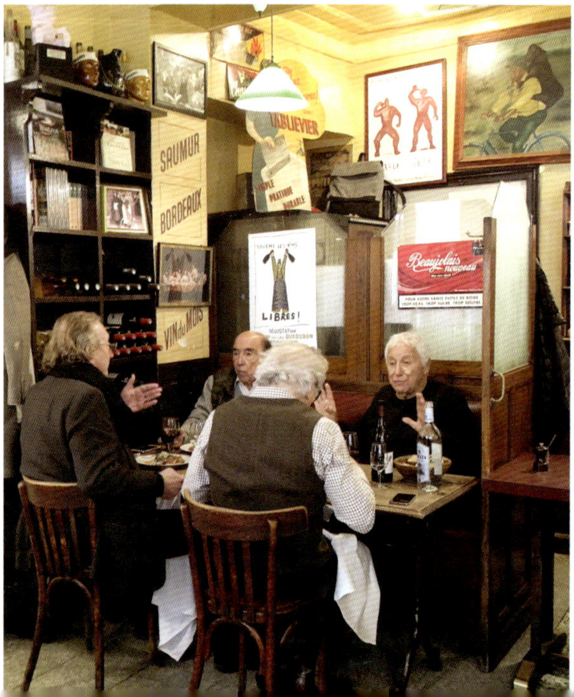

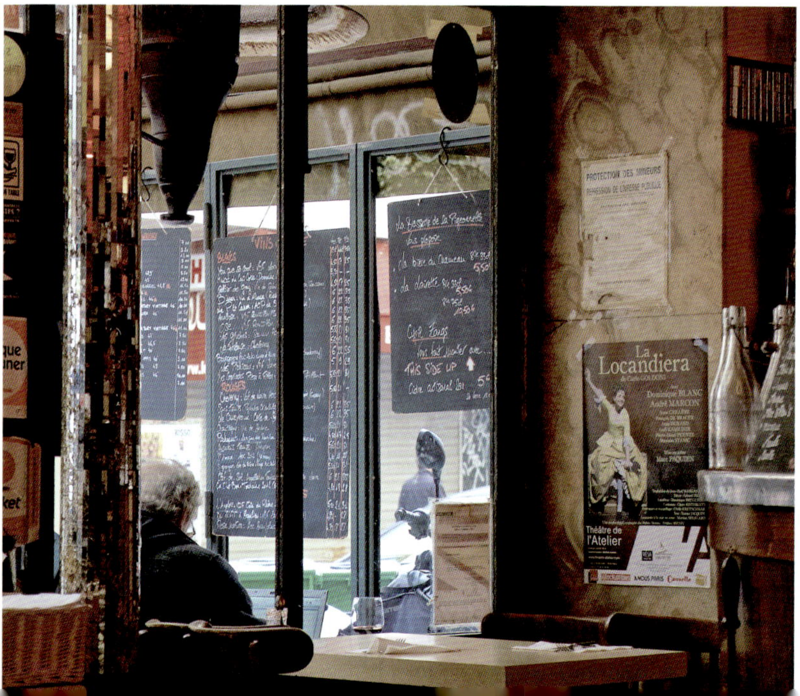

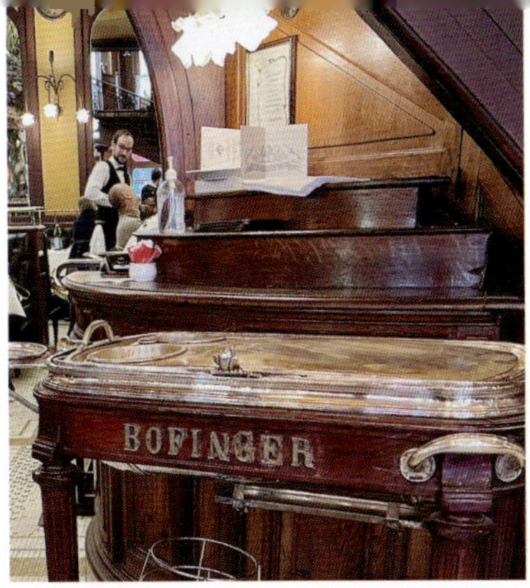

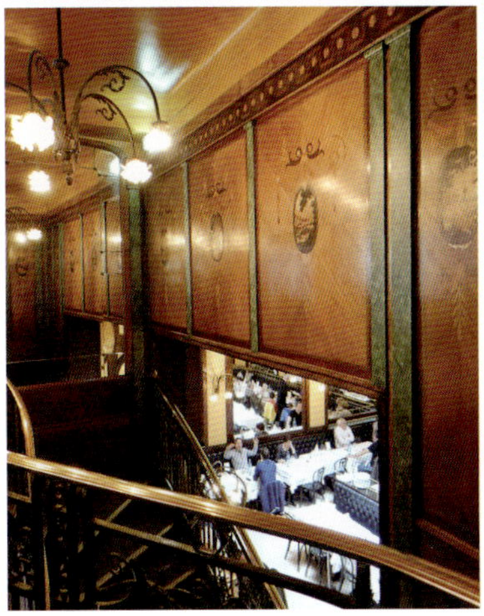

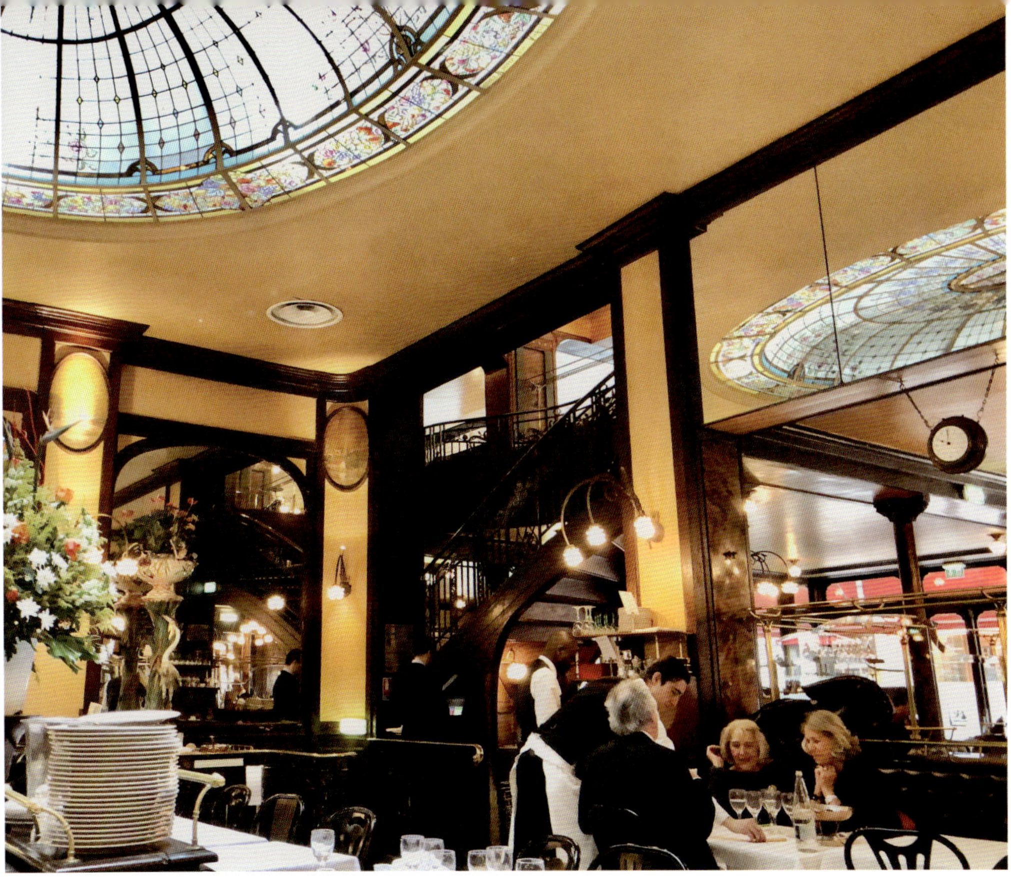

Alsatian Frédéric Bofinger opened the first brasserie in Paris in 1864. A few years later, in 1871, after the Franco-Prussian War, Bofinger evolved into the glorious archetype of a Paris brasserie. Elegantly remodeled during the Belle Époque, Bofinger has been further embellished through the years. The current formidable dining space recalls another era, one filled with writers, academics, and politicians. Almost every French president and prime minister of modern times has eaten here, often regularly. Along with many other historic brasseries, Bofinger is now owned by a corporation that is fortunately sensitive enough to preserve its aesthetics and Alsatian cuisine.

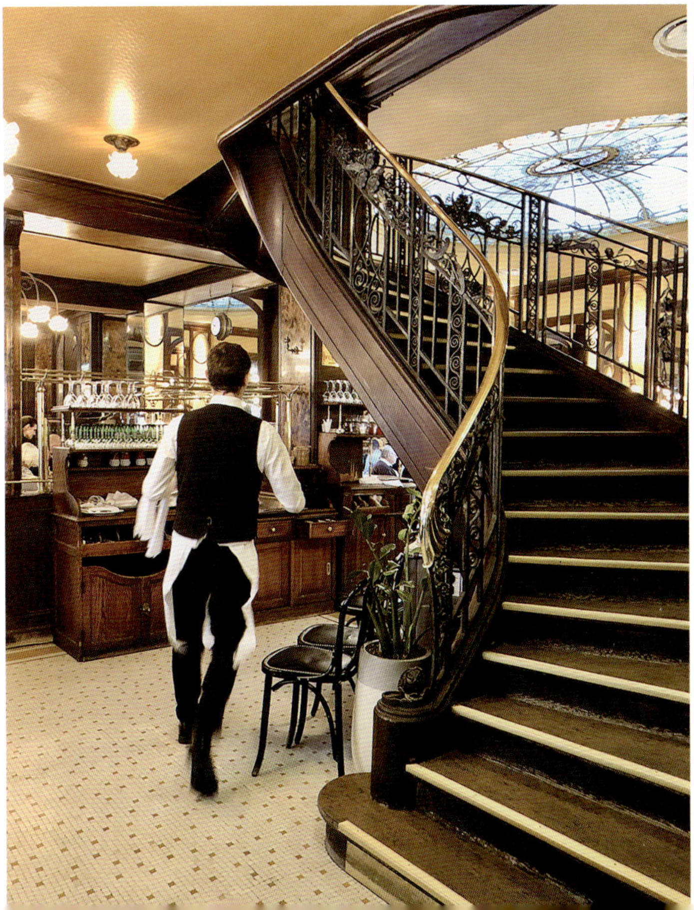

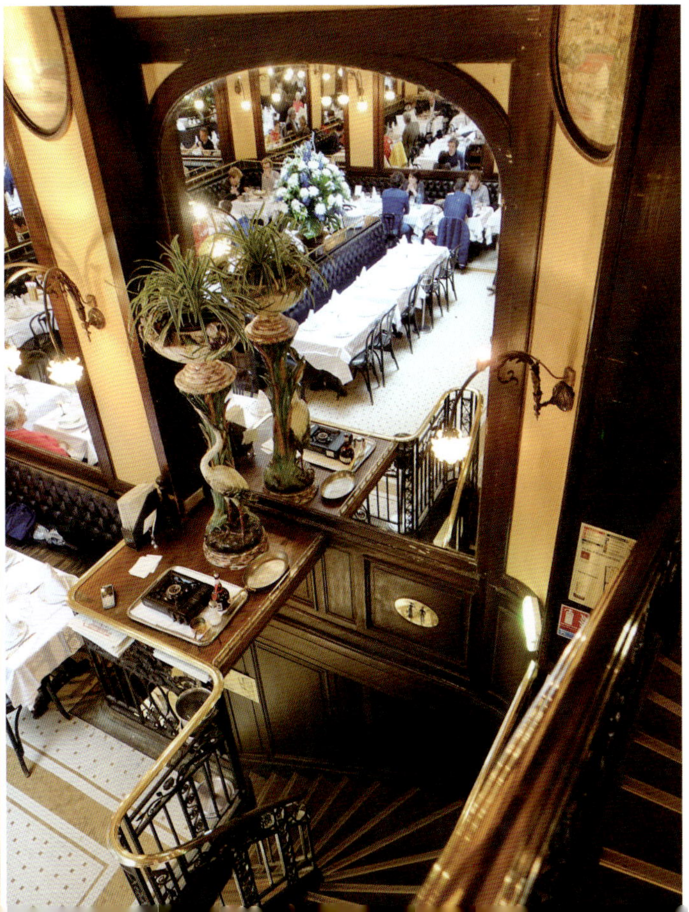

All Around Town: Cafés du Quartier

"Paris was the most stimulating city in the world, with its painters, its writers, its energy, its café life envied everywhere."
Jean-Paul Sartre

Wandering back through time, we see that the trendy cafés of the day have shifted from the Left Bank to the Right Bank, then back and forth until today when they can be found on both sides of the Seine. In our time, along with the renowned Parisian watering holes in well-known neighborhoods, each of Paris's 20 arrondissements is replete with divine cafés, bistros, and brasseries. However, some arrondissements have a greater volume of quality establishments. It seems that almost every corner in every arrondissement in Paris has its corner café, *café du coin*, each a far cry from the ubiquitous Starbucks on every corner in the US (and the four corners of the globe). Flourishing since the late 1900s, food critics now frequently disparage the *cafés du coin* for serving mediocre microwaved food and inferior espresso. While many fall into this category, others serve *fait maison* ("made in-house") menus and are beautiful to boot. Of course, cafés are not only located on corners but rather, everywhere imaginable, on the street and off, including in parks and museums.

It is interesting to note that Parisians historically and even now prefer staying in their quartier, which has every amenity they need for everyday life. Rarely do they travel across town to dine or drink. Instead, most go to their neighborhood hangouts. A comfortable gathering place for everyone, from habitués seated at the same table daily to children enjoying their *chocolat chaud* and *frites* after school, everyone is "at home" in their local café. Often these neighborhood haunts, some simple, others elegant, are the most memorable for tourists. You can discover the gems by strolling the streets, following your nose, and, if you must, cross-referencing with online research. Then, reinforce your choice by reading the menus posted outside and checking out the neighborhood crowds inside and out. Often it is more exciting and fun to fall upon something unplanned rather than spending hours checking reviews.

With a full view of the Centre Pompidou, Café Beaubourg (BELOW) has a terrace that offers a full-length movie of passing life.

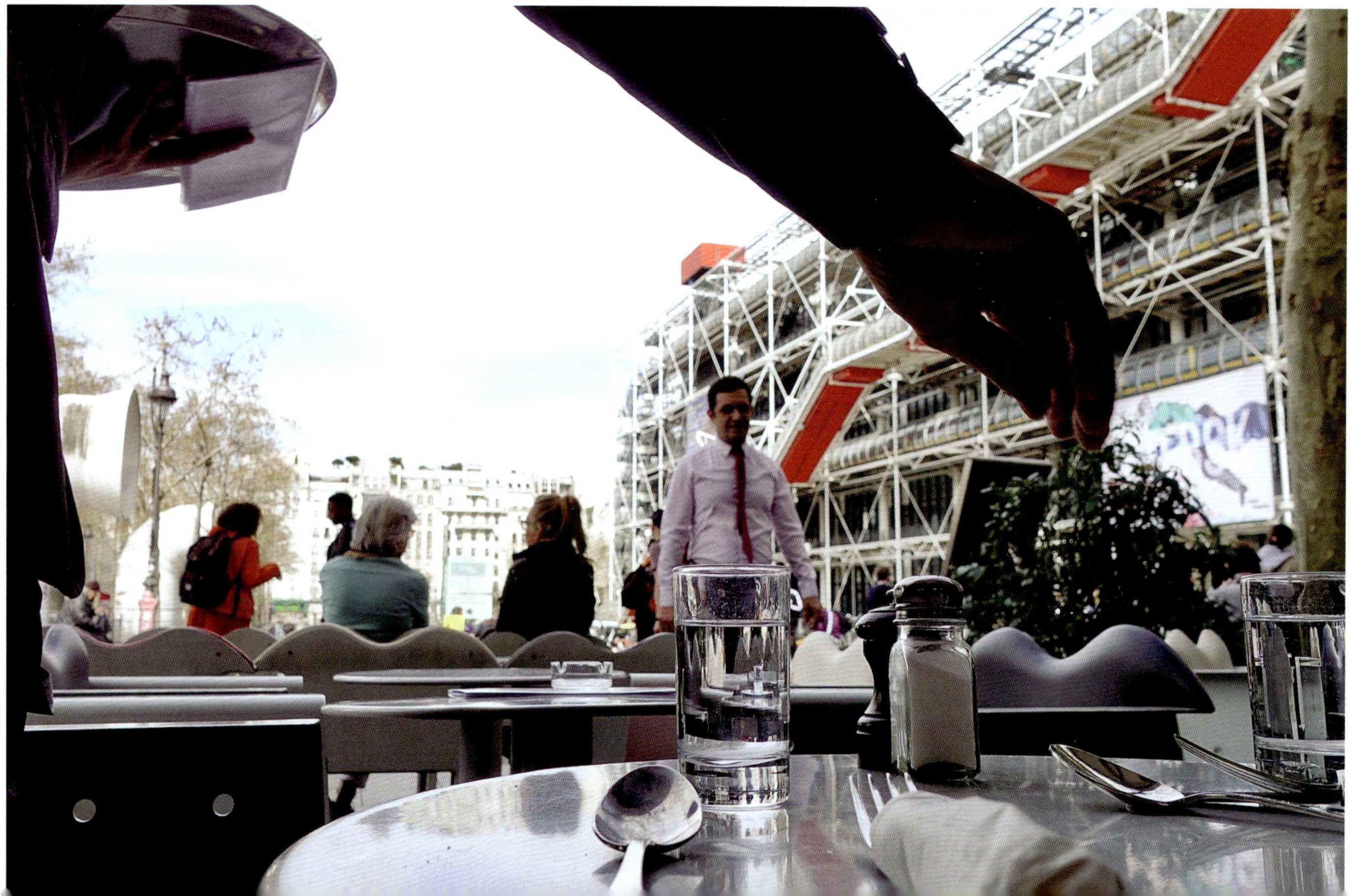

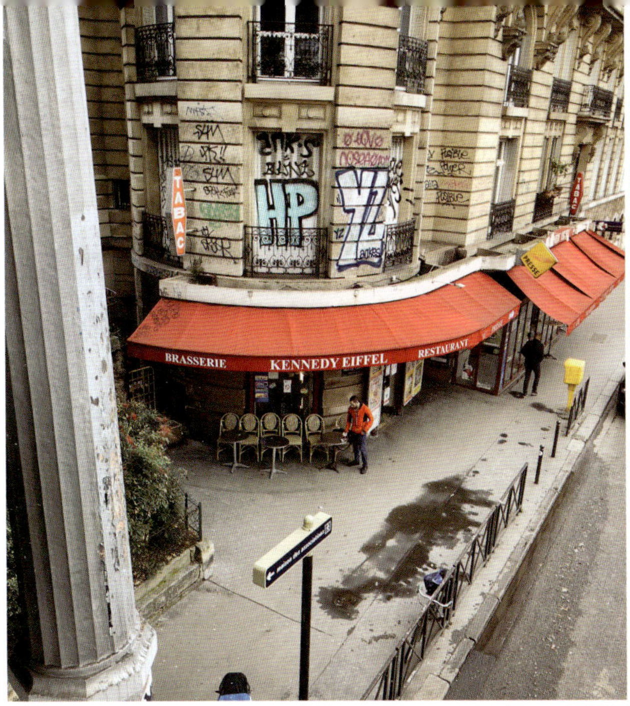
BRASSERIE
KENNEDY EIFFEL
RESTAURANT

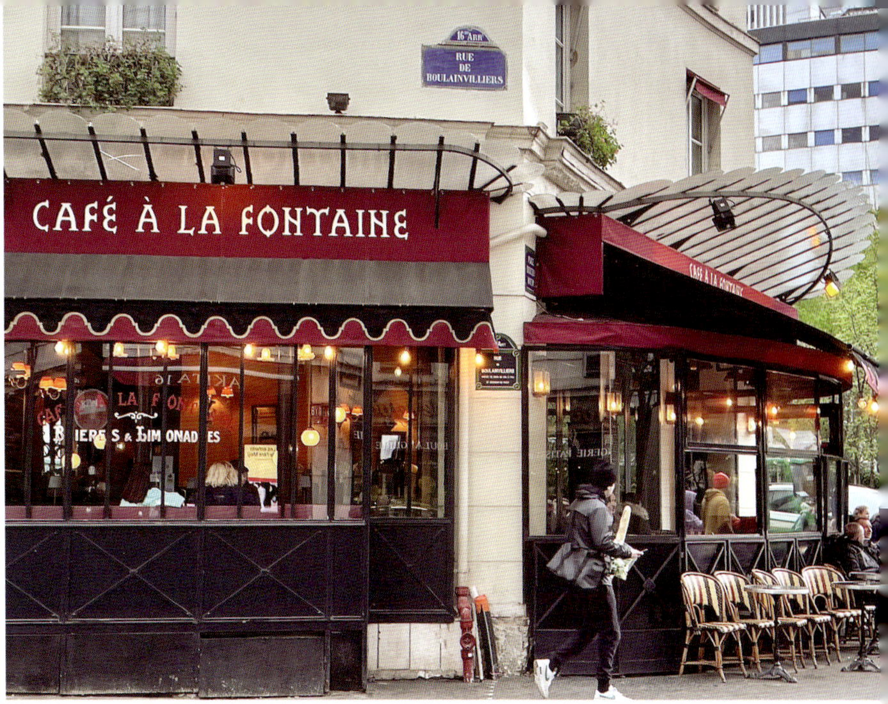
RUE DE BOULAINVILLIERS
CAFÉ À LA FONTAINE

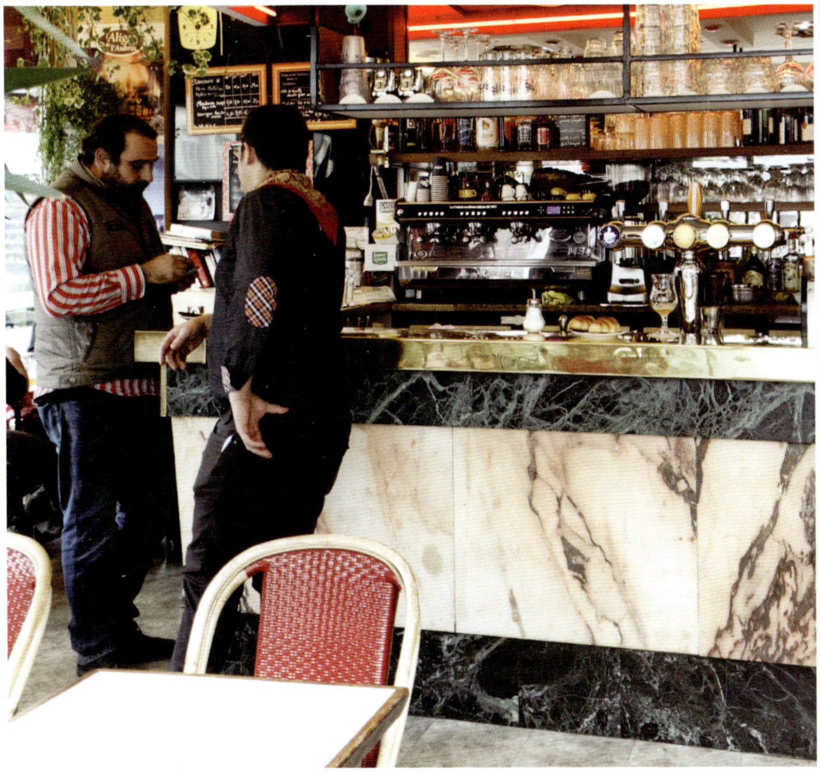

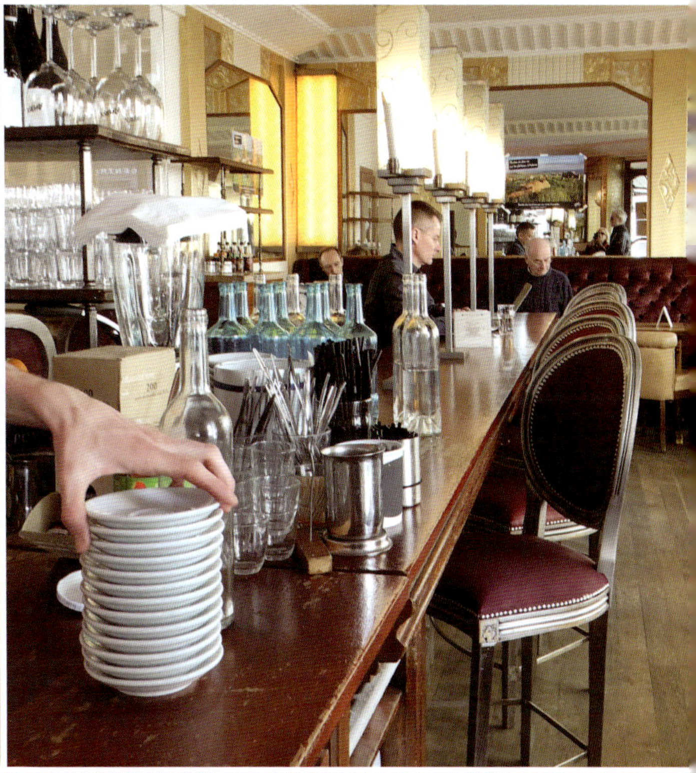

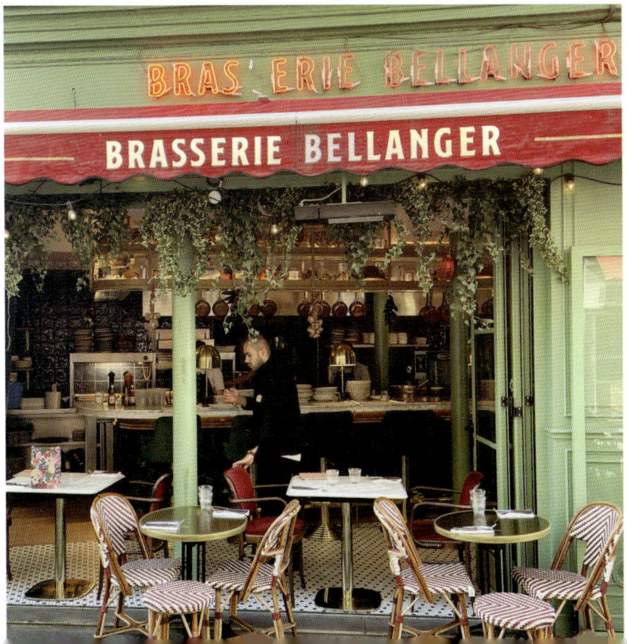
BRASSERIE BELLANGER
BRASSERIE BELLANGER

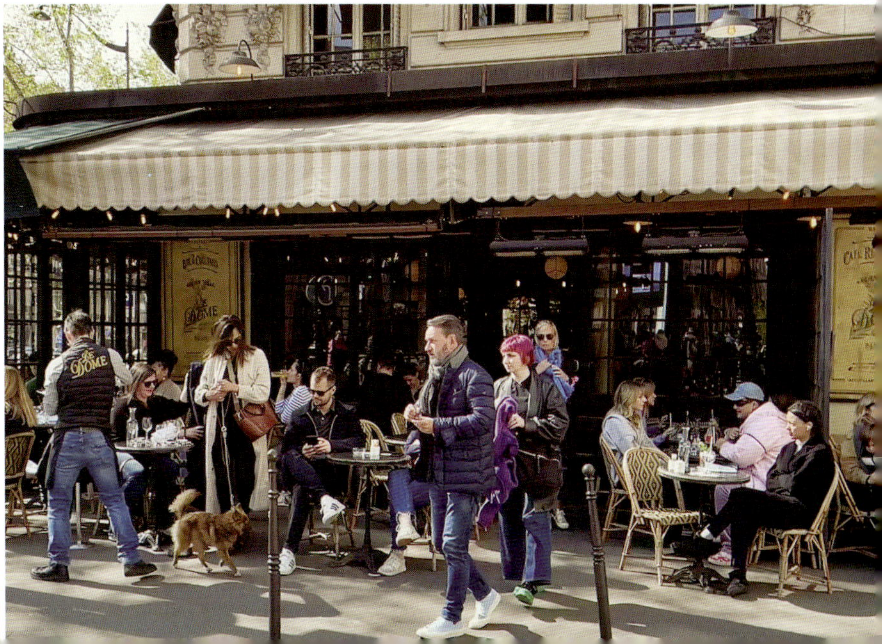

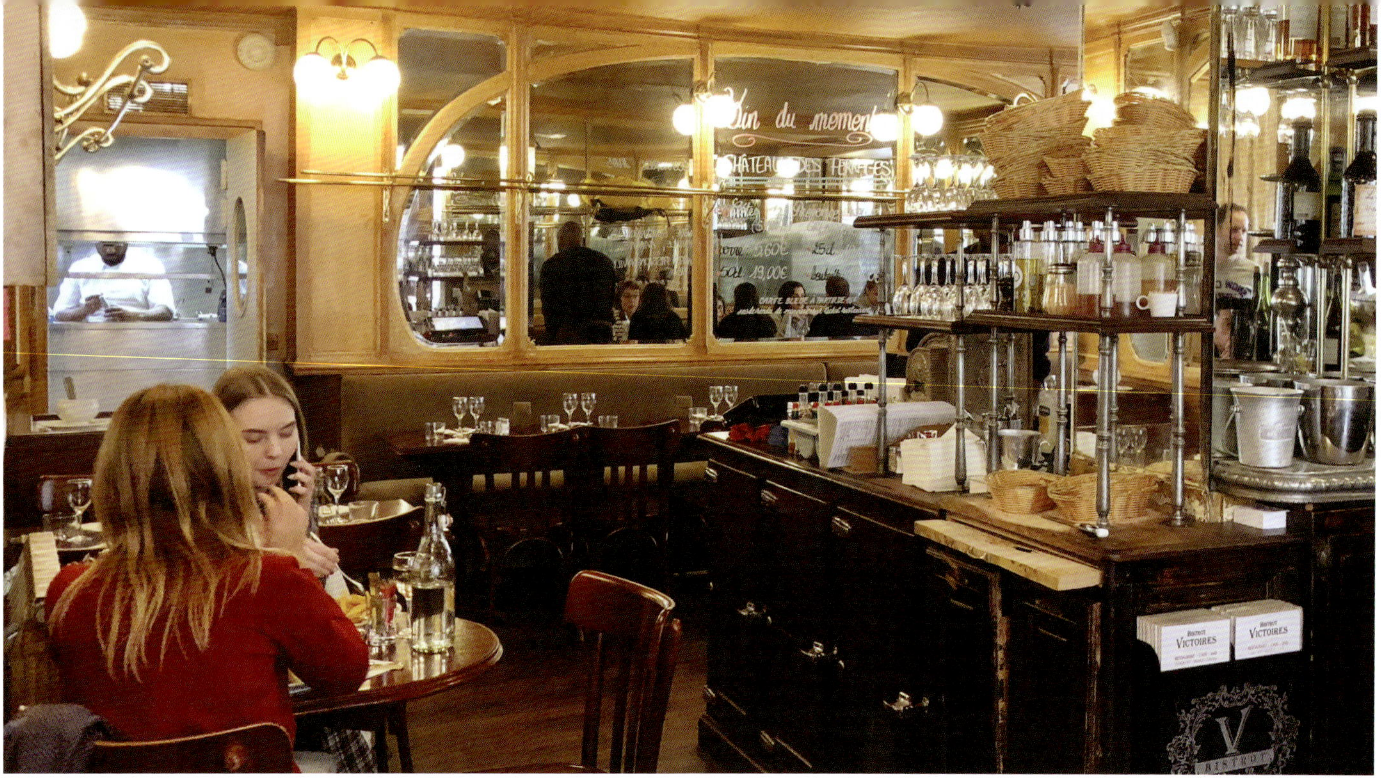

Not accepting reservations but worth the wait, Bistrot Victoires, near the elegant Place des Victoires, retains its authentic 19th-century style and serves a classic menu with reasonable prices and portions. Guide books across the globe have broadcast this gem, so it's best to come off-hours or be patient waiting in the queue.

With a prime location at the tip of the heavily tourist trafficked Île Saint-Louis, facing Notre Dame de Paris, La Brasserie de l'Isle Saint-Louis is a rare full-on, old-time brasserie that remains independently held. Formerly La Taverne du Pont-Rouge in the nineteenth century, later L'Oasis and Le Café des Sports, it has been owned and managed by three generations of the Guépratte family since the '50s. Revealing a perfect terrace view of the Seine and an interior with all the character of another era, it's a favored stop on the island. Café St. Regis, on Île Saint-Louis, has exterior signage in the old-style (not original) and a French/Italian/American menu, including eggs benedict; a popular if not entirely authentic spot.

There are around 130 museums in Paris, large and small, many famous, others beneath the radar, almost hidden on side streets. It isn't only the tourists who flock to the museums, sometimes standing in line for hours in frosty temps—even after buying tickets online—but the French as well. The Parisians follow the exhibitions in earnest and are usually first in line. Doesn't it go without saying that museum-goers must rest their eyes and feet at some point, and what better place to do this than a café? Some significant museums have both formal restaurants and casual cafés, often displaying Paris's best café design.

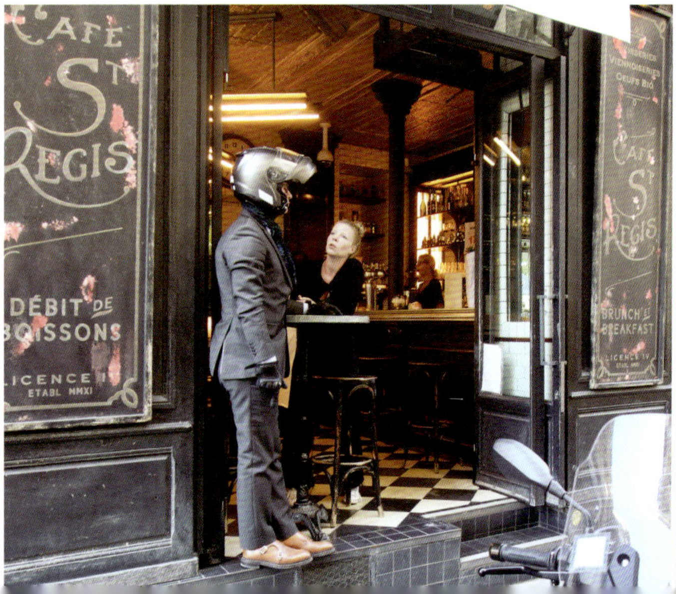

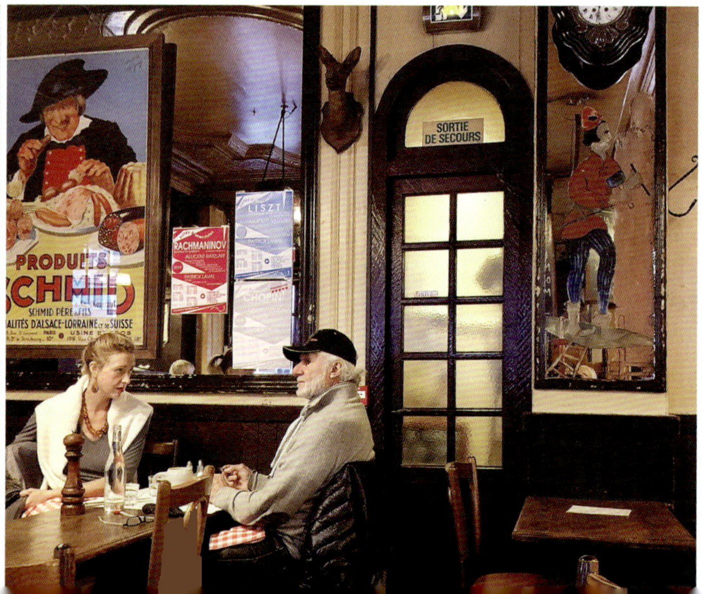

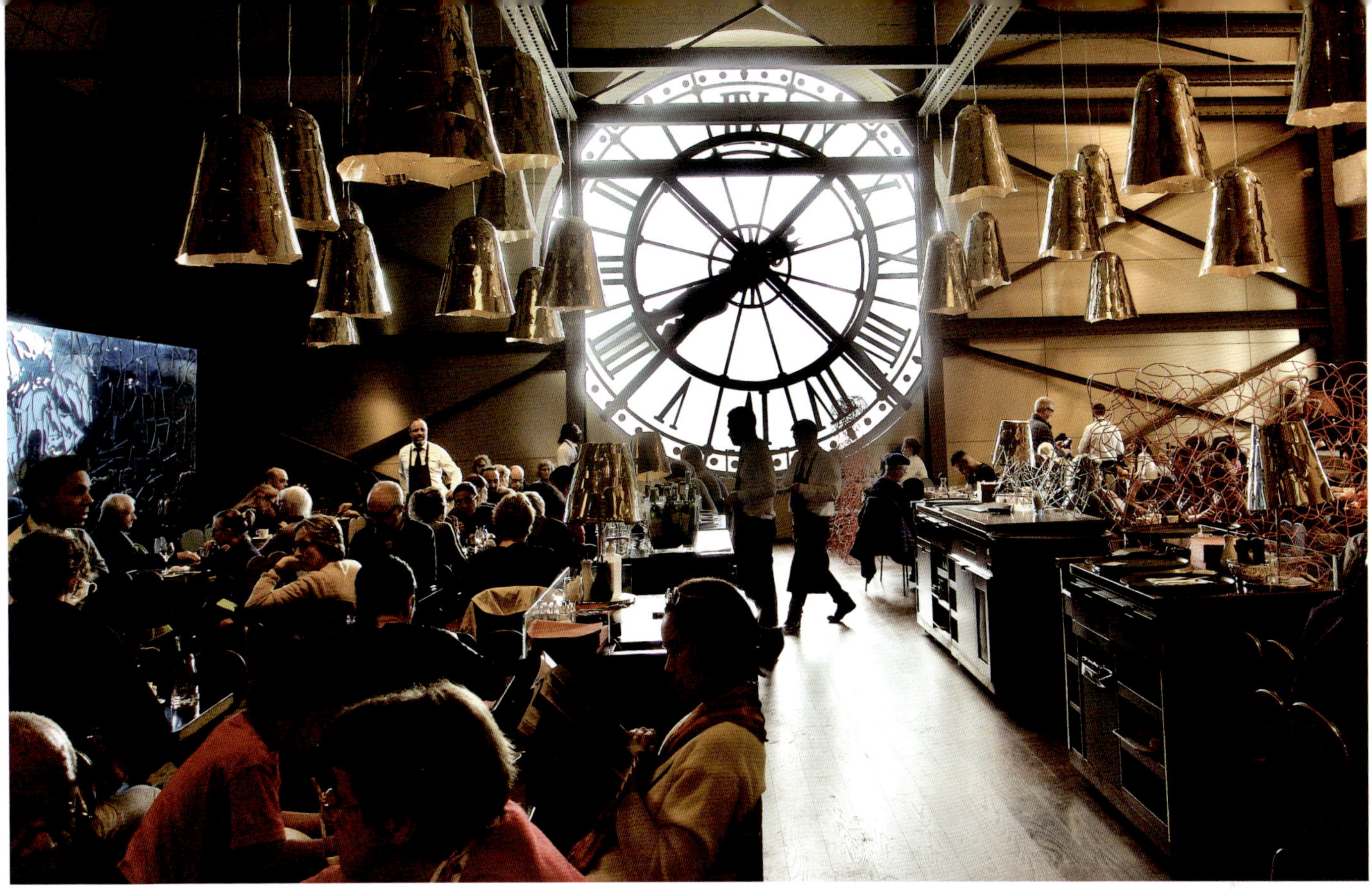

Opened in 2011, Café Campana, with a close-up view of the iconic Musée d'Orsay clock, was designed by Brazilian brothers Fernando and Humberto Campana. Its innovative, festive design is itself a work of art.

Another jewel, with panoramic views of Paris to rival the Eiffel Tower, Georges at the top of the Pompidou, was brilliantly designed by Dominique Jakob and Brendan MacFarlane for the Costes brothers. Open from lunch until late into evening hours, it is a perfect rest stop between taking in the art or a post-museum renewal with a city lights vista.

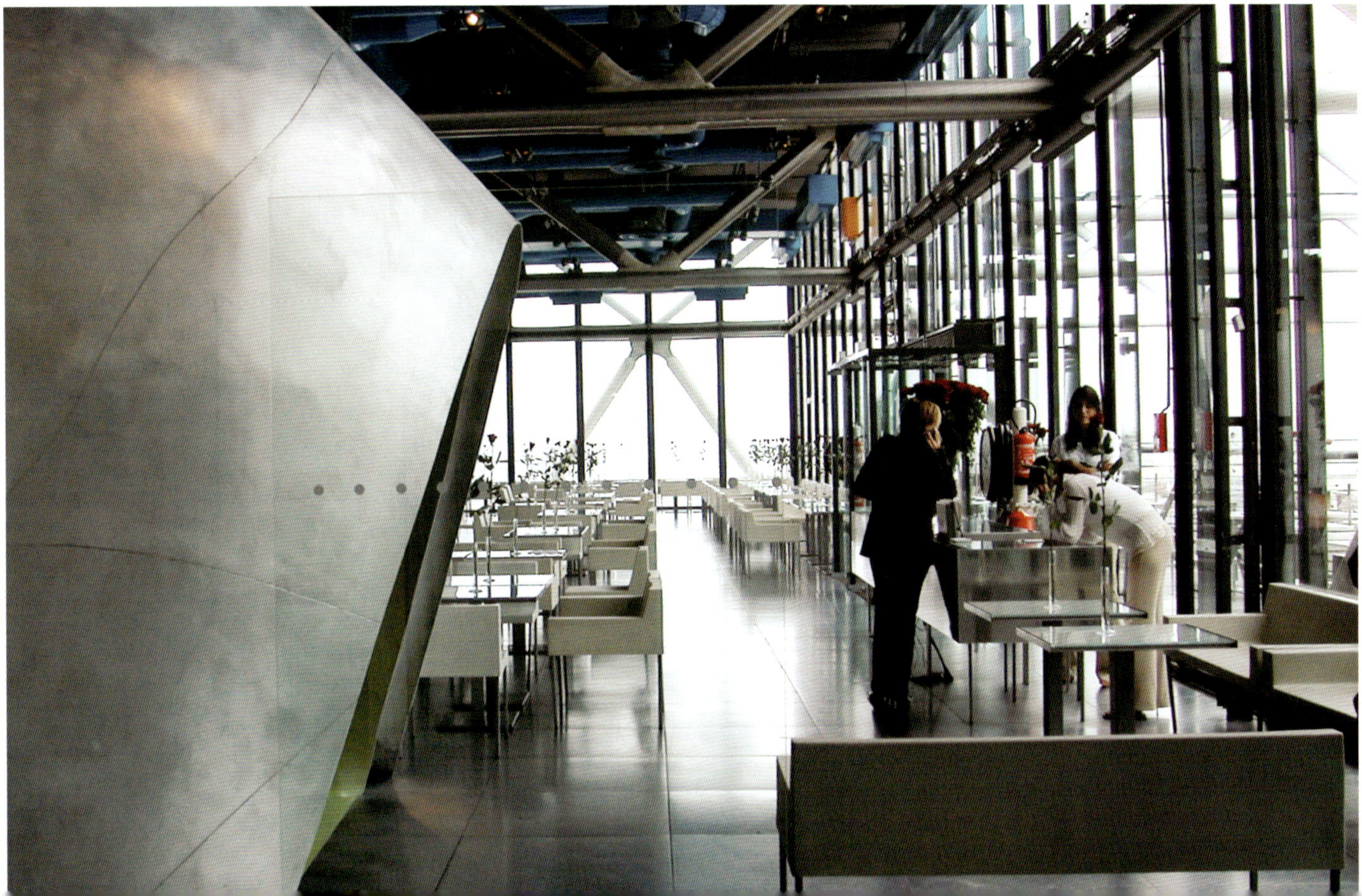

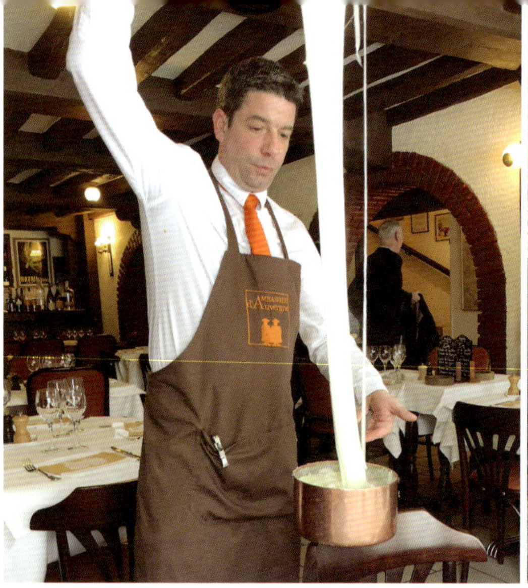

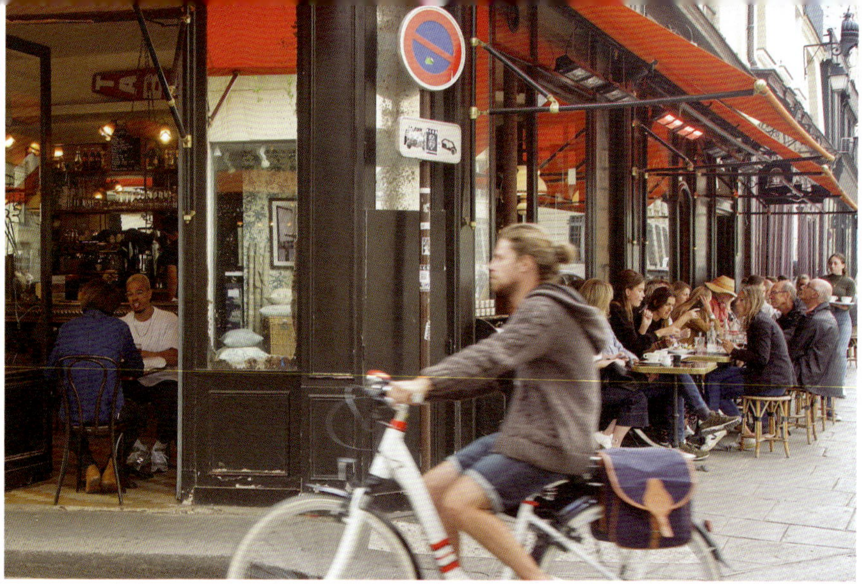

Ambassade d'Auvergne (ABOVE LEFT), located in a 17th-century building that once housed an inn, opened in 1966 and is now run by *Maître Restaurateur* Didier Desert, who preserves and promotes the best traditions of the Auvergne juxtaposed with a lighter, modern touch. Not to be missed is the very traditional cheesy, buttery, creamy aligot, served at the table with great fanfare—a perfect gastronomic splurge before or after a long promenade.

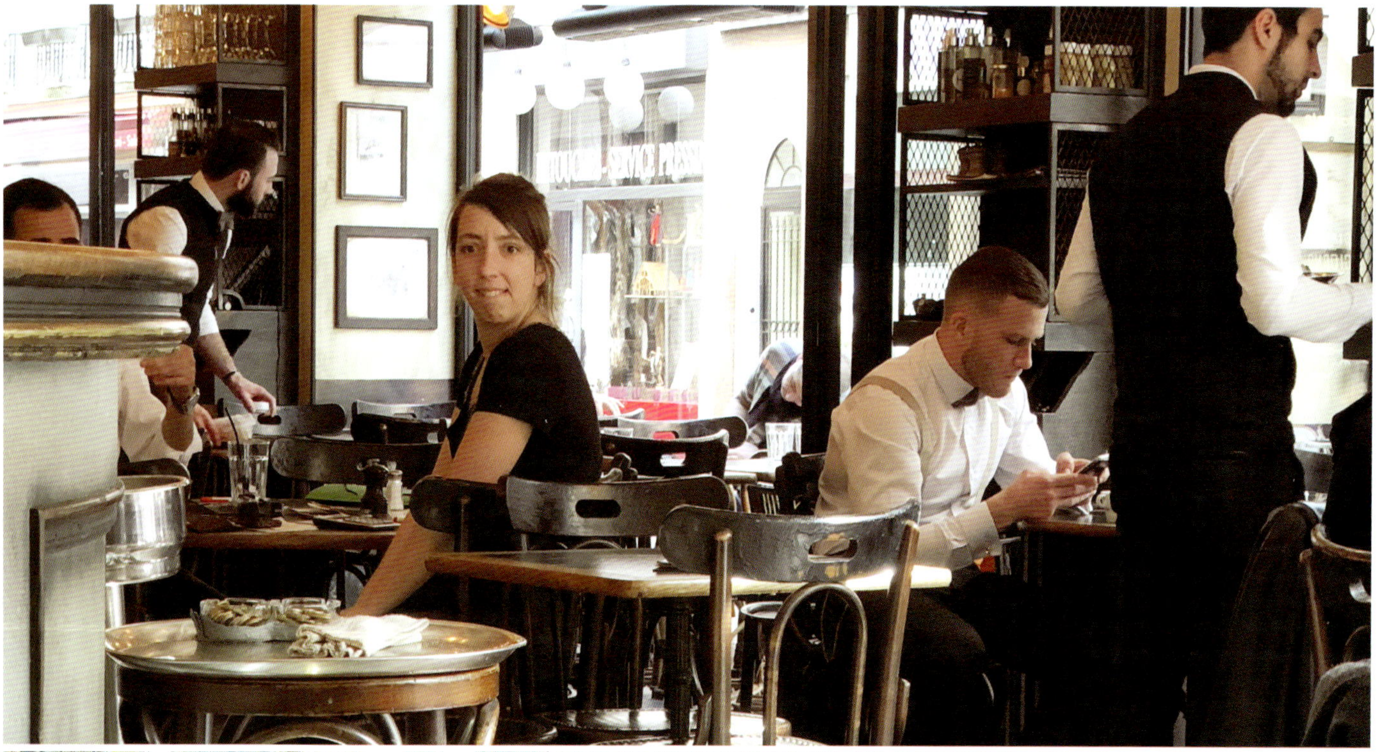

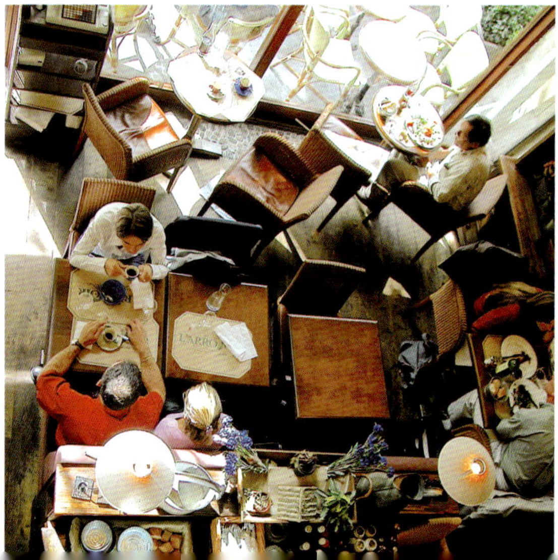

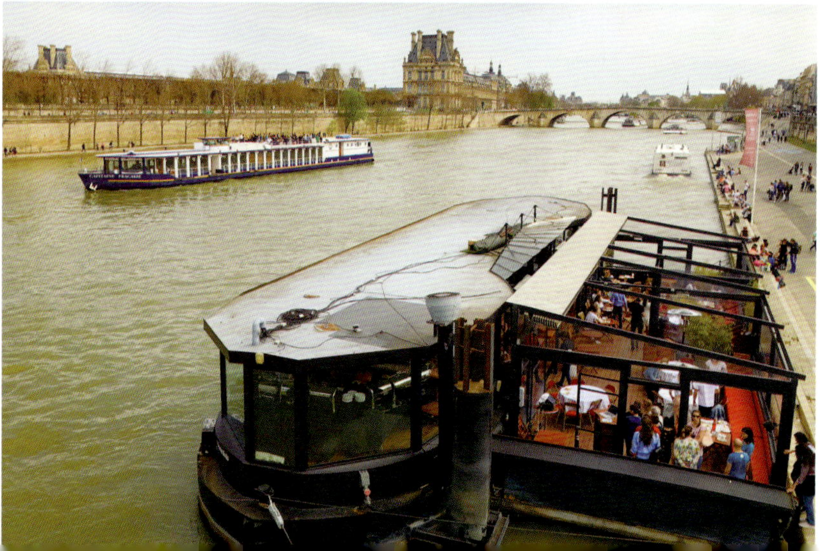

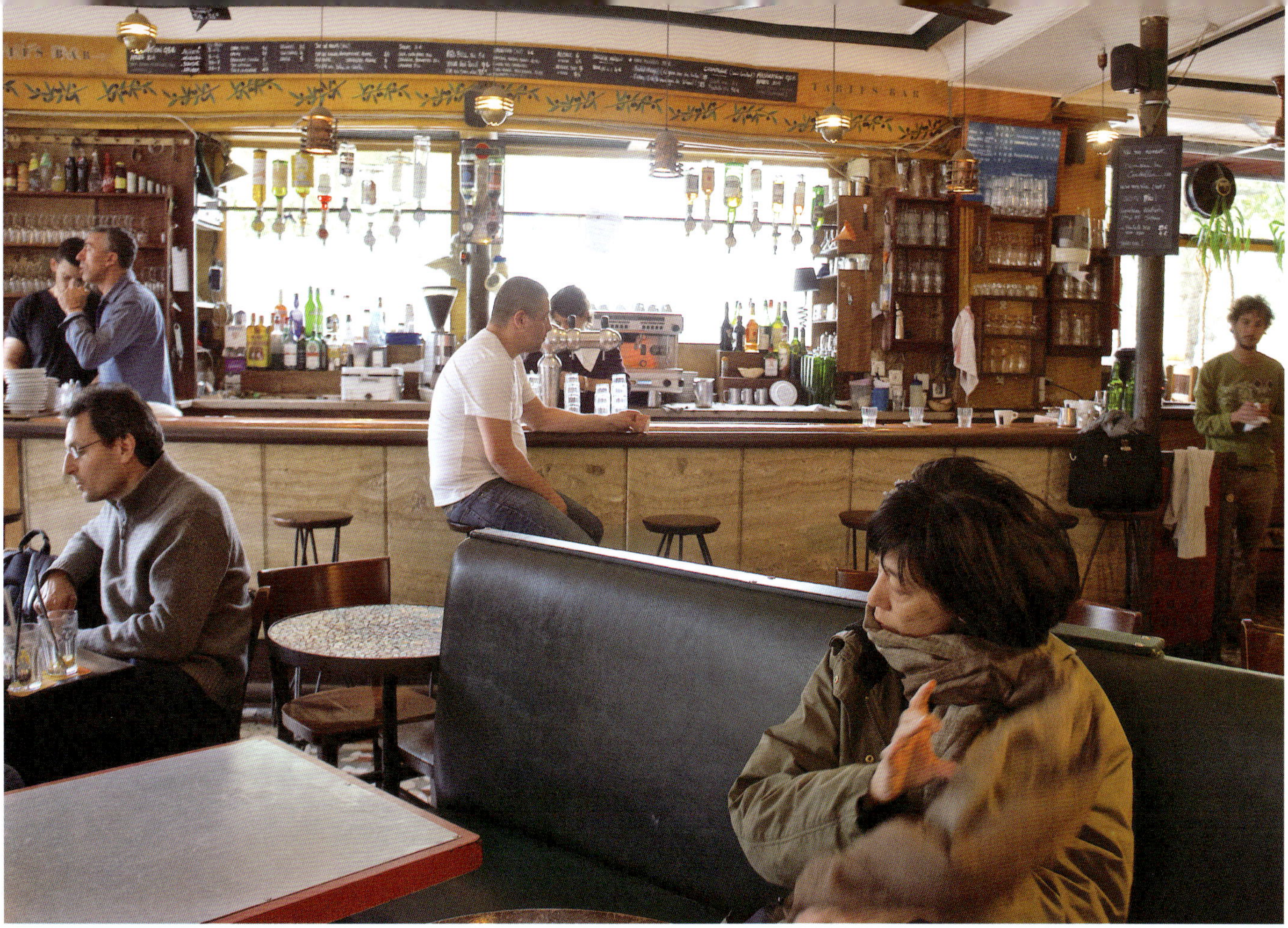

Edgy, funky, affordable, bobo (*bourgeois bohême*) Chez Prune, in the trendy 10th arrondissement on the oh-so-bobo and graffiti adorned Canal Saint-Martin, is typically filled with young Parisians. With an evocative working-class café interior and a terrace facing the canal, it is an ultra-cool spot for a drink or light meal at any time of the day. Stroll along the canal, commissioned by Bonaparte in 1802, and watch the locks swing to let the boats pass through.

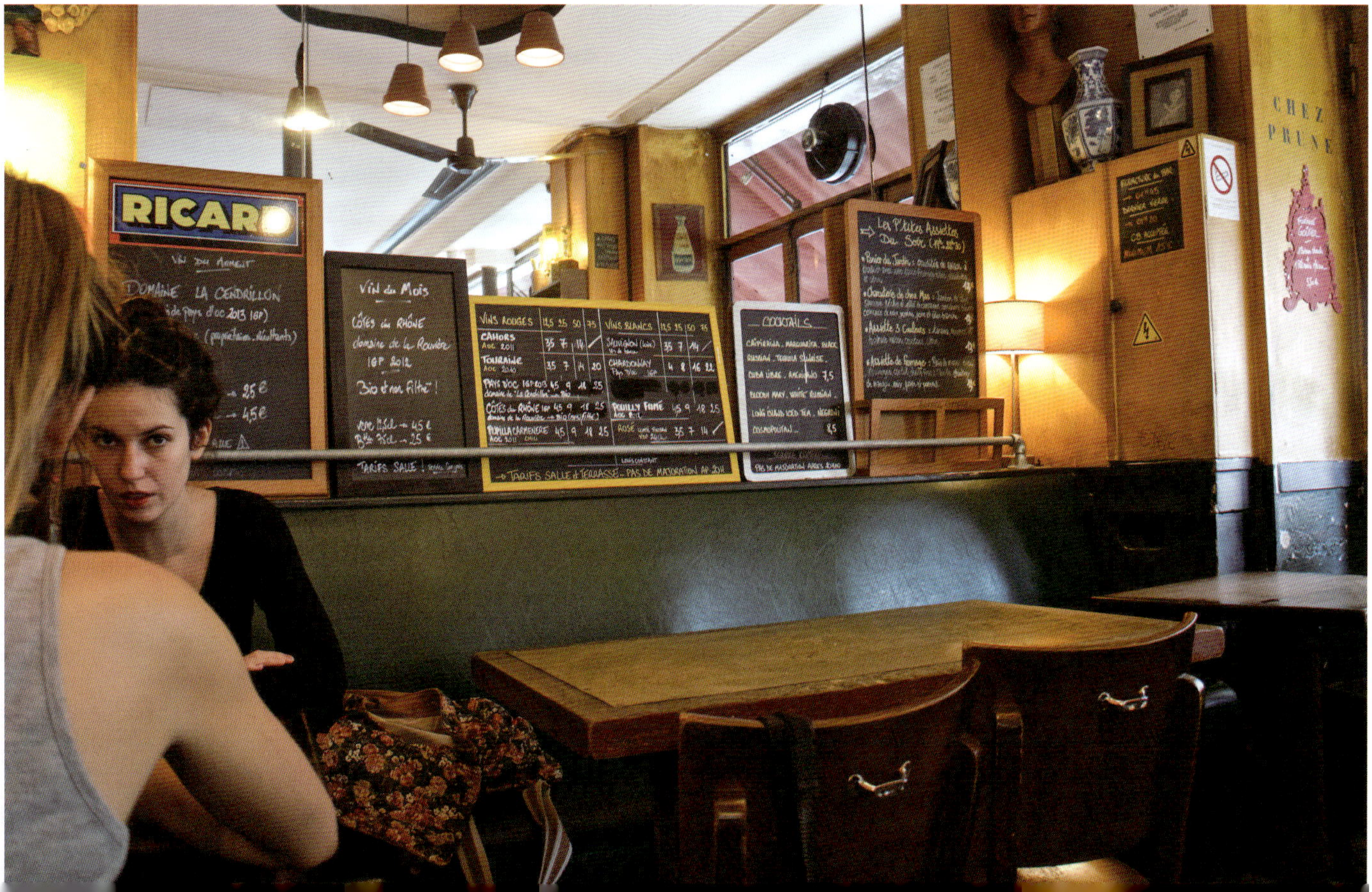

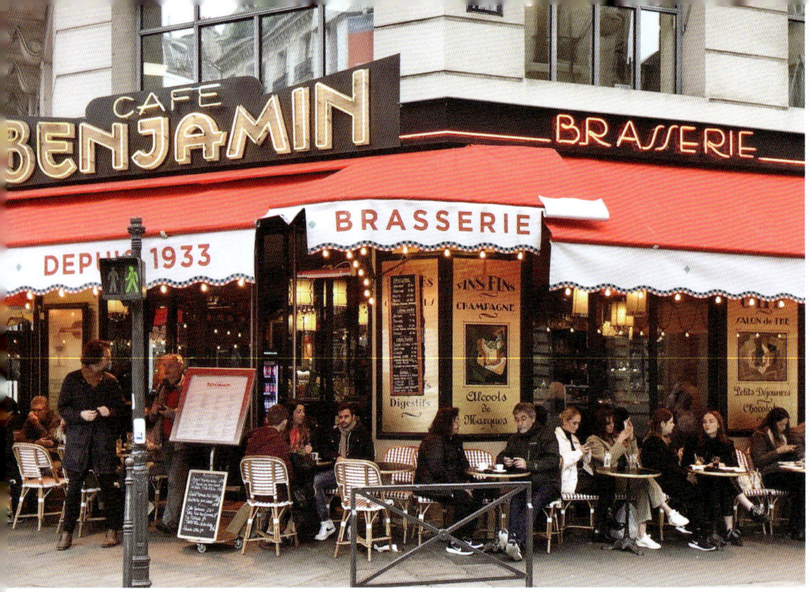
CAFE
BENJAMIN
BRASSERIE
BRASSERIE

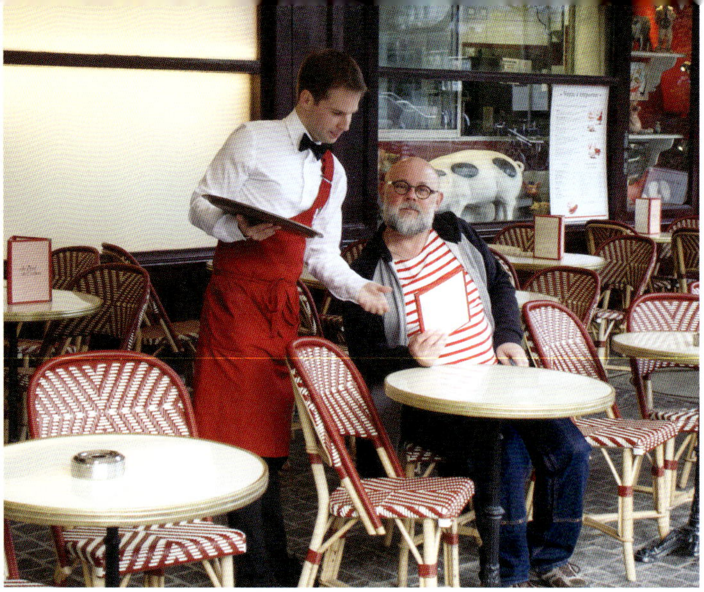

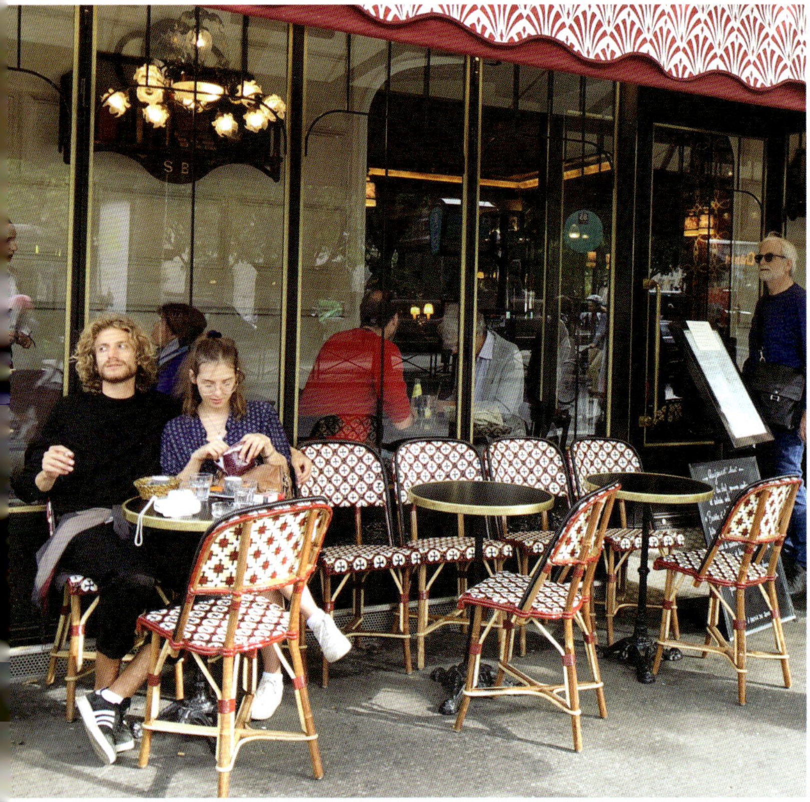

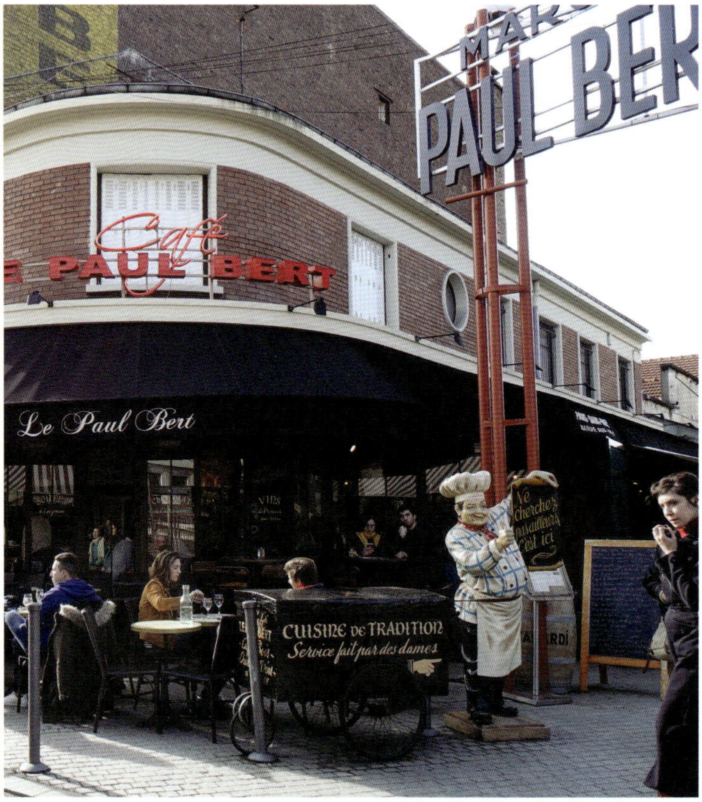
PAUL BERT
Café
Le Paul Bert
CUISINE DE TRADITION
Service fait par des dames

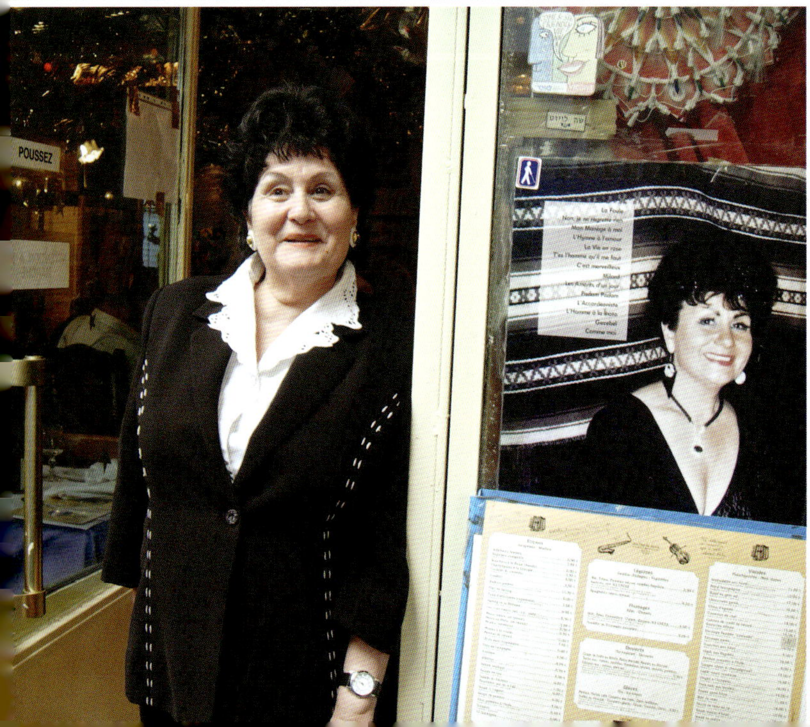
POUSSEZ

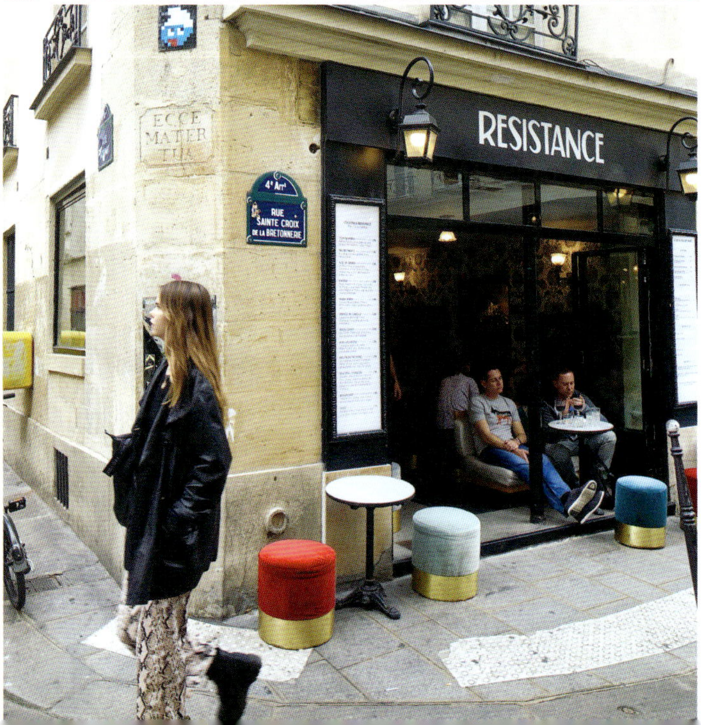
RESISTANCE
RUE SAINTE CROIX DE LA BRETONNERIE

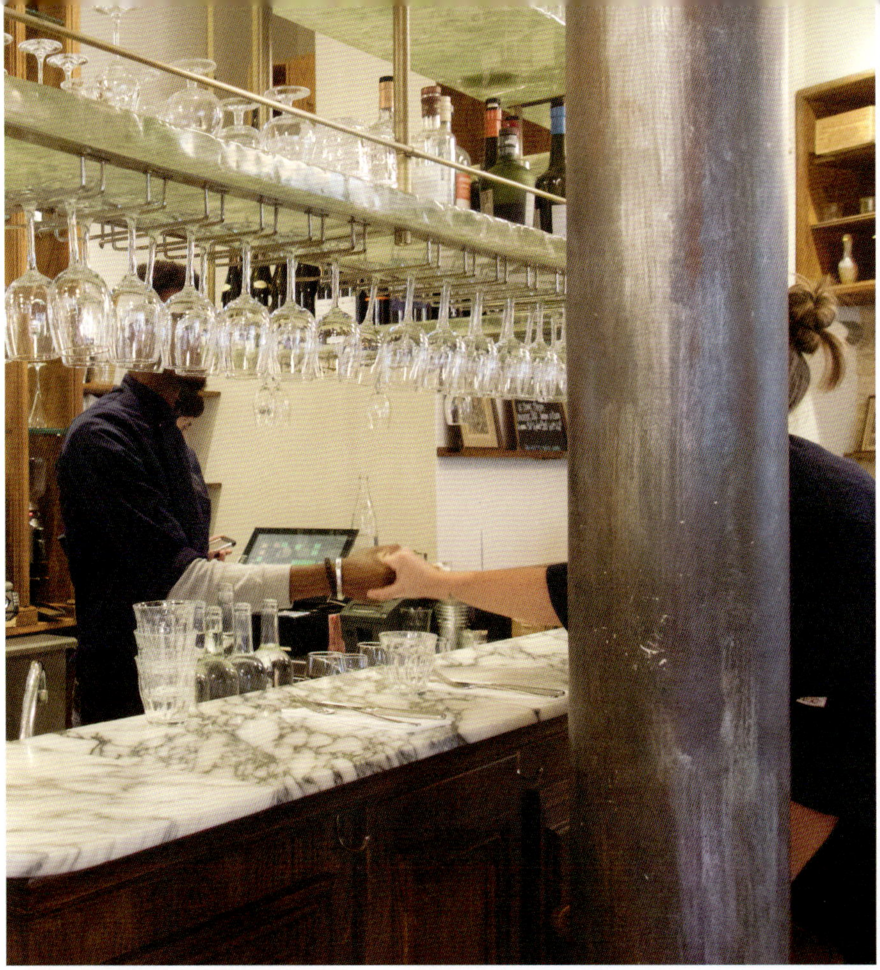

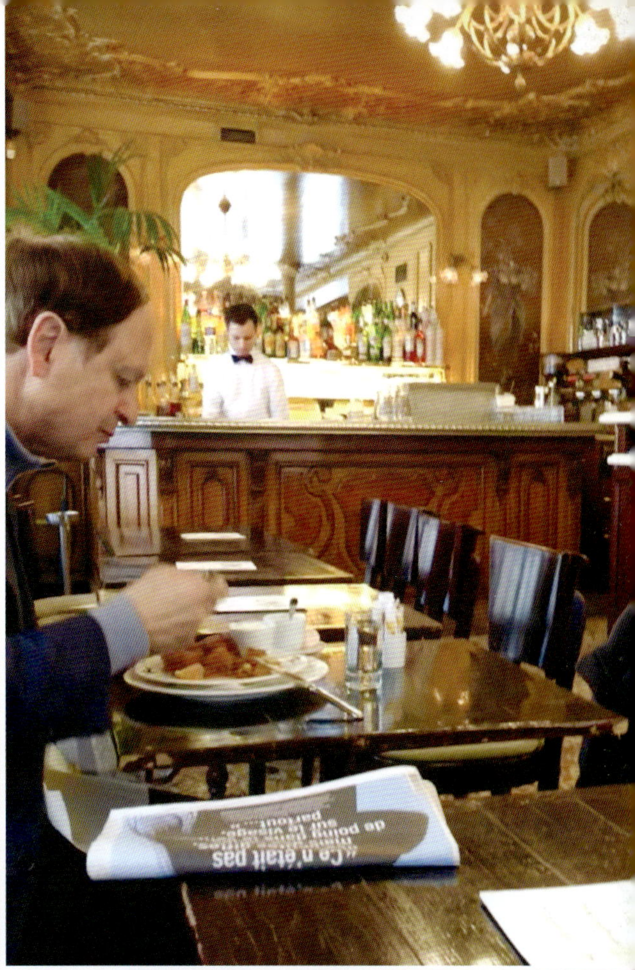

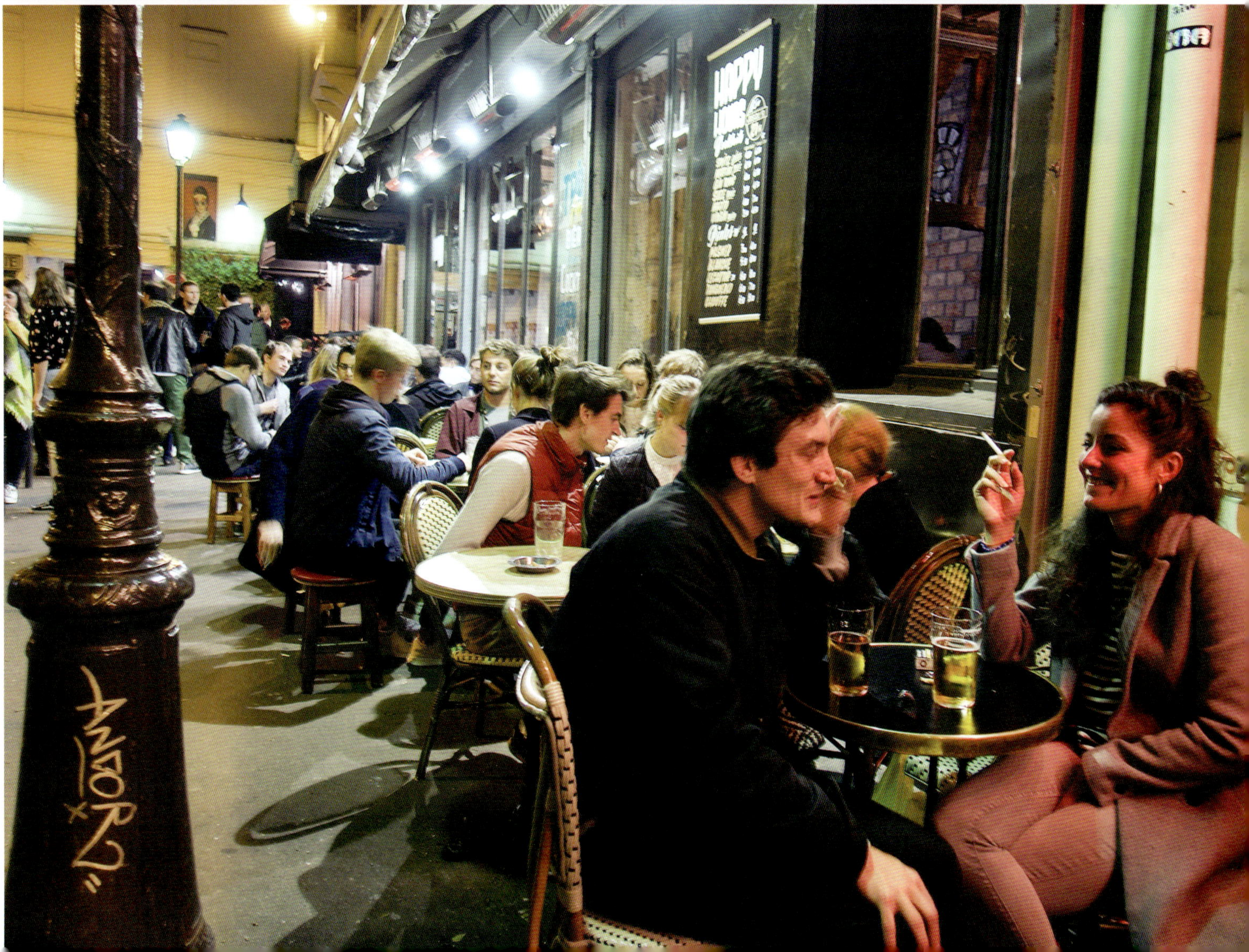

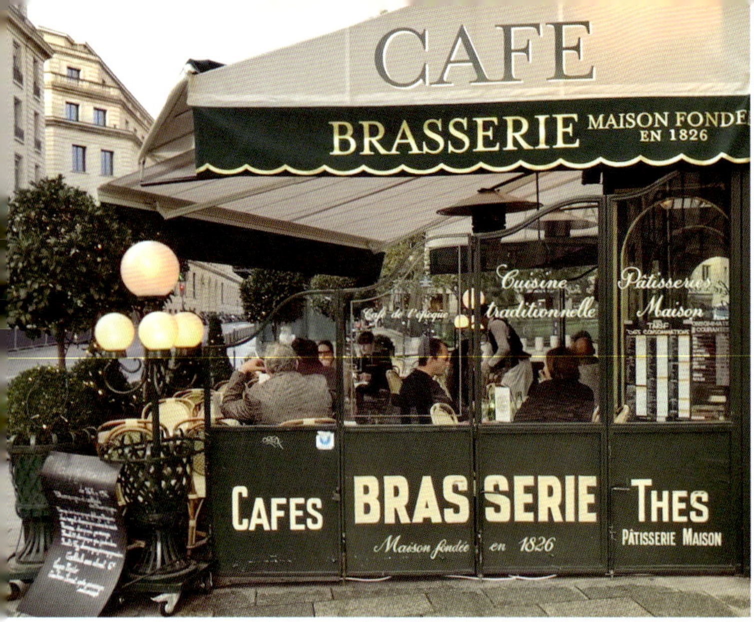
CAFE
BRASSERIE
MAISON FONDE
EN 1826
Cuisine traditionnelle
Pâtisseries Maison
CAFES BRASSERIE THES
Maison fondée en 1826
PÂTISSERIE MAISON

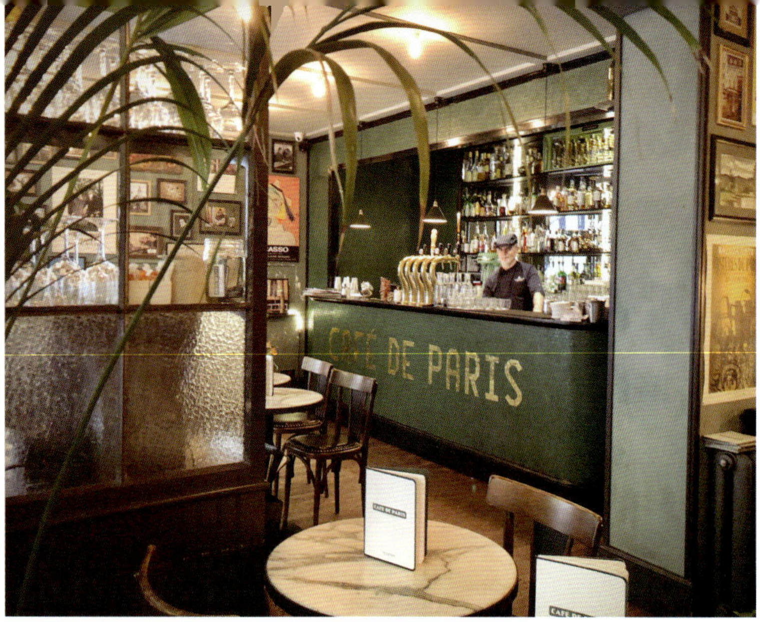
CAFÉ DE PARIS

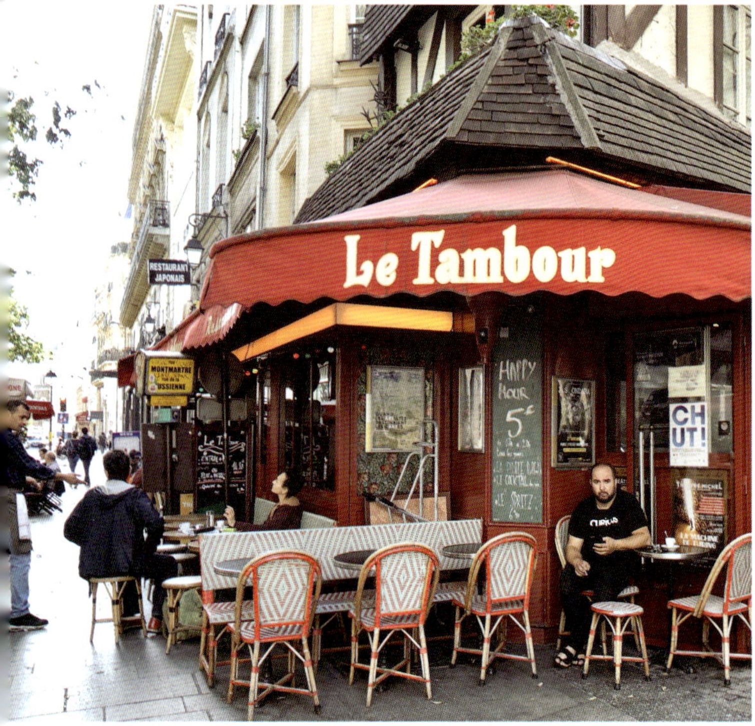
Le Tambour
HAPPY Hour
5€
CHUT!

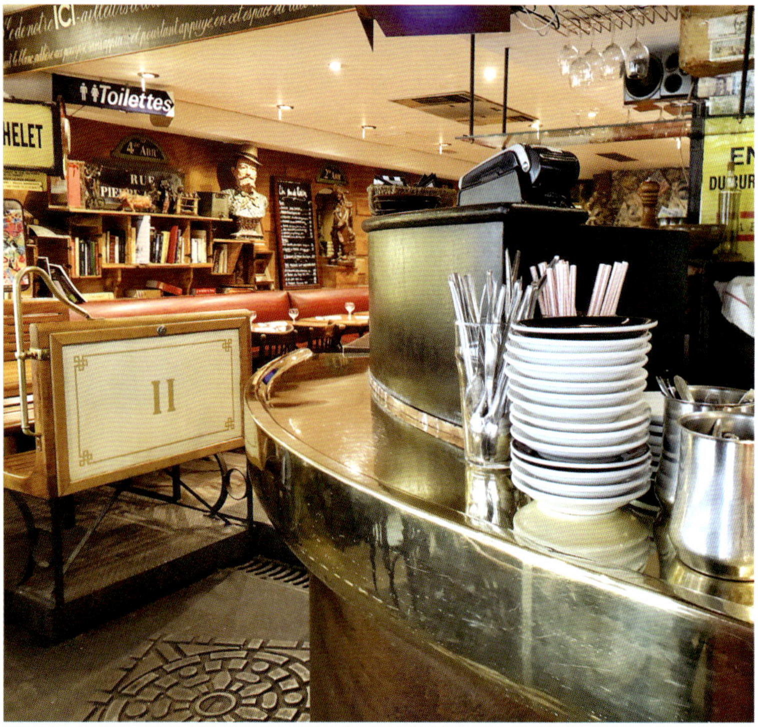
Toilettes
II

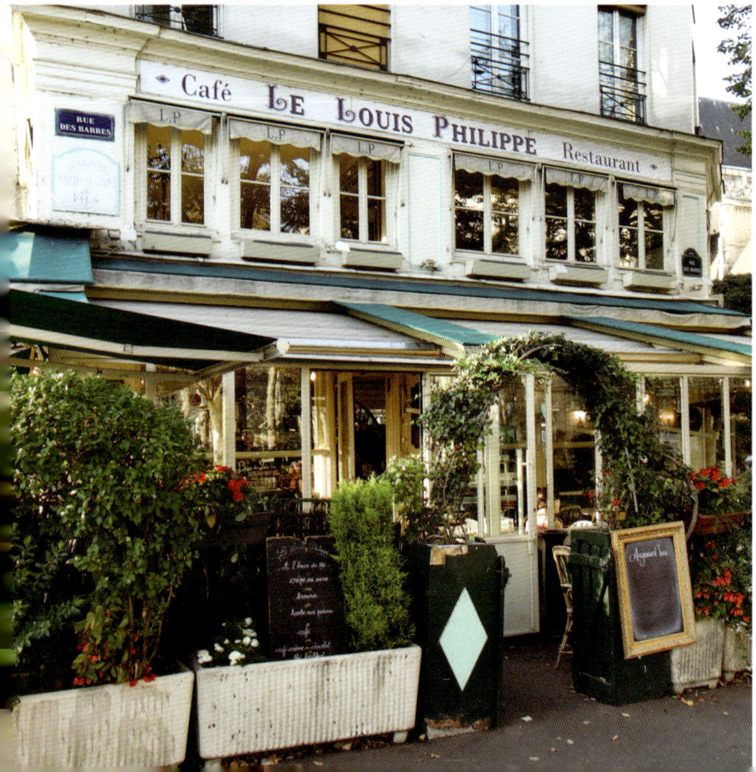
Café LE LOUIS PHILIPPE Restaurant
RUE DES BARRES

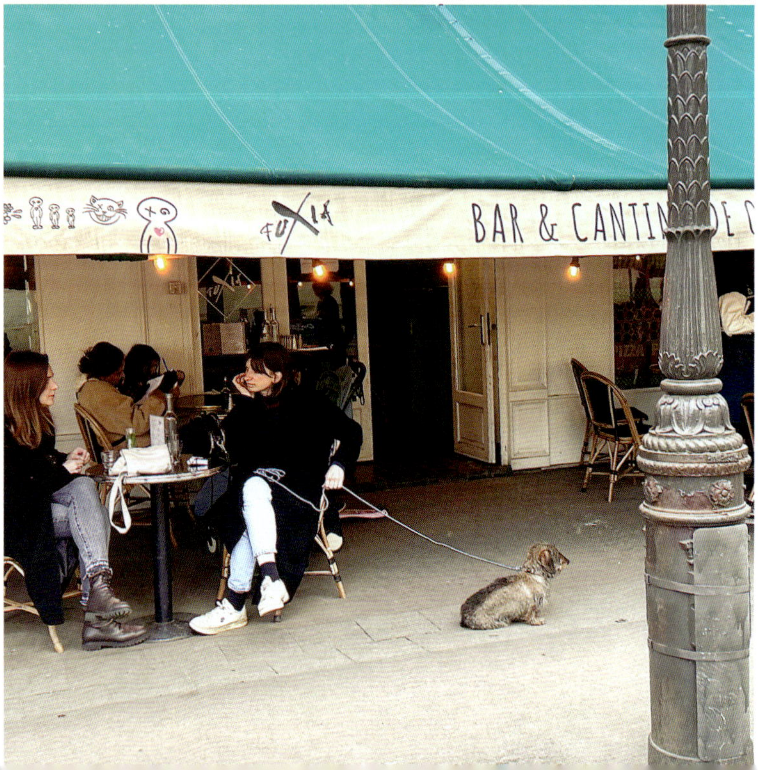
BAR & CANTIN

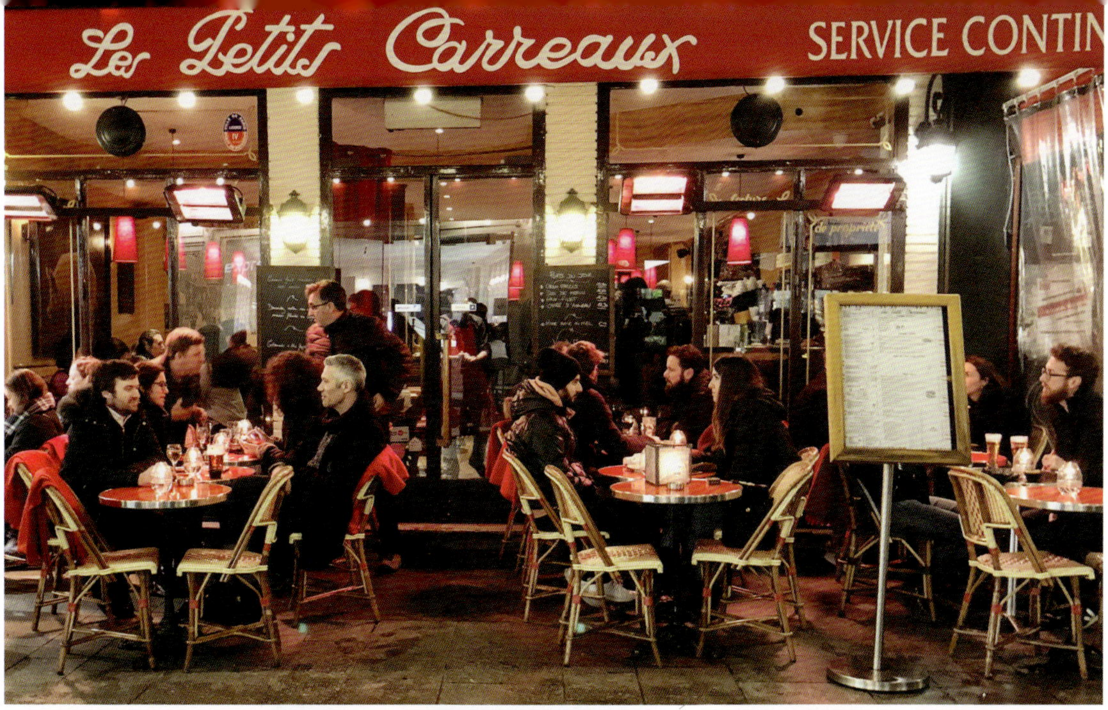
Les Petits Carreaux
SERVICE CONTIN

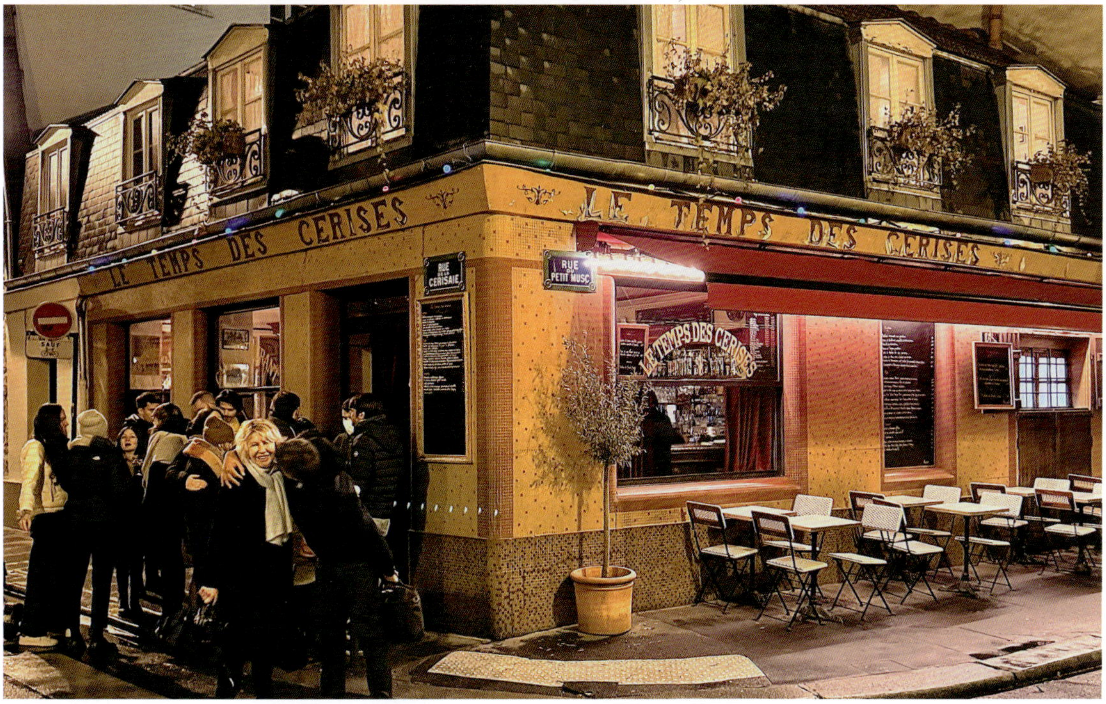
LE TEMPS DES CERISES
LE TEMPS DES CERISES
RUE CERISAIE
RUE PETIT MUSC
LE TEMPS DES CERISES

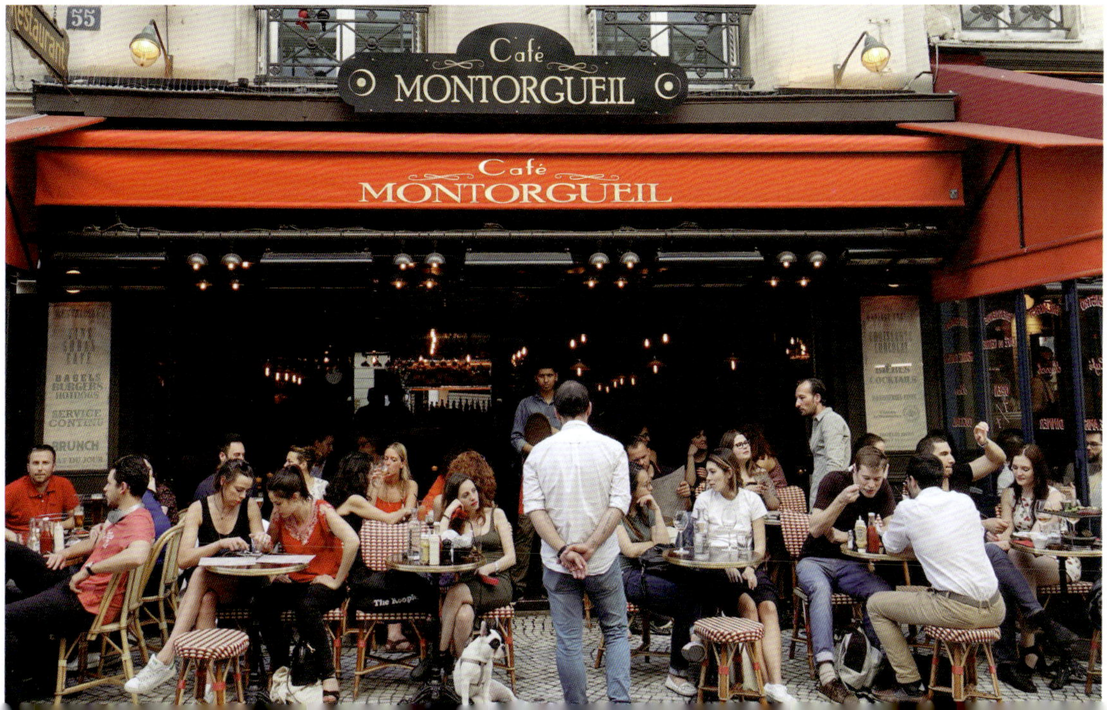
55
Café
MONTORGUEIL
Café
MONTORGUEIL

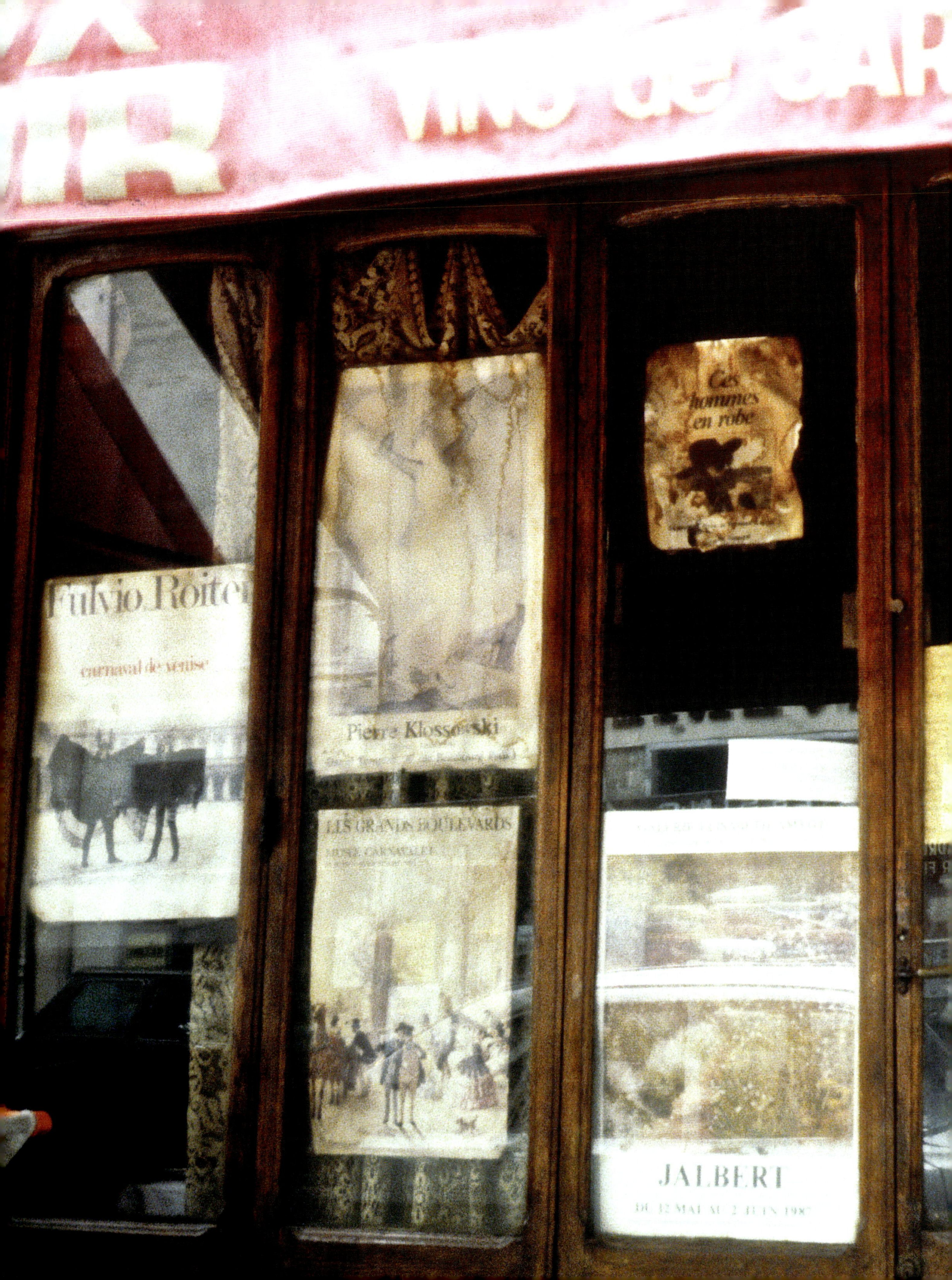
Ces hommes en robe
Fulvio Roiter
carnaval de venise
Pierre Klossowski
LES GRANDS BOULEVARDS
MUSÉE CARNAVALET
JALBERT

PART 9 In Search of Lost Time

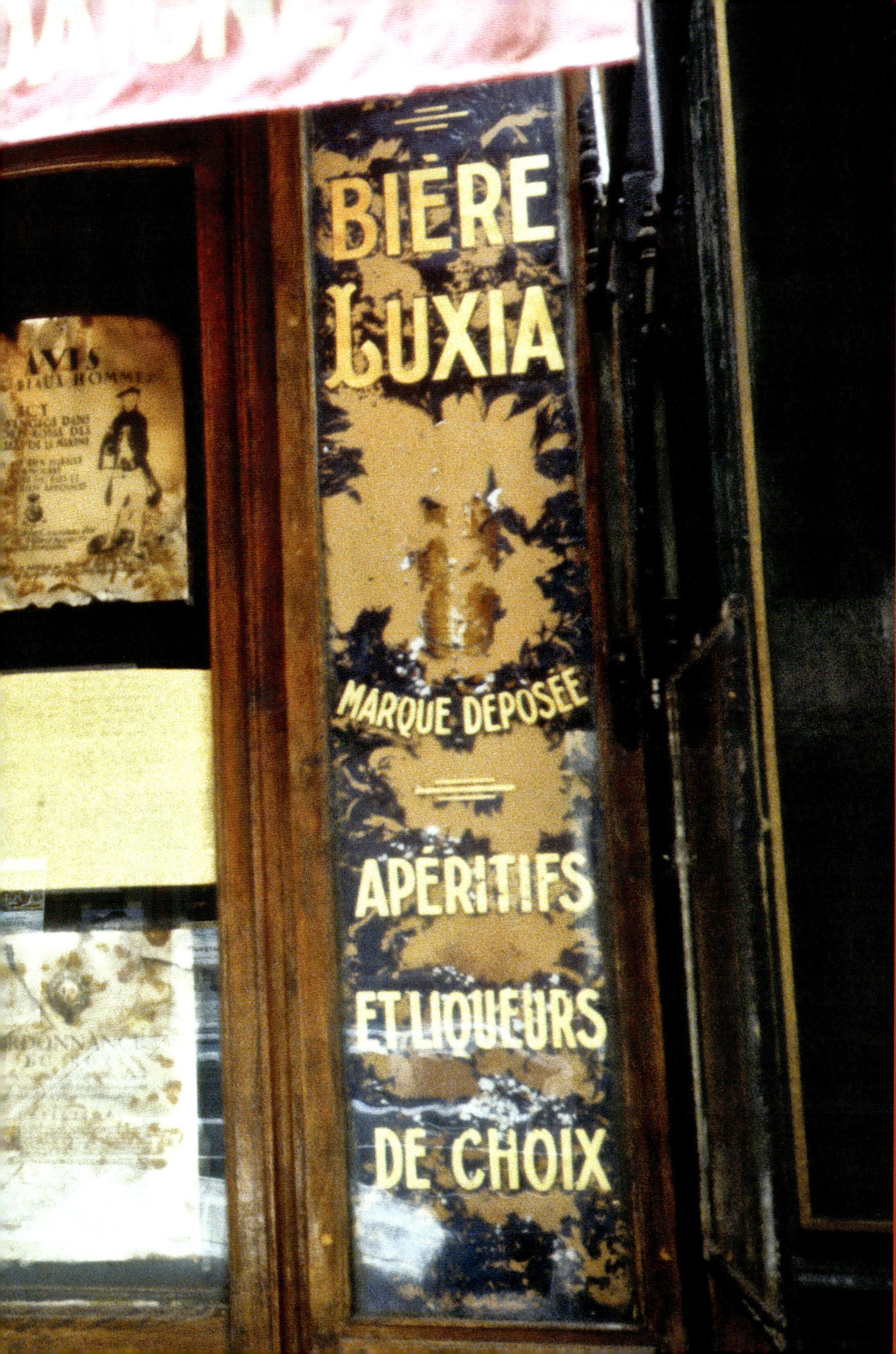

Now & Then: Time Regained

"If you are lucky enough to have lived in Paris as a young man,
then wherever you go for the rest of your life, it stays with you, for Paris is a moveable feast."

Ernest Hemingway, *A Moveable Feast*

It is said that the French hate change but love revolution. Change, *bien sûr*, is inevitable, even for the French. From the Neanderthals to the Celtic Parisii, the Gauls, Romans, Huns, Vikings, and more—conquerors, traders, immigrants, neighbors, and travelers have influenced the country's culture and cuisine. Whereas some classic French dishes are centuries old, reaching as far back as the Roman Empire and Renaissance Italy, perpetual international influences, innovation, and the love of good food and wine have fostered epicurean revolutions and evolutions, lending a grand diversity to the French table.

European trade and colonialism scattered crops, spices, herbs, and recipes from and to every continent across the globe: chocolate, corn, tomatoes, potatoes, and avocados from the Americas, sugar, citrus, coffee (and cafés) from Asia via Islam, spices from Asia and Africa. The French planted these riches at home and in their colonies, in accordance with the climate and the soil, cultivating ingredients that changed everything.

This rich culinary history, coupled with the country's diverse and fertile topography enabling a variety and abundance of food to be grown within its borders, along with its meticulously trained chefs, make French gastronomy one of the world's great cuisines. In 2010, UNESCO included the French gastronomic meal as part of the Intangible Cultural Heritage of Humanity.

Cities constantly reinvent themselves, and Paris delights with creativity in all aspects of art, life, and food. Along with exciting, innovative change, it is heartening that some venerable Parisian icons, including its quintessential gastronomic institutions, remain intact. The storied food establishments that continue to serve up beloved classic dishes, frequently with a twist, often in beautifully preserved surroundings, are a gift. It is comforting and thrilling to dip into the past in these authentic cafés, bistros, and brasseries and wistfully imagine them through the years, with illustrious patrons *à table*. Too many of the oldies but goodies have disappeared or have been poorly remodeled rather than refreshed. We celebrate those that remain and retain or regain their quality and hope they endure.

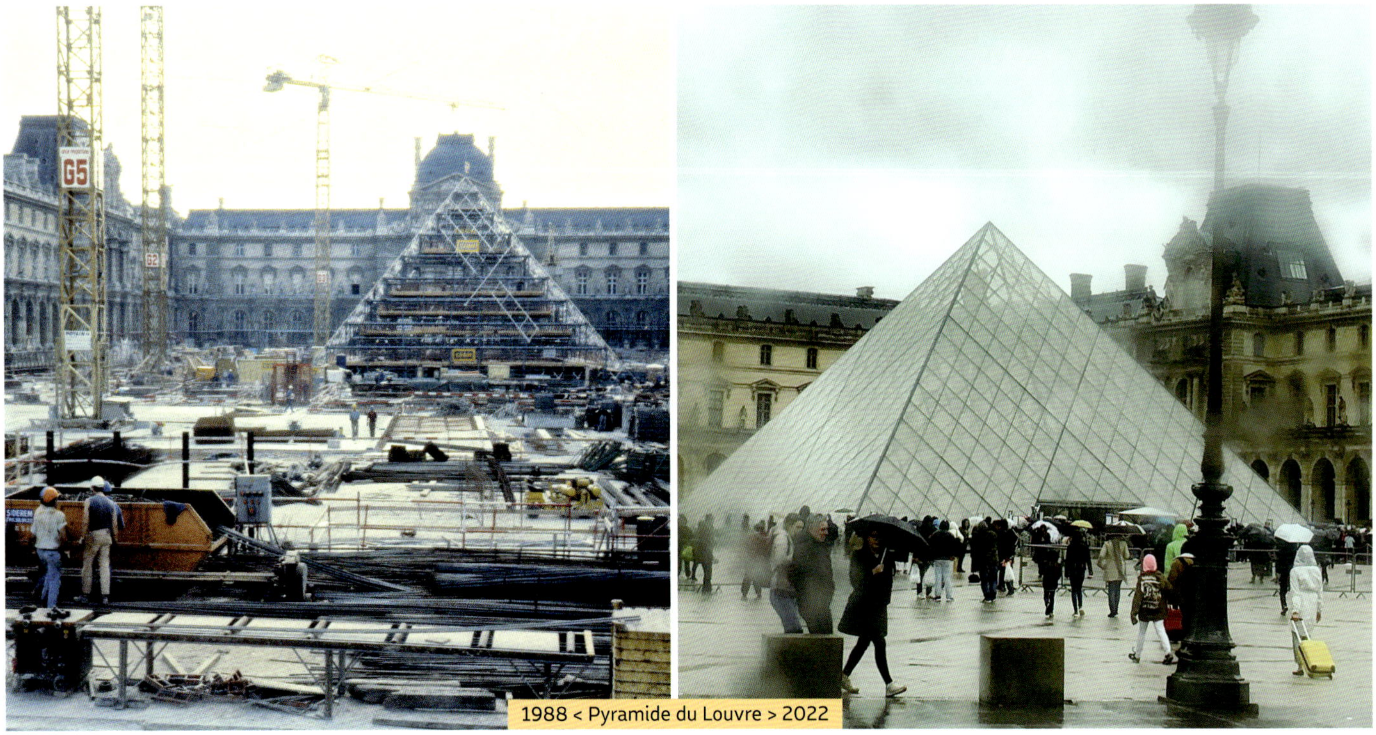

1988 < Pyramide du Louvre > 2022

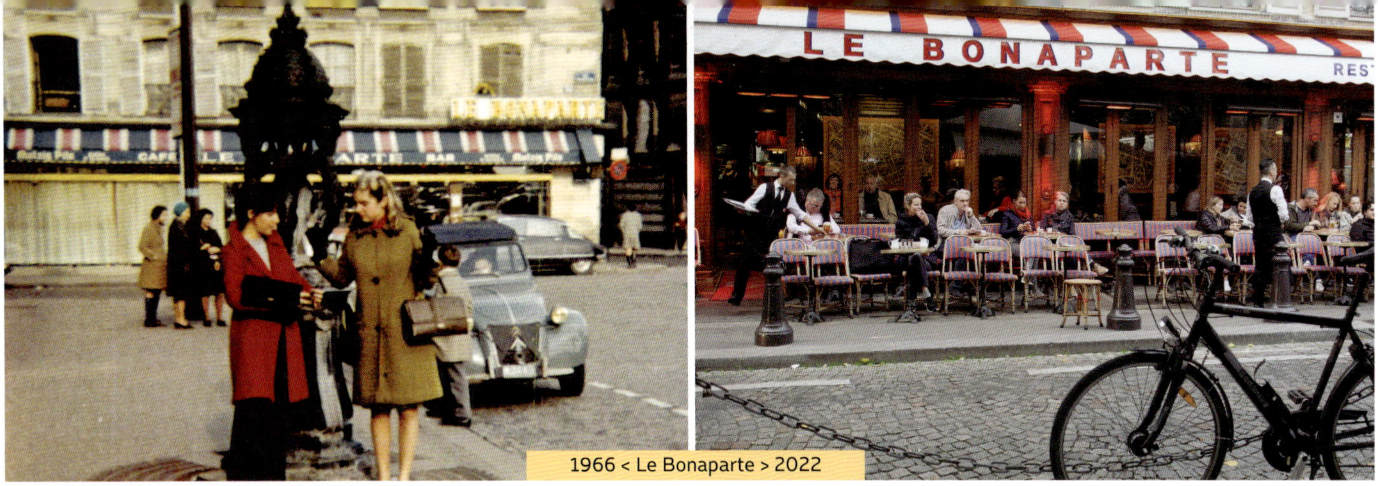

1966 < Le Bonaparte > 2022

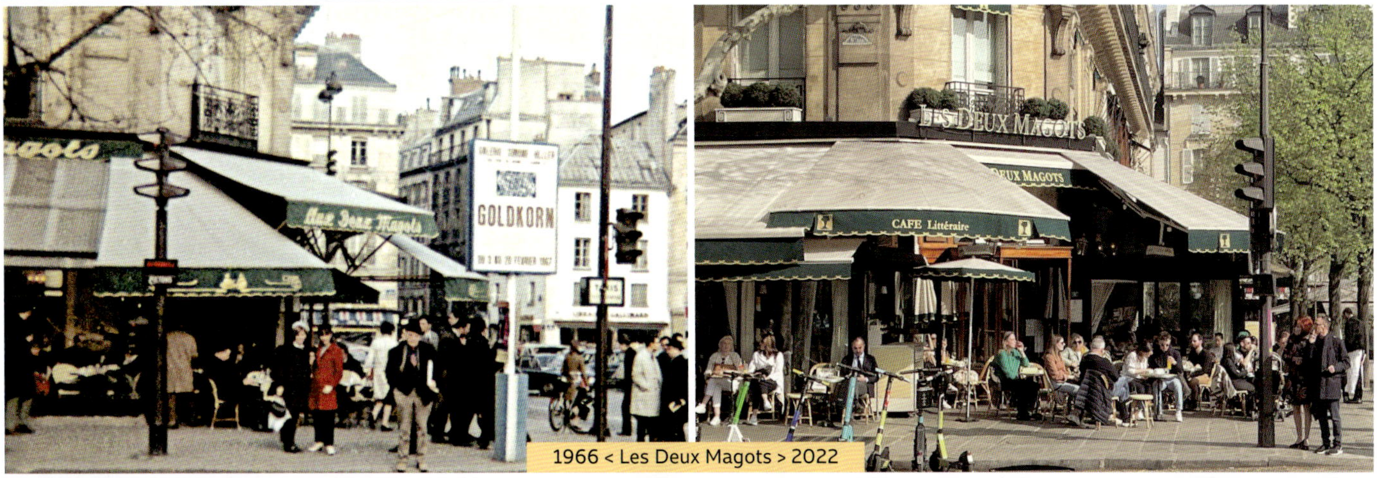

1966 < Les Deux Magots > 2022

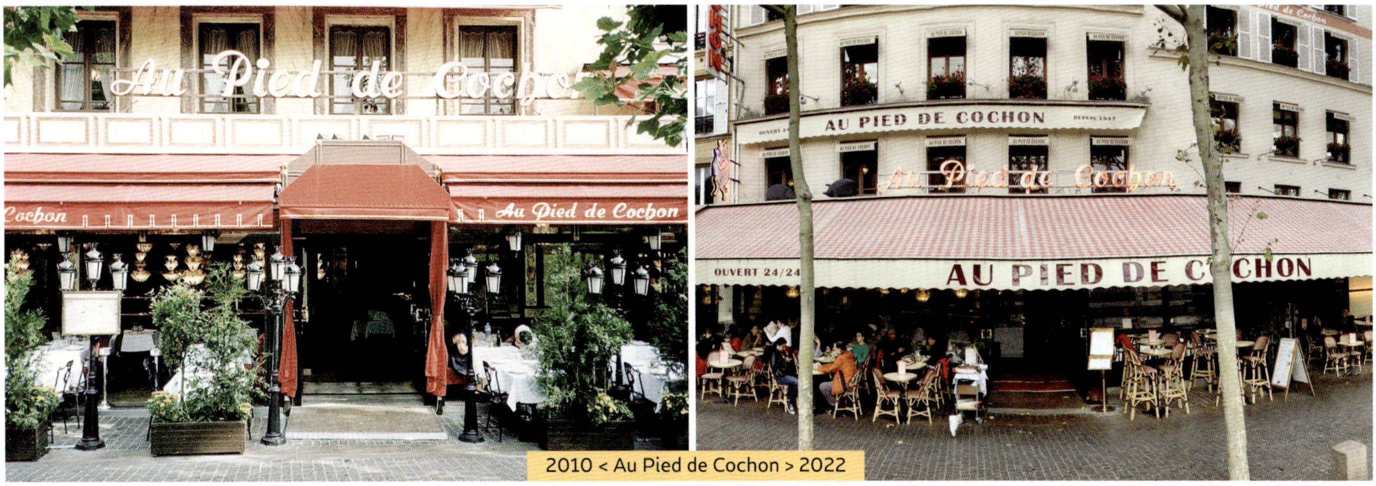

2010 < Au Pied de Cochon > 2022

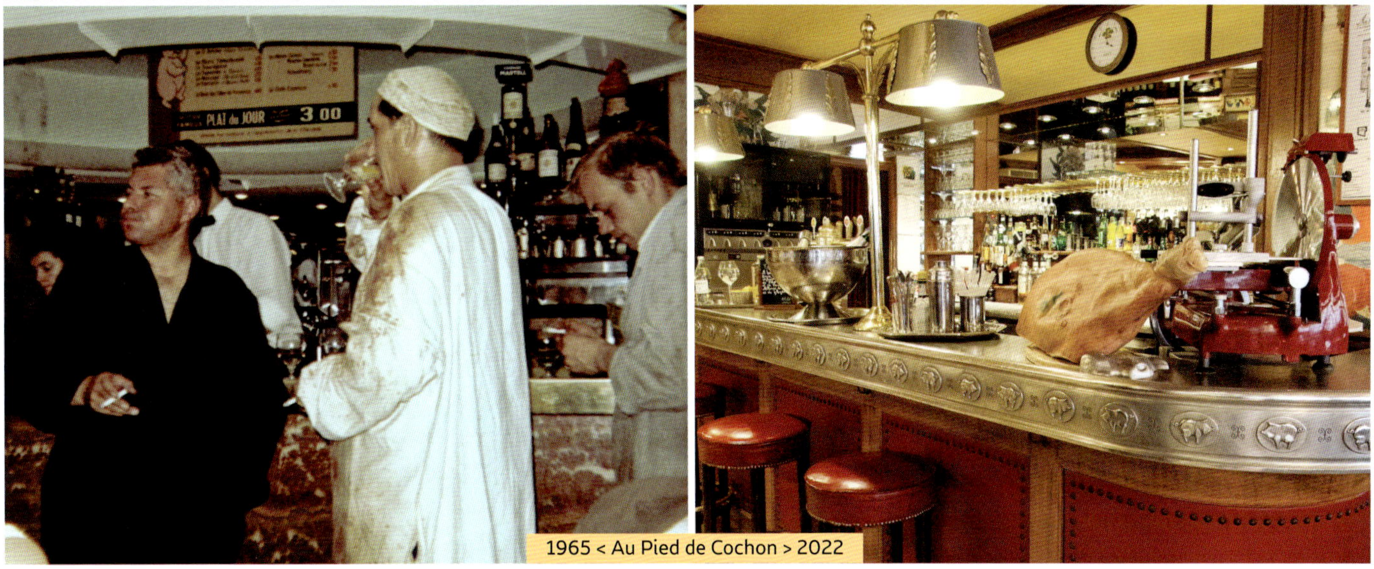

1965 < Au Pied de Cochon > 2022

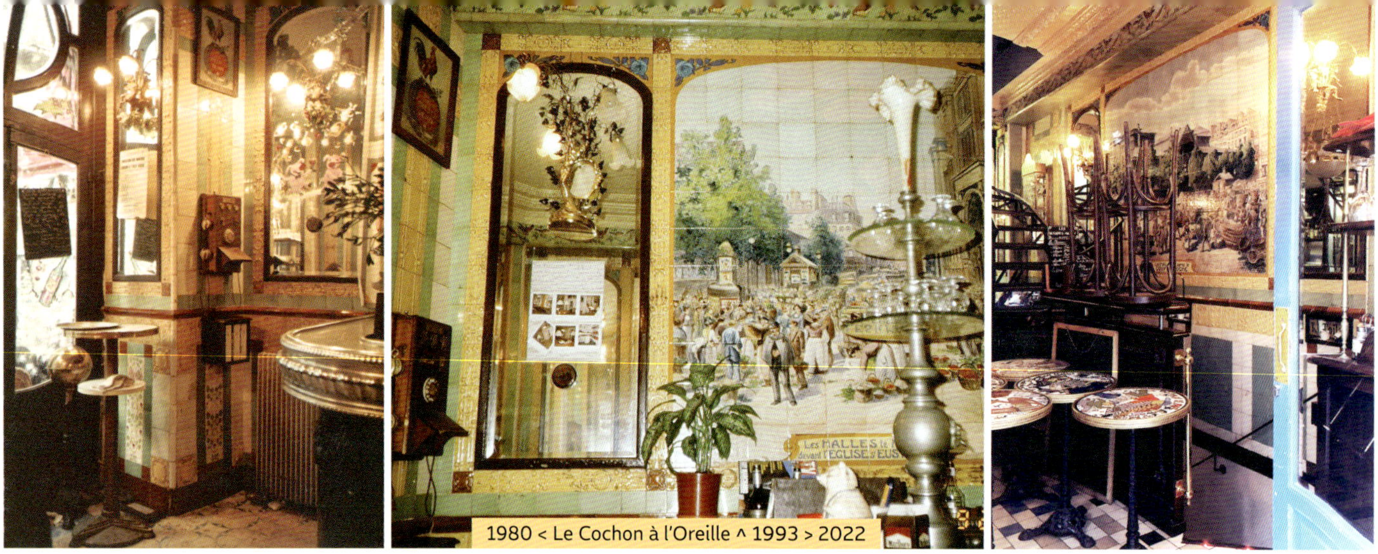
1980 < Le Cochon à l'Oreille ^ 1993 > 2022

Le Cochon à l'Oreille (The Pig's Ear, ABOVE), dating back to 1890, was originally a working-class café. Still encrusted with tile murals depicting the now defunct Les Halles food market, this tiny café is a historic monument.

Legendary Brasserie, La Coupole (OPPOSITE), with the dome or cupola over a rotating sculpture by Louis Derbré (added in 1993), and its Bar Americain, retains its 1927 flavor in every aspect of its design, food, and service. Nothing here is trendy; timeless is the key. With a stellar literary, artistic, and intellectual history dating back to *Les Années Folles* (aka "The Crazy Years," "The Roaring Twenties," or "the Jazz Age"), this illustrious institution entertained *Le Tout Paris* regularly. Still now, the luminaries stop in for the copious platters of *fruits de mer* and legendary lamb curry, elegantly served at the table from a cart by a *serveur* in appropriate attire.

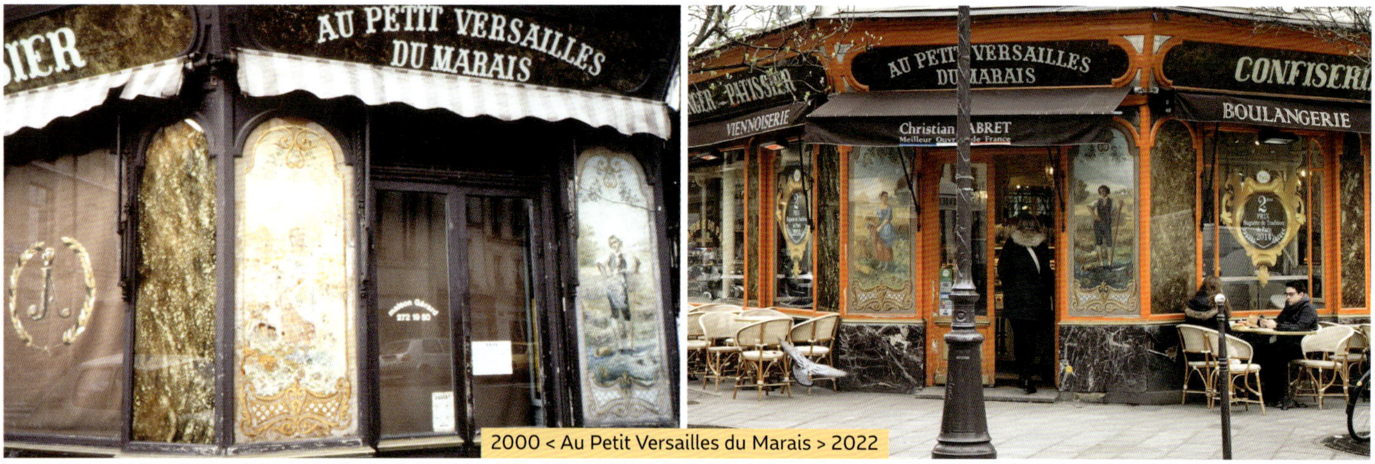

2000 < Au Petit Versailles du Marais > 2022

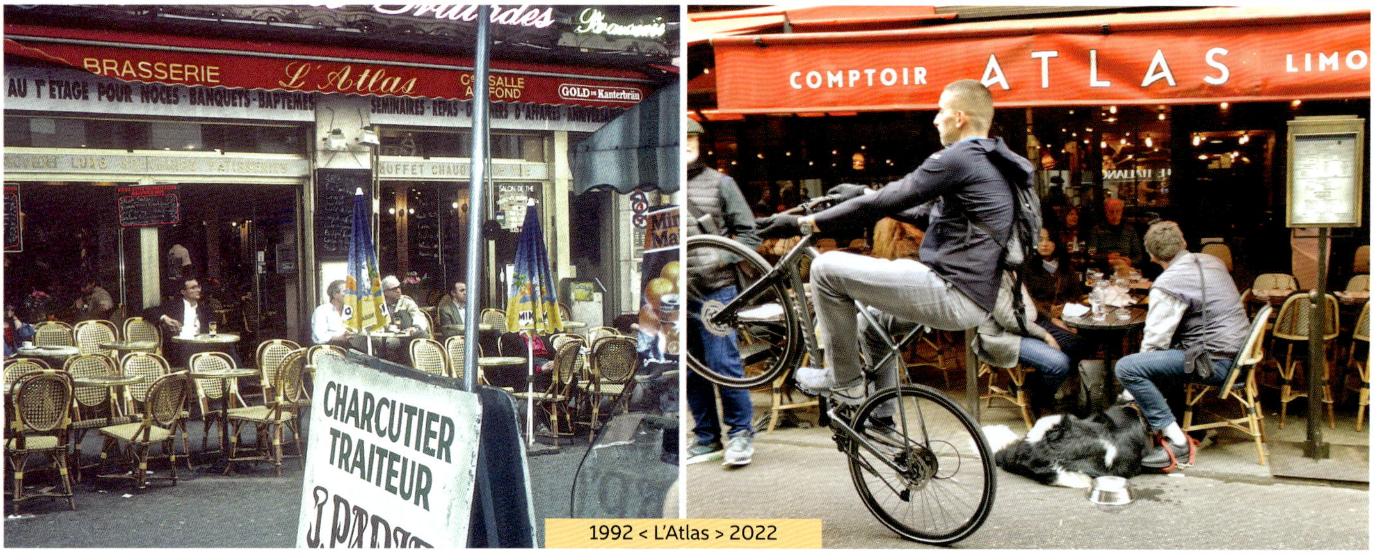

1992 < L'Atlas > 2022

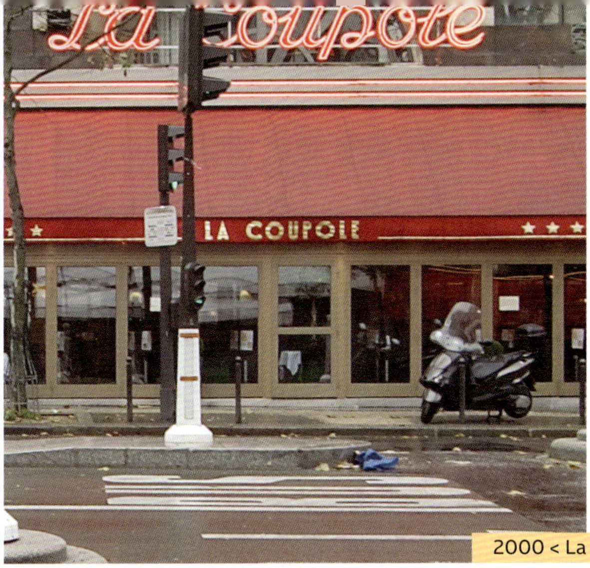

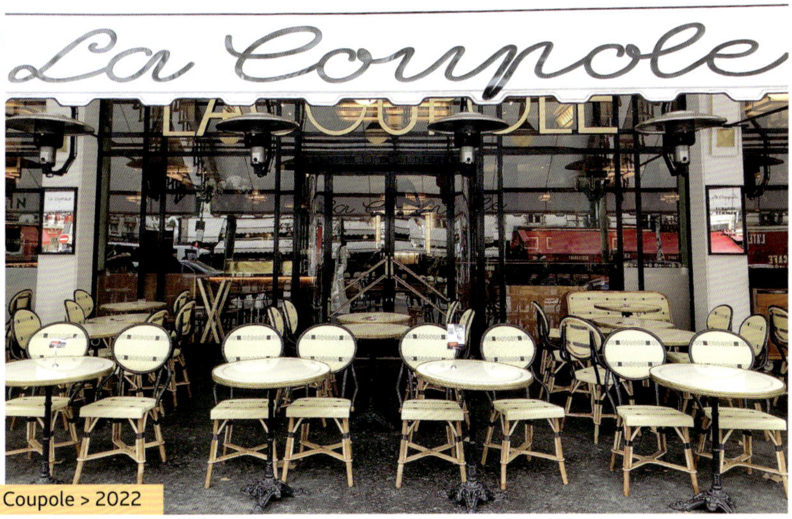

2000 < La Coupole > 2022

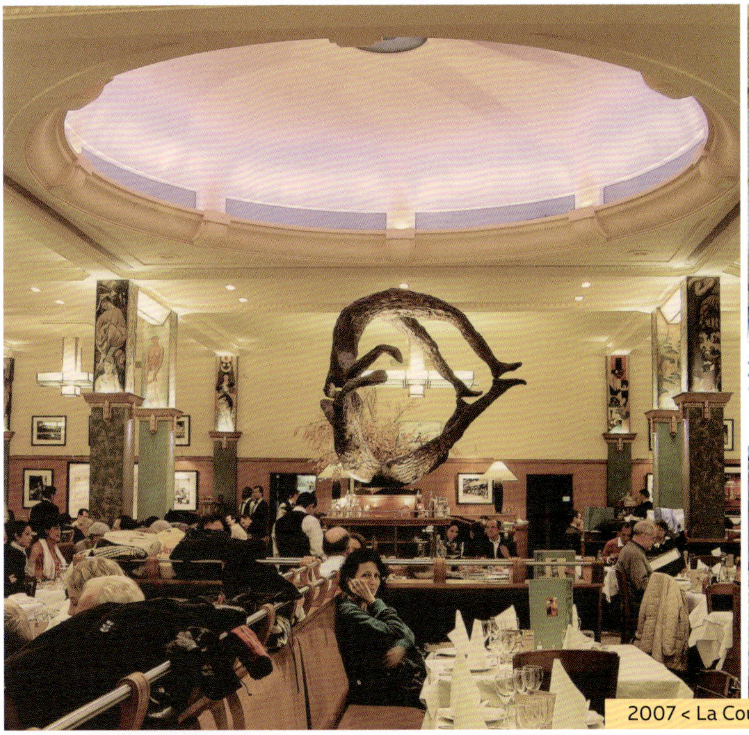

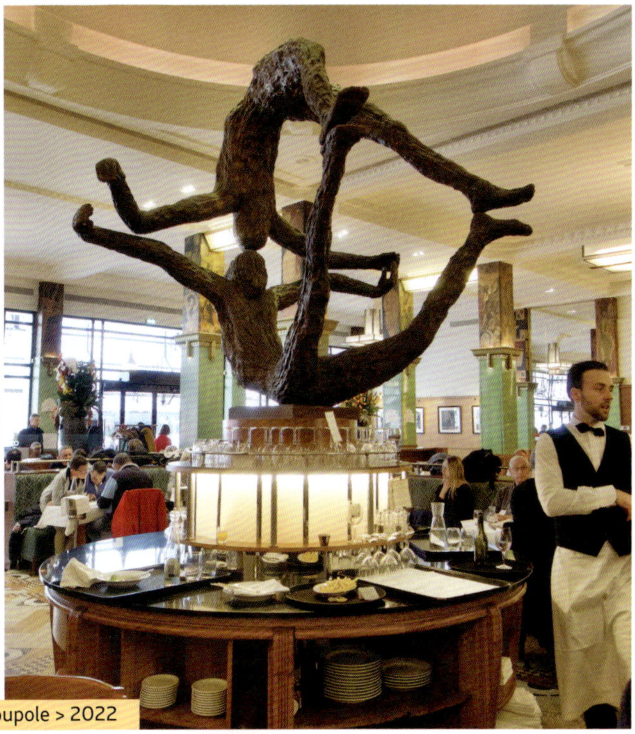

2007 < La Coupole > 2022

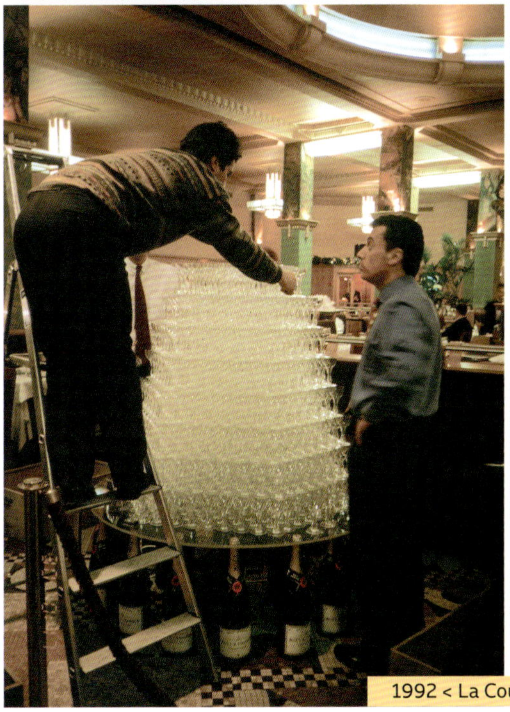

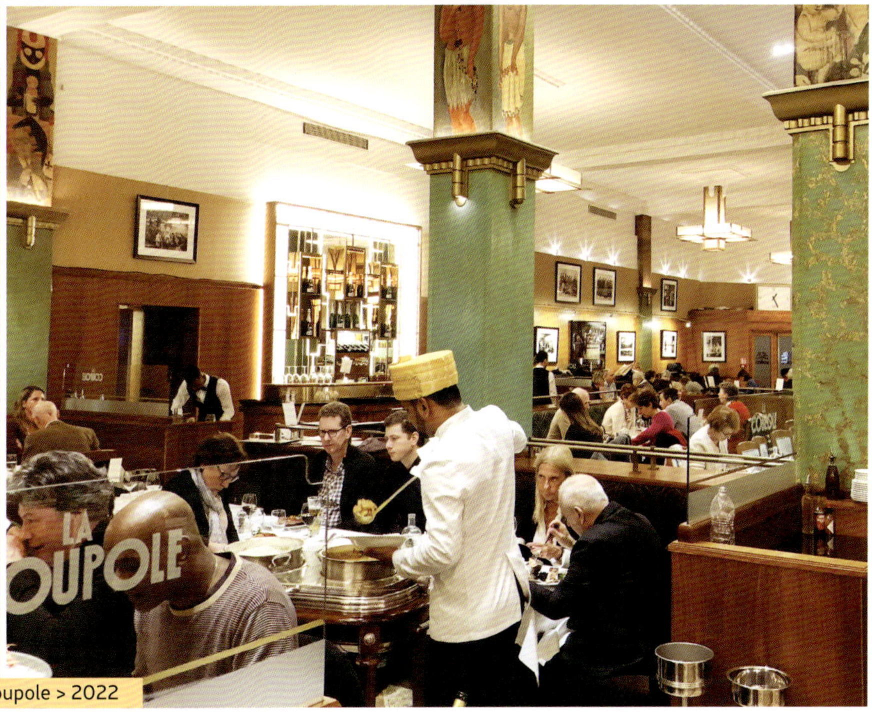

1992 < La Coupole > 2022

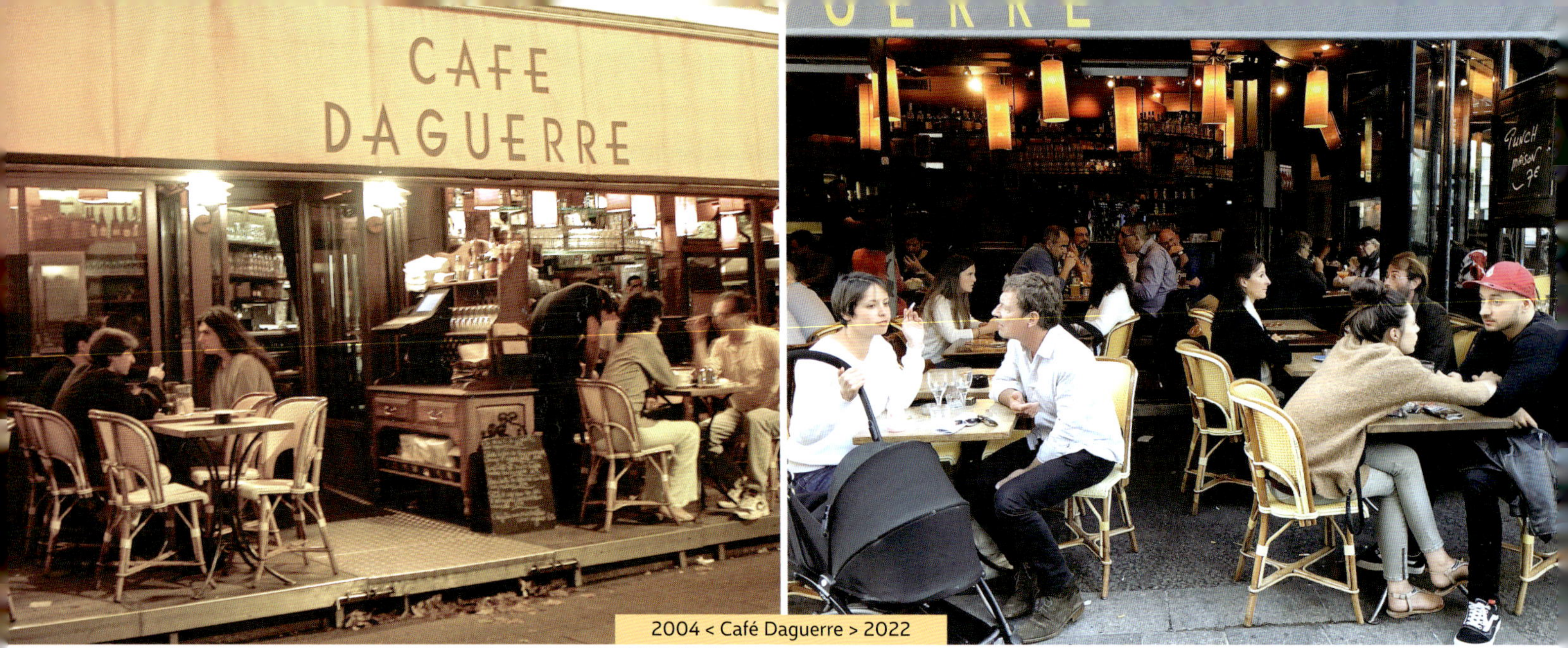

2004 < Café Daguerre > 2022

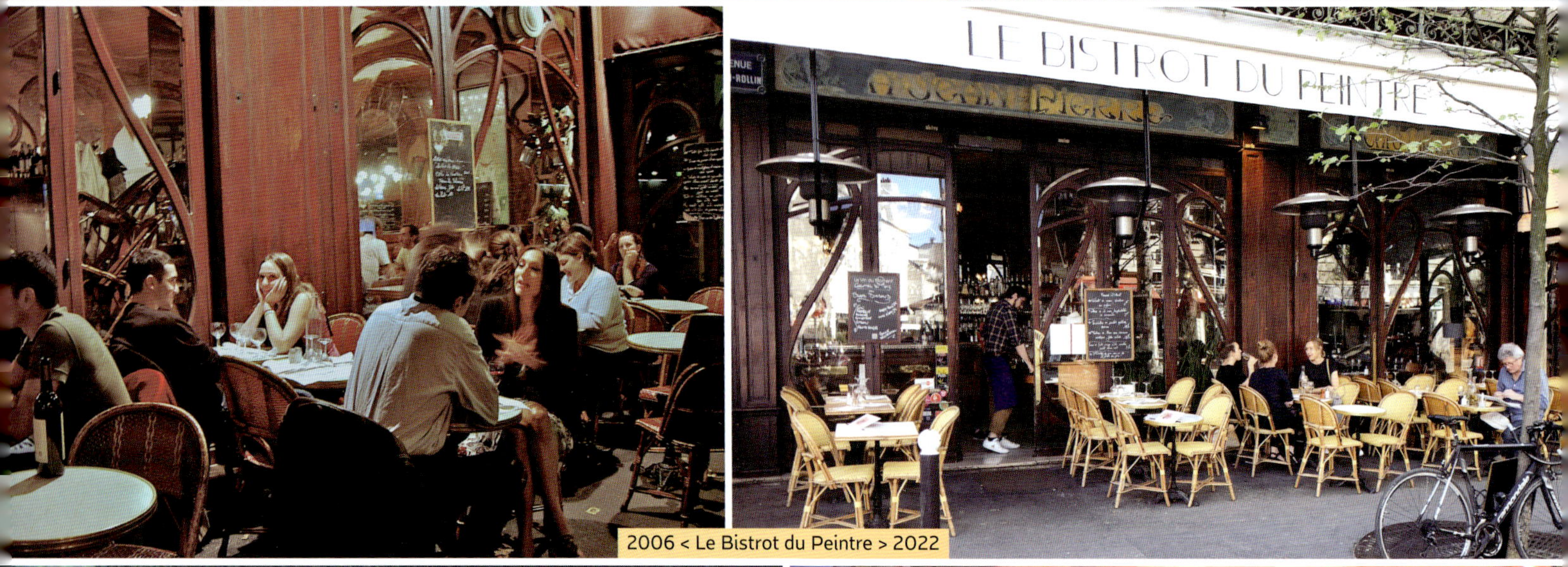

2006 < Le Bistrot du Peintre > 2022

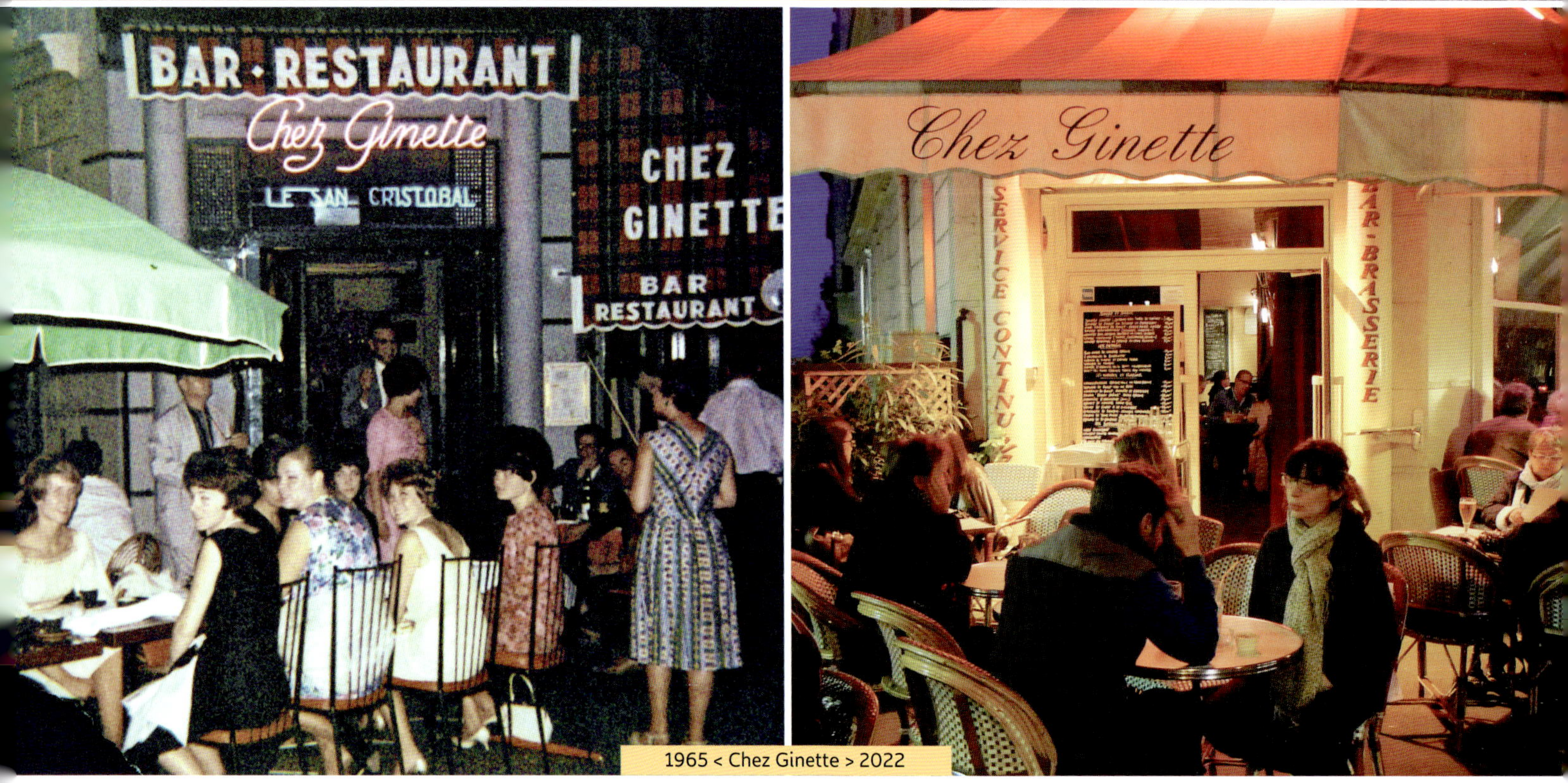

1965 < Chez Ginette > 2022

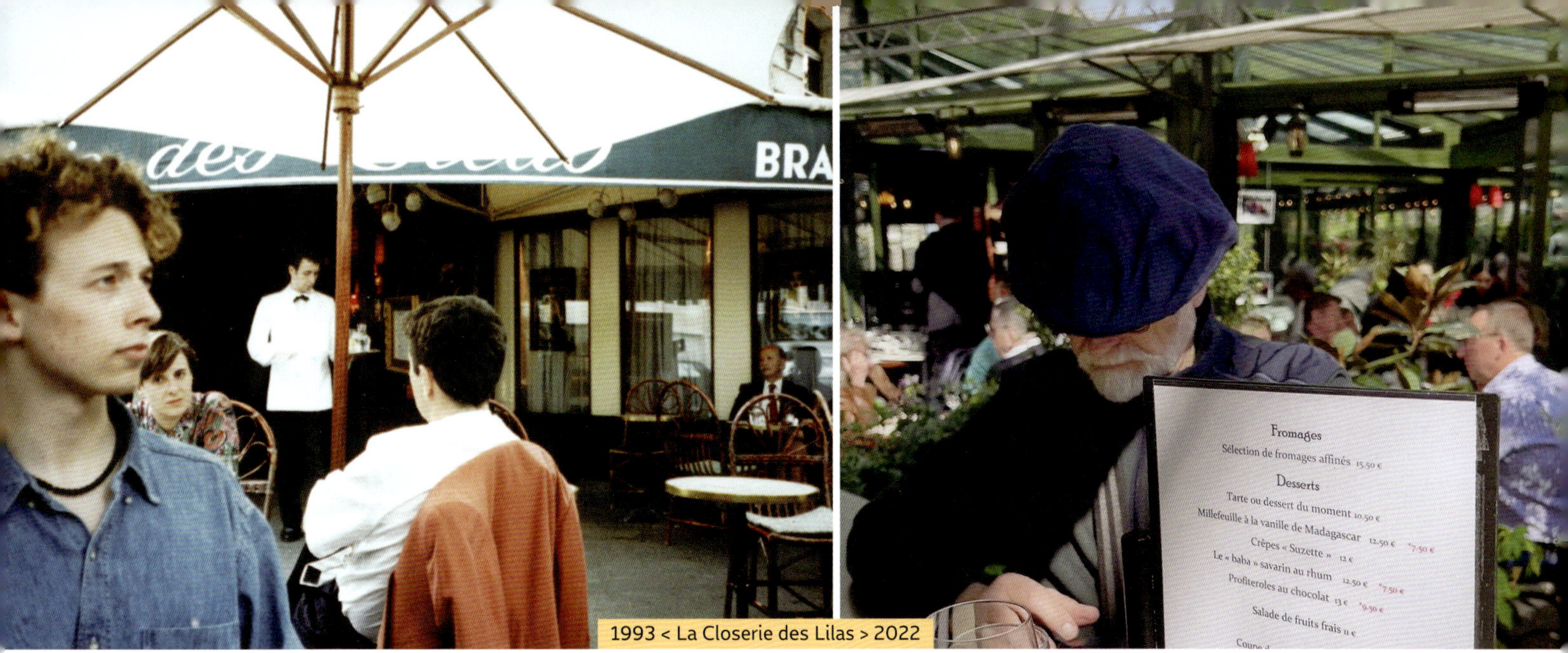

1993 < La Closerie des Lilas > 2022

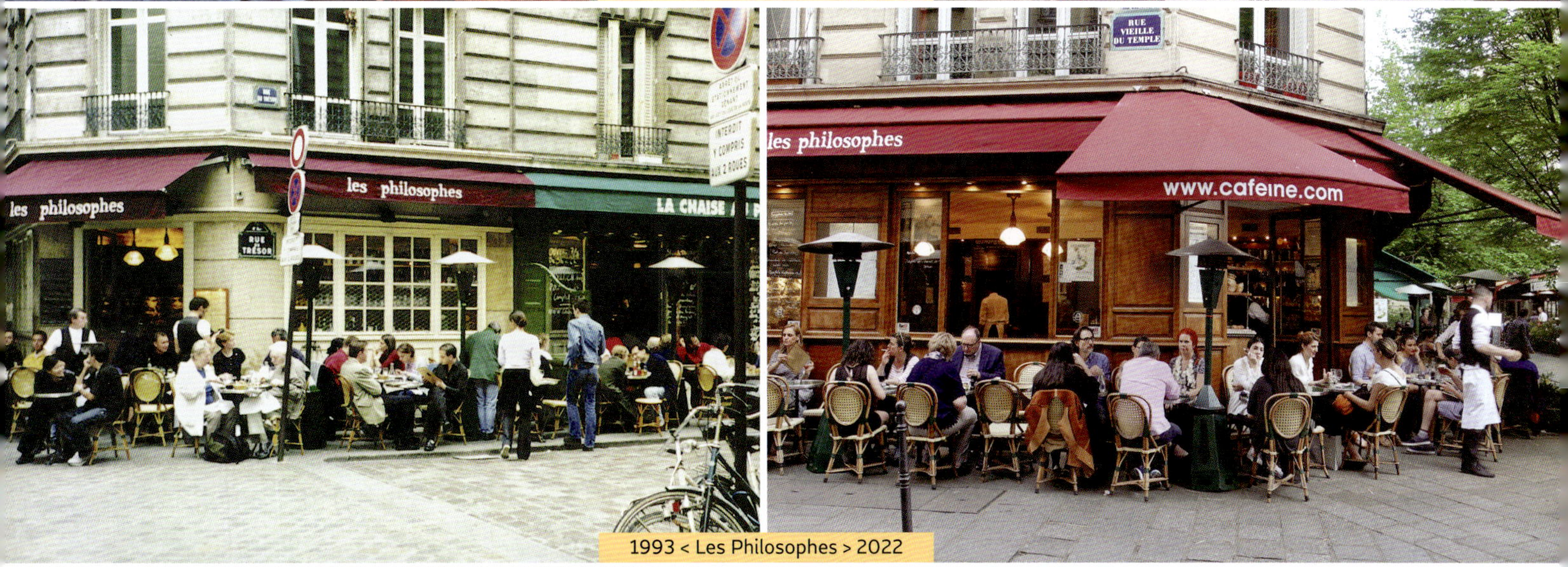

1993 < Les Philosophes > 2022

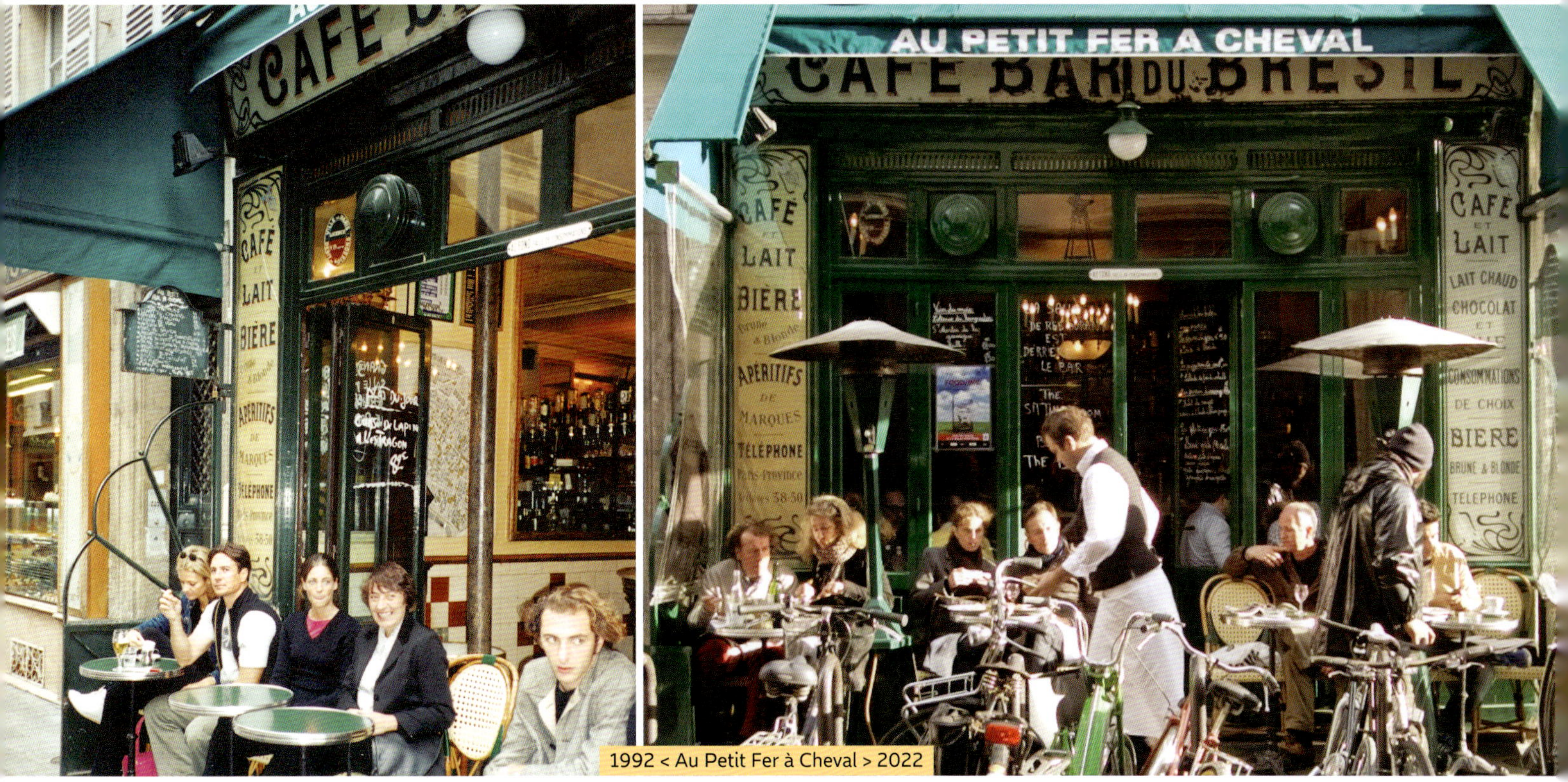

1992 < Au Petit Fer à Cheval > 2022

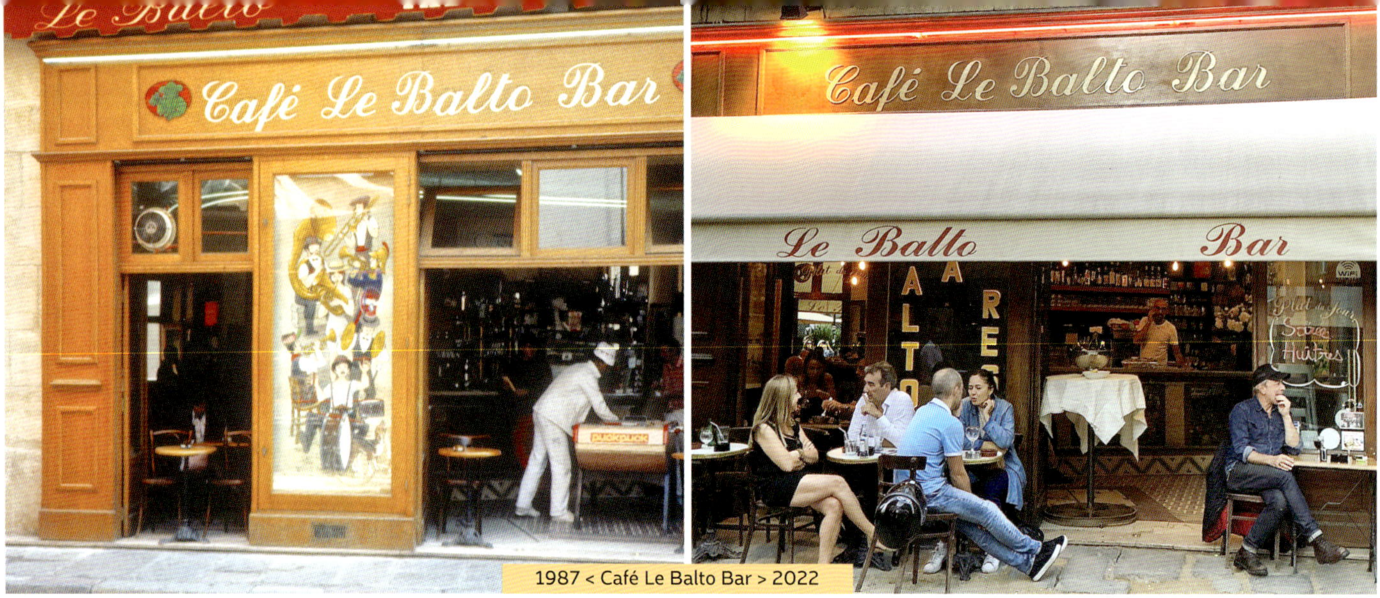

1987 < Café Le Balto Bar > 2022

Le Balto no longer has a *tabac*, nor can you play foosball there, yet this café-bar-*tabac* maintains the flavor of an earlier day when café-goers drained their wine or espresso and puffed their cigarettes, all the while playing foosball.

Established in 1846 and still flourishing, Au Rocher de Cancale is located in a 17th-century building on the marvelous food-focused cobblestone walking street, rue Montorgueil. Positioned near Les Halles' bustling food markets, it was initially renowned for its oysters, its regulars (including Alexandre Dumas, Baudelaire, and Balzac), and its epicurean feasts. Balzac was not only a habitué, but he chose to seat the characters in some of his novels at Cancale. Here is an extract from *La Rabouilleuse* ("The Human Comedy"): "Find Paris! Do you know what it is, O Parisians? It is to rediscover…the cuisine of Rocher de Cancale…for gourmets who know how to appreciate it because it is only done in Montorgueil."

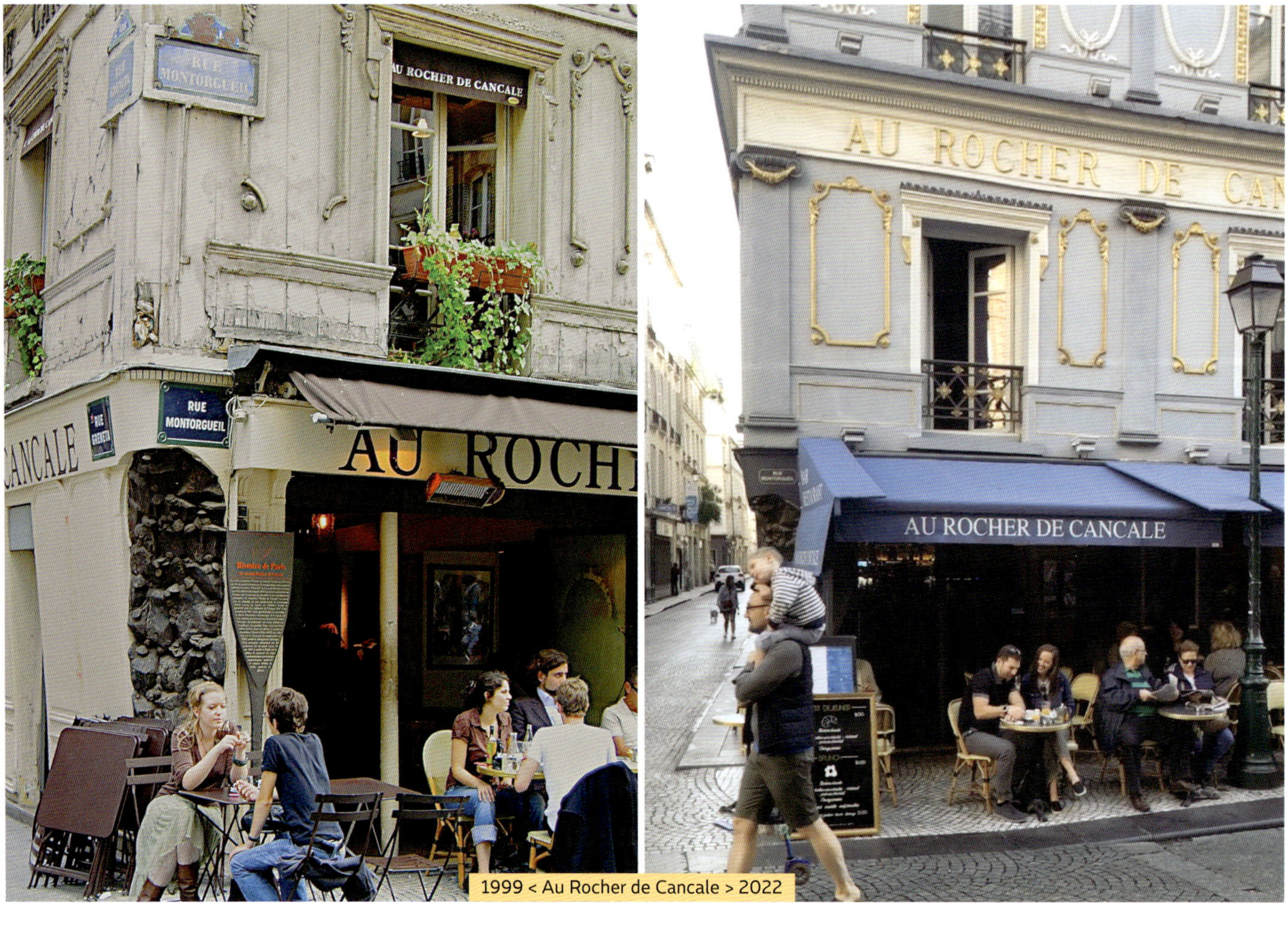

1999 < Au Rocher de Cancale > 2022

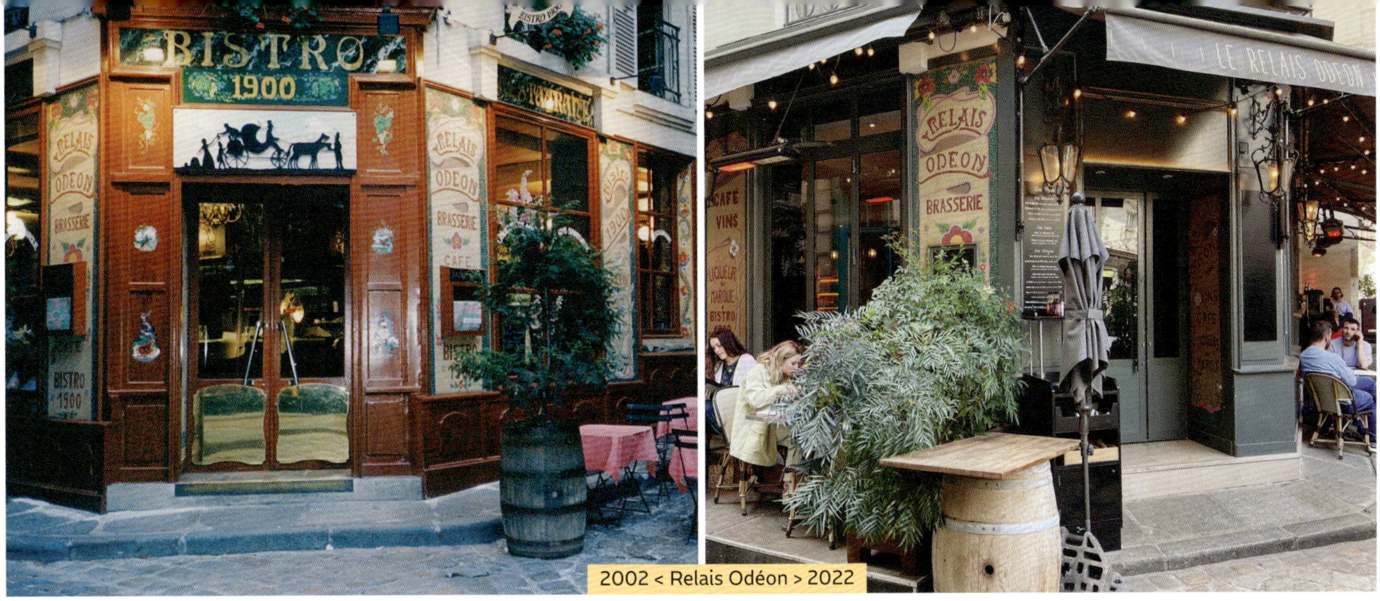

2002 < Relais Odéon > 2022

Relais Odéon's original 1900 façade (that covered all culinary bases with "Café, Bistro, Brasserie, Restaurant 1900" beautifully embedded in its tile façade) has not changed dramatically over the years: just a bit of paint, new awnings, and lighting. The interior, however, is altered beyond recognition. The warm, elegant design is gone, stripped clean, the beautifully painted stairway with its graceful sweeping form lost to history—obscured by white paint. The juxtaposition between the interior and the exterior is jarring. Photos on the upper and lower right show it now—an example of a remodel without preservation. We can wistfully imagine a more refined time when Lenin, Trotsky, Joyce, and Einstein dined here.

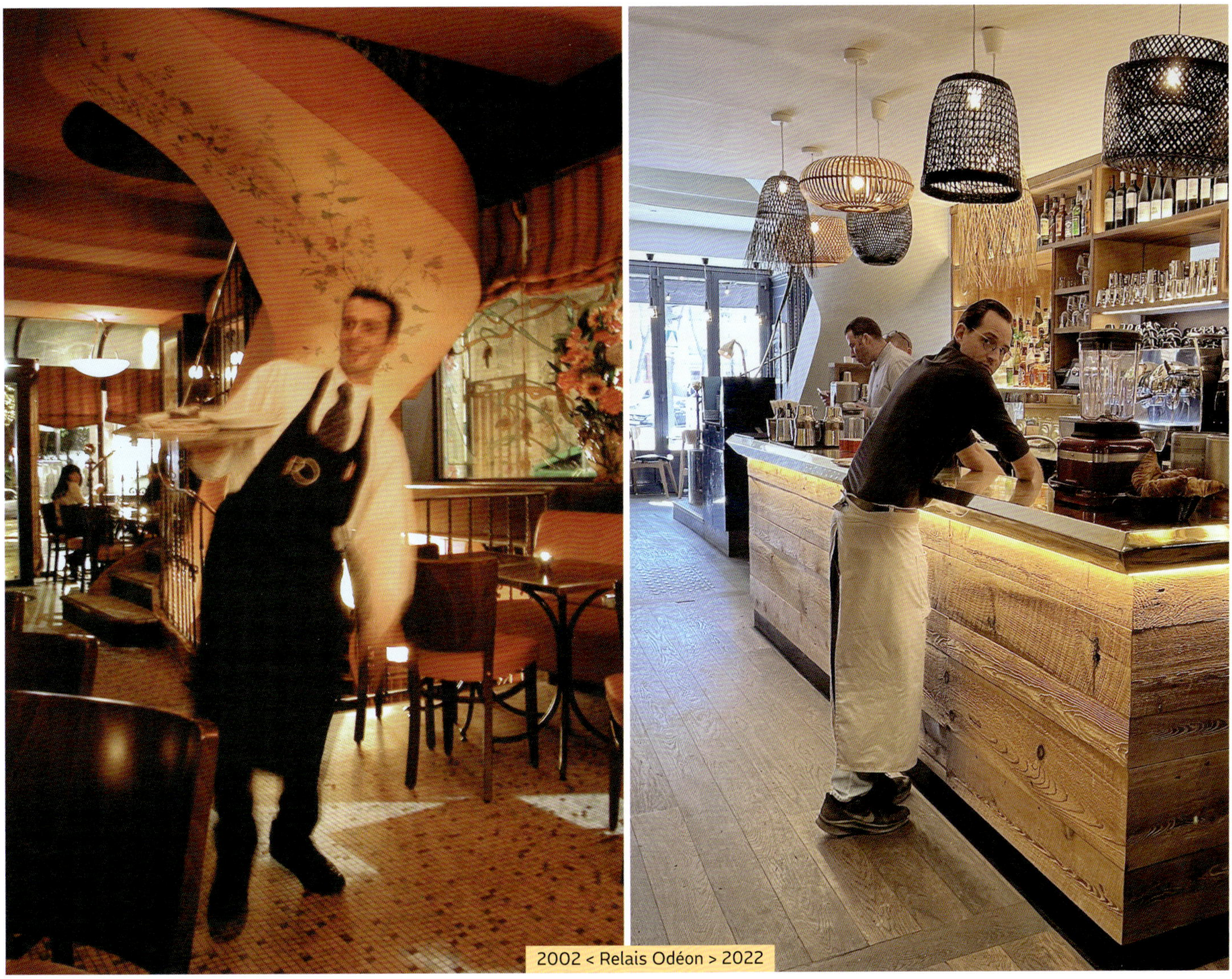

2002 < Relais Odéon > 2022

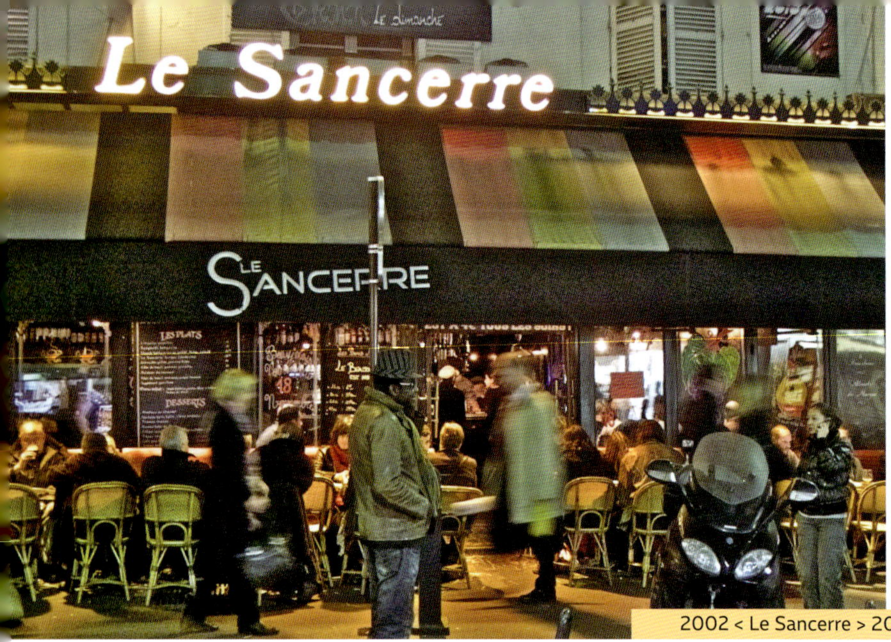

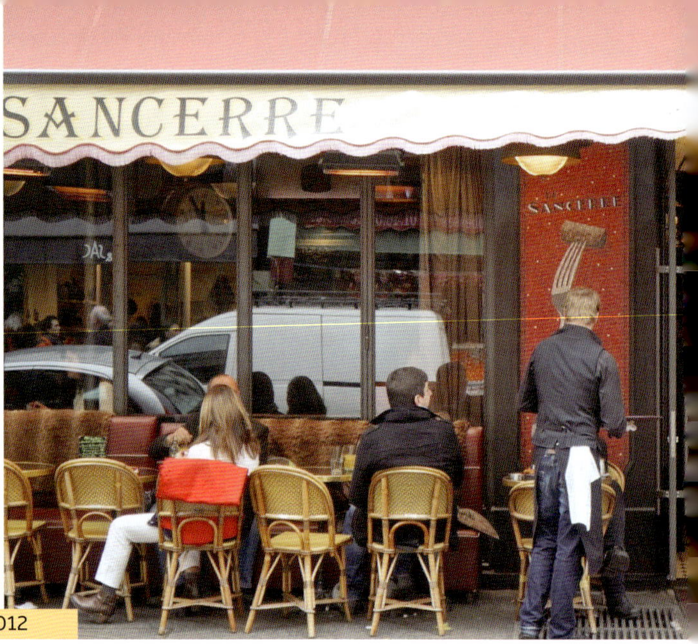

2002 < Le Sancerre > 2012

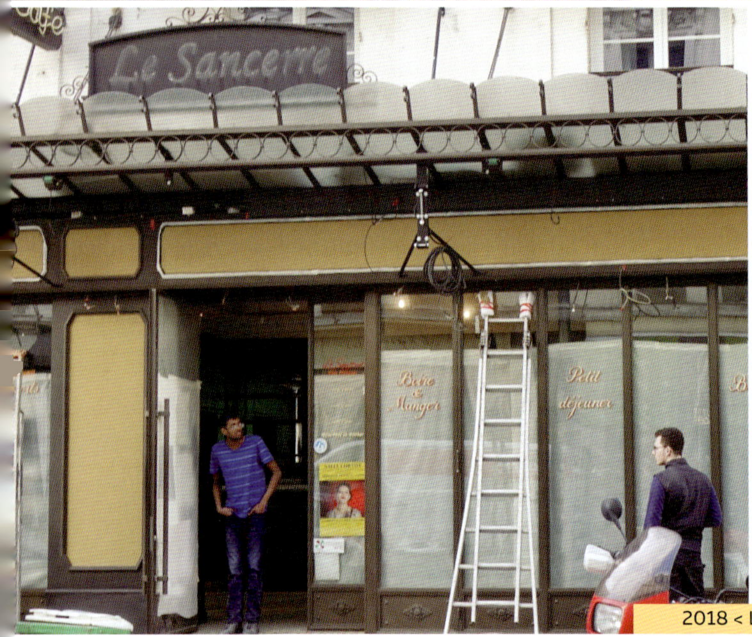

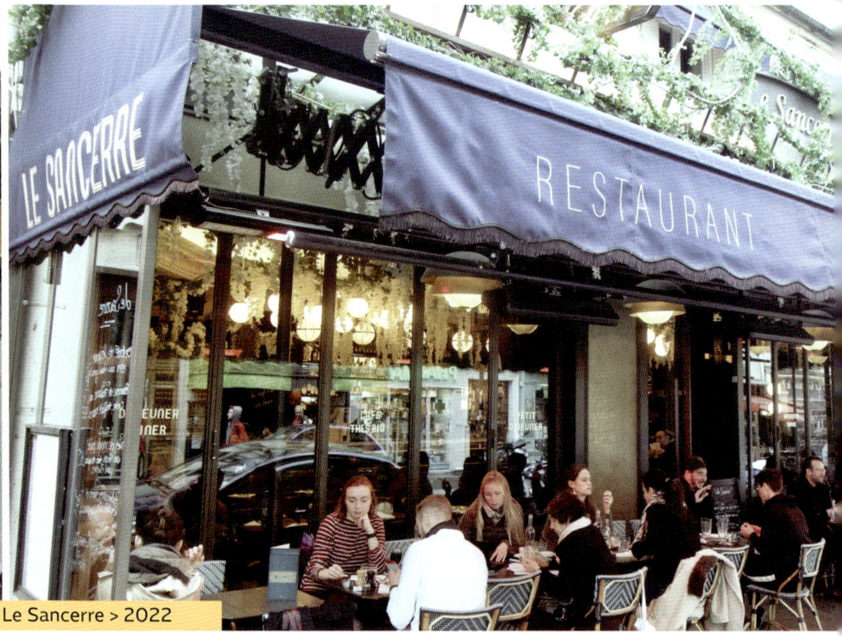

2018 < Le Sancerre > 2022

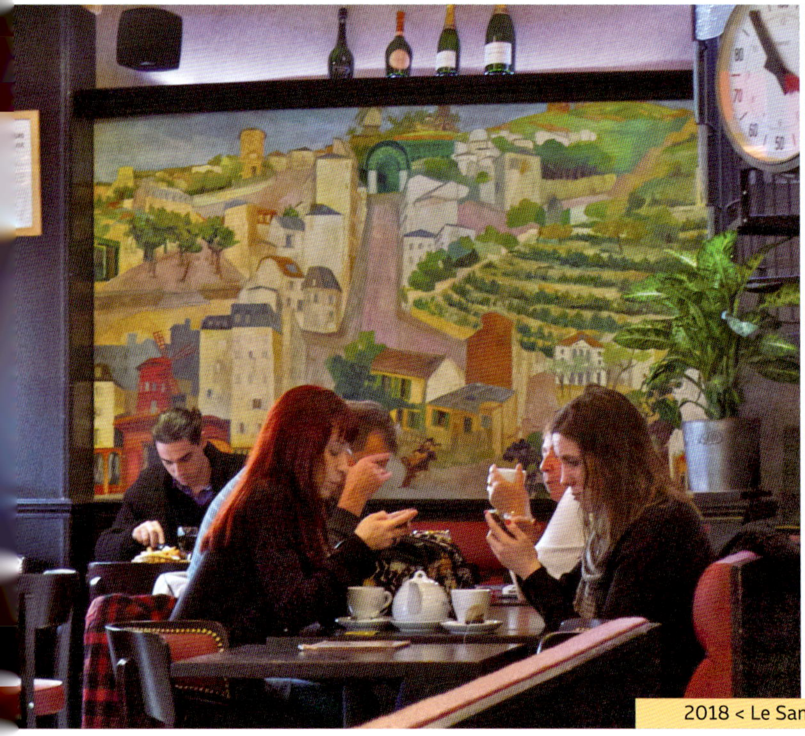

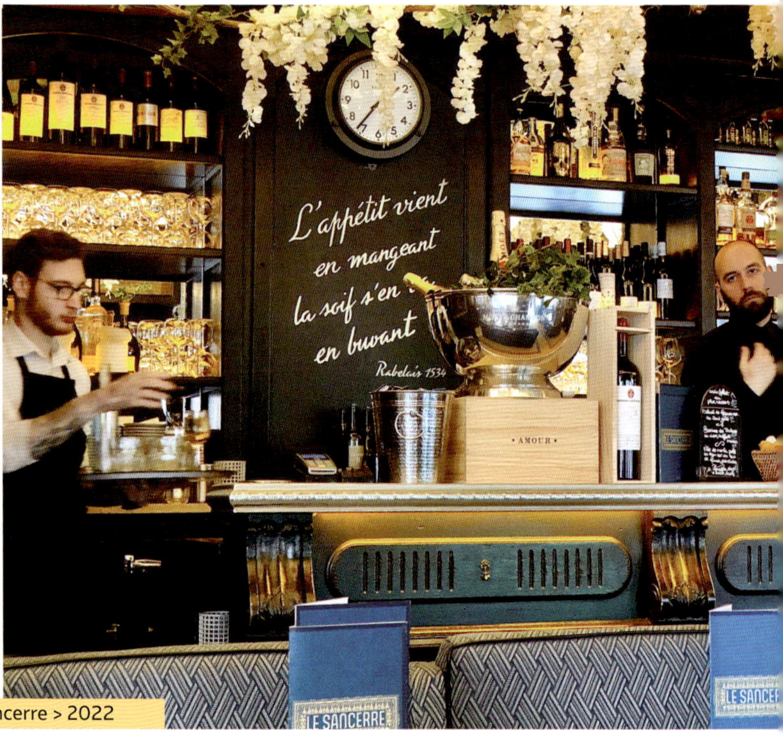

2018 < Le Sancerre > 2022

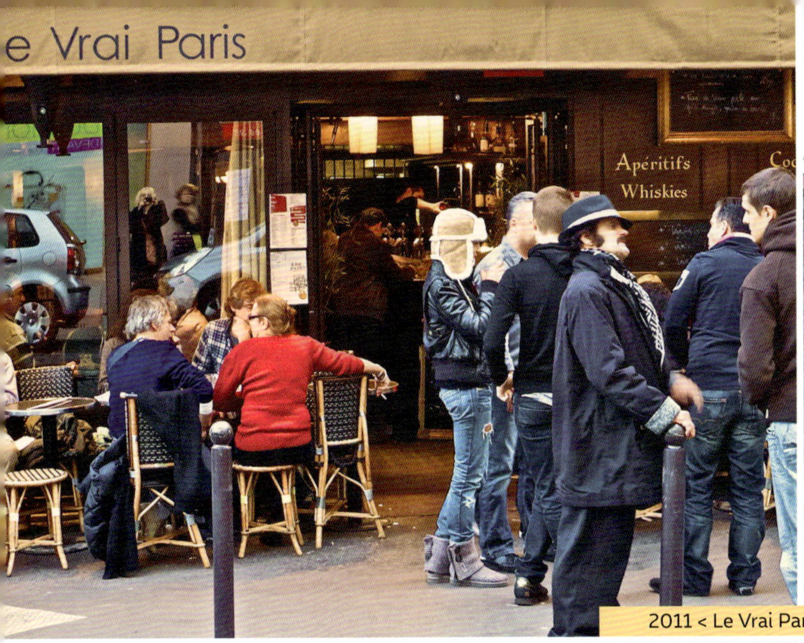

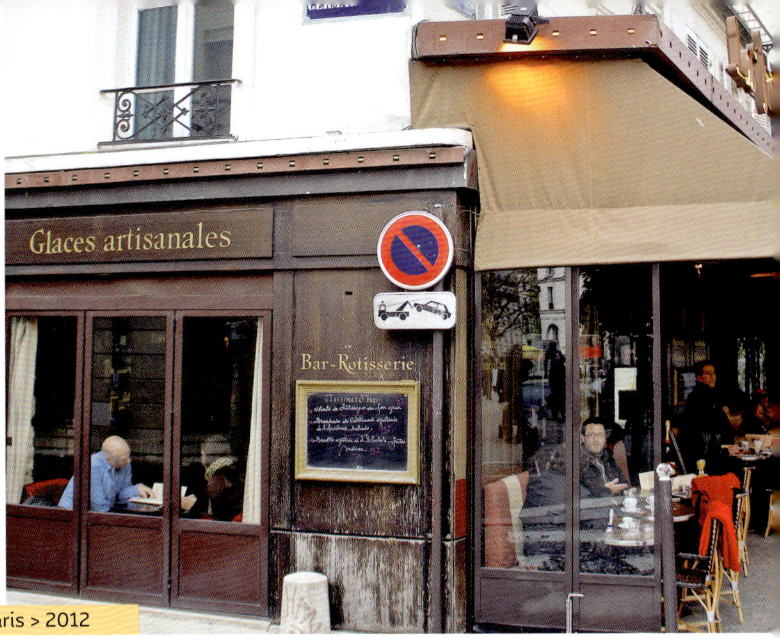

2011 < Le Vrai Paris > 2012

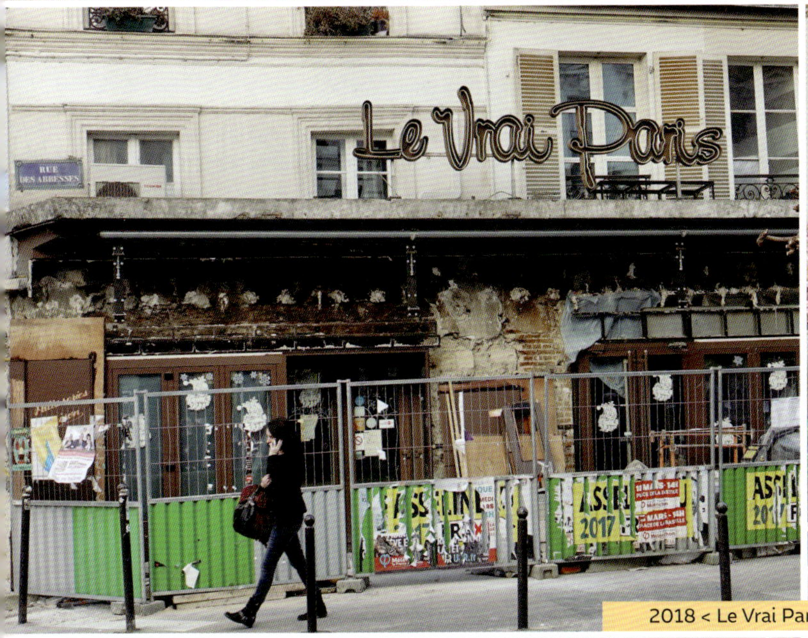

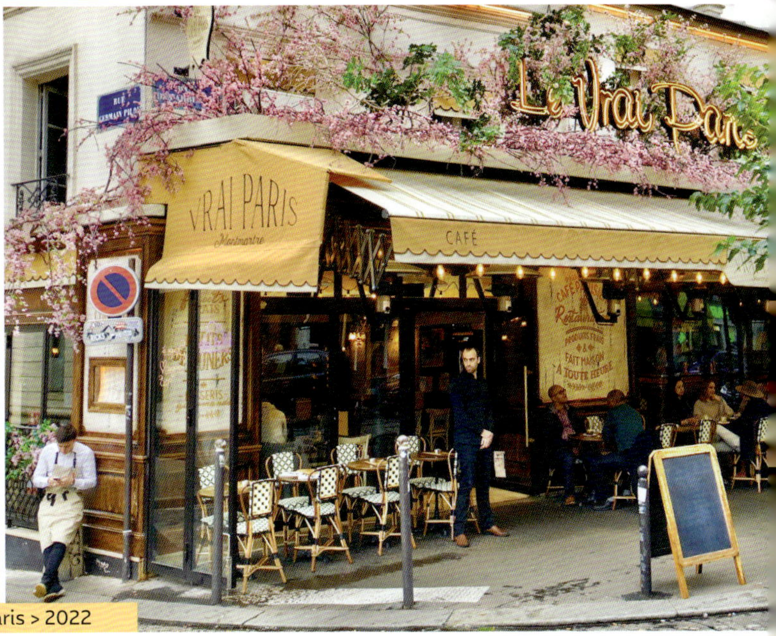

2018 < Le Vrai Paris > 2022

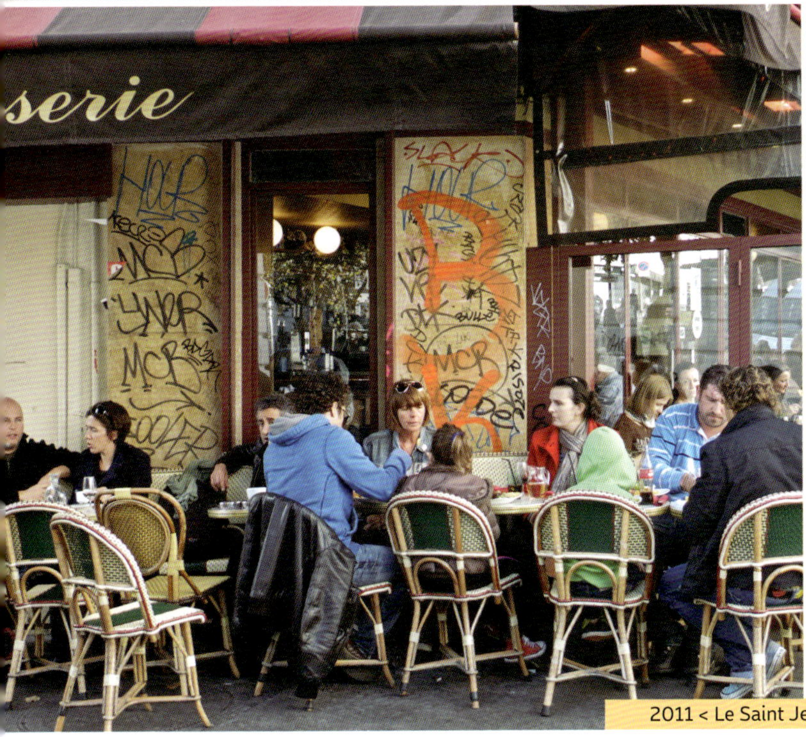

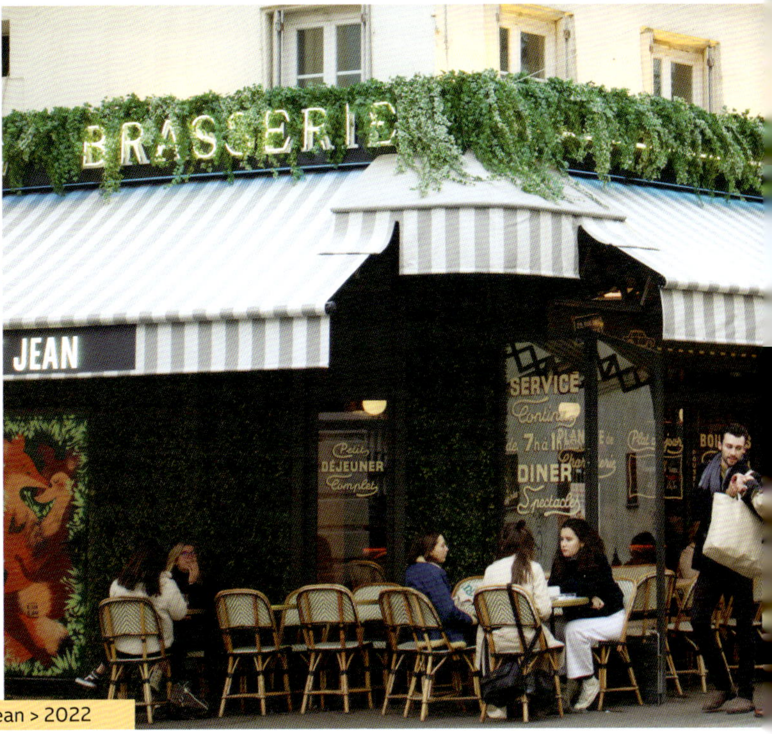

2011 < Le Saint Jean > 2022

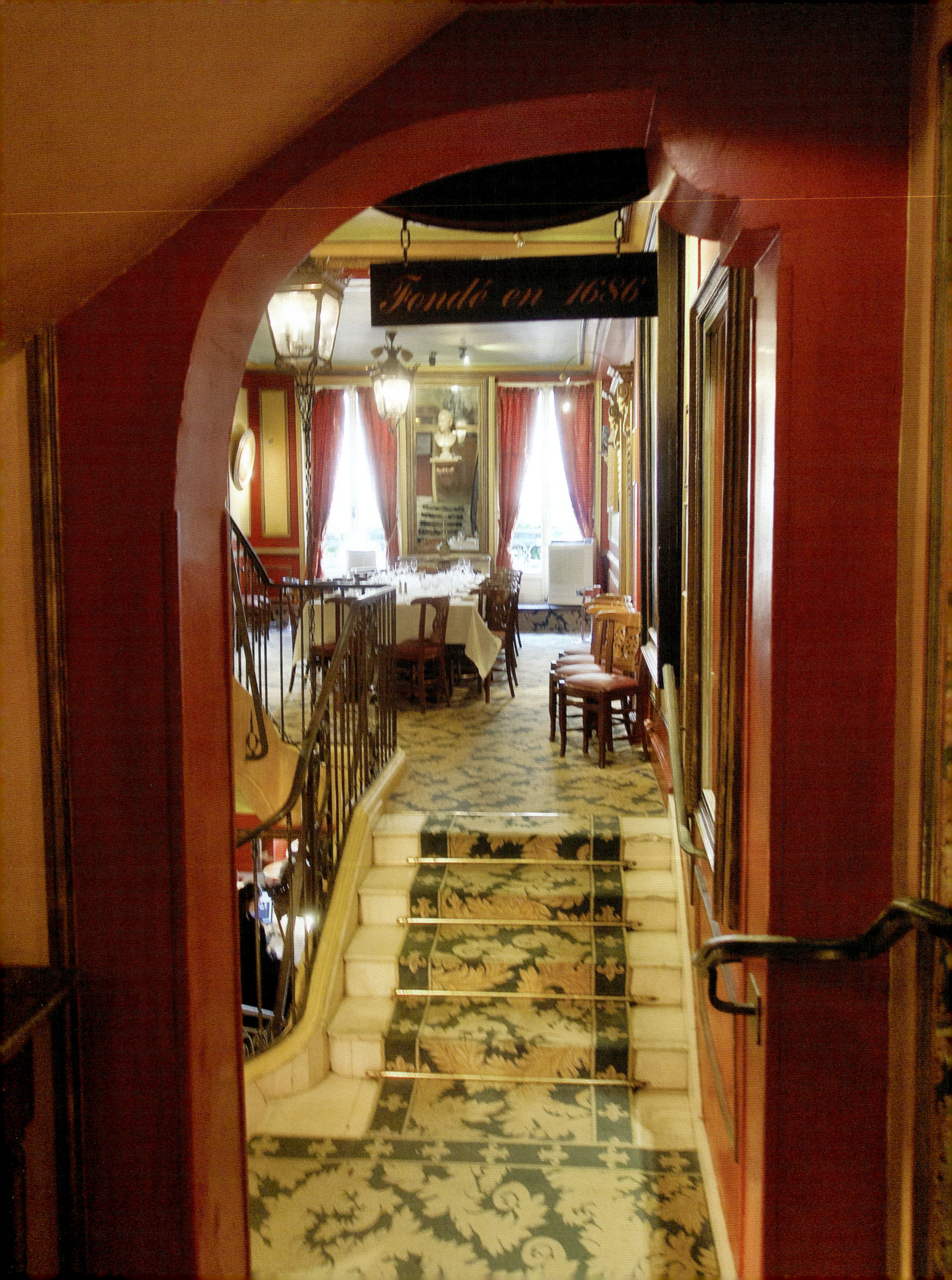
Fondé en 1686

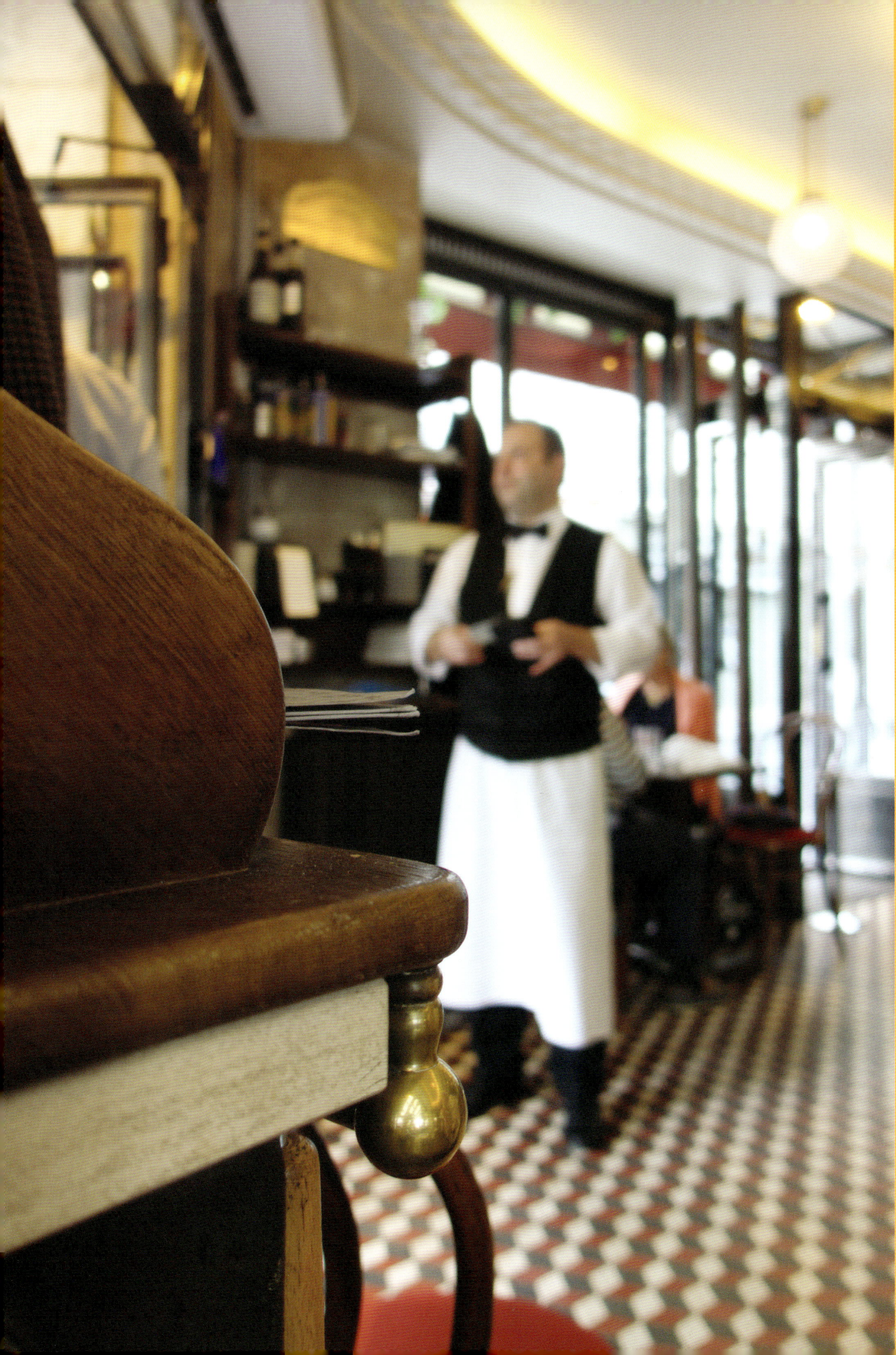

PART 10 The Paris Café in the Early 21st Century

Poof: The *Disappearing* Cafés & Bistros

"The English pub is a very different animal, and the American bar is profoundly different again...(The French café is) the most egalitarian society in the world because the price of one cup of coffee or glass of wine buys you the day at the table, and you can write, you can do anything...That's where the intellectual life really blazes."

George Steiner

With travel and trade flowing across borders, much is gained in sharing goods, services, ideas, technology, and friendships. Nonetheless, in today's world, an unfortunate side effect is that the same branded boutiques, fast-food chains, and takeaway shops are now in cities across the globe. New and original fads can be refreshing; however, do we want to continue to lose cities' and villages' unique character and charm by having the same ubiquitous brands everywhere?

Fast food, takeout, Nespresso's popular inexpensive espresso machines, and the high cost of real estate and rents are some current trends threatening the future of the beloved iconic Parisian café. In the 1800s, there were 45,000 cafés in Paris, 15,000 in 1938; today, there are fewer than 5,000. Bistros suffer the same fate. In 2022, only 14% of the food establishments are authentic bistros, whereas 50% of them were the real thing twenty years ago. The days of finding a bistro or café—the lifeblood of the Parisian lifestyle—on every street corner, where neighbors gathered and socialized, are long gone.

Two events this century that have shaken Paris and the world demonstrate the relevance of cafés and bistros in Paris. In November 2015, at La Belle Équipe, shooters opened fire, and 19 people were killed. Shortly after this terrible event, Parisians crowded onto the terraces, and the hashtags #jesuisenterrace, "I am on the terrace of a café," and #tousaubistrot, or "Everyone to the bistro," exploded on social media. Four months later, owner Grégory Reidenberg, whose wife was killed at the bistro, reopened a remodeled bistro and said, "we need to protect bistros. What happens inside is life itself."

And then there was COVID. In the 20th century, even during WWI and WWII, cafés remained open in Paris. During the 21st-century pandemic, they closed for several months in 2020 and 2021, and Paris was not itself. When the cafés reopened in May 2021 after a six-month coronavirus shutdown, there was jubilation in the streets as Parisians flocked to their beloved café terraces. Rain, hail, thunder, and lightning could not deter the joyful return of essential Parisian café life. President Emmanuel Macron and prime minister Jean Castex were seen celebrating at Café Beauvau, near the Élysée; finance minister Bruno Le Maire took a selfie at a café and tweeted, "l'art de vivre à la Française!" Ten minutes after opening, every seat was taken at the legendary Café de Flore and the neighboring Les Deux Magots. The mood was so buoyant that some masked waiters were even seen dancing. It was a day to remember; the day quotidian life returned to Paris and its cafés.

During COVID, many cafés and bistros closed, remodeled, or updated their physical spaces and websites; some for the better, others not. Other changes to the food scene that began during the pandemic have become permanent, including the temporary café terraces set up in the city's streets. Summer Terraces, open from the beginning of April to the end of October, can carve out up to three parking spots for tables. Annual Terraces, occupying no more than one parking spot, are open all year round. A boon to cafés and customers, the new arrangement adds to a greener, bicycle-and-pedestrian-friendly Paris. However, neighbors complain about the noise, and motorists are livid—losing up to 60,000 parking spaces.

The Association Bistrots et Terrasses de Paris works with the Association Française des Maîtres Restaurateurs (AFMR), both supported by the mayor of Paris and the president of the republic, to protect the cafés and bistros of Paris and all of France, thus preserving the French *art de vivre*. The city continues to be a movable feast, ready to delight with the shock of the new, hopefully without the loss of any more authentic cafés and bistros. Why not revere the past, celebrate the present, embrace the future, and preserve these beloved only-in-Paris institutions for generations to come? Paris would not be Paris without its classic cafés and bistros.

THE DISAPPEARED

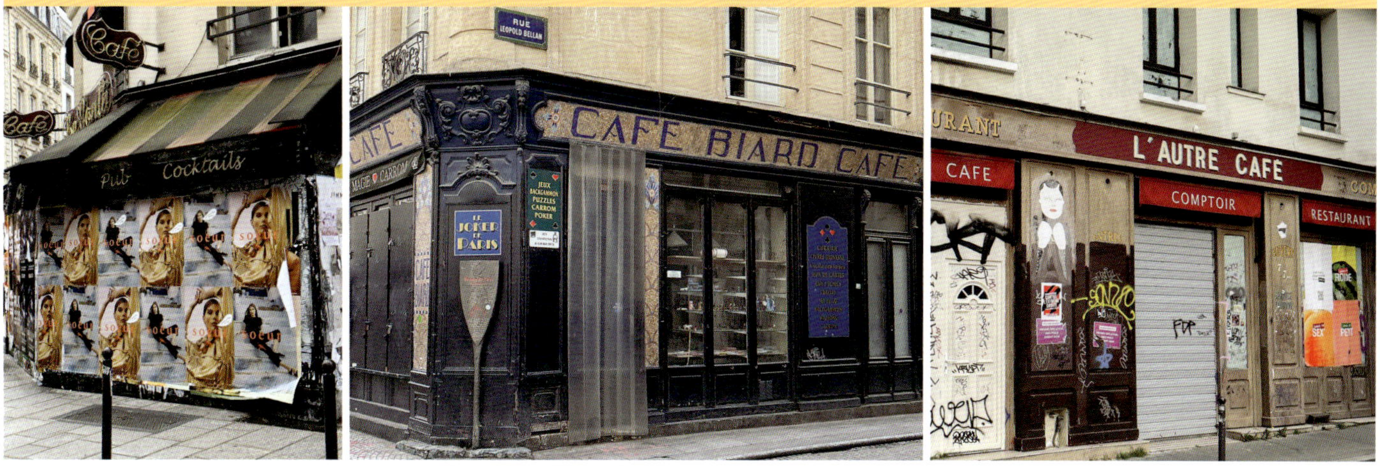

THE REPLACEMENTS

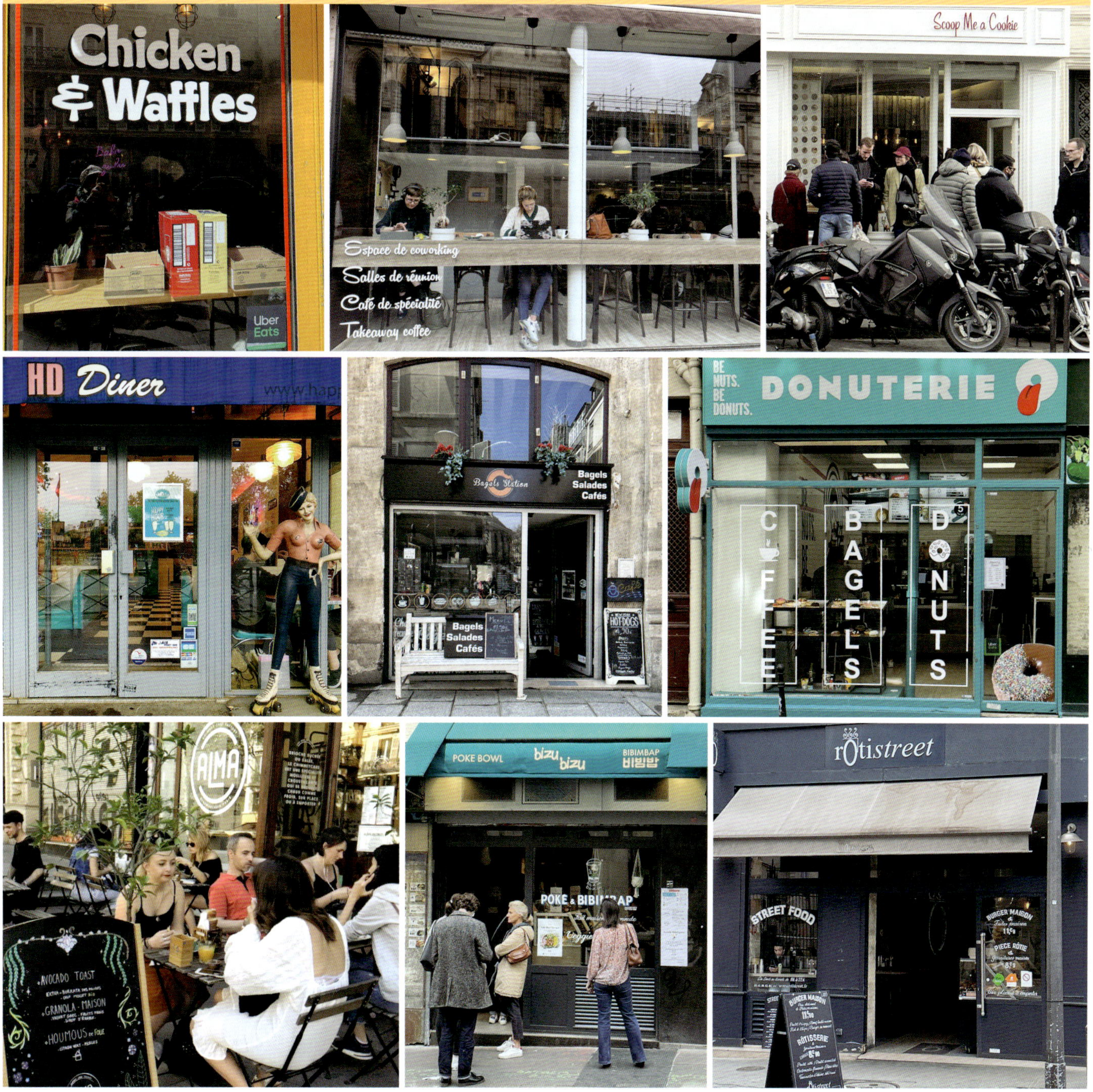

A Café is not a Coffee Shop

"The last time I saw Paris, her heart was warm and gay. I heard the laughter of her heart in every street café."

Oscar Hammerstein II

Make no mistake, Paris cafés are not coffee shops that commonly serve coffee drinks, pastries, and, perhaps, sandwiches and salads. While the early Parisian cafés *were* coffee-centric coffee houses, a bonified Parisian café has a complete kitchen offering a varied menu with meals served any time of day, a full bar, and a selection of wines.

Beginning in 1994, when the Columbus Café chain came to town, followed by Starbucks 10 years later serving coffee concoctions in large paper cups to-go, coffee houses re-entered Paris. Next came twenty-first-century third-wave coffee shops like La Caféothèque offering up specialty coffee and roasting beans from all over the world. These serious specialty coffee houses are now multiplying daily, popping up in every arrondissement, attracting a crowd who prefer quality Arabica coffee over the inferior coffee served in most authentic cafés. Even the ubiquitous Cafés Richard, supplying beans, cups, and espresso machines to many classic Parisian cafés since the 1950s, has opened specialty coffee shops.

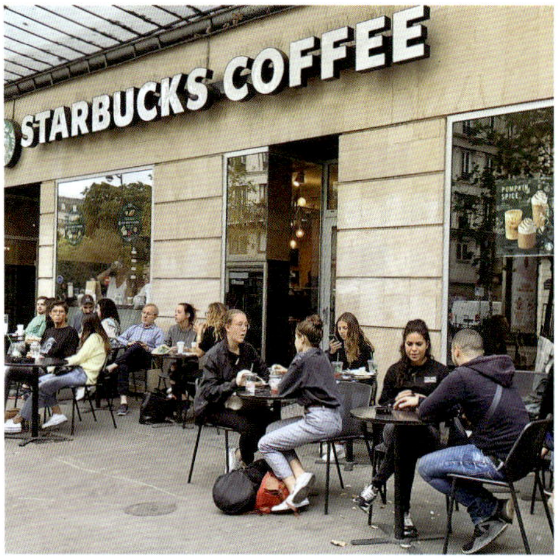

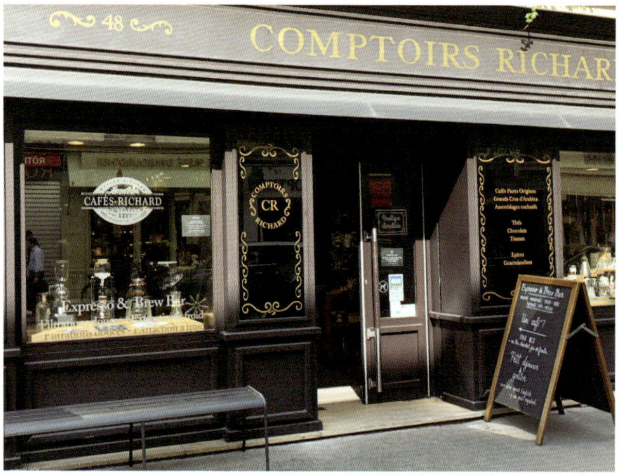

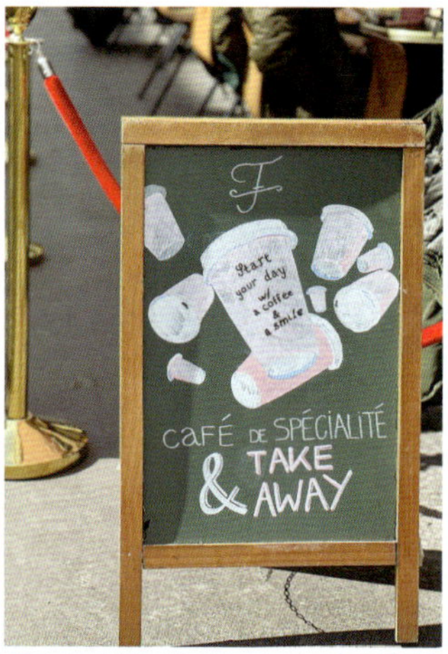

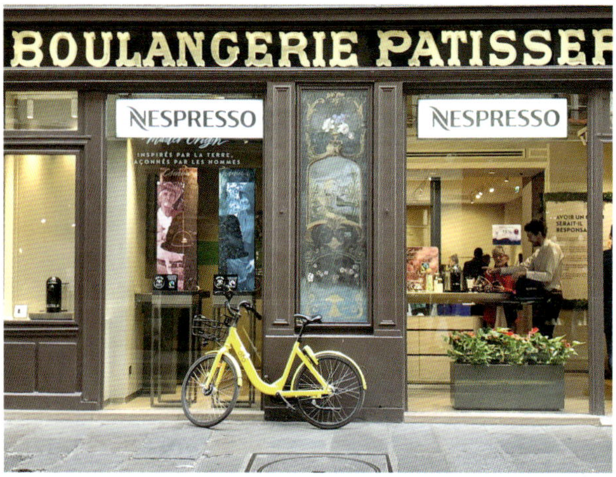

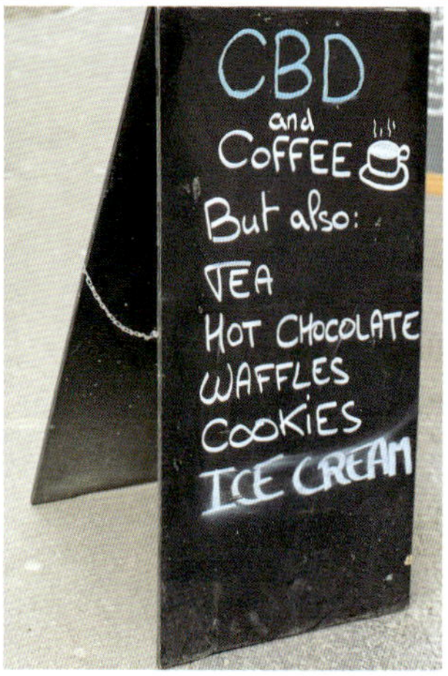

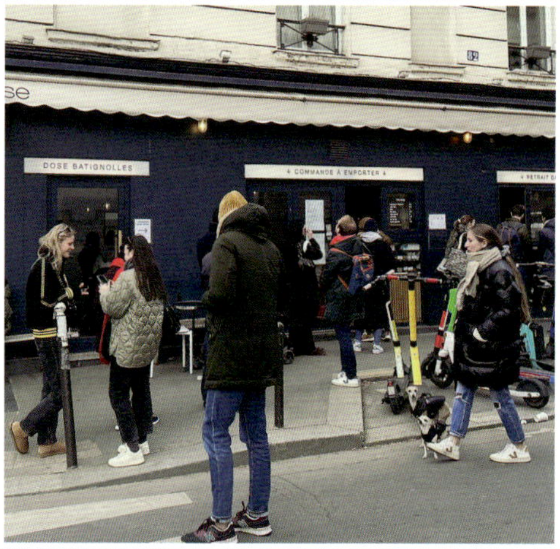

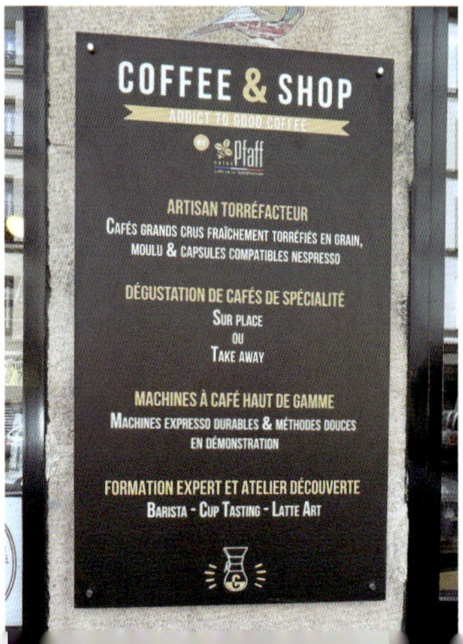

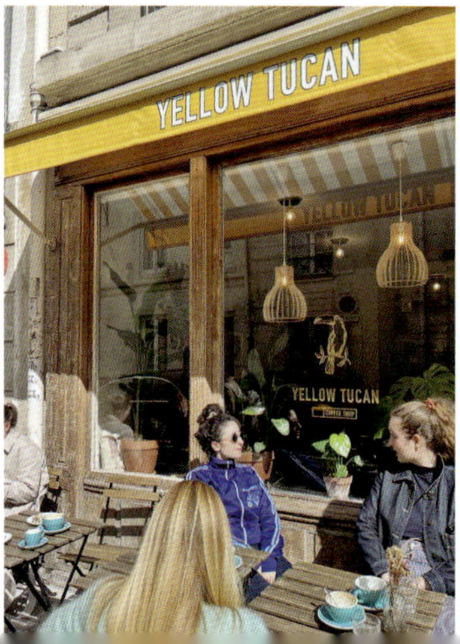

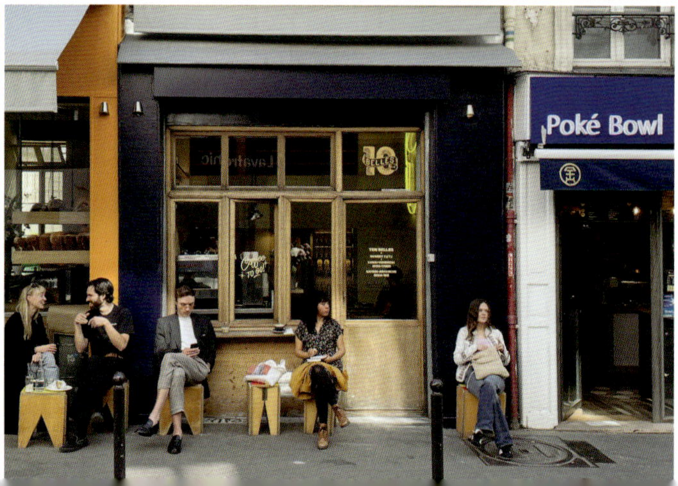

The Specialty Coffee House

"I have always been completely indifferent to American-style cafés, the sort where you have to queue up for a tall drink served to you in a paper cup by a 'trained' barista, a scenario that to me is reminiscent of a bourgeois soup kitchen."

Oliver Ferry

The proliferation of specialty coffee in Paris, often driven by English-speaking entrepreneurs, is an exciting trend to follow. Unlike Italy, where a shot of exquisite espresso at a caffé bar takes but a minute to down, the Paris café is, historically, far less about the quality of the coffee, and more about leisurely hours nursing an (often mediocre) espresso, a glass of wine, or a full meal while enjoying the café lifestyle. Specialty coffee, in the Italian tradition, takes care in sourcing and roasting the beans, as well as preparing and serving the beverage. Coffee is now nicely elevated to an epicurean level, along with wine and chocolate.

The vibe in the trendy coffee houses is usually casual, informal, and welcoming, with spare, white minimal design, and it can seem more like being in Brooklyn or Berkeley than Paris. Sometimes there is a bit of snobbery palpable in these young third-wave establishments: *"Décaféiné? Absolument pas!"* Hmmm. There is room for cafés and coffee shops; one need not supplant the other. And it is becoming in vogue for genuine cafés to serve specialty coffee and coffee houses to become more café-like. Hopefully, a more significant number of classic Parisian cafés, inspired by the excellence of Italian coffee and specialty coffee houses, will serve quality coffee; and the new coffee houses will evolve into genuine cafés with full kitchens, decaf espresso, and more interesting design. For a bit of café/specialty coffee house fusion, try Café Charlot in the 3rd, La Fontaine de Belleville in the 10th, and Craven in the 16th.

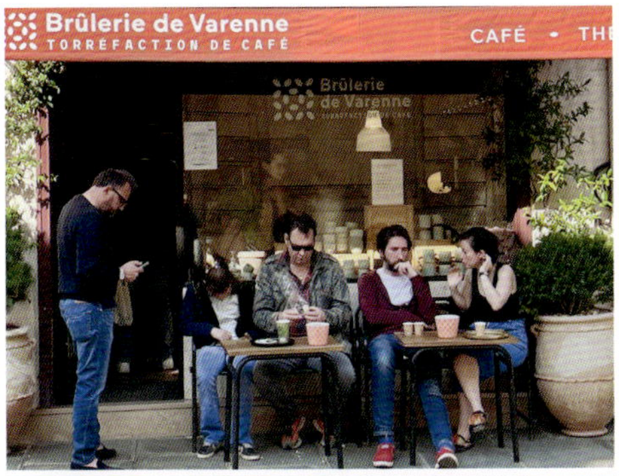

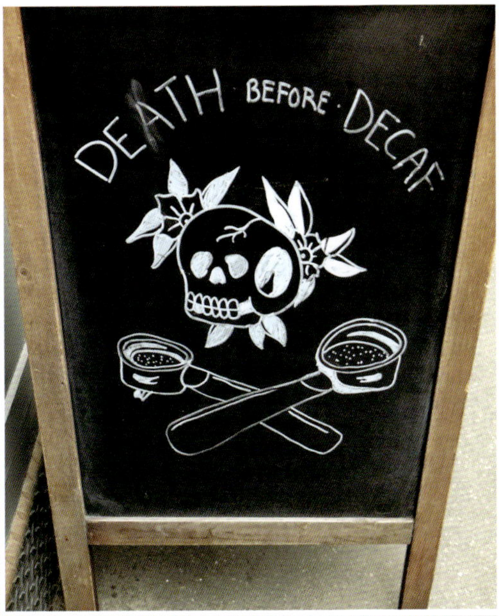

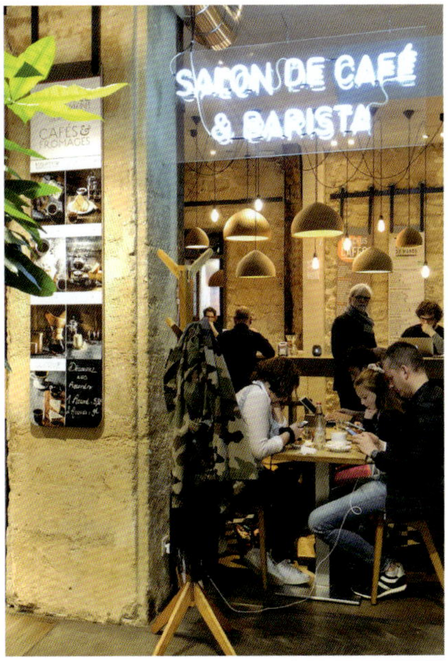

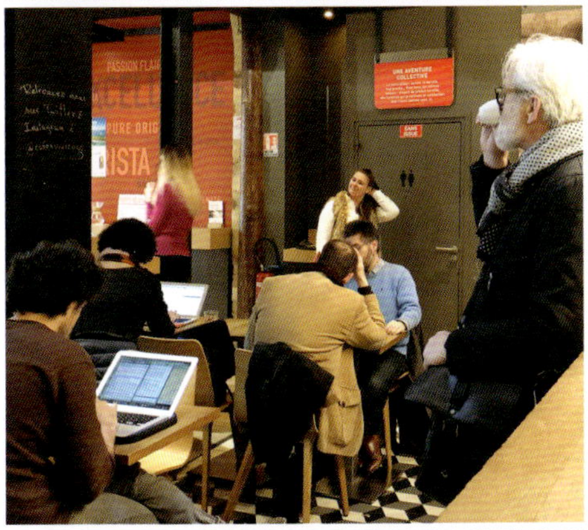

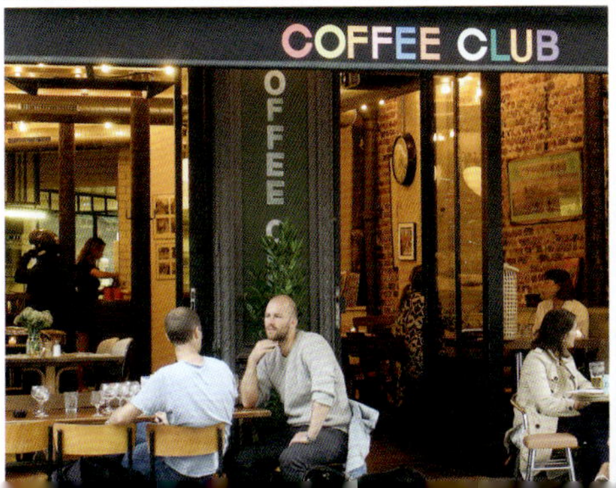

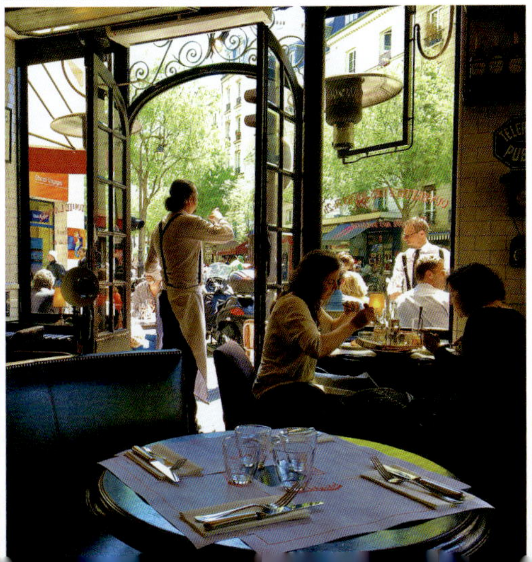

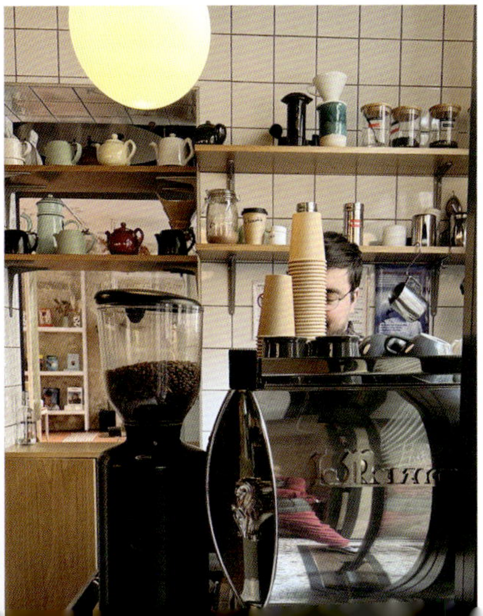

The Burgering of Paris

"Paris, as always, is swarming with Americans, and these days, it's also swarming with hamburgers. Oddly, though, it's not typically the Americans who are pursuing the perfect burger on the perfect bun with the obligatory side of perfect coleslaw; the Americans are pursuing the perfect blanquette de veau."

Robert Gottlieb

Joining the universal pizzeria on every corner, burgers are commonplace on Parisian menus these days. MacDonald's and Burger King may have started it all, but there is no end in sight. France is MacDonald's second most profitable market, and hamburgers are a popular choice for French diners—not just at MacDonald's. Burgers are ubiquitous, appearing on 85% of menus, including stylish cafés, bistros, and restaurants. The French order them, with *frites*, regularly. Granted, some are haut burgers with grass-fed beef and all sorts of gourmet ingredients and condiments, including foie gras, and are eaten with knives and forks. Still, it's strange to see sophisticated diners ordering burgers when a selection of more exciting and intricate dishes is on the bill of fare. We will have to wait to see whether this import from Hamburg via the US is a passing trend or a fundamental staple.

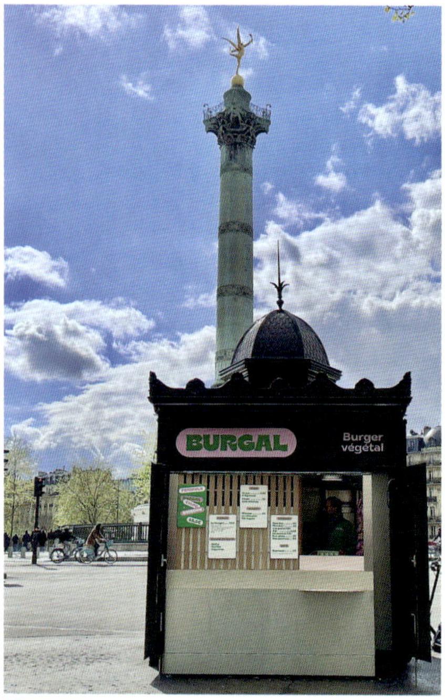

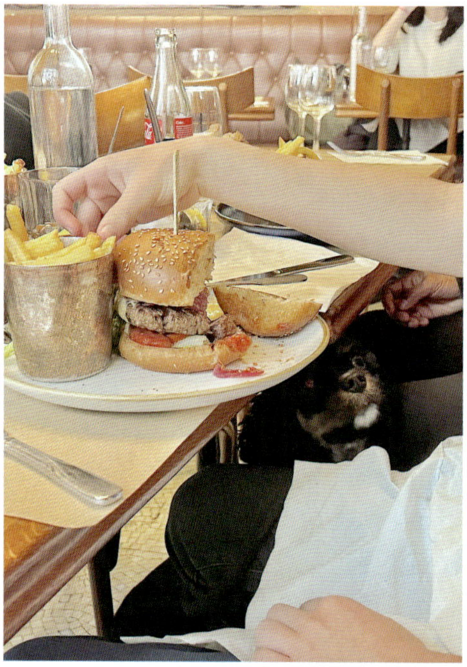

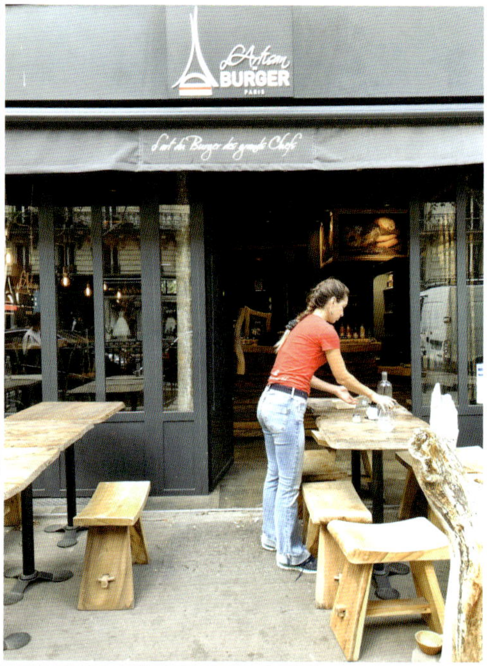

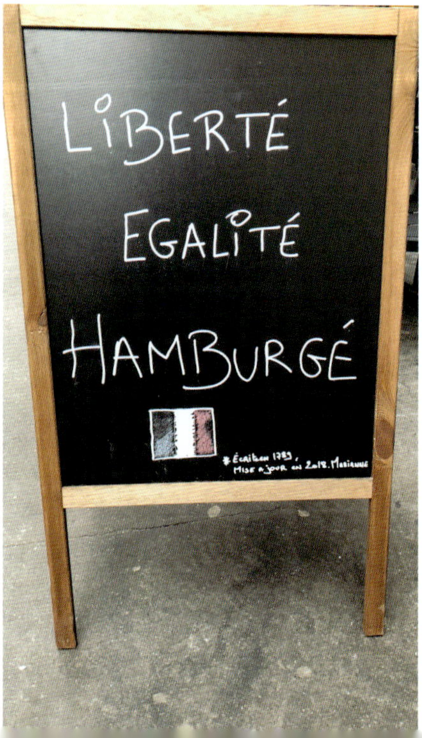

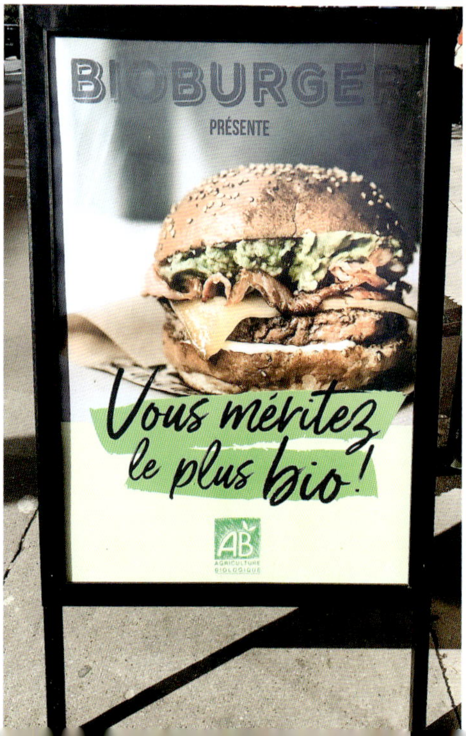

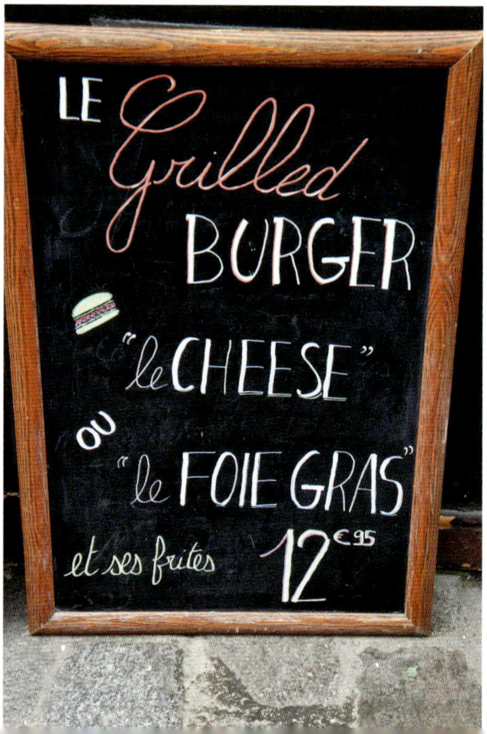

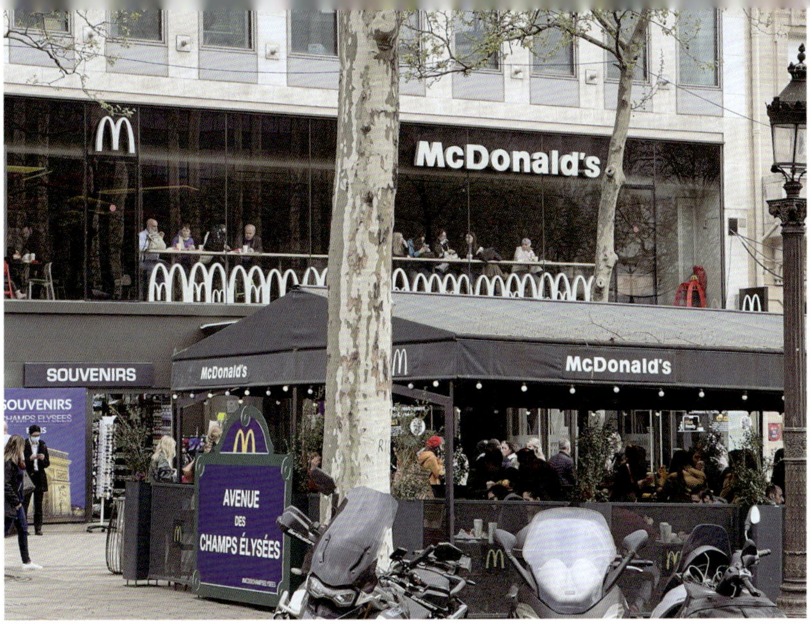
McDonald's
SOUVENIRS
McDonald's
McDonald's
AVENUE DES CHAMPS ÉLYSÉES

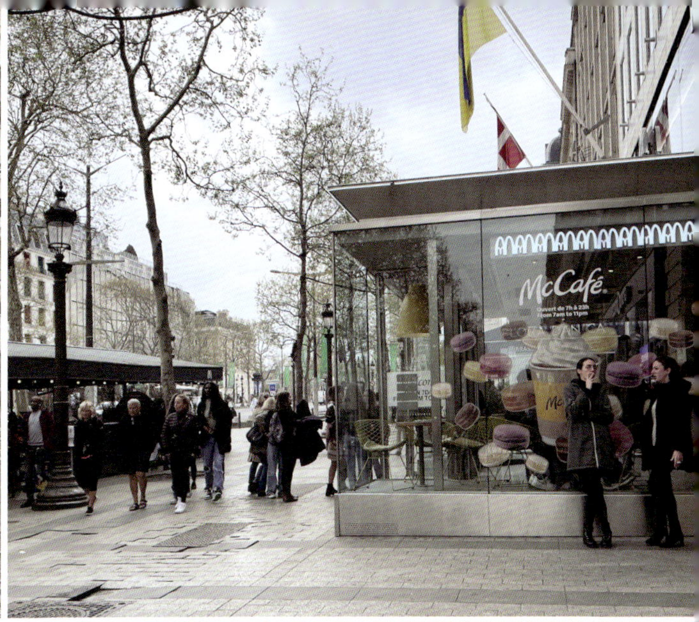
McCafé

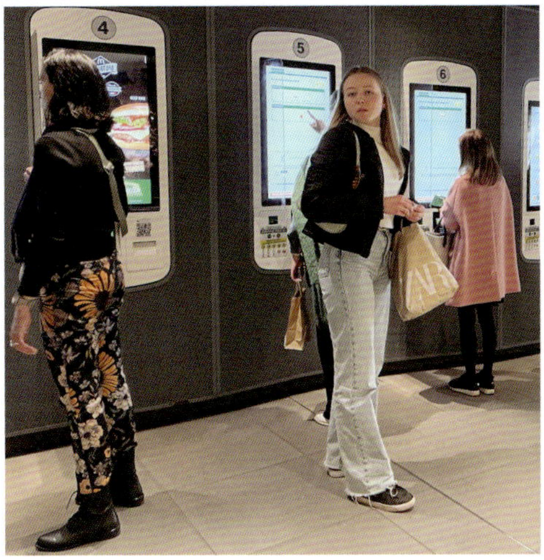

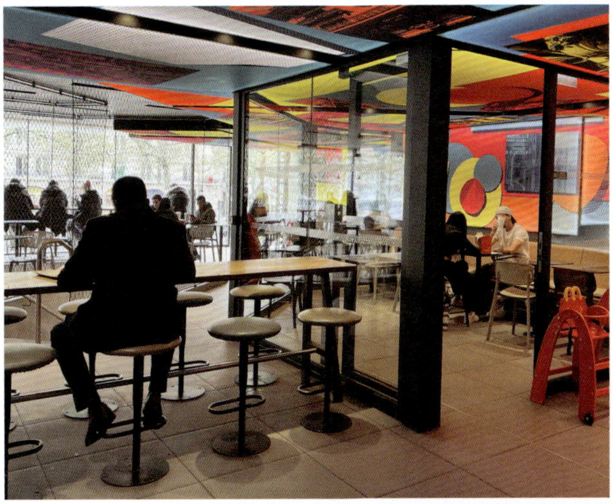

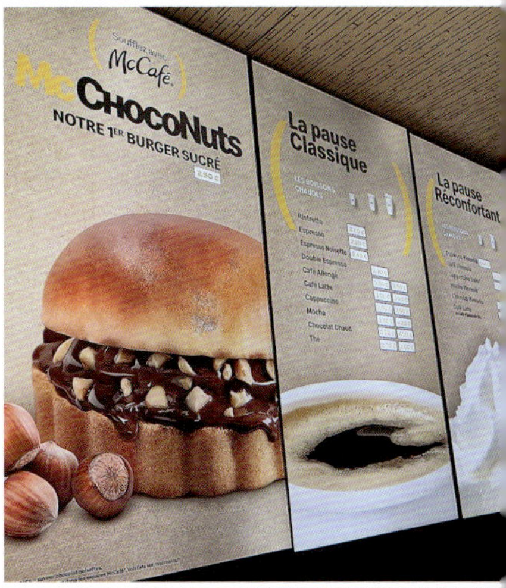
McCafé
ChocoNuts
NOTRE 1er BURGER SUCRÉ
La pause Classique
La pause Réconfortant

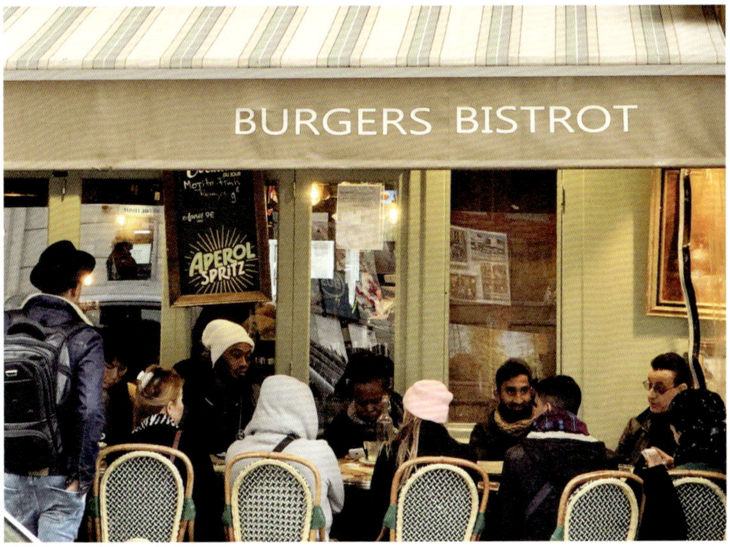
BURGERS BISTROT
APEROL SPRITZ

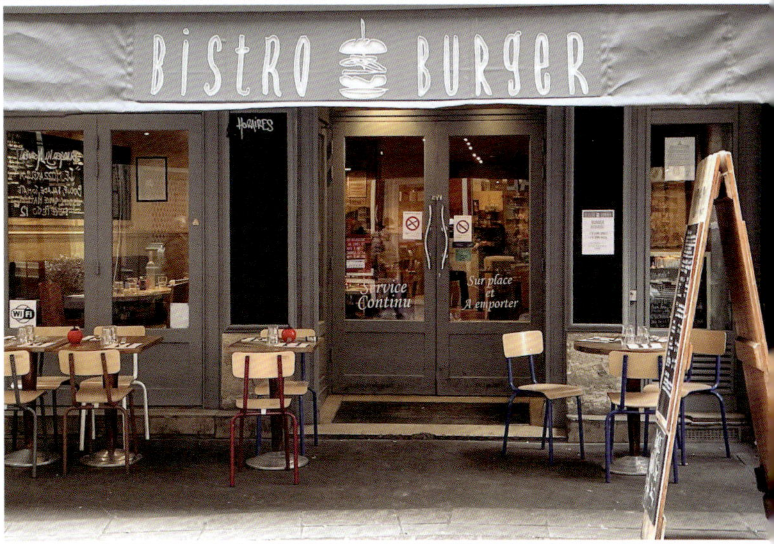
Bistro Burger
Service Continu
Sur place et A emporter

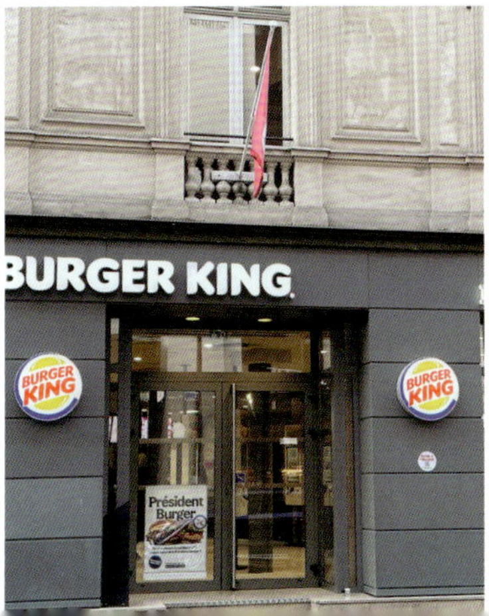
BURGER KING
BURGER KING
BURGER KING

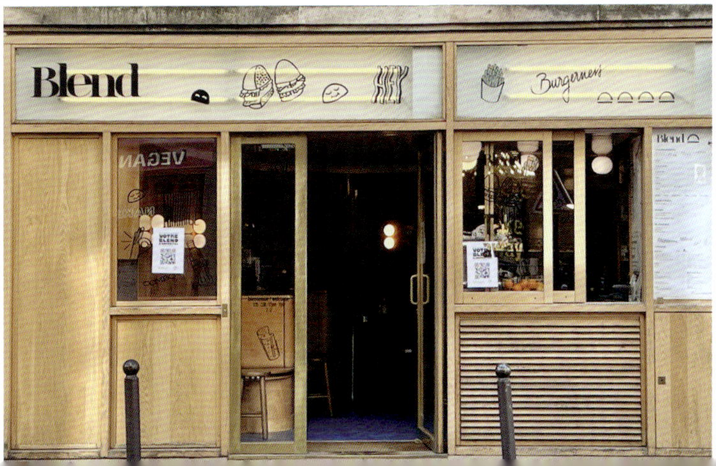
Blend
Burgermen

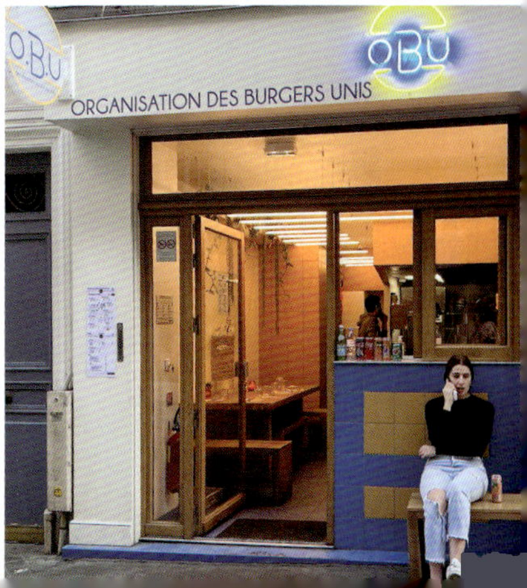
OBU
ORGANISATION DES BURGERS UNIS
OBU

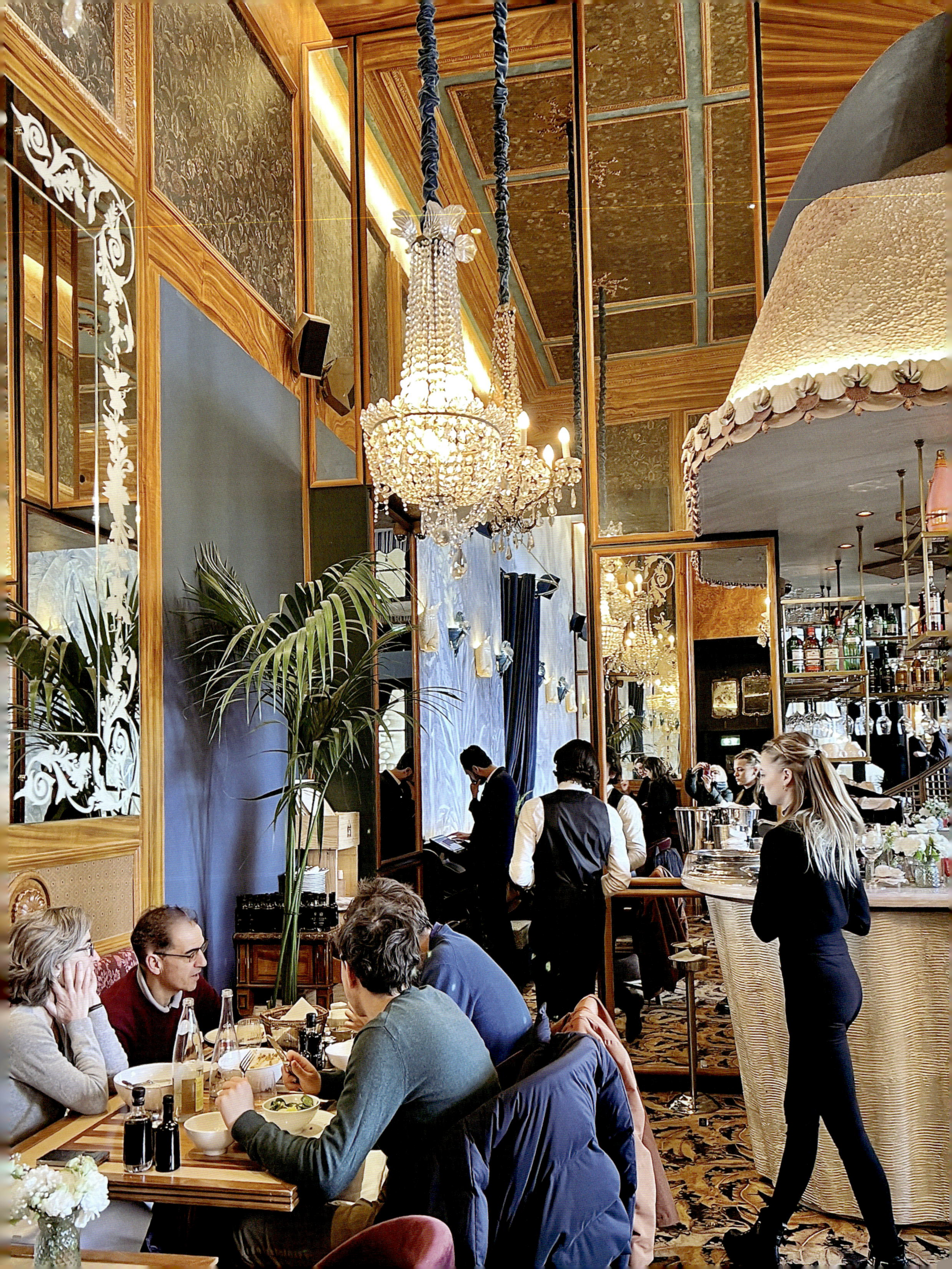

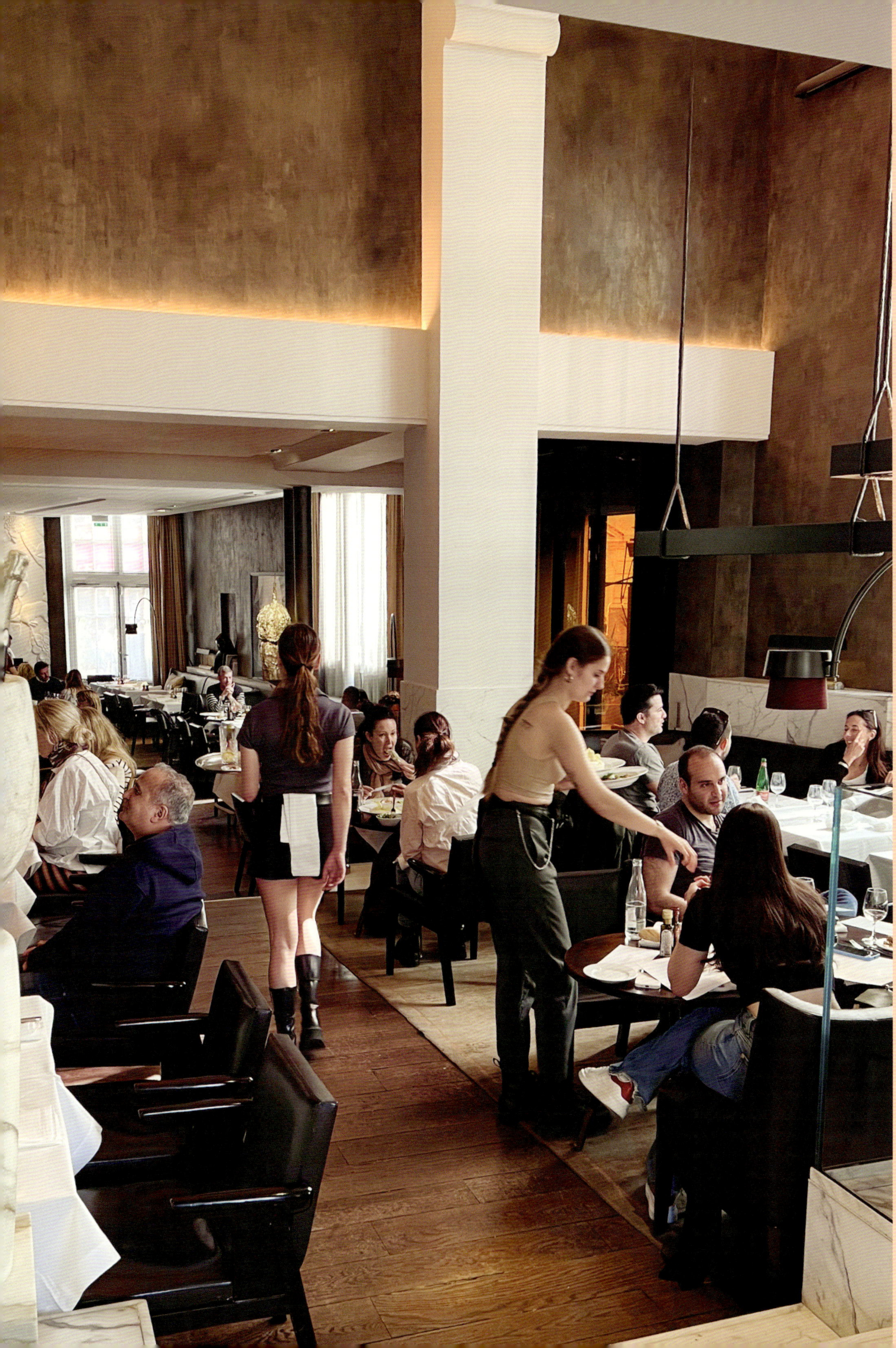

PART 11 Looking Forward: Trendy in a Good Way

L'art de Vivre is Alive and Well

"You can't escape the past in Paris, and yet what's so wonderful about it is that the past and present intermingle so intangibly that it doesn't seem a burden."

Allen Ginsberg

Like other major cities in the world, Paris is home to a multitude of cuisines from other countries. Films, TV, the internet, podcasts, social media, and the ease of modern travel spread trends and fads across the globe: boba, craft beer, craft cocktails, natural wine, specialty coffee, matcha, juice bars, burgers, avocado toast, kale chips, pork-belly, food trucks, pizza, tacos, bagels, poke, falafel, sushi, plant-based, vegan, small plates, carb-free, lactose-free, gluten-free, etc. Some fads will fade; others are here to stay.

In contrast to cookie-cutter fast food and coffee shop chains proliferating in Paris for the last several decades, some proprietors, eternally creative in the pursuit of good food, beauty, and craft, have fashioned cafés and bistros that are as exciting in our time as those of the Belle Époque were in theirs. Countless new cafés and bistros usher in new ways of cooking, presenting, and surprising the world with delicious culinary concepts in intriguing settings. When traditions endure and morph by design, something extraordinary often results; these newbies are as diverse as the arrondissements and can be simple, colorful, elegant, classic, funky, austere, retro, or cutting edge. Some will fizzle, while others, assuredly, will become the classics of their time.

Mention must be made of the "Neo-Bistro" or "Bistronomy" movement, a synthesis of "bistro" and "gastronomy" coined by the journalist and food critic Sébastien Demorand in 2004, naming a trend that began in the 1990s. Often attributed to chef Yves Camdeborde (mentored at the Ritz by Christian Constant), who in 1992, at the age of 27, opened La Régalade in the 14th and remained at the helm for twelve years before moving on to his Comptoir empire in the 6th. Michelin-starred chefs soon followed, expanding into less expensive satellites, adding fresh, simpler dishes to their repertoire served in a more casual ambiance. The movement has inspired a renaissance in French cooking with worldwide food influences, seasonal ingredients, and combining old and new in food and design. The best of the lot offers diners an injection of texture, youth, creativity, and innovation for the eye and palate. The new establishments prompt the owners and chefs of established cafés, bistros, and brasseries to refresh their game and step up to the (new) plate. Classicism, too, lives on and thrives in historic dining rooms and brand new classic-style bistros.

Young French chefs, joined by chefs from around the world, continue to build on the Neo-Bistro trend by launching new eateries and taking over some stalwarts—serving up locally sourced, natural ingredients and inspirations from all corners of the globe. Several current Parisian food trends are imported from California Cuisine's fusion and use of fresh, seasonal, local, and sustainable fare. Flashback to fifty years ago when Alice Waters, inspired by provincial France's cuisine, opened Chez Panisse in Berkeley, California, delivering quality, natural, flavorful, farm-to-table ingredients, simply prepared with no need to be sauced up. From France to California and back again, California cuisine and bistronomy was (and is) all about the three S's: Seasonal, Sourced, Sustainable; ingredients and menus that change with the seasons, rather than being fixed forever.

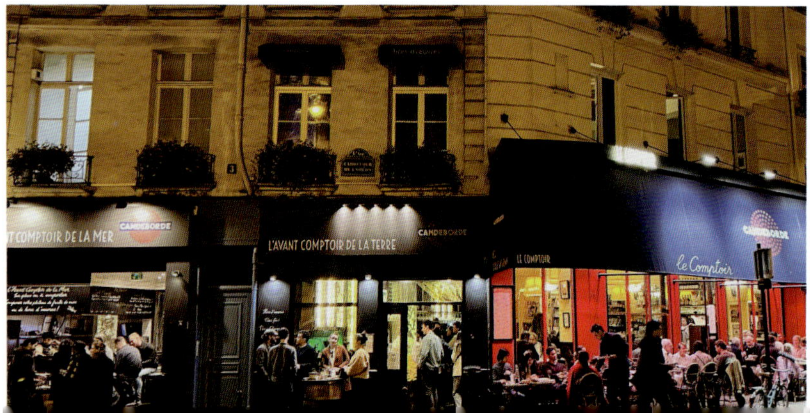

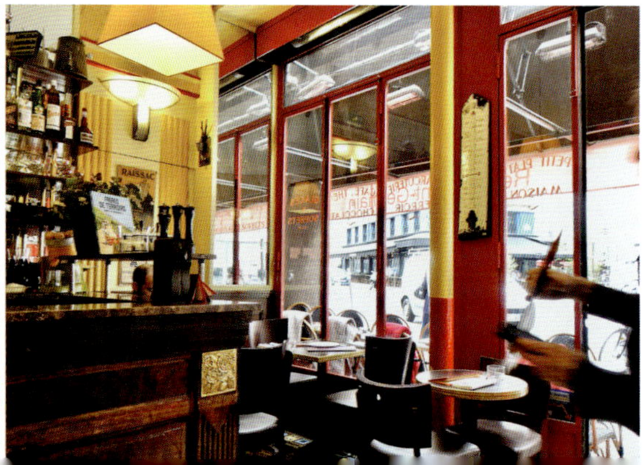

Add the in-vogue buzzwords: fusion, small-plates, bio, plant-based, vegetarian, vegan, lactose-free, gluten-free, fait maison, biodynamic wines, craft beer, craft cocktails, happy hour, third-wave coffee shops, fresh, (not ready-made or frozen). Mix with world cuisine prepared by creative young chefs from France and around the globe, frequently infusing French classics with Asian, Anglo, Italian, Spanish, and other influences. Beef it up with an embrace of vegetables as a central element in this historically meat-centric country. Throw in a bit of co-working, caves à, mangers, take-away, and delivery options like Deliveroo and Uber Eats—expanded by necessity during the COVID pandemic—and voilà, a lively, modern culinary scene emerges.

Neo-Bistro interiors range from industrial or minimal—sometimes so spartan as to be uncomfortable—to those elegantly designed by top contemporary designers. You may find servers in their classic black-and-white attire or those sporting jeans and warm smiles, carrying pretty plates with dots and flowers—good optics are a French tradition. To be clear, Neo-Bistros are not always healthy organic, bio, vegetarian, vegan, detox, or gluten-free; often, they serve riffs on traditional dishes with cream, butter, salt, and plenty of red meat. And there are opponents as well as proponents, with a variety of complaints regarding everything from the less-than-hearty portion size (nothing new in Paris) to strangely concocted dishes, made to look pretty but not very tasty. Neos are also criticized for being restaurants pretending to be bistros, particularly those with *prix fixe* tasting menus, celebrity chefs, and prices to match.

Initially heralded as a rebellion against the rigor of the Michelin Guide, in 2020, Michelin has since responded by introducing the Michelin Green Star that awards sustainability, local and ethical ingredient sourcing, and recycling. The first twenty-four Parisian chefs were anointed with green stars in 2021. Since the early 2000's Le Fooding, a youthful alternative to the Michelin Guide has been touting bistronomy; in 2018, Michelin bought a significant stake in Le Fooding. Thus Michelin has embraced the Neo-Bistro revolution and has institutionalized the integration of the old and the new.

Alongside the rise of the Neo-Bistro and the specialty café movement in Paris comes the revival of brasseries and bouillons, two 19th -and early 20th-century institutions that became nearly extinct by the end of the 20th century. The few surviving early brasseries and bouillons are often gorgeous temples of Art Nouveau or Art Deco design; grand spaces with high ceilings, mirrors, and embellished surfaces. The new (neo) brasseries and bouillons, though less opulent, are most undoubtedly fashionable. Charles Compagnon, a young French chef, coffee roaster, and sommelier, has been instrumental in revitalizing and popularizing the neo-brasserie movement. He opened his first neo-brasserie, L'Office, in 2011, followed by Le Richer, Le 52, and in 2021, Café Compagnon, each a grand success. Other neo-brasseries continue to spring up. However, the word brasserie on a food establishment can be misleading as many display the name without proof of concept.

The flâneur on the streets of Paris is forever on the lookout for something new and exciting as well as tried and true; invariably foraging for cafés and bistros laced with good food and design, be it classic French with a twist or something completely novel and delicious to the eye and the palate. Talented designers, craftspeople, artists, chefs, entrepreneurs, *bistrotiers*, and *cafetiers*, eternally creative in the pursuit of beauty and *l'art de vivre*, are alive and well in the cafés, bistros, brasseries, and bouillons of Paris.

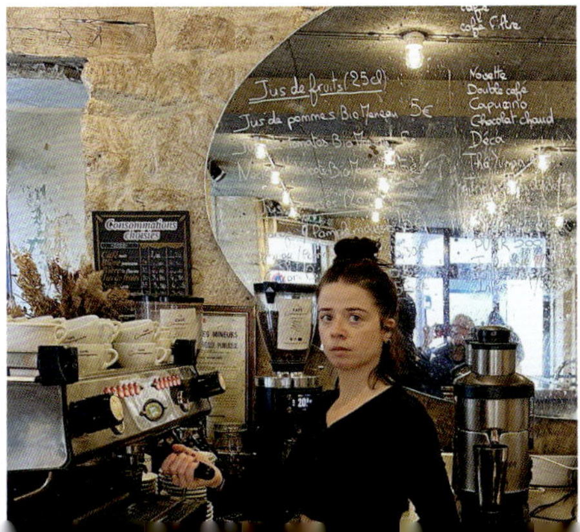
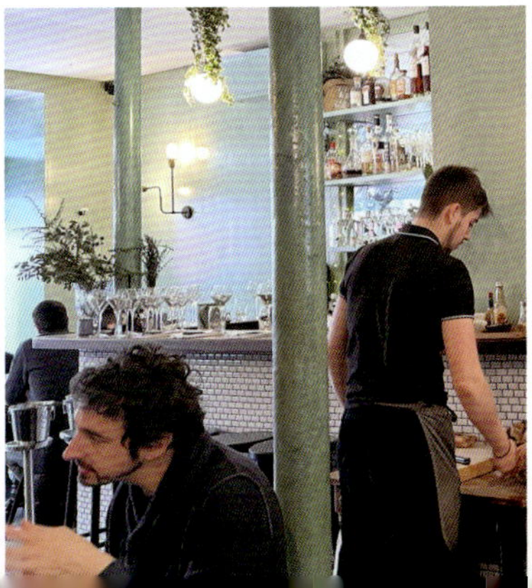
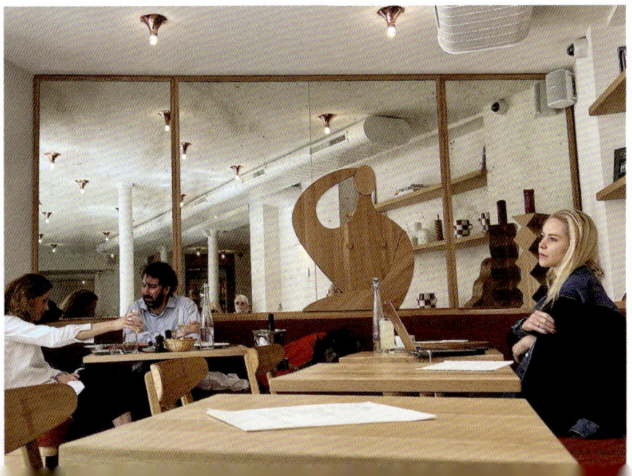

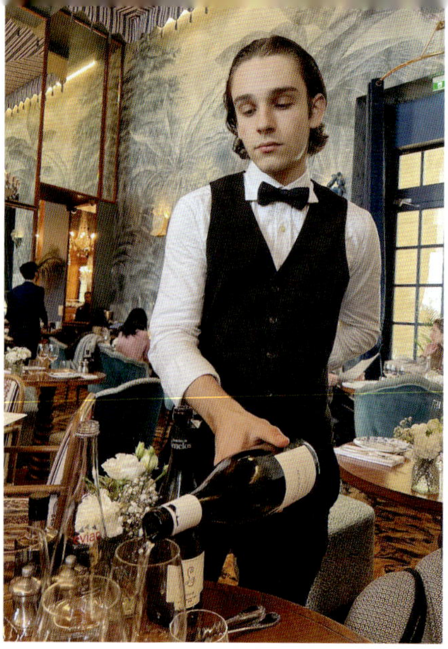

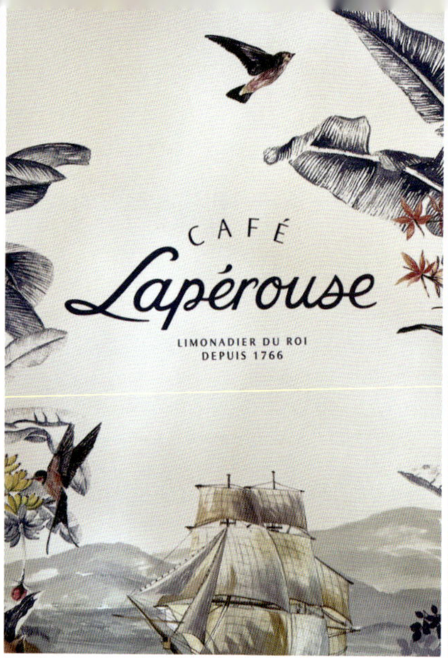

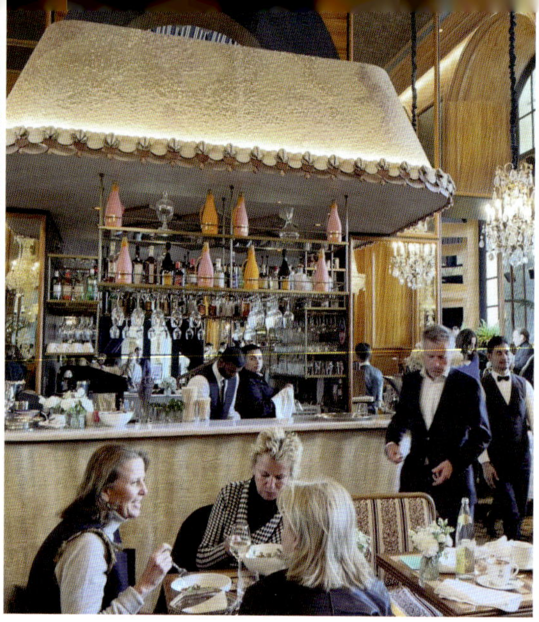

Benjamin Patou, the owner of Lapérouse—the 250-year-old Rive Gauche establishment that was the first restaurant awarded three Michelin stars in 1933—opened gorgeous Café Lapérouse in 2021, located in the newly restored Hôtel de la Marine at Place de la Concorde. Patou partnered with Antoine Arnault, the CEO of luxury men's accessory company Maison Berluti and head of communications for LVMH, and Cordélia de Castellane, the artistic director of Dior Maison and Baby Dior, who designed the interiors. The bistronomy menu and interiors pay homage to sailors, including explorer Jean-François de Galaup, Comte de La Pérouse (*voila* Lapérouse), a navigator and wine merchant who established his business in the building in 1766.

Gregory Marchand, known as "Frenchie," the nickname bestowed by Jamie Oliver, started training at the age of 16 in Brittany and worked in Marbella, London, New York, and Hong Kong before moving to Paris with his wife and partner Marie in 2008. He launched the much-heralded bistronomic Frenchie, now sporting one Michelin star, on the rue du Nil in 2009. The Marchand family now runs Frenchie Restaurant, Frenchie Bar à Vins, FTG (Frenchie To Go), Frenchie Caviste, all on the rue du Nil—which is essentially an alley. He sources many ingredients from a bakery, a fishmonger, a butcher, a coffee roaster, and a bean-to-bar chocolate shop (inspired by Dandelion Chocolate in San Francisco), which now line both sides of the street.

Opened in 2021, Bouillon République takes no reservations and sports long lines with those hungry for its traditional and affordable dishes. The shared large tables on the ground floor make for a convivial feast. Those who prefer more private conversations can dine upstairs. Three courses with generous portions, prepared with quality ingredients, can tally up to less than 25 euros. In the 18th, Bouillon Pigalle is a sister establishment in the same mode, both reviving the classic bouillon tradition.

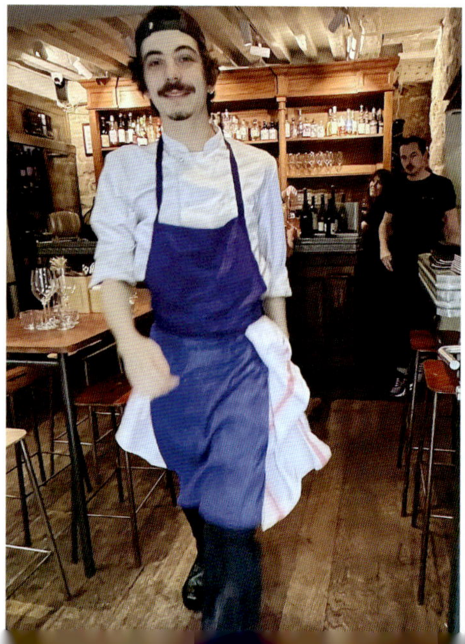

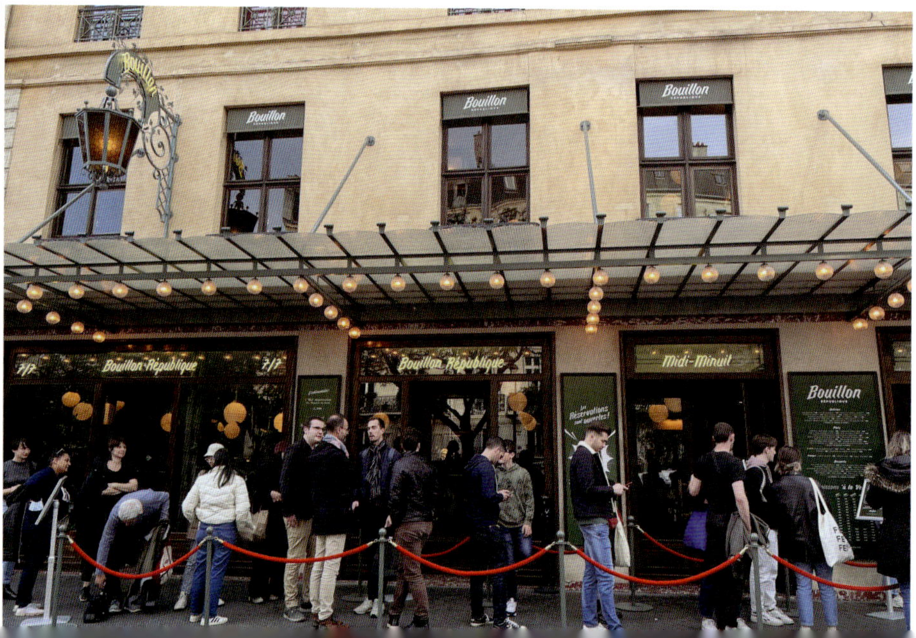

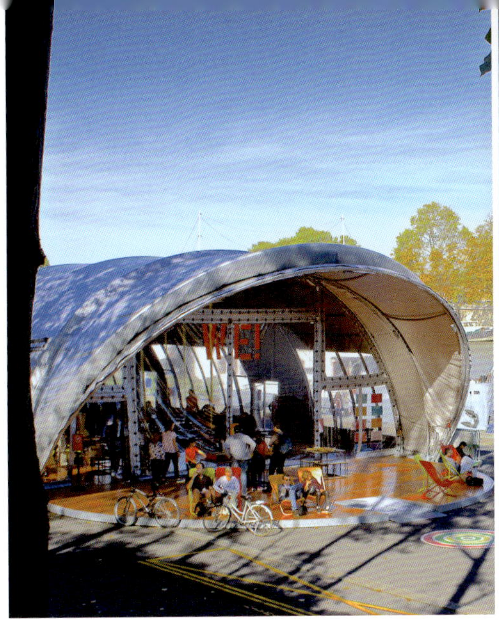

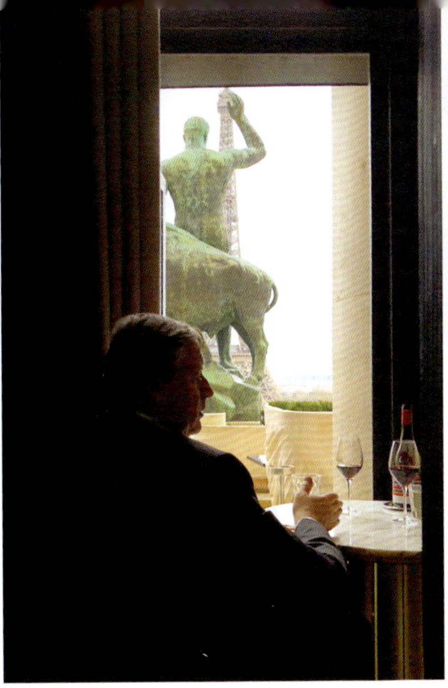

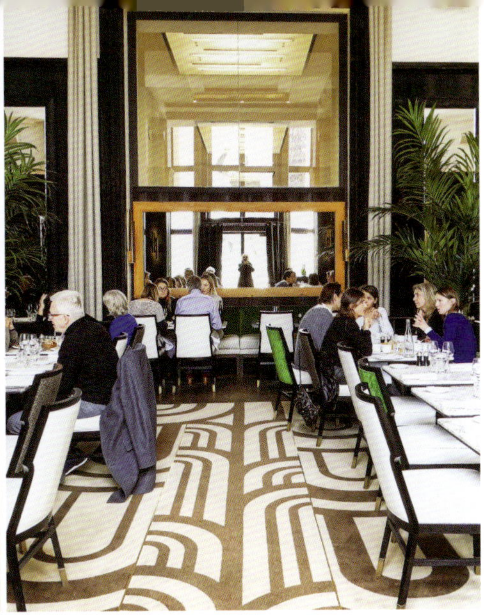

On the Seine, a festive food and entertainment scene is thriving. Harking back to a lively past are historic and brand-new cabarets and guinguettes, where you can enjoy food, drink, and dancing. Come to the cabaret!

Café de l'Homme, which opened in 2015 in the Palais de Chaillot at Trocadero, boasts a terrace that looks out onto one of the best views in Paris—the Eiffel Tower straight-on—and features a beautiful 30s-deco-style interior in concert with the building's Art Deco architecture. Here the menu is as exquisite as the elegant design and panorama.

Crowds flock to the Marais' Café Charlot, housed in a former bakery, for its simply good bistro food, high-quality (specialty) coffee, *comme il faut* design, and friendly ambiance.

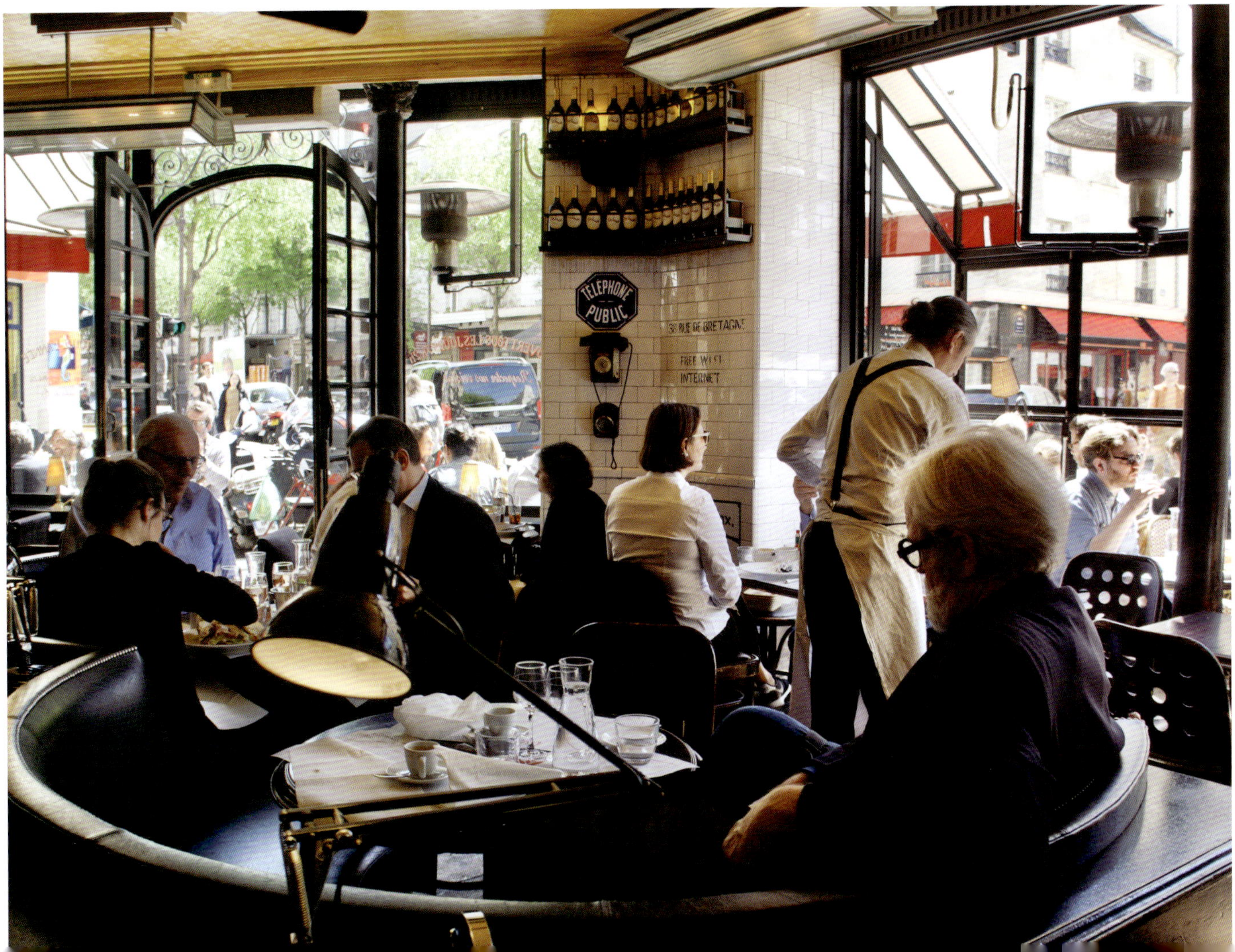

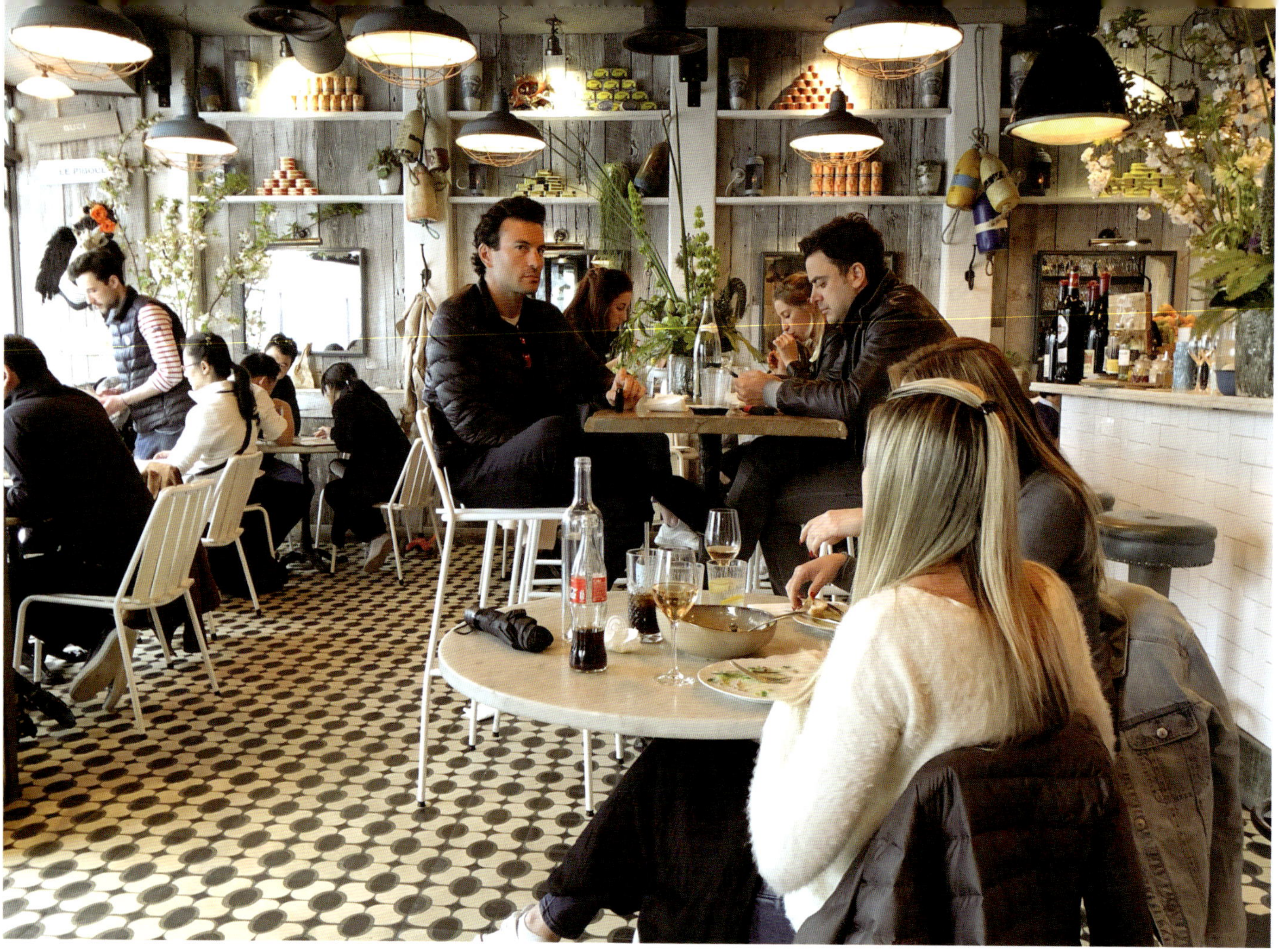

Right in the center of Paris's dynamic Saint-Germain/Buci neighborhood, Restaurateur Olivier Flotte's Huguette is a lively fresh seafood bistro in the style of a 21st-century fisherman's hut. Sit upstairs, downstairs, or enjoy the terrace on bustling rue de Seine and taste the catch of the day. Reservations are a must during busy times.

Often hailed as the best of bistronomy, Septime, with its prix fixe menu and haut pricing, is difficult to classify as a bistro. In multicultural Paris, a café can also be a caffé. The Big Mama group was founded in 2013 by two Frenchmen, Tigrane Seydoux and Victor Lugger, who work in the Italian style with a modern French twist. Opening Big Love Caffé in the Marais and a host of trattorias all around Paris, the food and design are so inviting and the prices so fair that their establishments often have a street-side line-up and are always worth the wait.

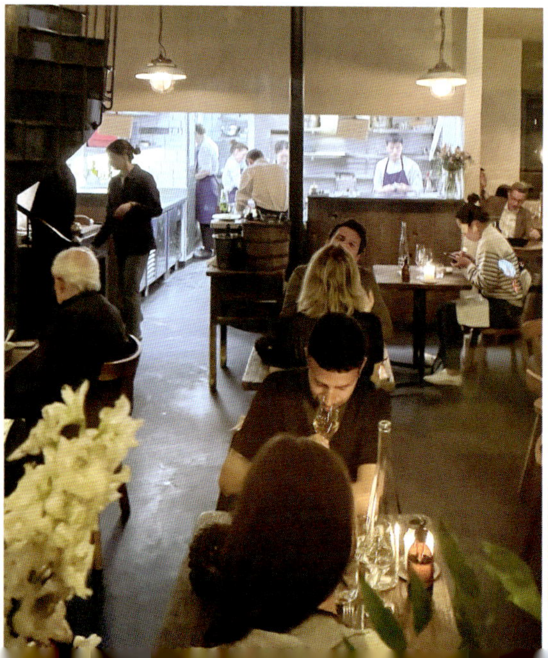

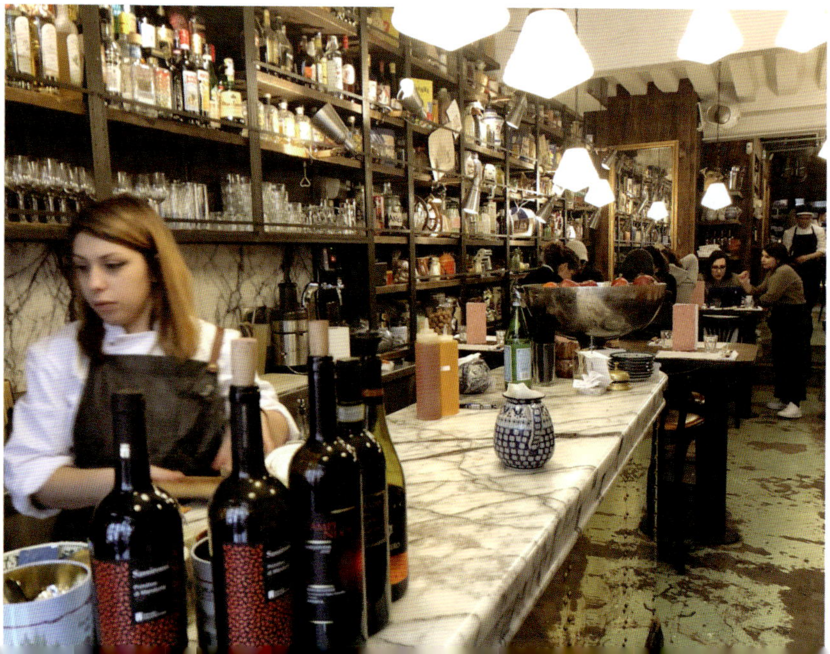

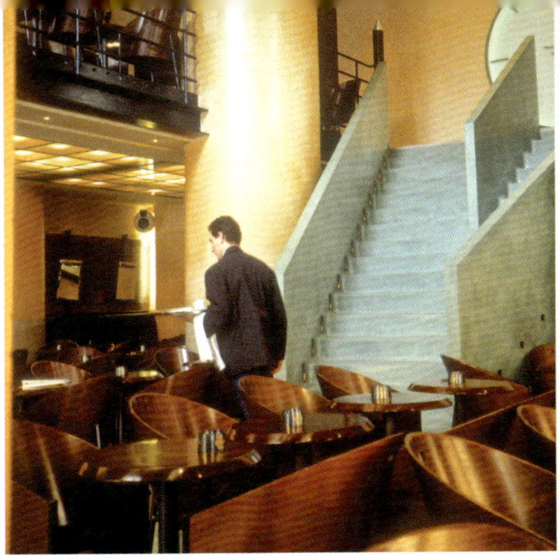

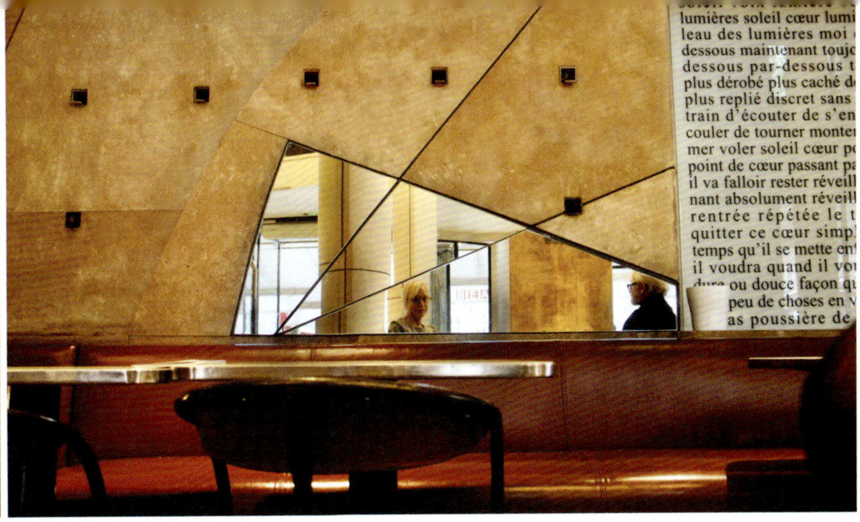

Coming to Paris from the Aveyron and starting as waiters, the Costes brothers, Jean-Louis & Gilbert, like the many Auvergnats before them, opened a café. Groundbreaking Café Costes, designed by a young, little-known Philippe Starck, opened in 1984 and closed just ten years later. Short-lived for a café, but astonishing nevertheless. From the architectural space to the chairs, the design of every element was like nothing ever before seen in Paris. Modern had beautiful new forms. Café Costes cemented the careers of Philippe Starck and the Costes brothers, who continue to create a multitude of wonders. By hiring top designers, the Costes brought sophisticated design to numerous Parisian bistros, cafés, and hotels, including Café Beaubourg in the 1980s, Café Marly in 1994, Georges in 2000, and a slew of others in the late-20th- and early 21st-century. Every venue is a unique delight, designed with a refined avant-garde sensibility that adds glamour to the cafés and bistros of contemporary Paris.

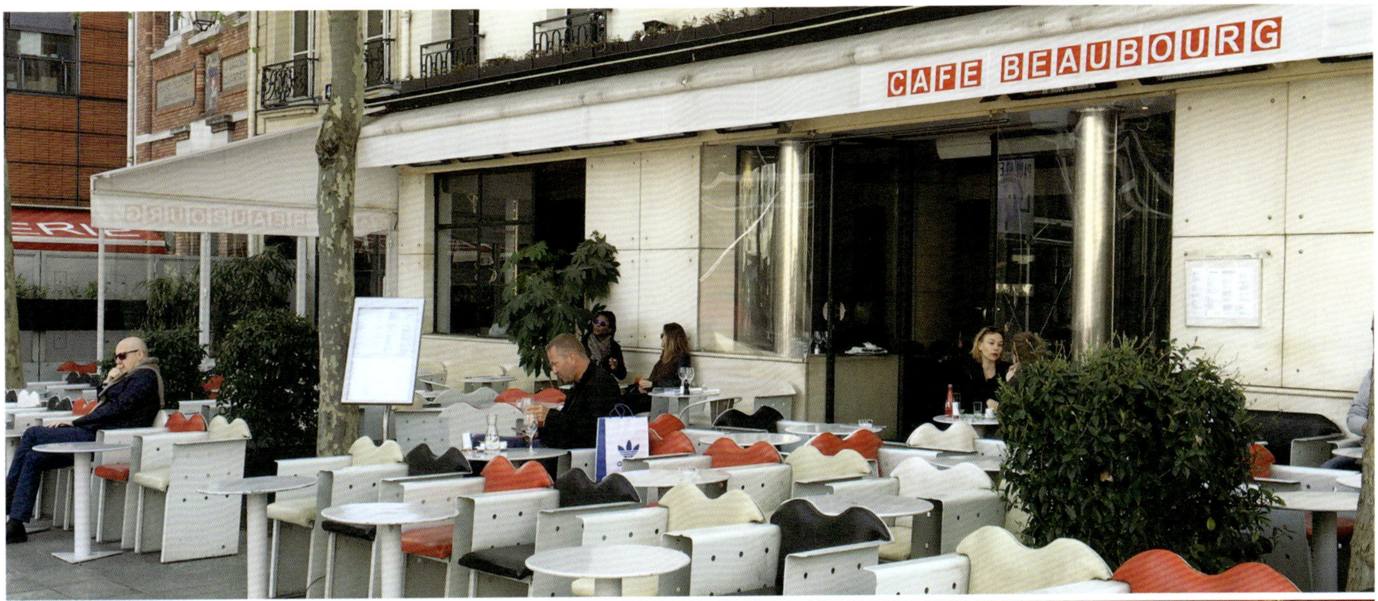

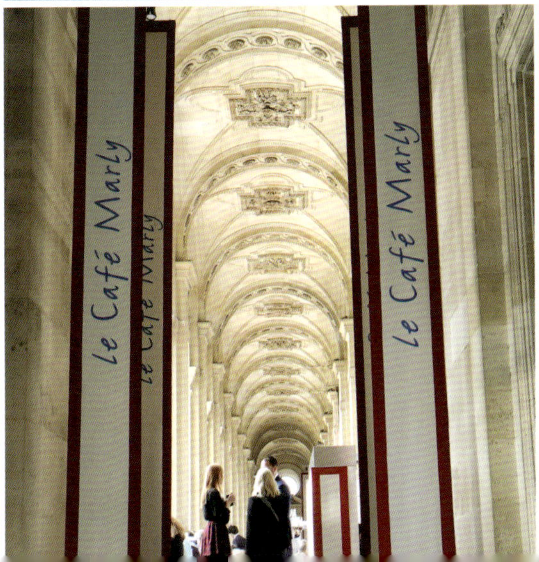

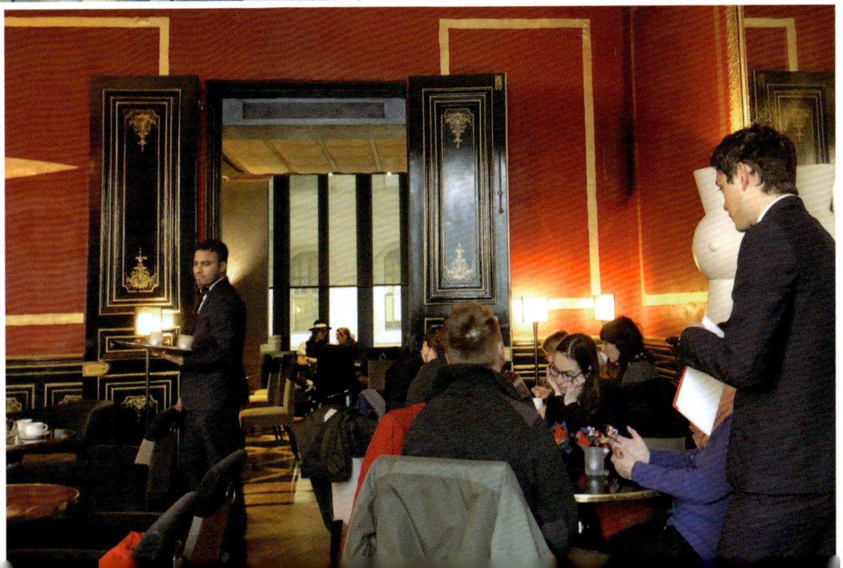

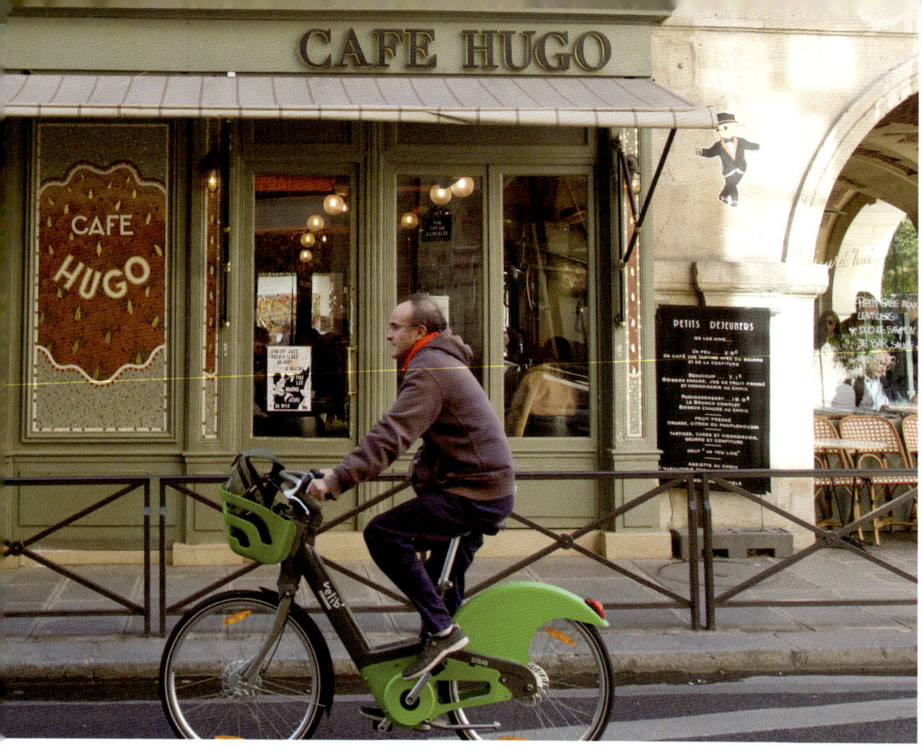

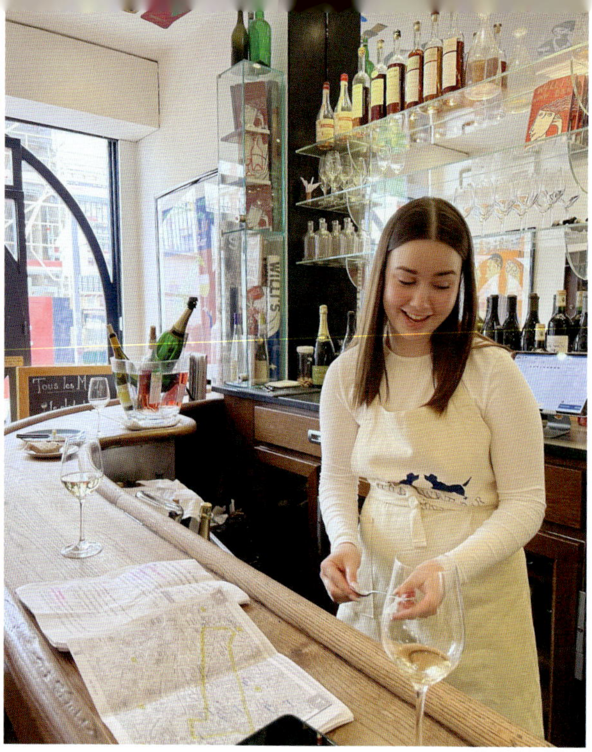

Boissonnerie, a fish haven in Saint-Germain by New Zealander Drew Harré and American Juan Sanchez, along with their other haunts—nearby Semilla, Cosi, and Freddy's—serves fresh, seasonal dishes to a sophisticated crowd. English speakers feel at home here. Located at the historic Place des Vosges, near the Victor Hugo Museum (his former residence), Café Hugo provides a perfect respite. Order just a cappuccino or a simple meal; open your computer or rest your eyes on the garden. Whatever the mood, all's well.

British expat Mark Williamson's Willi's Wine Bar (ABOVE RIGHT) heralded the modern Parisian Wine Bar in 1980. Enjoy a glass or bottle of expertly curated wine, with or without a light, delicious meal. Willi's is another haven for English speakers.

With its playful clown theme, the Clown Bar (OPPOSITE TOP LEFT), located in the former pump room of nearby Cirque d'Hiver in the Haut Marais, opened as a café for circus performers in 1907 and is now a neo-bistro. The historic monument's joyful ceramic walls and painted glass ceiling portray depictions of clowns, while the kitchen prepares seasonal dishes and serves the requisite natural wine.

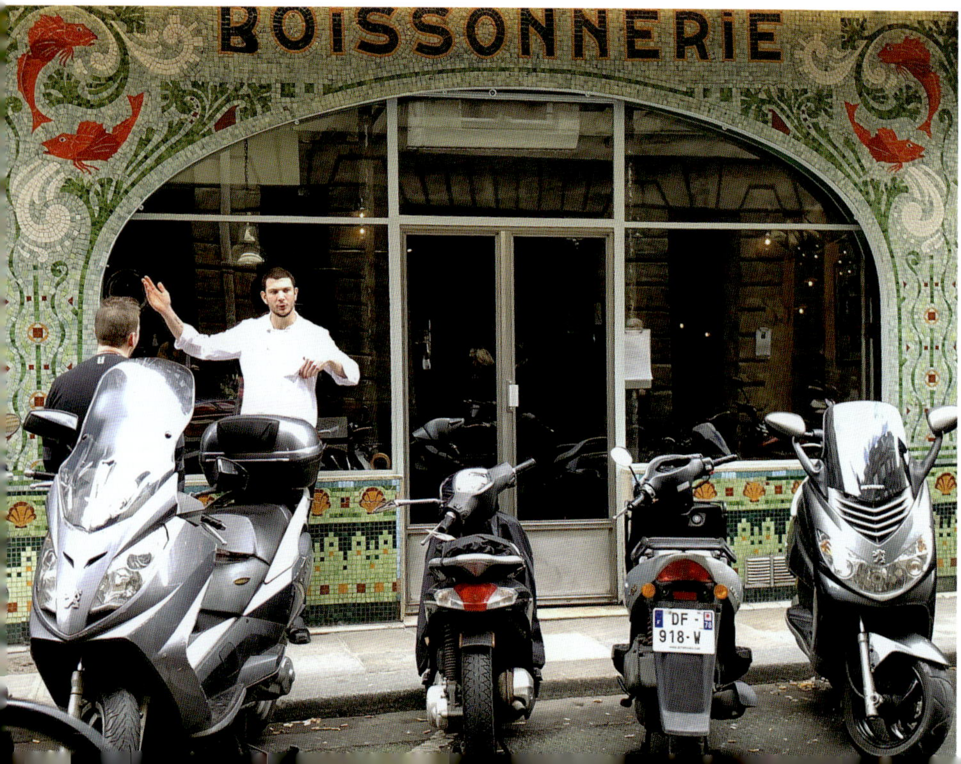

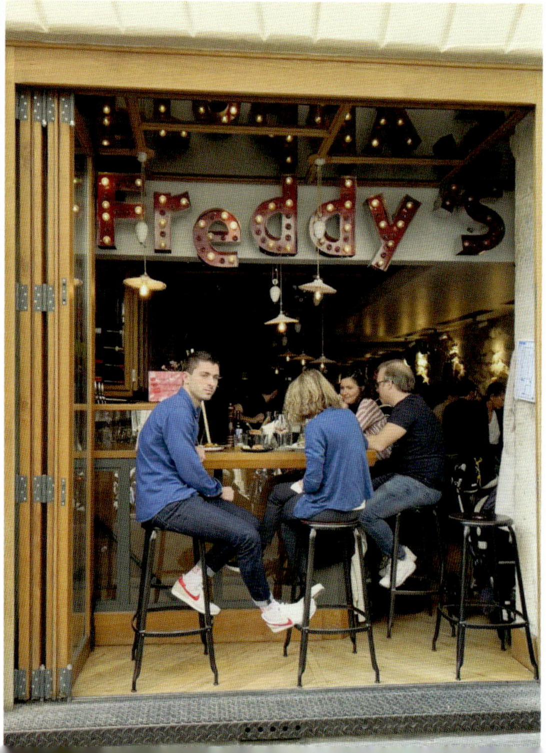

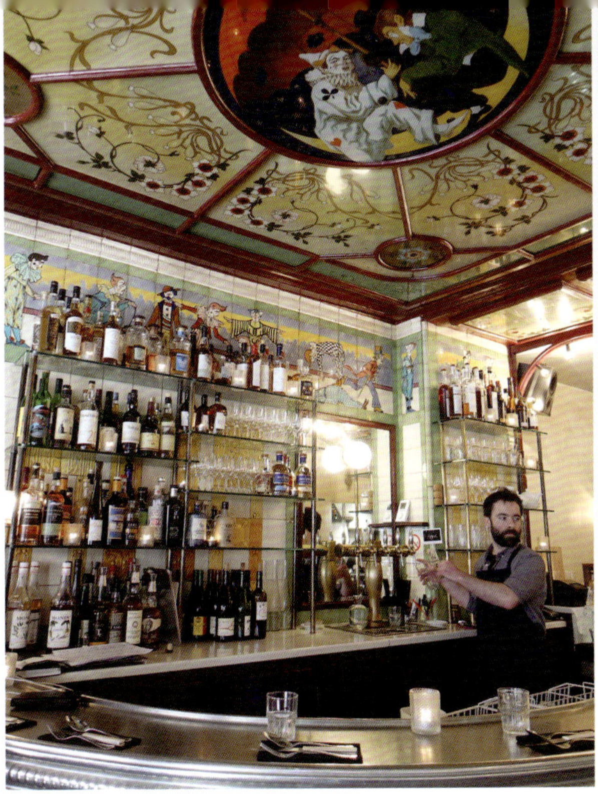

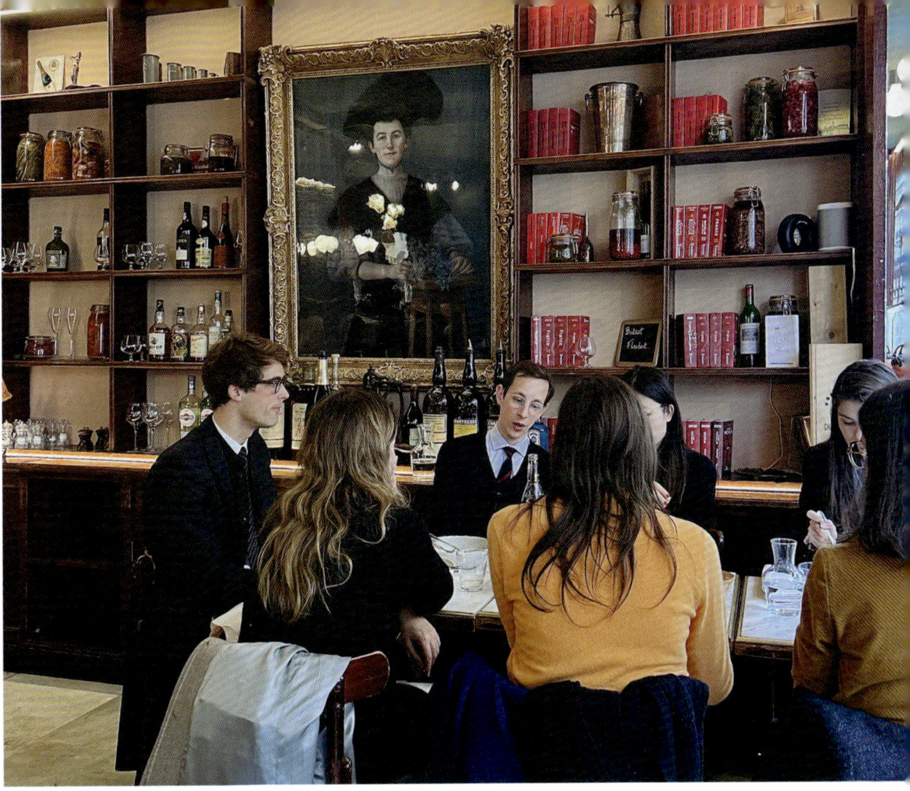

When cooking traditions organically evolve, something magical can result, with patrons the fortunate recipients. In Paris, time-honored cafés and bistros—some glued to tradition, others introducing innovative twists—exist next door to new ones, their inventive menus a welcome addition. As always, democracy rules: just as everyone is welcome in a café and bistro, every café and bistro is welcome in Paris. One of the first bistros Michel Rostang opened in 1987, Le Bistrot d'à Côté Flaubert, along with Bistrot Flaubert (ABOVE RIGHT) next door, has been handed over to his sous-chef, Nicolas Baumann, and Stéphane Manigold in 2020. The vibe at á Côté is classic with a modern, friendly twist. The food is carefully sourced and prepared with excellent old-school wines that you can purchase right off the walls.

Cyril Lignac, who owns several restaurants in Paris, has preserved and polished the interior of Le Chardenoux (BELOW), the designated historic monument which opened in 1908. The showpiece is a long undulating bar inlaid with 14 varieties of marble topped by a zinc counter. The cuisine is classic with a creative twist, and it is open every day.

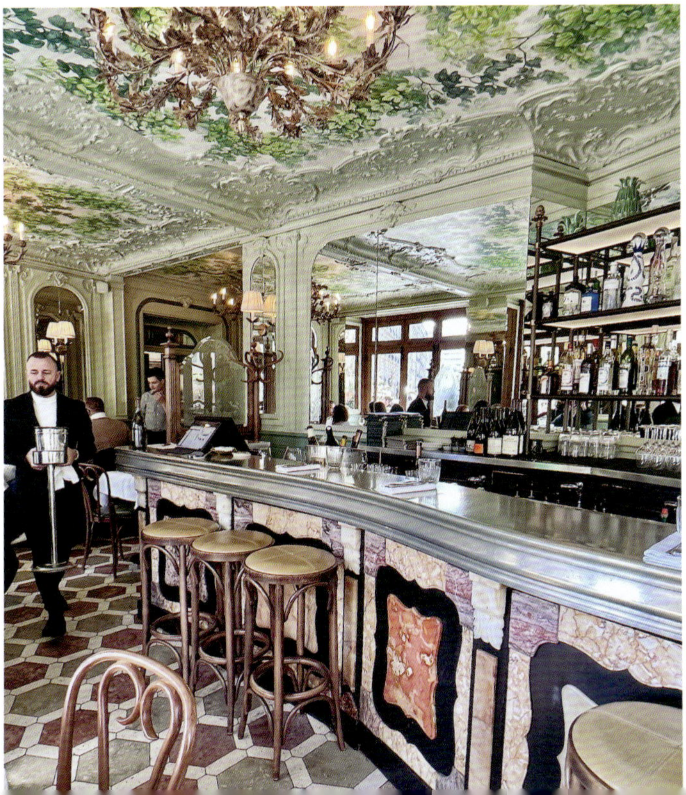

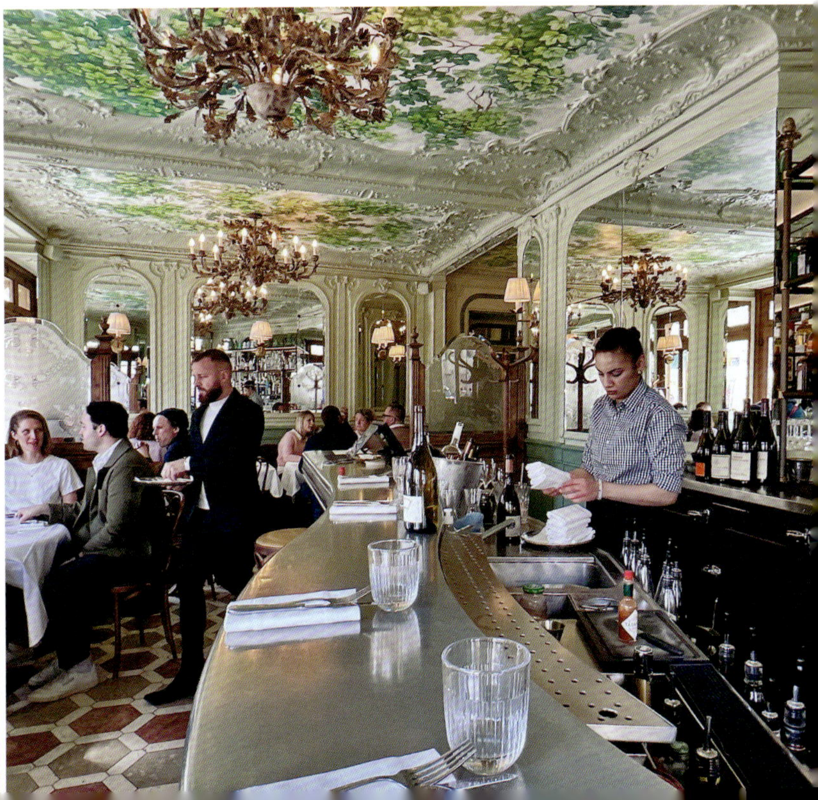

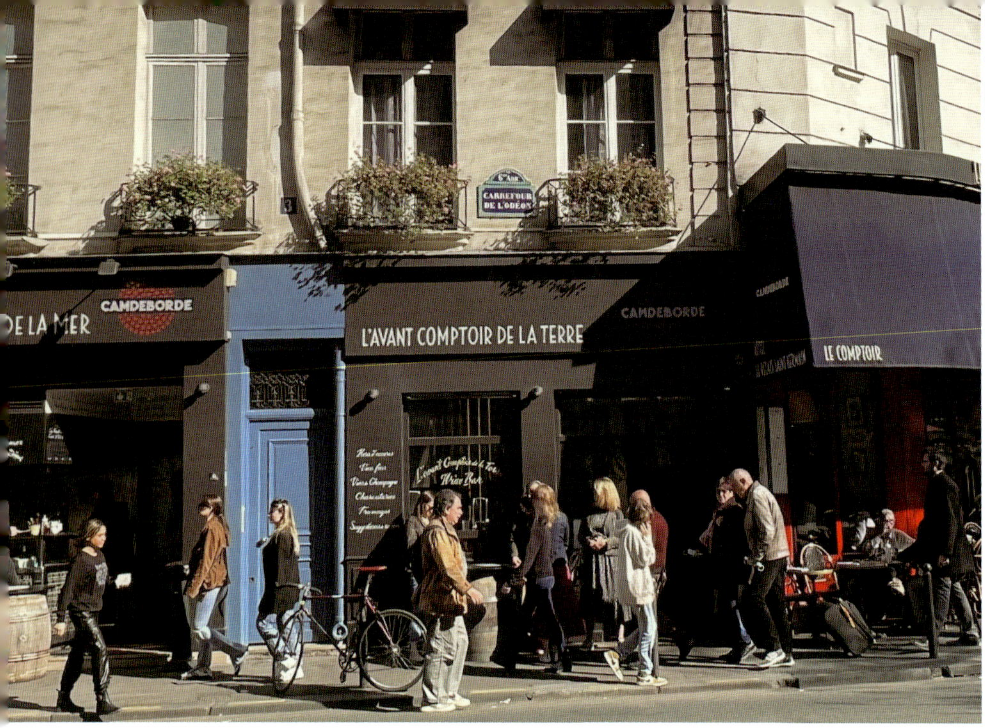

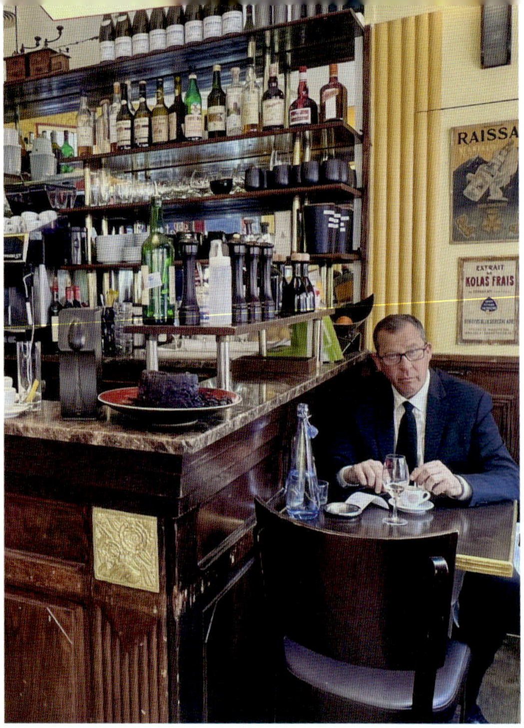

Carrefour de l'Odéon has two opposite-facing, very different bistros. Yves Camdeborde's (the father of bistronomy) Le Comptoir serves naturally-sourced ingredients—often procured directly by Camdeborde—in a tiny interior space and terrace. Right next door at L'Avant Comptoir de la Terre and L'Avant Comptoir de la Mer, it's standing room only. Without reservations, fans line the street. Open every day from noon to 11 pm.

Across the broad Odéon intersection, Carrefour de l'Odéon, is Les Éditeurs, a contemporary café whose name pays homage to the literary past of rue de l'Odéon. On this street, Adrienne Monnier opened her bookshop, La Maison des Amis des Livres in 1915, and American Sylvia Beach launched her English bookshop, Shakespeare and Company, in 1919. After establishing a bookstore, lending library, and sometimes crash pad renowned as a sanctuary for great expat writers, Beach made literary history in 1922 by publishing James Joyce's *Ulysses*. The institution was forced to close shop in 1941 when the Germans occupied Paris. At the end of WWII, Ernest Hemingway personally "liberated" Shakespeare and Co. (along with the Ritz Bar), but it never reopened.

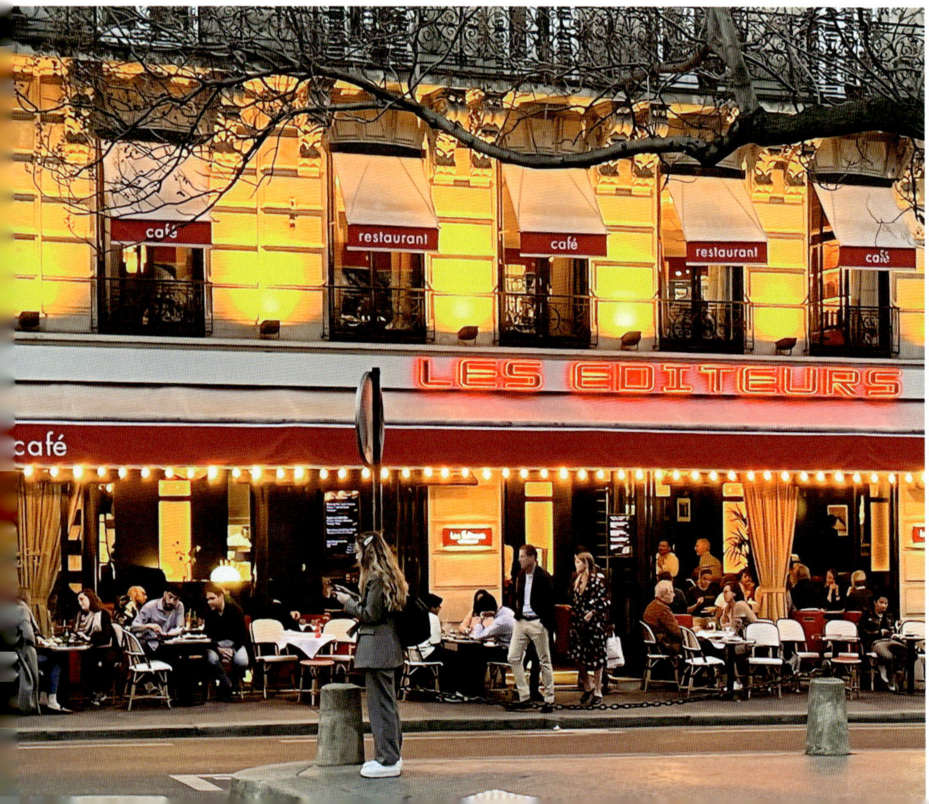

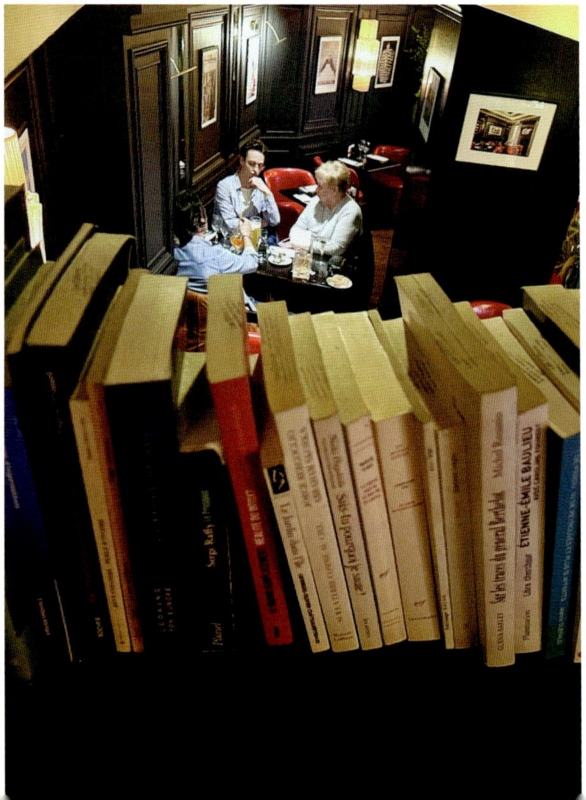

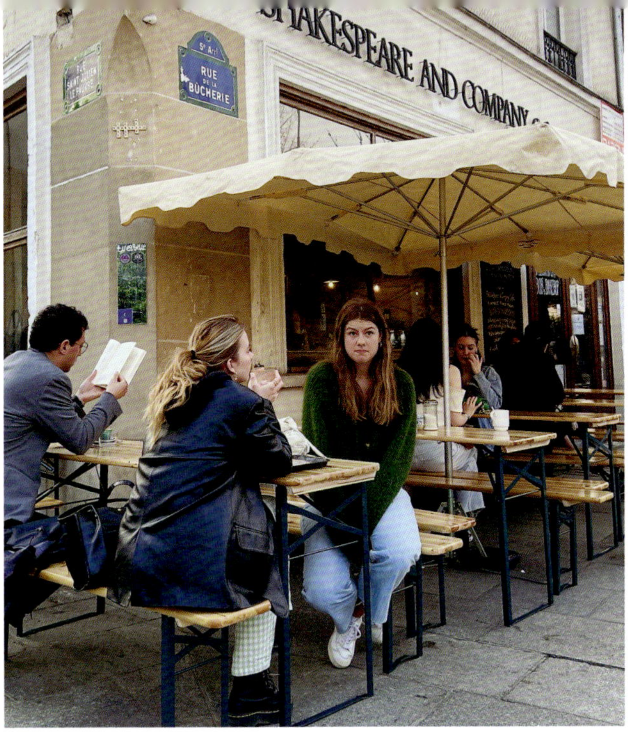

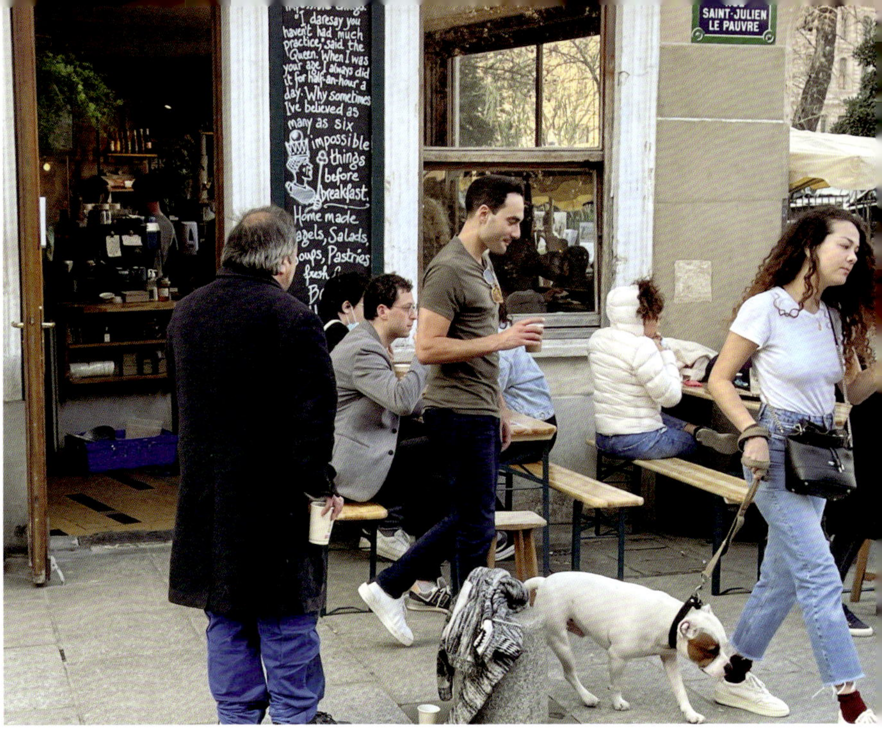

George Whitman carried on the tradition in 1964 when he changed the name of his Le Mistral bookstore to Shakespeare and Company in honor of Sylvia Beach. He later named his daughter Sylvia, and she is now in charge of preserving the heritage. Adding a café to the bookstore in 2015 was a triumph for Sylvia after her father had unsuccessfully tried for decades to convince the owner next door to let him open a literary café. "Coffee and books go so well together," says Sylvia, and a sign over the door declares, "Open door, open books, open mind, open heart." This revered venue remains a destination, with lines forming at both the bookstore and the café. With a simple coffee house menu—mostly food to accompany beverages and 5,000 books, she hosts literary and jazz events to recall the literary history of the original on rue de l'Odéon. Whitman's Shakespeare and Company is located opposite Notre Dame at 37 rue de la Bûcherie.

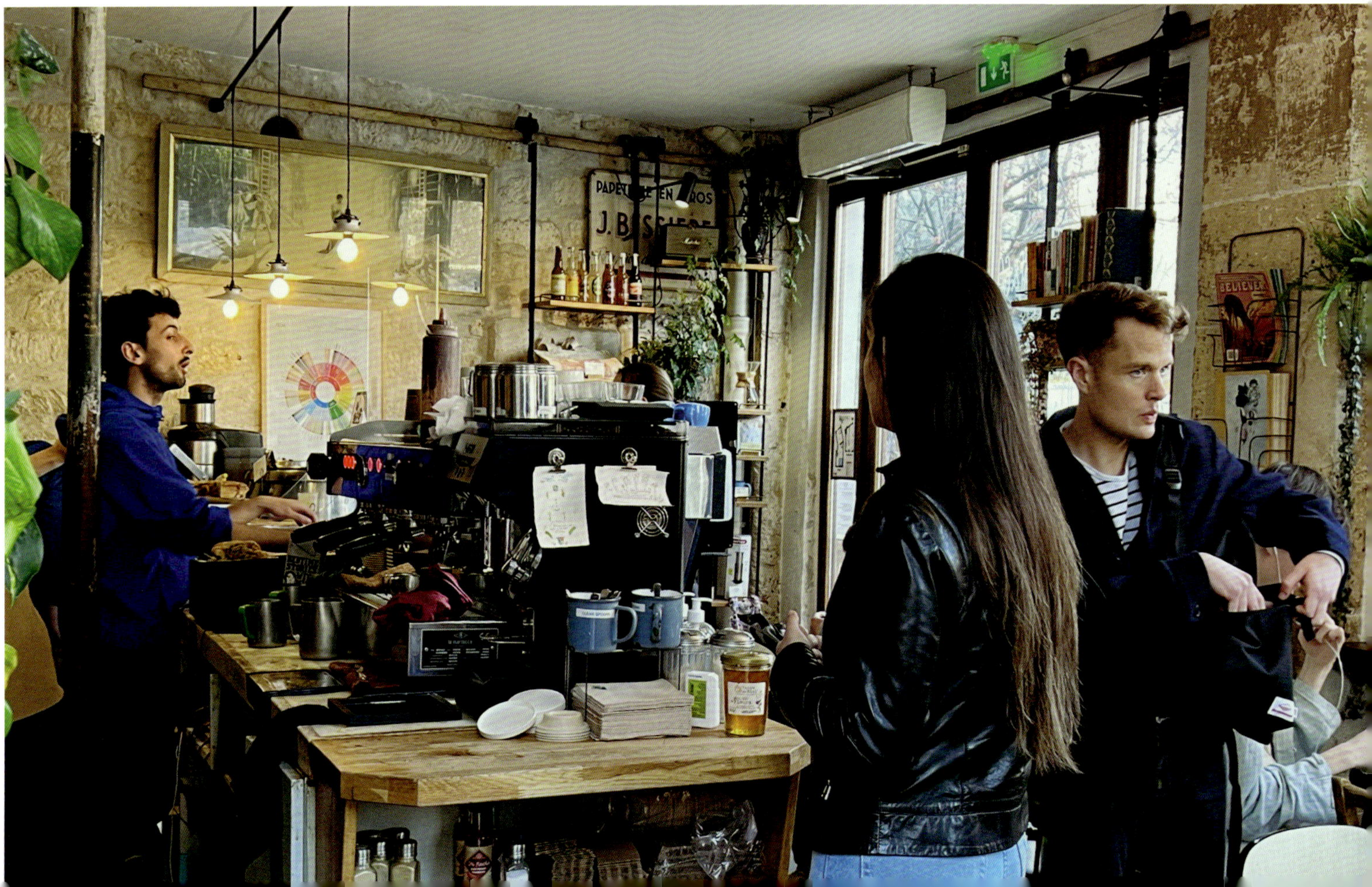

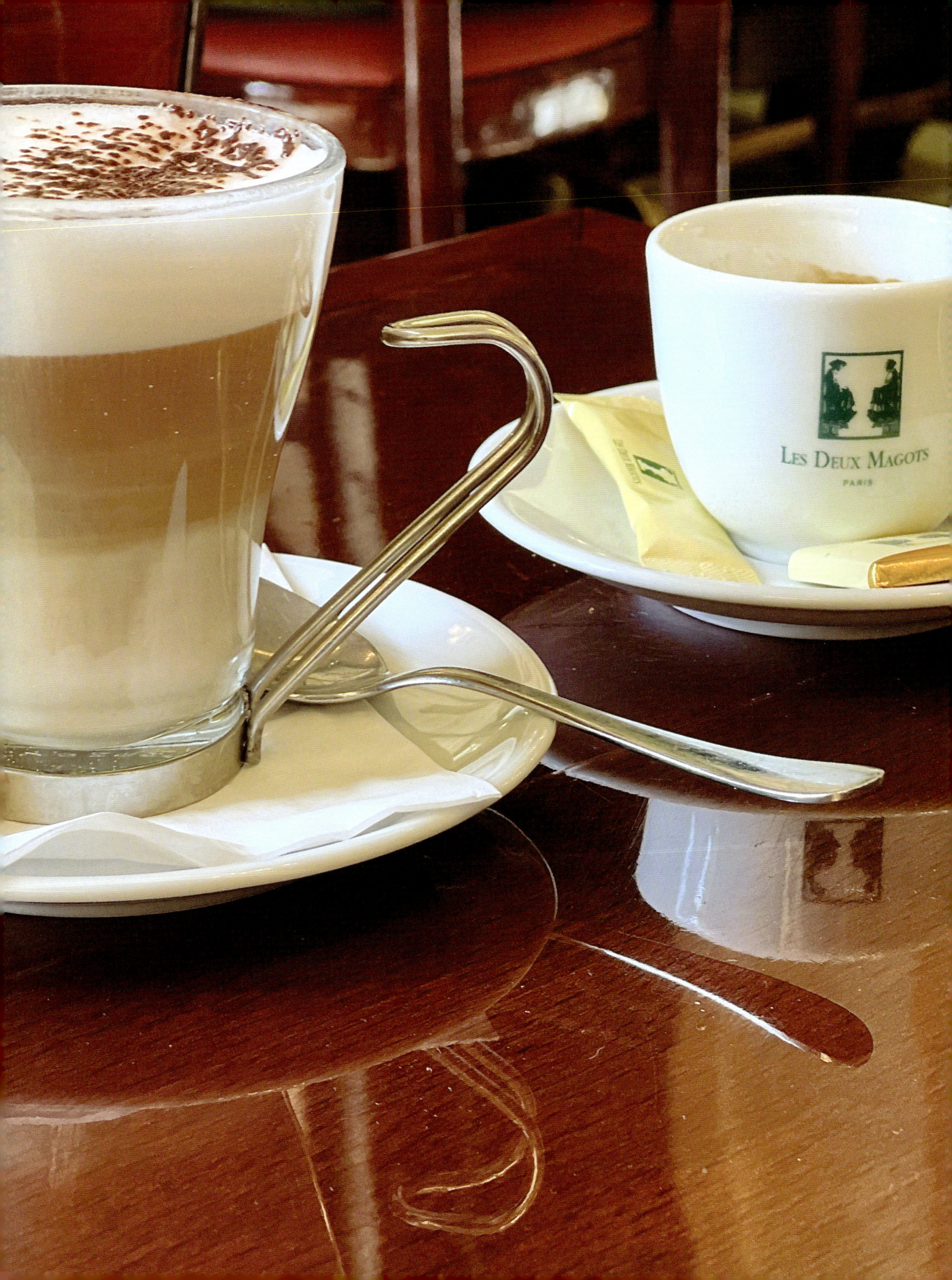
LES DEUX MAGOTS
PARIS

PART 12 A Little History: From Coffee to Café

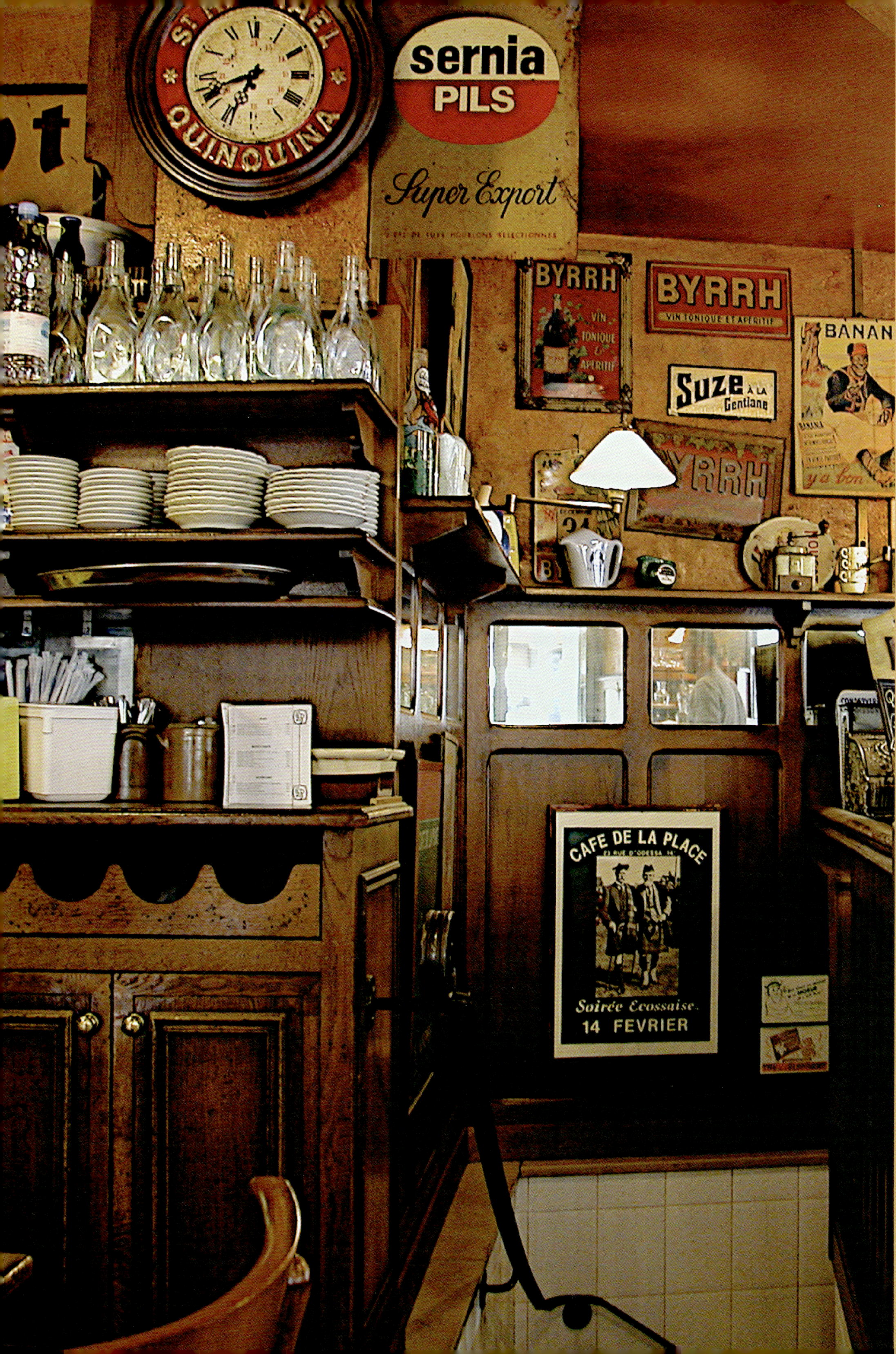

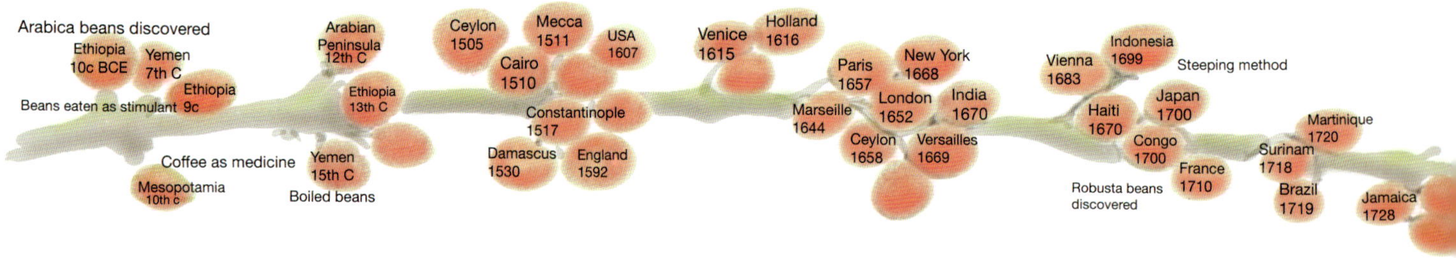

History of Coffee

"It caresses your throat and sets you going. Ideas come crowding in... the artillery of logic advances, shafts of wit fly through the air."

Balzac, who drank coffee by the pint

Today, the coffee trade is second only to crude oil in global commodities. Where and when was the first bean discovered, the first coffee tree (intentionally) planted? When was its first use as a beverage? What is the difference between the Arabica and the Robusta bean? How did coffee spread worldwide and evolve into the sophisticated, individualized drinks we now enjoy?

The movement of coffee beans, changing preparation methods, and tastes through the centuries, over the earth and seas, have led to a delightful ritual the world over. Yet, the history surrounding the discovery and diffusion of coffee remains as muddy as a cup of the brew. It is a long and often contentious story awash with inaccuracies, debates, legends, myths, little documentation, and anecdotes too numerous to include here. Whether coffee as a beverage was first enjoyed in Ethiopia or Yemen is one bone of contention. The current consensus is that coffee, primarily boiled, mixed with fat, and chewed rather than brewed, originated in central Ethiopia, perhaps, as far back as the 10th century BCE. In the 6th or 7th century CE, coffee trees were planted in southern Arabia, now Yemen, and the bean became known as Arabica. Coffee scholars agree that around 1438, Sufis in Yemen boiled the beans and drank the brew as a stimulant to stay alert during their religious devotions. From the very beginning, preparation methods have varied dramatically for extracting the essence of coffee from the bean by grinding, soaking, boiling, steaming, heating, filtering, and pressurizing.

Having spread throughout the Middle East, by the 16th century coffee became a substitute for wine (which was banned by Islam). It was given the name *qahwa* or *kahve*—literally, "wine of Arabia." Trade between the Ottoman Empire and the Venetians brought coffee to Venice around 1615. The Italians first called the beverage *cavee*, translated from the Arabic *kahve*, which later morphed into caffè, then café in French, and coffee in English.

In the 18th century, the Robusta bean was cultivated in Africa's sub-Saharan regions, such as the Belgian Congo (now the Democratic Republic of Congo) and Uganda. Production spread to Asia and South America and is currently exceptionally high in Indonesia and Vietnam. More "robust" than Arabica, Robusta beans have a less refined flavor—some say bitter—partially due to their high caffeine content, but can grow in warmer climates, which is advantageous as the earth warms. In France, Robusta beans, traditionally imported from the French colonies, still account for around 50% of French coffee and thus the inferior coffee flavor found in many cafés. While Arabica beans are favored for their quality and taste, Robusta beans are sometimes mixed with Arabica in blends. Unsurprisingly, 100% Arabica is a marketing strategy, even in Robusta accustomed Paris. While sugar, milk, chocolate, and other more trendy ingredients are popular, purists will only drink dark, rich, and strong Arabica coffee. This coffee timeline notes some significant markers in a long continuum that continues to evolve.

*Myth: An Ethiopian herdsman named Kaldi observed his goat, frolicking in quite a chipper mood near a bush. Subsequently the goat chewed on the red berries and let out an exuberant "Baaaaaaahhh!"

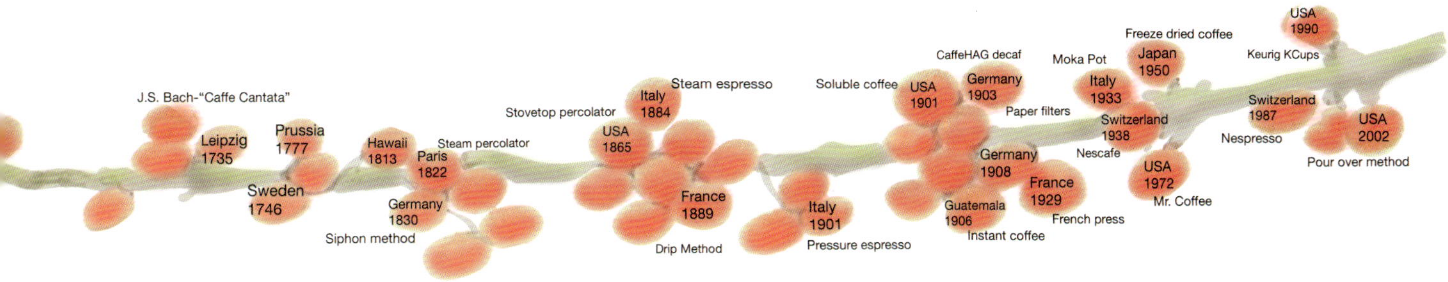
J.S. Bach-"Caffe Cantata"
Leipzig 1735
Prussia 1777
Sweden 1746
Hawaii 1813
Paris 1822
Germany 1830
Siphon method
Steam percolator
Stovetop percolator
USA 1865
Italy 1884
Steam espresso
France 1889
Drip Method
Italy 1901
Pressure espresso
Soluble coffee
USA 1901
CaffeHAG decaf
Germany 1903
Paper filters
Guatemala 1906
Instant coffee
Germany 1908
France 1929
French press
Moka Pot
Italy 1933
Switzerland 1938
Nescafe
Freeze dried coffee
Japan 1950
USA 1972
Mr. Coffee
Keurig KCups
USA 1990
Switzerland 1987
Nespresso
USA 2002
Pour over method

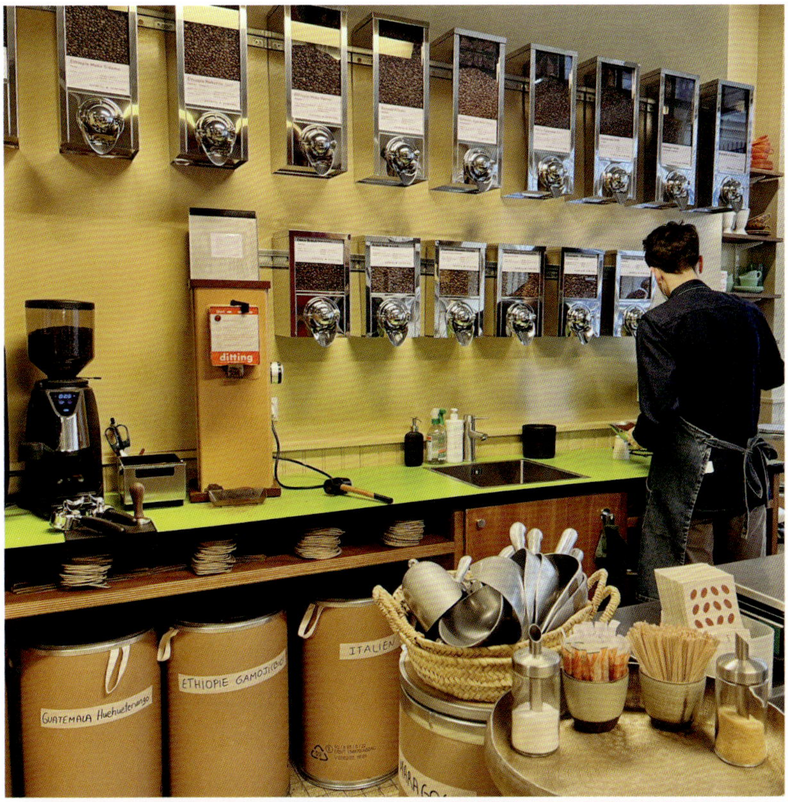
ditting
ITALIEN
ETHIOPIE GAMOJIBOWE
GUATEMALA Huehuetenango

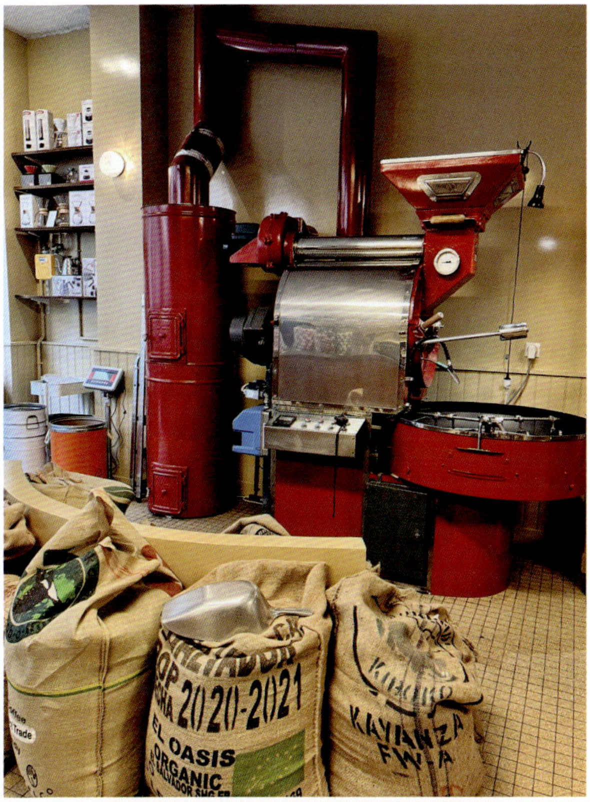
2020-2021
EL OASIS
ORGANIC
KAYANZA

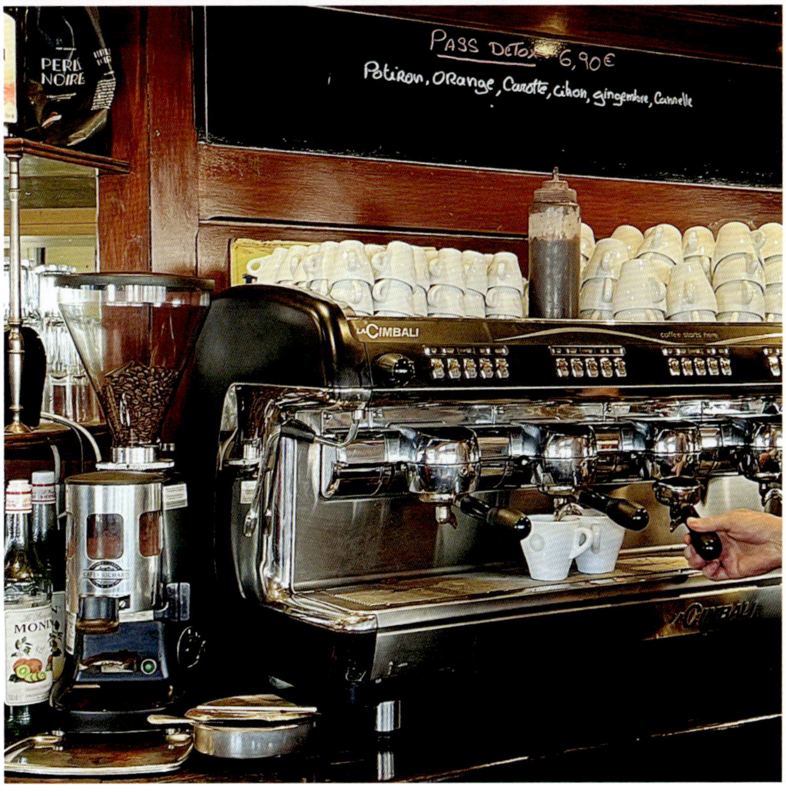
PASS DETOX 6,90€
Potiron, Orange, Carotte, Citron, gingembre, Cannelle
LA CIMBALI

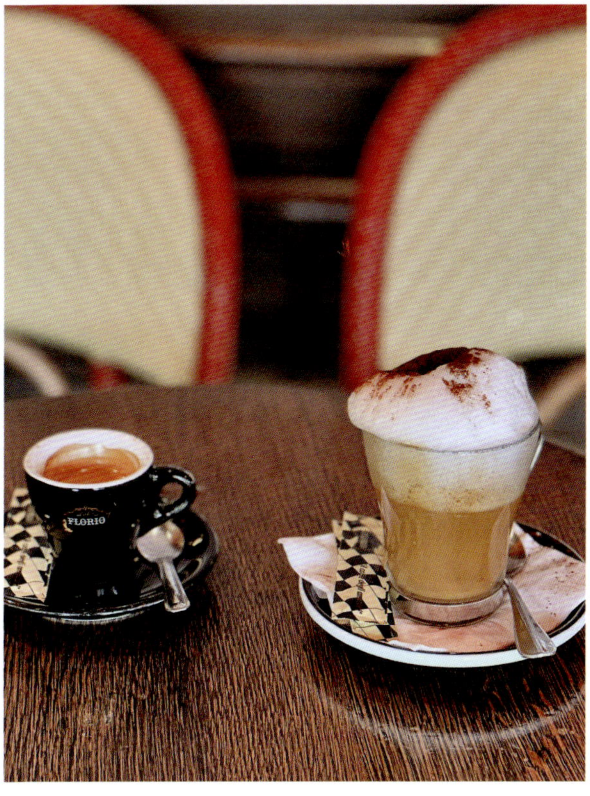
FLORIO

1475 Constantinople Kiva Han
1530 Damascus Café of the Roses
1638 Venice Il Rimedio
1651 Oxford The Angel
1664 The Hague Korte Voorhout
1670 Boston London Coffeehouse
1672 Paris Marché St Germain
1679 Hamburg English Coffeehouse
1680 London Jonathan's Coffehouse
1686 Vienna Zur Blauen Flasche
1686 Paris Café Procope
1688 London Lloyd's Coffeehouse
1696 New York The King's Arms
1697 Boston The Green Dragon
1706 London Tom's Coffeehouse
1714 Prague The Golden Snake
1720 Venice Caffè Florian
1720 St. Petersburg Chetyre Fregata
1723 Leipzig Café Zimmerman
1749 Paris Café de Foy
1760 Rome Antico Café Greco
1779 Lisbon Café Nicola
1782 Lisbon Café Martinho da Arcada
1797 Cairo El-Fishawy Café
1825 Berlin Café Kranzler
1829 Lviv Videnska Kavyarnia
1848 Budapest Café Pivlax
1858 Buenos Aires Café Tortoni

History of World Cafés

"When café life thrives, talk is a shared limberness of the mind that improves appetite for conversation: an adequate sentence maker is then made good, a good one excellent, an excellent one extraordinary."

Vivian Gornick

A bit like the history of coffee, the history of cafés is often replete with squabbles among researchers and historians, resulting in dissimilar determinations of fact. The lore surrounding them is as rich and complex as the food and beverages they serve. It's challenging to discern precisely where and when the first coffee house or the first café opened and where it originated (note that coffee house and café are not synonymous). Still, with plenty of qualifications, there is some agreement and approximate dates.

The first known coffee house may have been the Kiva Han that opened in Constantinople (Istanbul) in 1475; however, others have been noted earlier in Constantinople and Arab cities like Damascus, Mecca, and Medina. It seems that it took almost two centuries after Kiva Han for the first café to reach Europe when Il Rimedio (known as Grancaffè Quadri from 1775 to the present), a *botega da caffè*, was opened in Venice in 1638. After that, coffee, coffeehouses, and cafés spread quickly throughout Italy and Europe and were firmly established by the mid-1600s. Even in London, coffee became the favored beverage aside from beer before the East India Company imported, exported, and promoted tea. Indeed, Thomas Twining, the founder of the well-known tea dynasty, bought Tom's Coffee House on the Strand from Thomas D'Aeth in 1706 and, of course, served coffee along with tea. Storied institutions were born in London coffee houses, including the London stock exchange at Jonathan's Coffee House in 1680, and Lloyd's of London, founded by Edward Lloyd at his coffee house in 1688.

From the 17th century on, coffee houses and cafés flourished across Europe, with Vienna becoming one particularly notable haven for coffee culture after Turkey's failed Siege of Vienna. The story here is that when the Turks abandoned their efforts to capture Vienna in 1683, they left behind numerous bags of coffee beans brought to stay alert during battle. Following the first coffee houses in Vienna, the Viennese-style coffee house quickly spread and thrived throughout the many countries in the Austro-Hungarian Empire.

For various interesting yet strange reasons, coffee and cafés were banned by religious and political rulers in several countries between the 16th and the 19th centuries. The primary motivation of these rulers? Fear of the unknown (what is this coffee?) and the fear of losing control of their people. Here are but a few examples: In 1511 Mecca (and many other countries during these centuries), those in power thought that coffee stimulated radical thinking and had to be forbidden. In Europe, Christian clergymen considered it Satanic and therefore taboo. The Ottoman ruler outlawed coffee in 1623 and penalized those who disobeyed. In 1746 it was prohibited in Sweden, with convicted murderers "forced" to drink coffee while doctors monitored how long the brew would take to kill them. Despite all the attempts to eliminate coffee and cafés, coffee became known as the fuel for democracy, and cafés are sometimes credited with catalyzing the Enlightenment in Europe.

This timeline delineates some of the noteworthy cafés that may just have changed the world.

1862 New Orleans Café du Monde
1876 Vienna Café Central
1884 Prague Café Slavia
1888 Madrid Grand Café Gijón
1894 Rio de Janerio Confeitaria Colombo
1894 Budapest New York Café
1897 Barcelona Els Quarte Gats
1899 Vienna Café Muséum
1905 Lisbon Café de Brasileira
1911 Tokyo Café Paulista
1912 Prague Municipal House Café
1914 Nazareth Café Abo Salem
1921 Tangier Café Hafa
1921 Porto Café Majestic
1923 Istanbul Fazil Bey
1927 Hong Kong Olympia Graeco
1927 Rabat Le Grand Café de Paris
1927 New York Café Reggio
1928 Melbourne Café Florentino
1938 Rome Sant' Eustachio il Café
1940 Tel Aviv Café Tamar
1956 Seoul Hakrim Dabang
1956 San Francisco Café Trieste
1966 Berkeley Peet's
1970 Montreal Café Olimpico
1971 Seattle Starbucks
1976 Amsterdam The Bulldog
2001 San Francisco Blue Bottle

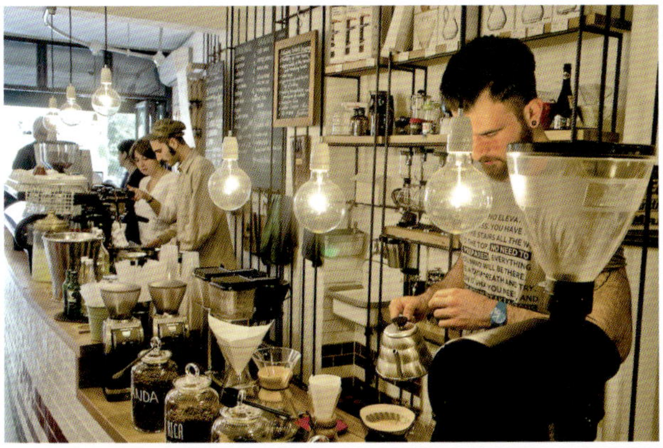

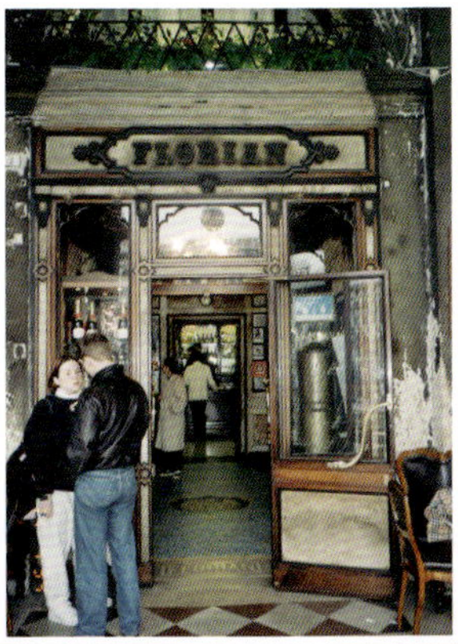

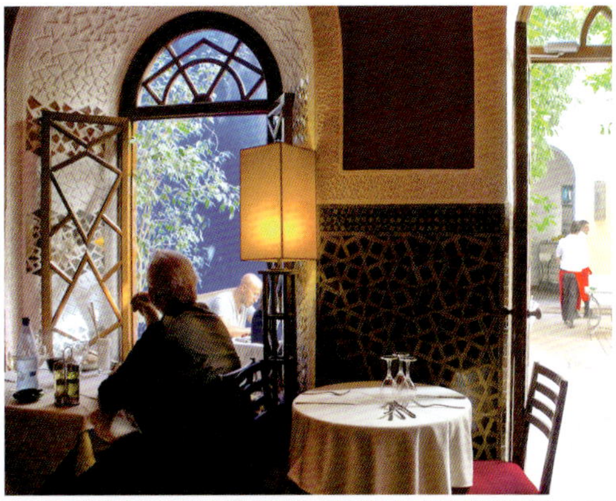

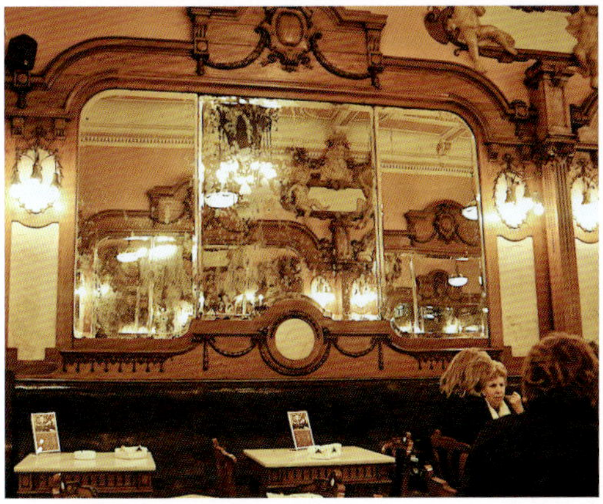

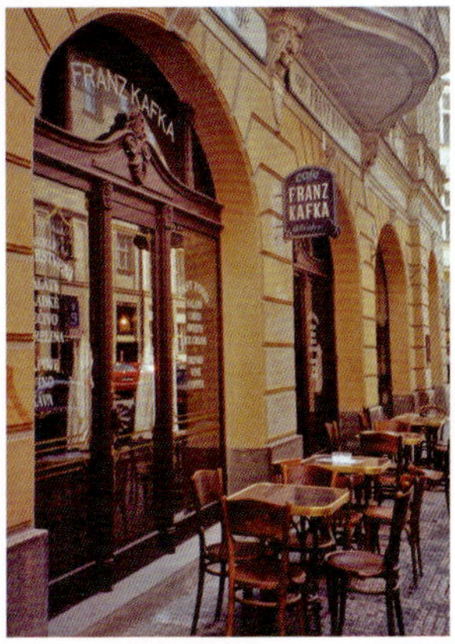

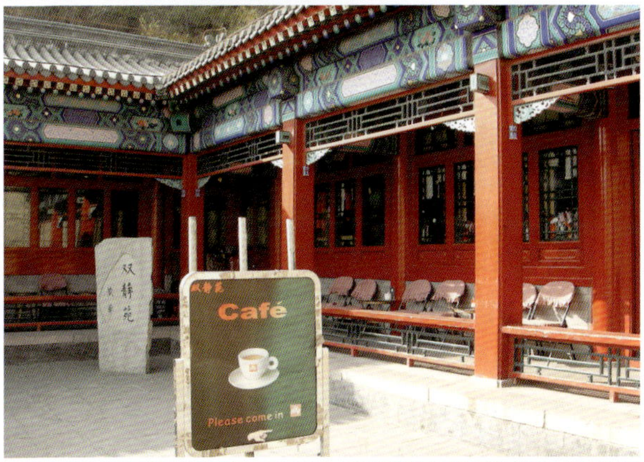

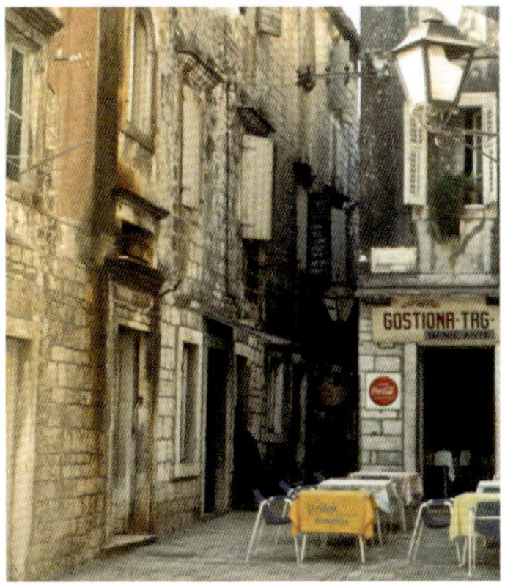

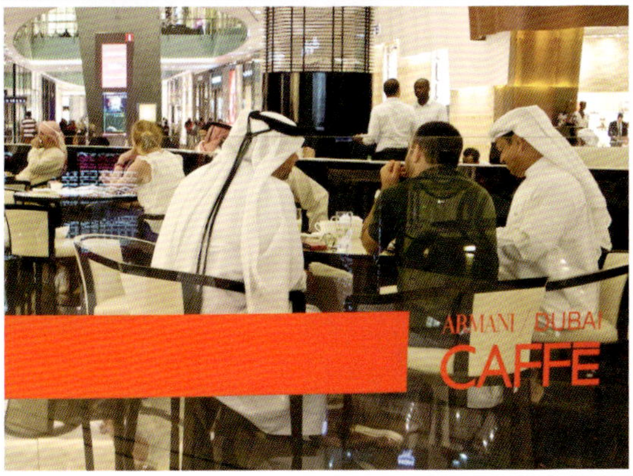

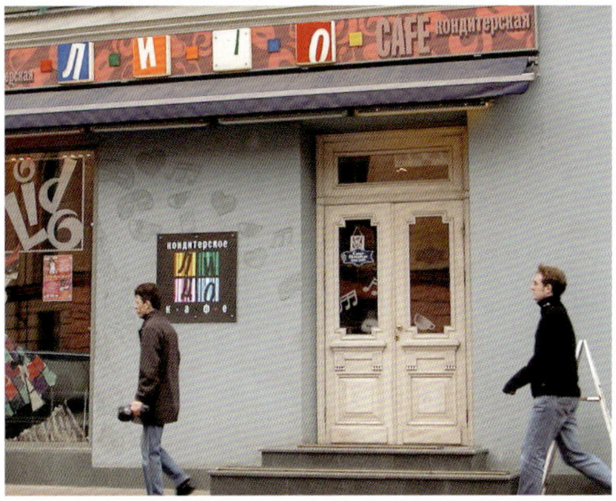

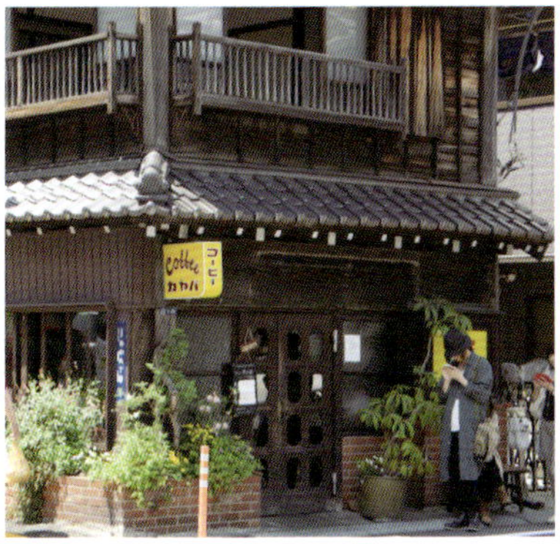

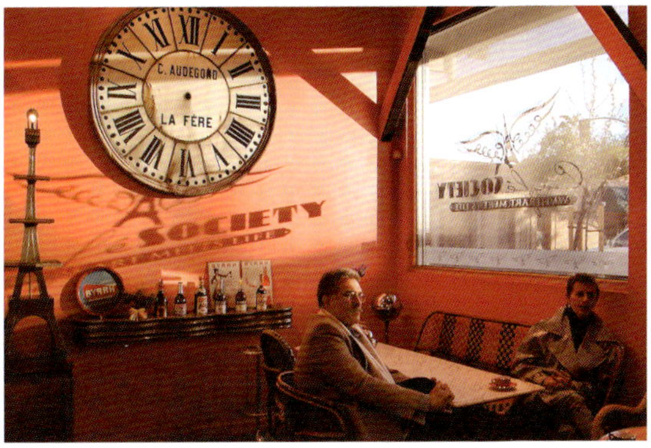

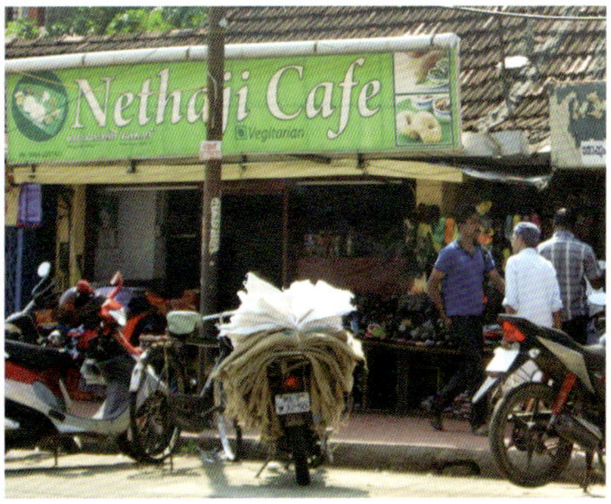

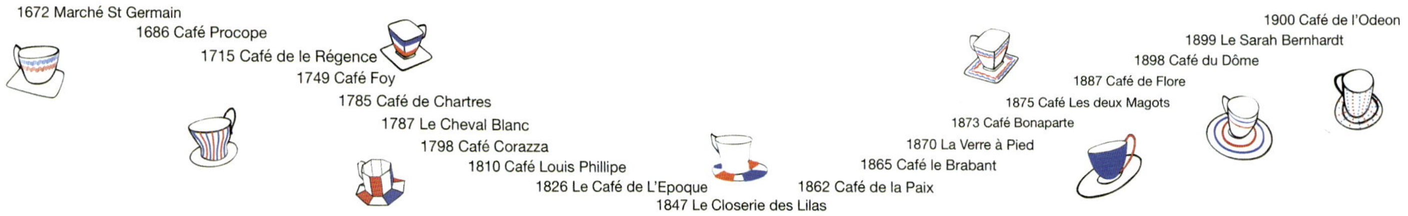

History of Paris Cafés

"Everyone had their private cafés where they never invited anyone and would go to work, or read or to receive their mail...It was nothing like the organization of the Montparnasse quarter centered about the Dôme, Rotonde, Select and later the Coupole or the Dingo bar which you read about in the books of early Paris."

Ernest Hemingway

In France, coffee and cafés began with Louis XIV and Marie Antoinette in 1669 when Soliman Aga, the Turkish Ambassador, introduced coffee to the Court. Only three years later, in 1672, coffee entrepreneur Pasqua Rosée, whose heritage is recorded as Armenian, Turkish, or Greek, sold coffee to the Parisian public from a tent at the Marché Saint-Germain and Turkish waiters peddled cups of coffee to passersby on the streets of Paris. Before arriving in Paris, an ambitious Rosée plied his wares in England and Holland (opening the first British café in Oxford in 1651).

In 1686, Sicilian Francesco Procopio opened the first authentic café in Paris, the elegant Café Procope, where he developed an illustrious clientele. Coffee, lemonade, and Italian ice cream served on porcelain with silver service in a luxurious café drew the likes of Marie Antoinette, Napoleon, and other notables--both the distinguished and the infamous. Procope became a model for other cafés throughout Europe and is a Paris institution still in operation today.

Originally the Parisian café, like cafés throughout Europe and the Ottoman Empire, was usually a coffee house without a kitchen. Over time, French proprietors added full kitchens and cafés as we know them were born. Opulent cafés spread from Procope on the Left Bank to the more fashionable (at that time) Right Bank, then back to the Left Bank in the mid-19th century, until they were popping up all across central Paris. Cafés for every political, social, and professional segment of the population multiplied and flourished. Simple worker cafés, as well as embellished showplaces, became the *Parisiens'* meeting place, the home of social networking and café society. Today cafés of all manner of design and culinary choices are in each of Paris's 20 arrondissements, though their numbers are diminishing in the late 20th and early 21st centuries.

Everyone is welcome in the democratic cafés of Paris, but it wasn't always smooth sailing. In Paris and most cafés across the globe, it was only in the late 19th century that women were welcome, if accompanied by a male escort or serving food and drink. Furthermore, those in power wanted to end any democratic rumblings by banning cafés as a threat—to religion, authoritarianism, or family values. It's interesting that every time the bans were inevitably overturned, cafés flourished more than ever.

The story of coffeehouses and cafés is brimming with flavor and mystique. So many stories unfolding, so many books, paintings, musical scores, plays, love affairs, political discussions and revolutions, innovations, and creations, happening at a table on the terrace, in the interior, or standing at the iconic zinc bar.

This timeline highlights some of the noteworthy cafés dotting the map of Paris. The narrative continues to unfold in our time.

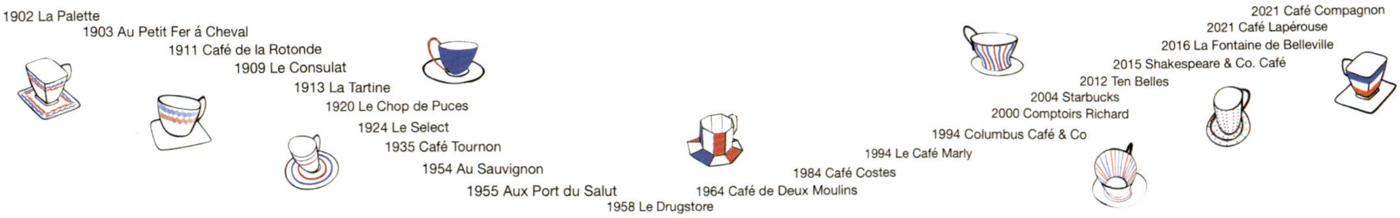
1902 La Palette
1903 Au Petit Fer á Cheval
1911 Café de la Rotonde
1909 Le Consulat
1913 La Tartine
1920 Le Chop de Puces
1924 Le Select
1935 Café Tournon
1954 Au Sauvignon
1955 Aux Port du Salut
1958 Le Drugstore
1964 Café de Deux Moulins
1984 Café Costes
1994 Le Café Marly
1994 Columbus Café & Co
2000 Comptoirs Richard
2004 Starbucks
2012 Ten Belles
2015 Shakespeare & Co. Café
2016 La Fontaine de Belleville
2021 Café Lapérouse
2021 Café Compagnon

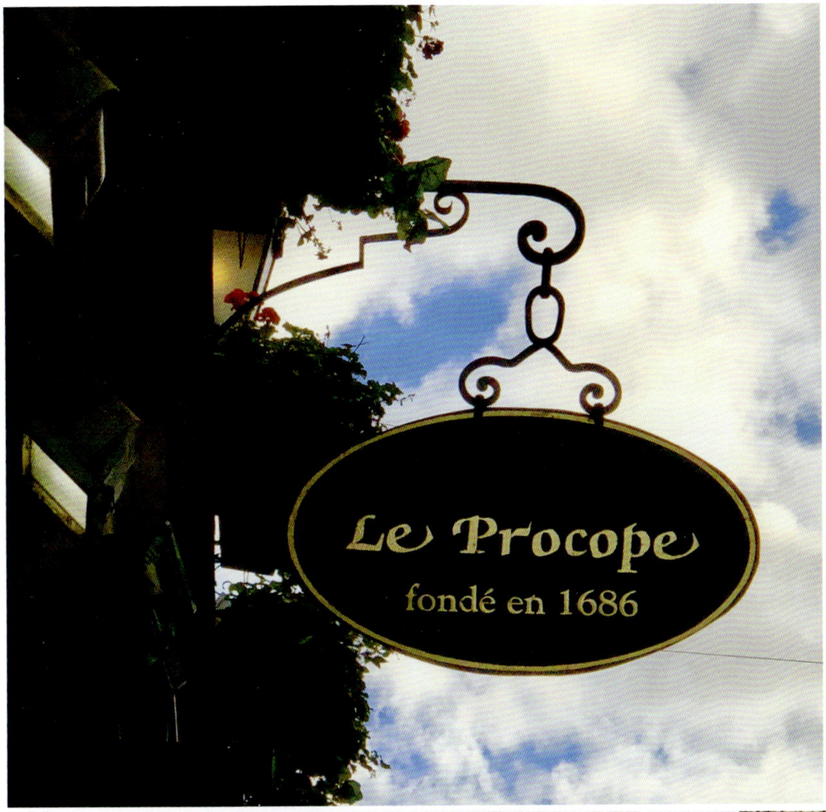
Le Procope
fondé en 1686

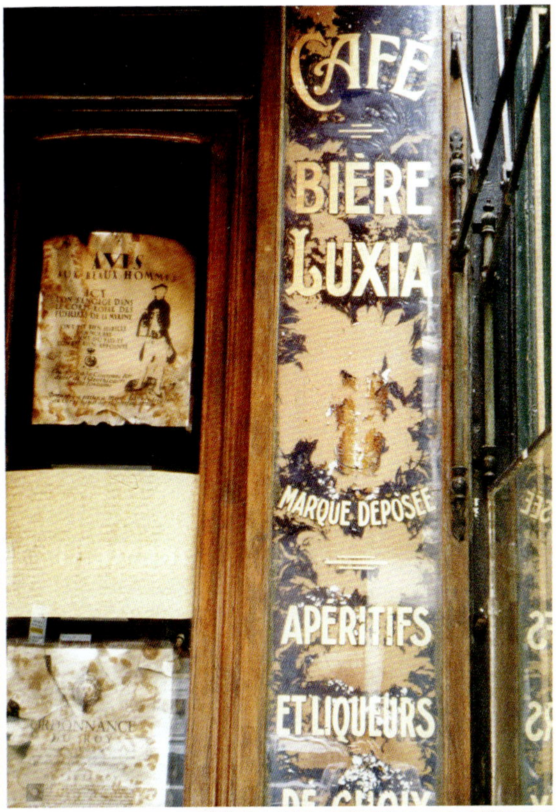
CAFÉ
BIÈRE
LUXIA
MARQUE DÉPOSÉE
APÉRITIFS
ET LIQUEURS

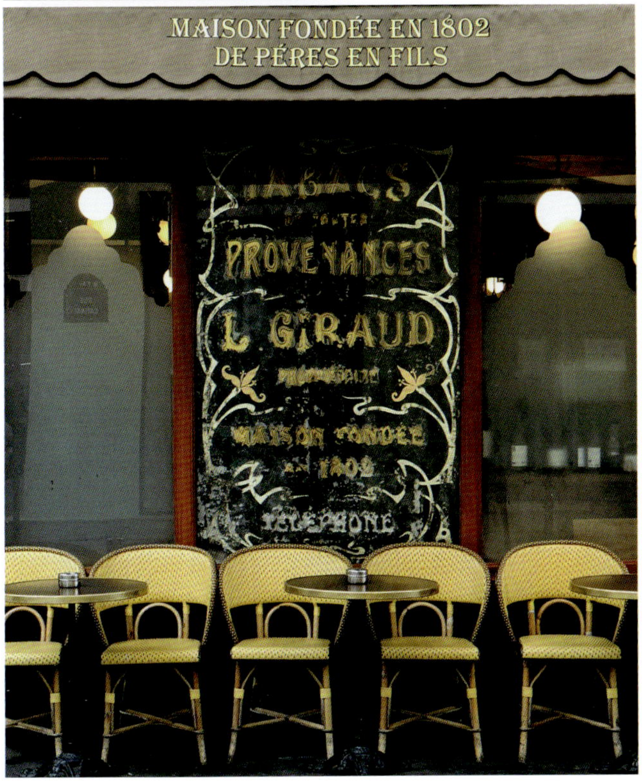
MAISON FONDÉE EN 1802
DE PÉRES EN FILS
PROVENANCES
L. GIRAUD

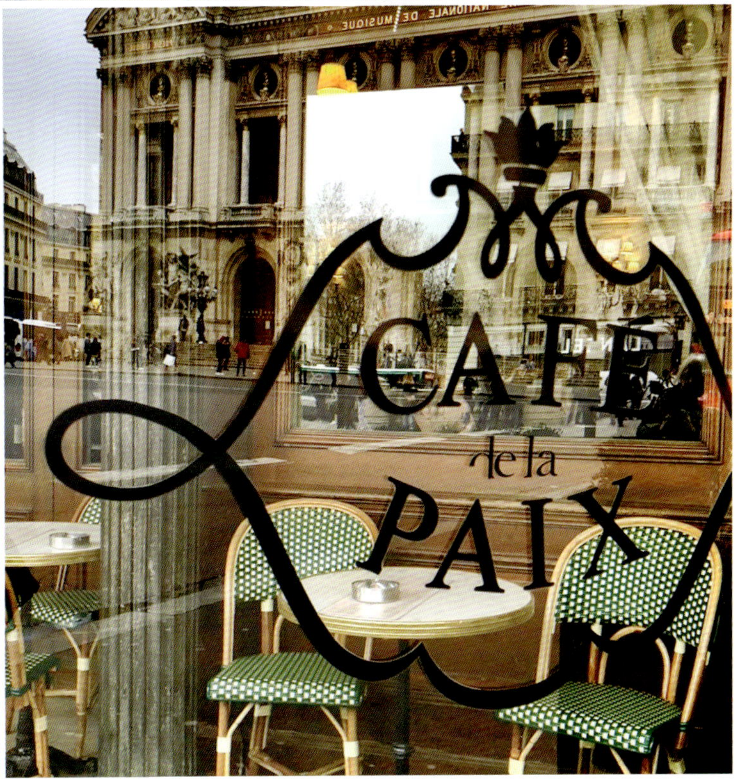
CAFÉ
de la
PAIX

1802 Bistro Victoires
1826 Bistro Vivienne
1830 Le Temps de Cerises
1832 L'Escargot Montorgueil
1845 Le Polidor
1847 La Closerie des Lilas
1848 Au Rocher de Cancale
1863 Café Charbon
1864 Bofinger
1896 Le Zimmer

1876 Le Gallopin
1878 Brasserie Vagenende
1880 Brasserie Lipp
1881 Le Wepler
1886 Brasserie Balzar
1890 Au Lyonnais
1890 Le Cochon à l'Orielle
1893 Maxim's
1895 Brasserie Mollard

1896 Le Boullion Chartier
1899 Fouquet's
1900 Chez Paul
1900 Le Grande Colbert
1900 L'Européen
1901 Le Train Bleu
1902 Bistro du Peintre
1902 Chez Julien
1903 Le Boullion Chartier Montparnasse

History of Paris Bistros and Brasseries

"Bistro cooking is good, traditional food, earnestly made and honestly displayed. It is earthy, provincial, or bourgeois; as befits that kind of food, it is served in ample portions."

David Liederman

What about the three B's: bistros, brasseries, and bouillons? These Parisian culinary traditions were launched in the span of the mid- to late 19th century. Parisian bistros and worker cafés originated around the mid-19th century when fifty percent of Parisian workers were manual laborers living in apartments without kitchens. Many were immigrants from the Auvergne or Aveyron of the Massif Central. Some of these Bougnats or Auvergnats were entrepreneurs who began selling water (before Paris had a water supply network), firewood, coal (charbon), wine, lemonade, and later simple one-dish meals from a cart. They worked hard, saved their money, and bought shops that became the bistros and cafés of mid- to late 19th-century Paris, which continued to thrive in the 20th and 21st centuries. Even now, some old (or former) cafés display worn signs: "*Vins et Charbons*." These bistros, not luxurious but relatively simple, provided places for struggling workers, artists, and writers to have inexpensive *cuisine de grand-mère*, prepared by husband-and-wife owners presiding over a zinc bar. The iconic zinc bar is so much a part of the French bistro DNA that some bistros are still referred to as "*le zinc*."

The mid-19th century also saw the emergence of bouillons. These food venues served a single dish—a bouillon or soup—to the workers of the market halls. By 1900, they served a more diverse but still simple menu, and Paris boasted nearly 250 bouillons. Although they had become sumptuous Art Nouveau showplaces, they still served affordable food. Toward the end of the 19th century, brasseries arrived in Paris when French entrepreneurs from Alsace fled after the Franco-Prussian war of 1870. Initially, just breweries (brasserie is the French word for brewery), later serving beer, then beer and Alsatian food, and finally a variety of beverages along with massive platters of seafood and Alsatian dishes. All in spacious and stunning Art Nouveau and Art Deco dining rooms.

In the early 20th century, bouillons almost vanished, there were fewer brasseries, and by the 21st century, many bistros had also disappeared from Paris. Over the decades, too many extraordinary bistros, brasseries, and bouillons, as well as cafés, have been lost to history. While we honor these historic institutions, especially those that have survived, we are pleased new ones are opening. Whether classic or with a contemporary twist, creative new eateries are dotting the streets of Paris, appearing on back streets as well as grand boulevards. Proprietors and chefs today, many young, some from around the world, are as dedicated and talented as ever before. It is not easy to predict which of these will become part of the history of Paris, but it is most important that these Parisian traditions are preserved.

These timelines include only a wee sampling of the historically significant classic and inventive establishments from the earliest days to the 21st century.

*Myth: The Russian Cossacks who occupied Paris following the Napoleonic Wars demanded that the food be served "bistro bistro!" (Fast, fast!) Since the word bistro did not appear until the end of the 19th century this amusing story is an urban legend.

1906 Boullion Racine
1907 Le Clown Bar
1907 Le Square Trousseau
1908 La Fontaine de Mars
1908 Le Chardenoux
1909 Brasserie Floderer
1912 Benoit
1913 Le Zeyer
1914 Le Cyrano
1918 Brasserie Vaudeville

1920 Au Chien Qui Fume
1921 Le Bœuf sur le Toit
1925 Terminus Nord
1926 La Coupole
1930 La Tartine
1930 Chez l'Ami Jean
1932 Allard
1935 La Poule au Pot
1947 Au Pied de Cochon
1953 La Brasserie de l'Isle Saint-Louis

1956 Astier
1958 Le Drugstore
1970 Le Rubis
2005 Le Comptoir du Relais
2000 Bistro Paul Bert
2003 Le Mesturet
2008 Le Chateaubriand
2009 Frenchie
2012 Le Richer
2015 Le Bourse et la Vie

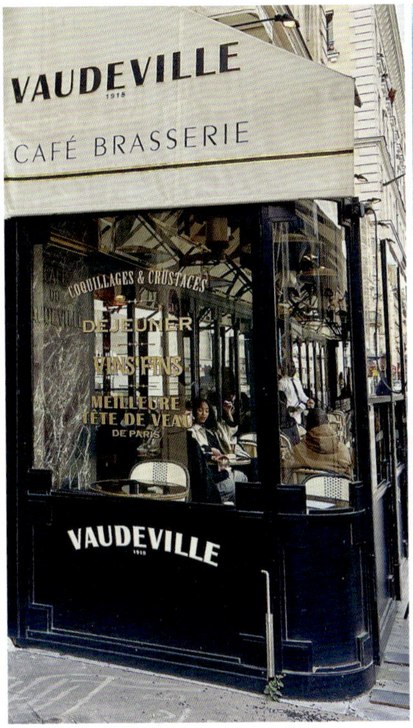

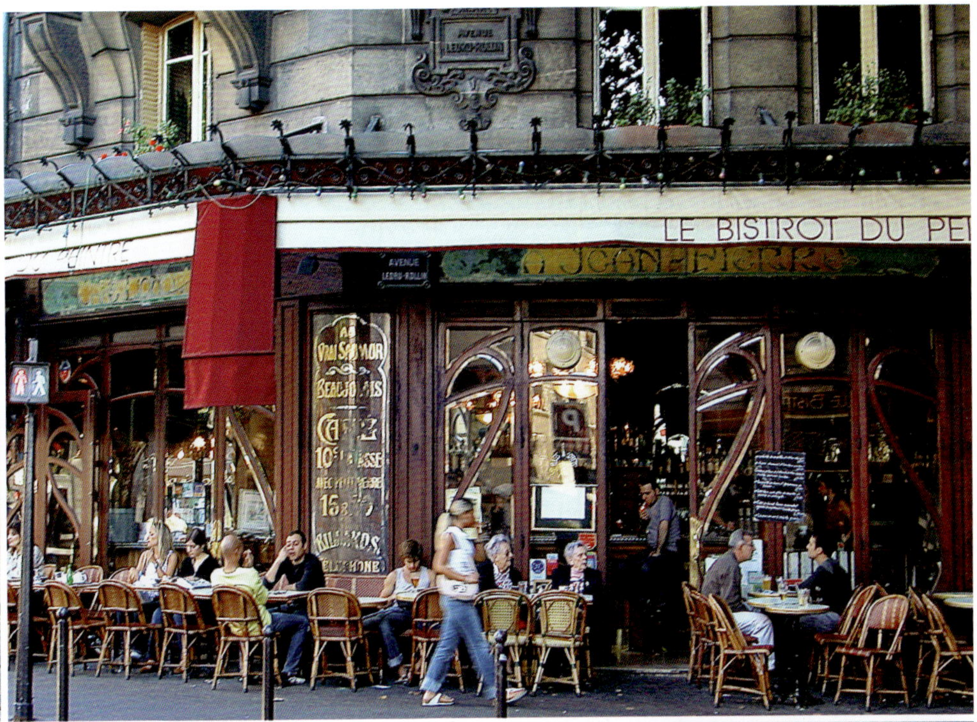

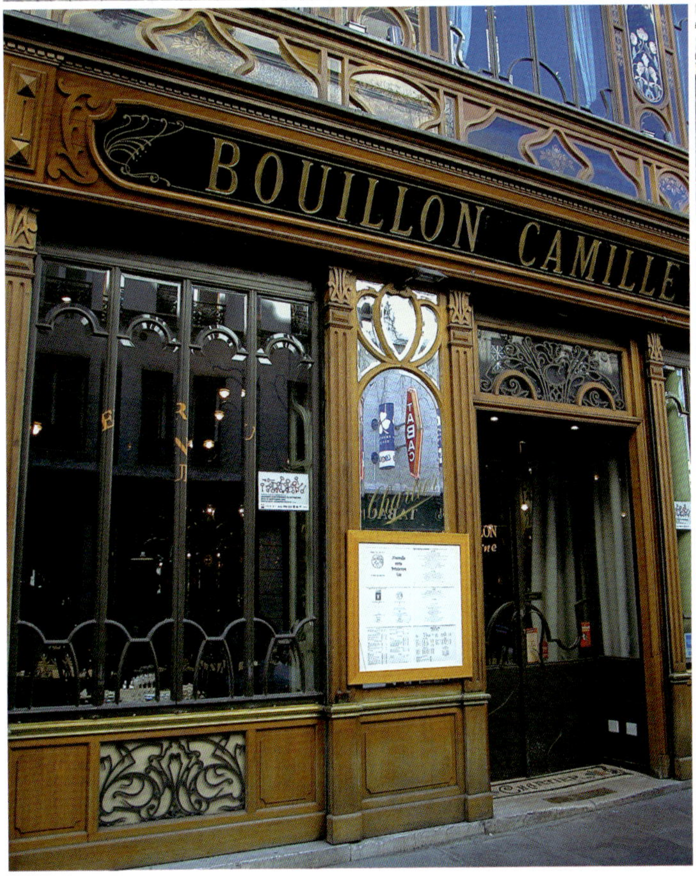

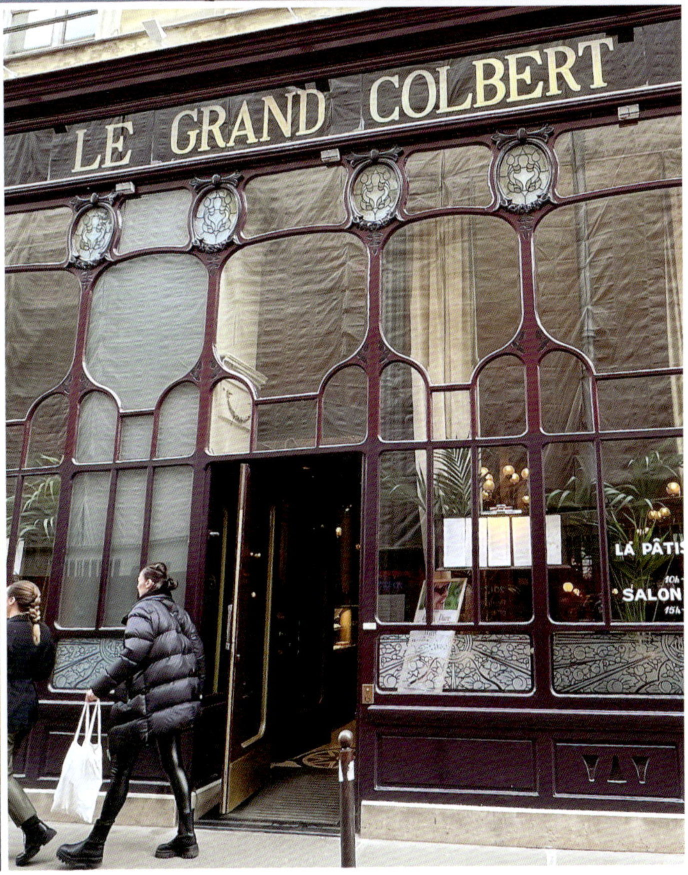

Au revoir...et à bientôt!

"J'ai deux amours, Mon pays et Paris"
Josephine Baker

Whether a first-time tourist, a regular visitor, an expat, or Parisian born, strolling the streets of Paris *en flâneur* is magical and stopping in a café is natural. Life on the streets and in the cafés, bistros, and brasseries is full of energy, of movement, of flow. Nothing is static or dull. The Parisians walk fast with purpose on the boulevards, and the servers move like lightning in the cafés. It is an elegant dance of life lived in real-time.

Parisian café society is about suspending time, being in the moment, meeting family, friends, and co-workers, or blissfully being alone, out in the world, in the café. From their beginnings as social networks where revolutions were fomented to the present day, where cell phones are in hand, along with the food and drink, the café is a convivial gathering place for conversation and contemplation. The alchemy of the Paris café is like nowhere else on earth.

The people who make café society dazzle—the designers, artisans, farmers, food purveyors, entrepreneurs, chefs, servers, and customers—are the people who help make Paris, Paris. Whether local or historic, classic or neo, Parisian cafés celebrate the past as well as the present, and their role in daily life is immeasurable.

Vive the Paris café and *l'art de vivre* Parisian!

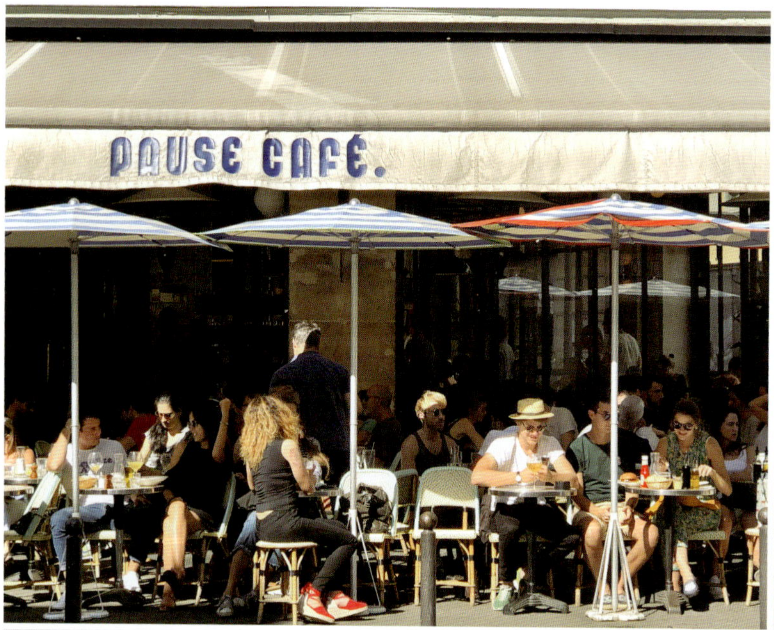

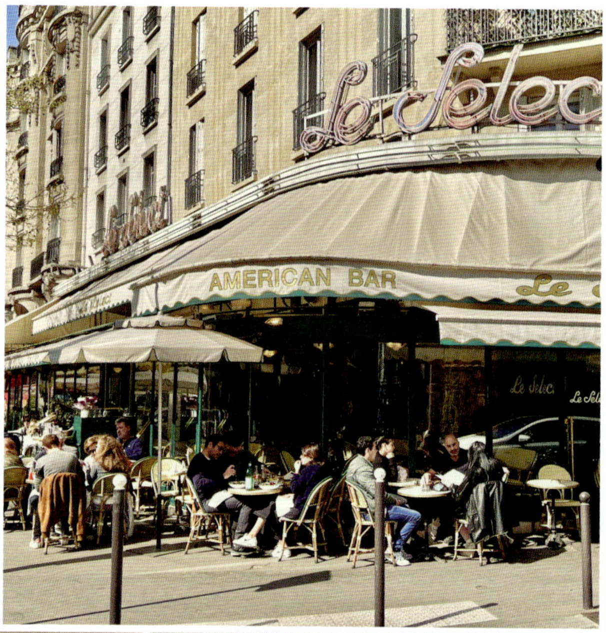

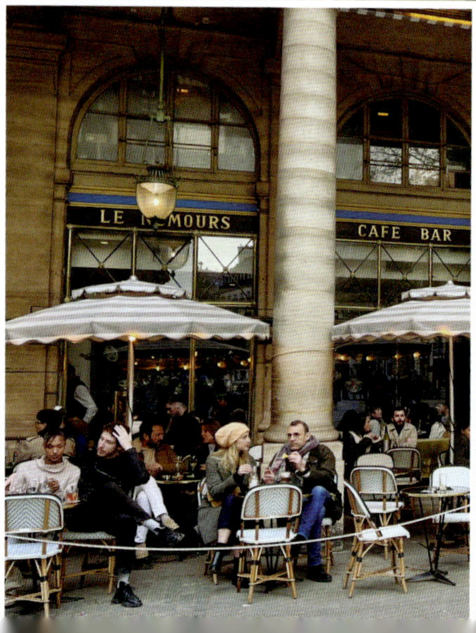

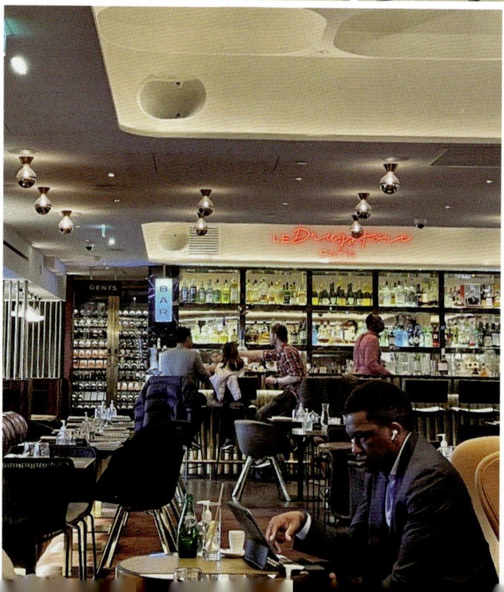

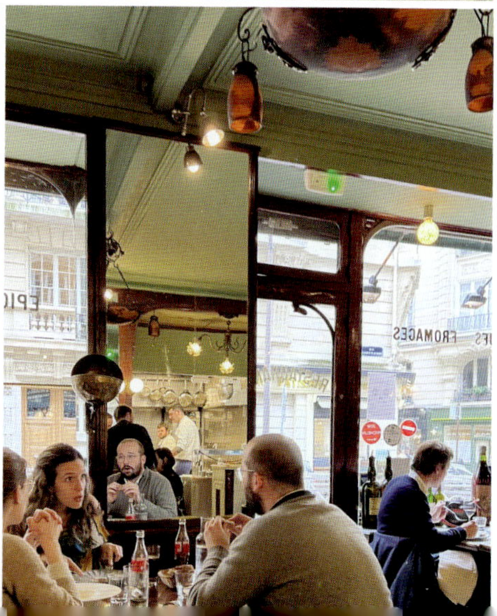

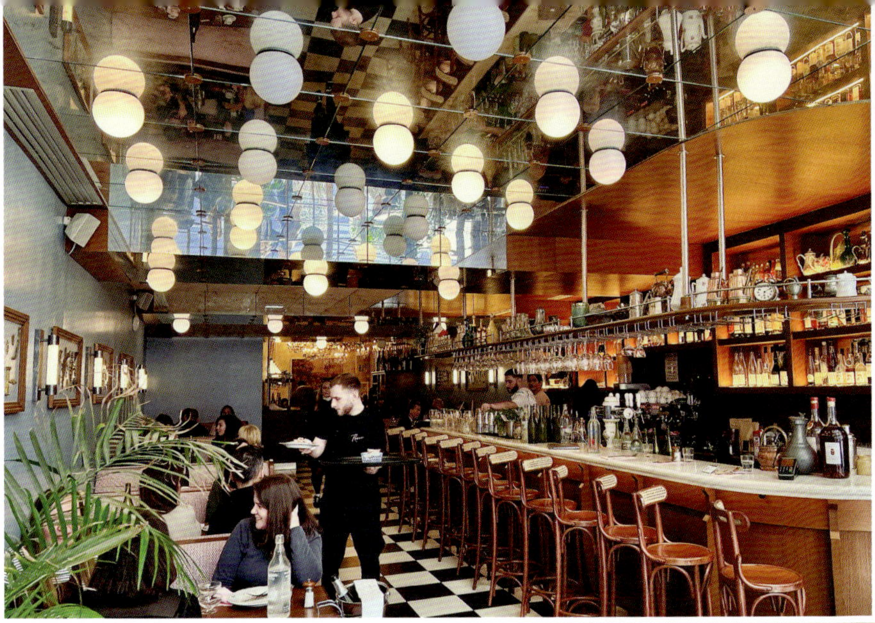

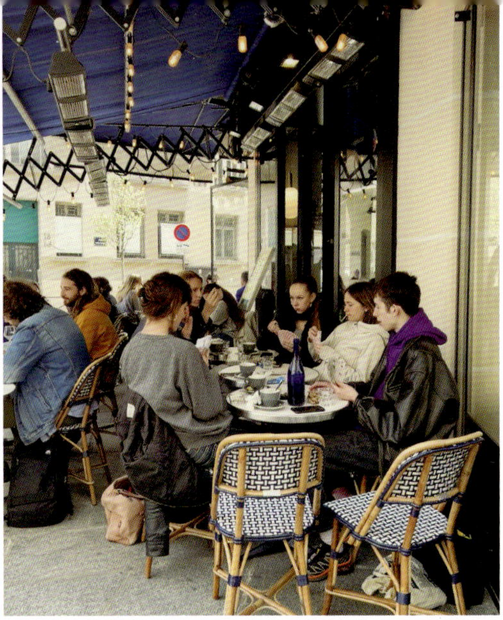

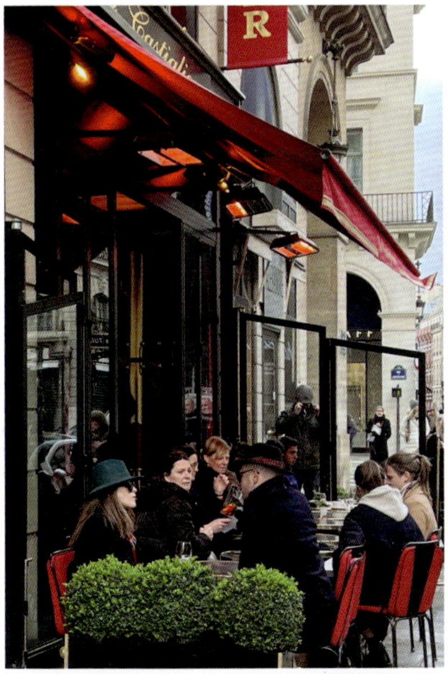

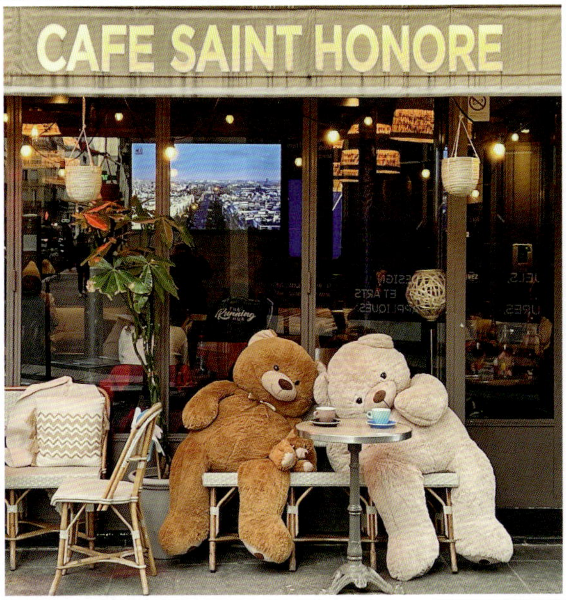
CAFE SAINT HONORE

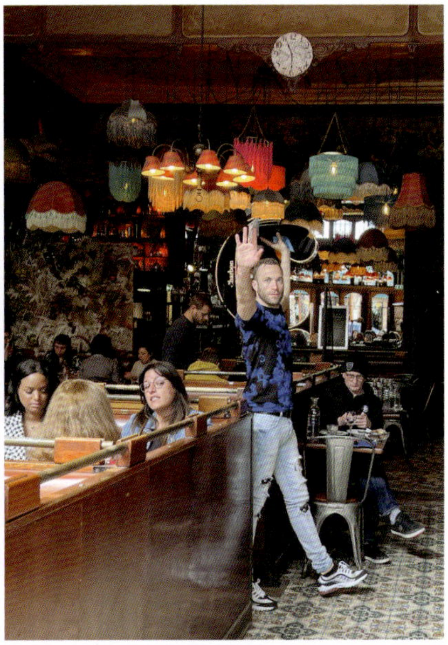

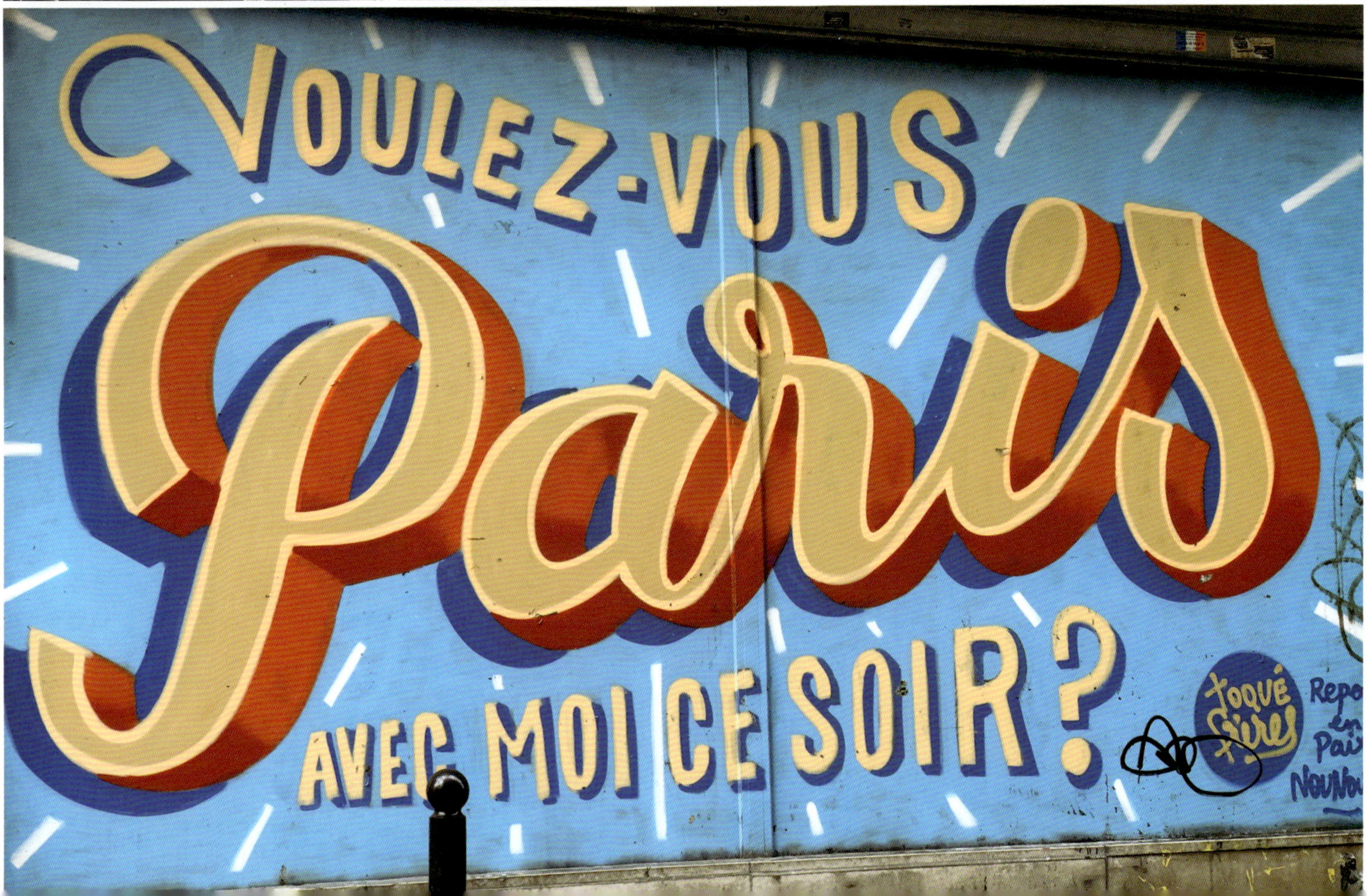
VOULEZ-VOUS
Paris
AVEC MOI CE SOIR?

ADDRESSES

1er PALAIS ROYAL, LOUVRE

Au Chien Qui Fume, 33 rue du Pont Neuf, M° Louvre-Rivoli
49

Au Pied de Cochon, 6 rue Coquillière, M° Les Halles
190, 197

Bistrot Victoires, 6 rue de la Vrillière, M° Bourse
33, 38, 102, 125, 186, 233

Café de la Comédie, 157 rue St-Honoré, M° Palais Royal
88, 91, 127

Café Saint Honoré, 194 rue St-Honoré, M° Palais Royal
237

L'Escargot Montorgueil, 38 rue Montorgueil, M° Étienne Marcel
36

Le Café de l'Époque, 2 rue du Bouloi, M° Palais Royal
83, 192

Le Café Marly, 93 rue de Rivoli, M° Palais Royal
73, 221

Le Castiglione Café, 235 rue St-Honoré, M° Concorde
236, 237

Le Cochon à l'Oreille, 15 rue Montmartre, M° Les Halles
198

Le Grand Véfour, 17 rue de Beaujolais, M° Pyramides
144, 145

Le Nemours, 2 pl. Colette, M° Palais Royal-Louvre
33, 143, 236

Le Petit Crème, 28 rue Montorgueil, M° Étienne Marcel
123

Le Rubis, 10 rue du Marché Saint-Honoré, M° Pyramides
42

Salon Proust, **Hôtel Ritz**, 15 pl. Vendôme, M° Madeleine
121

Willi's Wine Bar, 13 rue des Petits-Champs, M° Bourse
103, 222

2e MONTORGUEIL, BOURSE

Au Rocher de Cancale, 78 rue Montorgueil, M° Étienne Marcel
202

Bistrot Vivienne, 4 rue des Petits-Champs, M° Bourse
147

Brasserie Les Petits-Carreaux, 17 rue des Petits-Carreaux, M° Bourse
132, 193

Brasserie Vaudeville, 29 rue Vivienne, M° Bourse
27, 35, 74, 234

Café Compagnon, 22 rue Léopold Bellan, M° Sentier
65, 217

Café du Centre, 57 rue Montorgueil, M° Sentier
29, 33, 67, 111

Café Montorgueil, 55 rue Montorgueil, M° Sentier
193

Frenchie, 5 rue du Nil, M° Sentier
218

Le Compas, 62 rue Montorgueil, M° Sentier
17, 68

Le Grand Colbert, 2 rue Vivienne, M° Bourse
235

Le Mesturet, 77 rue de Richelieu, M° Quatre-Septembre
6, 61, 109

Le Moulin de la Vierge, 10 pl. des Petits-Pères, M° Bourse
33, 103, 120, 188

Le Tambour, 41 rue Montmartre, M° Étienne Marcel
192

Père et Fils, 86 rue Montmartre, M° Sentier
28

3e HAUT MARAIS

Ambassade d'Auvergne, 22 rue du Grenier-Saint-Lazare, M° Étienne Marcel
188

Big Love, 30 rue Debelleyme, M° Filles du Calvaire,
220

Bouillon République, 39 bd. du Temple, M° République
218

Café Charlot, 8 rue de Bretagne, M° Filles du Calvaire
43, 90, 104, 106, 219

Café des Musées, 49 rue de Turenne, M° Chemin Vert
81

Grand Café Tortoni, 45 rue Saintonge, M° Filles du Calvaire
102

4e MARAIS, HÔTEL-DE-VILLE

Au Petit Fer à Cheval, 30 rue Vieille-du-Temple, M° Saint-Paul
27, 37, 49, 88, 99, 111, 137, 139, 178, 201

Au Petit Versailles du Marais, 1 rue Tiron, M° Saint-Paul
198

Berthillon, 31 rue Saint-Louis-en-l'Île, M° Pont Marie
13, 62

Bofinger, 5-7 rue de la Bastille, M° Bastille
124, 183

Café Beaubourg, 43 rue Saint-Merri, M° Rambuteau
184, 221

Café Benjamin, 53 rue de Rivoli, M° Châtelet
190

Café Hugo, 22 pl. des Vosges, M° Chemin Vert
65, 174, 175, 222

Café Louis Philippe, 66 quai de l'Hôtel-de-Ville, M° Pont Marie
37, 192

Café Saint-Régis, 6 rue Jean-du-Bellay, M° Pont Marie
186

Chez Julien, 1 rue du Pont Louis-Philippe, M° Saint-Paul
100

Comptoir des Archives, 41 rue des Archives, M° Chemin Vert
28

Georges, 6e ét. Centre Georges Pompidou, M° Rambuteau
187

L'Éléphant du Nil, 125 rue Saint-Antoine, M° Saint-Paul
83

L'Esmeralda, 2 rue du Cloître-Notre-Dame, M° Cité
134

La Brasserie de l'Isle Saint-Louis, 55 quai de Bourbon, M° Saint-Paul
80, 186

La Chaise au Plafond, 10 rue de Trésor, M° Hôtel de Ville
179

La Résistance, 16 rue Sainte-Croix-de-la-Bretonnerie, M° Hôtel de Ville
190

La Tartine, 24 rue de Rivoli, M° Saint-Paul
38, 177

Le Pick Clops, 16 rue Vieille-du-Temple, M° Saint-Paul
176

Le Sarah Bernhardt, 2 pl. du Châtelet, M° Hôtel de Ville
55, 99, 190

Le Temps des Cerises, 31 rue de la Cerisaie, M° Sully-Morland
34, 98, 125, 193

Le Voltigeur, 45 rue des Francs-Bourgeois, M° Saint-Paul
69

Les Philosophes, 28 rue Vieille-du-Temple, M° Saint-Paul
128, 129, 179, 201

Ma Bourgogne, 19 pl. des Vosges, M° Chemin Vert
174

5e QUARTIER LATIN

Au Port du Salut, 163 bis rue Saint-Jacques, M° Luxembourg
150

Aux Doux Raisin, 29 rue Descartes, M° Cardinal Lemoine
149

Brasserie Balzar, 49 rue des Écoles, M° Cluny-La Sorbonne
82, 151

Café de la Nouvelle Mairie, 19 rue des Fossés-Saint-Jacques, M° Luxembourg
77, 133

Café Delmas, 2 pl de la Contrescarpe, M° Cardinal Lemoine
148

Café Panis, 21 quai de Montebello, M° Saint-Michel,
122

La Contrescarpe, 57 rue Lacépède, M° Place Monge
29, 75, 148

Le Mouffetard, 116 rue Mouffetard, M° Censier-Daubenton
149

Le Sorbon, 60 rue des Écoles, M° Cluny-La Sorbonne
151

Le Verre à Pied, 118 rue Mouffetard, M° Censier-Daubenton
148

Shakespeare and Co Café, 35 rue de la Bûcherie, M° Saint-Michel
225

6e ODÉON, SAINT-GERMAIN-DES-PRÉS

Allard, 41 rue Saint-André-des-Arts, M° Saint-Michel
107

Au Chai de l'Abbaye, 26 rue de Buci, M° Saint-Germain-des-Prés
84, 136

Au Chien Qui Fume, 19 bd du Montparnasse, M° Duroc
18, 42, 43, 45

Au Père Louis, 38 rue Monsieur-le-Prince, M° Odéon
18, 83, 102

Au Vieux Colombier, 65 rue de Rennes, M° Rennes
76

Balto Bar, 15 rue Mazarine, M° Mabillon
47, 133, 202

Bar du Marché, 75 rue de Seine, M° Saint-Germain-des-Prés
94, 131, 132, 136

Bouillon Chartier Montparnasse, 59 bd. du Montparnasse, M° Notre-Dame-des-Champs
39

Bouillon Racine, 3 rue Racine, M° Odéon
150

Brasserie Lipp, 151 bd. Saint-Germain, M° Saint-Germain-des-Prés
65, 112, 164

Café de Flore, 172 bd. Saint-Germain, M° Saint-Germain-des-Prés
30, 34, 40, 75, 82, 88, 92, 93, 116, 117, 119, 130, 166, 167

Café de la Mairie, 8 pl. Saint-Sulpice, M° Saint-Sulpice
16, 33, 132, 171

Café Madame, 25 rue de Vaugirard, M° Rennes
29

Café de Paris, 10 rue de Buci, M° Mabillon
192

Café du Metro, 67 rue de Rennes, M° Saint-Sulpice
133

Café Procope, 13 rue de l'Ancienne-Comédie, M° Mabillon
140, 141, 206, 233

Freddy's, 54 rue de Seine, M° Mabillon
222

Huguette, **Bistro de la Mer**, 81 rue de Seine, M° Mabillon
99, 220

L'Atlas, 11 rue de Buci, M° Mabillon
131, 172, 198

L'Avant Comptoir, 3 carrefour de l'Odéon, M° Odéon
224

La Boissonnerie, 69 rue de Seine, M° Saint-Germain-des-Prés
222

La Closerie des Lilas, 171 bd. du Montparnasse, M° Vavin
162, 163, 201

La Palette, 43 rue de Seine, M° Mabillon
21, 24, 40, 80, 91, 92, 137, 173

La Rotonde, 105 bd. du Montparnasse, M° Vavin
32, 156

La Société, 4 pl. Saint-Germain-des-Prés, M° Saint-Germain-des-Prés
170, 215

Le Bonaparte, 42 rue Bonaparte, M° Saint-Germain-des-Prés
31, 80, 165, 197

Le Comptoir des Saints-Pères, 29 rue des Saints-Pères, M° Mabillon
29, 45

Le Comptoir du Relais, 9 carrefour de l'Odéon, M° Odéon
27, 118, 216, 224

Le Germain, 25 rue de Buci, M° Saint-Germain-des-Prés
118

Le Hibou, 16 carrefour de l'Odéon, M° Odéon
71

Le Mabillon, 164 bd Saint-Germain, M° Mabillon
120, 126

Le Nemrod, 51 rue du Cherche-Midi, M° Sèvres-Babylone
43, 54, 70, 87, 136

Le Pré, 4-6 rue du Four, M° Mabillon
46

Le Pré aux Clercs, 30 rue Bonaparte, M° Saint-Germain-des-Prés
23, 131, 170

Le Relais Odéon, 132 bd. Saint-Germain, M° Odéon
23, 124, 203

Le Rostand, 6 pl. Edmond Rostand, M° Odéon
29

Le Select, 99 bd. du Montparnasse, M° Vavin
77, 85, 99, 113, 120, 121, 138, 158, 159, 236

Le Tournon, 18 rue de Tournon, M° Odéon
20, 171

Les Deux Magots, 6 pl. Saint-Germain-des-Prés, M° Saint-Germain-des-Prés
4, 32, 62, 77, 83, 89, 90, 92, 95, 116, 117, 126, 168, 169, 197, 226

Les Éditeurs, 4 carrefour de l'Odéon, M° Odéon
70, 137, 170, 224

Maison Sauvage, 5 rue de Buci, M° Mabillon
60, 77, 101, 172,

Polidor, 41 rue Monsieur-le-Prince, M° Odéon
150

7e TOUR EIFFEL, INVALIDES

Au Sauvignon, 80 rue des Saints-Pères, M° Sèvres-Babylone
54, 64, 118, 133, 170

Café Campana @Musée D'Orsay, 1 rue de la Légion d'Honneur, M° Solférino
187

Café du Marché, 38 rue Cler, M° École Militaire
23

Café Varenne, 36 rue de Varenne, M° Rue du Bac
43, 64, 79, 89, 92, 93, 99, 108, 207

La Fontaine de Mars, 129 rue Saint-Dominique, M° École Militaire
108

Le Vin Bellechasse, 20 rue de Bellechasse, M° Solférino
105, 107, 119

8e ARC DE TRIOMPHE, CHAMPS-ÉLYSÉES

Brasserie Mollard, 115 rue Saint-Lazare, M° Saint-Lazare
26, 41, 83

Café Lapérouse Concorde, 2 pl. de la Concorde, M° Concorde
96, 214, 218

Fouquet's, 99 av. des Champs-Élysées, M° George V
77

Le Drugstore, 133 av. des Champs-Élysées, M° George V
236

9e MONTORGUEIL, BOURSE

Bouillon Camille Chartier, 7 rue du Faubourg-Montmartre, M° Grands Boulevards
235

Café de La Paix, 5 pl. de l'Opéra, M° Opéra
87, 146, 233

Le Brebant, 32 bd. Poissonnière, M° Grands Boulevards
147

L'Office, 3 rue Richer, M° Poissonnière
217

Le Bon Georges, 45 rue Saint-Georges, M° Saint-Georges
107

Le Richer, 2 rue Richer, M° Poissonnière
217

10e CANAL ST MARTIN

Brasserie Bellanger, 140 rue du Faubourg-Poissonnière, M° Gare du Nord
185

Brasserie Floderer, 7 cour des Petites Écuries, M° Château d'Eau
37, 54

Chez Prune, 36 rue Beaurepaire, M° Jacques Bonsergent
189

Hôtel du Nord, 102 quai de Jemmapes, M° Goncourt
48, 101

P'tite Bougnate, 85 bd. de Magenta, M° Gare de L'Est
130

Ten Belles, 10 rue de la-Grange-aux-Belles, M° Goncourt
210

Terminus Nord, 23 rue de Dunkerque, M° Gare du Nord
39

11e LA BASTILLE, OBERKAMPF

À La Renaissance, 87 rue de la Roquette, M° Voltaire
47, 182

Aux Deux Amis, 45 rue Oberkampf, M° Parmentier
29

Bistrot Les Sans Culottes, 27 rue de Lappe, M° Bréguet-Sabin
41, 44-45, 83, 182

Bistrot Paul Bert, 18 rue Paul Bert, M° Charonne
37, 71, 101, 182

Brasserie Rosie, 53 rue du Faubourg-Saint-Antoine, M° Ledru-Rollin
237

Café Charbon, 109 rue Oberkampf, M° Parmentier,
38, 237

Café du Temple, 14 rue du Faubourg-du-Temple, M° République
176

Café Rey/Café Milou, 1 rue du Faubourg-Saint-Antoine, M° Bastille
124

Chez Gaston, 112 bd. Richard-Lenoir, M° Oberkampf
132

Chez Paul, 13 rue de Charonne, M° Ledru-Rollin
81, 97, 182

Clown Bar, 114 rue Amelot, M° Filles du Calvaire
223

La Fée Verte, 108 rue de la Roquette, M° Voltaire
55, 123

Le Bastille, 8 pl. de la Bastille, M° Bastille
180

Le Bistrot du Peintre, 116 av. Ledru-Rollin, M° Ledru-Rollin
25, 26, 34, 88, 93, 100, 101, 126, 180, 181, 200, 235

Le Café des Chats, 9 rue Sedaine, M° Bréguet-Sabin
113

Le Chardenoux, 1 rue Jules Vallès, M° Charonne
101, 223

Le Pure Café, 14 rue Jean-Macé, M° Charonne
182

Pause Café, 41 rue de Charonne, M° Charonne
236

Septime, 80 rue de Charonne, M° Charonne
220

12e BERCY, VINCENNES

Brasserie Café Jardin L'Arrosoir, 75 av. Daumesnil, M° Gare de Lyon
188

Chez Charlette, 11 rue d'Aligre, M° Ledru-Rollin
130

Le Charlois, 15 rue de Cotte, M° Gare de Lyon,
21

Le Square Trousseau, 1 rue Antoine Vollon, M° Ledru-Rollin
35, 191

14e MONTPARNASSE

Café Daguerre, 4 av. du Général-Leclerc, M° Denfert-Rochereau
200

Café de la Place, 23 rue d'Odessa, M° Edgar Quinet
108, 227

La Coupole, 102 bd. du Montparnasse, M° Vavin
27, 56, 65, 90, 121, 122, 135, 160, 161, 199

Le Bullier, 22 av. de l'Observatoire, M° Port-Royal
18, 119, 134

Le Dôme, 108 bd. du Montparnasse, M° Vavin
28, 89, 116, 134, 157

Le Lithographe, 234 bd. Raspail, M° Raspail
85

Le Plomb du Cantal, 3 rue de la Gaité, M° Edgar Quinet
69

My Baar, 152 bd. du Montparnasse, M° Raspail
73

15e VAUGIRARD, GRENELLE

À la Tour Eiffel, 96, rue du Commerce, M° Commerce
54, 122

Au Roi de Café, 59 rue Lecourbe, M° Sèvres-Lecourbe
44, 185

Le Café du Commerce, 51 rue du Commerce, M° Commerce
99

16e PASSY, AUTEUIL

Café à La Fontaine, 12 rue de Bougainvilliers, M° Ranelagh
185

Café de l'Homme, 17 pl. du Trocadéro et du 11 Novembre, M° Trocadéro
219

Kennedy Eiffel Café, 16 av. du Président-Kennedy, M° Passy
185

17e BATIGNOLLES, MONCEAU

Breizh Café, 31 rue des Batignolles, M°Rome
123

Dose, 82 pl. du Docteur-Félix-Lobligeois, M° Pont Cardinet
210

Fuxia, 69 pl. du Docteur-Félix-Lobligeois, M° Pont Cardinet
192

Le Bistrot d'à côté Flaubert, 10 rue Gustave-Flaubert, M° Courcelles
223, 236

Le Cabanon, 75 pl. du Docteur-Félix-Lobligeois, M° Pont Cardinet
121

Le Dôme Villiers-Paris, 4 av. de Villiers, M° Villiers
93, 185

Millésimes, 110 rue de Courcelles, M° Courcelles
91

18e MONTMARTRE

Au Clarion des Chasseurs, 3 pl. du Tertre, M° Lamarck-Caulaincourt
154

Au Petit Montmartre, 16 pl. des Abbesses, M° Abbesses
153

Café Bruant, 59 rue des Abbesses, M° Abbesses
152

Café des Deux Moulins, 15 rue Lepic, M° Blanche
155

Café Francoeur, 129 rue Caulaincourt, M° Jules Joffrin
155

Chez Ginette, 101 rue Caulaincourt, M° Lamarck-Caulaincourt
200

Le Chinon, 49 rue des Abbesses, M° Abbesses
153

Le Consulat, 18 rue Norvins, M° Abbesses
153

Le Nazir, 56 rue des Abbesses, M° Abbesses
154

Le Progrès, 7 rue des Trois Frères, M° Abbesses
153

Le Relais de la Butte, 12 rue Ravignan, M° Abbesses
68, 154

Le Saint Jean, 23 rue des Abbesses, M° Abbesses
72, 111, 155, 205

Le Sancerre, 35 rue des Abbesses, M° Abbesses
64, 86, 89, 92, 155, 204

Le Village, 36 rue des Abbesses, M° Abbesses
137

Le Vrais Paris, 33 rue des Abbesses, M° Abbesses
154, 205

Lux Bar, 12 rue Lepic, M° Blanche
23, 69

MARCHE AUX PUCES, SAINT-OUEN BUTTE-CHAUMONT, LA VILLETTE

Chez Louisette, 130 av. Michelet, M° Porte de Clignancourt
190

La Chope des Puces, 122 rue des Rosiers, M° Porte de Clignancourt
110

Le Paul Bert, 20 rue Paul Bert, M° Porte de Clignancourt
190

ACKNOWLEDGMENTS

In gratitude, I want to express my appreciation for everyone who has helped me one way or another in the making of this book, beginning with the hard-working and talented bistrotiers, cafetiers, servers, and barmen and women, who, after initially viewing me as "another American tourist," graciously allowed me to freely photograph the daily life in their cafés, bistros, and brasseries.

Here's to the chefs. Thank you to Maître Restaurateur Alain Fontaine, whose generous Foreword and continued support are greatly appreciated. Not only does Alain work tirelessly at his fabulous bistro, Le Mesturet, but he also spearheads a vigorous campaign to honor the cafés and bistros of Paris as a UNESCO heritage.

To Maître Restaurateur Didier Desert, for informing my knowledge of the history of the Auvergenats who brought bistros and *le zinc* to Paris. His Ambassade d'Auvergne is a fresh 21st-century ode to these formidable ancestors.

I cannot thank enough Louise Brody, my brilliant book designer, whose professionalism, talent, and expertise, along with her invaluable first-hand knowledge of the French language and Parisian life, have shaped this handsome book.

A nod to American expat Terrance Gelenter, who, in the tradition of social networking at Paris cafés, offers an open invitation to his café gatherings every Sunday.

Thanks to Noa Bar for taking time from her multiple endeavors to provide edits and cheer.

Many thanks to everyone at Goff, especially Jake Anderson, who has provided invaluable encouragement and guidance.

I am grateful to Anne Hidalgo, the mayor of Paris, whose appreciation and support for this book is a great honor.

A special thanks to my friends and family, whose enthusiasm has kept me going through the writing, photographing, editing, organizing, and forming of this book. Especially Blake, Indu, and Nikolai for their suggestions and encouragement and for being the wonderful, lovable people they are. Above all, an eternal thank you to my architect husband and traveling companion, Steven, who, in addition to superbly cooking our meals and supporting me in this and every endeavor, put together the addresses and created the timeline graphics for the book. My hero, indeed.

And last but not least, thank you to the city of Paris itself with its cafés, bistros, and brasseries that invite us to celebrate every moment dwelling in these divine only-in-Paris haunts.

Goff Books
Published by Goff Books. An Imprint of ORO Editions
Gordon Goff: Publisher

www.goffbooks.com
info@goffbooks.com

Author: Joanie Osburn
Photography: Joanie Osburn
Foreword: Alain Fontaine
Design: Louise Brody
Editor: Noa Bar
Managing Editor: Jake Anderson

10 9 8 7 6 5 4 3 2 1 First Edition

ISBN: 978-1-954081-77-2

Color Separations and Printing: ORO Group Ltd.
Printed in China.

Goff Books makes a continuous effort to minimize the overall carbon footprint of its publications. As part of this goal, Goff Books, in association with Global ReLeaf, arranges to plant trees to replace those used in the manufacturing of the paper produced for its books. Global ReLeaf is an international campaign run by American Forests, one of the world's oldest nonprofit conservation organizations. Global ReLeaf is American Forests' education and action program that helps individuals, organizations, agencies, and corporations improve the local and global environment by planting and caring for trees.

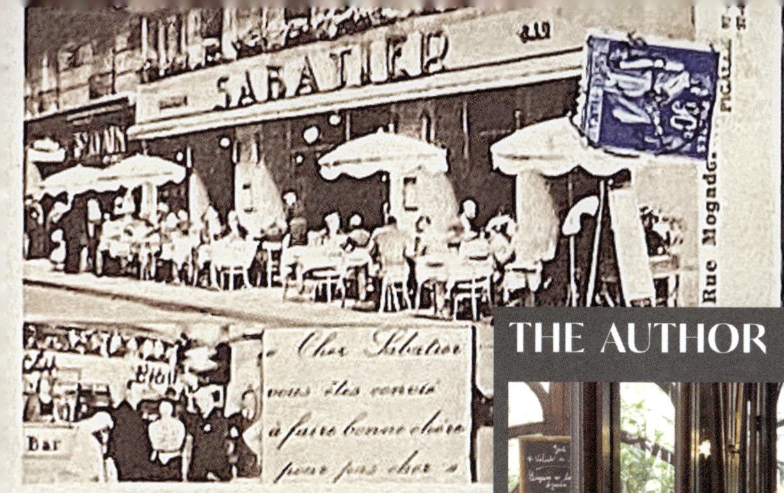

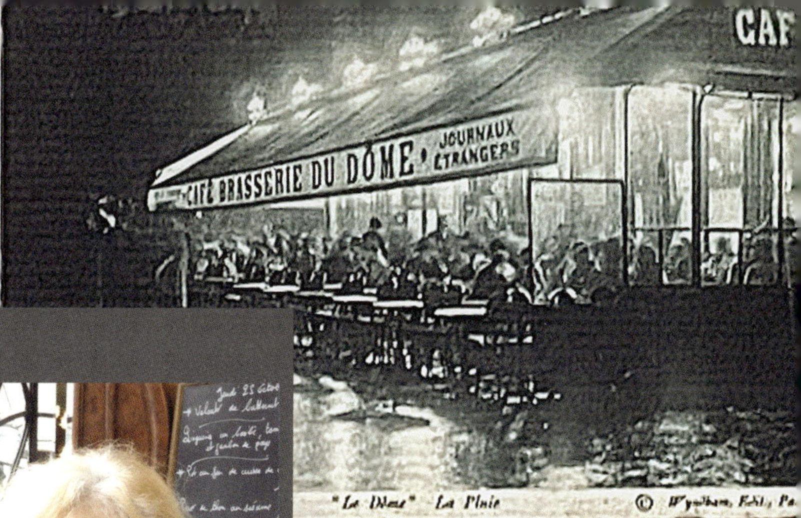

THE AUTHOR

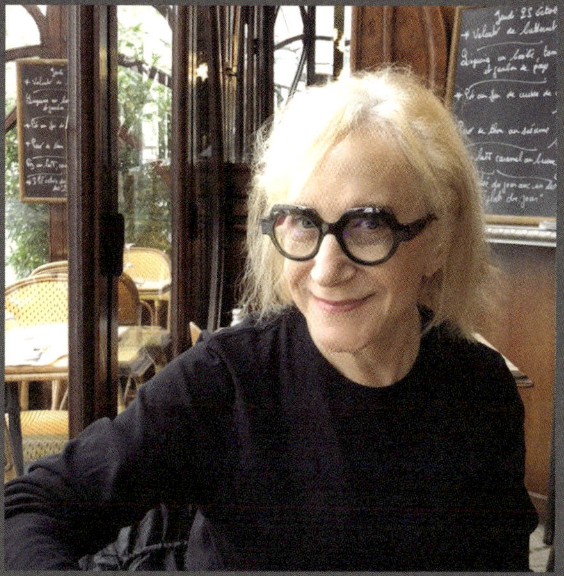

Joanie Osburn is an award-winning interior designer, artist, and photographer based in San Francisco, CA. After receiving a bachelor of arts degree from the University of California at Berkeley, she studied painting and photography in Paris and Cal Arts in Los Angeles, and interior design and architecture at the Rudolph Schaeffer School of Design in San Francisco—receiving a degree in Interior Design and Color. In partnership with her husband, Steven Osburn, she has had an award-winning design and architecture studio and showroom at the San Francisco Design Center, a Parisian café in their Parisian shop in Napa, CA, and a webstore purveying French café furniture, furnishings, and antiques.

Joanie's art has been exhibited in galleries and museums across the U.S., and her interior design projects and writing have been featured in magazines, newspapers, and books, including *The Wall Street Journal*, *The Washington Post*, *Architectural Digest*, *The San Francisco Chronicle*, *The Los Angeles Times*, *House Beautiful*, *Sunset Magazine*, *Graphis Product Design 2*, *Habitat*, and *La Mia Casa*. Television appearances include The Discovery Channel, PBS, and HGTV.

Osburn's first-hand experience living and working in Paris and meeting with French artisans, vendors and factory owners give insight into the people and products behind the look and feel and the life of the Parisian café. Having lived and studied in Paris and traveling there each year, her passion for the French café and *l'art de vivre* while exploring the latest trends is ongoing.

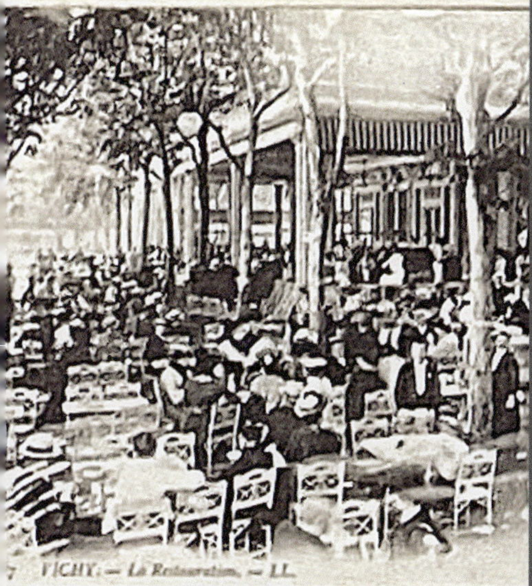

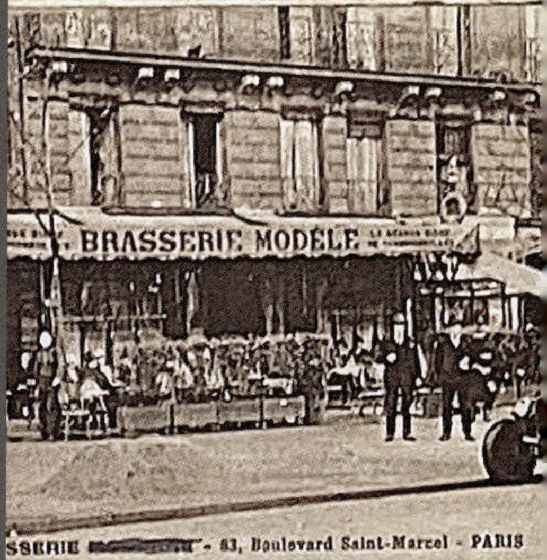

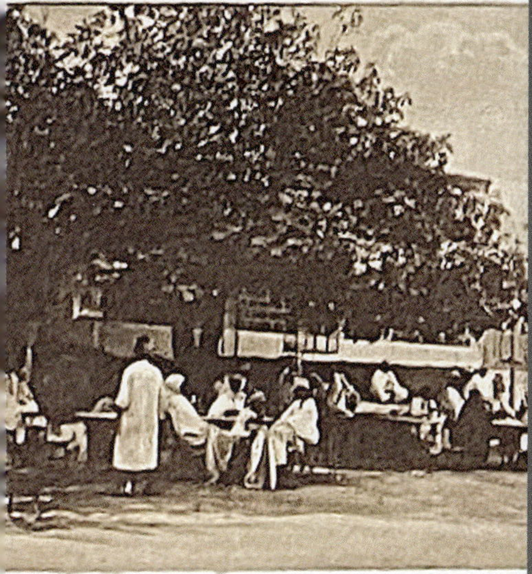

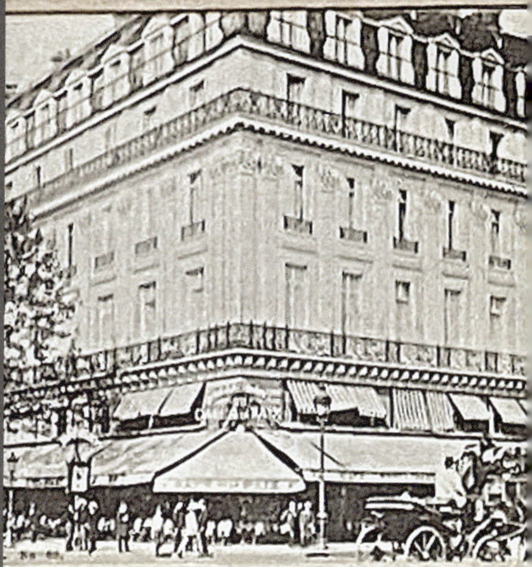

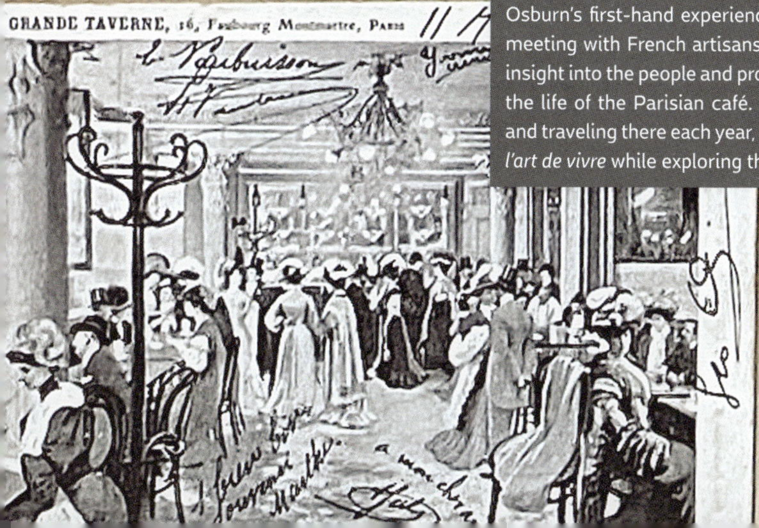

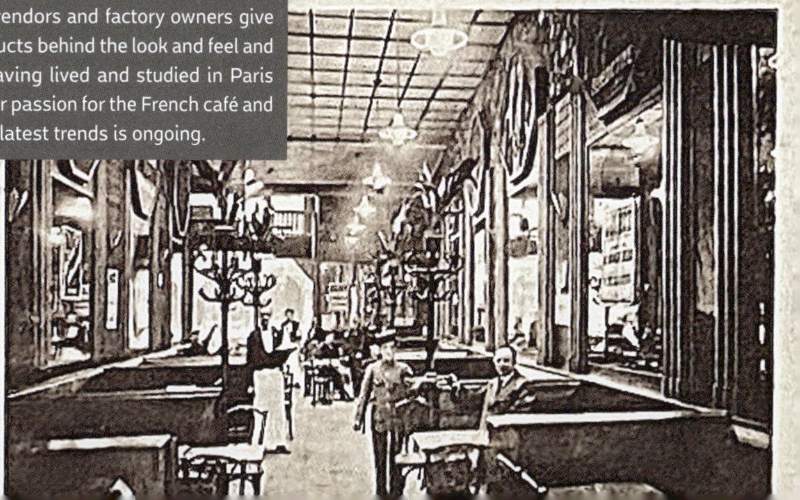

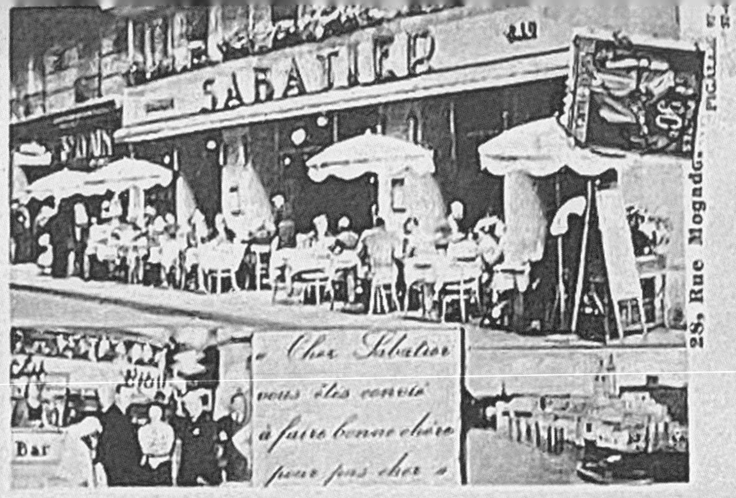
SABATIER
28, Rue Mogador
Chez Sabatier
vous êtes convié
à faire bonne chère
pour pas cher
Bar

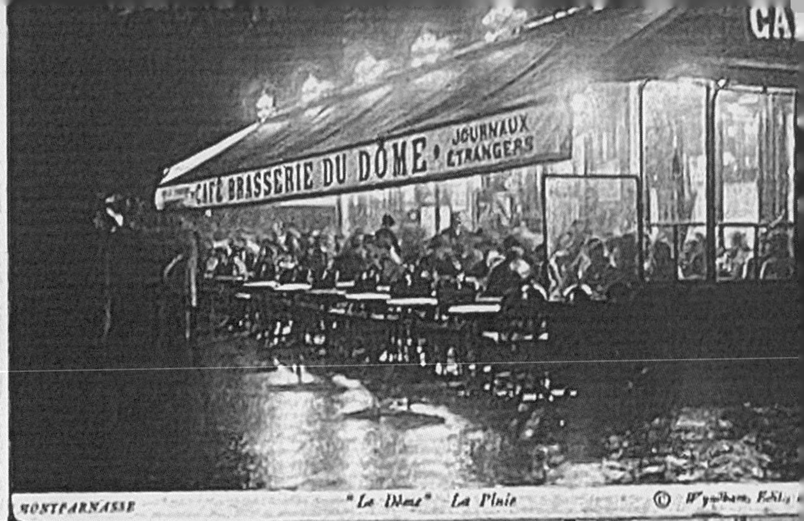
CAFÉ BRASSERIE DU DÔME
JOURNAUX ÉTRANGERS
MONTPARNASSE
"Le Dôme" La Pluie

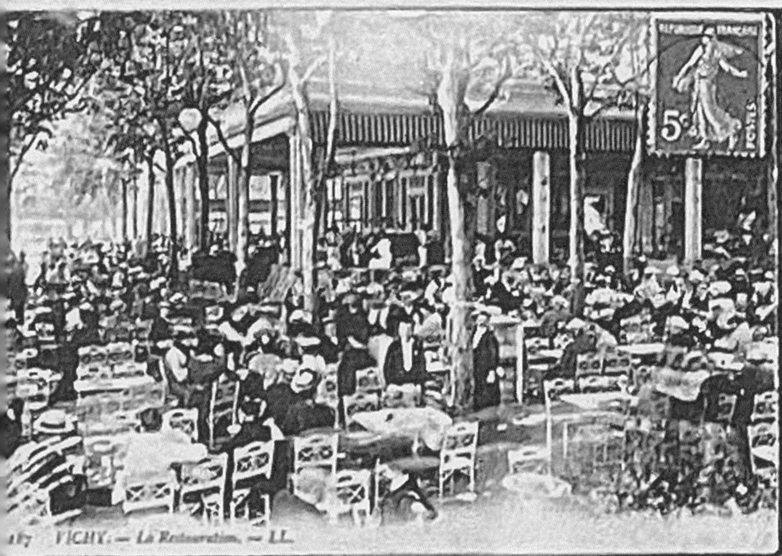
VICHY. — La Restauration. — LL.

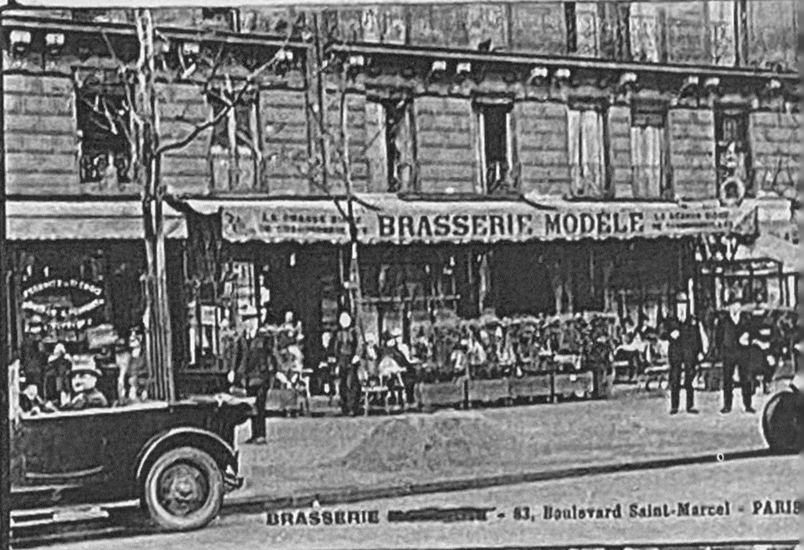
BRASSERIE MODÈLE
BRASSERIE [redacted] - 83, Boulevard Saint-Marcel - PARIS

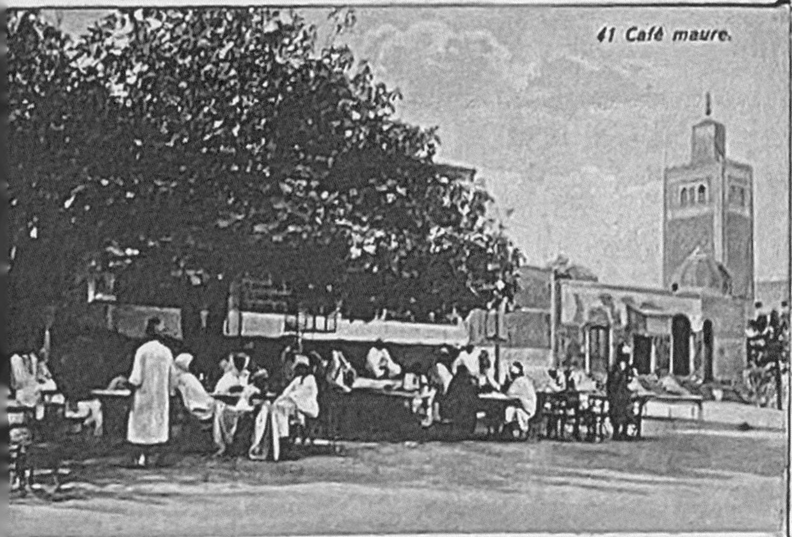
41 Café maure.

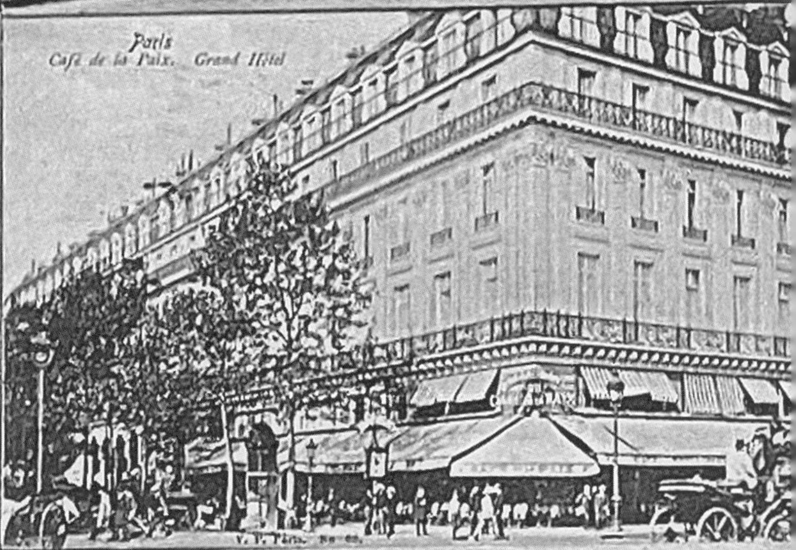
Paris
Café de la Paix. Grand Hôtel

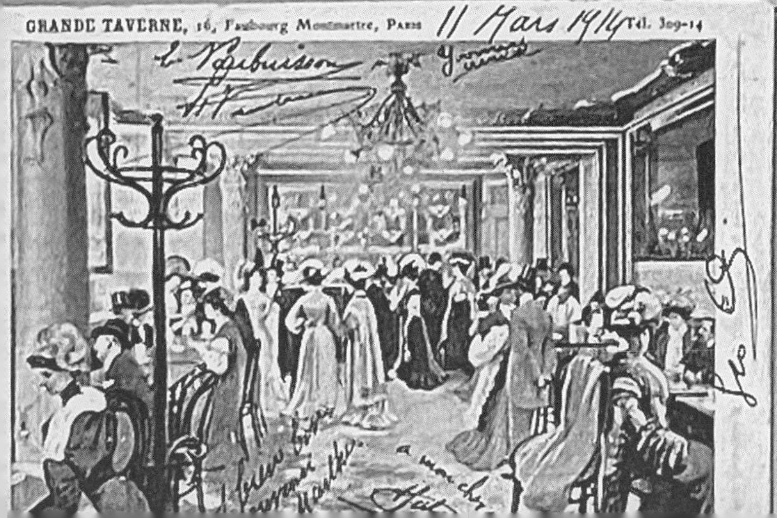
GRANDE TAVERNE, 16, Faubourg Montmartre, PARIS
11 Mars 1914
Tél. 309-14

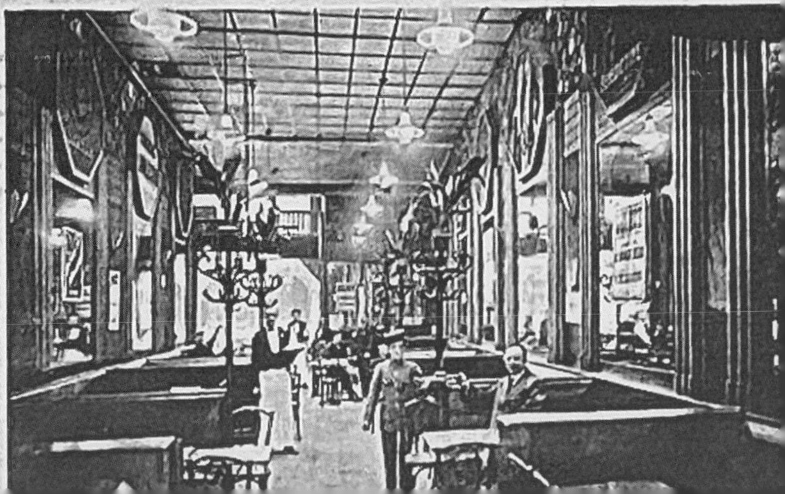